Contemporary Archaeology in Theory

Contemporary Archaeology in Theory

The New Pragmatism

Second Edition

Edited by

Robert W. Preucel and Stephen A. Mrozowski

A John Wiley & Sons, Ltd., Publication

Blackwell Publishing was acquired by John Wiley & Sons in February 2007. Blackwell's publishing program has been merged with Wiley's global Scientific, Technical, and Medical business to form Wiley-Blackwell.

Registered Office
John Wiley & Sons Ltd, The Atrium, Southern Gate, Chichester, West Sussex, PO19 8SQ, United Kingdom

Editorial Offices
350 Main Street, Malden, MA 02148-5020, USA
9600 Garsington Road, Oxford, OX4 2DQ, UK
The Atrium, Southern Gate, Chichester, West Sussex, PO19 8SQ, UK

For details of our global editorial offices, for customer services, and for information about how to apply for permission to reuse the copyright material in this book please see our website at www.wiley.com/wiley-blackwell.

Library of Congress Cataloging-in-Publication Data

Contemporary archaeology in theory : the new pragmatism / [edited by] Robert W. Preucel and
    Stephen A. Mrozowski. – 2nd ed.
        p.   cm.
    Includes bibliographical references and index.
    ISBN 978-1-4051-5832-9 (hardcover : alk. paper) – ISBN 978-1-4051-5853-4 (pbk. : alk. paper)
    1. Archaeology. I. Preucel, Robert W. II. Mrozowski, Stephen A.
    CC173.C66 2010
    930.1–dc22
                                                                    2009054212

A catalogue record for this book is available from the British Library.

Set Set in 9.5/11pt Minion by SPi Publisher Services, Pondicherry, India
Printed in Singapore by Ho Printing Singapore Pte Ltd

01   2010

For Leslie and Ammie

Contents

List of Tables and Figures

Tables

Figures

List of Contributors

Arjun Appadurai is Goddard Professor of Media, Culture, and Communication at New York University, NY

Sonya Atalay is an Assistant Professor of Anthropology at Indiana University, Bloomington, IN

Zainab Bahrani is the Edith Porada Professor of Ancient Near Eastern Art and Archaeology at Columbia University, New York

Kelly P. Bannister is Assistant Professor in the School of Environmental Studies at the University of Victoria, BC

Michael L. Blakey is Professor of Anthropology and American Studies at the College of William and Mary, Williamsburg, VA

Eleanor Conlin Casella is Lecturer in the School of Arts, Histories, and Cultures at the University of Manchester, UK

Jean Comaroff is Bernard E. and Ellen C. Sunny Distinguished Service Professor of Anthropology at the University of Chicago, IL

John L. Comaroff is Harold H. Swift Distinguished Service Professor of Anthropology at the University of Chicago, IL

Margarita Díaz-Andreu is a Reader in the Department of Archaeology at Durham University, UK

Marcia-Anne Dobres is Adjunct Faculty in Anthropology at the University of Maine at Orono, ME

Roger Echo-Hawk is a historian, writer, and composer based in Longmont, CO

Clark L. Erickson is Associate Professor of Anthropology and Associate Curator of South America at the University of Pennsylvania, Philadelphia, PA

Russell G. Handsman is Project Consulant at the Mashantucket Pequot Museum and Research Center, Mashantucket, CT

Ian Hodder is the Dunlevie Family Professor of Anthropology at Stanford University, Palo Alto, CA

Audrey Horning is a Reader in Historical Archaeology in the School of Archaeology and Ancient History at the University of Leicester, UK

Tim Ingold is Professor of Social Anthropology at the University of Aberdeen, UK

Siân Jones is Senior Lecturer in the School of Arts, Histories and Cultures at the University of Manchester, UK

Rosemary A. Joyce is Professor of Anthropology at the University of California, Berkeley, CA

Webb Keane is Professor of Anthropology at the University of Michigan, Ann Arbor, MI

Trudie Lamb Richmond is Director of Public Programs at the Mashantucket Pequot Museum and Research Center, Mashantucket, CT

Kent G. Lightfoot Professor of Anthropology at the University of California, Berkeley, CA

Antoinette Martinez is Assistant Professor of Anthropology, California State University, Chico, CA

Lynn Meskell is Professor of Anthropology at Stanford University, Palo Alto, CA

Barbara J. Mills is Director of the School of Anthropology and Professor of American Indian Studies at the University of Arizona and Curator of Archaeology at the Arizona State Museum, Tucson, AZ

Sarah M. Nelson is Professor Emeritus of Anthropology at the University of Denver, CO

George P. Nicholas is Associate Professor of Archaeology and Anthropology at Simon Fraser University, Burnaby, BC

Timothy R. Pauketat is Professor of Anthropology at the University of Illinois, Urbana-Champaign, IL

Kenneth E. Sassaman is Associate Professor of Anthropology at the University of Florida, Gainesville, FL

Ann M. Schiff is a retired member of the Archaeological Research Facility, Department of Anthropology, University of California, Berkeley, CA

Peter R. Schmidt is Professor of Anthropology at the University of Florida, Gainesville, FL

Paul A. Shackel is Director of the Center for Heritage Resource Studies and Professor of Anthropology at the University of Maryland, College Park, MD

Carla M. Sinopoli is Professor of Anthropology and Director of the Museum of Anthropology at the University of Michigan, Ann Arbor, MI

Paul S. C. Taçon is Professor of Anthropology and Archaeology in the School of Arts at Griffith University, Queensland, Australia

Lauren E. Talalay is Curator of Education at the Kelsey Museum at the University of Michigan, Ann Arbor, MI

Barbara L. Voss is Associate Professor of Anthropology at Stanford University, Palo Alto, CA

Jonathan R. Walz is a Lecturer in the Honors Program at the University of Florida, Gainesville, FL

LouAnn Wurst is Associate Professor of Anthropology at the University of Western Michigan at Kalamazoo, MI

Alison Wylie is Professor of Philosophy at the University of Washington, Seattle, WA

Larry J. Zimmerman is Professor of Anthropology and Museum Studies at Indiana University-Purdue University Indianapolis, IN

Preface

If edited books are collaborative projects, edited Readers are even more so. Throughout the process of organizing and writing this Reader, we have explored our own deeply held commitments and challenged each other to broaden our horizons. Given our backgrounds in prehistoric and historical archaeologies, we were particularly intrigued by the idea of breaking down these categories and exploring the implications of deep time and the search for a deeper history. In addition, we both have considerable experience working with Native American communities and are strong advocates of indigenous archaeologies. We are both committed to increasing the numbers of Native American archaeologists as well as transforming our profession in ways that acknowledge the rights and interests of Native American peoples. In many ways, our collaboration has been and continues to be a transformative process. We would be remiss, however, if we didn't thank the person who brought us together, namely Craig Cipolla. Craig was a Masters student with Steve at the University of Massachusetts at Boston and is currently a doctoral candidate with Bob at the University of Pennsylvania. Craig's interest and enthusiasm for all things theoretical helped to spark discussions between us that led to our collaboration on this book.

We are especially grateful to the individual authors who have agreed to allow their publications to be reprinted in our book. They have been extremely supportive and generous without any knowledge of exactly how we would represent their work. We have chosen to use their writings to provide a context for exploring the articulation of different theories and their real-world applications and consequences. But, in the end, these chapters must stand on their own. They were not produced for this Reader, but rather for different contexts – a specific book, a given journal article, a particular interview. We have extracted them for our purposes and used them to make specific points about what we are calling "the new pragmatism," the increasing professional commitment to the practice of socially relevant archaeology. But because of their preexistence, they retain the ability to "talk back" and actively resist the interpretations we offer. This quality can be understood as their partial objectivity.

We thank Rosalie Roberston at Wiley-Blackwell for her strong commitment to this project. Rosalie has been extremely patient, and always understanding with several unavoidable delays. We thank Julia Kirk for skillfully steering us through the various stages of the production process. Finally, we thank Justin Dyer, our copy-editor, for his superb attention to detail.

Each of us has had a deep interest in theoretical questions during the course of our careers. Throughout that journey we have been influenced by our peers, our students, and our mentors. Each of us has incurred special debts we would like to acknowledge. Bob would like to thank Asif

Agha, Herman Agoyo, Woody Aguilar, Wendy Ashmore, Ofer Bar-Yosef, Alex Bauer, Alexis Boutin, K. C. Chang, Christopher Chippindale, Craig Cipolla, Meg Conkey, Linda Cordell, Ann Dapice, Terry Deacon, Harold Dibble, Tim Earle, Roger Echo-Hawk, Clark Erickson, T. J. Ferguson, Kathy Fine-Dare, Richard Ford, John Fritz, Yosef Garfinkle, Pamela Geller, Joan Gero, Chris Gosden, Richard Grounds, Suzan Harjo, Julie Hendon, Michael Herzfeld, Jim Hill, Ian Hodder, Mark Johnson, Matthew Johnson, Rosemary Joyce, Sergei Kan, Webb Keane, Mark Leone, Richard Leventhal, Matt Liebmann, Randy McGuire, Desirée Martinez, Randy Mason, Frank Matero, Lynn Meskell, Barbara Mills, Koji Mizoguchi, Melissa Murphy, Simon Ortiz, Tom Patterson, Tim Pauketat, Robert Paynter, Steve Pendery, Bernie Perley, Colin Renfrew, Uzma Rizvi, Diego Romero, Mateo Romero, David Rudner, Jeremy Sabloff, Dean Saitta, Bob Schuyler, Rus Sheptak, Tad Shurr, Michael Silverstein, Daniel Smail, Monica Smith, Laurajane Smith, James Snead, Edward Soja, Matthew Spriggs, Miranda Stockett, Joseph Suina, Greg Urban, Joe Watkins, Mike Wilcox, Gordon Willey, Lucy Williams, Alison Wylie, and Larry Zimmerman.

Steve wishes to thank Ping-Ann Addo, Susan Alcock, Douglas Armstrong, Christa Baranek, Mary Beaudry, William Beeman, Douglas Bolender, Joanne Bowen, Kathleen Bragdon, Marley Brown, Eleanor Casella, Craig Cipolla, Meg Conkey, Christopher DeCorse, Jim Deetz, James Delle, Amy Den Ouden, Roger Echo-Hawk, Arturo Escobar, Maria Franklin, Jack Gary, Rae Gould, Richard Gould, Martin Hall, David Harvey, Kat Hayes, Ian Hodder, Audrey Horning, Dan Hicks, Matthew Johnson, Martin Jones, Rosemary Joyce, Kenneth Kvamme, David Landon, Heather Law, Henri Lefebvre, Mark Leone, Kent Lightfoot, Lynn Meskell, Barbara Little, Kevin McBride, Thomas McGovern, Randy McGuire, Richard McNeish, Jose Martinez-Reyes, Christopher Matthews, Kathleen Morrison, Daniel Mouer, Paul Mullins, Michael Nassaney, Charles Orser, Marilyn Palmer, Gisli Palsson, Tom Patterson, Tim Pauketat, Robert Paynter, Guido Pezzarossi, Virginia Popper, Colon Renfrew, Krysta Ryzewski, Dean Saitta, Ken Sassman, Peter Schmidt, Bob Schuyler, Paul Shackel, Stephen Silliman, Theresa Singleton, James Snead, Edward Soja, John Steinberg, Christopher Tilley, Heather Trigg, Bruce Trigger, Diana Wall, Joe Watkins, Michael Way, Laurie Wilkie, Christopher Witmore, LouAnn Wurst, and Judith Zeitlin.

As our work on this book has unfolded, the individuals we have turned to most often for advice and feedback were our spouses. Leslie Atik and Anne Lang Mrozowski have provided invaluable editorial input as well as forthright critiques that have been instrumental in maintaining the project's momentum and direction. As a small measure of our appreciation for their enthusiastic encouragement and unfailing support, we dedicate this book to them.

Acknowledgments

The editors and publisher gratefully acknowledge the permission granted to reproduce the copyright material in this book:

Chapter 1: Tim Ingold, "The Temporality of the Landscape," pp. 152–74 from *World Archaeology* 25:2 (1993). Reprinted with permission of Taylor & Francis Group and the author.

Chapter 2: Paul S. C. Taçon, "Identifying Ancient Sacred Landscapes in Australia: From Physical to Social," pp. 33–57 from *Archaeologies of Landscapes: Contemporary Perspectives*, ed. Wendy Ashmore and A. Bernard Knapp (Oxford: Blackwell Publishers, 1999). Reprinted with permission of Blackwell Publishers.

Chapter 3: Eleanor Conlin Casella, "Landscapes of Punishment and Resistance: A Female Convict Settlement in Tasmania, Australia," pp. 103–30 from *Contested Landscapes of Movement and Exile*, ed. Barbara Bender and Margot Winer (Oxford: Berg Publishers, 2001). Reprinted with permission of Berg Publishers Oxford via A C Black.

Chapter 4: Clark L. Erickson, "Amazonia: The Historical Ecology of a Domesticated Landscape," pp. 157–83 in *The Handbook of South American Archaeology*, ed. Helaine Silverman and William Isbell (New York: Springer, 2008). Reprinted with permission of Springer.

Chapter 5: Timothy R. Pauketat, "Practice and History in Archaeology: An Emerging Paradigm," pp. 73–98 from *Anthropological Theory* 1 (2001). Reprinted with permission of Sage.

Chapter 6: Marcia-Anne Dobres, "Technology's Links and *Chaînes*: The Processual Unfolding of Technique and Technician," pp. 124–45 from Marcia-Anne Dobres and Christopher R. Hoffman (eds) *The Social Dynamics of Technology: Practice, Politics, and Worldviews* (Washington, DC: Smithsonian Institution Press, 1999). Copyright © Marcia-Anne Dobres, 1999. Reprinted with permission of the author.

Chapter 7: Kenneth E. Sassaman, "Structure and Practice in the Archaic Southeast," pp. 79–107 from Timothy R. Pauketat and Diana DiPaolo Loren (eds) *North American Archaeology* (Oxford: Blackwell Publishers, 2005). Reprinted with permission.

Chapter 8: Kent G. Lightfoot, Antoinette Martinez, and Ann M. Schiff, "Daily Practice and Material Culture in Pluralistic Social Settings: An Archaeological Study of Culture Change and Persistence from Fort Ross, California," pp. 199–222 from *American Antiquity* 63:2 (1998). Reprinted with permission of the Society for American Archaeology and the author.

Chapter 9: Alison Wylie, "Good Science, Bad Science, or Science as Usual? Feminist Critiques of Science," pp. 29–55 from Lori D. Hager (ed.) *Women in Human Evolution* (London: Routledge, 1997). Reprinted with permission of Taylor & Francis Books UK.

Chapter 10: John L. Comaroff and Jean Comaroff, "On Personhood: An Anthropological Perspective from Africa," pp. 267–83 from *Social Identities* 7:2 (2001). Reprinted with permission of the publisher (Taylor and Francis Group http://www.informaworld.com).

Chapter 11: Rosemary Joyce "Girling the Girl and Boying the Boy: The Production of Adulthood in Ancient Mesoamerica," pp. 473–83 from *World Archaeology* 31 (2000). Reprinted with permission of the publisher (Taylor and Francis Group http://www.informaworld.com).

Chapter 12: Barbara L. Voss, "Domesticating Imperialism: Sexual Politics and the Archaeology of Empire," pp. 191–203 from *American Anthropologist* 110:2 (2008). Reprinted with permission of the American Anthropological Association and the author.

Chapter 13: Sarah M. Nelson, "The Politics of Ethnicity in Prehistoric Korea," pp. 218–31 from Philip L. Kohl and Clare Fawcett (eds) *Nationalism, Politics, and the Practice of Archaeology* (Cambridge: Cambridge University Press, 1995). Reprinted with permission of Cambridge University Press and the author.

Chapter 14: Siân Jones, "Historical Categories and the Praxis of Identity: The Interpretation of Ethnicity in Historical Archaeology," pp. 219–32 from Pedro Paulo A. Funari, Martin Hall, and Siân Jones (eds) *Historical Archaeology: Back from the Edge* (London: Routledge, 1999). Reprinted with permission.

Chapter 15: Roger Echo-Hawk and Larry J. Zimmerman, "Beyond Race: Some Opinions about Racialism and American Archaeology," pp. 461–85 from *The American Indian Quarterly* 30:3–4 (2006). Reprinted with permission of the University of Nebraska Press.

Chapter 16: LouAnn Wurst, "A Class All Its Own: Explorations of Class Formation and Conflict," pp. 190–206 from Martin Hall and Stephen Silliman (eds) *Historical Archaeology* (Oxford: Blackwell Publishers, 2006). Reprinted with permission.

Chapter 17: Webb Keane, "Money Is No Object: Materiality, Desire, and Modernity in an Indonesian Society," pp. 65–90 from Fred Myers (ed.) *The Empire of Things: Regimes of Value and Material Culture* (Santa Fe: School of American Research Press, 2001). Reprinted with permission of SAR Press.

Chapter 18: Barbara Mills, "Remembering while Forgetting: Depositional Practices and Social Memory at Chaco," pp. 81–108 from Barbara J. Mills and William Walker (eds) *Memory Work: Archaeologies of Material Practices* (Santa Fe: School of American Research Press, 2008). Reprinted with permission of SAR Press.

Chapter 19: Paul A. Shackel, "Public Memory and the Search for Power in American Historical Archaeology," pp. 655–70 from *American Anthropologist* 103:3 (2001). Reprinted with permission of the American Anthropological Association and the author.

Chapter 20: Peter R. Schmidt and Jonathan R. Walz, "Re-Representing African Pasts through Historical Archaeology", pp. 53–70 from *American Antiquity* 72:1 (2007). Copyright © 2007 by the Society for American Archaeology. Reprinted with permission of the Society for American Archaeology and the authors.

Chapter 21: Margarita Díaz-Andreu, "Archaeology and Nationalism in Spain," pp. 39–56 from Philip L. Kohl and Clare Fawcett (eds) *Nationalism, Politics, and the Practice of Archaeology* (Cambridge: Cambridge University Press, 1995). Reprinted with permission of Cambridge University Press.

Chapter 22: Carla M. Sinopoli, "Echoes of Empire: Vijayanagara and Historical Memory, Vijayanagara as Historical Memory," pp. 17–33 in Ruth M. Van Dyke and Susan E. Alcock (eds) *Archaeologies of Memory* (Oxford: Blackwell, 2003). Reprinted with permission.

Chapter 23: Zainab Bahrani, "Conjuring Mesopotamia: Imaginative Geography and a World Past," pp. 159–74 from Lynn Meskell (ed.) *Archaeology under Fire: Nationalism, Politics and Heritage in the Eastern Mediterranean and Middle East* (London: Routledge, 1998). Reprinted with permission of Taylor and Francis (UK) Books.

Chapter 24: Russell G. Handsman and Trudie Lamb Richmond, "Confronting Colonialism: The Mahican and Schaghticoke Peoples and Us," pp. 87–118 from Peter R. Schmidt and Thomas C. Patterson (eds) *Making Alternative Histories: The Practice of Archaeology and History in Non-Western Settings* (Santa Fe: School of American Research Press, 1995). Reprinted with permission of SAR Press.

Chapter 25: Arjun Appadurai, "The Globalization of Archaeology and Heritage: A Discussion with Arjun Appadurai," pp. 35–49 from *Journal of Social Archaeology* 1 (2002). Reprinted with permission of Sage.

Chapter 26: Lynn Meskell, "Sites of Violence: Terrorism, Tourism, and Heritage in the Archaeological Present," pp. 123–46 from Lynn Meskell and Peter Pels (eds) *Embedding Ethics* (Oxford: Berg, 2005). Reprinted with permission of Berg Publishers c/o A C Black.

Chapter 27: Michael L. Blakey, "An Ethical Epistemology of Publicly Engaged Biocultural Research," pp. 17–28 from Junko Habu, Clare Fawcett, and John M. Matsunaga (eds) *Evaluating Multiple Narratives: Beyond Nationalist, Colonialist, Imperialist Archaeologies* (New York: Springer, 2008). Reprinted with permission.

Chapter 28: Audrey Horning, "Cultures of Contact, Cultures of Conflict? Identity Construction, Colonialist Discourse, and the Ethics of Archaeological Practice in Northern Ireland," pp. 107–33 from *Stanford Journal of Archaeology* 5 (2007). Copyright © Audrey Horning 2007. Reprinted with the kind permission of the author.

Chapter 29: Sonya Atalay, "No Sense of the Struggle: Creating a Context for Survivance at the NMAI," pp. 597–618 from *The American Indian Quarterly* 30:3–4 (2006). Reprinted with permission of the University of Nebraska Press.

Chapter 30: Lauren Talalay, "The Past as Commodity: Archaeological Images in Modern Advertising," pp. 205–216 from *Public Archaeology* 3 (2004). Reprinted with permission of Maney Publishing.

Chapter 31: Ian Hodder, "The Past as Passion and Play: Çatalhöyük as a Site of Conflict in the Construction of Multiple Pasts," pp. 124–39 from Lynn Meskell (ed.) *Archaeology under Fire: Nationalism, Politics and Heritage in the Eastern Mediterranean and Middle East* (London: Routledge, 1998). Reprinted with permission of Taylor and Francis UK.

Chapter 32: George P. Nicholas and Kelly P. Bannister, "Copyrighting the Past? Emerging Intellectual Property Rights Issues in Archaeology," pp. 327–50 from *Current Anthropology* 45:3 (2004). Reprinted with permission of the University of Chicago Press.

Part I
The New Pragmatism

NEW EDITIONS OF TEXTBOOKS OR READERS are generally of two kinds. Typically, they stay close to the structure of the first edition and add in new material to acknowledge the ways in which the field has changed since its original publication date. Less frequently do they represent a complete rewrite or a new engagement with the field. This second edition of *Contemporary Archaeology in Theory* is of this latter kind and, indeed, it is why we have chosen to add the subtitle *The New Pragmatism*.

The first edition, edited by Robert Preucel, an American Southwesternist, and Ian Hodder, a British prehistorian, was an attempt to review the landscape of archaeological theory circa 1995 (Preucel and Hodder 1996). We began by acknowledging the challenges and risks of the project. Readers are a distinctive publication genre. They bind together a group of essays written by diverse scholars for different purposes into a single volume where their common threads are highlighted by the editors. There is a sense of authority and completeness about them that is exciting when they first come out, but that quickly fades with passage of time. Because each reader brings his or her own experience and knowledge to bear in the process of reading, we wished our Reader to be fluid and open to multiple interpretations. We were aware that our introductory essays and our essay selections could be perceived as an attempt to establish a canon, even though this was certainly not our intention.

We then discussed possible ways of organizing the Reader to emphasize the point that organizational decisions are not neutral and they have an effect upon interpretation. Some of the possible organizational structures we reviewed included dividing the book by historical periods (antiquarianism, culture-historical archaeology, processual archaeology, postprocessual archaeology), by types of societies (band, tribe, chiefdom, state), or by subject and national origin (Paleolithic archaeology, Roman archaeology, Chinese archaeology). We then raised the question of whether it was possible to develop an organizational schema that does not suffer from an evolutionary or imperialist bias. We concluded that while there can be no definitive account of theory in archaeology, there can nonetheless be productive engagements that are forged through a process of discourse and dialogue. This perspective requires a commitment to a more democratic archaeology where all views and positionalities have the right to be included in the discourse (which is, of course, not the same thing as saying that all views are equally valid). This is the basis for doing applied anthropology as well as a socially committed or action archaeology.

This second edition, edited by Preucel and Stephen Mrozowski, an American historical archaeologist, adopts a somewhat different approach. It is not so much a review of the field as it is an investigation of a particular movement or spirit in the human sciences. We have called this investigation the "new pragmatism." This spirit does not refer to the dominance of any one theory, but rather to the more explicit integration of archaeology and its social context in ways that serve contemporary needs. While it is true that archaeology has always had a social purpose, it is becoming clear that archaeology and the social are inextricably intertwined. It is no longer possible to hold that archaeology is an objective science first and a social practice second. Archaeology is irreducibly both at the same time. Archaeologists are increasingly asking the following questions: How can archaeology better contribute to broader dialogues concerning the myriad social challenges humanity faces at this point in its history? What is archaeology's role in the development of social theory? What are the practical consequences of holding a particular theory? Does archaeology matter?

In the past 15 years, there has been a growing emphasis on the social and an interest more generally in establishing the relevance of social sciences to the modern world. In philosophy, this has meant the reemergence of pragmatism and the importance it places on self-referential knowledge and its practical application to contemporary social issues (Baert 2005). In archaeology, this is perhaps exemplified by the emergence of postprocessual archaeologies and the gradual incorporation of questions of identity, meaning, agency, and practice alongside those of system, process, and structure. This development, of course, should not be interpreted to mean that process or structure has been superseded. The social must always be positioned within a long-term trajectory and linked to the cognitive.

Rather, it means that in terms of the doing of archaeology, there are increasingly more studies deploying social categories in pursuit of a past that holds relevance in today's world. It is no longer possible to justify archaeology on some abstract terms; rather, the ethics of archaeology now require that we join diverse interest groups in the common project of understanding the multiple meanings of the past for the present. The obvious question to ask is why is this happening now? This Reader is an attempt to interrogate this question from several different, but interrelated, directions.

Disciplinary Anxieties

All fields and disciplines undergo periodic reevaluations when they take stock of their current situation and chart possible courses for the future. This is a healthy thing since knowledge grows and interests shift. In anthropological archaeology, one such reevaluation took place in the 1960s and early 1970s and turned on the degree to which positivism was an appropriate epistemology for the scientific investigation of past cultures and societies (Fritz and Plog 1970; Watson et al. 1971; Flannery 1973, Renfrew 1982). Ironically, this reevaluation came precisely at the moment that philosophers of science were moving away from positivism and advocating alternative approaches, some of which came to be called postpositivism (Rorty 1979, 1982; Wylie 1981, 2002). This "epistemic delay" is typical of those social sciences, like archaeology, that have attempted to emulate the physical sciences. There is now a growing sense that there are multiple legitimate ways of knowing the world. Indeed, science studies scholars have concluded that, as important as it is, science cannot be claimed on philosophical grounds to be a privileged enterprise (Latour and Woolgar 1979; Pickering 1995; Barnes et al. 1996; Knorr Cetina 1999). Rather, science is but one among many ways of knowing, each of which serves particular social purposes. This is not a statement in favor of relativism, since all forms of knowledge acquisition are manifestly not equivalent. It simply means that knowledge claims must be continually justified against one another in discourse and dialogue. This conclusion is central to a pragmatic archaeology.

In the 1960s, Lewis Binford and his students at the University of Chicago introduced an explicitly scientific approach to explaining the past known as the "new archaeology." What was new was the placement of theory building, particularly systems theory, ecological theory, and evolutionary theory, at the core of the archaeological agenda (Binford 1962; Flannery 1972). The ultimate goal was for archaeology to take its place along other empirical, law-generating sciences and apply itself to explaining the past as a predictable trajectory. This new focus contrasted with the particularistic nature of standard traditional or culture-historical archaeology and had the advantage of directly linking archaeology to other newly reformulated sciences, such as evolutionary ecology, sociology, and human geography. David Clarke (1968) at Cambridge University offered a somewhat different, but largely congruent, version of the new archaeology that emphasized quantitative and analytic methods borrowed from many of these same sciences. Enthusiasm among archaeologists was high and some even touted this movement as a "paradigm shift" in the Kuhnian sense (Kuhn 1962) because it was perceived as marking a radical break with the approaches and methods of culture-historical archaeology (Sterud 1973).

The excitement of the new archaeology, however, was short-lived and internal critiques quickly came to the surface. Although occasionally forgotten, these early critiques would, in some instances, presage changes that would shape the field as a whole. One area of dispute was the nature of scientific explanation. John Fritz and Fred Plog (1970) promoted the hypothetico-deductive method as devised by Hempel and Oppenheim (1948) in their classic account of the logic of scientific explanation. Patty Jo Watson, Steven LeBlanc, and Charles Redman (1971) observed that this method would bring archaeology in line with other sciences. Colin Renfrew (1982), however, questioned the appropriateness of a strict allegiance to positivism, and Merrilee and Wesley Salmon proposed the statistical-relevance model in place of the covering-law model (Salmon and Salmon 1979; Salmon 1982).

A second topic of debate was the integrity of the archaeological record and the impact of "site formation processes." Michael Schiffer (1976) critiqued the new archaeologists who had naively assumed that the archaeological record was a "fossil record" of past behavior. He introduced a discussion of post-depositional processes, pointing out that they often introduced patterns of their own which "distorted" the record. A proper explanation of a given problem must thus proceed first by identifying natural and cultural transforms and then factoring them out to reveal the underlying behavior of interest. Binford (1980) quickly took issue with Schiffer, arguing that he assumed the "Pompeii premise," namely the existence of some real past waiting to be discovered. For Binford, the record is the normal consequence of the operation of dynamic living systems and is generated continuously. This important insight challenged the standard opposition of past and present and foreshadowed the dialectical arguments by postprocessualists (Shanks and Tilley 1987a, 1987b).

Schiffer and his University of Arizona colleagues, J. Jefferson Reid and William Rathje, responded to this intellectual fragmentation by offering "behavioral archaeology" to unify the field into a coherent program (Reid et al. 1975; Schiffer 1995). The basic premise of behavioral archaeology is the belief that the proper goal of archaeology is the study of the relations between people and material culture at all times and places. The unification of archaeology was to be accomplished through the integration of four distinct research strategies (Reid et al. 1975). Strategy 1 was devoted to using material culture produced in the past to answer specific questions about past human behavior. Strategy 2 focused on contemporary material culture to derive laws of human behavior useful for explaining the past. Strategy 3 was the use of past material culture to generate laws of human behavior. Strategy 4 was the use of present material culture to explain present human behavior. According to this framework, Strategies 2 and 3 were the nomothetic or law-generating strategies and Strategies 1 and 4 were the idiographic or law-using ones. This approach, with some modifications, is still influential today (Schiffer 1995, 1999; Skibo and Schiffer 2008).

Yet another debate turned on the proper role of analogy (see Wylie 1985). Binford (1967) argued that analogy was to be used not for explanation, but rather for the construction of hypotheses about the past that could then be tested against the archaeological record. Explanation was thus a two-step process involving hypothesis generation and hypothesis testing. Left unresolved, however, was the stopping point, the stage of testing at which an analogy might be considered validated. In the late 1970s, Richard Gould offered a pessimistic view on the use of analogy. He felt that archaeology could never hope to address more than a "limited and rather unimportant part of the story of the human species" because of its reliance on material culture (Gould 1980:3). For Gould (1980), symbolic behavior, the most important and interesting aspects of human behavior, could only be understood in contemporary human societies. This meant that ethnography could only be used negatively to identify anomalies, the so-called "spoiler approach." Patty Jo Watson (1982), on the other hand, took the more positive view that the archaeological record could be used to confront scientific hypotheses. Binford (1985) critiqued Gould, claiming that he ignored the role of theory, specifically how it provides a context for interpretation. Gould (1985) responded by arguing that theory alone was not sufficient and that empirical research was essential for the building of middle-range theory, of what he called operational theory (Gould 1990). This debate is particularly interesting in that it contains elements of a social constructivist position. While arguing for greater objectivity, Binford explicitly acknowledged that our theories and assumptions fundamentally condition what we accept as fact.

What underlay processual archaeology, and its variants, was the view that archaeology could be divorced from its social context. One does archaeology first and then attends to its social contexts and consequences. The implication here is that the doing of archaeology can be separated off from its social uses and that only the former was true archaeology. Some prescient archaeologists did challenge aspects of this view and raised issues of relevance. As John Fritz and Fred Plog (1970:411–412) put it, "We suspect that unless archaeologists find ways to make their research increasingly relevant to the modern world, the modern world will find itself increasingly capable of getting along without archaeologists." Their justification for this statement was that archaeology is largely funded by the public in the form of federal grants and programs. Fritz (1973) later drew attention to how archaeology had the potential to help provide a deeper understanding of poorly assimilated technological change, unchecked population growth, environmental mismanagement, and social disintegration. Similarly, Richard Ford (1973) held that a scientific archaeology had the potential to promote a universal humanism.

In the 1980s, "postprocessualism" emerged as a new and forceful critique of processual archaeology. Ian Hodder and his students at Cambridge University were the main leaders of this movement. Significantly, Hodder, a student of David Clarke, was an early advocate of the new archaeology, and was particularly interested in the spatial organization of human behavior (Hodder and Orton 1976; Hodder 1978). And like Binford, Hodder took up ethnoarchaeology to study the relationship between material culture patterning and behavior. However, unlike Binford, he drew the conclusion that social boundaries were dynamic and fluid, always in the process of negotiation (Hodder 1979, 1982c). He interpreted material culture as actively constituting social action and not merely passively reflecting it. This perspective drew support from the work of historical archaeologists working in both North America and Africa who stressed that the meaning attached to material culture could only be understood by examining material practices in their cultural-historical contexts (see Hodder 1982c:229). In 1984, Hodder introduced the term "postprocessual" to describe an archaeology that takes greater account of meaning, the individual, culture, and history (Hodder 1984). He later extended the term to encompass a variety of alternatives to processualism, including neo-Marxist, indigenous, and feminist perspectives (Hodder 1986). Christopher Tilley (1989a:185) has heralded this development and not the rise of the new archaeology as the true paradigm shift in archaeological theory.

At the same time, a group of scholars inspired by Marxist approaches developed their own critiques of processual archaeology. Some of these individuals identified with classical historical materialism and argued that class relations were the driving force for culture change (Spriggs 1984; Gilman 1989; McGuire and Paynter 1991; Muller 1997). Others were more interested in Althusser and Foucault and issues of ideology and power (Leone 1982, 1984; Miller and Tilley 1984; Shanks and Tilley 1987a, 1987b). Despite their common Marxist lineage, these two directions were not entirely congruent. Indeed, the classical Marxists possessed certain affinities with processualists and the neo-Marxists shared many interests with postprocessualists. There were tensions between the advocates of Marxist and neo-Marxist perspectives, and these tended to be expressed over notions of agency, class, structure, and meaning. Bruce Trigger (1985), for example, critiqued the neo-Marxists for what he saw as tendencies toward relativism (see also Patterson 1989). The main area of overlap, however, was the common belief in an emancipatory archaeology, the idea that archaeology has a transformative role to play in the modern world.

Perhaps the most important development of this period was the archaeology of gender. Margaret Conkey and Janet Spector published the first widely read feminist piece in Anglo-American archaeology in 1984. Their review article was essentially a call to arms, an attempt to introduce gender as a legitimate topic of archaeological research and to draw attention to the status inequalities of women in the profession (Conkey and Spector 1984). Contemporaneous with this was Joan Gero's (1983, 1985) work on how our Western ideological construction of womanhood affects the research and funding opportunities of women in archaeology and the sciences. Her results pointed to clear discrepancies in the funding of male and female scholars by the National Science Foundation. In 1988, Gero and Conkey (1991) organized the Wedge Conference at the Wedge Plantation in Georgetown, South Carolina, as the first group effort to explore different approaches to women and production in prehistory. They invited a range of women and men, some of whom had never before considered the implications of feminism and gender in archaeology. As an example of the fresh insights that this new approach could bring, Patty Jo Watson revisited the origins of agriculture in North America and exposed the logical contradictions between its standard presentation as the result of male bias and the general acceptance that women were gatherers (Watson and Kennedy 1991). A year later, the archaeology of gender was the theme of the annual Chacmool Conference in Calgary, drawing a large number of participants (Walde and Willows 1991). This conference helped legitimize gender as a research topic and united various strands of feminist theory.

Processual archaeology has now diversified broadly in response to both internal and external critiques. A good example of this is "cognitive processual archaeology," an approach closely associated with the work of Colin Renfrew at Cambridge University. Renfrew (1994a:5) has characterized cognitive archaeology in general terms as the study of the "specially human ability to construct and use symbols" in order to understand how cognitive processes operated in specific contexts. It draws from palaeoanthropology, animal ethology, evolutionary psychology, artificial intelligence, neuroscience, and cognitive science. While there is, as yet, no clear theoretical consensus, it is heuristically useful to differentiate "evolutionary studies" from "cognitive processual studies." The former encompasses the origins and evolution of human cognitive abilities, particularly consciousness, language, and tool using (Mellars 1991; Wynn 1991; de Beaune et al. 2009). The latter addresses the identification of cognitive processes of past modern peoples and their relationships to general cognitive principles (Flannery and Marcus 1993; Zubrow 1994). What unites these approaches, then, is their refutation of the standard processualist thesis that the mind is epiphenomenal and their methodological commitment to some form of positivism.

Gender studies have also proliferated, and exhibit a considerable range of diversity from empirical to idealist, from positivist to hermeneutic. These studies indicate the evolution of feminist thinking from dichotomous models of sex and gender to a concern for multivalent issues of identity, embodiment, and subjectivity. Here the work of Judith Butler (1990, 1993) and her ideas of performativity have been particularly important (Perry and Joyce 2001). The categories of sex and sexuality have been interrogated and retheorized (Meskell 1999; Joyce 2000a, 2000b; Schmidt and Voss 2000; Wilkie

and Hayes 2006). Women have been placed at the center of new models of human evolution (Zihlman 1989; Hagar 1997). Special symposia and sessions at professional meetings are routinely devoted to such topics as equity issues, career development, and historical struggles (see Siefert 1991; Claassen 1992; Claassen and Joyce 1994; Nelson et al. 1994; Geller and Stockett 2006). Special committees and workgroups have been established within the professional associations. There is now a journal devoted to women in archaeology (*Kvinner in Archaeologi*) and a handbook on gender in archaeology (Nelson 2006). This interest in feminism and gender research is now firmly established at the international level, most notably in England (Braithwaite 1982; Moore 1986, 1988, 2007; Gibbs 1987; Gilchrist 1994, 1999), Norway (Dommasnes 1992; Dommasnes et al. 1998; Englestad 1991, 2004), and Australia (du Cros and Smith 1993).

Evolutionary approaches have also diversified. One of these, known as "selectionism" or "Darwinian archaeology," is associated with Robert Dunnell (1980, 1989) and his students at the University of Washington. They have offered the controversial view that culture change can be modeled in Darwinian terms. More specifically, they claim that natural selection is responsible for functional variation in cultural traits. Neutral or stylistic traits are those traits that are conditioned only by the processes of cultural transmission. Robert Leonard and George Jones (1987) have expanded Dunnell's approach by introducing the notion of "replicative fitness." For them, there is an important distinction to be made between individuals, who have differential reproductive success, and the traits of those individuals, which have only replicative success. Each trait can thus be considered to have its own fitness value, which may or may not affect the fitness of the bearer of that trait. Michael O'Brien and R. Lee Lyman (2000, 2002) have developed this approach even further, arguing that artifacts are to be treated analytically as phenotypic manifestations of cultural traits and that their differential replicative fitness is probabilistic, not deterministic. Thus whether or not a human population evolves along with them is contextually specific. However, other scholars have offered sharp critiques of selectionism, arguing that it betrays a misunderstanding of the role of phenotypic variation and, in particular, behavioral variation in the evolutionary process (Boone and Smith 1998; Preucel 1999; Bamforth 2002; Gabora 2006).

Perhaps the most exciting area of evolutionary research is the evolution of mind. Several major syntheses have now been published by archaeologists or by scholars strongly influenced by archaeology. Merlin Donald (1991) has proposed the thesis that symbolic thought emerged from a pre-symbolic form through the gradual embedding of new representational systems. He writes that "the functional locus of 'consciousness' can shift, depending on the representational system currently in command" (Donald 1991:369). Terrence Deacon (1997) takes as his starting point the problem of reference. He holds that reference is fundamentally hierarchical in nature: more complex forms are built up from simpler ones. More specifically, symbolic reference depends upon indexical reference, which, in turn, depends upon iconic reference. This means that in order to understand symbolic reference one needs to start with icons and work upwards to indexes and then symbols. Steven Mithen (1994, 1996) has proposed that the key event in the evolution of the modern mind is the shift from specialized intelligence to "cognitive fluidity" during the Middle/Upper Paleolithic transition. As with Donald, he adopts a modified version of the developmental model as it is used in current psychology. He then introduces the analogy of a cathedral as a means of understanding the architecture of mind. He notes that just as it is impossible to separate out the influences of the architectural plan and the building environment on the cathedral, so, too, it is impossible to separate out the effects of genes and the developmental environment in the mind (Mithen 1996:66).

An important recent development is the rise of "postcolonial archaeologies." Postcolonialism refers to the critique of the Western canon by such preeminent scholars as Frantz Fanon (1963, 1965), Edward Said (1978), Gayatri Spivak (1988), and Homi Bhabha (1994), among others. This critique has highlighted issues of representation in the fields of history and literary criticism and emphasized power differentials between colonists and the colonized, particularly in the context of Africa, the Caribbean, Palestine, and India. In archaeology, this critique is associated with the rise of postprocessual archaeologies, which singled out the colonial origins of archaeology and the unacknowledged biases underlying its practice in non-Western contexts (Gosden 2001; Shepherd 2002a). As Hodder (1986:157) puts it, "Western archaeologists working in non-industrialized societies, particularly in the post-colonial era, became increasingly confronted with the idea that the pasts they were reconstructing were 'Western' and with an articulate rejection of those pasts as being politically and ideologically motivated." The relationships between postcolonial theory and archaeology are complex and nuanced and linked to indigenous rights movements worldwide (Dean and Levi 2003). Matthew Liebmann (2008:4) advocates postcolonial theory on the grounds that it has the potential to contribute to archaeology in three ways: (1) interpretively, in the investigation of past cases of colonization and colonialism; (2) historically, in the study of archaeology's role in the construction and deconstruction of colonial discourses; and (3) methodologically, as an aid to the decolonization of the field as part of ethical practice.

Related to postcolonialism is the international movement championing indigenous knowledge and decolonizing methodologies that has come to be called "indigenous archaeology" (Nicholas and Andrews 1997; Watkins 2001; Smith and Wobst 2005; Atalay 2006; Silliman 2008). These indigenous archaeologies represent the interests of different indigenous communities and their multiple articulations with archaeology. They are now beginning to be expressed in New Zealand, Australia, Africa, Bolivia, Canada, and the United States. Indigenous archaeologies are thus relatively new developments on the archaeological landscape and parallel the growing national and international acknowledgment of indigenous rights. Because of their newness, they are still in the process of establishing their agendas and priorities. Perhaps the most widely cited definition is due to George Nicholas and Thomas Andrews (1997:3), who state that indigenous archaeology is archaeology conducted "with, for, and by Indigenous peoples."

Indigenous archaeology is more than indigenous people learning the methods of Western archaeology or Western archaeologists collaborating with indigenous communities. It raises fundamental questions about Western ways of knowing and offers radically different ontologies grounded in indigenous conceptions of space, time, and social being (see Cajete 1999, 2004).

The theory debates, so prominent in the 1980s, have now become muted by the debates over archaeology's disciplinary status. These debates are revisiting the distinctively American thesis that archaeology is a form of anthropology, as Phil Phillips (1955:246) and Robert Braidwood (1959:79) originally argued. They are intimately related to the current critiques of the "four-field approach," which was an approach that was first outlined in 1904 by Franz Boas, who proposed that the discipline properly embraced "the biological history of mankind in all its varieties; linguistics applied to people without written language; the ethnology of people without historic records; and prehistoric archeology" (Boas 1904:35). In the decades that followed, anthropology became institutionalized with the establishment of a national anthropological organization and the creation of anthropology departments at major universities. Although few scholars were ever fluent in all four fields, anthropologists nonetheless regarded their field as a holistic scientific enterprise, and argued for its place among other disciplines and its role in intellectual life and public discourse (Stocking 1995).

In some ways, anthropology has been a victim of its own success. Its steady growth has led to considerable subdisciplinary specialization and the attendant disputes and rivalries. In 1995, George Stocking observed that the American Anthropological Association consisted of 15 subsidiary societies (including the ethnological, humanistic, linguistic, medical, psychological, urban, visual, Latin American and European, as well as consciousness and work). There were ten associations (including Africanist, Black, feminist, political and legal, senior and student), as well as several regional associations and one devoted to the practice of anthropology. There are three "councils" (education, museum, nutrition). Finally, there were two sections (biology and archaeology). In addition, the circulation of the

American Anthropologist, the official journal of the association, had declined from over 11,000 subscribers to fewer than 8,000 and was taken by less than half of the membership (Stocking 1995). Some anthropologists regard this situation as indicating the "fragmentation" of the field and have pointed to the increasing difficulty that scholars have in talking across their subdisciplinary specializations.

Contributing to this anxiety is the loss of control over the culture concept. Once the proud domain of anthropology, it has been appropriated in different ways by cultural studies, women's studies, African American studies, Native American studies, among many others. Scholars in economics, political science, and sociology are focusing on globalization, transnationalism, diaspora, and so on. In addition, there is a growing gap between anthropologists studying human evolution and those favoring applied approaches addressing the interests and needs of contemporary communities. Related to this latter focus is a new ethically based concern with the relationship between anthropologists and the people whom anthropologists study. Some see the idea of an "informant" as a holdover from a colonialist-era anthropology. Informants must now be acknowledged as "co-producers of knowledge" (Mills 1995:7). These critiques have caused many scholars to question whether anthropology is now too dispersed to meet the needs of the discipline, to educate key audiences within and beyond the academy, to attract "diverse voices to the discipline, to foster the use of anthropological knowledge in the public policy process" (Cornman 1995:6).

The iconoclastic nature of the current critique is captured by the title of the recent book *Unwrapping the Sacred Bundle: Reflections on the Disciplining of Anthropology* (Segal and Yanagisako 2005). Daniel Segal and Sylvia Yanagisako (2005), its editors, are skeptical of the unitary goals for anthropology and hold that advocates of the four-field approach seek to establish a normative science in the Kuhnian sense which closes down the possibility of critical dialogue across different knowledge domains. James Clifford (2005) takes this argument even further, suggesting that the discipline should be "disestablished" on the grounds that its object of study (primitive societies), method (fieldwork), interpretive paradigm (culture), and *telos* (Man) have all been subjected to critique so that their articulation is no longer self-evident. This argument must perhaps be taken with a grain of salt since Clifford is not a member of a Department of Anthropology, but rather a member of the History of Consciousness Department at the University of California at Santa Cruz. Michael Silverstein (2005) sees a blurring of identity between the subfields such that some are losing their distinctive status. He suggests that linguistic anthropology is "sociocultural anthropology with a twist, the theoretical as well as instrumental (via 'discourse' or 'the discursive') worrying of our same basic data, semiosis in various orders of contextualization" (Silverstein 2005:119).

As the only archaeologist in Segal and Yanagisako's volume, Hodder (2005) poses a series of sharp questions about the current status of anthropological archaeology. He asks, "Why are there only four fields in anthropology?" and, "Is archaeology better served outside of anthropology?" He favors a discourse consisting of independent disciplines, each with its own expertise and questions, coming to the table as equals. This questioning was given dramatic expression in 1998 when Hodder's own department at Stanford University split in two, creating a Department of Anthropological Science and a Department of Cultural and Social Anthropology. Many scholars drew attention to the fact that this split took place on epistemological lines (positivism and postpositivism) and not subdisciplinary ones (archaeology, linguistic anthropology, cultural anthropology, biological anthropology). For example, there were archaeologists in each of the new departments. However, it is equally true that this reorganization was the result of personality disputes. Similar disputes have also led to the creation of a Department of Anthropology and a Department of Human Evolutionary Biology at Harvard University. Somewhat ironically, the impact of the Stanford situation has recently diffused. Owing to budgetary reasons, the university reunited the department in 2007.

Some of Hodder's concerns were raised previously at professional conferences. In 2000, Susan Gillespie and Deborah Nichols organized a session at the Society for American Archaeology (SAA) meetings entitled "Archaeology is Anthropology" (Gillespie and Nichols 2003). This was followed a year later by Douglas Price's session at the SAA meetings on the topic of an autonomous archaeology, separate from anthropology (Wiseman 2001, 2002). This session motivated responses from Robert Kelly (2002) and Susan Lees (2002) in defense of anthropological archaeology. Also in 2001, Joseph Schuldenrein and Susan Gillespie organized a session at the American Anthropological Association meetings entitled "Teaching Archaeology at the Dawn of the Millenium: Is Anthropology Really Necessary?" At the same meeting, William Longacre gave the distinguished Archaeology Division lecture entitled "Archaeology as Anthropology Revisited." Longacre (1964), of course, was one of the early advocates of anthropological archaeology, and played a key role in the establishment of processualism.

These critiques of and arguments for anthropological archaeology are certainly very useful. They challenge our underlying assumptions and offer new ways of thinking about archaeology. However, up to this point they have been disciplinocentric, in the sense that they have been more about preserving the integrity of archaeology as a profession (either within anthropology or apart from it) than about considering the social consequences of the debates for diverse communities and interest groups. Largely absent from these discussions has been any acknowledgment that they also have real consequences for the public. For example, T. J. Ferguson (2003) has made a compelling case for an anthropological archaeology based upon the premise that its focus on language, culture, the body, and material culture best serves the contemporary interests of Native peoples.

If we are to retain the "sacred bundle" metaphor, then we might acknowledge that such bundles are not static; they are always renewed through ritual practice serving a specific social need. When sacred bundles are opened, ritual specialists examine their contents and repair or replace old objects with new ones as appropriate. There is no reason that we cannot acknowledge our four "sacred arrows" while we simultaneously seek to transcend them by developing new alliances and collaborations that crosscut traditional fields and disciplines and incorporate different publics. This pragmatic spirit can be seen in historical archaeology, a theoretically robust part of anthropology. In fact, we believe an argument can be made that, in some respects, historical archaeology, as it is currently constituted, presents a healthy model for contemporary archaeology.

Historical Archaeology in Theory

The case of historical archaeology presents some intriguing parallels with and departures from the field of archaeology as a whole. Although its earliest practitioners were formulating agendas in the 1930s, historical archaeology did not emerge as a subdiscipline of anthropological archaeology until the early 1960s (see South 1994; South and Deagan 2002). After an initial period of identity anxiety in which questions circulated concerning whether it should be history or anthropology, or whether it should be separate from or a part of the larger enterprise of archaeological research, the field entered a relatively bland period of "normal science" in the later 1960s and early 1970s. Our use of the term "bland" to describe this period is purposeful because much of the work in the field revolved around technical discussions of identifying material culture and the issue of reconciling text and material evidence. In contrast to these rather quotidian pursuits, some historical archaeologists chose instead to explore theoretical avenues that presaged what would later emerge as postprocessual archaeology.

One of the more noteworthy theoretical divides that characterized the early years of historical archaeology revolved around the differences between the processual agenda of Stanley South (1977) and the structuralist approach of James Deetz (1977). Deetz acknowledged the inspiration for his foray into structuralism as coming from the work of folklorist and architectural historian Henry Glassie (1969, 1972, 1975; see Deetz 1972, 1977, 1993). Although there is little doubt that this was true, it belies Deetz's (1965, 1967) own work with the idea of material culture as language and his early contribution to what would eventually be termed the linguistic turn in archaeology. These theoretical fault lines were played out in the plenary of the 1979 meetings of the Society for Historical Archaeology in a session aptly called "Star Wars." In one of the more memorable comments, William Kelso noted that South's quantitative approach seemed to provide the perfect set of methods to achieve what Deetz sought in his own work, a better understanding of the ideational changes that accompanied the growth of modernity, although no one used the term in the session.

Deetz's work inspired Peter Schmidt (1978), who was developing a similar approach in Tanzania. Using structural analysis to interrogate local oral histories, Schmidt was able to link oral testimony to early iron-smelting technologies that could be traced back more than 2,500 years. This allowed him to expand the scope and usefulness of this kind of analysis while exploring change and continuity in local historiographies. Schmidt also drew from the work of the English Africanist Merrick Posnansky (1966, 1969). Posnansky (1959, 1968) subsequently influenced the growth of historical archaeology across the continent (see Posnansky and DeCorse 1986; DeCorse 1987, 1989, 2001a, 2001b; Reid and Lane 2004a, 2004b; Schmidt 2006). These studies by Deetz, Glassie, and Schmidt, as well as others by Leland Ferguson (1977) and Mark Leone (1977), were acknowledged by Hodder (1982c:229) as a model that had already been successfully applied to the study of the past. This seldom-examined link between structuralism and postprocessualism is just one of several examples of historical archaeology anticipating changes that would influence the field of archaeology as a whole.

Another noteworthy example is the early work of Charles Fairbanks in the field of African American archaeology. As early as 1958, Fairbanks took the courageous step of arguing that archaeology had the potential to address issues of identity politics as they were being played out over the issue of civil rights in the American South. At a time when the civil rights movement was in its formative stages, Fairbanks (1958) put forth the provocative idea that archaeology could help retrieve a forgotten history. His anthropological training resulted in a program of research that strongly shaped the direction of historical archaeology in its formative years (South and Deagan 2002). Fairbanks (Fairbanks and Ascher 1971; Fairbanks 1984) inspired an entire generation of students who established what is today the archaeology of the African diaspora (e.g. Ferguson 1977, 1991, 1992; Otto 1984; Singleton 1985, 1999, 2006). This research also benefited from the Africanist perspective brought to the topic by Posnansky (1999) and his students working both in Africa (Kelly 1997, 2004; DeCorse 1999) and in the Caribbean (Armstrong 1985, 1990, 1999, 2003; Agorsah 1994; Armstrong and Kelly 2000). By focusing on the forging of new identities in colonial contexts, Fairbanks also inspired other students, most notably Kathleen Deagan (1973, 1974, 1983, 1995), to examine the growth of creole cultures in the southeastern United States and the Caribbean. In so doing, Fairbanks and his students have contributed important theoretical perspectives surrounding the manner in which colonialism and slavery shaped the growth of creole cultural practices. This notion of creolized cultural practices would subsequently inform research in other colonial contexts in which the lives of Europeans, Native Americans, and African Americans became intertwined (Deagan 2003; Lightfoot 2003; Trigg 2005; Hayes and Mrozowski 2007).

A third and perhaps most visible example of historical archaeology's contribution to contemporary theoretical discourse is its focus on the growth of capitalism and its links to colonialism, globalization, and modernity. The studies by Mark Leone and Robert Paynter were particularly influential. In his seminal 1982 article "Some Opinions About Recovering Mind," Leone acknowledges the theoretical sophistication of the structuralist approach employed by both James Deetz in New England and Henry Glassie in Virginia, but questions the efficacy of this approach for identifying evidence of the contradictions that he correctly assumes were part of New England and Virginian society (Leone 1982:749). In a subsequent article, he more explicitly explores the manner in which the work of Deetz (1977) and Glassie (1975) can contribute to a better understanding of the cultural and ideological dimensions of 18th-century, mercantile capitalism (Leone 1988). In seeking to answer this question, Leone makes an important argument for the potential of historical archaeology to explore the history of capitalism and its ideological structures (Leone 1988). Paynter (1988) expanded this by suggesting that

the massive assemblages that historical archaeologists were recovering from their sites were a testament to the success of capitalist production. Paynter (1988, 1989; McGuire and Paynter 1991) also noted that capitalist production involved more than just material culture; it also involved the production and reproduction of the social relations of production and the inequalities they engendered. A group of historical archaeologists influenced by Marx, Eric Wolf (1982), Fernand Braudel (1981, 1982, 1985), and Immanuel Wallerstein 1974, 1980) set themselves the task of tracing the history of capitalist development and the impact it had in shaping the modern world (e.g. Leone 1984, 1988, 1995; McGuire 1988, 1991; Orser 1988, 1996; Mrozowski 1991, 1996; Johnson 1993, 1996; Shackel 1993, 1996; Leone and Potter 1994, 1999; Little 1994; Mrozowski et al. 1996; Shackel et al. 1998).

In pursing the historical development of capitalism as a central research topic, historical archaeologists began placing more emphasis on the event, particularly the industrial revolution. Although there was new interest in agency in terms of cultural expression (e.g. Beaudry et al. 1991; Ferguson 1991, 1992), this did result in a loss of focus on structure. Indeed, historical archaeologists were among the first to critically examine the manner in which material culture served to reinforce notions of power and hierarchy (see Leone 1984, 1988; Orser 1988). The notion of structure and its material expression would be an important component of research that sought to place events such as industrialization and colonialism in a larger historical context with an appreciation of the long term as their focus. This turn toward history, with an emphasis on power, structure, and agency, was also embraced by postprocessual theorists (Hodder 1987; Conkey 1991).

Mark Leone's contributions to the archaeology of capitalism also extended to the introduction of a critical theory approach. In 1982, Leone noted the importance of accounting for the ideological context in which research is carried out. He states that "since we are members of a capitalist society with an ideology of its own and since we know that one way ideology operates is to make the present look inevitable by making the past look like precedent for modern conditions, then to what degree does our modern archaeology create the past in its own image?" (Leone 1982:750). He drew inspiration from the work of Christopher Tilley (1981), David Meltzer (1981), Carmel Schrire (1980), and Russell Handsman (1980), who, like Leone, were beginning to examine the role of contemporary ideologies in the shaping of archaeological interpretations. Leone was particularly interested in exposing what Marx called "vulgar histories" or histories "written without awareness of how knowledge is related to the context of its creation" (Leone 1982:754). He later used critical theory to examine how archaeology and history were used to present Annapolis's colonial past (Leone et al. 1987). In examining archaeology's ideology, Leone was exploring theoretical questions that were parallel to those of postcolonial scholars both in Africa and in Australia who questioned how their links to a colonialist ideology affected their research (e.g. Hall 1984; Smith 2000, 2001; Shepherd 2002b, 2003). Randall McGuire has extended this work to a critique of capitalism as a structuring force in US and Latin American archaeology in an attempt to create the conditions for a more humane world (McGuire 1992, 2006, 2008).

Today historical archaeology is a global pursuit that examines the growth of the modern world (e.g. Orser 1996; Funari et al. 1999; Paynter 2000a, 2000b; Hall and Silliman 2006; Hicks and Beaudry 2006). Although it has often been perceived as a North American invention, in various forms historical archaeology has been a part of the archaeology of Africa, Europe, and Britain for an equally long period (Courtney 1999; Johnson 1999, 2006; Schuyler 1999; Hicks 2003; Reid and Lane 2004; Hicks and Beaudry 2006). In many respects, the historical archaeologies of Africa, Europe, and Britain stem from the close relationship that has always existed between history and archaeology in these parts of the world. As historical archaeology has grown, so has its theoretical breadth. One example is the growing focus on empire as a common theoretical focus linking recent explorations in the Middle East (Baram and Carroll 2000), Africa (Perry 1999; DeCorse 2001a), India (Dhavalikar 1999; Sinopoli 2006), Sri Lanka (Jayasena 2006), Europe (Horning 2000; Johnson 2006), and the New World (Mrozowski 2009). When combined with archaeology's more

traditional research on early empires, this investigation of more recent empires offers the potential to transcend the boundaries between those who study the recent and more distant pasts.

We believe that the role of historical archaeology in the history of archaeological theory remains underappreciated. This lack of appreciation has its roots in the broad rejection of history that accompanied the growth of processual archaeology, as Trigger (1978) observed more than thirty years ago. Culture process was emphasized at the expense of culture history, even though process and history are codependent. Today, there is a new appreciation of history as providing the essential context for understanding the manner in which meaning is attached to the material world both at the local level and over the long term (Johnson 1999). With its focus on the archaeology of capitalism, historical archaeology can contribute to larger debates concerning neo-colonialism, empire, and their connections to modern nations (e.g. Baram and Carroll 2000). It is thus well positioned to contribute to some of the more contentious debates that have confronted anthropology and, by extension, anthropological archaeology.

Living in a Material World

From its inception, archaeology has been defined with reference to "things," the things we humans use to make our living in the world. The word "archaeology" itself comes from the Greek word *arkhaiologia* and can be translated "discourse about ancient things" (Daniel 1981:13). However, the ways in which archaeologists have conceptualized things have varied considerably over time. Broadly speaking, these approaches differ on whether things are to be considered most like culture, like language, or as social networks. The "material culture" approach tends to equate artifacts with past cultures where the part metonymically stands for the whole. The "material language" approach regards artifacts as having properties similar to, but not identical with, language in the signaling of specific meanings. The relatively new "material network" approach regards humans and things as entangled in complex networks where the actors are human–thing hybrids. It is important to note that while these approaches do bear a chronological relationship with one another, versions of each are in use today. The focus on things under the heading of "materiality" is increasingly bringing together anthropological archaeology, social anthropology, sociology, and museum studies (Dant 2005; Miller 2005; Dudley 2009; Shove et al. 2009).

Archaeology became a science in the 18th century (Willey and Sabloff 1980; Daniel 1981; Trigger 2006). Its early focus was on constructing systematic typologies that had chronological and geographical significance. Specific artifacts came to be valued as horizon markers, indicating the temporal and spatial extent of archaeological cultures and permitting conclusions about diffusion and migration. This is the basis for the "material culture" approach. In Europe, for example, the Bell Beaker culture was defined by the common use of a distinctive pottery style, a beaker with an inverted bell-shaped profile possibly used in the consumption of alcoholic beverages and distributed across a large part of western Europe during the late third millennium BC (Nicholis 2001). In the United States Southwest, scholars mapped out the distribution of pottery types, equating them with past peoples. A good example is the Red-on-buff culture (now the Hohokam culture), which was defined on the basis of red-on-buff pottery found throughout the Sonoran desert area (Gladwin and Gladwin 1929).

The new archaeology extended the material culture approach beyond historical questions to address adaptive systems. Binford (1962) argued that a key flaw of traditional archaeology was its undifferentiated view of artifacts such that they were treated as equal and comparable traits. For him, artifacts have their primary functional context in the different operational subsystems of the total cultural system. Following Leslie White (1959), Binford famously defined culture as being composed of three subsystems and proposed that artifacts were articulated differently within each. He identified "technomic artifacts" (those artifacts having their primary function in coping with the physical environment), "sociotechnic artifacts" (those artifacts having their primary function in the social component of the cultural system), and "ideotechnic artifacts" (those artifacts having their primary function

in the ideological component of the social system) (Binford 1962:220–221). Schiffer (1976) regarded material culture studies as the centerpiece of his behavioral archaeology. He used it to redefine archaeology in universalist terms, from the study of past material traces to the study of material culture at all times and places. This reorientation gave archaeology an immediate relevance to the contemporary world (Gould and Schiffer 1981).

A parallel trajectory developing within processual archaeology was the "material language" approach, whereby things were understood as part of symbolic behavior that communicated adaptive information. In an influential paper, Martin Wobst (1977) proposed a relationship between stylistic behavior and information exchange. He reviewed the standard approaches to artifact style that typically distinguished form from function. Form was defined as that which was left over after function was explained. Wobst argued that style possessed certain functions, and suggested that stylistic studies should focus on the investigation of the ways form conveys information. He illustrated this point in an ethnographic analysis of clothing style in contemporary Yugoslavia. He found that individuals varied their dress far beyond what was needed to adapt to their environment. He interpreted this variation as a result of people making statements about their social affiliation.

Conkey (1978, 1980) adopted the material language approach in her study of the evolution of Paleolithic art. She argued that art can be understood as symbolic behavior involving culturally standardized systems of visual representation that function to order experience and organize it into discrete categories. Because the production of art is labor-intensive and competes with other activities, she suggested that it must have had some adaptive value for the individual artist as well as the group. For Conkey, those societies that maximized the intergenerational transmission of information through art may have enjoyed an adaptive advantage in terms of increased life spans, delayed maturation processes, and/or encoding strategies. She then reviewed the archaeological evidence for human evolution and suggested that an explosion of symbolic behavior occurred sometime after 70,000 years ago and perhaps as recently as

40,000 years ago. For Conkey, Paleolithic art can be seen as part of the diversification of symbolic behavior and represents an attempt to reduce the arbitrariness of symbols into manageable categories. She regards style in Paleolithic art to be an informational process that favors behavioral predictability and assists in the common organization of different behavioral domains. This, in turn, facilitates groups in establishing identities and maintaining social boundaries in relation to other groups.

A more recent example of the language approach is James Skibo and Michael Schiffer's study of the sale of pottery among the Kalinga in the Philippines. Their approach is based upon Schiffer's (1999) theory of material communication, which employs Ferdinand de Saussure's (1966) classic speech circuit model to describe the communicative process. Schiffer develops a formal model where each interactor plays three major roles, as sender, emitter, and receiver, and these roles typically involve performances with artifacts. For him, archaeology needs to explicate the changing character of person–artifact relationships. In their Kalinga case study, Skibo and Schiffer (2008:13) suggest that when potters with their wares come to a village it is possible to isolate different types of communication in the behavioral chain. The sender is the itinerant potter, the emitter is the pot for sale, and the receiver is the potential pottery consumer. The consumer can identify a particular kind of pot (e.g. a pot made in the Pasil Valley) based upon various visual performance characteristics based upon the potter's technical choices. After the sale and the pot enters its use life, the interactors shift. So, if a woman takes a pot to her field or to a funeral at another village, she is silently communicating to people that she is from or has an association with the Pasil River Valley.

Postprocessual archaeology developed a post-structural version of the material language approach in which things were regarded as text. Hodder (1986) originally proposed this idea in his book *Reading the Past*. He notes that the text analogy means "in association" or "in context." Artifacts are silent only when they are "out of their texts." That is to say, the network of relations between the artifact, its discovery locus, and other artifacts and features constitutes the essential field by which meaning can be read.

The important insight here is the structuralist view that meaning is a relational quality and not a transcendent one that inheres in the artifact through all time and space. Hodder later argued, following Paul Ricoeur (1971), that human action can be conceived as having the properties of discourse and text. He writes that "any material action, such as the forming of a pot or the discarding of an artifact, has a 'propositional' content which can be identified and reidentified as the same" (Hodder 1989:257). Here he extends Ricoeur's view of social action to incorporate the making of things. For Hodder, the archaeological implications of his textual approach are twofold: it reveals that material culture meanings are continually generated through practice, and it links power and social strategy with symbolic meaning.

Tilley (1991) further developed the text approach in his book *Material Culture and Text: The Art of Ambiguity*. Inspired by Jacques Derrida (1976), he begins with a comparison of material culture and writing and suggests that material culture is "written" through a practice of differentiation in just the same manner as phonetic writing. He suggests that "both result in the material fixation of meaning which by contrast to speech is indirectly communicated in the sense that I decorate a pot by dividing up the empty space of the clay or write a letter by inscribing marks on a blank sheet of paper and at some time in the future you read and interpret the visual medium, able by virtue of the material fixation to read what I have produced" (Tilley 1991:17). He notes, however, that material culture does not communicate in the same way as language or the written word; rather it is structured in an analogous fashion. In his later work, Tilley (1999) has emphasized the idea of material culture as "solid metaphor." Here he is referring to the idea that objects are not merely the product of human activity; they are rather created out of persons, where production can be regarded as a performance in which persons and objects co-create each other. He suggests that the artifact, through its presence, "speaks what cannot be spoken, writes what cannot be written, and articulates that which remains conceptually separated in social practice (Tilley 1999:103).

A variant of the material language approach is the view of things as discursive practice. Here material culture is viewed as text and symbol, active media in a larger social discourse. Drawing on a variety of theorists, including Roland Barthes (1957, 1964), Mary Douglas (1973; see also Douglas and Isherwood 1979), and Victor Turner (1974), Mary Beaudry, Lauren Cook, and Stephen Mrozowski (1991) conceptualize material things as critical elements in a public and private discourse in which social identities are negotiated. The unfolding of this discourse in various contexts raises questions concerning power and its ability to silence the voice of the oppressed. In arguing for a bottom-up, inside-out approach, Beaudry et al. counter the dominant ideology thesis of Louis Althusser (1971) in suggesting that material things can serve to mitigate power through the construction of individual and group identities. This approach has subsequently been incorporated into historical archaeology's expanding focus on the intersectionality of race, class, sexuality, gender, and ethnicity in the construction and negotiation of identity (Singleton 1999, 2006; Delle et al. 2000; Paynter 2000a, 2000b; Franklin 2001; Orser 2001, 2006; Mrozowski 2006; Voss 2006).

Recently, the discourse approach has expanded to consider how things actively mediate social relations. This view underlies "material engagement theory," a key component of cognitive archaeology. According to Renfrew (2001b, 2004), a new kind of human engagement with the material world emerged around 10,000 years ago. He writes that "it was when some of these materials themselves took on, or were led to take on, symbolic power that the process of engagement became a powerful driving force for social and economic change" (Renfrew 2001b:127). This new kind of engagement was facilitated by the development of a sedentary lifestyle. Material symbols were created through a process of "substantialization." Here Renfrew emphasizes that it is incorrect to presume that mind precedes practice and concept precedes material symbol. He writes that "symbols are not always just the reflection or 'materialization' of pre-existing concepts. The substantive engagement process brings the two forward together" (Renfrew 2001b:129). His material engagement theory is thus an attempt to join the physical and conceptual aspects of materiality, where the term "engagement" is used to indicate a unifying relationship that joins together the standard oppositions of mind and matter, symbol and referent, signified and signifier. For Renfrew (2004:30), the material culture of any society is a vast continuing engagement that defines the corporate life of that society.

This view of things as mediating social relations also underpins new developments in semiotic archaeology. These studies reveal that material culture, like language, often plays a central role in mediating social identities and relations (Preucel and Bauer 2001; Lele 2006; Preucel 2006; Watts 2009). However, they also show that material culture does not participate in the same kind of structured system as language. Objects are not words and there is nothing comparable to syntax or grammar. But because material culture has concrete form and substance, it has the power to fix meanings in ways that are not possible with language. Several scholars have been attracted to the version of semiotics developed by Charles Sanders Peirce and have applied it successfully in pragmatic anthropology (Daniel 1984; Singer 1984; Parmentier 1997; Keane 2003). This approaches enjoys certain compelling advantages over its Saussurian rival. It does not privilege language as the model for semiotics; rather it offers a more general model which incorporates language, social practices, and material culture, indeed all of culture. It addresses, in Peirce's words, the "outward clash" of the real world. This is to say that it is a pragmatic rather than an idealist philosophy.

The "material network" approach finds its origins in the critique of economic anthropology. In 1986, Arjun Appadurai, a cultural anthropologist, edited an influential book entitled *The Social Life of Things* (Appadurai 1986a) deriving from an Ethnohistory Workshop at the University of Pennsylvania. In his introduction, he argued that the standard distinction between gift and commodity is flawed because it treats these concepts as essentialist categories. A commodity is better regarded as a things in a certain situation, that is, in a "commodity state." Appadurai defined this state as "the situation in which its exchangeability (past, present, or future) for some other thing is its socially relevant feature" (Appadurai 1986b:13). Things move in and out of the commodity state and such movements can be slow or fast, reversible or terminal, normal or deviant. Appadurai makes the point that the commodity candidacy of things is a cultural process referring to the standards and criteria that define the exchangeability of things in any particular context.

Igor Kopytoff (1986) has approached the commoditization process by examining the boundaries between persons and things in the context of slavery. He suggests that slavery is a process by which people are commoditized and decommoditized. The process involves the removal of an individual from an original social setting, his or her commoditization, followed by his or her singularization in a new setting, and then the possibility of recommoditization (Kopytoff 1986:65). His point is that the slave is a commodity only during a relatively short period of time, after which he or she becomes more of a singular individual as he or she is integrated into the host community. While one can take issue with Kopytoff's view that slaves ever escape the commodity state within the institution of slavery, his idea that things may be usefully viewed from a biographical perspective is certainly valuable. The study of the social lives of things involves exploring the possibilities inherent in their "social status" and determining how these possibilities are realized (see Hoskins 1998). So, for example, in a culture contact situation what is significant in the adoption of European objects is not so much the fact that they are adopted, but rather they ways in which they are incorporated into the social order (Silliman 2005). This social life of things approach has captured the attention of many archaeologists, particularly those interested in Schiffer's behavioral chain analysis (Schiffer 1975; Skibo et al. 1995).

A key issue in the "material network" approach is the question of agency. Can things be understood as having a form of subjectivity all their own? Or is their agency a partial agency, lent to them by means of their human manipulators? Alfred Gell (1998) develops a sophisticated theory of the agency of art objects, which recognizes the partial agency of things. His basic thesis is that works of art can be treated as "person-like" in the sense that they are both the sources of and targets for social agency. This view involves a reengagement with animism, the belief in the spirit of things, which was a traditional topic of early anthropology and is of growing interest in indigenous archaeology. Gell suggests that people and things share certain attributes that do not necessarily collapse the categorical difference between them. This implies that it doesn't necessarily matter what a thing is, in and of itself. What matters is where it stands in a network of social relations. For Gell (1998:123), all that may be necessary for things to become "social agents" is that there be persons in their vicinity and not that they be biological entities themselves.

Several scholars have taken the issue of agency further and argued that we need to consider things as having their own ontological existence. Bjørnar Olsen writes that "although the textual analogy was important and productive, we come to ignore the differences between things and text: that material culture *is* in the world and plays a fundamentally different constitutive role for our being in this world than texts and language (Olsen 2003:90, his emphasis). He continues to say that things do more than express meanings; they act in the world. For this reason, he proposes a "symmetrical archaeology" where all physical entities are conceptualized as beings in the world alongside humans, plants, and animals. Here he draws inspiration from Actor Network Theory (ANT) (Latour 1996, 1999, 2005; Law and Hassard 1999) and its principle of generalized symmetry. ANT holds that human and non-human should be integrated into the same conceptual framework and accorded equal amounts of agency (Knappett and Malafouris 2009). According to Timothy Webmoor and Christopher Witmore (2005), symmetrical archaeology is an attempt "to re-characterize our relationships with what remains of the material past and contemporary things in ways that are not based upon the dualistic schemes characteristic of modernist thought ... by considering hybrids of humans and things in networks of being and becoming." Although sometimes characterized as a version of practice theory (Fine 2007), ANT nonetheless risks imposing a Euro-American preoccupation with society and technology onto non-European cultures (Strathern 1996:521). Moreover, ANT fails to consider adequately power relations and how networks based upon social interactions are maintained and made durable.

The idea of things as having agency is also a component of "thing theory," developed by the

English literature professor Bill Brown (1998, 2003, 2004). Brown is particularly interested in focusing attention "not just on things as such, but on the place things occupy in daily life; the place they occupy, if you will, in the history of human-being; the pressure they exert on us to engage them as something other than mere surfaces" (Brown 2003:12). He makes a distinction between history *of* things and history *in* things, where the former refers to the circulation of the object in different cultural fields and the latter describes the crystallization of the anxieties and aspirations that linger in the material object (Brown 1998). He asks, "What desires did objects organize? What fantasies did they provoke? Through what economies were they assigned new value? Through what epistemologies were they assigned meaning?" (Brown 2003:12). For Brown, the status of things is inseparable from the question of what they do, or what can be done with them. Hodder (2006) uses this approach to emphasize the codependencies and entanglements between humans and non-humans and posit that long-term change comes about through the dispersed interactions of these entanglements. He favors this theory because it is eclectic in the sense that it is congruent with aspects of many current theoretical agendas, from experimental and behavioral archaeology to neo-evolutionary and selectionist models. He also observes that it links these theoretical agendas with archaeometry and archaeological science. Indeed, such is the growing interest in thing theory that it was the inspiration for an entire session at the New York Theoretical Archaeology Group conference in 2008.

The Problem with Prehistory

The term "prehistory" occupies a privileged status in the history of archaeology. Indeed, it might be said to be the originary term. Archaeology has sometimes been characterized as the field that begins where history leaves off. Glyn Daniel's book *The Idea of Prehistory* (1962), although published later, is thus the logical precursor to R. G. Collingwood's book *The Idea of History* (1946). To his credit, Daniel was aware of some of the problems with the term. He wrote that some scholars "have complained that

prehistory ... was essentially a misnomer [since] there was, strictly speaking, no time in the past of man before he had any history" (Daniel 1964:10). More recently, George Nicholas and Tom Andrews (1997:xiv–xv) note that "the term prehistory is often misconstrued to mean 'without history,' implying that archaeologists present or support the view that Indigenous peoples had no history. What prehistory actually refers to is archaeology done without use of, or access to, written records by the investigators of past human societies – a tremendous difference and this meaning is conveyed by all standard archaeology textbooks." However, prehistory is not an impartial term. It is grounded in social evolutionary theory and the idea of the progress of civilization. Prehistory and its cousins, "pre-Columbian" and "premodern," have generated and continue to generate profoundly negative consequences for non-Western peoples.

Daniel Wilson is usually credited as the first scientist to use the term "prehistory" in the English language. In his book *The Archaeology and the Prehistoric Annals of Scotland* (Wilson 1851), he uses the term to refer to the races preceding the historically known nations of Northern Europe. He later extended the term as a general description of ancient and modern tribes without written records and which are known only through archaeology (Wilson 1862). Prehistory was thus conceived as an immature stage of human development. He writes that "the object [of archaeology] ... is to view Man, as far as possible, unaffected by those modifying influences which accompany the development of nations and the maturity of a true historic period" (Wilson 1862:vii–ix). Sir John Lubbock published his book *Pre-historic Times* in 1865. His goal was to describe "the principles of prehistoric archaeology" and to explicate "the conditions of man in primeval times" (Lubbock 1865:vi). While acknowledging the unity of the human race, he adopted an evolutionary perspective and held that the sufferings of the "savages" were alleviated by the benefits of civilization.

Recently, a number of scholars have offered pointed criticisms of the term "prehistory." In her book, *The Land of Prehistory*, Alice Kehoe presents an alternative account of the development of American archaeology. She writes,

"American archaeology . . . seemed a natural proceeding; it only extended an Old World prehistory that celebrated the power of industrial technology through a chronicle of artifacts absolutely alienated from their makers, the mute history of the proletariat whose role is to continue manufacturing, silently" (Kehoe 1998:208–209). In America, prehistory was equated with an arrested stage of development, since there was no Native industrial revolution or Native capitalism. The tacit assumption was that Native Americans never achieved a stage of civilization comparable to that of the colonizing societies, and this legitimized the latter's dominance over the former. Kehoe concludes by saying, "American archaeology is ready to be a mature science, one that accepts the primacy of its empirical data – for these can outlast theories – and the political and human ramifications of its actions as it reflectively constructs and compares interpretations" (Kehoe 1998:230).

Similarly, Stephen Lekson (2009) has critiqued the standard narrative of Southwestern archaeology for not adequately addressing what happened in the past. The standard narrative, which he says began in the 1880s and continues up to the present day, sees slow and steady progress in Pueblo Indian life culminating in the modern reservation communities. He observes that texts we write about the ancient Southwest are surprisingly dull and lifeless. They typically revolve around the narration of one of three great events: the adoption of agriculture, the formation of towns, and the abandonment of those same towns. He writes, "I don't think it happened that way. I think the Southwest had rises and falls, kings and commoners, wars and peace, triumphs and failures" (Lekson 2009:3). Lekson then offers his own version of Southwestern political history, one that unites Chaco Canyon, Aztec Ruin, and Paquimé in a broad political power shift involving the migration of elites from Chaco, first north to Aztec and then south to Paquimé (Lekson 1999). He proposes that the modern pueblo communities of Hopi, Zuni, and the Rio Grande developed as a reaction against the Chaco state, a conscious rejection of the earlier hierarchies. This is, as he puts it, "real history."

Ian McNiven and Lynette Russell have extended the critique of prehistory to Australian archaeology. They suggest that the colonial culture of Australian archaeology is responsible for the form and current state of the relationships between indigenous peoples and archaeologists (McNiven and Russell 2005). Unlike the United States, Australia has failed to enter into treaties with Australian Aborigines and the Torres Strait Islanders. McNiven and Russell identify a suite of negative tropes with deep historical roots in Western thought that have aided in dissociating indigenous people from their traditional lands and ancestral places. The tropes include the claims that the Aboriginal peoples are "living fossils," that they are not the "original inhabitants" of Australia, and that they have no history. They single out the notion of prehistory for special comment. and cite a member of the Tasmanian Aboriginal Land Council as saying that "from our perspective the claims that parts of our heritage belong to all 'mankind' and that they are of 'world significance' are one more example of the continuing appropriation of our land and our heritage" (McNiven and Russell 2005:215–216). Linda Burney (1999:54), an Aboriginal scholar, writes that "the point is that we find this term [prehistory] offensive, most particularly because of the related meanings of 'prehistoric,' such as 'primitive' and 'subhuman' – two of the most offensive stereotypes imposed on Aboriginal people since colonization." Steve Hemming (2002:60) notes that the use of prehistory has created a false dichotomy between contemporary Aboriginal peoples and their pre-European pasts. McNiven and Russell (2005:258) conclude that archaeology in settler colonies, such as Australia, Canada, and the United States, has served the interests of the colonial project to represent indigenous peoples and their past as the story of "a lesser people in possession of a lesser history."

Prehistory is often linked to a series of related terms that serve to divorce indigenous peoples from their lands. A particularly good example is "abandonment." This term runs counter to the deep spiritual attachments indigenous peoples have to sacred places (Watkins 2005). Much of Southwestern archaeology, for example, has focused on explaining the abandonments of Chaco Canyon or Mesa Verde (Cameron and Tomka 1993). Less frequently have scholars considered that the absence of permanent settlement does not necessarily mean abandonment since such regions may be used periodically or season-ally, often in the contexts of religious pilgrim-ages. What we see then is not the relinquishment of use, but rather a shift in the kind of use. In Western law, however, land's uses are ranked such that land improved though agriculture is valued over unimproved land. Another term often applied to Native American groups that contributes to a distorted view of their history is "marginal" (Doughton 1997). Native peoples are said to occupy marginal habitats, or to eke out marginal existences. The various policies of the Bureau of Indian Affairs and the Indian Agencies were typically justified on the grounds that they would raise the standard of living. The use of these terms has helped codify the idea that Native Americans are "peoples without history." Beyond the obvious problems such a notion would carry for any group, this idea also has concrete legal ramifications for indigenous people seeking recognition in land claim disputes.

Historians have been equally complicit in per-petuating the division between prehistory and history. The received view of history is that it begins with the rise of civilization in Egypt, Mesopotamia, or Greece, approximately 6,000 years ago. In this scenario, the Paleolithic is rele-gated to the status of a "prologue to history, humanity's apprenticeship" (Smail 2008:39). Historians have maintained prehistory as a buf-fer zone, keeping separate the biological evolu-tion of hominids and the origins of civilization. As Daniel Smail (2008) suggests, the deep gulf between the two was "humanity's Rubicon." Once it was crossed, sometime during the Neolithic, humanity embarked upon the path to civilization, and created history in the process. The myth of the Paleolithic was that it was a period of stasis, a timeless dystopia. To a large extent, this view still dominates the teaching of history today. Smail writes that "the deep past of humanity still plays a marginal role in the grand historical narrative as measured by the history curricula offered in secondary schools and colleges in the United States and the textbooks used to teach them" (Smail 2008:2). This is problematic since new archaeological and genetic studies are challenging the notion of the timeless Paleolithic. Smail notes that archaeolo-gists have made new discoveries that are

revealing late Paleolithic villages, long-distance trading networks, and aspects of social memory. He thus favors a "deep history" which places the Paleolithic and Neolithic alongside the Postlithic in order to acknowledge the full chronology of the human past.

The ideas of deep time and deep history res-onate with Native American oral historical tra-ditions. In Africa, North America, and Australia, concepts of history have relied heavily upon oral testimony that, in some instances, is of great antiquity (Echo-Hawk 2000). The idea of deep history is also proving useful for archaeologists working with North American Native groups engaged in disputes with the United States government concerning their recognition as fed-erally recognized tribal nations (Miller 2003; Daehnke 2007; Mrozowski et al. 2009). In North America there is a long history of colonial and federal governments raising questions con-cerning the persistence and authenticity of Native American groups. These problems still influence the political realities that confront many tribal nations (Den Ouden 2005; Raibmon 2005). In this regard, the replacement of prehis-tory with deep history serves two purposes: it provides a new focus for archaeological interpretation while, at the same time, acknow-ledging the contemporaneity of all humans across the globe.

Practice Makes Perfect?

Rethinking prehistory in its various manifest-ations is just one of several trends that are influencing the theoretical trajectory of contem-porary archaeology. A key development in archaeology and social theory in the past 20 years is the growing significance of theories of practice (Schatzki et al. 2001). These approaches have their origins in the critiques of functional-ism, structuralism, and Marxism put forward most notably by Pierre Bourdieu in social anthropology, and by Anthony Giddens in soci-ology. They typically emphasize the generative potential of individual agency and the guiding frameworks of social structure, specifically the routinized and performative character of action and its dependence on tacit knowledge and implicit understandings. Significantly, practice theory also bears a close relationship to pragmatism. Before turning to a discussion of different applications of practice theory, we begin with a historical review of its relationship to structuralism.

Structuralism is a way of thinking about the world in terms of structures that are themselves composed of individual entities organized in relations of mutual interdependence. It is based upon concepts of totality, self-regulation, and transformation common not only to linguistics and anthropology, but also to mathematics, physics, biology, psychology, and philosophy. It underpins such topics as general systems theory, ecosystems, network analysis, cybernetics, and information theory, which developed in the 1930s and 1940s. Structuralism is usually associated with the linguistic approach of Saussure (1966), who emphasized the study of deep structure, that is, rules, grammar, and models, in contrast to surface phenomena, such as speech acts, which he considered accidental and variable. This focus on structure, while valuable and important, had the effect of detaching language from its social context. In the 1950s and 1960s, Claude Lévi-Strauss (1963, 1966) and Roland Barthes (1957, 1964) elaborated Saussure's approach and applied it to the study of social and cultural phenomena. Largely due to their work, the language model spread rapidly across the humanities and social sciences in the 1970s and 1980s, in a movement that has been called "the linguistic turn" (Clark 2004). It was especially popular in literary theory and criticism (Culler 1975, 1981; Hawkes 2003). There are also strong associations with Freudian psychoanalysis and Marxist theory. Jacques Lacan (1977), for example, used Saussure's model to interrogate the Freudian unconscious.

The role of structuralism in the emergence of processual archaeology has not been fully appreciated (but see Hodder 1982b; Leone 1982, 1986; Wylie 1982; Conkey 1989; Gosden 1994). This is unfortunate since although never a main approach, structuralism closely articulated with the cognitive revolution and the interest in information theory. One of the earliest examples of structuralist archaeology is the work of James Deetz and his historical archaeology students at Brown University. In his popular book *Invitation to Archaeology* (Deetz 1967), he defined anthropological archaeology as the study of past peoples in terms of their physical, cultural, and psychological aspects. By identifying the psychological as a legitimate topic of investigation, he immediately broadened the focus of processual archaeology beyond its narrow adaptationalist agenda. He devoted an entire chapter to structure defined as the rules that produce artifacts and govern the combination of their attributes. Although he does not cite Saussure, Deetz's approach is clearly influenced by structural linguistics. In subsequent publications, Deetz (1972, 1977) was more explicit about the genesis of his interest in structuralism, citing the work of both Lévi-Strauss (1963, 1966) as well as that of folklorist Henry Glassie (1972, 1975).

Although not all of Deetz's students at Brown adopted his structuralist approach, many did and expanded upon his ideas. In her study of 18th-century English and American ceramics, Anne Yentsch (1991) argues that a culture/nature opposition underlying ceramic manufacture and use was part of the negotiation of social inequality. Her interpretation of the meaning of white and earth-toned pots is built up from associations and contrasts in the placing of ceramics in male and female, public and private parts of houses. She also draws parallels between changes through time in ceramic assemblages and changes in the use of space, and makes links to variation in the use of spices, the complexity of recipes, and the proliferation of knives, forks, and spoons (see also Yentsch 1994). These similarities and differences in apparently disconnected spheres are made sense of in terms of abstractions. For example, nothing obviously links the use of natural building materials to a lack of separation in the use of ceramics and in the use of space. But such a link is made possible by the concept of "organic solidarity." Yentsch uses the abstractions culture/nature and public/private to draw out the similarities in her covarying data. She goes on to argue that these abstractions were used as metaphors in the creation of inequality.

The primary deficiency of structuralism for postprocessual archaeologists was its failure to account for change. Hodder (1982a) and his students embraced aspects of Bourdieu's theory of practice and Giddens's structuration theory. Anthony Giddens developed his structuration theory as a way to recuperate the notion of the competent and knowledgeable actor without lapsing into subjectivism. For him, the basic domain of the social sciences is neither individual experience, nor any social totality, but rather social practices ordered across space and time (Giddens 1979, 1981, 1984). At the core of his theory is the idea of "duality of structure," the view that structure is both the medium and outcome of the practices that constitute the social system. Stated differently, social actions are not brought into being by social actors, but continually re-created by them by the very means by which humans express themselves as actors. In their activities, social actors reproduce the conditions that make their activities possible, an insight originally recognized by Marx. Bourdieu proposed his theory of practice as a critique of structuralism. He argued that practices cannot be deduced from the social conditions underlying their production (Bourdieu 1977). Rather, they can only be understood by being related to the objective structure defining those conditions and the particular state of that structure. For Bourdieu, *habitus* is naturalized history as it is reproduced through practice. Both of these perspectives, Giddens's and Bourdieu's, ultimately derived from critiques of Marx's notion of praxis, are attempts to overcome the classic oppositions of the individual and society, free will and determinism, functionalism and structuralism. Significantly, they also represent a shift in scale from grand theories of adaptation and conformity to local theories of negotiation and contingency.

John Barrett (1988, 1994, 2001) provided one of the earliest and most sustained considerations of structuration theory in archaeology. Following Giddens, he suggests that the domain of the social sciences (including archaeology) is neither the experience of the social actor, nor the existence of social totality, but rather social practices ordered across time and space (Barrett 2001:149). He argues that structures need to be considered not as constraining or determining action, but as fields of possibilities (cf. Barrett 1988). He makes a useful analogy with language, saying that it is both the medium and outcome of the practice of talking. This, then, is what Giddens means by the "duality of structure." It does not reinstate the opposition of agency and structure, but rather refers to the recursive

properties of social practices that effect particular outcomes and, in the process, instantiate structure. Barrett (2001) also draws inspiration from Bourdieu and his characterization of the generative potential of non-discursive knowledge. Practice thus involves both knowing the rules in a discursive sense and a practical mastery of "how to go on" (cf. Barrett 1988). Taking gift giving as an example, Barrett shows that human identities are objectified not only in the things exchanged, but also in the labor of making things in the first place (see Voss 2008). For him, materiality cannot be simply reduced to the archaeological traces of past practices. Rather, it must consider how materiality is engaged in the very structuring of those practices.

Closely related to practice theory is agency. Marcia-Anne Dobres and John Robb (2000) have reviewed the history of this concept in archaeology. They suggest that the interest in agency comes from four distinct sources. The first is the archaeology of gender and the study of gender dynamics. These studies typically emphasize the microscale and the role of the individual. The second is a greater appreciation of the sources of material culture variation. There is an increased focus on the contexts of negotiation and social action. The third is the influence of phenomenology and Giddens's structuration theory. They note that these approaches emphasize that structures are not fixed or static, but always "in process." The fourth is the study of social inequality. These studies show how the strategic pursuit of power can lead to long-term change. Dobres and Robb then identify a variety of views, ranging from the idea that agency is the constitution of an individual as a psychological entity, to the experience of individual action in creating a life story, the process of intersubjective engagement with the material world, and the successful deployment of discursive and non-discursive technological knowledge and skill (Dobres and Robb 2000:9). Agency is now even being applied to inanimate things, with somewhat unclear implications (Knappett and Malafouris 2009). One persistent problem with studies of agency is that they often neglect structure and assume that agency is identical with individual action or behavior.

Perhaps the most sophisticated use of practice theory in archaeology is the work of Charles

Orser, who applies the approach to the study of race. Orser (2007) builds on the work of Bourdieu in developing a framework to help understand how groups such as African Americans, Asian Americans, and Irish Americans were viewed as biologically inferior to mainstream white society. This process of racialization unfolded during a time when Western society was being shaped by colonialism, industrialization, and the rapid growth of urban communities. Orser contextualizes his discussion by noting the difficulties of understanding the way human agency articulates with larger societal structures (see Johnson 1989; Gero 2000). Drawing on the work of Donald Donham (1999), Orser distinguishes two forms of agency, historical agency and epochal agency. Historical agency refers to the struggle of groups to overcome structural inequalities, while epochal agency refers to the cumulative result of individual actions that contribute to the reproduction of those inequalities (Orser 2007:53). Orser also acknowledges the inspiration of Braudel's (1981) notion of the structures of everyday life as an example of the epochal agency that he incorporates in his study of race. In addition, he borrows from the work of microhistorians, such as Carlo Ginzburg (1980), in gaining a clearer picture of instances where individual beliefs or actions collide with those who use their power to perpetuate societal structures. The powerful often rely upon spatial structures to serve as their allies (Ashmore and Sabloff 2002; Delle 1998; Mrozowski 1999, 2006). In addressing the issue of space, Orser (2007) deploys the work of Edward Soja (1980, 1989) and Henri Lefebvre (1991) in arguing that space was often used to marginalize groups such as the Chinese and Irish in the United States during the 19th century.

By combining the concepts of historical agency and epochal agency with Bourdieu's concepts of *habitus*, *doxa* (being the beliefs that are taken for granted in a specific society), and *fields* (being the network of individuals and groups that join in support of the *habitus*), Orser is able to demonstrate the manner in which material culture and space were used to racialize the Chinese of California and the Irish of New York. He notes, for example, that the racialized discourse of 19th-century popular literature depicted the Chinese populations of California

as having insulated themselves from mainstream, white society so they could continue cultural practices that were viewed as indicative of a backward people. This is just one of the barriers that the Chinese faced in attempting to maintain some semblance of cultural identity while building new communities. The archaeological evidence indicates that, contrary to the view of a marginalized population, the Chinese purchased many of the same items that whites did, while at the same time purchasing patent medicines that Orser suggests helped them avoid local doctors who may have harbored racist views. Orser argues that from a pragmatic perspective the Chinese were able to adopt strategies that countered some of the epochal structures that racialized them as a group. Although they were not able to overcome the racism that they faced, the cultural practices evidenced in the archaeological record suggest they were able to mitigate some of the forces that sought to marginalize them. Orser makes a related argument concerning the New York Irish, who faced similar attempts at racialization. Here again space, in the form of segregation, served to marginalize the Irish. Like the Chinese of California the Irish were able to construct lives that were materially quite similar to the native-born populations of New York. Based on archaeological evidence, it is even possible to argue that the materiality of Irish often rivaled that of native-born working-class families, and, in some instances, those of middle-class families (see also Yamin 2000). Like the Chinese, the Irish of New York relied upon patent medicines; however, in this instance, it is not clear whether this is evidence that the New York Irish sought to minimize their contact with a racist medical establishment or whether economics limited access to adequate health care.

The Three R's: Repatriation, Reconciliation, and Restitution

We (the editors) live in a neoliberal society. Neoliberalism refers to global market-capitalism and free-trade policies that emerged in the first half of the 20th century (Patterson 2001; Harvey 2007). It is often used interchangeably with "globalization." But neoliberalism is not only about economics; it is also a social and moral philosophy qualitatively different from liberalism. It emphasizes such values as individual responsibility, deregulation, and privatization over the public good. These values have come to be expressed in specific ways in the Western discourses about heritage and culture resource management. In particular, heritage is typically globalized and regarded as an universal product belonging equally to all peoples (Cuno 2008). But this argument is a peculiarly Western conceit, one that appropriates other people's pasts under the pretext of a common humanism. It belies the fact that heritage is increasingly promoted as an economic development tool linked to tourism and elite consumption. From this perspective, heritage is a commodity, something to be traded, packaged, and marketed, just like any other resource.

Today, the neoliberal society is coming under sharp attack. The Western view of the world no longer holds the status that it once did, in part because of postcolonialism (Patterson 1997; Liebmann and Rizvi 2008). There is now a global heritage discourse increasingly attached to human rights issues that is having dramatic real-world consequences (Tunbridge and Ashworth 1996; Smith 2006). It is no longer possible to mount a museum exhibit and not consider issues of ownership and representation: how the museum acquired the objects, whether the objects should be returned to their home country, and whether the exhibit was curated with input from the relevant nations and/or descendant communities. Some important examples of different facets of this discourse include the Burra Charter in Australia, the creation of Nunavut in Canada, the passage of the Native American Graves Protection and Repatriation Act in the United States, the establishment of the Truth and Reconciliation Committee in South Africa, and the New York Metropolitan Museum of Art's return of the Euphronios vase to Italy, each of which we shall now discuss in turn.

One of the most influential documents providing for the care and conservation of heritage places is the Burra Charter (Walker and Marquis-Kyle 2004). In 1964, the Second International Congress of Architects and Technicians of Historic Monuments meeting in Venice approved principles guiding the preservation and restoration of ancient buildings (Sabloff 2008). These principles

came to be known as the "Venice Charter." While the charter provided an international framework, each country was responsible for implementing it within the framework of its own culture and traditions. The Congress also proposed the creation of an international non-governmental organization to coordinate international efforts for the preservation and appreciation of heritage sites. This resulted in the formation of the International Council of Monuments and Sites (ICOMOS). In 1977, the Australian branch of ICOMOS reviewed the Venice Charter and, in 1979, adopted the Charter for the Conservation of Places of Cultural Significance in a meeting in the historic mining town of Burra, South Australia. This document is commonly known as the "Burra Charter."

The Burra Charter has been widely accepted and adopted as the international standard for heritage conservation practice. This is due to its flexibility in acknowledging natural, indigenous, and historic places as possessing cultural values. Significantly, it sets a standard for various stakeholders, including owners, managers, and custodians. It encourages participation from people for whom the place has special associations and meanings, and people who have social, spiritual, or other cultural responsibilities for the place. Cultural significance is broadly defined as aesthetic, historic, scientific, social, or spiritual value for past, present, or future generations. It is embodied in the place itself, its fabric, setting, use, associations, meanings, records, related places, and objects. Significantly, the charter acknowledges that places may have a range of values for different individuals or groups. Conservation entails all the processes of looking after a place so as to retain its cultural significance. It is grounded in a respect for the existing fabric, use, associations, and meanings, and encourages a cautious approach to maintenance and repair. Maintenance refers to the continuous protective care of the fabric and setting of a place, while repair involves restoration or reconstruction. There is an intervention hierarchy whereby understanding cultural significance comes first, followed by the development of policy, and, finally, the management of the place in accordance with the policy.

The Burra Charter has had considerable influence on archaeological practice. A good example is the "archaeology under the canopy" approach in Maya archaeology. This approach was developed by Anabel Ford for the presentation of pre-Columbian Maya monuments at the archeological site El Pilar, an ancient Maya center on the border of Belize and Guatemala (Ford and Havrda 2006). Traditional approaches to the excavation of sites involve the removal of soil and foliage to record archaeological remains. After the excavation is complete, significant monuments are consolidated and left for public viewing and tourism. However, this approach exposes the monuments to wind, rain, and acid-producing microbes and causes extensive damage. The same soil processes that make the Maya forest fertile and underwrote the prosperity of the Maya civilization are now damaging exposed limestone structures. The "archaeology under the canopy" approach involves protecting monuments with rainforest foliage and strategic exposure of ancient structures. The majority of the monument is covered with plant foliage for stabilization. This practice protects the monument from the elements and insures its integrity for the future.

The most important international development in indigenous heritage and land rights was the creation of Nunavut as a territorial subdivision of the Northwest Territories in Canada. Nunavut translates as "our land" in the Inuktitut dialect of the Eastern Arctic Inuit. Nunavut is one of the most sparsely inhabited regions in the world, with settlement clustered in the coastal areas. The total land included in the subdivision is 2.1 million square kilometers. Nunavut is particularly important because it represents the Canadian government's acknowledgment of indigenous land rights. It was a process that took over 23 years. In 1973, the Inuit Tapirisat of Canada (now the Inuit Tapiriit Kanatami) entered into land claims negotiations with the Canadian government. They conducted a study of Inuit land use and occupancy to demonstrate the extent of Inuit aboriginal title in the Arctic. Three years later, the ITC proposed the creation of a Nunavut Territory as part of a comprehensive settlement of Inuit land claims in the Northwest Territories. On April 14, 1982, a plebiscite was held in the Northwest Territories, with a majority of the residents voting in favor of the resolution. The federal government gave a conditional agreement seven months later. The land claims agreement was decided in September 1992, and ratified by nearly 85 percent of the voters. On July 9, 1993, the Canadian Parliament passed the Nunavut Land Claims Agreement Act and the Nunavut Act, and the transition to indigenous control was completed on April 1, 1999. This was the largest land claim in Canadian history.

The Inuit Heritage Trust (IHT), established by the Nunavut Land Claims Agreement, is an indigenous organization dedicated to the preservation, enrichment, and protection of Inuit cultural heritage and identity embodied in Nunavut's archaeology sites, ethnographic resources, and traditional place names (IHT 2009a). The Trust's activities are based on the principle of respect for traditional knowledge and wisdom. The Trust has established a series of programs related to Nunavut sovereignty. One of these is the Nunavut Geographic Names Program, which preserves and promotes Inuit language and culture by providing official recognition to traditional Inuktitut place names. The program also provides technical support and financial assistance to communities for research and analysis of place names. Another program is the Nunavut Archaeology Program, responsible for the management and protection of the archaeological resources in Nunavut. Inuit Heritage Trust has developed a CD and website that presents Arctic peoples and archaeology in Nunavut. Ken Swayze initiated an archaeology field school in 2002 under contract with IHT, which continues to the present day (IHT 2009b). Yet another program is the Traveling Museum Project. It consists of two cases of reproduction artifacts, photographs, and text and is specially designed to travel to each Nunavut community. The exhibit tells the story of the Thule culture as it progressed from Siberia to Alaska and then to Nunavut. The exhibit is multilingual, presented in the Inuktitut, Inuinnaqtun, and English languages.

In the United States, the Native American Graves Protection and Repatriation Act (P.L. 101–601), known as NAGPRA, was signed into law by President George H. W. Bush in 1990. This act empowers Native American, Native Hawaiian, and Alaskan Native peoples by giving them information on the human remains, burial goods, and certain categories of objects held by museums and other institutions receiving federal funds. These categories include sacred objects and objects of cultural patrimony. Sacred objects are defined as specific ceremonial objects that are needed by traditional Native American religious leaders for the current practice of traditional Native American religions. An object of cultural patrimony is defined as an inalienable object having ongoing historical, traditional, or cultural importance central to the Native American group or culture itself, rather than property owned by an individual. Tribes must establish "cultural affiliation," that is to say that there must be a relationship of shared group identity between the present-day tribe or organization making the request and the tribe or group to which the deceased or objects belonged. In addition, the act has provisions for inadvertent discovery of Native American human remains and objects on federal or tribal land. These provisions require the notification of the Secretary of the Smithsonian and the appropriate tribe or Native Hawaiian organization. The act also prohibits the illegal trafficking in Native American human remains and objects. Finally, NAGPRA established a Review Board to adjudicate difficult cases.

The history of the passage of NAGPRA has yet to be adequately documented. Historically, it is part of Federal Indian law and must be considered alongside the American Indian Religious Freedom Act of 1978 (Trope and Echo-Hawk 2000). It is also related to the National Historical Preservation Act of 1966, the Archaeology and Historical Preservation Act of 1974, and the Archaeological Resource Protection Act of 1979. However, the available evidence shows that the law was not the result of benevolent legislators seeing restitution for past wrongs done to Native peoples. Rather, it was part of a plan to salvage the Museum of the American Indian, Heye Foundation. It was a carefully wrought agreement involving Walter Echo-Hawk, Director of the Native American Rights Fund, Suzan Shown Harjo, Executive Director of the National Congress of American Indians, Representative Ben Nighthorse Campbell of Colorado, and Robert McCormick Adams, Secretary of the Smithsonian Institution (Preucel et al. 2006). Harjo served on the board of the Heye Foundation. When it became clear that the Foundation did not have the financial resources to continue,

the board began exploring various options that culminated in the transfer of the collection to the Smithsonian and the creation of a new National Museum of the American Indian on the Mall in Washington, DC. One of the conditions of this transfer was the creation of legislation to facilitate the repatriation of Native American human remains from federally funded museums. Originally, the new National Museum was to be exempt from NAGPRA. Later, Native activists pointed out the injustice of retaining Native American human remains and grave goods in the new museum, and a separate amendment, known as the National Museum of the American Indian Act Amendment (P.L. 104-278), had to be passed in 1996 to bring it into compliance.

Initial responses to this legislation by the Society for American Archaeology and the American Association of Museums were strongly negative (Zimmerman 1989). There was a great concern that this law would shut down scientific research and empty out museums, compromising the possibility of putting on exhibits. Now, almost twenty years after the passage of the act, these fears have proven largely misguided. The most challenging case to date has been Kennewick man, a 10,000-year-old Native American man accidentally discovered on the banks of the Columbia River in Washington State. The case turns on the cultural affiliation and respectful treatment of an ancient ancestor and has implications for the origins of Native peoples on the American continent. Kennewick man has received considerable media coverage because of claims about his distinctive skeletal morphology (Thomas 2001; Watkins 2004). Unfortunately, the media made the scientifically invalid shift from Caucasoid features to Caucasian race and, for some people, this called the standard view of the peopling of the New World into question. Nonetheless, Kennewick does not characterize the entire repatriation discourse. It is now widely appreciated that NAGPRA has had a beneficial effect upon American archaeology, largely by increasing interactions between Native peoples, archaeologists, cultural anthropologists, and museum specialists. In some cases, it has inspired Native peoples to pursue careers in archaeology and museums.

How does a nation heal itself from apartheid? On April 27, 1994, the first multi-racial democratic election was held in South Africa. The African National Congress won 63 percent of the approximately 20 million votes cast. Nelson Mandela had been convicted by South African courts on charges of sabotage, as well as other crimes committed while he led the ANC in the movement against apartheid, and served 27 years in prison until his release in 1990. One of the most challenging issues he faced was addressing the abuses and human rights violations committed under apartheid. Accordingly, the new government passed the Promotion of National Unity and Reconciliation Act, which established a Truth and Reconciliation Commission to investigate and document the violations committed during the period from 1960 to 1994. The justification was that telling the truth about past human rights violations, from the perspectives of perpetrator and victim, facilitates the process of understanding, and the public acknowledgment of "untold suffering and injustice" (Preamble to the Act) helps to restore the dignity of victims and afford perpetrators the opportunity to come to terms with their own past. The Truth and Reconciliation Commission was designed to centralize and legitimize postapartheid state power (Wilson 2001). The Truth and Reconciliation process was used to establish South Africa's new political identity as a defender of human rights and liberal democracy. It secured popular support by linking human rights discourse to notions of restorative justice and *ubuntu* (or "African humanism") and thus to indigenous notions of justice (Wilson 2001).

Archaeology was part of the apartheid project and, in particular, linked to concepts of ethnic identity (see Hall 1984; Shepherd 2002b, 2003). The apartheid government of South Africa used archaeology and anthropology to legitimize its homeland policy by proving that the communities who lived in these artificial areas had always lived there. Archaeological research carried out during the early stages of the 20th century implicitly supported the notion that much of Southern Africa was barren of population until as late as the 18th century (Hall 1984). The idea that much of African history had been shaped by wave after wave of migrants provided a logical explanation for evidence of antiquity at important sites such as Great Zimbabwe by suggesting that they were the work of migrants to South

Africa, rather than of indigenous groups (Garlake 1982; see also Shepherd 2003). Eventually ideas such as this would be supplanted in the archaeological literature, but this created tensions with the government in Pretoria, which still held fast to the idea that white settlers had arrived to find a barren landscape, an idea that directly contributed to the emergence of a white, South African identity (Hall 1984; Shepherd 2003). Martin Hall (1984) also notes the influence of American archaeology in the idea of equating material assemblages with ethnic groups and identifying different expressions of ethnicity. However, Hall was not so much interested in arguing the virtues of one approach over another, as he was interested in the uses of the past in the present. His primary purpose was to demonstrate that archaeological methods and interpretations shared ideological connections to the politics that shaped much of Southern Africa in the colonial and early postcolonial periods (see also Hall 2000:152–162).

Hall's arguments are not without a sense of irony. They were published just after the political emergencies of the mid-1980s that would eventually result in the end of white rule and apartheid. Nonetheless, the white government continued to deploy historical events as part of an Afrikaner nationalist narrative (Hall 2000:153–155). The end of white rule brought with it many changes, among which, in the areas of archaeology and heritage, were the steps taken to construct new representations of South African history. Hall discusses District 6, a mixed neighborhood in Cape Town that was forcibly leveled in 1966 as part of government attempts to counter black South African nationalist aspirations. In 1997, the area became the focal point of a large museum project in which archaeology played an important role. The museum's mandate was to recover material evidence of this silenced community to build a new narrative of South African history (Hall 2000).

The antiquities trade has long been a contested arena where different notions of heritage, possession, and desire are played out (Renfrew 2001a). What can and cannot be legally sold reveals as much about a particular view of the nation-state as it does about cultural notions of beauty or art. On February 21, 2006, the Metropolitan Museum of Art and the Italian government signed a historic agreement resolving a 34-year conflict over the ownership of a famous Greek vase. The vase in question is a red-figured calyx krater from the sixth century BC painted by Euphronios and made by Euxitheos. Euphronios is widely regarded as the preeminent master of Greek vase painting, and only a small corpus of his work survives. The vase is quite large, standing 45.7 cm in height with a diameter of 55.1 cm, and depicts scenes from the Trojan war. One side shows Hermes overseeing Sleep (*Hypnos*) and Death (*Thanatos*) as they prepare to transport Sarpedon's body to Lycia for burial. Sarpedon, a son of Zeus and king of Lycia, was killed in single combat with Patroclus. The opposite side shows named Greek warriors arming for battle. The krater remained on display at the Met until January 2008, when it was returned to Italy. It is currently on display at the Villa Giulia in Rome.

The Met purchased the krater in 1972 from Robert Hecht, a dealer in antiquities, for $1 million (Atwood 2004). At the time, this was the most money ever paid for a Greek vase. Questions soon rose about its provenance and *The New York Times* published several pieces on the controversy. The Met claimed that there was no evidence that the object had been smuggled and that they had acquired it legally. But in 2005, photographs emerged showing the vessel and other looted objects in a Geneva storehouse owned by Giacomo Medici (Watson and Todeschini 2007). By then Italy had already begun a public campaign to claim antiquities in foreign museums that it suspected had been looted. Italian court documents indicate that the krater was looted from an Etruscan tomb in the Greppe Sant'Angelo near Cerveteri in 1971 (Silver 2009). After long negotiations, the Italian government brokered an agreement with the Met providing for the return of 21 antiquities, including the krater. The agreement also specified future long-term loans of objects of comparable value to the Met. In addition, Italy waived civil and criminal charges against the museum for its illegal acquisition of the objects. This agreement, while not perfect, is an important international model for other museums to consider in addressing their own histories of questionable collecting practices.

These cases are just a few of the many we could have selected to demonstrate how cultural heritage discourse is having real-world effects. Although these examples represent varied contexts and resolutions, what they signify is a new on-the-ground reality; the past is an increasingly contested political terrain (see Meskell 2005). This new reality has taken several forms. In some instances, it involves issues surrounding the actual ownership of specific artifacts or monuments. In others, it involves taking a stand on human rights issues, such as the return of sacred land or the repatriation of ancestors. Archaeologists today find themselves struggling to reinvent their profession in order to counter its colonial history of representing other people's pasts for Western interests. Museums are trying to find a balance between their traditional roles as the preservers of collections and their ethnical responsibilities to different publics, which sometimes require collections to be returned to their rightful owners. These questions of political relevancy are consistent with the precepts of pragmatism. The notion of knowledge as action stands as a prime example of a philosophical stance that dovetails nicely with growing calls for archaeologists to be more responsive to the political needs of nations, emerging nation-states, and indigenous communities around the world. Given the central role pragmatism plays in our framing of this book, it seems appropriate that we discuss its genealogy and potential for contemporary archaeology.

A Genealogy of Pragmatism

The new pragmatism incorporates two distinct, but intersecting, strands. The first is the renewed focus on social relevance, discussed above, and the second is the emphasis on epistemology. In order to understand this latter focus, it is useful to situate it within the historical context of American pragmatist philosophy. Pragmatism is the distinctive American philosophy that holds that the meaning of ideas or action can be determined by considering what idea or action it routinely generates, that is to say, its practical consequences. It is important to note that pragmatism was not in the past, and is not today, a unified approach. It was developed and modified in rather different ways by such noted philosophers as Charles Sanders Peirce, William James, John Dewey, and Richard

Rorty, among many others. It continues to be modified today by scholars such as Richard Bernstein, Christopher Hookway, Susan Haack, Jürgen Habermas, and Karl-Otto Apel. It seems significant that it has attracted the attention of both analytic and Continental philosophers. In our brief review, we pay special attention to those pragmatists cited by archaeologists.

Pragmatism is perhaps best known from the writings of William James, the Harvard psychologist and philosopher. James first introduced the concept in his California Union address "Philosophical Conceptions and Practical Results" in 1898 and in a series of lectures delivered at the Lowell Institute in 1906, and at Columbia University in 1907. James published these lectures in his book *Pragmatism: A New Name for Some Old Ways of Thinking* (James 1907). For him, pragmatism was a theory of truth that combined aspects of correspondence theory (how ideas match up with actual things in the world) and coherence theory (how well ideas hold together with one other). The former is an external property while the latter is an internal one. The truth of any particular idea can be verified by the observed results of the application of an idea to actual practice. As James (1907:97) puts it, truth is not a stagnant property inherent in an idea, rather it is something that happens to an idea as that idea is made true by events. James explicitly attributes the idea of pragmatism to his close friend Peirce. Their mutual interest in these issues grew out of their membership in a Cambridge salon known as the "Metaphysical club" (Menand 2001).

Peirce first published the idea of pragmatism in an article entitled "How to Make Our Ideas Clear" that appeared in *Popular Science Monthly* in 1878. Although the word "pragmatism" does not appear anywhere in the article, the theory is already well developed. His basic premise is that an idea is only clear if it produces the effect of recognition among a community of interpreters. A clear idea, then, is something that is widely understood by the general populace. Peirce saw his method of pragmatism as intimately associated with his view of semiosis. For him, all cognition is a semiotic process mediated by signs. To understand the meaning of a concept one needs to examine the various contexts in which it is used. However, this, by itself, is insufficient.

Meaning can only properly be understood with reference to those logical concepts that establish a belief that over time becomes a habit of thought. Peirce (1905), however, was not pleased with James's appropriation of his concept. He went so far as to change the name of his own view from "pragmatism" to the inelegant "pragmaticism" in order to disassociate himself from what he took to be the overly subjective aspects of James's position.

During the first part of the 19th century, John Dewey succeeded James as the foremost pragmatist (Boisvert 1988, 1998). Teaching first at the University of Chicago and then at Columbia, he made major contributions to philosophy, psychology, and education. Dewey was particularly critical of the Cartesian view of knowledge and the stark opposition between thought and fact. Inspired by Darwin, he argued that a naturalistic approach to the theory of knowledge was needed and that it must begin with the idea that knowledge is an adaptive human response to environmental conditions. He also rejected the "correspondence" theory of truth. He maintained that an idea can be said to agree with reality if and only if it is successfully employed in human action in pursuit of human goals and interests. For him, the world is not passively perceived and thereby known; rather the world is known through its active manipulation. Dewey (1925) developed what he calls "event ontology," the perspective that the world does not consist of things, but rather is composed of occurrences that are both particularistic and structured. He regards mind as an emergent issue of natural processes, the outcome of the interactive relationships between human beings and the world in which they live. Significantly, Dewey wrote extensively on social issues and was considered one of the leading social critics of his time. He called for the reconstruction of philosophy to assist in the public arena and espoused an enlightened educational process "in the search for the great community." His influence was only eclipsed by the emergence of analytic philosophy.

Richard Rorty was arguably the leading pragmatist of the 20th century. Teaching at Princeton and the University of Virginia, he developed a neo-pragmatic approach distinctive for its conversational and hermeneutic dimensions. Early in his career, he developed an influential critique of analytic philosophy and the representational view of knowledge (Rorty 1979). More specifically, he held that there is no foundational point on which truth can be grounded, no language that adequately describes the world, and no way to secure knowledge once and for all. He singled out for special critique the standard correspondence view of knowledge from Plato to Kant as corresponding to some external reality. In support of his thesis, he synthesizes the arguments of Willard van Orman Quine, Wilfrid Sellars, Thomas Kuhn, Ludwig Wittgenstein, and Donald Davidson to deconstruct the modern project of epistemology. But what is left? He suggests that we must give up our pursuit of security and acknowledge the contingency and irony of the human condition (Rorty 1989, 1991). We must "accept our inheritance from, and our conversation with, our fellow-humans as our only source of guidance" (Rorty 1982:166). This, he suggests, is the basis for truth without foundations (cf. Margolis 1986). Rorty was a socially committed liberal democrat, and this move allowed him to join his philosophy with his politics. For him, the task of the intellectual is not to develop new social theory, but rather to create community and awaken in all of us a sense of solidarity (Rorty 1998, 1999). Rorty was particularly critical of his own field of philosophy and felt that it should not be consulted for solutions to social ills. Indeed, he observes that past attempts to use philosophical theories of human nature to justify social and political action have done more harm than good. The best philosophers can do, he suggests, is to express our hopes for the world.

Until recently, there have been very few considerations of pragmatism in archaeology. One of the first was Christopher Gaffney and Vincent Gaffney's Theoretical Archaeology Group session in 1985 in Sheffield, England (Gaffney and Gaffney 1987a). This session was inspired by their observation that the processual/postprocessual debates of the 1980s appeared to split the field into two warring camps, "one bristling with paradigms and the other armed with mattocks, 'Ivory towers and empirical barricades'" (Gaffney and Gaffney 1987b:1). Of special note is that fact that their distinction is not between kinds of theory (processual versus

postprocessual), but rather between theory (processual and postprocessual) and practice (the actual doing of archaeology in the field). The Gaffneys also were concerned that archaeology was fragmenting into various "isms," the same concern that led Schiffer to develop his behavioral archaeology. While some diversity is to be expected, when the field becomes mired in unproductive debate, they argued that radical action is necessary. They thus sought to transcend these divides by gathering together people working with theory to solve pragmatically particular problems and then to determine from these case studies those domains in which theory "worked." For them, the problem of the relevance of archaeology and its justification in an uncertain world was a core issue.

In their conclusion to the conference proceedings, Ron Yorston and the Gaffneys (1987) offered a "manifesto for a pragmatic archaeology." They assert that their manifesto, while rather vague and incompletely articulated, nonetheless offers the potential for a productive way forward. They favor pragmatism because it "denies a fixed and restrictive theoretical stance, whilst providing an analytical base that cannot be simply labeled empiricist" (Yorston et al. 1987:107). They then articulate four principles for pragmatism in archaeology: it should be humanist, it should accept the context dependence of knowledge, it should be free in its use of hypotheses, and it should use theory as a "leading principle." Humanism acknowledges the central significance of the human element both in the formation of the archaeological record and in the interpretation of that record. Yorston and the Gaffneys write, "Perhaps we should note that site taphonomy continues through the postexcavation process and ends with the final distortion of the synthesist's pen" (Yorston et al. 1987:109). The context dependence of knowledge implies that there can never be a final answer to the questions of archaeology. This is because new generations of archaeologists will always find new theories based upon their present circumstances. The free use of hypotheses refers to the concern that the strict allegiance to the scientific method should not limit interpretation. Since the results of archaeological investigations are what matters, valid methods must be flexible and responsive to changing interests.

Finally, the idea of theory as a "leading principle" is associated with the idea that theory is only a tool that has meaning insofar as it provides an account which can be matched up against experience. That is to say, it must have a practical application.

In 2001, Robert Preucel and Alexander Bauer published an article called "Archaeological Pragmatics." This was one of the first archaeological engagements with the work of Charles Sanders Peirce (see also Gardin 1992). Preucel and Bauer argued that archaeological interpretation is an inherently semiotic process. Every stage of interpretation consists of the construction of new "signs"; in fact, interpretation is simply sign production. And since signs produce more signs in an endlesss chain of semiotic mediation, all methods used by archaeologists in the interpretive process are also signs. Metaphors, analogies, middle-range theories, and other such methods are signs that, in effect, stand for or represent the reality of the past that we are attempting to understand. The concern of archaeology has been to ask how the signs we create compare with the signs (or "meanings") that were part of a past reality that resulted in the creation of the archaeological record we study. This question is partially misleading, however, because every interpreter in the past as well as in the present is continuously in the process of creating signs. That said, some signs, or past meanings, are possible to comprehend. On one level, it seems safe to assume that chisel marks on stone building blocks "meant" the same thing to people in the past as they do to us today. But there are degrees of differences, and it is important to understand that, even synchronically, knowledge is situated (Haraway 1988), and will vary between "insiders" and "outsiders" as well as among members of different interpretive communities.

Dean Saitta (2003, 2007) has advocated a pragmatist sensibility as a way for archaeology to move beyond realism. Inspired by John Dewey and Richard Rorty, he identifies three core pragmatist principles. The first is that truth is belief justified by social need, rather than the way the things are in nature. This justifies experimentation with theory and method in order to achieve intersubjective consensus, rather than the rigid adherence to a particular theory and method.

The second principle is that experimental truths must be evaluated against experience. According to Saitta (2003:12), we must ask "what difference the claim [about the past] makes to how we want to live." More specifically, he asks us to consider the theoretical implications of evolutionary archaeology, interpretive archaeology, Marxist archaeology, and indeed all other approaches in current use. The third principle involves testing in the context of beliefs from different cultural traditions. Rather than testing by correspondence or coherence to some empirical reality, a pragmatist approach requires us to continually interweave different webs of belief so as to expand and deepen community. Saitta calls this a "measured relativism," which balances the commitment to evaluation against the commitment to cultural pluralism. He favors such a pragmatism as a way of subsuming Enlightenment critical rationality to more humanistic, regulative ideals (Saitta 2003:15). In addition, he sees it as converging with subaltern priorities and concerns, particularly in the area of the social consequences of knowledge claims.

In 2006, Preucel published *Archaeological Semiotics* to demonstrate the advantages of a pragmatic archaeology allied with pragmatic anthropology. Pragmatic anthropology refers to a movement that encompasses, in varying degrees, the subfields of linguistic and sociocultural anthropology and is largely associated with scholars who teach, or have received their training, at the University of Chicago. To a large extent, this movement can be seen as a measured response to the limitations of symbolic, structural, and cognitive anthropology. In addition, it is also a critique of certain excesses of poststructuralism, particularly the notion of radical ambiguity. Of special significance is the notion of indexicality, the sign mode that signals the contextual existence of an entity. This is a key topic in linguistic anthropology, where research has focused on deictics (Hanks 1990), referential language (Silverstein 1976; Parmentier 1994), and linguistic ideologies (Schieffelin et al. 1998; Kroskrity 2000). It is important in studies of identity and the relationships of self and society (Daniel 1984; Singer 1984; Munn 1986). Here scholars have seen Peirce's insights about distributed identity as a means of going beyond the Cartesian mind–body dualism. And indexicality is central in studies of how material culture mediates social relations (Parmentier 1987; Keane 1997). In this case, scholars approach material culture as distinct from, but complementary with, language in the semiotic mediation process.

Pragmatic archaeology, like pragmatic anthropology, is based upon the application of Peircian semiotics to language and culture. It is not to be confused with Saussurian semiotics, which underlies structuralism and its poststructural critique. A Peircian semiotic is superior to its Saussurian rival on several counts. It does not privilege language as the model for semiotics; rather it offers a more general model which incorporates language, social practices, and material culture, indeed all of culture (Parmentier 1997:xv; Keane 2003, 2005). Related to this, it addresses socialness of language and material practices without reducing the one to the other. The major contribution of pragmatic anthropology has thus been its pragmatic view of culture and its commitment to understanding the culturally specific ways in which sign relations mediate social being. Signs function not simply to represent social reality, but also to create it and effect changes in that reality. Signs thus have agency by virtue of their ability to generate other signs. The control of this process via strategic action permits the fixing of meanings, as sign combinations come to be interpreted together as semiotic ideologies. And yet, as Webb Keane (1997) points out, these strategies come with certain risks since semiotic ideologies can always be questioned and challenged; meaning is always unstable and constantly under negotiation.

The philosopher Patrick Baert (2005) has recently presented a compelling argument for pragmatism as a philosophical context for research in the social sciences. Of special interest is his analysis of anthropology and archaeology as two fields that have adopted a pragmatic spirit. For contemporary anthropology, this spirit is embodied in the "critical turn." The critical turn was initiated by the writings of George Marcus and Michael Fischer (1986) and James Clifford and Marcus (1986) in response to what they called the "crisis of representation." This is the wholesale reevaluation of anthropological method, theory, and practices, largely stimulated by feminist, neo-Marxist, and

postcolonial critiques. Baert notes that there is no dominant theory associated with the critical turn, only a willingness to experiment with methods and subject matter. Writing, for example, is no longer regarded as a neutral, transparent mechanism for the conveying of information, but is rather recognized as an active social practice with rhetorical qualities that affects interpretation. There is an acknowledgment that ethnographic truths are partial truths. This is the rationale for seeing the production of truth as a conversation composed of people from different cultural backgrounds speaking in different voices. The critical turn thus emphasizes the dialogical nature of knowledge and the relevance of anthropological knowledge to modern society.

Baert then turns to archaeology and identifies the pragmatic spirit with the rise of postprocessualism. He begins by contrasting processual and postprocessual archaeologies. Processualism, he suggests, was based upon a naturalist agenda which emphasized how cultural systems adapted to their environments. On this view, there was little place for human agency. Postprocessualism, by contrast, adopts a post-naturalist agenda, in the sense that the meanings people attribute to their worlds are the focus of research. Attributing meaning is not simply an issue of correspondence to the real world, but rather a creative process of interacting with the world. He writes, "They [postprocessualists] adopt a pragmatic stance, emphasizing how their method of inquiry may alter the present constellation of meanings. Knowledge is no longer conceived as something passive, but it is more like an action; it affects things" (Baert 2005:163). He also suggests that the reflexive turn in archaeology may be due to the increasing prominence of heritage in contemporary society. Archaeologists are now paying more attention to how power struggles in the present incorporate claims about the past. Baert notes that postprocessualists have critiqued museums because of their authoritarian structure, which reduces visitors to passive objects. This has caused archaeologists to be more explicit in critiquing the present and challenging our society's assumptions. Baert cites Tilley's (1989b:111) statement that "archaeologists have so far interpreted the past; they should undertake to change it in the service of the present." He concludes that archaeologists have become more open to critiquing their work and reconsidering their underlying assumptions.

We find Baert's overall scheme appealing, for several reasons. Like most pragmatists, Baert believes that self-referential knowledge can help in ridding Western science of some of its flaws and, in so doing, enable it to position itself to contribute to the dialogues surrounding contemporary social and political issues in meaningful ways. He provides a compelling critique of those analytic philosophers, such as Karl Popper and Carl Hempel, who have argued that natural science offers the most robust model for success in the social sciences. Baert argues that there are myths concerning Western science that, once acknowledged, undermine some visions of science. In particularly, there is no real unity to science in terms of either epistemology or methods. Rather, there exist collections of scholars who employ diverse methods to explore a variety of scientific questions. This is a point also made by increasing numbers of philosophers and scientists (see Margolis 1987; Galison and Stump 1996; Galison 1997). Instead of regarding this lack of unity as a weakness, Baert celebrates the diversity of methods and approaches. Indeed, it is precisely the disunity of science that gives it its strength and stability.

We also agree with his critique of the "spectator theory of knowledge" (Baert 2005:151). This notion, first proposed by Dewey, refers to the representational view of knowledge, the idea that the ultimate goal of science is to map the world as completely as possible. This approach, which Baert refers to as social cartography, assumes the ability of the researcher to acknowledge his or her own positionality and somehow control for it, which in turn allows him or her some objective view of an external world. He then suggests that many social theorists, including Roy Bhaskar (1978) and Giddens, are guilty of this perspective. He suggests that they attribute "a mysterious capacity to individual researchers to 'step outside history', to assume what [Willard van Orman] Quine called a 'God's eye view', stripped from the own culture, while subjects being investigated are portrayed as necessarily drawing upon a culturally specific framework to make sense of the world" (Baert 2005:152). He notes there is a curious

ontological asymmetry here where one view is applied to the researcher and another to the subject. For Baert, a shared intersubjectivity is a prerequisite for an understanding of the social.

Finally, we support Baert's argument for the centrality of a dialogical stance in the human sciences. This view is a clear rejection of foundationalism, the belief in a secure epistemological grounding upon which all knowledge can be based. Like many pragmatists, Baert does not believe that such a grounding is possible and, moreover, he feels it has led to entrenchment and intellectual rigidity. Even Quine (1981) rejected the idea of a First Philosophy, the possibility of a theoretical position standing outside of nature. In place of a foundationalist epistemology, Baert argues for social research as a conversation between observer and the observed that results in some new and meaningful understanding of the worlds they both inhabit. Ultimately, these new understandings will facilitate larger conversations that lead to social action. Knowledge production is thus not a representational process, but rather a form of action. We see this perspective as closely allied to Jürgen Habermas's (1984, 1989) theory of communicative action, although Baert would prefer to link Habermas to foundationalism.

Although there is much in Baert's pragmatism that we find compelling, we believe, as he does, that pragmatism is a work in progress. In fact, one of the unyielding principles of pragmatic philosophies is that they remain open, evolving projects that are wary of attempts to limit dialogue or to deny self-critique. Among the elements of pragmatism to which we adhere is that the human sciences, in this instance, archaeology, cannot escape the social. We are less interested in attempts to artificially segment the world in the Cartesian sense. Instead, we accept as a given that the external world is a non-essentialized reality that cannot be separated from the social. We agree with Baert, and other pragmatic philosophers, that the notion of detached spectator should be replaced with an emphasis on social action. There is, however, real value in attempting to map the social, to determine its contours over the long term, and to place our cartographies of the past in the service of the needs of the present. In this regard, we do not necessarily agree with Baert's characterizations of the work of Giddens, for example, as promoting a "God's eye view."

Where we find common ground with Baert is his idea that pragmatism should lead to meaningful social action. We thus advocate a pragmatic archaeology that continually challenges the usual distinctions between time (e.g. prehistoric archaeology, historical archaeology), space (e.g. settlement archaeology, urban archaeology, landscape archaeology), process (e.g. archaeology of capitalism, industrial archaeology), and people (e.g. the archaeologies of race, class, gender, ethnicity, sexuality, indigeneity, etc.). An archaeology that acknowledges the multiple imbrications of recent and distant pasts can more effectively address the problems of our day, many of which are the direct outgrowth of historical forces, such as colonialism, industrialism, and globalization. In our view, archaeology can only realize its full anthropological potential by reconfiguring itself, not as a detached science of the Other, but as a conscious, self-informed, socially active science of humanity.

Organization of the Reader

The essays in this Reader are testimony to the influence of the new pragmatism on contemporary archaeological theory and practice. We hasten to state that the individual authors do not necessarily consider themselves pragmatists in the philosophical sense. That is to say, they are not necessarily devotees of Peirce, James, Dewey, Rorty, or indeed, any other pragmatist. Nonetheless, most authors agree that archaeology must ask questions about what difference archaeological knowledge makes to the lives we want to live (Sabloff 2008). Archaeology and the social are inextricably intertwined. The central task of archaeology is thus to free us from our complacency by reminding us that current social relations are neither natural nor inevitable, but rather the creation of particular cultural traditions that have developed in specific ways over a long period of time. Once it is acknowledged that data are not only theory laden, but also politically laden, archaeologists can begin to negotiate the past in the present with different interest groups ranging from the lay public to indigenous peoples, and, in the process, open up

new options and possibilities for being-in-the-world. This, for us, is the core of a pragmatic sensibility.

We have found the selection process to be quite challenging since there are a large number of excellent studies that we could have included. In the end, we have made our selections to highlight how the personal is the professional. That is to say, we have considered issues of gender, sexuality, ethnicity, class, age, and so on, not only as topics to pursue in our studies of the past, but also as ways to think about how we define ourselves and interact with one another in the present. The categories, and the issues they raise, are problematic on a number of counts. But we believe that by taking them into consideration, rather than bracketing them off or holding them aside, we are strengthening the practice of archaeology. Archaeology is enriched by the asking of new kinds of questions from different vantage points and perspectives. This is because knowledge is produced from particular standpoints, only some of which enjoy hegemonic status. Alternative standpoints are forged in active political resistance to these hegemonic standpoints. These alternative perspectives uniquely have the potential to expose unacknowledged systems of oppression and are thus potentially liberating. This is what Alison Wylie (Kincaid et al. 2007) means in her discussion of a feminist "angle of vision" and Sandra Harding (1991) values in her "view from the margins."

Some of our colleagues may critique us on the grounds that we are two white males trained in the Western canon who, despite our best intentions, are still controlling the discourse (the assertion of the new pragmatism). There is some truth to this criticism. But while it is the case that both of us were trained as processual archaeologists, we have both challenged that canon in our work and have taken up, in different ways, pragmatic perspectives as we have engaged with and continue to engage with alternative views and perspectives. We are prepared to accept that alternative views, including non-Western perspectives, have the potential to call into question our own taken-for-granteds, and we embrace this as part of the democratic process of knowledge growth. Writing this Reader has been a learning process that continues to evolve, and, therefore, we take it as a given that a new generation of scholars will question the choices we have made and the reasons behind those choices. Accepting this reality is itself a reflection of the pragmatic philosophy that underlies much of what is presented in this volume. For us, archaeology is a part of a larger project that seeks to learn from the past to inform the future and to play an active role in the variety of current discourses.

We have organized the Reader into eight parts, not including this introduction. Part II is "Landscapes, Spaces, and Natures." It addresses how archaeology has moved away from deterministic models of human–land relations toward more constitutive models where humans transform and are transformed by land. In this sense, we see landscape and nature as non-essentialized realities that have been profoundly influenced by human action. Part III is "Agency, Meaning, and Practice." Here we feature some of the various permutations of practice theory with an emphasis on the manner in which they are interrelated. Meaning emerges at the intersections of agency, structure, and practice. Part IV is "Sexuality, Embodiment, and Personhood." Here we consider the nexus of gender and sexuality as a starting point for better understanding the ways humans construct both individual and group identities. We also show how feminist perspectives and gender studies, more than any other theoretical movement, have exposed the political nature of archaeology and made the case why knowledge is always situated. Part V is "Race, Class, and Ethnicity." These social constructs represent critical lines of demarcation that have shaped and continue to shape the character and tenor of human interaction. An objective archaeology is thus one that seeks not to remove biases, since these are precisely what facilitates interpretation, but rather to acknowledge them in the process of considering which are shared and which are interest-specific.

Part VI is "Materiality, Memory, and Historical Silence." This is a rich group of theoretical concepts that have played a major role in refining and reorienting archaeological practice. Materiality refers to the agentive quality of things in mediating and sometimes transforming social practices. The notion of historical silence has become a *raison d'être* for the many archaeologists who seek to understand why such silences are often perpetrated and how they

might be filled. The concept of memory also relates to what is remembered, what is forgotten, and why, and, not surprisingly, has become an important element of the theoretical repertoire of contemporary archaeology. Part VII is "Colonialism, Empire, and Nationalism." These concepts focus attention on the imperial enterprise and its political, economic, cultural, and environmental implications. As the voices of postcolonial scholars mingle with those of indigenous scholars, they call attention to the need for a critical examination of the manner in which historical forces such as colonialism, the growth of empire, and nationalism have helped to shape the modern world. They also remind us that colonialism and empire are not elements of the past; they are part of the present and continue to have a powerful influence over the events that define our lives. Part VIII is "Heritage, Patrimony, and Social Justice." This is a consideration of the legitimization of political structures through the selective invocation of the past. This section also raises important questions concerning who owns the past and the contentious terrain archaeologists are currently navigating. The final section, Part IX, is "Media, Museums, and Publics." Here we emphasize the multiplicity of publics and the different technologies of (re)presenting the past. Given that all archaeology ultimately results in representations of people's histories, the issues surrounding how those representations are constructed and communicated are vitally important.

The division of the book and the placement of readings in the individual parts is, to some degree, arbitrary. Some of the readings could have fit equally well into different sections. For example, Carla Sinopoli's piece on the elite manipulation of social memory at Vijaynagara in Part VII could just as easily been placed in Part V. Similarly, Barbara Voss's piece on sexual politics and the Spanish empire in Alta California in Part IV could have been placed in Part VI, and so on. This fuzziness is "real" and exposes the underlying problems of categorization and typology. As George Lakoff (1987) writes, there is nothing more basic than the categories we use in how we think and talk about things. Traditionally, we have treated categories as though they are empty containers to be filled up with things that possess certain attributes in common. However, new studies in philosophy and the cognitive sciences have called this assumption into question and revealed the complexities of making distinctions. Moreover, our introductions to the various parts intentionally overlap to demonstrate the ways in which social categories co-construct one another. For example, our discussion of heritage blends into our review of race, media, and colonialism and our discussion of race and ethnicity grades into our treatment of nationalism. As Lynn Meskell (2004:41) perceptively notes, taxonomies are artifacts. The process of classification cannot be separated from the practical motives of classification. There is not and, indeed, cannot be one best organization framework or scheme. Any attempt at bounding knowledge can only be partial and provisional. For this reason, we

encourage the reader to read across the divisions as well as within them.

We hope that this collection provides our students and colleagues with a stimulating group of papers that are testimony to the pragmatic spirit in contemporary archaeology. But beyond this, we also hope that our collaboration will "pay off" in a very pragmatic way; we hope that it will strengthen the discourse between those who seek to connect the distant past with the world we know today. In the end, our colleagues and students must evaluate the success of our endeavor. We thus take a pragmatic view of this Reader. If people with different interests and agendas find it interesting and useful, then we will be satisfied ... for the moment.

References

Agorsah, Kofi E., ed., 1994 Maroon Heritage: Archaeological, Ethnographic and Historical Perspectives. Barbados: Canoe Press.

Althusser, Louis, 1971 Ideology and Ideological State Apparatuses: Notes towards an Investigation. In Lenin and Philosophy and Other Essays. Louis Althusser, ed. Pp. 127–186. New York: Monthly Review Press.

Appadurai, Arjun, ed., 1986a The Social Life of Things: Commodities in Cultural Perspective. Cambridge: Cambridge University Press.

Appadurai, Arjun, 1986b Introduction: Commodities and Politics of Value. In The Social Life of Things: Commodities in Cultural Perspective. Arjun Appadurai, ed. Pp. 3–62. Cambridge: Cambridge University Press.

Armstrong, Douglas V. 1985 An Afro-Jamaican Slave Settlement: Archaeological Investigations at Drax Hall. In The Archaeology of Slavery and Plantation Life. Theresa A. Singleton, ed. Pp. 261–285. New York: Academic Press.

Armstrong, Douglas V. 1990 The Old Village and the Great House: An Archaeological and Historical Examination of Drax Hall Plantation, Jamaica. Urbana: University of Illinois Press.

Armstrong, Douglas V. 1999 Archaeology and Ethnohistory of the Caribbean Plantation. In "I Too Am America": Archaeological Studies of African-American Life. Theresa A. Singleton, ed. Pp. 173–192. Charlottesville: University of Virginia Press.

Armstrong, Douglas V. 2003 Creole Transformation from Slavery to Freedom: Historical Archaeology of the East End Community, St. John, Virgin Islands. Gainesville: University Press of Florida.

Armstrong, Douglas V., and Kenneth G. Kelly, 2000 Settlement Patterns and the Origins of African Jamaican society: Seville Plantation, St. Ann's Bay, Jamaica. Ethnohistory 47(2):369–397.

Ashmore, Wendy, and Jeremy A. Sabloff, 2002 Spatial Orders in Maya Civic Plans. Latin American Antiquity 13(2):201–215.

Atalay, Sonya, 2006 Decolonizing Archaeology. American Indian Quarterly 30(3–4):269–279.

Atwood, Roger, 2004 Stealing History: Tomb Raiders, Smugglers and the Looting of the Ancient World. New York: St. Martin's Press.

Baert, Patrick, 2005 Philosophy of the Social Sciences: Towards Pragmatism. Cambridge: Polity Press.

Bamforth, Douglas B., 2002 Evolution and Metaphor in Evolutionary Archaeology. American Antiquity 67:435–452.

Barnes, Barry, David Bloor, and John Henry, 1996 Scientific Knowledge: A Sociological Analysis. Chicago: University of Chicago Press.

Barrett, John C., 1988 Fields of Discourse: Reconstructing a Social Archaeology. Critique of Anthropology 7:5–16.

Barrett, John C., 1994: Fragments from Antiquity: An Archaeology of Social Life in Britain, 2900–1200 B.C. Oxford: Blackwell.

Barrett, John C., 2001: Agency, the Duality of Structure and the Archeological Record. In Archaeological Theory Today. Ian Hodder, ed. Pp. 141–164. Cambridge: Polity Press.

Barthes, Roland, 1957 Mythologies. Paris: Éditions du Seuil.

Barthes, Roland, 1964 Elements of Semiology. New York: Hill and Wang.

Baram, Uzi, and Lynda Carroll, eds., 2000 A Historical Archaeology of the Ottoman Empire: Breaking New Ground. New York: Kluwer/Plenum.

Beaudry, Mary C., Lauren J. Cook, and Stephen A. Mrozowski, 1991 Active Voices: Material Culture as Social Discourse. In The Archaeology of Inequality. Randall H. McGuire and Robert Paynter, eds. Pp. 150–191. Oxford: Blackwell.

Bhabha, Homi K., 1994 The Location of Culture. London: Routledge.

Bhaskar, Roy, 1978 A Realist Theory of Science. 2nd edition. Brighton: Harvester.

Binford, Lewis R., 1962: Archaeology as Anthropology. American Antiquity 11:217–225.

Binford, Lewis R., 1967 Smudge Pits and Hide Smoking: The Use of Analogy in Archaeological Reasoning. American Antiquity 32:1–12.

Binford, Lewis R., 1980 Behavioral Archaeology and the "Pompeii Premise." Journal of Anthropological Research 37:195–208.

Binford, Lewis R., 1985 "Brand X" versus the Recommended Product. American Antiquity 50:580–590.

Boas, Franz, 1904 The History of Anthropology. Science 20(512):513–524.

Boisvert, Raymond D., 1988 Dewey's Metaphysics. New York: Fordham University Press.

Boisvert, Raymond D., 1998 John Dewey: Rethinking Our Time. Albany: State University of New York Press.

Boone, James L., and Eric Alden Smith, 1998 Is It Evolution Yet? A Critique of Evolutionary Archaeology. Current Anthropology 39:141–173.

Bourdieu, Pierre, 1977 Outline of a Theory of Practice. Cambridge: Cambridge University Press.

Braidwood, Robert, 1959 Archeology and the Evolutionary Theory. In Evolution and Anthropology: A Centennial Appraisal. Betty J. Meggars, ed. Pp. 76–89. Washington, DC: Anthropological Society of Washington.

Braithwaite, Mary, 1982 Decoration as Ritual Symbol: A Theoretical Proposal and an Ethnographic Study in Southern Sudan. In Symbolic and Structural Archaeology. Ian Hodder, ed. Pp. 80–88. Cambridge: Cambridge University Press.

Braudel, Fernand, 1981 Civilization and Capitalism 15th–18th Century, vol. I. The Structures of Everyday Life. New York: Harper and Row.

Braudel, Fernand, 1982 Civilization and Capitalism 15th–18th Century, vol. II. Wheels of Commerce. New York: Harper and Row.

Braudel, Fernand, 1985 Civilization and Capitalism 15th–18th Century, vol. III. The Perspective of the World. New York: Harper and Row.

Brown, Bill, 1998 How to Do Things with Things (a Toy Story). Critical Inquiry 24(4):935–964.

Brown, Bill, 2003 A Sense of Things: The Object Matter in American Literature. Chicago: University of Chicago Press.

Brown, Bill, ed., 2004 Things. Chicago: University of Chicago Press.

Burney, Linda, 1999 Letter to the Editor. Australian Archaeology 48:54.

Butler, Judith, 1990 Gender Trouble: Feminism and the Subversion of Identity. London: Routledge.

Butler, Judith, 1993 Bodies That Matter: On the Discursive Limits of Sex. New York: Routledge.

Cajete, Greg, 1999 Native Science: Natural Laws of Interdependence. Santa Fe: Clear Light Books.

Cajete, Greg, 2004 Philosophy of Native Science. In American Indian Thought: Philosophical Essays. Ann Walters, ed. Pp. 45–57. New York: Wiley-Blackwell.

Cameron, Catherine M., and Steve A. Tomka, eds., 1993 Abandonment of Settlements and Regions: Ethnoarchaeological and Archaeological Approaches. Cambridge: Cambridge University Press.

Claassen, Cheryl, ed., 1992 Exploring Gender through Archaeology. Madison: Prehistory Press.

Claassen, Cheryl, and Rosemary A. Joyce, eds., 1997 Women in Prehistory: North American and Mesoamerica. Philadelphia: University of Pennsylvania Press.

Clark, Elizabeth Ann, 2004 History, Theory, Text: Historians and the Linguistic Turn. Cambridge, MA: Harvard University Press.

Clarke, David L., 1968 Analytical Archaeology. London: Methuen.

Clifford, James, 2005 Rearticulating Anthropology. In Unwrapping the Sacred Bundle: Reflections on the Disciplining of Anthropology. Daniel A. Segal and Sylvia J. Yanagisako, eds. Pp. 24–48. Durham, NC: Duke University Press.

Clifford, James, and George E. Marcus, 1986 Writing Culture: The Poetics and Politics of Ethnography. Berkeley: University of California Press.

Collingwood, R. G., 1946 The Idea of History. Oxford: Oxford University Press.

Conkey, Margaret W., 1978 Style and Information in Cultural Evolution: Toward a Predictive Model for the Paleolithic. In Social Archaeology: Beyond Subsistence and Dating. Charles L. Redman, Mary Jane Berman, Edward V. Curtin, William T. Langhorne, Jr., Nina M. Versaggi, and Jeffrey C. Wanser, eds. Pp. 61–85. New York: Academic Press.

Conkey, Margaret W., 1980 Context, Structure and Efficacy in Paleolithic Art and Design. In Symbol as Sense. Mary LeCron Foster and Stanley Brandes, eds. Pp. 225–248. New York: Academic Press.

Conkey, Margaret W., 1989 The Structural Analysis of Paleolithic Art. *In* Archaeological Thought in America. C. C. Lamberg-Karlovsky, ed. Pp. 135–154. Cambridge: Cambridge University Press.

Conkey, Margaret W., 1991 Contexts of Action, Contexts of Power: Material Culture and Gender in the Magdalenian. *In* Engendering Archaeology: Women and Prehistory. Joan M. Gero and Margaret W. Conkey, eds. Pp. 57–92. Oxford: Blackwell.

Conkey, Margaret W., and Janet Spector, 1984 Archaeology and the Study of Gender. *In* Advances in Archaeological Method and Theory, vol. 7. Michael B. Schiffer, ed. Pp. 1–38. New York: Academic Press.

Cornman, Jack, 1995 Can't Get There from Here. Anthropology News 36(5):1–6.

Courtney, Paul, 1999 "Different Strokes for Different Folks": The Transatlantic Development of Historical and Post-Medieval Archaeology. *In* Old and New Worlds. Geoff Egan and Ronald L. Michael, eds. Pp. 1–9. Oxford: Oxbow Books.

Culler, Jonathan D., 1975 Structuralist Poetics: Structuralism, Linguistics and the Study of Literature. London: Routledge and Kegan Paul.

Culler, Jonathan D., 1981 In Pursuit of Signs: Semiotics, Literature, Deconstruction. Ithaca, NY: Cornell University Press.

Cuno, James, 2008 Who Owns Antiquity? Museums and the Battle over Our Ancient Heritage. Princeton: Princeton University Press.

Daniel, E. Valentine, 1984: Fluid Signs: Being a Person the Tamil Way. Berkeley: University of California Press.

Daniel, Glyn E., 1962 The Idea of Prehistory. London: C. A. Watts.

Daniel, Glyn E., 1981 A Short History of Archaeology. London: Thames and Hudson.

Dant, Tim, 2005 Materiality and Society. Maidenhead: Open University Press.

Daehnke, Jon D., 2007 A "Strange Multiplicity" of Voices: Heritage Stewardship, Contested Sites and Colonial Legacies on the Columbia River. Journal of Social Archaeology 7(2): 250–275.

Deacon, Terrence W., 1997 The Symbolic Species: The Co-evolution of Language and the Brain. New York: Norton.

Deagan, Kathleen, 1973 *Mestizaje* in Colonial St. Augustine. Ethnohistory 20(1):53–65.

Deagan, Kathleen, 1974 Sex, Status and the Role of the *Mestizaje* of Spanish Colonial Florida. Ph.D. dissertation, Gainesville: University of Florida.

Deagan, Kathleen, 1983 Spanish St. Augustine: The Archaeology of a Colonial Creole Community. New York: Academic Press.

Deagan, Kathleen, ed., 1995 Puerto Real: The Archaeology of a Sixteenth-Century Spanish Town in Hispaniola. Gainesville: University Press of Florida.

Deagan, Kathleen, 2003 Colonial Origins and Colonial Transformations in Spanish America. Historical Archaeology 37(4):3–13.

Dean, Bartholomew, and Jerome Levi, eds., 2003 At the Risk of Being Heard: Indigenous Rights, Identity and Postcolonial States. Ann Arbor: University of Michigan Press.

de Beaune, Sophie A., Frederick L. Coolidge, and Thomas Wynn, eds., 2009 Cognitive Archaeology and Human Evolution. Cambridge: Cambridge University Press.

DeCorse, Christopher R., 1987 Historical Archaeological Research in Ghana, 1986–1987. Nyame Akuma 29:27–31.

DeCorse, Christopher R., 1989 Material Aspects of Limba, Yalunka and Kuranko Ethnicity: Archaeological Research in Northeastern Sierra Leone. *In* Archaeological Approaches to Cultural Identity. Stephen Shennan, ed. Pp. 126–140. London: Unwin Hyman.

DeCorse, Christopher R., 1999 Oceans Apart: Africanist Perspectives on Diaspora Archaeology. *In* "I Too Am America": Archaeological Studies of African-American Life. Theresa A. Singleton, ed. Pp. 132–155. Charlottesville: University of Virginia Press.

DeCorse, Christopher R., 2001a An Archaeology of Elmina: Africans and Europeans on the Gold Coast, 1400–1900. Washington, DC: Smithsonian Institution Press.

DeCorse, Christopher R., ed., 2001b West Africa during the Atlantic Slave Trade: Archaeological Perspectives. London: Leicester University Press.

Deetz, James, 1965 The Dynamics of Stylistic Change in Arikara Ceramics. Illinois Studies in Anthropology, No. 4. University of Illinois Press, Urbana, IL.

Deetz, James, 1967 Invitation to Archaeology. Garden City, NY: The Natural History Press.

Deetz, James, 1972 Ceramics from Plymouth, 1620–1835: The Archaeological Evidence. *In* Ceramics in America. Ian Quimby, ed. Pp. 15–40. Charlottesville: University of Virginia Press.

Deetz, James, 1977 In Small Things Forgotten. New York: Anchor Books.

Deetz, James, 1993 Flowerdew Hundred: The Archaeology of a Virginia Plantation 1619–1864. Charlottesville: University of Virginia Press.

Delle, James A., 1998 An Archaeology of Social Space. New York: Plenum.

Delle, James A., Stephen A. Mrozowski, and Robert Paynter, eds., 2000 Lines that Divide: Historical Archaeologies of Race, Class and Gender. Knoxville: University of Tennessee Press.

Den Ouden, Amy 2005 Beyond Conquest: Native Peoples and the Struggle for History in New England. Lincoln: University of Nebraska Press.

Derrida, Jacques, 1976 Of Grammatology. Baltimore: Johns Hopkins University Press.

Dewey, John, 1925 Experience and Nature. Chicago: Open Court.

Dhavalikar, Madhukar K., 1999 Historical Archaeology of India. New Delhi: Books and Books.

Dobres, Marcia-Ann, and John Robb, 2000 Agency in Archaeology: Paradigm or Platitude? In Agency in Archaeology. Marcia-Ann Dobres and John Robb, eds. Pp. 3–17. London: Routledge.

Dommasnes, Liv Helga, 1992 Two Decades of Women in Prehistory and in the Archaeology of Norway: A Review. Norwegian Archaeological Review 25(1):1–14.

Dommasnes, Liv Helga, Else Johansen Kleppe, Gro Mandt, and Jenny-Rita Naess, 1998 Women Archaeologists in Retrospect: The Norwegian Case. In Excavating Women: A History of Women in European Archaeology. Margarita Díaz-Andreu and Mary Louise Stig Sørensen, eds. Pp. 105–124. London: Routledge.

Donald, Merlin, 1991 Origins of the Modern Mind: Three Stages in the Evolution of Culture and Cognition. Cambridge: Cambridge University Press.

Donham, Donald, 1999 History, Power, Ideology: Central Issues in Marxism and Anthropology. Berkeley: University of California Press.

Doughton, Thomas L., 1997 Unseen Neighbors: Native Americans of Central Massachusetts, People Who Had "Vanished." In After King Philip's War: Presence and Persistence in Indian New England. Colin G. Calloway, ed. Pp. 207–230. Hanover, NH: University Press of New England.

Douglas, Mary, 1973 Introduction. In Rules and Meanings: Anthropology of Everyday Knowledge. Mary Douglas, ed. Pp. 9–13. Harmondsworth: Penguin.

Douglas, Mary, and Baron C. Isherwood, 1979 The World of Goods: Towards an Anthropology of Consumption. New York: Norton.

du Cros, Hilary, and Laurajane Smith, eds., 1993 Women in Archaeology: A Feminist Critique. Australian National University, Department of Prehistory Occasional Papers in Prehistory no. 23. Canberra: Australian National University.

Dudley, Sandra, 2009 Museum Materialities: Objects, Engagements, Interpretations. London: Routledge.

Dunnell, Robert C., 1980 Evolutionary Theory and Archaeology. Advances in Archaeological Method and Theory, vol. 7. Michael B. Schiffer, ed. Pp. 35–99. New York: Academic Press.

Dunnell, Robert C., 1989 Aspects of the Application of Evolutionary Theory in Archaeology. In Archaeological Thought in America. C. C. Lamberg-Karlovsky, ed. Pp. 35–49. Cambridge: Cambridge University Press.

Echo-Hawk, Roger C., 2000 Ancient History in the New World: Investigating Oral Traditions and the Archaeological Record of Deep-Time. American Antiquity 65(2):267–290.

Engelstad, Erika, 1991 Images of Power and Contradiction: Feminist Theory and Post-Processual Archaeology. Antiquity 65:502–514.

Engelstad, Erika, 2004 F-Word? Feminist Gender Archaeology. In Combining the Past and the Present: Archaeological Perspectives on Society. Terje Østigård, Nils Anfinset, Tore Sætersdal, and Randi Håland, eds. Pp. 39–45. Oxford: Archaeopress.

Fairbanks, Charles H., 1958 Anthropology and the Segregation Problem. In The Negro in American Society. Pp. 1–18. Tallahassee: Florida State University Studies no. 28.

Fairbanks, Charles H., 1984 The Plantation Archaeology of the Southeastern Coast. Historical Archaeology 18:1–14.

Fairbanks, Charles H., and Robert Ascher 1971 Excavation of a Slave Cabin, Georgia, U.S.A. Historical Archaeology 5:3–17.

Fanon, Frantz, 1963 The Wretched of the Earth. New York: Grove Press.

Fanon, Frantz, 1965 A Dying Colonialism. New York: Monthly Review Press.

Ferguson, Leland, ed., 1977 Historical Archaeology and the Importance of Material Things. Society for Historical Archaeology, Special Publication Series no. 2.

Ferguson, Leland, 1991 Struggling with Pots in Colonial South Carolina. In The Archaeology of Inequality. Randall H. McGuire and Robert Paynter, eds. Pp. 28–39. Oxford: Blackwell.

Ferguson, Leland, 1992 Uncommon Ground: Archaeology and Colonial African-America. Washington, DC: Smithsonian Institute Press.

Ferguson, T. J., 2003 Anthropological Archaeology Conducted by Tribes: Traditional Cultural Properties and Cultural Affiliation. In Archaeology is Anthropology. Susan D. Gillespie and Deborah L. Nichols, eds. Pp. 137–144. Arlington, VA: Archaeological Papers of the American Anthropological Association no. 13.

Fine, Arthur, 2007 Relativism, Pragmatism and the Practice of Science. In New Pragmatists. Cheryl Misak, ed. Pp. 50–67. Oxford: Oxford University Press.

Flannery, Kent V. 1972 The Cultural Evolution of Civilizations. Annual Review of Ecology and Systematics 3:399–426.

Flannery, Kent V., 1973 Archaeology with a Capital S. In Research and Theory in Current Archaeology. Charles L. Redman, ed. Pp. 47–53. New York: John Wiley and Sons.

Flannery, Kent V., and Joyce Marcus 1993 Cognitive Archaeology. Cambridge Archaeology Journal 3:260–269.

Ford, Anabel, and Megan Havrda, 2006 Archaeology under the Canopy: Imagining the Maya of El Pilar. *In* Tourism, Consumption and Representation: Narratives of Place and Self. Kevin Meethan, Alison Anderson, and Steve Miles, eds. Pp. 67–93. Wallingford: CAB International.

Ford, Richard I., 1973 Archaeology Serving Humanity. *In* Research and Theory in Current Archaeology. Charles L. Redman, ed. Pp. 83–93. New York: John Wiley and Sons.

Franklin, Maria, 2001 A Black Feminist-Inspired Archaeology. Journal of Social Archaeology 1(1): 108–125.

Fritz, John M., 1973 Relevance, Archaeology and Subsistence Theory. *In* Research and Theory in Current Archaeology. Charles L. Redman, ed. Pp. 59–82. New York: John Wiley and Sons.

Fritz, John M., and Fred T. Plog, 1970 The Nature of Archaeological Explanation. American Antiquity 35:405–412.

Funari, Pedro Paulo A., Siân Jones, and Martin Hall, 1999 Introduction: Archaeology in History. *In* Historical Archaeology: Back from the Edge. Pedro Paulo A. Funari, Siân Jones, and Martin Hall, eds. Pp. 1–20. London: Routledge.

Gabora, Liane, 2006 The Fate of Evolutionary Archaeology: Survival or Extinction? World Archaeology 38 (4):690–696.

Gaffney, Christopher F., and Vincent L. Gaffney, eds., 1987a Pragmatic Archaeology: Theory in Crisis? Oxford: BAR British Series 167.

Gaffney, Christopher F., and Vincent L. Gaffney, 1987b Introduction. *In* Pragmatic Archaeology: Theory in Crisis? Christopher F. Gaffney and Vincent L. Gaffney, eds. Pp. 1–8. Oxford: British Archaeological Reports 167.

Galison, Peter L., 1997 Image and Logic: A Material Culture of Microphysics. Chicago: University of Chicago Press.

Galison, Peter L., and David J. Stump, eds., 1996 The Disunity of Science: Boundaries, Contexts, and Power. Stanford: Stanford University Press.

Gardin, Jean-Claude, 1992 Semiotic Trends in Archaeology. *In* Representations in Archaeology. Jean-Claude Gardin and Christopher Peebles, eds. Pp. 87–104. Bloomington: Indiana University Press.

Garlake, Peter S., 1982 Prehistory and Ideology in Zimbabwe. Africa 52:1–19.

Gell, Alfred, 1998 Art and Agency: An Anthropological Theory. New York: Clarendon Press.

Geller, Pamela L., and Miranda K. Stockett, eds., 2006 Feminist Anthropology: Past, Present and Future. Philadelphia: University of Pennsylvania Press.

Gero, Joan M., 1983 Gender Bias in Archaeology: A Cross-Cultural Perspective. *In* The Socio-Politics of Archaeology. Joan M. Gero, David M. Lacey, and Michael L. Blakey, eds. Pp. 51–57. Amherst: University of Massachusetts, Department of Anthropology Research Report no. 23.

Gero, Joan M., 1985 Socio-Politics and the Woman-at-Home Ideology. American Antiquity 50:342–350.

Gero, Joan M., 2000 Troubled Travels in Agency and Feminism. *In* Agency in Archaeology. Marcia-Anne Dobres and John Robb, eds. Pp. 34–39. London: Routledge.

Gero, Joan M., and Margaret W. Conkey, eds., 1991 Engendering Archaeology: Women and Prehistory. Oxford: Blackwell.

Gibbs, Liv, 1987 Identifying Gender Representation in the Archaeological Record: A Contextual Study. *In* The Archaeology of Contextual Meanings. Ian Hodder, ed. Pp. 79–89. Cambridge: Cambridge University Press.

Giddens, Anthony, 1979 Central Problems in Social Theory. London: Macmillan.

Giddens, Anthony, 1981 A Contemporary Critique of Historical Materialism, vol. 1. Power, Property and the State. London: Macmillan.

Giddens, Anthony, 1984 The Constitution of Society. Berkeley: University of California Press.

Gilchrist, Roberta, 1994 Gender and Material Culture: The Archaeology of Religious Women. London: Routledge.

Gilchrist, Roberta, 1999 Gender and Archaeology: Contesting the Past. London: Routledge.

Gillespie, Susan D., and Deborah L. Nichols, eds., 2003 Archaeology is Anthropology. Arlington: Archaeological Papers of the American Anthropological Association no. 13.

Gilman, Antonio, 1989 Marxist Thought in American Archaeology. *In* Archaeological Thought in America. C. C. Lamberg-Karlovsky, ed. Pp. 63–73. Cambridge: Cambridge University Press.

Ginzburg, Carlo 1980 The Cheese and the Worms: The Cosmos of a Sixteenth-Century Miller. Baltimore: Johns Hopkins University Press.

Gladwin, Winifred, and Harold S. Gladwin 1929 The Red-on-Buff Culture of the Gila Basin. Medallion Papers no. 3. Pasadena: Privately Printed.

Glassie, Henry, 1969 Pattern in the Material Folk Culture of the Eastern United States. University of Pennsylvania Monographs in Folklore and Folklife. Philadelphia: University of Pennsylvania Press.

Glassie, Henry, 1972 Folk Art. *In* Folklore and Folklife: An Introduction. Richard M. Dotson, ed. Pp. 268–279. Chicago: University of Chicago Press.

Glassie, Henry, 1975 Folk Housing in Middle Virginia: A Structural Analysis of Historic Artifacts. Knoxville: University of Tennessee Press.

Gosden, Chris, 1994 Social Being and Time. Oxford: Blackwell.

Gosden, Chris, 2001 Postcolonial Archaeology: Issues of Culture, Identity and Knowledge. *In* Archaeological Theory Today. Ian Hodder, ed. Pp. 241–261. Cambridge: Polity Press.

Gould, Richard A., 1980 Living Archaeology. Cambridge: Cambridge University Press.

Gould, Richard A., 1985 The Empiricist Strikes Back: Reply to Binford. American Antiquity 50 (3):638–644.

Gould, Richard A., 1990: Recovering the Past. Albuquerque: University of New Mexico Press.

Gould, Richard A., and Michael B. Schiffer, eds. 1981: Modern Material Culture: The Archaeology of Us. New York: Academic Press.

Habermas, Jürgen, 1984 The Theory of Communicative Action, vol. 1. Reason and the Rationalization of Society. Boston: Beacon Press.

Habermas, Jürgen 1989 The Theory of Communicative Action, vol. 2. Lifeworld and System: A Critique of Functionalist Reason. Boston: Beacon Press.

Hagar, Lori D., ed., 1997 Women in Human Evolution. London: Routledge.

Hall, Martin, 1984 The Burden of Tribalism: The Social Context of Southern African Studies. American Antiquity 49(3):455–467.

Hall, Martin, 2000 Archaeology and the Modern World: Colonial Transcripts in South Africa and the Chesapeake. London: Taylor and Francis.

Hall, Martin, and Stephen W. Silliman, eds., 2006 Historical Archaeology. Oxford: Blackwell.

Handsman, Russell G., 1980 Studying Myth and History in Modern America: Perspectives for the Past from the Continent. Reviews in Anthropology 7 (2):255–268.

Hanks, William, 1990 Referential Practice: Language and Lived Space among the Maya. Chicago: University of Chicago Press.

Haraway, Donna J., 1988 Situated Knowledges: The Science Question in Feminism and the Privilege of Partial Perspective. Feminist Studies 14 (3):575–599.

Haraway, Donna J., 1991 Simians, Cyborgs and Women: The Reinvention of Nature. London: Routledge.

Harding, Sandra, 1991 Whose Science? Whose Knowledge? Thinking from Women's Lives. Ithaca, NY: Cornell University Press.

Harvey, David, 2007 A Brief History of Neoliberalism. Oxford: Oxford University Press.

Hawkes, Terrence, 2003 Structuralism and Semiotics. 2nd edition. London: Routledge.

Hayes, Katherine H., and Stephen A. Mrozowski, eds., 2007 The Historical Archaeology of Sylvester Manor. Northeast Historical Archaeology Vol. 36.

Hemming, Steve, 2002 Taming the Colonial Archive: History, Native Title and Colonialism. *In* Through a Smoky Mirror: History and Native Title. Mandy Paul and Geoffrey Gray, eds. Pp. 49–64. Native Title Research Series. Canberra: Aboriginal Studies Press.

Hempel, Carl G., and Paul Oppenheim, 1948 Studies in the Logic of Explanation. Philosophy of Science 15:135–175.

Hicks, Dan, 2003 Archaeology Unfolding: Diversity and the Loss of Isolation. Oxford Journal of Archaeology 22(3):315–329.

Hicks, Dan, and Mary C. Beaudry, 2006 Introduction: The Place of Historical Archaeology. *In* The Cambridge Companion to Historical Archaeology. Dan Hicks and Mary C. Beaudry, eds. Pp. 1–9. Cambridge: Cambridge University Press.

Hodder, Ian, ed., 1978a The Spatial Organisation of Culture. London: Duckworth.

Hodder, Ian, 1979 Social and Economic Stress and Material Culture Patterning. American Antiquity 44:446–454.

Hodder, Ian, ed., 1982a Symbolic and Structural Archaeology. Cambridge: Cambridge University Press.

Hodder, Ian, 1982b Theoretical Archaeology: A Reactionary View. *In* Symbolic and Structural Archaeology. Ian Hodder, ed. Pp. 1–16. Cambridge: Cambridge University Press.

Hodder, Ian, 1982c Symbols in Action: Ethnoarcheological Studies of Material Culture. Cambridge: Cambridge University Press.

Hodder, Ian, 1984 Archaeology in 1984. Antiquity 58:25–32.

Hodder, Ian, 1986 Reading the Past. Cambridge: Cambridge University Press.

Hodder, Ian, ed., 1987 Archaeology as Long-Term History. Cambridge: Cambridge University Press.

Hodder, Ian, 1989 This is Not an Article about Material Culture as Text. Journal of Anthropological Archaeology 8:250–269.

Hodder, Ian, 2005 An Archaeology of the Four-Field Approach in Anthropology in the United States. *In* Unwrapping the Sacred Bundle: Reflections on the Disciplining of Anthropology. Daniel A. Segal and Sylvia J. Yanagisako, eds. Pp. 126–140. Durham, NC: Duke University Press.

Hodder, Ian, 2006 Thing Theory: Towards an Integrated Archaeological Perspective. Scottish Archaeological Journal 28(2):v–vi.

Hodder, Ian, and Clive Orton, 1976 Spatial Analysis in Archaeology. Cambridge: Cambridge University Press.

Horning, Audrey, 2000 Urbanism in the Colonial South: The Development of Seventeenth-Century Jamestown. *In* Urban Archaeology in the South. Amy Young, ed. Pp. 52–68. Tuscaloosa: University of Alabama Press.

Hoskins, Janet, 1998 Biographical Objects: How Things Tell the Stories of People's Lives. London: Routledge.

Inuit Heritage Trust (IHT), 2009a Inuit Heritage Trust website: www.ihti.ca/eng/home-new.html.

Inuit Heritage Trust (IHT), 2009b Taloyoak – Stories of Thunder and Stone. www.taloyoaknunavut.ca/html/english/index.html.

James, William, 1898 Philosophical Conceptions and Practical Results. The Annual Public Address before the [Philosophical] Union [of the University of California] August 26, 1898. Berkeley: The University Press.

James, William, 1907 Pragmatism: A New Name for Some Old Ways of Thinking. New York: Longmans, Green and Co.

Jayasena, M. Ranjith, 2006 The Historical Archaeology of Katuwana, a Dutch East India Company Fort in Sri Lanka. Post-Medieval Archaeology 40 (1):111–128.

Johnson, Matthew, 1989 The Conception of Agency in Archaeological Interpretation. Journal of Anthropological Archaeology 8:189–211.

Johnson, Matthew, 1993 Housing Culture: Traditional Architecture in an English Landscape. London: University College London Press.

Johnson, Matthew, 1996 An Archaeology of Capitalism. Oxford: Blackwell.

Johnson, Matthew, 1999 The New Postmedieval Archaeology. *In* Old and New Worlds. Geoff Egan and Ronald L. Michael, eds. Pp. 17–22. Oxford: Oxbow Books.

Johnson, Matthew, 2006 The Tide Reversed: Prospects and Potentials for a Postcolonial Archaeology of Europe. *In* Historical Archaeology. Martin Hall and Stephen W. Silliman, eds. Pp. 313–331. Oxford: Blackwell.

Joyce, Rosemary A., 2000a Girling the Girl and Boying the Boy: The Production of Adulthood in Ancient Mesoamerica. World Archaeology 31:473–483.

Joyce, Rosemary A., 2000b A Precolumbian gaze: Male Aexuality among the Ancient Maya. *In* Archaeologies of Sexuality. Barbara Voss and Robert Schmidt, eds. Pp. 263–283. London: Routledge.

Keane, Webb, 1997 Signs of Recognition: Power and Hazards of Representation in an Indonesian Society. Berkeley: University of California Press.

Keane, Webb, 2003 Semiotics and the Social Analysis of Material Things. Language and Communication 23:409–425.

Keane, Webb, 2005 Signs Are Not the Garb of Meaning: On the Social Analysis of Material Things. *In* Materiality. Daniel Miller, ed. Pp. 182–205. Durham, NC: Duke University Press.

Kehoe, Alice Beck, 1998 The Land of Prehistory: A Critical History of American Archaeology. London: Routledge.

Kelly, Kenneth G., 1997 The Archaeology of African-European Interaction: Investigating the Social Role of Trade, Traders and the Use of Space in the Seventeenth- and Eighteenth-Century Hueda Kingdom, Republic of Benin. World Archaeology 28 (3):77–95.

Kelly, Kenneth G., 2004 The African Diaspora Starts Here: Historical Archaeology of Coastal West Africa. *In* African Historical Archaeologies. Andrew M. Reid and Paul J. Lane, eds. Pp. 219–241. New York: Kluwer/Plenum.

Kelly, Robert, 2002 Archaeology is Anthropology. The SAA Archaeological Record 2(3):13–14.

Kincaid, Harold, John Dupré, and Alison Wylie, 2007 Value-Free Science: Ideals and Illusions. Oxford: Oxford University Press.

Knappett, Carl, 2005 Thinking through Material Culture: An Interdisciplinary Perspective. Philadelphia: University of Pennsylvania Press.

Knappett, Carl, and Lambros Malafouris, eds., 2009 Material Agency: Towards a Non-Anthropocentric Approach. New York: Springer.

Knorr Cetina, Karin, 1999 Epistemic Cultures: How the Sciences Make Knowledge. Cambridge, MA: Harvard University Press.

Kopytoff, Igor, 1986 The Cultural Biography of Things: Commoditization as Process. *In* The Social Life of Things: Commodities in Cultural Perspective. Arjun Appadurai, ed. Pp. 64–91. Cambridge: Cambridge University Press.

Kroskrity, Paul V., ed., 2000 Regimes of Language: Ideologies, Politics, and Identities. Santa Fe: School of American Research Press.

Kuhn, Thomas S., 1962 The Structure of Scientific Revolutions. Chicago: University of Chicago Press.

Lacan, Jacques, 1977: Écrits, a Selection. London: Tavistock Publications.

Lakoff, George, 1987 Women, Fire and Dangerous Things: What Categories Reveal about the Mind. Chicago: University of Chicago Press.

Latour, Bruno, 1996: Aramis or the Love for Technology. Cambridge, MA: Harvard University Press.

Latour, Bruno, 1999 Pandora's Hope: Essays on the Reality of Science Studies. Cambridge, MA: Harvard University Press.

Latour, Bruno, 2005 Reassembling the Social: An Introduction to Actor-Network-Theory. Oxford: Oxford University Press.

Latour, Bruno, and Steve Woolgar 1979 Laboratory Life: The Social Construction of Scientific Facts. Los Angeles: Sage.

Law, John, and John Hassard, eds., 1999: Actor Network Theory and After. New York: Wiley-Blackwell.

Lees, Susan, 2002 Separation versus a Larger Vision. The SAA Archaeological Record 2(3):11–12.

Lefebvre, Henri, 1991 The Production of Space. Oxford: Blackwell.

Lekson, Stephen H., 1999 The Chaco Meridian. Walnut Creek, CA: AltaMira Press.

Lekson, Stephen H., 2009 A History of the Ancient Southwest. Santa Fe: School of American Research Press.

Lele, Veerendra P., 2006 Material Habits, Identity, Semeiotic. Journal of Social Archaeology 6:48–70.

Leonard, Robert D., and George Jones 1987 Elements of an Inclusive Model for Archaeology. Journal of Archaeological Research 6:199–219.

Leone, Mark P., 1977 The New Mormon Temple in Washington DC. In Historical Archaeology and the Importance of Material Things. Leland Ferguson, ed. Pp. 43–61. Society for Historical Archaeology, Special Publication no. 2.

Leone, Mark P., 1982 Some Opinions about Recovering Mind. American Antiquity 47:742–760.

Leone, Mark P., 1984 Interpreting Ideology in Historical Archaeology: Using the Rules of Perspective in the William Paca Garden in Annapolis, Maryland. In Ideology, Power and Prehistory. Daniel Miller and Christopher Tilley, eds. Pp. 25–35. Cambridge: Cambridge University Press.

Leone, Mark P., 1986 Symbolic, Structural and Critical Archaeology. In American Archaeology Past, Present and Future. David Meltzer, Donald Fowler, and Jeremy Sabloff, eds. Pp. 415–438. Washington, DC: Smithsonian Institution Press.

Leone, Mark P., 1988 The Georgian Order as the Order of Merchant Capitalism in Annapolis, Maryland. In The Recovery of Meaning: Historical Archaeology in the Eastern United States. Mark P. Leone and Parker B. Potter, eds. Pp. 235–261. Washington, DC: Smithsonian Institution Press.

Leone, Mark P., 1995 A Historical Archaeology of Capitalism. American Anthropologist 97(2):251–268.

Leone, Mark P., and Parker B. Potter, Jr., 1994 Historical Archaeology of Capitalism. Bulletin of the Society for American Archaeology 12(4):14–15.

Leone, Mark P., and Parker B. Potter, Jr., eds., 1999 Historical Archaeologies of Capitalism. New York: Kluwer.

Leone, Mark P., Parker B. Potter, Jr., and Paul A. Shackel, 1987 Towards a Critical Archaeology. Current Anthropology 28:283–302.

Lévi-Strauss, Claude, 1963 Structural Anthropology. New York: Basic Books.

Lévi-Strauss, Claude, 1966 The Savage Mind. Chicago: University of Chicago Press.

Liebmann, Matthew, 2008 Introduction: The Intersections of Archaeology and Postcolonial studies. In Archaeology and the Postcolonial Critique. Matthew Liebmann and Uzma Rizvi, eds. Pp. 1–20. Walnut Creek, CA: AltaMira Press.

Liebmann, Matthew, and Uzma Rizvi, eds., 2008 Archaeology and the Postcolonial Critique. Walnut Creek, CA: AltaMira Press.

Lightfoot, Kent G., 2003 Russian Colonization: The Implications of Mercantile Colonial Practices in the North Pacific. Historical Archaeology 37(4):14–28.

Little, Barbara J., 1994 People with History: An Update on Historical Archaeology in the United States. Journal of Archaeological Method and Theory 1:5–40.

Longacre, William A., 1964 Archeology as Anthropology: A Case Study. Science 144(3625):1454–1455.

Lubbock, John, 1865 Pre-Historic Times. London: Williams and Norgate.

McGuire, Randall H., 1988 Dialogues with the Dead: Ideology and the Cemetery. In The Recovery of Meaning: Historical Archaeology in the Eastern United States. Mark P. Leone and Parker B. Potter, Jr., eds. Pp. 435–480. Washington, DC: Smithsonian Institution Press.

McGuire, Randall H., 1991 Building Power in the Cultural Landscape of Broome Country, New York, 1880–1940. In The Archaeology of Inequality. Randall H. McGuire and Robert Paynter, eds. Pp. 102–124. Oxford: Blackwell.

McGuire, Randall H., 1992 A Marxist Archaeology. New York: Academic Press.

McGuire, Randall H., 2006 Marxism and Capitalism in Historical Archaeology. In The Cambridge Companion to Historical Archaeology. Dan Hicks and Mary C. Beaudry, eds. Pp. 123–142. Cambridge: Cambridge University Press.

McGuire, Randall H., 2008 Archaeology as Political Action. Berkeley: University of California Press.

McGuire, Randall H., and Robert Paynter, eds., 1991 The Archaeology of Inequality. Oxford: Blackwell.

McNiven, Ian J., and Lynette Russell, 2005 Appropriated Pasts: Indigenous Peoples and the Colonial Culture of Archaeology. Walnut Creek, CA: AltaMira Press.

Marcus, George E., and Michael J. Fischer, 1986 Anthropology as Cultural Critique: An Experimental Moment in the Human Sciences. Chicago: University of Chicago Press.

Margolis, Joseph, 1986 Pragmatism without Foundations: Reconciling Realism and Relativism. Oxford: Blackwell.

Margolis, Joseph, 1987 Science without Unity: Reconciling the Human and Natural Sciences. Oxford: Blackwell.

Mellars, Paul, 1991 Cognitive Changes and the Emergence of Modern Humans. Cambridge Archaeology Journal 1:63–76.

Meltzer, David J., 1981 Ideology and Material Culture. In Modern Material Culture, the Archaeology of US. Richard A. Gould and Michael B. Schiffer, eds. Pp. 113–125. New York: Academic Press.

Menand, Louis, 2001 The Metaphysical Club: A Story of Ideas in America. New York: Farrar, Straus and Giroux.

Meskell, Lynn, 1999 Archaeologies of Social Life: Age, Sex, et cetera in Ancient Eygpt. Oxford: Blackwell.

Meskell, Lynn, 2004 Object Worlds in Ancient Egypt: Material Biographies Past and Present. Oxford: Berg.

Meskell, Lynn, ed., 2005 Archaeology under Fire: Nationalism, Politics and Heritage in the Eastern Mediterranean and Middle East. London: Routledge.

Miller, Bruce G., 2003 Invisible Indigenes: The Politics of Nonrecognition. Lincoln: University of Nebraska Press.

Miller, Daniel, ed., 2005 Materiality. Durham, NC: Duke University Press.

Miller, Daniel, and Christopher Tilley, eds., 1984 Ideology, Power and Prehistory. Cambridge: Cambridge University Press.

Mills, Antonia, 1995 First Nations Help Create a Viable Human Future. Anthropology Newsletter 36(7):36.

Mithen, Steven, 1994 From Domain-Specific to Generalized Intelligence: A Cognitive Interpretation of the Middle/Upper Paleolithic Transition. In The Ancient Mind: Elements of Cognitive Archaeology. Colin Renfrew and Ezra B. W. Zubrow, eds. Pp. 29–39. Cambridge: Cambridge University Press.

Mithen, Steven, 1996 The Prehistory of the Mind: The Cognitive Origins of Art, Religion and Science. London: Thames and Hudson.

Moore, Henrietta L., 1986 Space, Text and Gender. Cambridge: Cambridge University Press.

Moore, Henrietta L., 1988 Feminism and Anthropology. Cambridge: Polity Press.

Moore, Henrietta L., 2007 The Subject of Anthropology: Gender, Symbolism and Psychoanalysis. Cambridge: Polity Press.

Mrozowski, Stephen A., 1991 Landscapes of Inequality. In The Archaeology of Inequality. Randall H. McGuire and Robert Paynter, eds. Pp. 79–101. Oxford: Blackwell.

Mrozowski, Stephen A., 1996 Nature, Society and Culture: Theoretical Considerations. In Historical Archaeology and the Study of American Culture. Lu Ann De Cunzo and Bernard L. Herman, eds. Pp. 447–472. Knoxville: University of Tennessee Press.

Mrozowski, Stephen A., 1999 Interdisciplinary Perspectives on the Production of Urban Industrial Space. In Old and New Worlds. Geoff Egan and Ronald L. Michael, eds. Pp. 136–146. Oxford: Oxbow Books.

Mrozowski, Stephen A., 2006 The Archaeology of Class in Urban America. Cambridge: Cambridge University Press.

Mrozowski, Stephen A., 2009 Pulling the Threads Together: Issues of Theory and Practice in an Archaeology of the Modern World. In Crossing Paths or Sharing Tracks? Future Directions in the Archaeological Study of Post-1550 Britain and Ireland. Audrey Horning and Marilyn Palmer, eds. Pp. 381–396. Woodbridge: Boydell and Brewster.

Mrozowski, Stephen A., Grace H. Zeising, and Mary C. Beaudry, 1996 Living on the Boott: Historical Archaeology at the Boott Mills Boardinghouses, Lowell, Massachusetts. Amherst: University of Massachusetts Press.

Mrozowski, Stephen A., Holly Herbster, David Brown, and Katherine L. Priddy, 2009 Magunkaquog Materiality, Federal Recognition and the Search for a Deeper Meaning. International Journal of Historical Archaeology 13(4): 430–463.

Muller, Jon, 1997 Mississippian Political Economy. New York: Plenum.

Munn, Nancy D., 1986 The Fame of Gawa. Cambridge: Cambridge University Press.

Nelson, Margaret C., Sarah M. Nelson, and Alison Wylie, eds., 1994 Equity Issues for Women in Archaeology. Arlington, VA: American Anthropological Association.

Nelson, Sarah Milledge, ed., 2006 Handbook of Gender in Archaeology. Walnut Creek, CA: AltaMira Press.

Nicholas, George P., and Thomas D. Andrews, 1997 Indigenous Archaeology in the Post-Modern World. In At a Crossroads: Archaeology and First Peoples in Canada. George P. Nicholas and Thomas D. Andrews, eds. Pp. 1–18. Burnaby: Archaeology Press, Simon Fraser University.

Nicolis, Franco, 2001 Bell Beakers Today: Pottery, People, Culture, Symbols in Prehistoric Europe. Toronto: Servizio Beni Culturali Ufficio Beni Archeologici.

O'Brien, Michael J., and R. Lee Lyman, 2000 Applying Evolutionary Archaeology. New York: Plenum.

O'Brien, Michael J., and R. Lee Lyman, 2002 Evolutionary Archaeology: Current Status and Future Prospects. Evolutionary Anthropology 11:26–36.

O'Brien, Michael J., R. Lee Lyman, and Michael B. Schiffer 2005 Archaeology as a Process: Processualism and Its Progeny. Salt Lake City: University of Utah Press.

Olsen, Bjørnar, 2003 Material Culture after Text: Re-Membering Things. Norwegian Archaeological Review 36(3):87–104.

Orser, Charles E., 1988 Toward a Theory of Power for Historical Archaeology: Plantations and Space. In The Recovery of Meaning: Historical Archaeology in the Eastern United States. Mark P. Leone and Parker B. Potter, Jr., eds. Pp. 313–343. Washington, DC: Smithsonian Institution Press.

Orser, Charles E., 1996 A Historical Archaeology of the Modern World. New York: Plenum.

Orser, Charles E., ed., 2001 Race and the Archaeology of Identity. Salt Lake City: University of Utah Press.

Orser, Charles E., 2006 Symbolic Violence and Landscape Pedagogy: An Illustration from the Irish Countryside. Historical Archaeology 40(2):20–36.

Orser, Charles E., 2007 The Archaeology of Race and Racialization in Historic America. Gainsville: University of Florida Press.

Otto, John S., 1984 Cannon's Point Plantation 1794–1860: Living Conditions and Status Patterns in the Old South. New York: Academic Press.

Parmentier, Richard J., 1987 The Sacred Remains: Myth, History, and Polity in Belau. Chicago: University of Chicago Press.

Parmentier, Richard J., 1994 Signs in Society: Studies in Semiotic Anthropology. Bloomington: Indiana University Press.

Parmentier, Richard J., 1997 The Pragmatic Semiotics of Culture. Semiotica 116.

Patterson, Thomas C., 1989 History and the Post-Processual Archaeologies. Man (N.S.) 24:555–566.

Patterson, Thomas C., 1997 Inventing Western Civilization. New York: Monthly Review Press.

Patterson, Thomas C., 2001 A Social History of Anthropology in the United States. Oxford: Berg.

Paynter, Robert, 1988 Steps to an Archaeology of Capitalism. In The Recovery of Meaning: Historical Archaeology in the Eastern United States. Mark P. Leone and Parker B. Potter, Jr., eds. Pp. 407–433. Washington, DC: Smithsonian Institution Press.

Paynter, Robert, 1989 The Archaeology of Equality and Inequality. Annual Review of Anthropology 18:369–399.

Paynter, Robert, 2000a Historical and Anthropological Archaeology: Forging Alliances. Journal of Archaeological Research 8(1):1–37.

Paynter, Robert, 2000b Historical Archaeology and the Post-Columbian World of North America. Journal of Archaeological Research 8(3):169–217.

Peirce, Charles Sanders, 1878 How to Make Our Ideas Clear. Popular Science Monthly 12: 286–302.

Peirce, Charles Sanders, 1905 What Pragmatism Is. The Monist 17:161–181.

Perry, Elizabeth, and Rosemary Joyce, 2001 Providing a Past for "Bodies that Matter": Judith Butler's Impact on the Archaeology of Gender. International Journal of Sexuality and Gender Studies 6(1/2): 63–76.

Perry, Warren, 1999 The Archaeology of Colonial Impact in Southern Africa 1500–1900. New York: Plenum.

Phillips, Philip, 1955 American Archaeology and General Anthropological Theory. Southwestern Journal of Anthropology 11:246–250.

Pickering, Andrew, 1995 The Mangle of Practice: Time, Agency and Science. Chicago: University of Chicago Press.

Posnansky, Merrick, 1959 The Progress and Prospects in Historical Archaeology in Uganda. Kampala: Uganda Museum Occasional Paper 4.

Posnansky, Merrick, 1966 Kingship, Archaeology and Historical Myth. Uganda Journal 30:1–12.

Posnansky, Merrick, 1968 The Excavation of Ankole Capital Site at Bweyorere. Uganda Journal 32:165–183.

Posnansky, Merrick, 1969 Myth and Methodology: The Archaeological Contribution to African History. Accra: Ghana University Press.

Posnansky, Merrick, 1999 West Africanist Reflections on African-American Archaeology. In "I Too Am America": Archaeological Studies of African-American Life. Theresa A. Singleton, ed. Pp. 21–37. Charlottesville: University of Virginia Press.

Posnansky, Merrick, and Christopher R. DeCorse, 1986 Historical Archaeology in Sub-Saharan Africa: A Review. Historical Archaeology 20(1):1–14.

Preucel, Robert W., 1999 Review of Evolutionary Archaeology: Theory and Application, edited by Michael J. O'Brien. Journal of Field Archaeology 26:93–99.

Preucel, Robert W., 2006: Archaeological Semiotics. Oxford: Blackwell.

Preucel, Robert W., and Alexander A. Bauer, 2001 Archaeological Pragmatics. Norwegian Archaeological Review 34:85–96.

Preucel, Robert W., and Ian Hodder, eds., 1996 Contemporary Archaeology in Theory. Oxford: Blackwell.

Preucel, Robert W., Lucy Fowler Williams, and Brian Daniels, 2006 Interview with Suzan Shown Harjo on the history of NAGPRA. Ms.

Quine, Willard van Orman, 1981 Theories and Things. Cambridge, MA: Harvard University Press.

Raibmon, Paige, 2005 Authentic Indians: Episodes of Encounter from the Late Nineteenth-Century Northwest Coast. Durham, NC: Duke University Press.

Reid, Andrew M., and Paul J. Lane, eds., 2004a African Historical Archaeologies. New York: Kluwer/Plenum.

Reid, Andrew M., and Paul J. Lane, 2004b African Historical Archaeologies: An Introductory Consideration of Scope and Potential. *In* African Historical Archaeologies. Andrew M. Reid and Paul J. Lane, eds. Pp. 1–32. New York: Kluwer/Plenum.

Reid, J. Jefferson, William L. Rathje, and Michael B. Schiffer, 1975 Behavioral Archaeology: Four Strategies. American Anthropologist 77:864–869.

Renfrew, Colin, 1982 Explanation Revisited. *In* Theory and Explanation in Archaeology: The Southampton Conference. Colin Renfrew, Michael J. Rowlands, and Barbara Abbott Seagraves, eds. Pp. 5–23. New York: Academic Press.

Renfrew, Colin, 1994a Towards a Cognitive archaeology. *In* The Ancient Mind: Elements of Cognitive Archaeology. Colin Renfrew and Ezra B. W. Zubrow, eds. Pp. 3–12. Cambridge: Cambridge University Press.

Renfrew, Colin, 2001a Loot, Legitimacy and Ownership. New York: Duckworth.

Renfrew, Colin, 2001b Symbol before Concept: Material Engagement in the Early Development of Society. *In* Archaeological Theory Today. Ian Hodder, ed. Pp. 122–140. Cambridge: Polity Press.

Renfrew, Colin, 2004 Towards a Theory of Material Engagement. *In* Rethinking Materiality: The Engagement of Mind with the Material World. Elizabeth DeMarrais, Chris Gosden, and Colin Renfrew, eds. Pp. 23–31. Cambridge: McDonald Institute for Archaeological Research.

Ricoeur, Paul, 1971 The Model of the Text: Meaningful Action Considered as Text. Social Research 38:529–562.

Rorty, Richard, 1979 Philosophy and the Mirror of Nature. Princeton: Princeton University Press.

Rorty, Richard, 1982 Consequences of Pragmatism. Minneapolis: University of Minnesota Press.

Rorty, Richard, 1989 Contingency, Irony, and Solidarity. Cambridge: Cambridge University Press.

Rorty, Richard, 1991 Objectivity, Relativism, and Truth: Philosophical Papers, vol. 1. Cambridge: Cambridge University Press.

Rorty, Richard, 1998 Achieving Our Country: Leftist Thought in Twentieth-Century America. Cambridge, MA: Harvard University Press.

Rorty, Richard, 1999 Philosophy and Social Hope. London: Penguin Books.

Sabloff, Jeremy A., 2008 Archaeology Matters: Action Archaeology in the Modern World. Walnut Creek, CA: Left Coast Press.

Said, Edward, 1978 Orientalism. New York: Vintage.

Saitta, Dean J., 2003 Archaeology and the Problems of Men. *In* Essential Tensions in Archaeological Method and Theory. Todd L. VanPool and Christine S. VanPool, eds. Pp. 11–16. Salt Lake City: University of Utah Press.

Saitta, Dean J., 2007 The Archaeology of Collective Action. Gainesville: University Press of Florida.

Salmon, Merrilee H., 1982: Philosophy and Archaeology. New York: Academic Press.

Salmon, Merrilee H. and Wesley C. Salmon, 1979 Alternative Models of Scientific Explanation. American Anthropologist 81:61–74.

Saussure, Ferdinand de, 1966 Course in General Linguistics. New York: McGraw-Hill.

Schatzki, Theodore R., Karin Knorr Cetina, and Eike von Savigny, eds., 2001 The Practice Turn in Contemporary Theory. London: Routledge.

Schieffelin, Bambi B., Kathryn A. Woolard, and Paul V. Kroskrity, eds., 1998 Language Ideologies: Practice and Theory. Oxford: Oxford University Press.

Schiffer, Michael B., 1975 Behavioral Chain Analysis: Activities, Organization, and the Use of Space. Fieldiana 65:103–74.

Schiffer, Michael B., 1976 Behavioral Archaeology. New York: Academic Press.

Schiffer, Michael B., 1995 Behavioral Archaeology: First Principles. Salt Lake City: University of Utah Press.

Schiffer Michael B., 1999 Material Life of Human Beings. London: Routledge.

Schmidt, Peter R., 1978 Historical Archaeology: A Structural Approach in an African Culture. Westport, CT: Greenwood Press.

Schmidt, Peter R., 2006 Historical Archaeology in Africa: Representation, Social Memory and Oral Traditions. Walnut Creek, CA: Altamira Press.

Schmidt, Robert A., and Barbara L. Voss, eds., 2000 Archaeologies of Sexuality. London: Routledge.

Schrire, Carmel, 1980 Hunter-Gatherers in Africa. Science 210:890–891.

Schuyler, Robert L., 1999 The Centrality of Post-Medieval studies to General Historical Archaeology. *In* Old and New Worlds. Geoff Egan and Ronald L. Michael, eds. Pp. 10–16. Oxford: Oxbow Books.

Segal, Daniel A., and Sylvia J. Yanagisako, eds, 2005 Unwrapping the Sacred Bundle: Reflections on the Disciplining of Anthropology. Durham, NC: Duke University Press.

Shackel, Paul A., 1993 Personal Discipline and Material Culture: An Archaeology of Annapolis. Knoxville: University of Tennessee Press.

Shackel, Paul A., 1996 Culture Change and the New Technology: An Archaeology of the Early American Industrial Era. New York: Plenum Press.

Shackel, Paul A., Paul R. Mullins, and Mark S. Warner, 1998 Historical Archaeology in Annapolis, Maryland. Knoxville: University of Tennessee Press.

Shanks, Michael, and Christopher Tilley, 1987a Re-Constructing Archaeology. Cambridge: Cambridge University Press.

Shanks, Michael, and Christopher Tilley, 1987b Social Theory and Archaeology. Cambridge: Polity Press.

Shepherd, Nick, 2002a Heading South, Looking North: Why We Need a Postcolonial Archaeology. Public Archaeology 3(4):248–256.

Shepherd, Nick, 2002b The Politics of Archaeology in Africa. Annual Review of Anthropology 31:189–209.

Shepherd, Nick, 2003 State of the Discipline: Science, Culture and Identity in South African Archaeology, 1870–2003. Journal of Southern African Studies 29 (4):823–844.

Shove, Elizabeth, Frank Trentmann, and Richard Wilk, 2009 Time, Consumption and Everyday Life: Practice, Materiality and Culture. Oxford: Berg.

Siefert, Donna J., ed., 1991 Gender in Historical Archaeology. Historical Archaeology 25(4):1–155.

Silliman, Stephen W., 2005 Culture Contact or Colonialism? Challenges in the Archaeology of North America. American Antiquity 70:55–74.

Singer, Milton, 1984 Man's Glassy Essence: Explorations in Semiotic Anthropology. Bloomington: Indiana University Press.

Singleton, Theresa A., ed., 1985 The Archaeology of Slavery and Plantation Life Orlando: Academic Press.

Singleton, Theresa A., ed., 1999 "I Too Am America": Archaeological Studies of African-American Life. Charlottesville: University of Virginia Press.

Singleton, Theresa A., 2006 African Diaspora Archaeology in Dialogue. In Afro-Atlantic Dialogues: Anthropology in the Diaspora. Kevin A. Yelvington, ed. Pp. 249–287. Santa Fe: School of American Research Seminar Series.

Skibo, James M., and Michael B. Schiffer, 2008 People and Things: A Behavioral Approach to Material Culture. New York: Springer.

Skibo, James M., William H. Walker, and Axel E. Nielsen, eds, 1995 Expanding Archaeology. Salt Lake City: University of Utah Press.

Silver, Vernon, 2009 The Lost Chalice: The Epic Hunt for a Priceless Masterpiece. New York: William Morrow.

Silliman, Stephen W., ed., 2008 Collaborative Archaeology at the Trowel's Edge: Learning and Teaching in Indigenous Archaeology. Tuscon: University of Arizona Press.

Silverstein, Michael, 1976 Shifters, Linguistic Categories, and Cultural Descriptions. In Meaning in Anthropology. Keith Basso and Henry Selby, eds. PP. 11–55. Albuquerque: University of New Mexico Press.

Silverstein, Michael, 2005 Languages/Cultures are Dead! Long Live the Linguistic-Cultural! In

Unwrapping the Sacred Bundle: Reflections on the Disciplining of Anthropology. Daniel A. Segal and Sylvia J. Yanagisako, eds. Pp. 99–140. Durham, NC: Duke University Press.

Sinopoli, Carla M., 2006 Imperial landscapes of South Asia. In Archaeology of Asia. Miriam T. Stark, ed. Pp. 324–348. Oxford: Blackwell.

Smail, Daniel Lord, 2008 On Deep History and the Brain. Berkeley: University of California Press.

Smith, Claire, and H. Martin Wobst, eds., 2005 Indigenous Archaeologies: Decolonizing Theory and Practice. London: Unwin Hyman.

Smith, Laurajane, 2000 "Doing Archaeology": Cultural Heritage Management and Its Role in Identifying the Link between Archaeological Practice and Theory. International Journal of Heritage Studies 6 (4):309–316.

Smith, Laurajane, 2001 Archaeology and the Governance of Material Culture: A Case Study from South-Eastern Australia. Norwegian Archaeological Review 34(2):97–105.

Smith, Laurajane, 2006 Uses of Heritage. London: Routledge.

Soja, Edward, W., 1980 The Socio-Spatial Dialectic. Annals of the Association of American Geographers 70:207–225.

Soja, Edward W., 1989 Postmodern Geographies: The Reassertion of Space in Critical Social Theory. London: Verso.

South, Stanley, 1977 Method and Theory in Historical Archaeology. New York: Academic Press.

South, Stanley, ed., 1994 Pioneers in Historical Archaeology: Breaking New Ground. New York: Plenum.

South, Stanley, and Kathleen Deagan, 2002 Historical Archaeology in the Southeast, 1930–2000. In Histories of Southeastern Archaeology. Shannon Tushingham, Jane Hill, and Charles McNutt, eds. Pp. 35–50. Tuscaloosa: University of Alabama Press.

Spivak, Gayatri Chakravorty, 1988 Can the Subaltern Speak? In Marxism and the Interpretation of Culture. Cary Nelson and Lawrence Grossberg, eds. Pp. 271–313. Urbana: University of Illinois Press.

Spriggs, Matthew, ed., 1984 Marxist Perspectives in Archaeology. Cambridge: Cambridge University Press.

Sterud, Eugene, 1973 A Paradigmatic View of Prehistory. In The Explanation of Culture Change: Models in Prehistory. Colin Renfrew, ed. Pp. 3–17. London: Duckworth.

Stocking, George W., Jr., 1995 Delimiting Anthropology: Historical Reflections on the Boundaries of a Boundless Discipline. Social Research 62(4):933–966.

Strathern, Marilyn, 1996 Cutting the Network. Journal of the Royal Anthropological Institute (N.S.) 2:517–535.

Thomas, David Hurst, 2001 Skull Wars: Kennewick Man, Archaeology and the Battle for Native Identity. New York: Basic Books.

Tilley, Christopher, 1981 Conceptual Frameworks for the Explanation of Sociocultural Change. In Pattern of the Past: Studies in Honour of David Clarke. Ian Hodder, Glynn Isaac, and Normand Hammond, eds. Pp. 363–386. Cambridge: Cambridge University Press.

Tilley, Christopher, 1989a Interpreting Material Culture. In The Meaning of Things. Ian Hodder, ed. Pp. 185–194. London: Unwin Hyman.

Tilley, Christopher, 1989b Archaeology as Socio-Political Action in the Present. In Critical Traditions in Contemporary Archaeology: Essays on the Philosophy, History and Socio-Politics of Archaeology. Valerie Pinsky and Alison Wylie, eds. Pp. 104–116. Cambridge: Cambridge University Press.

Tilley, Christopher, 1991 Material Culture and Text: The Art of Ambiguity. London: Routledge.

Tilley, Christopher, 1999 Metaphor and Material Culture. Oxford: Blackwell.

Trigg, Heather B., 2005 From Household to Empire: Society and Social Interactions in Early-Colonial New Mexico. Tuscon: University of Arizona Press.

Trigger, Bruce G., 1978 Time and Traditions: Essays in Archaeological Interpretation. New York: Columbia University Press.

Trigger, Bruce G., 1985 Marxism in Archaeology: Real or Spurious. Reviews in Anthropology 12:114–123.

Trigger, Bruce G., 2006 A History of Archaeological Thought. 2nd edition. Cambridge: Cambridge University Press.

Trope, Jack F., and Walter R. Echo-Hawk, 2000 The Native American Graves Protection and Repatriation Act: Background and Legislative History. In The Repatriation Reader: Who Owns American Indian Remains? Devon A. Mihesuah, ed. Pp. 123–168. Lincoln: University of Nebraska Press.

Tunbridge, John E., and Gregory J. Ashworth, 1996 Dissonant Heritage: The Management of the Past as a Resource in Conflict. New York: Wiley.

Turner, Victor, 1974 Dramas, Fields and Metaphors: Symbolic Action in Human Society. Ithaca, NY: Cornell University Press.

Voss, Barbara, 2006 Engendered Archaeologies: Men, Women and Others. In Historical Archaeology. Martin Hall and Stephen W. Silliman, eds. Pp. 107–127. Oxford: Blackwell.

Voss, Barbara L., 2008 The Archaeology of Ethnogenesis: Race and Sexuality in Colonial San Francisco. Berkeley: University of California Press.

Walde, Dale, and Noreen D. Willows, eds., 1991 The Archaeology of Gender: Proceedings of the 22nd Annual Chacmool Conference. Calgary: The Archaeological Association of the University of Calgary.

Walker, Meredith, and Peter Marquis-Kyle, 2004 The Illustrated Burra Charter: Good Practice for Heritage Places. Burwood, Vic.: Australia ICOMOS.

Wallerstein, Immanuel, 1974 The Modern World System I: Capitalist Agriculture and the Origins of the European World-Economy in the Sixteenth Century. New York: Academic Press.

Wallerstein, Immanuel, 1980 The Modern World System II: Mercantilism and the Consolidation of the European World-Economy, 1600–1750. New York: Academic Press.

Watkins, Joe, 2001 Indigenous Archaeology: American Indian Values and Scientific Practice. Walnut Creek, CA: AltaMira Press.

Watkins, Joe, 2004 Becoming American or Becoming Indian? Journal of Social Archaeology 4(1):60–80.

Watkins, Joe, 2005 Through Wary Eyes: Indigenous Perspectives on Archaeology. Annual Review of Anthropology 34:429–449.

Watson, Patty Jo, 1982 Review of Living Archaeology by Richard Gould. American Antiquity 47:445–448.

Watson, Patty Jo, and Mary C. Kennedy, 1991 The Development of Horticulture in the Eastern Woodlands of North America: Women's Role. In Engendering Archaeology: Women and Prehistory. Joan M. Gero and Margaret W. Conkey, eds. Pp. 255–275. Oxford: Blackwell.

Watson, Patty Jo, Steven A. LeBlanc, and Charles L. Redman, 1971 Explanation in Archaeology: An Explicitly Scientific Approach. New York: Columbia University Press.

Watson, Peter, and Cecilia Todeschini, 2007 The Medici Conspiracy: The Illicit Journey of Looted Antiquities from Italy's Tomb Raiders to the World's Greatest Museums. New York: Public Affairs Books.

Watts, Christopher M., 2009 On Mediation and Material Agency in the Peircean Semeiotic. In Material Agency: Towards a Non-Anthropocentric Approach. Carl Knappett and Lambros Malafouris, eds. Pp. 187–207. New York: Springer.

Webmoor, Timothy, and Christopher Witmore, 2005 Symmetrical Archaeology. Metamedia, Stanford University (http://humanitieslab.stanford.edu/23/Home).

White, Leslie A., 1959 The Evolution of Culture. New York: McGraw-Hill.

Wilkie, Laurie A., and Katherine H. Hayes, 2006 Engendered and Feminist archaeologies of the Recent and Documented Pasts. Journal of Archaeological Research 14:243–264.

Willey, Gordon R., and Jeremy A. Sabloff, 1980 A History of American Archaeology. 2nd edition. San Francisco: W. H. Freeman.

Wilson, Daniel, 1851 The Archaeology and Prehistoric Annals of Scotland. Edinburgh: Shetland and Knox.

Wilson, Daniel, 1862 Prehistoric Man. London: Macmillan.

Wilson, Richard A., 2001: The Politics of Truth and Reconciliation in South Africa: Legitimizing the Post Apartheid State. Cambridge: Cambridge University Press.

Wiseman, James, 2001 Declaration of Independence. Archaeology 54(4):10–12.

Wiseman, James, 2002 Archaeology as an Academic Discipline. The SAA Archaeological Record 2 (3):8–10.

Wobst, H. Martin, 1977 Stylistic Behavior and Information Exchange. *In* Papers for the Director: Research Essays in Honor of James B. Griffin. Charles E. Cleland, ed. Pp. 317–342. Ann Arbor: University of Michigan Museum of Anthropology, Anthropological Papers no. 61.

Wolf, Eric, 1982 Europe and the People without History. Berkeley: University of California Press.

Wylie, Alison, 1981 Positivism and the New Archaeology. Unpublished Ph.D. dissertation. Department of Philosophy, State University of New York at Binghamton.

Wylie, Alison, 1982 Epistemological Issues Raised by a Structuralist Archaeology. *In* Symbolic and Structural Archaeology. Ian Hodder, ed. Pp. 39–46. Cambridge: Cambridge University Press.

Wylie, Alison, 1985 The Reaction against Analogy. *In* Advances in Archaeological Method and Theory, vol. 8. Michael B. Schiffer, ed. Pp. 63–112. New York: Academic Press

Wylie, Alison, 2002 Thinking from Things: Essays in the Philosophy of Archaeology. Berkeley: University of California Press.

Wynn, Thomas, 1991 Tools, Grammar and the Archaeology of Cognition. Cambridge Archaeological Journal 1:191–206.

Yamin, Rebecca, ed., 2000 Tales of Five Points: Working-Class Life in Nineteenth-Century New York, 7 vols. West Chester, PA: John Milner Associates.

Yentsch, Anne E., 1991 The Symbolic Divisions of Pottery: Sex-Related Attributes of English and Anglo-American Household Pots. *In* The Archaeology of Inequality. Randall H. McGuire and Robert Paynter, eds. Pp. 192–230. Oxford: Blackwell.

Yentsch, Anne E., 1994 A Chesapeake Family and Their Slaves. Cambridge: Cambridge University Press.

Yorston, Ron, with Christopher F. Gaffney and Vincent L. Gaffney, 1987 A Manifesto for Pragmatic Archaeology. *In* Pragmatic Archaeology: Theory in Crisis? Christopher F. Gaffney and Vincent L. Gaffney, eds. Pp. 107–114. Oxford: British Archaeological Reports 167.

Zihlman, Adrienne L., 1989 Woman the Gatherer: The Role of Women in Early Hominid Evolution. *In* Gender and Anthropology: Critical Reviews for Research and Teaching. Sandra Morgen, ed. Pp. 21–40. Washington DC: American Anthropological Association.

Zimmerman, Larry, 1989 Made Radical by My Own: An Archaeologist Learns to Accept Reburial. *In* Conflict in the Archaeology of Living Traditions. Robert Layton, ed. Pp. 60–67. London: Unwin Hyman.

Zubrow, Ezra B. W., 1994 Knowledge Representation and Archaeology. *In* The Ancient Mind: Elements of Cognitive Archaeology. Colin Renfrew and Ezra B. W. Zubrow, eds. Pp. 107–118. Cambridge: Cambridge University Press.

Part II

Landscapes, Spaces, and Natures

ONE OF THE MAJOR DEVELOPMENTS in archaeological theory has been a transformation in how the environment is conceptualized. Although archaeologists have been collecting environmental data since the founding of the field, it was the work of American anthropologist Julian Steward during the 1950s that established a theoretical baseline for what would later be labeled "cultural ecology" (Steward 1955:4). Typified by the interdisciplinary research carried out by archaeologists such as Richard MacNeish (1978) and Robert Braidwood (1974), cultural ecology was an attempt to integrate detailed environmental reconstructions along with regional studies of settlement patterns as a means of understanding human adaptation to the environment. Cultural ecology was given a political twist by Karl Wittfogel's (1957) hydraulic hypothesis, which proposed that managerial states emerged wherever irrigation required centralized control; in these cases, the government monopolized political power and dominated the economy (see Sanders and Price 1968).

With the rise of processual archaeology, ecological concepts, such as carrying capacity, feedback loops, and scheduling, became an integral part of an archaeological theory that cast the environment as a major, and sometimes determining, variable in the process of culture change (Flannery 1972). The borrowing of middle-range theoretical concepts from fields such as evolutionary biology (Krebs and Davies 1978) and ecological anthropology (Hardesty 1977) was seen as part of a broader program of strengthening the scientific rigor of archaeology. Fundamental to this new ecological thinking was the view that environment can be modeled as an ecological system, hence the term "ecosystem." There was an assumption that while the environment was dynamic and could influence cultural change, it was itself an essentialized reality. In other words, it was a separate, external reality standing outside the realm of human society. Some processual archaeologists went so far as to say that culture change could only come from sources outside the cultural system (e.g. Hill 1977:76).

In the past 20 years, landscape archaeology has challenged this view of nature and explored the multiplicity of ways in which landscape is constructed, conceptualized, and contested (Ashmore and Knapp 1999). In many ways, landscape archaeology is the intellectual heir of Gordon Willey's (1953:1) influential settlement pattern approach, the study of how "man disposed himself over the landscape on which he lived." It is a particularly significant research program because it crosscuts traditional theoretical boundaries. One of the most exciting theoretical contributions was Christopher Tilley's *The Phenomenology of Landscape* (1994). This book was the first systematic consideration of the phenomenological approach in archaeology and drew attention to the importance of past and present sensory experience of landscapes and locales (cf. Tilley 2004, 2008). Of equal importance, but less often noted, is the fact that Tilley linked his study of the British Neolithic to the modern world. He suggested that there was a major disconformity between capitalist and precapitalist uses of space. In precapitalist societies, space is sanctified and communal. In capitalist societies, it is secularized and commodified. The land is thus stripped of meaning and people's experiences are changed.

Landscape has been and continues to be a key focus in historical archaeology. Much of the early work focused on the interpretation of gardens and landscapes as instruments of both cultural expression and power (Leone 1984; Kelso and Most 1990). Mark Leone (1984; Leone et al. 2005), for example, analyzed the garden of William Paca, a signatory of the Declaration of Independence. Leone argues that Paca used the garden to help support his status in Chesapeake society and to emphasize continuity in a time of great social change. Another example is the work of Matthew Johnson (1996, 2006), who has examined the enclosure of the English countryside as a key strategy of power in the transition from feudalism to capitalism. Drawing inspiration from British historian W. G. Hoskins, whose seminal book *The Making of the English Landscape* (1955) shaped the trajectory of landscape studies in Britain, Johnson (2006) explains how the survey and map were the first steps in the enclosure movement and the dispossession of peasant farmers. Still another example is the work of James Delle (1998, 1999), who incorporated concepts of space developed by French social theorist Henri Lefebvre (1991) into his analysis of Irish and Jamaican plantation landscapes. More recently, landscape studies have served as a vehicle for examining the convergence of landscape, materiality, power, and heritage (e.g. Hicks et al. 2007).

The idea of nature as standing outside of culture has been critiqued by a broad range of disciplines, including political ecology, historical ecology, and historical geography. William Balée, a historical ecologist, and Clark Erickson, an archaeologist, have challenged landscape ecology on the grounds that it views humans as just another species within the ecosystem (Balée 1989; Erickson 2000; Balée and Erickson 2006a, 2006b). They favor the perspective that humans can be seen as a "keystone species" and that human agency is responsible for sophisticated land-use strategies that sometimes enhance species diversity and ecological richness. David Harvey (1996), a geographer, emphasizes the idea that humans are to be conceptualized not as things in an environment, but rather as nodes in a relational network without determined spatial and temporal structures. There is thus no boundary to be drawn between people and the environment. Sarah Whatmore (2002) has recently introduced the idea of hybrid geographies to reconfigure the human/nature debate. Such geographies, informed by Latour's Actor Network Theory, involve explicating the heterogeneous entanglements of social life. Arturo Escobar (1999), a leading political ecologist, has challenged the view of nature as an independent variable and developed an approach that attempts to combine a recognition of nature as a "biophysical reality" with a more contextually based perception of nature. Nature thus exists simultaneously both as an empirical reality and as a cultural reality. Stephen Mrozowski (1996, 1999, 2006a, 2006b) has incorporated these views in his studies of the urban landscape and the natures of capitalism.

Here it is useful to acknowledge the Red–Green debate that ultimately led to the "greening" of Marxism (Benton 1996) and the emergence of ecological Marxism (O'Conner 1998) and political ecology (Escobar 1999). The growth of these related fields of study occurred despite the early rejection of Marxism by Green politicians in Europe, who pointed to the terrible environmental record of industry in socialist countries (see Benton 1989:51–52). Marxists also had deep

reservations about Green politics because of the emphasis placed on global environmental concerns at the expense of issues such as labor exploitation. The emphasis on the global was seen by Marxists as an attempt to abstract environmental concerns to the point where environmentalists were ignoring the maximization of profits so central to capitalism rather than confronting it as a problem. Some of these reservations stemmed directly from the work of Marx and Engels and their early ambivalence toward the environment and nature (Martinez-Altier 1995). But a more important factor was that many Marxists saw environmentalism as an essentially middle-class, elitist cause that ignored the obvious connections between the growing power of capitalism and social and ecological inequality (Benton 1989:51–52; Martinez-Altier 1995:70). By the 1990s, however, these concerns began to evaporate as environmentalists and social theorists attempted to bridge their differences.

Tim Ingold is one of the leaders in developing a more sophisticated understanding of the spatial and temporal scales of landscape. In his influential chapter "The Temporality of the Landscape," he argues for the unity of archaeology and social-cultural anthropology. In calling for this unity, he asserts two fundamental principles that underlie his research program: that human history has unfolded over a long period of time, and that as a process this history has resulted in the creation of a landscape. In contrast to a nature/culture divide, he offers what he calls a "dwelling perspective," the view that humans have dwelt in places and have left a record of their history in those places. Therefore, embedded within the landscape are the residues of past activities that are akin to stories that archaeologists can attempt to reconstruct. Although the dwellers who created these landscapes and the archaeologists who interpret them differ, both seek the past in the landscape and as such are doing essentially the same thing. Hunters must have knowledge of their terrain, and this they gain through experience. The same is true of archaeologists, who spend their time getting to know a landscape and the archaeological remains that are part of that landscape.

Ingold's argument is based on four ideas. The first is that landscape is neither nature, nor land, nor space. In making this claim, he rejects the notion of a division between an external world and the mind, suggesting that they are in fact two elements of the same reality. He follows this with a discussion of temporality and the concept of "taskscape," which encompasses the activities that are played out on the landscape. In presenting his ideas concerning both of these concepts he explains first what they are not. Landscape, for example, is not land. Land is a quantity, but you cannot quantify a landscape. It is not nature, because it cannot be separated from the inner world of the mind. Yes it exists outside the mind, but that world is not the world we encounter. Finally, landscape is not space. Drawing on the analogy Ferdinand de Saussure gives of the sign as being comprised of thought and sound as two sides of the same piece of paper, Ingold argues that you cannot cut one without cutting the other. This is a critical point for Ingold because for him landscape is analogous to thought in that it is what we see. Taskscapes are the actions performed on the landscape and, as such, are analogous to sound, or what we might hear on the landscape. For Ingold, landscape is not space because it cannot be cut out of the larger environment in the way space can. He goes on to argue that landscape is about form in the same manner that the concept of the body is about form, rather than how the body functions. In this sense, the body and landscape are very similar concepts and are in some senses interchangeable. Ingold also notes that just as the body moves though a life-cycle, it may be possible to identify a corresponding series of cycles that result in landscape.

In defining temporality, Ingold notes that it is neither chronology nor history. Chronology is a series of time intervals and history is the events that take place during that time. Ingold's discussion of the difference between notions of time, history, and temporality hinges on the idea that time is inherent in the passage of events, but events can also be treated as isolated moments like beads on a thread. Temporality refers to the unfolding of social life over both time and space. Taken together, the concepts of temporality and landscape make up the taskscape. Ingold's presentation of taskscape builds upon Marx's concept of value. He argues that in the same manner that Marx contrasted exchange-value and use-value, human action or work is not carried out in a vacuum. Work can only be understood within its social context in the same manner that value is determined by the worth placed upon it by people. The notion of taskscape thus comprises the interlocking of all of the tasks that people carry out and the social context in which they are embedded. As such, tasks are embedded in the social. Therefore, taskscape is to labor what landscape is to land and combined they form a record on the land of the tasks carried out on that landscape.

In his effort to combine these concepts into a more comprehensive notion of landscape, Ingold turns to an orchestra analogy, noting that musicians do not dwell on the difference between what they are playing, what the others are playing, and what the conductor is instructing them to do. In drawing this analogy, he notes that social time is not metronomic; it runs in cycles, and these cycles vary in several ways and yet combine to produce something that is coherent and has direction. So the taskscape is not linked to a chronological temporality that is consistent, but rather it varies, and therefore time is conceived according to tasks, and ultimately these tasks, in collapsed form, constitute an element of the landscape. It is in this sense that Ingold argues that the landscape is what we see around us and the the taskscape is what we hear. An important corollary to this is that taskscape is interactive because it is humans who transform the environment into a landscape. Ingold ends by using Pieter Bruegel the Elder's painting *The Harvesters* to illustrate how the concept of taskscape allows one to interpret the many elements that contribute to the formation of landscape.

Paul Taçon offers an indigenous Australian view of landscape in his discussion of rock art and sacred landscapes. He focuses on the manner in which landscapes are transformed into sacred landscape by the creation of places of meaning. Like Ingold, Taçon notes that landscapes are described by humans and, as such, are both socialized and conceived. He distinguishes between instances where rock art serves to depict both internal and external meanings. The former are typically the spatial relations of clan lands, while the latter are parts of mythical stories related to the body parts of supernatural beings. In his quest to determine the process whereby landscapes become sacred places, Taçon notes that some of these landscapes inspire awe, for example mountain ranges, valleys, gorges, locations of sudden elevation changes, or unusual outcrops such as peaks or places where panoramic views can be seen. In some instances, these awe-inspiring places are believed to contain concentrations of power. In Australia, these types of locations also serve as entry points to other areas where vistas are visible, and these two are interwoven into the broader fabric of the spiritual landscape. Taçon also notes that there are levels of knowledge that allow one to access the spiritual landscape, and for the uninitiated access is often restricted.

To interpret Australian Aboriginal sacred landscapes, Taçon turns to Dreaming Tracks: those tracks that link landscapes, people, and supernatural beings across time and space. Although specific clans may be responsible for certain sites along the tracks, all clans share a common interest in their protection and maintenance. Taçon also explains how Dreaming Tracks serve as media for communicating origin myths and codes of conduct that, in turn, often inspire art. He describes Rainbow Serpents, mythical creatures who are believed to possess great power and combine elements of both male and female. They dissect much of the country and serve as points along spiritual tracks that help those who travel them to know where they can expect to find help and places that should be avoided. Representations of these beings are found throughout Australia and are still created today.

Taçon then turns to a consideration of what are considered the oldest examples of rock art in Australia, the cup-shaped engravings often called "cupules." He notes that these sites are found in landscapes dominated by rivers and they seem to follow paths that humans must have been traveled for thousands of years. In this sense, the earliest sites seem to be linked to the natural landscape, thereby representing a layering of human meaning. This interpretation, then, is not an example of the use of ethnographic analogy and the direct historical method since Western notions of time and space are conflated. Taçon believes that it is still possible to grasp the spiritual meaning of the art because of the integral place it holds on the landscape. In the end, this is what makes the study of such landscapes so important; it links us to a different way of viewing space and reveals the spiritual

significance it once held and continues to hold for the Aboriginal peoples of Australia today.

Eleanor Casella discusses a radically different kind of landscape, a woman's prison in Tasmania. Here the landscape was comprised of spaces that served the particular needs of the prison. In reading their arrangement and use, Casella is able to see the way space functioned as an instrument of power, as well as instances where resistance could circumvent that power. This is, of course, an argument originally put forth by Foucault (1977). In this sense, Casella is less interested in landscapes than she is in the manner in which space is deployed to serve social ends. The prisons of Tasmania provide an intriguing case because they maintained English concepts of incarceration that were originally based on the idea of workhouses. Convicts were viewed primarily as labor. The class-laden ideology that served as the foundation for many of England's prisons was extended to women, as Casella demonstrates. Yet gender was far from the only variable that served to differentiate status and space. The power hierarchy of the prison itself was also maintained through the use of space.

The Australia prisons reinforced dominant social categories, particularly those addressing gender and class. Space was broken down by gender, but was also part of tightly controlled systems of both time and space; where someone was allowed to be depended upon the time as much as the place. The social differentiation between convicts and prison staff was reinforced by spatial differences that controlled behavior in both subtle and overt ways. The prison hierarchy was both reflected and reinforced by a spatiality of power. Materiality played an important role as well. The various forms of housing that were supplied for the prison's staff were, as Casella describes, a material expression of class differences. There were several tiers of workers and supervisory staff as well as convicts, and each of these groups had their own space that was set off from the others. This demarcation employed a variety of instruments, including finer materials used in the decoration of supervisory personnel housing. There was also great symbolism interwoven into the prison landscape, with the chapel, for example, visible from the workroom.

The prison contained a variety of spaces in which convicts both lived and worked. Depending upon the severity of the crimes that had been committed, some inmates were allowed to move with relative freedom between living- and work-space while others were placed in solitary confinement in which their days were spent contemplating their mistakes. By comparing the material traces found in living- and workspaces throughout the prison, Casella was able to discover signs of behavior that did not fit the assumed strictures on prison inmates. As she notes, there is evidence to suggest that black-market activities were a part of prison life as well as evidence that even the most stringent prison rules were being circumvented. It is this combining of archaeological evidence and its spatial context that affords Casella the opportunity to offer a more nuanced picture of what life in these spaces of domination and control was actually like.

Clark Erickson provides a useful overview of the emerging field of historical ecology in his consideration of Amazonia. He begins with a discussion of the succession theory in traditional plant ecology. Succession is the view that plant communities evolve through a series of regular stages, with the final climax stage representing an equilibrium state with a stable composition of plant species. Although wildfires or other natural disasters may damage the community, it is eventually assumed to return to homeostasis. Erickson then introduces the ecological movement known as the "new ecology," which is critical of the stability concept and conservation measures to protect nature from change. Instead, it favors the idea that perturbations are an integral part of ecosystem health and actively contribute to biodiversity. The creation of patches, mosaics, and edge habitats, for example, provides new environments in which species can grow and thrive. Historical ecologists draw from these insights, and apply them to the study of anthropogenic change. They observe that, unlike natural disturbances, human disturbances to the landscape are highly structured and patterned. Some of these include burning, erosion, settlement, roads, and so on. Such disturbances halt plant succession and promote secondary, rather than primary, forest growth. This in turn may promote biodiversity and ecosystem heterogeneity.

Erickson illustrates the value of historical ecology by using it to deconstruct a number of popular myths about Amazonia. He notes that the romantic imagery of Amazonia as a natural wilderness belies a very different reality, namely that of a land domesticated by humans. In formulating his argument, he examines the history of human agency in shaping the Amazonian landscape. The standard view was that the environment was an immutable given to which humans had to adapt. So the assumption was that poor environments produced simple societies. Erickson proposes historical ecology as offering an important alternative to this view. It looks at the history of human/environment interaction and focuses on the notion of landscape as the intentional results of human action and the logic of indigenous knowledge. He goes on to state that archaeology permits scholars access to a deep record that shows that humans have also been beneficial to the environment and contributed to biodiversity. In Amazonia, native peoples created a domesticated landscape resulting from both intentional and unintentional actions. They have managed the environment through a variety of techniques, including transplanting, culling, and controlled burning. Rather than viewing Amazonia as a pristine form of nature, it is more accurate to conceive it in the same manner that we would a garden.

References

Ashmore, Wendy, and A. Bernard Knapp, eds., 1999 Archaeologies of Landscape: Contemporary Perspectives. Oxford: Blackwell.

Balée, William A., 1989 The Culture of Amazonian Forests. Advances in Economic Botany 7:1–21.

Balée, William A., and Clark L. Erickson, eds., 2006a Time and Complexity in Historical Ecology: Studies in the Neotropical Lowlands. New York: Columbia University Press.

Balée, William A., and Clark L. Erickson, 2006b Time, Complexity, and Historical Ecology. In Time and Complexity in Historical Ecology: Studies in the Neotropical Lowlands. William A. Balée and Clark L. Erickson, eds. Pp. 1–20. New York: Columbia University Press.

Benton, Ted, 1989 Marxism and Natural Limits: An Ecological Critique and Reconstruction. New Left Review 178:51–86.

Benton, Ted, 1996 The Greening of Marxism. New York: Guilford.

Braidwood, Robert J., 1974 The Jarmo Project. *In* Archaeological Researches in Retrospect. Gordon R. Willey, ed. Pp. 59-83. Cambridge, MA: Winthrop Publishing.

Delle, James, 1998 The Archaeology of Social Space. New York: Plenum.

Delle, James, 1999 Extending Europe's Grasp: An Archaeological Comparison of Colonial Spatial Processes in Ireland and Jamaica. *In* Old and New Worlds. Geoff Egan and Ronald L. Michael, eds. Pp. 106–116. Oxford: Oxbow Books.

Erickson, Clark, 2000 An Artificial Landscape-Scale Fishery in the Bolivian Amazon. Nature 408:190–193.

Escobar, Arturo, 1999 Steps to an Antiessentialist Political Ecology. Current Anthropology 40(1):1–16.

Flannery, Kent V., 1972 The Cultural Evolution of Civilizations. Annual Review of Ecology and Systematics 3:399–426.

Foucault, Michel, 1977 Discipline and Punish: The Birth of the Prison. London: Penguin.

Hardesty, Donald L., 1977 Ecological Anthropology. New York: Wiley.

Harvey, David, 1996 Justice, Nature, and the Geography of Difference. Oxford: Blackwell.

Hicks, Dan, Laura McAtackney, and Graham Fairclogh, eds., 2007 Envisioning Landscape: Situations and Standpoints in Archaeology and Heritage. Walnut Creek, CA: Left Coast Press.

Hill, James N., ed., 1977 The Explanation of Prehistoric Change. Albuquerque: University of New Mexico Press.

Hoskins, W. G., 1955 The Making of the English Landscape. London: Penguin.

Johnson, Matthew, 1996 An Archaeology of Capitalism. Oxford: Blackwell.

Johnson, Matthew, 2006 Ideas of Landscape: An Introduction. Oxford: Blackwell.

Kelso, William, and Rachel Most, eds., 1990 Earth Patterns: Essays in Landscape Archaeology. Charlottesville: University of Virginia Press.

Krebs, John R., and Nicholas B. Davies, eds., 1978 Behavioural Ecology: An Evolutionary Approach. Oxford: Blackwell.

Lefebvre, Henri, 1991 The Production of Space. Oxford: Blackwell.

Leone, Mark P., 1984 Interpreting Ideology in Historical Archaeology: Using the Rules of Perspective in the William Paca Garden in Annapolis, Maryland. *In* Ideology, Power and Prehistory. Daniel Miller and Christopher Tilley, eds. Pp. 25–35. Cambridge: Cambridge University Press.

Leone, Mark P., James M. Harmon, and Jessica L. Neuwirth, 2005 Perspective and Surveillance in Eighteenth-Century Maryland Gardens, Including Willam Paca's Garden on Wye Island. Historical Archaeology 39(4):138–158.

MacNeish, Richard S., 1978 The Science of Archaeology? North Scituate, MA: Duxbury Press.

Martinez-Alier Joan, 1995 Political Ecology, Distributional Conflicts, and Economic Incommensurability. New Left Review 211:70–88.

Mrozowski, Stephen A., 1996 Nature, Society, and Culture: Theoretical Considerations. *In* Historical Archaeology and the Study of American Culture. Lu Ann De Cunzo and Bernard L. Herman, eds. Pp. 447–472. Knoxville: University of Tennessee Press.

Mrozowski, Stephen A., 1999 The Commodification of Nature. International Journal of Historical Archaeology 3(3):153–166.

Mrozowski, Stephen A., 2006a The Archaeology of Class in Urban America. Cambridge: Cambridge University Press.

Mrozowski, Stephen A., 2006b Environments of History: Biological Dimensions of Historical Archaeology. *In* Historical Archaeology. Martin Hall and Stephen W. Silliman, eds. Pp. 23–41. Oxford: Blackwell.

O'Conner, James, 1998 Natural Causes: Essays in Ecological Marxism. New York: Guilford.

Sanders, William T., and Barbara Price 1968 Mesoamerica: The Evolution of a Civilization. New York: Random House.

Steward, Julian, 1955 Theory of Culture Change: The Methodology of Multilinear Evolution. Urbana: University of Illinois Press.

Tilley, Chris, 1994 The Phenomenology of Landscape: Places, Paths and Monuments. Oxford: Berg.

Tilley, Chris, 2004 The Materiality of Stone: Explorations in Landscape Phenomenology. Oxford: Berg.

Tilley, Chris, 2008: Body and Image: Explorations in Landscape Phenomenology 2. Walnut Creek, CA: Left Coast Press.

Whatmore, Sarah, 2002 Hybrid Geographies: Natures, Cultures, Spaces. London: Sage.

Willey, Gordon R., 1953 Prehistoric Settlement Patterns in the Virù Valley, Peru. Bureau of American Ethnology Bulletin 155. Washington, DC: Smithsonian Institution.

Wittfogel, Karl 1957: Oriental Despotism: A Comparative Study of Total Power. New Haven: Yale University Press.

1

The Temporality of the Landscape

Tim Ingold

Prologue

I adhere to that school of thought which holds that social or cultural anthropology, biological anthropology and archaeology form a necessary unity – that they are all part of the same intellectual enterprise (Ingold 1992a: 694). I am not concerned here with the link with biological or 'physical' anthropology, but what I have to say does bear centrally on the unifying themes of archaeology and social-cultural anthropology. I want to stress two such themes, and they are closely related. First, human life is a process that involves the passage of time. Second, this life-process is also the process of formation of the landscapes in which people have lived. *Time* and *landscape*, then, are to my mind the essential points of topical contact between archaeology and anthropology. My purpose, in this article, is to bring the perspectives of archaeology and anthropology into unison through a focus on the temporality of the landscape. In particular, I believe that such a focus might enable us to move beyond the sterile opposition between the naturalistic view of the landscape as a neutral, external backdrop to human activities, and the culturalistic view that every landscape is a particular cognitive or symbolic ordering of

Tim Ingold, "The Temporality of the Landscape," pp. 152–74 from *World Archaeology* 25:2 (1993). Reprinted with permission of Taylor & Francis Group and the author.

space. I argue that we should adopt, in place of both these views, what I call a 'dwelling perspective', according to which the landscape is constituted as an enduring record of – and testimony to – the lives and works of past generations who have dwelt within it, and in so doing, have left there something of themselves.

For anthropologists, to adopt a perspective of this kind means bringing to bear the knowledge born of immediate experience, by privileging the understandings that people derive from their lived, everyday involvement in the world. Yet it will surely be objected that this avenue is not open to archaeologists concerned with human activities in the distant past. 'The people', it is said 'they're dead' (Sahlins 1972: 81); only the material record remains for their successors of our own time to interpret as best they can. But this objection misses the point, which is that *the practice of archaeology is itself a form of dwelling*. The knowledge born of this practice is thus on a par with that which comes from the practical activity of the native dweller and which the anthropologist, through participation, seeks to learn and understand. For both the archaeologist and the native dweller, the landscape tells – or rather *is* – a story. It enfolds the lives and times of predecessors who, over the generations, have moved around in it and played their part in its formation. To perceive the landscape is therefore to carry out an act of remembrance, and remembering is not so much a matter of calling up an internal image, stored in the mind, as of engaging perceptually with an environment that is itself pregnant with the past. To be sure, the rules and methods of engagement employed respectively by the native dweller and the archaeologist will differ, as will the stories they tell, nevertheless – in so far as both seek the past in the landscape – they are engaged in projects of fundamentally the same kind.

It is of course part of an archaeological training to learn to attend to those clues which the rest of us might pass over (literally, when they are below the surface), and which make it possible to tell a fuller or a richer story. Likewise, native dwellers (and their anthropological companions) learn through an education of attention. The novice hunter, for example, travels through the country with his mentors, and as he goes, specific features are pointed out to him. Other things he discovers for himself, in the course of further forays, by watching, listening and feeling. Thus the experienced hunter is the *knowledgeable* hunter. He can tell things from subtle indications that you or I, unskilled in the hunter's art, might not even notice. Called upon to explicate this knowledge, he may do so in a form that reappears in the work of the non-native ethnographer as a corpus of myths or stories, whereas the archaeologist's knowledge – drawn from the practices of excavation rather than hunting – may appear in the seemingly authoritative form of the site report. But we should resist the temptation to assume that since stories are stories they are, in some sense, unreal or untrue, for this is to suppose that the only real reality, or true truth, is one in which we, as living, experiencing beings, can have no part at all. Telling a story is not like weaving a tapestry to *cover up* the world, it is rather a way of guiding the attention of listeners or readers *into* it. A person who can 'tell' is one who is perceptually attuned to picking up information in the environment that others, less skilled in the tasks of perception, might miss, and the teller, in rendering his knowledge explicit, conducts the attention of his audience along the same paths as his own.

Following that preamble, I shall now go on to lay out the burden of my argument. This is presented in four principal sections. In the first two, I attempt to specify more precisely what I mean by my key terms – landscape and temporality. I argue that temporality inheres in the pattern of dwelling activities that I call the taskscape. In the third section I consider how taskscape relates to landscape and, ultimately by dissolving the distinction between them, I proceed to recover the temporality of the landscape itself. Finally, I draw some concrete illustrations of my arguments from a well-known painting by Bruegel, *The Harvesters*.

Landscape

Let me begin by explaining what the landscape is *not*. It is not 'land', it is not 'nature', and it is not 'space'. Consider, first of all, the distinction between land and landscape. Land is not something you can see, any more than you can see the weight of physical objects. All objects of the most diverse kinds have weight, and it is possible to express *how much* anything weighs relative to any other thing. Likewise, land is a kind of lowest common denominator of the phenomenal world, inherent in every portion of the earth's surface yet directly visible in none, and in terms of which any portion may be rendered quantitatively equivalent to any other (Ingold 1986a: 153–4). You can ask of land, as of weight, how much there is, but not what it is like. But where land is thus quantitative and homogeneous, the landscape is qualitative and heterogeneous. Supposing that you are standing outdoors, it is what you see all around: a contoured and textured surface replete with diverse objects – living and non-living, natural and artificial (these distinctions are both problematic, as we shall see, but they will serve for the time being). Thus at any particular moment, you can ask of a landscape what it is like, but not how much of it there is. For the landscape is a plenum, there are no holes in it that remain to be filled in, so that every infill is in reality a reworking. As Meinig observes, one should not overlook 'the powerful fact that life must be lived amidst that which was made before' (1979a: 44).

The landscape is not 'nature'. Of course, nature can mean many things, and this is not the place for a discourse on the history of the concept. Suffice it to say that I have in mind the rather specific sense whose ontological foundation is an imagined separation between the human perceiver and the world, such that the perceiver has to reconstruct the world, in consciousness, prior to any meaningful engagement with it. The world of nature, it is often said, is what lies 'out there'. All kinds of entities are supposed to exist out there, but not you and I. We live 'in here', in the intersubjective space marked out by our mental representations. Application of this logic forces an insistent dualism, between object and subject, the material and the ideal, operational and cognized, 'etic' and 'emic'. Some writers distinguish between nature and the landscape in just these terms – the former is said to stand to the latter as physical reality to its cultural or symbolic construction. For example, Daniels and Cosgrove introduce a collection of essays on *The Iconography of Landscape* with the following definition: 'A landscape is a cultural image, a pictorial way of representing or symbolising surroundings' (1988: 1).

I do not share this view. To the contrary, I reject the division between inner and outer worlds – respectively of mind and matter, meaning and substance – upon which such distinction rests. The landscape, I hold, is not a picture in the imagination, surveyed by the mind's eye; nor, however, is it an alien and formless substrate awaiting the imposition of human order. 'The idea of landscape', as Meinig writes, 'runs counter to recognition of any simple binary relationship between man and nature' (Meinig 1979b: 2). Thus, neither is the landscape identical to nature, nor is it on the side of humanity *against* nature. As the familiar domain of our dwelling, it is *with* us, not against us, but it is no less real for that. And through living in it, the landscape becomes a part of us, just as we are a part of it. Moreover, what goes for its human component goes for other components as well. In a world construed as nature, every object is a self-contained entity, interacting with others through some kind of external contact. But in a landscape, each component enfolds within its essence the totality of its relations with each and every other. In short, whereas the order of nature is explicate, the order of the landscape is implicate (Bohm 1980: 172).

The landscape is not 'space'. To appreciate the contrast, we could compare the everyday project of dwelling in the world with the rather peculiar and specialized project of the surveyor or cartographer whose objective is to *represent* it. No doubt the surveyor, as he goes about his practical tasks, experiences the landscape much as does everyone else whose business of life lies there. Like other people, he is mobile, yet unable to be in more than one place at a time. In the landscape, the distance between two places, A and B, is experienced as a journey made, a bodily movement from one place to the other, and the gradually changing vistas along the route. The surveyor's job, however, is to take instrumental measurements from a considerable number of places, and to combine these data to produce a single picture which is *independent* of any point of observation. This picture is of the world as it could be directly apprehended only by a consciousness capable of being everywhere at once and nowhere in particular (the nearest we can get to this in practice is by taking an aerial or 'bird's-eye' view). To such a consciousness, at once immobile and omnipresent, the distance between A and B would be the length of a line plotted between two points that are simultaneously in view, that line marking one of any number of journeys that could potentially be made (cf. Bourdieu 1977: 2). It is as though, from an imaginary position above the world, I could direct the movements of my body within it, like a counter on a board, so that to say 'I am here' is not to point from somewhere to my surroundings, but to point from nowhere to the position on the board where my body happens to be. And whereas actual journeys are made through a landscape, the board on which all potential journeys may be plotted is equivalent to space.

There is a tradition of geographical research (e.g. Gould and White 1974) which sets out from the premise that we are all cartographers in our daily lives, and that we use our bodies as the surveyor uses his instruments, to register a sensory input from multiple points of observation, which is then processed by our intelligence into an image which we carry around with us, like a map in our heads, wherever we go. The mind, rather than reaching into its surroundings from its dwelling place within the world, may be likened in this view to a film spread out upon its exterior surface. To understand the sense of space that is implicated in this cartographic view of environmental perception, it is helpful to draw an analogy from the linguistics of Ferdinand de Saussure. To grasp the essence of language, Saussure invites us to picture thought and sound as two continuous and undifferentiated planes, of mental and phonic substance respectively, like two sides of a sheet of paper. By cutting the sheet into pieces (words) we create, on one side, a system of discrete concepts, and on the other, a system of discrete sounds; and since one side cannot be cut without at the same time cutting the other, the two systems of division are necessarily homologous so that to each concept there corresponds a sound (Saussure 1959: 112–13). Now when geographers and anthropologists write about space, what is generally implied is something closely akin to Saussure's sheet of paper, only in this case the counter-side to thought is the continuum not of phonic substance but of the surface of the earth. And so it appears that the division of the world into a mosaic of externally bounded segments is entailed in the very production of spatial meanings. Just as the word, for Saussure, is the union of a concept with a delimited 'chunk' of sound, so the place is the union of a symbolic meaning with a delimited block of the earth's surface. Spatial differentiation implies spatial segmentation.

This is not so of the landscape, however. For a place in the landscape is not 'cut out' from the whole, either on the plane of ideas or on that of material substance. Rather, each place embodies the whole at a particular nexus within it, and in this respect is different from every other. A place owes its character to the experiences it affords to those who spend time there – to the sights, sounds and indeed smells that constitute its specific ambience. And these, in turn, depend on the kinds of activities in which its inhabitants engage. It is from this relational context of people's engagement with the world, in the business of dwelling, that each place draws its unique significance. Thus whereas with space, meanings are *attached to* the world, with the landscape they are *gathered from* it. Moreover, while places have centres – indeed it would be more appropriate to say that they *are* centres – they have no boundaries. In journeying from place A to place B it makes no sense to ask, along the way, whether one is 'still' in A or has 'crossed over' to B (Ingold 1986a: 155). Of course, boundaries of various kinds may be drawn in the landscape,

and identified either with natural features such as the course of a river or an escarpment, or with built structures such as walls and fences. But such boundaries are not a condition for the constitution of the places on either side of them; nor do they segment the landscape, for the features with which they are identified are themselves an integral part of it. Finally, it is important to note that no feature of the landscape is, of itself, a boundary. It can only become a boundary, or the indicator of a boundary, in relation to the activities of the people (or animals) for whom it is recognized or experienced as such.

In the course of explaining what the landscape is not, I have already moved some way towards a positive characterization. In short, the landscape is the world as it is known to those who dwell therein, who inhabit its places and journey along the paths connecting them. Is it not, then, identical to what we might otherwise call the environment? Certainly the distinction between landscape and environment is not easy to draw, and for many purposes they may be treated as practically synonymous. It will already be apparent that I cannot accept the distinction offered by Tuan, who argues that an environment is 'a given, a piece of reality that is simply there', as opposed to the landscape, which is a product of human cognition, 'an achievement of the mature mind' (Tuan 1979: 90, 100). For that is merely to reproduce the dichotomy between nature and humanity. The environment is no more 'nature' than is the landscape a symbolic construct. Elsewhere, I have contrasted nature and environment by way of a distinction between reality *of* – 'the physical world of neutral objects apparent only to the detached, indifferent observer', and reality *for* – 'the world constituted in *relation* to the organism or person whose environment it is' (Ingold 1992b: 44). But to think of environment in this sense is to regard it primarily in terms of *function*, of what it affords to creatures – whether human or non-human – with certain capabilities and projects of action. Reciprocally, to regard these creatures as organisms is to view them in terms of their principles of dynamic functioning, that is as organized systems (Pittendrigh 1958: 394). As Lewontin succinctly puts it (1982: 160), the environment is 'nature organised by an organism'.

The concept of landscape, by contrast, puts the emphasis on *form*, in just the same way that the concept of the body emphasizes the form rather than the function of a living creature. Like organism and environment, body and landscape are complementary terms: each implies the other, alternately as figure and ground. The forms of the landscape are not, however, prepared in advance for creatures to occupy, nor are the bodily forms of those creatures independently specified in their genetic makeup. Both sets of forms are generated and sustained in and through the processual unfolding of a total field of relations that cuts across the emergent interface between organism and environment (Goodwin 1988). Having regard to its formative properties, we may refer to this process as one of embodiment. Though the notion of embodiment has recently come much into fashion, there has been a tendency – following an ancient inclination in Western thought to prioritize form over process (Oyama 1985: 13) – to conceive of it as a movement of *inscription*, whereby some preexisting pattern, template or programme, whether genetic or cultural, is 'realized' in a substantive medium. This is not what I have in mind, however. To the contrary, and adopting a helpful distinction from Connerton (1989: 72–3), I regard embodiment as a movement of *incorporation* rather than inscription, not a transcribing of form onto material but a movement wherein forms themselves are generated (Ingold 1990: 215). Taking the organism as our focus of reference, this movement is what is commonly known as the life-cycle. Thus organisms may be said to incorporate, in their bodily forms, the life-cycle processes that give rise to them. Could not the same, then, be said of the environment? Is it possible to identify a corresponding cycle, or rather a series of interlocking cycles, which build themselves into the forms of the landscape, and of which the landscape may accordingly be regarded as an embodiment? Before answering this question, we need to turn to the second of my key terms, namely 'temporality'.

Temporality

Let me begin, once again, by stating what temporality is *not*. It is not chronology (as opposed to history), and it is not history (as opposed to chronology). By chronology, I mean any regular system of dated time intervals, *in which* events are said to have taken place. By history, I mean any series of events which may be dated in time according to their occurrence in one or another chronological interval. Thus the Battle of Hastings was an historical event, 1066 was a date (marking the interval of a year), and records tell us that the former occurred in the latter. In the mere succession of dates there are no events, because everything repeats; in the mere succession of events there is no time, as nothing does. The relation between chronology and history, in this conception, has been well expressed by Kubler: 'Without change there is no history; without regularity there is no time. Time and history are related as rule and variation: time is the regular setting for the vagaries of history' (1962: 72).

Now in introducing the concept of temporality, I do not intend that it should stand as a third term, alongside the concepts of chronology and history. For in the sense in which I shall use the term here, temporality entails a perspective that contrasts radically with the one, outlined above, that sets up history and chronology in a relation of complementary opposition. The contrast is essentially equivalent to that drawn by Gell (1992: 149–55) between what he calls (following McTaggart) the A-series, in which time is immanent in the passage of events, and the B-series, in which events are strung out in time like beads on a thread. Whereas in the B-series, events are treated as isolated happenings, succeeding one another frame by frame, each event in the A-series is seen to encompass a pattern of retensions from the past and protentions for the future. Thus from the A-series point of view, temporality and historicity are not opposed but rather merge in the experience of those who, in their activities, carry forward the process of social life. Taken together, these activities make up what I shall call the 'taskscape', and it is with the intrinsic temporality of the taskscape that I shall be principally concerned in this section.

We can make a start by returning for a moment to the distinction between land and landscape. As a common denominator in terms of which constituents of the environment of diverse kinds may be rendered quantitatively comparable, I compared land with weight. But I could equally have drawn the comparison with *value* or with *labour*. Value is the denominator of

qualitative/not quantitative

commodities that enables us to say how much any one thing is worth by comparison with another, even though these two things may be quite unlike in terms of their physical qualities and potential uses. In this sense, the concept of value (in general) is classically distinguished from that of *use*-value, which refers to the specific properties or 'affordances' of any particular object, that commend it to the project of a user (Ingold 1992b: 48–9, cf. J. Gibson 1979: 127; Marx 1930: 169). Clearly, this distinction, between value and use-value, is precisely homologous to that between land and landscape. But if we turn to consider the work that goes into the making of useful things, then again we can recognize that whilst the operations of making are indeed as unlike as the objects produced – involving different raw materials, different tools, different procedures and different skills – they can nevertheless be compared in that they call for variable amounts of what may simply be called 'labour': the common denominator of productive activities. Like land and value, labour is quantitative and homogeneous, human work shorn of its particularities. It is of course the founding premise of the labour theory of value that the amount of value in a thing is determined by the amount of labour that went into producing it.

How, then, should we describe the practices of work in their concrete particulars? For this purpose I shall adopt the term 'task', defined as any practical operation, carried out by a skilled agent in an environment, as part of his or her normal business of life. In other words, tasks are the constitutive acts of dwelling. No more than features of the landscape, however, are tasks suspended in a vacuum. Every task takes its meaning from its position within an ensemble of tasks, performed in series or in parallel, and usually by many people working together. One of the great mistakes of recent anthropology – what Reynolds (1993: 410) calls 'the great tool-use fallacy' – has been to insist upon a separation between the domains of technical and social activity, a separation that has blinded us to the fact that one of the outstanding features of human technical practices lies in their embeddedness in the current of sociality. It is to the entire ensemble of tasks, in their mutual interlocking, that I refer by the concept of *taskscape*. Just as the landscape is an array of related features, so – by analogy – the

taskscape is an array of related activities. And as with the landscape, it is qualitative and heterogeneous: we can ask of a taskscape, as of a landscape, what it is like, but not how much of it there is. In short, the taskscape is to labour what the landscape is to land, and indeed what an ensemble of use-values is to value in general.

Now if value is measured out in units of money, and land in units of space, what is the currency of labour? The answer, of course, is *time* – but it is time of a very peculiar sort, one that must be wholly indifferent to the modulations of human experience. To most of us it appears in the familiar guise of clock-time: thus an hour is an hour, regardless of what one is doing in it, or of how one feels. But this kind of chronological time does not depend upon the existence of artificial clocks. It may be based on any perfectly repetitive, mechanical system including that (putatively) constituted by the earth in its axial rotations and in its revolutions around the sun. Sorokin and Merton (1937), in a classic paper, call it 'astronomical' time: it is, they write, 'uniform, homogeneous; ... purely quantitative, shorn of qualitative variations'. And they distinguish it from 'social time', which they see as fundamentally qualitative, something to which we can affix moral judgements such as good or bad, grounded in the 'rhythms, pulsations and beats of the societies in which they are found', and for that reason tied to the particular circumstances of place and people (1937: 621–3). Adopting Sorokin and Merton's distinction, we could perhaps conclude that whereas labour is measured out in units of astronomical time, or in clock-time calibrated to an astronomical standard, the temporality of the taskscape is essentially social. Before we can accept this conclusion, however, the idea of social time must be examined a little more closely.

In my earlier discussion of the significance of space, I showed that in the cartographic imagination, the mind is supposed to be laid out upon the surface of the earth. Likewise in the chronological perspective, time appears as the interface between mind and 'duration' – by which is meant an undifferentiated stream of bodily activity and experience. Taking time in this sense, Durkheim famously likened it to 'an endless chart, where all duration is spread out before the mind, and upon which all possible events can be located in relation to fixed and determinate guidelines' (1976[1915]: 10). Rather like Saussure's sheet of paper, it could be compared to a strip of infinite length, with thought on one side and duration on the other. By cutting the strip into segments we establish a division, on the one hand, into calendrical intervals or dates, and, on the other hand, into discrete 'chunks' of lived experience, such that to every chunk there corresponds a date in a uniform sequence of before and after. And as every chunk succeeds the next, like frames on a reel of film, we imagine ourselves to be looking on 'as time goes by', as though we could take up a point of view detached from the temporal process of our life in the world and watch ourselves engaged now in this task, now in that, in an unending series of present instants. Whence, then, come the divisions which give chronological form to the substance of experience? Durkheim's answer, as is well known, was that these divisions – 'indispensable guidelines' for the temporal ordering of events – come from *society*, corresponding to the 'periodical recurrence of rites, feasts, and public ceremonies' (ibid.). Thus for Durkheim, time is at once chronological *and* social, for society itself is a kind of clock, whose moving parts are individual human beings (Ingold 1986b: 341).

This is not, however, the way we perceive the temporality of the taskscape. For we do so not as spectators but as participants, in the very performance of our tasks. As Merleau-Ponty put it, in reckoning with an environment, I am 'at my task rather than confronting it' (1962: 416). The notion that we can stand aside and observe the passage of time is founded upon an illusion of disembodiment. This passage is, indeed, none other than our *own* journey through the taskscape in the business of dwelling. Once again we can take our cue from Merleau-Ponty: 'the passage of one present to the next is not a thing which I conceive, nor do I see it as an onlooker, I *effect it*' (1962: 421, my emphasis). Reaching out into the taskscape, I perceive, at this moment, a particular vista of past and future; but it is a vista that is available from this moment and no other (see Gell 1992: 269). As such, it *constitutes* my present, conferring upon it a unique character. Thus the present is not *marked off* from a past that it has replaced or a future that will, in turn,

replace it; it rather gathers the past and future into itself, like refractions in a crystal ball. And just as in the landscape, we can move from place to place without crossing any boundary, since the vista that constitutes the identity of a place changes even as we move, so likewise can we move from one present to another without having to break through any chronological barrier that might be supposed to separate each present from the next in line. Indeed the features that Durkheim identified as serving this segmenting function – rites, feasts and ceremonies – are themselves as integral to the taskscape as are boundary markers such as walls or fences to the landscape.

The temporality of the taskscape is social, then, not because society provides an external frame against which particular tasks find independent measure, but because people, in the performance of their tasks, *also attend to one another*. Looking back, we can see that Durkheim's error was to divorce the sphere of people's mutual involvement from that of their everyday practical activity in the world, leaving the latter to be carried out by individuals in hermetic isolation. In real life, this is not how we go about our business. By watching, listening, perhaps even touching, we continually feel each other's presence in the social environment, at every moment adjusting our movements in response to this ongoing perceptual monitoring (Ingold 1993: 456). For the orchestral musician, playing an instrument, watching the conductor and listening to one's fellow players are all inseparable aspects of the same process of action: for this reason, the gestures of the performers may be said to *resonate* with each other. In orchestral music, the achievement of resonance is an absolute precondition for successful performance. But the same is true, more generally, of social life (Richards 1991; Wikan 1992). Indeed it could be argued that in the resonance of movement and feeling stemming from people's mutually attentive engagement, in shared contexts of practical activity, lies the very foundation of sociality.

Let me pursue the analogy between orchestral performance and social life a little further since, more than any other artistic genre, music mirrors the temporal form of the taskscape. I want, by means of this analogy, to make three points. First, whilst there are cycles and repetitions in music as in social life, these are essentially rhythmic rather than metronomic (on this distinction, see Young (1988: 19)). It is for precisely this reason that social time, *pace* Durkheim, is *not* chronological. A metronome, like a clock, inscribes an artificial division into equal segments upon an otherwise undifferentiated movement; rhythm, by contrast, is intrinsic to the movement itself. Langer has argued that the essence of rhythm lies in the successive building up and resolution of tension, on the principle that every resolution is itself a preparation for the next building-up (1953: 126–7). There may of course be rests or sustained notes within a piece, but far from breaking it up into segments, such moments are generally ones of high tension, whose resolution becomes ever more urgent the longer they are held. Only our last exhalation of breath is not a preparation for the next inhalation – with that, we die; similarly with the last beat the music comes to an end. Social life, however, is never finished, and there are no breaks in it that are not integral to its tensile structure, to the 'ebb and flow of activity' by which society itself seems to breathe (Young 1988: 53).

My second point is that in music as in social life, there is not just one rhythmic cycle, but a complex interweaving of very many concurrent cycles (for an exemplary analysis of 'the rhythmic structures of economic life', see Guyer (1988)). Whilst it reflects the temporal form of social life, music in fact represents a very considerable simplification, since it involves only one sensory register (the auditory), and its rhythms are fewer and more tightly controlled. In both cases, however, since any rhythm may be taken as the tempo for any of the others, there is no single, one-dimensional strand of time. As Langer puts it: 'life is always a dense fabric of concurrent tensions, and as each of them is a measure of time, the measurements themselves do not coincide' (1953: 113). Thus the temporality of the taskscape, while it is intrinsic rather than externally imposed (metronomic), lies not in any particular rhythm, but in the network of interrelationships between the multiple rhythms of which the taskscape is itself constituted. To cite a celebrated anthropological example: among the Nuer of southern Sudan, according to Evans-Pritchard, the passage of time is 'primarily the succession of [pastoral] tasks *and their relations to one another*' (1940: 101–2; my

emphasis). Each of these relations is, of course, a specific resonance. And so, just as social life consists in the unfolding of a field of relationships among persons who attend to one another in what they do, its temporality consists in the unfolding of the resultant pattern of resonances.

Third, the forms of the taskscape, like those of music, come into being through movement. Music exists only when it is being performed (it does not pre-exist, as is sometimes thought, in the score, any more than a cake pre-exists in the recipe for making it). Similarly, the taskscape exists only so long as people are actually engaged in the activities of dwelling, despite the attempts of anthropologists to translate it into something rather equivalent to a score – a kind of ideal design for dwelling – that generally goes by the name of 'culture', and that people are supposed to bring with them into their encounter with the world. This parallel, however, brings me to a critical question. Up to now, my discussion of temporality has concentrated exclusively on the taskscape, allowing the landscape to slip from view. It is now high time to bring it back into focus. I argued in the previous section that the landscape is not nature; here I claim that the taskscape is not culture. Landscape and taskscape, then, are not to be opposed as nature to culture. So how are we to understand the relation between them? Where does one end and the other begin? Can they even be distinguished at all? If music best reflects the forms of the taskscape, it might be thought that painting is the most natural medium for representing the forms of the landscape. And this suggests that an examination of the difference, in the field of art, between music and painting might offer some clues as to how a distinction might possibly be drawn between taskscape and landscape as facets of the real world. I begin by following up this suggestion.

Temporalizing the Landscape

At first glance the difference seems obvious: paintings do not have to be performed, they are presented to us as works that are complete in themselves. But on closer inspection, this contrast appears more as an artefact of a systematic bias in Western thought, to which I have already alluded, that leads us to privilege form over process. Thus the actual work of painting is subordinated to the final product; the former is hidden from view so that the latter alone becomes an object of contemplation. In many non-Western societies, by contrast, the order of priority is reversed: what is essential is the act of painting itself, of which the products may be relatively short-lived – barely perceived before being erased or covered up. This is so, for example, among the Yolngu, an Aboriginal people of northern Australia, whose experience of finished paintings, according to their ethnographer, is limited to 'images fleetingly glimpsed through the corner of their eyes' (Morphy 1989: 26). The emphasis, here, is on painting as *performance*. Far from being the preparation of objects for future contemplation, it is an act of contemplation in itself. So, too, is performing or listening to music. Thus all at once, the contrast between painting and music seems less secure. It becomes a matter of degree, in the extent to which forms endure beyond the immediate contexts of their production. Musical sound, of course, is subject to the property of rapid fading: speeding outwards from its point of emission, and dissipating as it goes, it is present only momentarily to our senses. But where, as in painting, gestures leave their traces in solid substance, the resulting forms may last much longer, albeit never indefinitely.

Returning now from the contrast between music and painting to that between taskscape and landscape, the first point to note is that no more than a painting is the landscape given ready-made. One cannot, as Inglis points out, 'treat landscape as an object if it is to be understood. It is a living process; it makes men; it is made by them' (1977: 489). Just as with music, the forms of the landscape are generated in movement: these forms, however, are congealed in a solid medium – indeed, to borrow Inglis's words again, 'a landscape is the most solid appearance in which a history can declare itself' (ibid.). Thanks to their solidity, features of the landscape remain available for inspection long after the movement that gave rise to them has ceased. If, as Mead argued (1977[1938]: 97), every object is to be regarded as a 'collapsed act', then *the landscape as a whole must likewise be understood as the taskscape in its embodied form*: a pattern of activities 'collapsed' into an

array of features. But to reiterate a point made earlier, the landscape takes on its forms through a process of incorporation, not of inscription. That is to say, the process is not one whereby cultural design is imposed upon a naturally given substrate, as though the movement issued from the form and was completed in its concrete realization in the material. For the forms of the landscape arise alongside those of the taskscape, within the same current of activity. If we recognize a man's gait in the pattern of his footprints, it is not because the gait preceded the footprints and was 'inscribed' in them, but because both the gait and the prints arose within the movement of the man's walking.

Since, moreover, the activities that comprise the taskscape are unending, the landscape is never complete: neither 'built' nor 'unbuilt', it is perpetually under construction. This is why the conventional dichotomy between natural and artificial (or 'man-made') components of the landscape is so problematic. Virtually by definition, an artefact is an object shaped to a pre-conceived image that motivated its construction, and it is 'finished' at the point when it is brought into conformity with this image. What happens to it beyond that point is supposed to belong to the phase of use rather than manufacture, to dwelling rather than building. But the forms of the landscape are not pre-prepared for people to live in – not by nature nor by human hands – for it is in the very process of dwelling that these forms are constituted. 'To build', as Heidegger insisted, 'is itself already to dwell' (1971: 146). Thus the landscape is always in the nature of 'work in progress'.

My conclusion that the landscape is the congealed form of the taskscape does enable us to explain why, intuitively, the landscape seems to be what we *see* around us, whereas the taskscape is what we *hear*. To be seen, an object need do nothing itself, for the optic array that specifies its form to a viewer consists of light reflected off its outer surfaces. To be heard, on the other hand, an object must actively emit sounds or, through its movement, cause sound to be emitted by other objects with which it comes into contact. Thus, outside my window I see a landscape of houses, trees, gardens, a street and pavement. I do not hear any of these things, but I can hear people talking on the pavement, a car passing by, birds singing in the trees, a dog barking some-where in the distance, and the sound of ham-mering as a neighbour repairs his garden shed. In short, what I hear is *activity*, even when its source cannot be seen. And since the forms of the taskscape, suspended as they are in move-ment, are present *only* as activity, the limits of the taskscape are also the limits of the auditory world. (Whilst I deal here only with visual and aural perception, we should not underestimate the significance of touch, which is important to all of us but above all to blind people, for whom it opens up the possibility of access to the landscape – if only through proximate bodily contact.)

This argument carries an important corollary. Whilst both the landscape and the taskscape presuppose the presence of an agent who watches and listens, the taskscape must be popu-lated with beings who are themselves agents, and who reciprocally 'act back' in the process of their own dwelling. In other words, the taskscape exists not just as activity but as *inter*activity. Indeed this conclusion was already foresha-dowed when I introduced the concept of reson-ance as the rhythmic harmonization of mutual attention. Having said that, however, there is no reason why the domain of interactivity should be confined to the movement of human beings. We hear animals as well as people, such as the birds and the dog in my example above. Hunters, to take another example, are alert to every sight, sound or smell that reveals the presence of ani-mals, and we can be sure that the animals are likewise alert to the presence of humans, as they are also to that of one another. On a larger scale, the hunters' journeys through the landscape, or their oscillations between the procurement of different animal species, resonate with the migratory movements of terrestrial mammals, birds and fish. Perhaps then, as Reed argues, there is a fundamental difference between our perception of animate beings and inanimate objects, since the former – by virtue of their capacity for autonomous movement – 'are *aware* of their surroundings (including us) and because they *act* on those surroundings (includ-ing us)' (Reed 1988: 116). In other words, they afford the possibility not only of action but also of interaction (cf. J. Gibson 1979: 135). Should we, then, draw the boundaries of the taskscape around the limits of the animate?

Though the argument is a compelling one, I find that it is ultimately unsatisfactory, for two reasons in particular. First, as Langer observes, 'rhythm is the basis of life, but not limited to life' (1953: 128). The rhythms of human activities resonate not only with those of other living things but also with a whole host of other rhyth-mic phenomena – the cycles of day and night and of the seasons, the winds, the tides, and so on. Citing a petition of 1800 from the seaside town of Sunderland, in which it is explained that 'people are obliged to be up at all hours of the night to attend the tides and their affairs upon the river', Thompson (1967: 59–60) notes that 'the operative phrase is "attend the tides": the patterning of social time in the seaport follows *upon* the rhythms of the sea'. In many cases these natural rhythmic phenomena find their ultimate cause in the mechanics of planetary motion, but it is not of course to these that we resonate. Thus we resonate to the cycles of light and darkness, not to the rotation of the earth, even though the diurnal cycle is caused by the earth's axial rota-tion. And we resonate to the cycles of vegetative growth and decay, not to the earth's revolutions around the sun, even though the latter cause the cycle of the seasons. Moreover these resonances are *embodied*, in the sense that they are not only historically incorporated into the enduring fea-tures of the landscape but also developmentally incorporated into our very constitution as bio-logical organisms. Thus Young describes the body as 'an array of interlocking (or interflow-ing) cycles, with their own spheres of partial independence within the solar cycle' (1988: 41). We do not consult these cycles, as we might consult a wrist-watch, in order to time our own activities, for the cycles are inherent in the rhythmic structure of the activities them-selves. It would seem, then, that the pattern of resonances that comprises the temporality of the taskscape must be expanded to embrace the totality of rhythmic phenomena, whether animate or inanimate.

The second reason why I would be reluctant to restrict the taskscape to the realm of living things has to do with the very notion of animacy. I do not think we can regard this as a property that can be ascribed to objects in isolation, such that some (animate) have it and others (inanimate) do not. For life is not a principle that is separately installed inside individual organisms, and which sets them in motion upon the stage of the inanimate. To the contrary, as I have argued elsewhere, life is 'a name for *what is going on* in the generative field within which organic forms are located and "held in place"' (Ingold 1990: 215). That generative field is constituted by the totality of organism – environment relations, and the activities of organisms are moments of its unfolding. Indeed once we think of the world in this way, as a total movement of becoming which builds itself into the forms we see, and in which each form takes shape in continuous relation to those around it, then the distinction between the animate and the inanimate seems to dissolve. The world itself takes on the character of an organism, and the movements of animals – including those of us human beings – are parts or aspects of its life-process (Lovelock 1979). This means that in dwelling in the world, we do not act *upon* it, or do things *to* it; rather we move along *with* it. Our actions do not transform the world, they are part and parcel of the world's transforming itself. And that is just another way of saying that they belong to time.

For in the final analysis, everything is suspended in movement. As Whitehead once remarked, 'there is no holding nature still and looking at it' (cited in Ho 1989: 19–20). What appear to us as the fixed forms of the landscape, passive and unchanging unless acted upon from outside, are themselves in motion, albeit on a scale immeasurably slower and more majestic than that on which our own activities are conducted. Imagine a film of the landscape, shot over years, centuries, even millennia. Slightly speeded up, plants appear to engage in very animal-like movements, trees flex their limbs without any prompting from the winds. Speeded up rather more, glaciers flow like rivers and even the earth begins to move. At yet greater speeds solid rock bends, buckles and flows like molten metal. The world itself begins to breathe. Thus the rhythmic pattern of human activities nests within the wider pattern of activity for all animal life, which in turn nests within the pattern of activity for all so-called living things, which nests within the life-process of the world. At each of these levels, coherence is founded upon resonance (Ho 1989: 18). Ultimately, then, by replacing the tasks of human dwelling in their proper context within the process of becoming of the world as a whole, we can do away with the dichotomy between taskscape and landscape – only, however, by recognizing the fundamental temporality of the landscape itself.

The Harvesters

In order to provide some illustration of the ideas developed in the preceding sections, I reproduce here a painting which, more than any other I know, vividly captures a sense of the temporality of the landscape. This is *The Harvesters*, painted by Pieter Bruegel the Elder in 1565 (see Figure 1.1). I am not an art historian or critic, and my purpose is not to analyse the painting in terms of style, composition or aesthetic effect. Nor am I concerned with the historical context of its production. Suffice it to say that the picture is believed to be one of a series of twelve, each depicting a month of the year, out of which only five have survived (W. Gibson 1977: 147). Each panel portrays a landscape, in the colours and apparel appropriate to the month, and shows people engaged in the tasks of the agricultural cycle that are usual at that time of year. *The Harvesters* depicts the month of August, and shows field hands at work reaping and sheafing a luxuriant crop of wheat, whilst others pause for a midday meal and some well-earned rest. The sense of rustic harmony conveyed in this scene may, perhaps, represent something of an idealization on Bruegel's part. As Walter Gibson points out, Bruegel was inclined to 'depict peasants very much as a wealthy landowner would have viewed them, as the anonymous tenders of his fields and flocks' (1977: 157–8). Any landowner would have had cause for satisfaction in such a fine crop, whereas the hands who sweated to bring it in may have had a rather different experience. Nevertheless, Bruegel painted during a period of great material prosperity in the Netherlands, in which all shared to some degree. These were fortunate times.

Rather than viewing the painting as a work of art, I would like to invite you – the reader – to imagine yourself set down in the very landscape depicted, on a sultry August day in 1565. Standing a little way off to the right of the group beneath the tree, you are a witness to the scene unfolding about you. And of course you hear it too, for the scene does not unfold in silence. So accustomed are we to thinking of the landscape as a picture that we can look *at*, like a plate in a

Figure 1.1 *The Harvesters* (1565) by Pieter Bruegel the Elder. Reproduced by permission of the Metropolitan Museum of Art, Rogers Fund (19.164). Image copyright © 2007 The Metropolitan Museum of Art / Art Resource / Scala, Florence.

book or an image on a screen, that it is perhaps necessary to remind you that exchanging the painting for 'real life' is not simply a matter of increasing the scale. What is involved is a fundamental difference of orientation. In the landscape of our dwelling, we *look around* (J. Gibson 1979: 203). In what follows I shall focus on six components of what you see around you, and comment on each in so far as they illustrate aspects of what I have had to say about landscape and temporality. They are: the hills and valley, the paths and tracks, the tree, the corn, the church, and the people.

The hills and valley

The terrain is a gently undulating one of low hills and valleys, grading off to a shoreline that can just be made out through the summer haze. You are standing near the summit of a hill, from where you can look out across the intervening valley to the next. How, then, do you differentiate between the hills and the valley as components of this landscape? Are they alternating blocks or strips into which it may be divided up? Any attempt at such division plunges us immediately into absurdity. For where can we draw the boundaries of a hill except along the valley bottoms that separate it from the hills on either side? And where can we draw the boundaries of a valley except along the summits of the hills that mark its watershed? One way, we would have a landscape consisting only of hills, the other way it would consist only of valleys. Of course, 'hill' and 'valley' are opposed terms, but the opposition is not spatial or altitudinal but kinaesthetic. It is the movements of falling away from, and rising up towards, that specify the form of the hill; and the movements of falling away towards, and rising up from, that specify the form of the valley. Through the exercises of descending and climbing, and their different muscular entailments, the contours of the land-scape are not so much measured as *felt* – they are directly incorporated into our bodily experience. But even if you remain rooted to one spot, the same principle applies. As you look across the valley to the hill on the horizon, your eyes do not remain fixed: swivelling in their sockets, or as you tilt your head, their motions accord with the movement of your attention as it follows its course through the landscape. You 'cast your eyes' first downwards into the valley, and then upwards towards the distant hill. Indeed in this vernacular phrase, to 'cast one's eyes', common-sense has once again grasped intuitively what the psychology of vision, with its metaphors of ret-inal imagery, has found so hard to accept: that movement is the very essence of perception. It is *because*, in scanning the terrain from nearby into the distance, your downward glance is followed by an upward one, that you perceive the valley.

Moreover someone standing where you are now would perceive the same topographic pan-orama, regardless of the time of year, the weather conditions and the activities in which people may be engaged. We may reasonably suppose that over the centuries, perhaps even millennia, this basic topography has changed but little. Set against the duration of human memory and experience, it may therefore be taken to establish a baseline of permanence. Yet permanence, as Gibson has stressed, is always relative; thus 'it is better to speak of persistence under change' (J. Gibson 1979: 13). Although the topography is invariant relative to the human life-cycle, it is not itself immune to change. Sea-levels rise and fall with global climatic cycles, and the present contours of the country are the cumulative out-come of a slow and long drawn out process of erosion and deposition. This process, moreover, was not confined to earlier geological epochs during which the landscape assumed its present topographic form. For it is still going on, and will continue so long as the stream, just visible in the valley bottom, flows on towards the sea. The stream does not flow between pre-cut banks, but cuts its banks even as it flows. Likewise, as we have seen, people shape the landscape even as they dwell. And human activities, as well as the action of rivers and the sea, contribute

significantly to the process of erosion. As you watch, the stream flows, folk are at work, a landscape is being formed, and time passes.

The paths and tracks

I remarked above that we experience the con-tours of the landscape by moving through it, so that it enters – as Bachelard would say – into our 'muscular consciousness'. Reliving the experience in our imagination, we are inclined to recall the road we took as 'climbing' the hill, or as 'descending' into the valley, as though 'the road itself had muscles, or rather, counter-muscles' (Bachelard 1964: 11). And this, too, is probably how you recall the paths and tracks that are visible to you now: after all, you must have travelled along at least some of them to reach the spot where you are currently standing. Nearest at hand, a path has been cut through the wheat-field, allowing sheaves to be carried down, and water and provisions to be carried up. Further off, a cart-track runs along the valley bottom, and another winds up the hill behind. In the distance, paths criss-cross the village green. Taken together, these paths and tracks 'impose a habitual pattern on the move-ment of people' (Jackson 1989: 146). And yet they also arise out of that movement, for every path or track shows up as the accumulated imprint of countless journeys that people have made – with or without their vehicles or domestic animals – as they have gone about their everyday business. Thus the same move-ment is embodied, on the side of the people, in their 'muscular consciousness', and on the side of the landscape, in its network of paths and tracks. In this network is sedimented the activ-ity of an entire community, over many gener-ations. It is the taskscape made visible.

In their journeys along paths and tracks, however, people also move from place to place. To reach a place, you need cross no boundary, but you must follow some kind of path. Thus there can be no places without paths, along which people arrive and depart; and no paths without places, that constitute their destinations and points of departure. And for the harvesters, the place to which they arrive, and whence they will leave at the end of the day, is marked by the next feature of the landscape to occupy your attention. ...

The tree

Rising from the spot where people are gathered for their repast is an old and gnarled pear-tree, which provides them with both shade from the sun, a back-rest and a prop for utensils. Being the month of August, the tree is in full leaf, and fruit is ripening on the branches. But this is not just *any* tree. For one thing, it draws the entire landscape around it into a unique focus: in other words, by its presence it constitutes a particular place. The place was not there before the tree, but came into being with it. And for those who are gathered there, the prospect it affords, which is to be had nowhere else, is what gives it its particular character and identity. For another thing, no other tree has quite the same configuration of branches, diverging, bending and twisting in exactly the same way. In its present form, the tree embodies the entire history of its development from the moment it first took root. And that history consists in the unfolding of its relations with manifold components of its environment, including the people who have nurtured it, tilled the soil around it, pruned its branches, picked its fruit, and – as at present – use it as something to lean against. The people, in other words, are as much bound up in the life of the tree as is the tree in the lives of the people. Moreover, unlike the hills and the valley, the tree has manifestly grown within living memory. Thus its temporality is more consonant with that of human dwelling. Yet in its branching structure, the tree combines an entire hierarchy of temporal rhythms, ranging from the long cycle of its own germination, growth and eventual decay to the short, annual cycle of flowering, fruiting and foliation. At one extreme, represented by the solid trunk, it presides immobile over the passage of human generations; at the other, represented by the frondescent shoots, it resonates with the lifecycles of insects, the seasonal migrations of birds, and the regular round of human agricultural activities (cf. Davies 1988). In a sense, then, the tree bridges the gap between the apparently fixed and invariant forms of the landscape and the mobile and transient forms of animal life, visible proof that all of these forms, from the most permanent to the most ephemeral, are dynamically linked under transformation within the movement of becoming of the world as a whole.

The corn

Turning from the pear-tree to the wheat-field, it is no longer a place in the landscape but the surrounding surface that occupies your attention. And perhaps what is most striking about this surface is its uniformity of colour, a golden sheen that cloaks the more elevated parts of the country for as far as the eye can see. As you know, wheat takes on this colour at the particular time of year when it is ripe for harvesting. More than any other feature of the landscape, the golden corn gathers the lives of its inhabitants, wherever they may be, into temporal unison, founded upon a communion of visual experience. Thus whereas the tree binds past, present and future in a single place, the corn binds every place in the landscape within a single horizon of the present. The tree, we could say, establishes a vivid sense of duration, the corn an equally vivid sense of what Fabian (1983: 31) calls *coevalness*. It is this distinction that Bachelard has in mind when he contrasts the 'before-me, before-us' of the forest with the 'with-me, with-us' of fields and meadows, wherein 'my dreams and recollections accompany all the different phases of tilling and harvesting' (Bachelard 1964: 188). You may suppose that the sleeper beneath the tree is dreaming of corn, but if so, you may be sure that the people and the activities that figure in his dream are coeval with those of the present and do not take him back into an encounter with the past. (Note that the distinction between coevalness and duration, represented by the corn and the tree, is not at all the same as the classic Saussurian dichotomy between synchrony and diachrony: the former belongs to the perspective of the A-series rather than the B-series, to the temporality of the landscape, not to its chronology (Ingold 1986b: 151).)

Where the corn has been freshly cut, it presents a sheer vertical front, not far short of a man's height. But this is not a boundary feature, like a hedge or fence. It is an interface, whose outline is progressively transformed as the harvesters proceed with their work. Here is a fine example of the way in which form emerges through movement. Another example can be seen further off, where a man is engaged in the task of binding the wheat into a sheaf. Each completed sheaf has a regular form, which arises out of the co-ordinated movement of binding. But the completion of a sheaf is only one moment in the labour process. The sheaves will later be carried down the path through the field, to the haycart in the valley. Indeed at this very moment, one woman is stooped almost double in the act of picking up a sheaf, and two others can be seen on their way down, sheaves on their shoulders. Many more operations will follow before the wheat is eventually transformed into bread. In the scene before you, one of the harvesters under the tree, seated on a sheaf, is cutting a loaf. Here the cycle of production and consumption ends where it began, with the producers. For production is tantamount to dwelling: it does not begin here (with a preconceived image) and end there (with a finished artefact), but is *continuously going on.*

The church

Not far off, nestled in a grove of trees near the top of the hill, is a stone church. It is instructive to ask: how does the church differ from the tree? They have more in common, perhaps, than meets the eye. Both possess the attributes of what Bakhtin (1981: 84) calls a 'chronotope' – that is, a place charged with temporality, one in which temporality takes on palpable form. Like the tree, the church by its very presence constitutes a place, which owes its character to the unique way in which it draws in the surrounding landscape. Again like the tree, the church spans human generations, yet its temporality is not inconsonant with that of human dwelling. As the tree buries its roots in the ground, so also people's ancestors are buried in the graveyard beside the church, and both sets of roots may reach to approximately the same temporal depth. Moreover the church, too, resonates to the cycles of human life and subsistence. Among the inhabitants of the neighbourhood, it is not only seen but also heard, as its bells ring out the seasons, the months, births, marriages and deaths. In short, as features of the landscape, both the church and the tree appear as veritable monuments to the passage of time.

Yet despite these similarities, the difference may seem obvious. The church, after all, is a *building.* The tree by contrast, is not built, it grows. We may agree to reserve the term 'building' for any durable structure in the landscape whose form arises and is sustained within the current of human activity. It would be wrong to conclude, however, that the distinction between buildings and non-buildings is an absolute one. Where an absolute distinction is made, it is generally premised upon the separation of mind and nature, such that built form, rather than having its source within nature, is said to be superimposed by the mind upon it. But from the perspective of dwelling, we can see that the forms of buildings, as much as of any other features of the landscape, are neither given in the world nor placed upon it, but emerge within the self-transforming processes of the world itself. With respect to any feature, the scope of human involvement in these processes will vary from negligible to considerable, though it is never total (even the most 'engineered' of environments is home to other species). What is or is not a 'building' is therefore a relative matter; moreover as human involvement may vary in the 'life history' of a feature, it may be *more or less* of a building in different periods.

Returning to the tree and the church, it is evidently too simple to suppose that the form of the tree is naturally given in its genetic makeup, whereas the form of the church pre-exists, in the minds of the builders, as a plan which is then 'realized' in stone. In the case of the tree, we have already observed that its growth consists in the unfolding of a total system of relations constituted by the fact of its presence in an environment, from the point of germination onwards, and that people, as components of the tree's environment, play a not insignificant role in this process. Likewise, the 'biography' of the church consists in the unfolding of relations with its human builders, as well as with other components of its environment, from the moment when the first stone was laid. The 'final' form of the church may indeed have been prefigured in the human imagination, but it no more issued from the image than did the form of the tree issue from its genes. In both cases, the form is the embodiment of a developmental or historical process, and is rooted in the context of human dwelling in the world.

In the case of the church, moreover, that process did not stop when its form came to match the conceptual model. For as long as the building remains standing in the landscape, it will continue – as it does now – to figure within the environment not just of human beings but of a myriad of other living kinds, plant and animal, which will incorporate it into their own life-activities and modify it in the process. And it is subject, too, to the same forces of weathering and decomposition, both organic and meteorological, that affect everything else in the landscape. The preservation of the church in its existing, 'finished' form in the face of these forces, however substantial it may be in its materials and construction, requires a regular input of effort in maintenance and repair. Once this human input lapses, leaving it at the mercy of other forms of life and of the weather, it will soon cease to be a building and become a ruin.

The people

So far I have described the scene only as you behold it with your eyes. Yet you do not only look, you listen as well, for the air is full of sounds of one kind and another. Though the folk beneath the tree are too busy eating to talk, you hear the clatter of wooden spoons on bowls, the slurp of the drinker, and the loud snores of the member of the party who is outstretched in sleep. Further off, you hear the swish of scythes against the cornstalks and the calls of the birds as they swoop low over the field in search of prey. Far off in the distance, wafted on the light wind, can be heard the sounds of people conversing and playing on a green, behind which, on the other side of the stream, lies a cluster of cottages. What you hear is a taskscape.

In the performance of their particular tasks, people are responsive not only to the cycle of maturation of the crop, which draws them together in the overall project of harvesting, but also to each other's activities as these are apportioned by the division of labour. Even within the same task, individuals do not carry on in mutual isolation. Technically, it takes only one man to wield a scythe, but the reapers nevertheless work in unison, achieving a dance-like harmony in their rhythmic movements. Similarly the two women carrying sheaves down into the valley adjust their pace, each in relation to the other, so that the distance between them remains more or less invariant. Perhaps there is less co-ordination between the respective movements of the eaters, however they eye each other intently as they set about their

repast, and the meal is a joint activity on which all have embarked together, and which they will finish together. Only the sleeper, oblivious to the world, is out of joint – his snores jar the senses precisely because they are *not* in any kind of rhythmic relation to what is going on around. Without wakeful attention, there can be no resonance.

But in attending to one another, do the people inhabit a world of their own, an exclusively *human* world of meanings and intentions, of beliefs and values, detached from the one in which their bodies are put to work in their several activities? Do they, from within such a domain of intersubjectivity, look at the world outside through the window of their senses? Surely not. For the hills and valley, the tree, the corn and the birds are as palpably present to them (as indeed to you too) as are the people to each other (and to you). The reapers, as they wield their scythes, are *with* the corn, just as the eaters are *with* their fellows. The landscape, in short, is not a totality that you or anyone else can look *at*, it is rather the world *in* which we stand in taking up a point of view on our surroundings. And it is within the context of this attentive involvement in the landscape that the human imagination gets to work in fashioning ideas about it. For the landscape, to borrow a phrase from Merleau-Ponty (1962: 24), is not so much the object as 'the *homeland* of our thoughts'.

Epilogue

Concluding an essay on the ways in which the Western Apache of Arizona discover meaning, value and moral guidance in the landscape around them, Basso abhors the tendency in ecological anthropology to relegate such matters to an 'epiphenomenal' level, which is seen to have little or no bearing on the dynamics of adaptation of human populations to the conditions of their environments. An ecology that is fully *cultural*, Basso argues, is one that would attend as much to the semiotic as to the material dimensions of people's relations with their surroundings, by bringing into focus 'the layers of significance with which human beings blanket the environment' (Basso 1984: 49). In rather similar vein, Cosgrove regrets the tendency in human geography to regard the landscape in narrowly utilitarian and functional terms, as 'an impersonal expression of demographic and economic forces', and thus to ignore the multiple layers of symbolic meaning or cultural representation that are deposited upon it. The task of decoding the 'many-layered meanings of symbolic landscapes', Cosgrove argues, will require a geography that is not just human but properly *humanistic* (Cosgrove 1989: 120–7).

Though I have some sympathy with the views expressed by these writers, I believe that the metaphors of cultural construction which they adopt have an effect quite opposite to that intended. For the very idea that meaning *covers over* the world, layer upon layer, carries the implication that the way to uncover the most basic level of human beings' practical involvement with their environments is by stripping these layers away. In other words, such blanketing metaphors actually serve to create and perpetuate an intellectual space in which human ecology or human geography can flourish, untroubled by any concerns about what the world means to the people who live in it. We can surely learn from the Western Apache, who insist that the stories they tell, far from putting meanings upon the landscape, are intended to allow listeners to place themselves in *relation* to specific features of the landscape, in such a way that their meanings may be revealed or disclosed. Stories help to open up the world, not to cloak it.

And such opening up, too, must be the objective of archaeology. Like the Western Apache – and for that matter any other group of people who are truly 'at home' in the world – archaeologists study the meaning of the landscape, not by interpreting the many layers of its representation (adding further layers in the process) but by probing ever more deeply into it. Meaning is there to be *discovered* in the landscape, if only we know how to attend to it. Every feature, then, is a potential clue, a key to meaning rather than a vehicle for carrying it. This discovery procedure, wherein objects in the landscape become clues to meaning, is what distinguishes the perspective of dwelling. And since, as I have shown, the process of dwelling is fundamentally temporal, the apprehension of the landscape in the dwelling perspective must begin from a recognition of its temporality. Only through such recognition, by temporalizing the landscape, can we move beyond the division that has afflicted most inquiries up to now, between the 'scientific' study of an atemporalized nature, and the 'humanistic' study of a dematerialized history. And no discipline is better placed to take this step than archaeology. I have not been concerned here with either the methods or the results of archaeological inquiry. However to the question, 'what is archaeology the study *of*?', I believe there is no better answer than 'the temporality of the landscape'. I hope, in this article, to have gone some way towards elucidating what this means.

References

Bachelard, G. 1964. *The Poetics of Space*. Boston: Beacon Press.

Bakhtin, M. M. 1981. *The Dialogic Imagination: Four Essays* (trans. C. Emerson and M. Holquist; ed. M. Holquist). Austin: University of Texas Press.

Basso, K. 1984. 'Stalking with stories': names, places, and moral narratives among the Western Apache. In *Text, Play and Story: The Construction and Reconstruction of Self and Society* (ed. E. M. Bruner). Washington, DC: American Ethnological Society, pp. 19–55.

Bohm, D. 1980. *Wholeness and the Implicate Order*. London: Routledge & Kegan Paul.

Bourdieu, P. 1977. *Outline of a Theory of Practice*. Cambridge: Cambridge University Press.

Connerton, P. 1989. *How Societies Remember*. Cambridge: Cambridge University Press.

Cosgrove, D. 1989. Geography is everywhere: culture and symbolism in human landscapes. In *Horizons in*

- explain difference between land & landscape more.
- too philosophical for me
- contours of landscape is felt (A)
- cycle
  landscape – activity – landscape
- reciprocity of terms
- deeper meaning – not just interpreting layers as if they are untouched & unaffected
- what do you think of the article?

Gell, A. 1992. *The Anthropology of Time: Cultural Constructions of Temporal Maps and Images*. Oxford: Berg.

Gibson, J. J. 1979. *The Ecological Approach to Visual Perception*. Boston: Houghton Mifflin.

Gibson, W. S. 1977. *Bruegel*. London: Thames & Hudson.

Goodwin, B. 1988. Organisms and minds: the dialectics of the animal – human interface in biology. In *What is an Animal?* (ed. T. Ingold). London: Unwin Hyman, pp. 100–9.

Gould, P. and White, R. 1974. *Mental Maps*. Harmondsworth: Penguin.

Guyer, J. 1988. The multiplication of labor: gender and agricultural change in modern Africa. *Current Anthropology*, 29: 247–72.

Heidegger, M. 1971. *Poetry, Language, Thought* (trans. A. Hofstadter). New York: Harper & Row.

Ho, M-W. 1989. Reanimating nature: the integration of science with human experience. *Beshara*, 8: 16–25.

Inglis, F. 1977. Nation and community: a landscape and its morality. *Sociological Review*, 25: 489–514.

Ingold, T. 1986a. *The Appropriation of Nature: Essays on Human Ecology and Social Relationships*. Manchester: Manchester University Press.

Ingold, T. 1986b. *Evolution and Social Life*. Cambridge: Cambridge University Press.

Ingold, T. 1990. An anthropologist looks at biology. *Man* (N.S.), 25: 208–29.

Ingold, T. 1992a. Editorial. *Man* (N.S.), 27: 693–6.

Ingold, T. 1992b. Culture and the perception of the environment. In *Bush Base: Forest Farm. Culture, Environment and Development* (eds E. Croll and D. Parkin). London: Routledge, pp. 39–56.

Ingold, T. 1993. Technology, language, intelligence: a reconsideration of basic concepts. In *Tools, Language and Cognition in Human Evolution* (eds K. R. Gibson and T. Ingold). Cambridge: Cambridge University Press, pp. 449–72.

Jackson, M. 1989. *Paths Toward a Clearing: Radical Empiricism and Ethnographic Inquiry*, Bloomington: Indiana University Press.

Kubler, G. 1962. *The Shape of Time: Remarks on the History of Things*. New Haven, Conn.: Yale University Press.

Langer, S. K. 1953. *Feeling and Form: A Theory of Art*. London: Routledge & Kegan Paul.

Lewontin, R. C. 1982. Organism and environment. In *Learning, Development and Culture* (ed. H. C. Plotkin). Chichester: Wiley, pp. 151–70.

Lovelock, J. E. 1979. *Gaia: A New Look at Life on Earth*. Oxford: Oxford University Press.

Marx, K. 1930. *Capital*, Vol. I (trans E. and C. Paul, from 4th German edn of *Das Kapital*, 1890). London: Dent.

Mead, G. H. 1977 [1938]. The process of mind in nature. In *George Herbert Mead on Social Psychology* (ed. A. Strauss). Chicago: University of Chicago Press, pp. 85–111.

Meinig, D. W. 1979a. The beholding eye: ten versions of the same scene. In *The Interpretation of Ordinary Landscapes* (ed. D. W. Meinig). Oxford: Oxford University Press, pp. 33–48.

Meinig, D. W. 1979b. Introduction. In *The Interpretation of Ordinary Landscapes* (ed. D. W. Meinig). Oxford: Oxford University Press, pp. 1–7.

Merleau-Ponty, M. 1962. *The Phenomenology of Perception* (trans. C. Smith). London: Routledge & Kegan Paul.

Morphy, H. 1989. From dull to brilliant: the aesthetics of spiritual power among the Yolngu. *Man* (N.S.), 24: 21–40.

Oyama, S. 1985. *The Ontogeny of Information: Developmental Systems and Evolution*. Cambridge: Cambridge University Press.

Pittendrigh, C. S. 1958. Adaptation, natural selection and behavior. In *Behavior and Evolution* (eds A. Roe and G. G. Simpson). New Haven, Conn.: Yale University Press, pp. 390–416.

Reed, E. S. 1988. The affordances of the animate environment: social science from the ecological point of view. In *What is an Animal?* (ed. T. Ingold). London: Unwin Hyman, pp. 110–26.

Reynolds, P. C. 1993. The complementation theory of language and tool use. In *Tools, Language and Cognition in Human Evolution* (eds K. R. Gibson and T. Ingold). Cambridge: Cambridge University Press, pp. 407–28.

Richards, P. 1991. Against the motion (2). In *Human Worlds are Culturally Constructed* (ed. T. Ingold). Manchester: Group for Debates in Anthropological Theory.

Sahlins, M. D. 1972. *Stone Age Economics*. London: Tavistock.

Saussure, F. de 1959. *Course in General Linguistics* (trans. W. Baskin). New York: Philosophical Library.

Sorokin, P. A. and Merton, R. K. 1937. Social time: a methodological and functional analysis. *American Journal of Sociology*, 42: 615–29.

Thompson, E. P. 1967. Time, work-discipline and industrial capitalism. *Past and Present*, 38: 56–97.

Tuan, Y-F. 1979. Thought and landscape: the eye and the mind's eye. In *The Interpretation of Ordinary Landscapes* (ed. D. W. Meinig). Oxford: Oxford University Press, pp. 89–102.

Wikan, U. 1992. Beyond words: the power of resonance. *American Ethnologist*, 19: 460–82.

Young, M. 1988. *The Metronomic Society: Natural Rhythms and Human Timetables*. London: Thames & Hudson.

2

Identifying Ancient Sacred Landscapes in Australia
From Physical to Social

Paul S. C. Taçon

Introduction

Debates about what makes us human have focused on our tool-making abilities, language, the production of "art," the use of symbols, and our genetic heritage. In most cases, similarities rather than differences from other species are highlighted and it seems that, in terms of behaviors such as tool use, language and art, humans are the creatures that practice these things to the extreme. Our physical selves are aided by our material culture and symbolic communication but it is the concept of "landscape" that is integral to this process. Other species have home-ranges, preferred travel routes, or dwellings used by many generations of individuals, but with humans landscape use, modification and manipulation have become obsessions. Our oldest ancestors initiated the process of transforming natural wilderness into cultural places and spaces many thousands of years ago, by the mythologizing, marking and mapping of landscapes (Cosgrove 1989; 1993; Taçon 1994). Today there are few areas of the world that have not been built upon, mapped, marked, or other-wise modified for human use. Indeed, a driving urge for many people is to be the first to conquer the last few remaining areas of what they perceive to be "wilderness" – supposed but perhaps now mythical places untouched by humankind. Yet what we perceive to be wilderness is also landscape, with some people going to great lengths to preserve these "places." However, "wilderness" too is sectioned off, marked, mapped, and mythologized into networks of national parks or reserves, becoming another type of humanly defined landscape in the process.

There are many definitions of landscape and even more perceptions and conceptions (e.g., Bender 1993; Cosgrove and Daniels 1988; Gosden and Head 1994; Ingold 1993). "Landscape is a term which both invites and defies definition" (Gosden and Head 1994: 113) – consequently, there is a vast body of landscape literature that attempts to dissect the very essence of landscape use and understanding, but ultimately we are forced to conclude that landscape as a concept is infinitely variable. Landscape, like "beauty," is in the mind of the beholder and, as such, varies widely from one personal or cultural perspective to the next. Experience, history, value systems, relationships, circumstance, and individual choices all play a part in how landscapes are seen or described. The important point is that they are seen and described from a human perspective – often personified, deified and/or defined in terms of

Paul S. C. Taçon, "Identifying Ancient Sacred Landscapes in Australia: From Physical to Social," pp. 33–57 from *Archaeologies of Landscapes: Contemporary Perspectives*, ed. Wendy Ashmore and A. Bernard Knapp (Oxford: Blackwell Publishers, 1999). Reprinted with permission of Blackwell Publishers.

production patterns

human history and exploitation. Landscapes are socialized; landscapes are conceived. But are there certain physical landscapes that share common features which make them recognizably special, sacred or sublime, no matter what one's cultural background? For example, Nash (1997) makes a case for archetypal landscapes founded in nature. How have humans responded to these places, converting them from physical to social landscapes? And what of the world's earliest surviving human landscapes? Is there good evidence that humans have always been obsessed with socializing large-scale landscapes?

In order to answer these questions we must turn to rock art, that great body of enduring human-made marks produced with both symbolic and aesthetic intent. For it is this form of ancient human activity that is most directly linked to early perceptions of landscape – the very location and organizational structure of rock art speaks of human relationships to places and spaces (see Hodder 1993 and Tilley 1994 for definitions and other relationships between material culture and landscapes). We will never be able to decipher the full meaning of ancient rock art, but we can define its structure and organizing principles (Chippindale and Taçon 1998). These, in turn, can be related to the larger landscapes of which they are a part. As Richard Bradley (1995: 107) notes for the "Atlantic" style of rock art found on natural surfaces from Scotland to Spain: "It is a scheme based largely on geography." Many other forms of rock art are similarly structured, with striking examples found in some parts of Australia, the Americas, and southern Africa. In all these regions one of the earliest surviving forms of rock art consists of cup-shaped marks known as "cupules" (Parkman 1995; Taçon et al. 1997). It is these that may give us insight into very early landscape use at the symbolic level (Figure 2.1).

However, in Australia (Figure 2.2) there is also a large body of ethnographic evidence to consult about landscape perceptions and conceptions. Furthermore, visual art and landscape feature prominently in modern politics, from urban "multi-cultural" to remote "traditional" settings. For instance, Luke Taylor (1988: 381) has shown that some "X-ray" paintings from the remote region of Arnhem Land:

Figure 2.1 Large panels of cupules, such as this one at Jinmium, Northern Territory, are found scattered across the northern portions of Western Australia and the Northern Territory (photo: Paul Taçon).

encode "inside" meanings relating to the spatial relationship between topographic features of clan lands. At an "outside" level these paintings are also interpreted to show the body parts and internal organs and bones of ancestral beings. The metaphors of these paintings express the way Kunwinjku conceive of the spatial organization of sites in their lands in terms of an abstract model of the divided yet organically related body parts of the ancestral being that created those lands. Such sites are described as transformations of the actual body parts of the ancestral being, and all the sites thus created are considered to be intrinsically connected. The association between body parts and landscape is developed principally within the Mardayin ceremony and in X-ray paintings used in the Mardayin. Paintings interpreted to show X-ray features occur in a number of contexts in this ceremony.

According to Djon Mundine (1992: 11), similar layered levels of relationship between people and places underpin Indigenous urban art, even though the specific ways in which they are expressed and the particular meanings are quite different:

As in ancient times, Aboriginal people are returning to a multi-layered artistic culture: to interactive forms of song, dance, literature, and newer forms in film and video. Through their expansion of subject matter and range of work, employing new media alongside ones long-used, Aboriginal people are again finding ways to access their inner, vital, dynamic spirit. They are giving voice to a wounded history but also

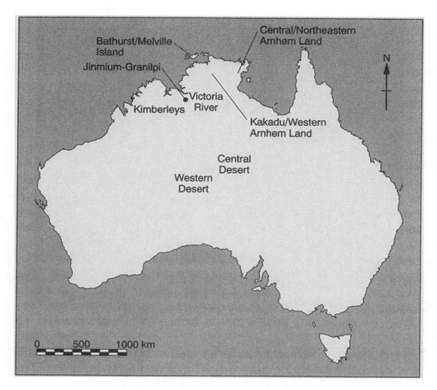

Figure 2.2 Map of Australia showing places mentioned in the text.

reaching beyond anger, speaking again with pride about the land called Australia and their long, strong, enduring and once again confident relationship to it.

Sacred Landscapes, Sacred Sites

In areas of the world where ethnographic or historic information is available we know that certain landscape features invoke common responses in human beings – feelings of awe, power, majestic beauty, respect, enrichment among them. Most commonly these subjective feelings occur in response to perceiving four types of places: (a) where the results of great acts of natural transformation can be best seen, such as mountain ranges, volcanoes, steep valleys or gorges (Figure 2.3); (b) at junctions or points of change between geology, hydrology, and vegetation, or some combination of all three, such as sudden changes in elevation, waterfalls, the places where rainforest meets other vegetation

(Figure 2.4); (c) where there is an unusual landscape feature, such as a prominent peak, cave, or hole in the ground that one comes upon suddenly (Figure 2.5); and (d) places providing panoramic views or large vistas of interesting and varied landscape features (Figure 2.6). Often these are places where concepts of an upper world, a lower world and the earth plain come together visually in a striking manner. These are places where the center of the world may be experienced, where an *axis mundi* is located (Eliade 1964; 1978; Ouzman 1998; Paper 1990), for it is at these places that it is claimed a powerful connection between different levels and states of existence can be encountered. For Indigenous people of northern Australia:

> Most often, these nodes or focal points are unusual or outstanding aspects of the natural landscape, such as the tops of hills or raised areas, the centres of plains, areas marking the interfaces of water, rock, earth and sky (i.e., the underworld, middle world and skyworld),

Figure 2.3 Outstanding and unusual geological features, such as those that define Rainbow Valley in central Australia, are important landscapes associated with the activities of Ancestral Beings who created, shaped, and formed the land in the ancient eras of the Dreamtime (photo: Paul Taçon).

waterfalls, darkened deep pools of permanent water surrounded by rock, unusually sculptured and eroded geological forms or shaped boulders and rocky outcrops and areas in general. At some of these locations, the power is believed to be so concentrated that it is dangerous for all but those initiated into the highest levels of religious knowledge to approach them. At others, correctly conducted rituals or observances, such as rock painting, song, ceremonies, and blowing water in Australia … allow individuals to tap into the power of places or to be protected from it. (Taçon 1990: 13)

The ancient Greeks, Romans, Maya, Chinese, Vikings, and peoples of Southeast Asia, among others, responded similarly to these powerful landscape nodes, as is evidenced by their stories, literature, visual art, and architecture. Indeed, places of worship are invariably modeled on the more striking features of geology, with temples, cathedrals, churches, and monasteries placed in relation to mountains or pillars of stone or shaped to resemble them. Often their insides re-create a cave or cavern-like environment and water invariably features in some of the rituals performed inside. Physical manifestations of upper, lower, and middle worlds can be found in the architecture, highlighting aspects of belief systems founded on landscape qualities. These human-made sacred places are also richly adorned with elaborate imagery – with symbols and senses of aesthetics that reflect the unique identities and experiences of their makers. Ouzman (1998) argues that southern African rock art sites represented physical and conceptual places where upper, lower, and middle worlds believed to exist by San communities intersect. Vastokas and Vastokas (1973) have argued similarly for many North American rock art sites. Thus we see a common pattern – human-made sacred places modeled on a core set of natural places but embellished with unique artistry to reflect the cultural distinctiveness of given groups of people.

Similar patterns may be observed with many Australian rock art sites. First of all, rock art sites may be situated near naturally defined "sacred" locations, but usually they do not occur right at them. Instead, they more often overlook, indicate the approach to, or mark the limits of the more sacred and restricted landscape zones.

Figure 2.4 Waterfalls, permanent pools and other liminal places where there is visual evidence of transformation between water, geology, and vegetation are usually considered to be sacred places. They may have either open or restricted stories and access depending on their context within larger Dreaming Tracks. This example is of an open site within Kakadu National Park but there are other closed, dangerous places nearby (photo: Paul Taçon).

Secondly, rock art sites are invariably located not far from water, whether the sites were once places of habitation or not. Thirdly, the rock shelters or platforms that were most extensively used for painting and/or engraving are those with prominent, often magnificent, panoramic views. In other words, significant stretches of what may be perceived to be powerfully charged or "beautiful" landscapes can be seen from the sites or vantage points nearby. It is almost as if people were situating themselves to take advantage of the visual results of nature's creativity in order to produce or enhance their own.

And this connection did not end with death for an important feature of secondary mortuary ceremonies in northern Australia is the reintegration of the deceased with the special, more sacred parts of the land. Many of the significant locations chosen for rock art were also used to house human remains, often painted with ochre. In areas where the geology is such that there are few suitable rocky locations other sorts of significant landscapes were chosen. For instance, among the Tiwi of Bathurst and Melville Islands the transitional spaces between eucalypt and rainforest were used to inter human remains, with elaborately carved and painted Pukumani poles erected to memorialize the dead (Figure 2.7; Goodale 1959; Mountford 1958: 60–118; Spencer 1914: 238–9).

In Australia, most other important rituals and ceremonies that emphasize rites of passage or intensification were and, in some areas, continue to be performed in these sorts of powerful, unusual, and visually striking natural places. In the process, "the rituals effectively bonded people with nature, with geography and with the landscape ... people anchored themselves in both space and time and gained insight and direction" (Taçon 1990: 30). Ultimately this is conceived and expressed as a religious experience and cultural practice, with divine knowledge, insight, or encounters a primary feature. When practices continue at the same locations over many generations these places and their surrounding landscapes become increasingly symbolically charged, patterned, and contextualized – traditions of landscape experience and enrichment are perpetuated and expressed as "Ancestral Law."

Finally, it should be noted that there are many levels of sacredness used to define and describe landscapes, with some more sacred than others. Often these are related to issues of restriction and access, powerlessness and authority, initiate and initiated. As people move through different levels of knowledge acquisition, access to more varied sacred sites – hence landscapes – becomes culturally possible. It is because of the power perceived to exist and believed to be directly experienced at some locations that restrictions of access are made but it also has to do with the power and authority of those already initiated into the secrets of those unusual places. This is true not only for Indigenous Australians but also for many other, if not most, peoples of the world. It is said to protect both uninitiated individuals

Figure 2.5   Near the Mann River this unusual geological feature is said to mark the spot where a Rainbow Serpent turned to stone (photo: Paul Taçon).

Figure 2.6   Meredith Wilson records rock paintings at a site that has magnificent panoramic views. These places were often marked with rock art imagery from a number of different periods (photo: Paul Taçon).

Figure 2.7 Tiwi burial grounds on Melville and Bathurst Islands were traditionally liminal spaces where rainforest meets eucalypt (photo: Paul Taçon).

and the nature of special places. This process began with natural places but continues with sacred architecture across the globe.

However, as Paper (1990: 44) notes for North America, there is a fundamental difference between Western and Indigenous religions in terms of the understanding of the natural world and landscape: "In western religions, the earth itself is not sacred; it is created by the sacred, by God. In Native American religions, the landscape is sacred; it is deity." Paper further notes that sacred space is "delineated from the standpoint of center and periphery" in Native American religions. This can be said of Indigenous Australian religions as well but there is an important difference in that a large number of centers may be linked together along *Dreaming Tracks*, routes that define the journeys of the *First People* – Ancestral Beings that shaped the land into its present form.

Dreaming Tracks

Dreaming Tracks, popularized as "Songlines" by Bruce Chatwin (1988), are the key to understanding Australian landscapes. For Aboriginal people it is these vast stretches of landscape that link particular individuals and language groups to other people, to the past, to other

creatures and to the land itself. Individuals or clans may be responsible for particular sacred sites along Tracks but there is a shared interest in their safeguarding and maintenance by all people associated with the routes. Often individuals of different backgrounds would come together at nodal points along Tracks to engage in a joint ceremony, make contact with the power of Ancestral Beings and the landscapes they created, as well as to reaffirm human relationships. In many cases, the stories associated with Dreaming Tracks are used to describe human origins, codes of conduct, and the nature of landscapes in their present form – they also inspire great works of contemporary art (e.g., Morphy 1991; Ryan 1989). Often the most powerful involve Beings collectively referred to as Rainbow Serpents – gigantic, powerful snake-like creatures that combine elements of male and female, lower world, middle world, and upper world, and features of the land's more significant animals, in both its perceived physical form and its behavior. The key elements of earth, water, rock, and air are also brought together in the Rainbow Serpent stories (Taçon 1989a; 1989b; Taçon et al. 1996; Taylor 1987; 1990).

In the western Arnhem Land region of Australia's Northern Territory, for example, it is believed there once were many Ancestral Beings and Heroes, all originally with human form, but it was a form of Rainbow Serpent, the most powerful of all Ancestral Beings, that was responsible for the birth of human beings and other creatures, as well as much of the land as it exists in its present form. This Being is described as a Rainbow Snake/Woman called *Yingarna* by the Kunwinjku, a Woman named *Imberombera* or *Warramurrungundji* by Gagudju and Iwaidja people, and an Ancestral Woman that turned into the powerful Rainbow Serpent *Almudj* according to the Gundjeibmi (Taçon 1989b: 239). Today she is depicted in either Rainbow Serpent or human female form, often carrying dilly bags full of babies or shown with a womb full of developing children (Figure 2.8). This Ancestral Woman/Rainbow Serpent came from the sea northeast of the Cobourg Peninsula and the various tribes and clans of western Arnhem Land trace her travels through their territories (Spencer 1928: 742). She created *Bininj*, people, and told the different tribes which language they should speak. She also prepared the land, told people what foods they could eat, and began the process of human reproduction by depositing spirit children at ten different localities in the landscape. Most of these are permanent clan wells, significant and sacred water holes surrounded by unusual rocky outcrops and other powerfully charged features of the land. At these locations spirit children are said to resemble small fish, or bundles of rainbow color (Taçon 1989a; 1989b). All subsequent Ancestral Beings who passed through the region, forming, shaping, and modifying landscapes in the process, are said to have derived their powers from the great Woman/Rainbow Snake "and were supposed to be acting under her instructions in everything they did" (Chaloupka et al. 1985: 75).

Spencer (1928: 753) credits *Imberombera* with making "creeks, hills, animals and plants," but contemporary Aborigines explain many features of landscapes as having been shaped by other Beings. Ultimately, however, they derived their power from her and the changes they made can be considered an indirect result of her activities. As well, many animals arose more as a result of some of her activities rather than as a matter of accident. Indeed, *Yingarna* or her son *Ngalyod* are said to have later killed or transformed other Ancestral Beings and humans by sending great storms and floods or through swallowing them whole. Regurgitated Beings, or their bony remains, are believed to form many of the region's escarpments and rock outliers. At other locations Ancestral Beings were turned to stone on the spot for igniting the Rainbow Serpent's fury. In some cases, they were transformed from their human-like forms into the animal species that now populate the region by the Serpent flooding or otherwise transforming vast stretches of land. In its most general sense the Rainbow Serpent is a symbol of the creative and destructive forces of the universe, what Western peoples refer to as *nature* or *Mother Nature*.

Rainbow Serpent Dreaming Tracks dissect much of Australia but other powerful Beings, such as the *Wandjina* of the Kimberley, *Bula* from southern Arnhem Land, or *Biaime* and others from the greater Sydney region of New South Wales also transformed and linked together great and vast landscapes. A variety of lesser Beings and Cultural Heroes formed other tracks, such as those associated with the native cat that runs north–south through central Australia (Gunn 1997; Taçon 1994). Taken together they map the more significant parts of the entire Australian continent, highlighting both places integral to human survival and those best avoided.

The Oldest Surviving Rock Art

At many sites Ancestral Beings are said to have left images of themselves behind when they entered rock walls, and some old, sizable, and more elaborate rock art is attributed to them. Other old painted art is said to have been made by tall, thin human-like spirit beings, such as the Mimi of Arnhem Land, who taught the first humans about physical and spiritual survival in newly settled landscapes. Rock art sites are common along major Dreaming Tracks and many motifs, whether believed to be human or divinely inspired, are said to relate to the oral histories that surround the Beings of the Tracks, as well as that of the creatures and peoples that followed. In this sense rock art is intimately related to both landscape and history for contemporary knowledgeable elders, rock art sites are described as Aboriginal history books that highlight

Figure 2.8 Thompson Yulidjirri painting *Yingarna*, the most powerful Rainbow Serpent, in her human female form. Dilly bags hanging from her shoulders carried babies that became the first people and ancestors of Aboriginal clans (photo: Paul Taçon).

continuing environmental, social, and landscape change (Taçon [2001]).

Of course, these contemporary readings of rock art sites, and the landscapes of which they are an integral part, may differ widely from those of the past. However, not only do they provide analogies based on oral history worth testing as explanatory devices, but they also suggest landscape organizing principles or structures that may have both great antiquity and an archaeological signature (e.g., Taçon et al. 1997).

As noted earlier, the oldest surviving form of Australian rock art consists of cup-shaped engraved marks known as "cupules" (see Figure 2.1). They are purposely made circular depressions constituting one of the world's most widespread and universal forms of rock art, second perhaps only to hand stencils and prints in both distribution and antiquity (see Taçon et al. 1997). In northern Australia, these round, cup-like marks, arranged in clusters of up to several thousand, are unanimously recognized to be

the region's oldest surviving form of rock art (Chaloupka 1993; Flood 1996; 1997; Taçon and Chippindale 1994; Walsh 1994; Welch 1992), in some instances dating to many tens of thousands of years ago (Fullagar et al. 1996; Taçon et al. 1997). They are found on vertical and sloping shelter walls, horizontal ledges, boulders, and large slabs of sloping or horizontal pavements (Figure 2.9). They were made by pecking and pounding and are not to be confused with grinding hollows that resulted from food processing – thousands of cupules were often arranged to cover vertical surfaces in orderly, tightly packed rows and could not be the by-products of non-symbolic, purely practical activities. On wall panels, the average diameter of cupules ranges between 26 and 34 mm, while on boulders they average 58 to 66 mm.

Cupules were not used to define figures, such as animals or humans. Rather, they tend to be more related to the nature of the surface they were pecked and/or abraded into, their extent often conforming to or accentuating the surface's natural cracks, crevices, and boundaries. Occasionally, a symmetrical geometric shape was defined with an orderly arrangement of a dozen or more cupules, but this is rare. For the most part, the cupule designs are abstract in appearance and enigmatic in meaning.

Landscapes, Art, and Meaning

We may never know exactly why cupules were made on an individual or widespread basis or much of the specific meaning these marks had for their makers. Many plausible reasons for their existence can be suggested, some of which are not mutually exclusive, such as use in ritual, in communicating ideas about places, as decoration and so forth; it is probable that cupules were made, used, or interpreted in many ways at particular times and over time. Indeed, it is likely that a number of levels of meaning could be derived from cupule arrangements when they were in common use, just as has been found with more recent Aboriginal art (e.g., Morphy 1984; 1991; Munn 1966; 1973; Taçon 1989a; 1989b; Taylor 1987; 1990).

Because the detailed study of patterning at cupule sites is preliminary, only general

Figure 2.9 The main Jinmium, N.T., cupule panels are located on the inner walls of two shelters that face in opposite directions. The marks not only signify that the location is important but also relate to the Dreaming story of the site and the Track on which it lies (photo: Paul Taçon).

observations can be made. What is clear, however, is that cupule-covered wall panels lie close to the major river systems, from central Arnhem Land to the western Kimberley; are found mainly on plains rather than plateaus; are among a given region's more prominent geological features; and that today many lie on important Dreaming Tracks. For instance, the Jinmium–Granilpi complexes – the best studied to date – lie on a major Rainbow Serpent Dreaming Track that runs from the coast near the Northern Territory–Western Australia border, through and across Keep and Victoria Rivers, and on to the Gulf of Carpentaria. The track links many diverse language groups together, just as does the *Yingarna/Imberombera* Rainbow Serpent Track of western Arnhem Land. Many cupule sites can be found along the track but they are not exclusive to it (Fullagar et al. 1996; Taçon et al. 1997).

The most important result of an analysis of cupule distribution at sites is that they are found to be organized very particularly in relation to natural signs and features of rock surfaces.

Whether the cup-shaped marks resulted from ritual activities, record keeping, art making, decoration, communication, or some unknown pastime or activity, they were placed in accordance with natural marks and boundaries. At Jinmium and Granilpi, for instance, cupules most commonly were used to infill sizable portions of rock shelter wall panels, with natural cracks, crevices, and contours defining the limits of their execution (4 localities); to mark high points on the tops of geological features (up versus down; 4 localities); to mark the edges of shelter floors and shelter limits (inside versus outside; 5 localities); and to mark/accentuate the outside edges of natural holes/tunnels/passageways through the rock but not the insides (outside versus inside versus other side; 12 localities). Sometimes rows of cupule-covered boulders link different locations within sites or across landscapes, and massive, shaped boulders with hundreds of cupules oriented in all directions dominate some shelters (Taçon et al. 1997). Although not fully investigated, similar patterns of cupule placement can be found in Kakadu

National Park and Arnhem Land to the west and the Kimberley region to the east, at sites thought to be of comparable antiquity. Perhaps then the oldest enduring human-made symbolic marks in Australia are structured by natural landscape features rather than by random or an organizing principle that overrides or ignores the nature of place and space, such as the placement of marks on surfaces in a disfiguring manner rather than one that enhances surfaces. There is evidence to suggest this occurred on both macro (landscape) and micro (panel/site) scales.

Many of the forms of rock art that followed cupules in Australia were arranged differently but retain a landscape focus in terms of marking and signifying important spaces, places, and landscapes and in regard to subject matter. For example, in the engraved, painted or beeswax rock art of Australia, the most common subjects are tracks of animals, humans or Ancestral Beings, as would be seen on the land; the key animals, such as macropods, large birds or fish, from and of the land and its waterways (Figure 2.10); Ancestral Beings that created the land; and human beings – the people who were born on, lived in, fought over, and died on the land (e.g., Flood 1997; Layton 1992; Taçon and Chippindale 1994). Even some more abstract motifs, such as circles and concentric circles, are said to represent camp sites, sacred sites, caves, trees, water holes, or other significant places – sometimes more than one or all of these at once (Dussart 1988; Munn 1966; 1973; Taçon 1994). Contemporary Aboriginal art continues the process with most bark painting, central Australian acrylic painting on canvas, and urban art of a variety of media (e.g., prints – see McGuigan 1992) directly or indirectly relating to land or dispossession from it:

Aboriginal art is strong in country and law: that is both its politics and blood. In its present form, this art is born of white colonisation and dispossession of Ancestral land. The weight and chains of *kardiya* (white) control and oppression have left their mark. Although some may see it as the colonisers' plaything, art is a means of empowerment for its makers, a political tool in the fight to regain sovereignty over the land. Beneath most Aboriginal paintings lie the principles of Land Rights. (Ryan 1993: 60)

Coming to terms with landscapes

The whole history of Australian Aboriginal art includes an emphasis on coming to terms with changing landscapes. This is true of both rock art and recent music, performance, and visual art. Furthermore, I contend that when people first arrived on the continent, whether 40,000 (Allen and Holdaway 1995), 60,000 (Roberts et al. 1993), or 120,000 (Fullagar et al. 1996) years ago, there was a need not only to colonize but also to humanize and socialize what may have been perceived as a hostile landscape. On a grand scale, vegetation was transformed through burning practices (Haynes 1985; Head 1994; Jones 1969; 1975; 1980), animal populations were changed through hunting practices (Flannery 1994), and geological places were socialized through rock art and ritual, including cupule marking. Places were also socialized through stories – the Dreamtime sagas of landscape creation and adventure. In many ways the journeys recount or relate to some of the initial colonization of the continent but they also describe subsequent changes to land experienced during the many millennia of human occupation – from volcanic eruptions to the great flooding that occurred at the end of the last glaciation.

Much contemporary art tells about further changes to landscapes and people, brought about by visits of Macassans in the north and invasions of Europeans initially through the country's south. And across the continent, contemporary Indigenous peoples reaffirm their connections to landscapes through art and ritual as a vital part of both their physical and spiritual survival. But this is done differently in various parts of the country, partly as a reflection of the particular landscapes and terrain people grew up in and partly as a reflection of the nature of their social networks. For instance, it is believed the geographic, hydrological, vegetation, and food resource differences between central Australia and the Top End of the Northern Territory led to differences in each region's social networks, and that these differences are mirrored in the art systems of each area. This is argued for both ancient rock art, that is non-figurative "Panaramittee" versus figurative (Smith 1992a; 1992c), and contemporary painting, such as acrylic on

Figure 2.10   Recent panels of polychrome rock paintings in the "Top End" of the Northern Territory are dominated by depictions of Ancestral Beings that created the land, animals seen on the land, and humans that manage the land. This site in Kakadu National Park has paintings over earlier cupules, showing two very distinct and separated periods of landscape marking (photo: Paul Taçon).

canvas versus ochres on bark (Ryan 1993; Smith 1989; 1992b; 1992c). As Smith (1992c: 44) explains:

> Art in fertile regions, characterised by high population densities and relatively high levels of territoriality, is more heterogeneous than art in infertile regions characterised by low population densities and low levels of territoriality. Style in ethnographic Aboriginal art can serve to both delineate territory and to create cohesion between groups ...

In relatively fertile regions such as that of northern Australia, it is likely that the increased regionalisation of rock art sequences through time reflects a change from open to closed social networks. Open social networks were essential to the colonisation of the continent, but after a threshold in population numbers had been reached at some stage in the mid-Holocene (and this would vary according to the region), social networks in infertile regions, such as the Western Desert, would have remained open as such networks are essential to the effective exploitation of resources in such regions.

In more precisely defining some of these differences, Ryan (1993: 62) adds: "If bark paintings generally are site-specific, narrow verticals, then large desert canvas[es] enclose the viewer in the vastness of the continent, leading him or her through a succession of named sites – on journeys of wandering." This is the key difference in the art of each region: the northern art features focused, clan-specific landscapes while that to the south addresses expansive tracts that have significance for many clans and linguistic groups. But in each art body, connections to landscapes are emphasized and elaborately expressed, as are specific Ancestral Beings that created the varied landscapes and the particular creatures that dwell in them. In turn, individual and corporate identity reaffirmed. In some cases the connection is so strong "they learn to see their own body as a metaphor of the topographic organization of their clan lands, features such as birthmarks on their body being seen as equivalent to sacred sites within their clan lands" (Taylor 1988: 384). Valuable lessons about land management are also often emphasized. Importantly, urban art, although more heterogeneous in style, form, and media and often made by people of mixed descent, features the same themes, but with the added political element of loss of land and invasion by foreigners (Kleinert 1997; Mundine 1992; Ryan 1993; Taçon 1996).

This sense of roots, belonging to land and taking responsibility for it, has developed over a lengthy period of time in Australia and it is because of this that many non-Aboriginal people, recent arrivals, have difficulty grasping the full significance or consequence of this form of bonding. Having severed their own roots and transformed their own landscapes into thoroughly artificial places, cities and cityscapes being the most poignant (Cosgrove 1993 argues that "Wilderness," "Garden" and "City" are distinct archetypal landscapes with differing concerns and mythologies), they have long been bent on doing the same to Indigenous lands. A driving concern is to not "waste" land, to see its full potential through "development," something seen to be of value in Western eyes. This is at odds with the Indigenous perspective, which instead focuses on managing and caring for land by way of burning practices, hunting restrictions, food-sharing responsibilities, art and ritual. But above all else the Indigenous perspective is expressed through knowledge

of and relations to land – and thus to other people, plants, and animals. Knowledge about a landscape's past – its creation, transformations, and particular history – is fundamental. Thus it is not only the human past that is of interest or importance but also the landscape past. For it is the web and chains of past landscape relationships, as expressed by Dreaming Tracks and so forth, that define present human relationships alongside those of kinship and language.

In Aboriginal English, "my mother's country," "my father's country" are two common descriptions that express this strong link between human kinship and landscape, but it is reaffirmed at much deeper levels as well – with connections to animals through totem systems or restricted ceremonies that honor specific creatures or Ancestral Beings responsible for the creation and sustenance of both people and places. Indeed, as Indigenous Australian Kumantjayi Ross (1994: vii) has emphasized at the beginning of his foreword to a book about the Central Land Council: "Aboriginal spirituality, culture and society can be defined in one word: land." However, although land has always been important to Indigenous Australians, the specific ways and meanings in which this has been expressed vary over time and across space – resulting in a heritage consisting of a mosaic of metaphoric landscape meaning and relationship, in need of continual visual display and reaffirmation. Obviously, the power of place can never be understated for Indigenous Australians, for without it the world would not exist.

References

Allen, J., and Holdaway, S. 1995: The contamination of Pleistocene radiocarbon determinations in Australia. *Antiquity*, 69, 101–12.

Bender, B. (ed.) 1993: *Landscape: Politics and Perspectives*. Oxford: Berg.

Bradley, R. 1995: Rock carvings and decorated monuments in the British Isles. In K. Helskog and B. Olsen (eds), *Perceiving Rock Art: Social and Political Perspectives*, Oslo: Instituttet for Sammenlignende Kulturforskning, 107–29.

Chaloupka, G. 1993: *Journey in Time*. Sydney: Reed Books.

Chaloupka, G., Kapirigi, N., Nayidji, D., and Namingum, G. 1985: *Cultural Survey of Balawurru, Deaf Adder Creek, Amarrkananga, Cannon Hill and the Northern Corridor: A Report to the Australian National Parks and Wildlife Service*. Darwin: Australian National Parks and Wildlife Service and the Museum and Art Galleries Board of the Northern Territory.

Chatwin, B. 1988: *The Songlines*. London: Picador.

Chippindale, C., and Taçon, P. S. C. (eds) 1998: *The Archaeology of Rock-Art*. Cambridge: Cambridge University Press.

Cosgrove, D. 1989: Geography is everywhere: culture and symbolism in human landscapes. In D. Gregory and R. Walford (eds), *Horizons in Human Geography*, London: Macmillan, 118–35.

Cosgrove, D. 1993: Landscapes and myths, gods and humans. In B. Bender (ed.), *Landscape: Politics and Perspectives*, Oxford: Berg, 281–305.

Cosgrove, D., and Daniels, S. (eds) 1988: *The Iconography of Landscape: Essays on the Symbolic Representation, Design and Use of Past Environments*. Cambridge: Cambridge University Press.

Dussart, F. 1988: Women's acrylic paintings from Yuendumu. In M. West (ed.), *The Inspired Dream: Life as Art in Aboriginal Australia*, South Brisbane: Queensland Art Gallery, 35–8.

Eliade, M. 1964: *Shamanism: Archaic Techniques of Ecstasy*. New York: Pantheon.

Eliade, M. 1978: *A History of Religious Ideas*, Volume 1: *From the Stone Age to the Eleusinian Mysteries*, transl. W. R. Trask. Chicago: University of Chicago Press.

Flannery, T. 1994: *The Future Eaters: An Ecological History of the Australasian Lands and People*. Chatswood (Sydney): Reed Books.

Flood, J. 1996: Culture in early Australia. *Cambridge Archaeological Journal*, 6, 3–36.

Flood, J. 1997: *Rock Art of the Dreamtime*. Sydney: Angus and Robertson.

Fullagar, R., Price, D., and Head, L. 1996: Early human occupation of northern Australia: archaeology and thermoluminescence dating of Jinmium rock-shelter, Northern Territory. *Antiquity*, 70, 751–73.

Goodale, J. 1959: The Tiwi dance for the dead. *Expedition*, 2 (1), 3–13.

Gosden, C., and Head, L. 1994: Landscape – a usefully ambiguous concept. *Archaeology in Oceania*, 29, 113–16.

Gunn, R. G. 1997: Rock art, occupation and myth: the correspondence of symbolic and archaeological sites within Arrernte rock art complexes of central Australia. *Rock Art Research*, 14 (2), 124–36.

Haynes, C. D. 1985: The pattern and ecology of mun-wag: traditional Aboriginal fire regimes in north-central Arnhem-land. *Proceedings, Ecological Society of Australia*, 13, 203–14.

Head, L. 1994: Landscapes socialised by fire: post-contact changes in Aboriginal fire use in northern Australia, and implications for prehistory. *Archaeology in Oceania*, 29, 172–81.

Hodder, I. 1993: The narrative and rhetoric of material culture sequences. *World Archaeology*, 25, 268–82.

Ingold, T. 1993: The temporality of the landscape. *World Archaeology*, 25, 152–74.

Jones, R. 1969: Fire-stick farming. *Australian Natural History*, 16, 224–8.

Jones, R. 1975: The Neolithic, Palaeolithic and the hunting gardeners: man and land in the antipodes. In R. P. Suggare and M. M. Creswell (eds), *Quaternary Studies*, Wellington: Royal Society of New Zealand, 21–34.

Jones, R. 1980: Hunters in the Australian coastal savanna. In D. R. Harris (ed.), *Human Ecology in Savanna Environments*, New York: Academic Press, 107–46.

Keinert, S. 1997: Aboriginal landscapes. In G. Levitus (ed.), *Lying about the Landscape*, North Ryde, Sydney: Craftsman House, 82–99.

Layton, R. 1992: *Australian Rock Art: A New Synthesis*. Cambridge: Cambridge University Press.

McGuigan, C. 1992: *New Tracks Old Land: Contemporary Prints from Aboriginal Australia*. Surry Hills (Sydney): Aboriginal Arts Management Association.

Morphy, H. 1984: *Journey to the Crocodile's Nest*. Canberra: Australian Institute of Aboriginal Studies.

Morphy, H. 1991: *Ancestral Connections: Art and an Aboriginal System of Knowledge*. Chicago: University of Chicago Press.

Mountford, C. P. 1958: *The Tiwi – Their Art, Myth and Ceremony*. London: Phoenix House.

Mundine, D. 1992: "If my ancestors could see me now." In B. Murphy (ed.), *Tyerabarrbowaryaou: I Shall Never Become a White Man*, Sydney: Museum of Contemporary Art, 4–11.

Munn, N. 1966: Visual categories: an approach to the study of representational systems. *American Anthropologist*, 68, 936–50.

Munn, N. 1973: *Walbiri Iconography*. Ithaca: Cornell University Press.

Nash, R. 1997: Archetypal landscapes and the interpretation of meaning. *Cambridge Archaeological Journal*, 7, 57–69.

Ouzman, S. 1998: Toward a mindscape of landscape: rock-art as expression of world-understanding. In C. Chippindale and P. S. C. Taçon (eds), *The Archaeology of Rock-Art*, Cambridge: Cambridge University Press, 30–41.

Paper, J. 1990: Landscape and sacred space in Native North American religion. In J. Vastokas (ed.), *Perspectives of Canadian Landscape: Native Traditions*, North York: York University, 44–54.

Parkman, E. B. 1995: "California Dreaming": cupule petroglyph occurrences in the American West. In J. Steinbring (ed.), *Rock Art Studies in the Americas*, Monograph 45, Oxford: Oxbow, 1–12.

Roberts, R., Jones, R., and Smith, M. A. 1993: Optical dating at Deaf Adder Gorge, Northern Territory, indicates human occupation between 53,000 and 60,000 years ago. *Australian Archaeology*, 37, 58.

Ross, K. 1994: Foreword. In *The Land is Always Alive: The Story of the Central Land Council*, Alice Springs: Central Land Council, vii–ix.

Ryan, J. 1989: *Mythscapes: Aboriginal Art of the Desert.* Victoria: National Gallery of Victoria.

Ryan, J. 1993: Australian Aboriginal art: otherness or affinity. In B. Luthi and G. Lee (eds), *ARATJARA – Art of the First Australians,* Dusseldorf: Kustsammlung Nordrhein-Westfalen, 49–63.

Smith, C. 1989: Designed Dreaming: assessing the relationship between style, social structure and environment in Aboriginal Australia. BA (Honors) thesis, University of New England, Armidale.

Smith, C. 1992a: Colonising with style: reviewing the nexus between rock art, territoriality and the colonisation and occupation of Sahul. *Australian Archaeology,* 34, 34–42.

Smith, C. 1992b: The articulation of style and social structure through Australian Aboriginal art. *Aboriginal Studies,* 1, 28–34.

Smith, C. 1992c: The use of ethnography in interpreting rock art: a comparative study of art from the Arnhem Land and Western Desert regions of Australia. In M. J. Morwood and D. Hobbs (eds), *Rock Art and Ethnography,* Melbourne: Occasional AURA Publication, No. 5, 39–45.

Spencer, W. B. 1914: *Native Tribes of the Northern Territory of Australia.* London: Macmillan.

Spencer, W. B. 1928: *Wanderings in Wild Australia.* London: Macmillan.

Taçon, P. S. C. 1989a: Art and the essence of being: symbolic and economic aspects of fish among the peoples of western Arnhem Land, Australia. In H. Morphy (ed.), *Animals into Art,* London: Unwin Hyman, 236–50.

Taçon, P. S. C. 1989b: From Rainbow Serpents to "x-ray" fish: the nature of the recent rock painting tradition of western Arnhem Land, Australia. PhD dissertation, Australian National University.

Taçon, P. S. C. 1990: The power of place: cross-cultural responses to natural and cultural landscapes of stone and earth. In J. Vastokas (ed.), *Perspectives of Canadian Landscape: Native Traditions.* North York: York University, 11–43.

Taçon, P. S. C. 1994: Socialising landscapes: the long-term implications of signs, symbols and marks on the land. *Archaeology in Oceania,* 29, 117–29.

Taçon, P. S. C. 1996: Indigenous modernism: betwixt and between or at the cutting edge of contemporary art? *Bulletin of the Conference of Museum Anthropologists,* 27, 33–55.

Taçon, P. S. C. 2001: Australian indigenous rock art – the human story. In D. Whitley (ed.), *The Handbook of Rock Art Research,* San Francisco: AltaMira Press.

Taçon, P. S. C., and Chippindale, C. 1994: Australia's ancient warriors: changing depictions of fighting in the rock art of Arnhem Land, N.T. *Cambridge Archaeological Journal,* 4, 211–48.

Taçon, P. S. C., Fullagar, R., Ouzman, S., and Mulvaney, K. 1997: Cupule engravings from Jinmium-Granilpi (Northern Australia) and beyond: exploration of a widespread and enigmatic class of rock markings. *Antiquity,* 71, 942–65.

Taçon, P. S. C., Wilson, M., and Chippindale, C. 1996: Birth of the Rainbow Serpent in Arnhem Land rock art and oral history. *Archaeology in Oceania,* 31, 103–24.

Taylor, L. 1987: "The same but different": social reproduction and innovation in the art of the Kunwinjku of western Arnhem Land. PhD dissertation, Australian National University.

Taylor, L. 1988: Seeing the "inside": Kunwinjku paintings and the symbol of the divided body. In H. Morphy (ed.), *Animals into Art,* London: Unwin Hyman, 371–89.

Taylor, L. 1990: The Rainbow Serpent as visual metaphor in western Arnhem Land. *Oceania,* 60, 329–44.

Tilley, C. 1994: *A Phenomenology of Landscape: Places, Paths and Monuments.* Oxford: Berg.

Vastokas, J. M., and Vastokas, R. 1973: *Sacred Art of the Algonkians: A Study of the Peterborough Petroglyphs.* Peterborough: Mansard Press.

Walsh, G. 1994: *Bradshaws: Ancient Rock Paintings of Australia.* Geneva: Édition Limitée.

Welch, D. 1992: The Early Rock Art of the Kimberley, Australia. Paper presented in Symposium F, Second AURA Congress, Cairns.

3

Landscapes of Punishment and Resistance
A Female Convict Settlement in Tasmania, Australia

Eleanor Conlin Casella

Introduction

In January 1851, a letter was intercepted en route to Jane Walker, an inmate of the women's prison establishment at Ross, Van Diemen's Land. Written by Catherine Cass, possibly a sister-in-law, the note assured Jane that she 'will be well don [*sic*] for':

> Jane your uncal sends you a pound note and you may expect to see littel John ... and he will tell you all about your uncal ... Dear Jane your box will be up as soon as the letter so I hope you keep up your spirits and do not fret for the time will soon come Dear Jane I must conclud with my Kind love to you and hope to see you soon ... (Mitchell Library, Tasmanian Papers, Number 104)

After seizing this letter, the prison Superintendent forwarded the forbidden communication to the Comptroller-General of the Convict Department, who annotated the margins with orders to improve perimeter security at the Ross Establishment so as to prevent future communications, and to intercept any box illicitly traded into the prison.

Eleanor Conlin Casella, "Landscapes of Punishment and Resistance: A Female Convict Settlement in Tasmania, Australia," pp. 103–30 from *Contested Landscapes of Movement and Exile*, ed. Barbara Bender and Margot Winer (Oxford: Berg Publishers, 2001). Reprinted with permission of Berg Publishers Oxford via A C Black.

When considered together, the presence of this letter and the reaction of the institutional authorities demonstrate overlapping landscapes of penal domination and inmate resistance that operated to create this site. Why was Jane denied access to her relatives outside the perimeter wall of the prison? Who enjoyed the privilege of access? And how did convicts intentionally circumvent and penetrate these disciplinary boundaries? This chapter is concerned with the spatial dynamics of such questions.

The Administration of Female Convicts in Van Diemen's Land

From 1803 to 1854, over 74,000 British convicts were transported to Van Diemen's Land, an island penal colony isolated from the southern coast of mainland Australia by the treacherous Bass Straits (Eldershaw 1968: 130). Approximately 12,000 of these felons were women, primarily convicted of petty theft of goods stolen from their domestic employers (Oxley 1996). Upon their colonial arrival, most spent time incarcerated within the Female Factory System, a network of women's prisons scattered across the island (Brand 1990).

Named 'factory' as a contraction of the word 'manufactory', these penal institutions were designed along the model of the British Workhouse System, a nineteenth-century form of public social welfare which required standard-ized rates of labour from all inmates to hasten their social and moral salvation from delin-quency, idleness and poverty (Driver 1993). Upon entry into a colonial Factory, female con-victs were assigned to the 'Crime Class', and incar-cerated for a minimum of six months. While serving this probationary sentence, the women were intended to 'reform' through Christian prayer and forced training in acceptably feminine industries, including sewing, textile production, and laundry work. Recalcitrance was punished through lengthy periods of confinement in Soli-tary Treatment cells, accompanied by severe reduction of food rations. Once they successfully served their probationary period, the 'reconsti-tuted' women were reclassified into the 'Hiring Class', and awaited assignment to local properties, completing their convict sentences as domestic servants for free colonists (Ryan 1995; Oxley 1996; Damousi 1997; Daniels 1998).

The Ross Female Factory

Located on the southern edge of the Ross Town-ship in the rural midlands of the island (renamed Tasmania in 1855), the Ross Female Factory operated from 1848 through 1854, when Britain ceased convict transportation to the Van Diemen's Land colony. The Ross site was then transferred to civilian management, and experienced a series of municipal and domestic occupations. It was gazetted as an historic reserve in 1980, and is now administered through the Cultural Heritage Branch of the Tasmanian Parks and Wildlife Service, Australia. Since 1995, the site has become the focus of historical, geophysical and archaeo-logical research (Casella 1999). This chapter pre-sents results from the Ross Factory Archaeology Project by integrating multidisciplinary evidence for coexisting landscapes of penal domination and female inmate resistance that created and shaped the Factory site.

A cultural landscape of containment

In his analysis of gendered landscapes among the Berbers of Kabylia, Algeria, Pierre Bourdieu noted the role of segregated space in forming gender relations:

The reason why submission to the collective rhythms is so rigorously demanded is that the temporal forms or the spatial structures struc-ture not only the group's representation of the world but the group itself, which orders itself in accordance with the representation: this may be clearly seen, for example, in the fact that the organization of the existence of the men and women in accordance with different times and different places constitutes two interchangeable ways of securing separation and hierarchization of the male and female worlds, the women going to the fountain at an hour when the men are not in the streets, or by a special path, or both at once. (Bourdieu 1977: 163)

The segmentation of space and time not only creates the disciplined bodies of institutional inmates, it also creates and reinforces a hier-archy of male and female spaces, through a temporal and physical ordering of their locales. Emphasizing a reflexive relationship between gender and the built environment, architect Daphne Spain similarly argued that the 'initial status differences between women and men create certain types of gendered spaces and that institutionalized spatial segregation then reinforces prevailing male advantages' (Spain 1992: 6).

Through the demarcation of spaces within the Ross Factory landscape, inmates were limited to occupying appropriate interior locales at appro-priate times. With functionally specific locales architecturally identified throughout the institu-tion, the nature of boundaries and forbidden territories depended upon the exact classification of the inhabitant. Both Factory staff and inmate movements through the prison were strictly ordered through spatial and temporal regula-tions and procedures. As these inhabitants moved through the various segregated spaces of the Factory, they reiteratively mapped relation-ships of unequal social status onto the penal landscape. Thus, through the segregation of interior spaces, convict administrators fabricated an institutional landscape of order and reforma-tion. Through this segmentation of movement in space and time, the threat of delinquency was – seemingly – eradicated and replaced by meticulously choreographed activity within the bounded institution (Foucault 1977: 150–1).

Mapping domination: the geography of Factory staff

Not only did differentiated places within the Ross Factory order the inhabitants, the segregation of space also exerted social control by materially expressing relationships of dominant and subordinate status. Both subtle and overt statements of social inequality infused the monumental architecture of nineteenth-century Britain. Designs for institutions ranging from prisons and workhouses (Driver 1993; Evans 1982) to schools and museums (Seaborne 1971; Peponis and Hedin 1982) reflected and reified the unequal status of genders, races and social classes (Markus 1993). Thus, Factory fence lines, pathways, and entrance porches cemented the social hierarchy of this penal site.

A geography of occupant movement within the Ross Factory revealed subtle layers of differential status infused throughout the institutional landscape. This 'cultural map of political power' (Rodgers 1993: 48) began within the ranks of the Ross Factory staff. At the top of the hierarchy, the Factory Superintendent and Matron, hired as a married couple, lived outside the Factory compound. Historical research suggested they occupied a house within the Ross township (Scripps and Clark 1991: 14). Besides encouraging their access to the outside colonial world, that location would have offered them a privileged degree of privacy from the Factory.

As the principal representative of the establishment, the Superintendent mediated the junction point between the inner world of the Ross Factory and the exterior colonial world of Van Diemen's Land. He provided all communication with the outside world, submitting frequent reports to the Comptroller-General of Convicts, hosting regular inspections by the Visiting Magistrate, and responding to all correspondence directed to the Factory. Arriving at the prison at 5:30 a.m., his hours of duty ended after the last, or 'silence', bell had rung at 8:30 p.m. At night, he was explicitly instructed to 'receive the [Factory] Keys and take them over to [his] house with [him]' (AOT MM 62/24/ 10774). Twice a week, he conducted surprise night-time inspections of the institution. As chief medical officer, the Superintendent directed activities in the Hospital Ward, classified and treated the health of inmates, regulated all medical supplies, and oversaw all births.

His personal interaction with female inmates was regulated by the Factory Matron, his wife. She maintained direct responsibility for all women within the institution, controlling interactions with both inmates and female officers. The Matron was required to accompany all dormitory inspections conducted by male officers, and 'attend to any just complaint of the women and if necessary bring the case before the Superintendent or Visiting Magistrate' (AOT MM 62/ 24/10774). Thus, issues of gender infused the political map of the Ross Factory. While the Superintendent controlled access between the institutional and free worlds, he was expected to inhabit only the administrative and hospital wards of the Factory. His wife controlled access to all locales directly related to the female inmates.

On the next tier of this hierarchical landscape were the Assistant Superintendent and Assistant Matron, also hired as a married pair. They lived within the boundaries of the Factory institution. Historic plans identified two rooms inside the Main Compound as the Assistant Superintendent's Quarters (Scripps and Clark 1991). This region was identified as Area B, and excavated during the 1997 season of the Ross Factory Archaeology Project (Casella 1997). Architectural and stratigraphic evidence suggested that the building had earthen floors, as no physical remains of stone or suspended wooden floors were recovered during excavation, and the two rooms contained compacted layers of sandy-silt containing high densities of nineteenth-century artefacts (Casella 1999). Since these brick quarters were relatively small, earthen-floored, and located inside the main compound of the prison, historians have suggested they functioned as an administrative office for the Assistant Superintendent, rather than as a primary residence for himself and the Assistant Matron (Terry 1998: 39).

Regardless of the exact function of this brick structure, the hierarchical status of the Assistant Superintendent's Quarters was materially emphasized by the introduction of a sandstone-flagged pathway delineating the entrance to the structure. Archival documents suggest this structure was installed sometime between 1848,

*landscape &
class
- castles & servants
quarters*

when the Ross Female Factory was opened, and 1851, when the pathway first appeared in plans at the northern face of the Assistant Superintendent's Quarters. As with most convict-built architectural features, this sandstone pathway could be functionally interpreted as a labour-intensive construction scheme designed to occupy the male convict workers. The feature could also have been laid for safety or sanitary purposes within this densely occupied Establishment. However, this sandstone pathway also physically segmented space, and probably operated as a status marker within the cultural landscape of the Factory (Markus 1993: 95). Given a consistently inadequate supply of shoes for female inmates (AOT MM 62/28/12161: Scripps and Clark 1991: 51), winter musters within the pebble-packed earthen courtyards of the convict wards would have been cold, wet, and muddy experiences of institutionalized subordination for the women convicts. The presence of a sandstone pathway for access to and from the Assistant Superintendent's Quarters could easily have provided physical communication between hierarchically ordered places within this penal environment (Markus 1993; Praetzellis and Praetzellis 1992).

The institutional duties of the Assistant Superintendent and Assistant Matron located them within the boundaries of the Factory. Whereas the Superintendent commanded the articulation of the prison with the external free colony, his Assistant regulated the internal boundaries and segmentations of this institution. Charged with the maintenance of Factory stores, he strictly governed the allocation of all non-medicinal resources, including daily food rations, firewood for cooking and heating, building materials used for additions and repairs, and water carried up from the nearby Macquarie River. He took charge of the keys at mealtimes, and evaluated the portions of food issued to inmates according to a March 1848 official scale of food rations (Scripps and Clark 1991). Each morning he would issue out quantities of wool, and every evening would meticulously collect, inventory, and secure unused portions of raw wool and all finished quantities of combed, carded, spun, and woven textile produced by the Crime Class inmates that day. Regulating the segmentation of time within the Factory, the Assistant

Superintendent supervised the bells for morning rise, morning muster call, dinner, evening muster, and night silence. He identified and categorized all prison inmates, ensuring the completion of:

> ... proper lists of the names of women in Crime Class with their sentence and ships, and of women in Nurseries and the Passholders ward and that this list is pasted on boards and hung up in each ward and corrected when required and that lists of the scale of rations for each ward is hung up in it, also that the name, sentence crime & c. of each woman in Solitary is hung up on door of her Cell. (AOT MM 62/24/10774)

Like the Matron, the Assistant Matron regulated interactions with the female inmates. However, her locale was limited to the Nurseries and Hiring Class, where she was directly responsible for 'preserving order, seeing [the wards] kept clean, the children, more especially the orphan children, properly provided for as regards nourishment and to see that those women who in the Nurseries may have Probation of work to do accomplish it ....' (AOT MM 62/24/10774). Again, gender and status intersected within the spatial hierarchy of the penal landscape.

The Male and Female Overseers and Constables formed a third tier in the Staff hierarchy. As the lowest-ranking employees of the Convict Department, their movements around the institutions were restricted to specific wards. Since the conjoined Georgian cottages immediately west of the Main Compound were identified as 'Staff Quarters' in archival plans, the Overseers probably resided within the boundary of the Factory, near the Assistant Superintendent and Assistant Matron. The Female Overseer escorted Crime Class inmates from their Dormitory to the Work Rooms, and chaperoned their labour. She accompanied them to dinner, to 'see they take their meals properly and that they use nothing which is not allowed' (AOT MM 62/24/10774). Using the lists created by the Assistant Superintendent, the Female Overseer called morning and evening musters to physically account for all inmates. Duties of the Male Overseer focused on the accommodation and supervision of the male convict labourers assigned to the Factory. He also appeared to play a coercive role within the Factory Main Compound, assisting the Constables to restrain female prisoners during violent altercations (AOT MM 62/26/11931; AOT MM 62/26/11946). Constables resided in the Guard House immediately north of the Main Gate. They exerted immediate disciplinary control over the female convicts through visual surveillance and physical coercion. Because of their immediate interaction with the inmates, and their role as purveyors of direct physical force, the Constables and Male Overseer occupied lower rungs of the Staff hierarchy (Foucault 1977: 153–6).

Convict labourers constituted the lowest rank of Factory staff. 'Turnkeys' were Factory inmates selected from the promoted Hiring Class. They provided unwaged supervisory labour, and held privileged positions within the Factory. As convicts, their unfree labour was assigned to a specific task within a specific locale, such as night watch inside the Crime Class Dormitory, or childcare in the Nurseries. They were expected to occupy the Hiring Class ward when not on duty. Approximately twelve male convicts were assigned to the Ross Factory (Rayner 1980: 20). These men were accommodated in a fortified stone cottage at some undocumented location within the nine acres of gardens attached to the Factory. No remains of this structure were discovered during the Ross Factory Archaeology Project. The anonymous male convicts served as manual labourers and field hands for the Ross Establishment. By situating the men away from the main compound, the Ross Superintendent ensured strict sexual segregation of inmates, thereby enforcing a central tenet of post-medieval penal reform schemes.

Mapping subordination: the documentary image of inmate geography

Incarcerated inmates also moved through segregated spaces, mapping their moral descent and redemption through the cultural landscape. Upon arrival, convict women entered the Factory by descending the steep slope of the alluvial terrace. Assigned to the Crime Class, they resided in one of two dormitories in the northwest ward of the Main Compound. By 9 a.m., after morning muster and breakfast, they were escorted across the Main Compound, past the enclosed Nursery Wards, out the southern side of the prison quadrangle. Marched to the Gothic-style sandstone Chapel, located on an elevated rise south of the Main Compound, they ascended the stairs for morning prayers. At 9:30 a.m. they descended from the House of God, and were escorted back across to the Main Compound.

Their days were spent either in the Work Room where they laboured at textile production, meeting predetermined Scales of Taskwork (AOT CO 280/699/268 p. 162), or in the Wash House, where they processed laundry for the institution and local private contracts. Six large rectangular windows were set into the southern wall of the Work Room. This architectural element was typical for nineteenth-century institutional designs, as the presence of large windows provided free light for work spaces. However, since the Work Room was located on the southern edge of the Main Compound, the commanding view from those windows was of the structures immediately south of the Main Compound (see Figure 3.1). While labouring at textile production, convict women gazed over a landscape of damnation and redemption – the topographically elevated Chapel towering over the bank of solitary punishment cells. At 5:30 p.m. their daily labour was assessed, and all unprocessed materials counted, weighed, and secured in a locked storeroom by the Assistant Superintendent. They were escorted back to the Chapel for an hour of evening prayers. Descending once again from the monumental structure, they re-entered the Main Compound, marched past the secluded Nursery wards, and reassembled in the Crime Class Yard for evening muster at 6:30 p.m. After dinner, the inmates were encouraged to attend literacy classes in their Dormitories. Although this indulgence was not a mandatory requirement, attendance was noted, and regular attendance did appear to factor into evaluations of a particular inmate's morality. At 8 p.m., the silence bell was rung. All inmates were incarcerated within their assigned Dormitory, and expected to occupy their assigned bunk.

If a female convict deviated from this template, she was punished by a period of Solitary Confinement. Exiled from the Main Compound,

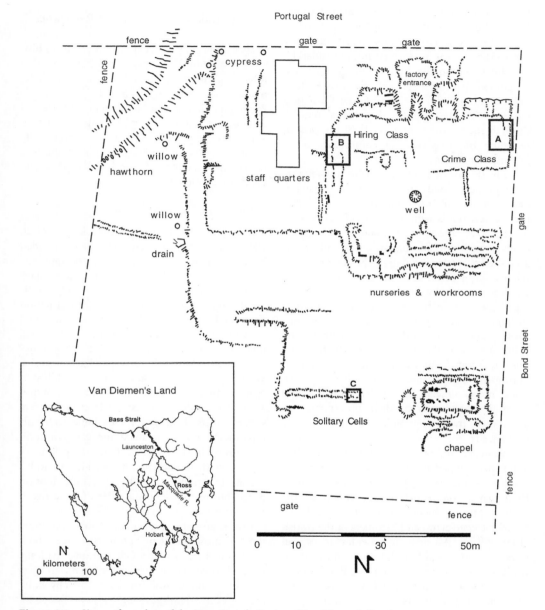

Figure 3.1 Site surface plan of the Ross Female Factory, Van Diemen's Land.

she descended to the block of cells located on the southern side of the Factory, at the base of the alluvial terrace, approximately 3 metres below the Work Rooms. After serving her transformational sentence, she ascended the slope to rejoin the collective group of Crime Class inmates within the Main Compound. Once she had exhibited frequent enough performances of obedient behaviour to convince authorities of her compliance (Scott 1990: 29), she earned reclassification into the Hiring Class. This promoted ward was located immediately next to the Assistant Superintendent's Quarters, west of the Crime Class, in the northern half of the rectilinear quadrangle. While waiting for assignment to unwaged domestic labour for one of

the local pastoral properties, she held the position of Turnkey within the prison. Intended to
encourage reform of other prisoners through her
good example, she performed limited supervisory duties within the Factory. When domestic
assignment had been secured, the Ross Factory
inmate completed her circle of transformation
by ascending the slope of the alluvial terrace,
through the northern Main Gate of the prison,
rejoining the free colonial community on a
probationary basis.

Both the movement of prison inhabitants
through segregated spaces and the material
demarcations of those locales communicated
hierarchical status within the Ross Factory. Different classifications of inhabitants, the various
ranks of both staff and inmates, were entitled to
access specified locales within the prison. Their
relative status determined the proximity of their
residence to the institution, and provided varying degrees of spatial privilege and restriction
throughout the segregated wards, workrooms,
yards, and pathways of the prison. Furthermore,
as female inmates processed through the rectilinear quadrangle, they constituted a spatial map
of transformation (Parham and Noble 1994: 72).
Their moral descent and redemption became
physically performed in their movements up
and down the topographic elevations of the
Factory site.

This geography of domination and subordination was mapped from surviving documentary
evidence – the letters, proclamations, architectural plans, and regulations generated by the
Factory Superintendent, staff of the colonial
Convict Department, and members of the British
Home Office. As such, it provides an official
transcript for an ideal cultural landscape of
institutional boundaries and regulated social
control through the segmentation and classification of prison spaces. To consider the
hidden transcript of inmate resistance, we
must turn to alternative sources of evidence.
Through the distribution of illicit objects within
the Ross Factory site, we can map an alternate
covert landscape. We can interpret the maintenance of a distinct and coexisting geography
forged by the female convict inhabitants as
they transgressed segmented spaces and moved
through disciplinary boundaries of the ideal
penal landscape.

Doing Trade: A Landscape of Resistance

This chapter will now explore the relationships
among clothing buttons, alcohol bottles, and
tobacco pipes, as evidence for a thriving black-
market trade economy within the Ross Female
Factory an illicit form of networking that created
an alternate and coexisting landscape of alliances
and enemies within the Ross Factory site
(Daniels 1998) and powerfully linked this site
to the shadowy convict world of Van Diemen's
Land penal colony.

On the distribution of buttons

During the Ross Factory Archaeology Project.
104 square metres were excavated, divided
between three different areas of the site: the
Crime Class, the Hiring Class, and the Solitary
Cells (Casella 1997). After analysing the stratigraphic data, a number of female convict period
deposits were identified, and their artefactual
contents were subjected to further study. I will
now turn to my analysis of the 67 buttons recovered from these female-convict-related deposits.
Since my research considered the possibility of
non-clothing-related functions for the button
assemblage. I developed an abstract typological
system for its classification (see Table 3.1). This
three-tiered system enabled the categorization
of buttons by their fabric type, their fastener
type, and their diameter dimensions in milli-
metres. I then examined the spatial distribution
of the button types through the three wards of
the Factory site.

Constituting 47.7 per cent of the Ross collection,
the two most prevalent button types were both
large four-hole sew-through buttons, typically
manufactured as fastenings for men's trousers
and shirts, and for woollen jackets worn by either
men or women (Lydon 1993; 1995) (see Table 3.2).
The third most common type consisted of small
shell mother-of-pearl four-hole buttons, objects
identified within industry catalogues as providing
fastening for both men's shirts and women's
dresses (Claassen 1994; Iacono 1996). Whether
used in the standard regulation convict uniform,
or related to non-uniform clothing, these buttons
could easily have entered the site on laundry
contracted from the local free community. Their
presence might have represented accidental

Table 3.1 Ross Factory Archaeology Project.

Button Typology – three-tiered coding system:

1. Fabric type	2. Fastener type	3. Diameter dimensions
1. Ferrous	a. 4 hole	i. 8–12mm
2. Copper-alloy	b. 3 hole	ii. 13–16mm
3. Bone	c. 2 hole	iii. 17–20mm
4. Shell	d. 1 hole (button core)	iv. 21–24mm
5. Glass	e. 5 hole	v. 25–28mm
6. Other	f. shank loop	vi. 29–32mm
	g. shank sew-through (pedestal)	vii. diameter undetermined (broken or too decayed to measure)
	h. unknown	

Table 3.2 Distribution and frequency of button assemblage.

Description	Area A	Area B	Area C	Total	Per cent
Ferrous large 4hole trouser buttons (1.a.iii)	3	1	10	14	20.9
Ferrous other			1	1	1.5
Copper 4hole 'sinkies' (2.a.ii & 2.a.iii)	1	2	1	4	6.0
Copper shank loop (2.f.iii)	1	1		2	3.0
Copper 2hole base for textile buttons (2.c.ii)		2		2	3.0
Copper other		2		2	3.0
Bone large 4hole trouser buttons (3.a.iii)		17*	1	18	26.8
Bone small 4hole shirt buttons (3.a.i)	1	2	2	5	7.4
Bone small 3hole (3.b.i)			3	3	4.5
Bone 1hole core (3.d.i)			1	1	1.5
Bone 5hole (3.e.ii)		1		1	1.5
Bone other		1	1	2	3.0
Shell small 4hole shirt buttons (4.a.i)	3	2	1	6	8.9
Shell small 2hole shirt buttons (4.c.i)		3		3	4.5
Shell shank loop (4.f.ii)			1	1	1.5
Shell other		1		1	1.5
Glass small 4hole shirt buttons (5.a.i)		1		1	1.5
Totals	9	37	21	67	100

*Note: 15 of these artifacts constituted special find 575.

deposition during taskwork. The simple presence of these buttons at the Ross Factory site is in itself rather unremarkable. However, the artefact distribution pattern is potentially more revealing.

The largest number and greatest diversity of buttons were recovered from Area B. It contained both the Hiring Class and the Assistant Superintendent's Quarters. The earthen floors of this latter structure contained evidence of mixing between pre- and post-Factory periods of site use (Casella 1999). Erected in 1833 to accommodate male convict labourers during construction of the Ross Bridge, the brick structure was subsequently reoccupied by the Factory Assistant Super-intendent after minimal modification of the original earthen floors. In addition to artefacts related to both pre-Factory and Factory periods of use, an 1866 Victorian penny was also recovered during excavation of these floors. Thus, artefacts from Area B could be least strongly related to the Factory period of site occupation.

In contrast, the stratigraphic, architectural, and documentary evidence from Areas A and C suggested that the Crime Class Dormitory and Solitary Cells both contained a number of floor and underfloor deposits more directly associated with the Female Factory period of site occupation (Casella 1997: 83–4; Casella 1999). Extensive modifications of the Crime Class Dormitory floors during establishment of the Female Factory directly linked underfloor deposits of this structure to the Female Factory occupation period. Archival documents indicate that construction of the Solitary Cells occurred in Area C during the Factory period: no historic or archaeological evidence was recovered to suggest substantial re-use of the cellblock after closure of the Factory in 1855. Thus, artefactual assemblages recovered from Areas A and C could be stratigraphically related to the female convict inmates with a reasonable degree of certainty.

Returning to Table 3.2, if results from Area B are disregarded because of problems with stratigraphic association, the remaining data suggest that both a greater quantity and a greater diversity of buttons were recovered from the Solitary Cells compared to those found at the Crime Class Dormitory of the main penal compound. As only 16 square metres were excavated in Area C, compared with 48 square metres in Area A, these results could also suggest that a greater density of buttons was present within the Solitary Cells.

As detailed earlier within this chapter, a landscape of disciplinary segregation divided interior locales of the Ross Factory into strictly defined functional regions. The workrooms were isolated from living and punishment quarters by a series of locked gates, courtyards, and nine-foot-high timber post and rail fences. Given this landscape of social, temporal, and spatial control, the presence of non-uniform related buttons in substantial quantities in the Crime Class Dormitory and Solitary Cells may reflect intentional transport and possession, rather than accidental deposition during taskwork.

Particularly the Solitary Cellblock, by virtue of its intrinsic purpose, was strictly segregated from the work-related wards of the prison. While undergoing 'separate treatment' the female convict was supposed to be silently engaged in moral reflection and disciplinary social isolation. She was not engaged in laundry- or sewing-related

taskwork. Thus, the significant presence of buttons, particularly non-uniform decorative buttons, in the Solitary Cells may represent evidence of non-clothing-related functions for this artefact assemblage.

It is significant to note the presence of two particularly unusual button types within the Solitary Cells. The one isolated occurrence of a bone button core within Factory-related deposits was recovered from Area C. These single-holed discs were used as the rigid core of a silk-thread decorative button, the colorful threads wrapped around the core, and a few loops left dangling for attachment to the article of clothing. Furthermore, all three specimens of a three-hole small bone button (Type 3.b.i) were recovered from occupation layers inside the Solitary Cells. Preliminary comparative examinations of contemporary Australian archaeological sites have only located occurrences of this unusual button type within settlements occupied by male convicts, ex-convict labourers, and/or Aboriginal communities (Birmingham 1992; Greg Jackman, Nadia Iacono, Susan Lawrence, personal communications).

In her 1992 report on archaeological excavations at Wybalenna, the 1840s Tasmanian Aboriginal settlement on Flinders Island in the Bass Straits, Judy Birmingham argued that the high frequency of bone and ferrous four-hole sew through buttons in occupation contexts related to the buttons' function as gaming tokens (Birmingham 1992: 110). By interpreting this particular function, Birmingham offered an alternative social and economic function for this class of artefacts. Extending this idea of the buttons as socio-economic objects, could they have held an exchange value in themselves? Could they have served as economic tokens? And if the buttons are trade tokens, what valued commodities would have fuelled the black-market economy of this convict landscape?

Illicit objects: the distribution of bottles and 'baccy

My distribution analysis of artefacts related to tobacco and alcohol consumption also demonstrated some significant patterns (see Table 3.3). While the presence of the recreational indulgences on most archaeological sites would be unremarkable, at the female factories of Van

Table 3.3 Distribution of illicit objects.

Description	Crime Class	Solitary Cells
Total glass assemblage	2751 g	406g
Olive glass alcohol bottle fragments	1529g (55%)	312g (77%)
Minimum number of vessels	15	10
Total ceramic assemblage	4,416g	1.547g
Kaolin clay tobacco pipe fragments	23g (0.5%)	74g (5%)
Minimum number of vessels	5	10
Total area excavated	48 square metres	16 square metres

Diemen's Land possession of alcohol and tobacco was strictly forbidden for prisoners. Thus, these two artefact assemblages were identified as 'illicit objects' within the specific context of the Ross factory.

Table 3.3 presents data on the frequency distributions of these objects recovered from the underfloor deposits of the Crime Class Dormitory, and the earthen floors of the Solitary Cells. As a common container for wine, beer, and gin during the nineteenth century, olive glass bottles were specifically selected as a material representation of alcohol consumption because an insufficient number of diagnostic shards of clear glass were recovered to differentiate between vessels for alcoholic spirits (most commonly whisky) and food containers. In Table 3.3, the presence of kaolin clay tobacco pipe fragments and olive glass bottle fragments is demonstrated in terms of total weight (in grams) and percentage by weight of the total artefact fabric category. The minimum number of vessels (MNV) present in each context was also calculated, and is presented within this table.

Results of this analysis suggest that in terms of both relative frequency and MNV counts, more illicit materials existed within the Solitary Cells than in the Crime Class dormitory. A greater estimated number of kaolin clay tobacco pipes was found within the excavated solitary cells; these forbidden objects also comprised a higher percentage of the overall ceramic assemblage recovered from cell interiors. While a greater minimum number of olive glass bottles was recovered from the Crime Class dormitory, three times more area had been excavated in this region than in Area C. Therefore, while a larger number of illicit grog bottles was

recovered from the Crime Class underfloor deposits, they occurred much less frequently than within the Solitary Cells. Comprising 77 per cent of the glass assemblage from Area C, olive bottle glass constituted only 55 per cent of the glass recovered from Area A.

These results could have been affected by such factors as occupation density, differential preservation of the record, and depositional processes. The greater presence of these artefacts within the earthen floors of the Solitary Cells might also have reflected the limited options for disposal of incriminating evidence. In her study of the glass assemblage from the Boott Mills of Lowell, Massachusetts, Kathleen Bond noted the significantly high quantity (by weight) of undiagnostic smashed glass artefacts in the courtyards that surrounded the workers' boarding-houses (Bond 1989). She suggested that this occurrence might indicate a 'smash and scatter' strategy employed by the mill girls to safely disperse all incriminating evidence of their illegal alcohol consumption. The lower frequency of tobacco pipes and alcohol bottles within the Crime Class Dormitory underfloors might indicate that a greater variety of options was open to those inmates for disposal of their 'indulgences'. But this archaeological evidence could also suggest an increase in prohibited activities within the Cells.

Subversion: The Convict Landscape

As places of ultimate punishment, the Solitary Cells were architecturally fabricated to discipline repeat offenders. Research by historians such as Kay Daniels (1998) and Joy Damousi (1997) has located these women at the apex of the underground economy of the Female Factories. The higher frequencies of tobacco- and alcohol-related materials within the Ross Factory Solitary Cells might reflect the flourishing of illicit trade within this edifice of confinement and punishment. While under solitary sentence, the factory 'incorrigibles' continued to maintain their access to forbidden indulgences, relieving the monotonous boredom, cold, and hunger of disciplinary confinement with a pipe and a bottle. Thus, when examined together, the significantly higher frequency and density of both illicit artefacts and buttons within the Solitary Cells may be related. These results archaeologically suggest a focal point within the black-market network. While inmates of the Crime Class actively engaged in economic 'trade', the most potent covert paths of this penal world seem to lead directly to the Solitary Cells, the very region of the prison designed for strictly bounded isolation. As inmate Mary Haigh noted in her 1842 deposition to the Parliamentary Committee of Inquiry, 'I have been in the dark Cells. That is bad punishment but even there Tea Sugar and etc [sic] can be obtained ...' (AOT CSO 22/50). Thus, through black-market trade, the female convicts created an alternate and coexistent landscape of socio-economic networks. They negotiated the disciplinary segregation and classification of penal spaces through their movement of illicit materials around the bounded institutional landscape.

Conclusion

Inhabitants of the Ross Female Factory occupied a landscape of strictly defined and hierarchically organized locales. These places were spatially and temporally organized to maintain relationships of domination and subordination within the ranks of both staff and inmate inhabitants. However, the ideal organization of this institutional landscape was only partially realized. Archaeological evidence suggests that an alternate landscape simultaneously coexisted at the Ross Factory site. Networks of underground exchange subverted the documented institutional template (Daniels 1998; Damousi 1997). Through the covert landscape of barter and exchange, inmates and illicit materials circulated through the various bounded locales of the Factory site. Remarkably, archaeological evidence appears to suggest a dramatic inversion of the ideal template, with the dominant node of the black-market network located within the Solitary Cells – that region of the prison officially intended for strict isolation and disciplinary separation of female inmates. The Ross Female Factory never existed as one static cultural landscape. Through surviving documents and material culture, we can map the simultaneous and overlapped landscapes of both institutional domination and inmate resistance, as they negotiated, conflicted, and intertwined to create this penal site.

References

Primary sources:

Mitchell Library. Tasmanian Papers, Number 104.

AOT CO 280/699/268, p. 162. Colonial Office records. Revised Scale of Task Work ... 29 December 1849.

AOT CSO 22/50. Colonial Secretary's Office. 1841–1843 Committee of Inquiry into Female Convict Prison Discipline.

AOT MM 62/24/10774. Miscellaneous Microfilm. October 1848. Duties of the Staff at the Ross Female Factory.

AOT MM 62/26/11931. Miscellaneous Microfilm. May 1849. Letter from Visiting Magistrate Stuart to Comptroller-General of Convicts.

AOT MM 62/26/11946. Miscellaneous Microfilm. May 1849. Investigations of Allegations made by Constable Taylor.

AOT MM 62/28/12161. Miscellaneous Microfilm. July 1849. Report by Visiting Magistrate to the Comptroller-General of Convicts.

Secondary sources:

Birmingham, J. 1992. *Wybalenna: The Archaeology of Cultural Accommodation in Nineteenth Century Tasmania.* Sydney: The Australian Society for Historical Archaeology Incorporated.

Bond, K. 1989. The medicine, alcohol, and soda vessels from the Boott Mills boardinghouses, in M. Beaudry and S. Mrozowski (eds) *Interdisciplinary Investigations of the Boott Mills, Lowell, Massachusetts, Volume 3.* Cultural Resources Management Study, No. 21. Boston: National Park Service, North Atlantic Regional Office.

Bourdieu, P. 1977. *Outline of a Theory of Practice.* Cambridge: Cambridge University Press.

Brand, I. 1990. *The Convict Probation System: Van Diemen's Land, 1839–1854.* Hobart: Blubber Head Press.

Casella, E. 1997. 'A large and efficient Establishment': preliminary report on fieldwork at the Ross Female Factory. *Australasian Historical Archaeology* 15: 79–89.

Casella, E. 1999. Dangerous Girls and Gentle Ladies: Archaeology and Nineteenth Century Australian Female Convicts. Unpublished PhD dissertation. Department of Anthropology, University of California, Berkeley.

Claassen, C. 1994. Washboards, pigtoes, and muckets: historic musseling in the Mississippi watershed. *Historical Archaeology* 28(2).

Damousi, J. 1997. *Depraved and Disorderly.* Cambridge: Cambridge University Press.

Daniels, K. 1998. *Convict Women.* Sydney: Allen & Unwin.

Driver, F. 1993. *Power and Pauperism: The Workhouse System, 1834–1884.* Cambridge: Cambridge University Press.

Eldershaw, P.R. 1968. The Convict Department. *THRA* 15(3): 130–49.

Evans, R. 1982. *The Fabrication of Virtue.* Cambridge: Cambridge University Press.

Foucault, M. 1977. *Discipline and Punish.* London: Penguin.

Foucault, M. 1980. *Power/Knowledge: Selected Interviews and Other Writings 1972–1977.* Colin Gordon (ed.). New York: Pantheon Books.

Iacono, N. 1996. Cumberland/Gloucester Streets Site Archaeological Investigations 1994: Artefact Report, Miscellaneous. Unpublished report for the Sydney Cove Authority, Godden Mackay Heritage Consultants.

Lydon, J. 1993. Task differentiation in historical archaeology: Sewing as material culture, in H. du Cros and L. Smith (eds) *Women in Archaeology: A Feminist Critique.* Canberra: Department of Prehistory. Research School of Pacific Studies, the Australian National University. *Occasional Papers in Prehistory*, No. 23. 129–33.

Lydon, J. 1995. Boarding-houses in the Rocks: Mrs Ann Lewis' privy. *Public History Review* 4: 73–88.

Markus, T. 1993. *Buildings and Power.* London: Routledge.

Oxley, D. 1996. *Convict Maids.* Cambridge: Cambridge University Press.

Parham, D. and Noble, B. 1994. Convict Probation Stations Archaeological Survey. Unpublished report to the Tasmanian Archaeological Society and the Philip Smith Education Centre.

Peponis, J. and Hedin, J. 1982. The layout of theories in the Natural History Museum, *9H* 3: 21–5.

Praetzellis, M. and A. Praetzellis 1992. Faces and façades: Victorian ideology in Early Sacramento, in A. Yentsch and M. Beaudry (eds) *The Art and Mystery of Historical Archaeology.* Boca Raton, FL: CRC Press, 75–100.

Rayner, T. 1980. *Historical Survey of the Ross Female Factory Site, Tasmania,* Unpublished report prepared for Cultural Heritage Branch, Parks and Wildlife Service, Department of Environment and Land Management, Tasmania, Australia.

Rodgers, S. 1993. Women's space in a men's house: the British House of Commons, in S. Ardener (ed.) *Women and Space.* Oxford: Berg. 48–50.

Ryan, L. 1995. From stridency to silence: the policing of convict women 1803–1853, in D. Kirkby (ed.) *Sex, Power and Justice.* Melbourne: Oxford University Press.

Scott, J. 1990. *Domination and the Arts of Resistance: Hidden Transcripts.* New Haven and London: Yale University Press.

Scripps, L. and Clark, J. 1991. *The Ross Female Factory.* Department of Parks, Wildlife and Heritage, Tasmania, Australia.

Seaborne, M. 1971. *The English School: Its Architecture and Organisation, 1370–1870.* London: Routledge & Kegan Paul.

Spain, D. 1992. *Gendered Spaces.* Chapel Hill, NC: University of North Carolina Press.

Terry, I. 1998. Ross Female Convict Station Historic Site: Conservation Plan. Unpublished report for the Tasmanian Parks and Wildlife Service, Department of Primary Industries, Water and Environment. Hobart, Australia.

4

Amazonia
The Historical Ecology of a
Domesticated Landscape

Clark L. Erickson

Introduction

When one thinks of Amazonia, images of large towering trees, dark and humid forests, brightly colored frogs, and smiling native people decorated in paint and feathers come to mind. In addition to engaging public awareness, these popular images are used to raise funds for conservation, to advance green politics, and to promote cultural and ecotourism. They are updated versions of nineteenth-century imagery common in travel books and explorers' accounts of Amazonia as a Green Hell or as the Garden of Eden. Surprisingly, many colleagues in the natural sciences and conservation still hold similar notions about Amazonia. These romantic views of nature are contrasted to the reality of contemporary humans destroying the ecosystems of Amazonia through modern development. Loss of biodiversity, extinction of species, deforestation, erosion, pollution, and global warming are attributed to humans and their activities. Recent studies argue that humans have been involved in environmental degradation, ecological catastrophe, and global change throughout their existence.

Clark L. Erickson, "Amazonia: The Historical Ecology of a Domesticated Landscape," pp. 157–83 in *The Handbook of South American Archaeology*, ed. Helaine Silverman and William Isbell (New York: Springer, 2008). Reprinted with permission of Springer.

Traditional historical, geographical, anthropological, and archaeological perspectives on native Amazonia share these negative views. In the classic literature, past and present Amazonian cultures are considered to have been determined largely by the environment to which they adapted. What appears to be a lush, bountiful setting for human development is actually a counterfeit paradise according to some scholars (e.g., Meggers 1971). Environmental limitations, such as poor soils and a lack of protein, combined with a limited technology, few domestic animals, and abundant unoccupied land restricted social development. The simple societies of Amazonia did not evolve into what we recognize as civilization. In this traditional view, the environment is an immutable given or a fixed entity to which human societies adapt (or do not, and, thus, fail, and disappear). The basic assumption is that poor environments produce simple societies (band societies of hunters, gatherers, and fishers or tribal societies of subsistence farmers) and the corollary, that rich environments produce complex societies (chiefly and state societies of urban and rural folk).

Historical ecology provides a radical, alternative perspective for understanding human–environment interaction over the long term and the complex human histories of environments. Historical ecology focuses on *landscape* as the medium created by human agents through their interaction with the environment. Although landscapes can be the result of unintentional activities, historical ecologists focus on the intentional actions of people and the logic of indigenous knowledge, particularly the understanding of resource creation and management. Historical ecologists, borrowing from the new ecology, argue that disturbance caused by human activities is a key factor in shaping biodiversity and environmental health. Because much of human-environmental history extends beyond written records, the archaeology of landscapes plays an important role. Through the physical signatures or footprints of human activities, technology, engineering, and knowledge embedded in the landscape, historical ecologists have a historical perspective of over 11,000 years about human-environment interaction in Amazonia.

What Amazonian people did to their environment was a form of _domestication of landscape_ (Erickson 2006). Domestication of landscape implies all intentional and non-intentional practices and activities of humans that transform the environment into a productive landscape for humans and other species. Domesticated landscapes are the result of careful resource creation and management with implications for the diversity, distribution, and availability of species. Through their long-term historical transformation of the environment involving transplanting of plants and animals, selective culling of non-economic species and encouragement of useful species, burning, settlement, farming, agroforestry (forest management), and other activities discussed in this paper, humans created what we recognize and appreciate as _nature_ in Amazonia. Through the perspective of historical ecology, however, we see that nature in Amazonia more closely resembles a _garden_ than a pristine, natural wilderness. Rather than "adapt to" or be "limited by" the Amazonian environment, humans created, transformed, and managed cultural or anthropogenic (human-made) landscapes that suited their purposes. The cultural or anthropogenic landscapes range from the subtle (often confused with "natural" or "pristine") to completely engineered.

In this chapter, I introduce historical ecology, new ecology, landscape, and domestication of landscape as key concepts for understanding complex, long-term interactions between humans and the environment. I show how historical ecology challenges traditional assumptions and myths about Amazonia. Later, I survey examples of human activities that have created, transformed, and managed environments and their association to biodiversity.

In this chapter, I use the term _Amazonia_ to refer to the Amazon basin (the entire region drained by the Amazon River and its tributaries) and more loosely to refer to the tropical lowlands of South America or Greater Amazonia (cf. Lathrap 1970; Denevan 2001). As an anthropogenic environment and interacting culture area of considerable time depth, Amazonia is tied to the neotropics or tropical regions of the Americas.

Biodiversity

Any discussion of humans and the environment invokes debates about biodiversity. Dirzo and Raven define _biodiversity_ as "the sum total of all of the plants, animals, fungi, and microorganisms on Earth; their genetic and phenotypic variation; and the communities and ecosystems of which they are a part" (2003: 138). Biodiversity is measured through _alpha diversity_ or the number of species within a locality, _beta diversity_ or the change in the composition of species between adjacent areas, and _gama diversity_ or all species in a region. The highest biodiversity is found in tropical regions such as Amazonia.

Biodiversity is assumed to benefit ecosystem function by increasing biomass, resilience, and productivity – although this is under intense debate. Biodiversity provides humans with food shelter, medicines, fiber, fuel, and other services (drinking water, air, and purification of contaminants) and a vast gene pool for future use. Humans have contributed agrodiversity or domesticated biodiversity through genetic selection of useful plants and animals (Brookfield 2001). Although these selected plants and animals are only a small number of the total species on earth, they provide most of our food and other resources. Semi-domesticates and wild economic species such as medicines, spices, ornamentals, pets, and utilitarian plants also rely on humans for their protection, propagation, and availability; they are not usually considered in discussions of biodiversity but are significant.

Historical Ecology

At its most basic, historical ecology is about people and their interactions with the environment through time (Balée 1989, 1998, 2006; Balée and Erickson 2006b; Crumley 1994). Although the case studies presented here focus on the contributions of the archaeology of landscapes, historical ecology is inherently multidisciplinary with contributions from botany, zoology, linguistics, soil science, agronomy, anthropology, history, geography, ecology, genetics, demography, climatology, geology, soil science, and many other fields (for examples, Balée 1998; Balée and Erickson 2006a; Crumley 1994; Glaser and Woods 2004; Hayashida 2005).

In doing historical ecology of landscapes, archaeologists practice a form of *reverse engineering*. Recognizing fragmentary physical patterns in sites and landscapes as reflecting human culture, archaeologists carefully document and analyze the evidence within its temporal and spatial context for insights into original logic, design, engineering, and intentionality of human actions. Due to the incomplete nature of the archaeological record, interpretation relies on careful use of analogy to specific historical and ethnographic cases or general cross-cultural models about human behavior. In the case of historical ecology, reverse engineering helps reveal the infrastructure and strategies of environmental management embedded in landscapes. Using this approach, historical ecologists can document and evaluate the successes and failures of human strategies through an examination of continuity and disjuncture in the archaeological record. Distinguishing between natural and cultural (or anthropogenic) processes of environmental change is possible with careful contextual analysis.

Traditional perspectives on human-environmental interaction separate and oppose people and nature. Humans are said to either co-exist in harmony with nature or over-exploit and degrade nature. In cultural ecology, human ecology, cultural materialism, and evolutionary ecology, nature is a fixed given entity that humans interact with and adapt to and their success and failure are measured (Moran 1982; Sutton and Anderson 2004). In cultural evolution and cultural ecology, societies are assumed to pass through sequential stages of development from simple to complex. Increasing control of energy, elaboration of technology, population growth, and formation of political hierarchy are implicit to this lineal scheme as societies advance towards civilization. Differing degrees of human impact and transformation of the environment are attributed to each cultural evolutionary stage. Band societies are assumed to have low or minimal impact while states are understood to have high impact (e.g., Redman 1999; Sutton and Anderson 2004).

In contrast to evolutionary approaches where natural selection and ecological processes determine the course of interaction of the human species and environments, historical ecologists propose that "the human species is itself a principal mechanism of change in the natural world, a mechanism qualitatively as significant as natural selection" (Balée and Erickson 2006b: 5). While not ignoring evolutionary and ecological processes, historical ecologists prioritize the historical processes, temporal and geographic scales appropriate for study of humans (often multiple), and human agency (intentionality, innovation, aesthetics, and creativity). Rather than "adapt" to an environment, humans practice *resource management* through which they create the environment in which they live. Balée defines resource management as "the human manipulation of inorganic and organic components of the environment that brings about a net environmental diversity greater than that of so-called pristine conditions, with no human presence" (1994: 117).

The New Ecology

A basic principle of ecology is succession theory or ecological succession (Clements 1916). Nature is assumed to have an ideal state or "climax community". A community such as a forest evolves through a series of orderly stages. At its mature, final stage, a community is said to be in equilibrium with a stable composition of specific species. Although equilibrium can be thrown out of balance by natural phenomena (windstorms, landslides, and wildfires), the community is assumed to recover and return to its optimal state. Much of traditional ecology, environmental science, and conservation are based on the notion that equilibrium and stability are good for nature. The mature, age-old rainforests of Amazonia are rich with biodiversity and are considered prime examples of undisturbed, mature wilderness or a climax community.

In recent decades, *new ecologists* have questioned the assumptions of succession theory (Botkin 1990; Connell 1978) and criticized traditional conservation based on succession theory's idea that nature should be protected from disturbance, change, and people. In contrast to succession theory, the *new ecology* considers natural disturbances not only common, but integral to ecosystem health and biodiversity. The instability, non-equilibrium, and at times chaos created by disturbance encourage environmental heterogeneity through the creation of patches, mosaics, and edges of distinct habitats where diverse species can compete and thrive (Botkin 1990; Zimmerer and Young 1998).

Borrowing insights from the new ecology, historical ecologists focus on human activities as a major source of disturbance (Balée and Erickson 2006a; Stahl 2000, 2006; Zimmerer and Young 1998). In contrast to natural disturbances, human or anthropogenic disturbances are highly patterned in timing, frequency, intensity, scale, context, complexity, and diversity (Blumler 1998; Erickson 2006; Pyne 1998). Common examples of human disturbance are burning, erosion, settlement, roads, farming, and deforestation, but can also include subtle activities such as weeding, transplanting, cultivation, fertilizing, and seeding which encourage certain species over others and which may increase overall biodiversity and biomass. Despite the negativity implied, disturbance by humans usually involves intentionality and planning, although the long-term effects may be unknown and unintended when they occur.

Building on the findings of new ecologists that intermediate levels of disturbance are optimal for species diversity, Blumler (1998) suggests that a variety of disturbances and timing or *disturbance heterogeneity* are as important as intensity. Human disturbances keep the environment in a form of arrested succession and disequilibrium. Secondary rather than primary forest is encouraged, which may increase biodiversity, biomass, and ecosystem heterogeneity, especially of wild and domesticated species exploited by humans that thrive in such contexts.

Landscapes

Whereas most traditional archaeologists study *sites*, archaeologists doing historical ecology focus on the largely ignored space between sites or *landscape* (Ashmore and Knapp 1999). In the rural Andes and Amazon where I work, people do most of their daytime activities such as farming, building walls, visiting neighbors, sharing labor, and collecting wild resources in the landscape rather than within the confines of sites which are primarily used for eating and sleeping. Because the totality of people's lives in the past is important, archaeologists must include landscapes in their studies.

Because they are physical and created by repetitive activities through time, landscapes are ideal artifacts for historical ecologists. Archaeologists often apply the metaphor of "reading" landscapes in the sense that cultural patterns created through human activity have meaning and intent that can be deciphered through contextual analysis. Permanent improvements to the land are considered *landscape capital*, investments that are handed down generation after generation (Brookfield 2001). Later generations benefit from the labor and knowledge of their ancestors embedded in landscape. In a recursive relationship, their lives are often structured by roads, trails, paths, field boundaries, irrigation canals, and clearings for houses imposed on the landscape by past inhabitants. Multiple, often contrasting, landscape patterns, which represent different systems of land use and management, are often embedded in landscapes as palimpsests or layered, sequential traces.

Amazonia: Wilderness or Cultural Landscape?

The high-canopy tropical rainforest, famous for its complexity and biodiversity, is the focus of contemporary research and conservation. Many scholars and the public consider the mature, tropical rainforest to be the ideal natural state of Amazonia, a classic wilderness. In succession theory, mature rainforest is assumed to be the climax community in stable equilibrium. Because these rainforests are relatively devoid of humans today, one might assume that biodiversity is highest in environments undisturbed by humans.

Amazonia-as-wilderness is an example of the *Myth of the Pristine Environment* (Denevan 1992), the belief that the environments of the Americas were relatively untouched by humans prior to European conquest. Native people are believed to have been too few in number, technologically limited, or living harmoniously with the Earth to significantly impact nature. The assumption is also based on the *Myth of the Noble Savage* (or Ecological Indian) – that past and present native people lived in harmony with nature until Europeans and modern world systems arrived, which negatively and permanently transformed the previously pristine environment (Redford 1991).

Archaeologists, however, have demonstrated that much of Amazonia was occupied by dense populations of urbanized societies practicing intensive agriculture that significantly contributed to creating the environment that is appreciated today (Denevan 1992; Erickson 2006; Heckenberger 2005; Lehmann et al. 2003; Stahl 1996). Scholars now argue that much of the tropical rainforest is the result of a "rebound effect" created by the removal of these people and their activities by European diseases, civil wars, ethnocide, slavery, and resource expropriation. Without the insights of historical ecology, Amazonia is easily misinterpreted as pristine wilderness.

Contrary to popular notions, Amazonia is diverse in environments and was probably more so in the past. While rainforest covers approximately one third of the region, the majority of Amazonia is deciduous forest, palm forest, liana forest, forest island, savanna, and wetland (Goulding et al. 2003; Moran 1993; Smith 1999). Other classic distinctions include riverine (*várzea*) vs. upland (*terra firme*) and white, clear, and black water rivers.

In addition, historical ecologists argue that much of Amazonia's diverse ecological patchwork of diverse habitats is anthropogenic and historical (Balée and Erickson 2006a; Posey and Balée 1989). Before the native population collapse after 1492, archaeologists show that much of Amazonia was transformed by burning, settlement, roads, agriculture, and agroforestry into forest clearings, savannas, parkland, countryside, and forest islands (Denevan 1992, 2001; Erickson 2006; Heckenberger 2005; Heckenberger et al. 2003; Posey 2004; Stahl 2006). The "natural" fauna and flora composition were replaced by anthropogenic formations. Amazonia had fewer trees five hundred years ago and the existing forests were more similar to gardens, orchards, and game preserves than wilderness.

Amazonia: A Counterfeit Paradise or Anthropogenic Cornucopia?

Environmental determinism has a long history in anthropological studies since the nineteenth century. Scholars believed that races, cultural diversity, cultural stability and change could be explained by the environmental conditions under which these traits developed. In this view, the environment is treated as a given fixed context to which societies adapt or fail. In Amazonia, the limitations include soils, technology, protein, and catastrophic climate change. The main spokesperson of environmental determinism, Betty Meggers (1954, 1971, 2001) explained the presence of simple societies and relatively nomadic lifeways of Amazonian people in the historical and ethnographic accounts as evidence of environmental limitations imposed on human cultural development. According to her Theory of Environmental Determinism, societal development is encouraged or limited by the conditions to which humans have to adapt. In the case of Amazonia, the poor quality of tropical soils is said to have restricted agriculture to simple systems such as slash-and-burn (swidden) (Carneiro 1960; Meggers 1971). Adopting the idea from natural scientists and developers that the lush, rich vegetation of the tropical forests is actually a fragile ecosystem growing on poor soils, Meggers (1971) coined the term *counterfeit paradise* to describe Amazonia.

Swidden is the most common traditional agriculture today, involving clearing isolated patches of forest, drying and burning the felled vegetation, and planting crops among the ash. Crops are rotated for several years and the field is abandoned eventually as weeds and secondary growth increase labor (abandonment was originally thought to be due to soil exhaustion). Over a period of 10–20 years, secondary forest covers the plot. Because the farmer clears and burns another stand of forest every 3–5 years, a large area is needed and settlements are frequently relocated; thus, slash-and-burn agriculture is assumed to support low population densities. Without large populations, surplus to support non-farmers and class stratification, and cities, Amazonia could never develop civilization. Environmental determinists also point to primitive technology as a reason for simple agriculture: the wooden digging stick, stone ax, and wooden machete.

Others examined the lack of animal protein as an environmental limitation. According to the Hypothesis of Protein Limitations, scholars proposed that the availability of protein determined settlement, population density, and inter and intra-societal relationships in Amazonia (Gross 1975). Unlike societies in the Old World, Amazonian people had few domesticated animals to provide reliable protein; and thus they were assumed to have relied on unpredictable and easily overexploited hunting of wild animals. Based on ethnographic cases, scholars argued that typical settlement size, duration, and regional patterns could be explained by the lack of protein. In more extreme interpretations, Amazonian patterns of warfare, settlement spacing, and mobility, were explained by the fierce competition over limited hunting resources (Chagnon and Hames 1979).

Meggers (1979, 1995, 2001) proposes catastrophic climate change as a new element of environmental determinism to explain periodic settlement abandonment and changes in pottery styles in the archaeological record. She hypothesizes that cycles of mega-El Niño events throughout prehistory caused severe and extended floods and droughts that caused frequent societal collapse, encouraged nomadic patterns of settlement, and limited social development. Recent El Niño events have caused droughts and flooding in Amazonia, often resulting in large forest fires that have been exacerbated by uncontrolled development of the region. Pre-Columbian societies faced similar challenges and survived. However, the evidence presented for catastrophic climate change by mega-El Niños and its impact on humans has been challenged (e.g., DeBoer et al. 1996; Erickson and Balée 2006; Stahl 1991; Whitten 1979).

Few contemporary scholars support environmental determinism. Carneiro (1960) points out that slash-and-burn agriculture under careful management can be highly productive, yield surpluses, and sustain large, sedentary villages of 1000 to 2000 people. Others highlight the importance of bitter manioc, a crop that thrives on poor soils and can be converted into a storable surplus as dry flour (Heckenberger 1998; Lathrap 1974).

In the 1960s, scholars documented intensive agriculture in pre-Columbian Amazonia, including house gardens, river levee farming, raised fields, terraces, Amazonian Dark Earth (ADE), and anthropogenic forest islands (Denevan 2001; Denevan and Padoch 1988; Langstroth 1996; Lathrap 1970, 1987; Lathrap et al. 1985; Posey 2004). In contrast to low-energy, extensive agriculture such as slash-and-burn, which requires long periods of fallow during which fields regain fertility, intensive agriculture, which has little or no fallow period and fertility, is maintained through inputs of labor and organic matter. Archaeologists and geographers highlighted the potential of farming river levees and banks when floods recede (Hiraoka 1985; Smith 1999). Raised fields, terracing, and ADE (discussed below) are capable of continuous, high yields and are associated with dense populations, large permanent settlements, and complex society (Denevan 2001; Erickson 2006; Lehmann et al. 2003; Neves and Petersen 2006; Valdez 2006; Walker 2004). These strategies take advantage of patches of naturally fertile soil and technologies of soil creation, transformation, and management and negate environmental determinism. Slash-and-burn agriculture depends on metal axes and machetes to efficiently clear primary forest. These tools were unavailable until after 1492 (Denevan 2001). Pre-Columbian farmers, using digging sticks and stone axes, probably continuously cultivated fields and practiced agroforestry rather than clearing primary forest.

In critiquing the Hypothesis of Protein Limitation, scholars noted that most groups studied as examples of protein limitation live inland, far from major water bodies and fish. In fact, Amazonian people were primarily riverine cultures and relied on fish and other aquatic resources as the main source of protein rather than game animals (Beckerman 1979). In addition to rivers and lakes, fish were systematically harvested in large numbers using networks of fish weirs (Erickson 2000b). Furthermore, maize is a storable staple crop and provider of protein (Lathrap 1987; Roosevelt 1991) and other sources of protein were available, including nuts, fruits, and insects common in the humanized forests (Beckerman 1979).

Native Amazonian People: With or Against Nature?

Indigenous people of Amazonia have become the subject of an intense debate about whether native people enhance or degrade biodiversity and environmental health. In some more extreme critiques, Amazonian people are considered to be no better or worse than Westerners (Alvard 1995; Redford 1991). But modern Western society often views the relationship of native people to the environment as positive in contrast to its own. Assumed to be living in harmony with nature, it is thought that native people must have an innate conservation ethic and, thus, are considered the natural stewards of the environment. This powerful belief is the Myth of the Noble Savage. Much of the debate about native Amazonia focuses on documentation of over-hunting of game animals. Rather than being omniscient curators of their environment, it can be argued Amazonian people were environmentally friendly due to low, dispersed populations, plenty of resources, simple technology, and settlement mobility rather than an innate conservation ethic.

In studies debunking the myth, game animals are treated as a natural and immutable resource subject to unsustainable overexploitation. Historical ecologists point out that the important game animals feed heavily on fruits and nuts provided by the anthropogenic forests established by the past inhabitants of Amazonia. Oligarchy or forests of a single species, usually a tree valuable to humans and game animals, is attributed to past human management (Peters 2000). In addition, most contemporary hunter-gatherers rely on the economic species of anthropogenic forests, the landscape capital of their ancestors. Humans created the conditions for the "natural" resources that they are blamed for degrading.

While scholars debate humans as agents of conservation vs. humans as agents of degradation, historical ecologists eschew the distinctions and argue that humans are neither (Balée 1998; Balée and Erickson 2006b). Rather than possessing an innate conservation ethic of preservation, native Amazonians consciously exploited their environments for subsistence while practicing resource creation and management. The management, a form of multigenerational indigenous knowledge about the environment, is based on local practical indigenous knowledge. Some historical ecologists consider humans to be a keystone species: a species that plays a disproportionate role in ecosystem health and the abundance and availability of other species (Balée and Erickson 2006b).

Whether human activities degrade or enhance biodiversity often depends on how biodiversity and environmental health are defined and measured, the temporal and geographical scale used for comparison, and the standard or a benchmark to which altered environments can be compared and evaluated. Because the impact of human activities is so early, widespread, and profound in Amazonia, most historical ecologists argue that there is no appropriate pristine benchmark for comparison. In some cases, Amazonian people enhanced biodiversity and practiced environmentally sustainable practices; in other cases the diversity of species was reduced and environments degraded. What may have been negative impacts over the short term and locally may actually enhance biodiversity over the long term and at the regional scales and vice versa. In many documented cases, human creation, transformation, and management of the Amazonia over thousands of years resulted in the high biodiversity that is appreciated today.

Amazonian People: Adaptation to or Creation of Environments?

Culture ecologists emphasize the concept of adaptation, modified from natural science and evolution, to explain cultural variation and the success and failure of native societies in Amazonia (e.g., Meggers 1971; Moran 1982; Sutton and Anderson 2004). Cultural ecologists

Figure 4.1   Savanna management using fire in the Bolivian Amazon. Baures in 1999. (Clark Erickson)

consider adaptations to the environment through human culture (material culture, technology, social organization, and settlement patterns) that undergo selection with beneficial behaviors favored and passed to future generations. The adaptation concept treats the environment as a static, fixed, often limited resource to which humans adapt. The concept is also believed to explain human cultural diversity through reference to unique adaptations to the exigencies of their particular environmental context.

Historical ecologists reject the assumptions of adaptation. Rather than adapt or respond to the environment, Amazonian people created, transformed, and managed those very environments in which they lived and thrived through their culture and accumulated multigenerational knowledge and management practices (Balée 1989, 2006; Balée and Erickson 2006a; Erickson 2006).

Elements of a Domesticated Landscape

Evidence of landscape creation, transformation and management of domesticated, engineered,

humanized landscapes in Amazonia includes: anthropogenic burning, settlements and associated landscapes, mounds, anthropogenic forest islands, ring ditch sites, Amazonian Dark Earth (ADE), raised fields, transportation and communication networks, and water management, fisheries management, and agroforestry.

Anthropogenic burning

Fire is the oldest and most powerful technology of environmental creation, transformation, and management available to native people (Figure 4.1). Thousands of fires can be detected daily on satellite imagery of Amazonia. For most natural scientists and conservationists, fires caused by humans are considered to be the worst threat to Amazonian rainforests and biodiversity. Complex fire histories documented in lake sediment cores, soil stratigraphy, and archaeological sites suggest that humans regularly burned Amazonia in the past (Lehmann et al. 2003; Oliveira and Marquis 2002; Sanford et al. 1985). Anthropogenic fires are distinguished from natural fires by their regularity, context, timing, and patterns (Pyne 1998).

Figure 4.2   Amazonian house, clearing, work areas, and house garden. Fatima in 2006. (Clark Erickson)

Hunters and gatherers burn landscapes to remove old vegetation for new to attract browsing game, clear the understory for easier movement and harvesting of wild plants, encourage economic species attracted to light gaps and disturbance, and hunt game through cooperative drives employing fire and smoke. Farmers employ burning to clear and prepare fields, gardens, orchards, and settlements, fertilize fields, incinerate garbage, and reduce bothersome insects (Pyne 1998). Regular burning prevents runaway fires stoked by accumulated fuel. Burning and the production of charcoal is a key element in the formation of Amazonian Dark Earth (discussed below).

Most scholars now agree that fire plays a key role in the creation and maintenance of Amazonian environments, in particular savannas and dry deciduous forests that cover much of Amazonia (Langstroth 1996; Oliveira and Marquis 2002).

Settlement and associated landscape

Human settlements may be one of the most persistent and permanent transformations of the Amazonian environment. Scholars have recorded a wide variety of settlement types and regional settlement patterns for past and present Amazonian people (Denevan 1996; Durán and Bracco 2000; Erickson 2003; Heckenberger 2005; Neves and Petersen 2006; Roosevelt 1991; Wust and Barreto 1999). While most settlements were small (less than 1 ha), the archaeological site under the present-day city of Santarem in Brazil covers 4 km^2 and the Faldas de Sangay site in Ecuador is possibly 12 km^2 (Roosevelt 1999). Traditional communities had large, open, clean central plazas and streets along which houses were arranged in linear, grid, radial, or ring patterns.

The typical Amazonian house is a simple example of resource use and local landscape transformation (Figure 4.2). The foundation requires 4 to 6 upright wooden posts plus additional beams (each representing a tree). Earthen floors are often raised 10–20 cm for drainage during the wet season (1.5–3.0 m^3 for a 3 × 5 m house). Thick layers of palm and grass thatch cover the roof. A typical Pumé community would require 13,498 fronds of palm which is

Figure 4.3 The Amazonian settlement and adjacent landscape of gardens, fields, agroforestry, roads, paths, orchards, garbage middens, and forest regrowth at various stages. The dark circular feature in the center is a precolumbian ring ditch site. Jasiaquiri, Baures in 2006. (Clark Erickson)

replaced every 2 to 3 years, and 750,000 fronds from 125,000 palms for a large communal house of the Bari (Gragson 1992). Vegetation around the house is cleared to bare ground for protection against snakes and for aesthetic reasons. A small but densely packed house garden is established for spices, colorants and dyes, medicinal plants, tobacco, cotton, hallucinogens, and fish poisons. The garden is also a compost pile for kitchen waste. In humid tropical regions, houses last 5 to 10 years. In summary, the environmental impact of a single house is profound: rearranging and altering soils, accumulation of organic matter through garbage and human wastes, deforestation and opening of forest canopy, cutting of construction and roofing materials, replacement of natural vegetation with economic garden, crop, and orchard species, and mixing of the soil horizons. Denevan (2001) estimates a pre-European conquest native population of 6.8 million for Amazonia. Assuming 5 people per household, some 1,360,000 houses were required in a single moment. The

environmental impact described above for a single household is now multiplied by over one million houses across the landscape.

House gardens were associated with individual residences and there was a larger clearing for staple crops in the forest with raised fields in savannas and wetlands or on exposed river banks beyond the settlement. Stream channels and wetlands were criss-crossed with fish weirs (corrals for harvesting fish). Any standing forest within a 5-km radius was a managed forest. Pathways were hacked through the forest and roads within settlements were often raised or defined by earthen berms, and other infrastructure. In the savannas, large earthen causeways with adjacent canals served as roads and canoe paths. In addition, each settlement required firewood, game, fish, and other wild resources in quantity.

A community's permanent transformation of the environment for these basic needs and infrastructure is staggering (Figure 4.3). As a result, the forested environments that are typical today were scarce in the past and of a much different character. Based on the archaeology, these communities were stable, long-lived, and sustainable despite this impact.

Mounds

Many Amazonian cultures were impressive mound builders (Denevan 1966; Durán and Bracco 2000; Erickson and Balée 2006). Farmers built mounds in the Llanos de Mojos of Bolivia, Marajo Island and the lower and central Amazon basin and Pantanal of Brazil, the Llanos de Venezuela, Mompos basin of Colombia, Sangay in the Upano Valley and Guayas Basin of Ecuador, and the coastal plains of Guyana, Brazil, Uruguay, and Ecuador. Mounds were constructed of earth, with the exception of the *sambaquis* of coastal Brazil, which are primarily of shell. Excavations show that many mounds served multiple functions, often simultaneously. Mounds generally contain fill or layers of domestic debris (bones, shell, and other organic food remains, pottery, and stone tools) typical of settlements. Some mounds have such a high percentage of broken pottery that scholars apply the term "potsherd soils" (Langstroth 1996). Mounds were formed over considerable time through the collapse and leveling of wattle and daub buildings, accumulation of refuse and construction debris, and the intentional addition of fill from adjacent large borrow pits, often filled with water. Mounds in the Llanos de Mojos and on Marajo Island contain hundreds of human burials in which a large pottery urn with lid was used for a coffin (Nordenskiöld 1913; Roosevelt 1991). Other mounds were used as chiefly residences or ceremonial centers (Rostain 1999).

Although most are small, the Ibibate Mound Complex in the Bolivian Amazon covers 11 ha and is 18 m tall with over 250,000 m³ of fill (Erickson and Balée 2006). Mounds are often found in groups of up to 40 for Marajo Island (Roosevelt 1991), and more than 50 mounds for the Huapula site (Rostain 1999). Mounds, as highly visible monumental features on the landscape, were probably a source of civic pride, a place where ancestors were buried in urn coffins, and an elevated spot above annual floodwaters to establish residences, gardens, cemeteries,

ceremonial centers, elite complexes, and public space.

Mound construction required mass movement of soils, transformation of local topography, soil enrichment, and change in vegetation composition. Our study of the Ibibate Mound Complex in the Bolivian Amazon demonstrates that the biodiversity on the mounds was much significantly richer than that of the surrounding landscape and consists primarily of economic species, some 400 years after abandonment as a settlement (Erickson and Balée 2006).

Anthropogenic forest islands

Forest islands are common throughout the savannas and wetlands of Amazonia (Figure 4.4). Forest islands range in size from a few hectares to many square kilometers. Most are raised less than one meter and often surrounded by ponds or a moat-like ditch. Excavations in forest islands in the Llanos de Mojos and Pantanal document their anthropogenic origins and use for settlement, farming, and agroforestry (Erickson 2000a, 2006; Langstroth 1996; Walker 2004). In Bolivia, archaeologists estimate the existence of 10,000 forest islands (CEAM 2003; Lee 1995). The Kayapó of Central Brazil create forest islands (*apêtê*) of improved soils through additions of organic matter from household middens and recycling of crop debris for intensive cultivation of crops (Hecht 2003; Posey 2004). These anthropogenic features are known for their high biodiversity and agrodiversity.

Ring ditch sites

Ring ditch sites are reported in the Bolivian Amazon (Figure 4.5), Matto Grosso, Acre, and Upper Xingu River regions (Erickson 2002; Heckenberger 2005; Parssinen et al. 2003; Ranzi and Aguiar 2004). These sites consist of a closed or U-shaped ditched enclosure or multiple ditches. Heckenberger (2005) describes numerous sites with large open plazas and radial roads marked by earthen berms extending through residential sectors enclosed by deep semicircular moat-like ditches and embankments. Early explorers described villages that were protected by wooden palisades and moats. If palisaded, a typical ring

Figure 4.4   Forest island in the savanna, Machupo River, in 2006. (Clark Erickson)

Figure 4.5   Pre-Columbian ring ditch site. The main ditch is approximately 3 m deep. A smaller ditch can be seen to the left. Baures in 2006. (Clark Erickson)

ditch site would require of hundreds or thousands of tree trunks, a considerable environmental impact.

Ring ditch sites in Acre and the Bolivian Amazon, described as geoglyphs because of their impressive patterns (circular, oval, octagon, square, rectangle, and D-shapes), appear to be more ceremonial than residential or defensive (Figure 4.6). Some ring ditch sites are associated with ADE. Modern farmers in the Bolivian Amazon intensively farm these sites and those covered with forest are good locations for hunting game and gathering fruit.

Amazonian Dark Earth (ADE)

As discussed earlier, soils have been central in debates about environmental potential and cultural development in Amazonia and play a major role in enhancing resource biodiversity and biomass. Rather than adapt to limited soils, we now recognize the ability of Amazonian farmers to improve and manage marginal tropical soils through creation of settlement mounds, forest islands, raised fields, and Amazonian Dark Earth (ADE).

ADE or Indian black earth (*terra preta do indio*) is an important subclass of anthrosols or

Figure 4.6 An octagon-shaped ring ditch site in the Bolivian Amazon. The ditch measures 108 m in diameter and 2 m deep. Santiago, Baures in 2006. (Clark Erickson)

anthropogenic soils and associated with archaeological sites (Erickson 2003; Glaser and Woods 2004; Lehmann et al. 2003; Neves and Petersen 2006; Smith 1980). A lighter color ADE, *terra mulata*, often surrounds *terra preta*. ADE is estimated to cover between 0.1 to 10% or 6000 to 600,000 km^2 of the Amazon basin. ADE sites range from less than one hectare to as large as 200 ha in size. ADE was probably used for settlement, house gardens, and permanent fields rather than slash-and-burn agriculture, the common practice today. Scholars believe that these soils were created specifically for permanent farming. Today ADE is prized by farmers for cultivation and in some cases, mined as potting soil for markets in Brazilian cities.

ADE is rich in typical domestic debris found in archaeological sites including potsherds, bone, fish scales, shell, and charcoal. The extremely dark color and fertility is due to large quantities of charcoal and other organic remains that sharply contrast to the surrounding poor reddish tropical soils. In contrast to slash-and-burn agriculture, where complete combustion of felled forest is the goal, ADE farmers practiced "slash

and char," a technique to produce biochar or charcoal through low temperature, incomplete combustion in a reduced atmosphere. Biochar has been shown to be a high-quality soil amendment for enhancing and maintaining soil fertility over hundreds of years. In addition, ADE is a rich habitat for beneficial microorganisms. Once established, ADE is a living entity that may sustain and reproduce itself (Woods and McCann 1999). The presence of intact ADE after 400 to 500 years is evidence of its permanence, sustainability and resilience. Ethnobotanical studies document high biodiversity on ADE (Balée 1989; Smith 1980). The number of soil microorganisms in ADE alone may be quite large. Although understudied, potential contribution of microorganisms in ADE to overall biodiversity is substantial.

If ADE was formed as the simple unintentional byproduct of long-term residence in a locale, we would expect to find black earth sites at any location where past human occupation was dense and of long duration. Archaeological sites fitting these criteria are common throughout Amazonia but do not have ADE. This

Figure 4.7   Pre-Columbian raised fields, canals, and causeways in the Bolivian Amazon. The clearing is now a ranch and the causeways are used as paths. San Ignacio in 2006. (Clark Erickson)

suggests that ADE formation, which involves careful production of biochar and management of soil microorganisms, is intentional soil engineering. ADE is an excellent example of landscape domestication below the ground.

Raised fields

Raised fields are probably the most impressive example of landscape engineering at a regional scale in Amazonia (Denevan 1966, 2001; Erickson 1995, 2006; Walker 2004). Raised fields are large platforms of earth raised in seasonally flooded savannas and permanent wetlands for cultivating crops (Figure 4.7). Excavations and agricultural experiments suggest that raised fields served multiple functions, including drainage of waterlogged soils, improvement of crop conditions (soil aeration, mixing of horizons, and doubling of topsoil), water management (drainage and irrigation), and nutrient production, capture, and recycling in canals alongside each platform. Crop production in experimental raised fields is impressive and up to double that of non-raised fields (Erickson 1995, 2006;

Saavedra 2006; Stab and Arce 2000). Based on high productivity and substantial labor costs to construct, raised fields were probably in continuous production. In addition to traditional crop cultivation on the platforms, aquatic resources such as edible fish, snails, reptiles, and amphibians could be raised in the adjacent canals. Canals also trap organic sediments and produce organic "green manure" and "muck" that can be periodically added to the platforms for sustained cropping.

Raised field agriculture represents a massive landscape transformation at a regional scale through rearranging soils, changing hydrology, and imposing a heterogeneous micro-topography of alternating terrestrial and aquatic ecosystems on landscapes that originally were relatively flat and biologically homogeneous and of limited production. Landscape engineering of this magnitude substantially increased biodiversity and biomass in savannas and wetlands. The presence of raised fields in deep forests of the Bolivian Amazon suggests that the landscape was open savanna maintained by regular burning when the fields were used. After abandonment and

Figure 4.8 Four pre-Columbian causeways and canals connecting forest islands in the Bolivian Amazon. The palm covered causeways are 3 to 4 m wide and 1 m tall with adjacent canals of 2 to 3 m wide and 1 m deep. Baures in 2006. (Clark Erickson)

cessation of burning, forests returned with trees arranged in orchard-like rows on the eroded raised fields.

Transportation and communication networks and water management

Transportation and communication networks in the present and past have significant environmental impacts at the local and regional scale. Paths, trails, and roads connect settlements and people and, like modern roads, bring development and new settlements, expand farming, and cause environmental change. All Amazonian societies use elaborate networks of paths and trails and roads between settlements, gardens, fields, rivers, resource locations, and neighbors. The Kayapó maintain thousands of kilometers of paths (Posey in Denevan 1990). Posey (2004) documents subtle anthropogenic impact along Kayapó paths created by the discard of seeds from meals and snacks and transplanting of economic species along path clearings. These resources also attract game animals, making

them easier to find and hunt. The long linear disturbance and light gap created by clearing and maintenance of paths produces distinct anthropogenic vegetation communities that penetrate deep into the forest.

Some advanced Amazonian societies built impressive formal roads, causeways, and canals of monumental scale (Figure 4.8). Large and small sites in the Tapajós and the Upper Xingú regions are connected by traces of networks of straight roads with earthen berms suggesting hierarchical socio-political organization at a regional scale (Heckenberger 2005; Nimuendajú 1952). The earliest explorers of the Amazon River reported similar wide straight roads connecting large riverine settlements to the distant hinterlands (Denevan 1990).

The late pre-Columbian inhabitants of the Llanos de Mojos and Baures regions in the Bolivian Amazon completely transformed the environment into a highly patterned landscape of complex networks of raised earthen causeways and canals (Denevan 1990; Erickson 2001, [2009]). These earthworks had multiple functions including transportation and communication, water management and production of aquatic resources, boundary and territorial markers, and as monumental ritual and political statements. Their construction was often intended for water management and the creation of artificial wetlands at the local and regional scale. On near flat savanna, a causeway of 1 m tall and 2 km long between the high ground of two adjacent river levees could potentially impound 5 million m³ of water. Canals brought water for irrigation and provided drainage when necessary.

Amazonians are classic canoe people and transport and communication by water is a basic element of tropical forest culture (Lathrap 1970; Lowie 1948). Most Amazonian people would rather paddle a canoe than walk. Nordenskiöld (1916) pointed out that most of the major headwaters of Amazonian river drainages connect to the headwaters of adjacent river drainages. Some of these aquatic connections, such as the Casquiare Canal between the major Negro and Orinoco drainages and the Pantanal between the Guaporé and the Paraguay drainages, are partially anthropogenic. Artificial river meander short cuts are common in the Llanos de Mojos of the Bolivian Amazon, Amapá Region of the Central Amazon basin, and the Ucayali River of Peru (Abizaid 2005; Denevan 1966; Nordenskiöld 1916; Raffles and Winkler-Prins 2003). The large meander loops of typical rivers of Amazonia are challenges to canoeists, often requiring hours or even days of paddling to move short lineal distances. The problem is solved by cutting short linear canals or repeatedly dragging a heavy dugout canoe in the same location between the neck of a large looping meander to save travel time. In a number of cases, these anthropogenic canals created a new river course, dramatically and permanently changing the regional hydrology.

Inter-river canals are common in the Llanos de Mojos of Bolivia. Pinto (1987) describes a complex network of natural channels combined with artificial canals to allow canoe traffic over 120 km perpendicular to natural river flow. In other cases, artificial canals tapping the headwaters of two adjacent rivers diverted the flow of one into the other permanently transforming the hydrology of two drainage basins (CEAM 2003).

travelling by water (canoeing)

Fisheries management

Fishing is now recognized as the major traditional source of protein in the Amazon basin (Beckerman 1979; Chernela 1993; Erickson 2000b). In contrast to other civilizations that domesticated fish, Amazonian people artificially enhanced the natural habitats of wild fish to increase availability through creation of artificial wetlands and expanding the capacity of existing wetlands through construction of raised field canals, causeways and other water management techniques.

The Baures region of Bolivia is an excellent example of landscape domestication for the improvement of natural fisheries (Erickson 2000b). Low linear earthen ridges zigzag across the seasonally inundated savannas between forest islands with funnel-like opening located where the earthworks changed direction (Figure 4.9). These features are identified as fish weirs based on descriptions in the ethnographic and historical literature. Fish weirs are fences made of wood, brush, basketry, or stones that extend across bodies of water. Baskets or nets are placed in openings to trap migrating fish. Most fish weirs are simple ephemeral structures on a river or shallow lake. In contrast, the fish weirs of Baures are permanent earthen features covering more than 550 km². Small artificial ponds associated with the weirs are filled with fish and other aquatic foods when the floodwaters recede. These were probably used to store live fish. Through fisheries management, the native people of Baures transformed savannas and wetlands into a productive landscape capable of providing hundreds of tons of protein to sustain large populations.

Agroforestry

Countering the view of Amazonian forests as pristine and natural, historical ecologists show that these forests are, to a large degree, the cultural products of human activity (Balée 1989; Denevan and Padoch 1988; Posey 2004; Posey and Balée 1989). Amazonian people past and present practiced agroforestry: tree cultivation and forest management (Peters 2000).

Analysis of pollen, opal phytolith, and sediment from lakes documents local and regional

Figure 4.9 A network of pre-Columbian fish weirs in the Bolivian Amazon. The brush-covered fish weirs measure 1 m wide and 50 cm tall. Straight features at the top and bottom of the image are causeways and canals, and circular features are artificial fish ponds. Baures in 1999. (Clark Erickson)

anthropogenic disturbances of Amazonia over thousands of years, including burning, clearing, farming, and agroforestry (Mora 2003; Piperno and Pearsall 1998; Piperno et al. 2000). Much of what was originally misinterpreted as natural change due to climate fluctuations is now considered anthropogenic. Records show a steady increase of "weeds" and secondary forest species, many of which are economic species, and later domesticated crops that thrive in open conditions and heterogeneous mosaic of forest and savanna and intermediate states created by human disturbance. At the same time, the frequency of species characteristic of closed canopy forests decreases until the demographic collapse after 1492. Fire histories are also documented in association with the formation of the anthropogenic forest. Evidence of fruit and nut tree use and human disturbance is documented by 10,500 years ago in the Central Amazon (and see discussion of dates in the Colombian Amazon in Mora 2003; Roosevelt et al. 1996; see discussion of evidence for domesticated crops at some sites in Amazonia in Piperno and Pearsall 1998; Piperno et al. 2000).

The long-term strategy of forest management was to cull non-economic species and replace them with economic species. Sometimes, this involves simple thinning, planting, transplanting, fertilizing, coppicing, and weeding of valued species to enhance their productivity and availability. Many wild plants are often found outside their natural range due to transplanting, cultivation, and habitat improvements. In other cases, wild and domesticated trees are tended as orchards. Useful plants that in the distant past relied on natural forces now depend increasingly on humans for seed dispersal, survival, and reproduction.

Slash-and-burn agriculture is characterized by low labor inputs, limited productivity per land unit, and short period of cultivation followed by longer periods of fallow or rest. Historical ecologists point out that slash-and-burn fields are never truly abandoned and unproductive during fallow. In Amazonia, agriculture is combined with agroforestry. In the initial cutting and burning to clear a field or garden, certain economic species are left to thrive while unwanted species are removed. In addition to basic food crops, useful fruit and palms are often transplanted to the clearing. As fields fall out of cultivation because of weeds and forest regrowth, the plots continue to produce useful products, long after "abandonment".

Anthropogenic forests are filled with fruit trees, an important component of agroforestry. Eighty native fruit trees were domesticated or semi-domesticated in Amazonia. [...] Fruit trees, originally requiring seed-dispersing frugivores attracted to the juicy and starchy fruits, became increasingly dependent on humans through genetic domestication and landscape domestication for survival and reproduction. In addition, humans improved fruit tree availability, productivity, protein content, sweetness, and storability through genetic selection. Oligarchic forests, characterized by a single tree species, often a palm, provide mass quantities of protein and building materials, and food for the game animals. In the Bolivian Amazon, thousands of kilometers of the burití palm, the Amazonian tree of life, contributes protein and materials for buildings, basketry, weapons, and roofing. Forest islands of chocolate trees are agro-forestry resource legacies of the past inhabitants of the region (Erickson 2006).

Agroforestry and farming also attract game animals that eat the abundant crops, fruits, and nuts. Farmers often grow more food than necessary to attract game. As a result, "garden hunting" is a particularly efficient (Linares 1976). Many game animals of Amazonia would have a difficult time surviving without a cultural and historical landscape of human gardens, fields, orchards, and agroforestry. The biodiversity of animals can also be enhanced by domestication of landscape. In coastal Ecuador, Stahl (2000, 2006) reconstructs biodiversity and the character of the anthropogenic environment through the remains of diverse animals in garbage middens of 4,000-year old settlements. The majority of identified animals thrive in a disturbed mosaic environment with light gaps, edges, old gardens and field clearings.

Even hunters and gatherers contribute to anthropogenic forests. The nomadic Nukak of the Colombian Amazon change campsites 70 to 80 times a year (Politis 1996). When establishing a new location, a small number of trees are felled and hundreds of palm fronds are collected for construction of a simple lean-to structure. Wild fruits and nuts are collected and some end up discarded. After the camp is abandoned, palm seeds take root in the clearing and thrive. Repeated over hundreds of years, the selective cutting of trees for nomadic camps, creation of small light gaps or openings, and distribution of seeds can substantially change the forest composition to one rich in economic species of plants and animals.

While agroforestry focuses on management of certain economic species, studies show that overall biodiversity may be enhanced in anthropogenic forests (Balée 1994, 2006; Peters 2000). The Ibibate Mound Complex in the Bolivian Amazon is a well-studied case of a biologically diverse anthropogenic forest (Erickson and Balée 2006). Surveys of forest growing on pre-Columbian mounds abandoned 400 years earlier and non-mounds were compared showing a significantly higher biodiversity in forest on the mounds, in addition to non-local economic species. Economic studies show that anthropogenic forests are more valuable for sustainable collection of renewable resources than logging (Balick and Mendelsohn 1992).

Conclusions: Lessons from the Past?

Western environmental history is characterized by humans, especially those living in farming and urban societies, who overexploit and degrade the environment. Some scholars now argue that environmental catastrophes are an ancient rather than recent historical phenomenon. Other scholars contrast the environmental failures of Western civilization to non-Western societies practicing efficient, productive, and sustainable strategies. Another group declares this a myth and that all human activities are negative for the environment. Rather than assume that humans are either *Homo ecologicus* or *Homo devastans*, historical ecologists attempt to evaluate these debates through careful investigation of particular case studies at multiple scales of analysis.

Amazonian Dark Earths, agroforestry, raised field agriculture, transportation and communication networks, urban settlements, mounds, artificial forest islands, river cutoffs, water control,

Figure 4.10   Pre-Columbian domesticated landscape of settlements, mounds, forest islands, raised fields, causeways, canals, and agroforestry. (Artwork by The Monkey Project)

Figure 4.11   Pre-columbian raised fields under forest. When the fields were in use, the landscape was treeless. San Ignacio in 2006. (Clark Erickson)

and fisheries management are clear examples of landscape creation, transformation and management by pre-Columbian native people in Amazonia (Figure 4.10). Through the domestication of landscape, native people shaped the landscape as they wanted it and made it work for them. What they transformed was often less productive and biologically diverse than what resulted. In other cases, human activities reduced biodiversity. Most landscapes which are today appreciated for their high biodiversity have evidence of human use and management, even if those landscapes are relatively unoccupied today. Environments with high biodiversity are a result of, rather than in spite of, long human disturbance of the environment.

My Bolivian informants state that the best hunting and farmland is on pre-Columbian earthworks deep in the forests (Figure 4.11). Recognized as having the highest biodiversity in Bolivia, the Tsimane Indigenous Territory is covered with raised fields, causeways, canals, and settlements under what is now continuous forest canopy (Erickson and Walker 2009). These cases of present-day biodiversity, treasured by scholars and the public alike, were ironically created under conditions of intensive farming, urbanized settlement, and dense populations. Anthropologists have recently pointed out that regions

of high biological diversity tend to map onto high cultural diversity (Maffi 2005). These findings contradict the Myth of the Pristine Environment that biodiversity should be associated with an absence of humans. To historical ecologists, this association makes sense.

Were these native practices sustainable? Sustainability usually refers to rational continuous harvest of a resource without destroying the capacity of that resource to reproduce. According to Janzen, sustainable development is "living off the interests rather than consuming the capital" (1997: 413). The longevity of settlements, agriculture, and cultural traditions and the dense populations supported in what are now considered biologically diverse environments are evidence of sustainability.

Are the past strategies of environmental management defined by historical ecology applicable to the modern world? Many goals of pre-Columbian native people, modern inhabitants of Amazonia, scientists, planners, and the general public coincide: the management of environmental resources for a comfortable life and sustainable future in what most consider a fragile ecosystem. Increasingly, the reservoir of existing biodiversity is found in humanized landscapes. The failure of traditional solutions such as fencing off nature and excluding native people highlights the need for strategies that embrace the co-existence of nature and humans. Environmental management informed by time-tested strategies for specific landscapes may be more appropriate than existing solutions. Because humans played a role in the creation of present-day biodiversity, solutions will have to include people.

ADE as a means to mitigate global warming is an example of applied historical ecology. Low-temperature biochar or charcoal, the key ingredient of ADE, and ammonium bicarbonate produced from urban wastes are the byproducts of biofuel production. Burial of biochar treated with ammonium bicarbonate is an excellent nitrogen based organic fertilizer *and* an ideal form of carbon sequestration (Marris 2006). Controlled burning, traditionally considered degrading to the environment, is being re-introduced as a management strategy in many biodiversity reserves. Once removed from their homelands in the establishment of parks, native people are now integral participants in the management of some ecological reserves and indigenous territories (Chapin 2004; Posey 2004). Many small farmers living along the Amazon River continue to practice sustainable strategies from the past within a modern urban context (Smith 1999).

Conservationists seek to protect what they advertise as pristine wilderness. Therefore, many conservationists regard as dangerous and detrimental to their fundraising the idea that humans created, transformed, and managed biodiversity (Chapin 2004). Native rights advocates worry that Amazonian people will be viewed as "bad" by Westerners in terms of environmental stewardship and lose claims and control of indigenous territories (Chapin 2004; Conklin and Graham 1995; Redford 1991). Others declare that historical ecologists who argue against the ideas of the Amazon as a counterfeit paradise fan the flames of tropical rainforest destruction by encouraging reckless development of already transformed landscapes (Meggers 2001).

Historical ecologists respond that ignoring the complex human history of environments in Amazonia would be unwise. A vast indigenous knowledge spanning hundreds of generations about the creation, transformation, and management of environments is physically embedded in the landscape, encoded in the distribution and availability of plant and animal species, documented in historical and ethnographic accounts, and in some cases, still practiced by native Amazonians.

References

Abizaid, Christian, 2005, An anthropogenic meander cutoff along the Ucayali River, Peruvian Amazon. *The Geographical Review* 95 (1): 122–135.

Alvard, Michael S., 1995, Intraspecific prey choice by Amazonian hunters. *Current Anthropology* 36: 789–818.

Ashmore, Wendy and A. Bernard Knapp (eds.), 1999, *Archaeologies of Landscape: Contemporary Perspectives*. Blackwell, Malden, MA.

Balée, William A., 1989, The culture of Amazonian forests. *Advances in Economic Botany* 7: 1–21.

Balée, William A., 1994, *Footprints of the Forest: Ka'apor Ethnobotany – the Historical Ecology of Plant Utilization by an Amazonian People*. Columbia University Press, New York.

Balée, William A., (ed.), 1998, *Advances in Historical Ecology*. Columbia University Press, New York.

Balée, William A., 2006, The research program of historical ecology. *Annual Review of Anthropology* 35: 1–24.

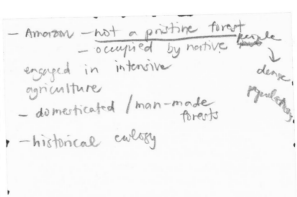

impacts in the Near East. In *Nature's Geography: New Lessons for Conservation in Developing Countries*, edited by Karl Zimmerer and Kenneth Young, pp. 215–236. University of Wisconsin Press, Madison.

Botkin, Daniel, 1990, *Discordant Harmonies: A New Ecology for the Twenty-First Century*. Oxford University Press, New York.

Brookfield, Harold, 2001, *Exploring Agrodiversity*. Columbia University Press, New York.

Carneiro, Robert, 1960, Slash and burn agriculture: a closer look at its implications for settlement patterns. In *Men and Cultures*, edited by Anthony Wallace, pp. 229–232. Philadelphia.

CEAM, 2003, *Moxos: Una Limnocultura*. Centre d'Estudis Amazonics, Barcelona.

Chagnon, N. and R. Hames, 1979, Protein deficiency and tribal warfare in Amazonia: new data. *Science* 203: 910–913.

Chapin, Mac, 2004, A challenge to conservationists. *World Watch* November-December pp. 17–31.

Chernela, Janet, 1993, *The Wanano Indians of the Brazilian Amazon: A Sense of Space*. University of Texas Press, Austin.

Clements, F. E., 1916, *Plant Succession: An Analysis of the Development of Vegetation*. Carnegie Institute of Washington, Washington, D.C.

Connell, Joseph H., 1978, Diversity in tropical forests and coral reefs. *Science* 199: 1302–1310.

Conklin, Beth A. and Laura Graham, 1995, The shifting middle ground: Amazonian Indians and eco-politics. *American Anthropologist* 97 (4): 695–710.

Crumley, Carole L. (ed.), 1994, *Historical Ecology: Cultural Knowledge and Changing Landscapes*. School of American Research, Santa Fe.

DeBoer, Warren R., Keith Kintigh, and Arthur Rostoker, 1996, Ceramic seriation and settlement reoccupation in lowland South America. *Latin American Antiquity* 7 (3): 263–278.

Denevan, William M., 1966, *The Aboriginal Cultural Geography of the Llanos de Mojos of Bolivia*. University of California Press, Berkeley.

Denevan, William M., 1990, Prehistoric roads and causeways in lowland tropical America. In *Ancient Road Networks and Settlement Hierarchies in the New World*, edited by Charles Trombold, pp. 230–242. Cambridge University Press, Cambridge.

Denevan, William M., 1992, The pristine myth: the landscape of the Americas in 1492. *Annals of the Association of American Geographers* 82: 369–385.

Denevan, William M., 1996, A bluff model of riverine settlement in prehistoric Amazonia. *Annals of the Association of American Geographers* 86 (4): 654–681.

Denevan, William M., 2001, *Cultivated Landscapes of Native Amazonia and the Andes*. Oxford University Press, Oxford.

Denevan, William M., and Christine Padoch (eds.), 1988, *Swidden-fallow Agroforestry in the Peruvian Amazon*. Advances in Economic Botany. Volume 5, New York Botanical Gardens, New York.

Dirzo, Rodolfo and Peter H. Raven, 2003, Global state of biodiversity and loss. *Annual Review of Environment and Resources* 28: 137–167.

Durán Coirolo, Alicia and Roberto Bracco Boksar (eds.), 2000, *La Arqueología de las Tierras Bajas*. Comisión Nacional de Arqueología, Ministerio de Educación y Cultura, Montevideo, Uruguay.

Erickson, Clark L., 1995, Archaeological perspectives on ancient landscapes of the Llanos de Mojos in the Bolivian Amazon. In *Archaeology in the American Tropics: Current Analytical Methods and Applications*, edited by Peter W. Stahl, pp. 66–95. Cambridge University Press, Cambridge.

Erickson, Clark L., 2000a, Lomas de ocupación en los Llanos de Moxos. In *La Arqueología de las Tierras Bajas*, edited by Alicia Durán Coirolo and Roberto Bracco Boksar, pp. 207–226. Comisión Nacional de Arqueología, Ministerio de Educación y Cultura, Montevideo, Uruguay.

Erickson, Clark L., 2000b, An artificial landscape-scale fishery in the Bolivian Amazon. *Nature* 408: 190–193.

Erickson, Clark L., 2001, Pre-columbian roads of the Amazon. *Expedition* 43 (2): 21–30.

Erickson, Clark L., 2002, *Large Moated Settlements: A Late Pre-Columbian Phenomenon in the Amazon*. Paper presented at the 2nd Annual Meeting of The Society for the Anthropology of Lowland South America (SALSA). St. Johns College, Annapolis, Maryland.

Erickson, Clark L., 2003, Historical ecology and future explorations. In *Amazonian Dark Earths: Origin, Properties, Management*, edited by Johannes Lehmann, Dirse C. Kern, Bruno Glaser, and William I. Woods, pp. 455–500. Kluwer, Dordrecht.

Erickson, Clark L., 2006, The domesticated landscapes of the Bolivian Amazon. In *Time and Complexity in Historical Ecology: Studies in the Neotropical Lowlands*, edited by William Balée and Clark Erickson, pp. 235–278. Columbia University Press, New York.

Erickson, Clark L., 2009, Agency, roads, and the landscapes of everyday life in the Bolivian Amazon. In *Landscapes of Movement: The Anthropology of Roads, Paths, and Trails*, edited by James Snead, Clark Erickson, and Andy Darling, University of Pennsylvania Museum of Archaeology and Anthropology Press, Philadelphia.

Erickson, Clark L., and William Balée, 2006, The historical ecology of a complex landscape in Bolivia. In *Time and Complexity in Historical Ecology: Studies in the Neotropical Lowlands*, edited by William Balée and Clark Erickson, pp. 187–234. Columbia University Press, New York.

Erickson, Clark L., and John H. Walker, 2009, Precolumbian roads as landscape capital. In *Landscapes of Movement: The Anthropology of Roads, Paths, and Trails*, edited by James Snead, Clark Erickson, and Andy Darling, University of Pennsylvania Museum of Archaeology and Anthropology Press, Philadelphia.

Glaser, Bruno and William Woods (eds.), 2004, *Explorations in Amazonian Dark Earths in Time and Space*. Springer-Verlag, Heidelberg.

Goulding, Michael, Ronaldo Barthem and Efrem Ferreira, 2003, *The Smithsonian Atlas of the Amazon*. Smithsonian Institution Press, Washington D.C.

Gragson, Ted L., 1992, The use of palms by the Pume Indians of Southwestern Venezuela. *Principes* 36: 133–142.

Gross, Daniel, 1975, Protein capture and cultural development in the Amazon Basin. *American Anthropologist* 77 (3): 526–549.

Hayashida, Frances, 2005, Archaeology, ecological history, and conservation. *Annual Review of Anthropology* 34: 43–65.

Hecht, Suzanna, 2003, Indigenous soil management and the creation of Amazonian Dark Earths: implications of Kayapó practices. In *Amazonian Dark Earths: Origin, Properties, Management*, edited by Johannes Lehmann, Dirse C. Kern, Bruno Glaser, and William I. Woods, pp. 355–372. Kluwer Academic Publishers, Netherlands.

Heckenberger, Michael J., 1998, Manioc agriculture and sedentism in Amazonia: the Upper Xingu example. *Antiquity* 72 (277): 633–648.

Heckenberger, Michael J., 2005, *The Ecology of Power. Culture, Place, and Personhood in the Southern Amazon A.D. 1000–2000*. Routledge, New York.

Heckenberger, Michael J., Afukaka Kuikuro, Urissapá Tabata Kuikuro, J. Christian Russell, Morgan Schmidt, Carlos Fausto, and Bruna Franchetto, 2003, Amazonia 1492: pristine forest or cultural parkland? *Science* 301: 1710–1714.

Hiraoka, Mario, 1985, Floodplain farming in the Peruvian Amazon. *Geographical Review of Japan*. 58 (Ser. B): 1: 1–23.

Iriarte, Jose, Irene Holst, Oscar Marozzi, Claudia Listopad, Eduardo Alonso, Andrés Rinderknecht, and Juan Montaña, 2004, Evidence for cultivar adoption and emerging complexity during the mid-Holocene in the La Plata basin. *Nature* 432: 614–617.

Janzen, Daniel H., 1997, Wildland biodiversity management in the tropics. In *Biodiversity II: Understanding and Protecting our Biological Resources*, edited by Marjorie Reaka-Kudla, Don Wilson, and Edward O. Wilson, pp. 411–431. Joseph Henry Press, Washington D.C.

Langstroth, Robert, 1996, Forest Islands in an Amazonian savanna of Northeastern-Bolivia. Ph.D. dissertation. Department of Geography, University of Wisconsin, Madison.

Lathrap, Donald W., 1970, *The Upper Amazon*. Praeger, New York.

Lathrap, Donald W., 1973, The antiquity and importance of long-distance trade relationships in the moist tropics of pre-Columbian South America. *World Archaeology* 5 (2): 170–86.

Lathrap, Donald W., 1974, The moist tropics, the arid lands, and the appearance of great art styles in the New World. *The Museum of Texas Tech University*, Special Publication No. 7, pp. 115–158. Lubbock.

Lathrap, Donald W., 1987, The introduction of maize in prehistoric eastern North America: the view from Amazonia and the Santa Elena Peninsula. In *Emergent Horticultural Economies of the Eastern Woodlands*, edited by William F. Keegan, pp. 345–371. Southern Illinois University, Center for Archaeological Investigations, Occasional Paper 7, Carbondale.

Lathrap, Donald W., A. Gebhart-Sayer, and Ann Mester, 1985, The roots of the Shipibo art style: three waves on Imiriacocha or there were Incas before the Incas. *Journal of Latin American Lore* 11 (1): 31–119.

Lee, Kenneth, 1995, Apuntes sobre las Obras Hidráulicas Prehispánicas de las Llanuras de Moxos: Una Opción Ecológica Inédita. Unpublished manuscript. Trinidad, Bolivia.

Lehmann, Johannes, Dirse C. Kern, Bruno Glaser, and William I. Woods (eds.), 2003, *Amazonian Dark Earths: Origin, Properties, Management*. Kluwer, Dordrecht.

Linares, Olga, 1976, "Garden hunting" in the American tropics. *Human Ecology* 4: 331–349.

Lowie, Robert, 1948, The tropical forest: An Introduction. In *Handbook of South American Indians Vol. 3: The Tropical Forest Tribes*, edited by Julian Steward, pp. 1–56. Smithsonian Institution Bureau of American Ethnology, Bulletin No. 143. Washington, D.C.

Maffi, Luisa, 2005, Linguistic, cultural, and biological diversity. *Annual Review of Anthropology* 29: 599–617.

Marris, Emma, 2006, Black is the new green. *Nature* 442: 624–626.

Meggers, Betty J., 1954, Environmental limitations on the development of culture. *American Anthropologist* 56: 801–824.

Meggers, Betty J., 1971, *Amazonia: Man and Culture in a Counterfeit Paradise*. Aldine, Chicago.

Meggers, Betty J., 1979, Climatic oscillation as a factor in the prehistory of Amazonia. *American Antiquity* 44: 252–266.

Meggers, Betty J., 1995, Amazonia on the eve of European contact: ethnohistorical, ecological, and anthropological perspectives. *Revista de Arqueología Americana* 8: 91–115.

Meggers, Betty J., 2001, The continuing quest for El Dorado: round two. *Latin American Antiquity* 12: 304–325.

Mora, Santiago, 2003, *Early Inhabitants of the Amazonian Tropical Rain Forest: A Study of Humans and Environmental Dynamics*. University of Pittsburgh Latin American Archaeology Reports, No. 3, Pittsburgh.

Moran, Emilio F., 1982, *Human Adaptability: An Introduction to Ecological Anthropology*. Westview Press, Boulder.

Moran, Emilio F., 1993, *Through Amazonian Eyes: The Human Ecology of Amazonian Populations*. University of Iowa Press, Iowa City.

Neves, Eduardo G. and James B. Petersen, 2006, Political economy and pre-columbian landscape transformation in Central Amazonia. In *Time and Complexity in Historical Ecology: Studies in the Neotropical Lowlands*, edited by William Balée and Clark L. Erickson, pp. 279–310. Columbia University Press, New York,

Nimuendajú, Curt, 1952, The Tapajo. *Kroeber Anthropological Society Papers*. 6:1–25.

Nordenskiöld, Erland, 1913. Urnengraber und Mounds im Bolivianischen Flachlande. *Baessler Archiv* 3: 205–255. Berlin y Leipzig.

Nordenskiöld, Erland, 1916, Die Anpassung der Indianer an die Verhältnisse in den Uberschwemmungsgebieten in Südamerika. *Ymer* 36. 138–155. Stockholm.

Oliveira, Paulo S. and Robert J. Marquis (eds.), 2002, *The Cerrados of Brazil: Ecology and Natural History of a Neotropical Savanna*. Columbia University Press, New York.

Pärssinen, Martti, Alceu Ranzi, Sanna Saunaluoma, and Ari Siiriäinen, 2003, Geometrically patterned ancient earthworks in the Rio Blanco Region of Acre, Brazil: new evidence of ancient chiefdom formations in Amazonian interfluvial *terra firme* environments. In *Western Amazonia-Amazônia Ocidental: Multidisciplinary Studies on Ancient Expansionistic Movements, Fortifications, and Sedentary Life*, edited by Martti Pärssinen and Antti Korpisaari, pp. 135–172. Helsinki: Renvall Institute Publications No. 14, Renvall Institute for Area and Cultural Studies, University of Helsinki.

Peters, Charles, 2000, Pre-Columbian silviculture and indigenous management of neotropical forests. In *Imperfect Balance: Landscape Transformations in the Pre-Columbian Americas*, edited by David Lentz, pp. 203–223. Columbia University Press, New York.

Pinto Parada, Rodolfo, 1987, *Pueblo de Leyenda*. Tiempo del Bolivia, Trinidad.

Piperno, Dolores R. and Deborah M. Pearsall, 1998. *The Origins of Agriculture in the Lowland Neotropics*. Academic Press, San Diego.

Piperno, Dolores R., Anthony J. Ranere, Irene Holst, and Patricia Hansell, 2000, Starch grains reveal early root crop horticulture in the Panamanian tropical forest. *Nature* 407: 894–897.

Politis, Gustavo, 1996, Moving to produce: Nukak mobility and settlement patterns in Amazonia. *World Archaeology* 27: 492–511.

Posey, Darrell A., 2004, *Indigenous Knowledge and Ethics: A Darrell Posey Reader*, edited by Kristina Plenderleith. Routledge, New York.

Posey, Darrell A., and William Balée (eds.), 1989, *Resource Management in Amazonia: Indigenous and Folk Strategies*. New York Botanical Garden, Bronx, NY.

Pyne, Stephen J., 1998, Forged in fire: history, land, and anthropogenic fire. In *Advances in Historical Ecology*, edited by William Balée, pp. 62–103. Columbia University Press, New York.

Raffles, Hugh and Antoinette Winkler-Prins, 2003, Further reflections on Amazonian environmental history: transformations of rivers and streams. *Latin American Research Review* 38 (3): 165–218.

Ranzi, Alceu and Rodrigo Aguiar, 2004, *Geoglifos da Amazônia: Perspectiva Aérea*. Faculdades Energia, Florianópolis.

Redford, Kent H., 1991, The ecologically noble savage. *Cultural Survival Quarterly* 15 (1): 46–48.

Redman, Charles, 1999, *Human Impact on Ancient Environments*. University of Arizona Press, Tucson.

Roosevelt, Anna C., 1991, *Moundbuilders of the Amazon: Geophysical Archaeology on Marajo Island, Brazil*. Academic Press, New York.

Roosevelt, Anna C., 1999, The development of prehistoric complex societies: Amazonia, a tropical forest. In *Complex Polities in the Ancient Tropical World*, edited by Elisabeth A. Bacus and Lisa J. Lucero, pp. 13–34, Archeological Papers of the American Anthropological Association, Number 9, Arlington, VA.

Roosevelt, Anna C., M. Lima da Costa, C. Lopes Machado, M. Michab, N. Mercier, H. Valladas, J. Feathers, W. Barnett, M. Imazio da Silveira, A Henderson, J. Sliva, B. Chernoff, D. S. Reese, J. A. Holman, N. Toth, and K. Schick, 1996, Paleoindian cave dwellers in the Amazon: the peopling of the Americas. *Science* 272: 373–384.

Rostain, Stéphen, 1999, Secuencia arquéologica en montículos del valle del Upano en la Amazonia ecuatoriana. *Bulletin de l'Institut Français d'Études Andines* 28 (1): 53–89.

Saavedra, Oscar, 2006, El sistema agrícola prehispánico de camellones en la Amazonia boliviana. In *Agricultura Ancestral. Camellones y Albarradas: Contexto Social, Uso, y Retos del Pasado y del Presente*, edited by Francisco Valdez, pp. 295–314. Editorial Abyaaylla, Quito.

Sanford, R. L., J. Saldarriaga, K. Clark, C. Uhl, and R. Herrera, 1985, Amazon rainforest fires. *Science* 227: 53–55.

Smith, Nigel J. H., 1980, Anthrosols and human carrying capacity in Amazonia. *Annals of the Association of American Geographers* 70 (4): 553–566.

Smith, Nigel J. H., 1999, *The Amazon River Forest: A Natural History of Plants, Animals and People.* Oxford University Press, New York.

Stab, Sabina and Julio Arce, 2000, Pre-hispanic raised-field cultivation as an alternative to slash-and-burn agriculture in the Bolivian Amazon: agroecological evaluation of field experiments. In *Biodiversidad, conservación y manejo en la región de la Reserva de la Biosfera Estación Biológica del Beni, Bolivia: Biodiversity, conservation and management in the region of the Beni Biological Station Biosphere Reserve, Bolivia,* edited by Olga Herrera-MacBryde, Francisco Dallmeier, Bruce MacBryde, James A. Comiskey, and Carmen Miranda, pp. 317–327. Smithsonian Institution, SI/MAB Biodiversity Program, Washington, DC.

Stahl, Peter W., 1991, Arid landscapes and environmental transformations in ancient southwestern Ecuador. *World Archaeology* 22 (3): 346–359.

Stahl, Peter W., 1996, Holocene biodiversity: an archaeological perspective from the Americas. *Annual Review of Anthropology* 25: 105–126.

Stahl, Peter W., 2000, Archaeofaunal accumulation, fragmented forests, and anthropogenic landscape mosaics in the tropical lowlands of prehispanic Ecuador. *Latin American Antiquity* 11 (3): 241–257.

Stahl, Peter W., 2006, Microvertebrate synecology and anthropogenic footprints in the forested neotropics.

In *Time and Complexity in Historical Ecology: Studies from the Neotropical Lowlands,* edited by William Balée and Clark Erickson, pp. 127–149. Columbia University Press, New York.

Steward, Julian H. (ed.), 1948, *Handbook of South American Indians, Vol. 3: The Tropical Forest Tribes.* Smithsonian Institution Bureau of American Ethnology, Bulletin No. 143. Washington, D.C.

Sutton, Mark O. and E. N. Anderson, 2004, *Introduction to Cultural Ecology.* AltaMira, Walnut Creek, CA.

Valdez, Francisco (ed.), 2006, *Agricultura Ancestral. Camellones y Albarradas: Contexto Social, Uso, y Retos del Pasado y del Presente.* Editorial Abya-Yala, Quito.

Walker, John H., 2004, *Agricultural Change in the Bolivian Amazon.* Latin American Archaeology Reports, University of Pittsburgh, Pittsburgh.

Whitten, Richard, 1979, Comments on the theory of Holocene refugia in the culture history of Amazonia. *American Antiquity* 44: 238–251.

Woods, W. and J. M. McCann, 1999, The anthropogenic origin and persistence of Amazonian Dark Earths. *Yearbook Conference of Latin Americanist Geographers* 25: 7–14.

Wust, Irmild and Christiana Barreto, 1999, The ring villages of central Brazil: a challenge for Amazonian archaeology. *Latin American Antiquity* 10 (1): 3–23.

Zimmerer, Karl and Kenneth Young (eds.), 1998, *Nature's Geography: New Lessons for Conservation in Developing Countries.* University of Wisconsin Press, Madison.

Part III

Agency, Meaning, and Practice

ONE OF THE KEY DIFFERENCES between processual and postprocessual archaeologies revolves around the issues of agency and structure. With its systemic view of culture, processual archaeology emphasized structure and system at the expense of agency and the individual (Binford 1965, 1972). Cultural change was commonly explained as the result either of an external force such as the environment, or of feedback loops by which the system adjusted to internal or external stimuli. The systemic view of culture was also part of the broader rejection of history in favor of evolutionary process. Lewis Binford (1967:235) famously denied that the reconstruction of the past should be a goal of archaeology since this would relegate it to being a particularistic, non-generalizing field. This view dominated processual archaeology despite Bruce Trigger's (1968, 1970) insistence on history as a legitimate topic that complemented processual archaeology's processual focus. The recent postprocessual embrace of agency and practice can, in some ways, be seen as a return to history. This is part of a larger movement in the human sciences inspired by developments in Continental philosophy and postmodernist theory (Schatzki et al. 2001). Among the more influential theorists are Anthony Giddens and Pierre Bourdieu. Although their approaches differ, each attempted to understand the articulation of larger societal structures and individual behavior.

Giddens's (1979, 1984) theory of structuration posits a recursive relationship between social structures and individual action that characterizes the potential of individuals to effect change in the larger, and often more powerful, structure. In this sense, Giddens differs from Marx, who focused more on the action of groups in his meta-theory of cultural change (Trigger 2006:469). Giddens incorporates some of Foucault's ideas concerning the various forms that power can take and its negative and positive consequences. His theory thus attempts to address the relationship between societal structures, their power, and individual action (Giddens 1979, 1984). He borrows from Marx the idea of dialectical relations and proposes that the relationship between the individual and societal structures is dialectical in character. From this perspective, he argues that the power

embedded within structures often weighs heavily in influencing individual behavior; however, the dialectical quality of the relationship also results in structural change brought about by individual action. It is this notion of individual agency in the face of large and powerful societal structures that has made Giddens's structuration theory particularly appealing to postprocessual archaeologists (e.g. Hodder 1982, 1986; Miller and Tilley 1984; Shanks and Tilley 1987; Johnson 1989).

Closely related to Giddens's structuration theory is Pierre Bourdieu's theory of practice. Like Giddens, Bourdieu (1977, 1984, 1990) was primarily interested in understanding the relationship between societal structures and individual practice. In this sense, Bourdieu's notion of practice is similar to Giddens's idea of individual action. However, Bourdieu has a much more explicit focus on the material world and the role it plays in the maintenance of *habitus*, a set of semi-conscious cultural predispositions that often characterize the choices made by a particular group. It is this material dimension that archaeologists have found so attractive. However, this is only part of Bourdieu's overall theoretical framework. Bourdieu also conceives of habitus as the product of history and the social relations that have developed over what is often a fairly long period of time. It is thus similar in many respects to the historical structures that Fernand Braudel (1981, 1982) describes as the structures of everyday life. Braudel (1982) explains how long-standing practices such as the baking of bread, the overall diet, and some economic relations become part of a broader societal structure that is subject to a far slower pace of change that that which affects other sets of practices, in particular those involving trade and commerce. Habitus expands the notion of structure to include several forms of capital through which it can be reproduced and perpetuated. One of the most important elements of habitus is the idea that it helps to routinize social difference in an effort to mask social inequality. Braudel describes three different forms of capital – political, social, and cultural – with the latter including his notion of symbolic capital. These various forms of capital are marshaled by different groups in the construction of narratives that reinforce social differences, especially those relating to class, but interestingly enough not race, and limit social mobility.

Bourdieu's concept of cultural capital is particularly important for archaeology because it includes material practices that are habitual. These types of practices and the cultural capital they often incorporate constitute what Bourdieu (1984:471) defines as "*doxa*," the adherence of practices that are so much a part of everyday practice that they are assumed to be self-evident. Materialized through space, in the form of landscapes, or in social practices involving material culture such as entertaining or other forms of display, the tangible elements of doxa offer archaeologists a theoretical scheme that helps bridge the evidentiary gap between the residues of daily life and the contextual structures that brought meaning to that life (Silliman 2004; Orser 2005, 2006). Combined with the idea of individual action, practice theory helps in articulating the relationship between structure and practice that is at the heart of much contemporary social inquiry. For archaeology, the joining of Bourdieu's notion of habitus with Giddens's idea of the duality of structure, its recursive quality, provides an important set of theoretical concepts that permit new interpretations of the material domain. They also provide one answer to the scale questions that have hampered attempts to resolve the relationship between daily practice and larger social structures (Dobres and Robb 2005).

A number of archaeologists have now engaged with theories of practice and agency in the process of theorizing both the composition and ideological elements of societal structures while at the same time suggesting potential avenues for individual action and their possible effectiveness in changing those very structures (Dobres and Robb 2005). We have already outlined Orser's (2007) discussion of epochal and historical agency and its importance in conceptualizing the societal structures addressed by both Giddens and Bourdieu. These studies, however, are not without their problems. They are not always explicit in defining precisely what kind of agency they are envisioning (Johnson 1989; Gero 2000). They also raise the problem of identifying the material correlates of agency in the archaeological record (Dobres and Robb 2005:163). The problem here, however, is not faulty

methodology, but rather the essentialist desire to identify an "agency signature" applicable to all cultures at all times and places. The cultural expression of agency varies across social contexts in relation to other kinds of affiliations and social identities, such as race, class, gender, and ethnicity. Practice theory provides one scheme that has aided archaeologists in confronting the challenge of identifying and understanding the cultural dynamics that characterize the interaction of past individuals and their worlds.

A promising new area of investigation is the study of microhistory, which focuses on just how individuals fit into and articulate with societal structures. Based upon the work of Carlo Ginzburg (1980, 1991, 1993; Ginzburg and Poni 1991), microhistory has developed into a powerful window into the interaction of individuals and the worlds in which they live (e.g. Davis 1983, 2006; Levi 1991; Revel 1995; Magnússon 2003; Brooks et al. 2008). By focusing on individuals located within social webs of various scales and powers, microhistorians have explored the scales of articulation, and in so doing have provided models for the character of that articulation. Historical archaeologists are beginning to draw on this literature in developing their own approaches to the study of agency and practice. Studies such as those by DeCorse (2008) and Lightfoot (2008) demonstrate how the use of documentary sources and oral histories can help in refining the methods archaeologists employ in the study of agency. Beaudry (2008) provides a particularly detailed study that demonstrates the importance of contextualizing material culture in order to understand stages in people's life-cycle. In this case, she insightfully interprets items that would have served as cultural capital in a habitus consistent with merchant families during the 18th century as the last residue of a group whose real social and political capital was in considerable decline.

Timothy Pauketat incorporates elements of practice theory in his argument for "historical processualism." He begins with a review of the strengths and weaknesses of neo-Darwinism (selectionism), cognitive processualism, and agency theory. He is particularly critical of the selectionist approach because of its dogged adherence to positivist philosophy that privileges science over history. He also questions the selectionists' narrow view of technology, which envisions change only in instances when a functional improvement results in its adoption by cultural groups. He offers a similar criticism of some forms of agency theory because, he argues, they stress the historical importance of a few, exceptional individuals who have been able to effect a change in the behavior of others. Instead, he favours the idea of cognitive processualism, which acknowledges that human action is often influenced by long-standing traditions. Pauketat sees value in such studies because their views of technologies as tradition-laden practices represent an important improvement over the reductionist, deterministic characterizations of tradition espoused by neo-Darwinists and selectionists.

Pauketat's main geographical focus is the greater Mississippi River basin. For him, this area represents a field, in the sense employed by Bourdieu, in which historical processes unfolded. To support his point, he draws upon his long-standing interest in the shell-tempered ceramics associated with the large settlement of Cahokia and its numerous satellite settlements. Pauketat chronicles the history of ceramic studies from this part of North America and their various interpretations. He notes, for example, that the spread of shell-tempered ceramics during the latter stages of the first millennium AD has usually been explained as a result of its stylistic appeal or because shell temper improved its durability. Instead, Pauketat argues that its spread was the result of its association with the growing influence of Cahokia and the rituals that were carried out in the town once it became the capital of a large polity. From this perspective, he argues that changes in practice, often at the micro or household scale, do not reflect the imposition of a set of cultural practices on the settlements surrounding Cahokia as much as they do the local emulation of an emergent cultural center. This subtle, but significant, difference is consistent with Pauketat's overall argument for the unfolding of historical processes that are not necessarily explained as being adaptive. In fact, he makes a compelling argument for the maladaptive qualities of shell-tempered pottery, which was nevertheless adopted for reasons having to do with the identities of the individuals living in Cahokia and the

surrounding region. In this sense, Pauketat argues that archaeologists would do well to break down the barriers between notions such as prehistory and history and look more carefully for evidence of changing practices at all scales in order to better understand how history actually happened.

Marcia-Anne Dobres has been among the most consistent contributors to the archaeological discourse on agency (e.g. Dobres 2000; Dobres and Robb 2000, 2005). In particular, she has examined the relationship between technologies and the gendered social contexts in which they are embedded. In her chapter, she addresses one of the weaknesses of agency theory: the lack of middle-range concepts to help in situating individual action in a larger, structural apparatus. In part to remedy this situation, she explores the analytical approach, developed by André Leroi-Gourhan, known as *chaîne opératoire* in her search for links between the production of technology and ideational maps or worldviews that formed the context of production. She outlines a picture of human technology as a transformative process in which raw materials are made into tools and other forms of material culture. The unfolding of this process takes a particular path that is in itself shaped by cultural traditions that reproduce broader structures of meaning. It is not just technological activities that unfold in this manner, but indeed all of work. The routine that structures labor is embedded within webs of meaning that extend to the items being manufactured. In this sense, Dobres is following the earlier work of Igor Kopytoff (1986) in arguing for an approach that situates the life-cycle of artifacts within deeper, but not static societal structures.

Dobres then turns to a consideration of identity and social agency in the Late Magdalenian. By employing the concept of *chaîne opératoire* to interpret bone and antler artifacts from eight sites, she is able to identify evidence of considerable variability in the production of these tools that runs counter to standard notions of widespread cultural conservatism for this time period. She finds that there was no one best way to create, modify, or repair harpoons, spear points, and needles across all sites. Rather, technical decisions were site-specific. What accounts for this variability? She suggests that the very practice of technology signaled identity; techno-gestures served as silent discourses of local salience. This variability, in turn, reveals a significant degree of choice in the production process. For example, at the site of La Vache, some harpoon barbs were either longer, sharper, or more curved, suggesting individualized strategies of manufacture. At Les Églises and Mas d'Azil, only a few bone needles were perforated; the majority showed a lack of refinement. These technogestural strategies would have materialized the identities and statuses of their makers. Dobres's analysis, while preliminary, is an important demonstration of the value of agency and its utility in studies of early, small-scale societies.

Kenneth Sassaman also presents a compelling example for the use of practice theory in interpreting, or, in this instance, reinterpreting, a range of archaeological data. Drawing upon an extensive review of artifact assemblages and landscape features ranging from mound and village complexes to coastal shell rings from the Southeastern United States, Sassaman makes a powerful argument for their role in the mediation of ethnic relations in emerging complex societies. He begins his discussion by challenging the egalitarianism and equality that are assumed to have characterized the Archaic societies of the American Southeast. In arguing for a nascent complexity during the Archaic period, Sassaman explores the idea that emerging polities likely incorporated a variety of groups that would have shared different histories and identities. He posits that as these processes began to unfold, individuals and groups invested greater energy in the production of material identities. This is how he chooses to interpret the caches of Dalton blades found in parts of the Southeast. Here he is arguing that the blades represent "primitive valuables" similar to items that represent cultural or possibly symbolic capital. He goes on to describe bannerstones as another class of hetertrophic items in arguing that the movement of people may have resulted in the increased production of such items as expressions of group identity.

Sassaman then turns his gaze to several classes of landscape features and suggests that as larger polities began to emerge, steps were taken to address the ethnic differences that were a growing part of daily life. The spread of societal structures that could have been economic, political, religious, or a combination of these fostered mechanisms to deal with the ethnic diversity that characterized such polities. Mound complexes, such as Poverty Point, may have served as gathering places in which rituals were performed that would have been designed to manage some of the tensions that likely characterized these complex societies. The spatiality of the various mound groups, as well as those of coastal shell rings, may have been integral to elite groups in the reproduction of the social hierarchies that supported them. Significantly, Sassaman does not limit his analysis to the large mound complexes alone. He also draws on evidence of outlying sites to argue that not all people would have been under the sway of these emerging powers. The extensive variability seen across the Southeast in the landscapes of village, shell ring, and mound complexes may speak to a level of fluidity and fragility in the maintenance of these early complex societies.

Agency and practice are also the subjects of Kent Lightfoot, Antoinette Martinez, and Ann Schiff's study of Fort Ross, a Russian outpost in Northern California. Here the dominating power of the Russians found its expression in the public spaces both inside the fort and in much of the surrounding area. The landscape of the fort itself and the area immediately surrounding it employed abstract notions of space to construct a rather symmetrical array of buildings and pathways. The architecture of many of the fort's buildings also reflected the cultural traditions of the Russians who planned and constructed them. These public spaces are contrasted with the interior spaces of multicultural households, often comprised of Native Alaskan men, whom the Russians brought with them to California to oversee the collection of furs, and local Native Californian women. Through their excavations, Lightfoot and his colleagues were able to determine that the foodways practices carried out in these households represented a blend of cultural traditions. Some food choices, such as sea mammals, appear to have been consistent with the dietary practices of the Native Alaskan men, while others, such as venison, were more typical of Native Californian women. In contrast to these food choices, the preparation of meals and the overall spatial ordering of the individual households appear to have been more consistent with the ethnohistorical accounts and oral traditions concerning Native Californian cultural practices.

Lightfoot and his colleagues also reveal the value of multi-scalar investigations that compare local practices with those at the settlement and regional levels. In their work at Fort Ross, it was essential that the evidence of daily activities at the household level was compared with that from the different neighborhoods that were associated with the fort. The interpretive significance of the evidence from the Russian, Native Alaskan, and Native Californian settlement areas was only truly understood once it was placed in the larger regional context. Only then was it possible to see that the cultural practices that formed the daily experience of the members of the individual households were an amalgam of traditions drawn from the historical experiences of their constituents. In this sense, the Fort Ross case represents an excellent example of how agency and practice converge to bring meaning to the lives of those who found themselves constructing new identities in the colonial encounter.

References

Beaudry, Mary C., 2008 "Above Vulgar Economy": The Intersection of Historical Archaeology and Micro-history in Writing Archaeological Biographies of Two New England Merchants. *In* Small Worlds: Method, Meaning and Narrative in Microhistory. James F. Brooks, Christopher R. N. DeCorse, and John Walton, eds. Pp. 173–198. Santa Fe: School of Advanced Research Press.

Binford, Lewis R., 1965 Archaeological Systematics and the Study of Culture Process. American Antiquity 31:203–210.

Binford, Lewis R., 1967 Comment. Current Anthropology 8:234–235.

Binford, Lewis R., 1972 An Archaeological Perspective. New York: Seminar Press.

Bourdieu, Pierre, 1977 Outline of a Theory of Practice. Cambridge: Cambridge University Press.

Bourdieu, Pierre, 1984 Distinction: A Social Critique of the Judgment of Taste. Cambridge, MA: Harvard University Press.

Bourdieu, Pierre, 1990 The Logic of Practice, Palo Alto, CA: Stanford University Press.

Braudel, Fernand, 1981 Civilization and Capitalism 15th–18th Century, vol. I. The Structures of Everyday Life. New York: Harper and Row.

Braudel, Fernand, 1982 Civilization and Capitalism 15th–18th Century, vol. II. Wheels of Commerce. New York: Harper and Row.

Brooks, James F., Christopher R. N. DeCorse, and John Walton, eds., 2008 Small Worlds: Method, Meaning and Narrative in Microhistory. Santa Fe: School of Advanced Research Press.

Davis, Natalie Z., 1983 The Return of Martin Guerre. Cambridge, MA: Harvard University Press.

Davis, Natalie Z., 2006 Trickster Travels: A Sixteenth-Century Muslim between Worlds. New York: Hill and Wang.

DeCorse, Christopher R. N., 2008 Varied Pasts: History, Oral Tradition and Archaeology on the Mina Coast. *In* Small Worlds: Method, Meaning and Narrative in Microhistory. James F. Brooks, Christopher R. N. DeCorse, and John Walton, eds. Pp. 77–93. Santa Fe: School of Advanced Research Press.

Dobres, Marcia-Anne, 2000 Technology and Social Agency: Outlining a Practice Framework for Archaeology. Oxford: Blackwell.

Dobres, Marica-Anne, and John E. Robb, eds., 2000 Agency in Archaeology. London: Routledge.

Dobres, Marcia-Anne, and John E. Robb, 2005 "Doing Agency": Introductory Remarks on Methodology. Journal of Archaeological Method and Theory 12 (3):159–166.

Gero, Joan M., 2000 Troubled Travels in Agency and Feminism. *In* Agency in Archaeology. Marcia-Anne Dobres and John Robb, eds. Pp. 34–39. London: Routledge.

Giddens, Anthony, 1979 Central Problems in Social Theory: Action, Structure and Contradiction in Social Analysis. London: Macmillian.

Giddens, Anthony, 1984 The Constitution of Society. Berkeley: University of California Press.

Ginzburg, Carlo, 1980 The Cheese and the Worms: The Cosmos of a Sixteenth-Century Miller. Baltimore: Johns Hopkins University Press.

Ginzburg, Carlo, 1991 Ecstasies: Deciphering the Witches' Sabbath. New York: Pantheon.

Ginzburg, Carlo, 1993 Microhistory: Two or Three Things That I Know about It. Critical Inquiry 20 (1):10–35.

Ginzburg, Carlo, and Carlo Poni, 1991 The Name and the Game: Unequal Exchange and the Historiographic Marketplace. *In* Microhistory and the Lost Peoples of Europe. Edward Muir and Guido

Ruggiero, eds. Pp. 1–10. Baltimore: Johns Hopkins University Press.

Hodder, Ian, 1982 Symbols in Action. Cambridge: Cambridge University Press.

Hodder, Ian, 1986 Reading the Past. Cambridge: Cambridge University Press.

Johnson, Matthew, 1989 Conceptions of Agency in Archaeological Interpretation. Journal of Anthropological Archaeology 8:189–211.

Kopytoff, Igor, 1986 The Cultural Biography of Things: Commodization as a Process. In The Social Life of Things. Arjun Appadurai, ed. Pp. 64–91. Cambridge: Cambridge University Press.

Levi, Giovanni, 1991 On Microhistory. In New Perspectives in Historical Writing. Peter Burke, ed. Pp. 93–113. University Park: Pennsylvania State University Press.

Lightfoot, Kent G., 2008 Oral Traditions and Material Things: Constructing Histories of Native People in Colonial Settings. In Small Worlds: Method, Meaning and Narrative in Microhistory. by James F. Brooks, Christopher R. N. DeCorse, and John Walton, eds. Pp. 265–288. Santa Fe: School of Advanced Research Press.

Magnússon, Siguròur G., 2003: The Singularization of History: Social History and Microhistory with the Postmodern State of Knowledge. Journal of Social History 36(3):701–735.

Miller, Danny, and Christopher Tilley, eds., 1984 Ideology, Power and Prehistory. Cambridge: Cambridge University Press.

Orser, Charles E., 2005 Violence, Resistance, and Symbol: The Vectors of Improvement in Early Nineteenth-Century Ireland. World Archaeology 37:392–407.

Orser, Charles E., 2006 Symbolic Violence and Landscape Pedagogy: An Illustration from the Irish Countryside. Historical Archaeology 40(2):20–36.

Orser, Charles E., 2007 The Archaeology of Race and Racialization in Historic America. Tallahasee: University of Florida Press.

Revel, Jacques, 1995 Microanalysis and the Construction of the Social. In Histories: French Constructions of the Past. Jacques Revel and Lynn Hunt, eds. Pp. 492–502. New York: New Press.

Schatzki, Theodore R., Karin Knorr Cetina, and Eike von Savigny, eds., 2001 The Practice Turn in Contemporary Theory. London: Routledge.

Shanks, Michael, and Christopher Tilley, 1987 Social Theory and Archaeology. Cambridge: Polity Press.

Silliman, Stephen W., 2004 Lost Laborers in Colonial California: Native Americans and the Archaeology of Rancho Petaluma. Tucson: University of Arizona Press.

Trigger, Bruce G., 1968 Beyond History: The Methods of Prehistory. New York: Holt, Rinehart and Winston.

Trigger, Bruce G., 1970 Aims in Prehistoric Archaeology. Antiquity 44:26–37.

Trigger, Bruce G., 2006 A History of Archaeological Thought. 2nd edition. Cambridge: Cambridge University Press.

5

Practice and History in Archaeology
An Emerging Paradigm

Timothy R. Pauketat

In archaeology today, history is a growing concern of more than just historical archaeologists. This concern may seem practical enough, as archaeology deals with long stretches of time. However, the archaeological study of the processes of history has been, well, a long time in coming. It is not that repeated calls to bridge history, ethnohistory, and archaeology have not been made; they have (e.g. Kohl, 1984; Trigger, 1982, 1984, 1989). Rather, there has been a reticence to abandon a commitment to science and ultimate causality for the less positivistic and proximate explanations of history. This is understandable, as many of today's practicing archaeologists were trained during a time when history was disdained as the antithesis of science, that stuff-left-over-after-explanation (e.g. Bamforth and Spaulding, 1982; Binford, 1983).

Nonetheless, today, American archaeologists, having once turned their backs on history, may now be ready to make a theoretical about-face. Historical archaeology, of course, has been gaining ground for some years now. In addition, a plethora of historically oriented approaches has emerged (Bintliff, 1991; Hodder, 1987; Knapp, 1992; Leone and Potter, 1988; Lightfoot, 1995; Lightfoot and Martinez, 1995; Little, 1994; McGuire, 1992; Rogers and Wilson, 1993;

Timothy R. Pauketat, "Practice and History in Archaeology: An Emerging Paradigm," pp. 73–98 from *Anthropological Theory* 1 (2001). Reprinted with permission of Sage.

Shackel and Little, 1992). There are even rumblings of returning in some fashion to the tenets of an older 'Culture-Historical Paradigm' (Barker and Pauketat, 1992; Lyman et al., 1997; Shennan, 1996). This is what one recent commentator called an emerging new paradigm – the study of historical processes – that promises to reunite American archaeology (Stein, 1998). Today, history matters in archaeology.

This emerging paradigm bridges the theoretical positions of the recent past and the present. A general willingness to reconcile disparate positions – a renewed spirit of inclusiveness – is archaeology's version of a bridge to the 21st century (see Maschner and Mithen, 1996; Schiffer, 1996). Certainly, the once common opposition of 'processual' archaeology's science to 'postprocessual' archaeology's interpretations has subsided (Cowgill, 1993; Hodder, 1995; Trigger, 1991; VanPool and VanPool, 1999). And rightly so, as anyone can observe that most archaeologists – whatever their position in the great processual – post-processual debate – study processes of one sort or another, and they tend to do this in a systematic manner.

Then again, if processualism and post processualism are not perceived to be so different any more, what is so distinct about an archaeology of historical processes to warrant calling it an emerging paradigm? The answer, I argue here, lies in its relocation of the locus of social change and, consequently, in what constitutes a satisfactory explanation. An older processualism (and some neo-Darwinism) relied on simple linear causality: a stimulus elicits a response. Usually, a functionalist logic ran through the entire causal chain. Material culture changed as a response to some human need, making it adaptive (but not creative). Material culture 'expressed' some process; archaeologists searched for 'material correlates' of those processes. Likewise, attributes of social life (e.g. leadership, subsistence, gender, etc.) were explained in terms of their roles in a larger social system (e.g. band-level, tribal, etc.). Centralized societies, for instance, were caused by inequities in resource distribution or by the innate tendency of growing populations to war, aggrandize, cultivate, or trade with remarkable efficacy. In this example, or in any such arguments, causality was somehow external to the historical settings in which centralization occurred. Archaeologists sought the 'system' behind individuals and their material culture even into the 1990s (see Brumfiel, 1992).

The new historical processualism is increasingly centered on a theory of practice (see later). From this perspective, people's actions and representations – 'practices' – are generative. As I will argue later, practices *are* the processes, not just consequences of processes. Thus, they generate change. That is, practices are always novel and creative, in some ways unlike those in other times or places. This means that practices are historical processes to the extent that they are shaped by what came before them and they give shape to what follows. These historical processes are quite different from what used to be called 'cultural processes' (Binford, 1965). Explaining history, most would agree, entails seeking the proximate causes of *how* a certain social feature, say centralization, developed in a particular time or place. What used to be called 'cultural processes' were abstract, law-like principles of *why* something occurred. These ultimate explanations tended to leapfrog over historical data, making them reductionist to the point of being trivial or easily debunked (e.g. Flannery, 1972).

An archaeology of historical processes, then, quite clearly involves a paradigmatic shift. This emerging historical-processual paradigm reorients the questions that we ask, relocates the processes that we seek to explain, and revises how we understand cause and effect. My purpose

here is to highlight this paradigmatic reorientation. I will begin by reviewing three archaeological approaches to explanation in the 1990s: neo-Darwinism, cognitive processualism, and agency theory. I am not concerned here with explicating in detail any of the three approaches. My purpose in examining them is to excise and discard problematic parts of the three contemporary approaches, the offending parts including functionalism, mentioned earlier, and essentialism, the reliance of explanations on irreducible phenomena ('essences') that themselves go unexplained. In this latter regard, 'behavior' is the principal bugaboo, antithetical as it is to an archaeology of historical processes. In discarding it, we are left with actions and representations that are best labeled 'practices'. The three reviewed approaches all share qualities with practice theory (following Bourdieu, 1977, 1990; Ortner, 1984). I highlight these shared elements and then, in order to illustrate the paradigmatic importance of a practice-based approach, I review explanations of pottery technological change and the emergence of Cahokia in the pre-Columbian midcontinental United States. I conclude with some thoughts on practice theory, proximate explanations, and the emerging historical-processual paradigm.

Neo-Darwinism, Cognitive Processualism, and Agency Theory

To begin, I will briefly review neo-Darwinian and cognitive-processual approaches to explanation. These, more than agency theory, have served both as a critique or revision of processualism and as a reaction to post-processualism (see Dunnell, 1980, 1992; Renfrew, 1994). Neither approach can claim to be an integrated program, especially cognitive-processualism, but both contribute to the construction of an archaeology of historical processes. Of the two, the neo-Darwinists have made the greatest strides in formulating and standardizing a research agenda. This is the case despite the fact that neo-Darwinists are actually a diverse lot of archaeologists that includes what I will label 'selectionists', 'individualists', and 'transmissionists' (see Barton and Clark, 1997; Maschner and Mithen, 1996; Teltser, 1995).

The selectionists are at once the most dominant and problematic of the three subgroups of neo-Darwinists. Selectionists espouse a rather strict adherence to Darwin's concepts of variation and selection as applied to human technologies. From their perspective, technologies change via selective forces that act on artifacts. Quite simply, the design or performance characteristics that best fit the conditions of use have selective advantages over other characteristics, and are disproportionately 'reproduced' through time (see Barton and Clark, 1997; Lyman and O'Brien, 1998; Neff and Larson, 1997; O'Brien and Holland, 1990, 1992; Rindos, 1989). To understand why change has occurred, however, they contend that the genealogy of a technology must first be understood. It seems largely irrelevant to selectionists whether or not selection was intentional or contingent on human agency or whether or not technological 'know-how' was affected by social change outside the technological dimension.

Human agency and social change are not considered by selectionists since, it is thought, these notions are reliant on 'essentialist' abstractions – i.e. those arbitrary constructs that are seen, erroneously, as real and irreducible entities (see Lyman and O'Brien, 1998; Lyman et al., 1997). In their words, 'only in rare cases can we, with any degree of certainty, know anything about how prehistoric peoples organized themselves socially and politically' (O'Brien and Wood, 1998: 2). Only inferences about the gradual (unintentional, uninstitutionalized) evolution of technology and the behavior that produced it are seen as legitimate in the selectionist agenda. Punctuated transformations in social life or technology, if these rely on higher-order changes in organizations or institutions, are not even thought possible (contrast Gould, 1987: 196). For instance, certain apparent shifts in pottery technologies in the Old and New Worlds, such as the spread of shell temper in the pre-Columbian Mississippi valley, have been explained as selection operating over centuries on chance, innovative, mechanical-performance characteristics (Dunnell and Feathers, 1991; Neff, 1992; Neff and Larson, 1997: 84; O'Brien and Holland, 1990, 1992; O'Brien et al., 1994). This gradualist, behaviorist agenda is not tenable from other viewpoints, not in the least part because it ignores data

(Clark, 2000; Gosselain, 1998; see Tempered Arguments, below).

Nonetheless, selectionism does possess conceptual advantages over other explanations of material change. In downplaying intentionality, selectionism begins to consider technological change in a way that is congruent with some definitions of 'practice' and 'cultural tradition'. Practice and tradition here are *not* the same things as essentialist notions such as ideologies, economic strategies, or political institutions and organizations.[1] Instead, practice and tradition are *what* people do and *how* they do it, with no strings attached to functionalist equations of why people do it. In paralleling such notions, selectionism also emphasizes change as historically contingent on that which has come before. Selection, in other words, *is* a historical process by virtue of the fact that change in arrays of some features of analytical interest is contingent on other and antecedent arrays. Moreover, selection is a universal process – present everywhere – even though any particular case of selection can only be explained with reference to a unique genealogy of change.

Conceptual advantages aside, however, the problem with the selectionist agenda lies in its extremely narrow approach to technology. While selection may be a historical process, it applies only to the 'functional attributes' of technologies. Non-functional 'stylistic' attributes, such as the decorative motifs on pots, are said to be inert (following Dunnell, 1978). In this instance, selectionism's processualist roots are bared: their stuff-left-over-after-explanation is style, not history. Selectionists arbitrarily isolate what *they* think are functional attributes, and then assume that such attributes are the result of behavior, the repetitive and invariate sets of actions that typify human beings. This is quite a leap of logic and one that essentializes behavior (Gosselain, 1998: 81). Indeed, it is the idea of behavior that allows selectionists, again like their older processual forerunners, to avoid thinking about the variability of human actions (which in turn might lead them to consider the higher-order origins of such variability). While selectionists recognize different kinds of behaviors, such as various pottery-making recipes within a single community, these behaviors are each seen, in essentialist terms, as real and internally homogeneous.

Consequently, behaviors are construed as something akin to phenotypes (O'Brien and Holland, 1990: 35). Selection at the level of behavior results in changing proportions of behaviors through time, but the phenotypes themselves do not change (except through innovations, which are compared to genetic 'mutations' [O'Brien et al., 1994: 294]).

The second group of neo-Darwinists – the 'individualists' – *are* concerned with human 'agency', at least as they define it. However, individualists are not concerned with the agency of *all* people, nor are they free of the behavioral essentialism that characterizes their selectionist counterparts. Individualists theorize that those few charismatic or aggrandizing individuals who competed for prestige were, by themselves, responsible for changing societies. These were the players of the past, those whose actions could affect scores to thousands of others. Perhaps it is no surprise that archaeologists studying the Northwest Coast and California, with its social ranking, competitive exchanges, and specialists, emphasize these few charismatic or aggrandizing players (Ames, 1995; Arnold, 1995; Hayden, 1995; Maschner and Patton, 1996). Perhaps it is also no surprise that individualists such as Maschner and Patton (1996) seek the ultimate explanations of aggrandizing behavior in sociobiology. However, in so doing, these particular neo-Darwinists abandon any claim to the study of historical processes by reducing change to a vitalistic equation: all populations naturally have aggrandizers who behave in predictable ways that, in turn, induce political complexity (see criticisms in Clark, 2000).

Agency is of concern to other neo-Darwinists who seek to isolate the mechanisms by which ideas were reproduced, transmitted, and transformed. Some of these neo-Darwinists, of course, explain idea transmission using abstract notions of 'fitness' and 'heritability', treating meanings – long recognized in cultural anthropology for their ambiguous, polysemic, and even 'maladaptive' character – as coded information subject to selection (see Barton and Clark, 1997; Mithen, 1997; Neff, 1992; but contrast Rappaport, 1979; Turner, 1967). However, other 'transmissionists' do not lose sight of symbols as the media of people's experiences and interpretations. Of the neo-Darwinists, transmissionists

come closest to a theory of practice, free of behavioral essentialism.

For Braun (1995) and Shennan (1993), human actions are not reduced to behaviors, then subject to selection. These transmissionists, particularly Shennan (1993), emphasize variation (in practice) over selection (of behavior) in a way that runs counter to the stated tenets of selectionism. Shennan (1993) recognizes human actions and representations, or 'practices', to be constrained in some ways by meanings, ideologies, identities, traditions, and various other 'macroscale' phenomena. These macroscale phenomena are not bounded things with a reality and a dynamic all their own, but – in various guises and at various scales (part of the reason why different concepts are used in different explanatory contexts) – are themselves products of practices. Practices in turn are not motivated by deep cultural meanings, but nonetheless enact or represent a cultural heritage or a tradition (Shennan, 1993: 58, drawing on Bourdieu, 1977, and Boyer, 1990). How this occurs is critical to our present consideration. To wit, words, shapes, gestures, dances, recipes, or even social spaces – what Shennan (1993) calls 'surface phenomena' – do not necessarily reveal their deep, meaningful referents – if indeed such referents exist – to the actors involved (see also Wagner, 1986). When one learns a language or performs a dance, for instance, one is perpetuating the surface form without necessarily understanding the ultimate meanings of the words or movements. This situation can produce variation in practices by actors who have imperfect or idiosyncratic understandings of what they do and the consequences of what they do.

This emphasis on variation in practice is shared with the loosely delineated 'cognitive processualists' (Renfrew and Zubrow, 1994). Unlike earlier processualists, tethered as they were to ecosystems explanations, the cognitive processualists profess a concern with how cultural information was 'transmitted', 'emulated', and 'transformed' from one point in time or space to another. In practice, understanding mechanisms of transmission often seems to take a back seat to simply demonstrating that archaeologists can deduce generic characteristics of religion and ideology from archaeological residues (Hill, 1994; Marcus and Flannery, 1994;

Renfrew, 1994). In so doing, these cognitive processualists are apt to rely on a teleological rationale when attempting ultimate explanations of social evolution. These attempts might begin with tool-manufacturing, artifact-distribution, or settlement-location evidence and extrapolate to the cognitive templates of whole populations (e.g. Zubrow, 1994). They might also explain how information was transmitted from group to group as a function of some macroscale behavioral system (e.g. Renfrew, 1987).

Then again, at its best, cognitive processualism breaks into the sequences of rudimentary human actions and sorts out the extent to which these actions were contingent on traditions, cognition, or the physical properties of that which was acted upon. These are the increasingly popular studies of technical-operational sequences, or chaînes opératoires (e.g. Dietler and Herbich, 1998; Dobres, 2000; Dobres and Hoffman, 1994 [also see Chapter 6, this volume]; Schlanger, 1994). Prime examples of this sort of study are Dietler and Herbich's (1989, 1998) and van der Leeuw's (1993, 1994) analyses of pottery production. Dietler and Herbich (1989, 1998), bordering on what could be termed practice theory, point to the macroscale implications of seemingly mundane pottery technological practices with respect to social identity. Van der Leeuw analyzes each step of production and the possible options available to the potters. Importantly, a point of reference for van der Leeuw's assessment of options is the pottery tradition – Michoacan, Mississippian, or otherwise – not abstract behavioral laws about technological efficiency (van der Leeuw, 1993: 241; contrast Schiffer and Skibo, 1997, for a behavioral approach to a similar level of analysis). In fact, he 'implies a complete dynamical redefinition' of the idea of tradition (van der Leeuw, 1993: 242). The analysis of operational chains tethered to such a 'dynamical' tradition concept can help us interpret technological change as change in traditional know-how at microscales – in the realm of practice – and at macroscales, in the milieu of cultural traditions.

Such analyses of technologies as routinized, cognized, tradition-bound practices are promising to free us from the problems of the behavioral essentialism and functionalist reductionism noted earlier to be lurking in some neo-Darwinian

and cognitive-processual approaches. Drawing on Ingold (1990), Lechtman (1993), Lemmonnier (1992, 1993), and others, Dobres and Hoffman (1994: 213) have linked the study of chaînes opératoires with a larger focus on technology, with the latter defined as 'a meaningful and socially negotiated set of material-based practices, as well as a technical means by which to make things' (emphasis in original). This view of technology, especially the 'meaningful and socially negotiated' part, is considerably different from a purely behavioral position (see also Dietler and Herbich, 1998; Dobres, 2000). For one thing, it implies that technology is not more readily accessible to archaeologists than 'prehistoric social and political organization, religious institutions, and the like' (contra O'Brien and Wood, 1998: 2–3). Human agency, social history, and traditions of various sorts exist simultaneously at microscales and macroscales (see especially papers in Stark, 1998). All are equally accessible to archaeologists!

This line of reasoning is testimony to the infiltration of ideas about human agency into archaeology. This is not to say that, today, there is a single, uniform agency approach in archaeology (following Archer, 1996; Giddens, 1979, 1984). Instead, there is a diversity of archaeological applications of the concept of human agency that have filtered in from various sources, especially political-economic ones (see Pauketat, 2000a). Various neo-Marxist, post-processual, and feminist studies have forwarded the notion that, to paraphrase Marx, people make their own history (e.g. Gero and Conkey, 1991; Hodder, 1986; Leone, 1985; McGuire, 1992; Nelson, 1997). Oddly, this intellectual heritage has produced a situation where merely invoking the idea of a human agent seems the criterion for being arrayed under the banner of agency theory (see Dobres and Robb, 2000). In some cases, those who have claimed to be using agency theory are doing nothing of the kind (Johnson, 1989; see respondents to Roscoe, 1993). These misguided claimants tend toward methodological individualism, often overlooking the central importance of the process of 'structuration', the continuous creation of the conditions that govern practice, as opposed to particular agents (see Giddens, 1979: 55, 66). Consequently, agency theory has been misconstrued as top-down and androcentric

(Gero, 2000), as exaggerating the roles of goal-oriented decision makers (Tainter, 1988), and as embodying post-processualism's rejection of science (Milner, 1996; but see Maschner and Mithen, 1996: 12; Shennan, 1993, 1996: x). These parallel older criticisms of 'action theory' by anthropologists more interested in 'symbolic action' and practice (see Cohen, 1974: 40–43; Ortner, 1984; Vincent, 1990: 341ff.).

A corrective to the theoretical ambiguity surrounding archaeological applications of 'agency' is the recent explicit focus on practice and structuration (e.g. Brumfiel, 1994; Dietler and Herbich, 1998; Dobres, 2000; Dobres and Hoffman, 1994; Emerson, 1997a; Hendon, 1996; Johnson, 1996; Jones, 1997; Lightfoot [Chapter 8, this volume]; Pauketat, 1994, 2000a; following Bourdieu, 1977 and Giddens, 1979, 1984). In the studies of technology already mentioned, Bourdieu's concepts – particularly his elaboration of 'habitus' (people's dispositions) – have found currency (see Dietler and Herbich, 1998; Dobres and Hoffman, 1994; Hegmon, 1998). His idea of 'doxa' – those second-nature, taken-for-granted ways of doing or knowing (which, when politicized, are heterodoxies and orthodoxies) – remains underdeveloped by archaeologists despite its promise alongside Foucauldian and Gramscian notions of 'power', 'governmentality', and 'hegemony' (see Bradley, 1996; Clark, 1998; Comaroff and Comaroff, 1991; Dietler and Herbich, 1998; Emerson, 1997a; Pauketat, 1994, 2000b; Pauketat and Emerson, 1999). However, there is no practice-theory cookbook, nor should archaeologists simply reify Bourdieu's concepts as ready-made interpretations rather than as jumping-off points for building theory.

The gist of both Bourdieu's (1977) practice theory and Giddens's (1979) agency theory is that all people enact, embody, or re-present traditions in ways that continuously alter those traditions (see also Archer, 1996). Alteration of tradition in this sense is not simply a tactical decision or a strategy. Here we need to disconnect the idea of strategy or behavior from the idea of intentionality in order to properly understand motivation, practice, and unintended consequences. The motivations to act were not the same as the end results that may be observed, so enacting, embodying, or representing traditions is not 'teleological' action as implied by the concept of behavior (Habermas, 1984). A teleological, behavioral view scientizes human actions. Cooking becomes 'cooking behavior'. Taking out the garbage becomes 'disposal behavior' (e.g. Schiffer, 1995). Behaviorism of this sort denies variable, situation-specific and culture-specific ways of doing or knowing even as it makes inferring 'dynamics' from 'static' remains a simple linear equation (see Binford, 1983).

Once we drop the pretense to invariate, goal-oriented action, behavior becomes practice (Hendon, 1996, exemplifies this nicely). As opposed to behavior, practices are, quite literally, the embodiment of people's 'habitus' or dispositions. Critical to practice theory is the realization that the dispositions that guide practice have 'doxic' referents ('unconscious', 'spontaneous', 'nondiscursive', 'practical', or 'commonsensical' forms of knowledge [Bourdieu, 1977, 1990; Giddens, 1979, 1984; see Comaroff and Comaroff, 1991: 22–7]). As Shennan (1993) has noted, such referents are the surface forms, not the deep cultural meanings. These doxic referents are, in a sense, non-ideological (but still cultural in the broadest sense of that term). Dispositions, in turn, are inculcated through one's experiences vis-à-vis these doxic referents in fields of action and representation ranging from relatively private, daily routines to colossal political rituals and mass media.

Importantly, the fields of action and representation, the dispositions of people, and practices themselves are not hermetically sealed. They are open to the potentially unpredictable circumstances, surroundings, and mix of participants (e. g. Sahlins, 1985). In this larger sense, practices are always 'negotiations' to the extent that power, the ability to constrain an outcome, pervades fields of action and representation (see Giddens, 1979; Foucault in Rabinow, 1984; Wolf, 1990, 1999: 4ff.). Negotiations, in turn, always recreate traditions. Traditions, in other words, are always in the process of becoming (Sztompka, 1991; e.g. Barth, 1987). They exist as 'real' entities only in practice (see Giddens, 1979: 5; Robb, 1998: 337), where they take any number of historical forms known to us elsewhere as accommodation, collaboration, communalization, creolization, domination, hierarchization, revitalization, syncretization, transculturation, etc. Any form of this practical, negotiative process of becoming is a historical process, and its explanation can only be made with reference to the genealogy of practices or the tradition of negotiations.

To be sure, seeing practices as both the medium of tradition and the medium of social change runs counter to the common assumption that, on the one hand, tradition (and ritual) is conservative while, on the other hand, political behaviors and technological innovations are dynamic (cf. Bell, 1997). So be it. From a historical-processual perspective, the essentialism wrapped up in the tradition – behavior dichotomy is simply untenable. Perhaps we should make a distinction here: there is tradition – the ex post facto rationalization of one's heritage (which is really more akin to Comaroff and Comaroff's [1991] definition of ideology) – and then there is tradition as I have used it here (see Pauketat, 2001). In this latter sense, tradition is the medium of change. In Bourdieu's (1977) terms, doxic elements of practice can be politicized to varying degrees, giving us 'orthodoxies' or, in other terms, cultural hegemonies or even ethnicities. Such co-optation of traditional themes is the lifeblood of politics (see Kertzer, 1988). Truly, tradition is part of a 'dynamical' process, even beyond van der Leeuw's (1993) more restricted meaning.

Once cleansed of essentialism, the three contemporary approaches to archaeological explanation do share a growing sense of urgency in considering the traditions of practice, the genealogies of production, and the proximate details of how things changed. There is a sense, among the practitioners discussed, that knowing how things changed will lead us toward more encompassing – dare I say ultimate – explanations of the cumulative effects of practice. Those cumulative effects, the cultural creations at microscales and macroscales, are what we typically call history.

Shell Temper, Cahokia, and Historical Processes

Lest one think the theoretical considerations of behavior, practice, tradition, and history insignificant for explanation, I will present an archaeological case in which change is alternately explained based on behavioral analogies versus homologous practices. The assumptions and explanations of each differ markedly, allowing us to distinguish an emerging paradigm of historical processes from the general background of contemporary approaches to archaeological explanation. There are two parts to this case study. The first part is a consideration of shell-tempered pottery technology in the central Mississippi valley, with special reference to the largest 'Mississippian' chiefdom, Cahokia. The second part is an elaboration of two alternate explanations of this pre-Columbian giant, one dependent on a behavioral theory of change, and the other historical, underlain by a theory of practice.

Tempered arguments

For well over a century, archaeologists have used crushed mussel shell temper (aplastic admixture) as a hallmark of 'Mississippian' tradition earthenwares in the American mid-continent (see Holmes, 1903; Milner et al., 1984; Morse and Morse, 1983; Phillips et al., 1951). During the twentieth century, the question of why shell temper was adopted across the Mississippi valley in the latter part of the first millennium AD was posed repeatedly. The answers focused either on style, shell temper being fashionable and widely emulated in the midcontinent and southeastern United States, or on function, as the chemical and mechanical properties imparted by mussel shell in certain ceramic pastes are thought to have improved pot utility and durability (Cobb and Nassaney, 1995; see Dunnell and Feathers, 1991; Morse and Morse, 1983: 208–10; Steponaitis, 1984).

For O'Brien and Holland (1990, 1992), shell temper was an innovative behavior introduced in southeast Missouri at or before AD 700. Whatever the origin for this innovation, the next several centuries saw the gradual diffusion of this behavior through the unintentional selection of the superior mechanical and chemical qualities by potters. By about AD 900, the argument goes, most potters had switched or soon would switch to this superior technology (see also Neff and Larson, 1997; O'Brien et al., 1994). I say most potters because, even as O'Brien et al. (1994: 295–6) realize, there were hold-outs in various pockets up and down the Mississippi river at AD 900 and later. In one area near modern-day St. Louis, the 'American Bottom', coeval traditions of shell temper users and non-shell temper users occupied the same floodplain for some two centuries (see Cobb and Nassaney, 1995; Kelly, 1990, 1993). From the selectionist camp, there is no explanation of this empirical problem, save the plea for more engineering studies and the speculation that localized clays or localized uses may have offset this otherwise desirable additive (O'Brien et al., 1994: 296–7).

This selectionist conundrum, rooted in an essentialist notion of behavior, does not consider technology as 'a meaningful and socially negotiated set of material-based *practices*, as well as a technical means by which to make things'. It ignores the other aspects of technology, the idea of cognitive processualists and agency theorists that technology is traditional know-how, and that this traditional know-how is transmitted and altered through the contingent contexts of negotiation. In other words, the selectionist explanation is too selective! The selectionist explanation, oddly, collapses centuries worth of context-contingent pottery production-and-use variability into one grand assertion about gradual behavioral change.

In fact, once we look closely at one locality's pottery-making history in the Mississippi valley (and base our observations on actual excavated data), we see anything but an even and gradual process of shell-temper adoption. The best documented archaeological case of this process in the Mississippi valley is that of the American Bottom's Mississippian emergence (AD 800–1050). In this well-documented case, and likely elsewhere in the valley, shell-tempered pottery was initially exotic and rare at AD 800 (Kelly, 1980, 1990). Local pottery manufacture and use practices featured distinctive cooking jars and bowls fashioned in localized microstylistic modes and tempered with grog, grit, and limestone. Whether the pots themselves or the know-how (and perhaps the potters) were exotic is uncertain at present (see Emerson and Jackson, 1984; Kelly, 1991; Pauketat, 2000a). In either case, however, a complicated process of technological hybridization was instigated by the exotic know-how, a technology that seems most closely associated with the Cahokia site proper (Pauketat, 1998a).

By AD 1000, shell-tempered wares comprised between 10 and 30 percent of those broken and discarded at most settlements in the vicinity of Cahokia, most of the shell-tempered pots probably being made in this same vicinity (e.g. Emerson and Jackson, 1984; Kelly, 1980; Pauketat, 1998a). However, around AD 1050, and within a span of a few decades at most, shell temper was adopted by most potters at large riverine settlements, especially Cahokia, where it comprises over 90 percent of all sherd assemblages (and 100 percent of some, see Holley, 1989; Milner et al., 1984; Pauketat, 1998a). Perhaps the most important sherd assemblages excavated to date are those from a series of rural sites several kilometers southeast of Cahokia (see Pauketat, 1996b, 1998b). Farmers at these 'Richland' settlements began emulating the early Cahokian shell-tempered technology within just a few years of Cahokia's abrupt beginning. They did this in over 75 percent of their cooking wares in spite of the preliminary evidence (seen in the especially high breakage rates) that the local ceramic fabric was not chemically or mechanically improved by the addition of crushed mussel shell (Alt, 1999).

To begin appreciating why a possibly 'maladaptive' attribute, in this instance shell temper at certain rural sites, might have been 'selected', we should be clear that, as Hendon (1996) notes, pottery is a part of an everyday dialogue in which power and tradition are negotiated through food preparation, distribution, and consumption. Gender, ethnicity, cosmology, and political allegiances are routinely negotiated in the contexts of pottery production, use, and discard. Such negotiations were 'microscale' to be sure, and yet even in the Cahokia-Richland settlements we begin to see the macroscale patterning associated with domestic practices as potters emulated an initially exotic and later politically potent technology (and perhaps one inseparable from the meanings and contexts of the foods with which the pots were associated).

With regard to understanding how a microscale process such as tempering or using a pot was related to macroscale change, Shennan (1993: 55) gives archaeologists a thoughtful application of the notion of practice. He states that the 'practices of which archaeology provides a record are at two extremes: important events which affected the way social space was structured and the routinized activity of individuals'. In so distinguishing, Shennan represents a stance diametrically opposed to the selectionist dismissal of people as active agents with their insistence on gradual change through selection. Shennan realizes that historical change may be punctuated and large-scale, like the building of Stonehenge, because transmission events – although microscale in a sense – have macroscale aspects as well. Recognizing such a punctuated, large-scale shift as practice 'does not necessarily imply a reduction of all social phenomena to a concern with individuals and their motivation, but it does imply a dependence of the higher levels on the level of the individual' (Shennan, 1993: 55). In fact, the elevation of the routine and everyday in a theory of history avoids an overly mechanical structure – agency feedback loop. What is transmitted through practice is not a whole cultural structure, an ideology, organization, or institution. Here, many of the agency theorists, cognitive processualists, and neo-Darwinists agree: incomplete and often unconscious bits of 'tradition' are reproduced, be they called technologies or something else (see Pauketat 2000a).

In the Cahokian case, the premier 'event' in which 'social space was structured' was the founding of a political capital in about AD 1050. Elsewhere I have discussed this dramatic regional change as having occurred within a short period of years in which capital grounds were constructed, the population was nucleated, villages were abandoned or relocated, and novel material symbols were produced, possibly under subsidized conditions (Pauketat, 1994, 1997a, 1997c, 1998b). Among the novel material-symbolic productions were pottery vessels, presumably including those used in the large-scale public events of the newly constructed central plazas. It is at this same time (roughly between AD 1050 and 1100) that shell-tempered pottery was rapidly adopted by Cahokians and by the Richland potters.

While a definitive 'causal' relationship between the centralized Cahokian changes and shell-tempered pottery production is not clear, it would seem ill advised to ignore – as does the selectionist story – the implications of evidence that the Mississippian chiefdom of Cahokia was consolidated over the same short span of time

that shell-tempered pottery technology was widely adopted in this pocket of the Mississippi valley. It also seems ill advised to ignore the evidence that shell-tempered wares (or perhaps the potters who made and used them) were among those featured in the large-scale collective rituals at places like Cahokia's Grand Plaza (Emerson, 1989; Pauketat, 1997b, 1998b; Pauketat and Emerson, 1991). In ignoring such matters, a historical process wherein microscale change is articulated with macroscale change is overlooked.

Alternative explanations of Cahokia

As the argument for an abrupt Cahokian consolidation is founded on multiple lines of largely independent survey and excavation evidence (see Dalan, 1997; Emerson, 1997a, 1997b; Pauketat, 1993, 1994, 2000a; Pauketat and Lopinot, 1997; Pauketat et al., 1998), the outline of events has been largely accepted even by researchers of other theoretical persuasions (e.g. Mehrer, 1995; Milner, 1998). Nevertheless, at present, there remains a vast gulf between researchers' explanations of these events. The distance between the two camps, those who favor an older processualist explanation (called 'minimalist' in Mississippian literature) and those who favor a revised historical-processual explanation, reveals the central importance of a theory of practice in an emerging paradigm of historical processes (Pauketat, 1998b: 52).[2] My presentation here is intended only to outline the explanatory rift relative to the problems of explanation.

Elsewhere, I have reviewed the general principles behind the older processualist mode of thought with reference to Cahokia in general (Pauketat, 1998b: 52–3):

[M]inimalist thought elevates local demographic and environmental factors as determinants in the development and dissolution of Cahokia, thereby projecting change as gradual, denying the possibility of a highly centralized political economy and minimizing the political and economic impacts of greater Cahokia beyond the American Bottom. [S]ubsistence-sufficient rural Mississippian farmers in the immediate vicinity of Cahokia could not have been reliant on or beholden to Cahokia; each farm family was politically autonomous (Mehrer, 1995, p. 164). In fact, for minimalists, political dynamics were irrelevant to long-term development, since communal organizations or adaptations were resistant to top-down change unless population or environmental pressures forced change upon people. Mississippianism, including the Cahokian variety, is seen as a uniform adaptation to floodplain environments across the Southeast regardless of variant regional conditions or iconographic manifestations (Milner, 1990; Muller, 1989; Muller and Stephens, 1991).

In this mode of thought, households are isolated as static features of pre-Mississippian and Mississippian society and assumed to have behaved according to universal agrarian rules of risk reduction and subsistence production (see Muller, 1997). Households 'on average would have aimed toward some overproduction as a cushion for lean years' (Milner, 1998: 175). This surplus, then, was available for expropriation by 'high-ranked people', gradually leading up to the founding of Cahokia (or any other such capital). Once established, such chiefdoms were unstable, subject to fracture along various old cleavage planes. Any physical-environmental problem of sufficient magnitude would provide the wedge to split the chiefdom into its component parts, those loosely articulated households with their low-order administrations. To stave off such political disasters, it is reasoned that chiefs must have taken on near-Machiavellian qualities (e.g. Milner, 1998).

This is a common political-behavioral model, akin to the models of Blanton et al. (1996), Earle (1991, 1997), Hayden (1995), and many others. This model's faults stem from the unquestioned acceptance of the idea of behavior such that (1) the actions and representations of people other than those 'high-ranked people' are irrelevant, (2) behaviors do not change, so that forces of change are external to people's actions and representations, and hence (3) all complex societies (including Mississippian chiefdoms) are seen to have been alike (Milner, 1998: 176). As to the causes of Cahokia's meteoric rise, the 'particular combination of circumstances that started Cahokia on the path to regional dominance *will never be known*' (Milner, 1998: 168, emphasis added).

Such a pessimistic assessment of causation is consistent with the older processualist disavowal of proximate causation and historical detail. These proximate details presumably were insignificant in the past, as 'Cahokia's chiefs owed their ultimate success largely to an especially favorable physical setting and the numerical superiority they enjoyed over similarly constituted groups elsewhere' (Milner, 1998: 168). However, the proximate causes and historical details of Cahokia's rise are not so unknowable and not so insignificant for all researchers, particularly those who do not begin with an essentialist view of human behavior.

A revised historical-processual explanation of Cahokia's emergence does not assume a standard set of pre-Mississippian household behaviors. In fact, even the idea of households as basal economic units cannot be assumed, much less their uniform behaviors (Pauketat, 2000b). Likewise, it is an error to seek the causes of Cahokia in the pre-Mississippian physical environment, subsistence 'system', or demographic profile. This is because, from a practice perspective, causes do not exist as abstract phenomena outside the realm of practices. The actions and representations of people at Cahokia *were* the processes that built Cahokia. Mound construction, for instance, was not a *consequence* of a process. Mound construction itself was part of the 'political' negotiation process (Pauketat, 1993, 1996a, 2000a).

The construction of the capital grounds, or any ritual landscape, would have constrained the practice of many people and would have continued to constrain future actions and representations contingent on how the space was continuously reconstructed (see Bradley, 1996). It is insufficient to conclude that such spaces were the 'expression' or 'materialization' of a pre-existing ideology (contra DeMarris et al., 1996). After all, construction events were dependent on coordinated action by people whose accommodation, resistance, or compliance shaped to some extent the meanings of the grounds. For instance, the construction of the central 'Grand Plaza' at Cahokia, which was undertaken as a short, large-scale labor project around AD 1050, was probably an integral part of the early Cahokian 'negotiations' in which incoming residents and rural visitors took part (see Dalan, 1997). The settings for such negotiations would have included, at a minimum, collective rites at which feasts, religious ceremonies, craft production, and plaza, mound, and building construction occurred (see Emerson, 1989; Pauketat, 1994, 1997a; Pauketat and Emerson, 1991). Given the scale of the central undertakings and the attendant, dramatic social shifts, these negotiations were likely enormous and continuous (Pauketat et al., n.d.).

We now have evidence of these rituals from the Cahokian capital's earliest phase. In a large stratified refuse pit adjacent to the Grand Plaza were piled the rich deposits of broken pots and animal parts from feasts along with remnants of magico-ritual plants and paraphernalia from the same public events (Pauketat, 1998b: 60; Pauketat et al., n.d.). Here, people deployed pottery vessels during large-scale collective rituals in ways that broadcast their meaning and would likely have enabled emulation by potters inside and, ultimately, outside the region (see also Renfrew, 1987). We also have evidence from rural localities of village abandonments and resettlements coeval with the founding of Cahokia and its plaza rituals (Pauketat, 1998b; Pauketat et al., 1998). Such abandonments and resettlements, especially if large-scale, would have broken up, reformed, or removed people who supported, accommodated, or resisted Cahokian centralization. Thus, these demographic reconfigurations constrained coordinated action and representation in ways that would have directly affected the giant ritual aggregations and, thus, the history of Cahokia.

That Cahokian history was affected in this way is further evident in the single most apparent characteristic of Cahokia: from house-life and craft goods to monuments, it seems, Cahokia was always in a state of becoming. It regularly incorporated the labor and cooperation of large segments of the regional population. Nothing was built or made just once. That is, Cahokian history – and the component actions and representations that defined it – was based on a continually redefined and revalued cultural logic (Pauketat, 1997a).

The upshot of this observation is that Cahokia cannot be explained with reference to an abstract behavioral logic, such as employed by Milner (1998), because that logic completely misplaces the locus of long-term change. The locus of change was practice, set in the context of a continually redefined and revalued tradition. If, in a counterfactual vein, we could somehow have changed the mix of actions and representations that gave shape to Cahokia, then Cahokia would have developed differently. The same applies to other peoples whose own histories were defined in some measure by contact with Cahokia (see Pauketat and Emerson, 1997b). The processes of Cahokia's emergence, and all such historical processes, must be understood through detailed and large-scale studies of who did what when and how. This historical view of Cahokia, that is, shifts the locus of explanation away from the invisible causes that 'will never be known' to the actual structuring events in which all people's actions and representations were brought to bear (following Sahlins, 1985). When this is done, the burden of explanation moves to the negotiations through which Cahokian social space was structured (Pauketat, 1998b). These negotiations themselves 'caused' Cahokia.

Toward a New Paradigm

Older processual explanations (of shell-tempered pottery and Cahokia), based on abstract notions of how people everywhere behaved, are untenable. Cultural processes from outside the field of human actions and representations do not set in motion a societal course independent of those actions and representations. The clear alternative to this older processualism is a historical-processual archaeology that adopts elements of a theory of practice. This alternative argues that how all people embodied their traditions, how they acted and represented themselves, shaped history (see Bradley, 1996; Burke, 1992; Hobsbawm and Ranger, 1983; Toren, 1999). The critical distinction boils down to the fact that behavior (abstract, goal-oriented human activity) is not practice (homologous actions and representations that vary between contexts or events even if the routinized forms – say cooking in pots – seem to remain the same). From a practice perspective, the locus of microscale *and* macroscale change is people acting out or representing their dispositions in social contexts. Even the selectionists and perhaps the individualists would agree that such processes of change are historical, contingent on the unique genealogies of development.

In recent years, others have considered the time-honored questions of archaeology in limited historical terms; the origins of agriculture, social inequality, and the state, for instance, are now commonly assumed to have been equifinal processes lacking single prime movers (e.g. Earle, 1991; Feinman and Marcus, 1998; Fritz, 1990). However, these and other diachronic questions still essentialize macroscale phenomena to the detriment of explaining historical processes. History is not a succession of cultural structures, institutions, or elite dynasties, and historical processes are not the abstract transitions or freak events between structures, institutions, and organizations.

History is the process of cultural construction through practice. Cultural construction may proceed in a relatively overt manner, as Polly Wiessner (1997: 173) explains for the !Kung San, whose intentional selection of traditionally meaningful beadwork represents their changing identities (see also papers in Costin and Wright, 1998 and Stark, 1998). Or it may operate less conspicuously, as Shennan (1993: 58) understands this process, in the realm of 'surface phenomena'. In either case, understanding history is a matter of understanding the undirected and creative negotiations of people whose dispositions were affected by their experiences (be they political, religious, gendered, technological, etc.). To study historical processes does mean accepting the commitment to the intensive study of homologies and regional, cultural-production genealogies (see Clark, 1998: 231; Shennan, 1993).[3]

A historical-processual paradigm in archaeology, combining the various approaches mentioned, pursues how change occurred – that is, how meanings or traditions were constructed and transmitted, not necessarily what those meanings or traditions were. A historical-processual paradigm rejects the use of behavioral analogies to infer the reasons that actions, representations, and technologies followed the courses that they did. It does not reject the search for causes as a legitimate goal of historical inquiry. However, answers to ultimate 'why' questions will be found only through the cumulative, painstaking, data-rich, multi-scalar studies of proximate causation (which, incidentally, tend to be more in demand by public audiences, see Weimer, 1995). The minimalist account of Cahokia, or

the continued comparative study of states – seeking political-behavioral regularities – is less productive than considering the historical processes of how cultural orthodoxies were created and resisted, or how a communal ethos or a corporate organization was co-opted or perpetuated through transformations of identity and scales of negotiation.[4]

In asking such proximate 'how' questions, the traditional boundaries between prehistoric archaeology and historical archaeology, or anthropology and history, are nearly invisible. In fact, the cross-fertilization of pre-Columbian archaeology and historical archaeology in the North American Southeast is one outstanding example of the utility of transcending those old boundaries (see Deagan, 1990; Ferguson, 1992; Little, 1994; Nassaney, 1992; Pauketat, 1998b, 2001; Rees, 1997). In these cases, while the historical contexts and scales of social change may be dramatically different in some ways, pre-Columbian, colonial, and post-colonial research is targeting a common problem: how were traditions appropriated within fields of social action to produce or resist central cultural orders? Few of these researchers reduce history to an ultimate explanation of why change occurred. But neither do they reconstruct cultural meanings or deep structures as if they caused long-term changes. Rather, they seek generalizations about processes that, perhaps counterintuitively, led to very different histories.

A theory of practice, I submit, makes perfect history. The idea of practice focuses attention on the creative moments in time and space where change was actually generated. This generative process assumes no essentialist organizations, institutions, or belief systems, but is located instead in microscale actions and representations. And yet, depending on the context of the practices, microscale processes exist simultaneously at macroscales as well. Such processes as domination, transculturation, communalization, creolization, and ethnogenesis are examples. We have seen how others – such as hybridization, emulation, revaluation, and construction – bridge the two scales in historical developments like Cahokia.

Clearly, to approach historical processes, archaeologists must grapple with the scales and histories of surface-phenomena transmissions, with technical-operational sequences, with negotiations, and with the *veneers* of uniform cultural structures that these transmissions, sequences, and negotiations did or did not produce (e.g. Braun, 1995). In archaeology, this means seeing material culture itself as the embodiment or active representation – intentional or unintentional – of cultural traditions. Material culture, as a dimension of practice, is itself causal. Its production – while contingent on histories of actions and representations – is an enactment or an embodiment of people's dispositions – a social negotiation – that brings about changes in meanings, dispositions, identities, and traditions.

In the new historical-processual archaeology, what people did and how they negotiated their views of others and of their own pasts *was and is* cultural process. This relocation of explanation may deprive archaeologists of direct and easy access to the ultimate *why* questions that we like to think we can answer. But in so doing, we will cease deluding ourselves that we can know – especially with our present limited databases – the ultimate truths behind complex histories simply by reifying the ideas of Darwin and Machiavelli. In realigning our theoretical basis for understanding long-term change, we will begin a new phase of theory building and regain the potential to explain the historical processes that affect all of humankind.

Notes

1 Ideologies, strategies, institutions, and organizations may be essentialist constructs of questionable utility when they are treated as if they exist outside the contexts of their continuous enactment and representation.
2 This does not make those who favor a historical-processual approach 'exaggerationalists' (as dubbed by Muller, 1997: 184).
3 It does not mean that anthropology ceases to be, in large part, a comparative enterprise. To the contrary, cross-cultural comparisons of technological change or global comparisons of political-cultural development (of the sort exemplified by the Cahokian case) enable the evaluation of historical significance. The comparative, analogical approach is also the only way to avoid the counterproductive forms of relativism and nihilism which hardly merit mention in this historical-processual scheme.
4 Chiefdoms or states, in the end, did not exist separate from such negotiations, and they never existed as static structures outside the continuous, active revaluations of tradition.

References

Alt, S. (1999) 'Tradition and Resistance in the Uplands', paper presented in the symposium, 'Resistant Traditions and Historical Processes in the Southeastern North America', organized by T. Pauketat for the 64th Annual Meeting of the Society for American Archaeology, Chicago.

Ames, K. M. (1995) 'Chiefly Power and Household Production on the Northwest Coast', in T. D. Price and G. M. Feinman (eds) *Foundations of Social Inequality*, pp. 155–87. New York: Plenum.

Archer, M. S. (1996) *Culture and Agency: The Place of Culture in Social Theory* (revised edition). Cambridge: Cambridge University Press.

Arnold, J. E. (1995) 'Social Inequality, Marginalization, and Economic Process', in T. D. Price and G. M. Feinman (eds) *Foundations of Social Inequality*, pp. 87–103. New York: Plenum.

Bamforth, D. B. and A. C. Spaulding (1982) 'Human Behavior, Explanation, Archaeology, History, and Science', *Journal of Anthropological Archaeology* 1: 179–95.

Barker, A. W. and T. R. Pauketat (1992) 'Introduction: Social Inequality and the Native Elites of Southeastern North America', in A. W. Barker and T. R. Pauketat (eds) *Lords of the Southeast: Social Inequality and the Native Elites of Southeastern North America*, pp. 1–10. Archaeological Papers of the American Anthropological Association, No. 3, Washington, DC.

Barth, F. (1987) *Cosmologies in the Making*. Cambridge: Cambridge University Press.

Barton, C. M. and G. A. Clark (1997) 'Evolutionary Theory in Archaeological Explanation', in C. M. Barton and G. A. Clark (eds) *Rediscovering Darwin:*

Evolutionary Theory and Archaeological Explanation, pp. 3–15. Archaeological Papers of the American Anthropological Association, No. 7, Washington, DC.

Bell, C. (1997) *Ritual: Perspectives and Dimensions.* Oxford: Oxford University Press.

Binford, L. R. (1965) 'Archaeological Systematics and the Study of Culture Process', *American Antiquity* 31: 203–10.

Binford, L. R. (1983) *Working at Archaeology.* New York: Academic Press.

Bintliff, J. (ed.) (1991) *The Annales School and Archaeology.* New York: New York University Press.

Blanton, R. E., G. M. Feinman, S. A. Kowalewski, and P. N. Peregrine (1996) 'A Dual-Processual Theory for the Evolution of Mesoamerican Civilization', *Current Anthropology* 17: 1–14.

Bourdieu, P. (1977) *Outline of a Theory of Practice.* Cambridge: Cambridge University Press.

Bourdieu, P. (1990) *The Logic of Practice.* Cambridge: Polity Press.

Boyer, P. (1990) *Tradition as Truth and Communication.* Cambridge: Cambridge University Press.

Bradley, R. (1996) 'Long Houses, Long Mounds and Neolithic Enclosures', *Journal of Material Culture* 1: 239–56.

Braun, D. P. (1995) 'Style, Selection, and Historicity', in C. Carr and J. E. Neitzel (eds) *Style, Society, and Person: Archaeological and Ethnological Perspectives*, pp. 124–41. New York: Plenum Press.

Brumfiel, E. M. (1992) 'Breaking and Entering the Ecosystem – Gender, Class, and Faction Steal the Show', *American Anthropologist* 94: 551–67.

Brumfiel, E. M. (1994) 'Factional Competition and Political Development in the New World: An Introduction', in E. M. Brumfiel and J. W. Fox (eds) *Factional Competition and Political Development in the New World*, pp. 3–13. Cambridge: Cambridge University Press.

Burke, P. (1992) *History and Social Theory.* Ithaca, NY: Cornell University Press.

Clark, J. E. (1998) 'The Arts and Govermentality in Early Mesoamerica', *Annual Review of Anthropology* 26: 211–34.

Clark, J. E. (2000) 'Towards a Better Explanation of Hereditary Inequality: A Critical Assessment of Natural and Historic Human Agents', in M.-A. Dobres and J. Robb (eds) *Agency in Archaeology*, pp. 92–112. London: Routledge.

Cobb, C. R. and M. S. Nassaney (1995) 'Interaction and Integration in the Late Woodland Southeast', in M. S. Nassaney and K. E. Sassaman (eds) *Native American Interactions: Multiscalar Analyses and Interpretations in the Eastern Woodlands*, pp. 205–26. Knoxville: University of Tennessee Press.

Cohen, A. (1974) *Two-Dimensional Man: An Essay on the Anthropology of Power and Symbolism in Complex Society.* London: Routledge and Kegan Paul.

Comaroff, J. and J. Comaroff (1991) *Of Revelation and Revolution.* Chicago: University of Chicago Press.

Costin, C. L. and R. P. Wright (eds) (1998) *Craft and Social Identity*, Archaeological Papers of the American Anthropological Association, No. 8, Washington, DC.

Cowgill, G. L. (1993) 'Distinguished Lecture in Archaeology: Beyond Criticizing New Archaeology', *American Anthropologist* 95: 551–73.

Dalan, R. A. (1997) 'The Construction of Mississippian Cahokia', in T. R. Pauketat and T. E. Emerson (eds) *Cahokia: Domination and Ideology in the Mississippian World*, pp. 89–102. Lincoln: University of Nebraska Press.

Deagan, K. A. (1990) 'Accommodation and Resistance: The Process and Impact of Spanish Colonization in the Southeast', in D. H. Thomas (ed.) *Columbian Consequences, Volume 1: Archaeological and Historical Perspectives on the Spanish Borderlands West*, pp. 297–314. Washington, DC: Smithsonian Institution Press.

DeMarris, E., L. J. Castillo and T. Earle (1996) 'Ideology, Materialization, and Power Strategies', *Current Anthropology* 17: 15–31.

Dietler, M. and I. Herbich (1989) '*Tich Matek*: The Technology of Luo Pottery Production and the Definition of Ceramic Style', *World Archaeology* 21: 148–64.

Dietler, M. and I. Herbich (1998) '*Habitus*, Techniques, Style: An Integrated Approach to the Social Understanding of Material Culture and Boundaries', in M. T. Stark (ed.) *The Archaeology of Social Boundaries*, pp. 232–63. Washington, DC: Smithsonian Institution Press.

Dobres, M.-A. (2000) *Technology and Social Agency: Outlining a Practice Framework for Archaeology.* Oxford: Blackwell.

Dobres, M.-A. and C. R. Hoffman (1994) 'Social Agency and the Dynamics of Prehistoric Technology', *Journal of Archaeological Method and Theory* 1: 211–58.

Dobres, M.-A. and J. Robb (eds) (2000) *Agency in Archaeology.* London: Routledge.

Dunnell, R. C. (1978) 'Style and Function: A Fundamental Dichotomy', *American Antiquity* 43: 192–202.

Dunnell, R. C. (1980) 'Evolutionary Theory and Archaeology', in M. B. Schiffer (ed.) *Advances in Archaeological Method and Theory* vol. 3, pp. 35–99. New York: Academic Press.

Dunnell, R. C. (1992) 'Archaeology and Evolutionary Science', in L. Wandsnider (ed.) *Quandaries and Quests: Visions of Archaeology's Future*, pp. 209–24.

Occasional Paper No. 20, Carbondale: Center for Archaeological Investigations, Southern Illinois University.

Dunnell, R. C. and J. K. Feathers (1991) 'Late Woodland Manifestations of the Malden Plain, Southeast Missouri', in M. S. Nassaney and C. R. Cobb (eds) *Late Woodland Stability, Transformation, and Variation in the Greater Southeastern United States*, pp. 21–45. New York: Plenum.

Earle, T. (1991) 'The Evolution of Chiefdoms', in T. Earle (ed.) *Chiefdoms: Power, Economy, and Ideology*, pp. 1–15. Cambridge: Cambridge University Press.

Earle, T. (1997) *How Chiefs Come to Power: The Political Economy in Prehistory*. Stanford: Stanford University Press.

Emerson, T. E. (1989) 'Water, Serpents, and the Underworld: An Exploration into Cahokia Symbolism', in P. Galloway (ed.) *The Southeastern Ceremonial Complex: Artifacts and Analysis*, pp. 45–92. Lincoln: University of Nebraska Press.

Emerson, T. E. (1997a) *Cahokia and the Archaeology of Power*. Tuscaloosa: University of Alabama Press.

Emerson, T. E. (1997b) 'Reflections From the Countryside on Cahokian Hegemony', in T. R. Pauketat and T. E. Emerson (eds) *Cahokia: Domination and Ideology in the Mississippian World*, pp. 167–89. Lincoln: University of Nebraska Press.

Emerson, T. E. and D. K. Jackson (1984) *The BBB Motor Site (11-Ms-595)* American Bottom Archaeology, FAI-270 Site Reports 6. Urbana: University of Illinois Press.

Feinman, G. M. (1995) 'The Emergence of Inequality: A Focus on Strategies and Processes', in T. D. Price and G. M. Feinman (eds) *Foundations of Social Inequality*, pp. 255–79, New York: Plenum Press.

Feinman, G. M. and J. Marcus (eds) (1998) *Archaic States*. Santa Fe: School of American Research Press.

Ferguson, L. (1992) *Uncommon Ground: Archaeology and Early African America*. Washington, DC: Smithsonian Institution Press.

Flannery, K. V. (1972) 'The Cultural Evolution of Civilizations', *Annual Review of Ecology and Systematics* 3: 399–426.

Fritz, G. J. (1990) 'Multiple Pathways to Farming in Precontact Eastern North America', *Journal of World Prehistory* 4: 387–435.

Gero, J. (2000) 'Troubled Travels in Agency and Feminism', in M.-A. Dobres and J. Robb (eds) *Agency in Archaeology*, pp. 34–9. London: Routledge.

Gero, J. M. and M. W. Conkey (eds) (1991) *Engendering Archaeology: Women and Prehistory*. Oxford: Basil Blackwell.

Giddens, A. (1979) *Central Problems in Social Theory: Action, Structure, and Contradiction in Social Analysis*. London: Macmillan.

Giddens, A. (1984) *The Constitution of Society*. Berkeley: University of California Press.

Gosselain, O. P. (1998) 'Social and Technical Identity in a Clay Crystal Ball', in M. T. Stark (ed.) *The Archaeology of Social Boundaries*, pp. 78–106. Washington, DC: Smithsonian Institution Press.

Gould, S. J. (1987) *Time's Arrow, Time's Cycle: Myth and Metaphor in the Discovery of Geological Time*. Cambridge, MA: Harvard University Press.

Habermas, J. (1984) *The Theory of Communicative Action*, vol. 1 Boston: Beacon Press.

Hayden, B. (1995) 'Pathways to Power: Principles for Creating Socioeconomic Inequalities', in T. D. Price and G. M. Feinman (eds) *Foundations of Social Inequality*, pp. 15–86. New York: Plenum Press.

Hegmon, M. (1998) 'Technology, Style, and Social Practices: Archaeological Approaches', in M. T. Stark (ed.) *The Archaeology of Social Boundaries*, pp. 264–79. Washington, DC: Smithsonian Institution Press.

Hendon, J. A. (1996) 'Archaeological Approaches to the Organization of Domestic Labor: Household Practice and Domestic Relations', *Annual Review of Anthropology* 25: 45–61.

Hill, J. N. (1994) 'Prehistoric Cognition and the Science of Archaeology', in C. Renfrew and E. B. W. Zubrow (eds) *The Ancient Mind: Elements of Cognitive Archaeology*, pp. 83–92. Cambridge: Cambridge University Press.

Hobsbawm, E. and T. Ranger (eds) (1983) *The Invention of Tradition*. Cambridge: Cambridge University Press.

Hodder, I. (1986) *Reading the Past: Current Approaches to Interpretation in Archaeology*. Cambridge: Cambridge University Press.

Hodder, I. (ed.) (1987) *Archaeology as Long-Term History*. Cambridge: Cambridge University Press.

Hodder, I. (1995) 'Fighting Back on the Plains', in P. Duke and M. C. Wilson (eds) *Beyond Subsistence: Plains Archaeology and the Postprocessual Critique*, pp. 235–9. Tuscaloosa: University of Alabama Press.

Holley, G. (1989) *The Archaeology of the Cahokia Mounds ICT-II: Ceramics*, Illinois Cultural Resources Study 11. Springfield: Illinois Historic Preservation Agency.

Holmes, W. H. (1903) *Aboriginal Pottery of the Eastern United States*. Bureau of American Ethnology, 20th Annual Report, Washington, DC: Smithsonian Institution.

Ingold, T. (1990) 'Society, Nature, and the Concept of Technology', *Archaeological Review from Cambridge* 9: 5–17.

Johnson, M. (1989) 'Conceptions of Agency in Archaeological Interpretation', *Journal of Anthropological Archaeology* 8: 189–211.

Johnson, M. (1996) *An Archaeology of Capitalism*. Oxford: Blackwell.

Jones, S. (1997) *The Archaeology of Ethnicity: Constructing Identities in the Past and Present.* London: Routledge.

Kelly, J. (1980) *Formative Developments at Cahokia and the Adjacent American Bottom: A Merrell Tract Perspective.* PhD dissertation, Department of Anthropology, Madison: University of Wisconsin.

Kelly, J. E. (1990) 'The Emergence of Mississippian Culture in the American Bottom Region', in B. D. Smith (ed.) *The Mississippian Emergence,* pp. 113–52, Washington, DC: Smithsonian Institution Press.

Kelly, J. E. (1991) 'The Evidence for Prehistoric Exchange and Its Implications for the Development of Cahokia', in J. B. Stoltman (ed.) *New Perspectives on Cahokia: Views from the Periphery,* Monographs in World Archaeology 2, pp. 65–92. Madison, WI: Prehistory Press.

Kelly, J. E. (1993) 'The Pulcher Site: An Archaeological and Historical Overview', *Illinois Archaeology* 5: 434–51.

Kertzer, D. (1988) *Ritual, Politics, and Power.* New Haven, CT: Yale University Press.

Knapp, A. B. (ed.) (1992) *Archaeology, Annales, and Ethnohistory.* Cambridge: Cambridge University Press.

Kohl, P. L. (1984) 'Force, History and the Evolutionist Paradigm', in M. Spriggs (ed.) *Marxist Perspectives in Archaeology,* pp. 127–34. Cambridge: Cambridge University Press.

Lechtman, H. (1993) 'Technologies of Power: The Andean Case', in J. Henderson and P. Netherly (eds) *Configurations of Power in Complex Societies.* Ithaca, NY: Cornell University Press.

Lemmonier, P. (1992) *Elements for an Anthropology of Technology,* Museum of Anthropology, Anthropological Papers No. 88. Ann Arbor: University of Michigan.

Lemmonier, P. (1993) 'Introduction', in P. Lemonnier (ed.) *Technological Choices: Transformation in Material Cultures Since the Neolithic,* pp. 1–35. London: Routledge.

Leone, M. (1985) 'Symbolic, Structural, and Critical Archaeology', in D. J. Meltzer, D. D. Fowler and J. A. Sabloff (eds) *American Archaeology Past and Future: A Celebration of the Society for American Archaeology 1935–1985,* pp. 415–38. Washington, DC: Smithsonian Institution Press.

Leone, M. P. and P. B. Potter, Jr. (eds) (1988) *The Recovery of Meaning: Historical Archaeology in the Eastern United States.* Washington, DC: Smithsonian Institution Press.

Lightfoot, K. G. (1995) 'Culture Contact Studies: Redefining the Relationship Between Prehistoric and Historic Archaeology', *American Antiquity* 60: 199–217.

Lightfoot, K. G. and A. Martinez (1995) 'Frontiers and Boundaries in Archaeological Perspective', *Annual Review of Anthropology* 24: 471–92.

Little, B. J. (1994) 'People with History: An Update on Historical Archaeology in the United States', *Journal of Archaeological Method and Theory* 1: 5–40.

Lyman, R. L. and M. J. O'Brien (1998) 'The Goals of Evolutionary Archaeology', *Current Anthropology* 39: 615–52.

Lyman, R. L., M. J. O'Brien, and R. C. Dunnell (1997) *The Rise and Fall of Culture History.* New York: Plenum.

Marcus, J. and K. V. Flannery (1994) 'Ancient Zapotec Ritual and Religion: An Application of the Direct Historical Approach', in C. Renfrew and E. B. W. Zubrow (eds) *The Ancient Mind: Elements of Cognitive Archaeology,* pp. 55–74. Cambridge: Cambridge University Press.

Maschner, H. D. G. and S. Mithen (1996) 'Darwinian Archaeologies: An Introductory Essay', in H. D. G. Maschner (ed.) *Darwinian Archaeologies,* pp. 3–14. New York: Plenum Press.

Maschner, H. D. G. and J. Q. Patton (1996) 'Kin Selection and the Origins of Hereditary Social Inequality: A Case Study from the Northern Northwest Coast', in H. D. G. Maschner (ed.) *Darwinian Archaeologies,* pp. 89–107. New York: Plenum Press.

McGuire, R. (1992) *A Marxist Archaeology.* San Diego: Academic Press.

Mehrer, M. W. (1995) *Cahokia's Countryside: Household Archaeology, Settlement Patterns, and Social Power.* DeKalb: Northern Illinois University Press.

Milner, G. R. (1990) 'The Late Prehistoric Cahokia Cultural System of the Mississippi River Valley: Foundations, Florescence, and Fragmentation', *Journal of World Prehistory* 4: 1–43.

Milner, G. R. (1996) 'The Muddled Mississippian: Agendas, Analogues, and Analyses', paper presented in the plenary session, Appropriate Theory in Archaeological Investigations, N. Yoffee (organizer), 61st Annual Meeting of the Society for American Archaeology, New Orleans.

Milner, G. R. (1998) *The Cahokia Chiefdom: The Archaeology of a Mississippian Society.* Washington, DC: Smithsonian Institution Press.

Milner, G. R., T. E. Emerson, M. W. Mehrer, J. A. Williams, and D. Esarey (1984) 'Mississippian and Oneota Period', in C. J. Bareis and J. W. Porter (eds) *American Bottom Archaeology,* pp. 158–86. Urbana: University of Illinois Press.

Mithen, S. (1997) 'Cognitive Archaeology, Evolutionary Psychology and Cultural Transmission, with Particular Reference to Religious Ideas', in C. M. Barton and G. A. Clark (eds) *Rediscovering Darwin: Evolutionary Theory and Archaeological Explanation,* pp. 67–74. Archaeological Papers of the American Anthropological Association, No. 7, Washington, DC.

Morse, D. F. and P. A. Morse (1983) *Archaeology of the Central Mississippi Valley*. New York: Academic Press.

Muller, J. (1989) 'The Southern Cult', in P. Galloway (ed.) *The Southeastern Ceremonial Complex: Artifacts and Analysis*, pp. 11–26. Lincoln: University of Nebraska Press.

Muller, J. (1997) *Mississippian Political Economy*. New York: Plenum Press.

Muller, J. and J. E. Stephens (1991) 'Mississippian Sociocultural Adaptation', in T. E. Emerson and R. B. Lewis (eds) *Cahokia and the Hinterlands: Middle Mississippian Cultures of the Midwest*, pp. 297–310. Urbana: University of Illinois Press.

Nassaney, M. S. (1992) 'Communal Societies and the Emergence of Elites in the Prehistoric American Southeast', in A. W. Barker and T. R. Pauketat (eds) *Lords of the Southeast: Social Inequality and the Native Elites of Southeastern North America*, American Anthropological Association, Archaeological Papers 3, Washington, DC, pp. 111–43.

Neff, H. (1992) 'Ceramics and Evolution', *Archaeological Method and Theory* 4: 141–93.

Neff, H. and D. O. Larson (1997) 'Methodology of Comparison in Evolutionary Archaeology', in C. M. Barton and G. A. Clark (eds) *Rediscovering Darwin: Evolutionary Theory and Archaeological Explanation*, pp. 75–94. Archaeological Papers of the American Anthropological Association, No. 7, Washington, DC.

Nelson, S. M. (1997) *Gender in Archaeology: Analyzing Power and Prestige*. Walnut Creek, CA: AltaMira Press.

O'Brien, M. J. and T. D. Holland (1990) 'Variation, Selection, and the Archaeological Record', *Archaeological Method and Theory* 2: 31–79.

O'Brien, M. J. and T. D. Holland (1990) 'The Role of Adaptation in Archaeological Explanation', *American Antiquity* 57: 3–59.

O'Brien, M. J., T. D. Holland, R. J. Hoard, and G. L. Fox (1994) 'Evolutionary Implications of Design and Performance Characteristics of Prehistoric Pottery', *Journal of Archaeological Method and Theory* 1: 259–304.

O'Brien, M. J. and W. R. Wood (1998) *The Prehistory of Missouri*. Columbia: University of Missouri Press.

Ortner, S. B. (1984) 'Theory in Anthropology since the Sixties', *Comparative Studies in Society and History* 26: 126–66.

Pauketat, T. R. (1993) *Temples for Cahokia Lords: Preston Holder's 1955–1956 Excavations of Kunnemann Mound*, Museum of Anthropology, Memoir 26. Ann Arbor: University of Michigan.

Pauketat, T. R. (1994) *The Ascent of Chiefs: Cahokia and Mississippian Politics in Native North America*. Tuscaloosa: University of Alabama Press.

Pauketat, T. R. (1996a) 'The Place of Post-Circle Monuments in Cahokian Political History', *Wisconsin Archaeologist* 77: 73–83.

Pauketat, T. R. (1996b) 'Resettled Rural Communities at the Edge of Early Cahokia', paper presented at the Southeastern Archaeological Conference, Birmingham, Alabama.

Pauketat, T. R. (1997a) 'Cahokian Political Economy', in T. R. Pauketat and T. E. Emerson (eds) *Cahokia: Domination and Ideology in the Mississippian World*, pp. 30–51. Lincoln: University of Nebraska Press.

Pauketat, T. R. (1997b) 'Mississippian from Top to Bottom', paper presented in the symposium 'New Evidence of Early Cahokian Provisions and Rituals', organized by T. Pauketat, Southeastern Archaeological Conference, November 5–9, Baton Rouge, Louisiana.

Pauketat, T. R. (1997c) 'Specialization, Political Symbols, and the Crafty Elite of Cahokia', *Southeastern Archaeology* 16: 1–15.

Pauketat, T. R. (1998a) *The Archaeology of Downtown Cahokia: The Tract 15A and Dunham Tract Excavations*. Illinois Transportation Research Program, Studies in Archaeology 1. Urbana: University of Illinois.

Pauketat, T. R. (1998b) 'Refiguring the Archaeology of Greater Cahokia', *Journal of Archaeological Research* 6: 45–89.

Pauketat, T. R. (2000a) 'The Tragedy of the Commoners', in M.-A. Dobres and J. Robb (eds) *Agency in Archaeology*, pp. 113–29. London: Routledge.

Pauketat, T. R. (2000b) 'Politicization and Community in the Pre-Columbian Mississippi Valley', in M.-A. Canuto and J. Yaeger (eds) *The Archaeology of Communities: A New World Perspective*, pp. 16–43. London: Routledge.

Pauketat, T. R. (2001) 'A New Tradition in Archaeology', in T. R. Pauketat (ed.) *An Archaeology of Traditions: Agency and History Before and After Columbus*. Gainesville: University Press of Florida.

Pauketat, T. R. and T. E. Emerson (1991) 'The Ideology of Authority and the Power of the Pot', *American Anthropologist* 93: 919–41.

Pauketat, T. R. and T. E. Emerson (eds) (1997a) *Cahokia: Domination and Ideology in the Mississippian World*. Lincoln: University of Nebraska Press.

Pauketat, T. R. and T. E. Emerson (1997b) 'Introduction: Domination and Ideology in the Mississippian World', in T. R. Pauketat and T. E. Emerson (eds) *Cahokia: Domination and Ideology in the Mississippian World*, pp. 1–29. Lincoln: University of Nebraska Press.

Pauketat, T. R. and T. E. Emerson (1999) 'Representations of Hegemony as Community at Cahokia', in J. Robb (ed.) *Material Symbols: Culture and Economy* in *Prehistory*, pp. 302–17. Carbondale: Center for Archaeological Investigations, Southern Illinois University.

Pauketat, T. R., L. S. Kelly, G. Fritz, N. H. Lopinot, and E. Hargrave (n.d.) 'Ritual Refuse from Cahokia'. Paper in possession of the authors.

Pauketat, T. R., and N. H. Lopinot (1997) 'Cahokian Population Dynamics', in T. R. Pauketat and T. E. Emerson (eds) *Cahokia: Domination and Ideology in the Mississippian World*, pp. 103–23. Lincoln: University of Nebraska Press.

Pauketat, T. R., M. A. Rees, and S. L. Pauketat (1998) *An Archaeological Survey of the Horseshoe Lake State Park, Madison County, Illinois*, Reports of Investigations, No. 55. Springfield: Illinois State Museum.

Phillips, P., J. A. Ford, and J. B. Griffin (1951) *Archaeological Survey in the Lower Mississippi Alluvial Valley, 1940–1947*, Papers 25. Cambridge, MA: Peabody Museum of American Archaeology and Ethnology.

Rabinow, P. (ed.) (1984) *The Foucault Reader*. New York: Pantheon Books.

Rappaport, R. A. (1979) *Ecology, Meaning, and Religion*. Berkeley, CA: North Atlantic Books.

Rees, M. A. (1997) 'Coercion, Tribute and Chiefly Authority: The Regional Development of Mississippian Political Culture', *Southeastern Archaeology* 16: 113–33.

Renfrew, C. (1987) 'Introduction: Peer Polity Interaction and Socio-Political Change', in C. Renfrew and J. F. Cherry (eds) *Peer Polity Interaction and Socio-Political Change*, pp. 1–18. Cambridge: Cambridge University Press.

Renfrew, C. (1994) 'Towards a Cognitive Archaeology', in C. Renfrew and E. Zubrow (eds) *The Ancient Mind: Elements of Cognitive Archaeology*, pp. 3–12. Cambridge: Cambridge University Press.

Renfrew, C. and E. Zubrow (eds) (1994) *The Ancient Mind: Elements of Cognitive Archaeology*. Cambridge: Cambridge University Press.

Rindos, D. (1989) 'Undirected Variation and the Darwinian Explanation of Cultural Change', in M. B. Schiffer (ed.) *Archaeological Method and Theory*, vol. 1, pp. 1–45. Tuscon: University of Arizona Press.

Robb, J. E. (1998) 'The Archaeology of Symbols', *Annual Review of Anthropology* 27: 329–46.

Rogers, J. D. and S. M. Wilson (1993) *Ethnohistory and Archaeology: Approaches to Postcontact Change in the Americas*. New York: Plenum.

Roscoe, P. B. (1993) 'Practice and Political Centralization', *Current Anthropology* 34: 111–40.

Sahlins, M. (1985) *Islands of History*. Chicago: University of Chicago Press.

Schiffer, M. B. (1995) *Behavioral Archaeology: First Principles*. Salt Lake City: University of Utah Press.

Schiffer, M. B. (1996) 'Some Relationships Between Behavioral and Evolutionary Archaeologies', *American Antiquity* 61: 643–62.

Schiffer, M. B. and J. M. Skibo (1997) 'The Explanation of Artifact Variability', *American Antiquity* 62: 27–50.

Schlanger, N. (1994) 'Mindful Technology: Unleashing the *Chaîne Opératoire* for an Archaeology of Mind', in C. Renfrew and E. B. W. Zubrow (eds) *The Ancient Mind: Elements of Cognitive Archaeology*, pp. 143–51. Cambridge: Cambridge University Press.

Shackel, P. A. and B. J. Little (1992) 'Post-Processual Approaches to Meanings and Uses of Material Culture in Historical Archaeology', *Historical Archaeology* 26: 5–11.

Shennan, S. (1993) 'After Social Evolution: A New Archaeological Agenda?', in N. Yoffee and A. Sherratt (eds) *Archaeological Theory: Who Sets the Agenda?*, pp. 53–9. Cambridge: Cambridge University Press.

Shennan, S. (1996) 'Foreword', in H. E. G. Maschner (ed.) *Darwinian Archaeologies*, pp. ix–x. New York: Plenum.

Stark, M. T. (ed.) (1998) *The Archaeology of Social Boundaries*. Washington, DC: Smithsonian Institution Press.

Stein, G. (1998) 'Diasporas, Colonies and World Systems: Rethinking the Archaeology of Inter-Regional Interaction'. Distinguished Lecture, Archaeology Division, 97th Annual Meeting of the American Anthropological Association, December 2–6, Philadelphia.

Steponaitis, V. P. (1984) 'Technological Studies of Prehistoric Pottery from Alabama: Physical Properties and Vessel Function', in S. E. van der Leeuw and A. C. Pritchard (eds) *The Many Dimensions of Pottery: Ceramics in Archaeology and Anthropology*, pp. 79–127. Universiteit van Amsterdam.

Sztompka, P. (1991) *Society in Action: The Theory of Social Becoming*. Chicago: University of Chicago Press.

Tainter, J. (1988) *The Collapse of Complex Societies*. Cambridge: Cambridge University Press.

Teltser, P. A. (ed.) (1995) *Evolutionary Archaeology: Methodological Issues*. Tucson: University of Arizona Press.

Toren, C. (1999) *Mind, Materiality and History: Explorations in Fijian Ethnography*. London: Routledge.

Trigger, B. G. (1982) 'Ethnohistory: Problems and Prospects', *Ethnohistory* 29: 1–19.

Trigger, B. G. (1984) 'Archaeology at the Crossroads: What's New?', *Annual Review of Anthropology* 13: 275–300.

Trigger, B. G. (1989) 'History and Contemporary American Archaeology: A Critical Analysis', in C. C. Lamberg-Karlovsky (ed.) *Archaeological Thought in America*, pp. 19–34. Cambridge: Cambridge University Press.

Trigger, B. G. (1991) 'Distinguished Lecture in Archeology: Constraint and Freedom – A New Synthesis for Archeological Explanation', *American Anthropologist* 93: 551–69.

Turner, V. (1967) *The Forest of Symbols*. Ithaca, NY: Cornell University Press.

van der Leeuw, S. E. (1993) 'Giving the Potter a Choice: Conceptual Aspects of Pottery Techniques', in P. Lemmonier (ed.) *Technological Choices: Transformation in Material Cultures since the Neolithic*, pp. 238–88. London: Routledge.

van der Leeuw, S. E. (1994) 'Cognitive Aspects of "Technique"', in C. Renfrew and E. Zubrow (eds) *The Ancient Mind: Elements of Cognitive Archaeology*, pp. 135–42. Cambridge: Cambridge University Press.

VanPool, C. S. and T. L. VanPool (1999) 'The Scientific Nature of Postprocessualism', *American Antiquity* 64: 33–53.

Vincent, J. (1990) *Anthropology and Politics*. Tucson: University of Arizona Press.

Wagner, R. (1986) *Symbols that Stand for Themselves*. Chicago: University of Chicago Press.

Weimer, M. B. (1995) 'Predictive Modeling and Cultural Resource Management: An Alternative View from the Plains Periphery', in P. Duke and M. C. Wilson (eds) *Beyond Subsistence: Plains Archaeology and the Postprocessual Critique*, pp. 90–109. Tuscaloosa: University of Alabama Press.

Wiessner, P. (1997) 'Seeking Guidelines Through an Evolutionary Approach: Style Revisited Among the !Kung San (Ju/Hoansi) of the 1990s', in C. M. Barton and G. A. Clark (eds) *Rediscovering Darwin: Evolutionary Theory and Archaeological Explanation*, pp. 157–76. Archeological Papers of the American Anthropological Association, No. 7, Washington, DC.

Wolf, E. R. (1990) 'Facing Power – Old Insights, New Questions', *American Anthropologist* 92: 586–96.

Wolf, E. R. (1999) *Envisioning Power: Ideologies of Dominance and Crisis*. Berkeley: University of California Press.

Zubrow, E. B. W. (1994) 'Knowledge Representation and Archaeology: A Cognitive Example Using GIS', in C. Renfrew and E. B. W. Zubrow (eds) *The Ancient Mind: Elements of Cognitive Archaeology*, pp. 107–18. Cambridge: Cambridge University Press.

6

Technology's Links and *Chaînes*
The Processual Unfolding of Technique and Technician

Marcia-Anne Dobres

Archaeological studies of technology have been revitalized significantly in recent years by the introduction of an analytic method known as *chaîne opératoire*. André Leroi-Gourhan was the first to name and apply this analytic technique to archaeological inquiry, and today *chaîne opératoire* analysis is employed to detail with extraordinary precision productive sequence(s) and decision-making strategies of raw material transformations, past and present. It is, however, far more than an analytic tool for identifying and describing the material "life history" of artifacts. *Chaîne opératoire* can be a powerful conceptual framework – a methodology – providing technology studies with both the empirical rigor they require and the human face they deserve. In this chapter I argue that *chaîne opératoire* is, at one and the same time, an interpretive methodology and analytic method capable of forging robust inferential links between the material patterning of technical acts and sociopolitical relations of production accounting for them. Although the analytic method of *chaîne opératoire* research is utilized most often to identify

Marcia-Anne Dobres, "Technology's Links and Chaînes: The Processual Unfolding of Technique and Technician," pp. 124–45 from Marcia-Anne Dobres and Christopher R. Hoffman (eds) The Social Dynamics of Technology: Practice, Politics, and Worldviews (Washington, DC: Smithsonian Institution Press, 1999). Copyright Marcia-Anne Dobres, 1999. Reprinted with permission of the author.

the prehistoric mental "maps" (or so-called world views) structuring rule-governed technical activities, as a conceptual methodology (and not simply an analytic method; distinction in Harding 1987), it can be especially helpful in considering the dynamic social milieus and artifice by which material acts were differentially pursued by technicians and variously organized work groups.

This discussion will, I hope, contribute to the revitalization of research on prehistoric technology in two ways. First, it directs attention to some of Mauss's long-forgotten views on technology, in particular his argument that technology is a "total social fact" encompassing more than the material and gestural actions transforming natural resources into cultural products. The next step is to infuse this redefinition with a healthy dose of contemporary social theory, by taking up the question of social agency (especially gender) that is implicated in expressions of self-interest and social identity through technical means. These ideas suggest some ways that the preservable traces of gestural acts of prehistoric artifact production and use can serve as an inferential link to the social agency of the technicians themselves. The discussion is substantiated with reference to a particular social formation of interest to much of archaeological inquiry, the communal mode of production (CMP). Contemporary examples include cases prominent in ethnoarchaeology, such as the !Kung San

(Ju/'hoansi), Chipewya, and Iñupiat, and also the Israeli *kibbutz*, which shares relevant structural commonalities. Two archaeological examples from the French Late Upper Palaeolithic round out the discussion.

The *Chaîne Opératoire* and What's Hidden in Black Boxes

To date, *chaîne opératoire* is primarily an analytic tool successfully applied to two fundamental kinds of research questions. The first and most basic is to identify the sequential technical operations by which natural resources were transformed into culturally meaningful and functional objects (Pelegrin et al. 1988). As a major interpreter of Mauss and Leroi-Gourhan for contemporary interests, Lemonnier (1989, 1992a) describes technical activity as the interplay of five heuristically separated elements: matter, energy, objects, gestures in sequence, and knowledge. Clearly, the first three elements share much in common with classic neo-evolutionary theory, wherein a cultural system is only considered as adaptive as its ability to transform matter and energy into efficient and viable cultural (survival) behaviors. The latter two elements of a technical activity, gestures in sequence and technical knowledge, derive from Mauss's concept of *enchaînement organique* (discussed next)[1] Taken together, the study of these five elements is supposed to permit an understanding of the sequential physical actions and decision-making strategies by which matter was transformed into culture-bearing objects. However, this chapter argues that only if we explicitly ask about social agency and the context-specific nature of social relations of material production can we comprehend the anthropological dynamics of technology (Dobres and Hoffman 1994).

Once the technical sequences by which artifacts were fabricated, used, and repaired are identified, *chaîne opératoire* research is employed most often to infer something of the abstract cognitive processes and underlying normative logic systems structuring those acts (see especially Pelegrin et al. 1988; Perlès 1992; essays in Renfrew and Zubrow 1994). Without doubt, the idea that preservable traces of artifact manufacture can be analyzed (through studying its technical chain) to identify deep-seated mental maps has provided archaeology with a major theoretical and analytic advance by researchers on both sides of the Atlantic (as in Lechtman 1977, 1984).

Nonetheless, a major strand in the web of interwoven social and material "threads" constituting technology lies somewhere *between* the sequential physical gestures of material culture production and use and the abstract cognitive frameworks structuring those activities. This particular thread concerns technicians, technical artifice, and dynamic interpersonal social relations of production (Dobres 1995a, 2000; Dobres and Hoffman 1994). For all the current focus on the structural "grammars" and the symbolic dimensions of prehistoric technologies, rarely do we explicitly theorize about the dynamic interactive social relationships through which all this symbolic and cognitive object-making and use took place. Even with more conventional interests in the "organization of technology" (typically pursued through cost–benefit analysis), explanatory models are rarely explicit on the dynamics of self-interested technical agents, the artifice of technical acts, much less the particular sorts of interpersonal relationships implied (Pfaffenberger 1988; Winner 1986). Without explicit attention to the socially constituted nature of technical acts and technical choice (those, for example, through which tacit mental maps were followed so faithfully or by which the physical and mechanical properties of raw materials were discovered or circumvented), neither the material nor mental processes involved will be adequately understood. Another way to think of this is that without attention to the hows and whys of everyday technical agency and the social contexts of those activities, descriptions will be little more than static (albeit sequential) rather than dynamic accounts of anthropological processes played out in and on the ancient material world.

Mauss's enchaînement organique *and technology: a total social fact*

Leroi-Gourhan's concept of *chaîne opératoire* derives from the ideas of the French ethnologist and sociologist Marcel Mauss (1935). As Durkheim's student, Mauss was interested in how social collectives articulated and maintained their mutually shared beliefs and traditional ways of acting in everyday life. Insightfully, he realized that technical acts were an integral part of the everyday way in which cultural traditions were maintained and passed on. At the same time, Mauss was interested in the body of collective knowledge underlying technical acts and how technical *connaissance* and *savoir-faire* were reaffirmed through routine physical gestures. For Mauss, then, technical knowledge involved more than understanding the physical properties (and limits) of raw materials and the practical knowledge enabling artifact production and use. It was also important to understand how technical *savoir-faire* was passed from generation to generation, embedded with value and significance, and reaffirmed through systems of kinship and apprenticeship. For Mauss, technology was dynamic and social to the core.

As an ethnologist, Mauss was especially interested in the *enchaînement organique* by which natural resources were sequentially transformed into useful cultural objects through bodily gestures practiced in socially constituted milieus. In keeping with Durkheim's lifelong interest in social solidarity, Mauss (1924) believed it necessary to move upward in analytic scale, from an understanding of the individual as *homo faber*, to that of the social collective and the enframing traditions within which individual techniques were practiced. He saw bodily techniques as integral to the everyday reproduction of society; thus he conceptualized technique as firmly embedded in normative cultural tradition (1935). Much like Heidegger (1977), Mauss argued the importance of understanding technical acts as they "unfolded," as they were in the process-of-becoming, for that was a key locus for the simultaneous production and reiteration of cultural meaning and practical action. This physical process of artifact-becoming-in-a-social-milieu is not only central to Mauss's concept of *enchaînement organique*. It is a physical link between artifactual and cultural reproduction that can be of special import to archaeologists. In sum, *chaînes opératoires* are of a decidedly social, collective, and material nature and show that technologies link together social, biological, gestural, and material transformative processes (Schlanger 1990).

Leroi-Gourhan: methodologist and evolutionist

It was André Leroi-Gourhan who provided these ideas with much-needed analytic rigor and introduced them into archaeology (Lemonnier 1992b). But in so doing, he also narrowed Mauss's total social fact to its more tangible side. As a student of Mauss, Leroi-Gourhan well understood that gestural sequences were rooted in ethnic traditions and entrenched in communal memory (Leroi-Gourhan 1964a:66). But as an archaeologist, he intellectualized technology at two vastly dissimilar scales: empirical traces of individual technical gestures, and macroevolutionary processes (Lemonnier 1992b:15–16; Pelegrin et al. 1988).

In his more philosophical reflections, Leroi-Gourhan explored the relationship between the somatics (or biology) of technical gestures and the technical act. In particular, he focused on the integration of bodily technogestures with the physicality of objects themselves (especially, 1943, 1945, 1964a, 1964b). But rather than explore how body and object integrated into an inseparable and total *social* phenomenon at the scale of everyday practice (as did his mentor), he concentrated on their evolutionary implications. For Leroi-Gourhan, the first meaningful act of distance and separation was between humans and their (material) technology, for example, in the evolutionary shift from the use of the hand *as* a tool to the hand *holding* a tool (Edmonds 1990:67). In contrast, Mauss focused on the ways *chaînes opératoires* were acquired through connections to the social body, through both direct and tacit education, *savoir-faire*, routinization, and even through self-awareness on the part of the working technician (see also Dobres 2000; Heidegger 1977; Ingold 1990, 1993a, 1993b).

Nonetheless, Leroi-Gourhan's introduction of *chaîne opératoire* into archaeological research began a critical and important shift away from the study of artifact morphology, typology, and function and toward an interest in the dynamic "life histories" of artifacts (see also Kopytoff 1986:84; Schiffer 1975, 1992b).

On the Social Agency of *Chaînes* and Links

Technologies are dynamic acts of social and material transformation: they serve as media through which social relations and world views are expressed and mediated; they materialize and make concrete people's attitudes about the right (and wrong) ways to make and use things; and, technologies take shape as they "take on" meanings and values by virtue of how technicians engage with each other while taking care of business. In my desire to infuse the archaeological use of *chaîne opératoire* with a more dynamic human face, I find it especially useful, indeed necessary, to bridge the artificial barriers separating the many disciplines interested in technology from one another and from archaeology (Dobres and Hoffman 1994; Dobres [2000]). Thus, I am in sympathy with philosophers, historians, sociologists, and sociocultural anthropologists who together define technologies as integrated *webs* weaving skill, knowledge, dexterity, values, functional needs and goals, attitudes, traditions, power relations, material constraints, and end-products together with the agency, artifice, and social relations of technicians.

For archaeologists, it is especially important to explore the parallel between technologies as acts of material transformation and technologies as acts of social transformation. As both Marx and Engels (1970:42–45) and Childe (1936) understood, through acts of material transformation people effect their own social transformation. And though this dialectic has long been recognized on a societal (evolutionary) level, theories of ancient technology have been relatively silent on how individual social identities were defined, expressed, and negotiated – that is, transformed – during technical acts. It is on this topic that *chaîne opératoire* can be of special methodological *and* interpretive value.

Contemporary theories of social agency can illuminate some of the above concerns by helping archaeologists understand how ancient technicians might have tried to situate themselves in relation to others while engaged in everyday technical pursuits (Dobres and Hoffman 1994; see also Cross 1990; Dobres 1995a, 1995b). In general, theories of social agency make sense of cultural practice as routinized and habitual actions in which women and men, children and elders engage on a day-to-day basis. As such, mundane and habitual social interaction lies at the heart of cultural practice and culture change.

Modeling daily life at the microscale, therefore, becomes necessary to understanding more macroscale cultural and transformative processes (Marquardt 1992). In the course of daily interaction, individuals express various kinds of interests, both personal and collective. In such arenas, the dynamics of interpersonal social relations inevitably lead to tensions and conflicts that require mediation and resolution. Nowhere is this *processual* dynamic more evident than in the daily practice of habitual technical activities.

For example, many ethnographic studies have shown how the agency of gender is inscribed onto the material world of resources and power, thereby affording certain individuals control of the objects produced, control of the technologies and technicians involved, control of the value systems that regulate the status of gendered technicians, and control of both esoteric and practical knowledge (see outstanding examples in Herbert 1993; McGaw 1996; MacKenzie 1991; Schwartz Cowan 1979). Therefore technologies are, at one and the same time, arenas in which agents construct social identities and forge power relations while also producing and using utilitarian objects for practical ends.

The conceptual framework of *chaîne opératoire* can link together the tangible and intangible dimensions of technological practice by regarding techniques as gestures undertaken in the "public" domain. At the same time, the analytic methods of *chaîne opératoire* research make it possible to link the archaeological record, comprised of static yet tangible remains of ancient technogestures, to the dynamic social milieus in which they were practiced. *Chaîne opératoire* research provides an excellent starting point for establishing such links, because it is specifically designed to identify and describe the material sequence(s) of gestural acts through which natural resources were modified (and remodified) into culturally useful objects. The idea in this chapter is that *while* undertaking productive activities, individuals create and localize personal and group identities, making statements about themselves that are "read" by others with whom they are interacting. Technical acts can thus be treated as a medium for defining, negotiating, and expressing personhood.

As Childs' ethnographic study (1999) illustrates, social identity, status, power, privilege, and access to important cultural objects are inseparably interwoven facets of a single complex dynamic. A Toro man cannot "buy" a wife until he has access not only to the means and forces of iron production, but also to the esoteric and practical knowledge and skills necessary to become a viable iron maker. Only when these factors come together in specific times and places in the life histories of individual men can they acquire wives, a living, and social status. Can we possibly understand the complexity of Toro ironworking without making these social dynamics and world views an integral part of materials analysis? Archaeologists need not restrict themselves to the observable present when asking about such processes. As an analytic method, *chaîne opératoire* provides the means for inquiring into such dynamics in prehistory.

Chaîne opératoire is explicit with respect to tracking the material and functional life history of artifacts. But as a corollary, *transforming natural resources into cultural products engenders the life history of technicians* (Dobres 1995b, 2000; Heidegger 1977). For example, as but one notable social identity cross-cut by many others, gender is not an immutable social category of person. What makes gender a cultural dynamic – that is, a process not an entity – is that it is *processed* throughout the life cycle (Moore 1986; Wolf 1974). Over the course of their lives, people move in and through salient cultural categories that conflate age, sex, and sexuality in complex ways: newborn, virgin girl, circumcised boy, pregnant wife, husband, skilled craftsman, father, mother-in-law, grandfather, divorcee, widow, and so forth. Gender, especially when conflated with age, has a sequential dimension not unlike a *chaîne opératoire*. Each gendered persona can, and typically does, confer new and different statuses on an individual. More to the point, gendered identities are processed, marked, and negotiated during one's life through the particular way individuals engage with one another while pursuing technical activities. Gender is, therefore, "manufactured" (de Lauretis 1987:9) in ways that resonate with the manufacture of material culture.

Attention to the ways individuals negotiate cultural categories does not ignore the fact that there are proscribed normative behaviors communities expect individuals to follow. Nor

does it have to mean that social identities are something people consciously negotiate with every breath they take. Here is where Bourdieu's (1977) concepts of *habitus* and routinization are useful. They suggest how the seemingly inconsequential, mundane, and everyday acts of producing and using artifacts serve to habituate individuals to the codified social categories on which expressions of personhood may rest. It is in balancing expressions of self-interest against cultural norms and expectations that the dynamics of social relations of production become especially salient.

The Dialectics of Gender and Technology

Once a conceptual parallel is established between making gender and making material culture, it becomes clear just how intertwined they are in everyday life. In particular, as McGaw (1996) and Pacey (1983) show, even what is defined a priori as "technology" stems in large part from gender ideologies and value systems, and that the two are inseparable:

> "Technology," like "economics," is a term conventionally defined by men to indicate a range of activities in which they happen to be interested.... Nearly all women's work, indeed, falls within the usual definition of technology. What excludes it from recognition is not only the simplicity of the equipment used, but the fact that it implies a different concept of what technology is about. Construction and the conquest of nature are not glorified, and there is little to notice in the way of technological virtuosity. (Pacey 1983:104)

There are few jobs that are not at least ideologically associated with particular genders, that do not differentially reward the players, and that do not also conjure up gender idioms. For example, in Western industrial societies men build and *mount* bridges, *erect* skyscrapers, and *man*-ipulate natural resources into cultural objects – all of which are unequivocal technical acts that simultaneously serve as powerful idioms of masculinity. In contrast, women's stereotypic share in codified divisions of labor turns on seemingly natural activities: having babies or nursing the young, sick, and elderly – none of which are typically thought of as technical per se, but which define femininity nonetheless.[2]

Significantly, until the advent of male-controlled Western reproductive technologies (in the sense of hard medical implements such as the speculum and, now, in-vitro fertilization), women's reproductive labor was thought of as natural and biological, but not necessarily technical. Yet even so-called natural childbirth has technical dimensions: to deliver a child safely and properly from the mother's womb requires a *chaîne* of biogestural techniques that vary cross-culturally. Such techniques combine esoteric and practical knowledge with practical skill and are supported by a particular configuration of social relationships (be they with midwives, nurses, doctors, nutritionists, or shamans). And as with any technology, the end-product is not limited to the production of a healthy baby; it includes new social positions for the mother and father, as well as the social and material power both gain within their community and from members of their immediate family (for examples, see Wolf 1974; also Childs 1999). Archaeological theory rests on the largely implicit premise that prehistoric lithic and ceramic production, big game hunting, and architecture all had their technical side. This "hard" concept of technology also suggests that less material and seemingly natural activities (such as childbirth and child rearing) were not properly technical. It is clear, here, that the primacy of the hard and the utilitarian conflates with contemporary gender value systems to define what counts as a prehistoric technology (Conkey and Spector 1984; Gero 1991; Lechtman 1993). This conflation is a prime example of what Whitehead (1927:73–86) called the "fallacy of misplaced concreteness."

reproducing labor itself (that is, biological reproduction) and related "domestic" activities (classic statement in Marx and Engels 1970:52). This distinction between material production and social reproduction, and between so-called political/public and domestic/private spheres, leads to another problematic corollary: the kinds of work in which women characteristically engage, such as child rearing and maintenance of the domestic sphere, are neither economic, political, nor all that technical (Hartmann 1987; Pateman 1987; Rosaldo 1980).

Because women's contribution to reproduction in the CMP has not been seen as properly economic, political, or technical, many of their everyday strategies for building networks of influence, prestige, and status have not attracted the same degree of academic interest as the "hard" techniques men practice (Ortner and Whitehead 1981; Rogers 1975). There is one important exception here: where women have been found to contribute significantly to *subsistence*, theorists have noted well that such activities serve as techniques of identity, status, and power. For example, in many post-colonial hunter-gatherer and foraging societies in South Africa and Australia, women have been found to contribute upward of 80 percent of the group's daily nutritional needs through plant gathering and more reliable techniques for hunting and trapping small animals (Hawkes et al. 1989; Lee 1979:253–272, table 9.3). And indeed, in many cases where women contribute the lion's share of daily foodstuffs, they often enjoy an important degree of autonomy and independence that women in other modes of production do not (Lee 1982; Sanday 1981:133–134; but see Bloch 1975 for a sobering counterexample).

Gender and technology in the communal mode of production

In the communal mode of production (CMP), the social organization of technological *production* (especially in terms of subsistence) involves material, economic, and political divisions of labor in which women and men differentially participate.[3] At the same time, *reproduction* in such societies involves divisions of labor that are said to derive from "natural" differences between the sexes, and is typically defined as activities

Rethinking Technology: Engendering the *Chaîne Opératoire*

Because the social agency of identity is implicated in people's lifelong engagement with their material world, the variety of technical activities individuals undertake should shed light on the sequential nature of their intertwined social and material lives. For archaeologists, making a conceptual link between the two sequences – one social, the other material – sets the stage for reasonable inferences about the production (and use) of social identities through material production (and use) activities. However, as we intertwine social and material life histories in our technical study of artifacts, we must also broaden what we mean by technology (Dobres and Hoffman 1994; Ingold 1988, 1990; Layton 1974).

For example, in suggesting that archaeologists study a broader set of factors impinging on the structure of hunting activities, as but one "properly" prehistoric technology, Gifford-Gonzalez (1993:190) cogently argues the "need to consider the imperatives of the household in driving field processing decisions." Another way to think of this, as feminist anthropologists have long argued, is that a separation of the "domestic" female sphere (thought to involve food processing, cooking, and care-taking) from the supposedly more "technical" and male-oriented world (of hunting) is a *construct* – a typological distinction arbitrarily separating reproduction from production (Rosaldo 1980). As Gifford-Gonzalez (1993:187–188) puts it, "the lack of attention to cooking and culinary end-products in zooarchaeology is, I believe, attributable to unconscious androcentric bias within the field. . . . This view favors hunting – especially male pursuit, dispatch, and butchery of prey – over just about any other activity involving animals." Following the logic of *chaîne opératoire*, ancient hunting techniques were inseparable from the antecedent value systems and material context(s) structuring them; thus the before, during, and after of "the hunt" was necessarily linked to concerns extending beyond physically killing game.

In a study of the contemporary Iñupiat (Inuit), Bodenhorn (1990:55) argues that "hunting cannot be reduced to the catching and slaughtering of animals, but rather includes a whole set of activities, both technical and symbolic, in which the interpendence [sic] of women and men is fundamental." Though whale hunting is described in the traditional anthropological literature as an exclusively male domain (because only men go to sea and actually spear whales), from an emic point of view Iñupiat women are directly implicated in and responsible for whale hunts. To ensure men's success on the open sea, the captain's wife must carefully comport herself in proscribed ways around their house; after all, "the whale comes to the whaling

captain's wife" (Bodenhorn 1990:61). As well, through her technical skill with an *ulu* (knife) she is charged with "calling up" the whale to be killed by men (Cassell 1988). It is thus the wife's job to attract the whale and, in Iñupiat terms, "to hunt" (Bodenhorn 1993:191). Ask a whaling captain and he will tell you: "I'm not the great hunter, my wife is" (Bodenhorn 1990).

As well, among the Chipewya, "the hunt" encompasses cosmological beliefs, gender ideologies, and gendered (not sexual) divisions of labor (Brumbach and Jarvenpa 1997; Sharp 1991:190). To the Chipewya, what is important about a hunt is not just the animal killed, but the tasks women perform to process and distribute meat and skins afterward. According to Chipewyan informants, it is the transformation of "raw" meat into cultural products (such as food and clothing) that is valued and gives value to hunting: acquisition techniques and the immediate end-product (meat) are of lesser importance (Sharp 1991). This example recalls Heidegger's emphasis on the "becoming" and processual nature of technology. It also shows why we need to broaden the current Western view of technology beyond practical concerns, efficiency, and material matters. By stressing the overlapping social and material acts of technique and technology, we are situated to put a human face to technological practices, past and present.

Politics, Identity, and Technology in the Communal Mode of Production

A key social dynamic that irrevocably links together material and social transformations is the politically charged nature of technological systems, technical acts, and end-products. Among other things, the politics of technology concern how the social labor of production is organized; who has access to the means, forces, and relations of production; what socioeconomic status(es) are at stake; and who is affected by their implementation (summarizing Bijker et al. 1987; Law 1991; Winner 1986). Studies of contemporary (industrial) technologies offer especially striking examples of technopolitics that link production, power, and personhood, but there is no basis for assuming a priori that such dynamics were not intertwined in the past as well (Bender 1989; Conkey 1991; Dobres 1995a; Gero 1991; Hayden 1994).

Knowledge and enskilment: a political basis for status

As a general rule, individuals in communally organized societies often gain status, prestige, influence, and power by demonstrating highly valued qualities for all to see. The possibility of a personal basis for position is, of course, offset by the proscribed roles individuals are expected to fill by virtue of their age, gender, kin and tribal affiliations, and so forth. Although fundamental social categories initially define one's identity(ies) and occupations, it is not through them alone that people find their place in the social collective. Such first-order identities are built upon and transformed by virtue of personality, level of skill and talents, personal history, reputation, and the possession and display of knowledge through technogestures. All of these can become the basis of social and material power (Keene 1991; examples in Ingold 1993c; Ridington 1988; Saitta and Keene 1990:205). Thus, in both tangible and intangible ways, technological practice is directly implicated in expressing political identity in egalitarian communities.

Knowledge, especially, figures prominently as a cross-cultural basis for leadership in nonhierarchical societies (Ingold 1993a, 1993b; Keene 1991), and it is worth reiterating that technology is the juncture of knowledgeable practice and practical knowledge (Ingold 1990; Schiffer and Skibo 1987). The *concrétisation* of ideas, values, and knowledge in technical practice and end-products provides an outward expression of the metaphors and world views central to, but not necessarily shared equally by, all members of a community (Childe 1956; Lechtman 1984; MacKenzie 1991; Simondon 1958). For example, one of the salient characteristics of most Canadian subarctic egalitarian societies (among them, Cree, Dene, Blackfoot, and Ojibwa) is that social status and the acknowledged capacity and right to leadership roles, however temporary and context-specific, are achieved through participation in vision quests and other forms of knowledge acquisition (Ridington 1988).

Moreover, contrary to both Rousseau's romanticized nineteenth-century view of primitive communism and Sahlins' (1972) neo-evolutionary concept of the original affluent society, people communally organized do *not* always work smoothly toward agreed-upon ends, even in egalitarian societies.[4] In particular, social tensions and acts of contestation during everyday routines of material production and use can become a means for expressing power and influence (Conkey and Gero 1991; Dobres 1995a). In a study of the organizational and power dynamics of production on the Israeli *kibbutz*, Keene (1991:377) shows that

> within the communal mode, the social group as a whole – the commune – serves as the basis for all productive activity. Access to necessary factors of production is guaranteed to all members, and all members participate in determining the division between necessary and surplus labor. *This pattern still leaves room for internal variation and does not necessarily demand material equality or equal access to the means of production.* (Emphasis added)

Anthropologists have paid considerable attention to the ways in which men in nonhierarchical societies develop social and material privilege, for example, through their skills as hunters (Hawkes 1993), through their exchange of women (Meillassoux 1981), and even through the production and subsequent hoarding of technical knowledge and skill (discussed next). Following Ingold (1993c), I suggest that the display and manipulation of cultural metaphors or practical knowledge signified outwardly in the performance of particular gestural techniques are also powerful "mechanisms" for negotiating social identity and status. Childs (1999), Hoffman (1999), and Pfaffenberger (1999) show how creating, possessing, and displaying technical knowledge and skill over the course of one's life can translate into social power and status. In communally organized societies, then, one need not have physical control "over" material techniques and products to exercise authority: differential access to techno-scientific knowledge (Schiffer and Skibo 1987), enskilment (Pálsson 1994), and technical virtuosity (Moore 1981; Root 1983) will do as well.

The Politics of Social Agency in Prehistoric Technology: Two Archaeological Examples

My comparative study of bone and antler technology at eight broadly contemporaneous Late Magdalenian sites in the French Midi-Pyrénées (ca. 14,000–11,000 years B.P.) identified extraordinarily variable sequential operations of artifact production, use, and repair around the region. Site-by-site, the actual choice of technical sequences used to manufacture, use, and repair harpoons, spear points, needles, and the like was structured *neither* by artifact physics *nor* by functional necessity. The guidelines for making, using, and repairing objects of the same raw material and even those of similar function were not based on objective conditions. Even among similar classes of artifacts retrieved from similar "site types" – such as needles at base camps and harpoons at upland seasonal ibex hunting sites – on-the-ground technical practices varied along almost every measurable attribute (Dobres 1996). Across the region there was no one "best" (or singularly "Magdalenian") way to make, use, decorate, or repair harpoons, points, and needles. Technical decisions were site-specific.

This evidence contradicts the notion that Late Magdalenian hunter-gatherers went about their daily lives faithfully following normative techno-cognitive maps maintained through a conservative cultural work ethic. Although they may have carried in their heads a roadmap of techniques to get a job done, *in practice* their strategies varied considerably. What, then, can account for these observable patterns?

When technical agents work in communal contexts, they are at least tacitly aware of each other's bodies and actions (Graburn 1976). And as Mauss recognized, when people are so engaged, even subtle bodily movements become a communicative medium. How individuals comport themselves while undertaking everyday technical activities, then, becomes a form of silent social discourse. "The very practice of a technique is itself a statement about identity: there can be no separation of communicative from technical behavior" (Ingold 1993b:438). People express interests of many kinds while making and using

material culture, and as a general rule, there is a cacophony of messages communicated through technical body language. Fortunately, ethno-archaeological and replicative experiments on the spatial patterning of material *chaînes opératoires* allow archaeologists to delimit with some precision the different contexts in which ancient artifacts were fabricated, used, and repaired on a site-specific basis. Because they were so often undertaken in what I like to call public contexts, where a variety of productive activities were going on simultaneously, ancient technical gestures were surely a total social fact. Intended or otherwise, technogestures so contextualized served as silent codes of discourse localizing identities of various sorts.

The gestural dimensions of Late Magdalenian organic technology can be understood as a sort of body language acted out in differently constituted contexts of social and material interaction. The technical evidence I have identified at individual sites in the Haute-Garonne and Ariège, specifically, attests to a significant degree of choice in how Magdalenian *chaînes* were actually practiced. It further points to the likelihood that in the day-to-day pursuit of such activities person-hood was mediated through material means. For example: at La Vache, the highly variable patterning of harpoon barb construction suggests that technicians had individualized strategies for making them either longer, sharper, more curved, or thinner than those of their neighbors; at Les Églises and Mas d'Azil, only a few bone needles show the successful completion of a highly skilled technique for piercing them with perfectly round eyes, while others betray an obvious lack of competence that those "in the know" could not have failed to observe; also at La Vache, only a few individuals (perhaps one) whittled an extra set of depressions on the base of their spear points, and through this, demonstrated materially (yet without recourse to overt self-aggrandizement) a special knowledge of hafting tricks learned over time. These subtle empirical variations in technical, functional, and morphological attributes imply an individualized level of *enchaînement organique* that would have been both visible and meaningful to one's neighbors, for as Graburn (1976:21) notes: "In small-scale societies where everything is everybody's business, there is little anonymity, and most people would know the details of style, the aesthetic choices, and even the tools of their contemporaries." It seems likely that the sorts of observable differences in Late Magdalenian techno-gestural strategies practiced on the ground contributed to localizing and materializing the identities and statuses of the technical agents performing them.

In the Paris Basin (also during the Late Magdalenian), French researchers have similarly suggested that technical knowledge was differentially practiced and shared under a system of tutelage they call apprenticeship (Karlin and Pigeot 1989; Olive and Pigeot 1992; Olive et al. 1991; Pigeot 1987, 1990). *Chaîne opératoire* research has been able to identify variable skill levels in blade production at Étiolles (Essonne) and their differential spatial distribution around discretely separated hearths. These data have been used to suggest that a hierarchy of interpersonal relationships (within family units) created and defined differential access to the practical and manual skills required to fabricate expert blades. Through the extraordinarily rigorous spatial mapping of variable qualities of blade manufacture, retouch, and repair "life" sequences, these mundane and practical endeavors have been resituated in something of their original social milieu. In turn, they have permitted reasonable inferences about the technical agency of ancient technological practice.

Discussion

In these two archaeological examples, the French analytic of *chaîne opératoire* research has been employed to identify a number of interrelated factors structuring Late Magdalenian organic and lithic technology. Keeping the focus on the contours of site-specific social interaction, both studies concentrate on empirical remains to infer the organizational dynamics accounting for them. While still in their infancy, these two attempts demonstrate that *chaîne opératoire* research can be helpful in elucidating the socially constituted and intertwined histories of artifacts and artifice, products and people, and material actions and sociotechnical agency. Analytically and

conceptually, we are now in an excellent position to establish even stronger anthropological links between static artifact patterns, traces of technogestural sequences, and the dynamic social contexts through which they materialized.

The preceding discussion has placed inordinate emphasis on the word *process*, arguing that social identities, subsistence activities, and artifact production all come about through sequentially organized technical activities. Allusion to the processing, or transformation, of both personhood and products is intentional, because technology always involves the recursive making of culture, agents, and material culture. For me, this means technical research needs to concentrate more on the *interrelationship* of social and material factors that combine to produce end-products, be they artifacts, the hunt, or individuals. Agents who move in and through specific material activities are embedded in, and thus bring with them, an extensive array of concerns and interests. The implications of technology's links and *chaînes* are ironic: while the material nature of the archaeological record often makes the dialectic of artifact and artifice hard to remember, it is also this tangible body of evidence that serves as our link to the intangible processes once involved.

Technology is no less than a materially grounded arena in which social interaction and contestation mediate the "becoming" of social agents and their artifacts. Thought of this way, technology is the sequential intertwining of social and material experiences best captured in the word *artifice*. Whereas artifacts and gestures take on their social life during productive sequences, social life is made meaningful and tangible through peoples' sequential processing of their material world. For all their daily and seemingly mundane repetition, ancient technogestures expressed the artifice of personal and group interests, reaffirmed collective memory, and materialized cultural sensibilities. Especially for prehistory, the conceptual framework underlying the pragmatics of *chaîne opératoire* research can be a powerful interpretive tool for understanding how social identities and relationships were constructed and transformed in the technological arena.

Notes

1 Quite independent of the French school. Anglo-American archaeologists have developed the notion of prehistoric technoscience (especially, Kuhn 1995; Schiffer 1992a: 134–138; Schiffer and Skibo 1987; see also Keller and Dixon Keller 1996 on "stocks" of technical knowledge).
2 In a later section I consider other less-than-technical (but typically "female-linked") activ-

ities, such as cooking and its relationship to "the hunt."
3 The CMP is not synonymous with hunting-gathering-foraging societies (extended discussion in Dobres 1995b:119–158).
4 On informal expressions of power and influence in egalitarian societies, see Cobb (1993), Flanagan (1989), and Keenan (1981), among others.

References

Bender, B. 1989 Roots of Inequality. In *Domination and Resistance*, edited by D. Miller, M. Rowlands, and C. Tilley, pp. 83–95. Unwin Hyman, London.

Bijker, W. E., T. P. Hughes, and T. K. Pinch (editors) 1987 *The Social Construction of Technological Systems: New Directions in the Sociology and History of Technology*. MIT Press, Cambridge, Mass.

Bloch, M. 1975 Property and the End of Affinity. In *Marxist Analyses and Social Anthropology*, edited by M. Bloch, pp. 203–228. John Wiley and Sons, New York.

Bodenhorn, B. 1990 "I'm Not the Great Hunter, My Wife Is": Iñupiat and Anthropological Models of Gender. *Inuit Studies* 14(1–2):55–74.

Bodenhorn, B. 1993 Gendered Spaces, Public Places: Public and Private Revisited on the North Slope of Alaska. In *Landscape Politics and Perspectives*, edited by B. Bender, pp. 169–204. Berg, Providence.

Bourdieu, P. 1977 *Outline of a Theory of Practice*. Translated by R. Nice. Cambridge University Press, Cambridge.

Brumbach, H. J., and R. Jarvenpa 1997 Ethnoarchaeology of Subsistence Space and Gender: A Subarctic Dene Case. *American Antiquity* 62(3):414–436.

Cassell, M. S. 1988 Farmers of the Northern Ice: Relations of Production in the Traditional North Alaskan Inupiat Whale Hunt. *Research in Economic Anthropology* 10:89–116.

Childe, V. G. 1936 *Man Makes Himself*. Watts, London.

Childe, V. G. 1956 *Society and Knowledge*. Harper and Brothers, New York.

Childs, S. T. 1999 "After All, a Hoe Bought a Wife": The Social Dimensions of Ironworking among the Toro of East Africa. In *The Social Dynamics of Technology: Practice, Politics, and Worldviews*, edited by M.-A. Dobres and C. R. Hoffman, pp. 23–45. Smithsonian Institution Press, Washington, DC.

Cobb, C. R. 1993 Archaeological Approaches to the Political Economy of Nonstratified Societies. *Archaeological Method and Theory* 3:43–100.

Conkey, M. W. 1991 Contexts of Action, Contexts for Power: Material Culture and Gender in the Magdalenian. In *Engendering Archaeology: Women and Prehistory*, edited by J. M. Gero and M. W. Conkey, pp. 57–92. Blackwell, Oxford.

Conkey, M. W., and J. M. Gero 1991 Tension, Pluralities, and Engendering Archaeology: An Introduction. In *Engendering Archaeology: Women and Prehistory*, edited by J. M. Gero and M. W. Conkey, pp. 3–30. Blackwell, Oxford.

Conkey, M. W., and J. D. Spector 1984 Archaeology and the Study of Gender. *Advances in Archaeological Method and Theory* 7:1–38.

Cross, J. R. 1990 *Specialized Production in Non-Stratified Society: An Example from the Late Archaic in the Northeast*. Unpublished Ph.D. dissertation, Department of Anthropology, University of Massachusetts at Amherst.

de Lauretis, T. (editor) 1987 *Technologies of Gender: Essays on Theory, Film, and Fiction*. Indiana University Press. Bloomington.

Dobres, M.-A. 1995a Gender and Prehistoric Technology: On the Social Agency of Technical Strategies. *World Archaeology* 27(1):25–49.

Dobres, M.-A. 1995b *Gender in the Making: Late Magdalenian Social Relations of Production in the French Midi-Pyrénées*. Ph.D. dissertation, Department of Anthropology, University of California at Berkeley. University Microfilms, Ann Arbor.

Dobres, M.-A. 1996 Variabilité des activités Magdaléniennes en Ariège et en Haute-Garonne, d'après les chaînes opératoires dans l'outillage osseux. *Bulletin de la Société Préhistorique Ariège-Pyrénées* 51:149–194.

Dobres, M.-A. 2000 *Technology and Social Agency: Outlining an Anthropological Framework for Archaeology*. Blackwell, Oxford.

Dobres, M.-A., and C. R. Hoffman 1994 Social Agency and the Dynamics of Prehistoric Technology. *Journal of Archaeological Method and Theory* 1(3):211–258.

Edmonds, M. 1990 Description, Understanding, and the Chaîne Opératoire. *Archaeological Review from Cambridge* 9(1):55–70.

Flanagan, J. G. 1989 Hierarchy in Simple "Egalitarian" Societies. *Annual Review of Anthropology* 18:245–266.

Gero, J. M. 1991 Genderlithics: Women's Roles in Stone Tool Production. In *Engendering Archaeology: Women and Prehistory*, edited by J. M. Gero and M. W. Conkey, pp. 163–193. Blackwell, Oxford.

Gifford-Gonzalez, D. 1993 Gaps in Ethnoarchaeological Analyses of Butchery: Is Gender an Issue? In *Bones to Behavior: Ethnoarchaeological and Experimental Contributions to the Interpretation of Faunal Remains*, edited by J. Hudson, pp. 181–199. Southern Illinois University Press, Carbondale.

Graburn, N. H. H. 1976 Introduction: Art of the Fourth World. In *Ethnic and Tourist Arts: Cultural Expressions from the Fourth World*, edited by N. H. H. Graburn, pp. 1–22. University of California Press, Berkeley.

Harding, S. 1987 Introduction: Is There a Feminist Method? In *Feminism and Methodology*, edited by S. Harding, pp. 1–14. Indiana University Press, Bloomington.

Hartmann, H. I. 1987 The Family as the Locus of Gender, Class, and Political Struggle: The Example of Housework. In *Feminism and Methodology*, edited by S. Harding, pp. 109–134. Indiana University Press, Bloomington.

Hawkes, K. 1993 Why Hunter-Gatherers Work. *Current Anthropology* 34(4):341–361.

Hawkes, K., J. F. O'Connell, and N. G. Blurton Jones 1989 Hardworking Hadza Grandmothers. In *Comparative Socioecology: The Behavioral Ecology of Humans and Other Mammals*, edited by V. Stande and R. A. Foley, pp. 341–366. Blackwell, Oxford.

Hayden, B. 1994 Competition, Labor, and Complex Hunter-Gatherers. In *Key Issues in Hunter-Gatherer Research*, edited by E. S. Burch Jr. and L. J. Ellanna, pp. 223–239. Berg, Providence.

Heidegger, M. 1977 *The Question Concerning Technology and Other Essays*. Translated by W. Lovitt. Garland, New York.

Herbert, E. W. 1993 *Iron, Gender, and Power: Rituals of Transformation in African Societies*. Indian University Press, Bloomington.

Hoffman, C. R. 1999 Intentional Damage as Technological Agency: Breaking Metals in Late Prehistoric Mallorca, Spain. In *The Social Dynamics of Technology: Practice, Politics, and Worldviews*, edited by M.-A. Dobres and C. R. Hoffman, pp. 103–123. Smithsonian Institution Press, Washington, DC.

Ingold, T. 1988 Tools, Minds, and Machines: An Excursion in the Philosophy of Technology. *Techniques et Culture* 12:151–176.

Ingold, T. 1990 Society, Nature, and the Concept of Technology. *Archaeological Review from Cambridge* 9(1):5–17.

Ingold, T. 1993a Technology, Language, and Intelligence: A Reconsideration of Basic Concepts. In *Tools, Language, and Cognition in Human Evolution*, edited by K. R. Gibson and T. Ingold, pp. 449–472. Cambridge University Press, Cambridge.

Ingold, T. 1993b Tool-Use, Sociality, and Intelligence. In *Tools, Language, and Cognition in Human Evolution*, edited by K. R. Gibson and T. Ingold, pp. 429–445. Cambridge University Press, Cambridge.

Ingold, T. 1993c The Reindeerman's Lasso. In *Technological Choices: Transformation in Material Cultures since the Neolithic*, edited by P. Lemonnier, pp. 108–125. Routledge, London.

Karlin, C., and N. Pigeot 1989 L'Apprentissage de la taille du silex. *Le Courrier du CNRS: Dossiers Scientifiques* 73:10–12.

Keenan, J. 1981 The Concept of the Mode of Production in Hunter-Gatherer Societies. In *The Anthropology of Pre-Capitalist Societies*, edited by J. S. Kahn and J. R. Llobera, pp. 2–21. Macmillan, London.

Keene, A. S. 1991 Cohesion and Contradiction in the Communal Mode of Production: The Lessons of the Kibbutz. In *Between Bands and States*, edited by S. A. Gregg, pp. 376–394. Southern Illinois University Press, Carbondale.

Keller, C. M., and J. Dixon Keller 1996 *Cognition and Tool Use: The Blacksmith at Work*. Cambridge University Press, New York.

Kopytoff, I. 1986 The Cultural Biography of Things: Commodization as a Process. In *The Social Life of Things*, edited by A. Appadurai, pp. 64–91. Cambridge University Press, New York.

Kuhn, S.L. 1995 *Mousterian Lithic Technology*. Princeton University Press, Princeton.

Law, J. (editor) 1991 *A Sociology of Monsters: Essays on Power, Technology, and Domination*. Routledge, New York.

Layton Jr., E. T. 1974 Technology as Knowledge. *Technology and Culture* 1531–41.

Lechtman, H. 1977 Style in Technology: Some Early Thoughts. In *Material Culture: Styles, Organization, and Dynamics of Technology*, edited by H. Lechtman and R. S. Merrill, pp. 3–20. West Publishing Co., St. Paul, Minn.

Lechtman, H. 1984 Andean Value Systems and the Development of Prehistoric Metallurgy. *Technology and Culture* 15(1):1–36.

Lechtman, H. 1993 Technologies of Power: The Andean Case. In *Configurations of Power in Complex Societies*, edited by J. S. Henderson and P. J. Netherly, pp. 244–280. Cornell University Press, Ithaca, N.Y.

Lee, R. B. 1979 *The !Kung San: Men, Women, and Work in a Foraging Society*. Cambridge University Press, Cambridge.

Lee, R. B. 1982 Politics Sexual and Non-Sexual in an Egalitarian Society. In *Politics and History in Band Societies*, edited by E. B. Leacock and R. B. Lee, pp. 37–59. Cambridge University Press, New York.

Lemonnier, P. 1989 Towards an Anthropology of Technology. *Man* 24:526–527.

Lemonnier, P. 1992a *Elements for an Anthropology of Technology*. Anthropological Papers No. 88. Museum of Anthropology, University of Michigan, Ann Arbor.

Lemonnier, P. 1992b Leroi-Gourhan: Ethnologue des techniques. *Les Nouvelles de l'Archéologie* 48–49:13–17.

Leroi-Gourhan, A. 1943 *Évolution et techniques: L'homme et la matière*. Albin Michel, Paris.

Leroi-Gourhan, A. 1945 *Évolution et techniques: Milieu et techniques*. Albin Michel, Paris.

Leroi-Gourhan, A. 1964a *Le geste et la parole II: La mémoire et les rythmes*. Albin Michel, Paris.

Leroi-Gourhan, A. 1964b *Le geste et la parole I: Technique et langage*. Albin Michel, Paris.

McGaw, J. A. 1996 Reconceiving Technology: Why Feminine Technologies Matter. In *Gender and Archaeology*, edited by R. P. Wright, pp. 52–75. University of Pennsylvania Press, Philadelphia.

MacKenzie, M. A. 1991 *Androgynous Objects: String Bags and Gender in Central New Guinea*. Harwood Academic Publishers, Chur, Switzerland.

Marquardt, W. H. 1992 Dialectical Archaeology. *Archaeological Method and Theory* 4:101–140.

Marx, K., and F. Engels 1970 *The German Ideology*. International, New York.

Mauss, M. 1924 *The Gift*. Translated by I. Cunnison (1967). W. W. Norton, New York.

Mauss, M. 1935 Les techniques du corps. In *Sociologie et psychologie, Parts II–VI*. Reprinted in *Sociologie et anthropologie*, pp. 365–386. Presses Universitaires de France, Paris, 1950; also in *Sociology and Psychology: Essays of Marcel Mauss*, Translated by B. Brewster, pp. 97–123. Routledge and Kegan Paul, London, 1979.

Meillassoux, C. 1981 *Maidens, Meals, and Money: Capitalism and Domestic Economy*. Cambridge University Press, Cambridge.

Moore, H. L. 1986 *Space, Text, and Gender: An Anthropological Study of the Marakwet of Kenya*. Cambridge University Press, Cambridge.

Moore, J. A. 1981 The Effects of Information Exchange Networks in Hunter-Gatherer Societies. In *Hunter-Gatherer Foraging Strategies*, edited by B. Winterhalder and E. A. Smith, pp. 194–217. University of Chicago Press, Chicago.

Olive, M., and N. Pigeot 1992 Les tailleurs de silex Magdaléniens d'Étiolles: Vers l'identification d'une organisation sociale complexe? In *La Pierre préhistorique*, edited by M. Menu and P. Walter, pp. 173–185. Laboratoire de Recherche des Musées de France, Paris.

Olive, M., N. Pigeot, and Y. Taborin 1991 *Il y a 13,000 ans à Étiolles*. Argenton-sur-Creuse, Paris.

Ortner, S. B., and H. Whitehead 1981 Introduction: Accounting for Sexual Meanings. In *Sexual Meanings: The Cultural Construction of Gender and Sexuality*, edited by S. B. Ortner and H. Whitehead, pp. 1–28. Cambridge University Press, New York.

Pacey, A. 1983 *The Culture of Technology*. MIT Press, Cambridge, Mass.

Pálsson, G. 1994 Enskilment at Sea. *Man* 29:901–927.

Pateman, C. 1987 Feminist Critiques of the Public/Private Dichotomy. In *Feminism and Equality*, edited by A. Phillips, pp. 103–126. Blackwell, Oxford.

Pelegrin, J., C. Karlin, and P. Bodu 1988 "Chaines opératoires": Un outil pour le préhistorien. In *Téchnologie préhistorique*, edited by J. Tixier, pp. 55–62. Notes et Monographies Techniques No. 25. CNRS, Paris.

Perlès, C. 1992 In Search of Lithic Strategies: A Cognitive Approach to Prehistoric Chipped Stone Assemblages. In *Representations in Archaeology*, edited by J-C. Gardin and C. S. Peebles, pp. 223–250. Indiana University Press, Bloomington.

Pfaffenberger, B. 1988 Fetishized Objects and Humanized Nature: Towards an Anthropology of Technology. *Man* 23:236–252.

Pfaffenberger, B. 1999 Worlds in the Making: Technological Activities and the Construction of Intersubjective Meaning. In *The Social Dynamics of Technology: Practice, Politics, and Worldviews*, edited by M.-A. Dobres and C. R. Hoffman, pp. 147–64. Smithsonian Institution Press, Washington, DC.

Pigeot, N. 1987 *Magdaléniens d'Étiolles. Débitage et organisation sociale* XXV Supplément à *Gallia Préhistoire*. CNRS, Paris.

Pigeot, N. 1990 Technical and Social Actors: Flintknapping Specialists at Magdalenian Étiolles. *Archaeological Review from Cambridge* 9(1):126–141.

Renfrew, C., and E. B. W. Zubrow (editors) 1994 *The Ancient Mind: Elements of Cognitive Archaeology*. Cambridge University Press. Cambridge.

Ridington, R. 1988 Knowledge, Power, and the Individual in Subarctic Hunting Societies. *American Anthropologist* 90:98–110.

Rogers, S. C. 1975 Female Forms of Power and the Myth of Male Dominance. *American Ethnologist* 2727–757.

Root, D. 1983 Information Exchange and the Spatial Configuration of Egalitarian Societies. In

Archaeological Hammers and Theories, edited by J. A. Moore and A. S. Keene, pp. 193–219. Academic Press, New York.

Rosaldo, M. Z. 1980 The Use and Abuse of Anthropology: Reflections on Feminism and Cross-Cultural Understanding. *Signs* 5(3):389–417.

Sahlins, M. 1972 *Stone Age Economics*. Aldine, Chicago.

Saitta, D. J., and A. S. Keene 1990 Politics and Surplus Flow in Prehistoric Communal Societies. In *The Evolution of Political Systems: Sociopolitics in Small-Scale Sedentary Societies*, edited by S. Upham, pp. 203–224. Cambridge University Press, Cambridge.

Sanday, P. R. 1981 *Female Power and Male Dominance: On the Origins of Sexual Inequality*. Cambridge University Press, New York.

Schiffer, M. B. 1975 Behavioral Chain Analysis: Activities, Organization, and the Use of Space. *Fieldiana* 65:103–174.

Schiffer, M. B. 1992a A Framework for the Analysis of Activity Change. In *Technological Perspectives on Behavioral Change*, edited by M. B. Schiffer, pp. 77–93. University of Arizona Press, Tucson.

Schiffer, M. B. 1992b *Technological Perspectives on Behavioral Change*. University of Arizona Press, Tucson.

Schiffer, M. B., and J. M. Skibo 1987 Theory and Experiment in the Study of Technological Change. *Current Anthropology* 28(5):595–622.

Schlanger, N. 1990 Techniques as Human Action. *Archaeological Review from Cambridge* 9(1):18–26.

Schwartz Cowan, R. 1979 From Virginia Dare to Virginia Slims: Womanhood and Technology in American Life. *Technology and Culture* 20:51–63.

Sharp, H. S. 1991 Dry Meat and Gender: The Absence of Chipewyan Ritual for the Regulation of Hunting and Animal Numbers. In *Hunters and Gatherers*. Vol. 2: *Property, Power, and Ideology*, edited by T. Ingold, D. Riches, and J. C. Woodburn, pp. 183–191. Berg, New York.

Simondon, G. 1958 *Du mode d'existence des objects techniques*. Aubier, Paris.

Whitehead, A. N. 1927 *Science and the Modern World*. Macmillan, New York.

Winner, L. 1986 *The Whale and the Reactor: A Search for the Limits in an Age of High Technology*. University of Chicago Press, Chicago.

Wolf, M. 1974 Chinese Women: Old Skills in a New Context. In *Women, Culture, and Society*, edited by M. Z. Rosaldo and L. Lamphere, pp. 157–172. Stanford University Press, Stanford, Calif.

Structure and Practice in the Archaic Southeast

Kenneth E. Sassaman

The Archaic period (10,000–3000 radiocarbon years before present [rcybp, hereafter B.P.]) of the American Southeast and the hunter-gatherer societies that existed during this time are being thoroughly redefined by archaeological discoveries that erode orthodoxy. New evidence for complex moundbuilding practices, circular-village plaza compounds, and symbolic action begs critical review of deeply entrenched assumptions about the sociality of small-scale societies. The Archaic period was long ago painted as a transitional stage between the big-game hunters of the Late Pleistocene, and farmers of the Woodland and Mississippian periods of the past two millennia. Archaeologists today acknowledge a great deal of variation among Archaic hunter-gatherers, even beyond the usual tripartite scheme that divides the Archaic into Early (10,000–8000 B.P.), Middle (8000–5000 B.P.), and Late (5000–3000 B.P.) periods. So many of the traits that originally defined and separated each of these periods have proven unreliable for evolutionary models but enormously fruitful for contemporary analyses of historical process. Archaeologists have much new data to digest.

Kenneth E. Sassaman, "Structure and Practice in the Archaic Southeast," pp. 79–107 from Timothy R. Pauketat and Diana DiPaolo Loren (eds) *North American Archaeology* (Oxford: Blackwell Publishers, 2005). Reprinted with permission.

As students of Archaic (pre)history come to grips with new data, several deeply entrenched ontological premises can be profitably abandoned. One is that Archaic societies are best understood as natural, not cultural phenomena. As with hunter-gatherers in general, Archaic societies have long been regarded as small scale, mobile, and simple formations whose settlement practices, subsistence choices, and ideologies were strongly influenced, if not determined, by the constraints and opportunities of nature. Ancillary to this premise is the logic that social formations were localized and self-contained, homeostatic systems that changed largely in response to imbalances between population and resource potential. A body of new ecological theory foregrounding the cultural and historical construction of nature (i.e., the cognized environment) has superseded the ecofunctionalist doctrine of the last century (Biersak 1999), and, happily, some of this new theorizing has begun to infiltrate Archaic studies.

A more recalcitrant premise is the notion that Archaic societies were constituted primarily on principles of egalitarianism and equality. Several threads of logic lead to this premise. First, from a behavioral ecological perspective, food-sharing and other means of alleviating inequality are beneficial to individuals in small-scale formations when the risk of failure from acting alone (e.g., hoarding) is greater than the costs of sharing with others (Kelly 1995:168–181). This logic establishes a threshold condition whereby a shift to less risky economic situations – be it through innovation (e.g., food production) or environmental change (e.g., stabilization of sea levels) – lifts the constraints on selfish behavior and opens the door to institutionalized social inequality (Hayden 1995). It also reifies egalitarianism as antecedent to complex society, a fundamental tenet of cultural evolutionism.

Throughout the world, societies are assumed to have become more complex through time as they have grown in size and become increasingly linked through institutions of religion, economics, and politics. Being antecedent to the Mississippian chiefdoms and Woodland tribes of the late precontact period, Archaic societies are assumed, *a priori*, to be somehow less complex than what followed. Whereas this is true on many levels, our sense of relative complexity is strongly influenced by the program of research in the 20th century that set out to establish the essential qualities of "primitive" societies through the study of modern foragers (Leacock and Lee 1982; Lee and DeVore 1976). The uniformitarian rationale for this effort was sound, but the program generally failed to recognize that the egalitarian structures of modern foragers were historically constituted through interactions with complex societies (Schrire 1984; Wilmsen 1989; Woodburn 1982), and thus could not be assumed to reflect the sociality of hunter-gatherers in a world of hunter-gatherers (i.e., the "primitive" state of humanity).

Following from this is a final problematic premise about the nature of cultural complexity. While most anthropologists today agree that so-called egalitarian societies are rife with inequalities (Flanagan 1989), many continue to distinguish such societies from chiefdoms and states because inequalities among the former were neither institutionalized nor of economic and political consequence. It is on this point that progress in our understanding of new data on the Archaic Southeast will turn. If we allow that relations of inequality, ranking, or even stratification can exist in cosmological or ideational realms without being manifest in structures of political authority or economic control, then the Archaic Southeast and "complex" hunter-gatherers in general have much to teach us about the origins of institutionalized inequality (Sassaman 2004a). Indeed, transformations in economy and polities must be

preceded by the cultural logic for differentiation, and I believe we can find this cultural logic deeply rooted in the practices of Archaic life. Transformations leading from Archaic to Woodland culture, and from Woodland to Mississippian culture, are certainly worthwhile research topics, but equally important are the sociohistorical structures that enabled these changes. It is my aim in this chapter to demonstrate that the cultural logic for ranked societies was in place throughout the Archaic period. To the extent they existed at all, egalitarian social formations of the Archaic period were a consequence of, and not a precondition for, sociohistorical structures of ranking or inequality.

The burden of proof for these bold assertions hinges as much on theoretical justification as it does on empirical validation. Indeed, it is not enough to argue that newfound data on Archaic complexity speak for themselves, for they do not. The body of theory known broadly as landscape archaeology provides insight into the myriad ways non-Western societies live *through*, and not simply *in*, environments, and how places, pathways, and resources are imbued with meaning through histories of movement, settlement, collective identities, group fissioning, and subsistence practices. Encoded in the built environments of Archaic mound complexes, for example, is the rationale for cultural identity and difference, inspired perhaps by the metaphors of nature, but constituted recursively by the actions of those engaged in their construction and use. This ongoing process of becoming was not likely a corporate affair in the sense that its participants were like-minded and self-identified as "one people." Rather, these were likely the consequence of collective actions involving people of somewhat different and perhaps contradictory histories, ethnic affiliations, and cultural traditions.

A historical process driven by the contradictions inherent to heterogeneous social formations encourages us to locate cultural difference where we expect none. It is difficult to justify the claim that Archaic societies were self-contained units of collectivism with so much material evidence for interactions among them. Intermarriage between communities that assert different cultural identities, for instance, results in multiethnic households whose internal contradictions in everyday practice were metaphors of (indeed the rationale for) social ranking at the community and regional scales (e.g., Grinker 1994). It follows that cultural differences in Archaic societies were transposed across a number of levels, from regional landscapes of power to local communities of practice. Negotiations of contradictions between these realms of experience – through group fissioning, shifting alliances, migration, and the like – were the forces of cultural change.

I cannot in this chapter provide a thorough exposition of the knowledge claims outlined above, for indeed that would take many more pages and much more data. My intent here is to simply tantalize the reader with some of the region's latest finds and novel ways of interpreting them. Above all, my intent is to show that the Archaic archaeological record needs to be redefined as the organization, reproduction, and transformation of cultural diversity. The unilineal logic of cultural evolutionism and the normative perspective of historical particularism are, for the most part, relics of a bygone era. In their place have come the rudiments of a social theory that foregrounds cultural identity, meaning, power, and history as core concepts (Pauketat 2001). As we will see, archaeological evidence for these dimensions of human experience is not often accessible, and even then, always cryptic. However, I would assert that much of the recent archaeological evidence of Archaic traditions and practice cannot be fully understood through the shopworn ontologies of cultural ecology and evolutionism. New discoveries require new ways of thinking (arguably, new discoveries *come* from new ways of thinking), and the Archaic Southeast, with its rich new data, is quickly becoming fertile ground for theoretical developments in anthropology at large.

Assertions of Identity

Archaic cultures are typically identified by the stone tools they made, the so-called diagnostic artifacts whose distribution in time and space allow archaeologists to recognize and compare different cultural traditions. Because diagnostic artifacts are generally portable, the geographic displacement of such items from the sources of raw material used to make them is a proxy for the physical and social scale of human activities across the landscape. Hence, the presence of

non-local lithic raw materials in archaeological assemblages is an indicator of interactions of personnel between communities.

The practice of long-distance exchange among Archaic societies has roots extending back to the Paleoindian era. Assemblages containing Paleoindian Clovis points, for instance, typically contain bifaces made on materials some 300 km or more from geological sources. However, many archaeologists argue that the geographic dispersal of toolstone signals long-distance movements by residential groups, not exchange between them (Meltzer 1989). The presumption here is that Clovis populations were too sparse and too transient to have experienced the need to assert boundaries amongst themselves and to reproduce those boundaries through alliance and exchange.

By some accounts, Paleoindians even lacked a sense of place, a historical connection to particular locations and landscapes. Kelly and Todd (1988) paint a picture of highly mobile hunters in the changing, unpredictable environments of the Late Pleistocene, relying on a storehouse of knowledge for tracking and dispatching large game. Their structuring principles centered on the behavior of migratory game, herds whose transient relationships with shifting grasslands and a retreating northern glacial front precluded the development of deeply inscribed land use patterns, and thus no ties to particular places. Plus, with open terrain to receive daughter communities as local populations grew and budded off, institutional boundaries among groups were unlikely, perhaps nonexistent. Of course, Kelly and Todd (1998), among others (Anderson 1990; Walthall and Koldehoff 1998), recognize the need for intergroup alliances for purposes of marriage, but the process is generally regarded as open-ended, flexible, and facilitated by seasonal aggregations among adjacent groups. The expansive distribution of Clovis points and the clinal patterns of its metric variances attest to unfettered flows of personnel across the Southeast.

This is a compelling model if Clovis-age people were indeed the first colonists of eastern North America. The growing body of evidence for precursors and contemporaries of Clovis populations throughout the New World suggests otherwise (Adovasio and Pedler, 2005). There is in fact good reason to believe that Clovis is a southeastern US original, and thus necessarily with local antecedents. It follows that Clovis populations in the Southeast had centuries of experience in the region under their collective cultural belt. The incredible number of Clovis points found in places like the middle Tennessee River valley argues convincingly for redundant, even permanent use of preferred locales. Indeed, such locales have been regarded as staging areas (Anderson 1990) for early populations, locations that were home to generations of Paleoindian bands. It follows that non-local raw material in Clovis assemblages of the Southeast could signify alliances between groups with long-term, routinized distributions across the landscape, that is, people of places.

Whereas the Clovis archaeological record remains ambiguous on the issue of intergroup dynamics, that of the succeeding Dalton period (10,500–10,000 B.P.) includes evidence that unequivocally speaks of boundaries and alliances. The rich Dalton archaeological record of the central Mississippi valley includes locations where unusually large and exotic lanceolate blades were cached (Gramly and Funk 1991; Morse 1997:17; Walthall and Koldehoff 1998). These hypertrophic blades measure up to 38 cm in length and exhibit remarkable workmanship on high-quality raw material (Figure 7.1). They have been found in over 30 locations along a 700 km stretch of the central Mississippi valley, from the American Bottom to northeast Arkansas. Most often they are isolated finds, but at least six caches of up to nine large blades each have been recorded in the southern half of this region (Walthall and Koldehoff 1998:260). Among the 146 Dalton points recovered from the Sloan site in northeast Arkansas are over two dozen described by Morse (1997:17–18) as "Large Daltons." All but two were made from non-local materials, and only six show signs of being used, damaged, and/or resharpened. These and other chipped stone artifacts were found distributed among 29 clusters or caches that Morse and colleagues (1997) convincingly argue were locations of human interment.

Burlington chert of the Crescent Quarries of east-central Missouri was a preferred material for making oversized Daltons (Walthall and Koldehoff 1998:263). Most of the isolated occurrences are located within 100 km of the Crescent Quarries, generally at locations along the Mississippi, Missouri, and Illinois rivers. Crescent Quarry

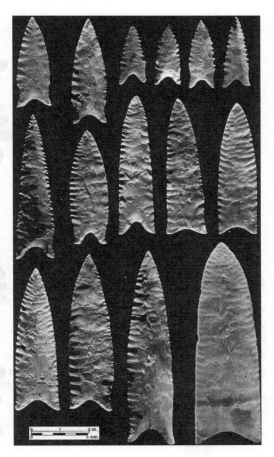

Figure 7.1 Examples of typical Dalton points (upper right) and oversized Dalton and Sloan points from the Sloan site in Arkansas (used with permission of Dan F. Morse).

chert was preferred for its superior quality, but it also occurs in blocks or boulders of up to 1 m in diameter, is located near the confluence of major rivers, and is thus readily accessible by boat (Walthall and Koldehoff 1998:263). About half of the oversized Daltons from the Sloan site were made from Burlington chert, at least seven from Crescent Quarries more than 300 km to the north (Morse 1997:17).

A similar pattern of hypertrophic biface production and exchange is seen in the Middle Archaic Benton tradition (ca. 5800–5200 B.P.) of the Midsouth (Johnson and Brookes 1989). Over 13 caches from five sites in northeast Mississippi have yielded examples of large, oversized

Benton bifaces, Turkey-Tail bifaces, and related cache blades, most made from blue-gray Fort Payne chert of the Tennessee River valley to the north. According to Johnson and Brookes (1989), some of these caches were likely mortuary. Hypertrophic bifaces and other elaborate artifacts are clearly associated with Middle Archaic burials (cremations) in the Duck River valley of Tennessee (Webb and DeJarnette 1942). Their use in mortuary ritual, according to Johnson and Brookes (1989), and following Brose (1979), is merely symbolic of secular exchange relationships that acted to buffer economic risk, a form of "subsistence insurance."

A parallel explanation for hypertrophic bifaces is proffered by Walthall and Koldehoff (1998:266) when they refer to oversized Daltons as "primitive valuables." The production and exchange of such valuables among hunter-gatherers is often viewed as a means of integrating groups into regional alliance networks for purposes of marriage, resource management, and information exchange. In this sense, the manipulation of valuables structures social interactions through ritual acts in the context of group aggregations. The inherent "power" of valuables resides in their function to reproduce social alliances (Walthall and Koldehoff 1998). Johnson and Brookes (1989) concur in their interpretation of Benton exchange.

This functionalist perspective on the manufacture and exchange of oversized Daltons and Bentons overlooks the possibility that possession and use of such items was intended to make a statement. The actual messages encoded in such items may never be revealed, but that is secondary to the structuring aspects of such actions, and in the consequences such uses may have to alter structure (to change history). Above all else, these were arguably assertions of identity, and, as such, they were clearly relational actions (i.e., multicultural or multiethnic).

One additional example of hypertrophy in Late Archaic polished stone technology helps to illustrate this point. In several cases regionwide, oversized bannerstones and grooved axes punctuate an otherwise pervasive record of mundane material culture (e.g., Fortier 1984; Hassen and Farnsworth 1987; Roper 1978). Among the better-dated examples are bannerstones of the middle Savannah River (Sassaman 1998; Figure 7.2). Presumed to be weights for spearthrowers, bannerstones are

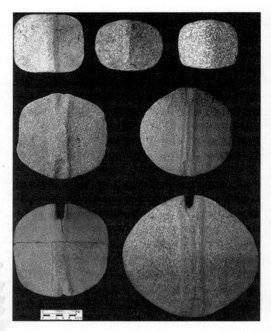

Figure 7.2 Examples of Southern Ovate (upper row) and Notched Southern Ovate bannerstones, including several preforms, the largest from Stallings Island (bottom right) (used with permission of the Peabody Museum, Harvard University).

polished stone objects whose large size, elaborate shape, or especially good workmanship transcend the technical requirements or tolerances for delivering spears (darts), and thus, in their elaborateness, likely encoded cultural significance beyond the act of hunting itself. Indeed, bannerstones of the middle Savannah River occasionally have exaggerated dimensions and intricate designs. Many examples of the so-called Notched Southern Ovate are over 20 cm in diameter and feature a deeply recessed spine that is drilled longitudinally, with wings on either side of the spine tapering to but a few millimeters thick, and delicate, tapered ridges along the medial edges of the wings, all highly polished (Knoblock 1939).

The specific timing and context of Notched Southern Ovate bannerstones in the middle Savannah region is linked to sustained contacts between groups of distinctive cultural identity and history. The forms are well dated to the Mill Branch phase of ca. 4200–3800 B.P. (Elliott et al. 1994; Ledbetter 1995). They are preceded by a smaller, related form, the Southern Ovate

(Knoblock 1939), dating to the Paris Island phase, ca. 4500–4200 B.P. (Elliott et al. 1994; Wood et al. 1986). Mill Branch culture is clearly derived from Paris Island culture, itself apparently derivative of indigenous roots in the region. In both its exaggerated bannerstones and comparatively large bifaces, Mill Branch culture evokes the image of Paris Island culture blown out of proportion.

Secure evidence links this moment of elaboration to the first sustained presence of interlopers from downriver, members of the early Stallings populations of the Atlantic Coast and lower Coastal Plain. Interaction between early Stallings groups and middle Savannah indigenes throughout the Paris Island phase is evidenced by the movement of soapstone from sources in the lower Piedmont and Fall Zone to the middle Coastal Plain. These existing relations apparently afforded the opportunity for certain early Stallings groups to relocate to the middle Savannah starting about 4200 B.P., the moment of transformation that led to the exaggerated material expressions of Mill Branch culture.

It is not altogether clear how elaborate bannerstones figured into interactions between indigenous peoples of the middle Savannah and their Coastal Plain neighbors, although there is little to recommend that they simply embodied reciprocal relations among social equals. As a transformation of Paris Island practice and tradition, the emergence of Mill Branch culture coincides with the sustained presence of a "foreign" people in their traditional land. Elaborate bannerstones may have been a medium of interaction between these groups, perhaps a form of wealth for brokering marriages and other alliances. In systems-serving terms, such interactions may have underwritten insurance against failure, a means to alleviate conflict, even divert tendencies for competition into economically inconsequential directions.

More likely, elaborate bannerstones signal efforts on the part of certain individuals or subgroups to assert identity in resistance to assimilation. Evidence for this may be seen in the circumstances surrounding the demise of bannerstones. Between 3800 and 3700 B.P., after a span of five centuries in the middle Savannah, the tradition of bannerstone-making was abandoned altogether. This is the time when Classic Stallings culture appears as a distinct archaeological culture (3800–3500 B.P.). Noted for its elaborate punctated pottery, Classic Stallings culture is likely the ethnogenetic consequence of interactions between Mill Branch and early Stallings groups, that is, the emergence of a new collective identity. On the geographical peripheries of this development we find other assertions of identity and alliance-building, notably the innovation of soapstone vessel technology and its exportation westward (Sassaman 1998). The roots of this development also lie in the ethnogenesis of Classic Stallings culture, but, in this case, as resistance to change by the displaced bearers of Mill Branch tradition (Sassaman 2001a).

I suspect that all cases of hypertrophic material culture discussed above were precipitated by the impingement of one group into another's culturally meaningful space (places). Whether this involves efforts on the part of some to engage interlopers in alliance, or rather, throw up boundaries of resistance to impingements on autonomy, or both, is not at all clear. However, there is ample reason to assert that hypertrophic forms arose as a declaration of identity among individuals resistant to assimilation or other impositions. These were likely acute responses to perceived threats, much in the same way that many Americans trumpeted the symbols of nationalism in the wake of the September 11 attacks.

In this sense hypertrophic actions were likely short-lived and perhaps expressive of only a segment of a population. But they were not terribly novel actions, as they drew inspiration from traditional practice. They signify efforts to reach back, through discourse and material symbol, into the past, and across space, to construct an image and sentiment that would shape people's motives and actions. And such actions were not simply the invoking of cultural symbols at the juncture and context of intergroup interaction. Rather, they embody divisions within groups as to how to engage the "other"; it is unlikely that all agreed upon any single stratagem, and thus such bold assertions of identity likely resulted occasionally in group fissioning.

The point of this discussion is that it may be erroneous to conclude that the actions of representation seen in the production and caching of hypertrophic items were corporate actions. Rather, such actions took place in multiethnic or multicultural contexts with claims and counterclaims over privilege, status, and identity.

Analysts of the later Mississippian period have begun to consider seriously how the multiethnic composition of communities was to a large extent the fuel of sociopolitical change (e.g., Blitz 1999; Pauketat 2003). Indeed, ethnic divisions were the basis for ranked dual organization of Mississippian chiefdoms, and they formed the cleavage planes along which polities coalesced and divided. This process is evident in the occupational sequences of places on the landscape that were imbued with history and ancestry and thus defined and redefined as places of origin. In their construction of mounds and monuments, as well as in their cemeteries and other vestments in place, societies of the Archaic Southeast inscribed this social logic on the landscape at least 5,000 years before the Mississippian era.

Shell Mound Archaic

A penchant for freshwater mussels and snails resulted in massive accumulations of shell among several distinct cultural traditions of the lower Midwest, the Midsouth, and peninsular Florida, known collectively as the "Shell Mound Archaic." Although the procurement of freshwater shellfish has great antiquity in the East, routine shellfishing and the formation of large middens/mounds along rivers of the Midsouth and lower Midwest began at about 7500 B.P. (Dye 1996) and ceased at about 3000 B.P. Mounds began to accumulate in Florida as early as 6000 B.P. and continued through the St. Johns tradition of the past three millennia. Human interments are common at many shell mounds across the East (Haskins and Herrmann 1996), owing, in part, to the excellent preservation afforded by the chemical composition of shell.

Through the 1980s, research on the Shell Mound Archaic centered on three related topics: (1) explaining the economic change of a seemingly expanded diet and intensified land use (e.g., Bender 1985; Brown 1985; Brown and Vierra 1983; Marquardt and Watson 1983); (2) reconstructing the patterns and mechanisms of long-distance exchange (e.g., Goad 1980; Marquardt 1985; Winters 1968); and (3) detecting social differentiation in burial practices (e.g., Rothschild 1979). More recently, Claassen (1991, 1992, 1996) has championed the notion that the Shell Mound Archaic

was primarily a mortuary tradition involving the use of shell as a medium for moundbuilding. Earthen mounds featuring ranked interments are a key feature of the Adena and Hopewell traditions of the Woodland period, and Late Archaic burial mounds in the lower Midwest have been interpreted as markers of corporate territories (Charles and Buikstra 1983). Mound construction for mortuary purposes is thus a hallmark feature of several regional traditions.

Nonetheless, Claassen's hypothesis has met with considerable resistance by those pointing out that most of the so-called "mounds" of the Shell Mound Archaic are merely midden deposits (Milner and Jefferies 1998) and that so many shell-bearing sites lack human interments (Hensley 1994).

While debate continues over the mortuary functions of shell-bearing sites in the mid-continent, shell mounds along the St. Johns River of northeast Florida provide unassailable proof that shell was mounded over human interments during the Archaic period. The best example thus far comes from Tick Island on the middle St. Johns River (Aten 1999). Burials salvaged by Bullen from a basal component of a shell-mound complex known as Harris Creek, dated to ca. 5500 B.P., were clearly set in a stratum of white sand beneath shell midden and a second mortuary layer dating to ca. 5300–5000 B.P. Successive layers of shell midden, clean shell, and earth spanning the ceramic Orange period (ca. 4200–3000 B.P.) capped the remnant of the mound. By all accounts, the overlying strata that were mined in the 1960s contained burials of St. Johns II age (post-1250 B.P.).

Ongoing research in Florida is bolstering the evidence from Tick Island for mortuary practices at shell mounds, although many related questions remain unanswered. As in the mid-continent, riverine shell mounds of Florida have yet to provide sufficient data on social structure and regional integration. The configuration and placement of mounds across the landscape is a potentially fruitful source of data in this regard, although perhaps unattainable given the widespread destruction of shell mounds over the past century. Fortunately, two other venues of Archaic moundbuilding in the East, each involving non-mortuary mound-plaza complexes, are providing new insight into social structure at both local and regional scales.

Mound Complexes in the Lower Mississippi Valley

Eleven earthen mound complexes in the lower Mississippi valley have been dated to the Middle Archaic period, and several others are likely that age or older (Russo 1996:table 1). At possibly over 7000 cal. B.P., Monte Sano in southern Louisiana is the oldest (Saunders 1994). Three of the better-documented complexes – Watson Brake (Saunders et al. 1997), Caney (Saunders et al. 2000), and Frenchman's Bend (Saunders et al. 1994) – are securely dated to 5600–5000 cal. B.P. (Figure 7.3). Four others apparently predate or are coeval with Watson Brake, Caney, and Frenchman's Bend, including the Lower Jackson mound near Poverty Point (Saunders et al. 2001). The latest Middle Archaic mound complex is Hedgepeth, dating to ca. 5200–4500 cal. B.P. Subsequent mound construction in the region leading up to Poverty Point at ca. 3400–2800 cal. B.P. is not well documented, although enough evidence exists to suggest that earth-moving traditions continued unabated through the Late Archaic period. In the words of one specialist, "the Mississippi Valley Archaic mound tradition, extending from the Middle Archaic to Poverty Point traditions, lasted longer than any later southeastern mound-building traditions dependent on horticulture or intensive agricultural production" (Russo 1996:285).

Of the confirmed Middle Archaic mound complexes, two are single mounds, four are paired mounds, and one each has three, five, six, and 11 mounds. All paired mounds include one in the range of 4–6 m in height, the other about 1.5 m. Distance between paired mounds varies from 50 to 200 m. The tallest mounds in complexes of three or more are also in the range of 4–6 m, with the exception of the 7.5 m-high Mound A at Watson Brake. All sites that have been adequately tested show evidence for staged construction in at least one mound. Finally, mounds excavated to date have included some sort of architectural components at their bases.

Below mounds at Monte Sano and Banana Bayou were burned surfaces (pyres?), the former accompanying the remains of a rectangular structure (Russo 1996:270; Saunders 1994). Postholes and thermal features were uncovered at the base of Mound A at Frenchmen's Bend (Saunders et al.

1994:141), and a burned post marked the initiation of Mound C construction at Stelly (Russo 1996:278). The significance of these finds lies in the fact that locations of mound erection were preceded by constructions that marked place. Each of the three well-documented complexes mentioned earlier (Watson Brake, Caney, Frenchman's Bend), and a fourth with possible Archaic origins (Insley), exhibits a series of spatial regularities that suggest they were constructed according to a common plan.

The most spectacular of the Archaic mound complexes is Watson Brake, an 11-mound elliptical complex some 370 m in length and 280 m wide, which has been well documented by Saunders et al. (1997). The largest mound (Mound A) is 7.5 m high. Opposite the largest mound, is a 4.5 m-high "backset" mound (Mound E). All the mounds, including nine subordinate mounds, are linked in a meter-high ridge defining an elliptical central plaza area. As is common to all of the complexes with a shared plan, Watson Brake is situated on the edge of an alluvial escarpment, in this case a Pleistocene-age terrace overlooking the Ouachita River.

Caney Mounds is a six-mound complex in an arc nearly 400 m in maximum dimension. First recorded in 1933, Caney has been investigated intermittently ever since (Gibson 1991), most recently by Saunders et al. (2000). Its plan duplicates the relative positions of the major mounds at Watson Brake. The third confirmed site, Frenchman's Bend (Saunders et al. 1994), bears some geometric similarity to Watson Brake and Caney, albeit with fewer mounds. Insley Mounds, located just south of Poverty Point (Kidder 1991), is an elliptical complex of 12 mounds with a plan highly reminiscent of Watson Brake. Although dating is uncertain and later Poverty Point and younger components are apparently present at the site, the overall similarity in plan between Watson Brake and the significantly larger Insley complex suggests initial mound construction dates to the Middle Archaic period.

A replicated plan of mound construction has been inferred from a series of proportional and geometric regularities at each site (Sassaman and Heckenberger 2004a, 2004b). In addition to these site-specific relationships, variations in the orientation of terrace lines and baselines with respect to cardinal directions suggest that individual

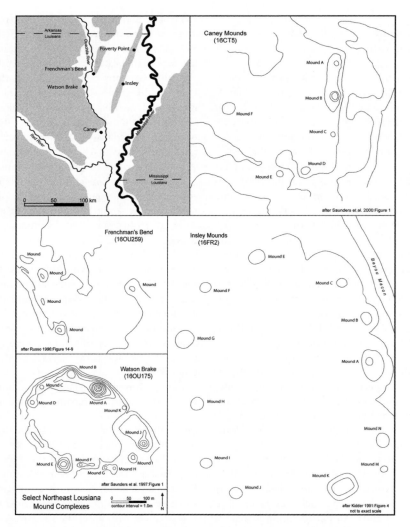

Figure 7.3 Topographic maps of the three known Archaic mound complexes and a sketch map of one suspected Archaic mound complex (Insley) in northeast Louisiana, with inset map to upper left showing locations of mound complexes in relation to Poverty Point.

complexes were part of a regional landscape of monument construction. In terms of scale, individual components were constructed on a ranked proportionality. Watson Brake and Frenchman's Bend are similar in size, but Caney is 20 percent larger and Insley twice the size of the first two.

Clark (2004) has successfully inferred the units of measurement employed to site mounds in each of the complexes, which, apparently, was also used to site complexes over the greater Archaic landscape. Given the apparent engineering behind all

this, it stands to reason that mounds were arranged for astronomical or calendrical purposes. However, the varied orientation of mound complexes to cardinal directions precludes such a possibility. Instead, a more complex arrangement across sites is suggested by the regional pattern of cardinality. Georeferencing all sites to the respective largest mounds and orienting each to magnetic north, a pattern of geometric integration is revealed (Sassaman and Heckenber 2004b). This arrangement clearly is not fortuitous. Rather, the integration of all four sites into a regional pattern of alignment suggests that entire landscapes of monumental architecture, and not just individual sites, were planned constructions.

Poverty Point

The relationship of Poverty Point to all of this is uncertain but provocative. Emerging after ca. 3700 B.P. and developing over several ensuing centuries, Poverty Point culture involved unprecedented levels of mound construction and interregional exchange centered on the type site, Poverty Point, a 3 km^2 complex of nearly 1 million cubic yards of mounded earth in six nested, elliptical half-rings, two massive bird-shaped effigies, and a few conical and flat-topped mounds (Ford and Webb 1956; Kidder 2002). Other settlements of Poverty Point affiliation were distributed across a 700-square-mile area centered on the type site, with more distant communities participating through exchange with core groups (see papers in Byrd 1991).

Resident population size and sociopolitical complexity are debated aspects of Poverty Point culture. Clearly an earth-moving project of this magnitude and sophistication, no matter how protracted over time, required not only a large pool of labor, but also formal orchestration. Ford and Webb (1956) asserted that Poverty Point was home to thousands of people, whose houses were distributed along each of the six nested ridges. Unfortunately, evidence for domestic architecture along ridges is cryptic at best, although midden accumulation at the site is sufficiently large to support an argument for repeated episodes of large-scale aggregation, if not continuous occupation.

Raw materials imported from as far away as the Great Lakes and the Appalachians, while impressive in volume and diversity, were often used to make mundane items: soapstone for cooking vessels; granite, basalt, and greenstone for celts; hematite and magnetite for plummets; and various cherts for projectiles and cutting tools, to name but a few. Coupled with the ubiquitous baked clay objects, hearths, pits, and midden accumulation, the inventory of subsistence technology strongly suggests that Poverty Point was a place of residence (Gibson 2000:157), but again, direct evidence for permanent residence remains elusive. no direct evidence

The regional integration of Poverty Point culture is likewise uncertain. Obviously, members of local populations were well connected to the outside world through trading partnerships stretching vast distances in virtually all directions. Communities in a 700-square-mile area centered on the type site shared many of the distinctively Poverty Point traits, yet the degree of similarity is not simply a function of distance from the core locale. This suggests that communities were economically and politically autonomous. Indeed, Gibson (2000) no longer subscribes to the chiefdom model of regional hierarchy, suggesting instead that Poverty Point culture was foremost a shared belief system, organized at a corporate level for public works and ritual, but underwritten by an egalitarian ethos.

The populations that built, occupied, and visited Poverty Point may have consisted of small-scale corporate groups whose internal sociality was based on principles of egalitarianism, but it is hard to defend the position that such constituent units were not ranked relative to one another. Poverty Point was a place of pilgrimage, and it drew from a pool of congregants with different histories, experiences, and know-how. People repeatedly traveled to Poverty Point from far-away places, bringing with them local materials that were left at the site or distributed locally. And they seem to have returned to their home lands with only ideas, as few of the material and objects entering the greater Poverty Point area appear to have left. In a sense, Poverty Point may have been the place of origin for all those who visited, but it is unlikely that all such persons could claim equal status. As in the origins myths of hunter-gatherers elsewhere, the sequential creations of different types of people are the rationale for ranking among the living.

Geometric patterning among Archaic mounds, including those of Poverty Point, is an archaeological fact whose significance lies not so much in the labor needed to erect them, but in the ideas needed to conceive of them. Arguably similar in function to diagrammatic mound centers of Mississippian society (Knight 1998), Archaic mound complexes may have served as sociograms, locations at which "public architecture [was] deliberately arranged in such a manner as to evoke and reinforce key social distinctions" (Knight 1998:60; see also DeBoer 1997). The central spaces or plazas

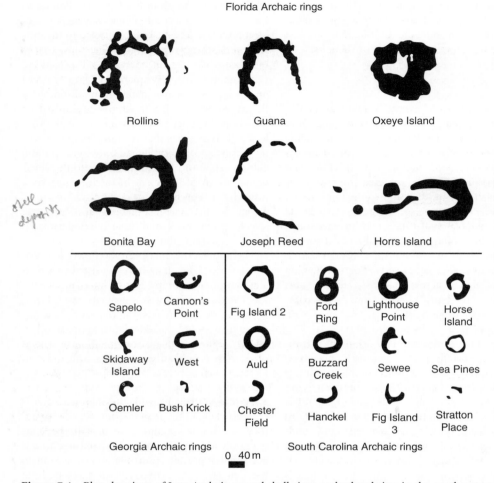

Figure 7.4   Plan drawings of Late Archaic coastal shell rings and related sites in the southeastern United States (used with permission of Michael Russo).

created by the circular or elliptical arrangement of mounds may have been especially significant in reproducing hierarchy, as they continue to do today among Xinguanos of central Brazil (Heckenberger 2004). Archaic shell rings on the Atlantic Coast may likewise have enabled the reproduction of hierarchical social relationships.

Coastal Shell Rings

Scores of shell deposits generally conforming to circular or semicircular shapes and ranging from tens to hundreds of meters in diameter have been

documented along the south Atlantic and Gulf coasts (Russo and Heide 2001; Figure 7.4). Although sites with arcuate shapes of shell-bearing middens formed well into the Woodland period on the Gulf Coast, sites referred to as shell rings on the south Atlantic Coast generally date from about 4500 to 3000 B.P., the Late Archaic period. Investigations through the 1980s led researchers to suggest that rings formed from the accumulation of refuse from communities arranged in a circle around an open public space (plaza). Trinkley's (1985) work at two small shell rings north of Charlestown, South Carolina, was particularly influential in shaping opinion that shell rings were simply accumulations of domestic refuse. Trinkley (1985) also championed the idea that the circular plan of shell rings reflected a community plan whose symmetry reinforced egalitarian relations among co-residents.

Recent fieldwork at shell rings by Michael Russo and Rebecca Saunders calls into question any simplistic claims about ring function and a presumed egalitarian social order. Detailed mapping, soil analysis, and excavation at several sites across the region have revealed much greater complexity in shell ring form and function than ever imagined. There is now abundant evidence that shell was deposited rapidly in large quantities, often over prepared surfaces or low sand mounds (Cable 1993; Russo 1991; Russo and Heide 2002; Saunders 2002). Deposits grew disproportionately across areas receiving shell, resulting in asymmetries in height and width. Russo (2002) and Saunders (2002) agree that large deposits of shell resulted from feasting activities, presumably competitive feasting.

Russo (2002) has focused on this complex geometry as a window into social ranking among shell ring feasters. Few that have been mapped are actually circular in plan; instead, they often assume asymmetrical forms that more than likely mirrored and reproduced social differentiation. Accepting that shell rings accumulated not haphazardly, but rather systematically, if not deliberately, Russo (2004) explores possible sociological implications of asymmetries in ring configuration. Often rings have one of more segments that are taller and broader at the base than other segments, and are rarely perfectly circular in plan.

The Fig Island site on the south Atlantic Coast of South Carolina exemplifies the complexity of shell ring formations (Saunders 2002). The site consists of three "rings" over some 5 hectares in an estuarine biome (Figure 7.5). Fig Island 2 is the closest to an actual ring, at some 77 m in diameter and about 2.5 m above the underlying marsh surface. Fig Island 3 is an arcuate midden about 50 m in maximum dimension that was connected to Fig Island 2 by a shell causeway. The largest feature, Fig Island 1, is a 157 m long, 111 m wide deposit some 5.5 m tall consisting of one large, steep-sided ring enclosing a small plaza and at least two small "ringlets" attached to the arc and enclosing additional small plazas.

The sheer complexity of Fig Island 1 leaves much to the imagination, but even the circular Fig Island 2 is actually structurally asymmetrical. As Russo (2002) notes, the ring is hexagonal in plan, with an opening to the southwest at the midpoint of one of its six sides. Opposite the opening are the widest and tallest segments of the enclosure; behind them is the causeway linking it with Fig Island 3, whose highest and widest aspect lies at one end of the arc. Russo (2002) reviews ethnographic literature of community plans to argue that either of the vertically accentuated features likely supported individuals of privilege or authority.

Fig Island is indeed among the more complex shell rings known, but it, along with others from South Carolina and Georgia, pales in size compared to several of those from Florida. Rings and arcuate structures at least 150 m and as much as 250 m in diameter have been documented at six sites in the state (Russo and Heide 2001; Russo et al. 2002). They typically have peaks at the top of the arcs, and those from south Florida (Horr's Island and Bonita Bay) have elongated U-shaped plans with associated sand/shell mounds.

Circular Village Plaza Complexes

As with Archaic mounds in general, evidence for domestic architecture at coastal shell rings is lacking. Russo (1991) documented an array of postholes in the open space bounded by mounds at Horr's Island in Florida, and Trinkley's (1985) work at Stratton Place revealed an array of features presumed to be associated with domestic space along the ring's outline, but few other data are available. Still, a community pattern of houses arranged in more or less circular fashion around an open space (plaza) can be inferred from the overall plan of most shell rings. Given Russo's (2002) line of argumentation for asymmetries in shell ring form and the general association of circular village plazas with hierarchy (Heckenberger 2004; Lévi-Strauss 1963), it stands to reason that inter-household comparisons, if they were possible, would reflect some measures of social differentiation. It is indeed frustrating that we cannot compare the residues of everyday life across households to see how routine practices reproduced and transformed structures of

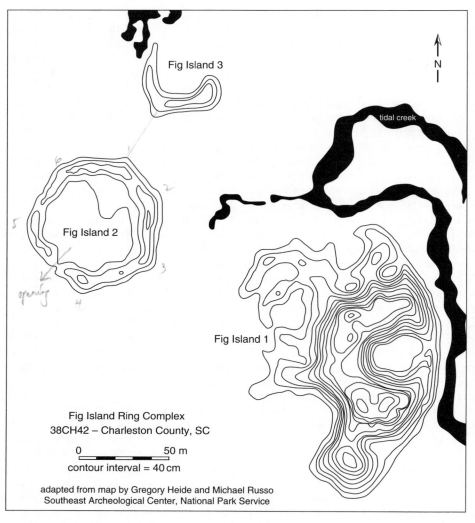

Figure 7.5 Topographic map of the Fig Island shell-ring complex, Charleston County, South Carolina (used with permission of Michael Russo).

inequality, or, alternatively, how the routines of everyday life contradicted such structures.

One venue of ongoing research is beginning to produce evidence for small circular village plazas. Direct evidence of a circular village plaza complex has been documented at one middle Savannah site and inferred indirectly from two other, contemporaneous sites of Classic Stallings cultural affiliation (ca. 3800–3500 B.P.). The best example comes from Mims Point, a small shell-bearing site on a ridge nose at the confluence of Stevens Creek and the Savannah River, 1 km north of

Stallings Island (Sassaman 1993). Middle Archaic and Late Woodland components interfere only slightly with an otherwise discrete Classic Stallings habitation. Although house floors were compromised by historic-era plowing, clusters of pit features attest to a circular village plaza configuration. Hand excavation of 364 m^2 exposed several of these feature clusters. The two best-preserved clusters include one or two deep storage pits, four to five shallow basins, and at least one hearth. Nearly all such features yielded punctated fiber-tempered pottery. The excavated space between major pit

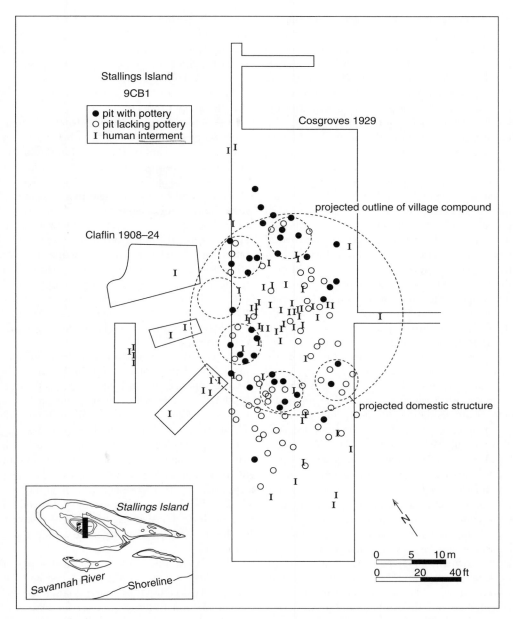

Figure 7.6 Plan schematic of the 1929 block excavation of Stallings Island, showing locations of pit features, burials, and projected domestic structures arrayed in circular fashion around a central plaza.

clusters was generally devoid of features. Those present in this central, plaza-like area some 16 m in diameter are mostly ephemeral and none contained Classic Stallings pottery. In sum, the evidence points to a circular compound of seven to nine structures, spaced 4–6 m apart, each defined by pit clusters 5–6 m in diameter. Indirect evidence for a circular village plaza complex of equal size has been uncovered at the nearby Ed Marshall site.

The Stallings Culture type site, Stallings Island, also has yielded evidence for a circular village plaza configuration, in this case with an interesting twist (Figure 7.6). Excavations at Stallings Island in 1929 exposed scores of pit features and burials, but no obvious evidence for house floors. Using unpublished field notes on the size, depth, and content of pits, Blessing and Sassaman (2001) were able to infer a pattern of settlement similar to Mims Point and Ed Marshall. Each of the five discernible pit clusters at Stallings Island contained at least one large storage pit, each placed to the right of the aspect (entrance?) facing the interior plaza, with one exception to the left. Frequency distributions of pit types across clusters were similar, lending further support to an inscribed, routinized practice of community layout.

Unlike those at Mims Point and Ed Marshall, the Stallings compound includes a sizeable burial population in the central plaza. The site-wide distribution of burials reveals an unequivocal non-random pattern for location within the projected plaza. Noteworthy in this distribution is the tendency for subadults to be placed on the north side of the central space, and for females to be located in the southeast quadrant. Small sample size notwithstanding, these tendencies give us cautious optimism that the layout of mortuary space was highly structured and thus indicative of social identity, possibly rank.

Stallings Island is the only site in the middle Savannah River valley to contain a large population of burials dating to Classic Stallings times, when circular village plazas were occupied. It is also the only site to produce a large fraction of sherds from carinated vessels (Sassaman 2004b). Using the Mississippian analog for carinated forms (Hally 1986), many of the Stallings Island vessels may have been used for serving in highly social contexts, perhaps mortuary feasting. In this regard Stallings Island was a special place on the landscape, and perhaps something of a center of a local settlement hierarchy. It remains for future work to compare middle Savannah community patterning with that of coastal shell rings to delve further into the symbolic and sociopolitical implications of circular village plazas.

Genesis of the "Powerless"

Lest the reader conclude at this point that the Archaic Southeast consisted exclusively of sedentary, moundbuilding societies structured by principles of hierarchy, allow me to briefly touch upon those unassuming, inconspicuous communities who occupied the interstitial spaces and "quiet" periods of the Archaic past. Indeed, the archaeological record of the Archaic Southeast is replete with evidence for societies whose generalized foraging, frequent mobility, and simple technology mirror the egalitarian formations of the ethnographic present.

The Morrow Mountain tradition of the Georgia-Carolina Piedmont is a case in point (Sassaman 2001a, 2001b). Sites of this tradition are highly redundant, showing little bias for particular locations of the landscape, limited midden accumulation, and nearly exclusive use of local raw materials for tool manufacture. In one sense, these features of the Morrow Mountain record are the expected long-term consequence of adaptation to the relatively homogeneous resource structure of the Piedmont, as Binford's (1980) model of forager settlement organization would predict. However, consideration of the deeper historical and cultural contexts of the Morrow Mountain tradition leads one to a more complicated scenario.

Roots of the Morrow Mountain tradition lie in major river valleys of the Mid-south, where the basal components of shell middens dating to ca. 7500 B.P. contain the tapered stemmed bifaces that is a hallmark of this tradition (Dye 1996). These strata signal the radical change in settlement organization that is the genesis of Shell Mound Archaic traditions. For the first time in the region, groups began to occupy riverine sites repeatedly, if not permanently, to intensify production to meet increasing economic demand, to inter their dead in shell deposits, and to routinely engage in long-distance exchange and perhaps warfare.

These conditions no doubt spawned scores of ethnogenetic events as groups coalesced and fissioned. The cultural boundaries asserted and redefined through alliances of marriage, exchange, and the like did more than simply demarcate one Shell Mound Archaic group from the next. They likewise excluded certain factions, and simultaneously, spurred some to resist impositions by asserting autonomy and new collective identity by relocating elsewhere.

Bearers of Morrow Mountain material culture appeared in the southern Piedmont shortly after 7500 B.P. and persisted in a virtually unchanging mode of generalized foraging for over 1,500 years.

results of fission

I have argued that, under these specific historical circumstances, the Morrow Mountain tradition had become a culture of resistance, asserting a new identity through practices that were antithetical to those of their immediate ancestors (Sassaman 2001a). By the time bearers of Morrow Mountain culture came to dominate the southern Piedmont landscape, the egalitarian relations they asserted were effectively reproduced for centuries through the routine practices of settlement mobility, food-sharing, generalized foraging, and expedient tool use. Because these practices were so well tuned to the local conditions of the Piedmont, it is easy to lose sight of the fact that the cultural logic underwriting them were historically derived from events and circumstances so distant in time and space.

Discussion and Conclusion

The empirical record of the Archaic Southeast has expanded dramatically in the past two decades to encompass traits hitherto deemed exclusive to food-producing societies of later times. The expanded purview of Archaic archaeology has generated a bit of controversy and skepticism (e.g., Russo 1994). Now that the archaeological community accepts the empirical reality of Archaic mounds, we face the tougher challenge of making sense of these new data. In this regard, a particularly interesting problem lies in the conflicting signals of complex ritual and the underpinnings of hierarchical structures with an archaeological record of everyday practice generally consistent with egalitarian practices. Rather than accept the need to retool conceptually to understand complexity among Archaic societies, the tendency on the part of some skeptics has been to argue that you do not need complex society to build mounds.

No matter what they say about daily practice, Archaic mounds and circular villages reflect and served to reproduce structures of ranking in Archaic cosmologies. The practices of mounding and village construction were institutions that transcended individual experiences and they involved esoteric knowledge that was unlikely to have been shared by all. There is little to suggest that the collectives involved in mound construction were corporations of like-minded people.

Rather, mound complexes may have been focal points for the negotiation and reproduction of diversity, and thus constantly in a state of becoming, never fixed or uncontested. For instance, cyclical movement through an integrated landscape of mound complexes, such as those of northeast Louisiana, could have reproduced a set of shifting ranked relationships among constituent parties with claims over origins at specific sites (stages) in the cycle, as in the concepts of sequential hierarchy (Johnson 1982) or heterarchy (Crumley 1987). Contrast this with Poverty Point, where arguably the entire regional landscape was telescoped down to the place of all origins, and where institutions of economic and political control would surely have emerged if only everyone stayed in residence long enough.

I submit that Archaic moundbuilding traditions embodied the root metaphors for hierarchical structures in the moundbuilding traditions of the Woodland and Mississippian traditions. In support of this assertion, I remind the reader of the need to separate the act of moundbuilding from the activities taking place on mounds (e.g., Knight 2001:302). Platform mounds of Mississippian chiefdoms were platforms for buildings of the elite and access to them was limited; they were explicitly about social differentiation. Similar constructions of the Middle Woodland period were locations of feasts and mortuary ritual, actions arguably serving to integrate, rather than to differentiate, social identities (Knight 2001; Lindauer and Blitz 1997). There are as yet few data on the activities taking place at Archaic mound complexes, but, given the absence of platform constructions, they were not likely used as ritual surfaces or residences per se. Thus, each of the major moundbuilding traditions involved different types of activities and most likely different structural relationships among mounds, ritual actions, and routine practice.

As we continue to understand how and why mound uses changed over the course of the pre-Columbian Southeast, we should not lose sight of the threads of continuity (or similarity) among the various moundbuilding traditions in the ways that mounds were conceived, sited, and erected. Mound construction was a staged process among all traditions. In Mississippian cosmology, mounds were earth symbols, and adding a stage was an action of renewing the earth

(Knight 1989). This same symbolism can be read into the staged construction of Woodland mounds (Knight 2001), and may very well have parallels in Archaic mounds.

In addition, all mound traditions of the Southeast involve locations with single mounds and contemporaneous locations with multiple mounds. Multi-mound complexes almost always involve mounds of variable size. Moreover, locations of three or more mounds across time were laid out according to replicated plans, with the largest mounds usually occupying prominent positions at the center or at the apex of an array of mounds. Such arrangements have been demonstrated to reflect social ranking or divisions in Woodland and Mississippian societies (DeBoer 1997; Knight 1998). Astronomical alignments have been implicated in many cases. Finally, mound complexes in Archaic, Woodland, and Mississippian traditions include examples with centrally enclosed space, typically regarded as plazas.

Given similarities in structural aspects of Archaic, Woodland, and Mississippian mound-building traditions, it is reasonable to expect continuity in the act of moundbuilding itself, even if the practices taking place on mounds changed repeatedly. Here the Archaic record seemingly belies continuity. The gap of over 1,000 years that separates the latest Middle Archaic mounds from Poverty Point is matched by a nearly comparable gap between the latest Poverty Point construction and those of the Woodland period.

However, like the time separating episodes of Woodland and Mississippian moundbuilding, these gaps are more apparent than real. If we expand the scale of observation beyond the Mississippi valley to include the entire eastern Woodlands, moundbuilding appears as a temporally continuous, albeit geographically discontinuous, phenomenon. From 4500 to 3500 B.P., when moundbuilding had slowed or ceased in the lower Mississippi valley, shell rings (mounds) were being built on the Atlantic and Gulf coasts, and the shell mounds of the middle St. Johns of Florida were expanding rapidly. We may likewise include here some sites of the interior Shell Mound Archaic, as well as Stallings circular village plazas, which date to the late centuries of this interval. The point is that once on the greater southeastern landscape, moundbuilding never ceased, and, of course, the mounds themselves became permanent fixtures on the landscape. The specific meanings of mounds indeed changed, as did activities associated with mounds, but the underlying principles of ranking and cyclical processes evident in their configuration and staged construction never disappeared.

Clark (2004) has suggested that the cultural logic for siting and building mounds was carried forward in everyday practice, in, for instance, the way houses were constructed and spaces arranged within, around, and between residences. I fully agree, but would add that potential contradictions between daily practice and ritual practice make it hard to imagine that the quotidian of Archaic life was always consonant with the proscriptions of sacred belief. I have two reasons for asserting this. First, the lack of secure evidence for large-scale, perennial occupations at Archaic mounds, shell rings, and even Poverty Point, means that middens and material assemblages accumulated from intermittent, transient visits by people who spent most of their time away from ritual centers. Poverty Point and sites of the Shell Mound Archaic suggest either that those visiting these locations came from great distances, or that visiting involved the travels of local residents to far-away places, or both. The beliefs these people carried with them as participants of Archaic religion(s) may not have squared with the experiences of living through such varied material circumstances. In other words, beliefs shaped the worlds that Archaic people experienced, but undoubtedly contradictions continuously arose between the ideal and the real in matters as mundane as the edibility of certain foods, the appropriateness of first-cousin marriages, and settlement near a swamp.

A related matter is the reality that Archaic moundbuilding ritual seems to have drawn in and integrated people of different cultural identity (ethnicity). Participants in group ritual no doubt filtered the deep structures of belief through the surface structures of their respective histories, and, in turn, altered deep structures through the routines of their daily lives. Put back into the context of aggregation at ritual centers, these altered structures no doubt fueled factionalization and ultimately the transformation of collective practice (at least in that one location).

Assertions of cultural identity permeated many aspects of social life in the Archaic, as they do in all times and places. These symbolic actions have too often been shrouded in theory aimed at emergent properties of social life (e.g., adaptation, mode of production), or reduced to essentialist dimensions of identity (e.g., an archaeological culture, consisting of methodological individuals). The instances of hypertrophy evident in the Archaic record provide an opportunity to investigate how material culture is manipulated, through tradition, to affect social identities and the links among them. But these instances of "culture blown out of proportion" are not singular in their potential to inform on historical process.

It is imperative that we continue to expand our methods for tracing the histories of population movements, interethnic encounters, and instances of ethnogenesis, for these are common causes of cultural variation and change, and they occurred repeatedly throughout the Archaic. And, in constructing a historical processualism (Pauketat 2001) for the Archaic Southeast, the next generation of researchers must jettison the received wisdom of their forebears who, in canonizing the Archaic as the antecedent to "complex" society, perpetuated the myth that little of interest took place. Clearly that was not the case.

References

Adovasio, James M., and David Pedler 2005 The Peopling of North America. In *North American Archaeology.* T. R. Pauketat and D. DiPaolo Loren, eds. Pp. 30–55. Oxford: Blackwell.

Anderson, David G., 1990 The Paleoindian colonization of eastern North America: A view from the southeastern United States. In *Early Paleoindian Economies of Eastern North America.* K. B. Tankersley and B. L. Isaac, eds. Pp. 163–216. Research in Economic Anthropology, Supplement 5. Greenwich, CT: JAI Press.

Aten, Lawrence, 1999 Middle Archaic ceremonialism at Tick Island, Florida: Ripley P. Bullen's 1901 excavation at the Harris Creek site. *The Florida Anthropologist* 52, 131–200.

Bender, Barbara, 1985 Emergent tribal formations in the American midcontinent. *American Antiquity* 50, 52–62.

Biersak, Aletta, 1999 Introduction: From the "New Ecology" to the new ecologies. *American Anthropologist* 101, 5–18.

Binford, Lewis R., 1980 Willow smoke and dogs' tails: Hunter-gatherer settlement systems and archaeological site formation. *American Antiquity* 45, 4–20.

Blessing, Meggan E., and Kenneth E. Sassaman, 2001 New perspectives on spatial patterning of Stallings communities. Paper presented at the 58th Annual Meeting of the Southeastern Archaeological Conference, Chattanooga.

Blitz, John H., 1999 Mississippian chiefdoms and the fission-fusion process. *American Antiquity* 64, 577–592.

Brose, David S., 1979 A speculative model on the role of exchange in the prehistory of the Eastern Woodlands. In *Hopewell Archaeology: The Chillicothe Conference,* D. S. Brose and N. Greber, eds. Pp. 3–8. Kent, OH: Kent State University Press.

Brown, James A., 1985 Long-term trends to sedentism and the emergence of complexity in the American Midwest. In *Prehistoric Hunter-Gatherers: The Emergence of Cultural Complexity.* T. D. Price and J. A. Brown, eds. Pp. 201–231. New York: Academic Press.

Brown, James A., and Robert Vierra, 1983 What happened in the Middle Archaic? Introduction to an ecological approach to Koster site archaeology. In *Archaic Hunter-Gatherers in the American Midwest.* J. L. Phillips and J. A. Brown, eds. Pp. 165–195. New York: Academic Press.

Byrd, Kathleen M., ed., 1991 *The Poverty Point Culture: Local Manifestations, Subsistence Practices, and Trade Networks.* Geoscience and Man, vol. 29. Baton Rouge: Louisiana State University.

Cable, John R., 1993 Prehistoric chronology and settlement patterns of Edisto Beach State Park. In *Cultural Resources Survey and Archaeological Site Evaluation of the Edisto Beach State Park, Colleton County, South Carolina.* Pp. 158–205. Report on file with South Carolina Department of Parks, Recreation, and Tourism, Columbia, South Carolina. Stone Mountain, GA: New South Associates.

Charles, Douglas, and Jane Buikstra, 1983 Archaic mortuary sites in the central Mississippi drainage: Distribution, structure, and behavioral implications. In *Archaic Hunter-Gatherers in the American Midwest.* J. L. Phillips and J. A. Brown, eds. Pp. 117–145. New York: Academic Press.

Claassen, Cheryl, 1991 New hypotheses for the demise of the Shell Mound Archaic. In *The Archaic Period in the Mid-South.* C. McNutt, ed. Pp. 66–72. Archaeological Report 24. Jackson: Mississippi Department of Archives and History.

Claassen, Cheryl, 1992 Shell mounds as burial mounds: A revision of the Shell Mound Archaic.

In *Current Archaeological Research in Kentucky*, vol. 2. D. Pollack and A. G. Henderson, eds. Pp. 1–12. Frankfort: Kentucky Heritage Council.

Claassen, Cheryl, 1996 A consideration of the social organization of the Shell Mound Archaic. In *Archaeology of the Mid-Holocene Southeast*. K. E. Sassaman and D. G. Anderson, eds. Pp. 235–258. Gainesville: University Press of Florida.

Clark, John, 2004 Surrounding the sacred. In *Signs of Power*, J. Gibson and P. Carr, eds. Pp. 162–213. Tuscaloosa: University of Alabama Press.

Crothers, George M., 1999 Prehistoric hunters and gatherers, and the Archaic period Green River shell middens of western Kentucky. Ph.D. dissertation, Department of Anthropology, Washington University, St. Louis.

Crumley, Carole L., 1987 A dialectical critique of hierarchy. In *Power Relations and State Formation*. T. C. Patterson and C. W. Gailey, eds. Pp. 155–159. Washington, DC: American Anthropological Association.

DeBoer, Warren, 1997 Ceremonial centers from the Cayapas (Esmeraldas, Ecuador) to Cillicothe (Ohio, USA). *Cambridge Archaeological Journal* 7(1), 1–15.

Dye, David H., 1996 Riverine adaptation in the Midsouth. In *Of Caves and Shell Mounds*. K. C. Carstens and P. J. Watson, eds., Pp. 140–158. Tuscaloosa: University of Alabama Press.

Elliott, Daniel T., R. Jerald Ledbetter, and Elizabeth A. Gordon, 1994 *Data Recovery at Lovers Lane, Phinizy Swamp and the Old Dike Sites Bobby Jones Expressway Extension Corridor Augusta, Georgia*. Occasional Papers in Cultural Resource Management 7, Georgia Department of Transportation, Atlanta.

Flanagan, J. G., 1989 Hierarchy in simple "egalitarian" societies. *Annual Review of Anthropology* 18, 245–266.

Ford, James A., and Clarence H. Webb, 1956 *Poverty Point, a Late Archaic Site in Louisiana*. Anthropological Papers, vol. 46, pt. 1. New York: American Museum of Natural History.

Fortier, Andrew C., 1984 *The Go-Kart Site*. American Bottom Archaeology, FAI-270 Site Reports 9. Urbana: University of Illinois Press.

Gibson, Jon L., 1991 Catahoula: An amphibious Poverty Point manifestation in eastern Louisiana. In *The Poverty Point Culture: Local Manifestations, Subsistence Practices, and Trade Networks*. K. M. Byrd, ed. Pp. 61–87. Geoscience and Man, vol. 29. Baton Rouge: Louisiana State University.

Gibson, Jon L., 2000 *The Ancient Mounds of Poverty Point: Place of the Rings*. Gainesville: University Press of Florida.

Goad, Sharon, 1980 Patterns of Late Archaic exchange. *Tennessee Anthropologist* 5, 1–16.

Gramly, Richard M., and Robert E. Funk, 1991 Olive Branch: A Large Dalton and Pre-Dalton encampment at Thebes Gap, Alexander County, Illinois. In *The Archaic Period in the Mid-South*. C. H. McNutt, ed. Pp. 23–33. Archaeological Report 24. Jackson: Mississippi Department of Archives and History.

Grinker, Richard Roy, 1994 *Houses in the Rainforest: Ethnicity and Inequality among the Farmers and Foragers in Central Africa*. Berkeley: University of California Press.

Hally, David J., 1986 The identification of vessel function: A case study from northwest Georgia. *American Antiquity* 51, 267–295.

Haskins, Valeria A., and Nicholas P. Herrmann, 1996 Shell Mound bioarchaeology. In *Of Caves and Shell Mounds*. K. C. Carstens and P. J. Watson, eds. Pp. 107–118. Tuscaloosa: University of Alabama Press.

Hassen, Harold, and Kenneth B. Farnsworth, 1987 *The Bullseye Site: A Floodplain Archaic Mortuary Site in the Lower Illinois River Valley*. Reports of Investigation 42. Springfield: Illinois State Museum.

Hayden, Brian, 1995 Pathways to power: Principles for creating socioeconomic inequalities. In *Foundations of Social Inequality*. T. D. Price and G. M. Feinman, eds. Pp. 15–86. New York: Plenum Press.

Heckenberger, M. J., 2004 *The Ecology of Power: Archaeology, History, and Memory in the Southern Amazon*. New York: Routledge.

Hensley, Christine, 1994 The Archaic settlement system of the Middle Green River valley. Ph.D. dissertation, Department of Anthropology, Washington University, St. Louis.

Hofman, Jack L., 1986 Hunter-gatherer mortuary variability: Toward an explanatory model. Ph.D. dissertation, Department of Anthropology, University of Tennessee, Knoxville.

Johnson, Gregory, 1982 Organizational structure and scalar stress. In *Theory and Explanation in Archaeology*. C. Renfrew, M. J. Rowlands, and B. Segraves, eds. Pp. 389–342. New York: Academic Press.

Johnson, Jay K., and Samuel O. Brookes, 1989 Benton points, turkey tails, and cache blades: Middle Archaic exchange in the Midsouth. *Southeastern Archaeology* 8, 134–145.

Kelly, Robert L., 1995 *The Foraging Spectrum: Diversity in Hunter-Gatherer Lifeways*. Washington, DC: Smithsonian Institution Press.

Kelly, Robert L., and Lawrence C. Todd, 1988 Coming into the country: Early Paleoindian hunting and mobility. *American Antiquity* 53, 231–244.

Kidder, T. R., 1991 New directions in Poverty Point settlement archaeology: An example from northeast Louisiana. In *The Poverty Point Culture: Local*

Manifestations, Subsistence Practices, and Trade Networks. K. M. Byrd, ed. Pp. 27–53. Geoscience and Man, vol. 29. Baton Rouge: Louisiana State University.

Kidder, T. R., 2002 Mapping Poverty Point. *American Antiquity* 67, 89–101.

Knight, Vernon J., Jr., 1989 Symbolism of Mississippian mounds. In *Powhatan's Mantle: Indians in the Colonial Southeast.* P. H. Wood, G. A. Waselkov, and M. T. Hatley, eds. Pp. 279–291. Lincoln: University of Nebraska Press.

Knight, Vernon J., Jr., 1998 Moundville as a diagrammatic ceremonial center. In *Archaeology of the Moundville Chiefdom.* V. J. Knight, Jr. and V. P. Steponaitis, eds. Pp. 44–62. Washington, DC: Smithsonian Institution Press.

Knight, Vernon J., Jr., 2001 Feasting and the emergence of platform mound ceremonialism in eastern North America. In *Feasts: Archaeological and Ethnographic Perspectives on Food, Politics, and Power.* M. Dietler and B. Hayden, eds. Pp. 311–333. Washington, DC: Smithsonian Institution Press.

Knoblock, Byron, 1939 *Bannerstones of the North American Indian.* LaGrange, IL: privately published.

Leacock, Eleanor, and Richard Lee, 1982 Introduction. In *Politics and History in Band Societies.* Eleanor Leacock and Richard B. Lee, eds. Pp. 1–20. Cambridge: Cambridge University Press.

Ledbetter, R. Jerald, 1995 *Archaeological Investigations at Mill Branch Sites 9WR4 and 9WR11, Warren County, Georgia.* Technical Report 3. Atlanta: Interagency Archeological Services Division, National Park Service.

Lee, Richard B., and Irven DeVore, eds., 1976 *Kalahari Hunter-Gatherers: Studies of the !Kung San and their Neighbors.* Cambridge, MA: Harvard University Press.

Lévi-Strauss, Claude, 1963 *Structural Anthropology.* New York: Basic Books.

Lindauer, Owen, and John Blitz, 1997 Higher ground: The archaeology of North American platform mounds. *Journal of Archaeological Research* 5, 169–207.

Marquardt, William H., 1985 Complexity and Scale in the Study of Fisher-Gatherer-Hunters: An example from the eastern United States. In *Prehistoric Hunter-Gatherers: The Emergence of Cultural Complexity.* T. D. Price and J. A. Brown, eds. Pp. 59–97. New York: Academic Press.

Marquardt, William H., and Patty Jo Watson, 1983 The Shell Mound Archaic of western Kentucky. In *Archaic Hunters and Gatherers in the American Midwest.* J. A. Phillips and J. A. Brown, eds. Pp. 323–339. New York: Academic Press.

Meltzer, David, 1989 Was stone exchanged among eastern North American Paleoindians? In *Eastern Paleoindian Lithic Resource Use.* C. J. Ellis and J. C. Lothrop, eds. Pp. 11–39. Boulder: Westview Press.

Milner, George R., and Richard W. Jefferies, 1998 The Read Archaic shell midden in Kentucky. *Southeastern Archaeology* 17(2), 119–132.

Morse, Dan F., 1997 *Sloan: A Paleoindian Dalton Cemetery in Arkansas,* Washington, DC: Smithsonian Institution Press.

Pauketat, Timothy R., 2001 Practice and History in Archaeology: An Emerging Paradigm. *Anthropological Theory* 1(1), 73–98.

Pauketat, Timothy R., 2003 Resettled farmers and the making of a Mississippian polity. *American Antiquity* 68, 39–66.

Roper, Donna C., 1978 *The Airport Site: A Multicomponent Site in the Sangamon Drainage.* Papers in Anthropology 4. Springfield: Illinois State Museum.

Rothschild, Nan, 1979 Mortuary behavior and social organization at Indian Knoll and Dickson Mounds. *American Antiquity* 44, 658–675.

Russo, Michael, 1991 Archaic sedentism on the Florida coast: A case study from Horr's Island. Ph.D. dissertation, Department of Anthropology, University of Florida, Gainesville.

Russo, Michael, 1994 Why we don't believe in Archaic ceremonial mounds and why we should: The case from Florida. *Southeastern Archaeology* 13, 93–108.

Russo, Michael, 1996 Southeastern Archaic mounds. In *Archaeology of the Mid-Holocene Southeast.* K. E. Sassaman and D. G. Anderson, eds. Pp. 259–287. Gainesville: University Press of Florida.

Russo, Michael, 2002 Architectural features at Fig Island. In *The Fig Island Ring Complex (38CH42): Coastal Adaptation and the Question of Ring Function in the Late Archaic.* R. Saunders, ed. Pp. 85–97. Report submitted to South Carolina Department of Archives and History under grant #45-01-16441.

Russo, Michael, 2004 Measuring shell rings for social inequality: Towards an understanding of circular community dynamics. In *Signs of Power.* J. Gibson and P. Carr, eds. Pp. 26–70. Tuscaloosa: University of Alabama Press.

Russo, Michael, and Gregory Heide, 2001 Shell rings of the southeast US. *Antiquity* 75(289), 491–492.

Russo, Michael, 2002 The Joseph Reed shell ring. *The Florida Anthropologist* 55(2), 67–88.

Russo, Michael, Gregory Heide, and Vicki Rolland, 2002 *The Guana Shell Ring.* Report submitted to the Florida Department of State Division of Historical Resources, Historic Preservation Grant F0126.

Sassaman, Kenneth E., 1993 *Mims Point 1992: Archaeological Investigations at a Prehistoric Habitation Site in the Sumter National Forest, South Carolina.* Savannah River Archaeological Research Papers 4. Occasional Papers of the Savannah River Archaeological

Research Program, South Carolina Institute of Archaeology and Anthropology. Columbia: University of South Carolina.

Sassaman, Kenneth E., 1998 Crafting cultural identity in hunter-gatherer economies. In *Craft and Social Identity*. C. L. Costin and R. P. Wright, eds. Pp. 93–107. Archeological Papers of the American Anthropological Association 8. Washington, DC: American Anthropological Association.

Sassaman, Kenneth E., 2000 Agents of change in hunter-gatherer technology. In *Agency in Archaeology*. M.-A. Dobres and J. Robb, eds. Pp. 148–168. London: Routledge.

Sassaman, Kenneth E., 2001a Hunter-gatherers and traditions of resistance. In *The Archaeology of Traditions: Agency and History Before and After Columbus*. T. Pauketat, ed. Pp. 218–236. Gainesville: University Press of Florida.

Sassaman, Kenneth E., 2001b Articulating hidden histories of the mid-Holocene in the southern Appalachians. In *Archaeology of the Appalachian Highlands*. L. P. Sullivan and S. C. Prezzano, eds. Pp. 103–121. Knoxville: University of Tennessee Press.

Sassaman, Kenneth E., 2004a Complex hunter-gatherers in evolution and history: A North American perspective. *Journal of Archaeological Research* 12, 227–280.

Sassaman, Kenneth E., 2004b Common origins and divergent histories in the early pottery traditions of the American Southeast. In *Early Pottery in the Lower Southeast*. R. Saunders and C. Hays, eds. Tuscaloosa: University of Alabama Press (in press).

Sassaman, Kenneth E., and Michael J. Heckenberger, 2004a Crossing the Symbolic Rubicon in the Southeast. In *Signs of Power*. J. Gibson and P. Carr, eds. Pp. 214–233. Tuscaloosa: University of Alabama Press.

Sassaman, Kenneth E., 2004b Roots of the theocratic formative in the American Southeast. In *Hunter-Gatherers in Theory and Archaeology*. G. M. Crothers, ed. Pp. 422–443. Carbondale: Center for Archaeological Investigations, Southern Illinois University.

Saunders, Joe W., Thurman Allen, and Roger T. Saucier, 1994 Four Archaic? Mound complexes in northeast Louisiana. *Southeastern Archaeology* 13, 134–153.

Saunders, Joe, Thurman Allen, Reca Jones, and G. Swoveland, 2000 Caney Mounds (16CT5). *Louisiana Archaeological Society Newsletter* 27(3), 14–21.

Saunders, Joe, Thurman Allen, Dennis LaBatt, Reca Jones, and David Griffing, 2001 An assessment of the antiquity of the Lower Jackson Mound. *Southeastern Archaeology* 20, 67–77.

Saunders, Joe W., Rolfe D. Mandel, Roger T. Saucier, E. Thurman Allen, C. T. Hallmark, Jay K. Johnson, Edwin H. Jackson, C. M. Allen, G. L. Stringer, Douglas S. Frink, James K. Feathers, Stephen Williams, Kristin J. Gremillion, M. F. Vidrine, and Reca Jones, 1997 A mound complex in Louisiana at 5400–5000 years before the present. *Science* 277, 1796–1799.

Saunders, Rebecca, 1994 The case for Archaic mounds in southeastern Louisiana. *Southeastern Archaeology* 13, 118–134.

Saunders, Rebecca, 2002 Summary and conclusions. In *The Fig Island Ring Complex (38CH42): Coastal Adaptation and the Question of Ring Function in the Late Archaic*. R. Saunders, ed. Pp. 4–159. Report submitted to South Carolina Department of Archives and History under grant #45-01-16441.

Schrire, Carmel, 1984 Wild surmises on savage thoughts. In *Past and Present in Hunter-Gatherer Studies*. Carmel Schrire, ed. Pp. 1–25. Orlando: Academic Press.

Trinkley, Michael B., 1985 The form and function of South Carolina's Early Woodland shell rings. In *Structure and Process in Southeastern Archaeology*. Roy S. Dickens, Jr., ed. Pp. 102–118. Tuscaloosa: University of Alabama Press.

Walthall, John, and Brad Koldehoff, 1998 Hunter-gatherer interaction and alliance formation: Dalton and the cult of the long blade. *Plains Anthropologist* 43, 257–273.

Webb, William S., 1974 *Indian Knoll*. Knoxville: University of Tennessee Press.

Webb, William S., and David L. DeJarnette, 1942 *An Archaeological Survey of Pickwick Basin in the Adjacent Portions of the States of Alabama, Mississippi, and Tennessee*. Smithsonian Institution Bureau of American Ethnology, Bulletin 129. Washington, DC.

Wilmsen, Edwin, 1989 *Land Filled with Flies: A Political Economy of the Kalahari*. Chicago: University of Chicago Press.

Winters, Howard D., 1968 Value systems and trade cycles of the Late Archaic in the Midwest. In *New Perspectives in Archaeology*. S. R. Binford and L. R. Binford, eds. Pp. 175–221. Chicago: Aldine.

Wood, W. D., D. T. Elliott, T. P. Rudolph, and D. B. Blanton, 1986 *Prehistory of the Richard B. Russell Reservoir: The Archaic and Woodland Periods of the Upper Savannah River*. Russell Papers. Atlanta: Interagency Archeological Services Division, National Park Service.

Woodburn, James, 1982 Egalitarian societies. *Man* 17, 431–451.

Daily Practice and Material Culture in Pluralistic Social Settings
An Archaeological Study of Culture Change and Persistence from Fort Ross, California

Kent G. Lightfoot, Antoinette Martinez, and Ann M. Schiff

Culture contact studies are well suited to evaluate and refine theoretical and methodological approaches to culture change and persistence in archaeology. In considering the implications of European exploration and colonialism in the Americas, these studies present unique opportunities to examine Native American encounters with European, African, and Asian peoples in early contact settings and to address the initial founding and development of multi-ethnic colonial communities. While recognizing the great potential for an archaeology of pluralism, two issues were raised recently about the theoretical models and methodological practices employed in the study of material culture in multi-ethnic contexts. The first issue concerned the development of more sophisticated "contextual" approaches to study pluralism, which can complement and broaden our current focus beyond artifact-based analyses (Lightfoot 1995:202–210). The second issue involved the promotion of multiscalar

Kent G. Lightfoot, Antoinette Martinez, and Ann M. Schiff, "Daily Practice and Material Culture in Pluralistic Social Settings: An Archaeological Study of Culture Change and Persistence from Fort Ross, California," pp. 199–222 from *American Antiquity* 63(2) (1998). Reprinted with permission of the Society for American Archaeology and the author.

research that may enable archaeologists to address not only macroscale processes of world systems and colonial policies, but also microscale practices of individual intentionality and social action that are critical components of "encounters" in pluralistic settings (Lightfoot and Martinez 1995:477–488).

The purpose of this paper is to develop an approach to the archaeology of pluralism that takes both of the above issues into account. We begin with a brief discussion of recent archaeological approaches employed in culture contact studies that focus primarily on artifact ratios and frequencies. We then present an alternative, but complementary, approach that considers the material remains of daily practices and use of space in pluralistic social settings. A critical component of this approach is the investigation of a suite of habitual practices in a multiscalar study that is broadly diachronic and comparative in scope. In the final section, we examine the nature and magnitude of culture change and persistence that took place in interethnic households at the nineteenth-century Russian colony of Fort Ross in northern California. We explore how cohabiting Native Alaskan men and Native Californian women constructed their own unique identities. We do so by examining the arrangement and use of space in built environments, the spatial patterning of trash disposal, and the organization of domestic activities.

Study of Culture Change and Persistence

A significant issue for archaeology is the development and refinement of approaches for the study of culture change and persistence using material remains. This issue is especially pertinent to archaeologists undertaking culture contact research in pluralistic settings. How does one evaluate the magnitude, direction, and meaning of change that may result from encounters between diverse peoples in multi-ethnic communities? Over the last three decades archaeologists in North America have experimented with various artifact-based approaches for measuring change and continuity before, during, and after culture encounters. The earliest studies employed ratios of European and native artifacts as straightforward measures of acculturation (e.g., Deetz 1963; Di Peso 1974). The proportion of European goods in Native American contexts was viewed as a direct reflection of the degree of culture change that had transpired over time as native peoples assimilated into the material world of Europeans or European Americans, while the proportion of traditional native materials was viewed as a proxy of cultural conservatism. The ratios of European to native materials were used in some regions (i.e., north-eastern North America) to seriate cultural deposits from native sites into chronological order, as it was commonly believed that the frequency of European goods increased over time at the expense of native manufactured items (see Smith 1987:24). As discussed in more detail elsewhere (Lightfoot 1995:206–207), the shortcomings of these pioneering approaches were soon recognized because they depicted passive and unidirectional models of acculturation, and they were unable to distinguish complex social processes underlying the synergism of multi-ethnic interactions.

The next generation of archaeological approaches is employing more sophisticated artifact-based analyses for measuring acculturation profiles and for undertaking artifact pattern analysis. Influenced by Quimby and Spoehr's (1951)

classic research on "acculturated" museum objects that had been modified through culture contact, acculturation profiles are constructed based on the percentage of traditional, hybrid, and imported artifact categories in archaeological assemblages (e.g., Farnsworth 1987, 1992; Hoover and Costello 1985; Smith 1987; White 1975). Farnsworth (1987, 1992), for example, measures the acculturation profiles of California mission assemblages by calculating the percentage of different artifact categories that combine local (native) and/or imported (European) artifact forms, raw materials, manufacturing processes, and functions. Artifact pattern analysis is used by Deagan (1983a, 1995a) and her coworkers to compare and contrast households of varying status, ethnicity, and wealth in the pluralistic Spanish colonies of St. Augustine, Florida, and Puerto Real, Haiti. Initially developed by South (1977) for the study of Anglo-American sites, the approach involves the systematic comparison of artifact types grouped into broad functional categories that include the kitchen, architecture (structural hardware), weaponry, clothing, personal items, activity-related items, furniture hardware, tools, harness and tack, and religion (see Deagan 1995b:441–444; Hoffman 1997:31; McEwan 1995:216–218). Artifact percentages provide measures for systematically evaluating similarities and differences in the material culture of households for each functional category and for the entire assemblage (see also Farnsworth 1987:510–575).

With the growing use and sophistication of artifact-based analyses in culture contact studies, more "contextual" approaches are needed to situate artifacts into the broader spatial organization of the archaeological record (Lightfoot 1995:207–209; Rogers 1990:100). This is not to imply that previous researchers have ignored archaeological context. Farnsworth (1987: 478–509) is careful to discriminate the cultural deposits within which he calculates acculturation profiles. Deagan (1983a, 1995a) and her colleagues employ artifact pattern analysis as but one component of a suite of investigations that consider diet, architecture layout, trash disposal practices, and settlement organization in colonial settings. Furthermore, Deagan (1995b:440–447) employs artifact pattern analysis to compare and contrast different kinds of social and economic contexts, such as the public sector, domestic-residential sites, and a commercial site at Puerto Real. Rogers (1990) analyzes artifact categories for three separate contexts (domestic earth lodges, ceremonial earth lodges, and burials) in his case study of Arikara contact with Europeans. Rather, our point is that the continued development of contextual approaches will complement current culture contact research through the explicit placement of artifacts into the "built environments" of pluralistic social settings.

Daily Practices and Material Culture

The approach we consider in this paper is predicated on theoretical implications involving the practice of day-to-day living. It is through daily practices – how space is structured, how mundane domestic tasks are conducted, how refuse is disposed of – that people both organize and make sense of their lives. The focus on daily practices and spatial organization is well suited to archaeology (see Kirch 1996; Moreland 1992; Roscoe 1993). It entails the investigation of "little routines people enact, again and again, in working, sleeping, and relaxing, as well as little scenarios of etiquette they play out again and again in social interaction" (Ortner 1984:154). These routine kinds of actions that dominate people's domestic lives produce much of the material culture we recover in the archaeological record. Furthermore, the performance of daily routines produces patterned accumulations of material culture that are often among the most interpretable kinds of deposits in archaeological contexts. The ordering of daily life may be observed in archaeological contexts by examining the arrangement and use of space in the built environment (both intramural and extramural areas), the organization of domestic activities (e.g., food preparation, cooking, tool production and maintenance), and the spatial pattern of refuse disposal.

With the development and elaboration of practice theory over the last 20 years, a growing theoretical corpus now exists on how the study of daily practices can provide insights into different people's worldviews, cultural meanings, and social identities (e.g., Bourdieu 1977, 1990;

Giddens 1979; Ortner 1984). The basic premise of practice theory is that the ordering of daily life serves as a microcosm of the broader organizational principles and cultural categories of individuals, as exemplified in Bourdieu's (1977) concept of the *habitus*. As Ortner (1984:154) succinctly states, all cultural practices "are predicated upon, and embody within themselves, the fundamental notions of temporal, spatial, and social ordering that underlie and organize the system as a whole." In other words, people repeatedly enact and reproduce their underlying structural principles and belief systems in the performance of ordering their daily lives.

The emphasis on daily practices is especially germane for culture contact studies. In case studies of Hawaiian, Fijian, and Maori contact with Europeans, Sahlins (1981, 1985, 1990) stresses how cultural practices often take on new interpretations and meanings in the process of encountering "others." In responding to new cultural orders, daily practices are often redefined or reinterpreted in order to be made meaningful in new social contexts. Cultural categories and values are not simply reproduced in daily practice, rather they are creatively modified during encounters with others (see Sahlins 1981:33–37). In the process of culture contact, people will reconstitute and reinterpret cultural practices in ways that both make sense of "others" and best suit their own interests. People sharing the same cultural orientation do not necessarily respond to "others" in a prescribed, uniform manner. Rather, they will seek new opportunities and social relationships in pluralistic contacts that are perceived as beneficial to their own or related interests, depending largely on their social status, political affiliations, kin relations, and gender (Brumfiel and Fox 1994; Cohen 1987; Lightfoot and Martinez 1995). For example, during early contact events in Hawaii, chiefs and commoners, both men and women, pursued very different courses of action with British seafarers that enhanced their respective positions in Hawaiian society (Sahlins 1981:36, 1985:28). Contact situations are often significant watersheds in reshaping cultural orders since they provide individuals from all walks of life with new opportunities to negotiate and redefine their social identities in the process of daily practice (e.g., Upton 1996).

From an archaeological perspective, we believe the study of change and persistence in multiethnic contexts pertaining to the construction of social identities may be best addressed by considerations of daily practices involving domestic life and the organization of space. We recognize that material culture may play an active role in the creation of social identities, depending largely on how materials are employed in daily practice. Material culture may be vested with special meanings in pluralistic contexts. Cultural practices that are often visible in the archaeological record, such as food preparation and the care of household space, may speak volumes about a person's social relations and identity in the community. The retention of traditional cultural practices or the adoption of novel ones can take on symbolic value in culture contact situations, as forms become "invested with a significance which they may have lacked in earlier incarnations" (Cohen 1987:96).

In considering the construction of social identities in pluralistic settings, it is important to examine a suite of different daily practices, since the ordering of some kinds of activities may be undertaken in a routine, almost subconscious manner, while others may be consciously manipulated to broadcast social relations and identities. By examining how residential space is laid out and maintained, how foods are prepared and cooked, how tools are manufactured and used, and how trash disposal is organized, one may observe the basic organizational principles of individuals in action. Some of the more routine, secluded activities, such as trash disposal practices in private residential space, may follow conventional cultural orderings, allowing us to identify individuals from specific homelands in archaeological contexts. The organization of other, more conspicuous cultural practices, such as the use and maintenance of extramural residential space or trash disposal practices outside the residence, may undergo transformations in the process of contact, providing insights on culture change and the creation of new social identities. For example, Deagan (1983b, 1990:240–241) stresses how activities in "public" or "private" space take on different meanings to Hispanic men and Native American women in mixed ethnic households in Spanish colonies.

The approach we advocate in our study of daily practices is broadly comparative in scope, diachronic, holistic, and multiscalar. A key consideration is to compare the suite of daily practices from different contexts in pluralistic sites with those of the homelands from which people came. This provides the necessary comparative framework for evaluating the nature and magnitude of culture change and persistence (see Lightfoot 1995:209–210). How were the organizational principles of individuals who once resided in homeland villages being transformed or reproduced in new, multi-ethnic settings? By examining multiple kinds of cultural practices from homeland contexts in a series of diachronic "windows" or points along a continuum spanning prehistoric, protohistoric, and historic times, one can build a comparative framework in which to evaluate critically how organizational principles and social identities were being actively constructed and transformed in pluralistic settings. The approach is holistic because information is drawn not only from archaeology, but also from relevant ethnohistorical and ethnographic sources, as well as native oral traditions.

Finally, it is critical to apply a multiscalar perspective in considering the suite of daily practices in both pluralistic and homeland contexts. Different scales of analysis may provide very different insights into the organizational principles, worldviews, and identities of individuals, groups, and communities. As Deagan (1995a: 195) notes, microscale studies of domestic activities in household contexts may be best suited for observing individual responses to colonial settings and encounters with others, while the layout of space at the broader community or regional scale may provide many insights on the overarching political hierarchy and organizational policies of colonizers. For example, under Spanish rule in St. Augustine and Puerto Real, the greater community pattern (layout of houses, streets, plazas) was highly structured by the precepts of colonial administrators (see Deagan 1983a:247–248; Williams 1995; Willis 1995). In interethnic households composed of Spanish men and Native American women, Spanish conventions were also followed in the more visible, public spaces of houses and extramural areas, whereas native ideals were employed in the less

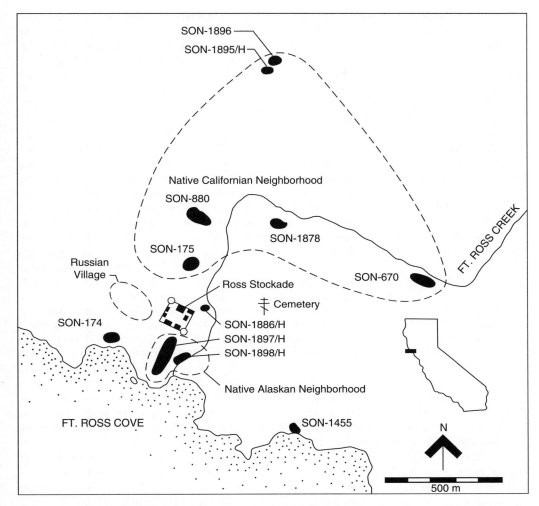

Figure 8.1 Spatial Layout of Fort Ross, including the Ross Stockade, the Russian Village, the Native Californian Neighborhood, the Ross Cemetery, and the Native Alaskan Neighborhood. (Illustration by Judith Ogden.)

visible, private sector of domestic life (Deagan 1983b; Ewen 1991; McEwan 1995).

Interethnic Households at Fort Ross

We employ the above approach in a case study on the creation of social identities in interethnic households at Fort Ross in northern California. At this colonial outpost established 110 km north of San Francisco Bay, the Russian-American Company dispatched a large contingent of Native Alaskan men (mostly Alutiiq men from Kodiak Island, Alaska) to harvest sea mammal furs and to serve as laborers in agricultural activities and manufacturing enterprises. While stationed at Fort Ross from 1812 to 1841, many of the men established joint households with local women from Native Californian tribes (primarily Kashaya Pomo, Coast Miwok, and Southern Pomo). Recent archaeological investigations at Fort Ross are focusing on the Native Alaskan Neighborhood (Figure 8.1), a residential zone of primarily interethnic households – the majority made up of

Alutiiq men and Kashaya Pomo women, according to census records in the early 1820s (Istomin 1992; Lightfoot et al. 1991:22–28).

Native Californian women left their homeland villages in the near and distant hinterland of Fort Ross to join their common-law husbands in establishing households in the Native Alaskan Neighborhood. Some Pomo and Miwok leaders apparently encouraged their daughters to live with foreigners (Golovnin 1979:163; Kotzebue 1830:124), an action probably calculated to cement alliances with the Russian-American Company and to establish kinship ties with the colonists. The domestic units that resulted from these unions were fragile, with couples often separating after only a short time together. Khlebnikov (1990:194) observed in 1824 that

> all the Aleuts have Indian women, but these relationships are unstable, and the Aleuts and the Indians do not trust each other. An Indian woman may live for a number of years with an Aleut and have children, but then, acting on a whim, will drop everything and run off to the mountains.

When husbands were transferred to other North Pacific colonies, Native Californian women frequently remained behind, although a few did accompany spouses to Alaska. In the 1820–1821 census listing of 11 Native Alaskan men who were transferred to other North Pacific colonies, two women accompanied their spouses to Sitka, two established new interethnic households in the Native Alaskan Neighborhood, and seven returned to their "homeland" or "native village" (Lightfoot and Martinez 1997:4–6). Census records indicate that in cases of divorce or separation, the status of children from mixed ethnic marriages was decided by the men, with male offspring frequently returning to Alaska to join their father's relatives and the female offspring remaining behind with their mothers in California (Istomin 1992:7).

The Native California women at Fort Ross entered a colonial world in which their identities, social roles, and status were somewhat ambiguous. The Russian-American Company imposed a colonial hierarchy that defined the status, work, pay, and even living arrangements of all its workers. While several factors were employed in defining an employee's position in the company (e.g., level of education, job skills, and overall motivation), ethnicity was the primary variable employed in defining four major "estates" or classes (see Fedorova 1975): (1) "Russians," (2) "Creoles," (3) "Aleuts," and (4) "Indians." At the apex of the colonial system were the elite Russian administrators, ship captains, and military officers, as well as lower-class clerks, navigators, and laborers. With mixed Russian and Native ancestry, Creoles comprised a rather nebulous second estate of employees who often served as middle-level managers, clerks, and skilled craftsworkers. The third major estate, Aleuts, was composed of Native Alaskans from the Aleutian Islands, Kodiak Island, and coastal Alaska who were marine mammal hunters, skilled craftsworkers, and laborers. They worked on commission (pay per sea otter pelt) or received daily or yearly salaries in scrip, a parchment token that could be exchanged for goods in the company store (Murley 1994; Tikhmenev 1978:144). Indians, the lowest estate in the colonial hierarchy, were local Native Californians (Kashaya Pomo, Coast Miwok, Southern Pomo) recruited primarily as seasonal agricultural workers. They were paid in kind (rather than salary) for their services, receiving food, tobacco, beads, and clothing from the Russians (Khlebnikov 1990:193–194; Kostromitinov 1974:9; Wrangell 1969:211).

It is not clear from the available documentary records just how Native Californian women in interethnic households were viewed or treated at Fort Ross (e.g., Parkman 1996–1997:359–362). Were they regarded simply as "Indian" women? Or were they perceived as the wives of "Aleut" men? Or were they, their husbands, and children appreciated as something new and different, perhaps a new ethnic group at Fort Ross similar to the mixed Creole estate? The underlying ambiguity suggests that different potentials and choices were available to Native Californian women in negotiating their social identities as members of interethnic households. As discussed below, they may have perpetuated and even enhanced their Native Californian heritage while residing in the Native Alaskan Neighborhood, or they may have emulated or created new identities that broadcast very different meanings and social relations within the colonial community.

Native Californian identities

Some Native Californian women may have maintained strong ties with their homeland villages, fostering social identities that clearly distinguished them from their Native Alaskan spouses. In reproducing their Native Californian identities at Fort Ross, these women could have employed conventional beliefs and values as practiced at home to respond to their new social setting. "Indian" identities would have been manifested in the organization of their daily lives, which may have been in part subconscious and routine, and in part deliberately created to distinguish themselves from other peoples at Fort Ross. In the process of cultural encounters, change most certainly would have taken place as they responded to their spouses, other workers, and Russian administrators at Ross. However, the incorporation of new cultural practices and material culture would have been highly selective, with their actions following perceived cultural categories of what they thought constituted "proper" Indian behavior (Kardulias 1990:29; Wilson and Rogers 1993:3–6). In such a manner, they may have attempted to reproduce their distinctive Indian identities while reacting to new contact conditions and undergoing transformations themselves (see also Simmons 1988:7–8).

New social identities

Members of mixed ethnic households may have also chosen to negotiate and create new social identities that served to assimilate them into other ethnic classes or estates for perceived social, political, or economic advantages. In reality, the imposed colonial estates were composites of diverse peoples from different homeland villages and kin groups, who often spoke distinct languages. Since these broad ethnic categories existed primarily in the minds of Russian administrators, the cultural practices associated with each of the different estates in the colonial hierarchy were somewhat enigmatic. There was considerable latitude for the creation of "invented traditions" at Fort Ross (e.g., Upton 1996:5). In order to be recognized as a member of the Indian, Aleut, or Creole estate, it was imperative that you "talk the talk" and "walk the walk" in the eyes of the Russian managers. In the

performance of daily practices, Native Californian spouses could have reconstituted themselves enough in the likeness of Native Alaskan women so that they were treated as one of the estate by the Russian-American Company. That is, daily routines and cultural practices could have been implemented in the image of Native Alaskan women, or at least the image as perceived by Russian administrators (e.g., dress, food preparation, craft production, ordering of residential space, and so on).

Another practice that may have been jointly implemented by Native Alaskan men and Native Californian women was the deliberate construction of Creole cultural identities. By initiating creative versions of Russian and native lifeways, they may have defined themselves as part of or associated with the Creole estate. Since this ethnic category remained rather ambiguous at Fort Ross, considerable leeway probably existed in initiating cultural practices that may have been perceived as "creolized" by Russian managers. This strategy may have become increasingly important to children of mixed ethnic households who could claim association with several different colonial estates at Fort Ross, depending largely on their creation of social identities.

Archaeological Study of Social Identities at Fort Ross

The study of pluralism at Fort Ross involves comparing and contrasting the spatial organization of daily practices of the interethnic households in the Native Alaskan Neighborhood with those of pertinent Kashaya Pomo villages in the vicinity of Fort Ross, and relevant Alutiiq residences on Kodiak Island, Alaska, and in other Russian outposts in the North Pacific. Specifically, we identify concordances and anomalies in a suite of daily practices involving the maintenance of residential space, the organization of trash disposal, the menu and preparation of food, the material culture from domestic contexts, and settlement layout. We attempt to detect the organizational principles of Native Californian women and Native Alaskan men in households, and to evaluate how their social identities were being constructed in interethnic households. The study and comparison of daily practices and organizational principles take place at the local (household, community), regional, and panregional scales.

Local scale

The field strategy we employed at the Native Alaskan Neighborhood was designed both to define the broader community pattern and to detect interpretable deposits that may have been produced by the daily practices of interethnic households. From 1988 to 1992 fieldwork focused on two sites: (1) the original village site containing Native Alaskan/Native Californian households, designated as the Native Alaskan Village site (CA-SON-1897/H), situated directly south of the Russian Stockade complex on a raised marine terrace and (2) the Fort Ross Beach site (CA-SON-1898/H), a complex midden deposit situated directly below the village in the Fort Ross Cove (Figure 8.1). As outlined in detail elsewhere (Lightfoot and Schiff 1997; Lightfoot et al. 1997a; Price 1997; Tschan 1997), the spatial organization of the Native Alaskan Neighborhood was defined by the topographic mapping of surface features, systematic surface collection and generation of artifact distribution maps, and geophysical investigations involving both magnetometer and soil resistance surveys. Remote sensing, in concert with the spatial patterning of surface features and artifacts, proved very useful in detecting house structures, fence foundations, communal spaces, and trash deposits (see Tschan 1997:116–126). We implemented an excavation strategy designed specifically to expose intramural and extramural space in and around houses and to identify contextually rich deposits within these areas.

The field program recorded a complex midden deposit and the remains of a bathhouse in the Fort Ross Beach site (Figure 8.2). Thirteen surface features were initially mapped at the Native Alaskan Village site (Figure 8.2), and subsequent excavations in and around two features unearthed portions of two pithouses (designated the East Central and South Pit features), a redwood fence line (outside the South Pit feature), and three deposits containing dense concentrations of faunal elements and artifacts (designated the East Central, South, and Abalone Dump "Bone Beds"). The bone beds are contextually

rich deposits that accumulated on intentionally created surfaces often in the fill of abandoned structures (Figures 8.3 and 8.4). The spatial distribution of surface features and artifacts, in combination with geophysical signatures, allowed us to detect abandoned houses with associated bone bed deposits.

Although we had intended to expose a more extensive area of internal and external residential space in and around pit features, the research design was modified so that we could carefully record and map the three-dimensional structure of the bone bed deposits. Field crews from the University of California, Berkeley, and the California Department of Parks and Recreation point-plotted thousands of abalone and mussel shells, bones of mammals (deer, sea lions, harbor seals, cattle, sheep, pigs), birds (common murre, cormorant, gull, pelican), and fish (cabezon, lingcod, rockfishes), fire-cracked rocks, and chipped-stone, ground-stone, glass, metal, and ceramic artifacts (see Lightfoot et al. 1997b:356–409). The spatial structure of the bone bed deposits, in combination with house foundations and exposed extramural space, provided many insights into the daily routines of domestic life in the Native Alaskan Neighborhood.

We interpret the bone beds as household dumps, where families from nearby residences deposited their trash. This interpretation is based on the shallow depth, modest size (less than 4 m in diameter), and the large number of refuse dumps that appear to be distributed across the residential space of the village site. By examining the toss pattern of faunal remains and artifacts, it appears that the deposits accumulated through the redundant disposal of materials from small containers, probably baskets (Lightfoot et al. 1997b:364–367). The presence of articulated fish bones, whole abalone shells and sea urchin spines, and clusters of animal bones from the same species indicates that the bone beds were covered with sediments shortly after deposition and that the refuse dumps were largely protected from trampling and other postdepositional processes. Bioturbation is minimal in the bone beds, in contrast to the majority of the other archaeological deposits excavated in the Native Alaskan Neighborhood and greater Fort Ross region. The dense accumulation of fire-cracked rocks and underlying

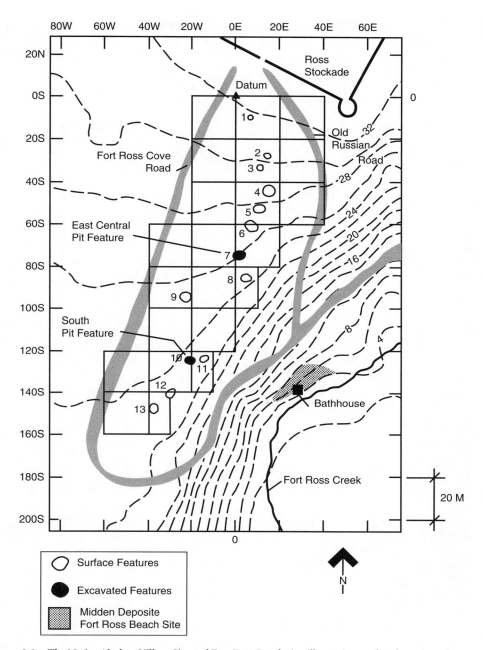

Figure 8.2   The Native Alaskan Village Site and Fort Ross Beach site, illustrating surface features and excavated structures (East Central Pit feature, South Pit feature, and Bathhouse). (Illustration by Judith Ogden.)

rock rubble used to raise and level the ground surface appears to have protected and even sealed the bone beds from intrusions by ubiquitous burrowing animals, especially gophers and voles (see especially Figure 8.4).

Regional scale

Class and status differences ingrained in the colonial hierarchy of the Russian–American Company were visibly constituted in the spatial

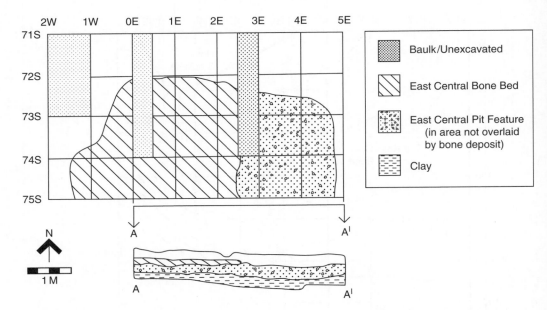

Figure 8.3 Excavation plan and profile of the East Central Bone Bed and East Central Pit feature. (Illustration by Judith Ogden.)

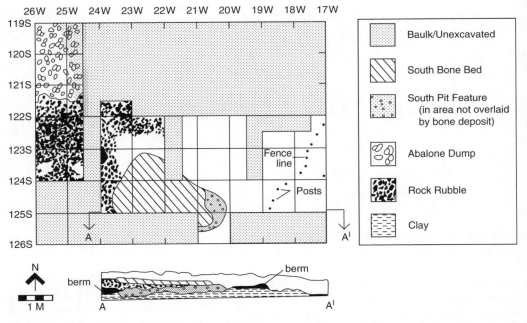

Figure 8.4 Excavation plan and profile of the South Bone Bed, South Pit feature, Abalone Dump, rock rubble, and redwood fence line. (Illustration by Judith Ogden.)

layout of the Fort Ross Colony, which comprised four "ethnic" neighborhoods and a cemetery (Figure 8.1). The Russian officials were the primary residents of the impressive stockade complex that was the center-piece and administrative hub of the colonial community. Enclosed within stout stockade walls were a manager's house, a warehouse and company store, chapel, kitchen, and other living quarters. The Native Alaskan Neighborhood was located a short distance to the south, outside the stockade walls. Directly west of the stockade complex was a "Russian Village," or *sloboda*, where the lower-class Russians and Creole workers and families lived in planked houses with gardens. In the northern hinterland of the stockade complex was the Native Californian Neighborhood, made up of a series of small villages or compounds where the Kashaya Pomo resided while working for the Russians, primarily during the harvest season. Finally, east of the stockade complex on a prominent knoll overlooking the Russian colony was the cemetery where people of the Russian Orthodox faith were buried.

In employing a combination of ethnohistorical accounts, native oral traditions, and archaeological research, one can construct a baseline for comparing and contrasting the different cultural practices reproduced in the four neighborhoods as enacted in the layout and maintenance of residential space, the spatial ordering of daily routines, the kinds of domestic chores undertaken, and the organization of trash disposal. There are excellent eyewitness descriptions and detailed archaeological investigations of elite "Russian" cultural practices in the stockade complex, information that has been synthesized by state park scholars in their reconstruction of imposing buildings and stockade walls (see Farris 1989, 1990). The cultural practices of households in the *sloboda* are not well documented in known archival sources, and little archaeological research has yet been undertaken here (Farris 1993). However, a recent analysis of archaeological remains along the north wall of the stockade provides provocative observations on the material culture of possible mixed ethnic households of Creole men and Native Californian women (Ballard 1995). Recent excavations to identify and document individual graves as part of the reconstruction of the Russian Orthodox

cemetery are providing new insights on the demographic parameters, ethnic classes, social identities, and gender and burial conventions of the Christians buried at Fort Ross (Goldstein 1992, 1995; Osborn 1992, 1997).

Much of our effort has focused on constructing a comparative baseline for examining culture change and persistence in the organization of Kashaya Pomo daily practices in prehistoric, protohistoric, and historic contexts. This baseline provides the diachronic perspective necessary to identify the presence of Kashaya Pomo women in mixed ethnic households in the Native Alaskan Neighborhood and to detail culture change and persistence taking place in the ordering of their daily lives and worldviews. Documentary information and native oral tradition are employed in the construction of this baseline: descriptions of houses and activities in the Native Californian Neighborhood and nearby environs recorded by Russian officials and other travelers to Fort Ross (Corney 1896; Kostromitinov 1974; LaPlace 1986; Lutke 1989; Wrangell 1974); Kashaya Pomo stories that describe their cultural practices at Fort Ross, as well as their observations of the Russians and Native Alaskans (Oswalt 1966); and later ethnographic reports that discuss the Kashaya Pomo in post-Russian times (Barrett 1908; Gifford 1967; Kennedy 1955). However, since detailed analyses of the spatial structure of Kashaya Pomo villages and residences in archaeological contexts are sparse (e.g., Lightfoot 1995:208–209), we initiated a program of archaeological fieldwork in the hinterland of Fort Ross to better establish the organization of Kashaya Pomo daily practices. We have undertaken survey work in the Fort Ross State Historic Park to locate village and processing sites, have completed surface collections and geophysical survey to define the spatial layout of settlements, and have initiated excavation strategies that detail the organization of residential space, activity areas, and trash deposits (Lightfoot et al. 1991, 1993; Martinez 1996, 1997a, 1997b).

Recent field investigations of one of the Kashaya Pomo villages is of special interest in our investigation. At the Tomato Patch site, a late prehistoric/historic village located on a ridge-top beyond the immediate Fort Ross community, Martinez (1996, 1997b) employed a similar field strategy as that used in the Native Alaskan Neighborhood to define the site structure and spatial organization of households. Surface features were carefully mapped, a systematic sample of surface materials was collected from which density maps of artifacts and faunal remains were generated, and both magnetometer and soil resistance surveys were conducted across the entire village. An excavation strategy was implemented in 1994 and 1995 to expose and document the layout of intramural and extramural residential space. The excavations unearthed portions of three structures, associated extramural space and features, and an extensive trash deposit situated downslope. The analysis of the field data is providing new perspectives on the spatial organization of Kashaya Pomo households and day-to-day routines involving food preparation and cooking, tool production, and trash disposal (e.g., Martinez 1997b:144–151).

Pan-regional scale

In constructing our comparative baseline, we are investigating the cultural practices of Native Alaskans in their tribal homelands and in other Russian-American Company colonies in the North Pacific where they were stationed. To date, this investigation has focused on the Alutiiq people of Kodiak Island, Alaska, since they made up the bulk of the residents who cohabited with Native Californian women in the Native Alaskan Neighborhood. We have assembled detailed ethnohistorical accounts and archaeological observations on the spatial organization of villages and the internal arrangements of houses and associated extramural space for late prehistoric and historic settlements on Kodiak Island (e.g., Clark 1974, 1984; Crowell 1994, 1997; Davydov 1977; Gideon 1977; Jordan 1994; Jordan and Knecht 1988; Knecht and Jordan 1985; Lisiansky 1814; Merck 1980); in Russian-American outposts on the Kurile Islands (Shubin 1990, 1994), where Alutiiq peoples made up much of the population; and at Fort Elisabeth on Kauai Island, Hawaii (Mills 1996). In addition, Crowell (1994:159–181) has summarized known accounts of interethnic structures in the North Pacific and described the excavation of a hybrid-style house that combined Native

Alaskan building techniques with Russian stylistic touches at the Three Saints Bay colony on Kodiak Island.

Daily Practices of Interethnic Households

The comparative approach employed in the study of the Native Alaskan Neighborhood indicates that both Kashaya Pomo and Alutiiq organizational principles were reproduced in the spatial ordering of daily practices, but at very different scales. At the microscale, it appears that the daily ordering of many domestic routines in individual households followed distinctly Kashaya Pomo conventions, at least for the house structures and refuse dumps we excavated. At the village scale, however, Alutiiq ideals apparently influenced the broader spatial layout of the neighborhood. As the findings are presented in detail elsewhere (Farris 1997; Gobalet 1997; Lightfoot et al. 1997b; Mills 1997; Ross 1997; Schiff 1997a, 1997b; Silliman 1997; Simons 1997; Wake 1997a, 1997b), we briefly summarize here the most significant observations on the organization of daily life and community structure in the Native Alaskan Neighborhood.

Residential space

Eyewitness accounts at Fort Ross indicate that a diverse range of architectural styles characterized the houses constructed in the neighborhood, ranging from Russian-style log or plank structures to the "flattened cabins" of the "Kodiaks" (Duhaut-Cilly 1946:10–11; Tikhmenev 1978:134). The East Central and South Pit features resemble in outline and depth the shallow, semisubterranean houses described by Shubin for the Alutiiq workers on the Kurile Islands. They also resemble the winter subterranean houses of the Pomo or Miwok observed by Corney (1896:33–34) and Kostromitinov (1974:8), although they are deeper and somewhat larger than the houses unearthed at the Tomato Patch Site. The excavated pit features in the neighborhood are at least 3.4 to 5 m in length, dug about .3 m below the historic ground surface. Both pit features were used before or during the 1820s and 1830s. The exposure of the house floors was limited (since much of our effort was spent documenting the overlying bone bed deposits), and we detected no internal pits or hearths. While the area exposed to the north and east of the East Central Pit feature revealed no extramural features (Figure 8.3), the extramural space north and east of the South Pit feature revealed a line of 12 redwood posts that appears to have been a fence, possibly containing a small garden plot or pen for small animals (Figure 8.4).

Spatial organization of trash disposal

Archaeological, ethnohistorical, and ethnographic observations of Alutiiq semisubterranean structures on Kodiak Island indicate that household trash accumulated within houses, specifically in the large central space that served as a combination living room, kitchen, and workshop. For example, Lisiansky (1814:212–214) observed the central rooms being used for dances, for the cleaning and drying of fish, for building *baidarkas* (skin boats), and for performing most domestic chores. He reported that they are "never cleaned, except that now and then some fresh grass is thrown over the floor, to give it a sort of decent appearance." Davydov (1977:154–155) commented that the Alutiiq house "is always dirty and presents an unpleasant spectacle to a European, for the food waste, fish bones, and shells are very rarely removed." Excavations of late prehistoric and early historic semisubterranean structures on Kodiak Island support the above accounts. The floor levels of the houses are often 20–30 cm thick, composed of highly compressed matrixes of vegetable matter, food bones, shellfish, matted grasses, hair, artifacts, wood chips, ash, charcoal, fire-altered rocks, and bits of fur (Clark 1974:155–156; Heizer 1956:18; Jordan and Knecht 1988:256–262; Knecht and Jordan 1985). These field investigations also indicate a pattern whereby old house floors and their accumulated trash were intentionally covered by new floors as part of the remodeling or reuse of house structures. Jordan and Knecht's (1988:256–262) excavation of one house structure uncovered 10 different house floors separated by thick deposits of floor debitage and sod roofs, while Clark (1974:155) revealed a house structure in which the floor refuse was capped by a "clean sand layer which evens up underlying irregularities and

overlay rubbly site deposits and midden." The frequent remodeling of houses and the construction of new floors over old trash appears to have been a creative means of trash disposal in Alutiiq villages.

In contrast, ethnohistoric and archaeological observations suggest that the Kashaya Pomo observed relatively strict rules for the disposal of trash in and around houses. Eyewitness accounts of Pomo and Miwok residences, as well as paintings illustrating the interior of dwellings, emphasize the Spartan contents of their dwellings and general tidiness or "orderly fashion" of their houses (Schabelski 1993:10; Wrangell 1974:3–4; also Tikhanov's 1818 watercolor in Wiswell 1979:337). For example, Kostromitinov (1974:8) described the sparse contents of Kashaya houses that included only clothing, bedding, "a bow, arrows, a large pot, and sometimes fishing nets."

Archaeological investigations of late prehistoric and historic Kashaya villages indicate the clear segregation of residential and midden space. Residential spaces, typically situated in elevated areas of sites, are relatively clean except for sparse scatters of lithic artifacts, while midden deposits located downslope contain dense concentrations of animal bones and shellfish remains (Lightfoot et al. 1991:116–119). The exposure of upslope house structures and associated extramural space at the Tomato Patch site revealed a light artifact scatter relatively free of food refuse, suggesting the regular maintenance and cleaning of both houses and surrounding space. Trash that was picked up appears to have been disposed of in discrete midden deposits more than 1 m deep situated downslope (Martinez 1997b:144–146).

Our investigation of the Native Alaskan Neighborhood suggests that some members of households were highly structured in their disposal of refuse. Few artifacts and faunal remains were found on the floors of the East Central and South Pit features, or the floor of the bathhouse, indicating that the buildings were periodically swept clean, at least before abandonment. The associated extramural space exposed around the houses was also in tidy order. The space to the north and east of the East Central Pit feature and along the fence line associated with the South feature was relatively sterile of material culture. Since fences can often serve as barriers in the accumulation of trash, this strongly suggests the latter area was intentionally cleaned.

We believe that Kashaya concepts of orderliness were enacted in some interethnic households, probably by Native Californian women. While the East Central and South Pit features may resemble the semisubterranean houses of Alutiiq workers excavated on the Kurile Islands or possibly the winter houses of Native Californians, it is clear that the day-to-day domestic practices involving the care and maintenance of these places followed the organizational principles of the Kashaya Pomo. Kashaya women, or individuals employing their ideals of cleanliness and order, swept houses clean on a regular basis and kept nearby extramural space clear of refuse. Food waste, workshop debris, and worn-out implements from kitchens and related residential space were probably scooped into containers whose contents were tossed into nearby refuse dumps established on artificially filled surfaces in abandoned house structures. In such a manner we believe the bone bed deposits accumulated as a direct consequence of the routine cleaning of nearby residential space. Other household refuse was also tossed over the edge of the marine terrace, creating much of the downslope midden deposit in the Fort Ross Beach site.

Innovative developments were also taking place in landscape modification and garbage disposal in the neighborhood. While traditional Alutiiq practices of covering refuse in house structures and other "old" surfaces with "new" surfaces (straw, clean sand, or other material) were not observed in our excavation, we suspect that Native Alaskan conventions were employed in the filling and leveling of abandoned house structures with rock rubble and dirt to create new surfaces (see Figure 8.4). These prepared surfaces were then incorporated into the Pomo worldview of order and hygiene as they were transformed into discrete refuse deposits.

Menu and food preparation

The sophisticated maritime Alutiiq peoples on Kodiak Island focused their culinary skills primarily on the preparation of marine mammals (whales, pinnipeds), pelagic (cod, halibut) and anadromous fish (salmon), seabirds, and

shellfish (Clark 1974:70–74, 1984:187–190; Haggarty et al. 1991:82–92; Lisiansky 1814:191–195). Meats were prepared in many ways: eaten raw, fermented in berry juices, boiled in native ceramic or metal vessels over fires or in watertight baskets using heated rocks, or barbecued or broiled directly over the fire (see Bolotov 1977:85; Davydov 1977:173–175; Lisiansky 1814:195; Merck 1980:106).

The Kashaya Pomo exploited a wide range of meats from the land and shore, including deer, elk, rabbit, terrestrial birds (quail), fish (coastal, anadromous, freshwater), and shellfish (Gifford 1967; Oswalt 1966). There is some debate among later ethnographers whether the Kashaya hunted marine mammals at the time of Russian contact (Gifford 1967:16–19; Loeb 1926:169). But, in any case, pinnipeds, cetaceans, and pelagic fish apparently did not play a major role in their traditional diet, an observation supported by recent archaeological excavations at the Tomato Patch site. Kashaya chefs prepared some meats and fishes raw, boiled meats in watertight baskets using heated stones, and cooked meats on coals and embers and in underground ovens (Barrett 1952:60–71; Gifford 1967:16–17; Kostromitinov 1974:8; Lutke 1989:276).

Our excavations in the Native Alaskan Neighborhood indicate that a new menu was served in interethnic households that was neither purely Kashaya nor purely Alutiiq. The men from Kodiak Island first experienced the regular taste of venison, abalone, and California rockfishes, while the Pomo were treated to seal, sea lion, and beef steaks that were not a regular part of their precontact diet. The bone bed deposits contain substantial information on the preparation and cooking of meat dishes. Steel tools were used to butcher mammal remains and fillet meat portions (Wake 1995, 1997b:284–290). The meat packages appear to have been cooked primarily using the "hot rocks" baking method of the Pomo and Miwok, as indicated by clusters of mostly unburned bones in association with medium- and large-sized "cooking" stones (fire-cracked rocks), small gastropods (probably from seaweed), and limited quantities of charcoal. This method, as vividly described by later ethnographers (e.g., Barrett 1952:61; Gifford 1967:19; Holmes 1975:22), involved the placement of alternating tiers of fired-hot rocks, protective layers of vegetable matter (such as seaweed), and meat packages in underground ovens that were covered and allowed to cook for five or more hours. The ovens were then opened and the meat contents removed and consumed. The remaining refuse was cleaned out of the ovens into containers and tossed as discrete clusters into the bone bed deposits.

The "hot rocks" baking method is well documented among the Pomo and Miwok in prehistoric and historic archaeological contexts (e.g., Beardsley 1954:30), including the excavation of a possible underground oven in the nearby Tomato Patch site. This method is not documented in either the archaeological or ethnohistorical literature, to the best of our knowledge, for the Alutiiq inhabitants of Kodiak Island in contact or precontact settings.

It appears that beef and mutton, meats not previously consumed by the Kashaya until the establishment of Fort Ross, were treated and cooked in the same manner as local black-tailed deer. What is somewhat unexpected is that marine mammals were treated in the same fashion as terrestrial game. Marine mammals and terrestrial game appear to have been cooked together in earth ovens, and both show similar dismemberment patterns and filleting marks (Wake 1995). Thus, Kashaya conventions were apparently used in the processing of marine mammals, as opposed to treating them separately and preparing them in a fashion more consistent with Alutiiq conventions. The one concession is that special cuts of meat were prepared for some meat dishes, especially flipper elements from harbor seals and sea lions, which are considered a great delicacy among Native Alaskan peoples (Wake 1995, 1997b:298–300). Other food refuse in the bone beds, such as sea urchins and sea birds, not commonly consumed by the Kashaya, but actively harvested by Alutiiq peoples in their native homeland, also appears to have been cooked in earth ovens according to local Native Californian practices.

Material culture from domestic contexts

The maritime-oriented Alutiiq peoples on Kodiak Island developed elaborate cultural practices for producing a complex assemblage of tools and domestic furniture from marine mammal and sea bird bone, ground slate, driftwood, basketry materials, and clays (see Clark 1974:112–127, 1984; Davydov 1977:187; Knecht and Jordan 1985). Chipped-stone tools are a relatively minor component of late prehistoric and historic sites on Kodiak Island (Clark 1974; Jordan and Knecht 1988:268; Knecht and Jordan 1985:29). In contrast, the Kashaya Pomo employed artifact assemblages of chipped stones, ground stones, terrestrial mammal bone, wood, and basketry materials in their homeland villages (Barrett 1952; Lightfoot et al. 1991; Martinez 1997b).

The excavations of the bone bed deposits in the Native Alaskan Neighborhood indicate refuse from non-food-related activities was also tossed into these household dumps, most likely from cleaning up nearby internal and external residential space. There is little evidence of Alutiiq household equipment or furniture as described in contemporaneous homeland villages on Kodiak Island, where houses typically contained stone lamps, ground slate ulus, adzes, and other accoutrements, bone spoons or ladles, native pottery or hollowed whale vertebrae platters (e.g., Clark 1974:112–127). The majority of Alutiiq practices observable in household refuse at the Native Alaskan Neighborhood are clearly oriented toward the production and maintenance of their sophisticated marine hunting and fishing equipment, as discussed by Wake (1995, 1997a). The worked-bone assemblage consists of large and small darts, harpoon arrow points, harpoon shaft (socket) pieces, and composite fishhooks. Other worked-bone implements include buttons, awls, fasteners, and plain and incised-bone tubes. The production of bone artifacts is amply demonstrated by cores of whale ribs, grizzly bear humerus and radius bones, and elk antlers; hundreds of chopping and carving flakes; amorphous worked-bone chunks; and handholds. The workshop debris represents the full sequence of reduction steps in the production of bone toolkits related to marine mammal hunting and fishing. The presence of bone conical points, awls, and large numbers of pinniped, common murre, gull, and cormorant remains suggests that the sewing of *kamleikas* (waterproof jackets) and birdskin parkas, as well as the repair of skin boats (*baidarkas* and *baidaras*), also may have taken place.

Other household refuse at the Native Alaskan Neighborhood includes chipped-stone and ground-stone artifacts and European/Asian materials, such as ceramic, glass, and metal objects. The chipped-stone assemblage consists of both formal tools (unifaces, bifaces), edge-modified flakes, and workshop debris primarily from local chert and obsidian obtained from sources in northern California (Schiff 1997a). Obsidian hydration dating of artifacts in the bone bed deposits suggests some were recycled as expedient tools from nearby prehistoric lithic scatters (Lightfoot and Silliman 1997:352–353). The residents of households were highly selective in choosing the prehistoric artifacts they recycled, primarily scavenging interior flakes and formal tools. Ground-stone tools in the bone bed deposits include handstones, pestles, basin milling stones, and slab milling stones, all common constituents of nearby Kashaya Pomo villages, including the Tomato Patch site (Schiff 1997a:230–233).

The European/Asian materials represent a relatively discrete assemblage in the neighborhood that dates primarily to the 1820s and 1830s (Farris 1997; Ross 1997; Silliman 1997). The ceramic assemblage consists mostly of refined earthenwares (e.g., hand-painted blue, transfer-print blue, and hand-painted polychrome), as well as some porcelains, stonewares, and yellowwares (Silliman 1997:140–153). Small, fragmentary pieces from many different ceramic vessels are represented. Windowpane and vessel glass artifacts are present, but are also highly fragmented into many small pieces. Most of the "black glass" pieces are probably from case-transported bottles that may have contained alcoholic drinks (Silliman 1997:153–160). Glass beads are frequent constituents of neighborhood deposits, most consisting of hot-tumbled, drawn, monochrome and polychrome, undecorated embroidery varieties. In other Pacific Coast contact sites, these inexpensive bead types are typically found in domestic contexts where day-to-day activities take place, in contrast to the more expensive, decorated beads that are often associated with ceremonial contexts where wealth displays and/or ritual activities occur (Ross 1997:202).

The absence of any complete or reconstructible ceramic or glass vessels strongly suggests a secondary context for these artifacts. While the fragmented remains of various vessel forms, such as ceramic plates, saucers, teacups, and other forms, as well as glass bottles, are represented in the bone beds, it does not appear that they served as table-wares or cooking wares in the residences associated with the refuse dumps (see Farris 1997:131–132; Silliman 1997:169–171). Rather, it appears that ceramic and glass fragments were scavenged from other Fort Ross locations, such as the stockade complex and *sloboda*, to be used as raw materials in the production of native artifact forms. Some ceramic sherds were modified into bead blanks, pendants, or other ornaments, while other glass bottle fragments and window glass pieces (to a lesser extent) were turned into flakes, scrapers, and bifaces (Silliman 1997:151, 160–161). We are currently exploring the possibility that some of the ceramic and glass pieces recycled from Fort Ross dumps by residents of the Native Alaskan Neighborhood were earmarked for distribution to outlying Kashaya homeland villages, such as the Tomato Patch site, which contain similar assemblages of highly fragmented ceramic and glass artifacts.

The metal assemblage is also in a fragmented state, consisting mostly of bent nails and largely defective metal items (e.g., iron spikes, lead bullet molds and sprues, pieces of buttons and button hooks). While residents of interethnic households may have been the primary users of these materials, at least some of the metal objects were probably recycled from other Fort Ross dumps or from nearby industrial areas of the colony and reused in new contexts. Some materials (e.g., ship-building tacks) appear to have been scavenged from the shipyard adjacent to the Fort Ross Beach site and then reused in the Native Alaskan Neighborhood as construction materials in houses or as raw material in the production of native artifact forms, such as fishhooks. Ongoing excavations of the blacksmith and carpenter shops associated with the shipyard are yielding a similar range of spikes, nails, and tacks as those recovered in the bone bed deposits (Allan 1997).

Settlement layout

Alutiiq winter villages on Kodiak Island tended to be located in slight embayments and coves generally along or near the outer coast with direct access to shellfish beds and good fishing (Clark 1987:124–129; Davydov 1977:155). Houses in these villages were arranged in a long linear pattern along an expansive beach or coastal strip (Jordan and Knecht 1988:232–236; Knecht and Jordan 1985:21–23). As Jordan (1994:148) notes, many subsistence-related tasks took place along the shore, while domestic, social, political, and ceremonial activities tended to occur in the central strip of structures. Early accounts state that Alutiiq peoples located houses so that they had clear views of the ocean. Men would climb the roofs and sit there scanning the sea, especially at sunrise when decisions were made to go to sea or to stay home (Clark 1984:191; Davydov 1977:156; Lisiansky 1814:182–184).

The Kashaya Pomo employed very different organizational principles in the placement and layout of their homeland villages. Late prehistoric settlements tend to be situated on ridges several kilometers from the coast at elevations several hundred meters above sea level. Village locations were chosen to provide protection from the fog and wind of the coast, to afford good sources of freshwater, and to take advantage of both coastal and interior resources (Lightfoot et al. 1991:112–115). When some Kashaya peoples began to aggregate near Fort Ross in the early nineteenth century to work in agricultural fields for the Russian-American Company, they relocated their villages from the top of ridges to the base of the ridges north of the stockade complex (Figure 8.1). However, similar kinds of organizational conventions were reproduced at these new places. Villages were reestablished some distance from the coast in secluded locations that still provided protection from wind and fog. The spatial arrangement of houses within Kashaya villages is variable in late prehistoric and early historic contexts. Houses tend to be arranged in a rough semicircular or circular manner with large assembly or "dance houses" situated in the center (Barrett 1975:45; Kniffen 1939:386). The spatial organization of the Tomato Patch site consists of a line of houses that follows the ridgeline in a roughly east–west direction.

The Native Alaskan Village site appears to have been organized according to spatial conventions of Alutiiq winter villages but contradicts many of the basic organizational principles of Kashaya villages in the nearby region. The village site is situated in a very exposed location on a marine terrace overlooking the Fort Ross Cove and the Pacific Ocean. The settlement is organized so that residents could place their houses, extramural work areas, and trash dumps along the eastern edge of the marine terrace with an unobstructed view of the sea below. The results of the fieldwork revealed a village plan in which houses paralleled the edge of the marine terrace in a roughly north–south line (Figure 8.2). Geophysical survey and subsurface testing suggest that only a row or two of houses were built in the north and central areas of the settlement and that an "open space" marked by little refuse and no evidence of house structures is found west of surface features 6, 7, and 8 in Figure 8.2. To the south, the geophysical survey suggests several rows of houses may have been constructed south of surface feature 9 and west of surface features 10 and 11 in Figure 8.2 (Lightfoot et al. 1997b:412–414; Tschan 1997:124–126).

The location of the Native Alaskan Village site differs in one significant respect from Alutiiq villages on Kodiak Island. Most Alutiiq houses would probably have been situated along the beach and creek of Fort Ross Cove, rather than on the elevated terrace directly adjacent to the stockade complex. The close placement of the village site under the guns of the Ross stockade may have been dictated by Russian administrators who wanted to keep an eye on the sea-mammal hunters, and/or the high location may have been chosen for its defensible position, similar to the "refuge rocks" used on Kodiak Island (Aron Crowell, personal communication 1997). The location also may have been influenced by the employment of the cove area as a shipyard and industrial zone, thereby precluding residential use of the area.

Summary

A significant finding of our study is that the world-views and structuring principles of Russian-American Company administrators, Alutiiq sea-mammal hunters, and Kashaya

Pomo spouses were reproduced at different scales of organization at Fort Ross. The imprint of Russian managers on the Ross landscape is most evident at the scale of the overall colonial spatial structure, where principles of class and status were employed in an attempt to segregate people into discrete "ethnic" neighborhoods, a practice observed at other Russian-American Company colonies in the North Pacific (Crowell 1994, 1997). At the scale of individual neighborhoods, company policies were relatively flexible in allowing residents to lay out and maintain their own communities. Alutiiq principles were employed in the spatial organization of the Native Alaskan Village site, which consisted of a linear arrangement of houses and work space along the eastern edge of the marine terrace. This spatial configuration provided the hunters with clear views of the Pacific horizon, as well as their *baidarkas* and hunting/fishing gear stored below in the Fort Ross Cove.

At the scale of individual households (at least the ones we examined), it appears that Kashaya conventions were reproduced in the daily practices of domestic life. These routinized practices include the preparation and cooking of meat dishes in earth ovens, the regular cleaning of house space and associated extramural locations, the tossing of refuse into specially prepared dumps, and the primary use of Native Californian material culture (e.g., milling stones, pestles, chipped-stone tools) in homes.

Another significant finding of our study is that it appears that the Native Californian women and Native Alaskan men attempted to maintain their own distinct social identities in interethnic households. Outside the individual home and its maintained extramural space, Alutiiq men's marine-oriented world was reproduced in their selection of house locations with unobstructed views of the water, in the maintenance of their sophisticated maritime hunting and fishing tool-kits, in the continued consumption of seafoods, and in the use of skin boats that allowed them ready access to the sea. On the other hand, Kashaya women – who left their homeland villages and moved into the already built environment of the Fort Ross colony – were able to assert their Native Californian identities in the daily practices of domestic life centering on the house. While the placement of houses and

work space was probably established by others, the Kashaya spouses broadcast their own unique identities in the manner in which they used this space. Kashaya conventions were largely re-created in the care and maintenance of residential space, foodways, domestic toolkits, and the organization of trash disposal.

Yet in the process of reproducing conventional cultural categories and worldviews in interethnic households, cultural transformations took place as Native Alaskan men and Native Californian women responded to one another and accommodated themselves to a new social setting. Their encounters produced new cultural practices: new foods were consumed by both spouses; new foodways were developed as marine mammals, terrestrial game, and domesticated animals were cooked together for the first time in earth ovens, along with special cuts of meat (seal flipper elements); new raw materials (ceramic, glass, metal) were used in the production of native artifact forms; and innovations took place in landscape modification practices and refuse disposal on specially prepared surfaces.

However, the process of culture change appears to have been very directed, as residents created cultural innovations that "fit" largely within their perceptions of what constituted proper "Kashaya" or "Alutiiq" behavior in the new social context. The recycling of ceramic and glass objects to manufacture conventional native artifact forms exemplifies this behavior. While Native Californian women may have been performing new tasks, such as cooking beef and marine mammals and sewing birdskin parkas, it appears they employed Kashaya organizational principles in the ordering of these daily practices. There is little evidence that they were implementing strategies of social mobility that would identify them as Native Alaskan women to Russian administrators. Furthermore, in the archaeological sample we examined, there is little evidence that the residents of mixed ethnic households deliberately constructed "creolized" cultural practices that creatively combined Russian and Native American lifeways. European uses of material culture, as exemplified by the elite Russians residing in the stockade complex, were not actively replicated in interethnic households. For example, there is no evidence that ceramic tablewares and glass beverage bottles were employed to set a "European" table among the Alutiiq and Kashaya couples.

In retrospect, there is a very good reason why Native Californian women would have reproduced social identities at Fort Ross that linked them directly to nearby Kashaya villages. It is clear from both our archaeological, and ethnohistorical research that the Russian-American Company provided little direct support to their native workers and especially to Native Californian women who remained at Fort Ross when their Alutiiq spouses were away on extended hunting trips. Correspondence from the 1820s indicates that, when by themselves, women and children experienced food shortages and that some families "ran away out of hunger and others endured terrible privation" (Khlebnikov 1990:131). This situation prompted Native Alaskan men to request that hunts be terminated early so they could return home to support their families. The deliberate maintenance of social relations and kin ties to homeland villages in the hinterland was probably critical for securing food, goods, and moral support during trying times. One facet of these extensive social networks was probably the recycling of ceramic, glass, and metal objects from Fort Ross dumps for redistribution to the outlying Native Californian community.

Conclusion

The purpose of this paper is to consider daily practices and the organization of space in a contextual approach that may complement current artifact-based analyses in culture contact research. The approach builds on a crucial tenet of practice theory – that individuals will enact and construct their underlying organizational principles and world-views in the ordering of daily life. By examining the organization of daily life in archaeological contexts the spatial layout of residential space, the ordering of domestic tasks, the structure of trash disposal – we can critically evaluate the nature and magnitude of culture change and persistence in contact settings. In developing such an approach, we emphasize that the study of habitual routines should be undertaken in a broadly diachronic and comparative framework by examining daily practices from a multiscalar perspective.

In applying this approach to the study of interethnic households at Fort Ross, we found that the organizational principles of the dominant colonizers were reproduced at the scale of the broader colonial landscape (layout of "ethnic" neighborhoods), while the worldviews and conventions of the underclass were most visible in the community and household organization. Similar findings have been reported for very different colonial settings in Florida and the Caribbean (e.g., Deagan 1983a, 1995a). Native Californian women, who were the primary players in maintaining the residential space and refuse dumps we examined, constructed unique social identities that, on the one hand, were an accommodation to their spouses and the distinctive colonial setting of Fort Ross but, on the other, allowed them and their children to maintain strong connections to nearby homeland Kashaya villages.

A critical issue raised in this paper is whether daily practices of individuals can be observed and studied in the archaeological record. There is, of course, considerable debate about whether the events and activities of individuals or even households can be discriminated in archaeological contexts. Some scholars argue persuasively that most archaeological deposits are palimpsests that are best viewed as "places" with limited temporal resolution (e.g., Binford 1982; Smith 1992).

We recognize that some archaeological contexts will be more pertinent to the investigation of daily practices on the scale of individuals and households than others. Admittedly, the archaeology of pluralism at Fort Ross is facilitated by the relatively short occupation of the Native Alaskan Neighborhood (less than 30 years) and the minimal reuse of this archaeological place in subsequent years (see Farris 1997:133). However, we believe that the study of daily practices can probably be undertaken in a variety of other archaeological contexts, but it will involve the rethinking of how we view the archaeological record and how we conduct fieldwork (see Parkington 1993:96; Tringham 1994, 1995). Since the focus is on mundane routines that produce deposits of materials on a day-to-day basis, the critical resolution is that which defines meaningful changes in the patterns of daily practices – how space is organized, how domestic tasks are conducted, and how trash is deposited. Not only are large block excavation strategies needed to define the broader spatial patterning of intramural and extramural space (e.g., Lightfoot 1995:208–209), but a refined scale of resolution is needed to identify promising archaeological deposits that may distinguish habitual patterns of daily practices in structures, activity areas, and trash dumps.

The study of daily practices is facilitated by making depositional events the units of analysis in excavation programs. The purpose is to define features and depositional events that accumulate as a consequence of the "little routines" people conduct over and over again, from one day to the next. Recent innovations in field techniques are providing better resolution for the study of the spatial structure of daily practices in archaeological contexts. Significant advances in the recording and interpretation of microstratigraphy and microformation processes are used to identify depositional events in archaeological contexts (e.g., Harris 1989; Harris et al. 1993; Kirch 1992; Stein 1992; Tringham 1995; Tringham et al. 1998). With the increasing sophistication of remote-sensing techniques, not only can the site structure be better defined, but archaeological contexts may be identified that yield high information content on daily practices, such as sealed deposits in association with residential space.

Our case study illustrates that trash deposits or middens in built environments can provide excellent contexts for the investigation of daily practices. While these deposits may be the "bread and butter" of most excavations, they are commonly treated as secondary refuse and mined for representative samples of artifacts and ecofacts using sondages and/or column samples. The time is right to recognize middens as contextually rich deposits that often accumulate through routinized behavior. We may greatly facilitate our investigation of patterns of daily practices in archaeological contexts by considering the spatial structure of these deposits and by defining discrete depositional events. In the study of trash disposal practices in villages and households, and the careful three-dimensional recording of midden deposits, we may obtain exceptional information on the practice and organization of day-to-day lifeways, a point exemplified in our study at Fort Ross. It is the detailed investigation of these kinds of daily practices, undertaken in broadly diachronic and comparative frameworks, that will provide a more sophisticated "contextual" approach for studying culture change and persistence in pluralistic settings.

References

Allan, J. M. 1997 Searching for California's First Shipyard: Remote Sensing Surveys at Fort Ross. In *The Archaeology of Russian Colonialism in the North and Tropical Pacific*, edited by P. R. Mills and A. Martinez, pp. 50–83. Papers No. 81. Kroeber Anthropological Society, Berkeley, California.

Ballard, H. S. 1995 *Searching for Metini: Synthesis and Analysis of Unreported Archaeological Collections from Fort Ross State Historic Park, California.* Unpublished senior honors thesis, Department of Anthropology, University of California, Berkeley.

Barrett, S. A. 1908 *The Ethno-Geography of the Pomo and Neighboring Indians.* Publications in American Archaeology and Ethnology No. 6. University of California, Berkeley.

Barrett, S. A. 1952 *Material Aspects of Pomo Culture, Part One and Two.* Bulletin No. 20. Public Museum of the City of Milwaukee, Milwaukee, Wisconsin.

Barrett, S. A. 1975 Pomo Buildings. In *Seven Early Accounts of the Pomo Indians and Their Culture*, edited by R. F. Heizer, pp. 37–63. Archaeological Research Facility, University of California, Berkeley.

Beardsley, R. K. 1954 *Temporal and Areal Relationships in Central California Archaeology, Parts One and Two.* Report No. 24. Archaeological Survey. University of California, Berkeley.

Binford, L. 1982 The Archaeology of Place. *Journal of Anthropological Archaeology* 1(1):5–31.

Bolotov, I. 1977 The Konyag (The Inhabitants of the Island of Kodiak) by Iosaf [Bolotov] (1794–1799) and by Gideon (1804–1807). Translated and edited by L. T. Black. *Arctic Anthropology* 14(2):79–108.

Bourdieu, P. 1977 *Outline of a Theory of Practice.* Cambridge University Press, Cambridge.

Bourdieu, P. 1990 *The Logic of Practice.* Stanford University Press, Palo Alto, California.

Brumfiel, E., and J. M. Fox 1994 *Factional Competition and Political Development in the New World.* Cambridge University Press. Cambridge.

Clark, D. W. 1974 *Koniag Prehistory: Archaeological Investigations at Late Prehistoric Sites on Kodiak Island, Alaska.* Tubinger Monographien zur Urgeschichte. Verlag W. Kohlhammer, Stuttgart, Germany.

Clark, D. W. 1984 Pacific Eskimo: Historical Ethnography. In *Handbook of North American Indians*, vol. 5, edited by D. Damas, pp. 136–148. Smithsonian Institution, Washington, D.C.

Clark, D. W. 1987 On a Misty Day You Can See Back to 1805: Ethnohistory and Historical Archaeology on the Southeastern Side of Kodiak Island, Alaska. *Anthropological Papers of the University of Alaska* 21:105–132.

Cohen, A. P. 1987 *Whalsay: Symbol, Segment and Boundary in a Shetland Island Community.* Manchester University Press, Manchester, England.

Corney, P. 1896 *Voyages in the Northern Pacific. Narratives of Several Trading Voyages from 1813 to 1818, Between the Northwest Coast of America, the Hawaiian Islands and China, With a Description of the Russian Establishments on the Northwest Coast.* Thomas G. Thrum, Honolulu.

Crowell, A. L. 1994 *World System Archaeology at Three Saints Harbor, An 18th Century Russian Fur Trade Site on Kodiak Island, Alaska.* Unpublished Ph.D. dissertation, Department of Anthropology, University of California, Berkeley.

Crowell, A. L. 1997 Russians in Alaska, 1784: Foundations of Colonial Society at Three Saints Harbor, Kodiak Island. In *The Archaeology of Russian Colonialism in the North and Tropical Pacific*, edited by P. R. Mills and A. Martinez, pp. 10–41. Paper No. 81. Kroeber Anthropological Society, Berkeley, California.

Davydov, G. I. 1977 *Two Voyages to Russian America, 1802–1807.* Translated by C. Bearne. Materials for the Study of Alaska History 10. Limestone Press, Kingston, Ontario.

Deagan, K. 1983a *Spanish St. Augustine: The Archaeology of a Colonial Creole Community.* University Press of Florida, Gainesville.

Deagan, K. 1983b The Mestizo Minority: Archaeological Patterns of Intermarriage. In *Spanish St. Augustine: The Archaeology of a Colonial Creole Community*, edited by K. Deagan, pp. 99–124. University Press of Florida, Gainesville.

Deagan, K. 1990 Sixteenth-Century Spanish-American Colonization in the Southeastern United States and the Caribbean. In *Columbian Consequences: Archaeological and Historical Perspectives in the Spanish Borderlands East*, vol. 2, edited by D. H. Thomas, pp. 225–250. Smithsonian Institution Press, Washington, D.C.

Deagan, K. 1995a *Puerto Real: The Archaeology of a Sixteenth-Century Spanish Town in Hispaniola.* University Press of Florida, Gainesville.

Deagan, K. 1995b After Columbus: The Sixteenth-Century Spanish-Caribbean Frontier. In *Puerto Real: The Archaeology of a Sixteenth-Century Spanish Town in Hispaniola*, edited by K. Deagan, pp. 419–456. University Press of Florida, Gainesville.

Deetz, J. 1963 Archaeological Investigations at La Purisima Mission. *Archaeological Survey Annual Report* 5:161–241. University of California, Los Angeles.

Di Peso, C. C. 1974 *Casas Grandes: A Fallen Trade Center of the Gran Chichimeca.* Vol 3. Amerind Foundation, Dragoon, Arizona.

Duhaut-Cilly, A. B. 1946 *An Episode from the Narrative of Auguste Bernard Duhaut-Cilly.* Translated by C. F. Carter. Silverado Press, Bohemian Grove, California.

Ewen, C. 1991 *From Spaniard to Creole: The Archaeology of Cultural Formation at Puerto Real, Haiti.* University of Alabama Press, Tuscaloosa.

Farnsworth, P. 1987 *The Economics of Acculturation in the California Missions: A Historical and Archaeological Study of Mission Nuestra Senora de la Soledad.* Unpublished Ph.D. dissertation, Interdepartmental Program in Archaeology, University of California, Los Angeles.

Farnsworth, P. 1992 Missions, Indians, and Cultural Continuity. *Historical Archaeology* 26(1):22–36.

Farris, G. J. 1989 The Russian Imprint on the Colonization of California. In *Columbian Consequences: Archaeological and Historical Perspectives on the Spanish Borderlands West*, vol. 1, edited by D. H. Thomas, pp. 481–498. Smithsonian Institution Press, Washington, D.C.

Farris, G. J. 1990 Fort Ross, California: Archaeology of the Old *Magazin*. In *Russia in North America: Proceedings of the 2nd International Conference on Russian America*, edited by R. A. Pierce, pp. 475–505. Limestone Press, Kingston, Ontario.

Farris, G. J. 1993 Life in the Sloboda: A View of the Village at Fort Ross, California. Paper presented at the Annual Meeting of the Society for Historical Archaeology, Kansas City, Missouri.

Farris, G. J. 1997 Historical Archaeology of the Native Alaskan Village Site. In *The Native Alaskan Neighborhood: A Multiethnic Community at Colony Ross*, edited by K. G. Lightfoot, A. M. Schiff and T. A. Wake, pp. 129–135. The Archaeology and Ethnohistory of Fort Ross, California, vol. 2. Archaeological Research Facility, University of California, Berkeley.

Fedorova, S. G. 1975 *Ethnic Processes in Russian America.* Translated by A. Shalkop. Occasional Papers No. 1. Anchorage Historical and Fine Arts Museum, Anchorage, Alaska.

Giddens, A. 1979 *Central Problems in Social Theory: Action, Structure and Contradiction in Social Analysis.* University of California Press, Berkeley.

Gideon, H. 1977 The Konyag (The Inhabitants of the Island of Kodiak) by Iosaf [Bolotov] (1794–1799) and by Gideon (1804–1807). Translated and edited by L. A. Black. *Arctic Anthropology* 14(2):79–108.

Gifford, E. W. 1967 Ethnographic Notes on the Southwestern Pomo. *Anthropological Records* 25:1–48.

Gobalet, K. W. 1997 Fish Remains from the Early 19th Century Native Alaskan Habitation at Fort Ross. In *The Native Alaskan Neighborhood: A Multiethnic Community at Colony Ross*, edited by K. G. Lightfoot, A. M. Schiff, and T. A. Wake, pp. 319–327. The Archaeology and Ethnohistory of Fort Ross, California, vol. 2. Archaeological Research Facility, University of California, Berkeley.

Goldstein, L. 1992 Spatial Organization and Frontier Cemeteries: An Example from a Russian Colonial Settlement. Paper presented at the 25th Annual Meeting of the Society for Historical Archaeology, Kingston, Jamaica.

Goldstein, L. 1995 Politics, Law, Pragmatics, and Human Burial Excavations: An Example from Northern California. In *Bodies of Evidence*, edited by A. L. Grauer, pp. 3–17. John Wiley, New York.

Golovnin, V. M. 1979 *Around the World on the Kamchatka 1817–1819.* Translated by E. L. Wiswell. Hawaiian Historical Society and University Press of Hawaii, Honolulu.

Haggarty, J. C., C. B. Wooley, J. M. Erlandson, and A. Crowell 1991 *The 1990 Exxon Cultural Resource Program: Site Protection and Maritime Cultural Ecology in Prince William Sound and the Gulf of Alaska.* Exxon Shipping Company and Exxon Company, Anchorage, Alaska.

Harris, E. C. 1989 *Principles of Archaeological Stratigraphy.* 2nd ed. Academic Press, San Diego, California.

Harris, E. C., M. R. Brown III, and G. J. Brown 1993 *Practices of Archaeological Stratigraphy.* Academic Press, San Diego, California.

Heizer, R. F. 1956 Archaeology of the Uyak Site Kodiak Island, Alaska. *Anthropological Records* 17(1):48–56. University of California, Berkeley.

Hoffman, K. 1997 Cultural Development in La Florida. *Historical Archaeology* 31(1):24–35.

Holmes, W. H. 1975 Pomo Reservation, Mendocino County (1902). In *Seven Early Accounts of the Pomo Indians and Their Culture*, edited by R. F. Heizer, pp. 21–23. Archaeological Research Facility. University of California, Berkeley.

Hoover, R. L., and J. G. Costello 1985 *Excavations at Mission San Antonio, 1976–1978.* Monograph XXVI. Institute of Archaeology. University of California, Los Angeles.

Istomin, A. A. 1992 *The Indians at the Ross Settlement According to the Censuses by Kuskov, 1820–1821.* Fort Ross Interpretive Association, Fort Ross, California.

Jordan, R. H. 1994 Qasqiluteng: Feasting and Ceremonialism among the Traditional Koniag of Kodiak Island, Alaska. In *Anthropology of the North Pacific Rim*, edited by W. W. Fitzhugh and V. Chaussonnet, pp. 147–173. Smithsonian Institution Press, Washington, D.C.

Jordan, R. H., and R. A. Knecht 1988 Archaeological Research on Western Kodiak Island, Alaska: The Development of Koniag Culture. In *Aurora: The Late Prehistoric Development of Alaska's Native People*, edited by R. Shaw, R. K. Harritt, and D. E. Dumond, pp. 225–306. Monograph Series, Vol. 4. Alaska Anthropological Association, Anchorage.

Kardulias, P. N. 1990 Fur Production as a Specialized Activity in a World System: Indians in the North American Fur Trade. *American Indian Culture and Research Journal* 14(1):25–60.

Kennedy, M. J. 1955 *Culture Contact and Acculturation of the Southwestern Pomo.* Unpublished Ph.D. dissertation, Department of Anthropology, University of California, Berkeley.

Khlebnikov, K. 1990 *The Khlebnikov Archive: Unpublished Journal (1800–1837) and Travel Notes (1820, 1822, and 1824).* Translated by J. Bisk. University of Alaska Press, Fairbanks.

Kirch, P. V. 1992 *Anahulu: The Anthropology of History in the Kingdom of Hawaii. The Archaeology of History*, vol. 2. University of Chicago Press, Chicago.

Kirch, P. V. 1996 Tikopia Social Space Revisited. In *Oceanic Culture History: Essays in Honor of Roger Green*, edited by J. M. Davidson, G. Irwin, B. F. Leach, A. Pawley, and D. Brown, pp. 257–274. New Zealand Journal of Archaeology, Dunedin.

Knecht, R. A., and R. H. Jordan 1985 Nunakakhnak: An Historic Period Koniag Village in Karluk, Kodiak Island, Alaska. *Arctic Anthropology* 22(2):17–35.

Kniffen, F. 1939 *Pomo Geography.* Publications in American Archaeology and Ethnology 36(6). University of California, Berkeley.

Kostromitinov, P. 1974 Notes on the Indians in Upper California. In *Ethnographic Observations on the Coast Miwok and Pomo by Contre-Admiral F. P. Von Wrangell and P. Kostromitinov of the Russian Colony Ross, 1839*, edited by F. Stross and R. Heizer, pp. 7–18. Archaeological Research Facility, University of California, Berkeley.

Kotzebue, O. V. 1830 *A New Voyage Round the World, in the Years 1823, 24, 25, and 26.* Vols. 1 and 2. Henry Colburn and Richard Bentley, London.

LaPlace, C. 1986 [1854] Description of a Visit to an Indian Village Adjacent to Fort Ross by Cyrille LaPlace, 1839. Translated and edited by G. Farris.

In *Cultural Resource Survey at the Fort Ross Camp-ground, Sonoma County, California*, by G. Farris, pp. 65–80. Cultural Heritage Section, California Department of Parks and Recreation, Sacramento.

Lightfoot, K. G. 1995 Culture Contact Studies: Redefin-ing the Relationship between Prehistoric and Histor-ical Archaeology. *American Antiquity* 60:199–217.

Lightfoot, K. G., and A. Martinez 1995 Frontiers and Boundaries in Archaeological Perspective. *Annual Review of Anthropology* 24:471–492.

Lightfoot, K. G., and A. Martinez 1997 Interethnic Relationships in the Native Alaskan Neighborhood: Consumption Practices, Cultural Innovations and the Construction of Household Identities. In *The Native Alaskan Neighborhood: A Multiethnic Com-munity at Colony Ross*, edited by K. G. Lightfoot, A. M. Schiff and T. A. Wake, pp. 1–22. The Archae-ology and Ethnohistory of Fort Ross, California, vol. 2. Archaeological Research Facility, University of California, Berkeley.

Lightfoot, K. G., and A. M. Schiff 1997 Archaeological Field Investigations at the Fort Ross Beach Site. In *The Native Alaskan Neighborhood: A Multiethnic Community at Colony Ross*, edited by K. G. Lightfoot, A. M. Schiff and T. A. Wake, pp. 23–41. The Archae-ology and Ethnohistory of Fort Ross, California, vol. 2. Archaeological Research Facility, University of California, Berkeley.

Lightfoot, K. G., A. M. Schiff, and L. Holm 1997a Arch-aeological Field Investigations at the Native Alaskan Village Site. In *The Native Alaskan Neighborhood: A Multiethnic Community at Colony Ross*, edited by K. G. Lightfoot, A. M. Schiff and T. A. Wake, pp. 42–95. The Archaeology and Ethnohistory of Fort Ross, California, vol. 2. Archaeological Research Facility, University of California, Berkeley.

Lightfoot, K. G., A. M. Schiff, A. Martinez, T. A. Wake, S. Silliman, P. Mills, and L. Holm 1997b Culture Change and Persistence in the Daily Lifeways of Interethnic Households. In *The Native Alaskan Neighborhood: A Multiethnic Community at Colony Ross*, edited by K. G. Lightfoot, A. M. Schiff and T. A. Wake, pp. 355–419. The Archaeology and Ethnohistory of Fort Ross, California, vol. 2. Arch-aeological Research Facility, University of California, Berkeley.

Lightfoot, K. G., and S. W. Silliman 1997 Chronology of Archaeological Deposits from the Fort Ross Beach and Native Alaskan Village Sites. In *The Native Alaskan Neighborhood: A Multiethnic Community at Colony Ross*, edited by K. G. Lightfoot, A. M. Schiff, and T. A. Wake, pp. 337–354. The Archaeology and Ethnohistory of Fort Ross, California, vol. 2. Arch-aeological Research Facility, University of California, Berkeley.

Lightfoot, K. G., T. A. Wake, and A. M. Schiff 1991 Introduction. The Archaeology and Ethnohistory of Fort Ross, California, vol. 1. Archaeological Research Facility, University of California, Berkeley.

Lightfoot, K. G., T. A. Wake, and A. M. Schiff 1993 Native Responses to the Russian Mercantile Colony of Fort Ross. Northern California. *Journal of Field Archaeology* 20:159–175.

Lisiansky, U. 1814 *A Voyage Round the World in 1803, 4, 5, and 6; Performed by Order of his Imperial Majesty, Alexander the First, Emperor of Russia, in the Ship Neva*. John Booth, London.

Loeb, E. M. 1926 *Pomo Folkways*. Publications in American Archaeology and Ethnology 19(2). Uni-versity of California, Berkeley.

Lutke, F. P. 1989 September 4–28, 1818. From the Diary of Fedor P. Lutke during his Circumnaviga-tion Aboard the Sloop Kamchatka, 1817–1819: Observations on California. In *The Russian American Colonies Three Centuries of Russian Eastward Expan-sion 1798–1867, Volume 3: A Documentary Record*, edited by B. Dmytryshyn. E. A. P. Crownhart-Vaughan, and T. Vaughan, pp. 257–285. Oregon Historical Society Press, Portland.

McEwan, B. G. 1995 Spanish Precedents and Domestic Life at Puerto Real: The Archaeology of Two Spanish Homesites. In *Puerto Real: The Archaeology of a Sixteenth-Century Spanish Town in Hispaniola*, edi-ted by K. Deagan, pp. 197–230. University Press of Florida, Gainesville.

Martinez, A. 1996 Hyphenated Identities. In *Proceed-ings of the Society for California Archaeology: Papers Presented at the 29th Annual Meeting of the Society for California Archaeology*, vol. 9, edited by J. Reed, pp. 5–8. Society for California Archaeology, San Diego.

Martinez, A. 1997a Animal Resource Acquisition in a Multi-Ethnic Contact Period Context. Paper pre-sented at the 62nd Annual Meeting of the Society for American Archaeology, Nashville, Tennessee.

Martinez, A. 1997b View from the Ridge: The Kashaya Pomo in a Russian-American Company Context. In *The Archaeology of Russian Colonialism in the North and Tropical Pacific*, edited by P. R. Mills and A. Martinez, pp. 141–156. Papers No. 81. Kroeber Anthropological Association, Berkeley, California.

Merck, C. H. 1980 *Siberian and Northwestern America 1788–1792: The Journal of Carl Heinrich Merck, Nat-uralist with the Russian Scientific Expedition Led by Captains Joseph Billings and Gavriil Sarychev*. Trans-lated by F. Jaensch. Limestone Press, Kingston, Ontario.

Mills, P. R. 1996 *Transformations of a Structure: The Archaeology and Ethnohistory of a Russian Fort in a Hawaiian Chiefdom, Waimea, Kaua'i*. Unpublished

Ph.D. dissertation, Department of Anthropology, University of California, Berkeley.

Mills, P. R. 1997 Slate Artifacts and Ethnicity at Fort Ross. In *The Native Alaskan Neighborhood: A Multiethnic Community at Colony Ross*, edited by K. G. Lightfoot, A. M. Schiff and T. A. Wake, pp. 238–247. The Archaeology and Ethnohistory of Fort Ross, California, vol. 2. Archaeological Research Facility, University of California, Berkeley.

Moreland, J. F. 1992 Restoring the Dialectic: Settlement Patterns and Documents in Medieval Central Italy. In *Archaeology, Annales, and Ethnohistory*, edited by B. A. Knapp, pp. 112–129. Cambridge University Press, Cambridge.

Murley, D. F. 1994 The Travels of Native Alaskan Marine Mammal Hunters in the Service of the Russian-American Company. Paper presented at the XXVII Annual Chacmool Conference, University of Calgary, Calgary, Alberta.

Ortner, S. B. 1984 Theory in Anthropology Since the Sixties. *Comparative Studies in Society and History* 26:126–166.

Osborn, S. K. 1992 Demographics of the Russian Colony at Fort Ross. California Derived from a Study of the Russian Cemetery. Paper presented at the 25th Annual Meeting of the Society for Historical Archaeology, Kingston, Jamaica.

Osborn, S. K. 1997 *Death in the Daily Life of the Ross Colony: Mortuary Behavior in Frontier Russian America*. Unpublished Ph.D. dissertation, Department of Anthropology, University of Wisconsin, Milwaukee.

Oswalt, R. L. 1966 *Kashaya Texts*. Publications in Linguistics No. 36. University of California, Berkeley.

Parkington, J. 1993 The Neglected Alternative: Historical Narrative Rather than Cultural Labelling. *South African Archaeological Bulletin* 48(158):94–97.

Parkman, E. B. 1996–1997 Fort and Settlement: Interpreting the Past at Fort Ross State Historic Park. *California History* 75(4):354–369.

Price, H. 1997 Site Formation Processes at the Native Alaskan Neighborhood. In *The Native Alaskan Neighborhood: A Multiethnic Community at Colony Ross*, edited by K. G. Lightfoot, A. M. Schiff and T. A. Wake, pp. 96–106. The Archaeology and Ethnohistory of Fort Ross, California, vol. 2. Archaeological Research Facility, University of California, Berkeley.

Quimby, G. I., and A. Spoehr 1951 *Acculturation and Material Culture – I*. Fieldiana: Anthropology Vol. 3 Pt. 6. Field Museum of Natural History, Chicago.

Rogers, J. D. 1990 *Objects of Change: The Archaeology and History of Arikara Contact with Europeans*. Smithsonian Institution Press, Washington, D.C.

Roscoe, P. B. 1993 Practice and Political Centralization: A New Approach to Political Evolution. *Current Anthropology* 34:111–140.

Ross, L. A. 1997 Glass and Ceramic Trade Beads from the Native Alaskan Neighborhood. In *The Native Alaskan Neighborhood: A Multiethnic Community at Colony Ross*, edited by K. G. Lightfoot, A. M. Schiff and T. A. Wake, pp. 179–212. The Archaeology and Ethnohistory of Fort Ross, California, vol. 2. Archaeological Research Facility, University of California, Berkeley.

Sahlins, M. 1981 *Historical Metaphors and Mythical Realities: Structure in the Early History of the Sandwich Islands Kingdom*. Special Publication No. 1, Association for the Study of Anthropology in Oceania. University of Michigan Press. Ann Arbor.

Sahlins, M. 1985 *Islands of History*. University of Chicago Press, Chicago.

Sahlins, M. 1990 The Political Economy of Grandeur in Hawaii from 1810 to 1830. In *Culture through Time: Anthropological Approaches*, edited by E. Ohnuki-Tierney, pp. 26–56. Stanford University Press, Palo Alto, California.

Schabelski, A. 1993 Visit of the Russian Warship *Apollo* to California in 1822–1823. Translated and edited by G. Farris. *Southern California Quarterly* 75(1):1–13.

Schiff, A. M. 1997a Lithic Assemblage at the Fort Ross Beach and Native Alaskan Village Sites. In *The Native Alaskan Neighborhood: A Multiethnic Community at Colony Ross*, edited by K. G. Lightfoot, A. M. Schiff and T. A. Wake, pp. 213–237. The Archaeology and Ethnohistory of Fort Ross, California, vol. 2. Archaeological Research Facility, University of California, Berkeley.

Schiff, A. M. 1997b Shellfish Remains at the Fort Ross Beach and Native Alaskan Village Sites. In *The Native Alaskan Neighborhood: A Multiethnic Community at Colony Ross*, edited by K. G. Lightfoot, A. M. Schiff and T. A. Wake, pp. 328–336. The Archaeology and Ethnohistory of Fort Ross, California, vol. 2. Archaeological Research Facility, University of California, Berkeley.

Shubin, V. O. 1990 Russian Settlements in the Kurile Islands in the 18th and 19th Centuries. In *Russia in North America: Proceedings of the 2nd International Conference on Russian America*, edited by R. A. Pierce, pp. 425–450. Limestone Press, Kingston, Ontario.

Shubin, V. O. 1994 Aleut in the Kurile Islands: 1820–1870. In *Anthropology of the North Pacific Rim*, edited by W. W. Fitzhugh and V. Chaussonnet, pp. 337–346. Smithsonian Institution Press, Washington, D.C.

Silliman, S. W. 1997 European Origins and Native Destinations: Historical Artifacts from the Native Alaskan Village and Fort Ross Beach Sites. In *The Native Alaskan Neighborhood: A Multiethnic Community at Colony Ross*, edited by K. G. Lightfoot, A. M. Schiff and T. A. Wake, pp. 136–178. The Archaeology and Ethnohistory of Fort Ross, California, vol. 2. Archaeological Research Facility, University of California, Berkeley.

Simmons, W. S. 1988 Culture Theory in Contemporary Ethnohistory. *Ethnohistory* 35:1–14.

Simons, D. D. 1997 Bird Remains from the Fort Ross Beach and Native Alaskan Village Sites. In *The Native Alaskan Neighborhood: A Multiethnic Community at Colony Ross*, edited by K. G. Lightfoot, A. M. Schiff, and T. A. Wake, pp. 310–318. The Archaeology and Ethnohistory of Fort Ross, California, vol. 2. Archaeological Research Facility, University of California, Berkeley.

Smith, M. E. 1992 Braudel's Temporal Rhythms and Chronology Theory in Archaeology. In *Archaeology, Annales, and Ethnohistory*, edited by A. B. Knapp, pp. 23–34. Cambridge University Press, Cambridge.

Smith, M. T. 1987 *Archaeology of Aboriginal Culture Change in the Interior Southeast: Depopulation during the Early Historic Period*. Ripley P. Bullen Series. University Press of Florida, Gainesville.

South, S. 1977 *Method and Theory in Historical Archaeology*. Academic Press, New York.

Stein, J. K. 1992 *Deciphering a Shell Midden*. Academic Press, San Diego.

Tikhmenev, P. A. 1978 *A History of the Russian-American Company*. Translated by R. A. Pierce and A. S. Donnelly. University of Washington Press, Seattle.

Tringham, R. 1994 Engendered Places in Prehistory. *Gender, Place, and Culture* 1(2):169–203.

Tringham, R. 1995 Archaeological Houses, Households, Housework and the Home. In *The Home: Words, Interpretations, Meanings, and Environments*, edited by D. Benjamin and D. Stea, pp. 79–107. Avebury Press, Aldershot, England.

Tringham, R., M. Stevanovic, and B. Brukner 1998 *Opovo: The Construction of a Prehistoric Place in Southeast Europe*. Contributions No. 58. Archaeological Research Facility, University of California, Berkeley.

Tschan, A. 1997 Sensing the Past and the Remoteness of the Future: A Soil Resistivity Survey at the Native Alaskan Village Site. In *The Native Alaskan Neighborhood: A Multiethnic Community at Colony Ross*, edited by K. G. Lightfoot, A. M. Schiff and T. A. Wake, pp. 107–128. The Archaeology and Ethnohistory of Fort Ross, California, vol. 2. Archaeological Research Facility, University of California, Berkeley.

Upton, D. 1996 Ethnicity, Authenticity, and Invented Tradition. *Historical Archaeology* 30(2):1–7.

Wake, T. A. 1995 *Mammal Remains from Fort Ross: A Study in Ethnicity and Culture Change*. Unpublished Ph.D. dissertation, Department of Anthropology, University of California, Berkeley.

Wake, T. A. 1997a Bone Artifacts and Tool Production in the Native Alaskan Neighborhood. In *The Native Alaskan Neighborhood: A Multiethnic Community at Colony Ross*, edited by K. G. Lightfoot, A. M. Schiff and T. A. Wake, pp. 248–278. The Archaeology and Ethnohistory of Fort Ross, California, vol. 2. Archaeological Research Facility, University of California, Berkeley.

Wake, T. A. 1997b Mammal Remains from the Native Alaskan Neighborhood. In *The Native Alaskan Neighborhood: A Multiethnic Community at Colony Ross*, edited by K. G. Lightfoot, A. M. Schiff and T. A. Wake, pp. 279–309. The Archaeology and Ethnohistory of Fort Ross, California, vol. 2. Archaeological Research Facility, University of California, Berkeley.

White, J. R. 1975 Historic Contact Sites as Laboratories for the Study of Culture Change. *The Conference on Historic Site Archaeology Papers* 9:153–163.

Williams, M. 1995 Spatial Patterning and Community Organization at Puerto Real. In *Puerto Real: The Archaeology of a Sixteenth-Century Spanish Town in Hispaniola*, edited by K. Deagan, pp. 115–142. University Press of Florida, Gainesville.

Willis, R. F. 1995 Empire and Architecture at Puerto Real: The Archaeology of Public Space. In *Puerto Real: The Archaeology of a Sixteenth-Century Spanish Town in Hispaniola*, edited by K. Deagan, pp. 141–166. University Press of Florida, Gainesville.

Wilson, S. M., and J. D. Rogers 1993 Historical Dynamics in the Contact Era. In *Ethnohistory and Archaeology: Approaches to Postcontact Change in the Americas*, edited by J. D. Rogers and S. M. Wilson, pp. 3–15. Plenum, New York.

Wiswell, E. L. 1979 *Around the World on the Kamchatka, 1817–1819: V. M. Golovnin*. Hawaiian Historical Society and University Press of Hawaii, Honolulu.

Wrangell, F. P. V. 1969 [1833] Russia in California, 1833, Report of Governor Wrangel. Translated and edited by J. R. Gibson. *Pacific Northwest Quarterly* 60:205–215.

Wrangell, F. P. V. 1974 Some Remarks on the Savages on the Northwest Coast of America. The Indians in Upper California. In *Ethnographic Observations on the Coast Miwok and Pomo by Contre-Admiral F. P. Von Wrangell and P. Kostromitinov of the Russian Colony Ross, 1839*, edited by F. Stross and R. Heizer, pp. 1–6. Archaeological Research Facility, University of California, Berkeley.

Part IV

Sexuality, Embodiment, and Personhood

THE ARCHAEOLOGY OF GENDER marks a turning point in the history of anthropological archaeology and in archaeological theory more specifically. Largely inspired by feminist scholars such as Margaret Conkey, Joan Gero, and Alison Wylie in the mid- to late 1980s, it opened the field up to a host of new questions about the constitution of profession and the nature of archaeological interpretation. Initially, these questions focused on the implications of androcentric bias (Conkey and Spector 1984; Gero 1985; Watson and Kennedy 1991), the methods of identifying women in the archaeological record (Conkey and Spector 1984; Ehrenberg 1989; Barber 1994), and the investigation of women's roles in different kinds of societies (Mrozowski 1984; Hastorf 1991; Seifert 1991; Spector 1991; Spencer-Wood 1991; Wall 1994). Gender studies later broadened through engagement with third-wave feminism, particularly the work of Judith Butler, to explore the social construction of self with a focus on sexuality, embodiment, lifecourse, and personhood (Gilchrist 1994, 1999; Meskell 1999; Joyce 2000 and Chapter 11 in this volume; Schmidt and Voss 2000; Wilkie and Hayes 2006). Some studies incorporated perspectives from women of color who argued that the nexus of race, class, and gender warranted greater attention (e.g. hooks 1982; Mohanty 1988). This nexus is particularly salient in colonial and postcolonial contexts in which indigenous identities were constantly under attack by colonial administrators (e.g. McClintock 1995).

It is important to note at the outset that feminist archaeology and the archaeology of gender are not isomorphic (Gilchrist 1991). That is to say, it is certainly possible to be a feminist and not do the archaeology of gender. Similarly, it is possible to do the archaeology of gender and not be a feminist. However, taken together, feminist archaeology and the archaeology of gender have made and are continuing to make a major impact on the profession. They have led to new theoretical insights on objectivity, standpoint, and interpretation (Wylie 1991, 1992a, 1992b, 1996, 2000). They have broadened our understanding of identity, materiality, and social being (Meskell 1999, 2004; Joyce 2000 and Chapter 11 in this volume). They have caused us to reexamine women's technologies and craft production (Kehoe 1990; Gero 1991; Costin 1993, 1996). They have introduced new topics

such as the archaeology of children (Arden and Hutson 2006; Baxter 2005) and the archaeology of mothering (Wilkie 2003). They are helping rewrite the history of the profession through a consideration of women's lives and careers (Levine 1991, 1994; Joyce 1994; Preucel and Chesson 1994). They are developing feminist approaches to pedagogy (Conkey and Tringhan 1996; Romanowicz and Wright 1996; Arnold 2005; Hendon 2006), experimental writing (Spector 1991, 1994; Tringham 1991; Joyce 1994), and multimedia (Joyce et al. 2000; Wolle and Tringham 2000).

Feminist archaeologists challenged the purported objectivity of processual archaeology by explicitly joining the political with the professional. Two important developments were the founding of the Committee on the Status of Women in Anthropology (COSWA) as a subcommittee of the American Anthropological Association in 1975, and the Committee on the Status of Women in Archaeology in the Society for American Archaeology (SAA) in 1978. Conkey was the initial chair of COSWA and she oversaw its establishment within the SAA. These organizations provided intellectual leadership and valuable resources especially important for younger women joining the professional ranks. At the same time, several researchers started gathering statistics on the status of women in the profession with respect to career opportunities, citation circles, and grant success (Gero 1983, 1985, 1988; Beaudry 1994; Nelson et al. 1994). These studies revealed serious inequities and concerns, some of which are only now being redressed. Over the past 20 years, studies have shown that the percentage of women in the professional workforce has risen from 20 percent to more than 50 percent today (Zeder 1997:205). There is also a narrowing in the gap in salary between senior men and women with equivalent qualifications. However, the profession is still a long way from achieving gender equity. There remains a disturbing tendency for women in academia to be hired more frequently than their male colleagues in adjunct and non-tenure track positions.

Alison Wylie's chapter is an important introduction to feminism and its complex interrelationships with science. Although there is a wide range of positions among feminists today, she identifies three broad commitments characteristic of most versions of feminism. The first of these is that gendered categories, relations, and social structures are a fundamental dimension along which human life is ordered. Gender is not epiphenomenal; rather, it is central to what it means to be human. The second is that there is a pervasive gender hierarchy in Western society such that women tend to be systematically disadvantaged as compared to men. Gender roles typically delimit different ranges of opportunities, privileges, and resources. The third is that these inequities are unjust and need to be redressed. She then discusses the ambivalence of feminism and science. On the one hand, feminists need accurate information about the sex/gender system that they hope to reform. Because science is a powerful tool in gathering this information, it is also useful in achieving a gender-equitable world. On the other hand, however, there is a deep suspicion that science is permeated with androcentric values and interests. She notes that scientists often neglect issues of interest to women. Thus science has perpetuated the very inequality that feminists seek to overcome.

Wylie next turns to a discussion of the history of women in science. She notes that androcentrism was by no means a given at the beginnings of the field; it was the result of active strategies and practices by male scholars. There is a growing literature highlighting the many prominent women who contributed to science: for example, Queen Christina of Sweden, Laura Bassi, Margaret Cavendish, Madame du Châtelet, and Madeleine de Scudery. Wylie notes that the early European universities drew from a monastic tradition which, by its very nature, excluded women. Science grew up within this context and, while some learned women certainly had access to science, feminine concerns or interests were not admitted within the scientific process and women were often excluded from the most prestigious societies. For example, Marie Curie was denied membership to the Académie des Sciences after winning her first Nobel Prize and was only reluctantly admitted after winning her second. The US National Academy of Science admitted its first woman member in 1925 and, as of 1992, only 4 percent of its membership are women. These cases are typical of virtually all scientific institutions. Today, the situation is gradually changing such that more women are gaining employment as engineers and scientists. But women still account for only 16 percent of this workforce at a time when they constitute 45 percent of the entire workforce. Of special concern are "pipeline issues" which refer to the disproportionate loss of women in the educational process and science training programs.

What are the implications of the feminist critique for the future of science? Wylie highlights two areas. The first of these is that it enriches the questions asked and improves the uses of science for contemporary needs. This is perhaps best demonstrated in the case of health care. Feminists have pointed out that medical research has typically focused on the male ailments such as heart disease, rather than osteoporosis and breast cancer. In addition, medical researchers have often tended to assume that clinical drug trial results can be extrapolated to the entire population from tests on male subjects. Feminists have also revealed that science is not only inequitable in terms of whom it recruits and serves, but also in the worldview it produces. Rather than being unbiased and objective as it claims, it, in fact, reproduces the biases and interests of its male practitioners. It is thus possible to argue that feminist science has the potential to produce "better" science since it offers a fresh "angle of vision" and reveals things about research methods and interpretations that have heretofore been ignored.

Wylie has explored these issues in considerable detail in archaeology. One especially interesting question has to do with why archaeology was so slow compared to the other social sciences to take up feminism and gender issues. She argues that the delay in adopting feminist perspectives was in part due to the hegemony of positivism, which denied an explanatory role to social variables (Wylie 1991). She also questions the objectivity claimed by the new archaeology. She writes that "what you find, archaeologically, has everything to do with what you look for, with the questions you ask and the conceptual resources you bring to bear in attempting to answer them" (Wylie 2002:xiv). She advocates "feminist standpoint theory" both as a way of making archaeology more equitable and as a way of improving its interpretive goals. For her, the reason feminists are in a position to make these contributions is not only their interest in gender theory as a form of situated knowledge, but also their perspectives on the situatedness of all knowledge (Wylie 2001:34). As she puts it, "Those identified and socialized as women and, more generally, those who are subdominant or marginal on conventional sex/gender norms, are often effectively insider-outsiders when they enter traditionally male dominated domains" (Wylie 2000:245). This "epistemic situatedness" is the product of the divergent lived experiences that can also emerge from factors of race, class, and ethnicity.

John and Jean Comaroff begin their article with a seemingly simple question. Is our notion of the "autonomous person" a European invention, or is it broadly shared across cultures? They then pose a second, more controversial, question. If it is in some respects a European invention, does its absence among non-European peoples indicate some sort of failure or deficiency? This question is controversial because it contains within it an inherent evolutionary bias, namely the belief that communal forms of social identity are primitive and always and everywhere replaced by modern individualist ones. The Comaroffs offer a partial answer to these questions through a close analysis of an African case study, the Southern Tswana of the republic of Botswana. They note that the idea of individuality is present among all African groups; there is a place for "personal agency, property, privacy, biography, signature, and authored action upon the world." However, the notion of individualism is new. It is likely a product of the postcolonial period and emerged in concert with Protestant elites.

For the Tswana people, the self is intimately bound up with the social, such that the two are mutually constituting. Adult men were expected to "build themselves up" or "make themselves" as they negotiated their rank and status and sustained a strong centralized polity. Women were considered jural minors subject to their senior male kinsmen while being celebrated as the source of the most basic value, namely reproduction and human life. Slaves and servants were regarded as semi-people not having the right to own goods. The production of personhood was a social process that involved acts of making, doing, or causing things to happen. These acts or *tiro*, translated as "labor," produced value in

things, persons, and relations. Significantly, this labor was not what Marx would recognize since it could not be exchanged or sold and only existed in a relationship of interdependence between the servant and owner. What the Tswana called "great work" involved the extension of self through ties of interdependence often by means of objects, with cattle being the most prized form of property. The only way in which this could "be undone" was through sorcery and witchcraft. *Dirologa* referred to this coming undone and was actively resisted by Tswana people as they secured the safety of their homes and sometimes mounted preemptive attacks on their enemies, both real and imagined.

The Comaroffs favor the term "autoplexy," originally developed by Michael Welker, to signify the Tswana mode of personhood during the late colonial period. This mode involved "playing with" a multiplicity of shifting roles and identities to negotiate freedom of action and social position. For them, the idea of autoplexy seeks to acknowledge the complexity of African ideas of personhood. In addition, it encourages us to treat African personhood as parallel to European notions of the individual and not some precursor in an evolutionary scheme of being. This thesis has strong resonance with Marilyn Strathern's notion of the "dividual." She observes that in Melanesian societies, persons are as much dividually conceived as they are individually conceived. They contain a generalized sociality within. Indeed, persons are frequently constructed as the plural and composite site of the relationships that produce them (Strathern 1988:13).

Rosemary Joyce's chapter is a novel analysis of the social construction of Aztec personhood. She notes that most Aztec studies have typically taken the adult as the subject of analysis. In contrast, she examines how Aztec identities were gendered during childhood and throughout the life-course. Here she draws particular inspiration from the work of Judith Butler, a third-wave feminist theorist. Butler (1993) holds that embodied identities are the product of repeated performances of particular, socially valued ways-of-being that are themselves replicated through citational precedents. There is a disjuncture, however, between citational precedent and individual performance such that individuals never fully achieve the former. This gap is mediated through life-cyle rituals which involve a careful repetition of action. Joyce argues that Aztec children were gradually socialized through habitual action involving costume and ornaments. There were three socially approved genders: potentially reproductive male, potentially reproductive female, and celibate. Children achieved their gender identities in their early teens when they adopted one of these genders.

According to Nahuatl texts, Aztec infants were conceptualized as raw materials that needed to be worked into specific adult forms. This "working" involved the use of material and verbal metaphors in specific ritual contexts. Before and after birth, the newborn child was equated with a precious necklace or a precious feather and considered to be a gift from god. During the burial of the umbilical cord, the child was described as a sprouting plant, a flake of stone, and a wild bird in a nest. At the child's formal bathing ritual, the child was given specific gender-related objects. Sahagun (1969) writes that these were "for the boy 'a little shield, a little bow, little arrows … his little loincloth, his little cape', for the girl, 'the equipment of women – the spinning whorl, the weaving sword, the reed basket, the spinning bowl, the skeins, the shuttle, her little skirt, her little shift.'" At four years of age, an ear-piercing ceremony took place. This ritual marked the transition from an infant's carefree existence to a child's structured training, when "children were grabbed by the neck to make them grow tall." Significantly, it accustomed children to singing, dancing, feasting, drinking, and bloodletting, all social practices that would be with them throughout their lives. These ritual acts combining verbal rhetoric and material objects initiated the process of "girling" of the girl and the "boying" of the boy.

Joyce has incorporated some of these ideas in her analysis of human figurines from northwest Honduras. These figurines, exemplifying the Playa de los Muertos style, were carefully detailed and exhibit a wide diversity of hairstyles and body ornaments. Joyce categorized these figures based upon differences in hair treatment, a feature significant in Aztec accounts of the life-course, and was able to distinguish four classes in which posture, dress, and ornamentation varied predictably along with hairstyle. Two of the

classes clearly denote relative age, indicating infants and the elderly. The remaining classes of figurines vary with respect to hair treatment. Joyce considers these to be stylized representations of transitions in bodily appearance at different points of the life-cycle. The long hair of childhood was modified by shaving, beading, braiding, and binding into the elaborate fashions of young adulthood. These figurines reveal that the materialization of adult bodies was already the subject of standardized practices in Mesoamerica's earliest villages.

Barbara Voss investigates the sexual politics underlying empire. Most scholars regard heterosexual marriage and the household as central to colonization. However, few people have fully addressed the relationships between colonial households and sexual politics of colonial institutions. Voss suggests that two areas in particular warrant closer attention – colonial indigenous intermarriage and the idea of Native American women as cultural brokers. For her, the focus on heterosexual marriage is somewhat misplaced since it characterized a relatively low proportion of colonial households. She argues that concubinage, slavery, and servitude were the most common ways in which colonial households incorporated Native Americans and Africans of both genders. She observes that the new studies of Native women as cultural brokers have been valuable because they give agency to women. Native women were the primary agents of acculturation and were responsible for many changes in Spanish colonial culture. However, this view has also tended to "domesticate imperialism" by situating colonial processes within the household and does not consider the effects of colonial institutions and labor regimes. It has not adequately addressed how Native women were forced into concubinage, servitude, and marriage.

In her case study of El Presidio de San Francisco, Voss examines recruitment practices, ethnosexual conflict, the architecture of sexual control, sexualization of military conflict, gendered labor regimes, and colonial ethnogenesis. Sexuality was a flashpoint in the relationships between colonial and indigenous peoples. Colonial settlers were selected for their compliance with European gendered and sexual norms. Indigenous sexual practices, in stark contrast, included not only monogamous heterosexual marriage, but also polygamy, premarital sex, same-sex sexuality, and transgendered practices. At the San Francisco mission, women's barracks (*monjeríos*) were established for all unmarried Native Californian women to both regulate their sexuality and protect them from sexualized warfare. Sexual violence was used as a tool of conquest. Voss notes that rape functioned as "an unofficial but widely deployed military tactic." This kind of sexualized warfare produced gendered labor regimes. Native Californians seized in battle were separated into two groups, with the women and children sent to the nearest mission and the men sent to El Presidio de San Francisco, where they were sentenced to hard labor. The practices served to support the emergence of a new Californio identity consisting of people of mixed European, Indian, and African heritage that referenced Alta California and Spanish descent (see Voss 2008).

Today, sexual violence remains a major problem in Native American communities. One of the leading activists on this issue is Native American scholar Andrea Smith. Smith (2005) suggests women of color live at the dangerous intersection of gender and race. On the one hand, survivors of sexual violence are encouraged by women's organizations to speak out against their perpetrators, who are often members of their immediate family. But, on the other hand, communities of color often advise them to keep silent in order to provide a united front against racism. She argues that the solution is not simply to provide services to survivors of sexual violence. Rather, strategies must also address how sexual violence is a legacy of empire and due, in large part, to the fact that colonial practices have become tribally internalized. In 2000, she established INCITE! Women of Color Against Violence, a national activist organization of radical feminists of color advancing a movement to end violence against women of color and their communities.

References

Arden, Traci, and Scott Hutson, eds., 2006 The Social Experience of Childhood in Ancient Mesoamerica. Boulder: University Press of Colorado.

Arnold, Bettina, 2005 Teaching with Intent: The Archaeology of Gender. Archaeologies 1(2):83–93.

Barber, Elizabeth Wayland, 1994 Women's Work: The First 20,000 Years. New York: Norton.

Baxter, Jane Eva, 2005 The Archaeology of Childhood: Children, Gender, and Material Culture. Lanham, MD: Rowman and Littlefield.

Beaudry, Mary, 1994 Cowgirls with the Blues? A Study of Women's Publication and the Citation of Women's Work in Historical Archaeology. *In* Women in Archaeology. Cheryl Claassen, ed. Pp. 138–158. Philadelphia: University of Pennsylvania Press.

Butler, Judith, 1993 Bodies That Matter: On the Discursive Limits of Sex. New York: Routledge.

Conkey, Margaret W., and Janet D. Spector, 1984 Archaeology and the Study of Gender. *In* Advances in Archaeological Method and Theory, vol. 7. Michael Schiffer, ed. Pp. 1–38. New York: Academic Press.

Conkey, Margaret W., and Ruth E. Tringham, 1996 Cultivating Thinking/Challenging Authority: Some Experiments in Feminist Pedagogy in Archaeology. *In* Gender and Archaeology. Rita P. Wright, ed. Pp. 224–250. Philadelphia: University of Pennsylvania Press.

Costin, Cathy Lynne, 1993 Textiles, Women, and Political Economy in the Late Prehispanic Andes. Research in Economic Anthropology 14:3–28.

Costin, Cathy Lynne, 1996 Exploring the Relationship among Craft Production, Gender, and Complex Societies: Methodological and Theoretical Issues of Gender Attribution. *In* Gender and Archaeology. Rita P. Wright, ed. Pp. 111–142. Philadelphia: University of Pennsylvania Press.

Ehrenberg, Margaret, 1989 Women in Prehistory. Norman: University of Oklahoma Press.

Gero, Joan M., 1983 Gender Bias in Archaeology: A Cross-Cultural Perspective. *In* The Socio-Politics of Archaeology. Joan M. Gero, David M. Lacy, and Michael L. Blakey, eds. Pp. 51–57. Research Reports 23. Amherst: Department of Anthropology, University of Massachusetts.

Gero, Joan M., 1985 Socio-Politics of Archaeology and the Woman-at-Home Ideology. American Antiquity 50:342–350.

Gero, Joan M., 1988 Gender Bias in Archaeology: Here, Then and Now. *In* Feminism within the Science and Health Care Professions: Overcoming Resistance. Sue V. Rosser, ed. Pp. 33–43. Oxford: Pergamon Press.

Gero, Joan M., 1991 Genderlithics: Women's Role in Stone Tool Production. *In* Engendering Archaeology: Women and Prehistory. Joan M. Gero and

Margaret W. Conkey, eds. Pp. 163–193. Oxford: Blackwell.

Gilchrist, Roberta, 1991 Women's Archaeology? Political Feminism, Gender Theory and Historical Revision. Antiquity 65:495–501.

Gilchrist, Roberta, 1994 Gender and Material Culture: The Archaeology of Religious Women. London: Routledge.

Gilchrist, Roberta, 1999 Gender and Archaeology: Contesting the Past. London: Routledge.

Hastorf, Christine A., 1991 Gender, Space, and Food in Prehistory. In Engendering Archaeology: Women in Prehistory. Joan M. Gero and Margaret W. Conkey, eds. Pp. 132–163. Oxford: Blackwell.

Hendon, Julia A., 2006 Fact or Speculation? How a Feminist Perspective Can Help Students Understand What Archaeologists Know and Why They Think They Know It. Archaeologies 1(2):21–32.

hooks, bell, 1982 Ain't I a Woman? Black Women and Feminism. London: Pluto Press.

Joyce, Rosemary A., 1994 Dorothy Hughes Popenoe: Eve in an Archaeological Garden. In Women in Archaeology. Cheryl Claassen, ed. Pp. 51–66. Philadelphia: University of Pennsylvania Press.

Joyce, Rosemary A., 2000 A Precolumbian Gaze: Male Sexuality among the Ancient Maya. In Archaeologies of Sexuality. Barbara Voss and Robert Schmidt, eds. Pp. 263–283. London: Routledge.

Joyce, Rosemary A., Carolyn Guyer, and Michael Joyce, 2000 Sister Stories. New York: New York University Press.

Kehoe, Alice B., 1990 Points and Lines. In Powers of Observation: Alternative Views in Archaeology. Sarah Nelson and Alice B. Kehoe, eds. Pp. 23–38. Archaeological Papers of the American Anthropological Association no. 2. Washington, DC: American Anthropological Association.

Levine, Mary Ann, 1991 A Historical Overview of Research on Women in Anthropology. In The Archaeology of Gender, Proceedings of the 22nd Annual Chacmool Conference. Dale Walde and Noreen Willows, eds. Pp. 177–186. Calgary: The Archaeological Association of the University of Calgary.

Levine, Mary Ann, 1994 Creating Their Own Niches: Career Styles among Women in Americanist Archaeology between the Wars. In Women in Archaeology. Cheryl Claassen, ed. Pp. 9–40. Philadelphia: University of Pennsylvania Press.

McClintock, Anne, 1995 Imperial Leather: Race, Gender, and Sexuality in the Colonial Contest. London: Routledge.

Meskell, Lynn, 1999 Archaeologies of Social Life: Age, Sex, Class Etcetera in Ancient Egypt. Oxford: Blackwell.

Meskell, Lynn, 2004 Object Worlds in Ancient Egypt: Material Biographies Past and Present. Oxford: Berg.

Mohanty, Chandra T., 1988 Under Western Eyes: Feminist Scholarship and Colonial Discourse. Feminist Review 30:61–88.

Mrozowski, Stephen A., 1984 Prospects and Perspectives on an Archaeology of the Household. Man in the Northeast 27(1):31–49.

Nelson, Margaret C., Sarah M. Nelson, and Alison Wylie, eds., 1994 Equity Issues for Women in Archaeology. Washington, DC: Archaeological Papers of the American Anthropological Association.

Preucel, Robert W., and Meredith Chesson, 1994 Blue Corn Girls: A Herstory of Three Early Women Archaeologists at Tecolote, New Mexico. In Women in Archaeology. Cheryl Claassen, ed. Pp. 67–84. Philadelphia: University of Pennsylvania Press.

Romanowicz, Janet V., and Rita P. Wright, 1996 Gendered Perspectives in the Classroom. In Gender and Archaeology. Rita P. Wright, ed. Pp. 199–223. Philadelphia: University of Pennsylvania Press.

Sahagun, Bernardino, 1969 Florentine Codex, Book 6 – Rhetoric and Moral Philosophy. Arthur J. O. Anderson and Chalres E. Dibble, trans. School of American Research Monographs, no. 14, part VII. Salt Lake City: University of Utah Press.

Schmidt, Robert A., and Barbara Voss, eds., 2000 Archaeologies of Sexuality. London: Routledge.

Seifert, Donna, J., ed., 1991 Gender in Historical Archaeology. Historical Archaeology 25(4).

Smith, Andrea, 2005 Conquest: Sexual Violence and American Indian Genocide. Cambridge, MA: South End Press.

Spector, Janet, 1991 What This Awl Means. In Engendering Archaeology: Women in Prehistory. Joan M. Gero and Margaret W. Conkey, eds. Pp. 388–406. Oxford: Blackwell.

Spector, Janet, 1994 What this Awl Means: Feminist Archaeology at a Wahpeton Dakota Village. St. Paul: Minnesota Historical Society Press.

Spencer-Wood, Suzanne M., 1991 Toward an Historical Archaeology of Materialistic Domestic Reform. In The Archaeology of Inequality. Randall H. McGuire and Robert Paynter, eds. Pp. 231–286. Oxford: Blackwell.

Strathern, Marilyn, 1988 The Gender and the Gift: Problems with Women and Problems with Society in Melanesia. Berkeley: University of California Press.

Tringham, Ruth, 1991 Households with Faces: The Challenge of Gender in Prehistoric Architectural Remains. In Engendering Archaeology: Women and Prehistory. Joan M. Gero and Margaret W. Conkey, eds. Pp. 93–131. Oxford: Basil Blackwell.

Voss, Barbara L., 2008 The Archaeology of Ethnogenesis: Race and Sexuality in Colonial San Francisco. Berkeley: University of California Press.

Wall, Diana, 1994 The Archaeology of Gender: Seperating Spheres in Urban America. New York: Plenum.

Watson Patty Jo, and Mary C. Kennedy, 1991 The Development of Horticulture in the Eastern Woodlands of North America: Women's Role. *In* Engendering Archaeology: Women and Prehistory. Joan M. Gero and Margaret W. Conkey, eds. Pp. 255–275. Oxford: Blackwell.

Wilkie, Laurie, 2003 The Archaeology of Mothering: An African-American Midwife's Tale. London: Routledge.

Wilkie, Laurie, and Katherine H. Hayes, 2006 Engendered and Feminist Archaeologies of the Recent and Documented Pasts. Journal of Archaeological Research 14:243–264.

Wolle, Anna C., and Ruth Tringham, 2000 Multiple Catalhoyuks on the World Wide Web. *In* Towards a Reflexive Method in Archaeology: The Example at Catalhoyuk. Ian Hodder, ed. Pp. 207–218. Cambridge: MacDonald Institute for Archaeology.

Wylie, Alison, 1991 Gender Theory and the Archaeological Record. *In* Engendering Archaeology: Women and Prehistory. Margaret W. Conkey and Joan M. Gero, eds. Pp. 31–54. Oxford: Blackwell.

Wylie, Alison, 1992a The Interplay of Evidential Constraints and Political Interests: Recent Archaeological Work on Gender. American Antiquity 57:15–34.

Wylie, Alison, 1992b Feminist Theories of Social Power: Some Implications for a Processual Archaeology. Norwegian Archaeological Review 25(1): 51–68.

Wylie, Alison, 1996 The Constitution of Archaeological Evidence: Gender Politics and Science. *In* The Disunity of Science: Boundaries, Contexts, and Power. Peter Galison and David J. Stump, eds. Pp. 311–343. Stanford: Stanford University Press.

Wylie, Alison, 2000 Standpoint Matters, in Archaeology For Example. *In* Primate Encounters: Models of Science, Gender, and Society. Shirley C. Strum and Linda M. Fedigan, eds. Pp. 243–260. Chicago: University of Chicago Press.

Wylie, Alison, 2001 Doing Social Science as a Feminist: The Engendering of Archaeology. *In* Feminism in Twentieth-Century Science, Technology, and Medicine. Angela N. H. Creager, Elizabeth Lunbeck, and Londa Schiebinger, eds. Pp. 23–45 Chicago: University of Chicago Press.

Wylie, Alison, 2002 Thinking from Things: Essays in the Philosophy of Archaeology. Berkeley: University of California Press.

Zeder, Melinda, 1997 The American Archaeologist. Walnut Creek, CA: AltaMira Press.

9

Good Science, Bad Science, or Science as Usual?
Feminist Critiques of Science

Alison Wylie

Introduction

I am often asked what feminism can possibly have to do with science. Feminism is, after all, an explicitly partisan, political standpoint; what bearing could it have on science, an enterprise whose hallmark is a commitment to value-neutrality and objectivity? Is feminism not a set of personal, political convictions best set aside (bracketed) when you engage in research as a scientist? I will argue that feminism has both critical and constructive relevance for a wide range of sciences, and that feminism has much to gain from the sciences, including at least some of those that even the most querulous of my interlocutors would dignify as "real" science.[1] I will concentrate here on the critical import of feminism for science, but will identify constructive implications as I go.

But first, some ground work. Let me begin with some brief comments about what it is I take feminism to be, and why feminists have been interested in science – why they have undertaken to comment on, scrutinize, and actively engage in science. In the body of this chapter I want to disentangle several quite distinct kinds of feminist

Alison Wylie, "Good Science, Bad Science, or Science as Usual? Feminist Critiques of Science," pp. 29–55 from Lori D. Hager (ed.) *Women in Human Evolution* (London: Routledge, 1997). Reprinted with permission of Taylor & Francis Books UK.

critiques of science. I will conclude with some suggestions about what feminism and science have to offer one another that could be, indeed that is, already proving to be very substantially enriching for both a range of scientific disciplines and for feminism.

What is Feminism?

On a cross-country drive in December 1994 I spent one evening in a roadside motel watching, with horrified fascination, a late-night edition of "Firing Line," in which a wildly incongruous assemblage of public figures debated the proposition "Is feminism as a movement dead?" Betty Friedan spoke first; she made a plug for her new book, evidently supporting the "not dead" position by ostentation: if she, a founding mother of the contemporary women's movement, was still publishing and active clearly feminism could not be dead. She was teamed up with, among others, Camille Paglia, who used the debate as an occasion to promote her bad girl image; she believed feminism was still alive, if not well, despite its unfortunate affiliation with a variety of women and men who identify as feminist. And on the "feminism is dead" side were arrayed William F. Buckley Jr., the feminist historian Elizabeth Fox-Genovese, and Arianna Huffington, prominent right-wing advocate from California. Buckley began by reading a passage from a feminist tract that firmly located pornography on a continuum of sexual harassment and violence against women; it was of the genre, "pornography is the theory; rape is the practice." He wanted to know what this could possibly mean. On one thing he was quite clear. However incoherent this passage might be, on Buckley's view it represented, in its most virulent form, precisely the sort of threat to principles of free speech (and to an implied subsidiary right to consume whatever appeals to you) that he finds most abhorrent in contemporary political movements like feminism. I was unclear how this was supposed to establish that feminism is dead. It seemed more an exercise in wishful thinking on Buckley's part: if feminism is not dead, it should be.

Fox-Genovese was, by contrast, full of regret that feminism had not realized its promise, that it had passed away before its time. On one hand, she objected that contemporary feminism had been derailed by its elitism and its failure to address the real bread-and-butter issues of concern to most (non-elite) women in the world: childcare, poverty, education, health care. But on the other hand, making common cause with at least some of those on the other side of the "firing line," she insisted that if feminists had just followed Betty Friedan's sensible lead (e.g., as set out in Friedan 1983), second-wave feminism would still be a viable political movement. Fox-Genovese made no mention of the vast range of feminist literature and activism that repudiates Friedan's liberal feminism as a chief exemplar of precisely the narrowness of vision she was calling into question, a narrowness that has alienated many from the popular women's movement in North America because it privileges, as normative, the frustrations and ambitions of class- and race-privileged women who found themselves, in the 1960s, unfulfilled by Friedan's "feminine mystique" (see, e.g., hooks' 1984 discussion of Friedan). The women Friedan spoke to and for were justifiably outraged at the squandering of their human talent but, as a great many feminists have objected since 1963 (when *The Feminine Mystique* appeared), they were also systematically uninformed about the needs and interests and agendas of the vast majority of women who, for example, never have had the option of staying home in suburbia, much less of demanding a more fulfilling "career" as an alternative to the stifling domestic roles open to them in "Father Knows Best" America.

The rear was brought up by Huffington, who opened her remarks with the observation that she and Buckley had been on opposing teams years ago in a debate at the Oxford Union; she was grateful to be aligned with him now and was eager to endorse his main points. In her view the defining flaw of contemporary feminism is that its main proponents are, at bottom, naive little girls who expect big government, a substitute for Dad, to make things all right; in this she seemed to be targeting, from another direction, the formal equality liberal feminists (of roughly the 1960s and 1970s) that Fox-Genovese also took to be definitive of contemporary feminism.

It was one of those late-night shows you cannot bear to watch, and cannot bear to turn off. Certainly it was one of the most frustrating discussions of contemporary feminism I have ever witnessed although, in many respects, it was all too familiar. Sweeping claims were made about what "feminism" has done, or failed to do, for women or for society as a whole, with almost no consideration of specific positions or programs of activism, or political gains or failures that might be attributed to (or blamed on) feminists in the more than thirty years since Friedan's *Feminine Mystique* was published. Some of the sharpest exchanges came between those who might otherwise have found themselves on the same "team." There was some pleading that Fox-Genovese should change sides since she is a feminist after all, and I suspect Friedan would have been pleased to pass Paglia off to Buckley. But wherever they found themselves positioned on the question of whether feminism is dead (yet), clearly everyone was engaging something – some set of ideas, political stances, policies, programs, laws, influences, collective actions – that was impinging on their lives in a significant way, whether welcome or abhorrent, disappointing or still bright with promise. I found myself thinking of Mark Twain: "the reports of my death are greatly exaggerated" (1897).

While this seemed hopeful, at the same time I found the general disarray of the debate – the sense of it being a mad tea-party replete with non sequiturs and gross incoherences – deeply disconcerting. For the most part it was an exercise in futility. There was virtually no contact, no exchange between parties to the debate; indeed, there was no real debate. Advocates and critics of feminism (on both sides of the official debate) were talking past one another, jousting with the most grotesque and reductive stereotypes of "feminism" and of "feminists." The one sane voice, in my estimation, was Helen Weinstein, a third party to the "not dead" side of the debate (a lawyer and Long Island representative to the New York State Assembly). She began her position statement with the objection that this sort of point-winning confrontation was really not very productive. She was sternly reprimanded by the moderator; evidently comments on the "Firing Line" debate format are not allowed. She took a different tack. She drew attention to the implausibility of various of the stereotypes that were defining the terms of the debate. She cited examples of feminist activism on child support and daycare issues and, as I remember, of feminist anti-poverty activism and involvement in the wages for housework movement to counter the claim that feminists are all anti-family radicals who have never taken seriously the interests and needs of the normative "ordinary" woman (for Huffington, it seemed, women committed to their roles as mothers and wives; for Fox-Genovese, non-elite women more generally). She noted the contradiction involved in condemning feminists for being too extreme in their anti-establishment politics, on one hand, and objecting, on the other (as Huffington had done), that they are perpetual dependants on the good offices of patriarchal institutions, lacking initiative and naively invested in a "liberal" faith in formal remedies and big government. She drew attention to the vibrant, deep-rooted traditions of feminist and womanist activism that have long flourished outside the narrow circle of privileged women addressed by Friedan in the early 1960s – for example, in the Black and Hispanic and Native communities in North America, and in Latin American, Eastern European, Middle Eastern, Asian/South Asian, and African contexts – countering the erasure perpetuated by claims that contemporary feminism is exclusively a movement of white, middle-class women, that it begins and ends with Friedan's brand of "American" liberal feminism. She could, as well, have challenged Buckley's selective and reductive reading of the anti-pornography literature by drawing attention to the enormous diversity of positions feminists have taken on pornography and to the vast array of initiatives they have taken in combating violence: violence against women, violence against children and, indeed, violence in general (when you consider the close ties between the women's movement and the peace movement). In short, Weinstein pointed out just how diverse a range of positions and actions and policies is encompassed by the term "feminism."

What was very largely missing from this debate – what Weinstein challenged all parties to the debate to consider – was an appreciation that feminism is quite different from many of the movements we dignify as "political" in North America. Both its strengths and its weaknesses lie in its grassroots diversity, its diffuseness, its multi-fronted, situational, and local/personal brand of political activism. The fact is, the women's movement is nothing more or less than women in movement, and women of all kinds have been "in movement" as women for a very long time, on many different fronts and in many different contexts, arguing and acting against gender-based inequities from positions that lie across the whole length and breadth of the social and political spectrum. Contemporary feminism, the "second wave women's movement," does not fit the monolithic stereotypes that the parties to the "Firing Line" type of debate eagerly declare dead or hopefully promote as alive. No wonder there was so little meaningful exchange across this particular "Firing Line."

Given this diversity – a vision of feminism as a grassroots movement, vigorously alive in many different local niches and configurations – it would seem that feminism must escape the confines of any clear-cut definition. I am reminded of Rebecca West's famous statement: "I myself have never been able to find out precisely what feminism is: I only know that people call me a feminist whenever I express sentiments that differentiate me from a doormat . . .".[2] I am inclined to this view, especially in face of definitions of feminism that involve a specification of what one must be or belive to be a feminist; the essentialism immanent in many such definitions seem to me inimical to the enterprise (although, unfortunately, it is by no means foreign to feminism). Nonetheless, I think it is possible to distinguish three general types of claim or commitment that are characteristic of a broad range of feminisms.

First, feminists typically hold that gender categories, gender relations, gendered social structures are a crucial, even a fundamental, dimension along which our lives are organized. This does not necessarily mean that feminists consider gender to be the sole or most important of structuring principles, or that it is autonomous of other factors, although there certainly are feminists who have embraced positions of this sort. It does mean that feminists are inclined to be suspicious of positions that categorically reduce gender to other factors, naturalizing it or rendering it epiphenomenal. Typically, too, feminists believe that sex/gender systems are to some degree amenable to change or, at least, to revaluation.

Second, feminists hold that those categorized as women under existing sex/gender conventions tend to be, in varying ways and to different degrees, systematically disadvantaged as women, compared to men who otherwise share their status or social location. That is to say, gender categories and relations are typically hierarchically structured. In many areas they do not simply define different but equal or complementary roles and identities; rather they delimit for individuals quite different ranges of opportunities, privileges, resources, and rewards depending on their gender.

Third, feminists believe that these gender-based inequalities are unjust or otherwise unacceptable (morally or politically), and they are committed to changing these inequities.

It is important to note two things about this core of defining commitments. First, they contain two very different kinds of claim: empirical claims about the way the social, political world actually is (various components of the first two tenets); and a normative or explicitly evaluative commitment about the acceptability of this world, so understood (the third tenet). Philosophers are fond of saying that you cannot get an "ought" (a normative conclusion) from an "is" (empirical premises) and, in fact, it is perfectly possible to accept some version of the first two claims while yet rejecting the third. The famous sociobiologist E. O. Wilson does just this.[3] In *On Human Nature* (1978) he argues that, where humans are concerned, the enormous volume of evidence he had compiled of ways in which our biological inheritance shapes

our behavior establishes that "at birth the twig is already bent a little" (1978: 132). But he acknowledges that these relatively "modest genetic differences [that] exist between the sexes" at birth (1978: 129) – the "slight biological component" he discerns in sexually dimorphic patterns of behavior (1978: 132) – must be substantially amplified (e.g., by "later psychological development by cultural sanctions and training," 1978: 129) to arrive at the strongly marked differences we associate with existing gender roles and identities. The biological tilt he documents cannot be said to uniquely or strictly determine the complex array of sex/gender differentiated behaviors we associate with masculine vs. feminine roles, sensibilities, psychology, patterns of interaction, and so on (see chapter 6, "Sex," in Wilson 1978; reprinted in Jaggar and Rothenberg 1984: 99–104).[4] Nevertheless, Wilson concludes that even if sex/gender systems are not an exclusively biological legacy – even if they are contingent and plastic enough that they could be changed "through an exercise of will" (1978: 196) – they are by now so entrenched in the fabric of our society that it would be enormously costly (both in energy and individual freedom) to change them. Thus he agrees with much that has been central to feminist argument: that sex/gender systems are fundamental, structural features of virtually all contemporary societies; that they are often inequitable; and that they are not an unalterable given. But he insists that these considerations do not necessarily justify challenging or changing gender inequities. At just the point where feminists argue, as a matter of moral, political commitment, that we must redress gender inequities, Wilson argues for conservative caution; one option that must be weighed by any society contemplating such change is that the greater good may be better served by allowing the status quo to persist, even if this means sacrificing the interests (and capabilities) of those who are disadvantaged by existing conditions.

A second feature of the central tenets I have identified is that they leave enormous room for divergence among feminists on a number of fronts. Feminists disagree on empirical questions about just what sort of structuring principle gender is. They diverge on the question of whether biological sex differences are in any sense separable from gender constructs and whether, if so, biology makes a difference (perhaps a positive difference) in women's sensibilities and capabilities that feminists must reckon with in formulating programs for change. Even those who agree that sex/gender systems are entirely social, historical constructs frequently disagree about how malleable sex/gender systems are. And feminists disagree, crucially, on how gender systems relate to other dimensions of social organization, especially class and race, sexual identity, ethnicity, nationality, and disability. In recent years the central focus of debate among feminists has been questions such as whether it is ever meaningful to analyze the effects of sex/gender systems independently of these other structuring principles and dynamics, and whether there is anything at all common to women's experience as women across all these other dimensions of difference (see, for example, contributions to Mohanty, Russo, and Torres 1991; Bannerji 1993; Hirsch and Keller 1990).

Feminists also disagree in their empirical assessment of how consistently or seriously, and in what areas, existing gender structures disadvantage women, and in their understanding of how and why gender structures have emerged – what generated and what sustains them, and therefore how amenable to change they may be. Some take the position that "sex/gender" structures have "organized social life throughout most of history and in every culture today"; that they are "an organic social variable ... not merely an effect of other more primary causes, that limits and creates opportunities within which are constructed the social practices of daily life, the characteristics of social institutions, and of all our patterns of thought" (Harding 1983: 312). Some argue that it remains an open question, to be settled by close examination of particular historical and social contexts, just how important a role is played by "sex/gender" structures, compared with other structuring principles. And many insist that there is no such thing as "gender" that is separable from the specific forms that gender relations or ideologies or identities take in particular social locations defined, for example, by race and by class, by sexual orientation, and by a wide range of other key factors and affiliations.

Given these differences in empirical understanding, it is not surprising that feminists also hold widely divergent moral and political views about the sorts of change we should be trying to make: what kinds of feminist ideals we should be striving to realize, what aspects of existing gender inequity are unacceptable and should be the primary target for political action, and what strategies are appropriate for making change. The result is a broad spectrum of feminist positions including the stereotypic liberal feminism that was centrally at issue in the "Firing Line" debate (with its focus on achieving equity before the law and within existing political and economic structures), as well as a range of socialist and "radical" feminisms (which call for more fundamental change in these encompassing structures), alongside various forms of "cultural" and spiritual feminism (some of which retain existing gender stereotypes and seek to valorize rather than transform the "feminine" principle they articulate). There are, as well, a great many other distinctive traditions of feminist activism and theory which incorporate elements of these political stances but rarely fit neatly into any of them: "womanism," Black and Hispanic feminism (see, e.g., Collins 1990 on "Black feminist thought"), lesbian feminism, various forms of feminist separatism, and issue-specific feminist alliances (e.g., the shelter movement, women against violence against women and the anti-pornography movement, wages for housework, pay and employment equity activism, reproductive rights groups, and so on), as well as a constantly evolving panoply of deliberately hybrid positions. So, contrary to much popular wisdom and the caricatures that dominated the "Firing Line" debate, "feminism" is not a monolithic entity that could plausibly be judged "dead" or "alive" as a singular whole. Neither is it an entirely arbitrary collection of individual "points of view." It is a family of positions that depend on quite specific empirical claims and normative commitments, some of which have a bearing on the enterprises we identify as scientific.

So Why Are (Some) Feminists Concerned about Science?

I believe there are really two sorts of reasons why feminists have concerned themselves with science. One is that if we are committed to making change in the world, as feminists, it matters a great deal that we understand with accuracy, subtlety, and explanatory precision, the nature and extent and sources of the inequitable sex/gender systems we hope to transform;[5] we need detailed and reliable knowledge of the conditions and forces we oppose. Scientific modes of inquiry are among the most powerful tools we have for doing this; indeed, one of the chief motivations for much science – its Enlightenment legacy – is precisely the commitment to ground action, including political action, in a sound empirical understanding of the human, social, biological, and natural conditions that impinge on our lives. So feminists have a prima facie interest in the sciences and in scientific methods as, in principle, a crucial source of just the kind of understanding we need to proceed effectively in the pursuit of our goals of creating a gender-equitable world.

At the same time, however, feminists have long been suspicious of science as a bastion of male privilege, as male-dominated, as infused with masculinist values and interests, and as an important source and ground of men's gender privilege and control over women's lives. Consider Virginia Woolf on the subject: "science it would seem is not sexless; he is a man, a father and infected too" (as cited in Harding 1986: 135). Despite their reputation for an all-consuming curiosity about the world and for unflinching objectivity in pursuing this curiosity, scientists often betray, at best, a pervasive disinterest in the questions of concern to women and to feminists. At worst, several decades of close analysis and critique reveal that the most relevant sciences for feminist purposes – the social and life and medical sciences – often reproduce and legitimize precisely the ideology of gender inequity that feminists find they have reason to question. So the second reason feminists have taken an interest in the sciences is because these disciplines of inquiry are, in various ways, part of the problem. They are one important locus and source of the inequalities that feminists mean to challenge at the same time as they are a resource for addressing this problem.

Let me now consider, first, some of the ways in which feminists have found the institutions of science to be inequitable and then turn to some of the implications that these inequities may have for the practice and content of science, and for the kinds of knowledge they have provided us for navigating the social and natural worlds.

Equity Issues in Science

In a recent popular discussion, Michael Schrage begins an assessment of the current status of women in the natural sciences and engineering with the observation that "historically, culturally, and economically, science and technology are overwhelmingly male enterprises ... there's the occasional Madame Curie and Ada, Countess of Lovelace, but they're atypical to the point of anomaly" (Schrage 1990). In fact, although this is true of the broad sweep of science as it has developed in Euro-American contexts in the last 300 years, women did play an important role in the founding of science, and a great many talented women have since contributed to the development of a whole range of sciences – from astronomy, physics, and chemistry through to anatomy, biology, and, later, the social sciences – despite the substantial institutional barriers they have had to overcome. There is a growing historical literature which shows that the overwhelmingly masculine profile of science as it has developed was by no means a given; it was a deliberately enforced and closely protected institutional construct.

Londa Schiebinger, a key contributor to this literature, argues that, in the seventeenth and eighteenth centuries, the emerging New Science "st[ood] at a fork in the road" with respect to the inclusion of women (Schiebinger 1989: 100). Women had been active both in the craft traditions and in the learned circles of aristocrats out of which emerged early modern science. The best known of these women are noblewomen, not surprisingly, and they included such prominent figures as Queen Christina of Sweden (who commissioned Descartes to draw up regulations for a scientific academy she sought to establish in the mid-seventeenth century); Laura Bassi, a professor of physics at the University of Bologna in the mid-eighteenth century who was known for her innovative early experimentation with electricity (Italy was an exception in allowing women to teach in universities); Margaret Cavendish,

Duchess of Newcastle, who was active in science circles that included many members of the Royal Society in London, and who visited the Society in the late seventeenth century but was never admitted to it; the physicist Madame du Châtelet (Emilie du Châtelet; a prominent mathematician and Newtonian physicist in eighteenth-century French science circles), and her seventeenth-century predecessor Madeleine de Scudery, both of whom were denied membership of the French Académie Royale but were admitted to Italian academies (see Schiebinger 1989, among others, for a much-expanded catalogue of women who contributed substantially to the development of science).

By contrast with these craft and aristocratic traditions, however, most of the European/English universities in which the sciences were to become established drew on monastic traditions that systematically excluded women. Schiebinger argues that, in the seventeenth and eighteenth centuries, when science was still a "new enterprise forging new ideals and institutions," its proponents could either have affirmed the presence and contributions of elite women and craft specialists, or followed the conventions of the universities and excluded them. For the most part those building the formal academies and other institutional bases that came to define science as we know it chose the latter path. Despite the presence of learned women, women who had had "access to the tools of science" and had put them to good use, women and, more generally, all things "feminine" were purged from the emerging traditions of modern science (Schiebinger 1989: 9, chapter 8).

With few exceptions the major academies of science maintained strict policies of not admitting women. In fact, Marie Curie was denied membership of the prestigious Académie des Sciences after winning her first Nobel Prize, and was admitted reluctantly only after becoming the first person ever to win two Nobel Prizes (Ramey 1992); no other woman was elected to the Académie until 1979, "more than three hundred years after it first opened its doors" (Schiebinger 1989: 2). The US National Academy of Sciences did not admit its first woman until 1925, and even now just 4 per cent of its members are women (this is a calculation based on data reported in a review article in the *Washington Post*: Ramey 1992). A similar story can be told

not only about other prestigious science academies, but about virtually all of the institutions that have trained and employed scientists since they formed their first formal associations and these policies of exclusion were adopted.

The view that science is a largely male enterprise, both literally and ideologically, is by no means unique to feminists. As Schiebinger has argued in historical terms, and Evelyn Fox Keller with reference to contemporary science (most influentially in Keller 1985), the conception of science as a masculine domain has been an essential feature of its self-definition, and the literal exclusion of women from scientific institutions is by no means anomalous or inadvertent given this self-definition. There are numerous examples of founding figures and pre-eminent practitioners who have been quite explicit about this. Bacon is famous for advocating, in the early seventeenth century (at the dawn of the New Science), a thoroughly masculine (and British) natural philosophy – an "active, virile, generative" science, distinguished by its commitment to the experimental method from the "passive, speculative, and effeminate [natural] philosoph[ies]" of antiquity and of the continent (Schiebinger 1989: 137). He made liberal use of rape metaphors to characterize this new scientific methodology: "you have but to follow and as it were hound nature in her wanderings, and you will be able when you like to lead and drive her afterward to the same place again" (an argument for the experimental replication of results); "neither ought a man to make scruple of entering and penetrating into these holes and corners, when the inquisition is his whole object" (an argument for regarding nature not as sacred or inviolate but as something to be explored and exploited to its fullest potential) (as quoted in Merchant 1980: 168). More recently Richard Feynman, a Nobel Prize laureate, is cited by Harding, among others, as having described the theory that brought him recognition as a mistress he had originally loved with youthful abandon, who had grown old and unattractive, but proved nonetheless to be a solid workhorse of a wife who had borne him a number of "very good children" (Harding 1986: 120).

While these metaphors may be dismissable as extrinsic to the actual content and practice of science, they are often aligned with quite literal claims to the effect that women are inherently incapable of doing science, or that it is inappropriate for them to try. Their intellects are too weak, or if exercised, will drain energy from their ovaries, rendering them infertile, and their presence is disruptive for those who are equipped to do science: "female company so enervates and relaxes the mind, and gives it such a turn for trifling, levity, and dissipation, as renders it altogether unfit for that application which is necessary in order to become eminent in any of the sciences" (William Alexander 1779, as quoted by Schiebinger 1989: 152–153). Clearly here the subject position of the scientist is not only gendered male, as it is in the case of Bacon's and Feynman's statements, but the capacity of the scientist to exercise his faculties to the fullest is understood to depend on eliminating "feminine" distractions and weaknesses. Moreover, closing the circle, the life and social and psychological sciences have often, themselves, been used to rationalize the exclusion of women from scientific and other preeminently masculine domains by "demonstrating" that they (along with criminals, members of the "lower" classes, and members of a shifting catalogue of despised "other" cultures, ethnicities, and races) are inherently less intelligent than the race- and class-privileged men who have predominantly done science.

Despite devastating critiques brought against the conceptual foundations of these sorts of racialist and sexist research programs over many years, due to such prominent figures as Steven J. Gould (e.g. Gould 1983), they are now enjoying a resurgence of popularity (see, e.g., Herrnstein and Murray 1994, and the commentaries assembled by Jacoby and Glauberman 1995). And one of their effects is to reinforce widely held "pre-judgements" to the effect that science is no place for a woman, a conviction that has proven to have considerable powers of self-realization since the time it was entrenched in the sciences in the seventeenth and eighteenth centuries. Taking stock of where we now stand, it is clear that since the beginnings of organized science in the Euro-American tradition, women have figured predominantly as technicians and assistants, they have had walk-on roles which were usually gender-stereotypic (see Rossiter 1982, especially chapter 3, "'Women's Work' in Science"). Those who did excel and make

significant original contributions are, indeed, remarkable exceptions and typically they were quickly forgotten, their accomplishments often, it is turning out, attributed to husbands, fathers, colleagues.[6]

Certainly some things have changed, and are changing, for the better. With the substantial, if uneven, inroads that women (largely middle-class, white women) have made in a whole range of disciplines and professions since their first admission to universities and colleges in the 1860s, women have improved their position in the sciences – especially in the last couple of decades. In the 1920s, figures reported in the publication *American Men of Science* (Cattell 1906; see Rossiter 1982: 326 note 59, and 358 note 3) indicate that under 5 per cent of all scientists working in the US were women (including engineering and technology, physics, mathematics, the life sciences). By the 1940s, according to Margaret Rossiter, there were "thousands of ... women working in a variety of fields and institutions, whereas sixty or seventy years earlier there were about ten at a few early women's colleges" (Rossiter 1982: xviii; see also discussion by Harding 1986: 60). This was an achievement realized by "the best efforts of a host of talented women, who, seeing how both science and women's roles were changing around them, took steps to carve out a legitimate place for themselves in the new order" (Rossiter 1982: xviii). And despite being vulnerable to reversal as this "new order" was itself reshaped – there was a sharp downturn in women's training and employment in the sciences in the 1950s – women have continued to build on these gains, doubling and quadrupling their representation in college and graduate programs in science, and among employed scientists and engineers.[7]

Today women account for easily twice as many employed engineers and scientists in the US as in the 1940s, but this is still just 16 per cent of the employed science and engineering workforce at a time when women constitute 45 per cent of the employed workforce in the US (Alper 1993: 409). And their numbers remain comparatively low in the "training pipeline" for scientists, compared to other professional and graduate training programs. Women are still awarded less than a quarter of the advanced degrees granted in the sciences on the most generous construal.

Between 36 per cent and 50 per cent of PhDs go to women in various of the social/human sciences (this figure is inflated by psychology, in which 50 per cent of new PhDs are awarded to women if you include clinical and applied psychology), while the typical percentage of women among new PhDs in the natural sciences is as low as 8 per cent for engineering, and well under 20 per cent for mathematics, computer science, physics, and environmental science (Alper 1993: 409). This is in an era in which over 50 per cent of the undergraduate student body in the US and Canada has been women since the mid-1980s (taking all fields of study together); in which women have proven to have a higher completion rate for undergraduate degrees than their male counterparts, and now take roughly half of all Master's degrees and over a third of PhDs (all fields); and in which between 30 per cent and 40 per cent of completing students in law and medicine are women. Only biology and chemistry approach this level of representation for women PhDs among the natural sciences and engineering (35 per cent and 24 per cent respectively; Alper 1993: 409). As Schrage observes, in the article I referred to earlier, the persistently low number of women in many sciences serves to "reinforce [a long-established] historical pattern ... women probably have greater influence over the future of baseball than they do over emerging technologies" (1990: D1) – a sobering thought, given the current state of baseball.

Just as disturbing is an increasing body of evidence that these statistics cannot altogether be attributed to women's lack of natural "aptitude" for science and mathematics or, indeed, to a lack of preparatory training in science. As Rossiter observes, "th[e] great growth [in the participation of women in the sciences seen in the first half of the century] ... occurred at the price of accepting a pattern of segregated employment and under-recognition which, try as they might, most women could not escape" (Rossiter 1982: xviii, see also discussion by Harding 1986: 60). Women who do succeed in getting trained in the sciences find themselves disproportionately unemployed and underemployed. A recent Canadian report describes a situation that seems endemic to the sciences: "although jobs for all highly trained scientists [have been] in short supply [since the mid-1970s], women

particularly have had a difficult time finding permanent jobs ... the percentage of women with PhDs [in science and engineering] form a pool that seems to be at least twice as great as the percentage of women hired as professors" (Dagg 1985: 74; see Flam 1991 for a comparable discussion of the status of women in astronomy and physics in the US). Even more worrisome, women are disproportionately deflected from the training programs that feed the job market for scientists in the academy, in industry, and in the public sector, not only at the level of preliminary training, but at various points where they already have the qualifications to go on in science but choose other fields. As declared by the title of a contribution to the 1993 *Science* special feature on "Women in Science," "The Pipeline is Leaking Women All the Way Along" (Alper 1993; this special feature is entitled, as a whole, "Gender and the Culture of Science").

This 1993 *Science* article on "pipeline" issues echoes the title and central theme of a Presidential Address that was presented to the AAAS (American Association for the Advancement of Science) by Sheila Widnall in 1988. Her title was "Voices from the Pipeline" and her point of departure was a review of statistics that were then a matter of serious concern to the various agencies and policy-makers in the US who monitor demographic trends in science and technology. Evidently the number of qualified students with BSc and engineering degrees who were choosing to go on to doctoral work in the sciences had dropped dramatically (from 12 per cent to 6 per cent since the mid-1960s) and showed no signs of reversing themselves; a further 26 per cent decrease was projected by the turn of the century. What Widnall juxtaposed with these statistics are the results of a number of studies which suggest that this loss of qualified candidates from the training pipeline is especially high for women, and for foreign and "minority" students. Focusing on women Widnall identified two major points at which women drop out of "the pipeline": at entry to college and mid-way through graduate school, between masters and doctoral programs.

Taking 2,000 girls and 2,000 boys beginning public school as a comparison group, she reports that 220 girls, compared to 280 boys, get the necessary high-school training in mathematics and science to go on to college science programs. Given Widnall's figures, this means that fully 44 per cent of those qualified for science programs in college are girls (14 per cent of the cohort of boys who begin school together, compared to 11 per cent of girls, complete high school with the qualifications to go on in the sciences). But, most striking, of these science-qualified high-school students, three times as many young men as women choose science programs in college. Widnall reports that only 44 women, compared to 140 men of the original cohort (that is, less than 20 per cent of the qualified women, compared to half of the men), continue their training in science at a college level. She observes that women more than hold their own through college; the figures she cites suggest that half of the women who start science programs in college finish with a BSc, compared to a third of the men. Moreover, roughly the same proportion of women as men who complete their BSc decide to go on to science programs in graduate school. The second sharp drop in the representation of women comes at the point when they are mid-way through their graduate studies (when they have completed an MSc) and must decide whether or not to continue on to a PhD in science or engineering. Just 1 woman compared to 5 men, of the original cohort of 2,000 girls and 2,000 boys, will emerge at the end of the pipeline with a doctoral degree in these fields. That is, as the 1993 *Science* article reports, just 20 per cent of new PhDs in science and engineering will be women: this is less than half the proportion of women among the high-school students who are qualified to go on in science programs (i.e., where Widnall's figures suggest 44 per cent of science-qualified high-school students are girls).

On Widnall's account, then, the persistently low number of women in the sciences and engineering cannot be attributed solely or even primarily to their failure, at early stages in their education, to get the necessary qualifications to do science at an advanced level. Rather, it seems that when women reach the point of entering college and PhD programs, a disproportionate number of those who have the training to go on in the sciences and engineering choose against these programs. To account for this pattern of "leakage" of women from the training pipeline, especially in graduate school, Widnall turns to various student surveys (specifically ones done at MIT and Stanford in the mid-1980s) and argues on the basis of their findings that one crucial factor must be what she calls the "environmental" conditions women encounter in science – what the 1993 *Science* feature on "Women in Science" refers to as the "culture of science."

A graduate career is, Widnall says, a process of "continuous testing and trial of one's academic and personal characteristics" that shapes and reshapes your career aspirations as you proceed. As an "apprenticeship in research," much depends on the "quality of interaction with the advisor" and on the role students have an opportunity to play as members of a research team. While "white male students benefit from the self-reinforcing confidence that they belong" which they acquire in part through "self-identification with [largely] white male faculty" for others – women, minority and foreign students – "acceptance is not a presumption, the environment is not so reinforcing" (Widnall 1988: 1744). Widnall finds this reflected in a whole series of measures of self-esteem, confidence, comparisons between "objective" test results and subjective estimates of one's own capabilities and performance relative to that of peers. Instructors evidently expect less from their women students; women students find that their instructors spend less time with them than with their male peers; they report strikingly low rates of assignment to roles of responsibility on research teams (20 per cent of men, compared to 6 per cent of women); and roughly half of the women report various forms of sexual harassment. Not surprisingly, these women come to doubt their capabilities (they routinely report much lower self-assessments of how well they have done or will do than male students who achieve the same results on objective tests and other measures of their performance as students). And as their confidence is eroded, they lower their career aspirations – entering a downward spiral that is reflected in disproportionately high attrition rates among women in graduate programs.

Setting these contemporary experiences and their consequences in historical perspective, I believe that what Widnall reports is the deep-rooted legacy of precisely the masculinist vision of science that, on Schiebinger's account, a great many founders of modern science were intent on establishing; the attributes of personal style and patterns of interaction, the social dynamics and the culture that are valorized in the sciences are pervasively gendered male.[8] As such, they are systematically undermining for individuals who are otherwise inescapably women. Insofar as we do not fit the male mould we are not easily seen as authoritative, as part of "the team," much less as hard-driving, self-starting, dynamic, independent leaders. And often we do not see ourselves in this picture, at least not without considerable conflict and great cost to our own (highly gendered) sense of self and integrity.

Clearly, then, although much has changed, the exclusion (or loss) of women from science is not yet an historical artifact. Widnall's argument for taking seriously the need to turn this situation around – in particular, her argument that we must create a more hospitable environment for women and a great many others who are marginalized in the sciences – is not primarily inspired by a concern with the injustices done to those who are denied the opportunity to "be the best they can" and to make a contribution in the fields they have chosen. Rather, her central concern is that the US as a whole, and the research establishment in particular, cannot afford any more to squander the trained "human resources" represented by those (most especially women) who are so persistently "leaking" from the training pipeline. In this Widnall echoes the concern voiced by Madeleine du Châtelet more than two hundred years ago, when she objected that it was a terrible shame to waste the talents and potential contributions of women to the emerging sciences. In 1735 du Châtelet insisted that "women deserve the same education as men," adding that if she were king, she would "reform an abuse which cuts off ... half the human race ... [and ensure that] women participate [fully] in the rights of humankind, and above all in those of the intellect" (as quoted by Schiebinger, 1989: 65).

I would add to Widnall's assessment the argument that this pattern of exclusion of women exacts a cost not only from women and from the larger communities of which we are a part, but also from the sciences themselves. Our sciences are not all they could be, measured against their own ideals of empirical rigour and explanatory power, when they deflect the insights and contributions of those potential science practitioners who could be drawn from well over "half

the human race," if you consider not only the exclusion of women but of all those who constitute the so-called "minority" groups that Widnall finds excluded as well.

Implications for Science: Content Critiques

The most controversial form of critique that feminists have levelled against the sciences is that it would be astonishing if the domination of science by men and by a highly masculinized culture did not have an impact on the doing of science – and, ultimately, on the content and results of science. The most straightforward of these critiques focuses on the questions asked and the uses made of scientific inquiry. Key examples often come from the medical sciences where, for example, feminists have objected that research tends to focus on the ailments of men rather than those of women, for example, on heart disease rather than osteoporosis and breast cancer.[9] But as important as these critiques are in practical terms, they leave untouched the conviction that the content and practice of science is value- and interest-neutral. The objection here is that reliable, empirically substantiated knowledge is being produced, but in areas that are of special interest to, or that stand to benefit, the members of one gender-defined group rather than another.

More challenging are critiques which purport to show that science is not only inequitable in who it recruits and rewards as practitioners and in who it serves, but that the understanding of the world it produces reflects, in its content, the social status, identities, and interests – in short, the standpoint – of its practitioners.[10] For many this is a radically counter-intuitive claim. In considering what such a claim might mean, it is important to recognize that it can be formulated in more and less radical terms, and that it has quite different import for the various disciplines we identify as scientific.

For one thing, the ways in which the content and practice of a science is gender-biased (either intentionally or inadvertently) are bound to be very different for sciences whose subject-matter is inherently or projectively gendered than for those that deal with seemingly non-gendered subjects. While some feminists have argued that the whole orientation of mathematics and theoretical physics is ideologically masculine (e.g., in their preoccupation with abstraction and control), it is not altogether clear how specific practices or results in these fields might reflect gender bias. To quote Schrage's popular discussion, however, this should not be taken to foreclose the question of whether the study of non-gendered subjects sustains gender bias:

[The natural sciences and engineering raise] a fascinating question: Does gender matter in scientific research? Do women, because of their temperaments and backgrounds, bring ... different sensibilit[ies] to scientific research than their male counterparts? Talk with people at Johns Hopkins, Stanford, and MIT's Whitehead Institute, and it's immediately clear that the influx of women in molecular biology has influenced the nature of research ... [but] unless there are fundamental changes in society and the engineering infrastructure ... we may never know just what sort of a sensibility women can bring to the various disciplines of engineering. (Schrage 1990: D1)

Certainly a number of sociologists of science argue that class and national bias are evident not just in notorious instances of propagandistic science (the favourite examples are Nazi and Soviet science), but in much of the natural science and mathematics that was acclaimed as the best of its kind in its day. It may be that these seemingly pure exemplars of scientific objectivity reflect the gendered interests of their makers in ways we cannot fully comprehend, being located as we are within a culture permeated both by the authority of science and by sex/gender constructs that are thoroughly naturalized.

By contrast, it is by now well established that the gendered standpoint of practitioners has had a profound impact on the content of the social sciences and many of the life sciences. But even here critiques of androcentrism – of gender bias – take a number of different forms depending on where this bias is located, how it is understood to arise, how pervasive it is, and how deeply rooted it proves to be. Here are some examples that illustrate this diversity.

First, feminists have identified pervasive domain definition bias in a number of social and life sciences; frequently research in these fields simply leaves women and gender out of account. One famous example is Lévi-Strauss's description of one morning's experience, entered in his field journal in the 1930s: "the entire village left the next day in about thirty canoes, leaving us alone in the abandoned houses with the women and children" (1936, as cited by Eichler and Lapointe 1985: 11). Another is the long tradition of anthropological research among "hunter–gatherers" that has characterized these societies almost exclusively in terms of the hunting activities of the men (e.g., as critiqued by Slocum 1975; see also contributions to Lee and DeVore 1968, and overviews by Dahlberg 1981, and Fedigan and Fedigan 1989). A third is Kohlberg's famous and influential study of moral development in children, which is fundamentally flawed, Gilligan has argued, by its dependence on samples comprised entirely of little boys (see Gilligan 1982; Kohlberg 1958, 1969).

A second, closely related form of bias, indeed one that is often a consequence of domain definition bias, is that of treating masculine attributes and activities as typical of, or normative for, humankind and society as a whole – the tendency to "count the part as whole." Alternatively, when gender is acknowledged as an important variable, a third tendency is to treat gender differences as a given, as absolute, and to characterize gender roles and identities in terms of stereotypes derived, uncritically, from our own society. For example, as Gilligan develops her critique of Kohlberg's account (Gilligan 1982), she was initially responding to the puzzle of why, on his model of moral development, female children should systematically test several stages behind males in the middle years of their development; here male experience was treated as normative for the population as a whole (the second form of bias). She argues that if you listen to the emerging moral "voice" of girls you will recognize in it a quite different pattern of development than is manifested by most of the boys of Kohlberg's samples (e.g., as discussed in Kohlberg 1958, 1969). Rather than seeing little girls as deficient or immature when they do not fit male-defined norms, she argues that we should recognize divergent paths to moral maturity. Boys later develop the capacity to think empathetically in terms of responsibilities and mutual connection that girls are developing in the middle stages of maturation, and girls later learn to manipulate principles and concepts of rights in the ways that become second nature for boys immersed in rule-governed schoolyard games in their middle years of development.

In a similar vein, detailed ethnographic studies of women's roles and activities in "hunter–gatherer" societies reveal that, among temperate, desert-dwelling, and subtropical groups, the small game and plant resources provided by women gatherers may account for as much as 70 per cent of the group's total dietary intake (see contributions to Lee and DeVore 1968); in many cases it is fundamentally misleading to characterize these groups in normatively male terms as "hunting" societies. In addition, women gatherers often proved to be highly mobile (not tied to a home base), to control their own fertility to an extent not previously acknowledged, and to take the lead in determining community movement and strategies for survival – by sharp contrast with the stereotypes of women's "natural" roles that were projected onto them when they did figure in traditional accounts of "hunter–gatherer" societies. These findings have profound implications not only for what we understand of contemporary "gatherer–hunter" or "foraging" societies (as they were renamed), but for models of human evolution that depend, in part, on ethnographic models of the subsistence patterns and social organization of such groups; they were the inspiration for corrective "woman the gatherer" models of human evolution. In a parallel development, androcentric theories of human evolution have also been undermined by the findings of largely female (although not always feminist) primatologists who have transformed our understanding of our nearest relatives: e.g., chimpanzees (Goodall), gorillas (Fossey), orangutans (Galdikas), and baboons (Fedigan). This quite recent tradition of research has demonstrated that, *contra* many deeply entrenched assumptions about what counts as "natural" in the domain of sex/gender relations, wild primate populations exemplify much greater diversity in social organization than previously recognized, that mother–infant bonds are often central in structuring primate social relations, and that the females of many species are not just the passive recipients of the attentions of dominant males but are

"endowed with sexual strategies of their own" (Morrell 1993: 429).

Cases like these have both depended on, and generated, a great deal of what has since come to be known as "remedial research." In the initial "add women and stir" phase of feminist research, as many now describe it, a great many women and men influenced by feminist critiques undertook to recover, in their various fields, what had been left out of account by research that had manifestly ignored women, that had treated male experience and activities as normative, or had characterized women in gender-stereotypic terms; this was an enterprise of recovering "women worthies, women victims, and women's contributions" (see Harding 1986, chapter 2). Very quickly, however, it became evident that the sorts of errors remedial researchers were bent on redressing had much deeper roots than they initially recognized and could not be corrected by simply augmenting existing accounts with details about women's lives and experiences. Broadening these various fields of inquiry to consider women all too often simply moved the reproduction of gender bias to a new level; the results were sexist or androcentric theories about women, or about a domain newly recognized to include gendered (specifically female) subjects.

Feminist researchers took up this deeper challenge as part of their program of critical inquiry. Soon after the advent of feminist programs of research in anthropology and primatology, history and psychology, the analysis of gender bias took a reflective turn, focusing on ways in which the underlying presuppositions of inquiry may embody ethnocentric, presentist assumptions not just about women, but about gender categories and social relations more generally. These include, for example, a growing body of critiques of Gilligan's continued dependence on a stage-schema model to characterize moral development; the presupposition of set stages and a dynamic of internally driven maturation begins to seem problematic when you expand the range of factors that make a difference in the moral "voice" of children beyond that of gender (see, e.g., Auerbach *et al.* 1985). They also include several powerful autocritiques published by feminist researchers within a decade of their initial critiques of androcentrism in their fields.

One is M. Z. Rosaldo (but see also Ringelheim 1985, and Nicholson 1983), who argued that her earlier work as a feminist was flawed by a failure to recognize the ethnocentrism of an implicit assumption that the non-industrialized societies she studied are structured by the same principles of sharp separation and opposition between gendered domains as is familiar from Euro-American contexts: the public domain of men, the private domain of women (Rosaldo 1980). Given this assumption she had held that the errors of androcentric accounts could be corrected by refocusing attention on the private, domestic domain of women. In fact, she came to argue, these dichotomous gender categories are highly specific to Anglo-American society, indeed, they are of quite recent origin (they date to the emergence of a middle class in the late nineteenth century) and cannot be projected onto cultures of other times and places. To do so is to retain precisely the androcentric and ethnocentric assumptions about gender roles that, as feminists, we should be prepared to question.

The turn to searching internal critique exemplified by Rosaldo is also evident in Fedigan's arguments that we should resist the tendency to replace "man the hunter" models of early hominid evolution with "female the gatherer" models; both betray the limitations of current taken-for-granteds about the fundamental and oppositional nature of gender difference and neither are adequate to the complexity of extant data (Fedigan 1986; see also Fedigan 1982; Sperling 1991). It is a mistake, Fedigan insists, to simply invert and revalue the categories central to our current sex/gender system; all indications are that our ancient ancestors lived in social groups, utilizing subsistence strategies, that are unlike any we know through historical, ethnographic, or primatological research. The compulsion to find elements of our own gender relations in the social lives of contemporary non-human primates, and to project these back onto our earliest (proto-human) ancestors, ignores the fact that evolutionary processes have as long a history for non-human as for human primates. In all cases it is as likely as not that paleontological populations were quite different in their behaviour and social dynamics from any of the forms we now know among their descendants. Finally, there have been numerous feminist critics within the social

sciences who have called into question simplistic assumptions to the effect that women in contemporary societies are everywhere disadvantaged, in the same ways and to the same degrees, by the sex/gender conventions that structure their lives. An early example in sociology/anthropology comes from those who had studied women in so-called "peasant" societies. Here the public subordination of women to men proved to be counterbalanced by the decisive control that women exercise over many aspects of family and community decision-making, so long as the domestic sphere in which they operate continued to be the primary locus of economic activity for such communities (see, e.g., Rogers 1975; Sanday 1974). To characterize these women as disenfranchised victims of an inequitable sex/gender system is to impose on them profoundly ethnocentric and, indeed, androcentric notions about what counts as power (for a more detailed discussion of this example see Wylie 1992).

In all of these cases, what began as an enterprise of adding a missing piece to a complex puzzle led to a reconfiguration of the puzzle as a whole. The central insight to emerge is that studies of literally or projectively gendered subject-matters are pervasively shaped by presuppositions which reflect our standpoint in a society structured by a range of deeply entrenched presuppositions about the nature and roles and capacities of those gendered female vs. male. These not only result in ignoring or stereotyping women but also determine, more generally, the range of variables we consider salient, the dimensions of the subject domain we document, the array of explanatory hypotheses we consider plausible enough to be worth testing, and even what we can recognize as "evidence" relevant for evaluating these hypotheses.

In the process, as the net of feminist critique is cast wider and turns up fresh examples of gender bias at increasingly fundamental levels, the question arises of just how deeply scientific practice is impugned. Certainly the case I have cited make it clear that many sciences are pervasively gender-biased in ways that have escaped attention until quite recently. But is this just a matter of human error – a failure to apply the tools of science carefully or widely enough – or are the tools themselves part of the problem, either in generating some of the biases that feminists document or, more modestly, in allowing bias to be reproduced, failing to be as thoroughly and automatically self-cleansing as we might have hoped? Is the problem we face one of correcting surprisingly widespread instances of "bad science," or must we reconsider the scope and powers of "science as usual," good science, even our best science (see Harding 1986: 19, 102–105)? A feminist biologist, Anne Fausto-Sterling, frames this question in particularly stark terms, after having described case after case in which it has been found that sex-difference researchers in psychology and physiology ignored negative results, failed to use appropriate control groups and generalized from inappropriately small samples, misapplied techniques of statistical analysis, manipulated variables to produce tautological results, and sometimes even falsified their data (Fausto-Sterling 1985: 7–9). Fausto-Sterling expresses considerable puzzlement over the "paradox" that much of this exceedingly bad research was done by "intelligent, serious men and women ... trained at the best institutions in the country. By all conventional measures, they are good scientists" who frequently built prestigious careers on results that are now proving to be seriously flawed, in terms they would have to respect (1985: 9). In the end she rejects the option of "denouncing the entire scientific enterprise as intellectually corrupt" (*ibid.*), not least, it would seem, because she wants to claim that the research by which feminists have called entrenched wisdom into question is *better* science, science enriched by the fresh "angle of vision" brought to bear by feminist researchers who notice "things about research methods and interpretations that many others have missed" (1985: 11).

I am sympathetic to Fausto-Sterling's position but would add that the cases I have cited – and many of those that she describes in *Myths of Gender* – seem to require a quite thoroughgoing reassessment of what we can reasonably expect of the tools of inquiry that have been honed by the sciences. These cases bring into view not just piecemeal error, but systematic error made possible by a misplaced confidence in the powers of scientific method to neutralize, to counter or wash out, the effects of the standpoint-specific interests that we inevitably bring to the endeavour of science. That range of "effects" born of the beliefs and practices that define sex/gender difference in contemporary society are just one example of the interests that impinge on science. Often these conventions are so completely transparent, especially to those who fit male norms and are privileged by existing sex/gender systems, that predominantly male science practitioners simply did not see the need to test framework assumptions about gender structures and were not alert to ways in which their research design and results might be biased by gendered presuppositions. It is perhaps not surprising that women who have become conscious of ways in which they are disadvantaged by contemporary sex/gender systems would be more sensitive to ways in which presuppositions about these systems structure our understanding, and would demand higher standards in these cases. Given this "angle of vision," they bring a critical perspective to bear that allows the quite literal discovery of errors and possibilities that had been overlooked. Not only do they use the existing tools of scientific inquiry more effectively in these cases, they often see more clearly the limitations of these tools and are creative in thinking around corners, exploring new ways of using them, and in some cases developing new tools.

The lesson I draw from the work of feminist practitioners and critics of science is that standpoint matters, in both a positive and negative sense. On the principle, "garbage in: garbage out," a great many of the framework assumptions that have informed scientific practice in the past must be subjected to critical scrutiny, especially in fields that study inherently or projectively gendered subject domains. We must become more accountable for the standpoint-specific assumptions we bring to inquiry, especially those that are so deeply entrenched we are barely aware that we hold them.

Conclusions

I close with three brief observations that I hope raise questions for discussion. First, the sort of bias in content I have identified suggests that inequities in who does science do have a bearing on how good science is. The argument is this: if bias is most likely to arise and persist where science is practiced by a fairly homogeneous group – a group whose values and interests are largely shared and unquestioned – then it would seem that a commitment to objectivity requires that we increase the diversity of those recruited to practice science (see Longino 1990:214). It is not just that the institutions of science should be more tolerant or accommodating of the diverse standpoints and perspectives of women, as just one among a whole range of groups who have traditionally been excluded from science, but that those who have been excluded in the past may well bring to the sciences quite unique, even transforming, insights and approaches. Our sciences stand to be better – more rigorous, more creative, more inclusive – if a greater diversity of people is involved in their practice.

Second, where feminism is a political perspective based on empirical presuppositions about the way the world actually is – about the role of gender as a structuring principle and the relative status of women vs. men – it is crucial that feminists not reject science as a mode of inquiry, however masculinist and inhospitable it has become as an institution. If we are to be effective in changing the inequities that women still face,

we need to make full use of the tools of science, and in the process transform them and the institutions that now control them.

Finally, a reflection that arises from conversation with Leo Block: I believe we should all enthusiastically endorse sunset clauses. My hope is that a genuinely feminist transformation of science and of society will realize a degree of human inclusiveness – intellectually, socially, economically – that will render feminism unnecessary both as a political movement and as a locus of intellectual, scientific engagement. The "Firing Line" debate brought home to me just how far we are from such a happy juncture. My own response to the framing proposition (that "feminism as a movement is dead") is that we have barely begun the task of dismantling the sex/gender systems that continue to limit the human potential, not just of women, but of men located in widely divergent contexts, including such traditionally masculine enterprises as science. *Pace* E. O. Wilson, this is a challenge that I believe we cannot afford not to meet.

Notes

1 Except when discussing the early modern founding of science (which pertains primarily to astronomy, physics, and mathematics) or "science and engineering" (a category used for statistical purposes which includes the natural and life sciences, as well as computing and some branches of psychology – cognitive science), I will use the term science to refer broadly to the whole range of disciplines committed to systematic empirical investigation of the human, social, and natural worlds that we now refer to as scientific.

2 Rebecca West (Cicily Isabel Fairfield) is widely cited as having made this statement in 1913, but I have been unable to find any more specific reference to it.

3 Wilson makes a case for taking this option seriously when he considers the responses open to a society that faces demands for change, e.g., given a growing and global "struggle for women's rights" (1978: 132).

4 Wilson calls for a "value-free assessment of the relative contributions of heredity and environment to the differentiation of behavioral roles between the sexes" (1978: 128–129), and urges that this can "help us to define the options and to assess the price of each" (1978: 132). Nonetheless he concludes that "the evidences of biological constraint alone cannot prescribe an ideal course of action" (1978: 132).

5 By way of a digression I am struck that just as "woman is not born, she is made" (de Beauvoir 1952), so too feminists are very largely not born but made. Often our feminism is inspired by evidence that shatters faith in the objectivity and fairness – specifically, the gender neutrality – of our educational and employment systems, and our social, economic, legal, and political institutions. At least, those who are privileged in other respects may have the luxury of growing up with the belief that if we work hard, get the right sorts of training, cultivate our talents, make ourselves useful, and otherwise contribute to society, we can expect, in these lands of opportunity, to achieve various sorts of success. We may believe, more specifically, that the crucial rights and freedoms underpinning these ideals were won for women by our mothers and grandmothers and that it is now up to us to make the most of the hard-fought freedoms and opportunities they have secured for us. In such cases the catalyst for exploring feminist analyses is often a growing realization that, no matter how talented or hard-working we are as individuals, being a woman can make a substantial difference to the opportunities that come our way, and to the rewards we can expect

242   ALISON WYLIE

in everything from the subtle reinforcement of full
integration into our communities and working
groups, through to the acknowledgement and com-
pensation we realize for our achievements and contributions. This is not an easy recognition. Often it
comes in agonizing response to a critical threshold
of evidence that renders inescapable some version
of the two empirical claims I have identified as
central tenets of feminism: that gender makes a
difference and that in many areas this difference is
not just an idiosyncratic, personal/circumstantial
problem, but a difference that systematically disadvantages those categorized as women, albeit in
widely varying ways.

6 For example, Émilie du Châtelet's key work in
Newtonian physics was claimed by her tutor as his
own (see Schiebinger 1989: 63), and by all accounts, Watson's and Crick's dismissive treatment
of the contributions made by Rosalind Franklin to
their discovery of the double helix – the work that
earned Watson and Crick the Nobel Prize – is still
by no means anomalous (Ramey 1992).

7 A more detailed discussion of these analyses of
the status of women in the sciences, and in colleges and universities more generally, is included
in Wylie (1995).

8 The sorts of issues Widnall raises, concerning
inhospitable teaching and working environments
in the sciences, are addressed more generally
in the growing literature on the "chilly climate"
that women confront not only in the sciences,
but in academia as a whole (see, e.g., Sandler
1986; Aisenberg and Harrington 1988; Chilly
Collective 1995).

9 In fact, recent news coverage suggests that medical
researchers have not always been very effective in
discerning sex/gender differences even in diseases
that have been extensively studied, as in the case of
heart disease.

10 I will focus here on critiques that consider the
gendered standpoint of practitioners, but a wide
range of counterpart critiques consider, as well,
the class, race, national identity, and other aspects
of standpoint.

References

Aisenberg, Nadya and Mona Harrington (1988)
  Women of Academe: Outsiders in the Sacred Grove,
  Amherst, Mass.: University of Massachusetts Press.
Alexander, William (1779) *The History of Women*,
  Vol. 1. London.
Alper, Joe (1993) "The Pipeline is Leaking Women All
  the Way Along," *Science*, special issue on "Women in
  Science '93," 260: 409–411.
Auerbach, Judy, Linda Blum, Vicki Smith and Chris-
  tine Williams (1985) "On Gilligan's *In a Different
  Voice*," *Feminist Studies* 11(1): 149–163.
Bannerji, Himani (ed.) (1993) *Returning the Gaze: Essays
  on Racism, Feminism, and Politics*, Toronto: Sister-
  Vision – Black Women and Women of Colour Press.
de Beauvoir, Simone (1952) *The Second Sex* (H. M.
  Parshley, trans.), New York: Bantam Books (origin-
  ally published in French, 1949).
Cattell, James McKeen (1906) *A Bibliographical
  Dictionary of American Men of Science*, Garrison,
  NY: Science Press (as discussed by Rossiter 1982).
Chilly Collective (1995) *Breaking Anonymity: The Chilly
  Climate for Women Faculty*, Waterloo, Ontario:
  Wilfrid Laurier University Press.
Collins, Patricia Hill (1990) *Black Feminist Thought*,
  New York: Routledge (originally Unwin Hyman).
Dagg, Anne Innis (1985) "The Status of Canadian
  Women PhD Scientists," *Atlantis* 11: 74.
Dahlberg, Frances (1981) "Introduction," in F. Dahlberg
  (ed.) *Woman the Gatherer*, New Haven: Yale University
  Press, pp. 1–33.

Eichler, Magrit and Jeanne Lapointe (1985) *On the
  Treatment of the Sexes in Research*, Social Sciences
  and Humanities Research Council of Canada, Ottawa.
Fausto-Sterling, Anne (1985) *Myths of Gender:
  Biological Theories about Women and Men*, New
  York: Basic Books.
Fedigan, Linda Marie (1982) *Primate Paradigms: Sex
  Roles and Social Bonds*, Chicago: University of
  Chicago Press.
Fedigan, Linda Marie (1986) "The Changing Role of
  Women in Models of Human Evolution," *Annual
  Review of Anthropology* 15: 25–66.
Fedigan, Linda Marie and Laurence Fedigan (1989)
  "Gender and the Study of Primates," in S. Morgan
  (ed.) *Gender and Anthropology: Critical Reviews for
  Teaching and Research*, Washington, DC: American
  Anthropological Association.
Flam, Faye (1991) "Still a 'Chilly Climate' for
  Women?," *Science* 252: 1604–1606.
Friedan, Betty (1983) *The Feminine Mystique*, New
  York: Laurel (originally 1963).
Gilligan, Carol (1982) *In a Different Voice: Psychological
  Theory and Women's Development*, Cambridge,
  Mass.: Harvard University Press.
Gould, Steven Jay (1983) *The Mismeasure of Man*,
  New York: W. W. Norton and Co.
Harding, Sandra (1983) "Why Has the Sex/Gender
  System Become Visible Only Now?" in Sandra Harding
  and Merrill B. Hintikka (eds) *Discovering Reality:
  Feminist Perspectives on Epistemology, Metaphysics,*

Methodology and Philosophy of Science, Dordrecht: Reidel, pp. 311–324.

Harding, Sandra (1986) *The Science Question in Feminism*, Ithaca: Cornell University Press.

Herrnstein, Richard J. and Charles Murray (1994) *The Bell Curve*, New York: Simon and Schuster.

Hirsch, Marianne and Evelyn Fox Keller (eds) (1990) *Conflicts in Feminism*, New York: Routledge.

hooks, bell (1984) *From Margin to Center*, Boston: South End Press.

Jacoby, Russell and Naomi Glauberman (eds) (1995) *The Bell Curve Debate*, New York: Times Books.

Jaggar, Alison M. and Paula S. Rothenberg (eds) (1984) *Feminist Frameworks*, New York: McGraw Hill, second edition.

Keller, Evelyn Fox (1985) *Reflections on Gender and Science*, New Haven, CT: Yale University Press.

Kohlberg, Lawrence (1958) "The Development of Modes of Thinking and Choices in Years 10 to 16," PhD dissertation, University of Chicago.

Kohlberg, Lawrence (1969) "Stage and Sequence: The Cognitive-Development Approach to Socialization," in D. A. Goslin (ed.) *Handbook of Socialization Theory and Research*, Chicago: Rand McNally.

Lee, Richard B. and Irven DeVore (eds) (1968) *Man the Hunter*, Chicago: Aldine.

Lévi-Strauss, Claude (1936) "Contributions a l'étude de la organisation sociale des Indiens Bororo," *Journal de la Société Américanistes de Paris* 28: 267–304.

Longino, Helen (1990) *Science as Social Knowledge: Values and Objectivity in Scientific Inquiry*, Princeton, NJ: Princeton University Press.

Merchant, Caroline (1980) *The Death of Nature: Women, Ecology, and the Scientific Revolution*, San Francisco: Harper and Row.

Mohanty, Chandra Talpade, Anne Russo and Lourdes Torres (eds) (1991) *Third World Women and the Politics of Feminism*, Bloomington: Indiana University Press.

Morell, Virginia (1993) "Seeing Nature Through the Lens of Gender," *Science* 260: 428–429.

Nicholson, Linda (1983) "Feminist Theory: The Private and the Public," in C. Gould (ed.) *Beyond Domination*, Totowa, NJ: Rowman and Allanheld, pp. 221–232.

Ramey, Estelle (1992) "A Look at Gender in Science," review of *The Outer Circle: Women in the Scientific Community*, Harriet Zuckerman, Jonathan R. Cole, and John T. Bruer (eds), *Washington Post*, April 21.

Ringelheim, Joan (1985) "Women and the Holocaust: A Reconsideration of Research," *Signs* 10(4): 741–761.

Rogers, Susan Carol (1975) "Female Forms of Power and the Myth of Male Dominance: Models of Female/Male Interaction in Peasant Society," *American Ethnologist* 2: 727–757.

Rosaldo, Michelle Z. (1980) "The Use and Abuse of Anthropology: Reflections on Feminism and Cross-Cultural Understanding," *Signs* 5: 389–417.

Rossiter, Margaret W. (1982) *Women Scientists in America: Struggles and Strategies to 1940*, Baltimore: Johns Hopkins.

Sanday, Peggy Reeves (1974) "Female Status in the Public Domain," in Michelle Z. Rosaldo and Louise Lamphere (eds) *Women, Culture and Society*, Stanford: Stanford University Press, pp. 189–206.

Sandler, Bernice R. (1986) *The Campus Climate Revisited: Chilly for Women Faculty, Administrators, and Graduate Students*, Project on the Status and Education of Women, Washington, DC: Association of American Colleges.

Schiebinger, Londa (1989) *The Mind Has No Sex?: Women in the Origins of Modern Science*, Cambridge, Mass.: Harvard University Press.

Schrage, Michael (1990) "Does it Matter if Women Aren't Into Physics? Well, Yes," *LA Times* July 5: D1.

Science (1993) special issue on "Women in Science '93," 260: 384–432.

Slocum, Sally (1975) "Women the Gatherer: Male Bias in Anthropology," in Rayna Reiter (ed.) *Toward an Anthropology of Women*, New York: Monthly Review Press, pp. 36–50. (Originally published under the name Sally Linton, in Sue-Ellen Jacobs (ed.) *Women in Perspective: A Guide for Cross-Cultural Studies*, Urbana: University of Illinois Press, pp. 9–21.)

Sperling, Susan (1991) "Baboons with Briefcases: Feminism, Functionalism, and Sociobiology in the Evolution of Primate Gender," *Signs* 17: 1–27.

Twain, Mark (1897) "Cable from London to the Associated Press," as cited in John Bartlett (ed.) *Familiar Quotations*, New York: Little Brown and Company, p. 625.

Widnall, Sheila (1988) "Voices from the Pipeline," *Science* 241: 1740–1745.

Wilson, E. O. (1978) *On Human Nature*, Cambridge, Mass.: Harvard University Press.

Wylie, Alison (1992) "Feminist Theories of Social Power: Some Implications for a Processual Archaeology," *Norwegian Archaeology*, 25: 51–68.

Wylie, Alison (1995) "The Contexts of Activism on Climate Issues," in The Chilly Collective (eds) *Breaking Anonymity: The Chilly Climate for Women Faculty*, Waterloo, Ontario: Wilfrid Laurier University Press, pp. 29–60.

On Personhood
An Anthropological Perspective from Africa

John L. Comaroff and Jean Comaroff

Prolegomenon

Is the idea of 'the autonomous person' a European invention?

This conundrum, posed to us by colleagues in philosophy and anthropology at the University of Heidelberg in June 1997, seems straightforward enough. Even ingenuous. But hiding beneath its surface is another, altogether less innocent question, one which carries within it a silent claim: to the extent that 'the autonomous person' *is* a European invention, does its absence elsewhere imply a deficit, a failure, a measure of incivility on the part of non-Europeans? And what of the corollary: is this figure, this 'person', the end point in a world-historical telos, something to which non-occidentals are inexorably drawn as they cast off their primordial differences? Is it, in other words, a universal feature of modernity-in-the-making, a Construct in the Upper Case? Or is it merely a lower case, local euroconstruct?[1]

We begin our excursion into African conceptions of personhood in a decentring, relativising voice, the voice often assumed by anthropologists to discomfort cross-disciplinary, transcultural, suprahistorical discourses about Western

John L. Comaroff and Jean Comaroff, "On Personhood: An Anthropological Perspective from Africa," pp. 267–83 from *Social Identities* 7:2 (2001). Reprinted with permission of the publisher (Taylor and Francis Group http://www.informaworld.com).

categories, their provenance and putative universality. From our disciplinary perspective, 'the *autonomous* person', that familiar trope of European bourgeois modernity (Taylor, 1989), *is* a Eurocentric idea. And a profoundly parochial, particularistic one at that.[2] To be sure, the very notion that this generic person might constitute a universal is itself integral to its Euro-cultural construction, a part of its ideological apparatus. What is more, '*the* autonomous person' – the definite, singular article – describes an *imaginaire*, an ensemble of signs and values, a hegemonic formation: neither in Europe, nor any place else to which it has been exported, does it exist as an unmediated sociological reality (Comaroff and Comaroff, 1991, 60f). Neither, of course, does the classical contrast between (I) the self-made, self-conscious, right-bearing individual of 'modern Western society', that hyphenated Cartesian figure epitomised in the Promethean hero of Universal History (Carlyle, 1842, p. 1), and (ii) the relational, ascriptive, communalistic, inert self attributed to premodern others. As we shall see, African notions of personhood are infinitely more complicated than this tired theoretical antinomy allows (Fortes, 1973; La Fontaine, 1985; Lienhardt, 1985).[3] So, too, is the telos of Afromodernity, which is not moving, in a fixed evolutionary orbit, toward Euromodernity. For one thing, the continent, as diverse as it is large, has spawned alternative moderni*ties* in which very different notions of selfhood, civility, and publicity have taken root (Comaroff and Comaroff, 1999a). For another, there is a strong counter-teleological case to be made: a case for the radically revisionist thesis that, in sociolegal terms at least, Europe is evolving toward Africa, not the other way around. But that is a story for another time.[4]

As this suggests, we shall call into doubt the universality of 'the autonomous person' by recourse to an anthropological insistence on cultural and historical specificity (see La Fontaine, 1985). But this does not exhaust either our objectives here or the interrogative that frames them: ... *a European Invention*? Phrased thus, the question mark points toward two further problems: is the idea of 'the autonomous person' properly regarded as an invention at all? If so, is it to be attributed to Europe? The first, patently, depends on the manner in which we understand processes of cultural production; the second, on the extent to which we allow that anything in European modernity was ever fabricated endogenously – rather than in hybridising encounters with significant, usually colonised, others. We shall return, in due course, to the historical dialectics underlying the rise of post-enlightenment Western constructions of selfhood and, with them, to the answers to these questions.

First, however, let us turn to Africa. Note that we do not seek to arrive at a generic account of '*the* African conception of personhood'. There is no such thing. Our purpose is to take one good, historically-situated case: that of the Southern Tswana peoples of South Africa during the late colonial period. As it happens, much of what we shall have to say about Tswana imaginings of being-in-the-world, and about their historical anthropology, has broad resonances elsewhere across the continent. But, more to the present point, by illuminating the contrasts and consonances between African and European discourses of personhood, this case casts a sharp, prismatic light on received Western notions of the modernist self and its antinomies.

Personhood and Society in the Interiors of South Africa

Among those peoples who, during the colonial encounter, came to be known as '*the* Tswana',[5]

personhood was everywhere seen to be an intrinsically social construction. This in two senses: first, nobody existed or could be known except in relation and with reference to, even as part of, a wide array of significant others;[6] and, second, the identity of each and every one was forged, cumulatively, by an infinite, ongoing series of practical activities. *Pace* Tönnies, selfhood was not ascribed: status and role were determined by factors other than birth or genealogy, although social standing was typically represented in genealogical terms (Comaroff and Roberts, 1981, pp. 37–46).[7] For reasons having to do with its internal workings – anthropologists have long noted that the coexistence of an ideology of patrilineal descent with endogamous marriage yields social orders of this sort[8] – the Tswana world of the time was at once highly communal and highly individuated. From within, it was perceived as a rule-governed, hierarchical, and ordered universe, and yet as an enigmatical, shifting, contentious one: a universe in which people, especially men, had to 'build themselves up' – to constitute their person, position, and rank – by acquiring 'wealth in people', orchestrating ties of alliance and opposition, and 'eating' their rivals. Potentially at least, selfhood and social status, which was reckoned in terms of agnatic seniority, was always negotiable, an observation which Gluckman (1963) once claimed to be true of all African 'tribal' societies. For Tswana of the colonial era, in sum, 'the person' was a constant work-in-progress; indeed, a highly complex fabrication, whose complexity was further shaded by gender, generation, class, race, ethnicity, and religious ideology. Among other things.

But we are running ahead of ourselves. A bit more background first. The Tswana peoples today compose one of the largest ethnic groupings in South Africa.[9] At least from the late eighteenth century onward, and probably for a good time before (Legassick, 1969, p. 98), the majority of them lived in expansive chiefdoms in the central, semi-arid interior of the country; although, for more than a hundred and thirty years, many have either migrated to cities and towns across the subcontinent or have lived in small decentralised rural communities (Schapera, 1953; Comaroff and Comaroff, 1991, p. 127). Until the colonial state went about subverting their autonomy, the chiefdoms were a substantial political presence on the landscape, their economies founded on cultivation, cattle, hunting, and trade (Shillington, 1985). Each was centred on a densely-populated capital, with thousands of residents ordered into family groups and wards, surrounded by fields and cattle-posts; polities (*merafe*) stretched as far as chiefs and their subjects could pasture and protect their animals (Comaroff and Comaroff, 1990). In the spaces between were tracts of 'bush', cross-cut by pathways that linked the capitals. These trails served as vectors of trade and alliance, of warfare and raiding, and of the exchange of cultural knowledge over long distances (Comaroff and Comaroff, 1997, p. 54).

With the arrival of Protestant evangelists and European settlers from the 1820s onwards, the region became increasingly populated. And contested. White farms, trading posts, and villages began to dot the countryside. Along with the missions – themselves augmented by schools, shops, and other structures – they soon asserted a visible presence on the 'bushveld'. Inexorably, roads and transport routes followed; inexorably, autochthonous populations found more and more of their land expropriated. With the mineral revolution, Southern Tswana, already schooled by the civilising mission in bourgeois ideas of property and progress, would learn the lessons of colonial capitalism at first hand. Many migrated as neophyte proletarians to the burgeoning mining settlements just beyond the edges of their territory; some benefited greatly from the opening up of markets for their produce and their services; all became embroiled in a rapid process of class formation, in which new patterns of social distinction and ideological difference, partly phrased in the polite language of the Protestant ethic, came to divide old communities. Finally, in the 1880s, overrule inserted the British state onto this terrain. Its structures and personnel located themselves either in the white towns at the hub of farming districts or in newly erected administrative centres, from which nearby 'natives' could be governed. Often these centres were sited close to Tswana capitals and brought in yet more Europeans, generally in pursuit of trade and business; the building of a railway line across the territory in the 1890s made it accessible to people and goods otherwise

unlikely ever to have entered it. Which, in turn, exacerbated the ingress of Southern Tswana into the racialised, class-fragmented world of colonial economy and society – with all that it entailed (see e.g. Shillington, 1985; Molema, 1966).

The most obvious thing it entailed was a complicated, contradictory sociology. On one hand, colonialism spawned relations that transected the lines of race, class, and culture, creating hybrid identities and unexpected patterns of consociation (Comaroff and Comaroff, 1997, pp. 24–25).[10] On the other, it came to be represented as a sharply sundered, Manichean world, in which the cleavage between black and white, ruler and ruled, African and European was cast in stone. Elsewhere (1997, pp. 24–29), we have argued that this schismatic reality was endemic to the construction of colonial societies. We have also shown that, in its representation here – wrought largely as a result of the encounter between Southern Tswana and colonial evangelists – this irredeemable opposition came to be phrased as a contrast between *sekgoa*, European ways and means, and *setswana*, their Tswana counterpart; each being reduced from a dynamic, evanescent, open-ended, historically expansive order of signs and practices to an ahistorical essence, a fetishised object, a tradition. A culture.

In point of historical fact, the content subsumed by these two constructs, by *setswana* and *sekgoa*, changed a great deal over time; that much is clear from the documentary record. However, they continued to stand in stark antinomy throughout the colonial epoch. To be sure, their residues persist today – even as they are encompassed within an increasingly heterotopic postcolonial cultural politics. It is out of this contrast that we may begin to draw our description of what personhood, as framed in *setswana*, may be taken to have meant during the late colonial period; to have meant, that is, both as a stereotypic representation and as a set of intersubjective practices.

Of being and becoming

As we said a moment ago, the Southern Tswana world was a socially fluid, evanescent field of social relations: one in which, despite the stress on genealogical placement, the onus was on citizens, especially adult males, to 'build themselves up', to protect themselves from their enemies and rivals, to negotiate their rank and status,[11] and to extend themselves across social space by accumulating wealth in people. Of course, not everybody was equal in this respect. For one thing, there were, until well into the colonial period, various forms of servitude to be found in most chiefdoms (Schapera, 1938; see Tagart, 1933). Slaves and servants, who were regarded as semisocial beings (Moffat, 1842, p. 383; Mackenzie, 1883, p. 57), lacked the right to own property or possessions – indeed, to be self-possessed. For another thing, women were jural minors, subject to the representation of their senior male kin. In the context of everyday social life, as well as in political processes that played themselves out away from the public eye, females were anything but inert or impotent; quite the opposite (J. L. Comaroff, 1987b). But, legally speaking, they lived in the passive voice: for example, where a man might marry (*go nyala*), a woman *was* married (*go nyalwa*). For a third thing, status made a difference. Kings and commoners, the rich and the poor, ritual experts and supplicants enjoyed varying capacities to act upon the world; not least, as we shall see, because the empowering activities of some people had the effect of reducing the potency and potentiality of others.

This qualification aside, however, most Southern Tswana adults found themselves engaged constantly in a praxis of self-construction. Given the scaffolding of their universe, it could not be otherwise. Either people acted upon the world or the world acted upon them. Or both, in some proportion. Every now and again this involved dramatic confrontations over property, possessions, or position. For the most part, however, it entailed the unceasing, quotidian business of cultivating relations and fields, of husbanding animals and allies, of raising offspring and avoiding the malign intentions of others, of gradually accumulating cultural capital and cash to invest in the future. Here, then, is the first principle of contemporary Tswana personhood: it referred not to a state of being but to a state of becoming. No living self could be static. Stasis meant social death.

The principle of personhood as a mode of becoming expressed itself in every aspect of social existence. Take, for instance, marriage, an ensemble of practices often treated as the site, *par excellence*, of social formation and reproduction.[12] Earlier generations of anthropologists were wont to say that, in Africa, wedlock was a process rather than 'an event or condition' (Radcliffe-Brown, 1951, p. 49); that, as Murray (1976, 1981) has observed of Lesotho, the salient question was not whether or not two people were married, but how much. Among Southern Tswana, the creation of a conjugal bond, and of the parties to it as fully social adults, took the form of a protracted, cumulative succession of exchanges, sometimes ending only after the death of the spouses. What is more, the status of that bond was always open to (re)interpretation – as casual sex, concubinage (*bonyatsi*), living together (*ba dula mmogo*), marriage (*nyalo*) – this being facilitated by the fact that the terms used between partners (*monna* [m], *mosadi* [f]) were unmarked; they might as well have referred to someone with whom an individual cohabited the night before as to a mate of long-standing. Nor, in the flow of everyday life, was any effort made to clarify such things: relations might go undefined because, in the normal course of events, they were growing, developing, becoming. As were the human beings involved in them. It was only at moments of rupture, when the continuing present came to an abrupt end, that there was any necessity to decide what they *had been*. Or, rather, had become. And this only because different kinds of partnership involved a different disposition of assets on dissolution (Comaroff and Roberts, 1981, pp. 151–53).

Much the same stress on becoming rather than being, on persons and relations as the unfolding product of quotidian social construction, was evident in patterns of inheritance as well. By contrast to European convention, the devolution of estates across the generations was not tied to death. It began, rather, as soon as an individual reached adulthood, set about establishing a conjugal union, and had children. And it continued, as an ongoing process, throughout the life cycle. Indeed, its success was measured not by how much of a residue of property one had at death, but by how much had been distributed before – and how little had been kept back to become the object of argument among heirs (Comaroff and Roberts, 1981, pp. 175–215).

Through the cumulative, gradual disposal of property, men and (to a lesser extent) women realised themselves as parents, spouses, citizens of substance, ancestors-in-the-making; by these means they insinuated, objectified, and embodied themselves in their offspring. And ensured their perpetuity as persons.

As this suggests, the foundational notion of being-as-becoming, of the sentient self as active agent in the world, was so taken-for-granted that it went largely unsaid. Throughout life (in embodied form) and even after death (as a narrated presence), the person was a subject with the potential to engage in the act of completing and augmenting him- or herself. Take just one, very mundane demonstration of the point:

> In 1970, in the course of doing ethnographic fieldwork in Mafikeng, we were sitting in a domestic courtyard with the family of a ward headman, Mhengwa Letsholo. An elderly female neighbour, obviously well past childbearing age, walked across the public meeting space just beyond the homestead wall. 'There goes Mme-Seleka', said the headman's wife, gesturing towards her. 'Mme-' denotes 'mother of', although its connotative fan is rather broad. Trying to place her in social space, one of us asked whether she had sons or daughters. 'Not yet', said the headman, 'No, not yet'. At face value, this seemed a refractory answer: there was no doubt that, given her age, Mme-Seleka was not about to fall pregnant. But it made perfect sense. For one thing, there were conventional means – such as the levirate and sororate – by which offspring might be 'born' to a person who could not physically produce them. But there was another, less pragmatic dimension to Mhengwa's response: to answer in the absolute negative would have been to consign the woman's active life to the past tense, to pronounce her socially dead. As long as she was a sentient being, as long as she was still in the process of becoming, some form of maternity was always possible. 'Not yet' implies the continuous present, just as 'no' puts closure to something that once may have been but now no longer is.

The only time that people stopped 'becoming' was when they fell victim to witchcraft or were 'eaten' by someone more powerful. In the former case, they were either immobilised by illness or mysteriously rendered inert, their capacity for productive activity negated (see Munn, 1986). In the latter, which implied feminisation, they were reduced to dependency and eventually lost all self-determination; typically, they ceased to toil on their own account, working instead at the behest of their masters and patrons. 'Absorbed by another personality' was the way in which one early nineteenth-century missionary-ethnographer described this state of arrested becoming (Willoughby, 1932, p. 227). A second observer, J. Tom Brown (1926, pp. 137–38), wrote an unusually vivid description of men who, having been thus consumed, suffered an eclipse of their personhood:

> When a man's relatives notice that his whole nature is changed, that the light of the mind is darkened and character has deteriorated so that it may be said that the real manhood is dead, though the body still lives; when they realise that ... the human is alienated from ... his kith and kin, they apply to him a name (sebibi or sehihi), which signifies that though the body lives and moves it is only a grave, a place where something has died or been killed. The essential manhood is dead. It is no uncommon thing to hear a person spoken of as being dead when he stands before you visibly alive. When this takes place it always means that there has been an overshadowing of the true relationships of life ...

Sefifi [sehihi], the term for this state of non-being, is the same as that for 'death pollution'. Interestingly, it describes a condition strikingly similar to the figure of the zombie, which has recently appeared in the South African countryside as part of a moral panic about joblessness in the postcolony (Comaroff and Comaroff, 1999b). It speaks of an erasure of self-determination; of empty shells of humanity who toil mindlessly for others; of a slippage into the passive, past tense. But how, by contrast, do sentient social actors construct themselves? Wherein lies their mode of producing personhood?

On producing personhood

The production of personhood here, we reiterate, was an irreducibly social process; this despite – or, perhaps, because of – the fact that, given the workings of the Southern Tswana social universe, initiative lay with individuals for 'building themselves up'. The emphasis on self-construction was embodied, metonymically and metapragmatically, in the idea of *tiro*, labour.[13] *Go dira*, in the vernacular, meant 'to make', 'to do', or 'to cause to happen'. It covered a wide spectrum of activities, from cultivation, cooking, and creating a family to pastoralism, politics, and the performance of ritual (J. Comaroff, 1985; Comaroff and Comaroff, 1991, 140ff). *Tiro* was, still is, generally translated as '[a] work' (Brown, 1931, p. 308), and accented the *act* of fabrication. It yielded value in the form of persons, things, and relations, although it might be undone by sorcery and other malign forces (see below). But *tiro* was not an abstract quality, a commodity to be bought or sold. It could not exist as alienable labour power. Southern Tswana often said that, in the past, even the energies of a serf were not to be exchanged, let alone purchased. They were only available to his or her master by virtue of a *relationship* of interdependence; hints, here, of Hegel. Work, in short, was the positive, relational aspect of human social activity; of the making of self and others in the course of everyday life.

Not only were social beings made and remade by *tiro*, but the product – namely, personhood – was inseparable from the process of production itself. As Alverson (1978, p. 132) has noted, 'an individual not only produce[d] for himself, but actually produce[d] his entitlement to be a social person'. This was captured in the various inflections of *go dira*. Its simple reflexive form, *go itira*, 'to contrive oneself' or 'to pose as', carried ambiguous moral implications. It spoke of antisocial, egocentric self-enhancement; hence the common usage *go itira motho* (lit. 'to make oneself a distinct person') connoted 'to be proud' or 'haughty'. *Go itira* contrasted with *go itirela* – the reflexive extension of *direla* ('work for') – which translated as 'to make (work, do) for oneself' in an affirmative sense. For Tswana in Botswana during the 1970s, according to Alverson (1978, p. 134), *itirela* still referred to the accretion of riches in family and social relations, in cattle and clients, in position and possessions; all of which was also held, hegemonically, to contribute to the common good. The creation of these forms of value was dubbed 'great work' – the effect of which was to extend the self through ties of interdependence, often by means of objects. Thus the significance of property, most notably beasts, was that it both indexed *and* capitalised leverage over people. By extension, power was taken here to be a measure of command within a complex, labile field of material and signal exchanges. Far from being understood in terms of individual autonomy or self-sufficiency, its signature was control over the social production of reality itself.

The concept of self-construction – of *tiro*, 'work' and *itirela*, 'to make [for] oneself' – then, projected a world in which the 'building up' of persons in relation to each other, the accumulation of wealth and rank, and the sustenance of a strong, centralised polity (*morafe*) were indivisible aspects of everyday practice. The object of that practice, minimally, was to avoid social death, to continue producing oneself by producing people and things; maximally, it was to do 'great works'. But just as individuals were presumed to be unequal in their capacity to construct themselves (see above), so not everyone was able to toil in the same kinds of way. Above all, male labour differed from female labour. Before the introduction of the plough – and after it, save for wealthy cultivators – women were associated primarily with agriculture, domesticity, and reproduction. The racial capitalism of the colonial state, and especially of the apartheid regime, played into this by coercing men into migrant wage employment away from home; concomitantly, their wives and daughters remained in the countryside. In addition to subsistence farming, these women were the source of the most basic value of all, human life. But their fertility also yielded polluting heat (*bothitho*) that could spoil the activities of their husbands, fathers, and brothers; even Christian converts evinced concern at this danger. Thus they were said to need physical confinement, denied an active role in the public sphere, and kept away from cattle, the most prized form of capital. Men, by contrast, were cool (*tshididi*): they had the qualities necessary for raising stock, for effective social production, and for the management of the commonweal. While wives did hold fields on their own account, had their own granaries, and exercised some control over the disposal of their harvest, their 'works' – the fruits of their labour pains and labour power (see Jeffery *et al.*, 1989) – provided the material base, the mundane commodities, on which male politics, law, and ritual depended. The point was made repeatedly in Tswana poetics: for example, the origin myth of the male initiation, the most comprehensive of their *rites de passage*, told how society was born when the raw fertility of females was domesticated by men and put to collective ends (J. Comaroff, 1985).

Personhood, negation, and self-defence

The ongoing process of self-construction was, as we said above, under constant threat of countervailing forces; forces inherent in the social world itself. Because men, especially agnatic rivals, sought to 'eat' one another, and because sorcery was an ever-present danger, work also involved protecting one's self and one's dependents from 'being undone'. *Dirologa*, the reversive extension of *dira*, described this mode of destruction. People took great pains to fortify their homesteads and fields against attack – and sometimes to attack their adversaries, real or imagined, before being hit themselves. Nor was this true only of 'traditionalists'. In the 1930s, Christian elites, deeply committed to 'private interest and competition', were observed – by a Tswana anthropologist – to deploy magical means to doctor their crops and cattle in order to safeguard them,[14] also, to 'get ahead'. We observed the same thing, sometimes fused with Christian ritual, in the 1970s.

Of all the available preventive measures against 'being undone', however, the most fundamental, and the most effective, lay in the fabrication of personhood itself. In anticipation of the postmodern stress on multiple subjectivity, and in a manner evocative of the partible *persona* described for Melanesia (see note 3), Southern Tswana were careful to fragment and refract the self in presenting its exteriors to the world. This derived from an ethnotheory of power/knowledge based on two foundational, if unspoken, axioms. First, because that self was not confined to the corporeal body – it ranged over the sociophysical space-time occupied by the sum total of its relations, presences, enterprises – anything that acted on its traces might affect it for good or ill; which is why human beings could be attacked through their footprints,

immobilised by curses, enabled by ancestral invocation, undermined or strengthened by magical operations on their houses, their clothes, or their animals. Second, to the degree that anyone was 'known' to others, she or he became vulnerable to their machinations, to being consumed by them. Conversely, empowerment, protective or predatory, lay in the capacity to conceal: to conceal purposes, possessions, propensities, practices – and, even more subtly, to conceal concealment, to hide the fact that anything at all was being hidden.

Put the two axioms together and the corollary is obvious: it made sense only to present partial, refractory aspects of one's person – of one's property, projects, interests – to the various others who shared the same coordinates of the life-world. Hence the people with whom an individual worked, or engaged in economic enterprises, were shown a single facet; political allies saw another; those with whom s/he prayed or played, yet another; and so on. Clearly, given the nature of everyday existence here, and the local predilection for gossip and scandal, there were inevitable overlaps; boundaries were breached, what was masked occasionally became transparent. Still, the effort to sustain the partibility of personhood, thus to empower the self and its undertakings, was a fundamental premise of being-through-becoming. So much so that it went utterly unremarked. But it was revealed, at the one moment in the life-cycle at which the coherence of biography was enacted: death. Echoes, *here*, of Sartrean existentialism.

The integration of the fractal human subject occurred toward the end of his or her funeral. In a public ceremony known as *tatolo*, people arose to narrate that part of the career of the deceased of which they, in particular, knew; and so, piece by piece, a composite portrait emerged, a life took shape from its shards. In the 1970s, we were told more than once that *tatolo* was the most engaging part of a burial – not least to mourning relatives, for whom the synoptic accounting was sometimes as much as a surprise as it was to relative strangers. In a universe in which social knowledge was a matter of insatiable interest and informational value, it is no wonder that *tatolo* held such fascination: it represented an existential *denouement*, the summation of a biography that had, until now, been an inscrutable work-in-progress. And was about to move onto an altogether different, even less scrutable plane. In the case of persons of power, the fascination grew exponentially: *tatolo* stood to reveal their ways and means, their secrets of being-and-becoming, in this complex, labyrinthine social world.

Conclusion: The Dialectics of Encounter

The Southern Tswana conception of personhood, in sum, was part and parcel of a distinct, historically-wrought universe of meaning and action; an Afro-modernist universe in which labour, the self, and the social were mutually constituting. Shades, here, of Marx. This conception was at once different and yet similar to its European counterpart. The latter had come to be represented, ideologically, in the liberal language of possessive individualism (Macpherson, 1962), a language alien to vernacular African experience – especially because it appeared to background the social, to relegate it to mere 'context'. But, *pace* the conventions of Western knowledge, the antinomy between Euro-individualism and African communitarianism, past and present, is profoundly misleading. For one thing, as anthropologists never tire of pointing out, personhood, however it may be culturally formulated, is *always* a social creation – just as it is *always* fashioned by the exigencies of history. This is as true in Europe and the USA as it is in Africa or Asia; as true of the eighteenth as it is of the twenty-first century. And it remains true under epochal conditions in which the very existence of Society is called into question. Or even, as in Britain of the Thatcher years (Tester, 1992; Comaroff and Comaroff, 1999a), flatly denied.

Similarly the stress on the social and communitarian foundations of African personhood. Nowhere in Africa were ideas of individuality ever absent (Lienhardt, 1985). Individual*ism*, another creature entirely, might not have been at home here before the postcolonial age; not, at least, outside of Protestant elites. But, each in their own way, African societies *did*, in times past, have a place for individuality, personal agency, property, privacy, biography, signature, and authored action upon the world. What differed was their particular substance, the manner

of their ontological embeddedness in the social, their ideological formulation. All of which ought to underscore, yet again, why crude contrasts between European and African selfhood – or the reduction of either to essentialising, stereotypic adjectives of difference – make little sense; why sociological and semantic similarities may be obscured by dissimilarities in languages of representation.

In this respect, Michael Welker has offered the term 'autoplexy' to signify the mode of personhood we describe for the late colonial Tswana world.[15] a mode of personhood, as he glosses it, which involved 'playing with' a multiplicity of shifting roles and identities to secure freedom of action and social position. This form of play in a fluid, intricate field of relations, Welker concludes, produced something analogous in Africa to the autonomous individual of the post-Enlightenment Western imagination. Perhaps. The more fundamental point, however, is that the idea of 'autoplexy', and the analysis to which it applies, seeks to pay due regard to the sheer complexity of African ideas of personhood. Also to treat them as parallel to, and commensurate with, their European counterpart; as their coeval rather than their benighted precursor.

We have situated this account in the late colonial period, not in 'traditional' Africa. As we intimated at the outset, no such thing exists, least of all in respect of the signs and practices of personhood. Among Southern Tswana, those signs and practices altered a great deal over the long run. In part, this was due to the encounter with Protestant missionaries, who evangelised the South African interior from the 1820s onwards, and who bore with them a strong commitment to liberal individualism and right-bearing selfhood. The Protestants essayed contradictory perceptions of Tswana subjectivity. On one hand, 'the natives' were described as 'primitive communists', savages with no individuality or sense of self; yet they were constantly accused of brute 'selfishness' and 'greed', even of a lack of 'natural affection' for others.[16] All of which made it necessary to instil in them a capacity for self-possession and an appreciation of refined individualism. For their part, Southern Tswana found the Europeans – whose idea of labour lacked the grammatical range and subtle semantic inflections of *tiro* – to be perverse in their insistence on private property and individual rights. To translate the discourse of toil into the vernacular, the Christians put *itira*, 'to contrive oneself' (in the morally ambiguous, self-seeking sense of the term) over *itirela*, 'to make oneself' in a positive, socially accountable manner. What is more, they stressed the value of contracts, titles, and deeds, a mode of textualising relations that, to the Africans, appeared to make humans into 'paper persons'; it also disembedded exchange from its social referents and rendered visible what ought to be concealed, thus opening people up to being 'eaten' more easily than before. To wit, the reduction of material transactions to these instruments of legality was referred to, by Tswana in the 1880s, as 'the English mode of warfare' (Mackenzie 1887, pp. 1, 80).

As this suggests, the dialectics of encounter were far from straightforward. For all the differences between European and Tswana sensibilities, Euro-Christian concepts of self and virtuous labour had strong resonances with indigenous notions of 'great work' and being-as-becoming. As a consequence, the transcultural discourse of personhood here bore within it a

number of legible, transitive signs; signs that pointed toward an ideological conjuncture for those who drew near to the church, adopted the practices of bourgeois civility, and entered the black elites spawned by colonial political economy. It also set in train a long conversation among Southern Tswana themselves about selfhood and civilisation (see e.g. Molema, 1920; Plaatje, 1996) – a conversation modulated by processes of class formation and social distinction. While some found the liberal individualism of *sekgoa* ('European ways') highly appealing and took on its terms, others repudiated it entirely, even while being affected by it. Yet others forged hybridity out of the antinomy. They still do.

The conversation continues today across the northern reaches of the South African countryside, albeit in altered circumstances. Indeed, it is has become more fervent as anxieties over the future of 'community' and 'culture', now named as such, grow into a populist postcolonial obsession. Amidst gathering talk of human rights and civil society, of the celebration of autochthony and authenticity, the vision of an African Renaissance arises to counter the rampant excesses of European modes of being-in-the world.

Notes

1 We are hardly the first to ask this question, of course. See, for just one example, Burridge (1979, p. 4). The individual, he says, lies 'at the center of our civilisation'. Is 'the development of [this figure] a universal in human experience, or is it in some sense culturally specific?'

2 Also one with a complex history, as Mauss ([1938] 1985) classically pointed out; see also MacFarlane (1978). Mauss, whose own characterisation of the development of personhood was distinctly evolutionary, took pains to point out that 'other societies have held very different notions of the self, and [that] each society's notion is intimately connected with its form of social organisation' (Carrithers *et al.*, 1985, p. vii); echoes here, too, of Durkheim, for whom the modern person is a 'product of specific social factors' (Collins, 1985, p. 63).

3 Similarly, for example, Melanesian notions of personhood, as Konrad (1998, p. 645) has recently reminded us, citing the seminal work of Strathern (1988) and Wagner (1991), among others; for a rather different, older account, however, see Read

(1955) – and, on the contrast between Melanesia and India, Busby (1997).

4 We make this point, albeit briefly and illustratively, in Bhabha and Comaroff (2002). We shall take it up in more detail in the near future.

5 On the ethnogenesis of 'the' Southern Tswana peoples during the early colonial period, see Comaroff and Comaroff (1997, pp. 387–95; 1991, pp. 306–8); also, more generally, on the construction of ethnic identity, see J. L. Comaroff (1987a).

6 The person, in short, was irreducible to an autonomous *individual*. A point of definitional clarification is in order here. As La Fontaine (1985, pp. 124–26) notes, orthodox anthropological usage has long distinguished the person from both the individual and the self. The individual refers to a biologically distinct, socially discrete, indivisible being, a unity of body and mind; the person, to an ensemble of social roles and relations; the self, to a unique identity. In analytic practice, however, this distinction is often blurred; to be sure, it is difficult to sustain – especially in the

West, where, given the ideological predominance of individualism (see MacFarlane, 1978; Dumont, 1970), there has long been a tendency to collapse the person into the individual, and both into the self. In late colonial Africa, there is the opposite tendency: to see the individual purely in terms of personhood.

7   The received opposition between ascription and achievement, like many of the great antimonies of modernist social theory, has played a major part in stereotypic (mis)perceptions of 'African personhood'; note, again, the spurious singular. We would argue that nowhere in Africa does an 'ascriptive' society (or, indeed, one of 'organic solidarity') exist outside of the imagination of social theorists (see J. L. Comaroff, 1978).

8   See, classically, Murphy and Kasdan (1959, 1967); also, Barth (1973) and Comaroff and Roberts (1981, pp. 31–33). For here, it is enough to note that unions among close kin have the effect of generating relations that are overlapping and inherently ambiguous, relations at once agnatic, matrilateral, and affinal. Among Tswana these forms of connection carried quite different, even inimical, social expectations; they had, therefore, to be reduced to one thing or another in the pragmatic course of everyday life – which, of necessity, made them an ongoing object of negotiation (see Comaroff and Comaroff, 1981).

9   They form the predominant population of neighbouring Botswana as well; but we are concerned here with those Southern Tswana who live in the Northwest Province of South Africa. Due to the unreliability of census data published by the apartheid regime, and to the fact that ethnic identities have long been somewhat malleable in this part of the world, it is impossible to establish the precise number of Tswana in the country. Somewhere in excess of 1.5 million is probably a fair estimate, however.

10 See, in this respect, Marks (1978) on Zululand.

11 For an account of the ways in which rules of rank and status were negotiated, see J. L. Comaroff (1978); also, see again note 8 for the effect of endogamous marriage practices on the ambiguity and negotiability of social ties.

12 It is striking how – at least until recently in the history of anthropological thought – marriage featured as *the* atom of social formation in all major theoretical traditions. Thus, for example, notwithstanding their differences, structural functionalist and structuralist approaches, in the guise of descent and alliance theory, agreed that marriage rules (especially prohibitions) were fundamental in the construction of non-Western societies; for foundational works, see e.g. Fortes (1953, 1969) and Lévi-Strauss (1969). Even revisionist Marxist approaches emphasised the significance of marriage and its prestations for structuring relations of production and exploitation in 'precapitalist formations' (see e.g. Meillassoux, 1964, 1972, 1981; Collier 1988).

13 Elsewhere (1987) we deal at length with the opposition between *tiro*, self-possessed labour, and *mmèrèkò* (from *bereka*, [Afrikaans]), wage work for others, usually whites. The contrast between these two terms – each had a broad fan of referents – was of enormous salience to Southern Tswana in the late colonial years. It underlay the way in which they imagined, and navigated, South African economy and society under apartheid.

14 See Comaroff and Comaroff (1997, pp. 153–54) for details. The anthropologist was Z. K. Matthews, one of South Africa's great black scholars and political figures, whose field notes are housed in the Botswana National Archives.

15 Welker outlined his concept of *autoplexy* to us in a letter (Heidelberg, 16 September 1998): 'a person's playing and shifting with a multiplicity of ascribed and assumed roles and identity patterns to secure individual freedom and importance, in short: to use this sort of complexity in analogous ways to the use of modern autonomy'. Clearly, the concept is intended to elide *autonomy* with *complexity*. We have paraphrased Welker's words here to fit more closely the terms of our own analysis.

16 For detailed references, see Comaroff and Comaroff (1991, 1997); also, for a specific case, Dachs (1972, p. 695).

References

Alverson, H. (1978) *Mind in the Heart of Darkness: Value and Self-Identity Among the Tswana of Southern Africa*, New Haven: Yale University Press.

Barth, F. (1973) 'Descent and Marriage Reconsidered', in J. Goody (ed.) *The Character of Kinship*, Cambridge: Cambridge University Press.

Bhabha, H. and J. L. Comaroff (2002) 'Speaking of Postcoloniality, in the Continuous Present: a Conversation between Homi Bhabha and John Comaroff', in D. T. Goldberg and L. A. Quayson (eds) *Relocating Postcolonialism*, Oxford: Basil Blackwell.

Brown, J. T. (1926) *Among the Bantu Nomads: a Record of Forty Years Spent among the Bechuana etc*, London: Seeley Service.

Brown, J. T. (1931) *Secwana Dictionary*, Tiger Kloof: London Missionary Society.

Burridge, K. (1979) *Someone, No One: an Essay on Individuality*, Princeton: Princeton University Press.

Busby, C. (1997) 'Permeable and Partible Persons: a Comparative Analysis of Gender and Body in South India and Melanesia', *Journal of the Royal Anthropological Institute* (N.S.), 3: 261–78.

Carlyle, T. (1842) *On Heroes, Hero-Worship, and the Heroic in History*, New York: D. Appleton.

Carrithers, M., S. Collins and S. Lukes (1985) 'Preface', in M. Carrithers, S. Collins and S. Lukes (eds) *The Category of the Person: Anthropology, Philosophy, History*, Cambridge: Cambridge University Press.

Collier, J. F (1988) *Marriage and Inequality in Classless Societies*, Stanford: Stanford University Press.

Collins, S. (1985) 'Categories, Concepts or Predicaments? Remarks on Mauss's Use of Philosophical Terminology', in M. Carrithers, S. Collins and S. Lukes (eds) *The Category of the Person: Anthropology, Philosophy, History*, Cambridge: Cambridge University Press.

Comaroff, J. (1985) *Body of Power, Spirit of Resistance: The Culture and History of a South African People*, Chicago: University of Chicago Press.

Comaroff, J. and J. L. Comaroff (1990) 'Goodly Beasts and Beastly Goods: Cattle and Commodities in a South African Context', *American Ethnologist*, 17: 195–216.

Comaroff, J. (1991) *Of Revelation and Revolution*, Volume I, *Christianity, Colonialism, and Consciousness in South Africa*, Chicago: University of Chicago Press.

Comaroff, J. (1997) *Of Revelation and Revolution*, Volume II, *The Dialectics of Modernity on a South African Frontier*, Chicago: University of Chicago Press.

Comaroff, J. (1999a) 'Introduction', in J. L. and J. Comaroff (eds) *Civil Society and the Political Imagination in Africa*, Chicago: University of Chicago Press.

Comaroff, J. (1999b) 'Occult Economies and the Violence of Abstraction: Notes from the South African Postcolony', *American Ethnologist*, 26 (3): 279–301.

Comaroff, J. L. (1978) 'Rules and Rulers: Political Processes in a Tswana Chiefdom', *Man* (NS), 13: 1–20.

Comaroff, J. L. (1987a) 'Of Totemism and Ethnicity: Consciousness, Practice and the Signs of Inequality', *Ethnos*, 52: 301–23.

Comaroff, J. L. (1987b) '*Sui Generis*: Feminism, Kinship Theory, and Structural Domains', in J. Collier and S. Yanagisako (eds) *Gender and Kinship: Essays Toward a Unified Theory*, Stanford: Stanford University Press.

Comaroff, J. L. and J. Comaroff (1981) 'The Management of Marriage in a Tswana Chiefdom', in E. J. Krige and J. L. Comaroff (eds) *Essays on African Marriage in Southern Africa*, Cape Town: Juta.

Comaroff, J. L. (1987) 'The Madman and the Migrant: Work and Labor in the Historical Consciousness of a South African People', *American Ethnologist*, 14: 191–209.

Comaroff, J. L. and S. A. Roberts (1981) *Rules and Processes: the Cultural Logic of Dispute in an African Context*, Chicago: University of Chicago Press.

Dachs, A. J. (1972) 'Missionary Imperialism: the Case of Bechuanaland', *Journal of African History*, 13: 647–58.

Dumont, L. (1970) *Homo Hierarchicus: an Essay on the Caste System*, translated by M. Sainsbury, Chicago: University of Chicago Press.

Fortes, M. (1953) 'The Structure of Unilineal Descent Groups', *American Anthropologist*, 55: 17–41.

Fortes, M. (1969) *Kinship and the Social Order: The Legacy of Lewis Henry Morgan*, London: Routledge & Kegan Paul.

Fortes, M. (1973) 'On the Concept of the Person Among the Tallensi', in G. Dieterlen (ed.) *La Notion de Personne en Afrique Noire, Paris 11–17 Octobre 1971*, Paris: Éditions du Centre National de la Recherche Scientifique.

Gluckman, M. (1963) *Order and Rebellion in Tribal Africa*, London: Cohen & West.

Jeffery, P., R. Jeffery and A. Lyon (1989) *Labour Pains and Labour Power: Women and Childbirth in India*, London: Zed Books.

Konrad, M. (1998) 'Ova Donation and Symbols of Substance: Some Variations on the Theme of Sex, Gender and the Partible Body', *Journal of the Royal Anthropological Institute* (N.S.), 4: 643–67.

La Fontaine, J. S. (1985) 'Person and Individual: Some Anthropological Reflections', in M. Carrithers, S. Collins and S. Lukes (eds) *The Category of the Person: Anthropology, Philosophy, History*, Cambridge: Cambridge University Press.

Legassick, M. C. (1969) 'The Sotho-Tswana Peoples before 1800', in L. M. Thompson (ed.) *African Societies in Southern Africa*, London: Heinemann Educational Books.

Lévi-Strauss, C. (1969) *The Elementary Structures of Kinship*, revised edn, translated by J. H. Bell, J. R. von Sturmer and R. Needham, London: Social Science Paperbacks in association with Eyre & Spottiswoode (first edition, 1949).

Lienhardt, G. (1985) 'Self: Public, Private. Some African Representations', in M. Carrithers, S. Collins and S. Lukes (eds) *The Category of the Person: Anthropology, Philosophy, History*, Cambridge: Cambridge University Press.

MacFarlane, A. (1978) *The Origins of English Individualism*, Oxford: Basil Blackwell.

Mackenzie, J. (1883) *Day Dawn in Dark Places: A Story of Wanderings and Work in Bechwanaland*, London: Cassell. Reprinted 1969; New York: Negro Universities Press.

Mackenzie, J. (1887) *Austral Africa: Losing It or Ruling It*, 2 volumes. London: Sampson Low, Marston, Searle & Rivington.

Macpherson, C. B. (1962) *The Political Theory of Possessive Individualism: Hobbes to Locke*, Oxford: Oxford University Press.

Marks, S. (1978) 'Natal, the Zulu Royal Family and the Ideology of Segregation', *Journal of Southern African Studies*, 4: 172–94.

Mauss, M. (1985) 'A Category of the Human Mind: the Notion of Person; the Notion of Self', translated by W. D. Halls, in M. Carrithers, S. Collins and S. Lukes (eds) *The Category of the Person: Anthropology, Philosophy, History*, Cambridge: Cambridge University Press (first published, 1938).

Meillassoux, C. (1964) *Anthropologie Economique des Gouro de Côte d'Ivoire*, Paris and The Hague: Mouton.

Meillassoux, C. (1972) 'From Reproduction to Production', *Economy and Society*, 1 (1): 93–105.

Meillassoux, C. (1981) *Maidens, Meal and Money: Capitalism and the Domestic Economy*, Cambridge: Cambridge University Press.

Moffat, R. (1842) *Missionary Labours and Scenes in Southern Africa*, London: John Snow. Reprinted 1969; New York: Johnson Reprint Corporation.

Molema, S. M. (1920) *The Bantu, Past and Present*, Edinburgh: W. Green & Son.

Molema, S. M. (1966) *Montshiwa, Barolong Chief and Patriot 1815–96*, Cape Town: Struik.

Munn, N. D. (1986) *The Fame of Gawa: A Symbolic Study of Value Transformation in a Massim (Papua New Guinea) Society*, Cambridge and New York: Cambridge University Press.

Murphy, R. F. and L. Kasdan (1959) 'The Structure of Parallel Cousin Marriage', *American Anthropologist*, 61: 17–29.

Murphy, R. F. (1967) 'Agnation and Endogamy: Some Further Considerations', *Southwestern Journal of Anthropology*, 23: 1–14.

Murray, C. (1976) 'Marital Strategy in Lesotho: The Redistribution of Migrant Earnings', *African Studies*, 35 (2): 99–121.

Murray, C. (1981) 'The Symbolism and Politics of *Bohali*: Household Recruitment and Marriage by Installment in Lesotho', in E. J. Krige and J. L. Comaroff (eds) *Essays on African Marriage in Southern Africa*, Cape Town: Juta.

Plaatje, S. T. (1996) *Selected Writings*, edited by B. Willan, Johannesburg: Witwatersrand University Press.

Radcliffe-Brown, A. R. (1951) 'Introduction', in A. R. Radcliffe-Brown and D. Forde (eds) *African Systems of Kinship and Marriage*, London: Oxford University Press for the International African Institute.

Read, K. (1955) 'Morality and the Concept of the Person among the Gahuku-Gama', *Oceania*, 25 (4): 233–82.

Schapera, I. (1938) *A Handbook of Tswana Law and Custom*, London: Oxford University Press for the International African Institute.

Schapera, I. (1953) *The Tswana*, London: International African Institute (revised edition, I. Schapera and J. L. Comaroff, 1991).

Shillington, K. (1985) *The Colonisation of the Southern Tswana, 1870–1900*, Johannesburg: Ravan Press.

Strathern, M. (1988) *The Gender of the Gift: Problems with Women and Problems with Society in Melanesia*, Berkeley: University of California Press.

Tagart, E. S. B. (1933) 'Report on the Conditions Existing among the Masarwa in the Bamangwato Reserve of the Bechuanaland Protectorate', *Official Gazette of the High Commissioner for South Africa*, 122 (1,661, 12 May).

Taylor, C. (1989) *Sources of the Self: The Making of Modern Identity*, Cambridge, MA: Harvard University Press.

Tester, K. (1992) *Civil Society*, London: Routledge.

Wagner, R. (1991) 'The Fractal Person', in M. Godelier and M. Strathern (eds) *Big Men and Great Men: Personifications of Power in Melanesia*, Cambridge: Cambridge University Press.

Willoughby, W.C. (1932) *Nature-Worship and Taboo: Further Studies in 'The Soul of the Bantu'*, Hartford, CT: The Hartford Seminary Press.

11

Girling the Girl and Boying the Boy
The Production of Adulthood in Ancient Mesoamerica

Rosemary A. Joyce

Introduction

Most Mesoamerican archaeology has taken adults as its representative subjects. Childhood is a significant focus in some demographic studies (Storey 1992). Mortuary analyses include discussion of burial treatment of infants and juveniles, rarely considering the experience of childhood or transitions in the life course. Some discussion of lifecycle rituals is embedded in historical accounts of specific Classic Maya rulers (Schele and Miller 1986: 114, 136–7, 148–50: Schele and Freidel 1990: 235–40, 470–1). Studies of figurines have led analysts to suggest connections with stages in the life course and life-cycle rituals (Cyphers Guillén 1993; Lesure 1997; Serra Puche and Durand 1998).

The most extensive discussions of childhood and the lifecycle in Mesoamerica, based on sixteenth-century ethnohistoric sources, examine the experience of childhood and adult concerns with control of children among the Aztecs (e.g. Calnek 1974, 1988, 1992; Clendinnen 1991; Kellogg 1995: 88–91). I use Aztec narratives about the social construction of adults to inform an understanding of archaeological artefacts and sites as media and settings for such lifecycle

Rosemary Joyce "Girling the Girl and Boying the Boy: The Production of Adulthood in Ancient Mesoamerica," pp. 473–83 from *World Archaeology* 31 (2000). Reprinted with permission of the publisher (Taylor and Francis Group http://www.informaworld.com).

transformations. These complex verbal and visual narratives describe events in the lives of infants, children and young adults of both sexes and a variety of social classes and occupational statuses.

I deliberately juxtapose discussion of early village sites in Mesoamerica, dating to the Formative period (c. 1500–500 BC), with the Aztec material because they were linked in an historical *longue durée*. The Mesoamerican *longue durée* was shaped not only by conservative reproduction of basic economic relations but also by conservatism in the reproduction of social personhood (Joyce 1998, 2000; compare Cobb 1991: 171–4; Smith 1992). While specific conjunctures within the *longue durée* experienced significant change, not all practices were equally transformed. I argue that social construction of the person, beginning within the household, was as conservative as subsistence technology. Mesoamerican archaeology provides abundant evidence of material practices through which basic ways of being in the world were continually re-created throughout this *longue durée* (Joyce 2000).

Aztec texts emphasize physical discipline of the body of the child to produce a properly decorous adult. This, I argue, is due to the social value placed on reproduction of embodied identification with tradition. Judith Butler (1993: 12–16, 101–19) describes the social production of embodied existence as resulting from repeated *performance* of particular ways of being that are represented within a society as *citational precedents*. The admonitions and physical discipline recorded in Aztec sources were directed towards instilling in youth a desire to match citational precedents presented by the examples and words of their elders. Lifecycle rituals involved careful repetition of actions, a compulsive iteration like that which Butler suggests is an inevitable outcome of consciousness of the unavoidable gap between a citational precedent and an individual performance (Butler 1993: 95, 107–9).

Presented at birth as raw materials like precious stones and feathers that were shaped into body ornaments, Aztec children were gradually socialized through habitual action, costume and ornaments. They achieved a peak of differentiated gender identity in the early teens, when three approved genders (potentially reproductive male, potentially reproductive female and celibate) were distinguished. Through lifecycle rituals, punctuating the continuous experience of embodied difference, individual chronological age was subordinated to socially recognized membership in common age-grades.

Sources for the Aztecs are unusually rich, allowing construction of a more complete narrative of lifecycle transformations than is possible for other Mesoamerican societies. Bodily markings and disciplines of work, worship and appearance were also deployed in lifecycle rituals described in much less detail in ethnohistoric accounts of Postclassic Yucatec Maya states (Joyce 1994). These late Aztec and Maya case studies suggest avenues for interpretation of material culture and social and political life of earlier societies. The conservative and repetitive nature of Mesoamerican lifecycle rituals results in their archaeological visibility as ordered material remains, for example, burials. The Mesoamerican emphasis on creating bodily signs as part of lifecycle rituals confers on even disordered material remains the potential to inform us about changes in the life course.

Items of costume should be considered as potential media for lifecycle transitions, and contrasts in their patterns of use evaluated in light of the possible importance of costume as a medium for materializing properly socialized embodied persons. Indeed, if distinctions in body modification like those described for the Aztec were already being employed earlier, then all distinctions in bodily appearance, as abstracted in representational media, must be considered potential evidence of lifecycle transitions. Finally, even understandings of the use of different spatial settings must be re-evaluated with the potential enactment of lifecycle rituals in mind.

Aztec Sources and Their Limits

Out of the sixteenth-century collision between European conquerors and native peoples came a literature reflecting the mutual task of understanding the other that united native peoples and Spanish newcomers. Because they served many purposes in dialogues about power, these texts cannot be uncritically treated as documentation about the prehispanic world, but must be read as products of interested writers (Gillespie 1998). I employ two major sources to examine Aztec life transitions. In the *Florentine Codex* (Sahagun 1951, 1953, 1954, 1961, 1969), Sahagun assembled texts in Nahuatl provided by elite male informants to native students trained to read Spanish and their own Nahuatl, and glossed them in Spanish (see Calnek 1974 and essays in Klor de Alva et al. 1988). It is believed that Sahagun made use of a questionnaire to elicit information, channelling responses. Surviving versions of the work assembled these already-structured responses in successive European orders. In the version represented in the *Florentine Codex*, we are faced with a document far from a straightforward description of life in the Aztec world. Obvious biases include substitution in the text of a normative male actor for mixed males and females (Brown 1983), and clerical concerns with labelling indigenous religious beliefs and practices as errors (Burkhart 1997: 27). Because lifecycle ceremonies were religious, these concerns affected the way they were recorded. Performance of lifecycle rituals was noted only where Sahagun's interests intersected the individual life course. Most information available about birth and marriage, both times of marked change in the life course, comes from speeches included only as examples of laudable rhetoric. A second issue is fragmentation. Text about transformations in the lifecycle comes from four volumes. There is no reason to think the aggregate description is ethnographically complete, since Sahagun was not trying to provide a single coherent account of everyday life.

Codex Mendoza is a pictorial document painted in 1541 by a master scribe trained in native traditions (see Berdan and Anawalt 1992, 1997: xi–xiii). It includes short glosses resulting from consultation with a group of Aztec elders and longer commentary. The section depicting childhood was a visual innovation without any preconquest model, which Calnek (1992) shows parallels texts collected by Sahagun. Like the *Florentine Codex*, the *Codex Mendoza* presented to the colonizing power an idealization of correct behaviour, and its just rewards, and of transgression and punishment. While this reduces their utility as accounts of everyday life, it makes them more useful sources for an investigation of attempts to define and impose norms through the life course.

The Existential Status of Aztec Children

Sixteenth-century Nahuatl texts describe Aztec infants initially as raw materials that needed to be worked into specific forms. Lifecycle rituals were the context where continued refinement of this raw material was effected. The natural background from which humans were to be differentiated was as much vegetal or mineral as animal (compare Clendinnen 1991: 153–67, 184–93, 223–8, 244–8, 250–3). In speeches to expectant mothers, children were characterized as the thorn that grows from the tip of the maguey leaf, and as maguey about to sprout and blossom (Sahagun 1969: ch. 25). Identification of the child with unmodified raw materials worked into valued forms within the household-based productive economy was emphasized by equating infants with feathers and precious stones. Before and at birth, the child was described as a product made by the gods:

> the one who has arrived, the precious necklace, the precious feather, the baby, which has been flaked off here. Our lord the creator, the master, Quetzalcoatl, flakes a precious necklace, places a precious feather, here on your neck, at your breast, in your hands he places a precious necklace. (Sahagun 1969: ch. 33)

During the ritual burial of the umbilical cord, the newborn child was still described as a sprouting plant, a chip of stone, and even as a wild bird in a nest (Sahagun 1969: ch. 31). A shift in balance toward symbols drawn from the social universe came with the reading of the calendrical fortune of the child's birthdate (Sahagun 1969: ch. 36). During the formal bathing ritual which followed, verbal rhetoric was given material form through the use of specific objects, for the boy 'a little shield, a little bow, little arrows ... his little loincloth, his little cape', for the girl, 'the equipment of women – the spinning whorl, the weaving sword, the reed basket, the spinning bowl, the skeins, the shuttle, her little skirt, her little shift' (Sahagun 1969: ch. 37). The midwife urged the baby to take and use small versions of adult tools. She named the baby and dressed it in small versions of adult clothing that had been provided, not the everyday garments of infants.

This verbal and material rhetoric of labour and dress began to impose distinct adult male and female statuses on the newborn, 'boying' and 'girling' (Butler 1993: 7–8) these as-yet unfixed human subjects. The initial act of dressing did not make adults of infants, a task that lasted many years. But it did begin to treat children as social beings of the same kind as adults with whom they shared this manner of dress. It began a sequence of changes in hair, costume and ornaments that gradually created distinct social identities, above all those of adult genders and labour roles.

Making Aztec Adults

The work of transforming the raw material of Aztec children into properly socialized adults was advanced through a series of lifecycle rituals, often including preparation for, or provision of, new forms of body modification. Kellogg (1995: 89–91) suggests that birth rituals involved gradually expanding groups of actors, from the midwife and parents present at birth, to kin who witnessed bathing and naming in the house compound, to non-kin at later, more public, ceremonies. Images in *Codex Mendoza* illustrate the actions of the midwife during the bathing ceremony (Berdan and Anawalt 1997: folio 57; compare Sahagun 1969: ch. 18: 1954: ch. 16:

1953: Appendix 4). A baby in a cradle is linked by a dotted line to an older woman labelled 'midwife' holding an infant near a pottery vessel full of water set on a mat. Footprints around the mat form a counterclockwise path. Two dotted lines link the baby to a shield and spears, and to a broom and spinning basket, alternative insignia of dichotomous adult genders in the *Florentine Codex* (see McCafferty and McCafferty 1988, 1991; Burkhart 1997: 33–8, 45–52; Brumfiel 1991). In the image, the male emblems are augmented by tools for woodworking, feather-work, scribal practice and metalworking, described as tools of the child's father's profession.

The parallel between the sources continues with dedication of the baby to either the religious schools, the *calmecac*, or the secular *telpochcalli* or 'house of youths' (Calnek 1988). Directly below the drawings of the bathing and naming ceremony, the cradled infant is shown in front of its parents (Berdan and Anawalt 1997: folio 57). Dotted lines link the cradle to two seated figures, labelled as the master of the *telpochcalli* and the priest who headed the *calmecac*. Sahagun noted that a feast accompanied the promise of a child to the *calmecac*, taking place in the temple precincts because the head priest could not enter houses of commoners. A feast for the masters of the house of youths was celebrated at the house of a child promised to the *telpochcalli*. On that occasion the Masters of Youths 'cradled [the child] in their arms to possess it, to make it forever their possession, until it reached a marriageable age' (Sahagun 1969: ch. 39).

In its first use, the either/or convention of the dotted line in *Codex Mendoza* differentiates the gender of the child. In its second use, it marks the institutional basis for the child's adult role. Assignment of children to the temple destined them to a life of chastity (Sahagun 1969: ch. 39). Through ceremonies of dedication to adult institutions, significantly different adult sexualities were predicted for newborn infants, conditioning the entire course of childhood towards these adult statuses.

Infants whose cultural shaping was initiated by these birth rituals underwent their next life-cycle ritual as early as 4 years old. Sahagun describes this ceremony in relative detail because it was tied to the civil calendar. Every fourth year in the month Izcalli a feast was held 'when children were grabbed by the neck to make them grow tall' (Sahagun 1951: ch. 37). It marked the transition from the freedom of infants to the structured training of older children. As Inga Clendinnen (1991: 189–92) noted, the timing of the feast at four-year intervals means the children participating were not all the same age. Izcalli rituals established an age-grade of four years.

The ceremony began at midnight at the local temple with piercing of the children's ears (Sahagun 1951: chs 37–8). At dawn the children and their sponsors, adult non-kin, returned to the house compound, initiating a round of feasting, drinking the intoxicating beverage *pulque*, singing and dancing. In the afternoon, the sponsors took the children to the temple again, bringing *pulque* and special child-size drinking vessels (Sahagun 1951: ch. 37). Everyone continued drinking throughout the day and, after returning to the house, throughout the evening.

Children who experienced the Izcalli ritual together were introduced to the repertoire of actions that would characterize all their later participation in religion: singing, dancing, ceremonial drinking and shedding sacrificial blood. They also began the process of expanding a perforation in the ear lobe to eventually allow use of adult ear ornaments. Sahagun, while emphasizing production of sacrificial blood from the ear as the goal of piercing, also explicitly notes that a cotton thread was placed in the pierced opening. This would have prevented it from closing again. A process of gradual expansion of these pierced holes would have to have ensued to ensure that young adults could later wear adult ear ornaments, whose shafts average over 2 cm wide.

Visual images in *Codex Mendoza* showing training of a boy and girl depict the introduction of serious adult expectations at the age when children would have completed the Izcalli ritual. Four-year-old children are shown beginning instruction in adult work. Between ages 7 and 8, children are shown subjected to punishments for the first time, including use of maguey spines to pierce the body. The 9-year-old boy is specifically shown with a spine inserted in his ear lobe, the site first pierced at Izcalli. The children between ages 4 and 7 depicted in *Codex Mendoza* were already beginning adult training. Only after age 7 were they subject to full discipline, and to forms of punishment that employed a method introduced as the bodily mark of passage through the Izcalli ritual. Discipline, both in the sense of regulation through punishment and of the creation of subjectivity through conformity to a norm, was a reality for Aztec children once they underwent this lifecycle event.

Bodily Discipline and the Achievement of Adult Status

Figures of speech relating Aztec children to precious raw materials used for ornaments evoke the symbolic importance of body ornaments as media that transformed and displayed age status. Approximately every four years from birth through the early teens, transitions in the lifecycle were visibly marked through changes in practices of body ornamentation and dress. Childhood was divided by these transitions into three uniform segments, followed by an adulthood of more individualized transitions. Through the coordination of social age-grades, lifecycle rituals reproduced individual performances of embodied subjectivity as citations of approved precedents (Butler 1993: 12–16). These precedents were so clear that they could be reproduced in visual and verbal records decades after their disruption.

With the dedication of children to the calmecac or *telpochcalli* the first body markings were directly applied to the flesh. Speeches made at the feast dedicating a child to the *calmecac* described the distinctive haircut of religious life that would be adopted with adulthood. In the meantime, the child's body was marked by ritual scarification on the hip and chest. For those destined to the non-religious life, 'to make it known that he belonged to the *telpochcalli*, the lip was pierced in order to place the lip plug there', although *use* of lip plugs was deferred until adulthood. Distinctions in adult destiny were literally marked on the bodies of children, prefigured in speech and anticipated through the provision of sites of body ornaments that would not be used until much later.

Modification of the body, begun for many in infancy, extended to all children by the time they were 8 years old, through the Izcalli ritual. The creation of the site to be occupied by the ear spools of adults was like the piercing of the lip for a labret that was not adopted until adulthood. *Codex Mendoza* depicts ear spools on a boy of age 15 going to the *telpochcalli*, and on a girl of the same age being married (Berdan and Anawalt 1997: folio 61). A later scene, glossed as a feast held by a newly married youth to beg leave from his peers in the *telpochcalli* for spending time away from them, shows six young men and the young bride, each with carefully detailed ear spools (Berdan and Anawalt 1997: folio 68). Use of labrets waited until the boy's achievements in warfare, marked by adoption of variants described in the *Florentine Codex* and shown in *Codex Mendoza*. Initial lip piercing or scarification and later ear piercing punctuated the continuous bodily development of the child, and prefigured adoption of adult practices. Ornamentation for which these sites were prepared were citations of practices visible to the child in the bodies of adults working to transform their infant raw material into disciplined social form. These piercings consequently had precisely the ambiguous status of the 'repetition of what cannot he recollected' that Butler (1993: 244) argues is central to materialization of embodied subjectivity.

A second set of disciplines of bodily materiality began with presentation of adult garments to the newborn infant. These symbolic garments were not the clothing of infancy. At age 3, the girl and boy each wore only the appropriate upper garment, the blouse or cape (Berdan and Anawalt 1997: folio 58). A skirt was added to the girl's costume at age 4, and a loincloth to the boy's costume by age 7 (Berdan and Anawalt 1997: folio 59). By the time they had passed through the Izcalli ritual, children were wearing the garments of adulthood and learning through them decorous postures and ways of moving of Aztec men and women.

The central action in wedding ceremonies reiterated use of clothing in birth ceremonies as synecdoches (Burkhart 1997: 46–7) for normative male and female subject positions:

> The mother of the man went to give gifts to the bride. She placed a blouse on her, and a skirt before her. And the mother of the woman also went to give gifts. She tied a cape on the groom,

but his breech clout she placed before him. ...
And the elderly matchmakers tied them together. They took the corner of the man's cape,
they drew up the woman's blouse, then they tied
these together. (Sahagun 1969: ch. 23; compare
Berdan and Anawalt 1997: folio 61)

Clothing served at life transitions as a form of
insistently stable gendered materiality that had
the power to impose particular ways of being
adult on children. Unlike the punctuated
changes of piercing for body ornaments, use of
static adult garments denied the gradual transformation of raw child to shaped adult, asserting
instead an essential stability of form.

Hair treatment was another aspect of bodily
materiality incorporated in Aztec lifecycle transitions. The hair of boys and girls is depicted as
identical, cropped short over the entire head,
through age 11. At age 12, the girl's hair is
noticeably long at the back, typical also of
depictions of sexually active young women
being punished for their transgressions (Berdan
and Anawalt 1997: folios 60, 61, 63). Images of
young men early in their training show a long
tail of hair indistinguishable from that of young
women (Berdan and Anawalt 1997: folios 60, 61,
62). This was named the 'young girl's lock of hair'
in a summary of Aztec noble women's appearance
and in admonitions to young men seeking their
first captive (Sahagun 1954: chs 15, 21).

Transformations of Aztec boys' hair are related
to their distinction as warriors:

> At first, while still a small boy, his hair was shorn.
> And when he was already ten years old, they then
> let a tuft of hair grow on the back of his head.
> And when he was fifteen years old, then the tuft
> of hair became long ... when he had nowhere
> taken captives. And if he took a captive ... then
> the lock of hair was removed. ... And when the
> tuft on the back of his head was removed, he was
> shorn so that he was left [another] lock: his hair
> dress kept, on the right side, the hair hanging
> low, reaching the bottom of his ear; to one side
> [only] was his lock of hair set. ... And he who
> then did not take a captive. ... might not remove
> his lock of hair. ... Thus was his hair shorn: it
> was cut like a ring-shaped carrying pad; they
> shaved only the crown of his head. (Sahagun
> 1954: ch. 21)

Men who continued as warriors were allowed a
new hairstyle when they captured their fourth
captive on their own.

Transformation of Aztec girls' hair is described
only briefly. Distinctions were noted between
noble girls with 'hair all cut the same length',
with the 'young girl's lock of hair', and with the
hairstyle of women 'wound about the head', but
neither the ages nor circumstances of these
changes are detailed (Sahagun 1954: ch. 15).
Commentary on another ethnic group, the
Otomí, characterized as having 'a civilized way
of life', describes their costume as comparable to
the Aztecs', and presents identical information
about male hair styles as for the Aztecs'. The
section on women's appearance provides details:

> When the women were still young girls, they cut
> their hair short; but when [they were] grown,
> when [they were] young women, the hair cov-
> ered their shoulders. ... And when one was a
> mature woman, when perhaps she also [had
> delivered] her child, the hair was bound around
> her head. (Sahagun 1961: ch. 29)

This suggests that the standard adult woman's
hair style (Berdan and Anawalt 1997: folio 68)
was adopted following childbirth, structurally
equated with the capture of prisoners in battle
that initiated new hair treatment for boys
(Sahagun 1969: chs 28, 30, 33).

For boys and girls alike, passage into adult
status was accompanied by adoption of a complex hairstyle that required continual maintenance, ensuring that, although the shared lifecycle
rituals of childhood were completed, each adult
would individually continue to perform disciplines of appearance that were major means
through which adult status was formalized,
internalized and externally signalled. Children's
bodies were worked as raw material by adult
authorities. Adults carried out their own regimes
of bodily control.

Discussion

Aztec childhood was divided through lifecycle rites
into phases. The bodies of children were systematically laden with signs of difference in gender,

achievement and status. Physical differences observable at birth had to be transformed through ritual and everyday action into socially interpretable forms. Youths were literally products of adult action, just as materials used to mark their bodies – items of clothing and ornaments – were. While appearance, achievement and destiny did not stop unfolding after childhood, marking of changes became less social and public and more private, personal and individual, as daily practices to maintain adult discipline replaced the punctuated experiences of childhood.

Material previously viewed simply as 'costume' must now be considered as active mechanisms for socialization and materialization of preferred forms of embodied subjectivity. The practices important for the Aztecs as means through which children were transformed into adults also vary by age in earlier Mesoamerican societies. The only consistent difference in use of costume ornaments in burials from several early village sites (dated 1500–400 BC) was the restriction of ear ornaments to adults, even when burials of children otherwise included the greatest number and diversity of goods, including other ornaments (Joyce 1999). I suggest that these children belonged to societies in which ear ornaments were media for lifecycle transitions, incomplete at the time of their death. This observation marks fragments of ear ornaments, routinely recovered in such sites, as possible evidence of lifecycle ceremonies. It draws attention to the relative stability of ear-ornament form over three millennia (Joyce 1998). Careful attention to distributions of ear spools of different diameters should allow documentation of the physical process through which children's ears were gradually made suitable sites for use of adult ornaments.

Contemporary with these burials, hand modelled figurines representing human subjects were created. Playa de los Muertos-style figurines from northwest Honduras were particularly carefully detailed, depicting a great diversity of hairstyles and body ornaments. Attempts to subdivide these figurines using traditional evolutionary criteria were unsuccessful (Agurcia 1978). By examining differences in hair treatment, a feature significant in Aztec accounts of the life course, I was able to subdivide the group into four classes in which posture, dress and ornamentation varied predictably along with hairstyle (Joyce 1997; compare Serra Puche and Durand 1998). Two of the classes feature physical marks of relative age, demarcating infant and elderly categories. The remaining figurines, neither infant nor elderly, vary in elaboration of hair treatment. I consider them stylized representations of transitions in bodily appearance at a point during the lifecycle when the long unornamented hair of infancy was transformed through shaving, beading, braiding and binding into elaborate fashions of young adulthood. Like contemporary burials, figurines document that the materialization of adult bodies was already the subject of standardized practices in Mesoamerica's earliest villages, practices deploying techniques of body modification that left behind substantial material traces.

Just as the Mesoamerican world of things is transformed by considering the use of objects as media for lifecycle rituals, so also the space of Mesoamerican sites must be reconsidered in light of these practices. Lifecycle rituals described in post-hispanic sources took place in and around the house compound. Entry into the house compound of neighbours, kin and fictive kin called to witness the events were occasions for hosting feasts and for formalized drinking. Recent discussions of the significance of feasting as a political tactic in Mesoamerica seldom consider what events provided occasions for employment of such strategies. Transitions in the lifecycle presented significant opportunities for hosting others without seeming overtly self-aggrandizing. On these occasions, the residential character of the house compound was thoroughly imbued with social strategizing. Facilities incorporated in house compounds – seating platforms, formal food-preparation facilities, domestic altars and sweatbaths – must be re-examined as conditioned not simply by economic requirements, but by the needs of effective and persuasive hosting of regularly timed, intimate rituals where the life of society intersected the biographies of individuals.

References

Agurcia, R. 1978. Las figurillas de Playa de los Muertos, Honduras. *Yaxkin*, 2: 221–40.

Berdan, F. F. and Anawalt, P. (eds) 1992. *The Codex Mendoza*. Berkeley: University of California Press.

Berdan, F. F. and Anawalt, P. 1997. *The Essential Codex Mendoza*. Berkeley: University of California Press.

Brown, B. A. 1983. Seen but not heard: women in Aztec ritual – the Sahagun texts. In *Text and Image in Pre-Columbian Art* (ed. J. C. Berlo). Oxford: BAR International Series 180, pp. 119–54.

Brumfiel, E. M. 1991. Weaving and cooking: women's production in Aztec Mexico. In *Engendering Archaeology* (eds J. Gero and M. Conkey). Oxford: Blackwell, pp. 224–51.

Burkhart, L. M. 1997. Mexica women on the home front. In *Indian Women of Early Mexico* (eds S. Schroeder, S. Wood and R. Haskett). Norman: University of Oklahoma Press, pp. 25–54.

Butler, J. 1993. *Bodies That Matter.* New York: Routledge.

Calnek, E. E. 1974. The Sahagun texts as a source of sociological information. In *Sixteenth-Century Mexico: The Work of Sahagun* (ed. M. Edmonson). Albuquerque: University of New Mexico Press, pp. 189–204.

Calnek, E. E. 1988. The Calmecac and the Telpochcalli in Pre-Conquest Tenochtitlan. In *The Work of Bernardino de Sahagun* (eds J. J. Klor de Alva, H. B. Nicholson and E. Quiñones Keber). Albany: Institute for Mesoamerican Studies, State University of New York, pp. 169–78.

Calnek, E. E. 1992. The ethnographic context of the third part of the *Codex Mendoza*. In *The Codex Mendoza, Volume 1: Interpretation* (eds F. Berdan and P. Anawalt). Berkeley: University of California Press, pp. 81–91.

Clendinnen, I. 1991. *Aztecs: An Interpretation.* Cambridge: Cambridge University Press.

Cobb, C. R. 1991. Social reproduction and the *longue durée* in the prehistory of the midcontinental United States. In *Processual and Postprocessual Archaeologies* (ed. R. W. Preucel). Carbondale: Center for Archaeological Investigations, Southern Illinois University, pp. 168–82.

Cyphers Guillén, A. 1993. Women, rituals, and social dynamics at Ancient Chalcatzingo. *Latin American Antiquity*, 4(3): 209–24.

Gillespie, S. D. 1998. The Aztec triple alliance: a post-conquest tradition. In *Native Traditions in the Post-conquest World* (eds E. H. Boone and T. Cummins). Washington, DC: Dumbarton Oaks, pp. 233–63.

Joyce, R. A. 1994. Looking for children in Prehispanic Mesoamerica. Presented at the annual meeting of the Society for American Archaeology, Anaheim, CA.

Joyce, R. A. 1997. Playa de los Muertos figurines and their predecessors. Ms.

Joyce, R. A. 1998. A Mesoamerican history of body ornamentation. Presented at the conference Thinking Through the Body, University of Wales, Lampeter.

Joyce, R. A. 1999. Social dimensions of pre-classic burials. In *Social Patterns in Pre-Classic Mesoamerica* (eds D. C. Grove and R. A. Joyce). Washington, DC: Dumbarton Oaks, pp. 15–47.

Joyce, R. A. 2000. High culture, Mesoamerican civilization, and the Classic Maya tradition. In *Order, Legitimacy, and Wealth in Early States* (eds J. Richards and M. Van Buren). Cambridge: Cambridge University Press, pp. 64–76.

Kellogg, S. 1995. *Law and the Transformation of Aztec Culture, 1500–1700.* Norman: University of Oklahoma Press.

Klor de Alva, J. J., Nicholson, H. B. and Quiñones Keber, E. (eds) 1988. *The Work of Bernardino de Sahagun.* Albany: Institute for Mesoamerican Studies. State University of New York.

Lesure, R. 1997. Figurines and social identities in early sedentary societies of coastal Chiapas, Mexico. In *Women in Prehistory: North America and Mesoamerica* (eds C. Claassen and R. Joyce). Philadelphia: University of Pennsylvania Press, pp. 227–48.

McCafferty, S. D. and McCafferty, G. G. 1988. Powerful women and the myth of male dominance in Aztec society. *Archaeological Review from Cambridge*, 7: 45–59.

McCafferty, S. D. and McCafferty, G. G. 1991. Spinning and weaving as female gender identity in Post-Classic Mexico. In *Textile Traditions of Mesoamerica and the Andes* (eds J. C. Berlo, M. Schevill and E. B. Dwyer). New York: Garland, pp. 19–44.

Sahagun, B. 1951. *Florentine Codex, Book 2 – The Ceremonies* (trans. A. J. O. Anderson and C. E. Dibble). School of American Research Monographs, number 14, Part III. Salt Lake City: University of Utah Press.

Sahagun, B. 1953. *Florentine Codex, Book 3 – The Origins of the Gods* (trans. A. J. O. Anderson and C. E. Dibble). School of American Research Monographs, number 14, Part IV. Salt Lake City: University of Utah Press.

Sahagun, B. 1954. *Florentine Codex, Book 8 – Kings and Lords* (trans. A. J. O. Anderson and C. E. Dibble). School of American Research Monographs, number 14, Part IX. Salt Lake City: University of Utah Press.

Sahagun, B. 1961. *Florentine Codex, Book 10 – The People* (trans. A. J. O. Anderson and C. E. Dibble).

School of American Research Monographs, number 14, Part XI. Salt Lake City: University of Utah Press.

Sahagun, B. 1969. *Florentine Codex, Book 6 – Rhetoric and Moral Philosophy* (trans. A. J. O. Anderson and C. E. Dibble). School of American Research Monographs, number 14, Part VII. Salt Lake City: University of Utah Press.

Schele, L. and Freidel, D. 1990. *A Forest of Kings*. New York: William Morrow.

Schele, L. and Miller, M. E. 1986. *The Blood of Kings*. Fort Worth TX: Kimball Art Museum.

Serra Puche, M. C. and Durand, K. R. 1998. Las mujeres de Xochitecatl. *Arqueologia Mexicana*, 5 (29): 20–7.

Smith, M. E. 1992. Rhythms of change in Postclassic Central Mexico: archaeology, ethnohistory and the Braudelian model. In *Archaeology, Annales and Ethnohistory* (ed. A. B. Knapp). Cambridge: Cambridge University Press, pp. 51–74.

Storey, R. 1992. Children of Copan: issues in paleopathology and paleodemography. *Ancient Mesoamerica*, 3: 161–7.

12

Domesticating Imperialism
Sexual Politics and the Archaeology of Empire

Barbara L. Voss

Archaeologists studying empire have long considered sexual relationships, especially heterosexual marriage, to be central to colonization. In particular, the archaeology of households formed through intermarriage has garnered considerable insights into the routines of daily life under imperialism. However, the household focus has at times "domesticated" imperialism by locating the processes and outcomes of colonization within interpersonal family relationships. Many archaeological studies have not fully addressed the relationship between colonial households and the sexual politics of colonial institutions. Research at the Spanish-colonial military settlement of El Presidio de San Francisco demonstrates that public sexual politics were integral to the imperial project and need to be considered in the archaeological interpretation of colonial sites.

The Household in Archaeologies of Empire

By excavating and analyzing the physical remains of household architecture, foodways, craft production, and material culture, archaeology has

Barbara L. Voss, "Domesticating Imperialism: Sexual Politics and the Archaeology of Empire," pp. 191–203 from *American Anthropologist* 110:2 (2008). Reprinted with permission of the American Anthropological Association and the author.

contributed a microscale focus on household life to the anthropology of empire. In the Spanish-colonial Americas, the archaeology of households has especially been used to investigate the ways that indigenous women responded to and influenced the outcomes of imperial projects. James Deetz's (1963) investigations of households at Mission La Purísima in Alta California concluded that indigenous women's activities showed continuity whereas indigenous men's roles changed dramatically as a result of their incorporation into colonial agriculture and craft production. Similarly, in the North American Southeast, Charles Fairbanks (1962) and Carol Mason (1963) interpreted continuity in indigenous ceramic traditions as evidence that Native American women "served as the thread of continuity from generation to generation and certainly were a powerful force for cultural conservatism" (Mason 1963:73). These early studies challenged conventional histories that either ignored indigenous women or portrayed them as passive victims of colonization.

In the 1970s, Kathleen Deagan's (1974, 1983) landmark research in the colonial town of St. Augustine in La Florida investigated the formation of "creole" colonial cultural patterns in the Spanish Americas. Deagan postulated that in colonial households,

> low-visibility, female-associated activities such as diet, food preparation, and other kitchen

activities would be expected to exhibit the strongest Indian characteristics, whereas such male-associated socially visible areas such as house construction, weaponry, and other military activities would be expected to exhibit the least Indian influences. (Deagan 1983:103)

This hypothesis was tested through excavation and analysis of five 18th-century households that represented a range of occupations and ethnicities. Deagan found that "regardless of the income or ethnic affiliation of a site's inhabitants, aboriginal influence is most strongly evident in the Kitchen (women's activity) group" (Deagan 1983:122). The one mestizo household in the sample, formed through the marriage of a colonial soldier with a local Guale woman, yielded a higher frequency of aboriginal ceramic wares and a wider range of local floral and faunal remains. This suggested that "an extremely potent force in acculturation and adaptive processes was Spanish–Indian intermarriage and *mestizaje*" (Deagan 1983:271), the latter term referring to racial and cultural mixing.

The findings of the St. Augustine investigations inspired new research on gender and domestic life in Spanish colonization of the circum-Caribbean. In Santa Elena, South Carolina, Stanley South (1988) postulated that locally made Indian pottery was an archaeological indication of households formed between Spanish men and indigenous women. Research at Puerto Real, Hispaniola, similarly documented the widespread presence of aboriginal vessels in colonial households (Deagan 1995; Ewen 1991). Bonnie McEwan concluded that "the most dramatic changes in material life at Puerto Real appear to have been in areas related to female activities. The scarcity of Spanish women in the colony resulted in the integration of Indian women into Spanish colonial households in a variety of legal and consensual capacities as was the case throughout the New World" (McEwan 1995:223).

Archaeologists studying households in other regions of the Spanish Americas have advanced different perspectives on the role of domestic life in the colonial encounter. Nan Rothschild's (2003) study of Spanish-colonial New Mexico reframes colonial–indigenous intermarriage as only one of several ways that colonists acquired Native American women's labor and services, including sexual services. Ross Jamieson's (2000) research on colonial households in Cuenca, Ecuador, demonstrated women's involvement in agriculture, business, and property ownership as well as domestic activities such as food preparation. Studies of Spanish-colonial households in Louisiana, Mexico, Peru, and Bolivia have shown that indigenous technologies and material culture were also incorporated into public arenas of colonial life such as architecture, dining, dress, and arms and armaments (Charlton et al. 2005; Charlton and Fournier 1993; Loren 1999; Rodríguez-Alegría 2005a, 2005b; Smith 1997a, 1997b; Van Buren 1999). Investigations at El Presidio de San Francisco in Alta California have found that colonial households there did not incorporate Native Californian material culture or dietary resources into their domestic routines, instead maintaining firm distinctions from local indigenous populations (Voss 2005, 2008a).

Although in this article, I focus on the Spanish Americas, the centrality of domestic life and indigenous women to colonization has also been investigated by archaeologists studying French, British, Russian, and Dutch imperial projects throughout the Americas (e.g., Frink 2007; Lightfoot et al. [Chapter 8, this volume]; Martinez 1994; Scott 1991; Spector 1993; Wagner 1998). Additionally, colonial–indigenous intermarriage and domestic practices are now commonly identified as central factors considered in comparative studies of empire (e.g., Lightfoot 2005; Rothschild 2003).

Intermarriage and Cultural Brokers

Half a century of archaeological research has shown that imperial projects relied on, and were transformed by, intimate and routine domestic practices. Two trends in this research warrant closer examination: (1) an emphasis on colonial–indigenous intermarriage and (2) the depiction of Native American women as cultural brokers.

Heterosexual marriage between colonial men and indigenous women has long been used by archaeologists as a literal and figurative explanation of the processes and outcomes of Spanish colonization. This is especially true in the circum-Caribbean region, where researchers have argued that the formation of a creole colonial culture was "achieved largely through intermarriage": "Through these unions, non-European and syncretic European American traits were incorporated into Spanish households on a regular basis" (Deagan 2002:34). This focus on intermarriage is puzzling because archival studies, often conducted by the same researchers, indicate that intermarriage only accounted for a low frequency of colonial households (generally two to ten percent, and rarely as great as 23 percent; Voss 2008b). Instead, concubinage, slavery, and servitude were likely to have been the most common means through which colonists incorporated Native Americans and Africans of both genders into their households.

In recent years several archaeological studies have concluded that Native American women played active roles as cultural brokers in colonial households (e.g., Deagan 2003; McEwan 1991; Trocolli 1992). The term *cultural broker* is an anthropological concept developed to describe individuals or groups who mediate seemingly irreconcilable tensions: between the state and the community; between tradition and modernity; and across religious, class, ethnic, or racial differences (Press 1969; Szasz 1994; Wolf 1956). Anthropological models suggest that cultural brokers gain power by facilitating financial and legal transactions; yet their roles as cultural innovators place them in marginal social positions because, "Janus-like, they face in two directions at once" (Wolf 1956:1076) and thus cannot be fully trusted by either community. In archaeological studies of colonization, portraying Native American wives and servants of colonial men as cultural brokers has been a way to consider the social agency of such women. These studies have emphasized that colonial lifeways were transformed by local material culture and foodstuffs that Native American women introduced into colonial homes: "Given their active participation in Spanish homes, non-Hispanic women served as the primary agents of acculturation and were mostly responsible for many of the changes identified in Spanish colonial culture" (McEwan 1991:40). That is, "whether as wives, concubines, or servants, [non-European] women were the brokers for European, Indian, and African exchanges within Spanish-American households and communities" (Deagan 2003:8).

Such interpretations seek to foreground the cultural influence and historical contributions of indigenous women who have often been portrayed as passive victims of colonization. However, the archaeological focus on intermarriage, and more recently, on cultural brokers, has served to domesticate imperialism by locating the processes and outcomes of colonization within households and interpersonal relationships. Such studies rarely discuss the effects of colonial institutions and labor regimes on colonized peoples or the fact that under colonial rule Native American women were at times coerced into concubinage, servitude, and marriage. As Rothschild (2003:31) notes, a "strong physical cruelty" often existed within the seeming intimacy of Spanish-colonial interethnic households.

Archaeological interpretations of colonization that emphasize intermarriage and cultural brokers also hazard replicating certain stereotypes of indigenous women. From Malintzin (La Malinche) to Matoaka (Pocahontas), one persistent cultural trope depicts sexually available indigenous women who assist colonial men in the domination of their own people. As postcolonial feminist scholars (e.g., Mohanty 1997; Powers 2002) have demonstrated, this sexualized trope of colonial domination continues to be reproduced in academic research and popular culture in the present day.

These imperial visions of colonial seduction also existed in the imaginations of colonial explorers. In the Spanish Americas, one prominent theme was the myth of Amazonia, a land of strong, usually dark-skinned, women warriors who horded great riches. On his first trip across the Atlantic Ocean, Christopher Columbus wrote in his journal that an Amazon island was located just east of Jamaica. Throughout Spain's subsequent explorations of the Americas, it was often rumored that Amazonia lay undiscovered just beyond the reaches of charted lands. For example, after the conquest of the Aztec Empire, Hernán Cortés requested funds to search for an island of Amazons in the Pacific Ocean to the west of present-day mainland Mexico. When Cortés's ships made landfall, the exploring party named the land "California" after Queen Calafia, a character in a chivalrous novel, *Las Sergas de Esplandián* (lit., *The Exploits of Esplandián*; Montalvo 2001).

The novel, first printed in Spain in 1510, was widely distributed in the Spanish Americas in the 1520s. The book describes an island of fierce but attractive black women who force men to mate with them and then kill them. The novel's hero, Esplandián, seduces and weds their ruler, Queen Calafia, and persuades her to be baptized. Calafia then renounces her pagan ways and relinquishes dominion of the island and its wealth to her new husband, who converts the rest of the Amazons and marries them to the men under his command. Through the sexual conquest of Calafia, Esplandián restores Catholic racial and gendered hierarchies to the conquered island (Bouvier 2001:6–12; Engstrand 1998; Hurtado 1999:xxvi; Polk 1991).

These lascivious tales were far from trivial. Colonial assumptions about indigenous sexuality were incorporated into the policies and practices of colonial institutions. In focusing on the domestic activities of indigenous women married or cohabitating with colonial men, archaeological research has unwittingly perpetuated these imperialist visions. Archaeologists have tended to frame domestic labor within consensual relationships such as marriage without full consideration of servitude and slavery as instrumental mechanisms used to appropriate and control the labor (incl. sexual and reproductive labor) of indigenous women. Additionally, despite the known range of genders and sexualities present in both Iberian and Native American cultures (Blackmore and Hutcheson 1999; Roscoe 1998), most studies presume that sexual relations and sexual identities were heterosexual. Finally, as in the late medieval tales of the Amazons, indigenous men are curiously absent from most archaeological accounts of the domestic politics of imperialism.

Sexuality beyond the Household

The challenge facing archaeological studies of empire is to integrate research on households with investigations of colonial institutions and labor regimes. The case of intermarriage provides an excellent example: Spanish-colonial institutions and resources were mobilized to shape the composition of colonial households to fit the goals of colonial administrators.

Intermarriage was initially promoted as a vehicle for cultural understanding. In 1503, Queen Isabela instructed the governor of Santo Domingo that "some Christians marry some Indian women and some Christian women marry some Indian men, so that both parties can communicate and teach each other" (Mörner 1967:26). Additionally, some high-ranking colonists were encouraged to marry into elite indigenous families to foster political and economic alliances. However, it was not until 1514 that a royal decree established the legality of marriages between colonists and Native Americans (Deagan and Cruxent 2002:221). That same year, the crown ordered that more Spanish women be transported to the American colonies to reduce the number of marriages between Spaniards and Native Americans (Mörner 1967:26–27).

In the 1620s, Spain adopted the Policy of Domestic Unity, which discouraged interracial marriages by providing funds to transport Spanish wives to American settlements and by offering incentives for single colonial men to marry Spanish women. In 1776, the Crown issued the Royal Pragmatic on Marriage, which prohibited "unequal" unions in the colonies (Castañeda 1993a). The effectiveness of these policies varied, but colonial endogamy was prevalent in most settlements. In cases when the colonial population had a highly skewed sex ratio, many male colonists elected to remain single rather than marry indigenous women (Voss 2008b).

Understanding the relationships between colonial policy, on one hand, and household composition, on the other hand, explodes the binary between "private" and "public" realms of colonial life. As Ann Stoler writes of European colonization more broadly, "Who bedded and wedded whom in the colonies of France, England, Holland, and Iberia was never left to chance" (2002:47). Throughout European colonial enterprises, ratios of colonial men to colonial women, and the prevalence of intermarriage between indigenous and colonial populations, followed from how colonial administrators felt sexuality should be managed and how racial categories were perceived. Household assemblages in the Spanish Americas must be interpreted by archaeologists as artifacts of imperial policy as well as the products of interpersonal relationships.

Case Study: El Presidio de San Francisco

The province of Alta California was established in 1769 as part of Spain's final northwest expansion of its North American empire. Alta California was divided into four districts (see Figure 12.1), each headed by a *presidio*, or military outpost. El Presidio de San Francisco, founded in 1776 to guard the mouth of the San Francisco Bay, was the northernmost of these. The settlement served as the military, administrative, and economic headquarters of the district, and it supervised

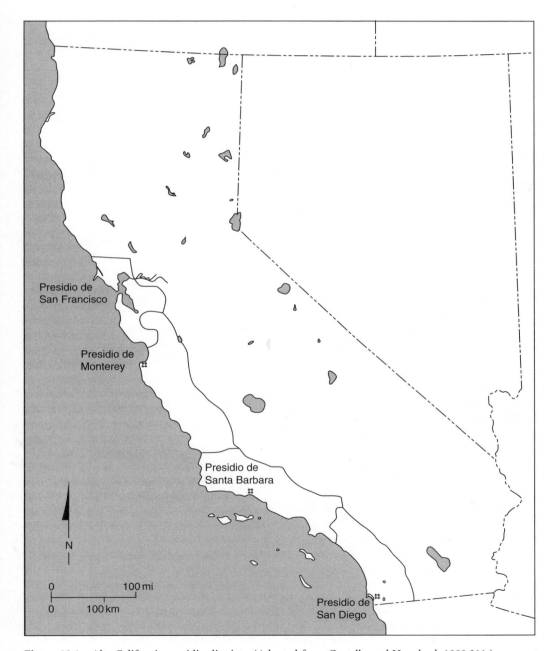

Figure 12.1   Alta California presidio districts. (Adapted from Costello and Hornbeck 1989:311.)

the establishment of six missions and two pueblos in the region (see Figure 12.2).

The archaeological site of El Presidio de San Francisco was first discovered in 1993 (Voss and Benté 1996) and has been under continuous investigation ever since. Research has included studies of the settlement's architectural history along with excavation of residential quarters, associated domestic midden deposits, and neighborhoods that formed outside the formal military settlement (Blind et al. 2004; Blind and Bartoy 2006; Simpson-Smith and Edwards 2000; Voss 2002, 2008a). Historic and ethnohistoric research provides specific information about the military colonial community as well as a broader regional context for site interpretation (e.g., Langellier and Rosen 1996; Milliken et al. 2005). Together these studies have garnered new perspectives on the sexual politics of San Francisco's colonization, including recruitment policies, ethnosexual conflict, architecture of sexual control, sexualization of military conflict, gendered labor regimes, and colonial ethnogenesis.

Recruitment practices

El Presidio de San Francisco was established by an expedition of 193 military settlers led by Juan Bautista de Anza, a prominent colonial military officer in northwest New Spain. Most of the settlers joined the frontier army during a special recruitment drive in the impoverished and war-torn provinces of Sinaloa and Sonora, today the region covering much of northwest Mexico. Promises of a steady income and opportunities for land ownership enticed the new recruits to leave their homelands for the most remote frontier of the Spanish-colonial empire.

Anza recruited not individual soldiers but entire families with demonstrated reproductive capabilities. He projected that each soldier and wife would bring six children with them to the new settlement (Chapman 1916). The actual figure was closer to four children per couple: 120 of the 193 settlers were dependent children (Langellier and Rosen 1996:191–193). The gendered and sexual composition of the new colonial settlement was thus set by state policy, and transgendered people, nonheterosexuals, and even unmarried heterosexuals were largely excluded from the colonial venture. As the

settlement matured, the colonial community was almost entirely endogamous. This was not simply a matter of personal choice: under frontier military regulations, marriages had to be approved by the presidio's commanding officer, who was charged with enforcing the Royal Pragmatic on Marriage. During 1776–1834, only six marriages between colonists and Native Californians were recorded in San Francisco. Most of these were among older widows and widowers whose first marriages had been within their community of origin (Milliken et al. 2005:128–129). The institutional character of Spanish colonial settlements such as El Presidio de San Francisco was such that colonists were under greater surveillance in sexual and gender matters on the frontier than they had been in the civilian towns from which they were recruited.

Ethnosexual conflict

From the expedition's first entry into the San Francisco Bay region, colonization was marked by ethnosexual conflict. This term, adapted from Joane Nagel (2003), is used here to refer to the clash between incompatible cultural beliefs and practices related to sexuality. Although colonization is generally understood as a conflict between different nations, ethnicities, races, or cultures, it is also a conflict between gendered and sexual systems (McClintock 1995; Stoler 2002).

San Francisco's military settlers and missionaries found Native Californians' appearance unsettling because most indigenous dress displayed, rather than concealed, the body's surface (Bouvier 2001:71–72; Hurtado 1999:10–12). The colonists were also simultaneously fascinated and repulsed by some indigenous gender identities and sexual practices. Native Californian cultures did not resemble the patriarchical society proscribed by Spanish religious and legal traditions. For example, both women and men held public and religions leadership positions. To the colonists, indigenous men appeared strangely feminine in their dress and occupations. Further, indigenous sexual relations included not only monogamous heterosexual marriage but also polygamy, premarital sex, same-sex sexuality, and transgendered practices; however, sexual modesty and restraint was valued and adultery was often

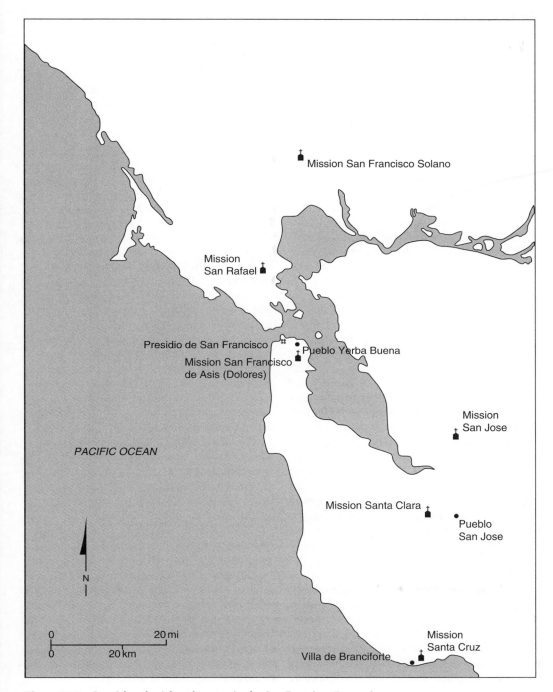

Figure 12.2   Spanish-colonial settlements in the San Francisco Bay region.

severely punished (Levy 1978; Margolin 1978; Milliken 1995). The perceived sexual savagery of the regions' inhabitants provided religious justification for initiating the colonial policy of *reducción*, through which Native Americans were removed from their home villages and aggregated at missions to be converted to Christianity and taught farming and other "civilized" occupations.

The first armed conflict between colonists and local indigenous people in San Francisco was in part spurred by cross-cultural sexual contact. El Presidio de San Francisco and its companion mission, San Francisco de Asís, were established within the territory of the Yelamu Ohlone. The Yelamu initially fled the area but began to slowly return in the fall to hunt waterfowl and trade with the colonists. In early December, the colonists began to experience these visits as threats. Father Palóu, head priest of the mission, wrote in his diary that the Yelamu men "began to disgrace themselves, now by thefts, now by firing an arrow close to the corporal of the guard, and again by trying to kiss the wife of a soldier" (Palóu 1926:136). In response, Sergeant Grijalva, the second highest-ranking officer at El Presidio de San Francisco, had a Yelamu man arrested and flogged. When the man's companions tried to rescue him, Grijalva's soldiers fired gunshots to frighten them off. The following day, Grijalva returned to the Yelamu campsite with additional soldiers, killing one Yelamu man, severely wounding another, and capturing and flogging two more (Palóu 1926:135–138).

This battle foreshadowed other campaigns to enforce colonial sexual and gender norms on colonized Native Californians. Like many Native American cultures, the Native Californian communities of the San Francisco Bay area recognized third and fourth genders that today are often called "two-spirits." Two-spirits were distinguished from other men and women by wearing clothing and doing work associated with the gender different from their physical sex. Marriage to, and sexual activity with, nontransgendered men and women was an integral part of two-spirit identity. Additionally, two-spirits in some California tribes had special responsibilities as healers, shamans, and undertakers (Holliman 1997; Katz 1976; Kroeber 1925; Williams 1986).

Spanish-colonial religious doctrine, military regulations, and civilian laws only recognized

two genders and condemned the two-spirits (whom the colonists called *joyas* and *amazonas*) as sodomites. In 1775, Alta California Governor Pedro Fages observed that there were two to three joyas in each village, and that all Indians were consequently addicted to "this abominable vice" (Williams 1986:87). Missionary Pedro Font wrote that the missions needed to eliminate these "sodomites [who are] dedicated to nefarious practices" (Font 1930:103). From that point forward, the colonists conducted a concerted campaign to eliminate two-spirits and same-sex sexual practices. By the 1820s, the missionaries reported that the once-numerous two-spirits were no longer present in missionized tribes, and as a result "this horrible custom is entirely unknown among them" (Williams 1986:139).

This violent suppression of two-spirits and same-sex sexuality was only part of the program of sexual control implemented by missionaries and military officials. With military support, missionaries also targeted premarital and extramarital sex, polygamy, and the use of birth control. As much as 25 percent of the annual mission budget for the Californias was used to purchase clothes to cover the Native California's "indecency" (Jackson 1999). Colonial policies about sexuality influenced the architecture of colonial settlements and the contents of supply shipments sent to the frontier from central New Spain. The archaeological record of Spanish colonial settlements was thus formed in part through the ongoing dynamics of ethnosexual conflict.

Architecture of sexual control

The stark differences between colonial and indigenous sexual ideologies meant that sexuality was a flashpoint of conflict throughout the colonization of Alta California. In San Francisco's missions, *monjeríos* (women's barracks) housed all unmarried Native Californian women and girls from late childhood until marriage. The monjeríos were particularly designed to prohibit premarital sex; abstinence was enforced by the priests with the aid of a matron.

Although the missionaries themselves considered the monjeríos to be benign institutions that protected indigenous women from lustful desires (Engelhart 1908–15:558), others were more critical. Foreign visitors (e.g., Kotzebue 1830) often described the monjeríos as unsanitary and crowded prisons that contributed to the spread of disease, a claim that has been substantiated by historical demographic studies (Bouvier 2001; Cook 1943; Jackson and Castillo 1995). Additionally, the monjeríos also increased indigenous women's vulnerability to sexual assault by priests and mission employees (Voss 2000).

Sexualization of military conflict

The monjeríos were only one element of the colonial landscape shaped by ethnosexual conflicts. Military conflict, in particular, was highly gendered and sexualized. Only men could enlist in the colonial military, a fact that was so widely accepted it was never codified into law. As a result, combat zones were highly masculinized regions of social life. Soldiers from the San Francisco presidio routinely attacked unmissionized Native Californians in their home villages in the coastal mountain ranges and the Central Valley. This created a region of colonial encounters in which colonial women were largely absent. Not coincidentally, military conflict within these inland zones was also sexualized. Rape functioned as an unofficial but widely deployed military tactic, creating "a disturbing pattern of wholesale sexual assault" against Native Californians (Castillo 1994:283; see also Bouvier 2001; Castañeda 1993b; Cook 1943; Jackson and Castillo 1995; Monroy 1990). Junípero Serra, the founding administrator-priest of the Alta California missions, described such campaigns:

> In the morning, six or more soldiers would set out together ... on horseback, and go to the distant rancherías [Indian villages] ... the soldiers, clever as they are with their lassoing cows and mules, would catch Indian women with their lassos to become prey for their unbridled lust. At times some Indian men would try to defend their wives, only to be shot down by bullets. (Jackson and Castillo 1995:75)

One Native Californian response to sexualized military violence was the spatial reorganization of village plans. Precolonial Native Californian villages in the San Francisco Bay area and in the Central Valley generally followed local topography and were loosely strung along a creek

bank or the bay shore. Archaeological research indicates that work areas for food processing, basket making, hide preparation, and other tasks usually performed by women were located on the periphery of these settlements. For example, Barbara Bocek's analyses of artifact distributions from village sites in the midpeninsula region revealed a central core that contained dwellings and food preparation areas. Tasks requiring flaked or groundstone tools, such as hide processing and acorn and seed processing, were performed in a peripheral zone to the east and south of this central region (Bocek 1991). Similarly, Thomas Jackson has found that bedrock mortar features, used for grinding seeds and acorns, were often located circa 50 meters away from housing areas in late prehistoric villages. Jackson suggests that grinding areas might have represented a "discrete women's space" separate from the mixed-gender main village area (Jackson 1991:315).

During the Spanish colonial era, the location of women's work areas on the periphery of indigenous villages left them especially vulnerable to ambush by colonial soldiers. Missionaries such as Pedro Font described Native Californian women fleeing from their work areas into their homes to avoid "the various excesses" of colonial soldiers (Castañeda 1993b). There are indications that at least some villages were deliberately reoriented to deter sexual assaults by colonial troops. For example, in 1797 Sergeant Pedro Amador reported that the Saclan village of Jussent had been reorganized into clusters of tightly packed thatch houses, with work areas located in the protected yards of each cluster. Further, new ditches around each housing cluster prevented colonial troops from riding into the village on horseback (Milliken 1995:157).

Military personnel were perceived as a sexual threat to Native Californians even within colonial settlements. Each mission housed four to eight soldiers who were charged with protecting the priests and preventing fugitivism. Initially, these troops were housed in the main quadrangle of each mission, next to Native Californian housing. However, by the 1790s most priests had ordered the construction of separate military housing outside the missions' main quadrangles (Bouvier 2001; Jackson and Castillo 1995). By the 1800s, the soldiers' residences were "always located on the opposite side of the quadrangle from the Indian dwellings" (Costello and Hornbeck 1989:310) to insulate Native Californian converts from the sexual abuses and secular influences of military settlers.

Gendered labor regimes

Sexualized warfare in San Francisco produced gendered labor regimes. After a successful battle, colonial soldiers separated their prisoners of war by age and gender, sending women and children to the nearest mission to be converted to Christianity. Native Californian men, however, were escorted to El Presidio de San Francisco, where they were sentenced to convict labor for several months to a few years. Native Californian male laborers at El Presidio de San Francisco worked primarily in construction and agriculture. Although war captives bore the harshest duties, the military command also obtained crews of adult male laborers from nearby missions and through labor contracts with leaders of unmissionized Native Californian villages. Over time, the number of adult male Native Californians working at El Presidio de San Francisco increased dramatically, from 5–20 workers in the 1780s to 60–70 workers in the 1790s to as many as 100 workers during the 1800–10s (Voss 2008a:77–83).

These gendered labor practices severely disrupted Native Californian family life, as men were separated from their wives and children for months and sometimes years at a time. Within the colonial settlement itself, archaeological evidence suggests that Native Californian men did not live in the main quadrangle, where most colonial families resided, but instead were probably housed in work camps north and east of the main quadrangle (Voss 2008a:159–163). This spatial segregation may have been intended to minimize interactions between the indigenous workers and the colonial women and children living in the settlement.

At El Presidio de San Francisco, these gendered labor regimes fostered situations in which colonial soldiers performed a form of masculinity derived from the control of other men's labor. This was particularly the case during the frequent construction projects that aimed to stabilize and expand the settlement's fragile mud-brick architecture. Designed by colonial

officers and implemented by rank-and-file soldiers who directed the Native Californian workers, architectural projects were social venues in which power differences between men were materially enacted through chain-of-command decision making and labor disciplines.

To date, there is little historic or archaeological evidence of Native Californian women's labor at El Presidio de San Francisco, suggesting that those who worked there were probably hired privately rather than contracted by the military command. In 1777, José Joaquín Moraga, commander of El Presidio de San Francisco, ordered, "If it is necessary to employ the Indian women to mill grain or do other chores, they are to do it outside the doorway, in plain view, without being permitted to go inside (as has been done until now), inasmuch as this kind of familiarity leads to grievances against both populations" (Milliken 1995:75–76). This short passage indicates that domestic workers were particularly vulnerable to sexual predation by their employers.

Colonial ethnogenesis

Ethnogenesis refers to the emergence and articulation of new ethnic identities. The military settlers who founded El Presidio de San Francisco were people of mixed Mexican Indian, African, and, to a much lesser degree, European heritage (Mason 1998). Under Spanish-colonial law, the settlers were classified according to the sistema de castas, an elaborate legal code that included as many as 40 different racial classifications. The fine gradations in the sistema de castas provided opportunities for individuals to shift their casta through court cases, marriages, patronage, migration, changes in personal appearance, and, in many cases, simply by declaration (Cope 1994; Mason 1998; Moorhead 1975; Mörner 1967). Several military settlers at El Presidio de San Francisco actively manipulated the sistema de castas to improve their and their families' status (Forbes 1983). But in the early 1800s, the military settlers went a step further by rejecting the sistema de castas altogether and claiming a new shared ethnic identity: Californios. This new ethnicity simultaneously referenced the region in which the colonial settlers lived and also emphasized Spanish ancestry at the expense of Mexican Indian and African identities.

Californio ethnogenesis was a complex, multistaged process (Voss 2008a:113–115). Throughout, the emergence of this new ethnic identity involved transformation of sexual codes and sexual relations. Ethnicity, race, and nationality have "sexual substructures" (Nagel 2000:109) through reference to actual or perceived shared ancestry, heredity, and kinship. In the Spanish-colonial Americas, *casta* designations were used to delineate honorable sexual relationships from dishonorable ones; and sexual relationships, in turn, produced the contested spectrum of racialized subjects that constituted the next generation of castas. The military settlers' rejection of casta rankings and the concomitant ethnogenesis of Californio identities must have had concurrent effects on gendered and sexual ideologies and practices.

The honor–shame complex provides a particularly useful lens through which to examine the intertwined transformation of ethnic, racial, and gendered practices. Within honor–shame ideologies, men's masculinity was gained through honor accrued through sexual conquests and by protecting the sexual virtue of female relatives. Honor and shame also differentiated between virtuous and fallen women, the latter of which were undeserving of protection from sexual assault. Masculinist ideologies of honor and shame likely contributed to the widespread patterns of sexual assault by some colonial men against some Native Californian women, as described above.

The architectural history of El Presidio de San Francisco's main quadrangle provides a material line of evidence of changing gender and sexual relations among the military settlers. In societies in which honor–shame ideologies are prominent, architecture is often used to support the preservation of feminine honor. Most commonly, residential architecture and public areas are partitioned or otherwise subdivided to create visual privacy and discrete enclosures, allowing women to conduct daily activities away from the public gaze. Formal spatial analysis of El Presidio de San Francisco's main quadrangle reveals significant changes in spatial partitioning and enclosure in colonial architecture (Voss 2008a:173–202). Initially, partitioned residential space was a privilege accorded to officers, who lived in multiroom dwellings with private walled yards, while rank-and-file soldiers and their families lived in small one-room houses. However, the quadrangle and its central plaza were not enclosed (as was required by military regulations) but instead stood completely open on its eastern side. In the 1810s, this configuration changed: later residences consisted of singleroom apartments, constructed in contiguous rows lining the central plaza. The plaza itself more than doubled in size, and for the first time the settlement was fully enclosed by a continuous exterior adobe wall (see Figure 12.3).

These changes signaled a transformation of spatial practices associated with the Californios' repudiation of casta classifications and the consolidation of their new shared ethnic identity. In the 1810s, practices related to honor and shame appear to have shifted from being a household-based elite practice to a paternalistic obligation of the military command toward the community at large. The newly rebuilt quadrangle allowed the settlers to physically control entrance to and egress from the settlement. The expanded, and fully enclosed, plaza offered a secure, visually protected interior space within which the military settlers could conduct their daily routines. In particular, this enclosure may have minimized contact between colonial women and the growing numbers of Native Californian men laboring at the settlement. This interpretation is supported by the artifactual evidence: almost no Native Californian artifacts have been found within the expanded quadrangle, although they are common in the extramural zones of the settlement (Voss 2008a:159–163). Californio ethnogenesis, it appears, involved the policing of the ethnosexual boundary between colonial women and indigenous men, and furthermore may have involved heightened surveillance of colonial women's conduct by the community as a whole.

Conclusion

I began this article by noting the prevalence of household studies of colonization in the Spanish Americas. Although the insights garnered by household-scale investigations have been valuable, this emphasis has at times domesticated imperialism by portraying colonization as an

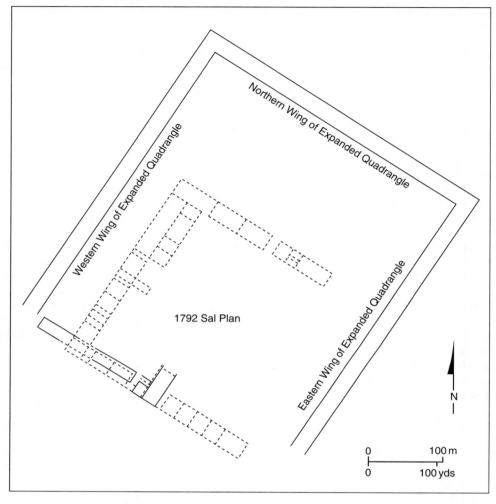

Figure 12.3 Schematic diagram showing relationship between El Presidio de San Francisco's earlier quadrangle (ca. 1792) and the later quadrangle expansion (ca. 1815).

interpresonal and consensual process. In Spanish-colonial San Francisco, the sexual politics of colonization were not located within marriages between colonial men and indigenous women. The colonial settlers were selected for their compliance with gendered and sexual norms and their proven reproductive capabilities. In the decades that followed the establishment of El Presidio de San Francisco, their new California identity emerged alongside heightened attention to differential masculinity and increased community surveillance of colonial women. The military settlers implemented colonial sexual policies that included violent campaigns against so-called sexual pagans and persecution of Native Californian two-spirits. Although not legally sanctioned, sexual assault was a patterned aspect of colonial–indigenous interactions, and gendered labor regimes profoundly disrupted the family lives of captive and conscripted Native Californians.

Although sexuality is sometimes treated as a trivial or private aspect of social life, the archaeology and ethnohistory of Spanish-colonial San Francisco demonstrates that sexual politics were central, rather than incidental, to the imperial project. The gender composition of the colonial population, and the forms that interracial sexual unions took, were conditioned in great part through the policies and regulations of the colonizing polity, rather than being a personal matter among private individuals. There were certainly cases in which intermarriage and the formation of interethnic households was an important element of the processes and outcomes of colonization. Yet these interpersonal relationships were influenced by and in turn participated in more public imperial sexual politics. Further, interracial sexual contact between colonizers and colonized was often violent, strategic, and public, rather than consensual, domestic, or private.

This and other research also indicates that there was considerable variability in the sexual politics of colonial ventures throughout the Americas. This should not be surprising, as Spain's imperial program in the Americas encountered an astounding range of cultures, economies, and polities. These ranged from powerful empires, such as the Aztec and Incan empires, to regions that contained sparsely populated mobile hunter–gatherers. The sexual practices and gender systems of American indigenous communities were as varied as their economic and political systems and religious beliefs. Further, the objectives of Spanish-colonial ventures varied as well, including different degrees of religious, commercial, and military involvement. It follows that the sexual components of conquest and colonization would have been shaped by all these factors. Although the institutional policies of the Spanish empire provided a degree of coherence in colonial settings throughout the Americas, nonetheless it seems advisable to refrain from assuming a uniformity of colonial sexual politics.

Household archaeology at Spanish colonial sites has made important contributions to scholarship on empire by drawing attention to the ways that colonization is implemented on the microscale. In the end, such household-level studies will provide the greatest insights when they are interpreted within a multiscalar context that includes investigations of colonial institutions, including the church, the military, and governmental and commercial economic enterprises. Sexual politics forge intimate relationships between the institutional and the personal, relationships that reverberate throughout many scales of cultural practice.

References

Blackmore, Josiah, and Gregory S. Hutcheson, eds., 1999 Queer Iberia: Sexualities, Cultures, and Crossings from the Middle Ages to the Renaissance. Durham, NC: Duke University Press.

Blind, Eric Brandon, Barbara L. Voss, Sannie K. Osborn, and Leo R. Barker, 2004 El Presidio de San Francisco: At the Edge of Empire. Historical Archaeology 38(3):135–149.

Blind, Heather, and Kevin Bartoy, 2006 Archaeological Investigations of the Mesa Room, Building 50 of the Officers' Club, El Presidio de San Francisco, San Francisco, California. Report to the Presidio Archaeology Center. Berkeley: Pacific Legacy.

Bocek, Barbara, 1991 Prehistoric Settlement Pattern and Social Organization on the San Francisco Peninsula, California. In Between Bands and States. S. A. Gregg, ed. Pp. 58–86. Carbondale: Southern Illinois University, Center for Archaeological Investigations.

Bouvier, Virginia M., 2001 Women and the Conquest of California, 1542–1840: Codes of Silence. Tucson: University of Arizona Press.

Castañeda, Antonia I., 1993a Marriage: The Spanish Borderlands. In Encyclopedia of the North American Colonies. Jacob E. Cook, ed. Pp. 727–738. New York: Maxwell Macmillan International.

Castañeda, Antonia I., 1993b Sexual Violence in the Politics and Policies of Conquest: Amerindian Women and the Spanish Conquest of Alta California. In Building with Our Hands: New Directions in Chicana Studies. Adela de la Torre and Beatriz M. Pesquera, eds. Pp. 15–33. Berkeley: University of California Press.

Castillo, Edward D., 1994 The Language of Race Hatred. In The Ohlone Past and Present: Native Americans of the San Francisco Bay Region. Lowell John Bean, ed. Pp. 271–295. Menlo Park, CA: Ballena.

Chapman, Charles Edward, 1916 The Founding of Spanish California: The Northwest Expansion of New Spain, 1687–1783. New York: Macmillan.

Charlton, Thomas H., Cynthia L. Otis Charlton, and Patricia Fournier-Garcia, 2005 The Basin of Mexico A.D. 1450–1620: Archaeological Dimensions. In The

Postclassic to Spanish-Era Transition in Mesoamerica: Archaeological Perspectives. Susan Kepecs and Rani T. Alexander, eds. Pp. 49–63. Albuquerque: University of New Mexico Press.

Charlton, Thomas H., and Patricia G. Fournier, 1993 Urban and Rural Dimensions of the Contact Period, Central Mexico, 1521–1620. In Ethnohistory and Archaeology: Approaches to Postcontact Change in the Americas. J. Daniel Rodgers and Samuel M. Wilson, eds. Pp. 201–220. New York: Plenum Press.

Cook, Sherburne F., 1943 The Conflict between the California Indian and White Civilization. Berkeley: University of California Press.

Cope, R. Douglas, 1994 The Limits of Racial Domination: Plebeian Society in Colonial Mexico City, 1660–1720. Madison: University of Wisconsin Press.

Costello, Julia G., and David Hornbeck, 1989 Alta California: An Overview. In Columbian Consequences, vol. 1: Archaeological and Historical Perspectives of the Spanish Borderlands West. David Hurst Thomas, ed. Pp. 303–331. Washington, DC: Smithsonian Institution Press.

Deagan, Kathleen, 1974 Sex, Status, and Role in the Mestizaje of Spanish Colonial Florida. Ph.D. dissertation, Department of Anthropology, University of Florida.

Deagan, Kathleen, 1983 Spanish St. Augustine: The Archaeology of a Colonial Creole Community. New York: Academic Press.

Deagan, Kathleen, ed., 1995 Puerto Real: The Archaeology of a Sixteenth-Century Spanish Town in Hispaniola. Gainesville: University Press of Florida.

Deagan, Kathleen, 2002 Artifacts of the Spanish Colonies of Florida and the Caribbean, 1500–1800, vol. 2: Portable Personal Possessions. Washington, DC: Smithsonian Institution Press.

Deagan, Kathleen, 2003 Colonial Origins and Colonial Transformations in Spanish America. Historical Archaeology 27(4):3–13.

Deagan, Kathleen, and José María Cruxent, 2002 Columbus's Outpost among the Taínos: Spain and America at La Isabela, 1493–1498. New Haven, CT: Yale University Press.

Deetz, James F., 1963 Archaeological Investigations at La Purisima Mission. UCLA Archaeological Survey Annual Report 5:165–191.

Engelhart, Zephyrin, 1908–15 The Missions and Missionaries of California. San Francisco: James H. Barry.

Engstrand, Iris H. W., 1998 Seekers of the "Northern Mystery": European Exploration of California and the Pacific. In Contested Eden: California before the Gold Rush. Ramon A. Gutierrez and Richard J. Orsi, eds. Pp. 78–110. Berkeley: University of California Press.

Ewen, Charles R., 1991 From Spaniard to Creole: The Archaeology of Cultural Formation at Puerto Real, Haiti. Tuscaloosa: University of Alabama Press.

Fairbanks, Charles H., 1962 Excavations at Horseshoe Bend, Alabama. The Florida Anthropologist 15 (2):41–56.

Font, Pedro, 1930[1776] Font's Complete Diary of the Second Anza Expedition. Herbert Eugene Bolton, ed. and. trans. Berkeley: University of California Press.

Forbes, Jack D., 1983 Hispano-Mexican Pioneers of the San Francisco Bay Region: An Analysis of Racial Origins. Aztlan 14:175–189.

Frink, Lisa, 2007 Storage and Status in Precolonial and Colonial Coastal Western Alaska. Current Anthropology 48(3):349–374.

Hollimon, Sandra E., 1997 The Third Gender in Native California: Two-Spirit Undertakers among the Chumash and Their Neighbors. In Women in Prehistory North American and Mesoamerica. Cheryl Claassen and Rosemary A. Joyce, eds. Pp. 173–188. Philadelphia: University of Pennsylvania Press.

Hurtado, Albert L., 1999 Intimate Frontiers: Sex, Gender, and Culture in Old California. Albuquerque: University of New Mexico Press.

Jackson, Robert H., 1999 Race, Caste, and Status: Indians in Colonial Spanish America. Albuquerque: University of New Mexico Press.

Jackson, Robert H., and Edward Castillo, 1995 Indians, Franciscans, and Spanish Colonization. Albuquerque: University of New Mexico Press.

Jackson, Thomas L., 1991 Pounding Acorn: Women's Production as Social and Economic Focus. In Engendering Archaeology: Women and Prehistory. Joan M. Gero and Margaret W. Conkey, eds. Pp. 301–328. Cambridge, MA: Basil Blackwell.

Jamieson, Ross W., 2000 Doña Luisa and Her Two Houses. In Lines That Divide: Historical Archaeologies of Race, Class, and Gender. James A. Delle, Stephen A. Mrozowski, and Robert Paynter, eds. Pp. 142–167. Knoxville: University of Tennessee Press.

Katz, Jonathan, 1976 Gay American History: Lesbians and Gay Men in the U.S.A. New York: Thomas Crowell.

Kotzebue, Otto von, 1830 A New Voyage Round the World in the Years 1823, 24, 25, and 26. London: H. Colburn and R. Bentley.

Kroeber, A. L., 1925 Handbook of the Indians of California. Washington, DC: Government Printing Office.

Langellier, John Phillip, and Daniel B. Rosen, 1996 El Presidio de San Francisco: A History under Spain and Mexico, 1776–1846. Spokane, WA: Arthur H. Clark.

Levy, Richard, 1978 Costanoan. *In* Handbook of North American Indians, vol. 8: California. Robert F. Heizer, ed. Pp. 485–495. Washington, DC: Smithsonian Institution Press.

Lightfoot, Kent G., 2005 Indians, Missionaries, and Merchants: The Legacy of Colonial Encounters on the California Frontiers. Berkeley: University of California Press.

Loren, Diana DiPaolo, 1999 Creating Social Distinction: Articulating Colonial Policies and Practices along the 18th Century Louisiana/Texas Frontier. Ph.D. dissertation, Department of Anthropology, Binghamton State University of New York.

McClintock, Anne, 1995 Imperial Leather: Race, Gender, and Sexuality in the Colonial Conquest. New York: Routledge.

McEwan, Bonnie G., 1991 The Archaeology of Women in the Spanish New World. Historical Archaeology 25(4):33–41.

McEwan, Bonnie G., 1995 Spanish Precedents and Domestic Life at Puerto Real: The Archaeology of Two Spanish Homesites. *In* Puerto Real: The Archaeology of a Sixteenth-Century Spanish Town in Hispaniola. Kathleen Deagan, ed. Pp. 197–229. Gainesville: University Press of Florida.

Margolin, Malcolm, 1978 The Ohlone Way: Indian Life in the San Francisco–Monterey Bay Area. Berkeley: Heyday Books.

Martinez, Antoinette, 1994 Native California Women as Cultural Mediators. Proceedings of the Society for California Archaeology 7:41–46.

Mason, Carol I., 1963 Eighteenth-Century Culture Change among the Lower Creeks. The Florida Anthropologist 16(3):65–80.

Mason, William Marvin, 1998 The Census of 1790: A Demographic History of Colonial California. Menlo Park, CA: Ballena.

Milliken, Randall, 1995 A Time of Little Choice. Menlo Park, CA: Ballena.

Milliken, Randall, Lawrence E. Shoup, and Beverly Ortiz, 2005 The Historic Indian People of California's San Francisco Peninsula: Draft Report: Prepared for the National Park Service, Golden Gate National Recreation Area. Oakland: Archaeological Consulting Services.

Mohanty, Chandra Talpade, 1997 Under Western Eyes: Feminist Scholarship and Colonial Discourses. *In* Dangerous Liaisons: Gender, Nations, and Postcolonial Perspectives. Anne McClintock, Aamir Mufti, and Ella Shohat, eds. Pp. 255–277. Minneapolis: Minnesota University Press.

Monroy, Douglas, 1990 Thrown among Strangers: The Making of Mexican Culture in Frontier California. Berkeley: University of California Press.

Montalvo, Garci Rodriquez de, 2001 [1510] La Conclusión del Amadis de Guala: Las Sergas de Esplandián.

Elroy R. Gonzalez Arguelles, ed. Potomac, MD: Scripta Humanistica.

Moorhead, Max L, 1975 The Presidio: Bastion of the Spanish Borderlands. Norman: University of Oklahoma Press.

Mörner, Magnus, 1967 Race Mixture in the History of Latin America. Boston: Little, Brown.

Nagel, Joane, 2000 Ethnicity and Sexuality. Annual Review of Sociology 26:107–133.

Nagel, Joane, 2003 Race, Ethnicity, and Sexuality: Intimate Intersections, Forbidden Frontiers. Oxford: Oxford University Press.

Palóu, Francisco, 1926 Historical Memoirs of New California, vol. 4. Herbert Eugene Bolton, ed. and trans. Berkeley, CA: University of California Press.

Polk, Dora Beale, 1991 The Island of California: A History of the Myth. Lincoln: University of Nebraska Press.

Powers, Karen Vieira, 2002 Conquering Discourses of "Sexual Conquest": Of Women, Language, and Mestizaje. Colonial Latin American Review 11 (1):7–32.

Press, Irwin, 1969 Ambiguity and Innovation: Implications for the Genesis of the Cultural Broker. American Anthropologist 71(2):205–217.

Rodríguez-Alegría, Enrique, 2005a Consumption and the Varied Ideologies of Domination in Colonial Mexico City. *In* The Postclassic to Spanish-Era Transition in Mesoamerica: Archaeological Perspectives. Susan Kepecs and Rani T. Alexander, eds. Pp. 35–48. Albuquerque: University of New Mexico Press.

Rodríguez-Alegría, Enrique, 2005b Eating Like an Indian: Negotiating Social Relations in the Spanish Colonies. Current Anthropology 46(4):551–573.

Roscoe, Will, 1998 Changing Ones: Third and Fourth Genders in Native North America. New York: Saint Martin's Press.

Rothschild, Nan A., 2003 Colonial Encounters in a Native American Landscape: The Spanish and Dutch in North America. Washington, DC: Smithsonian Institution Press.

Scott, Elizabeth M., 1991 A Feminist Approach to Historical Archaeology: Eighteenth-Century Fur Trade Society at Michilimackinac. Historical Archaeology 25(4):42–53.

Simpson-Smith, Charr, and Rob Edwards, 2000 San Francisco Spanish Colonial Presidio: Field and Laboratory Report for 1996, 1997, 1998, and 1999, with Stratigraphic Discussion. Aptos, CA: Cabrillo College Archaeological Technology Program.

Smith, Greg Charles, 1997a Andean and European Contributions to Spanish Colonial Culture and Viticulture in Moquegua, Peru. *In* Approaches to the Historical Archaeology of Mexico, Central, and

South America. Janine L. Gasco, Greg Charles Smith, and Patricia Fournier-Garcia, eds. Pp. 165–172. Los Angeles: Institute of Archaeology, University of California, Los Angeles.

Smith, Greg Charles, 1997b Hispanic, Andean, and African Influences in the Moquegua Valley of Southern Peru. Historical Archaeology 31(1):74–83.

South, Stanley, 1988 Santa Elena: Threshold of Conquest. *In* The Recovery of Meaning: Historical Archaeology in the Eastern United States. Mark P. Leone and Parker B. Potter Jr., eds. Pp. 27–72. Washington, DC: Smithsonian Institution Press.

Spector, Janet D., 1993 What This Awl Means: Feminist Archaeology at a Wahpeton Dakota Village. St. Paul: Minnesota Historical Society Press.

Stoler, Ann Laura, 2002 Carnal Knowledge and Imperial Power: Race and the Intimate in Colonial Rule. Berkeley: University of California Press.

Szasz, Margaret Connell, ed., 1994 Between Indian and White Worlds: The Cultural Broker. Norman: University of Oklahoma Press.

Trocolli, Ruth, 1992 Colonization and Women's Production: The Timucua of Florida. *In* Exploring Gender through Archaeology: Selected Papers from the 1991 Boone Conference. Monographs in World Archaeology, 11. Cheryl Classen, ed. Pp. 95–102. Madison, WI: Prehistory Press.

Van Buren, Mary, 1999 Tarapaya: An Elite Spanish Residence near Colonial Potosí in Comparative Perspective. Historical Archaeology 33(2):101–115.

Voss, Barbara L., 2000 Colonial Sex: Archaeology, Structured Space, and Sexuality in Alta California's Spanish-Colonial Missions. *In* Archaeologies of Sexuality. Robert A. Schmidt and Barbara L. Voss, eds. Pp. 35–61. London: Routledge.

Voss, Barbara L., 2002 The Archaeology of El Presidio de San Francisco: Culture Contact, Gender, and Ethnicity in a Spanish-Colonial Military Community. Ph.D. dissertation, Department of Anthropology, University of California, Berkeley.

Voss, Barbara L., 2005 From Casta to California: Social Identity and the Archaeology of Culture Contact. American Anthropologist 107(3):461–474.

Voss, Barbara L., 2008a The Archaeology of Ethnogenesis: Race and Sexuality in Colonial San Francisco. Berkeley: University of California Press.

Voss, Barbara L., 2008b Gender, Race, and Labor in the Archaeology of the Spanish-Colonial Americas: Reconsidering the St. Augustine Pattern. Current Anthropology 49(5):861–893.

Voss, Barbara L., and Vance G. Benté, 1996 Archaeological Discovery and Investigation of the Historic Presidio de San Francisco. Oakland, CA: Woodward-Clyde.

Wagner, Mark J., 1998 Some Think It Impossible to Civilize Them at All: Cultural Change and Continuity among the Early Nineteenth-Century Potawatomi. *In* Studies in Culture Contact: Interaction, Culture Change, and Archaeology. James Gregory Cusick, ed. Pp. 430–456. Carbondale: Center for Archaeological Investigations, Southern Illinois University.

Williams, Walter L., 1986 The Spirit and the Flesh: Sexual Diversity in American Indian Culture. Boston: Beacon Press.

Wolf, Eric R., 1956 Aspects of Group Relations in a Complex Society: Mexico. American Anthropologist 58(6):1065–1078.

Part V

Race, Class, and Ethnicity

RACE, CLASS, AND ETHNICITY have been and continue to be influential ways in which we categorize ourselves. Human "races" have been historically defined on the basis of a small number of superficial anatomical characteristics. These include most notably such traits as skin color, body type, and hair texture. Biological anthropologists, however, have demonstrated that all attempts to divide humanity into biological races are scientifically invalid (Goodman 1997). Supposed racial groups are largely cultural and historical constructs, the product of specific population movements and interactions. The present-day inequalities between so-called "racial groups" are due not to genetics, but rather to past and present social, economic, educational, and political circumstances (Shanklin 1993). This, of course, does not mean that race does not exist. To the contrary, "race discourse" is a very real part of the world we live in today (Harrison 1995; Jackson 2008). Similarly, ethnic groups are usually defined on the basis of a sense of collective identity based upon a shared geographical origin. They are often responses to nationalism as new political economies emerge and seek to transcend ethnic identities. Finally, class is usually regarded as category based upon kind of work and income level (Mrozowski 2006). Marx, of course, identified class as the key to his analysis of capitalism. For him, classes are defined and structured by the relations concerning work and labor and the ownership or possession of property and the means of production. In the United States, class identity swirls around differing notions about the meaning of the middle class.

In the United States, the archaeology of Native America is traditionally separated out from the archaeology of non-Native Americans as the domain of prehistoric archaeology. During the colonial period, however, it was not immediately accepted that Native Americans were the original inhabitants of America. This perspective is well illustrated by the so-called "Moundbuilder debate" (McGuire 1992; Orser 2004). As the country expanded west to what is now Ohio, West Virginia, and Illinois, displacing the local Indian inhabitants, settlers discovered remarkable mounds and earthworks. There was considerable speculation about the builders of these monuments. Some people argued that they were made by Native Americans, but many others proposed that they were the produce of more "civilized peoples." Popular speculation ran rampant and implicated the Lost Tribes of Israel, the Vikings, the Danes, the Welsh, among others. Early scholars and scientists played an active role in this debate, taking up sides. For example Caleb Atwater (1820), postmaster of Circleville, Ohio, and an amateur archaeologist, favored the idea that Hindus were responsible for the mounds. The telling evidence for him seems to have been a rather remarkable ceramic vessel with three effigy heads joined at the back to a central spout (what he called a triune vase). He interpreted this vessel saying "all the strong marks of the Tartar countenance are distinctly preserved, and expressed with so much skill, that even a modern artist might be proud of the performance" and went on to suggest that it represented the three chief gods of India: Brahama, Vishnu, and Shiva (Atwater 1820:271). This debate was not fully resolved until John Wesley Powell of the Bureau of American Ethnology hired Cyrus Thomas to conduct scientific investigations into the question. Thomas (1885) systematically evaluated the existing evidence and concluded that the mounds and earthworks were the work not of Europeans but of many different Native American communities.

The archaeology of African Americans, Chinese Americans, Hispanic Americans, Irish Americans, and so on, by contrast, has been the domain of historical archaeology. The standard approach to the study of the social categories of race, class, and ethnicity has been to address them individually in order to assess their influence in a particular context (Schuyler 1980). Vernon Baker (1980) conducted a comparative analysis of ceramics from the Lucy Foster and Parting Ways sites in Massachusetts and a slave cabin in Georgia. He hoped that his study would reveal patterns of material culture that were distinctive of African American behavior. However, he concluded that the ceramics were identical to those from Anglo-American sites. In the end, he could not determine whether the artifacts reflected poverty or ethnicity. Kathleen Deagan (1983) provided a pioneering study of colonial Spanish ethnicity and native acculturation at St. Augustine, Florida. She was able to identify the emergence of a distinctive Spanish-Indian culture facilitated by the practice of *mestizaje*. This new culture was not the replication of Iberian culture, but rather a composite with the public part more Iberian and the private more acculturated. She termed this a creole identity. These, and related studies, inspired the development of the archaeology of slavery (e.g. Singleton 1985, 1988) and plantation archaeology (e.g. Armstrong 1985, 1990).

Feminist scholars drew attention to the limitations of such one-dimensional approaches and began to investigate how these categories overlapped in the social construction of self and community (Conkey and Williams 1991; Gilchrist 1991, 1999). This critique paralleled developments in feminist theory (McCall 2005) and critiques by women of color (e.g. hooks 1982, 1984; Mohanty 1988). In response to these criticisms, feminist scholars have introduced the concept of intersectionality to foster the study of the intersection of social variables such as race, class, gender, sexuality, age, and ethnicity (see Collins 1991, 1993; Brewer 1993). Although archaeologists have not yet taken up intersectionality in any detail, they have begun to explore the relative effects of social categories in particular social contexts. Paul Mullins (1999, 2004) demonstrates the way class considerations appear to have been more important than race in influencing the purchasing choices of African Americans during the 19th century. Maria Franklin's (1997, 2001) research represents a successful attempt to examine the nexus of race and gender in the study of African American life. She has also examined the intersection of race and ethnicity (Franklin and Fesler 1999). Diana Wall (1994, 2000) has also explored the intersection of class, gender, and ethnicity by looking at families living in 19th-century New York. Orser (2001, 2004, 2007) has explored the way the identity of particular cultural groups is perceived through a convergence of race and class that results in these groups being racialized – a process in which particular sectors of a population are classified as essentialized groups who are perceived as biologically or socially inferior (Orser 2007). In the case of African American and Chinese American communities, racialization has revolved around constructed racial categories being conflated with ethnicity. For Irish immigrants living in the United States and Britain the intersection of class, ethnicity, and religion has conspired to result in their racialization as well (Delle 1998; Orser 2007). Examples such as these point to the power of race, class, and ethnicity as cultural and political forces in human relations.

The archaeology of class, by contrast, has lagged behind the study of other social categories (see McGuire and Paynter 1991; Duke and Saitta 1998; Wurst and Fitts 1999; Mrozowski 2006; Saitta 2007; McGuire 2008). This is due in part to the ambivalence toward class as a category of social inquiry. For much of the 20th century, class had held a position of prominence as a research focus in the social sciences. Despite its importance, however, class has remained an elusive concept to define. Depending upon the discipline, class is viewed as an abstract, often statistical, reality, as in the case of income groups, or as a form of social construction. One of the more difficult qualities of class is its relational quality. Class can be defined as a self-referential form of identity, or discursivity (Mrozowski 2006). These sorts of ambiguities were part of the reason class was supplanted by gender, sexuality, and ethnicity, as more meaningful markers of identity (Mrozowski 2006).

As archaeologists began to explore the topic of identity, class was rejoined as focus of social inquiry along with race, gender, sexuality, and ethnicity (Delle et al. 2000). Mrozowski (2006) has explored the way the meaning of class changed as mercantile capitalism was eclipsed by industrial and managerial capitalism between the 18th and early 20th centuries. As notions such as "the middling sort" gave way to more modern notions such as "middle class," the materiality of class became a driving force behind capitalism's mercurial rise to power as an economic regime. Yet what Mrozowski discovered was that material culture often masked class differences and helped in blurring the lines of difference. As a result he questioned the actual meaning of concepts such as middle class and working class. There seemed little question that class was real enough for the people who experienced it, but the materiality of class difference was far from clear. Where class differences were stark was at the biological level, the natures of capitalism. Here class differences resulted in decaying living and working conditions for the working class, while middle-class workers found their domestic space transformed into genteel spaces of ornamentation.

An archaeology of class thus involves the comparative study of the similarities and differences between ancient and modern lifeways as related to the social organization of production (Saitta 2007:110). It involves addressing groups that typically see themselves through the lens of identity and revealing that they share common class experiences. One of the most important archaeological studies to date is the Colorado Coalfield War project directed by the Ludlow Collective (2001; Saitta 2007; McGuire 2008). This is a collaborative project involving several institutions and a descendant community that includes members of the United Mine Workers of America, who own the Ludlow site. The site was the scene of a tragic massacre little noted in history books. In 1913, the coal miners in Ludlow, Colorado, struck for better wages and working conditions. Their demands were not met and Pinkerton detectives were called in to break up the strike. On April 20, 1914, this culminated in the burning of the small tent community established during the industrial action. Twenty people died in the conflagration, including 11 children. The archaeology of the site was able to discover the subterranean pits that served as homes for many of the miners and their families, including one in which a large number of the children died. Although the archaeology revealed much in the way of daily life in the tent community, its most powerful contribution was its rediscovery of the event and its giving new voice to the collective action of the workers and their families.

No discussion of ethnicity can fail to acknowledge its controversial history in European prehistory. The first use of the term has been attributed to the latter half of the 19th century and nationalist interests in the common origins of Indian and European languages and the migrations of specific social groups (Malina and Vasícek 1990). Rudolf Virchow used ceramics to distinguish between Slavic and Germanic occupation layers at hillforts in Lusatia. Oscar Montelius used the direct historical approach to trace the roots of Germanic people in Northern Europe to the Mesolithic period. Gustav Kossina equated culture and *ethnos* and held that the Germanic people were derived from a single origin in northern Germany and southern Scandinavia. Bettina Arnold (1990) has shown how the Nazi leaders used the work of Kossina as propaganda in the legitimization of the Aryan race. As Arnold notes, the National Socialist regime exaggerated and misrepresented archaeological evidence in various ways to support contemporary military and social agendas, ranging from invasion to genocide. Despite its connections with unpalatable forms of nationalism, however, ethnicity remains an important interpretive concept in contemporary European archaeology (see Shennan 1989; Dietler 1994; Jones 1997).

In some cases, the archaeology of ethnicity continues to be part of a nationalist agenda. Sarah Nelson examines the immense power ethnicity holds for archaeologists working in Korea. Questions of ethnic origin have been a major preoccupation of Korean history and archaeology. Korea differs from most countries in having a relatively homogeneous population. The standard narrative of Korean history and archaeology is that a single ancestral group migrated to Korea and that something like Koreanness existed within this group prior to their arrival on the Korean peninsula. Nelson explains that this and other interpretations have been dramatically influenced by relatively recent history. The modern division of the peninsula, for example, has resulted in dramatically different narratives that have shaped archaeological research. The emphasis on self-reliance on the part of North Korea has generated a narrative that will not entertain the possibility of a Chinese movement into the area. Similarly, in the South there is strong resentment of the Japanese colonization of the Korean peninsula. During the colonial period, Japanese archaeologists proposed that there was evidence to support a cultural connection between the two nations and this was used to justify the Japanese occupation. Not surprisingly, South Korean archaeologists rejected this idea and, like their counterparts in the North, maintained that the archaeological evidence of ethnic homogeneity tells a different story. Nelson provides an alternative interpretation that suggests that the present ethnic homogeneity was, in fact, forged out of past ethnic diversity. She concludes that the attempt to find wholeness in Korean culture has been detrimental to archaeological interpretation and prevented Korean

archaeologists from developing theories of ethnicity, even as ethnicity has remained a central
area of research.

Siân Jones concentrates on the role of ethnicity in historical archaeology. She begins by raising the question of the relationship between
historical documents and the archaeological
record. Generally speaking, historical studies
have privileged the written word over the artifact. Jones identifies two responses to this situation by historical archaeologists. The first is to
be skeptical of texts since they incorporate bias,
usually the point of view of the elite class. But
this reaction betrays a "fear of the emic," the
attempt to strip away subjectivity, rather than
engage with it (Beaudry et al. 1991:161). The
second is to treat them as separate lines of evidence independent of material culture. This
response is also associated with the retreat from
political history toward long-term social and
economic processes. However, some scholars,
like Martin Hall, have used text to refer to literary and material records where they are studied
together and neither is privileged.

Jones then offers a practice theory approach to
ethnicity. She notes that recent sociological and
anthropological studies have shown that ethnic
identity is not a straightforward reflection of a
group's culture or language. Rather, it is considerably variable and based upon the subjective
understanding of real or assumed shared culture
and/or common descent. It is often the case that
only some cultural practices are involved in the
expression of ethnic differences, while other cultural practices are widely shared. Jones then links
this back to her argument about the data of
historical archaeology. She concludes that rather
than thinking that archaeologists cannot consider ethnicity without historical texts, it is
more appropriate to argue that historians are
unable to study ethnicity without considering
material culture. The material thus complements
the discursive.

If race does not exist, why do we persist in
talking about it and celebrating the archaeology
of racial groups like Native Americans? This
question is the context for Roger Echo-Hawk
and Larry Zimmerman's provocative essay, constructed, in part, from contributions to an email
dialogue on an online discussion group known as
the Closet Chickens. One of the most interesting

aspects of the dialogue is Echo-Hawk and
Zimmerman's exchange about race. Echo-Hawk
initially challenged the members of the discussion
group for their unquestioned use of racial terms
and their advocacy of indigenous archaeology as a
new form of "racial archaeology" (this issue is
discussed in earlier threads). He singles out the
American Indian Quarterly, the publication venue
for the article, because it "cultivates racial Indianhood by devoting itself to uncritical perpetuation
of the basic ideas of race." Zimmerman responds
with an account of the anthropological deconstruction of the race concept and an acknowledgment of the power of race as a social construct. He
suggests that the persistence of race is, in part, due
to our universal human need to classify each
other. Echo-Hawk answers by saying that he sees
the Closet Chickens bonding over the notion of
race, rather than exploring the ways in which
race gives a false perspective on humankind.
Zimmerman then follows up by agreeing with
Echo-Hawk on the value of education and
acknowledging that we have a responsibility to
educate the public about the issue.

This debate has serious implications for society in general. What, in fact, would it mean to
live in a race-blind society of the future? But it
also has real implications for how racial minority scholars currently navigate the academy
today. Echo-Hawk worries about power relations, that decolonizing archaeology may be
seen as simply inserting Indians and Indian-
controlled archaeology into the structure of
white archaeology. He emphasizes the importance of historical process, instead of race, in
addressing identity. But this raises questions
about the pragmatic effects of contemporary
racial discourse. There may be circumstances
when race is a useful tool: for example, in
creating solidarity between Indian archaeologists (like in the Closet Chickens discussion
group) or dealing with racial inequities (like
affirmative action). One strategy that seems to
be emerging is Gayatri Spivak's (1987) notion of
"strategic essentialism," which refers to the ways
in which subordinate or marginalized social
groups may temporarily put aside local differences in order to forge a sense of solidarity
which permits them to come together in political movements. In this case, it might mean that
one could emphasize race in certain contexts for

specific purposes, and still critique it in other contexts for other purposes.

Issues of race and ethnicity are impossible to separate from the pervasive influence of class. Regardless of whether one is discussing the power of racism and racialization to foster prejudice and hate, the issue of class looms beneath the surface, just as large and just as pernicious. In her article dealing with class formation and conflict, LouAnn Wurst confronts many of the issues that have made the archaeological examination of class a contentious subject in its own right. Wurst notes that the academic community, like the United States society in general, has always felt somewhat ambivalent about pursuing class as a topic of research. This is due in a large measure to the misguided belief that class is less problematic in the United States than it is in Europe because of the lack of an aristocracy. But even in Europe, the rise of postmodernist theory and its emphasis on individual agency and identity has, as Wurst notes, marginalized the importance of class as a topic of social inquiry. Despite its recognition among some historical archaeologists, Wurst maintains that class is underdeveloped as a research focus.

Wurst suggests that one reason for the avoidance of class is that theories of class and class relations are somewhat unclear concerning just what class is and how it might be interrogated archaeologically. She draws attention to the two fundamental, but different, views of class: one that sees class as an objective reality based on a person's location within a socially constructed hierarchy; and another that sees class as a characteristic of the social relations of production. In her discussion of these two positions, she concentrates on the limitations of the structuralist view in articulating the interaction between individual and structure. This weakness stems from a reliance on postmodernist theories of individual agency which often fail to address the structure/individual dynamic and thus provide no basis for action. A relational view that draws more heavily on a Marxian dialectical method provides a very different point of entry for examining class relations. Wurst emphasizes that a dialectical approach to the totality of the social context is not the same as a universal explanation, so critiqued by postmodernists. For her, no other concept other than class has the potential to address issues of struggle and resistance in productive relations. Her suggestion is a particularly pragmatic one, namely that archaeologies of class should have as their goal social action. In an argument not unlike that posited by Jones, Wurst strives to clarify the theoretical discourse surrounding class and its utility for a socially active archaeology. In so doing, she argues that greater attention needs to be paid to the critical interrogation of concepts such as race, class, and ethnicity and their various intersections.

References

Armstrong, Douglas V., 1985 An Afro-Jamaican Slave Settlement: Archaeological Investigations at Drax Hall. In The Archaeology of Slavery and Plantation Life. Theresa A. Singleton, ed. Pp. 261–285. New York: Academic Press.

Armstrong, Douglas V., 1990 The Old Village and the Great House: An Archaeological and Historical Examination of Drax Hall Plantation, Jamaica. Urbana: University of Illinois Press.

Arnold, Bettina, 1990 The Past as Propaganda: Totalitarian Archaeology in Nazi Germany. Antiquity 64 (244):464–478.

Atwater, Caleb, 1820 Description of the Antiquities Discovered in the State of Ohio and Other Western States. Transactions and Collections of the American Antiquarian Society 1:105–207.

Baker, Vernon G. 1980 Archaeological Visibility of Afro-American Culture: An Example from Black Lucy's Garden, Andover, Massachusetts. In Archaeological Perspectives on Ethnicity in America: Afro-American and Chinese American Culture History. Robert L. Schuyler, ed. Pp. 29–37. Farmingdale, NY: Baywood.

Beaudry, Mary C., Lauren J. Cook, and Stephen A. Mrozowski, 1991 Active Voices: Material Culture as Social Discourse. In The Archaeology of Inequality. Randall H. McGuire and Robert Paynter, eds. Pp. 150–191. Oxford: Blackwell.

Brewer, Rose M., 1993 Theorizing Race, Class and Gender: The New Scholarship of Black Feminist Intellectuals and Black Women's Labor. In Theorizing Black Feminisms: The Visionary Pragmatism of

Black Women. Stanlie M. James and Abena P. A. Busia, eds. Pp. 13–30. London: Routledge.

Collins, Patricia H., 1991 Black Feminist Thought: Knowledge, Consciousness, and the Politics of Empowerment. New York: Routledge.

Collins, Patricia H., 1993 Toward a New Vision: Race, Class and Gender as Categories of Analysis and Connection. Race, Sex and Class 1(1):25–45.

Conkey, Margaret H., and Sarah H. Williams, 1991 Original Narratives: The Political Economy of Gender in Archaeology. In Gender at the Crossroads of Knowledge: Feminist Anthropology in the Postmodern Era. Micaela di Leonardo, ed. Pp. 102–139. Berkeley: University of California Press.

Deagan, Kathleen, 1983 Spanish St. Augustine: The Archaeology of a Colonial Creole Community. New York: Academic Press.

Delle, James A., 1998 An Archaeology of Social Space. New York: Plenum.

Delle, James A., Stephen A. Mrozowski, and Robert Paynter, eds., 2000 Lines That Divide: Historical Archaeologies of Race, Class and Gender. Knoxville: University of Tennessee Press.

Dietler, Michael, 1994 "Our Ancestors the Gauls": Archaeology, Ethnic Nationalism, and the Manipulation of Celtic Identity in Modern Europe. American Anthropologist 96:584–605.

Duke, Phillip, and Dean J. Saitta, 1998 An Emancipatory Archaeology for the Working Class. Assemblage 4. www.assemblage.group.shef.ac.uk/4/4duk_sai.html

Franklin, Maria, 1997 "Power to the People": Sociopolitics and the Archaeology of Black Americans. Historical Archaeology 31(3):36–50.

Franklin, Maria, 2001 A Black Feminist-Inspired Archaeology. Journal of Social Archaeology 1 (1):108–125.

Franklin, Maria, and Garrett Fesler, eds., 1999 Historical Archaeology, Identity Formation, and the Interpretation of Ethnicity. Williamsburg, VA: The Colonial Foundation Research Publications.

Gilchrist, Roberta, 1991 Women's Archaeology? Political Feminism, Gender Theory and Historical Revision. Antiquity 65:495–501.

Gilchrist, Roberta, 1999 Gender and Archaeology: Contesting the Past. London: Routledge.

Goodman, Allan H., 1997 The Problematics of "Race" in Contemporary Biological Anthropology. In Biological Anthropology: The State of the Science. Noel T. Boaz, ed. Pp. 221–243. Corvallis: Oregon State University Press.

Harrison, Faye V., 1995 The Persistent Power of "Race" in the Cultural and Political Economy of Racism. Annual Review of Anthropology 24:47–74.

hooks, bell, 1982 Ain't I a Woman? Black Women and Feminism. London: Pluto Press.

hooks, bell, 1984 Feminist Theory: From Margin to Center. Cambridge, MA: South End Press.

Jackson, John L., Jr., 2008 Racial Paranoia: The Unintended Consequences of Political Correctness. New York: Basic Books.

Jones, Siân, 1997 The Archaeology of Ethnicity: Constructing Identities in the Past and Present. London: Routledge.

Ludlow Collective, 2001 Archaeology of the Colorado Coal Field War, 1913–1914. In Archaeologies of the Contemporary Past. Victor Buchli and Gavin Lucas, eds. Pp. 94–107. London: Routledge.

McCall, Leslie 2005: The Complexity of Intersectionality. Signs: A Journal of Women in Culture and Society 30(3):1771–1799.

McGuire, Randall H., 1992 Archaeology and the First Americans. American Anthropologist 94 (4):816–836.

McGuire, Randall H., 2008: Archaeology as Political Action. Berkeley: University of California Press.

McGuire, Randall H., and Robert Paynter, eds., 1991 The Archaeology of Inequality. Oxford: Blackwell.

Malina, Jaroslav, and Zdenek Vasícek, 1990 Archaeology Yesterday and Today: The Development of Archaeology in the Sciences and Humanities. Cambridge: Cambridge University Press.

Mohanty, Chandra T., 1988 Under Western Eyes: Feminist Scholarship and Colonial Discourse. Feminist Review 30(Autumn):61–88.

Mrozowski, Stephen A., 2006 The Archaeology of Class in Urban America: Cambridge: Cambridge University Press.

Mullins, Paul R., 1999 Race and Affluence: An Archaeology of African-American Consumer Culture. New York: Kluwer Academic/Plenum.

Mullins, Paul R., 2004 Ideology, Power, and Capitalism: The Historical Archaeology of Consumption, In A Companion to Social Archaeology. Lynn Meskell and Robert W. Preucel, eds. Pp. 195–211. Oxford: Blackwell.

Orser, Charles E., ed., 2001 Race and the Archaeology of Identity. Salt Lake City: University of Utah Press.

Orser, Charles E., 2004 Race and Practice in Archaeological Interpretation. Philadelphia: University of Pennsylvania Press.

Orser, Charles E., 2007 The Archaeology of Race and Racialization in Historic America. Tallahasee: University of Florida Press.

Saitta, Dean J., 2007 The Archaeology of Collective Action. Gainesville: University Press of Florida.

Schulyer, Robert L., ed., 1980 Archaeological Perspectives on Ethnicity in America: Afro-American and

Chinese American Culture History. Farmingdale, NY: Baywood.

Shanklin, Eugenia, 1993 Anthropology and Race: Explanation of Differences. Boston: Wadsworth.

Shennan, Stephen, ed., 1989 Archaeological Approaches to Cultural Identity. London: Unwin Hyman.

Singleton, Theresa A., ed., 1985 The Archaeology of Slave and Plantation Life. New York: Academic Press.

Singleton, Theresa A., 1988 An Archaeological Framework for Slavery and Emancipation 1740–1880. In The Recovery of Meaning: Historical Archaeology in the Eastern United States. Mark P. Leone and Parker B. Potter, eds. Pp. 345–370. Washington, DC: Smithsonian Institution Press.

Spivak, Gayatri C., 1987 In Other Worlds: Essays in Cultural Politics. London: Taylor and Francis.

Thomas, Cyrus, 1885 Who Were the Moundbuilders? American Antiquarian and Oriental Journal 2:65–74.

Wall, Diana D., 1994 The Archaeology of Gender: Separating Spheres in Urban America. New York: Plenum.

Wall, Diana D., 2000 Family Meals and Evening Parties: Constructing Domesticity in Nineteenth-Century Middle-Class New York. In Lines That Divide: Historical Archaeologies of Race, Class and Gender. James A. Delle, Stephen A. Mrozowski, and Robert Paynter, eds. Pp. 109–141. Knoxville: University of Tennessee Press.

Wurst LouAnn, and Robert K. Fitts, 1999 Introduction: Why Confront Class? Historical Archaeology 33(1):1–6.

The Politics of Ethnicity in Prehistoric Korea

Sarah M. Nelson

Archaeology in Korea is viewed, as it is elsewhere in east Asia, as a branch of history rather than anthropology. One consequence of this position is that attention to the remote past has been focussed largely on Korean ancestors: who they were in reference to Chinese historic documents; and how and when they came to the Korean peninsula. By the time of the formation of states in the southern Korean peninsula and the Japanese islands, a fully Korean presence in the peninsula is assumed, and the identity of Koreans within the peninsula is complete.

Questions of ethnic origins have thus been paramount in terms of approaches to prehistory in Korea, and in the past answers have been found with reference to mythology and by appeal to ancient texts. More recently, archaeology has been asked to supply some answers to ethnic questions, or in some cases archaeology has been used to validate the established mythological or legendary constructs regarding the original ancestors. At this intersection of mythology, history, and archaeology lie many problems for the interpretation of the past. Political and nationalistic motivations for preferring one interpretation over another, although more covert than overt, are at the heart of these problems.

Although ethnicity is called upon to validate political claims in many places, Korea's particular variation on the theme helps to illuminate the way ethnicity in the past is and has been approached. Generally, Koreans look for a single ancestral antecedent, and implicitly assume that a Korean ethnic group existed outside the Korean peninsula before its migration to the peninsula.

Almost any archaeology or ancient history text makes clear that the purpose of archaeology in Korea is the search for Korean ethnicity, expressed as the history of the Korean people. An extended example of this approach to archaeology can be found in *Recent Archaeological Discoveries in the Republic of Korea*. Kim Won-yong, the doyen of Korean archaeology, devotes more than half of the introductory chapter to a summary of the Korean "race" and its derivation. The reader learns that the people are Tungusic Mongoloids, and the language belongs to the Altaic family, which also includes Mongolian, Turkic, and Tungusic. These statements are followed by a description of the Neolithic inhabitants of the Korean peninsula, who are said to be not Koreans but Palaeo-Siberians. The identity of the Palaeolithic people is left unspecified, but presumably they were also not Koreans.

Sarah M. Nelson, "The Politics of Ethnicity in Prehistoric Korea," pp. 218–31 from Philip L. Kohl and Clare Fawcett (eds) *Nationalism, Politics, and the Practice of Archaeology* (Cambridge: Cambridge University Press, 1995). Reprinted with permission of Cambridge University Press and the author.

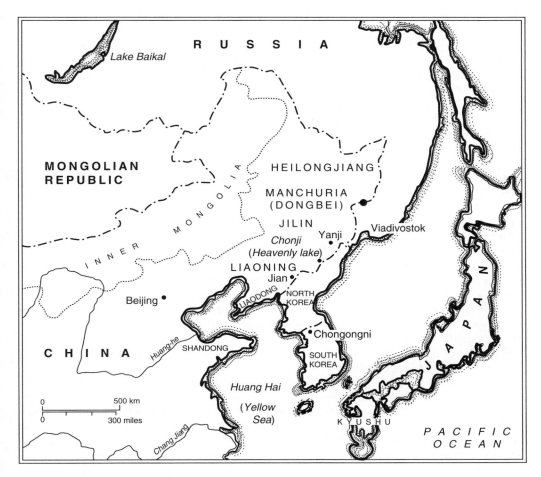

Figure 13.1 Northeast Asia and the Korean peninsula.

Next we learn about the real Koreans, who were called Yemaek (the Korean pronunciation of the Chinese characters Wei-Mo, or Kuai-Mo according to Kim). According to this scenario, the Yemaek entered Korea from Manchuria in about 1000 BC, bringing with them distinctive bronze swords, dolmens, stone cists, and new pottery types. Kim stresses the bear cult, and makes some linguistic comparisons to emphasize his point.

Kim also asserts that "the Yemaeks in northern Korea maintained their traditional nomadic pattern of life, but those who settled in southern Korea had become sedentary farmers by 300 BC." The nomadic notion is another theme which is emphasized in the formation of Korean ethnicity. This theme will be touched upon later.

The Three Kingdoms, traditionally dated from 57 BC to AD 668, are then all ascribed, despite their differences, to Yemaek descendants. Kim ends this section by summarizing: "Korean culture, however, retained its northern traits throughout her history largely due to a *remarkable ethnic homogeneity*" (Kim Won-yong 1983:2–3, emphasis mine).

This citation of Kim's work is not intended to call into question his enormous and important pioneering contributions to Korean archaeology, nor the right of Koreans to define their own archaeology in accordance with their own national goals. I also do not wish to leave the impression that every archaeologist in Korea subscribes equally to the ethnic theory I have outlined here, although it is very widespread, and examples could be multiplied. My point is, however, that an approach which begins with ethnic homogeneity and reads it into the past is incompatible with Western standards of archaeological interpretation, and makes discussion of archaeological evidence less than fruitful.

My own interpretations of Korean archaeology, which differ substantially from those described above (e.g. Nelson 1982, 1993), are not the point I wish to emphasize here. Rather, I wish to examine the concept of ethnicity as it is used as an interpretive device in Korea. I will explore the roots of this concept in the recent past, and consider the consequences of this approach for Korean archaeology.

There is no doubt that Korea is unusual in having a homogeneous population, with no national minorities or lingering aboriginals speaking different and unrelated languages, as is the case in both China and Japan. The Korean language has regional dialects, but they are mutually understandable throughout the peninsula and into the Korean Autonomous Region of Yanji, in Jilin Province, China. The Korean language is entirely congruent with people who consider themselves Koreans. Furthermore, although Korean is classified as a Tungusic language, among whose relatives is Manchu, it is distinct from the other languages, and clearly has had a long separate history (Miller 1980). Therefore, it is not the insistence upon Korean ethnicity in the present with which I wish to take issue, but rather I wish to consider the effect on interpretations of the past of reifying Koreanness.

The concept of a nation having a mixed background, with various ethnicities contributing to a new blend (for example the waves of immigration into the British Isles), is considered to be unlikely in the Korean case because of this apparent homogeneity of the present population. Generally, Korean archaeologists and historians, in seeking a single ancestral group which migrated into the peninsula, assume that something like Koreanness existed in the previous homeland. Although I have never seen this view explicitly stated, these ancestral Koreans are implicit in the model of the nomadic Yemaek people, who brought the Korean language and culture into the Korean peninsula. This emphasis on ethnic purity causes the interpretation of archaeological

evidence to be a history of population movements, only one of which (the last) is important because it is relevant to understanding the formation of the Korean people. However, a people can become homogeneous. The Korean homogeneity of the present could have been forged from diverse elements, as indeed the archaeology seems to indicate when viewed apart from this dominant ethnicity paradigm.

The causes of this emphasis on Korean ethnicity extending back into the mists of time are complex and historic. The most important of these reasons is probably the most recent: the present division of Korea into approximately equal halves – the south influenced by capitalism and the north by communism. While many deep differences divide the two Koreas, they are equally intent on reunification, and equally insistent that Koreans are the same wherever they may live. Divided Korea is uniquely a result of global Cold War politics – perhaps the last remaining vestige – and is unrelated to its prior history. A country which had done its best to avoid involvement in international affairs (once known as "The Hermit Nation" [Bishop 1905]) was caught up in a division, and later a war, for which there was no local agenda. The present condition of a divided Korea is thus an affront to the sensibilities of Koreans. Families affected by the division are a continuous theme of films, fiction, magazines, and newspapers.

The common wish for reunification, however, does not produce identical archaeological interpretations in North and South Korea. For example, the emphasis in the North on *juche*, self-reliance, spawns a rejection of any Chinese presence in the peninsula, while the South has few scholars who would dispute the Han dynasty Chinese commanderies (108 BC to 330 AD) as historical fact. Furthermore, while interpretations of Korean archaeology are somewhat influenced by evolutionism in the South and Marxism in the North, the underlying emphasis on eternal Koreanness makes the two archaeologies more alike than different.

A second root of the insistence on Korean ethnicity is the Japanese colonization of Korea from 1910 to 1945, which intensified a fierce national pride, especially in reaction to the sometimes derogatory Japanese accounts of ancient Korea. The first deliberate archaeology in Korea was done early in this century by Japanese scholars, who had their own agenda for the interpretations of the Korean past. Part of this involved justification of the colonization of Korea, which was understood as having "belonged" to Japan in the very ancient past. Among the many Japanese interpretations of Korean–Japanese relationships in the past, the worst affront to Korean sensibilities is the Japanese insistence that the Yamato state in Japan held part of southern Korea under the name of Mimana (Grayson 1977). The Koreans call this region Kaya (or Karak), and according to Korean histories it was a loose confederation of six small kingdoms, Korean to the core, which the Silla kingdom conquered one by one, completing the last conquest in 562.

The Kwanggaeto stele, a monument inscribed with Chinese characters extolling the exploits of a king of Koguryo (one of the Three Kingdoms) in AD 414, is widely believed in Korea to have been defaced by the Japanese who discovered and reerected it, so that the "mythical" (according to Koreans) invasions from Wa (the name for southern Japan in the Chinese chronicles) would be given historical validity (Hong 1988:231–6). The fact that no such polities as Korea or Japan existed at this time is irrelevant to the dispute, which is based on present national boundaries.

Other interpretations of Korean archaeology were based on Japanese perceptions as well. Because Japanese scholars were loath to recognize any debt to Korea in their own cultural past, they created an extremely short time depth for Korean state formation and denied a Korean Bronze Age. Furthermore, since bronze and iron appear to have been exported from Korea simultaneously into Kyushu, the southernmost island of Japan, in the Yayoi period, it was deemed necessary to declare that Korea likewise had no Bronze Age, but went directly from the Neolithic stage to the Iron Age. Japan and Korea were seen as simultaneously receiving an advanced culture from China, rather than that culture being seen as having been successively passed from China first to Korea and then to Japan. Western interpretations have more often followed Japanese than Korean models, perhaps because Western scholars tend to be more familiar with the Japanese view (Nelson 1989).

The third, most muted but still effective strand in the emphasis on Korean ethnicity is a Sinocentric view of history. Korea has stood in a dependent relationship to China at least since the Han dynasty commandaries on the Korean peninsula, 108 BC to AD 313. By the time Silla took control of the entire peninsula in 668 with the help of the Tang dynasty, China was seen as elder brother to the younger brother Korea, not interfering in internal affairs, but nevertheless validating the king's right to rule. Korea had looked to China originally for the civilizing influences of writing and religion. China's writing system long antedated Korea's alphabetic han'gul, and many facets of the governing system, the educational system, and even religion (Buddhism) and philosophy (Confucianism) came to Korea from China. Consequently, there is a strong dependence on China when it comes to historical interpretation. Furthermore, the earliest written references pertaining to Korea are found in Chinese sources, while the earliest Korean histories relate to the Three Kingdoms period, and are described in Confucian or Buddhist-influenced writings.

Thus, Korea has looked to Chinese documents more than to archaeology as the key to the ancient past. This led to a privileging of Chinese historical writings about archaeological discoveries. Myths, legends, and history are interwoven in these documents, as they are in Korea's own histories, the *Samguk Sagi* (History of the Three Kingdoms) and the *Samguk Yusa* (Memorabilia of the Three Kingdoms). Although these documents were written in the twelfth and thirteenth centuries, they were probably based on earlier documents now lost. One strand of archaeological interpretation, therefore, attempts to match archaeological discoveries with the written record.

Koreans have not been interested in world prehistory, nor in the comparative history of humankind, but in unearthing and validating their own past. The ethnogenesis of Koreans, however, is not the point, for Korean ethnicity is seen as eternal, not as an emergent process. Few archaeologists consider the *formation* of Koreanness within the Korean peninsula, for it is not possible to contemplate a time when Koreanness did not exist. Rather, Korean ethnicity is sought outside the peninsula, and the ethnic group which entered the peninsula is usually seen as a single people, entering relatively suddenly and spreading out quickly. Deriving from the "nomadic" fringes of China, the mythology demands that ethnic Koreans arrived with rice agriculture and bronze.

This insistence upon eternal Korean ethnicity might seem trivial, but there are consequences for archaeological method and theory, as well as for interpretations of the past. Furthermore, although there is no current bloodshed over the nationalism inherent in these ideas, implicit territorial claims are nevertheless staked (Sohn et al. 1987), ready to be acted upon under different circumstances. The interpretive implications will be considered first, in order to illuminate the consequences for method and theory.

In general stages in Korean prehistory are perceived as covering long stretches of time, and as being relatively static. Each stage is seen as a great event, superseded by the next event. The great stair steps of history occur in orderly progression. There is a tendency to emphasize similarities within a stage, masking both temporal and spatial variation, and to emphasize differences between adjacent stages. However, the search for the original homeland of Korean ethnicity plays out differently in different time periods.

I   The Siberian Connection

Since Palaeolithic and Neolithic sites are declared to represent Palaeo-Asiatics – that is, non-Koreans – until recently they have been less investigated than later sites and their study poorly financed. However, status accrued to Palaeolithic archaeology with the discovery of the site of Chon gongni, where a few classic handaxes challenged the previous dogma that northeast Asia was backward in the production of patterned stone tools (Movius 1948). Thereby the study of the Palaeolithic was legitimized, and the presence of stone tools "more developed" than those of China became a source of national pride, as well as the reported antiquity of the site. (The original age estimate was half a million years.)

The only scrap of legendary prehistory which might be said to apply to Korea in the Neolithic is the story of Tangun, preserved in the *Samguk*

Yusa (Ilyon 1972). The Tangun legend is a creation story, involving a tiger and a bear – both female, and both wanting to become the mother of humanity (or perhaps just the mother of Koreans, this distinction not being made). The bear wins by perseverance and adherence to ritually imposed sanctions, and becomes the mother of Tangun with the aid of the God of Heaven. Tangun teaches all good things, especially agriculture and sericulture; lives for one thousand years; and becomes a spirit presiding over Chonji. Heavenly Lake, a high crater lake which is found approximately in the middle of the current border between Korea and China. This is thin material for Neolithic reconstructions.

In contrast, the archaeological scenario for the Neolithic is based almost entirely on pottery. Both the pottery and the potters were traditionally assumed to have entered Korea from Siberia. Comb-marked pots made in simple conical shapes have been found in the vicinity of Lake Baikal in Siberia as well as in Korea, and the connection between the two was made without regard to what had been or might be found in the intervening territory. No concern was shown for establishing reasons for the migration, or for considering ecological similarities or differences between the reputed homeland and the ultimate destination. No interest in temporal differences is evident, either.

When this theory was established, it was believed that Palaeolithic evidence did not exist in Korea, making it imperative to derive Neolithic inhabitants from outside the peninsula. Even after a Palaeolithic presence in Korea had become well established, the Neolithic intrusion model has been sustained by the Palaeolithic Gap – a period of time in the early Holocene when Korea has had no archaeological evidence of human inhabitants. However the Palaeolithic Gap is rapidly closing. A surprising number of Mesolithic sites have recently been found in several different environmental settings, and sites with pottery are producing ever earlier dates. so that the gap is diminishing, and perhaps will turn out to have been only an artefact of the paucity of archaeological research in Korea. But the most telling point is that several of the prepottery sites are stratigraphically beneath pottery-bearing layers, with the continuity of stone tool types and food refuse strongly suggesting a continuity of culture. However, so far the discoveries of Mesolithic sites have had little effect on the Siberian hypothesis, which continues to be the official version of Korean prehistory.

Korean Neolithic pottery, although often called Chulmun, meaning "comb-marked," actually has a striking amount of variation in the beginning stages as judged by radiocarbon dates (Nelson 1992). This variation should serve as a caution to any interpretation of a single migration of a single pottery-using people into the peninsula. The earliest dated pottery is on the east coast. It has flat bases and is decorated on the shoulders with stamped or impressed motifs. In the southeast there is a large percentage of plain pottery, and in the northeast incised designs occur but they are not usually made with a toothed implement. None of these east coast ceramics bear much relationship to Siberian pottery, but more closely resemble widespread early coastal ceramics found in Japan and China. It is evident that boats were in use at the beginning of the Holocene in Japan (Ikawa-Smith 1986), so the mechanism for transmission is not mysterious. The coastal location of the earliest Korean sites is another reason to link these regions together.

Only the west coast pottery is properly designated Chulmun. It was made on conical, open-mouthed shapes with pointed or rounded bases. The west coast pottery resembles some Siberian pottery in its overall shape, but the inspiration for it can probably be found much closer at hand, across the Yellow Sea and in the Liaodong peninsula of China (Nelson 1990). Some of these sites have not only comb-incised and impressed pottery, but also square hearths bordered with cobbles, a characteristic found in most Korean sites. Recent discoveries in northeastern China produce ever earlier possible prototypes for Chulmun pottery.

II The Chinese Connection

Chinese writings include the names of four individuals or groups which are frequently claimed for Korean ancestors. The first of these is Kija (Jizi in Chinese), a member of the royal Shang clan who appears in the Zhou chronicles (Wu 1982:311). Owing to his meritorious behavior the Zhou conqueror granted Kija – despite his relation to the defeated Shang king – permission to take a retinue of followers to the northeast and found a new state called Choson. Kija has been claimed for Korea on these documentary grounds alone. If Choson was in the Korean peninsula, there is not a shred of archaeological evidence discovered so far. In particular, one would expect this prince of Shang to have brought with him bronze vessels and writing, both of which are noticeable by their total absence in Korea for several hundred years after the fall of the Shang dynasty. Possible evidence of Kija has been found in the Yan state, however, near modern Beijing, and it is sometimes argued that the territorial extent of Choson included the Liaodong peninsula and the region around Beijing (e.g. Yoon 1986).

The second group believed to be Korean ancestors by some scholars is the Dong-I, or Eastern Barbarians, who are most often located in Shandong (Hsu and Linduff 1988:14), on the basis of ancient Chinese writings. Some Koreans not only have claimed that the Dong-I were Koreans, but also have gone so far as to assert that the Shang dynasty was Dong-I and that, therefore, the Koreans invented the first Chinese writing (e.g., An 1974). Although oracle bones (without writing) have been found in Korea, a linguistic difficulty with this interpretation immediately springs to mind, for the oracle bone language is clearly Chinese, not merely in the ideograms but also in the grammatical structure. Pictograms and ideograms would be an unlikely vehicle for an agglutinative language like Korean.

Even leaving extravagant claims aside, there are few useful hypotheses regarding the Dong-I as Korean ancestors which could be tested archaeologically. However, if the Dawenkou culture in Shandong represents the Dong-I, as is the scholarly consensus, the Korean hypothesis becomes even less tenable, for tripod vessels, an important element in the Dawenkou complex, are not found in Korea until a millennium later.

The Dong-hu are yet another group named in Chinese documents and frequently claimed for Korean ancestors. Located in eastern Liaoning during the Zhou period, they were well placed for a Bronze Age sweep into Korea. Frequently they are equated with the Yemaek, listed at least once as a branch of the Dong-hu. Most often advanced as specifically Korean ancestors are the Yemaek themselves (as noted above), who are seen as a Tungusic tribal group. The Yemaek also appear once in Chinese documents as one of the nine tribes of the Dong-I, muddying the water a bit.

The *Wei Ji* (compiled 233–97) places the Yemaek in the Korean peninsula at the time of the Han commanderies in the first century BC (Parker 1890), giving them a specifically Korean identity at least by that time. These Yemaek are said to have had seven cities and forts. Obviously it is not easy to apply names from textual materials to archaeological sites. However, at least it seems likely that a group by this name occupied a part of northwestern Korea by Han dynasty times. The problem comes in the use of the name Yemaek to apply to Bronze Age peoples throughout the Korean peninsula as much as 1500 years earlier (Kim Won-yong 1986:19; Choi Mong-Iyong 1984). For example, Kim writes: "The Koreans of the Late Bronze Age were all the same Yemaek people, but historical records almost give us the impression that the southern Yemaek, called Han … were ethnically different from the northern nomadic Yemaek." A different interpretation sees the Yemaek as Koguryo ancestors, arising in southern Manchuria (which was the Koguryo homeland archaeologically as well as historically) by the ninth century BC (Rhee 1992).

Archaeological finds on the Korean peninsula suggest more complex origins for this time period just as they do for the Chulmun period. The Megalithic Age, sometimes problematically called the Bronze Age, begins with Mumun pottery accompanied or shortly followed by stone cist graves and dolmens. Rice agriculture and bronze may have entered the peninsula later, not recessarily together or even from the same direction (Kim Won-yong 1982). It is useful to examine each of these archaeological manifestations to see whether the Yemaek, or any single ethnic group, can reasonably be invoked as responsible for all of them.

Mumun or Plain Coarse pottery first appears in the southern coastal area of Korea at about 2000 BC in recalibrated radiocarbon dates (Nelson 1992). In this region Mumun has simple shapes with a round base and a wide mouth with a double rim. Necked jars and flowerpot-shaped plain pottery vessels appear in the north-west and center of the peninsula by 1500 BC, while jars with very small flat bases are found further to the northwest. There is clearly *not* a single diffusion of Mumun from the north. Regional styles are simply regional, and do not exhibit progressive changes or sequential time periods.

The change in Korean pottery styles from decorated to undecorated begins around 2000 BC in the south, and perhaps 1500 BC on the west coast. The pottery is thicker than Chulmun and appears to have different cultural roots, although some linear incising is found on Mumun vessels, a fact which has been argued to represent a vestige of Chulmun and therefore cultural continuity (Choe 1982). The stone tool inventory now includes polished forms almost exclusively. Well-made projectile points, semi-lunar knives, daggers, awls, chisels, axes, and adzes dominate the assemblages. Houses are larger than previous ones, and in a few places in west-central Korea longhouses have been excavated, with multiple hearths down the long axis. Villages are located on the sides of hills, as they are today, leaving the flatter land near rivers for growing crops.

Megalithic monuments are an important feature of the Mumun period. They consist mostly of dolmens, constructed like a rectangular house in the north, but consisting of only a large boulder above the ground in the southern form. The earliest C14 date from a dolmen is 2400 BC, but this date stands alone and is likely to be an error. From the bulk of C14 dates it would seem that the heyday of dolmen building was about 1500 to 500 BC. Most of the dolmens are burial markers. The ones shaped like stone houses (called *shipeng*, literally stone houses, in Liaoning) probably contained an above-ground burial. Southern dolmens were usually erected above a stone cist grave.

The Yemaek, as newcomers to the peninsula, must be found elsewhere. Manchuria (the Dongbei to Chinese) provides the putative homeland. Archaeological sites with broad similarities to Korean sites of the Megalithic period can be found in both Liaoning and Jilin provinces of China. The most obvious of these are the stone cist burial sites, which are widespread in both places. Contents of the cists are standardized in Korea, including one or two burnished red jars, polished stone daggers, and a necklace of tubular jades with a single *gokok*, or curved bead. Probably these burials represent an elite segment of the population, since there are not enough of them to account for burial of the entire population (Nelson 1993).

Dolmens are also found in Manchuria, as well as throughout Korea, but the Manchurian dolmens are fewer and tend to be more carefully constructed. There is no obvious reason to suppose that dolmens went from northeastern China to Korea instead of the other way around. In fact, if we assume that there is an evolution from crude to polished, then the Manchuria dolmens should be later than those in Korea. The complex of burial goods found in dolmens is distinctly Korean, yet there is a whole book dedicated to deriving the dolmens from outside Korea (Kim Byong-mo 1981). Again, the culture is seen as intrusive *in toto* rather than looking for a partially or totally indigenous base with multiple migrations from various places. The documented Yemaek area on the east coast is, in fact, the region with the *fewest* dolmens.

Rice is found in Korean sites definitely by 1000 BC and quite possibly a thousand years earlier (Choe 1991). Its movement into Korea is traced either by means of the distribution of semi-lunar reaping knives through northern China and Manchuria (Choe 1982), or according to finds of grooved adzes from southern China to Korea (Kim Won-yong 1982). The Yemaek along the east coastal strip of Korea are said to have raised the five cereals, including rice (Parker 1890), but of course this is much later than the identified archaeological rice.

Bronze is another element which is associated with Mumun pottery and dolmen burials. A particular style of bronze dagger, called Yoyong (Liaoning) style, has been found in southern Korea as well as in Liaoning. This is adduced as evidence that the Yemaek "tribe" formed in Manchuria and later moved into the Korean peninsula. Few Korean bronzes have been found in datable contexts, so typological analysis has substituted uneasily for firm dates, but recent dated excavations place the daggers in Korea about the same time as Liaoning – in the Spring and Autumn period of the Zhou dynasty (Rhee 1984).

Fixing on the Yemaek as the only tribal group that entered Korea in the Megalithic Bronze Age surely oversimplifies the case. The marked regional variation in both pottery and burial types suggests different ethnicities, although these differences are obscured by Korean terminology.

By the Warring States period (403–221 BC), the presence of Yen "knife money," which is found in far northwestern Korea, suggests the possibility of commerce, trade, or even Chinese settlers. Han dynasty writings indicate some northern Chinese settlement in the Korean peninsula, and even provide a motive – the Han monopoly on iron may have motivated traders to explore and locate sources of ore outside the Han jurisdiction. Wiman, a historical figure who founded a state referred to as "Wiman Choson" (to distinguish it from the earlier, more shadowy Ancient Choson), does not appear to have been a pedigreed Korean himself (Gardiner 1969). Some North Korean archaeologists, however, prefer to consider Wiman to have been a "pure" Korean. They even deny that the Han Chinese ever conquered any part of the Korean peninsula, instead seeing the rich graves of Lelang in Chinese style as those of noble Koreans with Chinese trade goods, copying upper-class Chinese (Pearson 1978).

After the Han dynasty established the Lelang Commandery on the Korean peninsula in 108 BC, Chinese chroniclers were able to have a closer view of southern Korea. Both the *Wei Ji* and the *Hou Han Shu* record ethnographic partial descriptions of the inhabitants of the south. These histories mention some similarities among various Korean groups, as well as a fair amount of diversity. As they formed, the Korean Three Kingdoms, which probably all spoke some form of proto-Korean, were separated by cultural differences and did not let their commonalities prevent them from waging wars of conquest among themselves. These differences, as we have seen above, have been explicitly denied.

III   The Japanese Connection

The migration of peoples continues to be an important theme in relation to Japan as well. From the Korean perspective, movement is seen only from north to south: Manchuria to Korea; and Korea to Japan. The emigrants from the peninsula established agriculture on Kyushu in early Yayoi times, exported a stratified society and warfare in later Yayoi, and brought enlightenment to the Kofun period. Thus the formation of early states in the Japanese islands is attributed in Korea to migratory Koreans. However, the Japanese presence on the peninsula in the Three Kingdoms period is hotly denied, especially in the form of the Mimana outpost (according to Japanese sources), as well as in the form of invading armies. The contorversy over the Kwanggaeto stele, noted above, is part of this contention.

IV   Conclusion

The insistence on migration as an explanation of the peopling of Korea to the virtual exclusion of other mechanisms for culture change has an important political dimension. Desire for reunification of the two Koreas probably underlies the emphasis on the exclusivity of the Korean culture in the past as well as in the present. Proposing the migration of the whole Korean people into the peninsula at one time from some other previously established homeland is an assertion that allows a kind of Koreanness to have been established from time immemorial. Perceiving the development of Korean culture from a number of diverse sources is not at all congenial to this perspective. Even if it had occurred a very long time ago, the formation of Korea from any amalgamation of peoples cannot be acknowledged. The Korean people simply are, and always have been.

The rejection of a theory that the Neolithic inhabitants might have practiced horticulture is related to the notion of real Korean ethnicity as well. Neolithic discoveries tend to be slighted, and their interpretation as anything other than a poor beginning is unwelcome. Why attribute any form of inventiveness to these non-ancestors?

Internal inconsistencies in the interpretation of the evidence is the result of these several strands of interpretation. For example, there is a certain shiftiness in the presentation of Tangun. As the progenitor of the Korean people, he needs to be assigned to the beginning period in the Korean peninsula, and so he is mythically described. This equates Tangun with the Chulmun or Neolithic period in Korea.

But as soon as a shift is made from myth to archaeology, inconsistencies appear. For example, since Neolithic inhabitants of the peninsula are not seen as Korean ancestors, but as a thin population that was soon overrun or possibly exterminated by the Yemaek invaders (Kim Won-yong 1982), Tangun cannot be one of those Palaeo-Asiatics. What happens to Tangun? He becomes one of the Yemaek. However, the association of Tangun with bear worship creates an awkwardness which is most often ignored, for the circumpolar bear cult is ascribed to Palaeo-Asiatics.

The asserted nomadism of the first Koreans is also part of the need to find Korean ethnicity outside the peninsula. It seems to be easier to conceive of a group moving in its entirety if it is nomadic to begin with, than to imagine people with land and crops making such a move. The reputed nomadism in Manchuria, however, is not substantiated with archaeological finds. In fact, permanent settlements are the norm in Manchuria for some seven thousand years (Nelson 1995).

I would like to conclude by suggesting that the political need to find distinctiveness and wholeness in Korean culture in the past, as well as in the present, has been detrimental to archaeological interpretation. In this climate it has been difficult, if not impossible, for Korean archaeologists to develop theory with regard to the formation of ethnicity, even though this is a major focus of interpretation in Korean archaeology.

This outcome is particularly disappointing, since theories of ethnicity in the prehistoric past are not well developed anywhere. Ethnicity is problematic even in ethnography, and it is even more difficult to understand using archaeological data. The origins of specific ethnicities, however, should be reachable with archaeological data (Auger et al. 1987).

Some suggestions have been made with regard to entry into this problem. For example, ritual and culinary practices may be reflected in archaeological finds (Santley et al. 1987), and continuity of house style (provided there is no environmental reason for the change) and cloth-ing may also reflect ethnic dimensions. Another promising line of inquiry would deal with styl-istic boundaries between non-functional arte-facts or decorative patterns on functional artefacts. Korean archaeology is in a position to make an important contribution to the develop-ment of theory regarding ethnicity in the past, if it can shed its insistence on ethnic Koreanness from time immemorial.

References

Auger, R., M. F. Glass, S. MacEachern, and P. H. McCartney (eds.) 1987 *Ethnicity and Cul-ture*. Proceedings of the Eighteenth Annual Chacmool Conference. The University of Calgary Archaeological Association.

Bishop, I. B. 1905 *Korea and Her Neighbours*. London: John Murray.

Choe Chong-pil 1982 The Diffusion Route and Chron-ology of Korean Plant Domestication. *Journal of Asian Studies* 41(3):519–30.

Choe Chong-pil 1991 A Critical Review of Research on the Origin of Koreans and Their Culture. *Han'guk Sangkosa Hakbo* 8:7–43.

Choi Mong-lyong 1984 Bronze Age in Korea. *Korea Journal* 24:23–33.

Florescu, A. 1966 Sistemul de Fortificare al Aşezarilor Cucuteniene din Moldova. *Archeologia Moldovei (Iaşi)* 4:23–37.

Gardiner, K. H. J. 1969 *The Early History of Korea*. Honolulu: University of Hawaii Press.

Grayson, J. H. 1977 Mimana: A Problem in Korean Historiography. *Korea Journal* 7(8):65–8.

Hencken, Hugh 1955 *Indo-European Languages and Archaeology*. American Anthropological Association Memoir 84.

Hong Wontack 1988 *Relationship between Korea and Japan in Early Period: Packche and Yamato Wa*. Seoul: Ilsimsa Publisher.

Hsu Cho-yun and K. M. Linduff 1988 *Western Chou Civilization*. New Haven and London: Yale Univer-sity Press.

Ikawa-Smith, F. 1986 Late Pleistocene and Early Holo-cene Technologies. In *Windows on the Japanese Past: Studies in Archaeology and Prehistory*, edited by R. J. Pearson, pp. 199–216. Ann Arbor: Center for Japanese Studies, University of Michigan.

Ilyon 1972 *Samguk Yusa: Legends and History of the Three Kingdoms of Ancient Korea*, trans by Tae-Hung Ha and Grafton K. Mintz. Seoul: Yonsei University Press.

Kim Byong-mo 1981 A New Interpretation of Mega-lithic Monuments in Korea. In *Megalithic Cultures in Asia*, edited by B. M. Kim, pp. 164–89. Seoul: Hanyang University Press.

Kim Won-yong 1982 Discoveries of Rice in Prehistoric Sites in Korea. *Journal of Asian Studies* 41(3):513–18.

Kim Won-yong 1983 *Recent Archaeological Discoveries in the Republic of Korea*. Tokyo: The Centre for East Asian Studies, UNESCO.

Kim Won-yong 1986 *Art and Archaeology of Ancient Korea*. Seoul: The Taekwang Publishing Company.

Kosso, Peter 1991 Method in Archaeology: Middle-Range Theory as Hermeneutics. *American Antiquity* 56(4):621–7.

Miller, D. 1980 Archaeology and Development. *Cur-rent Anthropology* 21:709–26.

Movius, H. 1948 The Lower Palaeolithic Cultures of Southern and Eastern Asia. *Transactions of the American Philosophical Society* 38(4):329–420.

Nelson, S. M. 1982 Recent Progress in Korean Archae-ology. In *Advances in Old World Archaeology*, vol. 1, edited by F. Wendorf and A. Close, pp. 99–149.

Nelson, S. M. 1989 Review of *Relationship Between Korea and Japan in Early Period*, by Won-taek Hong. *Journal of Asian Studies* 3:636–7.

Nelson, S. M. 1990 Neolithic Sites in Northeastern China and Korea. *Antiquity* 64:234–48. (Also trans-lated into Chinese.)

Nelson, S. M. 1992 Korean Archaeological Sequences from the First Ceramics to the Introduction of Iron. In *Chronologies in Old World Archaeology*, third edi-tion, edited by R.W. Ehrich, vol. 1, pp. 430–8; vol. 2, pp. 417–24. Chicago: University of Chicago Press.

Nelson, S. M. 1993 *The Archaeology of Korea*. Cam-bridge: Cambridge University Press.

Nelson, S. M. (ed.) [1995]. *The Archaeology of North-east China: Beyond the Great Wall*. [London: Routledge.]

Parker, E. H. 1890 On Race Struggles in Korea. *Trans-actions of the Asiatic Society of Japan* 23:137–228.

Pearson, R. 1978 Lolang and the Rise of Korean States and Chiefdoms. *Journal of the Hong Kong Archaeo-logical Society* 7 (1976–1978):77–90.

Rhee Song Nai 1984 Emerging Complex Society in Prehistoric Southwest Korea. Ph.D. dissertation, University of Oregon.

Rhee Song Nai 1992 Secondary State Formation: The Case of Early Korea. In *Pacific Northeast Asia in Prehistory: Hunter-Fisher-Gatherers, Farmers, and Sociopolitical Elites*, edited by C. M. Aikens and Rhee Song Nai Seattle: Washington State Univer-sity Press.

Santley, R. S., C. Yarborough and B. A. Hall 1987 Enclaves, Ethnicity, and the Archaeological Record at Matacapan. In *Ethnicity and Culture*, edited by R. Auger, M. F. Glass, S. MacEachern, and P. H. McCartney, pp. 85–100. Calgary: The University of Calgary Archaeological Association.

Sherratt, Andrew 1981 Plough and Pastoralism: Aspects of the Secondary Products Revolution. In *Pattern of the Past*, edited by Ian Hodder, G. Isaac, and N. Hammond, pp. 261–305. Cambridge: Cambridge University Press.

Sohn Pow-key, Pyon T'ae-sop, Han Yong-u, Yi Ki-dong, and Im Hyo-jai 1987 Reflections on Studies in Ancient Korean History: Colloquium of Five Historians. *Korea Journal* 27(12):4–22.

Wu, K.C. 1982 *The Chinese Heritage*. New York: Crown.

Yoon Nae-hyun 1986 *Ancient Korean History: A Reinterpretation*. Seoul: Ilchisa. (In Korean.)

14

Historical Categories
and the Praxis of Identity
The Interpretation of Ethnicity
in Historical Archaeology

Siân Jones

The interpretation of ethnic groups within historical archaeology has taken place within a narrative framework derived from surviving written sources and reflects the privileged status traditionally accorded to the written word over and above material culture in the study of 'historical periods'. This historical determinism has frequently resulted in a circular, self-referential use of documentary and archaeological evidence, and has led to the conflation of the material record with monolithic ethnic categories extracted from historical sources. In this chapter I explore some of the problems arising from such an approach in the context of recent debates about the value and use of historical versus archaeological evidence. However, rather than merely asserting the priority of one kind of evidence over another, an alternative approach is suggested based on a consideration of the ways in which material and written traditions are involved in the construction of ethnicity. Such an approach shows that attempts to seek out the archaeological correlates of historically known ethnic groups are flawed not only because they often ignore the situated and subjective nature of the historical sources, but also because they disregard qualitative differences in the manifestation

Siân Jones, "Historical Categories and the Praxis of Identity: The Interpretation of Ethnicity in Historical Archaeology," pp. 219–32 from Pedro Paulo A. Funari, Martin Hall, and Siân Jones (eds) *Historical Archaeology: Back from the Edge* (London: Routledge, 1999). Reprinted with permission.

of ethnicity in written sources and material culture. Recognition of these qualitative differences is essential for the development of an analytical framework for the analysis of ethnicity in which both archaeological and documentary evidence are 'seen as equal and potentially opposing elements in the dialectical process of knowledge' (Austin 1997: 35).

The Problem: The Interplay of Text and Material Culture in the Interpretation of Ethnic Groups

Trigger (1995: 277) has recently stated that ethnicity is a subjective concept which archaeologists cannot hope to study to any significant degree without specifically relevant historical or ethnographic data. This argument appears to hold sway among archaeologists and it is reflected in the number of studies of ethnicity carried out in historical as opposed to prehistoric archaeology. Historical archaeologists – those who study past societies for which we have written records available – spend a great deal of their time establishing the ethnic affiliation of the people who made and used the sites and objects which they are investigating. The question of ethnic association is particularly prominent in the colonial and post-colonial archaeology of countries such as the USA and Australia, but is also apparent in other regions and periods such as medieval Europe and Graeco-Roman Palestine. In contrast, since the demise of culture-history, there have been very few studies of prehistoric archaeology which are explicitly concerned with past ethnic groups.

This pattern of research reflects the assumption, prevalent among both historical and prehistoric archaeologists, that the study of ethnicity requires access to people's self-conscious reflections on identity, and that written records provide an authoritative source of information about such reflections. Historical sources are used to construct a narrative framework concerning the spatial distribution and movements of particular ethnic groups. Such information is then used to determine the ethnic status of particular regions and sites, and archaeologists then seek out material relating to that particular ethnic group. Moreover, this use of written sources is associated, for the most part, with a straightforward and commonsense notion of ethnicity which fails to take into account the complexity of the processes involved in the construction of such identities. The study of ethnic groups in historical archaeology usually involves the identification of material correlates – 'ethnic markers' – for particular groups. In almost all cases these 'ethnic markers' are themselves defined using historical documentation, and are then used to verify the historical sources, as well as to establish the ethnic status of sites for which there is no surviving historical evidence. The circularity of the process is self-evident and relies on a number of assumptions: (i) that historical sources can be taken as straightforward and valid statements concerning ethnicity; (ii) that there is a fixed relationship between particular styles of material culture (the 'ethnic markers') and a particular identity; (iii) that ethnic groups are homogeneous bounded entities.

Such an approach dominates the analysis of ethnicity in historical archaeology and is integral to the interpretation of a wide range of regions and periods. For instance, the identification of Jewish sites in Graeco-Roman Palestine is determined by historical references concerning the location of Jewish communities in association with a small number of supposedly diagnostic ethno-religious material traits, such as Jewish inscriptions, Jewish symbols, for example the menorah, and particular objects and structures, most notably ritual baths and synagogues. As pointed out by Rajak (1994: 239), 'non-Jewish' material on supposedly Jewish sites is frequently ignored or marginalized, interpreted either as evidence for the presence of other ethnic and religious groups, or as evidence for assimilation with an associated loss of Jewish culture and identity. Such modes of interpretation clearly assume that there was a fixed one-to-one relationship between particular types of material culture and Jewish identity, and that Jewish identity in antiquity was essentially homogeneous across different regions and periods, and different classes or social strata.

These assumptions about ethnicity are mirrored in the archaeology of other periods and regions. For instance, in the study of medieval Europe archeologists have unquestioningly pursued ethnic entities, such as the Franks, the Anglo-Saxons, the Danes and the Slavs, which are found in the written sources. Archaeological sites and artefacts have been labelled, for instance, as Anglo-Saxon simply because they are located in the areas where historical sources state that Anglo-Saxons settled. Furthermore, as in other periods, types of object which are not considered to represent Anglo-Saxon culture are ignored (for recent critical discussions see Lucy 1995; Austin 1997). Similarly, in the United States research on material from the post-European conquest period has been determined by historical sources and archaeologists have concentrated on the identification of 'ethnic markers', such as clay pipes for west coast Chinese (e.g. Etter 1980), and the controversial 'Colono Ware' pottery for Native American and Afro-American groups (e.g. Ferguson 1978). As in other regions, archaeologists have assumed a fixed one-to-one relationship between ethnic groups (both immigrant and native) and their respective cultures. Consequently, any changes in the relevant cultural assemblages have been interpreted in terms of assimilation and loss of identity (for recent critical discussions see Praetzellis, Praetzellis and Brown 1987; Rubertone 1989; Orser 1991; Burley, Horsfall and Brandon 1992).

Thus, the description and interpretation of material remains within historical archaeology is positively saturated with discourses of identity derived from written sources. The problem is that such discursive categories are rarely the subject of analysis themselves. Rather, they are accepted as given and constitute an *a priori* framework for description, classification and interpretation. As argued by Rajak with relation to studies of Jewish sites in ancient Palestine:

> to determine in advance what is Jewish and what is not (or even 'probably' not) is to operate with a pre-conception of Jewish identity when our task is, precisely, to seek to define that identity. (Rajak 1994: 239)

The same criticism can be made of the analysis of any other ethnic group. However, once identity becomes the subject of analysis itself, rather than an essential, taken-for-granted character, it becomes necessary to consider the nature of the social and cultural processes involved in the construction of ethnic identities. As yet, only a few historical archaeologists have considered the implications of recent research which reveals that ethnic identity is a dynamic, contested and multi-layered phenomenon (see below). Furthermore, even those who have emphasized the complexity of the processes involved in the construction of ethnicity for the most part still accept the written evidence as an authoritative and straightforward source of information about past identities (e.g. Kelly and Kelly 1980; McGuire 1982; Clark 1987). The relationship between written and material manifestations of ethnicity has not been in question. In contrast, in general terms, there has been much debate in the last ten to fifteen years concerning the relationship between archaeological and historical evidence, and the priority, if any, which should be accorded to one or the other.

Historical Archaeology: 'Handservant' of History or Objective Science?

The criticism that archaeology has been the 'handservant' of history is now well known and can be applied to the situation discussed here whereby historical sources have played a decisive role in the identification of ethnic entities, their geographical and chronological provenance and the material correlates associated with them. As in other areas of research, archaeological evidence has been slotted into a historical framework, thus confining interpretations of it to the perspectives represented in the documentary sources. As Leone and Potter have argued in a discussion of historical archaeology in general:

> the archaeological record and the documentary record are treated as if they are linked, with one a dependent version of the other. Rarely is this assumption made explicit or justified, but it leads the researcher to integrate documentary and archaeological materials in a single move, from one line of evidence to the other, and to do little more than search for extremely circumscribed information. (Leone and Potter 1988: 12)

The dominance of the written word over archaeological material has recently been challenged by the recognition that historical sources do not provide objective, absolute statements about the nature of past societies. Rather, they constitute partial and fragmented perspectives on the past, not only as a result of differential survival rates, but also because they represent the points of view of particular sections of society, frequently the dominant group (see Austin 1997: 12; Champion 1997). This realization has resulted in a number of positions. Some archaeologists (e.g. Rubertone 1989: 32, 38–9) are suspicious of the use of historical sources, arguing that archaeological material provides a more 'objective' source of evidence and suggesting that historical sources be relegated to a minor role in archaeological interpretation. Yet such an approach embodies what Beaudry, Cook and Mrozowski (1991: 161) have called a 'fear of the emic', attempting to strip away subjectivity (interests, politics, ideological factors and so on) rather than accept it and develop critical perspectives for examining subjective representations of the past. In effect this approach leads to a reversal of the deterministic relationship between historical and archaeological evidence; archaeological evidence is now accorded priority.

Another reaction is characterized by the argument that archaeological and historical evidence should be considered as independent and separate sources of evidence about the past (e.g. Dever 1977; Whitelam 1986; Leone and Potter 1988). For some, this argument has been associated with a shift away from the reconstruction of political history in favour of the analysis of long-term social and economic processes, and consequently archaeology and history tend to be regarded as complementary sources of information relating to distinct aspects of past social life. However, others (e.g. Leone and Potter 1988) have focused on issues such as identity and social status using the historical record to construct a descriptive grid and the archaeological record to explore ambiguity and contradiction, rather than as a source of complementary evidence. The argument that archaeological and historical evidence should not be conflated with one another is important, but neither of these approaches really addresses the issue of the subjectivity of historical sources. Furthermore, both tend to see archaeological evidence as a more 'objective' source of information.

As a number of people have recently argued, both archaeological and historical sources provide subjective perspectives on the past (e.g. Beaudry, Cook and Mrozowski 1991; Little 1992; Hall 1994). They are subjective both as a result of the processes involved in the production of literary and material remains, and in terms of their contemporary interpretation. For instance, Hall has used the notion of 'text' to refer to both literary and material remains:

> By viewing the past as a set of complex texts, intertwined to form a discourse, we can avoid privileging written documents over the archaeological record, or artefact assemblages over travellers' accounts, probate records and paintings. (Hall 1994: 168)

Furthermore, as Little (1992: 219) has suggested, meaning is ambiguous in texts, images and material culture; as in literary sources, meaning in material culture is 'neither fixed nor universal. Interpretation [in the past and the present] relies on social context and situation, not only of the author [or producer], but also of the reader and the listener.' Moreover, such ambiguity and subjectivity can provide an important source of information if subjected to critical analysis, so that, for instance, documents produced by the elite can be revealing about otherwise disenfranchised and/or inarticulate groups within society (see Beaudry, Cook and Mrozowski 1991; Hall 1994).

These approaches provide a useful basis for reconsidering the use of literary and archaeological remains in the analysis of past ethnicities. Textual sources themselves need to be subjected to in-depth analysis concerning their active involvement in the construction of past identities. Rather than being taken at face value, documentary sources should be considered in terms of the social and political contexts in which they were produced, the positions and interests of the authors and the audiences, and the active role which texts may have played in the construction and negotiation of cultural identity. For instance, as Kraabel (1985) has shown, representations of (diaspora) Jews in early Christian texts are not always as they seem. Jews in these texts are often fictional characters in disputes between Christian groups. References to Jewish practices do not necessarily indicate the presence of Jews, nor do they accurately represent Jewish practices. Such representations, he argues, are not dispassionate, 'objective' representations of Jews and Judaism (Kraabel 1985: 241). Once their subjectivity is acknowledged, such documents can provide important information about the cultural contexts of Jewish identification and the construction of 'Jewishness' by others in the early Christian period. However, recognition of the subjective and active role of written sources in the construction of ethnic identities does raise further questions about the relationship between material and literary manifestations of ethnicity. Can we expect to find the same kind of representations of ethnic identity in the archaeological record as we do in historical sources? I suggest that we cannot, and that we can obtain a better understanding of the ways in which historical and archaeological evidence can be used in the analysis of past ethnicities if we take into account the processes involved in the construction of ethnic identity.

A Theoretical Approach to Ethnicity

Over the last three decades a considerable body of research has been carried out in the human sciences which reveals that ethnic groups are not merely culture-bearing entities. That is, group identity is not a passive and straightforward reflection of a distinct culture and language.

Instead, ethnicity involves the subjective construction of identity on the basis of real or assumed shared culture and/or common descent, and groups have been studied by anthropologists and sociologists on the basis of self-definition and definition by others (e.g. Barth 1969: 10; Cohen 1978; Chapman, McDonald and Tonkin 1989; Ringer and Lawless 1989; Shennan 1994). In many instances, only certain cultural practices are involved in the perception and expression of ethnic difference, whilst other cultural practices and beliefs are shared across ethnic boundaries (see Hodder 1982). Furthermore, the processes involved in the construction of ethnic identities and the selection of particular cultural and linguistic characteristics as relevant symbols of identity take place in the context of social interaction and involve the ascription of identity vis-à-vis others (see Barth 1969; Roosens 1989; Eriksen 1992). In many instances, this active construction of identity is embedded in the negotiation of economic and political interests or what can be broadly termed power relations. For instance, it has been shown how individuals may shift identity in different situations or even permanently depending on their interests (e.g. Barth 1969; Eidheim 1969), and many studies have explored the ways in which ethnic groups have been formed in the context of resistance to colonial and state domination (see Comaroff and Comaroff 1992; Devalle 1992; Eriksen 1992).

Such an approach to ethnicity marks a significant departure from the traditional assumption that ethnic groups reflect discrete cultures and languages, an idea which has been central to a number of disciplines in the human sciences including archaeology. It can no longer be assumed, as in culture historical archaeology, that archaeological cultures reflect past peoples; a point which has been stressed from a variety of positions from the 1960s onwards (e.g. Binford 1962; Ucko 1969; Hodder 1978; Renfrew 1987; Shennan 1994). Certain aspects of material culture may have been involved in the expression of ethnic identities in the past, but many others may have been shared between groups. Indeed, a particular group's identity is unlikely to have been monolithic or homogeneous, and neither are the beliefs and practices which informed that identity. It is also likely that the relationships between particular ethnic identities and

particular types of material culture ('ethnic markers') were fluid and ambiguous and the expression of ethnicity may have changed in different contexts of social interaction. Thus, the adoption of 'western' style pottery by immigrant Chinese communities in the USA, or the adoption of Graeco-Roman architectural styles by Jewish communities in the late first millennium BC, does not *necessarily* represent evidence for acculturation or Hellenization. It is just as likely that such types of material culture were deliberately appropriated and redefined in the expression of Chinese or Jewish identity (and see Rubertone 1989: 36; Rajak 1994: 235).

Thus, recent theories of ethnicity in the human sciences present an important challenge to traditional techniques for identifying ethnic groups in archaeology. If we accept that ethnic identity is essentially based on self-conscious identification with a particular group (Shennan 1994: 14), such theories would appear to support the argument that archaeologists are dependent upon historical sources which provide access to people's self-conscious reflections on ethnicity. However, for the most part theories of ethnicity which emphasize the subjective, self-conscious aspects of identity fail to address the relationship between culture and ethnicity (see Jones 1997: 87–8). It has been convincingly demonstrated that there is not a one-to-one relationship between ethnic groups and cultures, but the precise relationship between actors' perceptions and expressions of ethnicity, and the cultural contexts and social relations in which they are embedded, has been neglected (e.g. Barth 1969; Glazer and Moynihan 1975; Ringer and Lawless 1989). Instead, culture has been reduced to an epiphenomenal and arbitrary set of symbols manipulated in pursuit of group interests in changing social and historical contexts (Eriksen 1992: 30, 44).

The relationship between people's consciousness of ethnicity and their cultural contexts can be explored through theories of practice which address the general relationship between the conditions of social life and people's subjective constructions of social reality (see Bentley 1987, 1991; Jones 1997). The anthropologist Pierre Bourdieu (1977) has argued that people possess durable, often subliminal, dispositions towards certain perceptions and practices (such as those relating to the sexual division of labour, morality, tastes and so on). Such dispositions become part of an individual's sense of self at an early age, and are generated by the conditions making up a particular social environment, such as modes of production or access to certain resources (Bourdieu 1977: 77–93). Bourdieu calls the totality of these dispositions the *habitus*. In contrast to traditional theories of culture, the *habitus* does not consist of a system of normative rules which exist outside of individual history (Bourdieu 1977: 72). Rather, the orientations of the *habitus* 'are at once "structuring structures" and "structured structures": they shape and are shaped by social practice' (Postone, LiPuma and Calhoun 1993: 4).

The concept of the *habitus* can be used to explain the way in which subjective ethnic classifications are grounded in the social conditions characterizing particular social domains. Ethnicity is not a passive reflection of similarities and differences in the cultural practices and structural conditions in which agents are socialized. Nor is ethnicity entirely constituted in the process of social interaction whereby epiphenomenal cultural characteristics are manipulated in the pursuit of economic and political interests. Rather, drawing on Bourdieu's theory of practice, it can be argued that the construction of ethnic identity is grounded in the shared subliminal dispositions of the *habitus* which shape, and are shaped, by commonalities of practice:

> [a] shared habitus engenders feelings of identification among people similarly endowed. Those feelings are consciously appropriated and given form through existing symbolic resources. (Bentley 1991: 173)

Furthermore, these 'symbolic resources', such as language, material culture, beliefs and so on, are not arbitrary. The cultural practices and beliefs which become reified as symbols of ethnicity are derived from, and resonate with, people's habitual practices and experiences, as well as reflecting the immediate conditions and interests which characterize particular situations. As Eriksen has argued, symbols of ethnicity

> are intrinsically linked with experienced, practical worlds containing specific, relevant meanings which on the one hand contribute to

shaping interaction, and on the other hand limit the number of options in the production of ethnic signs. (Eriksen 1992: 45)

Yet, the *habitus* and ethnicity are not directly congruent, as in the traditional equation of culture and ethnicity. There is a break between the cultural dispositions making up the *habitus* as a whole and the objectified representation of cultural *difference* involved in the expression of ethnicity. Shared habitual dispositions provide the basis for the recognition of commonalities of sentiment and interest, and the perception and communication of cultural affinities and differences, which ethnicity entails. However, a consciousness of ethnicity only emerges in the context of social interaction between peoples of differing cultural traditions. Such forms of interaction lead to a reflexive mode of perception involving a conscious rationalization of cultural practices which had previously constituted subliminal, taken-for-granted modes of behaviour. Such exposure to the arbitrariness of cultural practices, which had hitherto been taken as self-evident and natural, permits and requires a change 'in the level of discourse, so as to rationalize and systematize' the representation of those cultural practices and, more generally, the representation of the cultural tradition itself (Bourdieu 1977: 233). It is at such a discursive level that ethnic categories are produced, reproduced and transformed through the systematic communication of cultural difference with relation to particular 'ethnic others'.

There are numerous examples of this process in the ethnographic literature. For instance, in the process of interaction and communication between the Tswana people of southern Africa and evangelist missionaries, both groups began to recognize distinctions between them. In effect they began to *objectify* their world in relation to a novel other, and in the process they invented for themselves a self-conscious coherence and distinctness. This objectification of culture is not a fabrication, an entirely instrumental construction. Tswana ethnicity is based on the perception of commonalities of practice and experience in *Setswana* (Tswana ways) in opposition to *Sekgoa* (European ways). But it has also been fundamentally affected by the colonial situation which resulted in a break with pre-existing forms of identity. It was only as a result of the interaction between the Tswana and members of the colonial society that Tswana tradition was objectified as a coherent body of knowledge and practice uniting the Tswana people as an ethnic group. (For further discussion, see Comaroff and Comaroff 1992 [and also Chapter 10, this volume].)

Thus, the form which expressions of cultural difference take is constituted by the intersection of people's *habitus* with the social conditions constituting a particular historical context. These conditions include the prevailing modes of domination, and the relative distribution of the material and symbolic means necessary for the imposition of dominant regimes of ethnic categorization. The extent to which ethnicity is embedded in pre-existing cultural realities represented by a shared *habitus* is highly variable and contingent upon the cultural transformations engendered by the processes of interaction and the nature of the power relations between the interacting 'groups' (Comaroff and Comaroff 1992: 56). Moreover, expressions of ethnic difference are a product of the interrelation between the *particular* cultural practices and historical experiences activated in any given social context, and broader discourses of ethnicity. Consequently, the cultural content of ethnicity may vary substantively and qualitatively in different contexts, as may the importance of ethnicity (see Eriksen 1991 and 1992).

Such a theory accounts for the dynamic and contextual nature of ethnicity at the same time as addressing the relationship between people's perceptions of ethnicity and the cultural practices and social relations in which they are embedded. Furthermore, it suggests that there are likely to be significant differences between discursive literary representations of ethnicity and its manifestation in social practice which have important implications for the interpretation of ethnic groups in historical archaeology.

Practice and Representation

The theory of ethnicity proposed here suggests that archaeologists may not be able to find a reflection of the 'ethnic entities' represented in historical sources in the archaeological record (see also Miller 1985: 202, with relation to caste).

Indeed, it is possible to question the very existence of bounded, homogeneous ethnic entities except at an abstract conceptual level. Ethnic categories are based on a conscious reification of transient cultural practices taking place in different spatial and temporal contexts (cf. Bourdieu 1990: 84, on genealogy and mapping), and the 'group' only exists in the context of interpretation where it justifies and explains past practices and modes of interaction and informs future ones. In contrast, the praxis of ethnicity results in multiple transient realizations of ethnic difference in particular contexts. These practical realizations of ethnicity in many instances involve the production and consumption of distinctive styles of material culture. But they are a product of the intersection of the perceptual and practical dispositions of the people concerned and the interests and oppositions engendered in a particular social context rather than abstract categories of difference.

This distinction between abstract conceptual representations of ethnicity and the praxis of ethnicity is in some senses analogous to Connerton's (1989: 72–3) distinction between contexts of 'inscription' and 'incorporation'. Abstract representations of ethnicity are frequently found in 'inscribing practices', such as writing, art and other symbolic forms, which trap and hold information long after the 'author' has stopped informing. Whereas the praxis of ethnicity falls in the domain of 'incorporating practice', such as everyday practices, performative acts and bodily comportment which carry messages that a sender or senders 'impart by means of their current bodily activity, the transmission occurring only during the time that their bodies are present to sustain that activity' (Connerton 1989: 72).

These different forms of practice, inscriptive and incorpotating, should not be seen as exclusive, fixed categories; they overlap with one another and persist alongside one another in any particular socio-historical situation. However, they do represent a useful heuristic device in that they allow us to isolate qualitative differences in the manifestation of ethnicity in different contexts. As Connerton (1989: 4, 100–1) points out, interpretive history has traditionally taken inscription, most commonly textual inscription, as its privileged object of enquiry. In reconstructing past ethnic groups historians and archaeologists have colluded in giving precedence to literary representations of ethnicity and searching for an isomorphic reflection of such categories in the archaeological record. But to do so is to make the mistake of conflating qualitatively different manifestations of ethnicity. The archaeological record may provide evidence for some aspects of inscriptive practice, such as in symbolic motifs and architectural styles, but the vast proportion of the material recovered is the product of transient, but ongoing, cultural practices, some of which may have been involved in the recognition and expression of ethnic difference.

That is not to suggest that the vast majority of archaeological material is not relevant to the analysis of ethnicity. On the contrary, the analysis of such material can provide important information about the experienced, practical contexts with which inscriptive representations, or discourses, of ethnicity intersect and derive their power. Also, the study of material culture potentially provides access to multivocal practices which can be reduced to decontextualized, univocal, representations by certain forms of textual analysis (see Rappaport and Cummins 1994: 92). The point which I wish to emphasize here is the importance of recognizing the qualitative difference between objectified, inscriptive, representations of ethnicity and the praxis of ethnicity. Rather than the seemingly coherent ethnic categories which are produced at a discursive level, the praxis of ethnicity may be manifested in the archaeological record as a complex web of overlapping stylistic boundaries constituted by expressions of ethnic difference, expressions which were at once transient, but also subject to reproduction and transformation in the ongoing processes of social life.

Conclusions

Recent debates in historical archaeology have contributed to the development of a meaning-centred and contextual approach to the use of both historical and archaeological sources. In emphasizing the situated and subjective nature of historical evidence this work provides an important basis for exploring the active role of texts in the construction of past identities.

Beyond this, however, it is also important to consider the precise manner in which material and literary traditions are bound up in the construction of social reality. In exploring the ways in which literature and material culture are simultaneously involved in the construction of ethnicity it becomes clear that there are important qualitative differences between the representation of ethnicity in literature, and other forms of inscription, and expressions of ethnicity embodied in the cultural practices which contributed to much of the archaeological record. As a result archaeological and historical sources can provide both complementary and contradictory perspectives on past ethnicities.

Such an approach has important implications for the analysis of ethnic groups in historical archaeology. Neither archaeologists nor historians can continue to accept the ethnic categories represented in literary sources as straightforward representations of homogeneous ethnic entities with singular spatial and temporal co-ordinates. But conversely they should not disregard literary evidence in favour of supposedly more 'objective' archaeological analysis of long-term history, as has been the recent vogue. Whilst there is a place for the analysis of, for instance, long-term social and economic processes, there is also considerable scope for an archaeology of the social praxis of identities. In order to do this, it will be necessary to abandon the search for homogeneous, bounded ethnic groups and focus on the ways in which particular styles of material culture may have been involved in the active expression of ethnicity in different contexts. Moreover, through the analysis of spatial organization, modes of production, architectural styles and so on, archaeologists can explore the ways in which discursive systems of difference intersect with the values and modes of practice, the *habitus*, which characterized particular historical contexts.

Thus, contrary to the idea that archaeologists cannot hope to study ethnicity in the absence of historical sources, this approach suggests that historians cannot hope to study past ethnic groups without considering material culture. A contextual and meaning-centred approach to the archaeological analysis of ethnicity offers an essential counterpart to the critical study of textual representations of ethnicity. The praxis of ethnicity cannot be ignored in favour of analysing social identities as entirely discursive constructions, for as Norton points out:

> analysis of discursive processes tends to neglect the question of how meanings are socially experienced and lived. The equation of the social with the discursive seems often to flatten or impoverish the texture of social reality. (Norton 1993: 756)

In order to avoid such a flattening out of ethnicity, it is necessary to focus on the ways in which cultural discourses on identity are related to concrete social relations and activities, and the variable nature of the social existence of these discourses (*ibid.*). Archaeologists may not have easy access to the way in which people experienced life in the past, but they can certainly endeavour to explore the praxis of ethnicity, and the ways in which this intersected with the discursive systems of difference represented in historical sources, rather than accept the latter as straightforward representations of social reality.

References

Austin, D. 1997. The 'proper study' of medieval archaeology. In *From the Baltic to the Black Sea: studies in medieval archaeology*, D. Austin and L. Alcock (eds), 9–42. London: Routledge.

Barth, F. 1969. Introduction. In *Ethnic Groups and Boundaries*, F. Barth (ed.), 9–38. Boston, MA: Little Brown.

Beaudry, M. C., L. J. Cook and S. A. Mrozowski 1991. Artefacts and active voices: material culture as social discourse. In *The Archaeology of Inequality*, R. H. McGuire and R. Paynter (eds), 150–91. Oxford: Blackwell.

Bentley, G. C. 1987. Ethnicity and practice. *Comparative Studies in Society and History* 29, 24–55.

Bentley, G. C. 1991. Response to Yelvington. *Comparative Studies in Society and History* 33, 169–75.

Binford, L. R. 1962. Archaeology as anthropology. *American Antiquity* 28, 217–25.

Bourdieu, P. 1977. *Outline of a Theory of Practice.* Cambridge: Cambridge University Press.

Bourdieu, P. 1990. *The Logic of Practice.* Cambridge: Polity.

Burley, D. V., G. A. Horsfall and J. D. Brandon 1992, *Structural Considerations of Métis Ethnicity: an archaeological, architectural and historical study.* Vermillion: The University of South Dakota Press.

Champion, T. C. 1997. Medieval archaeology and the tyranny of the historical record. In *From the Baltic to the Black Sea: studies in medieval archaeology*, D. Austin and L. Alcock (eds), 79–95. London: Routledge.

Chapman, M., M. McDonald and E. Tonkin 1989. Introduction. In *History and Ethnicity*, E. Tonkin, M. McDonald and M. Chapman (eds), 1–21. London: Routledge.

Clark, L. 1987. Gravestones: reflectors of ethnicity or class? In *Consumer Choice in Historical Archaeology*, S. M. Spencer-Wood (ed.), 389–95. New York: Plenum Press.

Cohen, R. 1978. Ethnicity: problem and focus in anthropology. *Annual Review of Anthropology* 7, 379–403.

Comaroff, J. and J. Comaroff 1992. *Ethnography and the Historical Imagination.* Boulder, Co: Westview Press.

Connerton, P. 1989. *How Societies Remember.* Cambridge: Cambridge University Press.

Devalle, S. B. C. 1992. *Discourses of Ethnicity: culture and protest in Jharkhand.* London: Sage.

Dever, W. G. 1977. The Patriarchal traditions. Palestine in the second millennium BCE: the archaeological picture. In *Israelite and Judean History*, J. H. Hayes and J. M. Miller (eds), 70–120. London: SCM.

Eidheim, H. 1969. When ethnic identity is a social stigma. In *Ethnic Groups and Boundaries*, F. Barth (ed.), 39–57. Boston, MA: Little Brown.

Eriksen, T. H. 1991. The cultural contexts of ethnic differences. *Man* 26, 127–44.

Eriksen, T. H. 1992. *Us and Them in Modern Societies: ethnicity and nationalism in Mauritius, Trinidad and beyond.* London: Scandinavian University Press.

Etter, P. A. 1980. The west coast Chinese and opium smoking. In *Archaeological Perspectives on Ethnicity in America*, R. Schuyler (ed.), 97–101. Farmingdale, NY: Baywood Press.

Ferguson, L. 1978. Looking for the 'Afro' in Colono-Indian pottery. *The Conference on Historic Site Archaeology Papers* 12, 68–86.

Glazer, N. and D. P. Moynihan 1975. Introduction. In *Ethnicity: theory and experience*, N. Glazer and D. P. Moynihan (eds), 1–26. Cambridge, MA: Harvard University Press.

Hall, M. 1994. Lifting the veil of popular history: archaeology and politics in urban Cape Town. In *Social Construction of the Past: representation as power*, G. C. Bond and A. Gilliam (eds), 167–84. London: Routledge.

Hodder, I. 1978. Simple correlations between material culture and society: a review. In *The Spatial Organisation of Culture*, I. Hodder (ed.), 3–24. London: Duckworth.

Hodder, I. 1982. *Symbols in Action*. Cambridge: Cambridge University Press.

Jones, S. 1997. *The Archaeology of Ethnicity: constructing identities in the past and the present*. London: Routledge.

Kelly, M. C. S. and R. E. Kelly 1980. Approaches to ethnic identification in historical archaeology. In *Archaeological Perspectives on Ethnicity in America. Afro-Caribbean and Asian American culture history*, R. L. Schuyler (ed.), 133–43. New York: Baywood.

Kraabel, A. T. 1985. Synagoga Caeca: systematic distortion in Gentile interpretations of evidence for Judaism in the early Christian period. In *To See Ourselves as Others see Us: Christians, Jews, 'Others', in late antiquity*, J. Neusner and E. S. Frerichs (eds), 219–46. Chico, CA: Scholars Press.

Leone, M. P. and P. B. Potter 1988. Introduction: issues in historical archaeology. In *The Recovery of Meaning: historical archaeology in the eastern United States*, M. P. Leone and P. B. Potter Jr (eds), 1–22. Washington, DC: Smithsonian Institution Press.

Little, B. J. 1992. Texts, images, material culture. In *Text-Aided Archaeology*, B. J. Little (ed.), 217–21 Boca Raton, FL: CRC.

Lucy, S. J. 1995. The Anglo-Saxon cemeteries of East Yorkshire. Unpublished D.Phil. thesis, University of Cambridge.

McGuire, R. H. 1982. The study of ethnicity in historical archaeology. *Journal of Anthropological Archaeology* 1, 159–78.

Miller, D. 1985. *Artefacts as Categories: a study in ceramic variability in central India*. Cambridge: Cambridge University Press.

Norton, R. 1993. Culture and identity in the South Pacific: a comparative analysis. *Man* 28(4), 741–59.

Orser, C. E. 1991. The archaeological search for ethnicity in the historic United States. *Archaeologia Polona* 29, 109–21.

Postone, M., E. LiPuma and C. Calhoun 1993. Introduction: Bourdieu and social theory, In *Bourdieu: critical perspectives*, C. Calhoun, E. LiPuma and M. Postone (eds), 1–13. Cambridge: Polity.

Praetzellis, A., M. Praetzellis and M. Brown 1987. Artefacts as symbols of identity: an example from Sacramento's Gold Rush Era Chinese community. In *Living in Cities: current research in historical archaeology*, A. Saski (ed.), 38–47. Pleasant Hill, CA: The Society for Historical Archaeology.

Rajak, T. 1994. Inscription and context: reading the Jewish catacombs of Rome. In *Studies in Early Jewish Epigraphy*, J. Willem van Henten and P. Willem van der Horst (eds), 226–41. Leiden: E.J. Brill.

Rappaport, J. and T. B. F. Cummins 1994. Literacy and power in colonial Africa. In *Social Construction of the Past: representation as power*, G. C. Bond and A. Gilliam (eds), 89–109. London: Routledge.

Renfrew, C. 1987. *Archaeology and Language. The puzzle of Indo-European origins*. Harmondsworth: Penguin.

Ringer, B. B. and E. R. Lawless 1989. *Race, Ethnicity and Society*. London: Routledge.

Roosens, E. E. 1989. *Creating Ethnicity: the process of ethnogenesis*. London: Sages.

Rubertone, P. E. 1989. Archaeology, colonialism and 17th-century Native America: towards an alternative interpretation. In *Conflict in the Archaeology of Living Traditions*, R. Layton (ed.), 32–45. London: Unwin Hyman.

Shennan, S. J. 1994. Introduction. In *Archaeological Approaches to Cultural Identity*, S. J. Shennan (ed.), 1–32. London: Routledge.

Trigger, B. G. 1995. Romanticism, nationalism and archaeology. In *Nationalism, Politics and the Practice of Archaeology*, P. L. Kohl and C. Fawcett (eds), 263–79. London: Routledge.

Ucko. P. J. 1969. Ethnography and archaeological interpretation of funerary remains. *World Archaeology* 1, 262–80.

Whitelam. K. W. 1986. Recreating the history of Israel. *Journal for the Study of the Old Testament* 35, 45–70.

15

Beyond Racism
Some Opinions about Racialism and American Archaeology

Roger Echo-Hawk and Larry J. Zimmerman

The scrutiny of racism as a cultural practice is well established in scholarship and in American public discourse. The underlying problem of race itself is also a common topic in academic writings and is a matter of ever-increasing consensus in anthropology and biology. But the significance of race as an inherently flawed interpretation of human biological diversity has yet to register in many realms of scholarship and in the public mind. What does it mean that race has little or no biological reality?

In this essay we seek to encourage the expansion of the public discussion of race beyond racism and toward the broader problem of race itself.[1] It is not our intention to "solve" the problems of race, nor do we intend to add to the extant technical literature on the biology of race; rather, we hope to add a bit of clarity to a confusing and undeservedly obscure topic. Because the terminology surrounding race and associated issues is a quagmire as difficult to escape as the morass of race itself, it is important for us to define important terms as the basis for analyzing the cultural implications of the science of race. We proceed from there to explicitly scrutinize how the ideology and practice of racialism affects American archaeology and the people it studies.

Roger Echo-Hawk and Larry J. Zimmerman, "Beyond Race: Some Opinions about Racialism and American Archaeology," pp. 461–85 from *The American Indian Quarterly* 30:3–4 (2006). Reprinted with permission of the University of Nebraska Press.

Here we contend that even though many archaeologists say that they accept the long-held anthropological view that race is biologically unsupportable, they still embrace racialism in their methods and thinking, which has the typical result of confounding archaeological analysis related to issues of race. Archaeological racialism is damaging to archaeology and to the people archaeology studies because race distorts our understanding of humankind and human history. This outcome seriously undermines the ability of archaeology to contribute meaningfully to the ongoing construction of race in American culture. In short, archaeology accepts a warped status quo – a status quo that is common in scholarship in general and throughout American life. Nowhere is this made clearer than in the history of American Moundbuilder mythology and in the Ancient One/Kennewick case.[2]

The genesis of this paper stems from discussions by members of a Yahoo group, the Closet Chickens (a story in itself), in response to an online article that appeared in September 2004 – an article that touches on matters that parallel many of the issues surrounding the Ancient One case.[3]

Paul Rincon of BBC News Online wrote a piece titled "Tribe Challenges American Origins," which reports on the study of ancient human bones from Mexico by Dr. Sylvia Gonzalez.[4] Some of these bones were more than twelve thousand years old, and Gonzalez asserted that they were very different from Native American skulls. To her they represented a physical type that resembled "southern Asians, Australians and populations of the South Pacific Rim."

With this conclusion in hand, Gonzalez reportedly took the further leap of pondering what this might mean in racial terms, asserting that "[Native Americans] cannot claim to have been the first people there [in America]." Rincon noted the similarity of her findings to those of the scientists who "won" the Kennewick court case.

This essay will present pieces of the ensuing Closet Chicken discussion (used by permission of the authors). Since the group's inception in 2001, the Chickens have struggled with the concept of racialism and what it means in archaeology. This struggle illustrates the reality that race exists as a fundamental precept of American archaeology, but more important, the Closet Chicken dialogue on race has broader implications that deserve wide public attention.

A Dialogue on Race and American Archaeology

We start by relating the comments by the Closet Chickens regarding the Rincon news story.[5] Dorothy Lippert posted the article for the other Closet Chickens to read and commented:

I was trying to think of some clever comment about how this must be why I enjoyed visiting Australia so much – it's because I was going home, but really, all these theories that say variants of: "'[Native Americans] cannot claim to have been the first people there,' Dr Gonzalez said" are starting to get to me. Why is it so important to anthropologists to demonstrate that Native Americans weren't here first, or at least for a very long time before Europeans arrived?

Joe Watkins soon answered:

I feel as equally unsettled. It has become more political than scientific, as if "America" was always White until us heathens came along and somehow painted it red with a broad brush of blood, ochre, or something. The idea that we, as American Indians, are somehow lesser because we didn't have a separate biological origin or Genesis. The politics of the past have become news, especially since the scientists "won" [in the Kennewick decision].

Larry Zimmerman responded:

The researchers [in the Gonzalez story], as with the Kennewick plaintiffs, judges, politicians, and media folks (e.g., Leslie Stahl), don't get that it's not necessarily a claim of American Indian primacy on the continent that is important, but the issues associated with Indians being pushed off their lands, the ways in which it was done (i.e. broken treaties as much as anything), and matters of human rights. Somehow things get all warped into the notion that if Indians pushed other groups (especially if they possibly were "Caucasoid") out of the way, it was legitimate for EuroAmericans to push Indians out of the way. It also stems from an archaeological, scholarly (and to a degree public) bent for "oldest," "first," and "largest."

Sonya Atalay reacted:

Wow – this is quite upsetting. Not only what is being said, but as each of you has pointed out in different ways, it's HOW it is being framed. It's as if there is some huge paranoid conspiracy theory against the notion that Native People on this continent are not Indigenous. The motivation behind these kinds of inquiries is very interesting and, I think, is a new version of that old moundbuilders myth – "they" [Indians] couldn't have done it, "they" weren't here first, they are the real savages that killed off the moundbuilders (or in this case, the REAL first Americans), hence we are the rightful heirs to this land and our acts of genocide are justified.

As Atalay continued, her comment centered on the notion of skull measurements:

I wonder if there have been studies done in Europe and elsewhere globally that look at the changes in skulls and other human remains over long periods of time? I know that the human remains at Catalhoyuk are very different than modern populations – there was, after all something called the "Ottoman Empire" during which large [numbers] of people from various regions had opportunity to mix. Although they were all predominantly Caucasian, there was a great deal of difference between them. And the spread of the Ottoman Empire caused the mixing of those genetic groups, which led to major changes in facial structure and other skeletal changes. Humans adapt and change. Why is it assumed that Native People shouldn't have changed at all? One MAJOR difference here is that the Ottoman Empire was not colonization in the same way as we experienced on this continent. Yet even without the Ottoman Empire or colonizing efforts, 12,000+ years is a LOT of time for change to occur, particularly if we consider that there was a major climatic shift that took place during that period. Why should we look like we did 12,000+ years ago??????

So, perhaps focusing on the ways in which other groups have changed over time would be productive. Why are we as Native People still held to some notion of static and unchanging over time – is it the legacy of Edward Curtis coming back to essentialize us over and over again? ... I think one of the major themes we must be fighting against constantly in the media and among our colleagues (sadly) is this notion that our 500+ nations were all similar, without variation among us and between us, and that we should not have changed over 12,000 years. Also, we need to better educate people about the dramatic effects of the last 500 years of colonization – the change in diet, methods of preparation, health, disease, movement, change in our environments, boarding schools, intermarriage – all with dramatic effects on our bodies (not to mention other aspects of our daily lived experiences).

I know ... preaching to the choir ... but it is infuriating and I needed to vent.

Atalay suggested the possibility of writing something about the problem, and possibly offering it to *American Indian Quarterly*. This pushed Roger Echo-Hawk to respond:

Sonya has identified a point that I find interesting. When the Pawnee Nation disputed with the NMNH [National Museum of Natural History] in 1995 over the Caddoan identity of Steed-Kisker, I explored how Caddoan oral traditions matched the models put forward in various craniometric studies and other skeletal studies to support identification of Steed-Kisker as ancestral to Arikaras and South Band Pawnees. The NMNH Repatriation Review Committee found in our favor, but placed little credence in the craniometric evidence, following the views of Christy Turner, who felt that craniometrics

measures a very plastic substance (skull shape) that responds in unknown ways to environmental factors like diet. Turner felt that teeth are less amenable to such influences. Learning from this, I presume that one must utilize skull measurement comparisons with caution, particularly when looking at gross characteristics over time, such as whether a skull is deemed to be "long-headed" versus some other shape (I once looked at a book from circa 1930 that attached personality traits to head shape and featured drawings of numerous head shapes, including a quite square-headed – and very socially sensible – fellow). Several days ago I looked on the web for info about Silvia Gonzalez and found her vita. She's a bona fide scholar, but thinking back now, she doesn't appear to have any substantial specialty in craniometrics or such things. It would be useful to know more about what she actually said and where she got her opinions. I would suggest that the news article should be taken as a reflection of reporter Paul Rincon's opinions – a prime example of what I call shake-&-bake journalism, where a reporter conveys the impression of having become an instant expert on a complex topic. This is quite convincing to the consuming public, but typically just provides a vehicle for serving up whatever preconceptions are held by the reporter.

Echo-Hawk then leveled this criticism at the Closet Chickens:

In this case, the reporter has something in common with what I take to be the views of the Closet Chicken majority: an unshakeable faith-based belief in race, and that explaining human history through a racial model is a valid and appropriate way to understand even the ancient past (seeing white people, Caucasian, caucasoids vs. Indian, Native, Indigenes, etc, and accepting these gross groupings as unqualified biological groupings extending into the distant past). It is interesting to ponder how you Chickens have responded to this shake-&-bake journalism with a plan to approach the *"American Indian" Quarterly* [quotation marks around American Indian were intentional], a journal that cultivates racial Indianhood by devoting itself to uncritical perpetuation of the basic ideas of race. In other words, your plan involves a publication that explicitly has as its agenda a critical perspective on racism rather than on race. But what choice is there, really? It is difficult to avoid the thought that any such "choice" basically devolves to choosing to accept participation in race and its elaborate social mechanisms, or to choosing some other undefined path as a means to cultivate a useful outside perspective – or maybe to even go so far as to aim at some impossible form of non-participation. It is very difficult indeed to find an outside space to cultivate a critical eye on race, and few people have the luxury of withdrawing from the world. I suspect that my head-shape is, socially speaking, very, very far from square, so I'm always on the outside of things. I'm not interested in bonding with Chickenry on the false notions of race, so I hope no one minds if I choose instead to observe with genuine interest what manner of engagement your plans give rise to, and where you go in the world, and whatever happens next.

Echo-Hawk's critique of what he perceived as the Closet Chickens' views on race prompted this response from Zimmerman:

At the risk of going into anthro prof lecture mode, no Roger, you don't have it quite right that, "the reporter has something in common with what I take to be the views of the Closet Chicken majority: an unshakeable faith-based belief in race, and that explaining human history through a racial model is a valid and appropriate way to understand even the ancient past ... and accepting these gross groupings as unqualified biological groupings extending into the distant past." In fact, a primary anthropological tenet on race, based now on a century of scientific study, states exactly the opposite, that racial groups based on biological characteristics are unsupportable.[6] We understand that the visible (i.e. quantifiable) characteristics are based on adaptations to certain environments. Indeed, what we see for such traits are clines, that is, gradual variations as we move across space, environments, and time. So many factors can intervene to alter these characteristics.

At the same time, we understand that racial groups based on visible attributes are powerful social constructs that permeate virtually every aspect of (at least) American society and are mostly damaging to us; we must struggle constantly against racialism. In fact, even for those of us with such an understanding and training, race virtually is impossible to avoid, much as you point out in the last part of your missive.

At the moment, in fact, there is a major NSF-funded [American Anthropological Association] project to take this message more powerfully to the public. What that impact will be, who knows? In fact, I'm pretty skeptical about its success (and the $3 million they are spending on it!), but I suppose that the only way to change things is constantly to struggle with it.

The rub in all of this comes from what appears to be a universal human need to organize perceptions of the environment through classification, which is a foundation of all sciences. Scientists are trained to classify, as indeed all of us are as archaeologists, but we hope that our approaches are more carefully constructed and less biased than what a member of the public might use (hubris? probably). What guys like the Kennewick plaintiffs, and others are actually doing with craniometrics is measuring the clines and using statistical clusters or variations from the clusters to classify. Then they look at the broad categories (which they use in their forensic identifications), or, ... suggest, they think that they can tell "tribe" based on skull morphology (yes, this is an oversimplification). What happens to us in the process is that we conflate the results of our methods with the social constructions of race. This is almost inevitable, but something against which every scientist should guard. Unfortunately, most of us don't, which is something your statement strongly reminds us of, and in this particular instance, something of which Turner, Goodman, and others have also reminded us.

Now, Roger, about that square skull....

Echo-Hawk responded:

I didn't intend to give the impression that I accept the idea that racialism accurately describes human biological diversity among either present or past populations. Rather, I was trying to articulate my understanding of the majority Closet Chicken acceptance of race based on our ongoing dialogue on this issue – an acceptance I do not share.

In general, I don't really feel comfortable proselytizing on this issue, but I feel that anthropologists and scholars have an obligation to address the scholarship on race that you mention. I regard the Chickens as an important group that can and should provide leadership on the issue of race, but it has been my impression that the group has more generally sought to bond on race rather than delve into what it means that race gives us a false way to look at humankind.

Perhaps my effort to characterize Chicken opinions is misguided. I have often gotten the feeling that I have not been very effective in identifying the really important questions in my past emails on this subject. I failed to find a way to make race an issue of significance at the Denver Art Museum, and most recently failed to convince the Field Museum to introduce this topic in their popular public program on the Pawnees. There is lots of anthropological literature that shows why race is not useful as a means of characterizing human biological diversity, but this scholarship has not translated into visible forms of public discourse on the topic, which continues to focus on racism, rather than addressing the racialism that gives rise to racism.

The academic community has been very successful in helping to create public discourse on racism, but why haven't scholars succeeded in generating useful forms of public awareness and public discussion on race itself? I think part of the answer is that racialized elements of the academic community have been more intent on mining race as a source of social power than in defusing the power of race in our lives. What will the Chickens do, mine race or confront race?

I hope I find opportunities to make this a matter of public awareness and discourse, but as I said, I haven't found a venue so far. It's important to contribute to academic literature, but we really need to find ways to get the public involved in thinking about what it means that our cultural systems empower race rather than defuse it.

We have an obligation to either do something or, if you continue to accept and rely on race in your work, then perhaps you have some obligation to address what Larry has described as "a century of scientific study" and show why this heritage should be ignored and rejected. The choice is yours.

Zimmerman answered Echo-Hawk in this way:

Thanks for the clarifications, Roger. I don't disagree with you at all; the public is where it's at in terms of the issue. I happened to teach a course on Race and Ethnic Identity at the University of Iowa a couple of years ago. The class was mostly African-American and had expected an African-American professor. When this bald, white guy shows up, they were upset (not directly at me). I gave them traditional social science views of race/racism/racialism. Within a few days, the students were angry with me, at which point I stopped the class and just asked them what the problem was. One woman blurted out: "You're not teaching us the right stuff!" Others agreed. I asked what the right stuff was, and the response generally was that I wasn't teaching anything about their "feelings" about race.

The truth is, that every time a student opened his/her mouth, they "individuated" their experience: "What happened to me was . . .; what I think is.. . ." What this taught me is that we Americans don't want to give up our racism/ racialism. It's often how we define ourselves, and it's nearly unavoidable, because as I said earlier, race permeates American society. In the end, I told them that although their individual experiences and viewpoints are indeed important, they were not what the class was about. It was about what social sciences can tell us about race and its variants, which might explain the genesis of their individual experiences and feelings. I would only allow them to talk about individual situations if they put it in context of the social science. Truth is, it really helped, and I feel darned fortunate that by the end of class, only one student out of about 50 was still angry. Others were surprisingly capable of getting past the problems and really liked the class. The moral of this tale? Yes, it is imperative that academia confront the issue and educate the public on the matter. They are fully capable of understanding and incorporating our perspectives if we will communicate with them. But the pulls of individual experience and race as part of self-definition are extremely powerful and demand powerful, communicable information.

Now as for AIQ, the readership is mostly not anthropologists, so perhaps it is not so bad a venue for some of this. And non-anthro colleagues are indeed one of our "publics." I can even imagine stringing together some of the points made in our discussions about the matter as an "article" that might raise an eyebrow.

These Closet Chicken exchanges on race continued with other members chiming in with opinions and positions, and the group ultimately agreed to make the essence of this conversation on race public as a means of inviting a wider discourse. These exchanges are reflective of widespread attitudes toward race in America as well as current thinking about the science of race but particularly reveal how race, racialism, and racism affect American archaeology.

What follows is an examination of the key terms used in the Closet Chicken discussions. There is some repetition of ideas stated earlier, but hopefully the repetition strengthens key points.

The Quagmire of Race

"Race" is a term that subsumes a diverse set of cultural depictions and activities that aim at dividing humankind into groupings based on observable characteristics. Race permeates the American world to such an extent that most people don't even think about it – it's just another powerful force that people take for granted in American life. In this regard, American archaeology absolutely reflects American society. Because the vast majority of Americans have little or no awareness of the problems of racialism, it's extremely difficult for scholarship on race to translate from theory to practice. Moreover, to some degree, to act on the truth about race is to risk interesting forms of alienation from important core values that shape American society and personal identities.

It's important at the outset of this analysis to define our specific use of the terms "racialism" and "racism" as distinguishable aspects of race. These terms and their derivatives are often employed in various ways that frequently overlap, but our analysis of race in this paper flows in part from a careful delineation of the two terms as separate, interlocked ideas.

Racialism is the cultural idea that humankind is composed of racial groups that are biologically distinct. These groups are based on what seem to be long-term, received wisdom from straightforward observations of humanity: some skin colors are lighter or darker than others; some hair is straight and some tightly curled; the list of these attributes goes on and on.

Although we may intellectually understand these attributes to exist along an unbroken and indivisible continuum (that is, dark skin coloration grades into lighter coloration), most practitioners of race feel emotionally confident in implicitly assuming that one can know where to draw the arbitrary lines that separate racial groups. But where, for example, does light skin color stop and dark skin color start? This question can only be answered in a highly arbitrary fashion dictated more by accepted preconceptions than by any understanding of actual human biology. Racialism nevertheless promotes the idea that skin coloration provides a useful standard for creating discrete categories, typically interpreted as white, yellow, red, and black.

What has been more than adequately demonstrated is that these observable characteristics result from long-term adaptations – evident in a genotype, the internally coded, inheritable information of humanity – to particular sets of environmental circumstances. These result in phenotypic expression in an individual organism. In other words, what we see as differences in "race" are actually expressions of humanity's inherited characteristics from living in the world's multitudes of environments. As with the environments, each one of our physical traits exists along a cline, that is, gradual transitions across humankind from one observable characteristic to another. The clinal distribution of specific traits typically cuts across presumed human groupings in various ways rather than falling along clearly definable boundaries. The concept of biological "races" sharply delineates groups that are in reality highly nebulous with indistinct boundaries. This reality seriously undermines and discredits the whole enterprise of race. The creation of races is therefore a human cultural activity that bears little or no relationship with actual human biological diversity.

Creating categories or classifying things is something humans do well, a cognitive universal. We need this strategy to navigate our worlds. Classification rests at the core of science and most other ways of knowing. As such, creating categories is "natural." There is nothing at all wrong in doing so. In terms of race, the rub comes in actually enacting the notion that the stereotypical categories of race are "natural" and "true."

But biologically distinct racial groups are entirely cultural and arbitrary, so racialism is essentially a faith-based belief. Its primary tenet is that race depicts a valid representation of human diversity. Thus, if one believes in and accepts race and racial groupings, one is a *racialist*. When a journal like *American Indian Quarterly* employs the term "American Indian" as a matter of institutional self-definition, it deliberately practices and perpetuates racialism. When universities create "Indian studies" programs, they have consciously chosen to engage in racialism. When American archaeologists claim to study such artifacts of racial culture as "Native American prehistory" or "African American history," they act as purveyors of racialism. The vast majority of Americans are racialists. Being so is almost impossible to avoid.

Racism exists as a natural and common extension of racialism. When a person or group converts their racial categories from belief to action by preferentially ranking the groups, one is a *racist*. Thus, when museums deliberately segregate and exclude items by racial categories on a preferential basis, they reflect the systematic ranking of racism. When an academic journal employs race-based selection criteria to publish materials pertaining to a preferentially ranked racial group, it practices racism. When an archaeologist speaks of a racial group as excelling at communal psycho-social characteristics, such as indulging a special preference for bloodletting, such analysis is racist.

Because the current state of American racial ideology embraces the practice of racialism but sees racism as profoundly negative, our assessment here may sound much harsher than we intend. It is our intention to propound definitions that are useful in a critical sense and can be usefully applied to specific situations. As a matter of practice, Americans distinguish between non-desirable racism and desirable racism and attach value judgments accordingly.

It is therefore useful and important to distinguish between *unilateral racism* and *conjoint racism* as observable practices in American society. In the former, an individual or group has unilaterally enacted a form of preferential racial ranking, typically as a means of gathering and wielding social power to oppress and discriminate against other groups. In the latter, various groups have jointly agreed to enact forms of preferential racial ranking as the basis for wielding some form of social power on behalf of a selected group, as in developing a museum exhibit on "Indian art."

We can certainly assign value judgments as to the relative ethics involved in all such racist activities, but no form of racism is ever entirely benign. Racism, whether unilaterally imposed or conjointly sanctioned, inherently enacts and perpetuates the false and dehumanizing notions of racialism. It does so as a deliberate exercise of social power that is designed to exclusively benefit one racial group or as a means to discriminate against a selected racial group.

This raises an interesting question. Is it possible to employ racialism in a manner that serves a useful social purpose and does not do violence to human biology? Is it possible, for example, to divorce race from its origins as pseudo-biology and employ it strictly to classify cultural identity or ethnicity? We are skeptical that this is a workable option because it involves a circular logic that invariably returns to the assumption that racial categories somehow reflect human biology. This should be readily apparent. What, exactly, is African American culture or American Indian culture? Such constructions inherently assume something unwarranted about human biology.

The problem of race is a typical matter for scholars to wrestle with. It is common to rely upon race as a useful description even while recognizing its shortcomings. One might, for example, speak of how a Navajo or a Makah individual might prefer tribal identification over racial identification, but then when speaking of Navajos and Makahs as a group they become "Indians." In the pages of *American Indian Quarterly* and other such journals, scholars have continually emphasized that there is no such thing as a generalized "American Indian culture," but the convenience of race and its common usage makes racialism difficult to avoid in practice. The question remains, nevertheless, what are we practicing when we choose to employ the apparatus of race? Does race help clarify the doings of humankind, or does it obscure those doings? Can race ever be used without dehumanizing people?

Is it possible to define "Indians" according to citizenship in Indian tribes or First Nations? Again, it's difficult to achieve a workable definition without relying on unwarranted assumptions about race-as-biology.

As we noted, this is all a quagmire. Pulling free of it will not be a simple matter. Moreover, as the "anti-race" position becomes a discernible social movement in America – as we predict it will – it may readily fall into usage by some proponents as a way to undermine the quest for social justice by oppressed groups. Our intent here is not to promote that outcome, of course, but rather to encourage useful discussion about both the importance and the difficulties of negotiating the tangle, especially for archaeology.

The Epic Battlegrounds of Race

Archaeology's roots are colonial, with the world's first systematic archaeological excavations often attributed to Thomas Jefferson when he explored burial mounds on his estate.[7] Even before Jefferson's day, a dominant question in Europe and colonized America was the origin of the human populations of the New World. For a range of reasons, but especially because there was only a limited scientific tradition upon which scholars could draw, most people resorted to theological explanations. Too, by the time the colonizers got around to exploring the heartland of the continent, many resident populations had fallen victim to diseases that ravaged their cultures.

When the exploring colonizers encountered large, sophisticated earthworks such as burial mounds, temple mounds, and enclosures, they had no idea what to make of them. The fact that the cultures they encountered had undergone a variety of changes permitted the indulgence of colonial hubris. European colonists and their American heirs assumed that the now-racialized "Indian" residents of mid-America could not have made such monumental structures.

By the late 1700s, the imaginative colonizers had invented a disappeared race – the Moundbuilders – as the group that had built the earthworks and had devised the theory that this advanced race had later been destroyed by the bloodthirsty race of Indians. The Moundbuilders obviously were more sophisticated technologically and morally superior to the Indians the colonizers encountered.

The ancestry of the Moundbuilders was speculated to be everyone from the Lost Tribes of Israel to wandering Phoenicians, but almost always people with an Old World heritage, and almost always racially white. The implications of

this belief were many, but most important was that this epic tale of ancient America provided the colonizers with a sense of historical perspective on the land and implied a European priority in America. Thus, it became a rationale for taking Indian lands, a crucial component of Manifest Destiny.

In the early 1800s, the measurement of heads was all the rage. Phrenology, as it was called, believed that the skull derived its contours from the brain and its shape. By measuring its size, shape, and minor variations, the surface of the skull could be read as an index of various psychological tendencies.

By the mid-1800s phrenology was thoroughly discredited as science but lived on in the work of anthropologists bent on assessing race and other characteristics, such as intelligence, from skulls. A Philadelphia doctor, Samuel G. Morton (1799–1851), amassed a collection of three hundred Indian skulls, which along with those from other areas of the world became the basis for a comparative study of humankind. He assumed that cranial capacity was related to intelligence – capacity that he measured by filling skulls with shot and mustard seeds. His measurements, in step with incipient notions of unilinear evolution, seemed to confirm that there were inborn racial differences. African and Australian Aboriginals were of smallest cranial capacity and intelligence; American Indians were fourth; Southeast Asians and Polynesians, third; Chinese, second; and Europeans, first, with English at the top of the Europeans.

By 1900 the young scholarly discipline of scientific archaeology had discounted the Moundbuilder myth, recognizing that the ancestors of the Indians had indeed built the earthworks. Scholars also saw the limitations and flaws of works like Morton's. Both archaeology and ethnography gained rapid scientific sophistication, gathering more data about human history and culture, and by 1926 understood the deep antiquity of the human presence in the Americas. This long presence on the land had given people time to move around, time to adapt to a wide range of environments, and time to develop levels of substantial cultural diversity across the continents. By the late 1940s, the basic ideas anthropologists use to explain human cultural diversity in America were in place. These were concepts of multilinear evolution based on a cultural ecology – that groups adapt to natural and cultural environments in which they live – and the construct of "culture areas," which is the classification of cultures into a series of particular adaptations to particular environmental zones (Plains, Northwest Coast, Southwest, and the like).

Archaeologically, explanations for the origins of human populations in the New World became more sophisticated, and by the 1960s, the dominant hypotheses for human habitation of the Americas focused on the Bering Land Bridge. Beringia was a nearly 1,500-mile-wide connection between Siberia and North America, exposed as sea levels dropped during glacial advances. What it meant was that ancient Americans had an Asian origin, which seemed to fit various physical traits that appeared in populations on both continents, as evidenced by both living people and skeletal remains. The earliest American settlers were hunters of megafauna such as mammoth and were assumed to be part of a so-called Clovis culture arriving around twelve thousand years ago.

Physical anthropologists were part of these studies. At the start of the 1900s, in an effort to confront ideas about race by showing that physical form was malleable, Franz Boas suggested that exposure to the American environment was reflected in the measurements he took of the heads of nearly thirteen thousand European immigrants and their children. The dominant scholar in physical anthropology until the early 1940s was the Smithsonian's Aleš Hrdlicka. He was a conservative force when it came to the study of early habitation of the Americas, demanding high-quality evidence. Though he helped pioneer the use of body measurements, he was suspicious of advanced statistics, but after his death others were free to move the science along.

Physical anthropologists never lost interest in skulls, and by the late 1960s had developed a wide range of techniques, at least partly stemming from forensic anthropology, known as craniometrics. Though an over-simplification, the approach assumes that skull shape is at least partly genetically influenced and that approximately ninety measurements of the skull can be used to compare one skull to another. Skulls whose measurements statistically cluster are seen as stemming from the same general place

of origin, that is, race. Some specialists claim that the technique is 80 percent accurate. Within specific communities, some scholars claim to be able to assess what are essentially tribal connections, that is, that a skull found in an archaeological context can be placed with some degree of assurance within a broad tribal grouping. The technique and its racialist underpinnings have not gone without criticism.[8] For American archaeology the views about the early habitation of the Americas and craniometric assessment of race have coalesced in the Ancient One/ Kennewick remains.

By the late 1960s, a wide range of finds with early radiocarbon or stratigraphic dates began to call into question a Clovis age for the entrada of humans into the Americas. A few waves of migration across the land bridge could not account for all the evidence, and archaeologists began to suggest that the land bridge explanations were too simple. Some hypothesized that in addition to the land bridge crossings, people used boats to move around the glacial ice along Pacific coastlines. Claims of trans-Pacific migration became more frequent. Many of the claims were based on discoveries of skeletal remains whose skulls seemed craniometrically to share few characteristics with skulls of the ancestors of American Indians. By the time of the discovery of the Ancient One/Kennewick remains, there were more than ten of these early finds.[9] With the Kennewick discovery some archaeologists and physical anthropologists began to say that people were present in the Americas before the ancestors of Native Americans. When James Chatters, the first anthropologist to examine the Ancient One/Kennewick remains, suggested that the measurements and "look" of the skull were Caucasoid, the racialism of American archaeology became apparent.

The media further complicated matters by employing the terms "Caucasian" and "Caucasoid" interchangeably for the remains.[10] But when several physical anthropologists and archaeologists took legal action to stop repatriation of the remains under the Native American Graves Protection and Repatriation Act (NAGPRA), the politics of the situation turned to race as a cultural battleground – a battleground in which people were encouraged to view ancient populations in racial terms.

In a notable incident, Chatters and one of the scientists, physical anthropologist Douglas Owsley, were filmed as part of a CBS 60 *Minutes* segment with Leslie Stahl as host. Stahl pushed both scholars to say that the find challenged the priority of Native Americans on the continent, which she then noted would call into question treaties and even rights to run "lucrative casinos."

The willingness of the Kennewick scientists and their supporters to acquiesce in the racialization of Kennewick Man has had the effect of exploiting American racialism. The intention is explicitly designed to get governments – both federal and tribal – out of the way of science and archaeology, but it materially advances an anti-scientific acceptance of race. This is particularly interesting given the fact that one of the scientist-plaintiffs (C. Loring Brace) played a major role during the 1960s and later in raising challenges to race.

Whatever the strategy of the Kennewick scientist-plaintiffs and their supporters, they won massive national support in media editorial pages. Editorialists were quite taken with the idea that Kennewick Man might be white and might tell a story in which ancient racial whites were overcome by ancient racial Indians. Essentially Kennewick and similar remains had become revived Moundbuilders.

Losing control of the Ancient One in court, Indians and their supporters attempted in 2004 to introduce a slight modification to NAGPRA. This move was designed to see the Ancient One legally defined as "Native American," subject to treatment as culturally unidentifiable Native American human remains.[11] Intent on showing support for relationships between archaeologists and Indians, professional archaeology organizations like the Society for American Archaeology and the World Archaeological Congress announced their endorsement of this change in the law.

The Ancient One had lived and died without race. He entered the future as a prize to be won upon the racial battlegrounds of America. We ponder with interest how Indians, scientists, the media, professional archaeological organizations, and many other Americans have sought to move mountains to see that he gets race in some form.

It's interesting to consider what this signifies for science and scientific scholarship because all these developments have occurred in a time when race has been scientifically discredited. This observation, to be sure, seems oddly detached from our world, as if it applied to some other world than Planet Earth.

Race Is Dead; Long Live Race?

When Vine Deloria Jr. published his diatribe against archaeology, *Red Earth, White Lies*, the Ancient One/Kennewick remains had not yet been discovered.[12] Still, the volume challenges the approaches archaeology has taken toward the ancient origins of American populations. Deloria advocates the primacy of "red" oral traditions in explaining the ancient past, with "white" science relegated to an incidental support role. As a matter of social justice, this strategy is important because it takes aim at the long neglect of oral traditions in American scholarship and in archaeology. But in accordance with our definitions of racialism and racism, Deloria's model of historical inquiry is not simply racialist in design; it is inherently racist.

Deloria's role in shaping a national pan-Indian social agenda during the second half of the twentieth century assures him a prominent place at the pinnacle of the history of racial Indianhood during this era. His vastly influential writings and advocacy are clearly designed to counter white racism by advancing the social empowerment of Indians as a racial group. Toward this end, Deloria's attack on "white" archaeology is particularly interesting because it is designed to reverse the primacy of "white" scientific discourse over "Indian" epistemologies. There is an interesting kind of social justice in this strategy of using racism to defeat racism. We note that this has become a widespread strategy throughout Indian studies and in Indian social commentary.

In *Anti-Indianism in Modern America: A Voice from Tatekeya's Earth*, Elizabeth Cook-Lynn accuses archaeology of being anti-Indian in its interpretations.[13] This book – as with the Deloria book – features out-of-date sources and factual errors, but both books make important points about the poor way in which archaeologists sometimes present archaeology. In archaeology as a profession, practitioners have come to expect the charge from racialized Indians that racialized archaeology is fundamentally anti-Indian. This charge has an historical basis as a matter of identifiable archaeological practices – such as the history of minimal engagement with oral traditions and failing to work with descendant communities on important issues – but we reject the position that archaeological inquiry as a method of historical investigation is inherently anti-Indian. It is not.[14]

The "anti-Indian" critique, for all of its problems, has nevertheless played a meaningful role in encouraging self-assessment and recalibration of practice in archaeology. In response to the charge, the profession has embraced an "equal opportunity" model of opening up archaeology to Indian participation and aiming at partnerships with a politically empowered Native America. Toward this end, it is important for archaeology in the short term to counter its segregationist history of unilateral racism by deploying integrative forms of conjoint racism (such as by promoting "Native American" scholarship award programs), but what about the long term picture? Race is inherently dehumanizing, so we have an obligation to ultimately disempower its presence in our shared world.

Intellectuals like Deloria and Cook-Lynn do not simply accept the status quo of race. One major outcome of their analytical strategies is that the idea of race is uncritically perpetuated and kept alive in our world. Whether their intent is explicit or implicit, they are not alone in fostering this result. The effort to keep race intact lies at the heart of much of the American academic enterprise at present.

As a problem in scholarship, if race distorts the basic character of human biology, doesn't it also distort our models of human history? Writing about "the history of Indians" seems qualitatively very different from preparing scholarship on the "history of adherents to racial Indianhood."

This difference can be illustrated by comparison to the status of women in American history. Although the cultural status of women in American society at one time flowed from the idea that women were biologically and intellectually inferior to men, scholars do not write about American history as though it is populated by dumb women in the past. It would be inaccurate and dehumanizing to write "dumb women" histories rather than to aim at shedding light on historical American cultural ideology that is based on false biological models of gendered intelligence.

Following this insight, shouldn't we reconsider the status quo approach of writing about "Indians," whites," "blacks," and other racial groups? Shouldn't we instead start treating our racial history as an observable set of processes and circumstances in which people embraced the dehumanizing cultural ideas of race? As we see in the Moundbuilder mythology and in the Kennewick situation, belief in race leads to explanations of the human past that apply race and its terminological mechanisms uncritically to historical models – even extending into time periods preceding the invention of race as an idea. The Moundbuilder and Kennewick situations serve as obvious examples for how race distorts our views of the ancient past, but scholarship has yet to recognize how deeply the paradigm of race has colored our intellectual discourse.

The deracialization of academic study means that we must deracialize the concepts of "colonized" versus "Indigenous." In practice, these constructions have more to do with race than with any intention to accurately calibrate political and economic relationships among geopolitical entities. It is common, for example, to conflate the idea of European nations with "white people" and to distinguish nations "of color" as Indigenous peoples, again largely race-based.

There is considerable risk that readers will assume that the challenge of decolonizing archaeology is merely to insert "Indians" and "Indian-controlled" archaeology into the standard operating procedure of "white" archaeology. But decolonizing archaeology begs additional questions about decolonizing academia.

If we remove the distorting lens of race from analysis of colonialism and Indigenism, then it seems appropriate to rely wholly upon consideration of historical process rather than racial definition as a basis for making assignments of "colonial" identity and "Indigenous" identity. In this regard, what does it mean when a historian like Richard White characterizes the Sioux as a nineteenth-century colonizing empire in the Plains? What does this mean for their "Indigenous" status? What does it mean for sovereigns like the Pawnee Nation to participate in the conquest and occupation of the Sioux empire, Japan, Germany, Iraq, and other places in the world as allies of the U.S. military? How does this reconcile with their "Indigenous" status? The point is that an entire constellation of concepts needs to be challenged, not just those linked to archaeology.

Discussions of race and science are pointless if we decline to apply the outcome to our social world and our academic discourse. To be sure, applying the ideas in this essay to the intellectual legacy of the two coauthors, it is clear that we too have devoted considerable energy in our professional and personal lives to the perpetuation of race in the American world. Our analysis here is nothing if not introspective.

The task that seems meaningful to us is to give thought as to how one might best disengage from race and how best to contribute to the slowing of the headlong rush into race that forms the present and historical basis of the American journey. It is difficult to get people focused on the cultural implications of the science of race, but a new communal discourse on this topic is gradually evolving anyway, whether or not individuals and institutions choose to participate.

The forces that favor the perpetuation of race in American society show few signs of awareness of this coming dialogue about race. For the moment, it is accurate to observe that even though race has died as a matter of scientific consensus, it remains very much alive in the world.

In our view, archaeologists need to find more effective ways to present the nature of archaeology to the general public; this does not mean abandoning science for the purpose of appealing to the public. Archaeologists need a new discourse about race, and we should not wait to get overtaken by change – we must proactively acknowledge the problems of racialism and ponder together what these problems mean for the profession.

We need good ideas about how to escape the terminological clutches of race and the accompanying entrainment of ways of thinking about the presence of human diversity in the archaeological record. We must attend to racial social justice without surrendering our commitment to pursuing scholarship on racialism. We must be thoughtful about new efforts that may arise to racialize the community.

Bringing new voices into the discipline and creating new dialogue has resulted in the rise of the idea of "Indigenous archaeology." In our view, this presents an obvious and exciting opportunity to find ways to change and strengthen the profession. What will we make of it? The term "Indigenous" draws upon racialism for meaning, but can it find another sustaining source of meaning? Are alternate nonracial descriptive terms preferable?[15]

Addressing these issues will help to bring us into the next major paradigm for scholarship on humankind and scholarship on the archaeological evidence of our past doings. But make no mistake: it will be difficult to deal with entrenched powers that will not willingly relinquish race. Race reigns supreme in American society. Science brought race into being, and we must now deal with the consequence of this creation.

In the end, will our successors and intellectual heirs thank us or damn us for what we give them?

Notes

1 In this article, we purposely minimize usage of academic footnotes because it is our intention to promote a public dialogue rather than an academic discourse on race. We believe that this public dialogue must necessarily accommodate personal responses to the academic consensus on race – responses grounded in personal opinion and subjective feelings about racial identities. There are excellent books on race and associated notions, and academic consideration of the problems of racial ideologies is complex and long established. Several recent contributions of academic views aimed at the general public include Joseph L. Graves Jr., *The Race Myth: Why We Pretend Race Exists in America* (New York: Dutton, 2004), and Alexander Alland Jr., *Race in Mind: Race, IQ, and Other Racisms* (New York: Palgrave Macmillan, 2002). Interested readers may also wish to examine the American Anthropological Association's "Statement on 'Race'" from May 17, 1998, at

http://www.aaanet.org/stmts/racepp.htm (viewed December 31, 2005).

2 The Kennewick/Ancient One case has been debated for nearly a decade after 9,200-year-old human skeletal remains were found along the banks of the Columbia River near Kennewick, Washington, in 1996. The skull purportedly has physical characteristics different from those of remains more commonly seen as being American Indian. When the Corps of Engineers tried to repatriate the skeleton to the Umatilla, a group of osteological and archaeological scientists took legal action to stop the repatriation and to demand the right to study the remains. The case has seen several levels of judicial review. For the historical and legal facts of the case, the *Tri-City Herald's* Kennewick Man Virtual Interpretive Center presents a generally straightforward collection of information at http://www.kennewick-man.com (viewed January 21, 2005).

3 The Closet Chicken mysteries are shrouded in secrecy. Their formal origin story is known only to initiates, but it can be revealed that the group was founded in the wake of a May 2001 conference (titled "On the Threshold: Native American–Archaeologist Relations in the Twenty-First Century") organized by Deborah Nichols and Joe Watkins at Dartmouth College. Membership is granted only by consensual invitation of the group, and members participate in a listserv discussion group, hold an annual gathering every spring, bestow secret names upon one another, and devote themselves to esoteric studies in archaeology.

4 Paul Rincon, "Tribe Challenges American Origins," BBC News World Edition, http://news.bbc.co.uk/2/hi/science/nature/3634544.stm (viewed December 13, 2004).

5 We have taken most of the comments in the order that they appeared in the discussion. We have made minor editorial changes, deleting short segments but mostly making minor changes in grammar, spelling, and keyboarding errors. Readers are urged to understand that these comments were intended for online, chat room consumption, not to serve as finished academic work.

6 We find it disturbing that many people are not aware of this concept. We will not discuss this viewpoint in any detail in this paper, but for readers who desire more information, a huge body of literature exists on this subject, both technical and popular. A recent PBS series, *Race: The Power of an Illusion*, provides an excellent discussion of issues and provides a wide range of source materials on the accompanying website at http://www.pbs.org/race (viewed January 21, 2005).

7 For a good history of the pre-1990s in American archaeology, see Gordon Willey and Jeremy Sabloff, *A History of American Archaeology* (San Francisco: W. H. Freeman, 1993).

8 See Alan Goodman, "Racializing Kennewick Man," *Anthropology Newsletter* 38, no. 10 (1997): 3, for one example.

9 Whatever the flaws in his presentation of the Kennewick find and its politics, James Chatters's 2001 book *Ancient Encounters: Kennewick Man and the First Americans* (New York: Simon & Schuster) contains an excellent summary of current hypotheses about early human habitation of the Americas. Chatters's book is of additional interest in that it touches upon the problematic nature of race while at the same time relying heavily upon the ideas and terminology of racialism.

10 These terms are very confusing to most people. "Caucasoid," along with "Mongoloid," "Negroid," and "Australoid," are terms of racial classification for widely distributed groups, devised by European anthropologists of the seventeenth and eighteenth centuries, intended to distinguish observable characteristics such as skin color, hair type, body shape, and skull measurements. The terms have fallen into disfavor and may be considered by some to be offensive. "Caucasian" is generally understood as "white" or "European" and is more commonly used but should not be understood as a synonym for "Caucasoid." They mean very different things.

11 This proposed modification of NAGPRA originated as a suggestion in Paul Bender's July 14, 2004, testimony (see p. 12) before the Senate Committee on Indian Affairs. The testimony can be found at http://indian.senate.gov/2004hrgs/071404hrg/bender.pdf (viewed January 2, 2005). Bender's proposed modification added two words to the NAGPRA statutory definition of "Native American" – a definition grounded in race.

12 Vine Deloria Jr., *Red Earth, White Lies* (New York: Macmillan, 1995).

13 Elizabeth Cook-Lynn, *Anti-Indianism in Modern America: A Voice from Tatekeya's Earth* (Urbana: University of Illinois Press, 2001). Factual errors compromise the usefulness of this book. For example, she names Larry Zimmerman as Neal Zimmerman and presents a talk he gave on the Crow Creek Massacre in ways that didn't happen.

14 This "anti-Indian" accusation is most usefully asserted as a political position rather than as a useful critique because it lends itself very effectively to the politics of polarity. In this form of political discourse, a false enemy is demonized

not as a means of encouraging useful debate but rather as an announcement of political allegiance and as a means of attracting a core group of emotionally charged supporters. It is worth nothing that the demonization of "white" archaeology can serve political objectives only so long as one is willing to interpret history in racial terms and to perpetuate racialist social paradigms.

15   "Indigenous archaeology" could be reframed, for example, as "stakeholder archaeology" or as "integrative archaeology" or in some other way. We recognize that there are always problems with labels attached to categories. The term "stakeholder," for example, has been criticized by some who do not like the association with notions of property and capitalism.

16

A Class All Its Own
Explorations of Class Formation and Conflict

LouAnn Wurst

Introduction

Class is a curious concept. As an omnipresent aspect of the capitalist world, class has commonly been used as a way to classify and label groups of people, both in the present and in the past. And yet, while the word surrounds us in our everyday life, it is a concept that is supposed to have little salience to our world. Many pundits claim "class is dead"; while it was once one of the most important organizing concepts in sociology, class is thought to have little significance for understanding our postmodern world (Pakulski and Waters 1996). Other scholars argue that class has always been ignored in American society and scholarship and that class and class relations are rarely discussed openly (Aronowitz 1996; McNall et al. 1991). Similarly, Durrenberger (2001) argues that class is the only truly serious ethnographic problem and that we are all implicated in obscurantism by not addressing it. Ortner (1991:165) describes how class suffers from conceptual marginality in anthropology. For most, class is always with us but irrelevant.

We might expect historical archaeologists, who frame their discourse around the study of

LouAnn Wurst, "A Class All Its Own: Explorations of Class Formation and Conflict," pp. 190–206 from Martin Hall and Stephen Silliman (eds) *Historical Archaeology* (Oxford: Blackwell Publishers, 2006). Reprinted with permission.

capitalism (cf. Leone and Potter 1999), to have spent a lot more time talking about class. Indeed, the word "class" is commonly encountered in historical archaeological studies. However, while the term class is often mentioned, the concept of class has received very little attention in historical archaeology (Duke and Saitta 1998; Paynter 2000a; Wurst and Fitts 1999). This theoretical blindspot has been filled with other terms such as capitalism and modernity which are, perhaps, more benign. What minimal discussion exists tends to be contradictory and more than a little confusing. At one end of the spectrum, Duke and Saitta state that "one could argue that, to the extent that class is an axis of variability that crosscuts lines of gender, race, and ethnicity, it is arguably more important than these categories" (Duke and Saitta 1998:3). At the other extreme, Yentsch and Beaudry claim that class had no relevance for the early colonial period or to the cultures created through the colonial process, and they suggest that class "both conveys and exhibits the arrogance of the dominant class" (Yentsch and Beaudry 2001:223).

Statements by both the general populace and historical archaeologists seem to run a wide gamut: from class being the single most important aspect of social life to class being unimportant; from class as a structural location to class as a process; from an attribute of individuals to an analytical method; from a stale and outdated concept to a fresh approach that has seldom been operationalized; from a static evolutionary moment to a fluidly historical abstraction. So which is it? My glib answer is "yes"! I believe that our expectation that class can only be or do one thing has been damaging to the development of historical archaeology and our goal of understanding the modern world. Any simple example of a context where class is not the most important organizing principle has seemed sufficient for some to conclude that class is a poor concept upon which to build a rigorous archaeology. Any number of references that point to the importance of gender or race also seem to do the trick. We are assuaged from the conceptually difficult task of making sense of all of the conflicting statements and claims about class. Or are we? It would, perhaps, be wiser to assume that if class did not matter, there would be no need for such a copious literature (a theoretical form of "me thinks they doth protest too much").

A great deal of the confusion about class stems from the fact that the same term has been used in several very different ways. Wright (1994, 1997) divides these conceptions into gradational and relational views of class. Wood (1995:76) claims that there are only two ways to think about class: as a structural location and as a social relation. Williams (1983:60–69) presents a "classification" of class meanings that includes an objective group as in taxonomy, rank, or relative social position, and class as a formation or relationship. We can then define two major approaches to class: class as an objective entity, thing, or structural location based on a graduated scale, and class as a relation or formation. In what follows, I will contrast these two views to try to untangle the ways that historical archaeologists have used class.

Class as a Thing: Various Approaches

Class as an entity or thing on a graduated scale is the most familiar use of the term in capitalist society. From this perspective, class is defined as fixed rungs on a ladder of inequality, as in strata within an income distribution, occupation structure, or status variations (Wright 1994:89). These distinctions hinge on relative amounts in the quantity of defining resources, such as income, education, or occupational prestige that individuals possess (Fantasia 1988:13). In a gradational view, class is seen as a descriptive attribute of individuals (Zavarzadeh 1995:53), and classes represent the aggregate of individuals who share a particular descriptive quality. In this sense, classes are seen as fixed and immutable even though individuals can change their class standing by virtue of a change in occupation or increase or decrease in income.

One of the clearest symptoms of a gradational view is using class as an adjective to describe the location of an individual or group within a larger structural context. We commonly refer to "lower class," "middle class," "working class," or "elite." While not all of these terms are equivalent, historical archaeologists often use them as taxonomic units that define inclusion into a discrete group. For example, Wall (1999) distinguishes the working and middle classes of urban America based on whether individuals perform manual or non-manual labor. Hardesty (1994:131) described the class structure of western North American mining towns as comprised of the poor, unskilled, semi-skilled, and skilled workers, a middle class of professionals and managers, and an elite class of capitalists and managers. Three classes – upper, middle, and lower – are most commonly used, although some have defined as many as six (e.g., LeeDecker et al. 1987). All of these class titles are relative and are based on a view of class as ranked social position.

In historical archaeology these objective groups, based on either income or occupation, are most commonly linked to material culture through the study of socio-economic status, and historical archaeologists often use the terms class and status interchangeably (Baugher and Venables 1987; Shepard 1987). Archaeologists most often determine this relative social position by documentary evidence of wealth or occupation. Typically, historical archaeologists have then "tested" this document-derived status with material culture by calculating the amount of money expended on the items recovered from archaeological contexts. The vast majority of these consumer choice studies focus on ceramics (LeeDecker et al. 1987; Shephard 1987; Spencer-Wood and Heberling 1987), although some scholars have used faunal remains (Reitz 1987; Schultz and Gust 1983).

The focus on ceramics stems from their abundance and preservation on archaeological sites and from the pioneering work of George Miller (1991). Miller's index value for decorated white earthenwares compared to an undecorated common creamware (CC) baseline provides a standardized measure to compare the relative cost of ceramics from virtually any 19th-century context. Miller's research initiated a frenzy of studies attempting to relate the value of ceramic assemblages with status. At first, many archeologists treated this as an objective measure of socio-economic status; however, it soon became apparent that the correlation between ceramics and status was far from simple (Klein 1991:77). Studies showed that household size and structure (LeeDecker et al. 1987), as well as ceramic availability (Brighton 2001), affected the types of ceramics purchased. Noting that ceramics comprised a small percentage of a household's expenses when compared to the cost of housing, food, and other forms of material culture, some scholars even suggested that the focus on ceramics as indicators of wealth was misguided (Friedlander 1991:27; LeeDecker 1991). Other studies have documented that impoverished individuals used expensive ceramics, but in contexts that indicate that they were out of date and thus less desirable (Garman and Russo 1999; O'Donovan and Wurst 2001–02). These critiques represent significant improvements over earlier consumer choice studies based on a simple correlation between cost and status; however, few question the underlying assumption that equates economic wealth with social class and that uses material culture simply as the passive indicator of wealth. The socio-economic status approach in historical archaeology is a gradational view that sees class as a static, unchanging classification of reified persons and social roles.

The heyday of consumer choice and status studies has certainly ended in historical archaeology. I suspect that consumer choice and status models remain much more common in Cultural Resource Management (CRM) research, since they provide easily testable assumptions with ready-made interpretations. Other periodic forays can still be found. Monks (1999) proposes a "bottom up" perspective that builds from archaeological analysis toward the social concepts that can be accessed from it. Monks' approach is indeed different, but rather than challenge the idea that class is an entity, his critique simply states that we have not found the appropriate middle-range linking strategies. A more contemporary incarnation of class as a thing, the hallmark of a gradational view, can be detected in the way that many historical archaeologists have embraced the postmodern themes of individualism and agency. Since much recent work places the autonomous individual at the center of analytical focus, social formations such as class become blurred or invisible (Thomas 2002). With the active individual in the forefront of their efforts, postmodern-inspired archaeologists have produced a literature littered with statements about why the individual is the only actor capable of creating cultural change (Hodder 2000; Meskell 1999; Sweely 1999). These individual agents give meaning to the world around them and, in the end, the postmodern scholar tends to reduce their interpretations to the meanings given by individual agents.

Most postmodernist interpretations attempt to understand the interplay between individual subjectivities and structure, and yet, the dynamics of this articulation have not been fully realized (Dobres and Robb 2000:7). Since postmodernists begin with the individual, the social becomes an analytical problem – how do you get structure from the aggregate of discrete individuals? The solution has been to present structure as the sum total of experiences and practices. The sense of structure conveyed is fragmentary with little attention paid to the reality of the network of relations that joined individuals, social groups, and institutions, with little if any attention to class.

In historical archaeology, earlier consumer choice models have morphed into an emphasis on agency and the individual, and the terms "individual," "identity," and "agency" have become common. Mary Beaudry, Stephen Mrozowski, and Lauren Cook present one of the clearest statements of this new direction (Beaudry et al. 1991). In their study of the Boott Mills complex in Lowell, Massachusetts, they examine the artifacts found associated with factory workers and managers and interpret them as symbols that these groups used to give meaning to their lives. From this approach, class is an unchallenged category which people express through freely chosen material symbols (see Orser 1996 for an extended discussion of their case study, and Lodziak 2002 for a general critique).

A more recent statement by Wilkie and Bartoy (2000:748) provides some idea of the fruition of the individual agency trend in historical archaeology. They take aim at the so-called "Annapolis School" and argue that these archaeologists have failed to problematize basic concepts, including class. Wilkie and Bartoy emphasize that class relates to individual decision-making and choice. This focus can be clearly seen in their case study of the Freeman family of Oakley Plantation. Silvia Freeman worked as a cook on the plantation, and two of her daughters continued to live in the house after her death and worked as cook and domestic servant. According to Wilkie and Bartoy "their occupations clearly placed them in a social class distinct from that of the farming families" (Wilkie and Bartoy 2000:759). The descriptive adjectives that they use, "accept," "participation," "motive," and "choices," convey the sense that class is an attribute of individual identity – a choice that can be changed as simply as employment.

Many historical archaeologists clearly recognize that "identity" implies relationships. However, much of the actual analyses focus on individual actors that appear to have unconstrained freedom, a trend that is particularly evident in Wilkie and Bartoy (2000). In this approach, class has become an emblem of individual identity, like ethnicity, race, or gender, that individuals pick and choose from to create the identities they find most meaningful. Class has continued to be an attribute – a label designating where an individual stands in relative social standing.

This version of class also becomes tangled with what Eagleton (1996) calls the great triplet of gender, class, and race. Most historical archaeologists recognize the complex intersections between class, race, gender, and ethnicity (Delle et al. 2000; Orser 1996; Orser and Fagan 1995; Scott 1994), yet continue to identify all of these aspects as objective traits or attributes that characterize individual identity. Since these traits relate to individuals, these models assume that there is little room for the concept of class. If, as many archaeologists have assumed, seeing class

as an entity or thing were the only way of looking at class, I would have to reject it as well.

Many of the recent attacks on class can be understood as attacks on this perspective. For example, class as structural location is rejected theoretically since it cannot account for agency (either individual or social). It would also be impossible to coherently argue that ethnicity, race, or gender were unimportant to social life. Given the postmodern context, it is ironic that historical archaeologists have argued for a proliferation of identities, genders, races, and ethnicities, yet typically constrain class to a rigid triad of Upper, Middle, and Lower, or an exclusive duality of workers and capitalists. To quote Eagleton:

> we seem stuck with far too few social classes, whereas if the postmodern imperative to multiply differences were to be taken literally we should strive to breed as many more of them as we could, say two or three new bourgeoisies and a fresh clutch of landowning aristocracies. (Eagleton 1996:127)

Class as a Formation: The Rhetoric of Social Relations

In contrast to essentialized views that see class as a thing, relational views use class to designate the nature of the underlying social relations (Wright 1994:89). A relational view of class stems largely from the work of Karl Marx. Many have complained that Marx himself did not use the term class in a consistent way and never even provided an adequate definition. Pareto argued that Marx's words were like bats: appearing as both birds and mice (Ollman 1976:3). Many have railed against Marx's laxness – if class is indeed the most important concept to a viable critique of capitalism, how is it that the concept was never adequately defined? No wonder generations of scholars have thrown up their hands in frustration and futility!

To make sense of this, we need to understand that Marx used a dialectical method to study social relations. Marxism is often seen as a theory of internal relations, where the web of social relations makes up the whole, and the appearance of these relations is taken to be its parts (Ollman 1993:35). As McGuire (1992) notes, a theory of internal relations is not the only approach that uses the idea of relations. Relations are equally important within "commonsense" approaches that view class as a thing. The difference, however, is that these theories define concrete and objective entities, such as class, race, and gender, that interact in external relations. Using the dialectic implies that the relation actually defines what the entity will be and that the entity does not and cannot exist apart from that relation (Harvey 1996, 2000; McGuire 1992:94; Ollman 1976, 1993; Sayer 1987). One common example of a dialectical relation is husband–wife, neither of which can exist without the other. If the relation between husband–wife severs, as in divorce, both of these entities transform into ex-husband and ex-wife. In this simplified example, the internal relations define the surface appearance of the entity. To move this analogy to the social level, class is the surface appearance of the complex web of social relations of production.

Dialectical research emphasizes social totality and focuses on the whole of real lived experience. It proceeds by examining each part to see where it fits and how it functions within the social totality. The elements are defined through the process of abstraction, the simple recognition that all thinking about reality begins by breaking it down into manageable parts (Ollman 1993:24). According to Sayer (1987:147), this process begins with the use of concepts that are empirically open-ended and analytically capable of letting the real world in. This process eventually leads back to a fuller understanding of the whole with which we began (Ollman 1993:12).

It is in this context that we must evaluate Marx's use of class. Godelier (1986) has suggested that Marx used the term "class" in two different ways, specific and general. The specific use of class is restrictive and designates the relations of domination and exploitation between the social groups, which constitute modern capitalist society (Godelier 1986:245). In this specific usage, class is defined as strictly a capitalist formation. Marx, however, did not limit his use of class to this construction, and his general definition refers to the determinant role of the productive forces and relations of production in human history. Class is thus identified as

an organizing principle in the ancient and medieval worlds, as well as modern bourgeois society (Marx and Engels 1955). With this definition, the relations of production and differential group membership form the dynamic in any social context. Marx and Engels' famous quote, "The history of all hitherto existing society is the history of class struggles" (Marx and Engels 1955:9), refers to class in a general sense and points to the determinant role of the relations and forces of production.

It is also important to realize that Marx used the dialectic in two ways: as a social theory to account for the way the world works and, equally important, as a method of inquiry (Ollman 1993:12, see also Marquardt 1992). This dual usage has implications for a relational view of class, since class can be conceived as both an analytical concept and a concrete reality (McGuire 1992). As an analytical concept, class is used to classify, organize, and make sense of the complex web of social relations that form human society. However, real classes only exist in concrete historical contexts. Since the relations of production among people are not universally given, they can only be defined with reference to a particular historical context (Sayer 1987). As Sayer states, "to define a class – or any other social phenomenon – is, in the final analysis, to write its history" (Sayer 1987:22). To define a class, we must realize that class is not a thing we can find by sifting dirt or identify by a badge or insignia. Many historical archaeologists have tried to create predictive models of class by relating economic wealth or occupation to material patterns. This process "defines class" without examining the social relations present, and thereby reifies those categories. Sayer (1987) refers to this process as the "violence of abstraction." As Thompson writes: "When, in discussing class, one finds oneself too frequently commencing sentences with 'it', it is time to place oneself under some historical control, or one is in danger of becoming the slave of one's own categories" (Thompson 1978:85). From a relational approach, creating a firm and final list of the classes in any society is neither possible nor desirable. Ollman (1993:47) argues that "arriving at a clear-cut, once-and-for-all classification of capitalist society into classes" was not Marx's goal:

Rather than simply a way of registering social stratification as part of a flat description or as a prelude to rendering a moral judgment, which would require a stable unit, class helps Marx to analyze a changing situation in which it is itself an integral and changing part. (Ollman 1993:48)

Thus, class is an abstraction used for analytic purposes and the process of abstraction is the key to operationalizing a relational view of class. Ollman (1993) shows how Marx used abstraction in three different, but closely related, senses: abstraction of extension; abstraction of levels of generality; and abstraction of vantage point (see also O'Donovan 2002; Wurst 1999). One aspect of abstraction refers to delimiting both spatial and temporal boundaries around the subject of our studies. Unlike common temporal periodization schemes, abstractions of extension require abstracting relations or processes rather than simply events. Marquardt (1992) refers to this process as the dialectics of scale and notes that since individuals act on numerous different scales, our analyses must be multi-scalar. The patterns of human interaction identified will vary depending on what scale is examined. To be truly effective, Marquardt argues that multiple scales must be examined since different social relations come into focus at different scales (Marquardt 1992). Different scales affect how we abstract the class that any individual belonged to and, in fact, even the number of classes present in society (Ollman 1993:47). Marx's well-known allusion to capitalism as a two-class society is based on abstracting all groups in society into either workers or capitalists. On other occasions, Marx abstracted more limited extensions, which allowed him to refer to a variety of classes or class factions based on many social and economic differences.

Therefore, in a relational view, class is more than just a label for an objective reality. As an analytical abstraction, class becomes the most important concept to focus on issues of struggle, conflict, and contradictions in productive relations. The key aspect to a dialectical approach is an emphasis on relations and the explication of social totality – all social relations are intertwined into a complex web. Some may object to stating the primacy of class so boldly – indeed,

many have (Yentsch and Beaudry 2001). Yet, it is important to realize that class does not provide the only entry point into the analysis of this social totality; gender and race cannot be divorced from these social relations of production and can also provide an important starting place. Since none of these entities can be separated from their underlying social relations, and the social relations are completely intertwined, arguing over which "surface appearance" is paramount is non-productive.

Paynter and McGuire (1991:1) state that the archaeology of inequality "emphasizes the struggles among members of society over the exercise of social power." This emphasis on power relations and inequality fits nicely with a relational definition of class that focuses on the struggle between social groups over the means of production. Paynter and McGuire, and the associated articles in *The Archaeology of Inequality* (1991), persuasively argue for a relational view of class although most of the discussion is framed around the concepts of power and inequality rather than class. McGuire and Wurst (2002) present a similar discussion focused on the concept of struggle. In their view, the analytical emphasis on social relations of struggle has several components that include the real struggles of the past, scholars' struggles to know about the past, and uses of knowledge about the past to struggle in the present. These three aspects, in the context of archaeology, necessarily have temporal dimensions and components, and are best approached through the study of the production and reproduction of everyday life (Wurst and McGuire 1999). People must produce things to live and reproduce, but they must also reproduce themselves and their social relations that they enter into in order to engage in production. Understanding this for any context means understanding class.

Class as Relations in Historical Archaeology

Relational views of class in historical archaeology prove somewhat difficult to find, particularly since they are just as likely to avoid the term "class," use the term in a way that mimics a gradational approach, or use other terms from a relational perspective such as power, inequality, or struggle. As a result, I find it difficult to classify these studies into a manageable synthesis. Instead, I have decided to illustrate the potential of a relational view of class by organizing this discussion around several different scales that many historical archaeologists approach through their work. In particular, I will discuss studies that focus on what class analysis "looks like" at local, capitalist, and global scales of analysis. My goal here is not to be comprehensive, but to explore several examples that capture the complexity of class relations at each of these scales to help us think about class in a relational way. It is also important to keep in mind that these scales are not mutually exclusive realities; they comprise analytical categories that focus attention on different webs of relations.

Since real classes only exist in concrete historical contexts, much of the historical archaeology of class occurs at a local level. It is no surprise that one of the most common foci of explicit class analysis from a relational perspective has been on industrial labor contexts. Nassaney and Abel's (1993, 2000) study of the John Russell Cutlery factory in Turner's Falls, Massachusetts, deals with the struggles between workers and management over work regulation and hiring practices that resulted from the transformations of industrial production. Waste piles recovered from the factory led the archaeologists to ask whether the workers may have intentionally spoiled knives to resist imposed regulations and regain some autonomy over their production. Their analysis deals with the way that factory elites used space in both the workplace and the workers' homes to reinforce their positions of power and authority over workers' lives. The possibility that the workers resisted this control through their sabotage of the product of labor focuses attention on the relational and contested nature of class. This study, and others focusing on the relational aspects of class in industrial contexts (cf. Mrozowski 2000; Shackel and Larsen 2000), emphasize that labor relations are not separate from household ones, and that capitalists sought to create docile workers by controlling aspects of their workers' everyday lives. In these examples, class is not just our commonsense view of male workers in the industrial workplace.

conflict

Margaret Wood (2002a, 2002b) provides an excellent example of the relational aspects of class, gender, and ethnicity as seen through women's work in the coal town of Berwind, Colorado. Her work is part of the Colorado Coal Field Archaeology Project (McGuire and Reckner 2002; Wood 2002b) that has studied the 1913–14 Coal Field Strike and in particular the Ludlow Massacre. Wood examined material culture recovered from pre- and post-strike contexts in Berwind to examine how the social relations of women's domestic labor changed between 1900 and 1930. In particular, she focuses on women's role in boarding and food production to link women's communal labor to the shared experience of oppression. She argues that this was instrumental to the workers' effective organization during the 1913–14 strike. Wood's example reminds us that the social relations of class are as much about the home and domestic labor as the workplace, and enmesh class with commonsense classifications of gender, ethnicity, and race (see also Kruczek-Aaron 2002).

Instead of focusing on a single industrial context, my research in the small rural community of Upper Lisle, New York, looks at the dynamics of class relations within a single community (Wurst 1999, 2002). Contrary to common assumptions, rural communities included individuals involved in both agricultural and industrial economic spheres that exhibited a complex class structure. In Upper Lisle, this class structure included laborers in agriculture and industry, small commodity producers and farmers, merchants, wealthy farmers, and the Burghardt family who owned the tannery. Analysis showed that the Burghardts actively minimized the material differences between themselves and their workers in house architecture and gravestones, while their ceramics and disposal patterns showed striking differences. These material strategies denied the problematic nature of their class differences while constraining the Burghardts' material behavior.

These cases demonstrate several important aspects of a relational approach to class at a local scale. Class analysis crosscuts many of the dichotomies that structure commonsense ideas based on surface appearance. Class is about work and home, about men and women. In fact, it encompasses all social groups that lived within a particular historic context. These studies show that at the local level, class is lived everyday and thus plays out in all aspects of material existence. Finally, all of these studies, whether about a cutlery factory, a coal-mining town, or a small rural community, clearly link the class relations playing out at the local level with larger capitalist transformations.

One of the most valuable contributions of historical archaeology has been the analysis of class to elucidate the operations of capitalism itself. One research question at this scale has dealt with the "origin" of capitalism itself (Johnson 1996; Leone 1999; Orser 1996; Paynter 1988, 2000a). Other research has focused on the transformations of capitalism over the course of its oppressive history (McGuire 1991). Mark Leone has spent several decades elucidating these transformations. Building on ideas of worldview shift from folk society to Georgian order, Leone (1988) has demonstrated how these transformations expressed the development of capitalism in North America. In his work on Annapolis, Leone argued that an economic crisis in the area led to the adoption of the accouterment of Georgian order. While many have critiqued Leone for overemphasizing the elite and the role of dominant ideology (Hall 1992; Hodder 1986; Wilkie and Bartoy 2000), his work has been instrumental in focusing attention on class at a capitalist level.

Robert Paynter has also contributed to the archaeology of class at the scale of capitalism. Paynter (1988) presents a general framework to understand the material and organizational transformations of capitalism from the 18th through 19th centuries. He made us recognize the fact that capitalism is itself an abstraction of a dynamic formation defined by social relations characterized by temporal processes that vary from short-term business cycles to long-term cycles on the order of 200–300 years (Paynter 1988:415). The idea of capitalist transformation is also captured in Randy McGuire's (1988) research on gravestones from Binghamton, New York. These cemeteries embody the transformations from the early 19th-century ideal community that masked inequality, to the mid to late 19th-century material glorification linked to industrialization and the doctrine of

Social Darwinism, to the early 20th-century expansion of mass production, consumption, and the cult of individual success (McGuire 1988:461–464).

Class can also be a very powerful concept to deal with global-scale issues. Questions of globalization have been a key part of historical archaeology for decades (Falk 1991; Funari et al. 1999; Orser and Fagan 1995; Paynter 2000b). Orser (1996:27) defines historical archaeology itself as the study of "the global nature of modern life." Recently, several historical archaeologists have argued that "capitalism" is a poor organizing concept for the field of historical archaeology since it is based on an American focus and cannot account for non-capitalist contexts (Funari et al. 1999). Their first point is well taken; we need to guard against seeing all global processes from only the perspective of the United States. Paynter reminds us that "world-scale processes must be understood as the articulation of European and indigenous processes, and not simply the response of the imperatives of European political economies" (Paynter 2000b:9).

A dialectical view recognizes that capitalism is not a monolithic entity but a complex web of relations. Obviously, capitalism does not "play out" the same way in every global context (Hall 2000; Purser 1999), and the global stage is characterized as much by capitalist domination as "spaces of rupture" (Aronowitz and Gautney 2003:xxv). Warren Perry's (2000) discussion of the Zulu state in southeastern Africa, Martin Hall's (2000) comparison of South Africa and the Chesapeake, and contributors to *Historical Archaeology: Back from the Edge* (Funari et al. 1999) all provide prime examples of the intricacies of class formation on the global stage. Class analysis at the global scale provides the analytical tool to investigate the vagaries of capitalism as it spread throughout the world and articulates(d) with other modes of production.

A dialectical approach to class analysis makes it clear that class can be different things at different scales of analysis. People always make history, but, following Marx, we need to realize that the nature of class divisions, and even the number of classes we discuss, will be "determined" by the purpose of analysis. At the local level, terms such as working class and elite are of a particularistic nature, whether we are talking about John Russell, cutlery factory workers, coal miners and their wives, or the Burghardt family. When we shift the analytical lens to larger capitalist relations, the stark dialogue of capitalist and working class are necessarily of a significantly different nature to capture social relations at this scale. Discussions of class at the capitalist or global levels may well draw sharp contrasts, but their abstractions are necessary to understand the transformations of capitalism itself and its articulations on the global stage.

The One of Class

Many of the confusing statements about class, both within historical archaeology and without, are clarified when we recognize the two very different frameworks that structure the discourse about class. Class as an objective entity or essence has proven disappointing as a concept to understand human experience in the past. As has been pointed out, class in this sense cannot account for human agency or the complexity of the social relations of gender and race. This view of class is indeed dead – *requiem et pacem*.

However, we have barely begun to scratch the surface of the potential of a relational perspective of class. The goal of an archaeology based on a relational view is not to define as many classes as possible, but rather to understand the lived experience of the past and bring into focus aspects of the totality of social relations that would otherwise be invisible. Instead of using objective definitions of class that pigeonhole individuals into a narrow range of classes, we have to recognize that class is a relational, analytical, multi-scalar category. Much of the argument seems to deal with issues of scale – since we assume that class is an objective property, archaeologists believe that their views of class have to be the same at every scale, examining class at the local, capitalist, and global scales makes it clear that the abstraction of class can be drawn, and that the social relations "appear," very different at each of these scales. Recognizing, as Marx did, that class can be defined differently gives us a powerful tool to understand the social relations at each of these levels.

Given this, one of the most powerful aspects of a dialectical view of class is its insistence on social totality – the intricate whole of social relations. This means that class is not a male thing, a female thing, a workers' thing, a consumer thing, or any THING. Patterson argues that social totality has two aspects: "the phenomenal world of appearances – that is, everyday life – and the level of the unobservable processes and relations that are simultaneously revealed in the everyday as well as concealed by it" (Patterson 1993:91). Class is a concept that can help us understand the totality of the material conditions of human life in the past. This must include the everyday life of commoners as well as the elite. We also need to acknowledge the middle (managerial) class – the silent majority whose active role has been assumed but not subject to critical analysis (Bledstein and Johnston 2001; Praetzellis et al. 1988; Praetzellis and Praetzellis 2001). Archaeologists cannot, as mere mortals, study the totality of any social context, but we must recognize that we proceed with abstractions of the internal relations that form a totality.

Some readers may find this insistence on totality discomfiting. In this postmodern world, scholars have been trained to eschew any totalizing discourse in favor of diversity and difference. Yet, a dialectic approach emphasizing totality is not the same as a single universal explanation. We also need to ask what the postmodern "war on totality" does, and realize that this perspective does not challenge the dominant ideology of modern capitalism (Eagleton 1996; Zavarzadeh 1995:18). Larrain (1995) has suggested that the postmodern discourse plays an ideological role to conceal the true contradictions of advanced capitalist societies and thereby reproduces the ruling class interests. By emphasizing subjectivity, discontinuity, and difference, these theories conceal the elements of shared humanity and exploitation that exist in modern society (Larrain 1995). By denying any sense of totality, the universal, and objective reality, postmodernists provide no ground on which to act in order to change existing social relations (Eagleton 1996; Ebert 1995:128). Harvey claims that to turn our back on universals at this stage in our history, however fraught or even tainted, "is to turn our back on all manner of prospects for progressive political action" (Harvey 2000:94).

No other concept has the potential to explicate issues of struggle, conflict, and contradictions in productive relations. Leone and Potter's (1999) volume *Historical Archaeologies of Capitalism* represents one of the strongest statements characterizing American historical archaeology as political action. Wylie (1999) passionately argues that historical archaeologists have to study class and capitalism if we are to understand and provide alternatives to the present that is based on exploitative social relations. And this is exactly why we need to study class.

References

Aronowitz, Stanley, 1996 The Politics of Identity: Class, Culture, Social Movements. New York: Routledge.

Aronowitz, Stanley, and Heather Gautney, 2003 The Debate about Globalization: An Introduction. *In* Implicating Empire: Globalization and Resistance in the 21st Century World Order. Stanley Aronowitz and Heather Gautney, eds. Pp. xi–xxx. New York: Basic Books.

Baugher, Sherene, and Robert W. Venables, 1987 Ceramics as Indicators of Status and Class in Eighteenth-Century New York. *In* Consumer Choice in Historical Archaeology. Suzanne M. Spencer-Wood, ed. Pp. 31–53. New York: Plenum Press.

Beaudry, Mary C., Lauren J. Cook, and Stephen A. Mrozowski, 1991 Artifacts and Active Voices: Material Culture as Social Discourse. *In* The Archaeology of Inequality. Randall H. McGuire and Robert Paynter, eds. Pp. 150–181. Oxford: Blackwell.

Bledstein, Burton J., and Robert D. Johnston, eds., 2001 The Middling Sorts: Explorations in the History of the American Middle Class. New York: Routledge.

Brighton, Stephen, 2001 Prices that Suit the Times: Shopping for Ceramics at the Five Points. Historical Archaeology 35(3):16–30.

Delle, James A., Stephen A. Mrozowski, and Robert Paynter, eds., 2000 Lines That Divide: Historical Archaeologies of Race, Class and Gender. Knoxville: University of Tennessee Press.

Dobres, Marcia-Anne, and John E. Robb, 2000 Agency in Archaeology: Paradigm or Platitude? *In* Agency in Archaeology. Marcia-Anne Dobres and John E. Robb, eds. Pp. 3–18. London: Routledge.

Duke, Philip, and Dean Saitta, 1998 An Emancipatory Archaeology for the Working Class. Assemblage 4:1–7.

Durrenberger, E. Paul, 2001 On Class. Anthropology News 42, 5–6.

Eagleton, Terry, 1996 The Illusion of Postmodernism. Oxford: Blackwell.

Ebert, Teresa L., 1995 (Untimely) Critiques for a Red Feminism. *In* Post-Ality. Marxism and Postmodernism. Mas'ud Zavarzadeh, Teresa L. Ebert, Donald Morton, eds. Pp. 113–149. Washington, DC: Maisonneuve Press.

Falk, Lisa, ed., 1991 Historical Archaeology in Global Perspective. Washington, DC: Smithsonian Institution Press.

Fantasia, Rick, 1988 Cultures of Solidarity: Consciousness, Action, and Contemporary American Workers. Berkeley: University of California Press.

Friedlander, Amy, 1991 House and Barn: The Wealth of Farmers, 1795–1815. Historical Archaeology 25 (2):15–30.

Funari, Pedro P. A., Martin Hall, and Siân Jones, eds., 1999 Historical Archaeology: Back from the Edge. London: Routledge.

Garman, James C., and Paul A. Russo, 1999 'A Disregard of Every Sentiment of Humanity': The Town Farm and Class Realignment in Nineteenth-Century Rural New England. Historical Archaeology 33(1):118–135.

Godelier, Maurice, 1986 The Mental and the Material. London: Verso.

Hall, Martin, 1992 Small Things and the Mobile, Conflictual Fusion of Power, Fear, and Desire. *In* The Art and Mystery of Historical Archaeology. Anne Yentsch and Mary Beaudry, eds. Pp. 373–400. Boca Raton, FL: CRC Press.

Hall, Martin, 2000 Archaeology and the Modern World: Colonial Transcripts in South Africa and the Chesapeake. London: Routledge.

Hardesty, Donald L. 1994 Class, Gender Strategies, and Material Culture in the Mining West. *In* Those of Little Note: Gender, Race and Class in Historical Archaeology. Elizabeth M. Scott, ed. Pp. 129–145. Tucson: University of Arizona Press.

Harvey, David 1996 Justice, Nature and the Geography of Difference. Oxford: Blackwell.

Harvey, David 2000 Spaces of Hope. Berkeley: University of California Press.

Hodder, Ian 1986 Reading the Past: Current Approaches to Interpretation in Archaeology. Cambridge: Cambridge University Press.

Hodder, Ian 2000 Agency and Individuals in Long-Term Processes. *In* Agency in Archaeology. Marcia-Anne Dobres and John E. Robb, eds. Pp. 21–33. London: Routledge.

Johnson, Matthew 1996 An Archaeology of Capitalism. Oxford: Blackwell.

Klein, Terry, 1991 Nineteenth-Century Ceramics and Models of Consumer Behavior. Historical Archaeology 25(2):77–91.

Kruczek-Aaron, Hadley, 2002 Choice Flowers and Well-Ordered Tables: Struggling over Gender in a Nineteenth-Century Household. International Journal of Historical Archaeology 6(3): 173–185.

Larrain, Jorge, 1995 Identity, the Other, and Postmodernism. In Post-Ality: Marxism and Postmodernism. Mas'ud Zavarzadeh, Teresa L. Ebert, Donald Morton, eds. Pp. 271–289. Washington, DC: Maisonneuve Press.

LeeDecker, Charles H., 1991 Historical Dimensions of Consumer Research. Historical Archaeology 25 (2):30–45.

LeeDecker, Charles, H., Terry Klein, Cheryl Holt, and Amy Friedlander, 1987 Nineteenth-Century Households and Consumer Behavior in Wilmington, Delaware. In Consumer Choice in Historical Archaeology. Suzanne M. Spencer-Wood, ed. Pp. 233–259. New York: Plenum Press.

Leone, Mark P., 1988 The Georgian Order as the Order of Merchant Capitalism in Annapolis, Maryland. In The Recovery of Meaning: Historical Archaeology in the Eastern United States. Mark P. Leone and Parker B. Potter, Jr., eds. Pp. 235–261. Washington, DC: Smithsonian Institution Press.

Leone, Mark P., 1999 Setting Some Terms for Historical Archaeologies of Capitalism. In Historical Archaeologies of Capitalism. Mark. P. Leone and Parker B. Potter Jr., eds. Pp. 3–22. New York: Kluwer Academic.

Leone, Mark P., and Parker B. Potter, Jr., eds., 1999 Historical Archaeologies of Capitalism. New York: Kluwer Academic.

Lodziak, Conrad, 2002 The Myth of Consumerism. London: Pluto Press.

McGuire, Randall H., 1988 Dialogues with the Dead: Ideology and the Cemetery. In The Recovery of Meaning: Historical Archaeology in the Eastern United States. Mark P. Leone and Parker B. Potter, Jr., eds. Pp. 435–480. Washington, DC: Smithsonian Institution Press.

Marquardt, William H., 1992 Dialectical Archaeology. In Archaeological Method and Theory. Michael B. Shiffer, ed. Pp. 101–140. Vol. 4. Tucson: University of Arizona Press.

Marx, Karl, and Frederick Engels, 1955 The Communist Manifesto. New York: Appleton-Century-Crofts.

McGuire, Randall H., and Robert Paynter, eds., 1991 The Archaeology of Inequality, Oxford: Blackwell.

McGuire, Randall H., and Paul Reckner, 2002 The Unromantic West: Labor, Capital, and Struggle. Historical Archaeology 36(3):44–58.

McGuire, Randall H., and LouAnn Wurst, 2002 Struggling with the Past. International Journal of Historical Archaeology 6(2):85–94.

McNall, Scott G., Rhonda F. Levine, and Rick Fantasia, eds., 1991 Bringing Class Back In. Boulder, CO: Westview Press.

McNall, Scott G., Rhonda F. Levine, and Rick Fantasia, eds., 1991 Building Power in the Cultural Landscape of Broome County, New York 1880–1940. In The Archaeology of Inequality. Randall H. McGuire and Robert Paynter, eds. Pp. 102–124. Oxford: Blackwell.

McNall, Scott G., Rhonda F. Levine, and Rick Fantasia, eds., 1992 A Marxist Archaeology. San Diego: Academic Press.

Meskell, Lynn, 1999 Archaeologies of Social Life. Malden: Blackwell.

Miller, George, 1991 A Revised Set of CC Index Values for Classification and Economic Scaling of English Ceramics from 1787 to 1880. Historical Archaeology 25(1):1–25.

Monks, Gregory G., 1999 On Rejecting the Concept of Socio-Economic Status in Historical Archaeology. In Historical Archaeology: Back from the Edge. Pedro P. A. Funari, Martin Hall, and Siân Jones, eds. Pp. 204–216. London: Routledge.

Mrozowski, Stephen A., 2000 The Growth of Managerial Capitalism and the Subtleties of Class Analysis in Historical Archaeology. In Lines that Divide: Historical Archaeologies of Race, Class, and Gender. James A. Delle, Stephen A. Mrozowski, and Robert Paynter, eds. Pp. 276–305. Knoxville: University of Tennessee Press.

Nassancy, Michael S., and Marjorie R. Abel, 1993 The Political and Social Contexts of Cutlery Production in the Connecticut Valley. Dialectical Anthropology 18, 247–289.

Nassaney, Michael S., and Marjorie R. Abel, 2000 Urban Spaces, Labor Organization, and Social Control: Lessons from New England's Nineteenth-Century Cutlery Industry. In Lines that Divide: Historical Archaeologies of Race, Class, and Gender. James A. Delle, Stephen A. Mrozowski, and Robert Paynter, eds. Pp. 239–275. Knoxville: University of Tennessee Press.

O'Donovan, Maria, 2002 Grasping Power: A Question of Relations and Scales. In The Dynamics of Power. Maria O'Donovan, ed. Pp. 19–34. Carbondale: Center for Archaeological Investigations and Southern Illinois University.

O'Donovan, Maria, and LouAnn Wurst, 2001–02 Living on the Edge: Consumption and Class at the Keith Site. Northeastern Historical Archaeology 30–31:73–84.

Ollman, Bertell, 1976 Alienation. Cambridge: Cambridge University Press.

Ollman, Bertell, 1993 Dialectical Investigations. New York: Routledge.

Orser, Charles E., 1996 A Historical Archaeology of the Modern World. New York: Plenum Press.

Orser, Charles E., and Brian M. Fagan, 1995 Historical Archaeology. New York: HarperCollins.

Ortner, Sherry B., 1991 Reading America: Preliminary Notes on Class and Culture. In Recapturing Anthropology: Working in the Present. Richard G. Fox, ed. Pp. 163–189. Santa Fe, NM: School of American Research Press.

Pakulski, Jan, and Malcolm Waters, 1996 The Death of Class. London: Sage.

Patterson, Thomas C., 1993 Archaeology: The Historical Development of Civilizations. Englewood Cliffs: Prentice-Hall.

Paynter, Robert, 1988 Steps to an Archaeology of Capitalism. In The Recovery of Meaning: Historical Archaeology in the Eastern United States. Mark P. Leone and Parker B. Potter, Jr., eds. Pp. 407–433. Washington, DC: Smithsonian Institution Press.

Paynter, Robert, 2000a Historical Archaeology and the Post-Columbian World of North America. Journal of Archaeological Research 8(3):169–217.

Paynter, Robert, 2000b Historical and Anthropological Archaeology: Forging Alliances. Journal of Archaeological Research 8(1):1–37.

Paynter, Robert, and Randall H. McGuire, 1991 The Archaeology of Inequality: Material Culture, Domination and Resistance. In The Archaeology of Inequality. Randall H. McGuire and Robert Paynter, eds. Pp. 1–27. Oxford: Blackwell.

Perry, Warren R., 2000 The Divide in Post-Fifteenth-Century Southern Africa: Archaeology of the Color Line and White Settler History. In Lines that Divide: Historical Archaeologies of Race, Class, and Gender. James A. Delle, Stephen A. Mrozowski, and Robert Paynter, eds. Pp. 78–106. Knoxville: University of Tennessee Press.

Praetzellis, Adrian, and Mary Praetzellis, 2001 Mangling Symbols of Gentility in the Wild West: Case Studies in Interpretive Archaeology. American Anthropologist 103(3):645–654.

Praetzellis, Mary, and Adrian Praetzellis, and Marley Brown, 1988 What Happened to the Silent Majority? Research Strategies for Studying Dominant Group Material Culture in Late Nineteenth-Century California. In Documentary Archaeology in the New World. Mary Beaudry, ed. Pp. 192–202. Cambridge: Cambridge University Press.

Purser, Margaret, 1999 Ex Occidente Lux? An Archaeology of Later Capitalism in the Nineteenth-Century West. In Historical Archaeologies of Capitalism. Mark P. Leone and Parker B. Potter, Jr., eds. Pp. 115–141. New York: Kluwer Academic.

Reitz, Elizabeth J., 1987 Vertebrate Fauna and Socioeconomic Status. In Consumer Choice in Historical Archaeology. Suzanne M. Spencer-Wood. ed. Pp. 101–120. New York: Plenum Press.

Sayer, Derek, 1987 The Violence of Abstraction: The Analytical Foundations of Historical Materialism. Oxford: Basil Blackwell.

Schulz, Peter D., and Sherri M. Gust, 1983 Faunal Remains and Social Status in Nineteenth-Century Sacramento. Historical Archaeology 17(1):44–53.

Scott, Elizabeth M., ed., 1994 Those of Little Note: Gender, Race, and Class in Historical Archaeology. Tucson: University of Arizona Press.

Shackel, Paul A., and David L. Larsen, 2000 Labor, Racism, and the Built Environment in Early Industrial Harpers Ferry. In Lines That Divide: Historical Archaeologies of Race, Class, and Gender. James A. Delle, Stephen A. Mrozowski, and Robert Paynter, eds. Pp. 22–39. Knoxville: University of Tennessee Press.

Shephard, Steven J., 1987 Status Variation in Antebellum Alexandria. In Consumer Choice in Historical Archaeology. Suzanne M. Spencer-Wood, ed. Pp. 163–198. New York: Plenum Press.

Spencer-Wood, Suzanne M., and Scott D. Heberling, 1987 Consumer Choices in White Ceramics: A Comparison of Eleven Early Nineteenth-Century Sites. In Consumer Choice in Historical Archaeology: Suzanne M. Spencer-Wood, ed. Pp. 55–84. New York: Plenum Press.

Sweely, Tracy L., ed., 1999 Manifesting Power: Gender and the Interpretation of Power in Archaeology. London: Routledge.

Thomas, Julian S., 2002 Taking Power Seriously. In The Dynamics of Power. Maria O'Donovan, ed. Pp. 35–50. Carbondale: Center for Archaeological Investigations and Southern Illinois University.

Thompson, E. P., 1978 The Poverty of Theory and Other Essays. New York: Monthly Review Press.

Wall, Diana DiZerega, 1999 Examining Gender, Class, and Ethnicity in Nineteenth-Century New York City. Historical Archaeology 33(1):102–117.

Wilkie, Laurie A., and Kevin M. Bartoy, 2000 A Critical Archaeology Revisited. Current Anthropology 41, 747–777.

Williams, Raymond, 1983 Keywords: A Vocabulary of Culture and Society. Oxford: Oxford University Press.

Wood, Ellen M., 1995 Democracy Against Capitalism: Renewing Historical Materialism. Cambridge: Cambridge University Press.

Wood, Margaret C., 2002a Women's Work and Class Conflict in a Working-Class Coal-Mining Community. In The Dynamics of Power. Maria O'Donovan, ed. Pp. 66–87. Carbondale: Center for Archaeological Investigations and Southern Illinois University.

Wood, Margaret C., 2002b Fighting for Our Homes. Ph.D. dissertation, Department of Anthropology, Syracuse University.

Wright, Erik O., 1994 Interrogating Inequality: Essays on Class Analysis, Socialism and Marxism. London: Verso.

Wright, Erik O., 1997 Class Counts: Comparative Studies in Class Analysis. London: Cambridge University Press.

Wurst, LouAnn, 1999 Internalizing Class in Historical Archaeology. Historical Archaeology 33(1):7–21.

Wurst, LouAnn, 2002 Mobilizing Social Labor in Nineteenth-Century Rural America: A Power Play in Three Acts. In The Dynamics of Power. Maria O'Donovan, ed. Pp. 88–104. Carbondale: Center for Archaeological Investigations and Southern Illinois University.

Wurst, LouAnn, and Robert K. Fitts, 1999 Introduction: Why Confront Class? Historical Archaeology 33(1):1–6.

Wurst, LouAnn, and Randall H. McGuire, 1999 Immaculate Consumption: A Critique of the 'Shop till you Drop' School of Human Behavior. International Journal of Historical Archaeology 3(3): 191–199.

Wylie, Alison, 1999 Why Should Historical Archaeologists Study Capitalism? The Logic of Question and Answer and the Challenge of System Analysis. In Historical Archaeologies of Capitalism. Mark P. Leone and Parker B. Potter, Jr., eds. Pp. 23–50. New York: Kluwer.

Yentsch, Anne, and Mary C. Beaudry, 2001 American Material Culture in Mind, Thought, and Deed. In Archaeological Theory Today. Ian Hodder, ed. Pp. 214–240. Cambridge: Polity.

Zavarzadeh, Mas'ud, 1995 Post-Ality: The (Dis)Simulations of Cybercapitalism. In Post-Ality: Marxism and Postmodernism. Mas'ud Zavarzadeh, Teresa L. Ebert, and Donald Morton, eds. Pp. 1–75. Washington, DC: Maisonneuve Press.

Part VI

Materiality, Memory, and Historical Silence

MATERIALITY AND MEMORY are two new theoretical concepts, rapidly growing in popularity in contemporary archaeological discourse. And yet there is little agreement on what is meant by these terms. According to Lynn Meskell (2005:6), materiality refers to a set of dialectical practices implicating people and things. Victor Buchli (2002:18) approaches materiality as the various ways we materialize social being and the ways the process is challenged by rapid social change and our ephemeral interactions. For Tim Dant (2005:6), materiality is a context for human engagement: "Sometimes materiality remains environment; sometimes it is interacted with directly as distinct objects and sometimes material objects are taken up as tools that extend human instrumentality." Manuel Arroyo-Kalin (2004:74) defines materiality as the material objectification of the agent's social relations. He suggests that it is the product of materially mediated relationships both among and between agents. Taking these definitions together, materiality involves considering how humans construct their worlds and each other through material means and encompasses both physical and cognitive processes. In emphasizing the cultural construction of the material world, it bears certain similarities to the terms "temporality" and "spatiality," which refer to the cultural construction of time and space, respectively (Soja 1989, 1996).

Materiality is also a key topic in cultural anthropology. It finds its origins in Mary Douglas's study of consumption (Douglas and Isherwood 1979), Nancy Munn's (1986) views of cultural symbolism, Nicholas Thomas's (1991) notion of entangled objects, and Annette Weiner's (1992) ideas of inalienable possessions. Significantly, many of these formative studies are associated with the circulation of goods in Melanesian societies, particularly in the context of the Kula ring. These studies have been broadened out in terms of theory and geographical area by Daniel Miller (1985, 1987, 1998), who has been particularly interested in issues of consumption in Jamaica. Miller was one of Hodder's students at Cambridge and influential in the establishment of postprocessual archaeology (e.g. Miller and Tilley 1984). Also important has been the social life of things approach, as articulated by Arjun Appadurai (1986) and Igor Kopytoff (1986), and Alfred Gell's (1998) view of art and agency. These works have inspired edited volumes by Fred Myers (2001) and by Christopher Pinney and Nicholas Thomas (2001). More recently, Miller (2005) and Christopher Tilley et al. (2006) have drawn attention to the myriad ways in which materiality is implicated as a constitutive force in all aspects of social life. Not everyone, it should be said, has celebrated this newfound interest in materiality. Tim Ingold (2007), for example, has criticized this focus, claiming that it is moving us further away from a consideration of materials, their transformations and affordances (but see Jones 2004).

Memory, by contrast, is seemingly less controversial. It is usually regarded as the ability of an individual to store, retain, and retrieve information. It is an essential part of meaning construction. According to Maurice Halbwachs (1980), memory is not only individual, but also collective. It is a function of all of one's social interactions built up throughout one's life. Halbwachs (1980:23) notes that we are never alone since "we always carry with us and in us a number of distinct persons." These distinct others are imagined presences, mental representations of actual others and embodiments of our social relations with them. Similarly, Paul Connerton (1989) regards memory as a property of a group. He suggests that there are two different types of bodily based commemorative practices that generate social memory. These are inscribing practices and incorporating practices. The former includes all conscious activities that are used in the storage and retrieval of information: for example, photographing, writing, tape recording, and so on. The latter implies less conscious, more automatic skilled performances that are expressed by means of physical activity, such as a spoken word or gesture. Together these two kinds of inscriptive practices produce collective memory. De Certeau (1984) takes a slightly different tack, holding that practical memory receives its form from the external circumstances that call it into play. What is called up by memory is not something structured, but rather an improvisation. These views are a far cry from the idea of recalling information from a storage bank.

The key point here is that memory is not passive; it takes effort to remember some things and to forget others, and this effort often includes the production and/or destruction of material culture. Memory practices are well demonstrated by Susanne Küchler's (2002) studies of the New Guinea *malanggan*. *Malanggan* are wooden funerary effigies which are created to be ritually destroyed with the body in the funeral ritual. The carving process is known as "making skin" and instills the deceased's life-force in the object, which is to then be released in the mortuary ceremony (Küchler 2002:94-112). Forgetting is thus given a material expression and activated in cultural performance. Forgetting is also linked to the concept of historical silence as articulated in the work Michel-Rolph Trouillot. In his study of the Haitian revolt, Trouillot (1995) suggests that history contains silences that can be created at four different junctures: "the moment of fact creation (the making of *sources*); the moment of fact assembly (the making of *archives*); the moment of fact retrieval (the making of *narratives*); and the moment of retrospective significance (the making of *history* in the final sense" (Trouillot 1995:26, his emphasis). Silences thus exist in the narratives created by scholars for the public. In most instances these are not the result of commission as much as they acts of omission; they result from forgetting. Significantly, Trouillot (1995:150) cautions us that focusing on the past for its own sake often diverts us from acknowledging present injustices.

Recent archaeological studies are contributing to the literature on memory by demonstrating some of the different ways memory is made material in its social deployment. Two new edited volumes are particularly noteworthy. The first is *Archaeologies of Memory*, edited by Ruth Van Dyke and Susan Alcock (2003a), and the second is *Memory Work*, edited by Barbara Mills and William Walker (2008a). In their introduction to the first volume, Van Dyke and Alcock (2003b) suggest that social memory is an active and ongoing process: people remember or forget the past according to the needs of the present. The uses of memory, however, are quite varied. They can involve smoothing over social ruptures; they can create a sense of individual and community identity; or they can involve obliteration, as pasts are subsumed or destroyed. Van Dyke and Alcock note that these uses are neither straightforward, nor monolithic. Because of the dynamics of memory production and use, multiple

versions of specific narratives can coexist, often in support of the interests of competing groups. In their introduction to the second volume, Mills and Walker (2008b) outline a shift from collective memory to "memory work." For them, memory work is not just about studying the material traces of past activities; it is also about understanding the materiality of those past practices. These material traces are evidence for memory-making practices in different social settings. In addition, they identify memory work with the interpretive practices of contemporary scholars who study social memory. In this joining of the past and present, they are adopting aspects of a pragmatic perspective.

Webb Keane discusses the materiality of money and material objects at the cultural interstices of 20th-century capitalism. His focus is on exchange among the people of Sumba, an island of eastern Indonesia. The Sumbanese are caught up in a classic colonial contradiction between tradition and modernity, here expressed by costly and elaborate systems of ceremonial exchange and the growing importance of money. He notes that we cannot assume that the Sumbanese necessarily see money as hostile to their social values. Money with all its associations of modernity and commodification is deployed to revalidate native regimes of value and the material objects that circulate within them. This revalidation has two aspects, involving a dematerialization of the human world and a denial of the ways human subjects are enmeshed in the object world.

Keane begins with an account of a marriage negotiation he witnessed in the Anakalang district in 1986. He describes some trouble that occurred because of a misunderstanding of the local protocol. The bride's family from a neighboring district began the ceremonial exchange in the traditional way by sending over to the groom's family a dish on which they placed a cloth. The groom's family responded in kind by sending the dish back with a 100-rupiah note. Traditionally, they would have sent back gold objects known as *mamuli*. However, although both money and *mamuli* serve as material tokens to ground the formal speech that unites the two marriage partners, the mother of the bride objected to the money, saying that its use in this situation was inappropriate. After some discussion, the bride's party asked that the note be replaced with a 500-rupiah note. With this development, the spokesman on the groom's side spoke out, reminding them that when money is placed in the dish it is not to be treated as money. It is just like the gold *mamuli*. The bride's family reluctantly agreed to accept the dish once they were assured that it was not an insult. This case reveals the possibility that objects can slip across regimes of value and that the status of money is not stable since it too can take objective form.

One of Keane's most important contributions is his demonstration that material objects work in ways that differ from the standard Saussurian notion of the sign. For Saussure, material signs are arbitrary in the sense that their meanings are set by cultural convention. Their phenomenal properties, such as color or sound, are only significant in so far as they mark difference. However, this approach neglects the materiality of things. Objects are subject to scarcity since they must be obtained from somewhere. They possess physical qualities, such as the yellow color of gold, that predispose them to value and circulation. And objects have durability that allows them to extend the agency of their transactor. As Keane puts it, "The materiality of objects is a condition of possibility for their movement across social and semiotic domains."

The Sumbanese use of money in marriage negotiation finds a close parallel in the modern Tlingit potlatch of southeast Alaska. Potlatches (*koo.ex* in Tlingit) are memorial ceremonies usually held a year or two after the death of a clan member (Kan 1989). The basic principle of Tlingit social organization is the moiety, and all important social functions must be carried out and witnessed by members of the opposite moiety. Among the Tlingit, the moieties are the Eagles and the Ravens. Potlatches are also called "pay-off" parties because they involve paying off debts to members of the opposite moiety that assisted in the funeral. Prior to the start of the potlatch, the host clan collects sums of money from the guests. Guests typically give money, usually in small amounts, in honor of a deceased relative. During the potlatch, the donor and the honoree are publicly acknowledged and the money is ceremonially "killed" by being placed in a flow blue bowl or an upturned clan hat. It is then counted and redistributed to the guests in accordance with their rank and status, after which

they go home and use it to make their normal purchases. Money is thus transformed from a medium of exchange into a token of a social relationship and then back into a medium of exchange.

Barbara Mills draws attention to the centrality of forgetting in the process of remembering the past. The process of remembering-while-forgetting is a universal cognitive process characteristic of all humans at all times and not specific to Western thought. She demonstrates this point by introducing the New Ireland *malanggan* and the Zuni war gods (*Ahayu:da*), as examples of objects that construct memory, not through their preservation, but though their destruction. The processes underlying forgetting are quite variable. Some involve the hiding or secreting of objects as part of a ceremony. Others involve the ritual retirement of objects and spaces, through burning, filling in, and so on. Still others may involve imperfect reproduction or copying errors that result in the loss of information. These memory processes are often politically charged and sometimes linked to nationalist claims about the past. Ironically, acts of erasure, such as the Taliban's destruction of the Bamiyan buddhas, can often have a reverse effect, as in the mobilization of international support for the Afghan people (Meskell 2005).

Mills examines the processes of remembering-while-forgetting by analyzing variation in depositional practices in Chaco Canyon, New Mexico. She focuses on two contexts – offerings in ritual structures, commonly known as kivas, and deposits in Great House rooms. She regards the kiva offerings as examples of memory work that involve secrecy. Things acquire value through the process of gathering them up (bundling, to use Keane's term) and hiding them in architectural spaces. These depositions consist of finished ornaments and debris from ornament manufacture and are typically associated with architectural construction and termination in great kivas, court kivas, and room block kivas. Mills interprets these different kivas as being used by different social networks of varying size and inclusiveness. The deposits thus are an active part of commemorative performances working at different social scales.

Mills regards Great House deposits as examples of ritual retirement. This process refers to the deliberate caching and/or burial of altar pieces, staffs of office, and so on. In some cases, the objects are placed in rooms that are intentionally sealed, while in others they are placed in deep excavations beneath rooms. In still other cases, they are associated with mortuary remains. Mills draws attention to a Zuni example of the sealing off of a room upon the death of a ritual leader. The leader apparently used the room as a retreat when preparing himself for ceremonies. Significantly, people remembered this event long after the fact. Mills also cites the Hopi practice whereby certain ceremonial objects, considered to be communally owned, may be associated with particular houses over several generations. Senior males protect them, while senior females ceremonially feed them. Because the possession and proper care of these objects are associated with clan or lineage prestige, storage is a situated social practice that maintains and enhances social status.

Paul Shackel outlines some of the ways public memory is actively constructed in the context of race and power. He notes that public memory is more often a product of present political and social relations than it is a true representation of the past. In his work at Harpers Ferry, he observes that it is as if history stopped after the American Civil War. The dominant historical narrative emphasizes its role in the surrender of 12,500 Union troops to Stonewall Jackson and in the events surrounding John Brown. And yet, Harpers Ferry was a thriving industrial center up to the 1920s. According to Shackel, this silencing of the antebellum past was intentional. The postbellum industrial developers did little for the working class beyond supply low-paying jobs and take their rent. When they left the town by the late 1930s, the working class chose to forget their exploitation. This, then, is an example of the masking of a group history in the process of developing collective memory. Shackel goes on to provide other examples of memory practices, such as the commemoration of the Civil War Centennial and the Battle of Manassas and the Heyward Shepherd Memorial, where histories have been produced that do not address conflict, especially those surrounding issues of class or race.

Shackel points to several instances in which racist views remain active today despite all of the progress in the area of civil rights. In some cases, the racism is not necessarily overt or even conscious. Shackel describes, for example, how Civil War historians and enthusiasts see no reason to incorporate discussions of slavery into the commemoration of battlefield sites. These sites are viewed as hallowed ground, the scenes of heroism that should not be over-shadowed by extraneous issues. This approach runs counter to those who want to see the Civil War remembered for the inequities and conflict that gave rise to it in the first place. Shackel addresses some of these issues through the case of the Shaw Memorial in Boston, which was created in 1897 to commemorate the all-Black 54th Massachusetts Regiment that fought in the Civil War. The regiment was led by Colonel Robert Gould Shaw, a white man, who died along with many of the regiment during the attack on Fort Wagner in South Carolina. The plight of Shaw and his regiment were reported in the Boston newspapers as something akin to the attack on Bunker Hill during the American Revolution. At the time the memorial was created, it was heralded as the first example of a group depiction and for its heroic portrayal of members of the regiment. Yet as Shackel notes, this image belied a very different reality in which racial equality was not part of the contemporary discourse. When the monument was rededicated in 1997, several prominent African Americans, including Colin Powell and Henry Louis Gates, spoke and celebrated its tribute to the men of the regiment. Shackel notes that this performance helped solidify a new public meaning and memory and signify a willingness to include African American history within a common US heritage.

Peter Schmidt and Jonathan Walz offer an eye-opening critique of historical archaeology in Africa. They note the many examples in which Africa's history has been silenced by Euro-centric histories and its achievements masked. The long history of colonialism in Africa has resulted in a colonialist ideology that has held a powerful sway over the production of the continent's histories. Yet it is not just former colonial government officials or European metropolitan scholars who have purposely distorted the past to silence African achievement. According to Schmidt and Walz, archaeologists have also played a role, especially historical archaeologists, who have focused their attention on processes such as colonialism and industrialization and the groups caught up in these historical events. In addition they argue that historical archaeologists have privileged documentary history over oral history. They further note that the obsession with modernity and an archaeology of the modern world has in effect silenced the history of those in Africa who were not as dramatically touched by European colonialism or processes such as industrialization.

Schmidt and Walz follow this critique with a consideration of the some of the ways that archaeology can help in constructing alternative African histories. They argue that archaeologists need to look at the way theoretical frameworks limit the scope of the work they carry out. They suggest that anthropology should have as one of its goals the construction of histories that move beyond the confines of concepts such as prehistory. For them, prehistory serves as a barrier between the recent past and deeper histories. Prehistory is thus essentialized to the point where there is no connection with the present. Schmidt and Walz pay particular attention to the manner in which archaeology has been used to deepen the historicity of African oral traditions. Drawing on a series of case studies from different parts of Africa, they demonstrate how oral history can be proven to have historical veracity equal to that of written histories. They write that when oral texts are combined with materialities gleaned from archaeology, new, and in many instances alternative, histories can be constructed (Schmidt and Patterson 1995). These newly constructed histories have the potential the breach gaps in both geographies and temporal periods. It is these alternative histories that hold the greatest political relevance for the people of Africa.

References

Appadurai, Arjun, 1986 Introduction: Commodities and Politics of Value. In The Social Life of Things: Commodities in Cultural Perspective. Arjun Appadurai, ed. Pp. 3–62. Cambridge: Cambridge University Press.

Arroyo-Kalin, Manuel A., 2004 An Ongoing Outcome, a Surrounding World: Materiality, Agency, and History. In Rethinking Materiality: The Engagement of Mind with the Material World. Elizabeth DeMarrais, Chris Gosden, and Colin Renfrew, eds. Pp. 73–81. Cambridge: McDonald Institute for Archaeological Research.

Buchli, Victor, 2002: Introduction. In The Material Culture Reader. Victor Buchli, ed. Pp. 1–22. Oxford: Berg.

Connerton, Paul, 1989 How Societies Remember. Cambridge: Cambridge University Press.

Dant, Tim, 2005 Materiality and Society. New York: Open University Press.

de Certeau, Michel de, 1984 The Practice of Everyday Life. Berkeley: University of California Press.

Douglas, Mary, and Baron C. Isherwood, 1979 The World of Goods: Towards an Anthropology of Consumption. New York: Norton.

Gell, Alfred, 1998 Art and Agency: An Anthropological Theory. New York: Clarendon Press.

Halbwachs, Maurice, 1980 The Collective Memory. London: Harper and Row.

Ingold, Tim, 2007 Materials against Materiality. Archaeological Dialogues 14:1–16.

Jones, Andrew, 2004 Archaeometry and Materiality: Materials-Based Analysis in Theory and Practice. Archaeometry 46(3):327–338.

Kan, Sergei, 1989 Symbolic Immortality: The Tlingit Potlatch of the Nineteenth Century. Washington, DC: Smithsonian Institution.

Kopytoff, Igor, 1986 The Cultural Biography of Things: Commoditization as Process. In The Social Life of Things: Commodities in Cultural Perspective. Arjun Appadurai, ed. Pp. 64–91. Cambridge: Cambridge University Press.

Küchler, Suzanne, 2002 Malanggan: Art, Memory and Sacrifice. Oxford: Berg.

Meskell, Lynn, 2004 Object Worlds in Ancient Egypt: Material Biographies Past and Present. Oxford: Berg.

Meskell, Lynn, 2005 Introduction: Object Orientations. In Archaeologies of Materiality. Lynn Meskell, ed. Pp. 1–12. Oxford: Blackwell.

Miller, Daniel, 1985 Artifacts as Categories: A Study of Ceramic Variability in Central India. Cambridge: Cambridge University Press.

Miller, Daniel, 1987 Material Culture and Mass Consumption. Oxford: Blackwell.

Miller, Daniel, ed., 1998 Material Cultures: Why Some Things Matter. Chicago: University of Chicago Press.

Miller, Daniel, ed., 2005 Materiality. Durham, NC: Duke University Press.

Miller, Daniel, and Christopher Tilley, eds., 1984 Ideology, Power and Prehistory. Cambridge: Cambridge University Press.

Mills, Barbara J., and William H. Walker, eds., 2008a Memory Work: Archaeologies of Material Practices. Santa Fe: School for Advanced Research Press.

Mills, Barbara J., and William H. Walker 2008b Introduction: Memory, Materiality, and Depositional Practice. *In* Memory Work: Archaeologies of Material Practices. Barbara J. Mills and William H. Walker, eds. Pp. 3–23. Santa Fe: School for Advanced Research Press.

Munn, Nancy D., 1986 The Fame of Gawa. Cambridge: Cambridge University Press.

Myers, Fred R., ed., 2001 The Empire of Things: Regimes of Value and Material Culture. Santa Fe: School of American Research Press.

Pinney, Christopher, and Nicholas Thomas, eds., 2001 Beyond Aesthetics: Art and the Technologies of Enchantment. London: Berg.

Schmidt, Peter R., and Thomas C. Patterson, eds., 1995 Making Alternative Histories: The Practice of Archaeology and History in Non-Western Settings. Santa Fe: School of American Research Press.

Soja, Edward, 1989 Postmodern Geographies: The Reassertion of Space in Critical Social Theory. London: Verso.

Soja, Edward, 1996 Thirdspace: Journeys to Los Angeles and other Real-and-Imagined Spaces. Oxford: Blackwell.

Thomas, Nicholas, 1991 Entangled Objects: Exchange, Material Culture, and Colonialism in the Pacific. Cambridge, MA: Harvard University Press.

Tilley, Christopher, Webb Keane, Susanne Küchler, Mike Rowlands, and Patricia Spyer, eds., 2006 Handbook of Material Culture. London: Sage.

Trouillot, Michel-Rolph, 1995 Silencing the Past: Power and the Production of History. Boston: Beacon Press.

Van Dyke, Ruth M., and Susan E. Alcock, eds., 2003a Archaeologies of Memory. Oxford: Blackwell.

Van Dyke, Ruth M., and Susan E. Alcock, 2003b Archaeologies of Memory: An Introduction. *In* Archaeologies of Memory. Ruth M. Van Dyke and Susan E. Alcock, eds. Pp. 1–13. Oxford: Blackwell

Weiner, Annette B., 1992 Inalienable Possessions: The Paradox of Keeping-While-Giving. Berkeley: University of California Press.

Money Is No Object
Materiality, Desire, and Modernity in an Indonesian Society

Webb Keane

The distinction between what should and what should not have a price – between the alienable and the inalienable – is crucial to the ordering of relations among what Appadurai (1986) has called regimes of value, and it is central to Weiner's (1992) postulate about the creation of political hierarchies. Although often discussed with reference to so-called traditional exchange, the power and value of inalienables and of their supposed antitheses, commodities and money, are hardly restricted to "traditional" or "precapitalist" social or economic arrangements. In the contemporary United States, for instance, amid the efflorescence of free-market ideologies, the problem of confining the scope of alienability is evident in everything from debates over patenting genes and the question of child labor to the nervousness that often attends the circulation of money within the household.

As Miller (2001) cogently argues, inalienable value need not be restricted to elite or rare activities. What is at stake, rather, is the relationship between persons and things. Distinctions among kinds of objects and the ways they circulate matter, in part, because they have profound implications for the character of the humans who possess the objects and carry out transactions

Webb Keane, "Money Is No Object: Materiality, Desire, and Modernity in an Indonesian Society," pp. 65–90 from Fred Myers (ed.) *The Empire of Things: Regimes of Value and Material Culture* (Santa Fe: School of American Research Press, 2001). Reprinted with permission of SAR Press.

with them. After all, to be without a price is often taken, as it was by Kant (1956 [1785]), to define the human subject. Late in the twentieth century, most inhabitants of even the "freest" of market economies were still likely to feel that cash value stopped, or should stop, where the truly human began.[1] Market economies, then, do not do away with inalienables so much as they reorder the regimes of value in which they function (Carrier 1995; Miller 1994; Zelizer 1994). And contestations over these reorderings are not simply economic matters but are deeply concerned with the nature of persons as it is defined at the shifting boundaries between subjects and objects, boundaries whose particular configurations may define a historical epoch (Latour 1993).

In this chapter I address the unstable meanings of money and material objects at the margins of twentieth-century capitalism. In the process, I raise some general questions about the relations among materiality and abstraction, the values of persons and things, and the imagining of "modernity." For the last few generations, people in Sumba, an island of eastern Indonesia, have been involved in a classic confrontation between an elaborate, costly, and socially potent system of ceremonial exchange and the growing importance of money. We can no longer assume, as an earlier generation of anthropologists did, that people who practice ceremonial exchange will simply perceive money to be a threat to social values. It has become clear both that the advent of money may be welcomed even in so-called exchange societies and that it is not necessarily seen as inimical to the persistence of exchange (Akin and Robbins 1999). But certainly the growing availability of alternative regimes of value can give heightened visibility to certain cultural assumptions. Faced with money and its attendant discourses about modernity, freedom, and economic rationality, Sumbanese must try to account for the value things hold for people.

Their efforts to do so, I argue, often involve a certain dematerialization of the human world, a denial of the ways in which human subjects are enmeshed with material objects. But in an increasingly abstract world, where could value come from? One common site in which to locate the sources of value is the desires of the individual person. And it is money, issued by the state and linked to state discourses about modernity, that seems most to promote these desires. Thus, in dealing with money, people find themselves wrestling with a host of dilemmas raised by the tensions between the promises and threats of modernity.[2]

These tensions are especially prominent in local talk about "materialism." As their long-term interests, immediate concerns, and discursive circumstances variously incline them, Sumbanese may portray "the modern age" (I. *masa moderen*)[3] in terms of an increasing materialism in people's needs and economic activities – or in terms of disenchantment, as people lose their primitive and fetishistic over-investment in things such as ancestral valuables or bridewealth. New forms of production and circulation may be celebrated as bringing with them rationality and enlightenment. Conversely, money and commodities may be portrayed as corrosive agents that attack kinship, amity, spirituality, sociality, and virtue on all fronts. The relationship between modernity and "the materialist" (I. *materialis*) is a topic of anxious concern across Indonesia, whose ruling regime from 1966 until its fall in 1998 combined an aggressive emphasis on economic development with social conservatism and political authoritarianism. By conventional measures, until the crisis of 1997 the regime fostered rapid economic progress, although this progress may have seemed distant and of questionable value for many who

lived at the geographical and political margins of the nation.

On the island of Sumba, modernity, markets, and money appear in the context of a subsistence economy and a thriving system of ceremonial exchange.[4] Since Mauss's *The Gift* (1990 [1925]), scholars have tended to see money and ceremonial exchange as fundamentally opposed. The latter is distinguished from the former by the obligations between people that bind one moment of exchange to others, and by the spiritual links between people and the things that circulate between and, in marriage, along with them. Similar views on markets and exchange are found in local talk in many places like late-twentieth-century Sumba. Many Sumbanese tend to see money and markets as incipient challenges to the values supposedly embodied in exchange. Government officials and development experts worry, on the one hand, that ceremonial exchange is hindering economic development and, on the other, that the demise of exchange systems will have destructive consequences for social cohesion (Iskandar and Djoeroemana 1994). Nor are such worries new; in 1952 a Dutch missionary forecast that once Sumbanese came to see their traditional valuables in economic terms, possessions would "become a dangerous and threatening power" (Onvlee 1973:26). But the distinction between inalienable and alienable may not be so clear-cut. On examination, both money and ceremonial exchange present certain difficulties to any effort to explain the value of objects solely by appeal to their conventional sign value, mode of production, or innate ties to persons.

Meaning and the Motion of Things

Consider the following episode from a marriage negotiation I attended in 1986 in the Sumbanese district of Anakalang. Early in the initial stages of negotiation, trouble arose because the principals on the bride's side were from a neighboring district and thus unfamiliar with local procedural nuances. The bride's side initiated the exchange in the conventional way by sending over a dish on which they had placed a cloth, in order formally "to ask the purpose" of their guests' visit. The groom's side replied in an equally conventional manner by sending the dish back with a 100-rupiah note (a trivial sum even on Sumba – the smallest sum available in paper form, worth less than the price of a pack of cigarettes). The proper reciprocal to cloth is a gold ornament or its substitute, money. In either case, the object in the offering dish is an obligatory token that serves as a "base" to make the spoken words formal and binding. But the mother of the bride loudly rejected the note, saying the use of money in a formal exchange was inappropriate. After some discussion, the bride's party asked that the Rp 100 note be replaced with Rp 500. At this, the spokesman from the groom's side sharply berated them, explaining that when money is placed in the dish, it must not be treated as money. It is a token, just like a gold ornament. With a certain amount of grumbling, the bride's side was persuaded to accept this, on the condition that it was a proper procedure and not an insult, and the negotiation proceeded.

This incident took place at the highly fraught border between money and exchange, but are the two positions really clear-cut? The bride's side seems at first to be defending moral boundaries in a way familiar from received descriptions of spheres of exchange. From this point of view, they recognize the threat that money and the market-place pose to traditional moral values and the solidarity of precapitalist society. But when they retreat, they ask for an increase in the face value of the money, as if the insult had not been the intrusion of money after all, but rather the low price. In this, they reveal a possibility that always exists in exchange – that symbolic tokens might slip into alternative regimes of value. For, on the one hand, exchange valuables do not necessarily possess all the properties (inalienability, personality, morality) attributed to them by the model of the gift a priori (see Keane 1997). And on the other, the status of money itself is not entirely stable: in this case it serves as a formal token whose referent is confined to ceremonial exchange, yet it retains the potential for reinterpretation as cash value. In either case it is "symbolic," but its vulnerability to slippage is a function in part of its irreducible materiality. Even money shares with other objects the property of taking objectual form. Thus it can cross contexts and, being

semiotically underdetermined, is subject to reinterpretation. To make sense of the materiality and semiotics of money, however, first requires a look at the meaning and value of other objects that circulate in Sumba.

In Sumba, objects come most prominently into their own in formal exchanges between individuals or groups of people. Formal exchanges are the binding transactions at the heart of virtually all events of any importance; in the 1980s and 1990s the most prominent were marriage alliances. I have discussed these exchanges in detail in Keane (1997) Here, in order to compare the semiotics and materiality of valuables and money, I want briefly to return to one incident recounted in that book.

Ubu Tara had a large stone tomb carved for himself. By convention, when the capstone was dragged from the quarry to his village, his wife's kin provided two valuable textiles that were carried on top of it as banners. When Ama Koda, an important affine, was leaving the concluding feast, one of Ubu Tara's sons gave him one of the "banners," which by now were neatly folded up, to placate him in the wake of earlier hurt feelings. On arriving home, Ama Koda opened it up and discovered that he had only half a textile. On inquiry, it turned out that during the tomb dragging, the banner had snagged on a tree branch, and someone had cut off the tangled half. Once folded in the village, this was no longer apparent. Furious, Ama Koda sent the cloth back to Ubu Tara with the message, "I'm not yet so poor that I need a bit of cloth to cover my loins!" Great efforts were required to heal the rupture.

This episode shows some of vicissitudes to which material signs are prone. Ama Koda correctly placed great semiotic weight on the physical condition of the cloth, but that physical condition was subject to happenstance. Note the rapid series of roles through which the piece of cloth moved: by turns, it was a conventional obligation between affines, a figurative banner, a physical encumbrance tangled in a tree, a token of regard meant to placate an irate guest, a vehicle of insult, a metaphoric rag of poverty, and finally a rejected gift. In practical terms, this sequence of roles illuminates three things about objects as social media: that they are readily separated from the transactors and the context of the transaction; that they are available for multiple interpretations; and that throughout, they remain material objects and thus vulnerable to all that can happen to things.

These roles illustrate how both the value and possible meanings of objects are underdetermined. They call for speech, interpretive practices, and political strategies. This means they are necessarily caught up in the uncertainties of social action. Being material, objects are always subject to the forces of what Grice (1957) called "natural meaning" (signs based on causality, as a tear means the cloth was snagged in a tree). But as tokens within social action, they are also always subject to transformation into bearers of "non-natural meaning" (intentional signs, as a torn cloth means an insult). And this means the latter is always intertwined with the former. The meanings of things cannot be sharply disengaged from the ways in which they are embedded in the physical world. Thus the very materiality of objects means they are not merely arbitrary signs. Their materiality makes a difference both in the sources of their meanings and in their destinations, such that they are subject to shifting physical, economic, and semiotic contexts. Finally, insofar as objects often *seem* to carry their values and meanings on their sleeves, as it were, they can play critical roles at the intersections among these shifting contexts.[5] Their power and value emerge at the intersection of their character as conventional signs and their potential roles in a possibly unlimited range of contexts.

Ambiguous Attachments

In practice, Sumbanese formal exchanges stress the representative functions of objects, play down utility, and rigorously exclude money except as a symbolic piece of metal. Nonetheless, formal exchanges are embedded within a larger political economy of both social signs and usable things, and they take some of their meaning from the way in which they articulate with other "regimes of value." Explicit talk about "the real tradition" is one of the ways in which the barriers between exchange and its alternatives are regulated. Sumbanese can point to the coexistence of exchange with markets, barter,

usurious lending, and theft in order to insist on its distinctive moral value. For example, when Ubu Kura tried to impress upon me the superior morality of exchange, he said that the same pig that would get you five buffalo and five horses in marriage exchange would be worth the price of only one middling buffalo and a small horse if sold. In saying this, he was drawing on market values as a way to measure the heavy weight of the obligations imposed by proper exchange. (The claims of rational calculation cut both ways: the early Christian converts sought to discredit ancestral ritual for its wastefulness. As one proselytizer put it, the offerings "just use up chickens." Of course, by some understandings of sacrifice (e.g., Bataille 1988), that would be precisely the point.)

As elsewhere (Akin and Robbins 1999; Thomas 1991), such comparisons are part of the background against which exchange has long been carried out. They simultaneously represent formal exchange as morally elevated by virtue of its supposed exemption from the calculation and rationality of other transactions and as a difficult burden. The point of explicit comparisons between formal exchange and alternative regimes of value is usually to affirm the status and compulsory nature of "real custom" as a discrete domain of social action. Sumbanese who make this case may draw on the discourse of contemporary Indonesian national culture in order to contrast "real" and "politicized" custom. In reference to exchange, "politicized custom" denotes competition, calculation, and profit and confines these to the disorderly present. These are familiar themes in talk about capitalist relations (Bloch and Parry 1989; Hugh-Jones 1990). But I argue that they also manifest pervasive concerns about the potential detachment of objects from persons and thus about the boundaries of the subject and the ability to locate value in persons or in things.

One aspect of the comparison of exchange and its alternatives is an implicit claim about rank. Sumbanese frequently assert that market thinking is purely a recent development and (depending on the case they want to make) usually a deplorable one – that in the past, no one calculated the value of what they gave you. This is a part of the logic in talk about custom, which explicitly portrays both donors and recipients as acting not out of their own desires or willfulness but only because they are obligated by ancestral requirements. But, people say, now we live in a selfish era whose slogan is "as long as I (get mine)" *(mali nyuwa)*, an era in which people are driven by personal desires.[6] As a way of expressing and historicizing the difference between formal exchange and its alternatives, people sometimes talk about the economic irrationality of the past. For example, one man told me that people used to trade like quantities for like, regardless of the actual substance: one sack of rice would go for one much more expensive sack of coffee. He was suggesting that the folly of his forebears consisted in being taken in by the very materiality of things. They were unable to perform the symbolic operations embodied in money: exchange value in those days was inseparable from the things themselves (see Keane 1996). Part of the subtext here is that the ancestors' apparent folly is inseparable from their aristocratic disdain for haggling and calculation. The hierarchical implications of alternative regimes of value become explicit when some people observe that Sumbanese who engage in trade are usually of low rank, because, they claim, such people are naturally more clever at calculation. This is supposedly because they are unconstrained by the sense of honor, having little to lose.

Calculation implies a play on the relations between the object as a sign of something other than itself and as a source of value in itself, which is most evident at the boundaries between formal exchange and other kinds of transactions. The boundaries among kinds of transactions are permeable – if not conceptually then practically, for there are few exchange valuables that do not have some value in other contexts. For example, a horse received from Christian affines in marriage exchange can be sacrificed to "pagan" spirits or sold for cash. This permeability is both a resource and a threat, insofar as a skillful or simply powerful player can take advantage of it, but the existence of alternative schemes of value bears the increasingly real potential to undermine the status claims that are sustained by exchange, a threat at once logical, political, and economic.

Despite the traditionalist tendency to claim for the past the high values of ceremonial exchange and to confine less exalted alternatives to the present, all sorts of transactions have been available to Sumbanese, even before the introduction of markets and shops (compare Barnes and Barnes 1989). The most formal kinds of exchange impose the greatest constraints on potential interpretations. They do so in part by drawing on the social authority of elders to limit the kinds of objects involved and the functions they may serve, and by emphasizing the properties by which they serve as representations (signs) and representatives (of agents).

Material objects contrast in several ways to the familiar Saussurean model of the arbitrary sign, which signifies only by virtue of a social convention, and whose phenomenal qualities (such as color or sound) are relevant only as marks of difference from other signs. Objects cannot be produced at will but must be sought from somewhere – they are subject to scarcity and are relatively easy to quantify. Moreover, even exchange valuables bear physical properties in excess of their purely conventional attributes, which contributes to their potential for diversion into use or to alternative kinds of transactions. Finally, they have durability. Nonconsumables persist over time, across multiple transactions, passing through the hands of many people and taking on a range of possible functions. The materiality of objects is a condition of possibility for their movement across social and semiotic domains. For example, the charisma of the Thai monk, once it has been objectified in the form of an amulet, is able to enter into the mundane realm of distinctly nonascetic purposes, such as good luck in the lottery (Tambiah 1984:336). The multiple uses, mobility, and durability of objects allows them to extend the agency of their producers and original transactors. But the same properties entail the possibility that they will become detached from their transactors altogether.

One effect of the high formality of exchange events in Sumba is to help separate signification and utility, emphasizing the semiotic character of objects that also bear use and market values. Such formality is part of the ongoing effort it takes to keep gift and commodity distinct. It is reinforced by the ritual speech, which states explicitly that neither party desires the objects in question, but rather, each is compelled only by ancestral mandate. Acknowledging the possibility of misconstrual, people often say that marriage is not like going to the market. They insist that they seek objects not for the value or utility of the things themselves, as in purchase and sale, but as expressions of each party's value for the other. Underlining this insistence is the great attention they pay to the proper forms of transaction.

The insistent attentiveness given to tokens in offerings implies a latent alternative. People are aware of the possibility that the gift will become detached from the giver and the intent. Objects require the reflexive capacity of language if they are to serve as fully efficacious media of social relations. One pig, horse, or piece of cloth is pretty much like another of its kind: it is words that specify what kind of action is being performed, from whom the prestations come, to whom they are directed, and what kind of act they perform. As a result, the capacity of objects to serve semiotically as representations and economically as representatives of persons is unstable and requires constant effort to sustain. Recall the quarrel between Ama Koda and Ubu Tara over the torn banner. The conventional meanings that material signs convey are vulnerable to the accidents to which objects are prone. The insult is made possible in part by the way in which material signs expose semantics to objective circumstances, and in part by the way in which people's manipulation of objects constantly works to transform natural qualities into signs of persons. If a cloth really represents its transactors, how could a torn cloth fail to do so as well? If objects are parts of larger projects, then could the giving of a torn cloth be only an isolated incident?

Mauss's great insight was to challenge the Cartesian obviousness of the distinction between possessing subject and possessed object. But the very workings of exchange depend on the fact that the identity between the two is not seamless: their relation has a double character. For objects to be able to exteriorize and represent their possessors in circulation, they also must in some way be detachable from them. Like Mauss, Simmel saw possessions as extensions of the self: when a person acquires property, "the sphere of the individual extends beyond its original limits, and extends into another self which, however, is

still 'his'" (1990 [1907]:323). This capacity for "extension" exists only to the degree that the object is *not* fully identified with the subject. It follows from this double character of objects that the subject must engage actively with them, that possession is a form of action (Simmel 1990 [1907]:302–5).

The relentless work – and the formality, the politics, the talk, the attentiveness – demanded by Sumbanese exchange seems to be one way of responding to these circumstances. Exteriorization and objectification (see Miller 1987) work hand in hand with detachability and mobility. Therein lies both the promise and the risk posed by things, as vehicles of representation. Sent into circulation, they can extend the identity and agency of their transactors. By the same token, they may become lost to those whom they would serve, or be diverted into other regimes of value. The capacity of the prestation to stand for its owner over the course of its travels is not an inherent property of objects themselves but requires human efforts and interactions to sustain.

Enter Money

Since Mauss, systems of exchange like those in Sumba have come to stand for everything that the economic character of "modernity" supposedly lacks. The contrast is not restricted to Western scholars; for people in Sumba, as in many other places, the concept of "modernity" and the experience of the state that attends it are inseparable from the ubiquity of money. Sumbanese often experience modernity, strive for its promises, and resist its threats by way of their dealings with money. Like many of those who have written about modernity, Sumbanese often treat money as something with its own dynamic, something that, once introduced into society, has a rapid corrosive effect. The classic expression of this perspective remains that given by Marx (1976 [1867]:229), for whom money was a radical leveler, extinguishing all distinctions, because it never revealed which commodities had been transformed into it: "Circulation becomes the great social retort into which everything is thrown, to come out again as the money crystal." In this context, Sumbanese practices and discourses surrounding formal exchange are not simply remnants from an archaic past but are developing into strenuous and self-conscious responses to the world of money and markets. This response is both discursive, a vision of an alternative regime of value, and practical, an effort to control the circulation of value's objectified forms (compare Akin and Robbins 1999; Comaroff and Comaroff 1990; Ferguson 1985; Hutchinson 1996).

Here I focus on three aspects of money: its relations to abstraction, alienation, and production. I look at money not primarily as a component of an established system of commodity circulation but rather as currency in its phenomenal and imagined forms, ways in which it appears even in the absence of a full-fledged monetary economy. I am interested, that is, in local experiences of and ideas about money. For whatever the larger political economic context, as Guyer (1995:6) points out, money "is a vastly important reality to vast numbers of people, all but an infinitesimal number of whom have absolutely no idea of the official doctrines under which it 'makes sense,' but whose own constructions...are a necessary component of that 'sense' as it works out in practice." People, that is, cannot *not* have ideas about why and how money is valuable. Both money's fluidity and its limits – including the extent to which people trust it – are functions of those ideas.

Sumba is a useful place from which to look at money, because, being a relatively recent arrival and still scarce, money is far less taken for granted there than in more thoroughly monetized places. Until the twentieth century, the few coins that made it to Sumba were either treated like other inalienable valuables or melted down as raw materials for ornaments.[7] It was not until the 1920s and 1930s, with Dutch encouragement, that regular markets appeared, but trade was still carried out largely by barter (Versluys 1941:463–64). In Anakalang, the first petty traders, none of them Sumbanese, seem to have set up more permanent kiosks in the 1930s (Riekerk 1934). Beginning in 1911, the colonial government imposed a head tax, to be paid in cash (Couvreur 1914). But by the end of Dutch rule, just before the Japanese occupation, one study found that money had made little impact on

local society, being used largely as a unit of value for things of small worth (Versluys 1941:481).

Under the Indonesian state, monetization of Sumba lagged behind the rest of the nation, and large-scale government expenditure, the most important source of cash there, began only in the 1970s (Corner 1989:184; Iskandar and Djoeroemana 1994:67).[8] In the 1980s and 1990s, most Sumbanese still lacked a regular cash income. Everyday subsistence and most ceremonial needs were largely met by local production, barter, and other forms of exchange. Cash was required primarily for taxes, school fees, church offerings, and purchase of items such as medicine, kerosene, cooking oil, salt, sugar, coffee, tobacco, shirts, sandals, dishware, and bus fares. Only in the most recent decade or so have the most ambitious and well-heeled families begun to send children off the island for higher education, in the hope that they will land positions in the civil service. Funds for this are usually raised piecemeal by pooling the resources of many kinfolk – usually along links built through past ceremonial exchanges. In the 1990s, off-island schooling constituted perhaps the single greatest incentive for Sumbanese to sell cattle.

Money thus plays a limited and highly marked role on Sumba. Although the Indonesian rupiah is trusted, or at least was until the crisis of 1997 (in contrast to money in highly inflationary economies or weak states), in Sumba it does not flow freely or pervasively. Money's purchasing power is highly constrained; labor, land, and cattle, for instance, are more easily and legitimately acquired through kinship, patronage, or exchange.[9] Many people obtain money only for specific purposes (Vel 1994:70) such as paying taxes or school fees, and thus money runs through very tight circuits, without entering into investment or credit (compare Guyer 1995:9). When one person comes into some money, others are likely to make their claims on it; this is why some civil servants try to get themselves posted to parts of the island far from their kin. For those few people who have bank accounts, the main reason is to hide their money from others. As a result, money in Sumba does not always fully possess the properties of fluidity, impersonality, or abstraction, and, like exchange valuables, it often retains some indexical links to its sources and owners.[10]

The Value of Renunciation

Recall the use of money as a token in marriage exchange, in lieu of a gold ornament. This context suggests that gold and money have more in common than simply their properties. Both take their value in part from constraints on their materiality – the concrete particularity that for Marx defined the use-value of objects is played down in favor of semiotic abstraction. This is one reason money is so often compared to the quintessential arbitrary sign: "Like money, language manifests itself in material form, but in the former as in the latter the manifestation is external to the nature of the means and does not really matter" (Coulmas 1992:10). This negative property of money was described by Simmel as the result of a process of elimination or suppression: "It appears that even the most useful object must *renounce* its usefulness in order to function as money" (1990 [1907]:152). Only in this way can objects serve to symbolize simple quantities of value (yet the very uniformity that sustains money's abstractness has historically depended on the uniform, divisible, and durable properties of the materials out of which it is manufactured [Crump 1981:4]).

But this renunciation is incapable of fully abolishing its alternatives: even money, for example, to the extent that it retains a material form, may take on new functions. Coins may become jewelry or bullion – as Marx put it, "For a coin, the road from the mint is also the path to the melting pot" (1976 [1867]:222). Not only that, the very absence of one possibility is a critical component of the meaning of what remains: in Simmel's words, "the value that money has, and that allows it to perform its function, may be determined by those other possible uses which have to be forgone…. The perceived value of the developed function is constituted by … the exclusion of all other functions" (1990 [1907]:155).

So both gold and money, when placed in the dish, take their value from a similar basic structure of deferred value: everyone knows that the object in the dish is convertible to other forms. The Rp 100 could, of course, become money again. Gold and cloth, too, can be diverted from exchange. Indeed, their persistence as valuables can be seen as a continual refusal to allow them to return to their original state. As I argued earlier, it takes the work of ritualization to

maintain the boundary between the semiotics of exchange valuables and the alternative meanings and uses that things might possess in coexisting regimes of value.

Anakalangese descriptions of their world before "modernity" stress the absence of abstraction and a fetishistic clinging to the materiality of things. Anakalangese accounts of the naiveté of their forebears, however, contain an important subtext. People in the past ignored differences of quality because of their nobility. They eschewed such calculations because they refused to give in to their desires. Whereas for Marx the concrete particularities of things were important as the source of their use-values (1976 [1867]:230), the apparent empiricism that Sumbanese ascribe to exchange is a mark of people's relative *independence* from use-value. To follow ancestral rules is a demonstrative refusal to calculate utility, which can be understood only as a function of need or desire. Desire is something that separates one simultaneously from one's own best self (a loss of self-control) and from others (by attacking the moral bonds of community), and thus it threatens one's claims to high rank. By stressing the conventionalized semiotics of objects, formal exchange displays the players' imperviousness to the appeal of utility or their own wants.

The abstractness and fluidity that are supposed to characterize money, by contrast, appear to place desire in the foreground. Unlike inalienable valuables, money realizes its value neither in transaction as a social performance nor simply in being held, but only in that which it obtains in a future expenditure. To the extent that money is abstract and its uses unspecified – that is, as it is free both of particular qualities in itself and of the constraints of ancestral rules – any particular expenditure represents a choice among possible options. Therefore it seems to express, above all, the wishes of the person who spends it. And to legitimate those wishes is to challenge the principles by which people are valued and particular relations of domination sustained.

Alienation

The multiple uses, mobility, and durability of exchange goods allow them to extend the agency of their producers and original transactors.

But the same properties entail the possibility that they will become detached from their transactors altogether. This brings me to the second property of money, its relation to alienation. In most accounts of modernity, money is preeminently the instrument of alienation. It circulates promiscuously, without respecting persons or things. Ethnographic literature often describes it as dissolving the moral obligations that bind individuals into communities. Against this view of the multiply alienated conditions of modern life, Mauss saw the model of the gift as an attractive alternative.

Yet even Sumbanese exchange is never too far from the possibility of loss and alienation, both in practice and in fantasy. In practice, the capacity of objects to circulate threatens to become total detachment, a possibility that formal procedures and elaborate ritual speech work constantly to prevent. On the other hand, divergence from exchange can be an appealing fantasy, for even those who hold the greatest stakes in the play of exchange may chafe against the constraints it imposes on them, complaining, for instance, of the relatives who show up asking for help the moment one comes into a windfall. The alternative, a source of wealth free from social obligation, remains attractive. This, along with the risk that wealth will become detached from its possessor, is elaborated in a rich discourse about *yora*, the spirits of the wild who can become demonic patronesses of selected individuals. *Yora* have several features in common with those presented by market, money, and government development projects. The *yora* is a source of antisocial wealth that cannot reproduce itself, lead to social ties, or be transmitted to a person's children. It is also associated with illicit unions between men and women, thus exemplifying unrestrained desire. *Yora* represent the conjunction of wealth from beyond society with the threat of loss. It makes sense that such wealth is ephemeral, since it often manifests individual willfulness. The *yora*, like the government development project, is distinguished by the inexplicable entry of money from no comprehensible or stable source. The fact that this wealth is ultimately sterile parallels its lack of grounding in social interaction. Those who are considered most likely to deal with *yora* are either young, unmarried, adventurous men or, more rarely,

men so rich and powerful that they can hope to enter into such dealings with impunity.

The links between the idea of *yora* and the problems of modernity are especially evident in the following story, well known throughout Anakalang. The version I pass on here was told to me by Umbu Dewa Damaràka, a ritual specialist.

Ubu Nyali Malar was given a chicken by a yora. That chicken laid an egg which crowed from the inside. Once hatched from the egg, that rooster crowed continuously. As it grew, it kept on crowing. This crowing carried all the way to Java. Java over there heard that rooster crow. Now a man came from Java to Sumba wanting to buy that rooster. He wanted to buy it with money, but Ubu Nyali didn't want to sell it. He said, "Better than that, give me that gold ring on your finger." The man from Java really wanted that rooster, so in the end he gave up the ring. Now he had the rooster, which he brought home to Java. So that's why now the president is in Java. That ring is in Sumba. It had child after child, until they put it in the granary. The granary filled up with gold. Then Ubu Nyali's slave, Mùda, ran off with the ring. The ring kept having children. He put it in a granary, it filled up the granary; put it in another, filled that too. Finally put it in a cave, but that too filled. It's all gold in that cave. So now that's why in Java, it becomes the president, and in Sumba, we're rich in gold. So it's like that rooster: we hear that president wherever we are in Indonesia, otherwise, why is the president always from Java?

The fate of Ubu Nyali's gold displays both the promise and the hazards of antisocial sources of wealth. Reproducing on its own, it contains the possibility of autonomy and riches beyond the demands and politics of social interaction. Nonetheless it remains detachable from persons and thus vulnerable to loss. Once lost, it becomes the property of foreigners. This certainly accords with Sumbanese experience both historically and in everyday life in the 1990s. Sumbanese are reluctant to introduce money into dealings with clan fellows and affines, which are structured by formal exchange and informal debts, dependencies, and mutual assistance. In practice, most money is directly received from and paid back to non-Sumbanese, either the state or ethnically "foreign" traders (Vel 1994:68–69).

Even after Ubu Nyali's gold becomes a stolen good, it is wealth that reproduces itself independent of human agency. This foreign gold is unlike normal gold valuables, which, either as inalienable ancestral possessions held by clans or as tokens that circulate in ceremonial exchanges, are intimately linked to the social identity of their transactors. In contrast, this gold carries on regardless of proper ownership. As value uprooted from ancestry, it is alienable. As value that requires no reciprocity, it is self-contained.

Finally, the loss of the rooster forms an image of the colonial relations between Sumba and both Dutch and Indonesian rule. The rooster is a conventional Sumbanese image of masculine bravado, aggressiveness, and fame. With the rooster, Sumba surrenders power and self-esteem for wealth. Moreover, by Sumbanese standards, the very act of barter by which it is given away entails a suggestion of loss. Although barter in some form or other has long existed in Sumba, it is usually considered to be unworthy of proud people, since, unlike formal exchange, which is supposed to be dictated by ancestral mandates, it is visibly driven by personal, even bodily, needs or desires. It establishes no further relations, in contrast to the multigenerational ties of debt and ritualized obligations that are fostered by exchange. The result of Ubu Nyali's barter makes clear that local claims to wealth and authority now operate against a background of something that has been lost: the political control represented by the president will always be elsewhere, though his voice can be heard everywhere. Gold, self-reproducing and circulating without limit, enters as political autonomy departs.

Production

Yora represent not only antisocial wealth but also its uncanny sources. This brings me to the final feature of money, its peculiar relation to its own materiality as a product. Money seems to many Sumbanese to have sources not only distant in space but also at a remove from the labor and agency of humans. In 1912, a Dutch official recounted the following conversation:

A puzzle which our host would gladly have solved was why the "taoe djawa" (= foreign men, Europeans) came to have much money. He was asked what he thought himself. He said that in the foreign land three trees must grow, one which bears as fruit gold pieces (English pounds of which men on Sumba see much), another of silver (rijksdollars), and the third copper coins (2 ½ cent pieces). At a certain time, as soon as there is a need, the king or kings order a harvesting. Guilders and smaller silver money are nothing other than unripe rijksdollars, cents still undeveloped "gobangs" (2 ½ cent pieces). (Witkamp 1912:486; parentheses in the original)

Juxtaposed to the widespread interest in *yora*, this familiar story suggests that when people think about money, they think of uncanny origins that require no more labor than the plucking of fruit from a tree, a form of production requiring the minimal intervention of human agency. (This recalls Marx's satirical remark that those who fetishize capital assume it is "a property of money to generate value and yield interest, much as it is an attribute of pear trees to bear pears" [1967 (1894):392].)

But Sumbanese gold valuables also have uncanny and distant origins. People insist that "it wasn't *we* who made them" but rather the ancestors. Part of the value of gold, as I have suggested, derives from the fact that it is not produced locally, that it ultimately comes from nowhere in Sumbanese experience. Put another way, its value lies not in local control over the means of production but perhaps in the promise of an escape from the demands of production altogether, and in its capacity to supplement physical labor. In this respect money is like ancestral valuables to the extent that it represents the state as an absent origin. In a place like Sumba, money is one of the most pervasive everyday forms the state takes in most people's everyday experience. Money is legal tender because it is stamped with an inscription bearing the state's political authorization. The authority represented by money portrays itself on money's material substance: every coin or banknote carries some emblem of the state. It wears, in Marx's image, a "national uniform" (1976 [1867]:222; see Foster 1998; Hart 1986; Shell 1982). As a medium of alienation and an uncanny source of value beyond bodily labor, money is not always radically different from exchange valuables. Moreover, money is not necessarily even anti-social: like exchange, the use of money still requires trust (something made explicit, if socio-politically obscure, by the slogan "In God We Trust" on American currency). It is just that the object of that trust has shifted from exchange partners and the ancestors to the state. To that extent, money does not so much abolish society as it institutes a different kind of society. So wherein is the distinctive difference that makes for modernity?

The State of Desire

In contrasting the casualness of market transactions with the formality of exchange, Sumbanese express historical imagination in terminology that reflects contemporary national culture, but they also manifest more specific concerns about the potential detachment of objects from persons, concerns that are implicated in exchange itself. If the risk of loss has *always* haunted the ceremonies of exchange, then this risk has become inseparable from the dominant regime of value. In the modern world, the authority of ancestral mandates meets an alternative authority in the pervasive presence of money.

Money, of course, is issued and backed up by the state, but, as I have noted, Sumbanese often associate its appearance in their lives with the state in other ways as well. As in many subsistence economies, the need for money was initially produced by the state's demands for taxes. Today most money in Sumba ultimately derives from the state, either in salaries or from businesses whose income is due largely to government projects. More generally, the state has established itself as the chief promoter of capitalism and endeavored to do away with what it sees as the more irrational forms of local expenditure. Economic rationality has been the constant topic of government exhortations and directives. Finally, most states that issue money try to extirpate any competition with or restraints on the free movement of its currency – something that tends to meet resistance even in highly developed capitalist economies (Zelizer 1994).

What the state hopes money will come to mean may not fully determine how people understand it locally. Sumbanese understand money's threats and promises in terms of the virtues and frustrations of exchange. The ways Sumbanese handle and speak about money seem to be responses to a dilemma posed by the state project of development. This dilemma is that, to the extent that money's origin lies in the state, it seems to be the state that guarantees the play of individual desires. Sumbanese describe the present era with the Indonesian expression "free era" (I. *masa merdeka*). In national discourse, the "free era" usually refers to liberation from colonial rule. But Sumbanese often use the expression in speaking of the abolition of slavery and the resulting challenge to rank distinctions and the exchange system that helps support them. Depending on the speaker's social position, or the extent to which he or she is at home in the world of rank and exchange, this is not an unambiguous good. The "free era" means that Sumbanese live in a time dominated by "economic thinking," a time of rampant individualism. The ostentatious suppression of use-value and economic profit that is displayed in the forms of ceremonial exchange is supposed to manifest the participants' nobility and public display of honor. Like other familiar critics of money, many Sumbanese describe the present day as a time of antisocial stinginess, a ruthless calculating of costs and benefits unconcerned with honor or rank. The two aspects are combined in the assertion that now people get ahead by virtue of "brains" – by which people ambiguously refer to both the economic rationality that development should produce and the cleverness associated with devious former slaves, people who, it would seem, have no honor to lose or ancestry to sully.

Of course not everyone has the same stakes in the regimes of value and the social hierarchies that money seems to threaten. Former slaves and unmarried women, for instance, may benefit from the promise of freedom both from rank and from material dependence as reproduced in exchange. But even those who celebrate modernity and economic rationality must have some account of the respective values of exchange and money. This is where Christian discourses of interiority and materialism often come into play, discourses that help give expression to shifting distinctions between subject and object (Keane 1996, 1998). Talk about "materialism" seems to incite people to a certain dematerialization in their understandings of the world. This is evident, for instance, in the effort to treat material goods as merely symbolic. For example, Sumbanese Christians must often face the question, what is the value that is transacted in marriage exchange? Few are willing to reject exchange out of hand, yet they also cannot accept the world of ancestor spirits and rituals at its foundations. Nor are they entirely comfortable with the apparent identification of persons with things that marriage transactions seem to produce. One solution, which I often heard, is to explain marriage exchange in functionalist terms, as fostering social solidarity. Another explanation is provided in this newspaper essay by a Catholic high-school student (Witin 1997).[11]

> Bridewealth in the form of traditional valuables like ivory, gold, buffalo, is at base only a symbol (*simbol*) in order to raise a woman's value and dignity. Demands for bridewealth show that a woman must be honored, valued.... Bridewealth is only a symbol of the woman's self-respect.... It is proper that bridewealth be retained, on the basis of its essence as a symbol of woman's own value and dignity – and not tend toward business (*bisnis*) or "trade" in daughters. On the part of women themselves, the most important problem is as far as possible that she be able to guard her self-respect so that the demand for bridewealth which is to be discussed by her family doesn't put her to shame. One should value oneself by way of one's patterns of thinking, attitude, and praiseworthy behavior, before one is valued by others, especially the groom, by way of the bridewealth that will be discussed.

The author makes explicit something that is implicit in the social functionalist explanation as well – and that underlies many Western views, such as Polanyi's (1944:46), that assume a clear opposition between material and social values. Both accounts dematerialize exchange and treat material objects as merely signs of some immaterial value, whether that be social solidarity or self-worth. (The self-conscious modernity of this is evident in Witin's unusual appropriation of the English words "symbol"

and "business.") This dematerialization underwrites the world of money, in which the subject is supposed to be clearly separated from its objects and in which value can be fully abstracted from concrete practices and material forms. Yet in seeking to account for the value those objects hold for the subject, one is left with little but the willful and desiring subject itself.

Put in other words, the writer is describing how the modern subject must be the source of its own value. And there the subject encounters the promise and the threat of money, in the freedom that money seems to accord this subject. Money clearly proclaims a difficulty that other valuables also encounter, albeit more unobtrusively. It is hard to confine material objects to conventionalized symbolism and to constrain their motion to prescribed pathways. As the emblem of this social and semiotic fluidity, money bears a further implication. To the extent that it is abstract, it permits a potentially unconstrained range of choices among purchasable items. In coming to stand for those choices, for Sumbanese, it seems to point toward the desires that any given choice expresses.

But who stands behind money and its promises? Here the subject encounters the state, which, by authorizing money, seems to sponsor that willfulness. Yet certainly neither the state nor (for different reasons) most Sumbanese are willing to accept the consequences. The state's efforts to control willfulness and desire (as stimulated, for example, by elections or advertising) lie beyond the scope of this chapter. Sumbanese efforts are visible in the continued power of exchange in the 1990s. Recall again the use of money as an exchange valuable in the offering dish. To use money as a material token, emphasizing the underdetermined character of its materiality, is to deny the authorizing stamp on its face. To treat money as if it were gold is to deny the ultimate power of the issuing authority in favor of the semiotic value asserted by ancestral mandate. The use of the coin does not replace material use-values with symbolic values but rather asserts the primacy of one authorizing origin for signs over another. It asserts the superior power of exchange to suspend use-values in favor of claims to higher value. In the process, it seeks to deny the abstractness of money. Yet it does not necessarily do so by reasserting the materiality of meaningful objects. Rather, those objects are turned into signs of invisible values such as "social solidarity," "tradition," or "self-worth."

The tension between the two uses of money represents a tension between two sites of agency. In exchange, persons manipulate tokens of value in deference to the displaced agents of ancestral mandate. In commodity circulation, the state seems, unwittingly, to authorize the cleverness

of desiring selves and the endless possibilities that money affords them. The individual who can buy and sell with impunity bears the warrant of the state, which itself remains invisible except in its effects, in the form of "use"-less, circulating signs of itself. This rather implausible vision is, in turn, an effect of that aspect of the ideology of money that celebrates abstraction, denies social mediation, and imagines that signification offers the subject an escape from materiality.

Notes

1   At the boundaries of the properly salable in the United States we find things such as prostitution, fees charged for adopted children, the sale of body parts, and bribery. These are notable precisely for the discomfort, anxiety, or outrage they provoke. See Pietz (1997) for an insightful discussion of this problem as it was faced by the writers of liability laws for human deaths caused by machines in the early industrial age.

2   Albert O. Hirschman (1977) argued that the emergence of capitalism in the West was legitimated in part by the development of a conceptual distinction between the passions and the interests. The former were seen as destructive and irrational, the latter as subject to rational calculation. But like people in many other places in which other values are being challenged by the market, most Sumbanese find calculation and rationality themselves to be antithetical to social virtue.

3   Terms in the national language, Indonesian, are identified with an "I"; all other terms are in Anakalangese or cognate languages of Sumba.

4   Sumba, an island about the size of Jamaica, is dry, is sparsely populated, lies off the main trade routes across the archipelago, and itself offered little but sandalwood and slaves to attract traders. The Dutch took fairly light-handed control of the island in the first decades of the twentieth century. The postwar Indonesian state was too impoverished and distracted to attend to Sumba until the oil boom of the 1970s. What export and local trade now exists (in buffalo, horses, and local cloth) is controlled by ethnic Chinese, Arabs, and other off-islanders. Commerce in land is very recent and still highly constricted by the persistence of collective ownership and the general view that certain kinds of land should not be alienated. In the 1990s, most Sumbanese still depended on subsistence farming. Although there is considerable variation in systems of exchange and rank across the island, for pur-

poses of this chapter, these can be overlooked, and I will speak of "Sumba" rather than "Anakalang" (Keane 1997), Kodi (Hoskins 1993), Weyewa (Kuipers 1990), and so forth.

5   I do not discuss the iconographic and other metaphoric features of exchange valuables here. Having done so in detail elsewhere (Keane 1997), I argue that these are insufficient in most cases to make sense of either the practices surrounding objects or the values imputed to them.

6   The association of modernity with desire and desire with money is quite explicit in many parts of Indonesia. By the 1920s, the Minangkabau of Sumatra already contrasted the cooperative character they ascribed to traditional villages with the "desirousness" (I. *hawa nafsu*) that money induces in those who "eat wages" (I. *makan gaji*) (Kahn 1993:126). In Java, where conventionally it is women who handle money, people see both money and marketplace as stimulants to both sexual and material desire (Brenner 1995; Siegel 1986; for a Western analogy, see Hirschman 1977:9).

7   Even in parts of Indonesia where money and market production appeared much earlier than in Sumba, coins were often treated as valuables. In nineteenth-century highland Sumatra, for instance, pepper growers demanded payment only in Spanish "Carolus" dollars, whose high silver content was preferred for melting down into jewelry. Only coins with the full bust portrait of the king were acceptable for marriage payments, apparently for iconographic reasons (Steedly 1993:90–91).

8   In the 1990s, the most important sources of money for Sumbanese were government salaries paid to minor officials and schoolteachers. Some young unmarried men and women earned wages by working for non-Sumbanese merchants, but these were not sufficient to support a family. Other people engaged in petty trade in weekly markets, and a very small number sold everyday goods from tiny

kiosks. Reports from across Sumba gave the percentage of the population with access to cash at between 2 and 10 percent (Hoskins 1993:188; Vel 1994:47). Given Sumbanese resistance to outmigration (Iskandar and Djoeroemana 1994:57), remittance income was apparendy negligiable.

9 The anxieties raised by selling animals for money can be seen in the ritual precautions they provoke. If one sells a buffalo or pig that one has raised oneself, one should first pluck the eyebrows and place them under the household water pot so one retains a "cool corral." Otherwise the money will disappear or the remaining animals will not thrive.

10 When Sumbanese, at least in some districts, obtain a sum of money, it is not likely to enter into an existing stock of capital. Therefore, the sum obtained in a particular transaction tends to retain its identity. It is also likely to be earmarked for a specific expenditure. This has allowed Vel (1994:70–71) to rank spheres of money expenditure in parallel with spheres of exchange: one would sell a buffalo, for instance, only in order to raise money for something as important as university fees, but not for children's clothing. As Zelizer (1994) showed, earmarking is an extremely widespread means of constraining the abstraction and fluidity of money even in full-fledged market economies.

11 The author happens to be from the neighboring island of Flores, but the ideas she expresses are being propagated in churches and Christian schools across Sumba as well.

References

Akin, David, and Joel Robbins, eds., 1999 Money and Modernity: State and Local Currencies in Melanesia. Pittsburgh: University of Pittsburgh Press.

Appadurai, Arjun, 1986 Introduction: Commodities and the Politics of Value. In The Social Life of Things: Commodities in Cultural Perspective. Arjun Appadurai, ed. Pp. 3–63. Cambridge: Cambridge University Press.

Barnes, R. H., and R. Barnes, 1989 Barter and Money in an Indonesian Village Economy. Man (N.S.) 24:399–418.

Bataille, Georges 1988 The Accursed Share: An Essay on General Economy. Vol. 1, Consumption. Robert Hurley, trans. New York: Zone Books.

Bloch, Maurice, and Jonathan Parry, 1989 Introduction: Money and the Morality of Exchange. In Money and the Morality of Exchange. Jonathan Parry and Maurice Bloch, eds. Pp. 1–32. Cambridge: Cambridge University Press.

Brenner, Suzanne A., 1995 Why Women Rule the Roost: Rethinking Javanese Ideologies of Gender and Self-Control. In Bewitching Women, Pious Men: Gender and Body Politics in Southeast Asia. Aihwa Ong and Michael G. Peletz, eds. Pp. 19–50. Berkeley: University of California Press.

Carrier, James, 1995 Gifts and Commodities: Exchange and Western Capitalism since 1700. London: Routledge.

Cheal, David 1988 The Gift Economy. London: Routledge.

Comaroff, John, and Jean Comaroff, 1990 Goodly Beasts, Beastly Goods: Cattle and Commodities in a South African Context. American Ethnologist 17:195–216.

Corner, Lorraine, 1989 East and West Nusa Tenggara: Isolation and Poverty. In Unity and Diversity: Regional Economic Development in Indonesia since 1970. Hal Hill, ed. Pp. 178–206. Singapore: Oxford University Press.

Coulmas, Florian, 1992 Language and Economy. Oxford: Basil Blackwell.

Couvreur, A. J. L., 1914 Jaarverslag Afdeeling Soemba 1914 tevens memorie van Overgave. Typescript. Algemeen Rijksarchief, The Hague.

Crump, Thomas, 1981 The Phenomenon of Money. London: Routledge and Kegan Paul.

Ferguson, James, 1985 The Bovine Mystique: Power, Property, and Livestock in Rural Lesotho. Man (N.S.) 20:647–674.

Foster, Robert, 1998 Your Money, Our Money, The Government's Money: Finance and Fetishism in Melanesia. In Border Fetishisms: Material Objects in Unstable Places. Patricia Spyer, ed. Pp. 60–90. New York: Routledge.

Grice, H. P., 1957 Meaning. Philosophical Review 64:377–88.

Guyer, Jane I., 1995 Introduction: The Currency Interface and Its Dynamics. In Money Matters: Instability, Values, and Social Payments in the Modern History of West Africa. Jane I. Guyer, ed. Pp. 1–33. Portsmouth, NH: Heinemann.

Hart, K., 1986 Heads or Tails: Two Sides of the Coin. Man (N.S.) 21:637–656.

Hirschman, Albert O. 1977 The Passions and the Interests: Political Arguments for Capitalism before Its Triumph. Princeton, NJ: Princeton University Press.

Hoskins, Janet, 1993 The Play of Time: Kodi Perspectives on Calendars, History, and Exchange. Berkeley: University of California Press.

Hugh-Jones, Stephen, 1990 Yesterday's Luxuries, Tomorrow's Necessities: Business and Barter in Northwest Amazonia. *In* Barter, Exchange, and Value: An Anthropological Approach. Caroline Humphrey and Stephen Hugh-Jones, eds. Pp. 42–74. Cambridge: Cambridge University Press.

Hutchinson, Sharon E., 1996 Nuer Dilemmas: Coping with Money, War, and the State. Berkeley: University of California Press.

Iskandar, Margaharta, and Siliwoloe Djoeroemana, 1994 Kemiskinan dan Pembangunan: Kasus Kabupaten Sumba Barat. *In* Kemiskinan dan Pembangunan di Propinsi Nusa Tenggara Timur. Jakarta: Yayasan Obor Indonesia.

Kahn, Joel S., 1993 Constituting the Minangkabau: Peasants, Culture, and Modernity in Colonial Indonesia. Oxford: Berg.

Kant, Immanuel, 1956 [1785] Foundations of the Metaphysics of Morals. *In* Foundations of the Metaphysics of Morals and What is Enlightenment? Lewis White Beck, trans. Indianapolis: Bobbs-Merrill.

Keane, Webb, 1996 Materialism, Missionaries, and Modern Subjects in Colonial Indonesia. *In* Conversion to Modernities: The Globalization of Christianity. Peter van der Veer, ed. Pp. 137–170. New York: Routledge.

Keane, Webb, 1997 Signs of Recognition: Powers and Hazards of Representation in an Indonesian Society. Berkeley: University of California Press.

Keane, Webb, 1998 Calvin in the Tropics: Objects and Subjects at the Religious Frontier. *In* Border Fetishisms: Material Objects in Unstable Places. Patricia Spyer, ed. Pp. 13–34. New York: Routledge.

Latour, Bruno, 1993 We Have Never Been Modern. Catherine Porter, trans. Cambridge, Mass.: Harvard University Press.

Marx, Karl, 1967 [1894] Capital: A Critique of Political Economy. Vol. 3: The Process of Capitalist Production as a Whole. New York: International.

Marx, Karl, 1976 [1867] Capital: A Critique of Political Economy. Vol. 1: A Critical Analysis of Capitalist Production. Ben Fowkes, trans. New York: Penguin.

Mauss, Marcel, 1990 [1925] The Gift: The Form and Reason for Exchange in Archaic Societies. W. D. Halls, trans. New York: Norton.

Miller, Daniel, 1987 Material Culture and Mass Consumption. Oxford: Basil Blackwell.

Miller, Daniel, 1994 Modernity, an Ethnographic Approach: Dualism and Mass Consumption in Trinidad. Oxford: Berg.

[Miller, Daniel, 2001 Alienable Gifts and Inalienable Commodities. *In* The Empire of Things: Regimes of Value and Material Culture. Fred Myers, ed. Pp. 91–118. Santa Fe: School of American Research Press.]

Onvlee, L., 1973 De betekenis van vee en veebezit. *In* Cultuur als Antwoord. Verhandelingen van het Koninklijk Instituut voor Taal-, Land- en Volkenkunde 66. The Hague: Martinus Nijhoff.

Pietz, William, 1997 Death of the Deodand: Accursed Objects and the Money Value of Human Life. Res 31:97–108.

Polanyi, Karl, 1944 The Great Transformation: The Political and Economic Origins of Our Time. Boston: Beacon Press.

Riekerk, G. H. M., 1934 Grenregling Anakalang, Oemboe Ratoe Nggai. Typescript, no. H975 (2). Koninklijk Instituut voor Taal-, Land- en Volkenkunde, Leiden, Netherlands.

Shell, Marc, 1982 Money, Language, and Thought: Literary and Philosophical Economies from the Medieval to the Modern Era. Baltimore: Johns Hopkins University Press.

Siegel, James T., 1986 Solo in the New Order: Language and Hierarchy in an Indonesian City. Princeton: Princeton University Press.

Simmel, Georg, 1990 [1907] The Philosophy of Money. Tom Bottomore and David Frisby, trans. London: Routledge.

Steedly, Mary Margaret, 1993 Hanging without a Rope: Narrative Experience in Colonial and Postcolonial Karoland. Princeton, NJ: Princeton University Press.

Tambiah, Stanley J., 1984 The Buddhist Saints of the Forest and the Cult of the Amulets. Cambridge: Cambridge University Press.

Thomas, Nicholas, 1991 Entangled Objects: Exchange, Material Culture, and Colonialism in the Pacific. Cambridge, Mass.: Harvard University Press.

Vel, Jacqueline, 1994 The Uma-Economy: Indigenous Economics and Development Work in Lawonda, Sumba (Eastern Indonesia). Thesis, Agricultural University, Wageningen, Netherlands.

Versluys, J. I. N., 1941 Aanteekeningen omtrent gelden goederenverkeer in West-Soemba. Koloniale Studiën 25:433–483.

Weiner, Annette B., 1992 Inalienable Possessions: The Paradox of Keeping-While-Giving. Berkeley: University of California Press.

Witin, Fransiska, 1997 Belis dan Harga Diri Wanita. Dian, 1 August, p. 6.

Witkamp, H., 1912 Een Verkenningstocht over het Eiland Soemba. Tijdschrift van het Koninklijk Nederlandsch Aardrijkskundig Genootschap 30:484–505.

Zelizer, Viviana A., 1994 The Social Meaning of Money. New York: Basic Books.

Remembering while Forgetting
Depositional Practices and
Social Memory at Chaco

Barbara J. Mills

A central paradox of the study of social memory is that memories are made during a process that includes forgetting. The relationship of memory to its counterpart has been part of the Western philosophical tradition for millennia. As Adrian Forty (1999:16) points out, the ancient Greeks located the springs of Lethe (Forgetfulness) and Mnemosyne (Memory) next to each other so that one could drink from the first before the other. European philosophers from Proust to Heidegger have also recognized that "remembering is only possible on the basis of forgetting" (Forty 1999:12–13).

Susanne Küchler (1999, 2002) has persuasively shown that the interdependence of remembering and forgetting is not limited to Western society. Rather than a literal forgetting, her work deals with the practices that surround the memorialization of people, events, and places through the sacrifice of objects. Her work on *malanggan*, objects made for funerals that encapsulate social histories and are intentionally destroyed representations of the deceased, shows how memorialization occurs as part of rituals of sacrifice. Like Zuni War Gods, or Ahayu:da, malanggan are forms

Barbara Mills, "Remembering while Forgetting: Depositional Practices and Social Memory at Chaco," pp. 81–108 from Barbara J. Mills and William Walker (eds) *Memory Work: Archaeologies of Material Practices* (Santa Fe: School of American Research Press, 2008). Reprinted with permission of SAR Press.

that construct memories through their production and destruction, not through their preservation.

In this chapter I argue that forgetting is an important part of memory work, one that has been frequently used in the past. I outline several different ways in which forgetting contributes to memory work and then illustrate a few of these examples through a recontextualization of archaeological collections from Chaco Canyon, New Mexico.

Forgetting as Part of Memory Work

The practices that surround forgetting as part of memory work are widely divergent. One form of forgetting is through secrecy. Items may be secreted out of sight as part of different ritual practices such as the dedication and commemoration of structures. Social memories are constructed during the interactions between ritual participants and objects with particular qualities and origins as part of the commemorative performance. Although out of sight, sometimes permanently, the location of those objects may be remembered for long periods of time. Similarly, objects that are either deposited or destroyed during mortuary rituals, like malanggan, represent another form of forgetting while, at the same time, they are part of the creation of chains or networks of people through things in the present (Chapman 2000).

Other forms of forgetting transform and even deconstruct memories. For example, memory may be transformed through the imperfect reproduction or recollection of past practices, including what are called copying errors in the transmission literature (Mandler and Johnson 1977; Shennan 2002). Many of these so-called errors are now seen as potentially beneficial in the literature on cognitive psychology, because there are few who would choose to become like the character in Jorge Luis Borges's tale, "Funes the Memorious," who remembers every detail but cannot abstract or generalize (Gigerenzer 2005).

A more active deconstruction of memory may occur through the ritual retirement of objects no longer useful but too powerful and inalienable to be discarded like other objects (Mills 2004). Another manifestation of the active deconstruction of memory is the deconsecration of ritual spaces through burning, selective removal of architectural elements, and/or filling (Creel and Anyon 2003; Walker et al. 2000). In these cases, objects or spaces are filled, destroyed, or otherwise removed from circulation and use because they are considered too powerful to be preserved in situ once their use in specific contexts has ended.

The transformation of memory may have a more overt political or nationalistic motive. Memories may be transformed or reshaped as part of the invention of tradition (Hobsbawm 1983), in which new practices are replaced by others but are claimed to have great time depth to legitimize extant political forces. The transformation may be even more politically charged, as in the deconstruction of buildings, monuments, and groups of people, intended to end the reproduction of specific social memories and replace them with others, as seen with the Bamiyan Buddhas – examples of "past mastering" or "negative heritage" (Meskell 2002). Ironically, these examples of deconstruction often have results opposite to those intended. Through destruction, including the entombment of buildings, the defacing of statues and other monuments, and genocide, those who have attempted to erase the past make their marks more materially visible (especially archaeologically) and socially contested.

These examples illustrate how forgetting is an important part of memory work, along with recalling, reshaping, inventing, and coordinating.

Memory is a social practice (Halbwachs 1992), and it links people and things through time in the process of shaping history. Part of the study of memory must also look at how those links are transformed, broken, and replaced. To complement ways in which social memories have been constructed and reproduced through practice (Bourdieu 1977; Bourdieu and Wacquant 1992), I look at how these memories are reshaped through a variety of depositional practices that incorporate the placement of objects in spaces that were sequestered or sealed as well as those that were intentionally destroyed and/or removed from circulation for at least a portion of their biographies (Meskell 2004).

At Chaco Canyon the deposition of items took place in architectural spaces of different sizes and forms. These differences in the spatiality of memory work are one way that archaeologists can approach memory and materiality as they were constructed within different social networks. Different social groups inscribed their memories within these spaces as part of the performance of commemorative ceremonies, the storage of objects used in ritual performances, and the marking of spaces used for multiple interments. Chacoans also erased earlier structures, retired objects and spaces used in collective ceremonies, and removed objects from earlier deposits as part of the active transformation of social memories that illustrates how the multiple trajectories of forgetting are active parts of memory work.

Depositional Practices and Social Memory at Chaco

Discussions of the materiality of depositional practices are far less common than one might think, given that Chaco is considered a "rituality" (Yoffee 2001) or a place of "high devotional expression" (Renfrew 2001). Although several recent studies have called artifact deposits at Chaco "votive," "ritual," or "sacred" in some way, most of them do not talk about variation in the practices that produced these deposits. There has been little comparison of the overall content of different deposits in terms of who deposited them, in what contexts they were deposited, and how these practices were part of the materiality of Chacoan life. Analysts have specialized in particular material classes, and as a result we have excellent overviews of turquoise (Mathien 2001, 2003), wooden objects (Vivian et al. 1978), architecture (Lekson 2007; Van Dyke 2004), ceramics (Crown and Wills 2003; Toll 2001), chipped stone (Cameron 2001), and animal burials (Hill 2000; Kovacik 1998) but very little on different materials with shared contexts of deposition beyond the density of their spatial locations (Neitzel 2003). Yet at sites within the canyon, people inscribed their memories within different architectural spaces as part of the performance of commemorative ceremonies, the storage of objects used in ritual performances, and the marking of spaces used for multiple interments. Chacoans also erased earlier structures, retired objects and spaces used in collective rituals, and removed objects from earlier deposits as part of the active transformation of social memories in ways that illustrate how forgetting is an active part of memory work. The strategies and practices (de Certeau 1984) of memory work resulted in the deposition of large amounts of objects in architectural spaces at Chaco, especially at Chaco Canyon sites dating to the tenth through twelfth centuries. The peak use of Chaco by Ancestral Puebloans was shorter than a century, from 1030 to 1100 CE, sometimes called the Classic Bonito phase. Many of the practices seen in Chaco can be traced to contemporary Pueblo society – evidence of the efficacy of Puebloan ways of remembering while forgetting (for example, Kuwanwisiwma 2004).

Previous research on social memory at Chaco includes Kovacik's (1998) analysis of faunal materials and Van Dyke's (2003, 2004) interpretations of great house architecture. Kovacik compared the distribution of fauna in small site structures dating from 500 to 1180 CE, finding that there were continuities in the deposition of carnivores and bird of prey elements within architectural spaces. He argued that this was evidence of social memory over a long period of time, maintained through the renewal of buildings and the deposition of elements within floors and in the rafters. His analysis is important in that it also demonstrates that these practices bridged significant breaks in the occupational sequence of individual sites leading to the interpretation of continuities over

multiple generations. Van Dyke's work (2003, 2004) underscores how memory, meaning, and large-scale architectural constructions at Chaco were interrelated through the visible impact of buildings, their symmetry, and their locations on the landscape. Her work on the Late Bonito phase (1100–1140 CE), particularly, shows how great houses were transformed at the end of the canyon's occupation, and she argues that this is evidence of social memory at work. My analysis complements the above works on memory at Chaco. Like Kovacik, I focus on the depositional contexts and continuities of materials and their contexts, but I expand his approach to include a variety of materials. Like Van Dyke, I focus largely on great houses, but I look at how memory work inheres within architecture rather than how the buildings were perceived within the Chaco social and physical landscape.

Architectural contexts at Chaco include rectangular pueblo rooms, which are masonry rooms usually constructed in room blocks, and round rooms that were at least partially if not fully used for ritual practices (Lekson 1986, 2007). The latter include room block kivas, tower kivas, courtyard kivas, and great kivas. Room block kivas, round rooms that were constructed inside of pueblo rooms, are generally smaller than courtyard kivas. Tower kivas are room block kivas that were elevated through multi-story construction. Courtyard kivas, larger round rooms within plaza spaces rather than room blocks, are intermediate in size between round rooms and great kivas. Great kivas, the largest circular structures, may be in the plazas of pueblos or isolated, such as the great kiva at Casa Rinconada. They are identified on the basis of a specific constellation of floor features and their larger size; they are greater than 10 m and usually closer to 15–20 m in diameter. Courtyard kivas and great kivas were semi-subterranean, room block kivas were both subterranean and first-floor kivas, and tower kivas were elevated to two or three stories. Each of these spaces was constructed by members of different social groups who participated in different social fields. Each of the spaces also structured subsequent social interactions in terms of who and how many people could participate and view ceremonial events.

In looking at deposits at Chaco, I focus on offerings in several spatial contexts. The first are offerings in ritual structures of different sizes. I use these to look at how social memories are made through the deposition of objects in architectural features that mark different moments in the use of these spaces, especially their construction and termination. These are examples of memory work through the practice of secrecy in which things that are hidden acquire value through the acts of gathering them together and placing them in architectural cavities (Hendon 2000: Piot 1993). Secrecy is an important principle among contemporary Pueblos (Brandt 1980) and has clear historical continuities with Ancestral Pueblo material practices. I then look at deposits in Chaco great house rooms that are examples of the ritual retirements of objects used in Pueblo ceremonialism. These may be associated with the retirements of specific rooms or spaces within the pueblo but are more certainly the retirements of ceremonial objects, including altar pieces, staffs of office, and other objects that were intentionally buried and/or left behind, many of which were left in their ritual storerooms. I use these objects to illustrate how, through the active process of forgetting, they were used in the memory work of those who lived in and visited Chacoan great houses.

Dedicating and Dressing the House

The use of ornaments as offerings has a long history in the Southwest, but nowhere does it appear in the concentration and quantities present at Chaco during the Classic Bonito phase. Dedicatory and termination offerings in great kivas, court kivas, and room block kivas are overwhelmingly composed of finished ornaments and the debris from ornament working. Each of these ritual structures was used by different social networks of varying sizes and based on different principles of recruitment and degrees of inclusiveness. The deposits found in these structures illuminate the ways in which ornaments played a central role in commemorative performances and the construction of social memories on different scales at Chaco.

Although they occur over a broad area of the Southwest in various forms, circular roofed great kivas are closely associated with Bonito Phase architecture at Chaco Canyon (Vivian and Reiter

1960). They have a long history, dating at least to the Basketmaker III period (ca. 550–750 CE) at Chaco. Most are found at Chaco great houses, but a few are isolated from pueblos, such as the Casa Rinconada and Kin Nahasbas great kivas in Chaco Canyon (Figure 18.1).

Based on their size, great kivas were used by large segments of the community and may even have been places shared by members of multiple communities (Adler and Wilshusen 1990). Although they were not big enough to house the entire Chaco Canyon population, much less all of Chaco's nearby outliers, it is clear that they drew people from multiple social networks. As the largest structures constructed for ritual use, they are one of the most prominent forms of monumental architecture in the canyon. Their regular features, which became highly standardized during the Classic period (Van Dyke 2003), suggest a liturgical order to the performance of ritual. Because of their high visibility, their construction and reconstruction were points at which social memories were created for large segments of the community, whether or not they actually participated in the building events themselves.

The Chetro Ketl Great Kiva II, lying under Great Kiva I, provides one of the best examples of the materiality of dedicatory and termination/closing rituals at Chaco. This great kiva was constructed at the southern side of the Chetro Ketl plaza, where many of the late constructed rooms at the pueblo had been built (Lekson 1983:253). Ten niches were built into the lower wall of the structure, each measuring 15 × 25 cm and 45 cm deep (Hewett 1936; Vivian and Reiter 1960; Figure 18.2). The niches were planned by the builders based on their regular layout and incorporation within the initial construction of the wall. The entire construction of the wall appears to have been done over a relatively short period with no visible breaks in the circular wall. During the mid-1000s CE, Great Kiva II was reconstructed and expanded into Great Kiva I.

The niches in the Chetro Ketl Great Kiva II have stone lintels, like fenestration but with no opening to the exterior, which suggest they were intended to remain open for part of the use of the structure. However, when excavated by archaeologists, they were filled with masonry that was in a slightly different style from that of

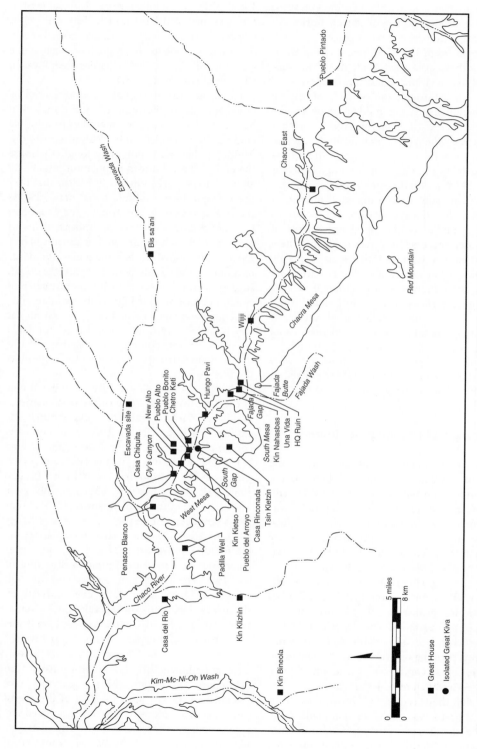

Figure 18.1 Chaco Canyon sites. (Chaco archives.)

Figure 18.2 Great Kiva II (below Great Kiva I), Chetro Ketl. (After Hewett 1936, courtesy of the University of New Mexico Press.)

the surrounding stonework. Before being closed with masonry, each niche was also filled with long strands of black and white beads and multiple turquoise pendants (Hewett 1936:90–92; Figure 18.3). The niches were sealed so that the stones were flush with the rest of the wall, and once the wall was plastered, the niches would have been completely out of sight – a symbolic forgetting that illustrates the importance of secreting away as a practice in Ancestral Pueblo memory work.

There are striking repetitions in these offerings. First, not only are they of the same materials, but the color, sizes, and forms of the beads are also highly regular. This repetition suggests a standardization or even habitualization in the acquisition and production of these objects in addition to their deposition. Second, the strands of beads are quite long; when restrung, they range from 2 to 5 m in length and include from 983 to 2,265 beads each (Table 18.1). Thus, it is likely that these strands were not made by a single person but represent the products of multiple hands within the network that participated

in the termination of the lower kiva and the construction and dedication of the overlying kiva in the mid-1000s.

The secreting or hiding of these necklaces was preceded by the construction of a series of social memories surrounding the life history of the objects, including their procurement, production, and finally their placement in niches. The closure of such a large building, its intentional filling, and then the construction of yet another great kiva in the same place would have been a memorable series of events for the community. Thus, even if the community members had not all witnessed the closure of the niches, because of the scale of the offerings and the amount of labor required to produce the objects, partially fill the lower structure, and construct an even more massive building and roof on top, the effort would have been one in which memory and materiality closely intersected.

Several other forms of offerings in the Chetro Ketl Great Kiva II were found in basal deposits lying below the pits for the massive upright roofing posts, in rectangular masonry floor vaults,

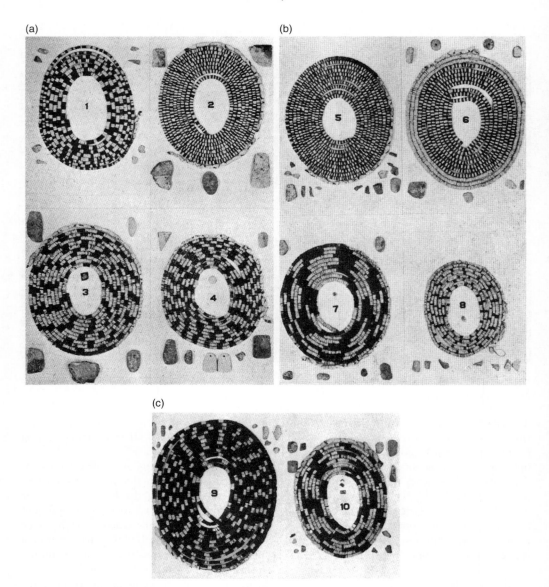

Figure 18.3 Contents of wall niches, Great Kiva II. (After Hewett 1936, courtesy of the University of New Mexico Press.)

and on the benches between remodeling episodes. Large stone disks were made for each of the four large postholes, also called seating pits (Vivian and Reiter 1960: Figure 15). One of these, the northeast seating pit, contained four large disks, which had been placed over four alternating layers of lignite and adobe (Vivian and Reiter 1960:Figure 16). One-third meter below the lower adobe layer, excavation of

a test pit revealed the remains of a leather bag containing turquoise. When the northwest seating pit was excavated, a similar offering was found.

The Chetro Ketl GK I/II east vault had a clean layer of sand above a flagstone floor. In this fill were deposited "numerous potsherds, turquoise fragments, 'anthracite' and calcite beads (singly), two pendants, and fragments of malachite-painted wood. Similar material

Table 18.1 Contents of niches in Chetro Ketl Great Kiva II.

Niche	Number of beads	Length of strand of beads (m)	Number of pieces of turquoise
1	1,724	3.8	8
2	1,538	3.2	5
3	1,797	4.3	5
4	1,940	3.6	9
5	1,770	3.7	13
6	1,745	4.	8
7	1,831	3.8	7
8	983	2.1	1
9	2,265	5.2	10
10	1,861	3.	16
Total	17,454	36.7	100

Modified from Hewett (1936:89).

was recorded from the west vault" (Vivian and Reiter 1960:36). These deposits were probably associated with GK II because of their depth and location near the base. When Chetro Ketl GK II was remodeled to construct Great Kiva I, 97 to 112 cm of fill were deposited, along with the raising of the walls of the floor features, construction of a new exterior wall and bench, and the removal and reconstruction of the massive roof. In the fill were found other deposits, including three coiled strands of beads, one uncoiled strand, and several other ornaments (Vivian and Reiter 1960:37). The bench also contained an offering of beads, although descriptions are not detailed. Like the offerings in the niches, these offerings served as both a closing of the earlier structure and dedication of the new one.

The objects placed in other great kivas appear to be primarily dedicatory offerings, and most are ornaments (Table 18.2). These include strings of shell, jet, and turquoise beads and pendants. Clearly, the construction of these buildings was one of the most important events to mark by depositing objects in parts of the building prior to their completion. As at Chetro Ketl the strands of beads were ways of ensuring that these structures would be ritually dressed throughout their lives.

Although items related to ornaments are more common, another pattern is repeated at smaller scales in other ritual structures. Kiva Q, a great kiva at Pueblo Bonito, contained a remarkably diverse assemblage of bone, slate, turquoise, and shell beads along with unworked minerals, fossils, pebbles, expertly crafted bifaces and flakes, sandstone jar covers, bone and ground stone tools, fragments of ceramic vessels, a fragment of a cloud blower, concretions, seeds, insect parts, and parts of the paws of a mountain lion, a bear, and a dog (Figure 18.4; Table 18.3). These items represent the widespread networks that Chaco residents were engaged in, with goods coming from as far as the Gulf of California (for example, olivella beads). Some of these objects were highly valued for their rarity and acquisition in distant places, as Helms (1993) has discussed in the context of Central America. But these objects and others may also have been selected for their physical or aesthetic properties (Hosler 1994; Pollard 2001; Pollard and Ruggles 2001) – as in the conundrum of a rock that looks like a shell in the case of the many fossils. Unlike the distant objects in Central America, these were not used within a prestige-goods economy, but in ritual consumption. They may be better viewed as a "gathering together" (Bradley 1990, 1998) of objects from multiple sources, marking what Pollard (2008) calls a geography of social relationships or what Chapman (2000) calls enchainment, linking people together through time.

Court kivas overlap in size with great kivas but do not have the same floor features. They do show a similar range of materials in dedicatory offerings (Tables 18.4 and 18.5), such as the one from Kiva D at Pueblo Bonito, where a white

Table 18.2 Ritual Deposits in Chacoan great kivas.

Site	Kiva	Feature/Context	Objects	Offering Type	Date (CE)	Reference
Chetro Ketl	Great Kiva II	Northeast seating pit	Leather bag with pulverized turquoise.	Dedicatory	Mid–late 1000s	Vivian and Reiter (1960)
Chetro Ketl	Great Kiva II	Northwest seating pit	Turquoise.	Dedicatory	Mid–late 1000s	Vivian and Reiter (1960)
Chetro Ketl	Great Kiva II	East vault	Sherds, turquoise fragments, jet and calcite beads, 2 pendants, and malachite-painted wood.	Dedicatory	Mid–late 1000s	Vivian and Reiter (1960)
Chetro Ketl	Great Kiva II	Niches 1–10	Jet and white shell bead necklaces, turquoise pendants.	Termination/renewal	Late 1000s	Hewett (1936); Vivian and Reiter (1960)
Chetro Ketl	Great Kiva I/II	Floor fill	4 strands of beads and other ornaments.	Termination/renewal	Late 1000s	Vivian and Reiter (1960)
Chetro Ketl	Great Kiva I	Bench	Beads.	Dedicatory	Late 1000s	Vivian and Reiter (1960)
Casa Rinconada	Great Kiva	Upper floor (south of firebox)	Sherds, 2 copper bells, 328 white (shell?) beads (probably strung).	Termination/renewal	Late 1000s	Vivian and Reiter (1960:24)
Casa Rinconada	Great Kiva	Subfloor trench (south of firebox)	Copper bell fragment.	Termination/renewal	Late 1000s	Vivian and Reiter (1960:24)
Aztec	Great Kiva	Western vault, pit	Worked turquoise (several), shell beads.	Dedicatory	1000s?	Morris (1921:133)
Aztec	Great Kiva	Western vault, pit	Shaped copper sphere, turquoise fragments.	Dedicatory	1000s?	Morris (1921:133)
Aztec	Great Kiva	Between floor resurfacings	Broken pottery vessels, turquoise from mosaic, strand of olivella shell beads with turquoise pendant.	Termination/renewal	1100s?	Morris (1921:126)
Pueblo Bonito	Kiva Q	Wall niche	Plant remains, shell ornaments and debris, fauna (black bear, dog, and mountain lion), chert and obsidian projectile points, chert knives, ground stone, worked bone (see Table 18.3 for detailed list).	Dedicatory	1040s (probable, earliest, possibly as late as the 1100–1150s (Windes 2003)	Judd (1954:323, Plate 90)

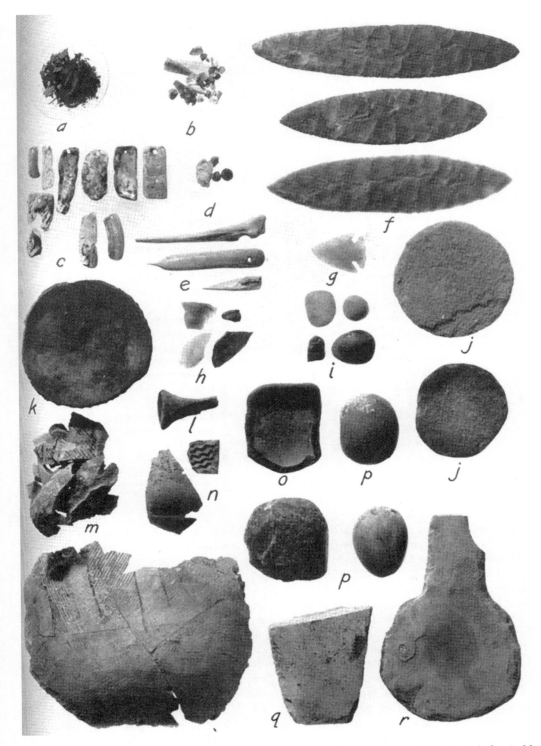

Figure 18.4 Contents of niche in Kiva Q, a great kiva at Pueblo Bonito (see Table 18.3). (After Judd 1954:Plate 90.)

Table 18.3   Objects from Kiva Q (great kiva) at Pueblo Bonito.

Number of objects	Description	Illustration (Judd 1954: Plate 90)	Number of objects	Description	Illustration (Judd 1954: Plate 90)
Numerous shreds	Juniper and rush	a	1	Sandstone worked concretion	a
3	Abalone shell scraps	a	3	Quartzite hammers	p
1	Twined fabric, possible sandal	a	1	Sandstone muller fragment	q
1	Chert arrowhead	b	1	Sandstone palette	r
2	Obsidian arrowheads	b	1	Turquoise pendant, fragment	–
1	Claystone tessera	b	2	Turquoise discoidal beads	–
4	Turquoise tesserae	b	6	Turquoise bead blanks	–
9	Abalone shell pendants	c	7	Turquoise worked fragments	–
1	Quartz crystal	d	6	Turquoise matrix fragments	–
3	Azurite pellers	d	2	Bone discoidal beads	–
3	Bone awls	e	1	State discoidal bead	–
2	Chert (brown) blades	f	2	Olivellas, spires removed	–
1	Quartzite blade	f	1	Squash seed	–
1	Chert knife blade	g	4	Wild grape seeds (*Vitis anizonica*)	–
2	Chert spalls (flakes)	e	1	Unidentified seed fragment	–
2	Quartzite spalls (flakes)	e	1	Spine of western locust (*Robinia neomexicana*)	–
2	Quartz pebbles	i	2	Mountain lion (*Felis concolor*) claws	–
2	Quartzite pebbles	i	178	Black bear (*Euarctos americanus*) digital bones and claws	–
2	Sandstone jar covers	j	28	Dog (*Canis familiaris*) digital bones and claws	–
1	Base of indented corrugated cooking jar	k			
1	Bowl of cloud blower	l			
1	Fragments of 2 black-on-white jars with hachure	m			
1	Fragment of 1 black-on-white bowl	n			

Laevicandium shell was nested inside a masonry box below the floor. Within the shell were worked and unworked shell and minerals, including four species of colorful shells along with azurite, turquoise, and hematite minerals. All were either finished ornaments or materials used in ornament production and from different areas of the Southwest. The selection of these materials is striking, as is the citation to all six of the colors used in historically documented Pueblo directional symbolism (for example, Cushing 1883; see also DeBoer 2005). The use of color as a geographical mnemonic linked people to places – an example of the spatiality of memory work.

Even the smallest ceremonial rooms had dedicatory offerings, but surprisingly, these room block kivas showed remarkable redundancy in their contents. Roofs in the Chacoan style room block kivas were built criblike, beginning on low pilasters. Each of the pilasters contained a short log in which offerings were placed before the roof was constructed. A small hollow was made in the pilaster logs, the offerings were placed inside, and then the receptacles were capped with sandstone or wood lids. The offerings, such as those from Room 161 at Pueblo Bonito, are primarily beads, production debris, or unworked turquoise. Each pilaster contained only a handful's worth, but they are highly similar from pilaster to pilaster and from room block kiva to room block kiva throughout the site.

Table 18.4 Ritual deposits in great kivas.

Site	Kiva	Feature	Objects	Offering type	Date (CE)	Reference
Chetro Ketl	Court kiva	Floor pit (sipapu?)	Unworked and worked turquoise, two white quartz pebbles, two brachiopods, several small bird bones, limestone polishing stone.	Dedicatory	Early 1000s	Vivian and Reiter (1960)
Pueblo Bonito	Kiva D	Masonry box in floor	Glycymeris bracelets and fragments, hematite cylinder, olivella shell, unworked and worked azurite, figure-8 shell beads, Haliotis shell, worked turquoise, worked spondylus shell.	Dedicatory	1000s?	Judd (1954:Plate 89); Judd (1964:184–186)
Pueblo Bonito	Kiva R	Pilasters and/or ceiling (2 deposits)	Bill of redhead duck (Nyroca americana); bone, shell, turquoise beads; broken pendants; shell bracelets (Glycymeris sp.).	Dedicatory	1000s?	Judd (1964:191–193); Judd (1954:322)
Pueblo Bonito	Kiva R	Wall niche	Shell trumpet (Murex sp.), black-on-white bowl.	Ritual retirement	1000s?	Judd (1964:192); Judd (1954:Plate 82, a and b)
Pueblo del Arroyo	Kiva C	Pilasters 1–8	Olivella shell beads, turquoise beads and pendants unworked turquoise and shell (see Table 18.4 for a more complete list).	Dedicatory	Mid–late 1000s (tree-ring date of 1067 + ×)	Judd (1959:60–62)
Pueblo del Arroyo	Kiva C	Fill above bench	Prairie falcon (Falco mexicanus).	Termination?	Late 1000s	Judd (1959:63–64)

Table 18.5 Contents of offerings in pilasters, Kiva C (great kiva), Pueblo del Arroyo.

Pilaster No.	Number of objects	Description
1	30	*Olivella* shell beads and fragments
	27	Oblong and figure-8 beads and fragments
	9	Discoidal beads and fragments
	10	Turquoise fragments
	1	Sandstone cover
2	12	Oblong and figure-8 beads
	2	Discoidal beads
	1	Turquoise pendant fragment
3	20	*Olivella* beads and fragments
	11	Oblong and figure-8 beads
	7	Abalone shell fragments
	3	Turquoise fragments
	1	Rib fragment, deer or antelope
4	2	Discoidal beads
	1	Turquoise pendant
5	18	*Olivella* beads and fragments
	26	Oblong and figure-8 beads and fragments
	6	Discoidal beads
	5	Abalone shell fragments
	2	Turquoise pendants and fragment
	3	Turquoise fragments
	1	"Cylindrical shell (?) bead, cross-drilled"
6	16	*Olivella* beads and fragments
	32	Oblong and figure-8 beads and fragments
	9	Discoidal beads and fragments
	1	Chama bead fragment
	2	Shell fragments
	4	Turquoise pendants and fragments
	6	Turquoise fragments
7	13	*Olivella* beads and fragments
	13	Oblong and figure-8 beads and fragments
	1	Discoidal bead
	1	Turquoise pendant fragment
8	5	*Olivella* beads
	70	Oblong and figure-8 beads and fragments
	7	Discoidal beads and fragments
	1	Oval shell bead fragment
	8	Discoidal turquoise beads
	7	Discoidal turquoise bead fragments
	4	Turquoise pendants and fragments
	1	Turquoise tessara
	47	Turquoise chips

Froin Judd (1959:61–62).

These different architectural spaces at Chaco are where performances were shared and "different forms of community" (Joyce and Hendon 2000) were made into historical facts. Each of the structures was used by a different network of people. The relationship of spatial proxemics to ceremonial performance might initially suggest that depositional practices in smaller spaces should be more variable than those that took place in larger spaces, but the Chaco room block kivas go against this expectation. Like the redundancy in the features themselves, the offerings are highly standardized from structure to structure. They illustrate a shared habitus – and a shared understanding and performance of what should be done in the construction of social memories associated with the dedication and termination of ritual structures that crosscut their membership. Like the practice of constructing the highly redundant forms of the structures themselves, including their internal arrangement of features, the practice of placing objects within architectural cavities was formalized through repeated construction and dedication. The frequency of building and rebuilding of these structures made these ritual practices canonical, a process in which strategies channelized practices (de Certeau 1984).

Although small in numbers, the contents of the room block kiva dedicatory offerings are like shorthand references to the larger deposits found in the court kivas and great kivas. In the case of the room block kivas, the performance of placing materials in the pilasters was a citation to the construction and dedication of larger structures – as well as previous structures of the same kind – linking people to different sites of memory within the canyon. Those sites of memory were other structures within the same building, such as Pueblo Bonito, but also other round structures within the canyon and its outlying great house communities.

The linkages between ornaments in ceremonial structures are also citations to what was considered the proper way to adorn a body, animating the ritual structure. Many strands of beads are depicted as hanging on kiva walls in later Pueblo IV-period murals, such as at Pottery Mound's Kiva 2 (Hibben 1975:Figure 17), attesting to the long-lived importance of ornaments in Pueblo ceremonial life and their use in dressing ceremonial rooms. In contemporary Pueblo society, jewelry is worn by individuals, but especially large pieces adorn kachinas. Jewelry is also worn by houses in Pueblo society. At Zuni, when dedicating a new house at Shalako, it is important to cover the walls with textiles and to hang the house's interior with jewelry. This makes the house beautiful and gives the house its identity.

These practices, seen in contemporary Pueblo society, can be traced to the numerous offerings containing shell, turquoise, jet, and other ornaments in Chaco Canyon buildings. Collectively, they show the importance of certain structures and afford glimpses of the materiality of Chacoan ritual practice. Ceremonial houses were adorned and made ready for use by depositing or "forgetting" ornaments in caches that marked the dedication and renewal of structures. Like the New Guinea malanggan, strands of beads and other ornaments were "produced to be discarded" (Strathern 2001:259) in Chacoan kivas. However, unlike the malanggan, they were secreted away rather than destroyed.

The entire process from production through deposition involved the producers in the process of memory construction. This process began with the planning and conception of the deposits that would be included, and continued with the acquisition of materials, the working of the stone or shell, the carrying of the beads to places where they were deposited, and their placement in kiva features that were then sealed off from view. Because of their association with ritual production, unworked turquoise, shell, and other materials, and the debris of production, were treated as equals of the finished products – not merely leftover bits or pieces, but part of the materiality of ritual practice. Although the presence of production debris is often interpreted as evidence of where the production took place, when the debris is found in sealed spaces within structures, it is clear that these spaces were not exactly where the materials were transformed into finished products, but where highly valued objects were placed because they were considered to be as valuable or inalienable as the finished objects. Their close association with other incorporative activities of memory construction was part of their consubstantiality, conferring value through the linkages made as parts of rituals of dedication.

The Memorialization of People and Places

A second set of deposits at Chaco illustrates additional ways in which memory and materiality were linked through depositional practice. A significant number of artifacts recovered from Pueblo Bonito and Chetro Ketl were used in ceremonial contexts but intentionally placed in rooms and then left behind when the occupants moved out. Many of them are preserved because the rooms had been intentionally sealed, while others were preserved because of their placement deep within the buildings.

Some of these room assemblages also contained mortuary deposits, which, as Nancy Akins noted, occur in two major clusters within Pueblo Bonito (Akins 2003; Neitzel 2003a, 2003b). Because human remains were present in nearby rooms, many of these objects have been interpreted as mortuary deposits. However, these deposits represent a range of depositional practices, some of which include the memorialization of ancestors. Other deposits more clearly were the result of other kinds of practices, such as the ritual retirement of powerful objects, the termination of ritual societies, and perhaps even the termination of the buildings themselves.[1] To distinguish among these different pathways. I look at some of the most well-known of the "caches" at Pueblo Bonito and Chetro Ketl to point out different ways that certain people, social groups, and perhaps a larger collective of Chaco were memorialized through the discard of large numbers of inalienable objects during moments of forgetting.[2]

The closing off of spaces associated with the death of a ritual leader is not unknown in Pueblo societies historically or today. For example, there is a room in Zuni Pueblo that was sealed upon the death of a particularly prominent religious leader. He had used the room as his retreat – a place to go to prepare for his participation in different ceremonies. What is particularly interesting about these closed-off spaces is that many people remember where they are long after the room has been sealed. One room near the retreat, completely sealed, was recently reopened when extensive renovations were done in the village. The intact roof was dated to the late 1690s, almost immediately after the Pueblo Revolt ended in 1692. Although this example was relatively recent, there are other similar spaces that had been in the collective memory of residents of Zuni Pueblo from previous room closures. These examples show that room spaces

in early established parts of long-occupied pueblos are often the spaces that are considered to be most sacred, especially when associated with specific persons, and may resonate in the social memories of a pueblo's residents.

In addition to these rooms, historic and contemporary pueblos contain other rooms where inalienable items used in individual and corporate rituals are stored (Beaglehole 1937; Mills 2000). While individually owned items are usually buried with the deceased, collectively owned items are passed down from one generation to another through flexible kinship networks that ensure the perpetuation of the religious society. These networks are often retained within specific lineages, and thus certain ceremonial objects may be associated with particular houses over several generations. Senior male members of the house are responsible for their guardianship, but senior female members may ceremonially feed them. The participation of household members in different societies as well as the relative ranking of different societites reproduces household status. Those households responsible for the maintenance of key ceremonial objects accrue considerable prestige. In this sense, storage is a situated practice (Hendon 2000) that contributes to social memory within the confines of designated spaces.

In multistoried pueblo buildings, such as Zuni Pueblo, ceremonial storage rooms are typically less accessible and located in back of living and other domestic rooms. In part this is because of the way that pueblo architectural additions are constructed with new living rooms on the exterior of the room block, but also because it is important to limit access to these rooms. Visitors and even some members of the household cannot view these objects because they are considered too dangerous. Some objects are considered to be so powerful that they are stored in ceramic vessels in these rooms (Mills 2004). Altar pieces of different ritual sodalities, such as medicine societies, are also stored in these rooms and then reassembled in ceremonial rooms when in use. These objects are not discarded but restored and repainted when needed. They are not generally buried with individuals because they are not individually owned. In Pueblo society, these are among the best examples of inalienable possessions (Weiner 1992) because they cannot be bought or sold; they belong to the group and are inherited to ensure the continuity of the society. Again, it would be unusual for these items to enter the archaeological record at all.

Given the ways in which collectively owned inalienable possessions are passed down in historic and contemporary Pueblo society, it is therefore surprising to see such large numbers of these items at Chaco. The quantity of material that by anyone's criteria can be called ritual or inalienable objects at Chaco Canyon sites far exceeds that from any other area of the Southwest. Collectively owned ceremonial objects such as altar pieces are present, but rare, from most other archaeological contexts across the entire Ancestral Pueblo area (Mills 2004).

The most spectacular of those at Chaco is a cache of wooden ritual artifacts found in a second-story room at the back of Chetro Ketl (Vivian et al. 1978). They were serendipitously found much later than Hewett's School of American Research/University of New Mexico excavations at the site, and only because a large area of the pueblo was undercut by a flood in the mid-twentieth century and required stabilization. Covering the floor of one room were hundreds of fragments of painted wood. Many of them had been broken, but when pieced together they are primarily parts of altars, headdresses, and wooden staffs and wands.

Besides the Chetro Ketl cache, it is clear that Pueblo Bonito has more objects that appear to have been ritually retired than any other site in the canyon, if not the rest of the Southwest. In contrast to all other great houses, Pueblo Bonito seems even more unusual than it did when the original excavators, Neil Judd (1954, 1964) and George Pepper (1920), reported their findings.

Besides the cache of objects that appears to have been ritually retired in Room 93 at Chetro Ketl, many other examples from Pueblo Bonito suggest the retirement of collectively owned objects. Two of these rooms, Rooms 10 and 13, contained the remains of many objects that are not clearly associated with individuals, including objects used in ornament and tool production, altar pieces, and whole and fragmentary shell trumpets (Pepper 1920:54–57, 67–69). Altar pieces and shell trumpets suggest use by a group, rather than an individual, and the large number of objects apparently intentionally broken in Room 10 is particularly interesting. Rooms 10 and 13 are both in the earliest-constructed portion of Pueblo Bonito, which dates to the 890s CE (Windes 2003:Figure 3.4). However, both were apparently left open and used for at least another 300 years before the final residents left.

Room 32, also in the north-central portion of Pueblo Bonito, contained over 300 wooden staffs, a wooden "design" board, many personal ornaments, and whole vessels (Pepper 1920:129–163; Plog, 2003; Figure 18.5). Although wooden staffs of office have been interpreted as individually owned, they are usually present archaeologically only in small numbers, and all are from mortuary contexts, such as the Magician's Burial near Flagstaff (McGregor 1943). At least one burial is present in this room, associated with a cloth-covered cactus stalk that resembles a badge of office. The staffs, also considered to be badges of office in historic Pueblo society, were found in a different portion of the room, however, and their numbers are out of proportion with the single burial. One would expect one or a few staffs with an individual, like the Magician's Burial. Instead, the staffs seem to represent the collective insignia of office of many members of a ritual society – not just one. In addition, the painted wooden board is a probable altar piece and would be considered to be collectively owned according to historic Pueblo practices. The room in which these objects were left was constructed and used between 1150 and 1250. The last use would have been during the Late Bonito period (and even into the post-Bonito period), when very few rooms were still in use at Pueblo Bonito.

Room 32 is adjacent to Room 33, a room with multiple burials that contained more objects than any other room at Pueblo Bonito (Neitzel 2003a). Together with Rooms 53 and 56 they are considered to be the north burial cluster, containing 24–28 different individuals (Akins 2003:Table 8.1, Figure 8.1). The number of human remains and the large number of ritual items suggested to Akins that these were the burials of highly ranked individuals with ascribed statuses based on ritual positions within the Pueblo Bonito hierarchy. The close biological affinity of the remains suggested to her some degree of familial relatedness, one that was different from the biological grouping in the

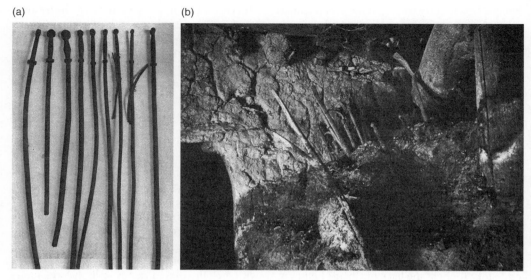

Figure 18.5 Wooden sticks from Room 32, Pueblo Bonito. (After Pepper 1920:Figures 52 and 53.)

west burial cluster. A recent reanalysis of the excavation notes by Plog and Heitman (2006) shows that there are both primary and secondary burials in Room 33. The ritual retirement of these items suggests the memorialization of these individuals and the place, and, as they argue, evidence of a "house society" (in the sense of Joyce and Gillespie 2000; see also Heitman and Plog 2005). The practice of placing objects in these rooms may have been a link to the founding families of Pueblo Bonito (such as discussed by Pauketat [2008] for the Southeast), whose remains were curated and redeposited in one of the oldest portions of the pueblo as part of the practice of ancestor veneration (see also Nielsen 2008).

The cache of cylinder jars from Room 28 at Pueblo Bonito more clearly falls into the category of ritual retirement unassociated with human remains (Figure 18.6). This room was constructed early in the building's history and has later tree-ring dates of 1071 and 1116 (http://www.chacoarchive.org/docs/dendrochronology.xls, accessed March 6, 2006). According to Windes (2003), the room remained in use until as late as 1150 to 1250 (and therefore into the post-Bonito period). In addition to the cylinder jars were sandstone jar covers, fragments of *Murex* shell trumpets, hammered copper, ceramic bowls and jars, ornaments, and many other objects (Pepper 1920:129–163). Of those vessels that were

painted, the decoration was in a style that has been dated to 1040 to 1125 CE (Toll 1990:285).

Crown and Wills (2003) observe that many of the cylinder jars were refurbished and compare these vessels to kivas during the Bonito phase. They interpret the intentional reslipping, repainting, and refiring of cylinder jars as symbolic of their use within rituals of renewal, similar to the way that ritual structures were renewed:

> By renewing these vessels through time, Chacoans maintained their continuity with the past while giving the vessels a new appearance. The hidden layers of designs probably added to the power of the latest design. Renewed by labor, imagination, slip, paint, and fuel, the vessels became repositories of collective memory and historical continuity between past and present. (Crown and Wills 2003:525)

Moreover, they draw on the idea that these pottery and kiva renewal rituals were ways in which identity was being maintained during a period of rapid change and population influx. These are examples of acts of forgetting through the painting over of ceramic surfaces and the rebuilding of structures that are closely associated with the production of ritual memories at different social scales.

Figure 18.6   Cache of cylinder jars in Room 28, Pueblo Bonito. (After Pepper 1920: Figure 43.)

As Toll (2001:63) has noted, the cylinder jars were made by many different producers and were probably brought to Chaco from different communities as representations of "membership in the community of communities" at Chaco during ritual pilgrimages. Unlike other caches of inalienable objects from Pueblo Bonito that were placed within interior rooms, Room 28 is adjacent to the western plaza. When these jars were taken out of the room, they would have been highly visible, and the room's proximity to the plaza and the number of jars suggest that their use was in this open space rather than in the room itself. Although other ritual caches at the site marked the termination of particular societies, memorialized the death of prominent leaders in lineages that maintained important ritual societies, or were part of a depositional practice associated with the maintenance of the "house," the use and deposition of the cylinder jars was a unique expression of Ancestral Pueblo materiality. The use of these vessels continued until the early twelfth-century reorganization, perhaps terminated by Pueblo Bonito's last ceremonial community, consisting of a dwindling population in the late 1100s.

Remembering while Forgetting in the Pueblo World

Objects found at Chaco had entangled histories (Thomas 1991) – associated with specific persons and their ritual officers, and used in multiple social fields. The deposition of large numbers of objects used in ritualizing practices, whether they were left in architectural cavities within ritual structures, interred with ritual leaders, or left behind in ritual storage rooms, was ceremonial discard on a grand order. These objects were placed out of sight during practices of dedication, renewal, memorialization, ritual retirement, and structure termination. Dedicatory and renewal practices were mostly in round rooms, used by ceremonial groups of different sizes. Objects used in ceremonial practices were stored in rectangular mortuary rooms and ritual storerooms within the pueblo. Burial clusters were used over long periods of time, some as long as 200 years or more, as the cumulative repositories of ritual items associated with specific areas of the site and with specific social groups. Still other objects were deposited in ritual storerooms during the life of the site when the pueblos' residents moved to other sites and/or the societies no longer were extant. Variation in the kinds of materials left in these storerooms, and in the different locations and accessibility of these rooms, suggests their use in different forms of ceremonial practice and what was considered to be of value to those who deposited them.

These forms of practice also illustrate the range of ways in which forgetting was a part of Chacoan memory work. Objects that were set into architectural spaces and then sealed, such as in kiva niches and pilasters, were placed out of sight and "forgotten" as part of the practice of secrecy. They memorialized the structures and were part of the materiality of Chaco ritual in ways that have been well described by Connerton (1989) as the process of inscription. The meters of shell beads that were placed in some of these spaces, such as in the great kiva at Chetro Ketl, were once highly visual artifacts that inscribed the value of the structures in the memories of those who participated and would have been remembered in subsequent ritual performances, despite being no longer visible. Smaller ritual structures received fewer and less visually performative objects, but even the smallest kivas contained shell, turquoise, and other materials that ornamented the foundations of the roof and the spaces in which altars were erected.

The intentional placement of large quantities of collectively owned objects with and near the members of high-ranking lineages at Pueblo Bonito also marks moments of remembering while forgetting. In this case, personal objects were placed with the deceased to reaffirm the position of their descendents. In other cases, collectively owned ritual objects either reached a point where they could not be renewed, or the societies in which they were used were no longer extant. Their ritual retirement was through discard in spaces considered different from more mundane locations. The stacking of hundreds of ceremonial staffs of office in the corner of one of the adjacent rooms was a way of marking the importance of those who were buried there. They would have been seen, and perhaps even used, by family members each time the room was accessed in new acts of deposition and burial in the adjacent room. These crypts and the

objects that they contained were places long remembered in the history of the site as evidenced by the repeated deposition of objects and people in the same areas of the site over many generations.

Another kind of forgetting was the intentional leaving behind of objects used in collective rituals, not in burial chambers, but in their storage rooms. No other site in the Southwest has as many of these rooms as Pueblo Bonito, nor so many deposits of inalienable objects. The cache at the nearby site of Chetro Ketl is exceptional for that site; together the remains from Chetro Ketl and Pueblo Bonito represent numerous cases of ritual retirement of ceremonial objects. I doubt that the presence of these objects was quickly forgotten by the sites' residents. Much as the empty rooms at Zuni were still remembered for several generations, even though sealed off and in some cases deeply buried within a mound of more recent rooms, the placement of powerful objects in these rooms would have ensured they were remembered by the pueblos' residents for many generations. The fact that many of these objects were interpreted by their excavators as intentionally broken before the rooms were naturally filled with sand and the walls of the structures collapsed is particularly intriguing in light of what we know about the end of the Pax Chaco and the sudden reorganization of Chaco society that led to its depopulation by the middle of the twelfth century. The breakage of these items may have been a "past mastering" on the part of those who were the last to leave or later visitors eager to rewrite the history of Chaco before it was buried.

A final form of forgetting may not have involved the residential population at all. At the end of Pueblo Bonito's use, residents from other sites and perhaps even outside the canyon continued to use the plaza and many of the kivas that ring the plaza. At least one ritual storage room was associated with this late use, in which objects that have no obvious precedents or antecedents – the ceramic cylinder jars – were brought out to be used in the plaza or in the plaza kivas. The objects marked the participation of multiple groups in the memory work of a larger community. Their final placement in a storage room commemorated this participation and the building itself. When these rituals were terminated, the objects were left behind as material manifestations of ritual engagements that were not needed in the next place, memorializing the building itself. Together, the deposits of dedication and termination illustrate the active ways in which people engaged with objects and how remembering and forgetting were part of the memory work of past and present societies.

Although the specific locations may not have remained part of Pueblo social memory, the practices at Chaco were reproduced by Pueblo society members at later sites throughout the Southwest. Painted wood, the deposition of turquoise, the use of shell and other materials from far-off places, and color symbolism are still important parts of Pueblo ritual practices today. In this way, they fit with Connerton's other process of social memory construction – incorporation. They became fundamental parts of ceremonial ritual practice through repeated social practices at multiple scales and were replicated at other settlements across the Ancestral Pueblo landscape.

The practices that I have described are part of long traditions of material practices within the Southwest. The memory of Chaco also resides in the historical narratives of contemporary Native Americans in the Southwest. As Leigh Kuwanwisiwma (2004) recounts, Chaco Canyon is the place called Yupköyvi to the Hopi. Not all clans trace their migration pathways from or through Chaco. Of those that do, there is a history of clan order and particularly memorable places where ceremonies were performed. This history, recounted over 800 years later, demonstrates the efficacy of Pueblo ways of remembering while forgetting, and how the Chacoan past became the present.

Notes

1 The retirement of ritual structures could also be approached in this way through the analysis of animal sacrifices found in the fill and in features. Hill (2000) compiles some of these data across the Southwest, and Creel and Anyon (2003) discuss this for Mimbres structures. Because of the lack of screening and the excavation methods used at Chaco for the earliest and most extensive excavations, the presence of these kinds of termination rituals are more difficult to identify, though they may be accessible through detailed analysis of the field notes.

2 I use the term "moments" recognizing that this term does not reflect the continuous phenomena that practice really is. However, many archaeological deposits do represent events rather than the kinds of depositional practices that would produce a more continuous record.

References

Adler, Michael A., and Richard H. Wilshusen, 1990 Large-scale Integrative Facilities in Tribal Societies: Cross-cultural and Southwestern U.S. Examples. World Archaeology 22:133–146.

Akins, Nancy J., 2003 The Burials of Pueblo Bonito. In Pueblo Bonito: Center of the Chacoan World, edited by Jill E. Neitzel, pp. 94–106. Smithsonian Institution Press, Washington, DC.

Beaglehole, Ernest, 1937 Notes on Hopi Economic Life. Yale University Publications in Anthropology No. 15. Yale University Press, New Haven.

Bourdieu, Pierre, 1977 Outline of a Theory of Practice. Translated by Richard Nice. Cambridge University Press, Cambridge.

Bourdieu, Pierre, and Loïc J. D. Wacquant, 1992 An Invitation to Reflexive Sociology. Polity Press, Cambridge.

Bradley, Richard, 1990 The Passage of Arms: An Archaeological Analysis of Prehistoric Hoards and Votive Deposits. Cambridge University Press, Cambridge.

Bradley, Richard, 1998 The Significance of Monuments: on the Shaping of Human Experience in Neolithic and Bronze Age Europe, Routledge, London.

Brandt, Elizabeth A., 1980 On Secrecy and Control of Knowledge. In Secrecy: A Cross-Cultural Perspective, edited by Stanton K. Tefft, pp. 123–146. Human Sciences Press, New York.

Cameron, Catherine M., 2001 Pink Chert, Projectile Points, and the Chacoan Regional System, American Antiquity 66:79–101.

Chapman, John, 2000 Fragmentation in Archaeology: People, Places and Broken Objects in the Prehistory of South Eastern Europe. Routledge. New York.

Connerton, Paul, 1989 How Societies Remember. Cambridge University Press, Cambridge.

Creel, Darrell, and Roger Anyon, 2003 New Interpretations of Mimbres Public Architecture and Space: Implications for Cultural Change. American Antiquity 68(1):67–92.

Crown, Patricia L., and W. H. Wills, 2003 Modifying Pottery and Kivas at Chaco Canyon: Pentimento, Restoration, or Renewal? American Antiquity 68 (3):511–532.

Cushing, Frank Hamilton, 1883 Zuni Fetiches. Second Annual Report of the Bureau of Ethnology. Smithsonian Institution, Washington, DC.

DeBoer, Warren R., 2005 Colors for a North American Past. World Archaeology 37(1):66–91.

de Certeau, Michel, 1984 The Practice of Everyday Life. Translated by Steven Rendall. University of California Press, Berkeley.

Forty, Adrian, 1999 Introduction. In The Art of Forgetting, edited by Adrian Forty and Susanne Küchler, pp. 1–18. Berg, Oxford.

Gigerenzer, Gerd, 2005 I Think. Therefore I Err (Errors in the Social Sciences). Social Research 72 (1):195–218.

Halbwachs, Maurice, 1992 On Collective Memory. Edited, translated, and with an introduction by Lewis Coser. University of Chicago Press, Chicago.

Heitman, Carolyn, and Stephen Plog, 2005 Kinship and the Dynamics of the House: Rediscovering Dualism in the Pueblo Past. In A Catalyst for Ideas: Anthropological Archaeology and the Legacy of Douglas W. Schwartz, edited by Vernon L. Scarborough, pp. 69–100. School of American Research Press, Santa Fe.

Helms, Mary, 1993 Craft and the Kingly Ideal: Art, Trade, and Power. University of Texas Press, Austin.

Hendon, Julia A., 2000 Having and Holding: Storage, Memory, Knowledge, and Social Relations. American Anthropologist 102(1):42–53.

Hewett, Edgar L., 1936 The Chaco Canyon and Its Monuments. University of New Mexico Press. Albuquerque.

Hibben, Frank C., 1975 Kiva Art of the Anasazi at Pottery Mound. KC Publications, Las Vegas.

Hill, Erica, 2000 The Contextual Analysis of Animal Interments and Ritual Practice in Southwestern North America Kiva 65(4):361–398.

Hobsbawm, Eric, 1983 Introduction: Inventing Traditions. In The Invention of Tradition, edited by Eric Hobsbawm and Terence Ranger. pp. 1–14. Cambridge University Press, Cambridge.

Hosler, Dorothy, 1994 The Sounds and Colors of Power: The Metallurgical Technology of Ancient West Mexico. MIT Press, Cambridge., MA.

Joyce, Rosemary A., and Susan D. Gillespie (editors), 2000 Beyond Kinship: Social and Material Reproduction in House Societies. University of Pennsylvania Press, Philadelphia.

Joyce, Rosemary A., and Julia A. Hendon, 2000 Heterarchy, History, and Material Reality: "Communities" in Late Classic Honduras. In The Archaeology of Communities: A New World Perspective, edited

by Marcel A. Canuto and Jason Yaeger, pp. 143–160. Routledge, London.

Judd, Neil M., 1954 The Material Culture of Pueblo Bonito. Smithsonian Miscellaneous Collections No. 124. Smithsonian Institution, Washington, DC.

Judd, Neil M., 1959 Pueblo del Arroyo, Chaco Canyon, New Mexico. Smithsonian Miscellaneous Collections Vol. 138, No. 1. Smithsonian Institution, Washington, DC.

Judd, Neil M., 1964 The Architecture of Pueblo Bonito. Smithsonian Miscellaneous Collections Vol. 147. No. 1. Smithsonian Institution, Washington, DC.

Kovacik, Joseph J., 1998 Collective Memory and Pueblo Space, Norwegian Archaeological Review 31(2):141–152.

Küchler, Susanne, 1999 The Place of Memory. In The Art of Forgetting, edited by Adrian Forty and Susanne Küchler, pp. 53–73. Berg. Oxford.

Küchler, Susanne, 2002 Malanggan: Art, Memory and Sacrifice. Berg, Oxford.

Kuwanwisiwma, Leigh, 2004 Yupköyvi: The Hopi Story of Chaco Canyon. In Search of Chaco: New Approaches to an Archaeological Enigma, edited by David Grant Noble, pp. 41–47. School of American Research Press, Santa Fe.

McGregor, John C., 1943 Burial of an Early American Magician. Proceedings of the American Philosophical Society 86(2):270–298.

Lekson, Stephen H. (editor), 1983 The Architecture and Dendrochronology of Chetro Ketl, Chaco Canyon, New Mexico. Reports of the Chaco Center No. 6. National Park Service, Division of Cultural Research, Albuquerque.

Lekson, Stephen H., 1986 Great Pueblo Architecture of Chaco Canyon. University of New Mexico Press, Albuquerque.

Lekson, Stephen H., 2007 Great House Form. In The Architecture of Chaco Canyon, New Mexico, edited by Stephen H. Lekson, pp. 7–44. University of Utah Press, Salt Lake City.

Mandler, Jean M., and Nancy S. Johnson, 1977 Remembrance of Things Parsed: Story Structure and Recall. Cognitive Psychology 9:111–151.

Mathien, F. Joan, 2001 The Organization of Turquoise Production and Consumption by the Prehistoric Chacoans. American Antiquity 66:103–118.

Mathien, F. Joan, 2003 Artifacts from Pueblo Bonito: One Hundred Years of Interpretation. In Pueblo Bonito: Center of the Chacoan World, edited by Jill E. Neitzel, pp. 127–142. Smithsonian Institution Press, Washington, DC.

Meskell, Lynn, 2002 Negative Heritage and Past Mastering in Archaeology. Anthropological Quarterly 75 (3):557–574.

Meskell, Lynn, 2004 Object Worlds in Ancient Egypt: Material Biographies Past and Present. Berg, Oxford.

Mills, Barbara J., 2000 Gender, Craft Production, and Inequality in the American Southwest. *In* Women and Men in the Prehispanic Southwest: Labor, Power, and Prestige, edited by Patricia L. Crown, pp. 301–343. School of American Research Press, Santa Fe.

Mills, Barbara J., 2004 The Establishment and Defeat of Hierarchy: Inalienable Possessions and the History of Collective Prestige Structures in the Puebloan Southwest, American Anthropologist 106(2):238–251.

Morris, Earl H., 1921 The House of the Great Kiva at the Aztec Ruin. Anthropological Papers of the American Museum of Natural History 26(2). New York.

Neitzel, Jill E., 2003a Artifact Distributions at Pueblo Bonito. *In* Pueblo Bonito: Center of the Chacoan World, edited by Jill E. Neitzel, pp. 107–126. Smithsonian Institution Press, Washington, DC.

Neitzel, Jill A., 2003b The Organization, Function, and Population of Pueblo Bonito. *In* Pueblo Bonito: Center of the Chacoan World, edited by Jill E. Neitzel, pp. 143–149. Smithsonian Institution Press, Washington, DC.

Nielsen, Axel E., 2008 The Materiality of Ancestors: *Chullpas* and Social Memory in the Late Prehispanic History of South America. *In* Memory Work: Archaeologies of Material Practices, edited by Barbara J. Mills and William Walker, pp. 207–232. School of American Research Press, Santa Fe.

Pauketat, Timothy R., 2008 Founders' Cults and the Archaeology of *Wa-kan-da*. *In* Memory Work: Archaeologies of Material Practices, edited by Barbara J. Mills and William Walker, pp. 61–80. School of American Research Press, Santa Fe.

Pepper, George H., 1920 Pueblo Bonito. Anthropological Papers of the American Museum of Natural History No. 27. New York.

Piot, Charles D., 1993 Secrecy, Ambiguity, and the Everyday in Kabre Culture. American Anthropologist 95(2):353–370.

Plog, Stephen, 2003 Exploring the Ubiquitous through the Unusual: Color Symbolism in Pueblo Black-on-White Pottery. American Antiquity 68 (4):665–695.

Plog, Stephen, and Carolyn Heitman, 2006 Microcosm and Macrocosm: Pueblo World View during the Chaco Era. Paper presented at the 10th Biennial Southwest Symposium, Las Cruces, New Mexico.

Pollard, Joshua, 2001 The Aesthetics of Depositional Practice. World Archaeology 33:315–333.

Pollard, Joshua, 2008 Deposition and Material Agency in the Early Neolithic of Southern Britain. *In* Memory Work: Archaeologies of Material Practices, edited by Barbara J. Mills and William Walker, pp. 41–59. School of American Research Press, Santa Fe.

Pollard, Joshua, and Clive Ruggles, 2001 Shifting Perceptions: Spatial Order, Cosmology, and Patterns of Deposition at Stonehenge. Cambridge Archaeological Journal 11(1):69–90.

Renfrew, Colin, 2001 Production and Consumption in a Sacred Economy: The Material Correlates of High Devotational Expression at Chaco Canyon. American Antiquity 66:14–25.

Shennan, Stephen, 2002: Genes, Memes and Human History: Darwinian Archaeology and Cultural Evolution. London: Thames and Hudson.

Strathern, Marilyn, 2001 The Patent and the Malanggan. *In* Beyond Aesthetics: Art and the Technologies of Enchantment, edited by Christopher Pinney and Nicholas Thomas. pp. 259–286. Berg, Oxford.

Thomas, Nicholas, 1991 Entangled Objects: Exchange, Material Culture, and Colonialism in the Pacific. Harvard University Press, Cambridge, MA.

Toll, H. Wolcott, 1990 A Reassessment of Chaco Cylinder Jars. *In* Clues to the Past: Papers in Honor of William H. Sundt, edited by Meliha S. Duran and David T. Kirkpatrick, pp. 273–305. Papers of the Archaeological Society of New Mexico No. 16.

Toll, H. Wolcott, 2001 Making and Breaking Pots in the Chaco World. American Antiquity 66:56–78.

Van Dyke, Ruth M., 2003 Memory and the Construction of Chacoan Society. *In* Archaeologies of Memory, edited by Ruth M. Van Dyke and Susan E. Alcock, pp. 180–200. Blackwell Publishers, Oxford.

Van Dyke, Ruth M., 2004 Memory, Meaning, and Masonry: The Late Bonito Chacoan Landscape. American Antiquity 69(3):413–431.

Vivian, R. Gordon, and Paul Reiter, 1960 The Great Kivas of Chaco Canyon and Their Relationships. Monograph No. 22. School of American Research Press, Santa Fe.

Vivian, R. Gwinn, Dulce N. Dodgen, and Gayle H. Hartmann, 1978 Wooden Ritual Artifacts from Chaco Canyon, New Mexico. Anthropological Papers of the University of Arizona Press, No. 32. University of Arizona Press, Tucson.

Walker, William H., Vincent M. LaMotta, and E. Charles Adams, 2000 Katsinas and Kiva Abandonments at Homol'ovi: A Deposit-Oriented Perspective on Religion in Southwest Prehistory. *In* The Archaeology of Regional Interaction, edited by Michelle Hegmon, pp. 341–360. University Press of Colorado. Boulder, Co.

Weiner, Annette, 1992 Inalienable Poussessions: The Paradox of Keeping-While-Giving. University of California Press, Berkeley.

Windes, Thomas C., 2003 This Old House: Construction and Abandonment at Pueblo Bonito. *In* Pueblo Bonito: Center of the Chacoan World, edited by Jill E. Neitzel, pp. 14–32. Smithsonian Institution Press, Washington, DC.

Yoffee, Norman, 2001 The Chaco "Rituality" Revisited. *In* Chaco Society and Polity: Papers from the 1999 Conference, edited by Linda S. Cordell, W. James Judge, and June-el Piper, pp. 63–78. Special Publication No. 4. New Mexico Archaeological Council, Albuquerque.

Public Memory and the Search for Power in American Historical Archaeology

Paul A. Shackel

Americans often turn to the past to explain current social conditions, to comfort themselves, to build self-esteem, and to create cultural pride. What aspects of the past are remembered and how they are remembered and interpreted are important issues that allow us to see how public memory develops. Memories can serve individual or collective needs and can validate the holders' version of the past. In the public arena they can be embedded in power to serve the dominant culture by supporting existing social inequalities. It is common for subordinate groups explicitly or implicitly to challenge the dominant meanings of public memories and create new ones that suit their needs. Often, the success of these challenges is situational, depending upon context and social and political power.

In 1925 Maurice Halbwachs formally introduced the concept of memory in the creation of history. He remarked that a collective memory develops when individuals seek the testimony of others in order to "validate their interpretations of their own experiences, to provide independent confirmation (or refutation) of the content of

Paul A. Shackel, "Public Memory and the Search for Power in American Historical Archaeology," pp. 655–70 from *American Anthropologist* 103:3 (2001). Reprinted with permission of the American Anthropological Association and the author.

their memories and thus confidence in their accuracy" (in Thelen 1989:1122). Other individuals are needed as a second reference in order to establish a frame of reference and to create recollection. People experience and remember or forget collectively, and they figure out how to interpret these experiences. They develop a collective memory by molding, shaping, and agreeing upon what to remember, although this process may not be always consciously planned. A collective memory becomes public when a group has the resources and power to promote a particular past. These histories mask or naturalize inequalities through material culture, such as memorials, museums, and the built landscape. Inequalities can be also promoted or challenged through commemoration ceremonies.

In archaeology some important works that critically evaluate the production of history include those written by Trigger (1989), Leone et al. (1987), and Shanks and Tilley (1987). These works evaluate the management and use of prehistoric and historic resources. They view the production of historical consciousness as an outcome of the struggle between groups. I found the production of a collective memory intriguing when examining the development of the industrial town of Harpers Ferry, West Virginia (see Shackel 1994b, 1999, 2000). For instance, until very recently, all of the town's histories written in the twentieth century stop document-ing the town just after the Civil War era. It is easy to come away with the impression that the town reached its economic zenith in the 1850s and 1860s and that the town had virtually disap-peared after the Civil War (Shackel 1996). Almost all of these histories proclaim that Harpers Ferry should be remembered only because of its role in the surrender of 12,500 Union troops to Stonewall Jackson and the events that surround John Brown (except Gilbert 1984, 1999). A historical archaeology of the town shows that it did survive and that it became a major regional industrial center until the 1920s. It thrives today as a tourist town (Shackel 1993, 2000). Many of the people who remained in Harpers Ferry after the Great Depression had a working-class background that extended into the Victorian era as all of the industrial entrepre-neurs were gone by the late 1930s. I think it is not an accident that Harpers Ferrians, mostly merchants and working-class families, ignored much of the town's Victorian industrial history. The postbellum industrial entrepreneurs who controlled the town's economy and labor oppor-tunities were northerners and did little for Harpers Ferry's working-class families, except to take their rent money and extract their labor at very low wages. While the town had industrial success, people chose to forget their exploitation as well as their relatives' (Shackel 1994a).

This phenomenon, masking a class or a group history when developing a collective memory, is well documented in other commu-nities. For instance, in Lawrence, Massachusetts, Sider (1996) describes a workers' history of resistance and strikes that has been repressed by community memory. In this mill commu-nity, the Strike of 1912, euphemistically called the "Bread and Roses Day," was branded by the Catholic Church as instigated by the most "unsavory immigrants" (quoted in Sider 1996:52). Strike leaders were intimidated through-out their lives by supervisors and industrialists. Community leaders focused on the strike, rather than the working conditions that provided the rationale for the strike. More important, the testimony of the factory working conditions by a 14-year-old girl in front of Congress was also suppressed from historical consciousness (Cameron 1993, 1996).

As these examples demonstrate, public mem-ory is more a reflection of present political and social relations than a true reconstruction of the past. As present conditions change socially, pol-itically, and ideologically, the collective memory of the past will also change. The control of a group's memory is often a question of power. Individuals and groups often struggle over the meaning of memory as the official memory is imposed by the power elite (Teski and Climo 1995:2). For instance, Handler and Gable's 1997 *The New History in an Old Museum* serves as an excellent example of deconstructing the pro-duction of history in an outdoor museum like Colonial Williamsburg. They reveal that the museum's interpretation of the colonial era is a way to reinforce social inequalities in contem-porary society. This sentiment, that the histories told at Colonial Williamsburg are a product of public memory, has been expressed by others (Leone 1981; Wallace 1981). Anthropologist Michel-Rolph Trouillot (1995:15) also produces a compelling argument about taking a critical approach to historical accounts. Taking accounts that range from Columbus Day to the Haitian revolution for independence, he notes that the past can only be understood in the context of the present. He recognizes that during the produc-tion of history power operates in a way that silences subaltern groups.

Historians, too, have seen memories as being subjective to group interests. Influential works by David Lowenthal (1985), Michael Frisch (1990), David Glassberg (1990), Michael Kammen (1991), John Bodner (1992), and Edward Linenthal (1993) have guided public historians into addressing issues that show the connected-ness between memory and power. These works show that we cannot assume that all groups, and all members of the same group, understand the past in the same way. The same historical and material representation may have divergent mean-ings to different audiences (Glassberg 1996:9–10; Lowenthal 1985). A struggle to create or subvert a past often develops between competing interest groups (see, for instance, Neustadt and May 1986; Peterson 1994). Different versions of the past are communicated through various institu-tions, including schools, amusements, art and literature, government ceremonies, families and friends, and landscape features that are designated as historical. Public memory does not solely rely on professional historical scholarship, but it is usually influenced by various individuals and institutions that support the collective memory.

In particular, I am interested in the various ways memory takes shape on the American landscape and how it is influenced by race and power. After the American Civil War sectional bitterness existed, and to some extent it continues today. By the end of Reconstruction the political importance of the war refocused (Foster 1987:68–69; McConnell 1992:108). Blue–Grey reunions from the 1880s became a form of selective memory rather than forgiveness (McConnell 1992:190). The African American memory of the war continually lost ground to a new and growing dominant ideology, led by people like Oliver Wendell Holmes Jr. and later Theodore Roosevelt. An integrated collective memory became unacceptable to the majority of white Americans. They interpreted the war as a test of a generation's valor and loyalty toward a cause. The Lost Cause mythology argued that the Confederacy was never defeated but, rather, was overwhelmed by numbers and betrayed by some key generals (Blight 2001).

While the Victorian era had been a healing period between the North and the South, greater schisms developed in this country that divided people along lines of class and ethnicity. The era is recognized by many as the "decade of patriotic offensives among native-born, white members of the American middle class" (McConnell 1992:207). Exclusionary groups dominated the era. Americans created clubs and organizations at a rate never seen before or after in U.S. history. Associations developed for group protection and the wealthy increasingly excluded other groups (Hobsbawm 1983:292–293). Social Darwinism and scientific racism became the popular paradigms in intellectual circles, and African American participation in society and their role in the Civil War minimized. Commemoration ceremonies of the war often celebrated the great white hero memorialized with statues of generals on horseback or a generic-looking single soldier that stood in a town center (O'Leary 1999).

Recognizing various types of power is valuable when examining issues related to the creation of public memory, race, and the American landscape. Eric Wolf (1990) describes four modes of power: "the first is power as the capability of a person; the second is power as the ability of a person to impose upon another interpersonally; the third is tactical power which controls social settings; and the fourth is structural power, which allocates social labor" (in Little 1994:23). The first mode is what Miller and Tilley (1984) describe as "power to" and the remaining they call "power over." Contextualizing the use of power in relationship to public memory allows us to recognize the complexity of the use of power and its connections to public memory.

Many of the studies in public memory can be viewed within the context of tactical power, which controls social settings. The control over the uses and meanings of material culture, and the exercise of "power over," can be accomplished in several ways. Memory can be about (1) forgetting about or excluding an alternative past, (2) creating and reinforcing patriotism, and/or (3) developing a sense of nostalgia to legitimize a particular heritage. These categories serve as an organizational point to see the relationship between power and the construction of public memory. They allow us to see that objects and landscapes that historical archaeologists and public historians often view have different meanings to different people and groups at different times. These categories are not mutually exclusive. The public memory associated with highly visible objects is always being constructed, changed, and challenged, and at all times power and the challenge to power are situational. Below, I provide background and a case study for each category, all from a Civil War context and related to how landscapes reflect and reinforce the ideals of race and power through heritage and patriotism.

An Exclusionary Past

Elements of the past remembered in common, as well as elements of the past forgotten in common, are essential for group cohesion (Glassberg 1996:13). While collective memory can be about forgetting a past, it often comes at the expense of a subordinate group. Those who are excluded may try to subvert the meaning of the past through alternative histories, or they may also strive for more representation in the form of a more pluralistic past. When Americans reflect on the traditional meanings associated with a collective national memory, it has focused on elites and traditional heroes. The perception of many is that American history is linear and straightforward. This uncomplicated story occurs only when we leave others out of the picture. This "sacred story with strong nationalist overtones ... derived much of its coherence from the groups it ignored or dismissed" (Leff 1995:833; also see Nash et al. 1998:100). Those who disagree with a multicultural history have claimed that

> it is difficult ... to see how the subjects of the new [social] history can be accommodated in any single framework, let alone a national and political one. ... How can all these groups, each cherishing its uniqueness and its claim to sovereign attention, be mainstreamed into a single, coherent, integrated history? (quoted in Nash et al. 1998:100–101)

I have seen this attitude among some historical archaeologists and historians who believe that the only reason for preserving Civil War battlefields is for commemorating the dead and for studying battlefield logistics. They refuse to see the relevance of incorporating social history to view the Civil War in its larger context. Multicultural perspectives, like addressing the issues of slavery at a national battlefield, are reprehensible to some Civil War scholars (see Smith 1999). There is the perception that the Civil War is all about loyalty to a cause, a sentiment that developed in the late nineteenth century that excluded African Americans from the Civil War story. It is a feeling that remains strong among many conservative scholars.

We often find that while accounts of ordinary people and subaltern groups do not necessarily find their way into official accounts, they can persist and create an alternative minority view. This view has a function to legitimize and stabilize a claim to a history (Fields 1994:153). While many federally funded museums extol the glories of economic and social progress as a result of industry, many working-class members view the preservation of old buildings and ruins as an attempt to save a degrading phase of

human history. Robert Vogel of the Smithsonian Institution notes, "The dirt, noise, bad smell, hard labor and other forms of exploitation associated with these kinds of places make preservation [of industrial sites] ludicrous. 'Preserve a steel mill?' people say, 'It killed my father. Who wants to preserve that?'" (quoted in Lowenthal 1985:403). Therefore, while individual dissenting views on the true benefits of industrialization exist, the federal government remains strong in supporting ideas of industrial progress at national parks such as Lowell and Saugus in Massachusetts and Hopewell and Steam Town in Pennsylvania. In many of these cases archaeology has played a major role in supporting the official history.

Following, I provide a case study of how a community created an official history of an event in the Civil War at the expense of another group. In particular, a white officer was commemorated in the form of a statue that minimized the role of the African American troops that he commanded. Only through protest and the rise of the Civil Rights movement did the forgotten history of the troops become part of the official memory.

Case Study: The Remaking of the Robert Gould Shaw Memorial

The Robert Gould Shaw Memorial sits on the Boston Common to commemorate the colonel who led the first African American Northern volunteer regiment into battle during the American Civil War. The memorial to Shaw with a representation of the 54th Massachusetts Infantry has stood for over a century with its meaning controlled by the white community. It demonstrates and reinforces the memory of their community's historic patriotic and abolitionist commitment.

On May 28, 1863, Shaw and the 54th Massachusetts Volunteer Infantry marched to Boston's Battery Wharf, where they sailed for the Sea Islands off Charleston, South Carolina. The world watched the soldiers since it was the first Northern-raised African American regiment. After a two-night march through rain and shifting sands, with insufficient rations, an exhausted Shaw accepted the order to lead an immediate attack on Fort Wagner. At dusk, on

July 18, the Massachusetts 54th led the assault. Six hundred troops charged across a narrow spit of sand against a strong earthwork. Shaw was one of the first to fall, but his troops pressed on. More than half reached the inside of the fort, and they were able to hold Wagner's parapet for an hour before being driven off by the Confederates. Other white regiments attacked that night, but they also failed. The assault on Fort Wagner that day left 1,515 Union casualties compared with 181 on the Confederate side.

News of the assault on Fort Wagner by the 54th Massachusetts became widely known in the North, and Shaw and the deeds of his fallen men were transformed into martyrdom. The *New York Tribune* wrote that the battle "made Fort Wagner such a name to the colored race as Bunker Hill had been for ninety years to the white Yankees" (from McPherson 1988:686). The *Atlantic Monthly* wrote, "Through the cannon smoke of that black night the manhood of the colored race shines before many eyes that would not see" (from McPherson 1969). The 54th had proven that African Americans could fight honorably. Shaw's death was a family loss and a moral contribution by Boston to preserve the Union and fight for emancipation.

Shaw became one of the Civil War's most celebrated legends. More than 40 poems have been written about Shaw and they helped to solidify his martyrdom. Plans for a Shaw monument began in 1865 with a formal meeting held in Boston. Many delays occurred as key proponents of the memorial died, but in 1884, a commission appointed a young, well-known artist, Augustus Saint-Gaudens, for the Shaw memorial project.

Saint-Gaudens labored sporadically on the monument for 13 years, and he finally unveiled it on "Decoration Day," May 31, 1897. At the ceremony 65 veterans of the 54th Massachusetts marched up Beacon Hill past the Robert Gould Shaw Memorial. It was the first soldier's monument to honor a group rather than a single individual, although an explicit hierarchy exists in the representation. The memorial places the colonel in the center among his troops. Shaw is on horseback with his fatigue cap on. The African American soldiers serve as a backdrop. They are ready for battle with rifles over their shoulders, and the procession is led by a drummer boy. Above them is an allegorical figure with laurel branches in one hand and poppies in the other. The work was immediately hailed as a great success by many art critics.

In 1916 Freeman Murry lauded the sculpture as a "memorial to man, race, and a cause." Murry remarked that Saint-Gaudens's work will "tower above the color line" (1916:166). Murry's interpretation – that the Shaw monument would help dismantle the racial boundaries that were so prevalent in the early twentieth century – puzzles some scholars. For instance, modern art scholars, like Albert Boime (1990), point out Saint-Gaudens's racist tendencies. He created the Shaw monument in the context of strong racial and ethnic tensions in the late-nineteenth-century United States. The development of Jim Crow legislation in the late nineteenth century made it increasingly difficult for African Americans to achieve equality – in the North and the South.

While creating the monument, Saint-Gaudens filled his studio in New York with African American subjects from the surrounding neighborhood. Reinforcing a contemporary stereotype, Saint-Gaudens wrote that "they are very likable, with their soft voices and imaginative, though simple, minds" (1913:334–335; see Boime 1990:208). Saint-Gaudens's son, Homer, describes an incident of his father's substandard treatment of African Americans. Homer noted, "I believe he could detect a change of two degrees from his favorite amount of heat, when woe betides the darkey who tended stove" (Saint-Gaudens 1913:133).

While contemporary critics claimed his sculpture as an act of "newborn American patriotism" (Taft [1924]1969: 304) and said that it would "tower above the color line" (Murry 1916:166), there were other contemporary voices that contested the meaning of the Shaw monument. Based on what we know about Saint-Gaudens's feelings about African Americans through his writings, it is difficult to see him as very sympathetic toward African Americans, and it becomes even more difficult to see his work as an expression of the abolitionist sentiment. The Shaw memorial is just that, a memorial to Robert Gould Shaw, and the African American troops serve as a background to the subject. It is a monument that remembers one of Boston's Brahman elite and the role that the elite played in the abolitionist movement.

A contemporary critic, Charles Caffin, wrote in 1913 that Saint-Gaudens "portrays the humble soldiers with varying characteristics of pathetic devotion. The emotion [is] aroused by intent and steadfast onward movement of the troops, whose dog like trustfulness is contrasted with the serene elevation of their white leader" (1913:11). There is no doubt that the white officer is the central figure in the monument. Shaw is elevated on horseback and "sharing the upper zone with the allegorical Angel of Death who bears Victory and Sleep" (Boime 1990:209). Shaw is portrayed as noble and sits erect in his saddle. Boime concludes that Saint-Gaudens was successful "in establishing a visual 'color-line' that guarded white supremacy" (1990: 211). The hegemony of the powerful is explicit and noticeable.

In the late twentieth century the tone and meaning associated with the monument have become even more muddled. A rededication of the monument in 1981 placed in stone on the back of the monument the names of the 281 African American soldiers who died in the assault of Fort Wagner. This act provides some recognition to the foot soldiers. Later that decade, the critically acclaimed movie *Glory* brought further recognition to the role of African Americans in the Civil War.

In May 1997, Boston held a public ceremony that celebrated the 100th anniversary of the unveiling of the Shaw memorial. Several prominent African Americans spoke at this 100th anniversary rededication. President Benjamin Payton of Tuskegee University, Professor Henry Louis Gates Jr. of the Du Bois Institute at Harvard University, and General Colin Powell all remarked on the splendid beauty of the monument and saw the portrayal of the troops in a positive and uplifting light (Blatt et al. 2000).

Art historian Kirk Savage remarked that the memorial is an excellent blend between soldier and general. Savage argued that they are not "listless," as described by Boime (1990) but, rather, determined. The troops do not lose their humanity. He notes that the soldiers look well drilled and each looks very different. They are individuals who wear their uniforms in various fashions. The horse glides and towers, and the soldiers are weighed down by their equipment as they lean forward: "Saint-Gaudens was able to elevate the white hero without demoting the black troops"

(Savage 1997:203). African Americans never had this representation of individuality before. While Saint-Gaudens was racist in his memoirs, Savage remarks, he made the infantrymen individuals, and the memorial is not a racist monument. Savage proposes that what Saint-Gaudens was thinking about had no bearing on his sculpture. He notes that Saint-Gaudens "treated racial differences openly and with dignity, asserting a 'brotherhood' of man. And yet it registered, compellingly and beautifully, the transcendence of the white hero in that of brotherhood" (1997:204). Savage does not believe that there can be different readings of the same piece of material culture and he claims that Caffin's (1913) and Boime's (1990) argument "cannot be sustained without a serious misreading of the sculpture itself" (Savage 1997:256 n. 97).

While Savage believes that there can only be one reading of the monument, I believe that the importance and significance of the Shaw memorial is that it can be read in various ways and different people will ascribe diverse meanings to it, depending upon the memory they have associated with the event. Saint-Gaudens created this statue in a racist era, and he used the white colonel to dominate the foreground of the memorial. He also gives African Americans significant representation in the memorial, a rare phenomenon for the era. The events of the civil rights movement of the mid- and late twentieth century, along with the Civil Rights Act, have given African Americans a greater representation in our public memory, and the Shaw memorial centennial celebration, backed by many prominent political and social figures, also helped to solidify and sanctify a new public meaning and memory of the memorial. For instance, the newspaper *USA Today* reported on the ceremonies, and it did not even mention Robert Gould Shaw when describing the memorial but, rather, only mentioned the 54th Massachusetts Infantry. No longer do public-funded institutions, like the National Park Service, speak only about the Robert Gould Shaw Memorial, but they now include the name of the 54th Massachusetts Infantry when referencing the monument. It is part of the dominant culture's changing view of the Civil War and its willingness to include African American history in the public memory of this country's heritage.

Commemoration and the Making of a Patriotic Past

Another way to control the past is to create a public memory that commemorates a patriotic past. The official expression is concerned with promoting and preserving the ideals of cultural leaders and authorities, developing social unity, and maintaining the status quo. Those in control of the official memory interpret the past and present reality in a way that helps to reduce competing interests (Bodner 1992:13). Government agencies have traditionally advanced the notion of "community of the nation while suppressing authentic local group memories and collective identities" (Glassberg 1996:12). The goal of the official public memory is to produce obedient, patriotic citizens. "The argument," remarks Michael Frisch, "has traveled a long way from its humanistic origins, arriving at a point where education and indoctrination – cultural and political – seem almost indistinguishable" (1989:1153).

The Enola Gay exhibit at the Smithsonian Institution is an excellent example of how the government suppressed an alternative view on the grounds that it was not patriotic. The original plans for the exhibit ran counter to the collective memory of powerful lobbying groups. The original draft text interpreted the horrors of the atomic bomb. Veterans' groups and lobbying groups convinced the U.S. Congress and the president of the United States to place political pressure on the Smithsonian Institution to change the exhibit. The revised exhibit conformed to the traditional patriotic view that claimed that it was necessary to drop the bomb to save American lives. The exhibit portrayed the flight crew as patriots and heroes (see *Journal of American History* 1995).

While collective memories are sometimes challenged, the ideals of the official memory must be supported through ceremonies and commemorations if their ideas and histories are to be long lived. One of the most popular commemorative events in U.S. history is the commemoration and reinterpretation of the American Civil War battlefields and landscapes. The struggle over which patriotic past the nation should celebrate was being settled by the end of Reconstruction, and it solidified through the early and mid-twentieth century. David Blight writes,

Historical memory . . . was not merely an entity altered by the passage of time; it was the prize in a struggle between rival versions of the past, a question of will, of power, of persuasion. The historical memory of any transforming or controversial event emerges from cultural and political competition, from the choice to confront the past and to debate and manipulate its meaning. (1989:1159)

From the late nineteenth century through most of the twentieth century, recognizing African American participation in the Civil War became increasingly limited as the southern revisionist movement gained momentum. Southern whites gained tremendous political and social power after Reconstruction, and they developed a southern patriotic past that could overcome historical humiliation. They created a glorious past of honor and dedication to a cause, while excluding African Americans from the story except to mention their faithfulness to the regime of the Old South (Aaron 1973:332–333).

Patriotism promotes and preserves the ideals of cultural leaders and authorities to develop social unity and maintain social inequalities in society. Officials in charge of creating patriotic histories present a past that reduced competing interests (Bodner 1992:13). They create the notion of community and heritage while suppressing the local memories of competing interest groups. The establishment of a patriotic past is evident with the development of the Civil War centennial movement.

Case Study: The Civil War Centennial and the Battle at Manassas

In the 1950s and 1960s Americans looked for a unifying theme that could bring some peace and tranquility to the growing antagonism between races and regions. The era was marked by violence and grief as racial issues tugged at the fragile seams that held this nation together. For instance, in September 1962 more than a thousand angry whites rampaged across the University of Mississippi campus to protest the admission of the campus's first black student. President Kennedy sent several hundred federal marshals to protect the student. The mob killed two men, more than two dozen marshals were wounded, and 120 people were wounded amid considerable property damage (Cohodas 1997). These were not isolated incidents, but they were indicative of race relations at the time.

During this era of racial tensions, Civil War Round Tables in 1957, successfully petitioned Congress to create a Civil War Centennial Commission. The commission used the anniversary of this historic event to promote nationalism and patriotism. It fashioned memories of past conflict and tried to transform them into symbolic struggles for unity. Abroe explains that the recollection of a heroic past could easily provide a diversion from the racial and political unrest sweeping through the country: "With citizens' attention fixed upon subversive threats – real or imagined – to democratic institutions, the vision of a United States tested and fortified in the crucible of civil conflict offered reassurance that the nation could meet any crisis and emerge victorious" (1998:22). President Eisenhower wrote the Civil War Centennial Commission and urged it to

> look on this great struggle not merely as a set of military operations, but as a period in our history in which the times called for extraordinary degrees of patriotism and heroism on the part of the men and women of both North and South. In this context we may derive inspiration from their deeds to renew our dedication to the task which yet confronts us – the furtherance, together with other free nations of the world, of the freedom and dignity of man and the building of a just and lasting peace. (1960a)

Karl Betts, who became the first executive director of the national commission, was joined by Ulysses S. Grant III. Both men had military backgrounds. At the Civil War Centennial meetings it is clear that the ideas of the Lost Cause were embedded in the national public memory of the Civil War. Grant explained that the Civil War could not be forgotten and that the Confederates were also Americans "who were heroically fighting for what they thought was right" (Minutes of the Civil War Centennial Commission 1960). Heroism allowed for the common foot soldier to be recognized, but it also provided an example of how ordinary

citizens followed the orders of their leaders. They fought for a larger political structure without question (Bodner 1992:209).

The opening ceremonies of the centennial celebration were held in New York City, where a group gathered at the Grant Memorial. There, Major General Grant gave a speech that stressed that the Civil War was important since it showed the ability of the country to reunite (*New York Times* 1961:1). That same day, opening ceremonies were held in Lexington, at Robert E. Lee's grave site. Congressman William Tuck of Virginia noted that after the war Lee urged Southerners to strengthen the Union (*New York Times* 1961:1).

Allan Nevis, a professional historian, and James I. Robertson, former editor of *Civil War History*, became the new commission leaders in 1961. Nevis declared the mission of the commission:

> Above all, our central theme will be unity, not division. When we finally reach the commemoration of Appomattox, we shall treat it not as a victory or a defeat, but as a beginning of a century of increasing concord, mutual understanding, and fraternal affection among all the sections and social groups. (Minutes of the Civil War Centennial Commission 1961)

The Civil War centennial celebrated dedication and loyalty to a cause while the issue of slavery played little or no role at all during commemoration events. The commission could not totally ignore the racial divisiveness within the country, and on September 22, 1962, it sponsored an event at the Lincoln Memorial to commemorate the centennial of the Emancipation Proclamation. The ceremonies marked more than the symbolic end to slavery, and white national unity became the overriding theme once again. The Kennedy administration was reluctant to take a major political stance at the event while racial tensions boiled in this country. At the time Kennedy contemplated reelection, and he did not want to offend white southerners. The audience did listen to a recording of President Kennedy. He emphasized patriotic themes and commended African Americans for working on civil rights issues within the framework of the Constitution. He praised African Americans for their struggle to make life better for their people: "He thought it remarkable that despite humiliation and depravation, blacks had retained their loyalty to the nation and 'democratic institution'" (*New York Times* 1962:1, 50; Bodner 1992:211).

Centennial celebrations occurred at many national parks, including Manassas National Battlefield Park on July 21, 22, and 23, 1961. Reenactment gatherings often attracted up to 100,000 spectators, and at Manassas, nearly 200,000 people observed the three-day event. In August 1960, President Eisenhower wrote the First Manassas Corporation that the event "will serve to remind all Americans that the bonds which now unite us are as precious as the blood of young men" (1960b). A 1961 pamphlet, called "Grand Reenactment," advertising the event described the importance of the battle in American history. It stated that the "reenactment will commemorate in action, sight, and sound the courage and devotion demonstrated here in 1861 and the need for similar dedication in the years to come."

The Centennial Commemoration program adopted the "Lost Cause" sentiment, claiming: "Today's commemorative spectacle has the objective of reminding you of our common heritage – and indeed of reminding the world – that our people have always been willing to fight and to die if need be for their beliefs – and their principles." Whether fighting for the Union or the Confederacy, "they were all deeply in love with their country. And the country they loved was America."

While the reenactment received praise from the press, others criticized the event as "a celebration rather than an event commemorating a tragic event in our history. The 'Coney Island' atmosphere that concession stands created behind the spectator section was objectionable" (see Volz 1961:12). Another citizen noted "that even though great pains were taken to present a historically accurate event, as it was, comparatively few people came away really understanding what took place" (see Volz 1961:12).

Manassas National Battlefield Park has always been about the history of the battles (the First Battle of Manassas and the Second Battle of Manassas), and National Park Service historians at the park have not been willing to expand the interpretation of the park to incorporate social history into the story of the park. The centennial celebrations were about Confederate victories and the reconciliation between whites. These celebrations ignored some of the broader issues surrounding the war, like slavery, emancipation, and the use of African American troops in the Civil War. These topics are still not fully addressed in the park today, and park cultural resource managers and historians have continued to take steps to reinforce and glorify a Confederate past by erasing any forms of African American history from the battlefield landscape (see Martin et al. 1997).

Nostalgia and the Legitimation of American Heritage

Another way to create memory is to develop a sense of heritage. Citizens of the early American republic resisted the development of an American collective memory and frowned upon the commemoration of a sacred past. Adherence to republican values in the early nineteenth century produced tensions between democracy and tradition. John Quincy Adams noted, "Democracy has no monuments. It strikes no medals. It bears the head of no man on a coin" (in Everett [1836] 1972:38). In the antebellum era, Americans saw the United States as a country with a future rather than a glorious past worth commemoration. They believed in the value of succeeding without patronage or family influence. Emerson wrote that Americans were "emancipated from history, happily bereft of ancestry, untouched and undefiled by the usual inheritances of family and race" (quoted in Lowenthal 1996:55).

Because of the resistance to create an American heritage, large-scale commemoration activities began slowly after the middle of the nineteenth century. The Mount Vernon's Ladies Association (formed in 1856) and the Ladies' Hermitage Association (1889) are important early preservation groups involved in the American historic, preservation movement. Women were the primary custodians of American heritage, and they took pride in demonstrating their care and, therefore, patriotism for America's past. Those who did not have ancestral roots could join other groups, like the Patriotic League of the Revolution (formed in 1894). Their goal was to "create and promote interest in all matters pertaining to American history, to collect and preserve relics of the period of the American Revolution, and to foster patriotism" (from Kammen 1991:267).

Until the 1890s the U.S. government did little to assist historic preservation or to create a national collective memory. From 1880 through 1886, eight bills were introduced to Congress to preserve historic lands, but none was enacted. In the 1890s Congress finally authorized the establishment of five Civil War battlefields as national military parks to be administered by the Defense Department – Chickamauga, Antietam, Shiloh, Gettysburg, and Vicksburg. Several Revolutionary War sites were also added. By 1906, protection became available for prehistoric ruins with the establishment of the Antiquities Act. These events are an important indication of America's growing need to create a useable heritage.

This national movement helped to develop and foster a collective memory and national heritage. Heritage creates a useable past and it generates a precedent that serves our present needs. More recently the political uses of heritage have been made very explicit within Western culture. We live in a society whose thirst for nostalgia seems unquenchable. Kammen (1991:214–219) calls the creation of Americans' consciousness for historic preservation since the 1950s the "heritage phenomenon." Heritage connotes integrity, authenticity, venerability, and stability. While "history explores and explains pasts it grows ever more opaque over time; heritage clarifies pasts so as to infuse them with present purposes" (Lowenthal 1996:xv).

Heritage is one way to create community and cultural continuity. A nation uses heritage to create a collective memory in order to look for more innocent and carefree days by selectively remembering. We remember what we perceive as good and forget the rest. False notions of the past may be upheld in order to create and sustain national mythology. For instance, David Lowenthal brings to our attention the myth behind the founding of Londonderry (Derry). Contrary to local belief, the city was not founded by St. Columba, and the famed siege of 1689 was only a blockade: "But Derry folk dote on these founding fables all the more because they are fabulous" (Lowenthal 1996: 129).

Closely linked with the idea of heritage is nostalgia. Nostalgia for things that are reminders of earlier days has replaced the early American republic's ideals for progress and development. Nostalgia is about nurturance and stewardship. Beleaguered by loss and change, Americans remember a bygone day of economic power. They have angst about the loss of community. In a throwaway society, people are looking for something more lasting (Lowenthal 1996:6). Massive migrations of the last 200 years have also sharpened our needs and feelings of nostalgia. Tens of millions of people have sought refuge outside of their native lands, fleeing hunger, violence, and hatred. Rural people have increasingly migrated to urban areas. People have been cut off from their own past, and they are increasingly seeking their roots (Lowenthal 1996:9).

The celebration of America's heritage can often be read from the American landscape, and it can be reinforced through material culture, such as museums and monuments. Following is an example of how a southern patriotic group used commemoration and a monument to reinforce nostalgia in order to legitimize southern bigotry. African American groups have challenged the placement of the monument is a visible and public place, and they have struggled to change the meaning of the event that the memorial commemorates.

Case Study: The Heyward Shepherd Memorial

After the Civil War, Southerners created more monuments to their defeat than any other civilization in history. It is their dedication to the Lost Cause, justifying their actions during the Civil War, that created the proliferation of these markers (McPherson 1982:488). The idea of the "Lost Cause" survived through the twentieth and now into the twenty-first century. It is kept alive by southern patriotic groups like the United Daughters of the Confederacy (UDC) and the Sons of Confederate Veterans (SCV). These southern heritage groups were, and still are, engaged in cultural warfare to establish a "Confederate tradition." This tradition focuses on the white South's view of history, appreciation for the rule by the elite, a fear of the enfranchisement of African Americans, and a reverence for the Confederate cause (Foster 1987:5). From the late nineteenth century, this paradigm has preached racial separation and the virtues of an aristocratic South. The Lost Cause mythology argued that the Confederacy was never defeated but, rather, they were over-whelmed by numbers and betrayed by some key generals. The Lost Cause has been compared to the Ghost Dance of the Plains Indians whereby southerners created "a dream of a return to an undefeated confederacy" (Foster 1987:47, 60). This mythology won in the battle to control the public memory of the Civil War (Blight 1989:1162–1163; Connelly and Bellows 1982; Holmes 1962:4–5, 76).

A monument to Heyward Shepherd, an African American killed by John Brown's raiding party on Harpers Ferry, is an important example of how one group consciously excluded another group's memory of the past. Brown, a famous abolitionist known for fighting against slavery in Kansas, had come to Harpers Ferry in October 1859. His goal was to capture the U.S. arsenal where guns were stored for the U.S. Army. Brown believed that once enslaved African Americans heard that he captured the arsenal they would abandon their plantations and come to his aid. Brown would supply escaped slaves with weapons and they would march south, free-ing slaves along the way. No slaves joined Brown's revolt; Brown and his men were captured, and many of his men were found guilty of treason and hanged.

It is ironic that Heyward Shepherd became the first casualty of Brown's raid. Although the stor-ies are not clear, it appears that he was shot in the back as he tried to flee from Brown's raiding party. The memory of Heyward Shepherd, con-trolled by the white press, became an important tool to justify the Lost Cause sentiment. The *Virginia Free Press* reported, "He was shot down like a dog. A humble negro as he was, his life was worth more than all of the desperadoes of the party, and his memory will be revered, when theirs will only be thought of with execution" (1859:2). The newspaper continually reinforced the martyrdom of a faithful African American who worked diligently in a white-dominated soci-ety (*Virginia Free Press* 1867, 1879, 1884).

The UDC decided in 1905 that a "Faithful Slave Monument" would be one way that south-erners could create and control a public memory of the conditions of slavery. A "Faithful Slave

Monument" was a vehicle to counter the mem-ory created by northerners about the South and the institution of slavery. The UDC believed that it was important to erect a monument "to the faithful old slaves who remained loyal and true to their owners in the dark days of the sixties and on through the infamous reconstruction period" (*Confederate Veteran* 1905:123). The monument would tell future generations "that the white men of the South were the negro's best friend then and that the men of the South are the negro's best friend today" (*Confederate Veteran* 1905:123–124).

During the beginning of the Great Depression there was a new sense of xenophobia that swept through the country, and African Ameri-cans found themselves further segregated and oppressed by Jim Crow legislation. In 1931, the town council in Harpers Ferry unanimously agreed to allow the "Faithful Slave Monument" to be erected in town. Ceremonies occurred in October 1931, and Henry T. McDonald, presi-dent of Storer College, an African American col-lege, participated in the unveiling of the memorial. The president general of the UDC, Elizabeth Bashinsky, spoke about her devotion to the Confederate flag and remarked how the "black mammy" loved her white "chilluns." She also believed that the slaves in the United States did not violently rise against their masters, like they did in Haiti, because they were well clothed, fed, and housed; treated kindly; and taught Christianity. Bashinsky noted that Heyward Shepherd "gave his life in defense of his employ-er's property, and in memory of many others of his race who were loyal and true during a period that tried men's souls. ... Heyward Shepherd's conduct was honorable, just, and true, and merits the praise we bring him" (*Confederate Veteran* 1931:411). After Bashinsky's speech the memorial was unveiled. Part of the memorial inscription reads:

As a Memorial to Heyward Shepherd,
Exemplifying The Character And
Faithfulness of Thousands Of
Negroes Who, Under Many
Temptations Throughout
Subsequent Years of War, So
Conducted Themselves That
No Stain Was Left Upon a Record
Which Is The Peculiar Heritage

of The American People, And An
Everlasting Tribute to The Best
in Both Races. (UDC 1931:58–59)

The inscription angered many African Americans, and McDonald's participation in the ceremonies was immediately attacked by several members of the African American community (Andrews 1931). Max Barber remarked that McDonald should have been "shocked and disgusted" at the statements made at the ceremony and that he erred in participating in an event coordinated by "a bunch of unregenerated rebels" (*Pittsburgh Courier* 1931). W. E. B. Du Bois wrote in *Crisis* (1932) that the dedication was a "proslavery celebration" and called McDonald's participation in the event "disgraceful."

In the 1950s the National Park Service (NPS) acquired the Heyward Shepherd Memorial along with the building it stood against in Lower Town Harpers Ferry. Funding became available for building renovations in the mid-1970s, and in 1976 the buildings adjacent to the Heyward Shepherd Memorial underwent construction. The NPS removed the memorial to its maintenance yard so it would not get damaged. In 1981 the Heyward Shepherd Memorial was moved back to its original location, although the NPS covered it with plywood when it received reports of possible plans to deface the monument (Meyer 1995:C2). The NPS found itself between two opposing organizations. The National Association for the Advancement of Colored People (NAACP) viewed the monument as offensive, and the UDC and the SCV wanted the monument uncovered and displayed to the public.

Mrs. Dewey Wood of the UDC believed that the message on the monument is clear in its meaning. She remarked, "Why should the NAACP be opposed to this? It is a monument to one of their people.... There were 40,000 slaves in Maryland, and none of them came to [John Brown's] support. They were loyal to their people.... I really don't know what they find offensive about it" (in White 1989:4). Efforts to have all groups – UDC, SCV, NAACP, and the NPS – reach a compromise to uncover the monument failed.

On January 13, 1994, Elliot Cummings, Commander, Maryland Division, SCV, wrote to Senator Jesse Helms, Republican, South Carolina, complaining that the monument, a form of southern heritage, was covered "for reason of political correctness." He argued against an interpretive sign next to the monument to explain its historical context: "This is the exact same line used by the perverters of history at the Smithsonian to justify a distorted story line about the Enola Gay.... This kind of thinking jeopardizes the heritage of all of us" (Cummings 1995).

The NPS received a congressional inquiry from Helms (Helms 1995) and political pressure forced it to remove the plywood covering. Beside the monument stands interpretive signage to create a context for the monument. The reaction to the inscription on the monument belies the oppressing memories this monument represents. Cummings demanded that the national park give the monument back to those who paid for it (the UDC and the SCV) or remove the interpretive wayside sign. "My position is that the monument should not be interpreted," said Cummings. "They should be allowed to exist as they are and people should be allowed to make whatever interpretation they want.... Do I get to put an interpretive plaque on the Lincoln Memorial saying this man was responsible for the deaths of 250,000 Southerners and usurped the Constitution?" (quoted in Bailey 1995:22).

While these southern heritage groups have fought to have the monument redisplayed in the national park, and are fighting to remove any contextual material associated with the object, blacks are arguing to remove the memorial from public display in order to erase some of the landscape reminders of the Jim Crow era. The president of the West Virginia chapter of the NAACP, James Tolbert, remarked, "I don't think it's history. I think it is a misrepresentation of the life and role of Heyward Shepherd. We don't think that the Daughters of the Confederacy and the Sons of the Confederacy had that much love for Negroes" (quoted in Deutsch 1995:1A). During its August meeting, the NAACP chapter passed a resolution that condemned the monument (Bailes 1995:A1). Tolbert later added, "I believe it should be taken by crane to the Potomac River and dropped at the river's deepest point" (quoted in Deutsch 1995:9A; *Jet Magazine* 1995:22–23).

The erection of the Heyward Shepherd Memorial is a way that the SCV and the UDC used nostalgia to legitimize southern bigotry. While African Americans were not pleased with the erection of the Heyward Shepherd Memorial in 1931, they continue to battle with the UDC and the SCV over the meaning of the monument and the memory of slavery. The presence of the memorial in lower town Harpers Ferry is a reminder of the racism that existed in America during the Jim Crow era, and its placement in the national park, on view to the public, threatens African Americans' wishes to remove these signs of bigotry on the American landscape. African Americans feel that the monument legitimizes a racist heritage and successfully excludes a memory of the cruelties of slavery. They fear that its meaning may become part of the official public memory. It is obvious that the lack of political clout has hampered the success of the West Virginia NAACP.

Conclusion

There is a growing literature related to how archaeology is used to create a particular memory and instill nationalism in almost all parts of the globe including Asia (Edwards 1991; Glover 1999; Ikawa-Smith 1999; Pai 1999; Pak 1999), the Pacific region (Spriggs 1999:109–121), the Middle East (El-Haj 1998:166–188), Mesoamerica (Mazariegos 1998), Scandinavia (Scott 1996), and Greece (Brown 1994; Hamilakis 1996, 1999). Archaeology has a long tradition of supporting national programs and creating a past that justifies national territories and/or particular pasts (Anderson 1991:163–185; Kohl 1998:225; Scham 1998; Trigger 1989). Using historical archaeology to help prop official histories is not new to Americans as many projects had their beginnings during times of instability or times of social and economic crises. For instance, a major historical archaeology project began in the United States in the late nineteenth century when labor increasingly challenged the practices of capitalism. In 1897, the Association for the Preservation of Virginia Antiquities, which owns portions of James Island, uncovered the brick foundations of the 1639 church at Jamestown, the first permanent English settlement in the New World. During the Great Depression, in 1934 the NPS initiated excavations at Jamestown with the main goal of architectural reconstruction. This work, undertaken by J. C. Harrington from 1936 through the 1940s, continued under the direction of John Cotter in the 1950s (Cotter 1958; Cotter and Hudson 1957).

Excavations at St. Mary's City, Maryland's first capital, were also begun in the 1930s, pioneered by H. Chandler Forman, who worked there intermittently from 1936 to 1965 after he left Jamestown (Shackel and Little 1994). While the first capitals of Virginia and Maryland received early attention by archaeologists, Virginia's second capital did as well. Sponsored by the Rockefeller Foundation, excavations at Williamsburg from the 1930s also catered to architectural restorations (Derry and Brown 1987; Noël Hume 1983:29).

Jamestown and Williamsburg, in particular, provide examples of government and private interest, respectively, in creating a memory of a historic past. For instance, at Jamestown the NPS presents the town not only as the first permanent English settlement in the New World but also as the birthplace of modern democracy. The first representative legislative assembly in America convened at Jamestown from 1619 until it was moved in 1699 to Williamsburg (Hudson 1985:48). At Williamsburg, the Rockefeller Foundation celebrates the ideals of the planter elite as timeless and inevitable American values (Wallace 1981: 68–78; Patterson 1986). While each site celebrates Anglo-American history, non-European (and other European) peoples whose histories were inextricably linked with the British (and other Europeans) have been largely ignored or glossed over. Neither American Indians nor African Americans figured in the initial vision of the Jamestown and Williamsburg restorations. However, in the 1980s the Colonial Williamsburg Foundation made substantial strides in incorporating the lives of those "others" (e.g., black slaves, servants, and women in general) in restoration, archaeology, research designs, and public presentations (Handler and Gable 1997). An increasing awareness exists among the public, probably through greater exposure to critical histories, that the ideals of the planter elite were not "natural" in the sense of being inevitable, or timeless, but were embedded in their own contemporary social and political realities.

There would be much less to say about historical archaeology in the Chesapeake were it not for the likes of the Rockefeller Foundation (Colonial Williamsburg), the Association for the Preservation of Virginia Antiquities (Jamestown), the Thomas Jefferson Memorial Foundation (Monticello), and the Mount Vernon Ladies Association (Mount Vernon). However, it is also very clear that all of these archaeologies help to reinforce the ideals of the official history and help to create stability and justify inequalities in society today.

The analysis of the construction of history and public memory has taken on a renewed interest, especially when dealing with memory of the recent past and justification for the present (see, for instance, Blake 1999; Daynes 1997; Peri 1999). Many scholars are paying considerable attention to the memory of a generation that is coming to a close, the histories associated with World War II (Epstein 1999; La Capra 1998), and the creation of modern Europe in the post-World War II era (Markovits and Reich 1997). Remembering the Vietnam era has also occupied the scholarship of memory in recent years (see, for instance, Hass 1998).

How we remember and reinterpret a past also serves to create ethnic identities for communities, such as African Americans (Bethel 1997; Fraser 1998), native peoples in Mexico (Florescano 1994), and people of rural Australia (Goodall 1999). Selective memory of the past has also been used by groups to create and justify racism and ethnic cleansing (Coslovich 1994; Larson 1999).

Memory can be about (1) forgetting about or excluding an alternative past, (2) creating and reinforcing patriotism, and/or (3) developing a sense of nostalgia to legitimize a particular heritage. These strategies become important for the construction and legitimation of social groups, particularly nation-states (Alonso 1988:40; Anderson 1991; Hobsbawm and Ranger 1983). It becomes important in creating national histories and in inspiring nationalism (see, for instance, Howe 1999; Nora 1999). Nation-states tend to be rooted in tradition, and this memory of the past appears to be "so 'natural' as to require no definition other than self assertion" (Hobsbawm and Ranger 1983:14). Official histories of a nation require consensus building and the construction of a history from multiple, often conflicting memories (Anderson 1991:163–185; Kohl 1998:225; Scham 1998; Trigger 1989).

Public memory can be viewed as tactical power that controls social settings. Competing groups ceaselessly battle to create and control the collective national memory of revered sacred sites and objects. Different group agendas often clash causing the established collective memories to be continuously in flux. Some subordinate groups can subvert the dominant memory, other groups compromise and become part of a multivocal history, while others fail to have their story remembered by the wider society. The tensions between and within groups who struggle for the control over the collective public memory is often situational and ongoing since the political stakes are high. Those who control the past have the ability to command the present and the future.

"Culture may be seen as memory in action as we live and enact our version of the real living world. Habitual ways of doing things are almost automatic, for we act as we have acted before, and ultimately as we have been taught to act" (Teski and Climo 1995:2). We learn through actual instruction and imitating patterns that we have observed as they surround us at all stages of life. Social actors actively know the way society operates and individuals act within a preexisting structure, or *habitus* (Bourdieu 1977; Giddens 1979). Habitus is the interaction between the unconscious and physical world that is learned and reinforced through interaction. Symbols play an important role in structuring relations of hierarchy and classification systems. Using past experience and the ability to read the meanings of objects allows one to accept or reject the use and meaning of the object and the creation of a particular past.

Material culture, in the form of statues, monuments, museums, artifacts, or landscapes, has some ascribed meaning – past and present – associated with it, and these meanings vary between individuals and interest groups. This material culture can be transformed into sacred objects when serving the goals and needs of any group. The three case studies presented above show how conflicting memories developed around the Heyward Shepherd Memorial, the Civil War Centennial and Manassas National Battlefield Park, and the Robert Gould Shaw Memorial. All of the case studies are about the situational use of power and the ability to use resources to control public memory. In none of these cases has a consensus been reached; rather, groups struggle to have their meaning become part of public history. In the case of the Heyward Shepherd Memorial groups like the UDC and the SCV, the NAACP, and the NPS are fighting over the control for the meaning of a particular past. In this case, NPS representatives placed the monument on display with an interpretive sign that provides some contextual information. A consensus was not reached between the different groups regarding a solution for redisplaying of the monument. The federal government imposed a solution and secured control over the interpretation of the monument. During the late 1950s and early 1960s, an era of great civil strife, the Civil War centennial commemorations became a vehicle to create the notion of obedience and loyalty to a cause. This message was reinforced through public displays and ceremonies. What became clear during these celebratory events was that African American issues played a subservient role to the larger issues of white reconciliation. At Manassas National Battlefield, as well as in many other national parks, African Americans have never had much of a voice at the national park. At the Robert Gould Shaw Memorial the African American community has been very successful in challenging the power of the meaning of the monument. The recent dedication has reaffirmed the power of the African American community and the meaning of the monument has become a memorial about the black soldiers rather than the white colonel. It is a monument that has become part an integral part of African American heritage related to the American Civil War.

In all of these case studies the power of the African Americans to assert themselves and become part of the official meaning varies significantly. While the civil rights movement and the Civil Rights Act allow blacks to gain some control over their official memory, it is important to look at the situational context of power. Blacks have had little power to claim representation at Manassas, a park that historically celebrated two Confederate victories. At Harpers Ferry, the NAACP struggles to gain control over the meaning of a UDC monument, although their efforts have not succeeded since they have had little political clout and they are fighting against an organization that has the backing of U.S. congressional leaders, like Senator Jesse Helms. In Boston, the presence of powerful black leaders like President Benjamin Payton of Tuskegee University, Professor Henry Louis Gates Jr. of the Du Bois Institute at Harvard University, and General Colin Powell gave legitimacy to the control of the meaning of the Shaw memorial.

While there is always a strong movement to remove subordinate memories from our national collective memory, minority groups continually struggle to have their histories remembered. The clash over the control of public history occurs in some of the most visible places on the landscape, like national monuments and national parks. They are the arenas for negotiating meanings of the past (see for instance Linenthal 1993; Linenthal and Englehardt 1996; Lowenthal 1996). The past is always in flux, with competing interests always trying to take control over the collective meaning. The meaning of the American landscape is continually being contested, constructed, and reconstructed.

References

Aaron, Daniel, 1973 The Unwritten War: American Writers and the Civil War. New York: Knopf.

Abroe, Mary Munsell, 1998 Observing the Civil War Centennial: Rhetoric, Reality, and the Bounds of Selective Memory: Understanding the Past. CRM 21(11):22–25.

Alonso, Ana, 1988 The Effects of Truth: Re-Presentations of the Past and the Imagining of Community. Journal of Historical Sociology 1(1):33–57.

Anderson, Benedict, 1991 Imagined Communities: Reflections on the Origins and Spread of Nationalism. London: Verso Press.

Andrews, Matthew Page, 1931 Letter to Henry T. McDonald. McDonald Collection Box 4, Folder 3. October 12. On file, Harpers Ferry National Historical Park, Harpers Ferry, WV.

Bailes, Marc, 1995 NAACP Seeks Response from Park Service, Calls Monument Offensive. The Journal, October 1:A1–A2.

Bailey, Rebecca, 1995 Harpers Ferry Sign Angers Some. Civil War News, August: 22–23.

Bethel, Elizabeth R., 1997 The Roots of African-American Identity: Memory and History in Free Antebellum Communities. New York: St. Martin's Press.

Blake, C. N., 1999 The Usable Past, the Comfortable Past, and the Civic Past: Memory in Contemporary America. Cultural Anthropology 14(3):423–435.

Blatt, Martin, Thomas Brown, and Donald Yacovone, 2000 Hope and Glory: Essays on the Legacy of the Fifty-Fourth Massachusetts Regiment. Amherst: University of Massachusetts and Massachusetts Historical Society.

Blight, David W., 1989 "For Something beyond the Battlefield": Frederick Douglass and the Struggle for the Memory of the Civil War. Journal of American History 75(4):1156–1178.

Blight, David W., 2001 Race and Reunion: The Civil War in American Memory. Cambridge, MA: Belknap Press of Harvard University Press.

Bodner, John, 1992 Remaking America: Public Memory, Commemoration, and Patriotism in the Twentieth Century. Princeton: Princeton University Press.

Boime, Albert, 1990 The Art of Exclusion: Representing Blacks in the Nineteenth Century. Washington, DC: Smithsonian Institution Press.

Bourdieu, Pierre, 1977 Outline of a Theory of Practice. Cambridge: Cambridge University Press.

Brown, K. S., 1994 Seeing Stars: Character and Identity in the Landscapes of Modern Macedonia. Antiquity 68:784–796.

Caffin, Charles H., 1913 American Masters of Sculpture: Being Brief Appreciations of Some American Sculptors and of Some Phase of Sculpture in America. New York: Doubleday, Page.

Cameron, Ardis, 1993 Radicals of the Worst Sort: Laboring Women in Lawrence, Massachusetts, 1860–1912. Urbana: University of Illinois Press.

Cameron, Ardis, 1996 Comments on "Cleansing History." Radical History Review 65:91–97.

Cohodas, Nadine, 1997 The Day the Band Played Dixie: Race and Liberal Conscience at Ole Miss. New York: Free Press.

Confederate Veteran, 1905 Monument to Faithful Slaves. Confederate Veteran 13 (March):123–124.

Confederate Veteran, 1931 Heyward Shepherd. Confederate Veteran 37 (November):411–414.

Connelly, Thomas L., and Barbara L. Bellows, 1982 God and General Longstreet: The Lost Cause and the Southern Mind. Baton Rouge: Louisiana State University Press.

Coslovich, Marco, 1994 I percorsi della sopravvivenza: Storia e memoria della deportazione della "Adriatisches Kustenland." Milan, Italy: Mursia.

Cotter, John L., 1958 Archaeological Excavations at Jamestown, Virginia. U.S. National Park Service Archaeological Research Series, 4. Washington, DC: National Park Service.

Cotter, John L., and Paul Hudson, 1957 New Discoveries at Jamestown. Washington, DC: Government Printing Office.

Cummings, Elliot G., 1995 Letter to Jesse Helms. Heyward Shepherd Folder. January 30. On file, Park Historian, Harpers Ferry National Historical Park, Harpers Ferry, WV.

Daynes, Gary, 1997 Making Villains, Making Heroes: Joseph R. McCarthy, Martin Luther King, Jr. and the Politics of American Memory. New York: Garland Publishing.

Derry, Linda, and Marley R. Brown III, 1987 Excavation at Colonial Williamsburg Thirty Years Ago: An Archaeological Analysis of Cross-Trenching behind the Peyton-Randolph Site. American Archaeology 6(1):10–19.

Deutsch, Jack, 1995 War of Words Erupts over Monument. Daily Mail, November 28:1A, 9A.

Du Bois, W. E. B., 1932 No title. Crisis 41 (January):467.

Edwards, Walter, 1991 Buried Discourse: The Toro Archeological Site and Japanese National Identity in the Early Postwar Period. The Journal of Japanese Studies 17:1–23.

Eisenhower, Dwight D., 1960a Letter to the Civil War Centennial Commission, 6 July 1959. In First Manassas (a Prospectus), a Commemorative Reenactment of a Great Moment in History, a Ceremony Officially Opening the Civil War Centennial Years 1961–1965. On file, Manassas National Battlefield Park, Manassas, VA.

Eisenhower, Dwight D., 1960b Letter to Major General James C. Fry, First Manassas Corporation. On file, Manassas National Battlefield Park, Manassas, VA.

El-Haj, Nadia Abu, 1998 Translating Truths: Nationalism, the Practice of Archaeology, and the Remarking of Past and Present in Contemporary Jerusalem. American Ethnologist 25(2):166–188.

Epstein, C., 1999 The Production of "Official Memory" in East Germany: Old Communists and the Dilemmas of Memoir-Writing. Central European History 32(2):181–201.

Everett, Edward, [1836]1972 Orations and Speeches on Various Occasions. New York: Arno Press.

Fields, Karen, 1994 What One Cannot Remember Mistakenly. In History and Memory in African-American Culture. Genevieve Fabre and Robert O'Meally, eds. Pp. 10–163. New York: Oxford University Press.

Florescano, E., 1994 Memory, Myth, and Time in Mexico: From the Aztecs to Independence. Albert G. Bork, trans. Austin: University of Texas Press.

Foster, Gaines M., 1987 Ghosts of the Confederacy: Defeat, the Lost Cause, and the Emergence of the New South, 1865 to 1913. New York: Oxford University Press.

Fraser, Gertrude J., 1998 African American Midwifery in the South: Dialogues of Birth, Race, and Memory. Cambridge, MA: Harvard University Press.

Frisch, Michael, 1989 American History and the Structure of Collective Memory: A Modest Exercise in Empirical Iconography. Journal of American History 75(4):1131–1155.

Frisch, Michael, 1990 A Shared Authority: Essays on the Craft and Meaning of Oral and Public History. Albany: State University of New York Press.

Giddens, Anthony, 1979 Central Problems in Social Theory: Action, Structure and Contradiction in Social Analysis. London: Macmillan Press.

Gilbert, David, 1984 Where Industry Failed: Water-Powered Mills at Harpers Ferry. Charleston, WV: Pictorial Histories Publishing.

Gilbert, David, 1999 Mills, Factories, Machines and Floods at Harpers Ferry, West Virginia, 1762–1991. Harpers Ferry, WV: Harpers Ferry Historical Association.

Glassberg, David, 1990 American Historical Pageantry: The Uses of Tradition in the Early Twentieth Century. Chapel Hill: University of North Carolina Press.

Glassberg, David, 1996 Public History and the Study of Memory. The Public Historian 18(2):7–23.

Glover, Ian C., 1999 Letting the Past Serve the Present – Some Contemporary Uses of Archaeology in Viet Nam. Antiquity 73(281): 587–593.

Goodall, H., 1999 Telling Country: Memory, Modernity and Narratives in Rural Australia. History Workshop Journal N47 (spring): 160–190.

Hamilakis, Yannis, 1996 Antiquities as Symbolic Capital in Modern Greek Society. Antiquity 70:117–129.

Hamilakis, Yannis, 1999 Stories from Exile: Fragments from the Cultural Biography of the Parthenon (or "Elgin") Marbles. World Archaeology 31(2):303–320.

Handler, Richard, and Eric Gable, 1997 The New History in an Old Museum: Creating the Past at Colonial Williamsburg. Durham, NC: Duke University Press.

Hass, Kristin A., 1998 Carried to the Wall: American Memory and the Vietnam-Veterans-Memorial. Berkeley: University of California Press.

Helms, Jesse, 1995 Letter to Marilyn Merrill. Heyward Shepherd Folder. April 3. On file, Park Historian, Harpers Ferry National Historical Park, Harpers Ferry, WV.

Hobsbawm, Eric, 1983 Introduction: Inventing Tradition. In The Invention of Tradition. Eric Hobsbawm and Terence Ranger, eds., Pp. 1–14. Cambridge: Cambridge University Press.

Hobsbawm, Eric, and Terence Ranger, eds., 1983 The Invention of Tradition. New York: Cambridge University Press.

Holmes, Oliver Wendell, 1962 Occasional Speeches. Mark DeWolfe Howe, comp. Cambridge, MA: Belknap Press of Harvard University Press.

Howe, Stephen, 1999 Speaking of '98: History, Politics and Memory in the Bicentenary of the 1798 United Irish Uprising. History Workshop Journal 47:222–239.

Hudson, Paul, 1985 Jamestown: Birthplace of Historical Archaeology in the United States. Journal of the Archaeological Society of Virginia 40(1):46–57.

Ikawa-Smith, Fumiko, 1999 Construction of National Identity and Origins in East Asia: A Comparative Perspective. Antiquity 73(281):626–629.

Jet Magazine, 1995 Monument to the First Black Killed at Harpers Ferry Raid Draws Criticism. Jet Magazine, September 18:22–23.

Journal of American History, 1995 History and the Public: What Can We Handle? A Round Table about History after the Enola Gay Controversy. Journal of American History 82:1029–1140.

Kammen, Michael, 1991 Mystic Chords of Memory: The Transformation of Tradition in American Culture. New York: Knopf.

Kohl, Philip L., 1998 Nationalism and Archaeology: On the Constructions of Nations and the Reconstructions of the Remote Past. Annual Review of Anthropology 27:223–246.

La Capra, Dominick, 1998 History and Memory after Auschwitz. Ithaca, NY: Cornell University Press.

Larson, P. M., 1999 Reconsidering Trauma, Identity, and the African Diaspora: Enslavement and History Memory in 19th-Century Highland Madagascar. William and Mary Quarterly 56(2):335–362.

Leff, Mark H., 1995 Revisioning United States Political History. American Historical Review 100:833.

Leone, Mark P., 1981 Archaeology's Relationship to the Present and the Past. In Modern Material Culture: The Archaeology of Us. Richard A. Gould and Michael B. Schiffer, eds. Pp. 5–14. New York: Academic Press.

Leone, Mark P., Parker B. Potter Jr., and Paul A. Shackel, 1987 Toward a Critical Archaeology. Current Anthropology 28(3):283–302.

Linenthal, Edward T., 1993 Sacred Ground: Americans and Their Battlefields. Urbana: University of Illinois Press.

Linenthal, Edward, and Tom Engelhardt, 1996 History Wars: The Enola Gay and Other Battles for the American Past. New York: Henry Holt.

Little, Barbara J., 1994 People with History: An Update on Historical Archaeology in the United States. Journal of Archaeological Method and Theory 1(1):5–40.

Lowenthal, David, 1985 The Past Is a Foreign Country. Cambridge: Cambridge University Press.

Lowenthal, David, 1996 Possessed by the Past: The Heritage Crusade and the Spoils of History. New York: Free Press.

Lowenthal, David, 1997 History and Memory. The Public Historian 19(2):31–39.

McConnell, Stuart, 1992 Glorious Contentment: The Grand Army of the Republic, 1865–1900. Chapel Hill: University of North Carolina Press.

McPherson, James M., 1969 Foreword. In A Brave Black Regiment: History of the Fifty-Fourth Regiment of Massachusetts Volunteer Infantry 1863–1865. New York: Arno Press and the New York Times.

McPherson, James M., 1982 Ordeal by Fire: The Civil War and Reconstruction. New York: Knopf.

McPherson, James M., 1988 Battle Cry of Freedom: The Civil War Era. New York: Oxford University Press.

Markovits, Andrei S., and Simon Reich, 1997 The German Predicament: Memory and Power in the New Europe. Ithaca, NY: Cornell University Press.

Martin, Erika, Mia Parsons, and Paul A. Shackel, 1997 Commemorating a Rural African-American Family at a National Battlefield Park. International Journal of Historical Archaeology 1(2):157–177.

Mazariegos, Oswaldo Chinchilla, 1998 Archaeology and Nationalism in Guatemala at the Time of Independence. Antiquity 72(276):376–386.

Meyer, Eugene L., 1995 As Civil War Monument Returns, So Does Controversy. Washington Post, July 10: C1, C2.

Miller, Daniel, and Christopher Tilley, 1984 Ideology, Power, and Prehistory: An Introduction. In Ideology and Power in Prehistory. Daniel Miller and Christopher Tilley, eds. Pp. 1–15. Cambridge: Cambridge University Press.

Minutes of the Civil War Centennial Commission, 1960 Records of the Civil War Centennial Commission. R.G. 79, Box 22, January 5, 1960. Washington, DC: National Archives.

Minutes of the Civil War Centennial Commission, 1961 Records of the Civil War Centennial Commission. R.G. 79, Box 21, December 4, 1961. Washington, DC: National Archives.

Murry, Freeman H. M., 1916 Emancipation and the Freed in American Sculpture: A Study in Interpretation. Washington, DC: Freeman Murry.

Nash, Gary B., Charlotte Crabtree, and Ross E. Dunn, 1998 History on Trial: Culture Wars and the Teaching of the Past. New York: Knopf.

Neustadt, Richard, and Ernst May, 1986 Thinking in Time: The Uses of History for Decision-Makers. New York: Free Press.

New York Times, 1961 No title. New York Times, January 9:1.

New York Times, 1962 No title. New York Times, September 22:1,50.

Noël Hume, Ivor, 1983 Martin's Hundred. New York: Alfred A. Knopf.

Nora, Pierre, 1999 Realms of Memory: Rethinking the French Past. Arthur Goldhammer, trans. New York: Columbia University Press.

O'Leary, Cecilia Elizabeth, 1999 To Die For: The Paradox of American Patriotism. Princeton: Princeton University Press.

Pai, Hyung, II, 1999 Nationalism and Preserving Korea's Buried Past: The Office of Cultural Properties and Archeological Heritage Management in South Korea. Antiquity 73(281):619–625.

Pak, Yangjin, 1999 Contested Ethnicities and Ancient Homelands in Northeast Chinese Archaeology. Antiquity 73(281):613–618.

Patterson, Thomas C., 1986 The Last Sixty Years: Toward a Social History of Americanist Archaeology in the United States. American Anthropologist 88 (1):7–26.

Peri, Yoram, 1999 The Media and Collective Memory of Yitzhak Rabin's Remembrance. Journal of Communication 49(3):106–124.

Peterson, Merrill, 1994 Lincoln in American Memory. New York: Oxford University Press.

Pittsburgh Courier, 1931 Heyward Shepherd Memorial. Pittsburgh Courier, October 24.

Saint-Gaudens, Homer, 1913 The Reminiscences of Augustus Saint-Gaudens. 2 vols. New York: Century Co.

Savage, Kirk, 1997 Standing Soldier, Kneeling Slaves: Race, War, and Monument in Nineteenth-Century America. Princeton: Princeton University Press.

Scham, Sandra A., 1998 Mediating Nationalism and Archaeology: A Matter of Trust? American Anthropologist 100(2):301–308.

Scott, Barbara G., 1996 Archaeology and National Identity: The Norwegian Example. Scandinavian Studies 68:321–342.

Shackel, Paul A., ed., 1993 Interdisciplinary Investigations of Domestic Life in Government Block B: Perspectives on Harpers Ferry's Armory and Commercial District. Occasional Report, 6. Washington, DC: Department of the Interior, National Capital Region Archaeology Program, National Park Service.

Shackel, Paul A., 1994a Archaeology in Harpers Ferry National Historical Park. West Virginia Archaeologist 1–2:1–11.

Shackel, Paul A., 1994b Memorializing Landscapes and the Civil War in Harpers Ferry. In Look to the Earth: An Archaeology of the Civil War. Clarence Geier and

Susan Winter, eds. Pp. 256–270. Knoxville: University of Tennessee Press.

Shackel, Paul A., 1996 Culture Change and the New Technology: An Archaeology of the Early American Industrial Era. New York: Plenum Publishing.

Shackel, Paul A., 1999 Public Memory and the Rebuilding of the Nineteenth-Century Industrial Landscape at Harpers Ferry. Quarterly Bulletin: Archaeological Society of Virginia 54(3):138–144.

Shackel, Paul A., 2000 Archaeology and Created Memory: Public History in a National Park. New York: Kluwer Academic/Plenum Publishing.

Shackel, Paul A., and Barbara J. Little, 1994 Archaeological Perspectives: An Overview of Chesapeake Historical Archaeology. In Historical Archaeology of the Chesapeake. Paul A. Shackel and Barbara J. Little, eds. Pp. 1–15. Washington, DC: Smithsonian Institution Press.

Shanks, Michael, and Christopher Tilley, 1987 Re-Constructing Archaeology. Cambridge: Cambridge University Press.

Sider, G. M., 1996 Cleansing History: Lawrence, Massachusetts, the Strike for Four Loaves of Bread and No Roses, and the Anthropology of Working-Class Consciousness. Radical History Review 65:48–83.

Smith, Steven, 1999 Preserving American Battlefields: What's the Point? Paper presented at "Commemoration, Conflict and the American Landscape: An Archaeology of Battlefield and Military Landscapes," University of Maryland, College Park, November 12.

Spriggs, Matthew, 1999 Pacific Archaeologies: Contested Ground in the Construction of Pacific History. The Journal of Pacific History 34(1):109–121.

Taft, Lorado, [1924]1969 The History of American Sculpture. New York: Arno Press.

Teski, Marea C., and Jacob J. Climo, 1995 Introduction. In The Labyrinth of Memory: Ethnographic Journeys. Marea C. Teski and Jacob J. Climo, eds. Pp. 1–10. Westport, CT: Bergin and Garvey.

Thelen, David, 1989 Memory and American History. Journal of American History 75(4):1117–1129.

Trigger, Bruce, 1989 A History of Archaeological Thought. Cambridge: Cambridge University Press.

Trouillot, Michel-Rolph, 1995 Silencing the Past: Power and Production of History. Boston: Beacon Press.

United Daughters of the Confederacy – National Chapter, 1931 Report of the Faithful Slave Memorial Committee. In Minutes of the Thirty-Eighth Annual Convention of the United Daughters of the Confederacy. Pp. 58–61. Jacksonville, FL, November 17–21.

Virginia Free Press, 1859 No title. Virginia Free Press, October 27:2.

Virginia Free Press, 1867 No title. Virginia Free Press, May 23:2.

Virginia Free Press, 1879 No title. Virginia Free Press, November 29:2.

Virginia Free Press, 1884 No title. Virginia Free Press, November 13:2.

Volz, J. Leonard, 1961 Draft Memorandum, from J. Leonard Volz, Regional Chief of Visitor Protection, to Regional Director. Critique – Reenactment of the Battle of First Manassas. August. On file, Manassas National Battlefield Park, Manassas, VA.

Wachtel, Nathan, 1986 Memory and History, Introduction. History and Anthropology 2 (October):2–11.

Wallace, Anthony, 1981 Visiting the Past: History Museums in the United States. Radical History Review 25:63–96.

White, Rodney A., 1989 The Monument in the Box. The Journal's Weekend Magazine, The Martinsburg Journal 12(23):4, 11.

Wolf, Eric, 1990 Distinguished Lecture: Facing Power – Old Insights, New Questions. American Anthropologist 92:586–596.

Re-Representing African Pasts through Historical Archaeology

Peter R. Schmidt and Jonathan R. Walz

In Africa there is a deep legacy of historical archaeologies that confront and remake metanarratives that misrepresent African pasts. Though these and other revisions of standard histories have made significant contributions to history making, African historical archaeologies have been mostly peripheral to a historical archaeology dominated by North American practitioners concerned first with European and Asian contact studies, and the impacts of colonialism and capitalism on indigenous societies and landscapes. Some of the latter studies open undeniably important insights into the dynamics of interaction between Eurasian and African societies. The historical archaeology of an African community contiguous to Elmina Castle on the coast of contemporary Ghana, for example, shows several striking continuities in foodways and architecture over time despite dominating European influence (DeCorse 2001), a testament to the resiliency of African identities under conditions otherwise resulting in culture change. While the Elmina study turns deserved attention to African responses to others, the framing of issues references European records and European observations.

Peter R. Schmidt and Jonathan R. Walz, "Re-Representing African Pasts through Historical Archaeology", pp. 53–70 from *American Antiquity* 72:1 (2007). Copyright © 2007 by the Society for American Archaeology. Reprinted with permission of the Society for American Archaeology and the authors.

Our goal here is to examine historical archaeologies of Africa that depart from the conventional foci on imperialism and colonialism, primarily but not exclusively a European phenomenon. We believe it is important to expand the way we think about and practice historical archaeology outside of our own historical settings, holding the concomitant ideal that a more international historical archaeology entails a renewed effort to develop perspectives that account for the histories of those without writing and those whose histories have been misrepresented. In the latter case we also address issues associated with misrepresentation of indigenous histories by outsiders, be they agents of colonialism, the church, or the academy. Such issues are significant for historical archaeology insofar as our practice must engage all historicities.

Inclusive or Exclusive Historical Archaeologies?

We question here how one is to make historical archaeologies out of groups that fall outside the margins of European ethnocentrism, colonialism, capitalism, and what Orser (1996) calls "modernity." Is it not contrary to the mission of anthropology to justify an ethnocentric practice of historical archaeology that denies local histories (McGuire and Paynter 1991; Schmidt and Patterson 1995b)? As Orser's (1996) modernity is framed, it is a European encapsulation and histories that escape this encapsulation fall outside the purview of historical archaeology. Orser (2001) more recently appears to recognize the resulting conundrum: that historicities of societies derive exclusively from entanglement with Europe. Such an orientation denies other modernities (Comaroff and Comaroff 1993; Piot 1999; Wolf 1982) and prevents North American historical archeologists from learning about peoples and settings divorced from modernities overwhelmingly influenced by Europe. While Mudimbe (1988) and Chakrabarty (2000) argue against our ability to "provincialize Europe" – in other words, to escape from European/Western paradigms when contemplating, say, Africa such standpoints *ipso facto* limit the gaze of historical archaeologists upon other societies and their pasts. Any obscuring condition carries with it profound ontological and epistemological issues, for knowledge production within the colonial experience unfolded within the colonial library with all of its biases and silences.

How has the practice of historical archaeology in Africa framed issues of historical representation? A historiography that stretches back more than a century as well as active practice over the last 40 years require both explication and a highlighting of examples that illustrate history making in Africa. African historical archaeologists often raise allied issues in contemporary praxis related to concerns taken up by critical historical archaeologists elsewhere (cf. Handsman and Leone 1989; Leone et al. 1987; Leone and Potter 1999; Potter 1994), particularly engaging publics and politics reflexively. They do so while addressing multiple historicities outside colonial libraries as well as the relevance of archaeology to remaking representations about pasts.

Our goal here is to examine historical archaeologies that *do not use* European contact or European colonialism as a framing mechanism. The latter, familiar school of thought has been reviewed in numerous venues over the last two decades (LaViolette 2004; Posnansky and DeCorse 1986). Rather, we want to explore a less-evident thread of historical archaeology that escapes the confines of a Eurocentric approach, focuses on historical representations about Africa, and employs local African historiographies as their frame of reference. Within this genre of

scholarship is Ann Stahl's (2001, 2004) research in Banda, Ghana. Stahl reopens an important discourse about the practice of historical archaeology and history making in Africa, proposing alternative ways of seeing and making histories within the context of African archaeology and history. She emphasizes the search for dissonant materialities and historiographies as well as building supplemental approaches as opposed to the additive approaches that continue to dominate historical archaeology in contact and colonial settings. A historical archaeology that incorporates dissonance is one that seeks contradictions, either to established historical narratives or between materiality and other evidence. An additive approach, on the other hand, simply adds to known historiographies, neither contradicting nor significantly altering conventional wisdom. A central feature of Stahl's project derives from Trouillot (1995), who argues that "mentions" in history actively create silences, an important lesson that warns against privileging one history over another. One of Stahl's themes is that we must understand, if we are to engage in history making, the interests and forces that stamp mentions and silences upon history and the landscape.

Following Trouillot (1995), Stahl posits that the mentions of history often represent vested interests and that once established, they obscure and gloss the historical context, the particulars from which the mentions arise. This concept is all the more important in settings where contests arise in the dynamic of oral representations and where scholars are involved actively in creating both mentions and silences. The politics of history making go beyond merely "constructing history"; researchers must reflexively accept responsibility for a historical product as "making history," a process that "more accurately captures the political process, also reflexively informed, inherent in giving voice to histories that have been silenced or erased" (Schmidt and Patterson 1995a:12–13).

There are other issues, however, that arise from Stahl's rendering of how material evidence is to be employed in history making. Among these is the use of tropes to represent materialities that are recursive constructions. Stahl (2001) argues, for example, that "*the* lived past" (emphasis added) can be accessed or envisioned from archaeological materials and other sources, yet in a manner that is seemingly remote from the interpreter's agency – an essentialization of the past as well as a positivist rendering (as something that can be known). Stahl's objective is to raise our consciousness about the usefulness of quotidian material evidence in making histories that valorize everyday life in history writing. The consequences of constructing a "lived past" – if we are to use the concept – must be examined reflexively. It is a powerful trope, a metonymy that animates and has the potential to transform and homogenize pasts by renaming them. Once reflexively aware of the tendency of "the lived past" to stand for the particulars of the quotidian evidence that we work with daily, we may then engage that evidence in our search for dissonance.

More recently Andrew Reid and Paul Lane (2004b) reference "the lived past" and Stahl's use of mentions and silences in their overview of historical archaeologies in Africa, raising our anticipation that these themes will play out in the case studies that comprise *African Historical Archaeologies*. This volume, however, highlights regions and periods with a preponderance of written texts – southern Africa and West Africa, with a tertiary focus on the East African coast and immediate hinterland. The use of European documents to frame much of the discourse clashes with the volume's philosophical framing – that African voices, expressing their own histories either in oral or written form, should be featured. We agree that if scholars are to assess change during the precontact period as well as African perspectives on change after contact, then unwritten sources must be an integral part of our method. One gets the definite impression, however, that something quite different is seen as defining the historical archaeology project when we are informed that "it is only in certain regions [southern African and the West African coast] that archaeologists have sought to engage their archaeology with historical texts and have actively used the term historical archaeology" (Reid and Lane 2004a:14–15).[1] An emphasis on these two regions, to the exclusion of any *extended* discussion about alternative sources, such as oral histories and traditions, or other regions, such as wider eastern Africa, submerges the possibility of reclaiming African voices and leads to texts comprised of voices arising from European

(and Islamic) colonial libraries. This leaves us with little that is "African" and much that is a reproduction of Europe in Africa (Asad 1987).

Reid and Lane are patently and refreshingly clear on the need to address issues that affect historical interpretations – one of the arguable short-comings of North American historical archaeology. They submit that, "Archaeology … can therefore provide an important foil to the thrusts of history, broadening and deepening our historical understanding" (Reid and Lane 2004a:15).[2] By this they mean that archaeology from any era – precontact, postcontact, or postcolonial – may be used to challenge and present alternative views to conventional historical thinking. A number of contributions in their volume feature this significant perspective, one that they acknowledge has been practiced in African historical archaeology for some time. Their emphasis on this school of thought makes an important contribution to global historical archaeology in its focus on the interaction – often the dissonance – between history and archaeology (Andrén 1998; Funari et al. 1999; Schmidt and Patterson 1995b).

The publication of the Reid and Lane volume opens an opportunity to explore an alternative practice of historical archaeology in Africa that goes beyond Eurocentric frames and additive approaches. Hence, we want to review here select literature that illustrates the dual themes of making alternative histories through the search for contradictory materialities and the valorization of indigenous historiographies, mostly oral-based and sometimes manipulated by certain Western interests. Most of these examples derive from East Africa and thus fall outside of the well-known "literary nexuses" that we earlier mentioned. We integrate several examples from the Reid and Lane volume that we believe best exemplify the making of alternative histories in Africa, a generally well-developed theme (Andah 1995a; Miller et al. 1989; McGuire and Paynter 1991; Schmidt and Patterson 1995b).

Addressing Questions that Count

We want to take this discussion beyond the traditional, taken-for-granted tropes and suggest that the practice of historical anthropology should address issues of historical representation – "questions that count" (Deagan 1988), whatever their temporal context or origins. Thus, an integrated historical archaeology – truly an historical anthropology, including archaeology and its attendant social theories – should address questions of historical representation. Historical anthropology cannot be disaggregated from historical archaeology, that nominally disappears under Stahl's (2001) treatment, but we focus on the latter because our praxis, the remaking of historical representations, arises with greater clarity when we find dissonance in materialities vis-à-vis other sources.

With these issues in mind, what direction might we take to recognize African histories, integrating oral traditions and histories, ethnographies, materialities, and written sources, among others? We want to highlight several intellectual trends, especially in eastern and southern Africa, that may stimulate further interchange and dialogue with researchers practicing historical archaeology elsewhere. In the meantime, we examine the intellectual genesis of archaeologies that impinge upon historical representations within Africa and their usefulness to historical archaeology on a global scale. These examples of African historical archaeologies offer possible paths that historical archaeologists in the Americas and Eurasia might take to reconfigure and fulfill their mission to address issues of significance.

Existing standard histories or master narratives may be derived from archaeological evidence that archaeologists normatively categorize as "prehistoric," even though many of the referenced ancient societies were within the orbit of written systems. Whether or not writing prevailed at the time or if written observations pertain to the society in question is not our interest. The critical issue is the interpretative narrative – the representations – that have developed out of archaeologically created materialities. When fresh perspectives arise out of oral history, as we will see in Helm's (2000, 2004) research, then the resulting dialectic compels a rethinking: a reworking of the narrative representation and engaging history making. We now want to turn to a number of studies that illustrate critical historical archaeologies addressing issues of historical representation that valorize African voices or materialities by accepting that they differ from and contradict standard

European histories of Africa. We suggest that what follows results from responding to "questions that count" in African history.

Re-representing oral narratives

We first turn to developments that have questioned Western interpretations of African histories, particularly those that have excluded or denigrated indigenous ways of seeing pasts. The limitations of oral traditions have been affirmed by some historians of Africa (Henige 1974, 1982; Miller 1980), but this perspective has developed strictly outside of archaeological treatments of the interplay between materiality and oral tradition. This skeptical view unfortunately has been amplified in wider archaeological circles through an ignorance of African case studies, a striking misunderstanding of the antiquity and usefulness of such traditions, and an ignorance of the contexts in which oral sources have been linked to monumental mnemonics (cf. Bradley 2004; Mason 2000).

To overcome these unwarranted treatments and enhance the potentials of oral traditions (Cohen et al. 2001), we emphasize a more sanguine and balanced approach that arose out the pioneering and innovative research of Lanning, Shinnie, and Posnansky in Uganda as well as Willett in Nigeria. This is scholarship that apparently affirmed Vansina's (1965) initial belief that archaeology had an important role to play in underwriting oral traditions, a position from which Vansina subsequently seems to have retreated (Vansina 1995; cf. Robertshaw 2000). In African settings oral traditions have come to be recognized as playing influential roles in local representations of history through royals and elites as well as commoners articulating competing views (Schmidt 1978; Stahl 2001). This approach may best be illustrated by re-examinations of well-known Cwezi oral traditions, oral texts that are mythological in structure and found in widely scattered regions of interlacustrine East Africa (Berger 1981; Tantala 1989).

A significant historiographic problem developed around the Cwezi as a historical dynasty dating to the mid-second century A.D. and associated with places such as alleged capital sites (Figure 20.1). Though most evidence points to the Cwezi as a religious cult with considerable

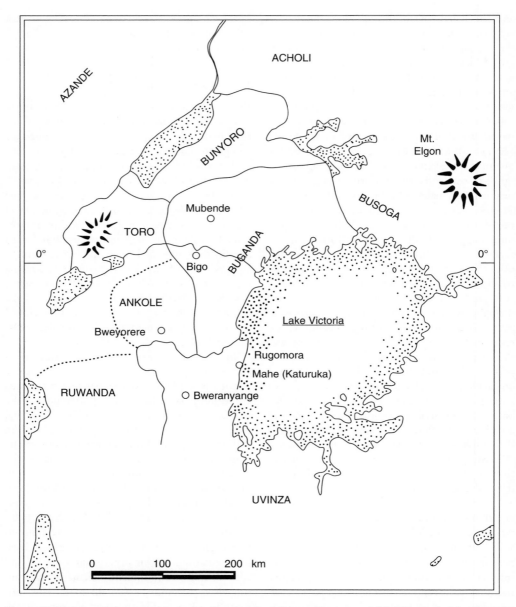

Figure 20.1   Map of sites associated with Cwezi oral traditions: Rugomora Mahe (Katuruka) in Tanzania; Bigo and Mubende [Hill] in Uganda.

political influence and direct control over the political economy in regions of what today are Uganda and Tanzania, the Cwezi state paradigm remains a popular standard history in East Africa. The first serious questioning arose during analysis of oral traditions about the Hinda dynasty and other social groups in Kyamutwara Kingdom in northwestern Tanzania. Structural

analysis showed that the oral traditions of king Rugomora Mahe had been significantly influenced by the structure (paradigmatic aspect) as well as sequencing and integration (syntagmatic aspect) of oral traditions linked to Cwezi rulers.

A comparison of royal and non-royal Cwezi oral traditions and an integrative tacking method between oral and archaeological clues revealed that the history of the king's royal capital was highly contested, exposing a hidden history. This sacred and very ancient Cwezi cult site had been co-opted by the foreign Hinda during the mid-seventeenth century as a means to gain legitimacy in their quest for hegemony over indigenous groups. Ritual pits created through performative displays during the Hinda occupation of this ancient shrine had been placed contiguous to ancient iron-working features dating to 2,500 years ago (Schmidt 1978, 1997); the contiguity of Hinda and Cwezi space affected by these seventeenth-century ritual features identified the Hinda, through metonymy, with etiological myth about an ancient iron tower. Succinctly, Hinda appropriation of sacred places unveiled historical manipulations during the seventeenth century A.D.

These discoveries directly challenged the canon that oral traditions had antiquity limited only to the last few hundred years while simultaneously opening up an understanding of the role of mnemonic monuments in social memory (Robertshaw 2000; Schmidt 1978, 1997, 2006) as well as historical insights into the play of sacred landscapes, political economies, power, and political legitimacy in Buhaya (a region of northwestern Tanzania). New interpretations about Cwezi oral traditions and their manipulations by Hinda royals over the last three centuries challenged well-ingrained, standard historical thinking on the origin of the state in East Africa, namely, that Cwezi oral traditions were first and foremost literal commentaries on a historic dynasty that ruled in Uganda about A.D. 1400–1500 (Schmidt 1978, 1990).

A subsequent outgrowth was an inquiry into the reliability of historical interpretations that represented the large earthwork site of Bigo in western Uganda as a Cwezi capital site. This idea was fixed as deeply as the historical notion held by whites in southern Africa in 1910 that Great Zimbabwe was built by the Queen of Sheba or Arabs, among others. Once evidence for a Cwezi capital at Bigo was examined closely, however, it was found that some oral traditions had been derived from outside groups and that others were ephemeral, undercutting standard historical interpretations for the origins of the state in Uganda, a phenomenon that grew out of colonial attempts to buttress the antiquity of

kingdoms administered by British indirect rule in Uganda.

Critical analysis of oral texts engages a comparative method that has long been a hallmark of historiographic analysis. Materialities derived from archaeology offer an additional dynamic as we tack among sources. Dissonance among oral testimonies may be amplified or resolved by material evidence, as was the case in Buhaya as well as in the Mosu area of Botswana (Reid 2005; Reid and Segobye 1999) (Figure 20.2), where the oral traditions of the Tswana claimed that a valley five kilometers south of the Sowa Pan marked the birthplace of Khama III, the father of modern Botswana in the late nineteenth and early twentieth centuries. Archaeologists located a series of walled enclosures along a one kilometer stretch of this hidden river valley (Reid 2005:365). Vitrified dung middens and putative grain platforms were excavated as an explicit verification exercise to confirm the link to the Tswana people. During their investigations, however, archaeologists became aware that oral traditions from a nearby Khoisan-speaking community provided a contradictory view: That the physical remains on the landscape were not Tswana. Instead, these remains corresponded to the amalgamation of an ancestral Khoisan group with a farming population named the Kalanga who had fled nineteenth-century social unrest to the east. This multiethnic community, known in the Kalanga language as Moojane, or "What shall we eat?", evidently blended their knowledge of resources and subsistence. The Khoisan community helped to identify food resources along the pan while the Kalanga community taught the Khoisan-speakers how to tend livestock and farm. Eventually, a Tswana polity extended its hegemony into this region, dispersing both the Kalanga and Khoisan-speaking groups.

Investigators understandably tend to privilege the importance of recognizing multiethnic communities within the Kalahari, but we believe there are equally important lessons to be derived for historical archaeology. A discursive analysis of different oral texts and materialities may isolate dissonance important to the making of new histories with compelling alternative narratives. In this case dominant Tswana representations of history were contradicted by extant oral traditions, held by a disenfranchised minority, that

Figure 20.2 Countries discussed in the text are shaded: Mali, Ghana, Sudan, Eritrea, Kenya, Tanzania, Uganda, Zimbabwe, Botswana, and South Africa.

better fit past materialities. Contradictions to taken-for-granted historical knowledge remade histories through the application of deconstructed oral traditions and reconfigured materialities, a dialectical process that led to a fuller practice of historical archaeology.

Transforming constructions of settlement

Increasingly, we are seeing historical archaeologies that address representations arising out of so-called ancient materialities, such as those

witnessed in Buhaya. David Edwards' (2004) self-identified historical archaeology in Nubia makes important contributions to evaluating standard histories that depend on perceived configurations in the material record. Edwards examines interpretations of the decline of Meroe based on a series of developments that for decades characterized the historical literature: (1) the replacement of pyramid-shaped royal tombs by tumulus-covered tombs; (2) the abandonment of urban/monumental centers; and (3), the rise of a new and distinct political order associated with Noba/Nubians. In an extensive exegesis Edwards meticulously demonstrates that fresh evidence for the materiality of the past in Nubia compels an alternative historical interpretation. First, there are clear continuities in burial forms that persist into the post-Meroitic "period," even within kingly burials. Archaeological research into settlement patterns further demonstrates that settlement in lower Nubia included far fewer people and greater settlement complexity than heretofore thought, with many sites abandoned and reoccupied. Edwards' recent investigations demonstrate that most settlements fall within an array of hamlets and small villages, not the large towns and villages that previously "characterized" the region. In other words, he provides viable alternatives to the standard history enshrined in popular historiography, a historical archaeology that engages questions that count. The re-representation of interpretations about ancient Nubia works from the same theoretical perspective developed in a critical historical archaeology of southeastern Kenya employing ancient materiality to confront, overturn, and rewrite historical narratives.

The literal construction of oral traditions arises as a problem in Kenya, where the research of Richard Helm (2004) shows how archaeology makes histories that challenge narrative hegemonies. Helm operates within a revisionist framework, deconstructing historical interpretations about the settlement history of the Kenyan hinterland, particularly the valorization of the Shungwaya myth by certain postcolonial scholars.[3] Helm argues that these oral traditions provided a persuasive account about the emergence of Bantu, Sabaki-speaking communities, particularly in their claim for southwards diffusion from the Tana River region in northern Kenya and differentiation into current ethnolinguistic communities (Helm 2004). Helm examines Spear's (1974, 1978) interpretation that Mijikenda[4] settlement was confined to nine kaya (defensive settlements often associated with sacred groves) until the nineteenth century by drawing on archaeological evidence for widespread settlement both prior to and during the second millennium A.D. – a substantive and direct challenge to the idea of a southerly sixteenth-century population movement into the Mijikenda hinterland. By producing evidence on settlement, subsistence, and

ceramics through archaeological research, Helm (2000) reinterprets the regional past. He builds a three-stage settlement history of the region attentive to alternative sources such as oral traditions associated with archaeological sites that indicate Spear failed to explore variations of the Shungwaya myth across groups (Helm 2004: 59–61). Instead, Helm argues that the Shungwaya origin myth simply "formed the basis of a cultural 'charter', helping to reinforce both their internal contemporary identity, and their external relationships with others" and thus should be viewed skeptically (Helm 2004:61).

Moreover, Helm recognizes a "crude correlation between the observed temporal periods of sites and the suggested structural order of the oral traditions," resulting in the following settlement outline: (1) a first millennium A.D. period of initial migration and settlement or, in Mijikenda traditions, a period of "how things became"; (2) a period from the late first millennium onwards demonstrative of gradual proliferation and a growing hierarchy of settlements or, to Mijikenda elders, a period of "things as they should be"; and (3) a period of decline in settlement size and hierarchy, or "things as they are" (Helm 2004:79–81). He concludes that the integration of archaeological data with oral traditions opens our understanding to alternative ways of perceiving this past, namely that Mijikenda settlement patterns and oral traditions work together to effectively question the established histories of origins and migration. This case study, drawing on finer and more nuanced research into variations of local oral traditions and more particular archaeological evidence for settlement in the coastal hinterland, results in a significant rejection of the extant historiography surrounding the Shungwaya construct. Helm's study overturns how historians have used oral tradition to represent the history of the region. In this regard his work bears significant affinities to how historical archaeology has challenged historical narratives about the Cwezi as well as peoples of so-called historical voids and geographical wastelands, as we shall see.

Paul Lane (2004) suggests that reasoned challenges to standard histories may develop from equitable attention to alternative interpretations, some of which arise out of ancient settlement patterning. His goal, like ours, is to develop a critical historical archaeology that can be applied across time frames to address historical representation. He explores the abandonment and aggregation of numerous Sotho-Tswana stone-built towns in Botswana, long held by historians to have resulted from the *difaqane* (or *mfecane*), a period of social conflict and demographic upheaval from circa A.D. 1790–1830 – a position amplified by archaeologists who employ the same explanation. Historians and archaeologists reason that conflict and raiding during this turbulent period forced population agglomerations to hilltops for defensive purposes. Lane suggests an alternative view, one that rejects the expansion of the Zulu state or the rise of commodity slavery as the only forces that might alter settlement patterns. He sees that the process of aggregation and abandonment in certain instances may be interpreted as a response to climatic cycles of drought that compelled relocation: "far from being an epiphenomenon arising from periodic warfare and unrest, settlement relocation was in fact an integral and long-standing aspect of Tswana land use strategies and settlement ecology" (Lane 2004:287). Such regular relocation, he infers, resulted from scarcity of water and depleted pasturage at any single locality through time.

Lane uses case studies from the settlements of Lepalong and Modipe to illustrate that histories of towns should be investigated independent of homogenizing paradigms. Lepalong and Modipe both contradict the anticipated trend of settlement location (hilltops) as projected from other areas impacted by the *difaqane*. Moreover, sites with hilltop or other settlement structures comprise phases that fall substantially outside the *difiqane* period, including previous occupations, raising additional questions about the *difiqane* as the primary cause of changes in the townscapes of all Sotho-Tswana. Lane's challenge to the standard history of the *difiqane* deconstructs this suspect use of historical generalization, a problem plaguing many histories of Africa.

Remaking temporal voids and disconnected geographies

Significant developments in southern Africa address historical representations about Khoisan-speakers in the Kalahari. The historical representation of the Kalahari as a culturally and environmentally isolated zone – widely recognized in the literature – is closely linked to stereotypic notions of an unchanged population that is ideal for understanding the behavior of hunter-gatherers in the past (Reid 2005). The issue of whether Khoisan-speakers were independent from surrounding pastoral and agricultural groups or were "encapsulated" within their sphere of influence has become a contentious debate in anthropology between the revisionist school and those opposed to the idea that the peoples of the Kalahari were integrated into a network of external contacts that stretches back more than a millennium (cf. Lee and Guenther 1991; Smith and Lee 1997; Solway and Lee 1990). Our concern here is only with the broader issue of historical representations of this region as lacking contact with the outside world until the nineteenth century, a representation related to the issue of Khoisan-speakers as remote from other influences.

The most elegant challenge to the notion of an ahistorical Kalahari comes from Edwin Wilmsen's (1989) meticulous and significant documentation of Kalahari relations with a broader world since Portuguese interactions with the continent, a perspective that defeats the notion of the Kalahari and its people as timeless. Archaeology enters the historical picture when one considers Denbow's (1984, 1990, 1999) research in the region. Using archaeological evidence, Denbow (1984) shows that there were significant communities on the eastern fringe of the Kalahari from A.D. 900–1300. Through his excavations in the Tsodilo Hills northwest of the Okavango Delta in Botswana, he additionally demonstrates that commerce between peoples of the Kalahari and the eastern coast of Africa dates back to the seventh century A.D. (Denbow 1990, 1999). The presence of glass beads via trade from the Indian Ocean and copper, likely derived from present-day Zambia, both testify to participation in far-flung trading systems. Reid (2005) persuasively argues that debates over encapsulation have severely obscured that large and significant communities were on the fringe of the Kalahari deep into the first millennium and that it is highly unlikely for mobile populations to have had no contact with these nearby societies. Central to our argument is that historical archaeology is not bound by the artificial literate/

nonliterate dichotomy. Historical representations of the Kalahari as outside the orbit of commerce and mercantile penetration have been permanently overturned by the application of compelling archaeological evidence that disproves the premise of remoteness and timelessness.

A striking historical parallel to the Kalahari is the representation of the arid, thorny scrubland in the immediate hinterland of eastern Africa known as *nyika*. Both regions have been misrepresented as peripheral wastelands in European texts. These characterizations emanate from environmental constructions that are tropes for the so-called sparseness of human history. The effect locates hunter-gatherers and pastoralists at the edge of European historicity. Archaeological questionings of the *nyika* as a cultural and historical wasteland began with Thorbahn's (1979) historical archaeology of the ivory trade, which focused on interaction between coastal and hinterland communities. Though his archaeological endeavors were modest, Thorbahn's survey results pointed to a presence of hinterland settlement and the interaction of populations across the wider region and beyond.

In the middle 1990s Helm began to investigate parallel issues pertaining to the so-called "settlement void" in the hinterland of Kenya, a characterization arising from Shungwaya representations, part of a historical interpretative package that included the ideas of the emergence of a coastal Swahili culture along the northern Kenya coast as well as "an apparent absence of archaeological evidence for settlement within the coastal hinterland, until the mid-second millennium AD" (Helm 2004:60). Helm's inquiries provided a substantive challenge to this widely accepted historical interpretation of East African history. His studies proved definitively that the coastal hinterland showed strong linkages with coastal culture (also Allen 1993; Mutoro 1987) – a situation that compelled deeper inquiry into the "existing standard history" (Helm 2004:60), and led to his schema for a regional settlement history that stretched over both the first and second millennia A.D.

More recently, Chapurukha and Sibel Kusimba (2005) have substantiated interaction and trade between hinterland communities in Tsavo National Park and coastal populations in southeastern Kenya through documentation of economic evidence in the archaeological record. Located as far as 150 kilometers from the coast, this region was an important source of Indian Ocean and coastal trade goods, such as ivory, rhinoceros horn, iron ore and bloom (raw iron), animal skins, and rock crystal. Surveys have identified 220 archaeological sites in addition to 150 already known. Sites include iron working localities, cairn burials, rockshelters, secondary interments, open-air sites, grinding hollows, and fortified refuges (Kusimba and Kusimba 2005). Excavations at 12 sites yielding more than 40 ^{14}C dates have now established a complex cultural history over the last 12,000 years as well as distinct spheres of influence in terms of resources exploited in trade with historical coastal communities (Chapurukha Kusimba, personal communication 2004).

The Kusimbas' research provides material evidence that erodes standard histories about the *nyika* as a cultural and physical wasteland. Their tacking among oral, archival, and archaeological evidence also illustrates that post-sixteenth-century Tsavo experienced periodic droughts punctuated by famine, disease, and warfare. Extensive oral traditions collected in the field offer insights into how, when, and where different groups utilized resources, including information over several centuries during which the region received only glossed, pejorative references in written documents. Of importance to their historical archaeology are oral testimonies recounting cattle raids, slaving, and shifts in settlement patterns during the turbulent eighteenth and nineteenth centuries (Kusimba 2004; Kusimba and Kusimba 2005:411).

In this case, tacking between oral evidence and the settlement record elucidates patterns of site abandonment as well as environmental change in the region. External demands for ivory and slaves as well as the local devastation caused by exploitative hunting practices, such as overkilling of elephants, and the accompanying shift from savannah grasslands to scrub woodlands, suggest that nineteenth-and early twentieth-century observations of a *nyika* void now enshrined in standard histories are the product of cultural and natural degradations initiated three centuries ago. The historical archaeology conducted by the Kusimbas poignantly suggests that *nyika* history must be recuperated and remade to incorporate multicultural, deep time human interactions with this landscape.

Working on similar issues in the adjacent hinterland of northeastern Tanzania, Walz (2001, 2005) has extended knowledge of coast and interior relations deeper in time by exploring historically known corridors of interaction identified in oral traditions and documents dating as early as the eighteenth century. After pinpointing archaeological sites from this era within the lower Ruvu/Pangani River basin, he employed them as analogical guideposts to trace much earlier evidence of regional settlement and interaction. Systematic fieldwork identified key ancient sites in the interior, such as Kwamgogo and Gonja Maore, with copious evidence of regional production and exchange, including marine shells, Eurasian glass beads, and coastal ceramics. Large interior sites dating to the late first millennium A.D. indicate recurrent utilization of the same general vicinities as more recent slave and ivory caravan stopping points. This historical archaeology erodes standard histories rooted in geographical dichotomies and an emphasis on written sources that amplify differences between the interior and the littoral – a separation that hinders understandings of genuinely regional histories. By bringing interior communities into the historical discourse, and thus working across geographical (coast/hinterland) and temporal (history/prehistory) dichotomies resulting from heretofore disparate epistemologies (history/ archaeology), we transform the history of the interior as well as the coast, making a more unified African history.

Challenging foreign foundations

Perhaps the most convincing examples of the power of ancient materiality to displace standard histories derive from challenges to paradigms of foreign foundation. By the mid-1970s, the use of historical archaeology to examine and reject standard historical representations in African history had become an active and conscious program among some archaeologists working in southern Africa (Garlake 1973, 1982; Hall 1984, 1990; Maggs 1976b). Peter Garlake's synthesis of research at Great Zimbabwe brought before a much wider audience the historical contests over the origins of Great Zimbabwe, confronting master narratives of foreign origins arising out of Cecil Rhodes's commissioned archaeology during the first part of the twentieth century and favored by racist settlers. Martin Hall (1984, 1990) elaborated Garlake's agenda when he addressed wider audiences about the fallacy of the myth of white superiority: that Great Zimbabwe was the creative genius of the Phoenicians or Portuguese rather than the ancestors of indigenous populations found in Zimbabwe. They work within a legacy that goes back to the groundbreaking research of D. R. MacIver (1906) and Gertrude Caton-Thompson (1931) – the earliest illustrations of the interplay between archaeology and history in sub-Saharan Africa.

Great Zimbabwe, of course, was not the only site or issue in southern Africa to attract historical archaeologists keen to confront and transform misleading historical representations – representations that, in some cases effectively denied cultural and human rights to contemporary Africans. Working within a heightened awareness of outmoded paradigms within southern African archaeology, Hall, for example, examined a number of historical myths about settlement, foremost of which was the apartheid-informed position that people of "white" descent were the first to inhabit an "empty" hinterland (Hall 1984; Maggs 1976a). Maggs and Hall reviewed chronological evidence for the presence of African communities dating to as early as the third century A.D. Synthesis of previous work formed a historical perspective that explicitly overturned the myth of white first arrival, undermining the white "prior claim" to land.

Also rooted in images that portray Eurasians as "civilizing" influences on Africans, the origins and histories of Swahili city-states have been effectively remade by scholars such as Allen (1974, 1993). Horton (1996). and Chami (1994, 1998), among others (for reviews, see Kusimba 1999: Spear 2000). Allen, a historian, and Horton, an archaeologist, examined the viability of the idea that Swahili culture and particularly urbanism. which arose along the coast of eastern Africa from A.D. 750 to 1500, were exclusively Near Eastern transplants: That central political authority and economic complexity were imports from Asia and not a product of local life

(Chittick 1974: Kirkman 1964). Using documents, oral histories and traditions, and ethnographic observations, Allen (1993) sought to provide local origins for Swahili culture rooted in African developments, namely the rise of an indigenous multiethnic state between coastal northern Kenya and southern Somalia. Although his conclusions remain contested. Allen's work spurred further investigations of regional populations and a fundamental remaking of pasts.

Alongside historical linguists who had demonstrated an early and indigenous origin for Swahili language, Horton (1996) and Chami (1994, 1998) produced critical material evidence of Swahili foundations and character tied to the continent. These archaeologies incisively confronted valorized oral traditions codified in coastal texts that identified the Swahili as a byproduct of links to the Shiraz region of contemporary of Iran. Archaeologists such as Horton and Chami transformed representations of littoral society as an Asian transplant by demonstrating continuities in settlement extending from earlier African communities to the principal periods of Swahili foundation (A.D. 600–1000) and florescence (particularly A.D. 1250–1500). Ceramics of Triangular Incised Ware (TIW), or Tana Tradition (TT), were central to arguments of African associations. These ceramics comprised more than 95 percent of vessel fragments recovered from early coastal urban settlements, the remainder being foreign and presumably articles of wealthy Islamic elites with overseas connections. Finds of wattle-and-daub structures predating coral and coral rag architecture, characteristic of ancient coastal towns, further supported African origins. More recently, archaeologists have continued to erode the colonialist model of the Swahili by utilizing ancient documents and material residues, binding together previously separate geographical entities (coast and hinterland) through materialities – ceramics and/or evidence of exchange with the African interior. This results in a better framework for understanding African regional social-economic developments rather than foreign-induced impacts (Abungu 1989; Haaland and Msuya 2000; LaViolette et al. 1989).

As with the standard histories of the East Africa coast, the dominant history of the Horn

of Africa since the eighteenth century has drawn on the idea that cultural complexity and civilization in the highlands of contemporary Ethiopia and Eritrea derived from Asian influences, in this case through direct contact with the Sabaeans of the Saba civilization (1000 B.C.–A.D. 300) in what is today Yemen (Fattovich 1997, 2004; cf. Schmidt 2002). The idea of a foreign source for political centralization and complexity first became popularized by the British explorer Theodore Bent, and was subsequently reiterated and reified by linguists and archaeologists. Amplified by documentation of Sabena-influenced artifacts such as votive altars as well as masonry structures – for example, at Yeha – the standard narrative alleges the Ethio-Sabaean state of Daamat arose from these imported influences. Subsequently, say the standard histories, these influences contributed to the rise of the Aksumite Empire from A.D. 150 forward (Schmidt 2002). This permutation of the foreign interaction paradigm has a much longer history than parallel renderings about Islamic influence in eastern Africa.

Starting in 1998, researchers and students at the University of Asmara began to document stonebuilt towns and large villages surrounding contemporary Asmara, the capital of present-day Eritrea (Schmidt and Curtis 2001). These large, settled, and demographically complicated agropastoral communities were clearly precursors to later urban developments found just 120 kilometers to the south dating to the mid-first millennium B.C. They also show unambiguous endogenous origins. The materialities of 800–400 B.C. challenge several centuries of dominant orthodox, not just standard, histories that attribute the origin of centralization, urbanism, and cultural complexity in the Horn to the foreign Sabaeans. The northern Horn of Africa certainly was within the orbit of Sabaean economic and religious spheres of influence and local African elites likely used symbolic materials to signal "Sabaean" identity for reasons of social differentiation (Curtis 2004), but the seeds of urbanism and local industry were planted locally long before. These examples vividly illustrate that the materiality of the past – regardless of its being precontact or postcontact – can empower historical archaeology if directed at questions that count.

Questioning ancient texts and the colonial library

The valorization and concretization of observations located in precolonial, colonial, and postcolonial documents is a problem that permeates African history and anthropology, perpetuating historical and historiographic myths that are often accepted without critical confrontation. Insoll (2004) questions one such representation in his historical archaeology of Gao, an ancient city in Mali, West Africa. Insoll's study of early representations through Arabic sources illustrates how later interpretations reify early observations, making the materiality of archaeology one of the few means by which challenges can be made to historical convention. Arabic descriptions from the late tenth and mid-eleventh centuries of two separate quarters of Gao, believes Insoll, reflect an exaggerated representation of "white" merchants and "black" Songhai on a geographical scale. The archaeological evidence does not substantiate such a view, yet recent historical interpretations amplify the ancient texts and ignore the archaeology (Insoll 2004: 179), a fallacy unmasked by Insoll's historical archaeology. This is a powerful cautionary tale for those who use historical archaeology in an additive manner rather than searching for dissonance.

Discord between sources can be uncovered by historical archaeologists taking a purposeful initiative to face histories heretofore reliant on ancient written sources alone. During the mid-1980s, archaeologists at the University of Dar es Salaam in Tanzania turned their collective attention to the littoral of East Africa (Schmidt et al. 1992), where historical interpretations favored a portrait of the immediate hinterland as an economic backwater and the populations along the littoral as recipients of trade materials and other cultural influences from abroad. A fixation on foreign influence and trade valorized by early first millennium trade histories, such as the *Periplus Maris Erythraei*, gave rise to an interpretative paradigm that reified these early accounts (Chittick 1968, 1974; Kirkman 1954, 1964). Under this historical narrative, scholars were silent about peoples who resided in vast areas of the interior not subject to coastal state authorities. This was an ideal opportunity for archaeology to bring to light the dynamic economies of ancient hinterland societies erased from ancient writings and ignored by colonial and postcolonial historians.

The documentary bias toward foreign goods in early trade records stood unchallenged until evidence was found for a prosperous and large iron production center close to the littoral south of Dar es Salaam, without a surrounding population sufficiently large to sustain demand (Chami 1992; La Violette and Fawcett 1990). With productive capacity beyond local needs, the only parsimonious explanation was exchange with contemporary traders in the western Indian Ocean who conveyed raw iron as far as the Arabian Peninsula for working and redistribution. This historical archaeology draws into question the completeness of nearly 2,000-year-old documents that were accepted as "accurate" portrayals of trade with East Africa for centuries. It also throws into considerable doubt all subsequent historical interpretations that reified the documents and their erasure of many locally manufactured products, such as shell beads and iron, in the hinterland and deeper interior of the region.

Lately, African archaeologists have made critical material discoveries extending models of interaction with the wider Indian Ocean deep into the past. Finds of pottery, beads, and early domesticated animal remains, including chicken and dog, connected to the Graeco-Roman world and southern Asia, not to mention the ancient Nile Valley (Chami 2006; Chami and Msemwa 1997), have directly challenged preexisting historical models that placed Africa outside of representations of ancient global connections. Discussions arising from African historical archaeological approaches and unique finds unearthed in eastern African, for example, on the island of Zanzibar and in the Rufiji Delta of southern Tanzania, are beginning to transform ancient Indian Ocean histories. That African archaeologies have spurred the rethinking of not only African histories, but of the connective histories to the Mediterranean, south Asia (cf. Kusimba et al. 1994), to mention only two, speaks directly to the power of African historical archaeologies to address questions that count: questions that have the ability to fundamentally transform historical conceptualizations and understandings and, in this case, assert Africans' agency in making world histories.

Yet, challenges to accepted texts need not focus on ancient periods. Heightening our knowledge of more proximal and, perhaps, controversial histories in key ways, van Schalkwyk and Smith (2004) portray dissonant histories of the 1894 Maleboho War in the Limpopo Province of South Africa, a war in which the government of the South African Republic (ZAR) fought the people (Hananwa) of Chief Leboho. The conflict erupted when white farmers fled north to find land and lives away from British rule, bringing them into conflict with settled Africans. The authors question the official historical accounts derived from white press stories, published diaries of missionaries and clergy, and reports of ZAR military staff. Such sources are filled with internal silences and inconsistencies about the conflict. Van Schalkwyk and Smith seek alternative perspectives of the war by locating new sources capable of developing an inclusive history.

Among the new sources are issues of an "unauthorized" newsletter written by disgruntled, English-speaking ZAR citizens conscripted to fight and a Hananwa praise poem that brands ZAR leaders as instigators of the conflict while glorifying Chief Leboho. Archaeological research into local rock art has also shown that Hananwa rock images portray the conflict from an indigenous perspective, allowing insights into local cultural slights directed at the enemy – humorous depictions of the ZAR soldiers and pictorial commentaries about battles. Complementing these sources is new archaeological information that shows hidden and defended African settlements, ZAR and allied forts, and evidence of the social devastation caused by ZAR forces (van Schalkwyk and Smith 2004). From these finds the authors interpret the contested nature of the conflict, ZAR abuses and military missteps, and Hananwa resistance – all elements of a more fulsome historical representation. Van Schalkwyk and Smith skillfully demonstrate that alternative sources can produce truly multivocal perspectives of the past that highlight previously silenced participants, whether Hananwa fighters, the general Hananwa populace, or conscripted ZAR troops.[5] A crucial further lesson derives from their work: landscapes often hold powerful narratives of local resistance that contradict official histories. Contradictory written sources, local oral traditions that provide a different point of view, and rock art converge to create an historical archaeology sensitive to indigenous representations.

Reflections and Conclusions

We have seen that there is a deep and rich African historiography that provides an interdisciplinary context for attempts at historical archaeology that operate outside the texts of the colonial library, yet often challenge the interpretations enshrined in that library about indigenous histories. Originating with MacIver and Caton-Thompson and later amplified by Posnansky, Garlake, Schmidt, and Hall and more recently by Lane, Denbow, Reid, Helm, Horton, Chami, Kusimba, and Edwards, among others, these alternative histories address the making of pasts, interplay of sources, rigorous interrogation of source-side and subject-side evidence for archaeological applications, and the politics of pasts rooted in representations.

We agree with Stahl's (2001) observation that we must find space to operate between history's materiality and the narrative formation of history, but we do not believe that it is necessary to privilege a materiality of quotidian life as "the lived past" – an approach that may submerge conflicts between historical sources and interpretations and thus the questions that count in historical archaeology. Questions that count inevitably arise out of narrative histories heretofore made from readings of archives, observations of the material record, ethnographies, and so forth. For example, it is when materialities and oral traditions confront and contradict historical or anthropological narratives that we make new histories, as we saw with the research of the Kusimbas and path-breaking studies of the Kalahari. This is a methodology with a long and enduring pedigree that should not be masked by tropes such as "the lived past" – a rhetorical device that renames methodologies and may run the risk of silencing earlier, parallel scholarship. Certainly the examination of quotidian life has an important role to play in our assessment of overlooked domains of archaeological inquiry, but we must not lose sight of how such evidence may be brought to bear in remaking narrative representations, whatever their derivation.

Missing from queries about how to reconcile various definitions of historical archaeology with its practice in Africa (commonly framed by contact or the impacts of colonialism and capitalism) is any consideration that historical archaeology will remain trapped in the conundrum of ethnocentrism until it accepts and values the integrity of African historicities. We must resist attempts to construct historical archaeologies that pertain only to colonial encounters no matter their chronological age (cf. Robertshaw 2004:388–389). Such a position homogenizes African histories into a metanarrative, dichotomizes peoples and pasts, ignores the dialectic of interaction between colonizers and colonized agents, and treats Africans as timeless entities to be made by Europe and the Islamic world (e.g., Comaroff and Comaroff 1993; Hall 2002; Wilmsen 1989; Wolf 1982).

An Africa-based historical archaeology is hardly a fresh idea: "One of the objectives of African History, once it freed itself from an over-dependence on sources in colonial archives, was to look at African history from an African viewpoint with sources rooted in Africa" (Posnansky 1969:19). If sites with evidence of Eurasian colonialism or the expanse of capitalism and modernity continue to be the primary framing mechanism of historical archaeology in Africa as well as elsewhere, then Posnansky's vision will not be realized and dynamic *African*, not to mention *Asian*, *Native American*, *Australian*, and *Pacific*, histories will remain inexcusably silenced by archaeologists unwilling to tackle questions that count, the questions that make histories of indigenous voices and materialities, indeed the questions that transform representations.

African historical archaeology, as critically constituted, can broaden and fundamentally transform local and global histories. One way to mediate the conundrum of a seemingly ever-present Europe is to practice historical archaeologies of Africa grounded in asking questions derived from African knowledge (Andah 1995b; Irele 1991). Such vibrant contests over representations of pasts, often entwined with equal consideration of African presents and futures as well as publics and politics, in many of our examples depends little or not at all on the colonial library as a framing context. Historical archaeologies, then, perhaps need not be imperialist, colonialist, or nationalist (Trigger 1984), although they may be appropriated as such. That they are Africa-based speaks to the capacity of historical archaeology to make representations of pasts that are genuinely revolutionary and that privilege African agencies rather than silencing them – the beginning of "provincializing Europe" and making truly African historical archaeologies.

Notes

1 It is indicative that most Africanist archaeologists labeling themselves as historical archaeologists are replicating the North American paradigm, which is most easily practiced in West Africa and southern Africa, where contact with western European cultures has been most pronounced and well recorded.
2 They are apparently using Stahl's (2001) reference to archaeology as a "foil."
3 Variants of the Shungwaya myth in local histories refer to a northerly place of origin (northern Kenya and southern Somalia) and the subsequent southerly dispersal of peoples into the immediate hinterlands of central and southern Kenya and northern Tanzania.
4 The Mijikenda live along the coast and its immediate hinterland and are a multiethnic population made up of closely related Bantu-speaking peoples.
5 The voices in this instance are not those of the archaeologists; rather, they are the voices of Hananwa and ZAR soldiers.

References

Abungu, George H. O., 1989 Communities on the Tana Delta, Kenya: An Archaeological Study of the Relations Between the Delta and the River Basin, 700–1890 A.D. Unpublished Ph.D. dissertation, Department of Archaeology, University of Cambridge.

Allen, James de Vere, 1974 Swahili Culture Reconsidered: Some Historical Implications of the Material Culture of the Northern Kenya Coast in the Eighteenth and Nineteenth Centuries. *Azania* 9:105–138.

Allen, James de Vere, 1993 *Swahili Origins: Swahili Culture and the Shungwaya Phenomenon*. James Currey, London.

Andah, Bassey W., 1995a Studying African Societies in Cultural Context. In *Making Alternative Histories: The Practice of Archaeology and History in Non-Western Settings*, edited by Peter R. Schmidt and Thomas C. Patterson, pp. 149–181. School of American Research Press, Santa Fe, New Mexico.

Andah, Bassey W., 1995b European Encumbrances to the Development of Relevant Theory in African Archaeology. In *Theory in Archaeology: A World Perspective*, edited by Peter J. Ucko, pp. 96–109. Routledge, London.

Andrén, Anders, 1998 *Between Artifacts and Texts: Historical Archaeology in Global Perspective*. Translated by Alan Crozier. Plenum Press, New York.

Asad, Talal, 1987 Are there Histories of Peoples without Europe?: A Review Article. *Comparative Studies in Society and History* 29(3):594–607.

Berger, Iris, 1981 *Religion and Resistance: East African Kingdoms in the Precolonial Period*. Musée Royal de l'Afrique Centrale, Tervuren, Belgium.

Bradley, Richard, 2004 The Translation of Time. In *Archaeologies of Memory*, edited by Ruth M. Van Dyke and Susan E. Alcock, pp. 221–227. Blackwell, Malden, Mass.

Caton-Thompson, Gertrude, 1931 *The Zimbabwe Culture: Ruins and Reactions*. Clarendon Press, Oxford.

Chakrabarty, Dipesh, 2000 *Provincializing Europe: Postcolonial Thought and Historical Difference*. Princeton University Press, Princeton, NJ.

Chami, Felix A., 1992 Limbo: Early Iron-working in South-Eastern Tanzania. *Azania* 27:45–52.

Chami, Felix A., 1994 *The Tanzanian Coast in the First Millennium AD: An Archaeology of the Iron-working, Farming Communities*. Studies in African Archaeology 7. Societas Archaeologica Upsaliensis, Uppsala, Sweden.

Chami, Felix A., 1998 A Review of Swahili Archaeology. *African Archaeological Review* 15(3):199–218.

Chami, Felix A., 2006 *The Unity of African Ancient History: 3000 BC to AD 500*. E & D, Dar es Salaam, Tanzania.

Chami, Felix A., and Paul Msemwa, 1997 A New Look at Culture and Trade on the Azanian Coast. *Current Anthropology* 38:673–677.

Chittick, Neville, 1968 The Coast before the Arrival of the Portuguese. In *Zamani: A Survey of African History*, edited by B. A. Ogot and J. A. Kieran, pp. 100–118. East African Publishing House, Nairobi, Kenya.

Chittick, Neville, 1974 *Kilwa: An Islamic Trading City on the East African Coast*. 2 vols. British Institute in Eastern Africa Memoir 5. British Institute in Eastern Africa, Nairobi, Kenya.

Cohen, David William, Stephan F. Miescher, and Luise White, 2001 Introduction: Voices, Words, and African History. In *African Words, African Voices: Critical Practices in Oral History*, edited by Luise White, Stephan F. Miescher, and David William Cohen, pp. 1–27. Indiana University Press, Bloomington.

Comaroff, Jean, and John Comaroff (editors), 1993 *Modernity and Its Malcontents: Ritual and Power in Postcolonial Africa*. University of Chicago Press, Chicago.

Curtis, Matthew C., 2004 Ancient Interaction across the Southern Red Sea: New Suggestions for Investigating Cultural Exchange and Complex Societies during the First Millennium BC. In *Trade and Travel in the Red Sea Region: Proceedings of Red Sea Project 1*, edited by Paul Lunde and Alexandra Porter, pp. 57–70. BAR International Series 1269. Archaeopress, Oxford.

Deagan, Kathleen, 1988 Neither History nor Prehistory: The Questions that Count in Historical Archaeology. *Historical Archaeology* 22(1):7–12.

DeCorse, Christopher, 2001 *An Archaeology of Elmina: Africans and Europeans on the Gold Coast, 1400–1900*. Smithsonian Institution Press, Washington D.C.

Denbow, James R., 1984 Prehistoric Herders and Foragers of the Kalahari: The Evidence for 1500 Years of Interaction. In *Past and Present in Hunter Gatherer Studies*, edited by Carmel Schrire, pp. 175–193. Academic Press, Orlando, Fla.

Denbow, James R., 1990 Congo to Kalahari: Data and Hypotheses about the Political Economy of the Western Stream of the Early Iron Age. *African Archaeological Review* 8:139–176.

Denbow, James R., 1999 Material Culture and the Dialectics of Identity in the Kalahari: AD 700–1700. In *Beyond Chiefdoms: Pathways to Complexity in Africa*, edited by Susan Keech McIntosh, pp. 110–123. Cambridge University Press, Cambridge.

Edwards, David, 2004 History, Archaeology and Nubian Identities in the Middle Nile. In *African Historical Archaeologies*, edited by Andrew M. Reid and Paul J. Lane, pp. 33–58. Kluwer Academic/Plenum Publishers, New York.

Fattovich, Radolfo, 1997 The Near East and Eastern Africa: Their Interaction. In *Encyclopedia of Precolonial Africa: Archaeology, History, Languages, Cultures, and Environments*, edited by Joseph O. Vogel, pp. 479–484. AltaMira Press, Walnut Creek, Calif.

Fattovich, Radolfo, 2004 The 'pre-Aksumite' State in Northern Ethiopia and Eritrea Reconsidered. In *Trade and Travel in the Red Sea Region: Proceedings of Red Sea Project I*, edited by Paul Lunde and Alexandra Porter, pp. 102–110. BAR International Series 1269. Archaeopress. Oxford.

Funari, Pedro Paulo A., Siân Jones, and Martin Hall, 1999 Introduction: Archaeology in History. In *Historical Archaeology: Back from the Edge*, edited by Pedro Paulo A. Funari, Martin Hall, and Siân Jones, pp. 1–20 Routledge, London.

Garlake, Peter S., 1973 *Great Zimbabwe*. Thames & Hudson, London.

Garlake, Peter S., 1982 Prehistory and Ideology in Zimbabwe. *Africa* 52(3):1–19.

Haaland, Randi, and Chiedel Msuya, 2000 Pottery Production, Iron Working, and Trade in the EIA: The Case of Dakawa, East-Central Tanzania. *Azania* 30:75–106.

Hall, Martin, 1984 The Burden of Tribalism: The Social Context of Southern African Iron Age Studies. *American Antiquity* 49(4):455–467.

Hall, Martin, 1990 'Hidden History': Iron Age Archaeology in Southern Africa. In *A History of African Archaeology*, edited by Peter Robertshaw, pp. 59–77. James Currey, London.

Hall, Martin, 2002 Timeless Time: Africa and the World. In *Archaeology: The Widening Debate*, edited by Barry Cunliffe, Wendy Davies, and Colin Renfrew, pp. 439–464. Oxford University Press, Oxford.

Handsman, Russell G., and Mark P. Leone, 1989 Living History and Critical Archaeology in the Reconstruction of the Past. In *Critical Traditions in Contemporary Archaeology: Essays in the Philosophy, History, and Socio-politics of Archaeology*, edited by Valerie Pinsky and Alison Wylie, pp. 117–135. Cambridge University Press, Cambridge.

Helm, Richard Michael, 2000 Conflicting Histories: The Archaeology of Iron-working, Farming Communities in the Central and Southern Coast of Kenya. Unpublished Ph.D. dissertation, Department of Archaeology, University of Bristol.

Helm, Richard Michael, 2004 Re-evaluating Traditional Histories on the Coast of Kenya: An Archaeological Perspective. In *African Historical Archaeologies*, edited by Andrew M. Reid and Paul J. Lane, pp. 59–89. Kluwer Academic/Plenum Publishers, New York.

Henige, David P., 1974 *The Chronology of Oral Tradition: Quest for a Chimera*. Clarendon Press, Oxford.

Henige, David P., 1982 *Oral Historiography*. Longman, New York.

Horton, Mark, 1996 *Shanga: The Archaeology of a Muslim Trading Community on the Coast of East Africa*. British Institute in Eastern Africa, London.

Insoll, Timothy, 2004 A True Picture?: Colonial and Other Historical Archaeologies. In *African Historical Archaeologies*, edited by Andrew M. Reid and Paul J. Lane, pp. 163–187. Kluwer Academic/Plenum Publishers, New York.

Irele, Abiola, 1991 The African Scholar: Is Black Africa Entering the Dark Ages of Scholarship? *Transition* 51:56–69.

Kirkman, James S., 1954 *The Arab City of Gedi*. Oxford University Press. London.

Kirkman, James S., 1964 *Men and Monuments on the East African Coast*. Praeger, New York.

Kusimba, Chapurukha M., 1999 *The Rise and Fall of Swahili States*. AltaMira Press, Walnut Creek, Calif.

Kusimba, Chapurukha M., 2004 Archaeology of Slavery in East Africa. *African Archaeological Review* 21:59–88.

Kusimba, Chapurukha M., and Sibel B. Kusimba, 2005 Mosaics and Interactions: East Africa, 2000 B.P. to the Present. In *African Archaeology: A Critical Introduction*, edited by Ann Brower Stahl, pp. 392–419. Blackwell, Malden, Mass.

Kusimba, Chapurukha M., David J. Killick, and Richard G. Cresswell, 1994 Indigenous and Imported Metals at Swahili Sites on the Coast of Kenya. In *Society, Culture and Technology in Africa*, edited by S. Terry Childs, pp. 63–77. MASCA Research Papers in Science and Technology, Supplement to Volume 11, Philadelphia.

Lane, Paul J., 2004 Re-constructing Tswana Townscapes: Toward a Critical Historical Archaeology. In *African Historical Archaeologies*, edited by Andrew M. Reid and Paul J. Lane, pp. 269–299. Kluwer Academic/Plenum Publishers, New York.

La Violette, Adria, 2004 Swahili Archaeology and History on Pemba, Tanznaia: A Critique and Case Study of the Use of Written and Oral Sources in Archaeology. In *African Historical Archaeologies*, edited by Andrew M. Reid and Paul J. Lane, pp. 125–162. Kluwer Academic/Plenum Publishers, New York.

La Violette Adria, and William B. Fawcett, 1990 Iron Age Settlement around Mkiu, South-eastern Tanzania. *Azania* 25:19–26.

La Violette, A., W. B. Fawcett, N. J. Karom, and P. Schmidt, 1989 The Coast and the Hinterland: University of Dar es Salaam Field Schools. 1987–88. *Nyame Akuma* 32:38–46.

Lee, Richard B., and Mathias Guenther, 1991 Oxen or Onions?: The Search for Trade [and Truth] in the Kalahari. *Current Anthropology* 32:592–601.

Leone, Mark P., and Parker B. Potter, Jr. (editors), 1999 *Historical Archaeologies of Capitalism*. Kluwer Academic/Plenum Publishers, New York.

Leone, Mark P., Parker B. Potter, Jr., and Paul A. Shackel, 1987 Toward a Critical Archaeology. *Current Anthropology* 28:283–302.

McGuire, Randall H., and Robert Paynter (editors), 1991 *The Archaeology of Inequality*. Basil Blackwell, Oxford.

MacIver, D. Randal, 1906 *Medieval Rhodesia*. Macmillan, London.

Maggs, Timothy M., 1976a *Iron Age Communities of the Southern Highveld*. Natal Museum, Pietermaritzburg. South Africa.

Maggs, Timothy M., 1976b Iron Age Patterns and Sotho History on the Southern Highveld. *World Archaeology* 7(3):318–332.

Mason, Ronald J., 2000 Archaeology and Native American Oral Traditions. *American Antiquity* 65(2): 239–266.

Miller, Daniel, Michael Rowlands, and Christopher Tilley (editors), 1989 *Domination and Resistance*. Allen & Unwin, London.

Miller, Joseph C., 1980 The *African Past Speaks: Essays on Oral Tradition and History*. Archon, Hamden, Conn.

Mudimbe, V. Y., 1988 *The Invention of Africa: Gnosis, Philosophy, and the Order of Knowledge*. Indiana University Press. Bloomington.

Mutoro, Henry, 1987 An Archaeological Study of the Mijikenda Kaya Settlements on the Hinterland Kenya Coast. Unpublished Ph.D. dissertation, Department of Anthropology, University of California, Los Angeles.

Orser, Charles E., Jr., 1996 *A Historical Archaeology of the Modern World*. Plenum Press, New York.

Orser, Charles E., Jr., 2001 The Anthropology in American Historical Archaeology. *American Anthropologist* 103:621–632.

Piot, Charles, 1999 *Remotely Global: Village Modernity in West Africa*. University of Chicago Press, Chicago.

Posnansky, Merrick, 1969 *Myth and Methodology – The Archaeological Contribution to African History*. Ghana Universities Press, Accra, Ghana.

Posnansky, Merrick, and Christopher R. DeCorse, 1986 Historical Archaeology in sub-Saharan Africa: A Review. *Historical Archaeology* 20(1):1–14.

Potter, Parker B., Jr., 1994 *Public Archaeology in Annapolis: A Critical Approach to History in Maryland's Ancient City*. Smithsonian Institution Press, Washington, D.C.

Reid, Andrew M., 2005 Interaction, Marginalization, and the Archaeology of the Kalahari. In *African Archaeology: A Critical Introduction*, edited by Ann Brower Stahl, pp. 353–377. Blackwell, Malden, Mass.

Reid, Andrew M., and Paul J. Lane, 2004a African Historical Archaeologies: An Introductory Consideration of Scope and Potential. In *African Historical Archaeologies*, edited by Andrew M. Reid and Paul J. Lane, pp. 1–32. Kluwer Academic/Plenum Publishers, New York.

Reid, Andrew M., and Paul J. Lane (editors), 2004b *African Historical Archaeologies*. Kluwer Academic/Plenum Publishers, New York.

Reid, Andrew M., and Alinah Segobye, 1999 The Archaeology of the Makgadikgadi Pans. Botswana. Paper presented at the 4th World Archaeological Congress. Cape Town, South Africa.

Robertshaw, Peter, 2000 Sibling Rivalry?: The Intersection of Archaeology and History. *History in Africa* 27:261–286.

Robertshaw, Peter 2004 African Historical Archaeolog(ies): Past, Present and a Possible Future. In *African Historical Archaeologies*, edited by Andrew M. Reid and Paul J. Lane, pp. 375–391. Kluwer Academic/Plenum Publishers, New York.

Schmidt, Peter R., 1978 *Historical Archaeology: A Structural Approach in an African Culture*. Greenwood Press. Westport, Conn.

Schmidt, Peter R., 1990 Oral Traditions, Archaeology and History: A Short Reflective History. In *A History of African Archaeology*. edited by Peter Robertshaw, pp. 252–270. James Currey, London.

Schmidt, Peter R., 1997 *Iron Technology in East Africa: Symbolism, Science, and Archaeology*. Indiana University Press, Bloomington.

Schmidt, Peter R., 2002 The Ona Culture of Greater Asmara: Archaeology's Liberation of Eritrea's Ancient History from Colonial Paradigms. *Journal of Eritrean Studies* I(1):29–59.

Schmidt, Peter R., 2006 *Historical Archaeology in Africa: Representation, Social Memory, and Oral Traditions*. AltaMira Press, Walnut Creek, Calif.

Schmidt, Peter R., and Matthew C. Curtis, 2001 Urban Precursors in the Horn: Early 1st Millennium BC Communities in Eritrea. *Antiquity* 75(290):849–859.

Schmidt, Peter, R., and Thomas C. Patterson, 1995a Introduction: From Constructing to Making Alternative Histories. In *Making Alternative Histories: The Practice of Archaeology and History in Non-Western Settings*, edited by Peter R. Schmidt and Thomas C. Patterson, pp. 1–24. School of American Research Press, Santa Fe, NM.

Schmidt, Peter R., and Thomas C. Patterson (editors), 1995b *Making Alternative Histories: The Practice of Archaeology and History in Non-Western Settings*. School of American Research Press, Santa Fe, NM.

Schmidt, P. R., N. J. Karoma, A. LaViolette, W. B. Fawcett, A. Z. Mabulla, L. N. Rutabanzibwa, and C. M. Saanane, 1992 *Archaeological Investigations in the Vicinity of Mkiu, Kisarawe District, Tanzania*. Archaeological Contributions of the University of Dar es Salaam, Occasional Paper I. Archaeology Unit, University of Dar es Salaam, Dar es Salaam, Tanzania.

Smith, Andrew B., and Richard B. Lee, 1997 Cho/ana: Archaeological and Ethnohistorical Evidence for Recent Hunter-Gatherer/Agropastoralist Contact in Northern Bushmanland, Namibia. *South African Archaeological Bulletin* 52:52–58.

Solway, Jacqueline S., and Richard B. Lee, 1990 Foragers, Genuine or Spurious?: Situating the Kalahari San in History. *Current Anthropology* 31 (2):109–146.

Spear, Thomas T., 1974 Traditional Myths and Historian's Myths: Variations on the Singwaya Theme of Mijikenda Origins. *History in Africa* 1:67–84.

Spear, Thomas T., 1978 *The Kaya Complex: A History of the Mijikenda Peoples of the Kenya Coast to 1900.* Kenya Literature Bureau, Nairobi, Kenya.

Spear, Thomas T., 2000 Early Swahili History Reconsidered. *International Journal of African Historical Studies* 33(2):257–290.

Stahl, Ann Brower, 2001 *Making History in Banda: Anthropological Visions of Africa's Past.* Cambridge University Press, Cambridge.

Stahl, Ann Brower, 2004 Making History in Banda: Reflections on the Construction of Africa's Past. *Historical Archaeology* 38(1):50–65.

Tantala, Renee Louise, 1989 *The Early History of Kitara in Western Uganda: Process Models of Religious and Political Change.* Ph.D. dissertation. University of Wisconsin. Madison, University Microfilms, Ann Arbor, Mich.

Thorbahn, Peter Frederic, 1979 *The Precolonial Ivory Trade of East Africa: Reconstruction of a Human-Elephant Ecosystem.* Ph.D. dissertation. University of Massachusetts, Amherst. University Microfilms, Ann Arbor, Mich.

Trigger, Bruce G., 1984 Alternative Archaeologies: Nationalist, Colonialist, Imperialist. *Man* (New Series) 19(3):355–370.

Trouillot, Michel-Rolph, 1995 *Silencing the Past: Power and the Production of History.* Beacon Press, Boston.

van Schalkwyk, J. A., and B. W. Smith, 2004 Insiders and Outsiders: Sources for Reinterpreting a Historical Event. In *African Historical Archaeologies,* edited by Andrew M. Reid and Paul J. Lane. pp. 325–346. Kluwer Academic/Plenum Publishers, New York.

Vansina, Jan, 1965 *Oral Tradition: A Study in Historical Methodology.* Aldine, Chicago.

Vansina, Jan, 1995 Historians, Are Archaeologists your Siblings? *History in Africa* 22:369–408.

Walz, Jonathan R., 2001 Prospects for Transforming the East African Past: Historical Archaeology in Lowland Northeastern Tanzania. Paper presented at Pathways to Africa's Past: Sources and Methods in African History, University of Texas, Austin.

Walz, Jonathan R., 2005 Mombo and the Mkomazi Corridor: Preliminary Archaeological Finds from Lowland Northeastern Tanzania. In *Salvaging Tanzania's Cultural Heritage,* edited by Bertram B. B. Mapunda and Paul Msemwa, pp. 198–213. Dar es Salaam University Press, Dar es Salaam, Tanzania.

Wilmsen, Edwin N., 1989 *Land Filled with Flies: A Political Economy of the Kalahari* University of Chicago Press, Chicago

Wolf, Eric R., 1982 *Europe and the People without History.* University of California Press, Berkeley.

Part VII

Colonialism, Empire, and Nationalism

COLONIALISM, EMPIRE, AND NATIONALISM are challenging concepts freighted with conflicting meanings in the modern world. Colonialism is usually defined as the control of people in one territory by a polity located in another territory. The colonizing polity is commonly an empire or nation-state and the colonial process, along with warfare, is the primary means of state expansion. Some of the relationships between colonialism and empire are highlighted in Bill Ashcroft, Gareth Griffiths, and Helen Tiffen's book entitled *The Empire Writes Back*. This book, while playing on the popular Star Wars trope, provides an account of the effects of colonization on imperial colonies such as India and the emergence of post-colonial literature. The authors observe that imperialism works "through" as well as "on" subjects and that colonizing polities wield oppression through the control of language (Ashcroft et al. 1989). This is manifest in a variety of ways; however, at its core, is the idea that as the language of the colonizers becomes the *lingua franca* of the colonized, all notions of identity are now recast and validated according to the ideological structure of the colonizing power (Parry 2004). The material world is part of that structure, whether it be architecture, landscape, or the body. Notions of empire are often reinforced through material expression and practice. It is through mediums such as language and landscape that empires attempt to codify their power.

Empire has become a key locus for cultural theory. Traditionally, empire was seen as synonymous with imperialism, and indeed the word "empire" is derived from the Latin *imperium*. An empire is a multiethnic state where the ruling class has politico-military jurisdiction over ethnically distinct peoples. Recently, Michael Hardt and Antonio Negri (2000) have argued that the nation-state is rapidly collapsing in the face of world capitalism and globalization. They suggest that it is being replaced by an acephelous supranational order they call "Empire." This term refers not to a territorial-based system where tribute flows from peripheries to cores, as with World Systems Theory (Wallerstein 1974, 1980), but rather to a more diffuse, anonymous network of the global world. This new order is generating a less dichotomous and more variegated pattern of inequality. Michael Strangelove (2005:14–16) has recently critiqued this deterritoralized view of

Empire. He writes that "the geographical mobility of capital, its ability to relocate from nation to nation has not diminished the significance of localized reality" (Strangelove 2005:115). He notes that Hardt and Negri view today's world as a complete rupture with the past. From this perspective, the history of Empire would seem to hold little value for understanding today's world. Yet any understanding of Empire depends upon our ability to know the historical trajectories of its various structures and practices. But what is that history?

Historical archaeologists have much to contribute to this topic. Most empires used colonies to expand their control, but not all colonies were necessarily part of coordinated imperial action (Johnson 2006). This subtle, but important difference is made all the more challenging because among postcolonial scholars colonialism and imperialism are often interchangeable (Parry 2004:107–108). Empire is often conceived as being sponsored by governments, but many scholars see capitalism as an imperial force (Parry 2004:108; Strangelove 2005:3–9; Johnson 2006: 314). From an archaeological perspective what makes the relationship between colonialism and empire so interesting is the manner in which Empire is both buttressed and perpetuated by its materiality. In contexts such as South Africa (Hall 2000) and Sri Lanka (Jayasena 2006) imperial power is projected through architecture, landscapes, and military installations such as forts. In South Africa, for example, Hall (2000:28–29), argues that urban landscapes of a city such as Cape Town were designed to serve as theaters in which imperial order was expressed through geometry. Even in a distant colony such as Jamestown, the façades of Empire took precedence over more practical pursuits. Rather than investing in technologies that might have aided the nascent colony to survive, public buildings were constructed that projected imperial power until they quickly fell into disrepair as the life of the colony dissipated (Horning 2000; Mrozowski 1999, 2009).

Archaeology is perhaps better known for its perspectives on ancient empires, particularly Egypt, Greece, Rome, China, and Mesopotamia. Recent research in this area has challenged many of our standard assumptions about colonies, colonization, colonialism, and culture contact

(Cusick 1998; Gosden and Knowles 2001; Lyons and Papadopoulos 2002; Gosden 2004; Murray 2004; Stein 2005a; Alcock et al. 2009). It has shown that unilinear models such as acculturation or World Systems Theory are too limiting. It has demonstrated that interacting complex societies must be seen as heterogenous entities composed of different interest groups whose goals are often in conflict. It has drawn attention to the importance of internal dynamics (economic, political, social, and ideological) in shaping the structure of the social network. Finally, it has stressed the centrality of human agency and the active role of material culture in the negotiation of social identities. Given that our contemporary knowledge of colonialism is dominated by the Western European experience, the study of comparative colonialisms thus offers the potential to broaden our perspective and help develop a more comprehensive understanding of colonial encounters (Stein 2005b:4).

Archaeologists and social anthropologists have also critiqued archaeology as a colonial project. According to Trigger (1984:360), colonialist archaeology is archaeology practiced "either in countries whose native population was wholly replaced or overwhelmed by European settlement or in ones where Europeans remained politically and economically dominant for a considerable period of time." This is well exemplified by the early archaeology of North America and the creation of the "Moundbuilder myth." Trigger (2006) demonstrates a very similar pattern in the archaeology of Australia, New Zealand, and colonialist Rhodesia (Zimbabwe). In these cases, colonialist archaeology seeks to deny the cultural achievements of colonized peoples as a rationalization for colonialism. Nadia Abu El-Haj (2001) has examined the relationships between the development of Israeli archaeology and the construction of the social imaginations and political orders in the Israeli state. She is particularly interested in the "formation and enactment of its colonial-national historical imagination and ... the substantiation of its territorial claims" (Abu El-Haj 2001:2). In the case of Zimbabawe and much of southern Africa, colonial ideology strongly influenced the trajectory of archaeological research (Garlake 1982; Hall 1984, 2000; Shepherd 2002a, 2003). In partial response to this history, there is a small, but growing, movement toward postcolonial archaeologies (Gosden 2001; Shepherd 2002b; Liebmann and Rizvi 2008). While these approaches are not a panacea for past injustices, they can nonetheless assist in providing a valuable material and historical basis for postcolonial studies (Liebmann 2008).

In the past 10 years, there has been a growing interest in the emergence of nationalist ideologies and the political tools used in their legitimization both in the past and in the present. The classic example is the case of Nazi Germany (Arnold 1990). However, all nation-states use archaeology and history in various ways to support their authority. In her chapter, Margarita Díaz-Andreu examines how Spanish nationalism influenced the emergence of archaeology as a scientific discipline. Her main thesis is that Spanish nationalism is properly conceived not as a single nationalism, but rather as three separate, but interrelated nationalisms: Catalan, Basque, and Galician.

Catalan nationalism emerged in the middle of the 19th century and was expressed by the cultural movement known as *Reinaixença* (Renassance). Enric Prat de la Riba played a key role in integrating archaeology and Catalan nationalism. He argued that the roots of Catalan culture could be found in the pre-Roman Iberian "*ethnos*" that extended from Murcia to the Rhone. The Roman conquest marked a temporary end to this *ethnos*, but it was revived by the medieval Catalan nation. Prat de la Riba established two institutions, the Institut d'Estudis Catalans and the Junta de Museus de Barcelona, both of which were important in Catalan archaeology. After Prat de la Riba's death in 1917, Pere Bosch Gimpera founded the Catalan school of archaeology. Like Prat de la Riba, he was a confirmed Catalan nationalist and regarded the prehistory of the Iberian peninsula as the direct precursor of multicultural Spain. He advocated an autonomous Catalan state within a federalist Spanish state. Bosh Gumpera was exiled at the end of the Spanish Civil War and his position was taken over by Martin Almagro Basch. Almagro Basch transformed Catalan archaeology into an archaeology in the service of the Franco state. In the 1960s and 1970s, the Catalan school was revived and became influenced by "modified positivism" and "pragmatic reformism."

Basque nationalism deployed archaeology largely to support the exceptionalism of the Basque people. During the first three decades of the 20th century, advocates of the Basque-Cantabrist theory held that the Romans had never conquered the Basque country. They argued that this failure accounted for the survival of the Basque people and the persistence of their language. At the same time, physical anthropologists initiated studies of human remains to demonstrate morphological difference between Basques and Romans. This was the primary aim of some excavations. One of the leaders was Father José Miguel de Barandiarán, who organized institutional support for archaeology, including the Laboratorio de Ethnologia y Folklore Euskera and the Seminario de Prehistoria Ikuska. Much like Bosh Gimpera, he advocated a direct relationship between prehistory and modern Basque culture. During and after the Civil War, archaeology came to a standstill and Barandiarán took refuge in France. When he returned in 1953, he reestablished Basque archaeology, creating new provincial institutions. Archaeology was first taught in a Basque university in 1964.

Galician nationalism, like Catalonian nationalism, was influenced by a cultural revitalization movement during the 19th century. It was known in Galicia as *Rexurdimento* and *Rexeneración* and based upon the view that the Celts were the origin of Galician race, language, and culture. Manuel Murguia was the principal exponent. This interest in Celtic heritage promoted the creation of new archaeological institutions such as the Sociedad Arqueologica de Pontevedra and informal social meetings devoted to these issues. In 1920 Vicente Risco y Agüero founded Nós, an organization devoted to ethnography and archaeology. He and his associates advocated the view that Galicia (including Portugal) was one of the seven Celtic nations, the others being Highland Scotland, the Isle of Man, Ireland, Wales, Cornwall, and Brittany. As in the other regions, the Civil War put a halt to archaeology. However, this lasted longer in Galicia than in the other two cases, and archaeology was not reestablished until 1967, when the Institute Padre Sarmiento founded its Department of Prehistory and Archaeology.

Carla Sinopoli's chapter highlights the material practices of empire. She addresses how elites manipulated historical knowledge in the context of the Vijayanagara empire and its aftermath. Vijayanagara was the name of both the capital city

and a remarkable empire founded by Sanagama kings and centered on the southern banks of the Tungabhadra river in modern Karnataka, India. Vijayanagara emerged in the early 14th century AD through a program of military conquest and lasted for three centuries until it was defeated by an alliance of three northern sultanates. In its heyday, it consisted of 25 million people who spoke three major Dravidian languages as well as several others. The empire incorporated people from a wide variety of religious traditions, including Jains, Muslims, and Hindus.

Sinopoli notes that the expansion of empire during the late 14th and early 15th centuries was directly associated with changes in the style and scale of temples. This style has been termed "revivalist" because it imitated the architecture of the Chola empire of the southeast coast. Architects and builders were imported from the Tamil region to construct these temples. The scale of temple architecture increased dramatically. Temple gateways (*gopura*), in particular, were transformed into towers that indexed the power of their benefactors. This southeast focus, however, belies the fact that Vijayanagara political and economic forms seem to derive from the upland Telugu and Kannada state traditions. Why this contradiction? Sinopoli suggests that the adoption of Chola style was a deliberate strategy that allowed Vijayanagara kings to create narratives of continuity and to associate themselves with the power and authority of the southern kingdom, thereby legitimizing their claim to universal kingship. In contrast to temple architecture, Vijayanagara courtly architecture expressed political ideologies based on present external relations. It was restricted to public and royal structures and drew its inspiration from the Deccani Sultanates. Some of the northern features include domes, vaulted chambers, and arches. A good example of this new style is the royal reception hall known as Lotus Mahal. This structure combines ornate Islamic-style arches with incised plaster motifs and a multi-tiered stone foundation and a stepped temple-like roof. As Sinopoli points out, this new architectural style is thus not a simple case of the imitation of northern styles, but rather an interpretation of them in ways that reflect new notions of kingship and royal ritual.

During the early 17th century, a series of successor states emerged in South India. The rulers of these states were descendants of the earlier regional rulers and they instituted a complex legitimization strategy that both acknowledged Vijayanagara's authority and resisted it. There is considerable evidence for the material referencing of the Vijayar past. Temple construction involved fully enclosing older structures within new ones so that the earlier structures were hidden from view. The core thus represented the past and the veneer the present. The temple gateways were highly elaborated and built in the form of towers. At the same time, the nayaka kings broke with Vijayanagara by introducing new representational forms, particularly sculpture. Rulers are depicted in Vijayanagara sculpture in highly stylized fashion. During the nayaka period, rulers are represented in portraiture. This is related to the idea of kings as "self-made" heroes in the origin stories. It is of interest to note that the royal rhetoric in architecture and elaboration in artistic representation occurs just at the time when state authority was at its weakest. None of the nayaka kings controlled polities that were anywhere near as extensive as Vijayanagara.

Zainab Bahrani provides a provocative explication of how the concept of "Mesopotamia" came to be appropriated by the West. She notes that the myth of Mesopotamia as the "cradle of civilization" became institutionalized during the mid-19th century. This is precisely the time when the major museums of London, Paris, and Berlin acquired their collections of Mesopotamian monuments and art objects. Significantly, these antiquities were not seen as the cultural heritage of Iraq, but rather as the remains of a mythical pre-European past. Sumerian, Babylonian, and Assyrian cultures were consciously separated out from the Islamic cultures of the region. Bahrani argues that this reconstructive act "severed 'Mesopotamia' from any geographical terrain in order to weave it into the Western historical narrative." Much as Edward Said (1978) has argued, the West was constructed in opposition to the Orient as Other. Bahrani suggests that the Otherness of the past, however, plays a complex double role: as the earliest stage in the universal history of humankind, and then as an example of the unchanging nature of the Orient.

Mesopotamia is popularly seen as the locus of firsts: the first writing, the first laws, the first architecture. This series of firsts represents the infancy of civilization. No less a distinguished scholar than Hegel defined Mesopotamia as the birthplace of civilization. Bahrani notes that there is a trick by which the "torch of civilization" is passed from Mesopotamia to the Greco-Roman world, neatly bypassing the Near East. The Bible and Classical texts were used to identify the Persians as presenting a constant threat to democracy and the worship of the Judeo-Christian God. This had a direct impact on Near Eastern archaeology. Bahrani argues that the earliest expeditions to Mesopotamia had two missions. The first was the search for the roots of Western civilization, and the second was to locate places mentioned in the Old Testament. This was certainly the justification underlying the University of Pennsylvania Museum's excavations at Nippur in 1890 (Kuklick 1996). Bahrani makes the important point that the myth of Mesopotamia is not a thing of the past, but is still regnant today. Indeed, it compromises Mesopotamian archaeology, where there has been little interest in self-reflexivity or any serious questioning of the internalized structure of the field and its practices. Bahrani interprets the few references to imperialism and Orientalism in some of the postcolonial literature as acting not to open up discourse, but rather to validate the status quo and neutralize counter-hegemonic debate.

Bahrani then presents a review of the Royal City of Susa exhibit at the Metropolitan Museum of Art which opened in 1992. Susa, located near modern Dizful, Iran, was the capital of the Elamite empire. It is mentioned in the Hebrew bible and was home to Daniel, Nehemiah, and Esther. It was successively incorporated into the Mesopotamian, Assyrian, Elamite, Babylonian, and Achaemenid empires. The Royal City of Susa exhibit contained over 200 objects from the Louvre, the most important being the Stele of Naramsin. Some of the Babylonian objects had been mutilated and carried to Susa by the Elamites as war trophies. The exhibit catalogue expressed dismay at these acts of destruction (Harper et al. 1993). Bahrani also noticed that nowhere in the exhibit did the word "Iran" and "Iraq" appear. She assumed that the rationale behind this choice was that the ancient names should appear prominently for didactic purposes.

But, as she points out, it is not standard museum practice to omit contemporary names of countries and it only contributions to the impression of Mesopotamia as a non-modern place, further distancing past and present. She then shows that the exhibit had an impact on popular discourse surrounding the US missile attack on Baghdad in 1993. The media was quick to link the despotism of past Mesopotamian rulers with the dictatorship of Saddam Hussein.

Archaeologists have begun to interrogate colonialism as a political practice underpinning the growth of social formations. Russell Handsman and Trudie Lamb Richmond offer a "counterhistory" of and against colonialism from the perspective of an archaeologist and Shaghticoke Indian scholar using colonial New England as their case study. Handsman and Lamb Richmond's analysis of the historiography of western Massachusetts shows that the first county histories celebrate the Stockbridge missionaries for their success in educating and Christianizing the Indians. At the same time, they praised the self-reliance of the colonial settlers and castigated Indians as being savage, uncivilized, and lazy. After 1850, large numbers of immigrants moved into the new cities of western Massachusetts. None other than W. E. B. DuBois commented that during his childhood in Great Barrington the Irish were greater targets of ridicule than he was. The growing influence and power of some of these new immigrants challenged the political power and social status of the white middle class, the gentry farmers, and factory owners. One response was for the elite to turn to the colonial past to justify their positions. They glorified the colonial past in pageants, such as the 1844 Berkshire Jubilee, and emphasized their genealogical connections to the colonial aristocracy. They also enthusiastically defended the more reprehensible actions of their ancestors, especially in their dealings with the Indians. They claimed a number of untruths, including the assertion that the Mahican were not permanent inhabitants of western Massachusetts and that they were unrelated to the evidence for prehistoric settlement since their occupation did not substantially predate that of the Europeans. This was a clear denial of their history.

Handsman and Lamb Richmond then identify two current archaeological models that contain elements of these views. One model regards the early inhabitants of the Connecticut River Valley as seasonal occupants who used the Berkshires only for hunting and fishing. Another model sees the historic Mahican settlement at Stockbridge as a recently arrived community of native traders, denying the archaeological evidence for settlement. Against these views, Handsman and Lamb Richmond juxtapose Mahican oral and written history. Mahican oral histories talks of these areas as their ancestral homelands and document multiple uses including hunting, fishing, and farming. These examples should cause archeologists to think more carefully about the kinds of interpretation they offer and, more specifically, about the historical relationships between past and present Native peoples.

Handsman and Lamb Richmond go on to reveal the hidden histories of the Mahican and Weantinock peoples in their homelands. They note that archaeologists have failed to acknowledge the presence and cultural meanings of Indian homelands. Instead, they write about decreased mobility, changes in the utilization of habitats, or the intensification of trade networks. Handsman and Lamb Richmond suggest that this abstract and distanced language inhibits a consideration of continuities in settlement and land use. Standard archaeology survey methods often miss low-density but widely distributed settlements. They also note that the colonists' deeds to land were often carefully negotiated agreements that preserved Indian rights to hunting, fishing, farming, and gathering wood. In a 1724 deed, the Mahican allowed the colonists to use a tract along the Housatonic River while preserving their rights to Skatehook, a traditional meeting place and sacred site. Forty years later, an act was passed to establish 10 new townships in the Berkshires. When the Mahican protested, a special committee found against them and a bribe was paid to keep them quiet.

As their homelands were dispossessed, some Indian peoples resisted by resettling at the edges of the colonial settlements. They took refuge in more inaccessible locations such as the tops of ridges and small upland valleys. These communities consisted of mixed groups of Native American and African American peoples and lasted up to the 20th century. This situation is very similar to the experiences of the Lenape of eastern Pennsylvania (Seldin et al. 2008). These communities are not well documented in the historical record. However, they do leave archaeological evidence. An example is the Pootatuck Wigwam site located on the Housatonic River in Southbury, Connecticut. This site contains native ceramics, quartz tools, pieces of cut brass and copper shaped into pendants, gun-flints used as scrapers, and European ceramics. Some archaeologists might interpret this assemblage as a prehistoric lithic scatter overlain by historic artifacts. However, the site actually is evidence for periodic contact with colonialists and the selective acceptance and modification of colonial material culture.

References

Abu El-Haj, Nadia, 2001 Facts on the Ground: Archaeological Practice and Territorial Self-Fashioning in Israeli Society. Chicago: University of Chicago Press.

Alcock, Susan E., Terence N. D'Altroy, Kathleen D. Morrison, and Carla M. Sinopoli, eds., 2009 Empires: Perspectives from Archaeology and History. Cambridge: Polity Press.

Arnold, Bettina, 1990 The Past as propaganda: Totalitarian Archaeology in Nazi Germany. Antiquity 64 (244):464–478.

Ashcroft, Bill, Gareth Griffiths, and Helen Tiffin, 1989 The Empire Writes Back: Theory and Practice in Post-Colonial Literatures. New York: Routledge.

Cusick, James G. (ed.) 1998: Studies in Culture Contact: Interaction, Culture Change, and Archaeology. Carbondale: Center for Archaeological Investigations, Southern Illinois University.

Garlake, Peter S., 1982 Prehistory and Ideology in Zimbabwe. Africa 52:1–19.

Gosden, Chris 2001: Postcolonial Archaeology: Issues of Culture, Identity and Knowledge. In Archaeological Theory Today, edited by Ian Hodder. pp. 241-261. Cambridge: Polity Press.

Gosden, Chris, 2004 Archaeology and Colonialism: Cultural Contact from 5000 BC to the Present. Cambridge: Cambridge University Press.

Gosden, Chris, and Chantal Knowles, 2001 Collecting Colonialism: Material Culture and Colonial Change. Oxford: Berg.

Hall, Martin, 1984 The Burden of Tribalism: The Social Context of Southern African Studies. American Antiquity 49(3):455–467.

Hall, Martin, 2000 Archaeology and the Modern World: Colonial Transcripts in South African and the Chesapeake. London: Routledge.

Hardt, Michael, and Antonio Negri, 2000 Empire. Cambridge, MA: Harvard University Press.

Harper, Prudence Oliver, Joan Aruz, and Francoise Tallon, eds., 1993 The Royal City of Susa: Ancient Near Eastern Treasures in the Louvre. New York: Metropolitan Museum of Art.

Horning, Audrey, 2000 Urbanism in the Colonial South: The Development of Seventeenth-Century Jamestown. In Urban Archaeology in the South. Amy Young, ed. Pp. 52–68, Tuscaloosa: University of Alabama Press.

Jayasena, M. Ranjith, 2006 The Historical Archaeology of Katuwana, a Dutch East India Company Fort in Sri Lanka. Post-Medieval Archaeology 40(1): 111–128.

Johnson, Matthew, 2006 The Tide Reversed: Prospects and Potentials for a Postcolonial Archaeology of Europe. In Historical Archaeology. Martin Hall and Stephen W. Silliman, eds. Pp. 313–331. Oxford: Blackwell.

Kuklick, Bruce, 1996 Puritans in Babylon: The Ancient Near East and American Intellectual Life, 1880–1930. Princeton: Princeton University Press.

Liebmann, Matthew, 2008 Introduction: The Intersections of Archaeology and Postcolonial Studies. In Archaeology and the Postcolonial Critique. Matthew Liebmann and Uzma Rizvi, eds. Pp. 1–20. Walnut Creek, CA: AltaMira Press.

Liebmann, Matthew, and Uzma Rizvi, eds., 2008 Archaeology and the Postcolonial Critique. Walnut Creek, CA: AltaMira Press.

Lyons, Claire, and John K. Papadopoulos, eds., 2002 The Archaeology of Colonialism. Getty Research Institute, Los Angeles.

Mrozowski, Stephen A., 1999 The Commodification of Nature. International Journal of Historical Archaeology 3(3):153–166.

Mrozowski, Stephen A., 2009 Pulling the Threads Together: Issues of Theory and Practice in an Archaeology of the Modern World. In Crossing Paths or Sharing Tracks? Future Directions in the Archaeological Study of Post-1550 Britain and Ireland. Audrey Horning and Marilyn Palmer, eds. pp. 381–396. Woodbridge: Boydell and Brewster.

Murray, Tim, ed., 2004 The Archaeology of Contact in Settler Societies. Cambridge: Cambridge University Press.

Parry, Benita, 2004 Postcolonial Studies: A Materialist Critique. London: Routledge.

Said, Edward, 1978: Orientalism. New York: Vintage.

Seldin, Abigail, Robert Red Hawk Ruth, and Shelley DePaul, 2008 In the Time of the Fourth Crow:

The Reemergence of the Lenape of Pennsylvania. Cultural Survival Quarterly 32(2):32–35.

Shepherd, Nick, 2002a The Politics of Archaeology in Africa. Annual Review of Anthropology 31:189–209.

Shepherd, Nick, 2002b Heading South, Looking North: Why We Need a Postcolonial Archaeology. Public Archaeology 3(4):248–256.

Shepherd, Nick, 2003 State of the Discipline: Science, Culture and Identity in South African Archaeology, 1870–2003. Journal of Southern African Studies 29(4):823–844.

Stein, Gil J., ed., 2005a The Archaeology of Colonial Encounters. Santa Fe: School of American Research Press.

Stein, Gil J., 2005b Introduction: The Comparative Archaeology of Colonial Encounters. In The Archaeology of Colonial Encounters. Gil J. Stein, ed. pp. 3-31. Santa Fe: School of American Research Press.

Strangelove, Michael, 2005 The Empire of the Mind: Digital Piracy and the Anti-Capitalist Movement. Toronto: University of Toronto Press.

Trigger, Bruce. G., 1984 Alternative Archaeologies: Nationalist, Colonialist, Imperialist. Man (N.S.) 19:355–370.

Trigger, Bruce G., 2006 A History of Archaeological Thought. 2nd edition. Cambridge: Cambridge University Press.

Wallerstein, Immanuel, 1974 The Modern World-System, vol. I. Capitalist Agriculture and the Origins of the European World-Economy in the Sixteenth Century. New York: Academic Press.

Wallerstein, Immanuel, 1980 The Modern World-System, vol. II. Mercantilism and the Consolidation of the European World-Economy, 1600–1750. New York: Academic Press.

21

Archaeology and Nationalism in Spain

Margarita Díaz-Andreu

The purpose of this chapter is to analyze the importance which the appearance of nationalism as a political doctrine had in the formation of archaeology as a scientific discipline in Spain. This question cannot be understood without first taking into account the complexity of the phenomenon of nationalism and the specificity of its development in Spain. Here a number of different nationalisms existed, and archaeological data were, therefore, interpreted from a nationalist perspective in a number of different and, to a certain extent, contradictory ways.

This article argues that in Spain, as in most of Europe, archaeology developed as the result of the need to find data which would permit the reconstruction of the remotest periods of the national past. The crystallization of the study of history for nationalist aims occurred in the nineteenth century, leading to the dramatic growth of historical studies in the universities, the creation of archives and libraries, and, finally, the funding of historical research, including archaeological excavations. However, one should not axaggerate the role of archaeology in the construction of national histories. Historical studies were centered fundamentally on the modern and medieval

Margarita Díaz-Andreu, "Archaeology and Nationalism in Spain," pp. 39–56 from Philip L. Kohl and Clare Fawcett (eds) Nationalism, Politics, and the Practice of Archaeology (Cambridge: Cambridge University Press, 1995). Reprinted with permission of Cambridge University Press.

periods. The Romantic movement drew on medieval times for inspiration. Nevertheless, to a lesser degree during the nineteenth century, and to a greater extent in the twentieth, the growth of historical studies affected ancient history and prehistory and led to a greater recourse to archaeological data. In this way archaeology became politically charged. Archaeologists were fully aware of this situation, yet after World War II this politicization was systematically denied. Only recently have some archaeologists rediscovered the influence of nationalism on archaeology.

National histories were not elaborated without difficulties. This is clear in the case of Spain. Here, the construction of a national history was more complex than in many other parts of Europe, because Spanish nationalism was challenged by other peripheral nationalisms in Catalonia, the Basque country and, to a lesser extent, Galicia. Hence, four distinct nationalisms, which developed antagonistic versions of the national past, were found within the same nation-state.

How was it possible for a political ideology like nationalism to foster the appearance of different interpretations of history, and why did this occur from the middle of the eighteenth century and most notably at the end of the nineteenth century? The word "nation" was employed before the term "nationalism." As the word itself came from Latin, it continued to be used throughout the old territories of the

Roman Empire. In the Middle Ages its meaning was more diffuse than today. "Nation" referred to sets of individuals related either because they lived in the same territory (a village, a town, or some more extensive area), or because they shared certain cultural traits. In some cases, the word "nation" was used to refer to people who were members of a concrete political unit.

The French Revolution of 1789 finally gave the term "nation" a political meaning, associating it with the concept of national sovereignty. A nation was conceived, in the words of Sièyes, as "a union of individuals governed by one law, and represented by the same law-giving assembly" (Kedourie 1988:5). Thus, this first political use of the term "nation," which some have referred to as political nationalism, did not consider its cultural origin. The French nation was simply seen as equivalent to the French state.

However, from the middle of the nineteenth century this politically based definition of nationalism was replaced by another definition which has become an integral part of what we now refer to as cultural or ethno-nationalism. This new definition of nation was based on two ideas: first, the world was divided naturally into cultures; and secondly, these cultures should ideally be political entities (Kedourie 1988). It was this essentialist interpretation of the nation which gave history an importance previously unknown. This enhanced importance stemmed from the fact that it now became necessary to justify the origin and formation of the nation from earliest times. Yet problems emerged when the attempt was made to delineate nations. As distinct from the French case where from the Parisian perspective the revolutionaries saw no problem in equating the nation with France, in other parts of Europe, like the German-speaking territories, a nation was not a political reality. The political potential that the term "nation" acquired in the French Revolution was then taken up by the supporters of this cultural definition of nation. The basis of the nation became cultural, and it was on the basis of this supposed cultural unity that the nationalists demanded political unity. But what did these people understand by culture? The emphasis on distinct factors – language, race, religion, or territory – made this term ambiguous. As in the case of Spain, these varying definitions were potential sources of bitter disputes on the identity and existence of a particular nation.

Together with France, Spain is one of the oldest political entities in Europe, given that the limits of its territory have varied little since the end of the fifteenth century. However, it only became a modern state in the eighteenth century, when several different kingdoms, which had until then only owed allegiance to the same king, were unified under Castilian law, Nevertheless, the concept of Spain[1] as a territory having a single history which differs from the histories of territories beyond the Pyrenees dates back at least to the Middle Ages (Maravall 1981). From the fifteenth century, when all the kingdoms of the Iberian peninsula, with the exception of Portugal,[2] were under the Habsburg Crown, the fact that individuals from different kingdoms fought in the same wars reinforced a consciousness of belonging to the same country.[3] This identification with Spain occurred despite the fact that most people also identified with their particular kingdoms or regions (Aragon, Castile, Catalonia, etc.).

The construction of a national history in Spain began in the mid-nineteenth century (Cirujano Marin et al. 1985). In contrast to developments in France, where there were few critics of the official version of the national history, in Spain dissident voices from the 1880s on were to be heard in Catalonia, the Basque country, and, to a lesser extent, Galicia. In the first two regions industrial growth resulted in the rise of a strong middle class which felt discriminated against by the Madrid central government. The fact that in both regions distinct languages were spoken, which the state's disastrous educational system was unable to undermine (as in France), intensified the consciousness of separate identities in these regions. Hence, they were also able to create national histories which justified the alternative nation's eternal existence. In all these cases archaeology contributed to the creation of the national myth.

I Spanish Nationalism and Archaeology

The appearance of nineteenth-century nationalism provoked a massive growth of interest in history, and therefore in archaeology. Yet it should be stressed that there existed, particularly from the Renaissance on, elements of nationalist sentiment and of the use of the past for pre-nationalist ends. In Spain some authors, such as Maravall (1981), detect already the existence of a consciousness of belonging to one single cultural unit, which sometimes corresponds with the desire to belong to one political unit, in the Middle Ages. One of the manifestations of this feeling, expressed after the fall of the Roman Empire, was remorse over the loss of Roman Hispania, when all the Iberian peninsula was united under the same rule.

In the sixteenth and seventeenth centuries the concept of Spain as a cultural and political unit was quite developed. It is significant that by the end of the sixteenth century the first *History of Spain*, written in 1598 by Father Mariana, had appeared. Likewise, literature reflected an interest in the past and a defense of Hispanic identity. A good example of this is the play, written by Cervantes in 1584, about Numantia, the Celtiberian town which heroically resisted the advances of the Romans in the second century BC.

From an archaeological perspective, what is important is that it was at this time that intellectuals began to look into the material culture of the past, especially that of the classical era. One reason for this was that possession of classical items and ruins reinforced the importance of a person or a locality. Therefore, the European intelligentsia, who had been fascinated since the fifteenth century by the classical period, proudly claimed ownership of the remains of the classical world located in their territories. In addition, Roman ruins were described by travellers and were included in engravings to emphasize the importance of cities. In Spain, ancient objects were systematically collected for the first time in the fifteenth century (Morán and Checa 1985:33). Roman sculptures and objects were used as decorations in noble houses. To cope with this new demand for antiquities, excavations of Roman sites began. Italica was one of the sites that were excavated at this time (Rodríguez Morales *et al.* 1991:95).

The new importance accorded the past also meant that it could become subject to manipulation. Forgeries of ancient objects provide clear examples of this tendency. It is worth emphasizing in this context the use of the past to try to resolve the ethnic conflict provoked by the presence of the *moriscos* (Moslems who had converted to Christianity) in Spain. One of the ways in which they fought for equality with the Old Christians was through the falsification of archaeological objects, such as the lead plates of Sacromonte in the sixteenth century.[4]

The appearance of political nationalism in the French Revolution at the end of the eighteenth century did not initially affect archaeology. This was because the main thrust of the movement toward political nationalism was not based on cultural identities. Consequently, although political nationalism was soon adopted in Spain, it was not this political philosophy which was behind the attention paid to the past by people such as King José I (Napoleon's brother). Bonaparte signed a decree which attempted to protect the Roman site of Italica (Rodríguez Hidalgo 1991:93). His intention was to protect an ancient site because of its antiquity, and not to save a symbol of the nation from destruction.

Ancient objects were not considered as part of the national heritage until the 1830s. As a result of the dissolution of the monasteries in these years the state acquired a vast quantity of works of art and archaeological objects, which were exhibited in newly created museums. These museums were no longer referred to as royal but, reflecting the new nationalist ideology, they were now called national or provincial. Provincial museums, which displayed archaeological remains, began to appear in the 1830s, and the National Museum, reserved for artistic objects, was opened in 1840 (Bouza Alvarez 1981). These museums needed curators. Therefore, from 1856 archaeology was taught in the *Escuela Superior de Diplomática* (Diplomatic School), where curators were trained (Pasamar Alzurí and Peiró Martín 1991:73). The last step in the creation of museums of archaeology was the opening of the National Archaeological Museum in 1867.

Nonetheless, one should not exaggerate the importance of nationalism at this time in Spain, nor of the study of archaeology in its elaboration. As against the powerful nationalist movements in France, Britain, or Germany, Spanish nationalism showed itself to be weak and hesitant. It should not be forgotten that at precisely the time when the major European powers were expanding their imperial possessions

Spain was to lose the remanants of her Latin-American empire. Given her weakened position, Spain had difficulty constructing the image of a glorious nation. Hence, other ways were found to exalt the national spirit. These included the identification of Spain with Castile, the War of Independence against Napoleon, the creation of a national historiography, and the attempts to overcome political tensions within Spain through military campaigns aimed at fostering a national spirit (García Casado 1987:41). In this glorification of the national past the heroic defense of pre-Roman cities like Saguntum and Numantia against their invaders was used, and was associated with the defense of the Spanish nation and the invincibility of the Spanish national spirit.

Because of the weakness of Spanish nationalism there was only a limited interest in the archaeological past in the nineteenth century. Two examples illustrate this fact. First, in comparison with other European countries, Spain's popular archaeological literature was underdeveloped (Olmos 1992a and 1992b:52). Secondly, attempts to create a national consciousness through the excavation and glorification of sites of interest for the construction of the national past were minimal. Moreover, even when efforts were made in this direction, they had little impact. The history of the excavation of the Celtiberian town of Numantia is significant in this respect. Initial excavations of Numantia were conducted briefly in 1803. These excavations were not published, and the collections from the excavations were lost (Gómez Santacruz 1935). In 1842, a cultural association tried to build a commemorative monument on the site as a means of awakening the national consciousness. This attempt could be seen as an example of Hobsbawm's "invention of tradition" (Hobsbawm 1983:7). But this commemorative monument was never finished, owing to a lack of funds. Some excavations were hurriedly carried out in 1853. In 1856 the Academy of History gave a subsidy for the excavations of the site, which were carried out between 1861 and 1867. However, at the end of the excavations, little use was made of the new data in terms of organizing a national mythical symbol. The results of the excavations were not presented as anything spectacular, and the site was not granted any special protection. Neither a monument identifying the

site, nor a provincial or special museum to display its collections was provided. Numantia lay abandoned for two decades until, in 1882, it was declared a national monument, forty years after the first monument had been given this status.[5] Despite the scant importance given to archaeology, the ancient past, nevertheless, was used in nationalist art, as seen, for example, in the painting of Alejo Vera, *The surrender of Numantia*, and in Manuel Dominguez's *The death of Seneca* (Reyero 1989:55).

The loss of the last colonies in 1898 forced Spaniards into a period of self-examination and, as Carr (1982:473) points out, into a debate on whether the catastrophe was explicable in terms of the Spaniard's incapacity to operate institutions imported from abroad, or whether Spain "had been excluded from those currents of progress which swept other nations towards prosperity and power." Intellectuals in Spain realized more than ever the necessity to create a national identity, but it was perhaps too late. Spanish nationalism had become more difficult to maintain as alternative Catalan, Basque, and Galician nationalisms had appeared. These peripheral nationalisms presented alternative ways of understanding the meaning of Spain.

The upsurge of Spanish nationalism in the twentieth century was reflected in archaeology. Myths such as those about Numantia were finally taken seriously. A memorial monument was set up on the site in 1905 by private initiative, and the king, Alfonso XIII, agreed to inaugurate it. The fact that just a few days earlier a German archaeologist, Adolf Schulten, had begun to excavate the site was considered a scandal. Schulten was prevented from working further on the excavation, and a Spanish expedition was charged with continuing the work. To examine the growing maturity of Spanish nationalism at this time, it is useful to compare the work carried out by the prestigious archaeologist José Ramón Mélida in the nineteenth century as against his later work in the twentieth century. In the nineteenth century Mélida studied mainly Egyptian archaeology. Yet, by the twentieth century his nationalism had developed to the point that he mentioned it expressly in his work. In 1906, Mélida was included in the team that excavated Numantia. His publications had a clear nationalist aim. For example, he began the report on the first excavation with the following remark: "The discovery of the remains of the heroic town of Numantia was a national duty." After some pages written in a similar tone, he admitted that the site had been excavated not only for scientific reasons but "to satisfy this historical duty, to make explicit through these relics the historical event of which our Fatherland is proud" (Mélida 1908:3, 10). Finally, in 1919 the Museo Numantino (Numantian Museum) was opened to keep and display the materials collected in the excavation; King Alfonso XIII inaugurated this museum.

From the beginning of the twentieth century stories about places such as Numantia and Saguntum, and about historical characters such as Viriatus, Indibilis and Mandonius, were included more and more frequently in didactic literature for children. These stories were also displayed in other media such as the *cromos culturales* printed in the 1930s. *Cromos culturales* were educational postcards for children, decorated with a national historical picture on one side and an explanation on the other (Olmos 1992a:20). The upsurge of Spanish nationalism was also reflected in the archaeological literature, for example in the attempt by Joaquín Costa to write three National Novels based on archaeology (Costa 1917 [probably written in 1908–9]), or in the novel *La novela de España* (*The Novel of Spain*) written in 1928 by the archaeologist Manuel Gómez-Moreno.

The institutional basis of Spanish archaeology was being organized at this time. In 1907 the Junta de Ampliación de Estudios or JAE (Commission for Further Studies) was created. The purpose of this official institution was "to train the future teaching body and to give to the present one the means and facilities to follow closely the scientific and pedagogical movements of the most cultivated nations" (foundation decree, quoted in Sánchez Ron 1988:6). The JAE had a leading role in Spanish archaeology. Some archaeological institutions depended on it. These included the Centro de Estudios Históricos (Center for Historical Studies), which, since the 1920s, has had an Archaeology section; the Escuela Española (Spanish School) in Rome, which had a short life owing to World War I; and the Comisión de Investigaciones Paleontológicas y Prehistóricas (Commission

for Palaeontologic and Prehistoric Research). The JAE also gave grants to post-graduates to study abroad, and thus the majority of the country's future staff spent some time in foreign universites, mainly in Germany. The importance that archaeology had acquired was also reflected in the passage of laws, such as the 1911 Excavations Act, and the 1933 Heritage Act. Through the first act the Junta Superior de Excavaciones y Antigüedades (High Commission for Excavations and Antiquities) was created.

The Spanish Civil War (1936–9) was, in a sense, a fight over two ways of understanding Spain as a nation. Some saw Spain as a multicultural unit, as it had been seen during the Spanish Second Republic (1931–6/9). Others, such as General Francisco Franco, viewed the country as a single cultural unit. Franco imposed this latter view between 1936/9 and 1975.

At the end of the Civil War archaeology still had a clear political role (Alonso del Real 1946). Julio Martinez Santa-Olalla, a falangist (the *Falange* was the Spanish fascist party), was put in charge of the reorganization of Spanish archaeology. Spanish nationalism in the Franco era drew its inspiration from the glories of Imperial Spain in the sixteenth and seventeenth centuries, and in the defense of the country's Catholic identity. Consequently after the Civil War, research on Spain under the Romans and under the Visigoths was encouraged. The Roman era was studied because it was argued by scholars that this was the first time Spain had been united, and that it was during this period that Spain learned how to act as an empire. Furthermore, it was during this time that Christianity entered Spain. The Visigothic period had also seen Spain united under one rule. Moreover, in the early years of Franco's rule, the Francoist ideologues admired Nazi Germany, and Spanish archaeologists tried to demonstrate an Aryan presence in Spain. This affinity led to close collaboration with teams of German archaeologists in the excavation of Visigothic sites (Werner 1946).

The end of World War II resulted in a gradual lessening of these extreme measures. Previously banned topics were discussed more openly. An example of this increasing openness was a seminar on the multiple roots of Spain given by the Catalan archaeologist Luis Pericot in the 1950s ([...] quoted in del Pino 1978:58).

Archaeology, however, began to lose its previous political power because of the appearance of "modified positivism" or "pragmatic reformism," a theory of scientific knowledge which argued that reality could be discerned through impartial, meticulous, and exhaustive observation. The goal of archaeology became, first, to impose order on the data and then to describe it. Progress in knowledge was measured by the increase of information accumulated and catalogued (Vicent 1982:31–2). The transformation of archaeology into endless lists of described objects and chronologies took archaeological data further and further away from the general public. Official archaeology became isolated and gradually lost the interest of those advocating nationalism.

Franco's death in 1975 led to a process of democratization in Spain. Once the constitution of 1978 came into effect, all regions were able to ask for autonomy. Consequently, by 1985 Spain had been divided into seventeen self-governed autonomies. The new territorial composition of Spain has greatly affected archaeology since each autonomy now administers its own cultural heritage as specified by the 1985 Heritage Act. Archaeology has not again been used to legitimize a single cultural Spanish nation. Nor is the past often used in defense of a present multi-cultural concept of Spain. This is based not on notions of the past, but on the modern concept of Spain as a democratic and developed country, a concept frequently mentioned in King Juan Carlos I's discourses.

II Catalan Nationalism and Archaeology

Catalan nationalism appeared toward the middle of the nineteenth century. Its clearest expression was the cultural movement called Reinaixença[6] (Renaissance). Catalan nationalism had little influence on archaeology during the nineteenth century, although intellectuals related to the Renaixença* movement, such as Joaquin Rubiói Ors and Francesc Martorell i Peña, included among their interests Catalan archaeology, These Intellectuals, however, did not use archaeology to legitimize the Catalan nation.

Enric Prat de la Riba was one of the first to describe Catalan archaeology in nationalist terms.

His book *La nacionalitat catalana** (The Catalan Nationality), written in 1906, was of great importance for the ulterior development of Catalan nationalism. Prat de la Riba based Catalan nationalism on the Catalan language (Prat de la Riba 1978:84). He believed that the roots of Catalonia were to be found in the pre-Roman Iberian "ethnos," as he saw it, the Iberian "nation" which extended from Murcia to the Rhône (p. 87). In this way he claimed as Catalan all the Catalan-speaking countries, i.e. apart from Catalonia itself, the French Roussillon, the Balearic islands, and Valencia. He even maintained from the study of Iberian-Roman coins that this area was characterized, even in the pre-Roman period, by a special phonetic system which seemed to be related to that of modern Catalan (p. 91). Prat de la Riba saw Roman conquest as a deep misfortune since, at this time, the Iberian nationality had disappeared. However, because the influence of the Roman culture on the population was only superficial, the Iberian "ethnos" – now transformed into the medieval Catalan "nation" – was revived once the Roman Empire came to an end (pp. 88–9). He saw the archaeological site of Empúries* (Emporion in Greek) as a kind of capital of the Iberian nation (p. 90). Prat de la Riba's aim, however, was not to gain political independence for Catalonia. He preferred the idea of Catalan self-government in a federal Spanish state (pp. 105–18).

In 1907 the Barcelona provincial government, directed by Prat de la Riba, created two institutions, the Institut d'Estudis Catalans* (Institute for Catalan Studies) and the Junta de Museus de Barcelona* (Commission of Barcelona Museums), both of which were important in the development of Catalan archaeology. The Institut d'Estudis Catalans,* an institution for the study of Catalan culture, was divided into several sections, One of these sections was devoted to archaeology. The excavation of Emporion began in 1908 under the direction of J. Puig i Cadafalch. In 1909 excavators uncovered two statues representing Venus and Aesculapius. Catalan nationalists were elated, and it was even argued that their finding had given Catalonia an ancient history and, therefore, consecrated the rebirth of the Catalan nation (d'Ors 1911:9).

Between 1909 and 1923 Catalonia achieved a very limited form of self-government called the Mancomunitat de Catalunya,* Prat de la Riba was the president until his death in 1917. He was succeeded by Puig i Cadafalch, the director of the Emporion excavation. In 1923 General Primo de Rivera imposed the first dictatorship of twentieth-century Spain and abolished the Mancomunitat. It is significant that no excavations were carried out in Emporion between 1924 and 1930.

The principal figure in Catalan archaeology during these years was Pere Bosch Gimpera. Between 1914 and 1939 he was able to organize in Catalonia the best infrastructure for archaeology in Spain. He was also the creator of what has been called the Catalan school of archaeology. Bosch Gimpera was a convinced Catalan nationalist. His thesis, written in 1915, dealt with the Iberian culture. This was, as we have seen in the case of Prat de la Riba, a subject of special interest for the elaboration of the Catalan national past. Bosch Gimpera saw the prehistory of the Iberian peninsula as the direct precursor of a multi-cultural Spain. This thesis was best expressed in his major work *Ethnology of the Iberian Peninsula* (1932). He intended to relate ancient "etnie" to modern cultures, and demonstrate that the cultural diversity of Spain had prehistoric roots. This finding allowed him to support a federal structure for the Spanish state, in which Catalonia had an autonomous status (Bosch Gimpera 1937).

However, Catalan archaeologists did not share a monolithic vision of the past. Some held a more Spanish nationalist position. For example, in 1934 Pericot, rather than emphasizing the cultural diversity of Spanish prehistory, maintained that the prehistoric period had been a time when all the races of the Iberian peninsula had intermingled and Spain had flourished as a center of European civilization. The evidence he cited to uphold such an argument was the cave art of the late Stone Age and the creation of the Beaker culture in the Iberian peninsula during the Copper Age, a culture later exported throughout Europe. Pericot did not see the Roman presence on the Iberian peninsula as a deep misfortune, as had Prat de la Riba. Rather, he believed that the Roman period was fundamental to Spanish history since it was at this time that Christianity arrived in Spain (Pericot 1934:14 and 18).

The end of the Civil War meant the exile of Bosch Gimpera. All his archaeological posts were taken over by Martín Almagro Basch. This intelligent, young non-Catalan archaeologist transformed Catalan archaeology into a discipline at the service of the Francoist state (Díaz-Andreu 1993). In the 1950s Almagro Basch moved to Madrid. Even though he was replaced by the Catalan Pericot, the Catalan School of Archaeology did not recover until the 1960s and 1970s (Marc-7 1986:227) when, with the return of other Catalans such as J. Maluquer de Motes (in 1959), M. Tarradell (in 1970), and P. Palol (in 1970), it flourished once more (Marc-7 1986b:228). However, in the 1960s and 1970s when the Catalan school had begun to be reorganized, archaeology had lost much of its power to affect nationalist thought since Catalan archaeology had also been influenced by "modified positivism" or "pragmatic reformism."

In 1982 Catalonia became self-governed. What effect does Catalan nationalism have on archaeology at present in a country in which nationalism has a strong presence? First, in contrast to what might be expected, there is no marked tendency to subsidize research on any particular period, as the annual reports, the *Memòrias dei Departament de Cultura** of the Generalitat clearly show. Secondly, nationalism in archaeology is demonstrated in other ways such as the language used to write scientific archaeological publications. These are written mostly in Catalan. Catalan is used to such a degree that papers written in Spanish, Castilian, English, or other languages are translated into Catalan (for example Shennan 1989 and Vicent 1990). However, this feature could be seen as consistent with a Spanish trend, given that foreign languages are also translated into Spanish in Spanish journals (Hodder 1987).

Catalan politicians rarely use archaeology to legitimize the Catalan nation. Nevertheless, Catalan symbols such as Emporion continue to have some power. One of the best examples was the arrival of the Olympic Torch at the port of Emporion at a time when there was an intense debate in Spain about the attempt to use the 1992 Olympic Games in Barcelona as a forum for Catalan propaganda to the world.

III Basque Nationalism and Archaeology

Basque identity and the use of the past to create it have a long tradition in the Basque country. Since the sixteenth century some intellectuals, such as Esteban de Garigay and the anonymous author of the Códice de Mieres, or, in the eighteenth century, the Jesuit Father Larramendi (Caro Baroja 1957 and Duplá and Emborujo 1991:107–8), had tried to explain the existence of the Basque language by linking it to the pre-Roman population. They saw Basque as one of the languages which had spread throughout the world after the fall of the Tower of Babel, Basque people were, therefore, considered to be the descendants of Tubal, who was himself a descendant of Noah.

The industrialization of the Basque country in the nineteenth century led to the immigration of large numbers of non-Basque speakers into the area. After this time, class differences were paralleled by linguistic differences; that is, there was a proletariat of non-Basque speakers (who were scornfully called maketos[**]) and a Basque middle class and peasantry. Basque nationalism first emerged in Bilbao, the Basque industrial heartland. Sabino de Arana Goiri (1865–1903) was its main ideologue and organizer, although he had some precursors, such as the Frenchman Joseph Augustin Chaho (1811–58) (García de Cortázar and Azcona 1991:17). De Arana Goiri's nationalism was based on a condemnation of the industrialization of the Basque country and an exaltation of traditional society. He passionately believed in the need to maintain the purity of the Basque race. His nationalism was represented by the slogan "God and Old Laws." He defended the independence of the Basque country, including not only the three official Spanish Basque provinces, but also Navarra and the three French Basque provinces. After de Arana Goiri's early death, Basque nationalism continued to grow and gradually broadened its popular base. The conversion, mostly during the 1920s, of large numbers of the lower clergy to Basque nationalism was extremely important.

Basque nationalism affected archaeological research in various ways. First, there was a debate between the opponents and the followers of the Basque-Cantabrist theory. This theory maintained that the Basque country had never been ruled by the Romans and that, therefore, the Basque race and language had been able to survive. The actual presence of Roman remains in the Basque country led to different interpretations of the same data. Nevertheless, Basque archaeologists maintained there was a racial and cultural division between Basques and Romans, and, in this way, they defended the purity of the Basque race and explained the survival of the Basque language (Duplá and Emborujo 1991; Ortiz de Urbina Montoya and Pérez Olmedo 1991). Secondly, the analysis of physical human remains became very important for scholars who wanted to study the relationship between the prehistoric and the modern Basque populations. This goal sometimes became the primary aim of excavations. Important work on physical anthropology was done at the end of the nineteenth century by Telesforo de Aranzadi. His thesis, written in the late 1880s on *El pueblo Euskalduna*[**] (the Basque people), tried to prove the racial uniqueness of the Basques. Later, in the first years of the twentieth century, he was to work in the field of archaeology.

Basque archaeology was highly nationalistic during the first three decades of the twentieth century. It seems to have been no accident that two of the three main representatives of Basque archaeology before the Civil War – Aranzadi and Eguren – were physical anthropologists, and that the other – Barandiarán – was a priest. The collaboration of these three men began in 1917. From 1918 on their works were subsidized by the nationalist institution Sociedad de Estudios Vascos, called in Basque Eusko Ikas-kuntza[**] (Society of Basque Studies).

Father José Miguel de Barandiarán was the crucial figure of Basque archaeology in the twentieth century. He began his training in archaeology (and in ethnology) as a pupil of Aranzadi. Unlike Aranzadi and Eguren, Barandiarán lived in the Basque country and, therefore, was the person who organized the infrastructure of Basque archaeology from 1916 onwards. He founded the Laboratorio de Ethnologia y Folklore Euskera[**] (Laboratory of Ethnology and Basque Folklore) (1916), and the Seminario de Prehistoria Ikuska[**] (Seminar of Ikuska Prehistory) (1921), later replaced by the Centro de Investigaciones Prehistóricas (Center of Prehistoric Research) (1925), which was dependent on the Sociedad de Estudios Vascos (Barandiarán 1988:44). He also promoted the reviews *Euskalarriaren Alde*** on prehistory and mythology from the First World War (del Pino 1978:72), and the *Anuario de Eusko-Folklore/*** (Annual Journal of Basque Folklore) (1921), which from 1927 included a section on prehistory. Like Bosch Gimpera in Catalonia, Barandiarán stressed a straightforward relationship between prehistoric and modern Basque culture (Barandiarán 1917, 1932 and 1934).

After the Civil War Barandiarán fled to the French Basque country and lived there until the 1950s. In his absence little archaeological work was done. However, some of the archaeological research carried out manifested signs of Spanish nationalism. An example of this was the excavation of a site located just 9 km from Guernica, a town of fundamental historical importance for Basque nationalism, and which was bombed by the Nazis during the Spanish Civil War. This excavation was used to document the presence of Celtic/Indo-European invasions of the Basque country. In this way the prehistory of the Basque people was equated with that of the rest of northern Spain (Taracena Aguirre and Fernández de Avilés 1945).

Barandiarán was allowed to return to the Basque territory in 1953. Basque archaeology was again institutionalized. The Servicio de Investigaciones Arqueológicas de la Diputación de Vizcaya (Department of Archaeological Research of the Vizcaya provincial government) (1958), Instituto de Investigaciones Arqueológicas Aranzadi (the Aranzadi Institute of Archaeological Research) (1962), and the Instituto Alavés de Arqueologia (the Archaeological Institute of the Province of Alava) (1966) were created (Barandiarán 1988). Archaeology began to be taught in a Basque university in 1964.

The Basque country achieved autonomous self-government in 1981. At present, Basque archaeology is quite similar to Catalan archaeology and, in fact, to the archaeology of the other Spanish autonomous regions with regard to the periods and subjects which archaeologists choose to study and for which they can get funding. There is no special attention paid to any period. The nationalist ideology adhered to

by archaeologists is reflected, as in Catalonia, in the language used in archaeological scientific publications. A great quantity of the publications are written in both Basque and Spanish. Basque is rarely chosen as the only language for publication, because not all Basques are able to read it and these articles would be absolutely incomprehensible to non-Basque speakers, as Basque is a non-Indo-European language. Nationalist ideology is also reflected in the decision made by some archaeologists to choose as an area of study the three French provinces, Navarra, and the three Spanish Basque provinces (for example Barandiarán 1988). Nationalist feelings are also seen in exhibitions such as *Gure herriaren lehen urratsak*** or *Ciento cincuenta mil años de prehistoria vasca* (*One Hundred and Fifty Thousand Years of Basque Prehistory*) (1982). The aim seems to be to root the present Basque country in an endless past.

IV Galician Nationalism and Archaeology

There was an upsurge of Galician identity around the middle of the nineteenth century. Before the 1840s the teaching of the Galician language had been supported by Fr. Martin Sarmiento, and, by 1843, the journalist and revolutionary Antolin Faraldo de Malvar saw Galicia as a nation (Beramendi 1981a:37). In his *History of Galicia*, published in 1838, José Verea y Aguiar, a liberal activist, stated that Galician history began with the Celts and Suebians (Beramendi 1981:35, 42, 182 note 10). The Suebians had been among the Germanic invaders who entered Hispania at the end of the Roman Empire during the early Middle Ages. They settled in a territory broadly coincident with Galicia. José Verea y Aguiar was the first president of the Diputación Arqueológica Gallega (Provincial Galician Archaeological Institute) created in Santiago de Compostela in 1843 (*Enciclopedia* 1924 (67): 1477).

The "Renaissance" movement in Galicia was called Rexurdimento*** or Rexeneración*** (1861–85), transformed later on into a nationalist movement called Rexioinalismo*** (1885–97) (the exact dates of these movements are still disputed). Although the cultural development of this movement was similar to that of

Catalonia, the political implications neither were felt as early nor were as important. This contrast can partially be explained by the underdevelopment of Galician industry and the resultant unimportance of the bourgeoisie. This situation limited nationalist aspirations to a small circle of intellectuals. Furthermore, Galician nationalism was poorly organized. There were constant disputes between nationalist leaders, Lamas Carvajal against Murguia, and later Murguia against Alfredo Brañas (Castelos Paredes 1990:41).

During the nineteenth century Galician nationalism was based on a belief in the Galician race, language, character, customs, and geography, as expressed by Manuel Murguia (Beramendi 1981a:50). The Celts were seen as being at the origin of the Galician race. This face was thought to have been renewed later on by Suebian blood (Murguia 1865 in Beramendi 1981a:51). The impact of these ideas on archaeology could be seen in the importance given to Celtic remains by archaeologists such as Leandro Saralegui y Medina (who in 1867 published *Studies on the Celtic Period in Galicia*), Pondal, Verea and Martinez Padin (Máiz 1984:46). The growing importance of archaeology in Galician life was shown by the creation of archaeological associations, such as the Sociedad Arqueológica de Pontevedra (the Pontevedra Archaeological Society) in the province of Pontevedra, which in 1895 promoted a provincial museum.

Nationalist cultural life at the beginning of the twentieth century included the *tertulias*, cultural meetings with friends, usually held once a week to debate subjects specially relevant for the participants. It seems significant that one of the best known of these *tertulias* adopted the name *La Cova céltica*[***] (the Celtic Cave), which had archaeological connotations.

In 1920 a group of Galician nationalist intellectuals created *Nós*[***]. The activities of this group included ethnography (Vicente Risco) and archaeology (Florentino López Cuevillas). The head of the group was Vicente Risco y Agüero, who actively participated in nationalist political life throughout the whole period. He carried on the myths formulated in the nineteenth century which described the origin of Galicia. According to these myths, Galicia was one of the seven Celtic nations which included

the Highlands of Scotland, Isle of Man, Ireland, Wales, Cornwall, Brittany, and Galicia (in which he included Portugal) (Beramendi 1981a:141–2). Only in this context can it be understood why some Galician archaeologists used their JAE grants not to go to Germany, as was usual, but to visit any of the previously mentioned seven "Celtic nations." Fermin Bouza Brey, for example, went to Portugal (1929) and Brittany (1933) (*Gran Enciclopedia* 1984 (4):31–2).

Galician cultural life was institutionalized in 1923 by the Seminario de Estudos Galegos[***] (Seminar of Galician Studies) (*Gran Enciclopedia* 1984 (28): 115–18), although there existed some previous associations, such as in archaeology the Xuntanza de Estudos e Investigacións Históricas e Arqueolóxicas[***] (Commission of Historical and Archaeological Studies and Research) of Pontevedra. Anthropologists/archaeologists, such as Fermin Bouza Brey and José Filgueira Valverde, were among its creators.

In 1926, it opened sections on "Prehistory" and "Archaeology and the History of Art," directed by Florentino López Cuevillas and Carro García respectively. After the Civil War the Seminario de Estudos Galegos[***] was replaced by the Instituto Padre Sarmiento (Father Sarmiento Institute) (*Gran Enciclopedia* 1984 (28): 115–18), which did not include archaeology until 1967. In that year the Institute established its Department of Prehistory and Archaeology.

Galicia obtained its autonomy in 1983. As in Catalonia and the Basque country, nationalism is reflected mainly through the use of the Galician language in publications. Nevertheless, Galician is not as widely used in archaeological works as is Catalan in Catalonia.

V Conclusions

This chapter has analyzed the relationship between nationalism and archaeology in Spain. A number of points have been stressed. First, it has been emphasized that the development of archaeology as a scientific discipline in the nineteenth century can only be understood in the context of the creation of a national history; that is to say a history directed at legitimizing the existence of a nation and, therefore, its right to constitute an independent state. Thus, in the case of Spain, the past was used in this way by all the nationalist movements – Spanish, Catalan, Basque, and Galician – without exception. This does not mean that archaeological interpretations were monolithic within each nationalism. Indeed a more detailed study would reveal different tendencies and nuances amongst the supporters of each nationalist movement.

Secondly, it seems clear that the relationship between archaeology and nationalism became most explicit in the first half of the twentieth century. It was also at this time that archaeologists laid down the basis for the institutionalization of their profession. Hence, new laws were passed; archaeologists were given a niche within the universities; and new institutions and associations were created. This institutionalization cannot be separated from the interest produced by archaeological discoveries, and, in particular, by the interpretations archaeologists made of these discoveries. In other words, archaeology attained an importance heretofore not experienced, allowing the discipline to become institutionalized because the data it produced were politically useful to elites dominated by a nationalist discourse. This explains why the study of archaeology grew most rapidly in Madrid, Catalonia, and the Basque country and, to a lesser extent, in Galicia.

Thirdly, after the Spanish Civil War, and particularly from the end of World War II, the academic work of intellectuals who attempted to pursue a scientific method slowly became depoliticized. Archaeology was no exception to this rule. This coincided with a decline in the social and political impact of nationalism. However, despite the current resurgence of nationalism, the type of discourse developed by archaeologists in the early twentieth century has not reappeared. Today few archaeologists would dare to write that they can see a relationship between the culture and identity of their own society and that of the prehistoric peoples they are studying, although it is true that on the margins of academic work, in the presentations and prologues of some publications, such a connection is still sometimes made. It is perhaps because of this lack of interest of archaeologists in nationalist interpretations that politicians have become less interested in archaeological research. This situation is reflected in the growing difficulties archaeologists have in getting their work subsidized by the autonomous governments which had at first heavily subsidized their labours.

Notes

1 This concept of Spain was the heir of Roman and Visigothic Hispania; i.e., it included Portugal.
2 Navarra was integrated only in 1512. Portugal only belonged to the Habsburg Crown between 1580 and 1640.
3 Some scholars even say that numerous examples show that wars transform a people into a nation (Shafer 1964:44).
4 It is in this context of ethnic conflict that the well-known falsification of the lead plates of Sacromonte should be placed. In 1588, when the old minaret of the Granada mosque was knocked down, a lead box was found on St Gabriel's day (Gabriel is the most important angel in Islam) with a statue of the Virgin Mary, a bone of St Esteban, and a parchment written in Arabic, Latin, and Castilian. The text contained a prophecy by St John, announcing the coming of Muhammad and Luther, with comments by St Cecilio, bishop of Iliberri. The forgers identified the ancient city of Iliberri with Granada. This identification was rejected by contemporary opinion, and was one of the arguments later used to deny the find's authenticity. Aware that the forgery had not been discovered, the forgers in 1595 went further and left a series of lead plates, inscribed with religious texts, on the Granada Sacromonte (Sacred Mount). These texts linked both Arabs and Christians to the origins of Christianity. The aim of these forgeries was to try to convince the Old Christians that Islam had played a key role in the preservation of Christianity. Thus, the forgers were attempting to resolve the ethnic conflict between the moriscos and the Old Christians and to integrate the moriscos into the dominant Christian society (Alvarez Barrientos and Mora Rodríguez 1985 and Caro Baroja 1992).
5 Reflecting the greater importance given to the medieval past in the creation of national sentiment, the first heritage monument to be protected as a national monument was the medieval León cathedral in 1844 (Hernández-Gil 1983:27).
6 The asterisks indicate the following languages: * Catalan, ** Basque (/** where the Basque name has been Hispanicized), and *** Galician.

References

Alonso del Real, C. 1946 Función social del arqueólogo. *Il Congreso Arqueológico del Sureste Español:* 33–43.

Alvarez Barrientos, J. and G. Mora Rodríguez 1985. El final de una tradición. Las falsificaciones granadinas del siglo XVIII. *Revista de Dialectología y Tradiciones Populares* 40:163–89.

Barandiarán, I. 1988 *Enciclopedia general ilustrada del Pais Vasco,* Vol. 1, *Prehistoria: paleolítico.* San Sebastián: Ed. Auñamendi.

Barandiarán, J.M. 1917 Investigaciones prehistóricas en la Diócesis de Vitoria. *Euskal Erria* 77:386–92, 431–42.

Barandiarán, J.M. 1932 Paralelo entre lo prehistórico y lo actual en el País Vasco. Investigaciones en Balzola y en Gibijo. *Anuario de Eusko-Folklore* 12.

Barandiarán, J.M. 1934 *Euskalerriko Lehen Gizona.* Colecc. Zabalkundea. Serie de Ciencias, Bellas Artes y Letras no. 3. Ed. Auñamendi.

Beramendi, J.G. 1981 *Vicente Risco no nacionalismo galego,* vol. I, *Das orixes a afirmación plena.* Santiago de Compostela: Edicions do Cerne.

Bosch Gimpera, P. 1915 *El problema de la cerámica ibérica.* Comision de Investigaciones Paleontológicas y Prehistóricas 7. Madrid.

Bosch Gimpera, P. 1932 *Etnologia de la Peninsula Ibèrica.* Barcelona: Ed. Alpha.

Bosch Gimpera, P. 1937 *"España."* Conferencia dada por Pedro Bosch Gimpera, rector de la Universidad de Barcelona. Valencia: Anales de la Universidad de Valencia.

Bouza Alvarez, J.L. 1981 *Introducción a la museologia.* Madrid.

Caro Baroja, J. 1957 Sobre ideas raciales en España. In *Razas, pueblos y linajes,* edited by J. Caro Baroja, pp. 141–54. Madrid: Ed. Revista de Occidente.

Caro Baroja, J. 1992 *Las falsificaciones de la Historia (en relación con la de España).* Biblioteca breve. Barcelona: Ed. Seix Barral.

Carr, R. 1982 *Spain 1808–1975,* second edition. Oxford: Oxford University Press.

Castelos Paredes, J. 1990 A aparición do rexionalismo na Galicia de fin de seculo, a sua estructura mental e o acondicionamiento social. *Dársena* 2:41–9.

Cirujano Marin, P., T. Elorriaga Planes, and J.S. Pérez Garzón 1985 *Historiografia y nacionalismo español 1834–1868* Madrid: Centro de Estudios Históricos. Consejo Superior de Investigaciones Científicas.

Costa, J. 1917 *Ultimo dia del paganismo y primero de . . . lo mismo.* Madrid: Biblioteca Costa.

Díaz-Andreu, M. 1993 Theory and Ideology: Spanish Archaeology under the Franco Regime. *Antiquity* 67:74–82.

Duplá, A. and Emborujo, A. 1991 El Vascocantabrismo: mito y realidad en la historiografia sobre el País Vasco en la antigüedad. In Arce and Olmos (1991), pp. 107–12.

Enciclopedia Universal Ilustrada Europeo-Americana 1924 Various volumes. Madrid, Barcelona: Ed. Espasa-Calpe.

García Casado, S. 1987 Algunas reflexiones acerca del problemático nacionalismo español. *Cuadernos de Alzate* 5:37–44.

Garcia de Cortázar, F. and Azcona, J.M. 1991 *El nacionalismo vasco.* Biblioteca Historia 16. Madrid: Ed. Historia.

Gómez Santacruz, S. 1935 *Numancia. Sus guerras. Exploración de sus ruinas.* El Museo Numantino. Soria.

Gran Enciclopedia Gallega 1984 Santiago de Compostela: Ed. Silveiro Cañada.

Hernández-Gil, D. 1983 Datos históricos sobre la restauración de monumentos. In *50 años de protección del patrimonio histórico artístico 1933–1983,* Madrid: Ministerio de Cultura.

Hobsbawm, E.J. 1983 Introduction: Inventing Traditions. In *The Invention of Tradition,* edited by E. Hobsbawm and T. Ranger, pp. 1–14. Cambridge: Cambridge University Press.

Hodder, I. 1987 La arqueología en la era postmoderna. *Trabajos de Prehistoria* 44:11–26.

Kedourie, E. 1988 [1966] *Nacionalismo.* Colección Estudios Políticos. Centro de Estudios Constitucionales. Madrid. [1979 *Nationalism.* London: Hutchinson.]

Khudyakov, M.G. 1931 Finnskaya expansiya v arkheologicheskoi nauke. *Soobshcheniya Gosudarstvennoi Akademii Materialnoi Kultury* 11–12:25–9.

Kidder, J.E. 1972 *Early Buddhist Japan.* London: Thames and Hudson. 1973. Asuka and the Takamatsuzuka Tomb. *Archaeology* 26(1):24–31.

Máiz, R. 1984 *Alfredo Brañas.* Vigo: Ed. Galaxia.

Maravall, J.A. 1981 *El concepto de España en la Edad Media.* Madrid: Centro de Estudios Constitucionales.

Marc-7 (Dupré, X., O. Granados, E. Junyent, X. Nieto, N. Rafel and F. Tarrats) 1986 L'arqueologia catalana – II. De la postguerra als anys setanta. *L'Avenç* 91:224–31.

Mélida, J.R. 1908 Excavaciones de Numancia. *Revista de Archivos, Bibliotecas y Museos* 8.

Morán, M. and F. Checa 1985 *El Coleccionismo en España.* Madrid: Ed. Cátedra.

Olmos, R. 1992a La realidad soñada. La recuperación del pasado en la novela arqueológica española del siglo XIX. *Arqcrítica* 3:18–20.

Olmos, R. 1992b La arqueología soñada. Una mirada a la novela arqueológica de raíz decimonónica. *Revista de Arqueología* 140:52–7.

d'Ors, E. 1911 Introducció al cicle de conferències d'Educació civil. *Revista Anyal* 7:7–12.

Ortiz de Urbina Montoya, C. and E. Pérez Olmedo 1991 La historiografía sobre Alvava romana en el siglo XIX. In *Historografía de la Arqueología y de la Historia Antigua en España (siglos XVIII–XX)*, edited by J. Arce and R. Olmos, pp. 113–16. Madrid: Ministerio de Cultura.

Pasamar Alzuría, G. and I. Peiró Martín 1991 Los orígenes de la profesionalización historiográfica española sobre la Prehistoria y la Antigüedad (tradiciones decimonónicas y tradiciones europeas). In *Historografía de la Arqueología y de la Historia Antigua en España (siglos XVIII–XX)*, edited by J. Arce and R. Olmos, pp. 73–8. Madrid: Ministerio de Cultura.

Pericot, L. 1934 *Historia de España: Geografía histórica general de los pueblos hispanos*, vol. 1, *Epocas primitiva y romana*. Barcelona: Instituto Gallach.

del Pino, F. 1978 Antropólogos en el exilio. In *El exilio español de 1939. 6. Cataluña, Euzkadi, Galicia*, edited by F. del Pino, V. Riera Llorca, A. Manent, M. de Ugalde, R. Martínez López, J. Campos, and J.L. Abellán. Biblioteca Poliítica Taurus 41. Madrid: Ed. Taurus.

Prat de la Riba, E. 1978 [1906]. *La nacionalitat catalana*. Barcelona: Edicions 62 i Caixa de Pensions.

Reyero, C. 1989 *La pintura de historia en España*. Cuadernos Arte Cátedra 26. Madrid: Ed. Cátedra.

Rodríguez Hidalgo, J.M. 1991 Sinopsis historiográfica del anfiteatro de Itálica. In *Historografía de la Arquelogía y de la Historia Antigua en España (siglos XVIII–XX)*, edited by J. Arce and R. Olmos, pp. 91–4. Madrid: Ministerio de Cultura.

Rodríguez Morales, A., B. Escobar Pérez and E. Garcia Vargas 1991 Historiografía de la estatuaria de Itálica. In *Historografía de la Arqueología y de la Historia Antigua en España (siglos XVIII–XX)*, edited by J. Arce and R. Olmos, pp. 95–8. Madrid: Ministerio de Cultura.

Sánchez Ron, J.M. 1998. La Junta para Amplición de Estudios e Investigaciones Cientificas. Ochenta años después. In *La Junta para Ampliación de Estudios e Investigaciones Científicas. Ochenta años despué* vol.1, edited by by J.M. Sánchez Ron, pp. 1–62. Madrid: CSIC.

Shafer, B. C. 1955 *Nationalism: Myth and Reality*. New York: Harcourt Brace and World.

Shennan, Stephen 1989 Tendències en l'estudi de la Prehistòria European Recent. *Cota Zero* 5:91–101.

Taracena Aguirre, B. and A. Fernández de Avilés 1945. *Memorias sobre las excavaciones enel Castro de Navárniz (Vizcaya)*. Vizcaya: Junta de Cultura de la Exma Diputación de Vizcaya.

Vicent, J. 1982 Las tendencias metodológicas en Prehistoria. *Trabajos de Prehistoria* 39:9–53.

Vicent, J. 1990 El debat postprocessual: algunes observacions "radicals" sobre una arqueologia "conservadora." *Cota Zero* 6:102–7.

Werner, J. 1946 Las excavaciones del Seminario de Historia Primitiva del Hombre en 1941, en el cementerio visigodo de Castiltierra (Segovia). *Cuadernos de Historia Primitiva* 1(1):46–50.

Wilkes, J. 1992 *The Illyrians*. Oxford: Basil Blackwell.

Echoes of Empire
Vijayanagara and Historical Memory, Vijayanagara as Historical Memory

Carla M. Sinopoli

Introduction

In the early fourteenth century AD southern India was in political turmoil. The sources for this disarray lay, in large part, in the late thirteenth to early fourteenth century incursions of the northern Sultanate of Delhi, as well as in various internal crises. I will not recount the complex political histories of the South Indian Kakatiya, Chola, Hoysala, Pallava, Yadava, Kampili, and Chalukya of Kalyani states – all powerful regional polities of the tenth through early-fourteenth centuries (see Stein 1998). Suffice it to say that by the 1330s, all of these large territorial polities had collapsed.

Emerging from this cataclysmic period was a small military state based at a sacred site on the southern banks of the Tungabhadra River in what is now central Karnataka. The founders of this state, brothers of the Sangama family, proved to be effective military and political leaders, and within a few short decades had consolidated control over a large area of the peninsula south of the Tungabhadra. The empire they ruled was named after their capital: Vijayanagara, Sanskrit for "City of Victory."

Carla M. Sinopoli, "Echoes of Empire: Vijayanagara and Historical Memory, Vijayanagara as Historical Memory," pp. 17–33 in Ruth M. Van Dyke and Susan E. Alcock (eds) *Archaeologies of Memory* (Oxford: Blackwell, 2003). Reprinted with permission.

The Vijayanagara empire dominated Southern India for three centuries under four successive dynasties until its collapse in the late seventeenth century.

The territories claimed by Vijayanagara's rulers were vast (ca. 360,000 sq.km) and diverse, encompassing areas that had been ruled by all of the pre-Vijayanagara states mentioned above. Environmentally, imperial territories included the rich river valleys and seacoasts of the southeastern peninsula, the semi-arid upland zone surrounding the imperial capital, and the mountainous forested zones of the western coastal ranges – sources of pepper, cardamom, and other spices essential for international commerce. Culturally, the region was even more complex. The empire's subjects (perhaps as many as 25 million people; Stein 1989) spoke the three major Dravidian languages of Kannada, Telugu, and Tamil, as well as other less common languages. They were Jains, Muslims, and Hindus; the latter grouped into numerous sects. Other "tribal" communities followed various local religious traditions. Vijayanagara's subjects also included diverse occupational communities, organized into numerous highly specialized hereditary castes or subcastes. Connections among these various localized occupational communities were forged through multiple higher order social and territorial associations. Such groups included merchant organizations and regional administrative councils, as well as various affiliations of low-status craft producers and agriculturalists (e.g., the right-hand and left-hand castes of Tamil Nadu).

The scale of Vijayanagara was far larger than that of any of the states that preceded it. Even the most expansive of the earlier polities were predominantly based within a single linguistic zone and in a more or less unitary ecological regime. The exception to this, the ninth- to thirteenth-century Chola empire of Tamil Nadu, did at times extend its rule over larger territories, but these did not approach the scale of Vijayanagara. As Vijayanagara territories expanded, through a program of military conquest and incorporation, the empire's rulers faced enormous challenges in consolidating their power and forging their state. In this paper, I employ architectural evidence and information on the Vijayanagara urban plan to explore one aspect of the construction of a Vijayanagara imperial identity – the acknowledgment and use of the past, and its denial. The relevant pasts that Vijayanagara's rulers remembered included both the deep past of the ancient Hindu epics and the more recent pasts of the states and empires that preceded Vijayanagara's ascendancy.

My focus for this exercise is largely on the imperial center and on imperial constructions, rather than on the peripheries of, or acts of resistance to, the empire. This is not because I do not think the latter are important or interesting: quite the contrary. But given the nature of present archaeological evidence, which comes primarily from the Vijayanagara capital and its immediate hinterland, and the elite-centered historiography of South India, it is difficult at this point to consider such issues (though see Morrison 2001 for an important exception). In some sense then, this paper is more about elite manipulation of historical knowledge, rather than about social responses to elite actions that may have been shaped by collective, or selective, memory. Nonetheless, the reasons that these manipulations were successful (at least for a time and among some of the empire's diverse communities) no doubt lie in the fact that the relevant memories that elites called upon had, or could be made to have, broad resonance among numerous South Indian communities. An additional factor, I would argue, for their success, lay in the fact that multiple, indeed contradictory, claims concerning Vijayanagara legitimacy often co-existed, in ways that allowed Vijayanagara's rulers to stake different positions in different contexts and to appeal to a broad array of social groups and political actors.

As I will elaborate upon below, Vijayanagara's elites creatively employed the sacred, mythic past associated with the region where their first capital lay, as well as sources of legitimacy derived from prior South Indian states, particularly the Chola empire of the productive riverine and coastal zones of the southeast peninsula. Yet simultaneously, in political and military domains, Vijayanagara practices were based on different, upland political traditions, and on creative borrowing and transformations of beliefs and practices of the Deccani Sultanates to their north (states that emerged in the wake of the withdrawal of the Delhi Sultanate). After I discuss the balance between remembered and new sources of legitimacy during the Vijayanagara period, I turn to the period following Vijayanagara's collapse, when the empire itself became an object of memory – representing past grandeur, a source of political legitimacy, and more recently, a focus of nationalist discourses.

Vijayanagara and Historical Memory

The Vijayanagara empire has often been viewed by scholars as marking a significant break from earlier political and cultural traditions of South India (e.g., Nilakanta Sastri 1966; Stein 1985) – and certainly this interpretation has considerable merit. Vijayanagara's armies employed new forms of cavalry-based warfare to build South India's largest expansionist polity; and the Vijayanagara period was a time of significant political and economic restructuring. More recent scholarship, however, has sought to explore both changes and continuities in a more nuanced way – to consider Vijayanagara state-building as both acknowledging the past and creatively transforming its present. Here, I want to consider under what contexts these two processes co-occurred in processes of state-building and imperial legitimation. Both of these patterns are evident in the architecture and layout of the imperial capital.

The Vijayanagara imperial capital

The city of Vijayanagara, the empire's first and longest-lived capital, is located on the southern banks of the Tungabhadra River in the modern state of Karnataka. This semi-arid region was comparatively densely settled during the much earlier South Indian Neolithic (third millennium BC) and early historic (ca. 500 BC–300 AD) periods, and pre-Vijayanagara temples and forts of the tenth – thirteenth centuries AD to the north of the river attest to some occupation in that period.

We do not at present have good estimates for local population densities immediately prior to the founding of Vijayanagara, but ten thousand people is not an unreasonable upper limit. With the formation of the empire, populations grew rapidly and dramatically, as individuals and entire communities flowed into the capital from throughout peninsular India. By the early 1400s, the city had approximately 100,000 inhabitants; by the early 1500s, the population had likely reached well over a quarter million and the city core extended over nearly 30 square kilometers (see Figure 22.1). The fortified suburban zone of the capital covered more than 600 square kilometers during the sixteenth century, and it contained numerous settlements and a range of other features amid areas of agricultural and craft production (see Morrison 1995; Sinopoli and Morrison 2008).

Shortly after reaching its greatest extent, Vijayanagara was abruptly abandoned. In 1565 AD, the combined forces of three of the northern sultanates defeated Vijayanagara's armies. The city's inhabitants fled and the site was briefly occupied by the victorious forces, as the Vijayanagara court shifted successively southwards – to Penukonda, Chandragiri, and finally to Vellore. Here I focus primarily on the empire's first and largest capital.

Sacred geographies

No doubt a range of factors contributed to the location of the first Vijayanagara capital. These included the fact that as the Vijayanagara state was forming in the 1330s and 1340s, this area was, to a significant extent, a political "no-man's land," not under the protection of any strong polity. Further, a bend in the Tungabhadra River provided a small arable zone in this otherwise semi-arid and rugged landscape (Morrison 1995). The region was also highly defensible; the high granitic outcrops of the southern extent of the Deccan Plateau both impeded movement and provided abundant raw materials for the construction of massive fortifications.

Along with the above-mentioned strategic reasons, it is also significant that the sparsely populated locale where Vijayanagara was founded was a place sacred to worshippers of both Shiva and Vishnu. These sacred associations were written on the landscape of the Vijayanagara region, inscribed in holy hills, the river, and other natural and constructed features, the latter including a Neolithic ash mound of the third millennium BC (believed to be the cremation ground of Vali, see below) and pre-Vijayanagara temples. These features provided a powerful source of memory and legitimation with which Vijayanagara's Sangama and subsequent kings sought to affiliate themselves.

As noted earlier, several small pre-Vijayanagara temples existed in the region where Vijayanagara was later founded. Most important of these was a complex of shrines dedicated to Virupaksha, a manifestation of the major Hindu deity Shiva. The earliest documented temple to Virupaksha, the "lord of Hemakuta," dates to the ninth-tenth centuries. Later shrines were added in the twelfth century ad, by which time the male Virupaksha was already linked with the goddess Pampa. The Virupaksha temple was expanded throughout the subsequent Vijayanagara period and remains today a major center of worship and pilgrimage.

By the Vijayanagara period, Virupaksha had become far more important in local religious traditions than his consort. Yet Pampa is the oldest documented deity of the area. The earliest inscriptional references to Pampa can be traced to the seventh century AD, and she was likely important long before then. Pampa appears to have been a local, aquatic goddess, associated with the Tungabhadra River, and with the power of a particular eponymous place on the river (modern Hampi). Verghese (1995:16–17) argues that this local, perhaps even "pre-Hindu," folk goddess, became Sanskritized, or brought into Hindu orthodoxy, during the pre-Vijayanagara period through her marriage to Shiva (Virupaksha).

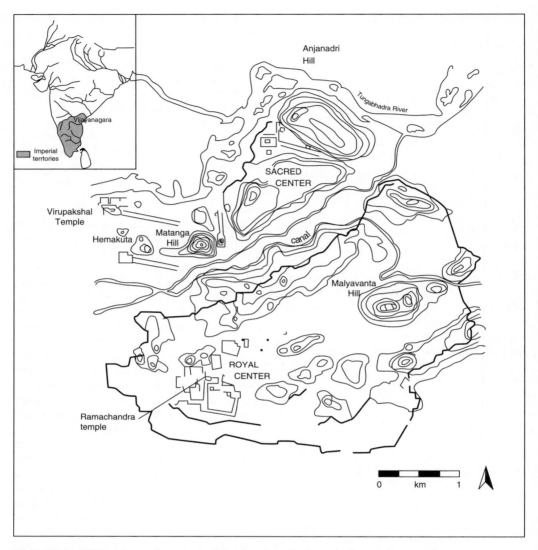

Figure 22.1 Vijayanagara urban core and key locations in the region's sacred geography.

Following this, her stature diminished as Virupaksha's rose, but (and I will return to this below), Pampa nonetheless remained important in local beliefs.

The second major sacred association of the Vijayanagara region lay with Vishnu, the other major deity of orthodox Hinduism, in his form (avatar) as the god-king Rama, whose adventures are recounted in the Ramayana epic. The relevant portion of this tale concerns Rama's exploits and travels as he tried to rescue his wife Sita, who had been kidnapped by the ten-headed demon Ravana and taken to (Sri) Lanka. In his quest, Rama and his brother Lakshmana came to Kishkinda, kingdom of the monkey deities. On top of a hill called Matanga he encountered Sugriva, the dispossessed lord of the monkey kingdom. Through his valor, Rama helped Sugriva to overthrow his rebellious brother Vali. After Sugriva's enthronement, his liege Hanuman traveled to Lanka and rescued Sita while Rama awaited her return atop Malyavanta Hill.

The recognition of the Vijayanagara region as Kishkinda is not as ancient as its association with the river goddess Pampa. Nor are there any pre-Vijayanagara period Ramayana temples or images at the site. However, Verghese (1995) has suggested that a small number of textual sources indicate that the Ramayana association had begun as early as the eleventh century. Nonetheless, it is not until the late fourteenth-early fifteenth-century Vijayanagara "building boom" in the region that these associations were made materially manifest and were mapped onto the landscape through the construction of temples and countless sacred images, as well as in urban plan. Key structures, routes of movement, and urban layout were linked with features of the sacred landscape, including Matanga Hill, Malyavanta Hill, Anjanadri (Hanuman's birthplace), and other sites linked with Ramayana events (Fritz 1986, 1992; Fritz and Michell 1989; see Figure 22.1).

Most striking of the structures associated with the Ramayana is an early fifteenth-century temple dedicated to Rama. This temple lies due south of Matanga Hill in the heart of the royal administrative and palace zone of the capital, which Fritz, Michell, and Nagaraja Rao (1985) have termed the "Royal Center" (see Figure 22.1). The Ramachandra temple was constructed relatively early in the empire's history, during the reign of a king of the first, Sangama, dynasty (the temple does not have a foundation inscription, but is believed to date to the reign of Devaraya I, 1406–1422 AD; Michell 1992a:17–20). It is a comparatively small temple complex, consisting of a walled enclosure containing the central temple, as well as subsidiary shrines, wells, and columned pavilions. The events of the Ramayana are depicted in a series of narrative friezes on the structure's exterior and on the interior compound wall (see Figure 22.2).

It is important to point out that the kings who were responsible for the construction of this temple were not primarily devotees of Rama. Instead, their tutelary deity was the Shaivite deity Virupaksha, discussed above. Even before the Sangamas sponsored the construction of a Rama temple, they had constructed a temple to Virupaksha in the Vijayanagara royal center. So why build a temple to Rama at all? And why place it at such a critical location in the city – at the nexus of key administrative and royal structures and the focus of multiple transport and processional routes?

As noted, no foundational inscription occurs on the temple. However, a fascinating, albeit brief, inscription on its principal shrine helps to date the shrine and to link the temple with the non-Ramayana dimensions of the sacred landscape. The Sanskrit inscription reads

As Vani blesses king Bhoka, Tripuramba king Vatsaraja, and Kali king Vikramarka, so does Pampa now bless Devaraya. (trans. Rajasekhara 1992:27)

In this text, the Vijayanagara king Devaraya is explicitly linked with three great kings of the distant past, each of whom was protected by a powerful goddess. Like those earlier rulers, Devaraya has a protector – Pampa, the ancient goddess of this place.

The Shaivite affiliations of the Sangama kings were well established. Through affiliating themselves with the expanding Rama cult, the Sangama rulers broadened their ties to encompass the powerful Vaishnava sects of the period, and associated themselves with a particular god – one linked with the land and with potent values concerning kingship and royal authority. However, by building a temple to Rama the Sangama kings did not disavow their prior loyalties. Indeed, the reference to Pampa in the above mentioned inscription demonstrates that these ties continued to be emphasized even as Vijayanagara's rulers added a new strand in their web of connections to the landscape, to the people they sought to rule, and to the sacred past. Construction of the Rama temple was an act of addition rather than replacement.

The increasing importance of the Ramayana and the expanded recognition of the Vijayanagara area as Kishkinda were not restricted to the political elite. Instead, this appears to have been a widespread phenomenon of the period. From the fourteenth through sixteenth centuries, hundreds (probably thousands) of images of Hanuman were carved on boulders and stone slabs throughout the Vijayanagara urban and suburban landscape. Representations of Hanuman significantly outnumber those of any other single deity at Vijayanagara and in its metropolitan region. Hanuman images occur in a broad array of

Figure 22.2   The Ramachandra temple.

contexts – along roads, near wells and agricultural features, and in countless small shrines in towns, villages, and rural settlements. These images vary considerably in artistic quality from finely wrought sculptures that follow classical conventions and proportions (e.g., Figure 22.3a) to more "folksy" images carved by less skilled artisans (e.g., Figure 22.3b). The extent to which the Vijayanagara kings encouraged the expansion of the Kishkinda cult in the capital is unknown, but it does seem clear that the explicit linking of the ruler with Rama, through the construction of the Ramachandra temple, was a deliberate act that had important consequences in legitimating their rule.

Temple architecture

The sacred geographies of the Vijayanagara region discussed above served to assert

connections between the Vijayanagara throne, the imperial capital, and the territories of the gods. In this section, I continue my focus on the religious realm, but from a somewhat different perspective. Rather than consider the *content* of Vijayanagara temples in terms of the deities worshipped, I address the *form* of temples, and how Vijayanagara sacred architecture provided an important context for the recognition and reconfiguration of the past through the creation of a distinctive imperial architectural style.

As noted earlier, a number of small temples in the Vijayanagara region date to the pre-imperial period, from the ninth–tenth through early fourteenth centuries. These temples are typically relatively small and simple, with pyramidal stone towers and simple unadorned exteriors. In form and construction, they belong to local architectural traditions of the inland and upland areas of the peninsula. The earliest Vijayanagara temples

(a)   (b)

Figure 22.3 a and b Hanuman sculpture in Vijayanagara metropolitan region. Image 22.3a is a finely wrought image, while 22.3b is a more folksy representation, with distorted proportions (the pigment is recent, indicating that this Vijayanagara period image is currently in worship).

of the mid- to late fourteenth century also adhere to this tradition. No radical changes in temple architecture corresponded with the initial founding of the city and empire; instead, architectural referents continued to be to local antecedents and traditions.

As Vijayanagara hegemony and claims to imperial status expanded beyond their upland core in the late fourteenth and early fifteenth centuries, a marked change occurred in both the scale and the style of temples. The result was a new and distinctive form of sacred architecture that spread across the empire and became increasingly elaborated over time. Architectural historian George Michell (1994:188) has described Vijayanagara imperial temple architecture as "revivalist," specifically, as imitating the architecture of the Chola empire, whose heartland lay in the fertile river valleys of the southeast coast. The Ramachandra temple (Figure 22.2, and above) is among the earliest

of the revivalist temples at Vijayanagara and its construction likely involved the importation of architects and master builders from Tamil-speaking regions to the imperial capital (Michell 1994:192). Over the next century, this revivalist style spread across imperial territories, producing a uniform and recognizable Vijayanagara temple style. Vijayanagara temples also increased in physical scale over time. By the sixteenth century, temple gateways, or *gopura*, towered over surrounding settlements, creating a distinctive and highly visible feature that marked the presence of the gods and their royal benefactors (see Figure 22.4).

Over the last decade, several historians of Vijayanagara (e.g., Stein 1989; Talbot n.d.) have argued that Vijayanagara political and economic forms are best understood as having evolved out of upland Telugu and Kannada traditions of state organization. This perspective stands in marked contrast to traditional understandings of

Figure 22.4   Sixteenth century temple *gopuram* (Kalahasti, Tamil Nadu).

Vijayanagara, which sought Chola roots for Vijayanagara practices (e.g., Nilakanta Sastri 1966; Stein 1980). If these more recent arguments are correct, and I believe they are, why then did temple architecture in particular draw on a distant southern tradition that lay hundreds of kilometers and several centuries removed from Vijayanagara, especially as other forms of complex and sculpturally elaborate temple architecture lay somewhat nearer to hand in Kannada- and Telugu-speaking zones that comprised the core of the empire?

Michell views the development of Vijayanagara revivalist temple style as the result of a deliberate strategy by the imperial rulers to make imperial claims. This was accomplished in two ways. First, adopting the style of an earlier empire allowed Vijayanagara's kings to call upon memories of past (Chola) grandeur to portray a message of continuity and legitimacy. Second, the style adopted was that of a physically *distant* empire in preference to more proximate available alternatives. Given the wide-ranging polity

that the Sangama kings were attempting to form, this emphasis on distance may have been part of a deliberate attempt to make a claim to universal status as rulers of the entire south. The result was a "temple style that would give expression to their imperial ambitions" (Michell 1994:195). In the sacred realm, then, the new Vijayanagara architectural style was grounded in the past.

New architectural forms and new forms of power

Reference to the Hindu and South Indian past was, however, not the only architectural mode through which Vijayanagara's rulers expressed their visions of empire. While temple architecture drew on historical knowledge and contexts, Vijayanagara administrative or "courtly" architecture expressed very different kinds of relations and political ideologies, based in the present rather than in memory. And while temple architecture involved the relations of political authority to sacred authority, Vijayanagara courtly architecture was mainly about the political; it was as Michell (1992b:168) described, "a means of defining the king's world."

The world of a Vijayanagara ruler was a large one. It included the polities and peoples of the south who had been variously incorporated into the empire. It also included other South Asian states and empires: particularly the five Deccani Sultanates to Vijayanagara's north and the large Hindu Gajapati state in Orissa, to its northeast. These polities were Vijayanagara's major enemies, and also its peers, and the relations among these states included warfare, trade, and diplomacy. Vijayanagara was also part of an international world; maritime commerce linked South India with East and Southeast Asia, the Middle East, and by the sixteenth century, directly with Europe.

Like temple architecture, Vijayanagara courtly architecture also entailed borrowing from other traditions. But here the references were not to the distant past, but to the newly configured political landscape and to new conceptions of kingship and authority that had emerged in the wake of the withdrawal of the Delhi Sultanate from the peninsula. As a result, the Vijayanagara king was a participant in a much broader political sphere than rulers of prior South Indian states. This had a dramatic impact on Vijayanagara political ideologies and political practices, with changes manifest in the emergence of new royal rituals, such as the "Robes of Honor" ceremony that was reported on by Portuguese visitors to the capital (Gordon 1996), as well as the adoption of new royal titles including the wonderfully multivalent "Sultan of the Hindu kings" (Wagoner 1996).

The new concept of kingly authority and royal ritual that emerged in South India during the Vijayanagara period drew creatively upon the political traditions and material forms of northern Muslim states. A distinctive Vijayanagara courtly architecture developed in the fifteenth and sixteenth centuries, and perhaps earlier (Michell, personal communications). It was restricted to public or royal structures, was found only at major imperial cities, and had clear associations with the architecture of the Deccani Sultanates (Michell and Zebrowski 1999). As such, Vijayanagara courtly architecture merged features from within and beyond imperial territories in the creation of an imperial style of public architecture.

Vijayanagara courtly architecture was distinctive in its building technologies as well as in external form. Structures in this category were built of small crudely cut stone blocks set in thick mortar and covered in plaster (Michell 1995:129), a marked contrast to the dry stone masonry technologies that characterized Vijayanagara temple and defensive architecture. Stylistic features derived from the north include domes, arches, and building layouts structured as a "geometric manipulation of one or more domed and vaulted chambers" (Michell 1992c:48). Features drawn from within the empire include stepped temple-like roofs, plaster decoration, and elaborately carved multi-tiered stone foundations. One of the best examples of this style at the capital is a structure in the royal center that is popularly referred to as the Lotus Mahal, which likely functioned as a reception hall (see Figure 22.5). This structure combines ornate Islamic style arches decorated with incised plaster motifs with a temple-like sculpted basement and tiered roof. Other structures of this distinctive style found at Vijayanagara and the later capitals of Chandragiri, Penukonda, and Vellore include palaces, watchtowers, baths or water-tanks, and administrative buildings.

It is important to stress that Vijayanagara courtly structures did not simply mimic northern styles; instead, this was something new and distinctive, expressing very different kinds of identities and relations than are evident in contemporaneous temple architecture. It is also important to emphasize that the kinds of transformations evident in courtly architecture are also evident in several other cultural spheres. These include military and administrative organization, as well as the patterns of royal dress and royal titles noted earlier, all of which also manifest an awareness of and participation in a political landscape extending far behind the bounds of the Vijayanagara empire. It is perhaps in this transformed political and ideological landscape where we see the most radical breaks with the past, and the creation of new and different memory communities. That these new alliances occur at the same time that very different communities and connections are being expressed through sacred architecture and in literary texts attests to the simultaneity of multiple constructions of Vijayanagara imperial

Figure 22.5   Vijayanagara courtly architecture: Pavilion in the Royal Center.

identities and the multiple audiences for those constructions.

Discussion

The discussion presented above paints a picture of a state very much in control of its "message," consciously manipulating existing beliefs, as well as new geopolitical situations, to meet specific ends. This is, to a large extent, a false picture. Certainly some of the processes described above, particularly the links made by Sangama kings to the God Rama, appear to have been the result of deliberate, conscious, political strategies by Vijayanagara elites. Other trends, such as changing elite clothing fashions and the emergence of new forms of Vijayanagara courtly architecture were likely far less deliberate, and emerged instead as a more gradual outgrowth of Vijayanagara's participation in an expanded and transformed political universe.

Vijayanagara as Memory

I noted earlier that the Deccani Sultanates were both peers and foes of Vijayanagara. In 1565, the foes won out. A major battle occurred to the north of the Vijayanagara capital that pitted Vijayanagara's armies against a confederation of three sultanates. Vijayanagara was defeated and its first capital was hastily abandoned. Over the course of the next century, Vijayanagara's rulers shifted ever further south to the cities of Penukonda, Chandragiri, and Vellore. Although each of these successive capitals was given the name Vijayanagara to link it to the former site of imperial grandeur, with each shift the empire became smaller and its authority weakened. As Vijayanagara declined (beginning even before the 1565 defeat), numerous smaller states rose to prominence across the empire's former territories. By the early seventeenth century (and even earlier in some areas), numerous large and small polities had emerged, with the largest and most effective of the successor states based in the southern and eastern parts of the former Vijayanagara territories. The rulers of these new "*nayaka*" states were the descendants of regional rulers or *nayakas*. The nayakas were military leaders, often from upland Telugu-speaking regions (modern Andhra Pradesh), who had risen to prominence as regional rulers in the Tamil-speaking south in the sixteenth century.

From the beginning, many of these rulers had sought independence from the empire and nayaka political ideologies from the sixteenth century on thus involved a complex dynamic that both acknowledged Vijayanagara authority and legitimated resistance to it. The decline of the empire following the 1565 battle provided the opportunity for that resistance to take hold and for the nayaka states to declare themselves as autonomous polities.

However, even as the empire was fragmenting, Vijayanagara as memory and source of authority became extraordinarily important. We see this most strongly in the courtly literature and temple architecture of the nayaka states of the seventeenth and eighteenth centuries. In a recent book on the period, the central paradox of nayaka kingship has been defined as "the tension between inflated claims, and the limited scale" of their polities (Narayana Rao, Shulman, and Subrahmanyam 1992:xi). These were small states compared to their predecessor and many were fragile and short-lived. Yet, their rhetoric of kingship was vast, entailing, in many cases, claims to the mantle of Vijayanagara's legitimacy.

This pattern is evident in the origin stories of several nayaka states. For example, the origin story of the Madurai nayaka state (which is preserved in several versions) involves a complex recounting of interactions between the archetypal great emperor of Vijayanagara, Krisnadevaraya (1509–1529 AD) and the first ruler of Madurai and his eldest son. Extant versions of this complicated story probably date to the early eighteenth century, 200 years after Krisnadevaraya's death, and involve murder, rebellion, and threats of patricide. The Madurai story recounts the tale of the warrior Nagama, a powerful nayaka who recaptured the Madurai region for Vijayanagara, but then refused to hand it over. Nagama's son Visvanatha remained loyal to the emperor and turned against his father to regain the land for Krisnadevaraya. Following his victory, Nagama brought his defeated father to stand judgment before the emperor. The ruler acknowledged the heroism of the son by releasing the father to his custody. And then, moved by the heroism and loyalty of Visvanatha, Krisnadevaraya told his courtiers that Visvanatha "deserves a throne equal to our own" (Narayana Rao, Shulman, and Subrahmanyam

1992:49). Thus, he offered Visvanatha kingship of the South, saying (as the story goes):

> You have saved my throne ... Moreover, we have said that we would create a kingdom for you equal to ours ... If you don't take control of the southern country, the situation won't be good. If it weren't for you the country would be without a king, and we would have to be reborn ourselves to struggle with those *palegallu*. You had best hurry south to be king. (Narayana Rao, Shulman, and Subrahmanyam 1992:51)

The "reluctant" Visvanatha agrees. However, to properly begin his rule, Visvanatha requests and is granted a gift from the king: the "protective goddess of Vijayanagara Durgamahalakshmi," who he installs in his capital of Madurai (Narayana Rao, Shulman, and Subrahmanyam 1992:51). As the Vijayanagara imperial center to the north declines and is abandoned, Madurai rises to glory, bearing the mantle of Vijayanagara's greatness.

This tale contains elements found in many origin stories associated with the nayaka kingdoms. These include accounts of the self-made nature of the nayakas, whose success is due to their heroic acts rather than to their lineage (which was, in fact, often undistinguished). Also present in these tales, though not discussed here, are references to the wealth and territory that these heroes' efforts yielded. A further critical component is the establishment of connections to higher sources of authority: most often to Vijayanagara. These linkages were not transferred through heredity, but through acts of personal loyalty, and through the transfer of the symbols and rights of legitimate rule from a past ruler to his successor.

Like the references to the Chola period found in Vijayanagara temple architecture, the nayaka historical references are restricted to a particular time and place in history. The place is the first city of Vijayanagara and the time is the reign of Krisnadevaraya, arguably the most effective, and certainly the most remembered of Vijayanagara kings. Krisnadevaraya's rule marked the political apogee of the empire, when it reached its greatest geographic extent and greatest unity and wealth. Thus, an important Telugu royal text of the early 1600s, the *Rayavacakamu* or "Tidings of the

King," was composed as if it had been written in the court of Krisnadevaraya, despite the fact that Krisnadevaraya had been dead for nearly 80 years by the time it was composed (Wagoner 1993). For the nayaka states, Vijayanagara had become the model and memory on which to build a state.

Nayaka architecture

Nayaka temple and administrative architecture also provides evidence for references to the Vijayanagara past, and for the exaggerated claims to power that dominated the period. Vijayanagara architectural forms continue, but become greatly elaborated in scale and ornateness. Many nayaka period constructions entailed expansions of existing temple complexes, either Vijayanagara or Chola constructions (or both). Often this involved fully enclosing the existing structures within new and elaborate enclosure walls or temple structures, so that the earlier structures were completely hidden from view. The past remained at the core of these structures, but the outward veneer was entirely of the present. In particular, the most visible part of temple complexes, the *gopura* or towered temple gateways of the nayaka period, were enormous; for example, the *gopuram* of the Tiruvannamalai temple (Tamil Nadu) built by the Thanjavur nayaka rulers reached a height of 66 meters (Michell 1995:91).

Sculptural elements also became greatly elaborated in scale and ornateness during the nayaka period. And it was during this time that portraiture – of rulers, their consorts, and elite temple donors – became well established. There are a small number of portrait sculptures from the Vijayanagara period, but most Vijayanagara depictions of rulers are highly stylized and do not make reference to specific individuals (that is, most often kings are depicted as small seated figures beneath a parasol, often shown as the endpoints of large processional scenes). By the seventeenth century, detailed, individualized, life-sized stone and bronze sculptural portraits had become widespread. Rulers and their queens were depicted in elaborate costume and with distinctive facial features. This new emphasis on portraiture is in keeping with the depictions of nayaka kings as "self-made" heroic leaders

evident in the origin stories discussed above, and also with the enormous claims to royal authority and power that characterize the period as a whole.

It is important to emphasize that all of the elaboration typical of the post-Vijayanagara period – in royal rhetoric, architectural forms, and artistic representation – occurs at precisely the time when state authority was at its weakest. As noted, while the polities that many nayaka kings ruled were small compared to Vijayanagara, their claims to universal rule and legitimacy were not. And many of these claims were based in the past, as nayaka kings traced their ascendancy to their service to the deceased emperors of Vijayanagara. This is, at the very least, a cautionary tale for archaeologists: the most monumental constructions of a state may refer as much to memories of power as to its actual presence.

Conclusions

This paper has addressed the deployment of the past and the constructions of new pasts during two periods in South Indian history. For the most part, my emphasis has been on acts of rulers and their courts and the creation of messages of state authority. The forms and content of messages created by political elites extended far beyond those considered in this paper. Music, theater, political ceremonies, and temple rituals, among others, all no doubt played important roles in creating and presenting images of imperial power. Here, I have focused on the material construction and (re)presentation of memory by examining landscape and urban layout, and temple and administrative architecture – dimensions that structured and constituted the spaces inhabited and experienced by Vijayanagara's residents. I have explored how Vijayanagara authority was linked to the sacred, mythic past of the region, incorporating South India's two major Hindu traditions, Vaisnavism and Saivism. This was a sacred landscape prior to Vijayanagara ascendancy, and Vijayanagara's rulers emphasized and expanded upon these sacred associations in support of their own legitimacy.

Vijayanagara temple architecture drew on the more recent memories of Chola imperial grandeur and architectural tradition, much as nayaka sacred architecture drew on those of Vijayanagara. In both of these cases, the past was used in claims of universality and legitimacy, and these claims were expressed in the universalizing idiom of the sacred domain. In administrative or "courtly" architecture, Vijayanagara's kings did not make claims on the past, but instead, with their northern neighbors, were involved in the creation of a very new architectural form. I have suggested that these forms were directed outward, toward the global political milieu in which Vijayanagara participated, and that they were part of broader political, economic, and ideological changes that affected all of peninsular India during the fourteenth through seventeenth centuries.

For the most part, I have not considered in detail who the audiences were for these various imperial constructions and messages, nor how they responded. Certainly, the audiences were diverse – rulers and elites of neighboring states, subject elites, powerful religious leaders and communities, and the many linguistic, ethnic, and caste communities that populated the empire.

At Vijayanagara, there is considerable evidence that the association of the city with the sacred landscape of Ramayana was widely accepted. However, we do not know the extent to which the diverse non-elite worshippers of Rama drew the associations between the god and the Vijayanagara king that the court clearly intended. While we have various monumental and textual routes to considering elite responses, much more archaeological research needs to be done beyond the bounds of the imperial capital to examine the multiple non-elites of the Vijayanagara period.

As I noted at the start of the this paper, memories of Vijayanagara continue to be important today in India, where they are deployed in various ways in national and regional political discourse. As in the past, these memories are multivocal and at times competing – involving diverse religious communities, multiple linguistic and ethnic communities (i.e., both Kannada and Telugu speakers lay claim to the empire), and the state, all with somewhat different claims to the memory of empire.

References

Fritz, J. M. 1986: Vijayanagara: authority and meaning of a south Indian imperial capital. *American Anthropologist* 88, pp. 44–55.

Fritz, J. M. 1992: Urban context. In *The Ramachandra Temple at Vijayanagara*, by A. L. Dallapiccola, J. M. Fritz, G. Michell and S. Rajasekhara. New Delhi: Manohar, pp. 1–14.

Fritz, J. M. and Michell, G. A. 1989: Interpreting the plan of a medieval Hindu capital: Vijayanagara. *World Archaeology* 19, pp. 105–29.

Fritz, J. M., Michell, G. A. and Nagaraja Rao, M. S. 1985: *Where Kings and Gods Meet: The Royal Center at Vijayanagara*. Tucson: University of Arizona Press.

Gordon, S. 1996: "Robes of honour:" A "transactional" kingly ceremony. *The Indian Economic and Social History Review* 33, pp. 227–42.

Michell, G. 1992a: Historical context. In *The Ramachandra Temple at Vijayanagara*, by A. L. Dallapiccola, J. M. Fritz, G. Michell and S. Rajasekhara. New Delhi: Manohar, pp. 17–23.

Michell, G. 1992b: Royal architecture and imperial style at Vijayanagara. In *The Powers of Art: Patronage* in *Indian Culture*, ed. B. S. Miller. Delhi: Oxford University Press, pp. 168–79.

Michell, G. 1992c: *The Vijayanagara Courtly Style*. New Delhi: Manohar.

Michell, G. 1994: Revivalism as the imperial mode: Religious architecture during the Vijayanagara period. In *Perceptions of South Asia's Visible Past*, ed. C. B. Asher and T. R. Metcalf. Delhi: Oxford and IBH, pp. 187–98.

Michell, G. 1995: *Architecture and Art of Southern India: Vijayanagara and the Successor States. The New Cambridge History of India* 1:6. Cambridge: Cambridge University Press.

Michell, G. and Zebrowski, M. 1999: *Architecture and Art of the Deccan Sultanates. The New Cambridge History of India* 1:7. Cambridge: Cambridge University Press.

Morrison, K. D. 1995: *Fields of Victory: Vijayanagara and the Course of Intensification*. Berkeley: Contribution 52, Archaeological Research Facility, University of California, Berkeley.

Morrison, K. D. 2001: Coercion, resistance, and hierarchy: local processes and imperial strategies in the Vijayanagara empire. In *Empires: Perspectives from Archaeology and History*, ed. S. E. Alcock, T. N. D'Altroy, K. D. Morrison and C. M. Sinopoli. Cambridge: Cambridge University Press, pp. 252–78.

Narayana Rao, V., Shulman, D. and Subrahmanyam, S. 1992: *Symbols of Substance: Court and State in Nayaka Period Tamil Nadu*. Delhi: Oxford University Press.

Nilakanta Sastri, K. A. 1966: *A History of South India from Prehistoric Times to Vijayanagara*. Madras: Oxford University Press.

Rajasekhara, S. 1992: Inscriptions. In *The Ramachandra Temple at Vijayanagara*, by A. L. Dallapiccola, J. M. Fritz, G. Michell and S. Rajasekhara. New Delhi: Manohar, pp. 27–30.

Sinopoli, C. M. and Morrison, K. D. 2008: The regional landscapes of the imperial city of Vijayanagara: Report on the Vijayanagara Metropolitan Survey Project. In *South Asian Archaeology 1999*, ed. E. Raven, pp. 561–574. Groningen: Egbert Forsten Publishing.

Stein, B. 1980: *Peasant State and Society in Medieval South India*. Dehli: Oxford University Press.

Stein, B. 1985: Vijayanagara and the transition to patrimonial systems. In *Vijayanagara: City and Empire*, ed. A. L. Dallapiccola and M. Z. Ave-Lallemant. Weisbaden: Franz Steiner Verlag, pp. 73–87.

Stein, B. 1989: *Vijayanagara. The New Cambridge History of India* 1:2. Cambridge: Cambridge University Press.

Stein, B. 1998: *A History of India*. Oxford: Blackwell.

Talbot, C. n.d.: *The Nayakas of Vijayanagara Andhra: A Preliminary Prosopography*. Unpublished ms. in possession of author.

Verghese, A. 1995: *Religious Traditions at Vijayanagara as Viewed through its Monuments*. New Delhi: Manohar.

Wagoner, P.B. 1993: *Tidings of the King: A Translation and Ethnohistorical Analysis of the Rayāvācakamu*. Honolulu: University of Hawaii Press.

Wagoner, P.B. 1996: "Sultan among Hindu kings:" Dress, titles, and the Islamicization of Hindu culture at Vijayanagara. *Journal of Asian Studies* 55, pp. 851–80.

Conjuring Mesopotamia
Imaginative Geography and a World Past

Zainab Bahrani

*Our familiarity, not merely with the languages of the peoples of the East but with
their customs, their feelings, their traditions, their history and religion, our capacity to
understand what may be called the genius of the East, is the sole basis upon which we are likely
to be able to maintain in the future the position we have won, and no step that can be taken to
strengthen that position can be considered undeserving of the attention of His majesty's
Government or of a debate in the House of Lords.*
(Lord Curzon, address to House of Lords, September 27, 1909)

Introduction

By 1909 the importance of the production of
knowledge for the British colonial enterprise in
the East was neither implicit in political rhetoric
nor subtly expressed. In Lord Curzon's words it
was "an imperial obligation ... part of the necessary furniture of Empire" (Said 1978: 214). The
need for this knowledge was stressed as an integral part of the process of colonisation, and one
that would facilitate the continuation of European authority over the East. It is my contention
that the development of the discipline of Mesopotamian archaeology and its discursive practices during this time cannot be isolated from
this colonialist enterprise. Nor can it be divorced
from the general Western historical narrative of
the progress of civilisation which was necessary
for the aims of a civilising imperial mission. I
argue here that this narrative of civilisation was

Zainab Bahrani, "Conjuring Mesopotamia: Imaginative
Geography and a World Past," pp. 159–74 from
Lynn Meskell (ed.) *Archaeology under Fire: Nationalism,
Politics and Heritage in the Eastern Mediterranean and
Middle East* (London: Routledge, 1998). Reprinted with
permission of Taylor and Francis (UK) Books.

heavily dependent upon a discourse of Otherness
which posited a "Mesopotamia" as the past of
mankind, and furthermore that the presencing of
Mesopotamia through this imperialist discourse
constitutes the ground whence today archaeologists continue to unearth what counts as "historical fact," and to decide upon its acceptable
mode of comprehension. First, in order to locate
Mesopotamia's position in the Euro-American
historical tradition I consider the historical dimensions of time and space as structuring horizons for
the framework of "Mesopotamia." Second, I argue
that this framework, which in Heidegger's words
"serves as a criterion for separating the regions of
Being" cannot be divorced from the cultural
abstraction most commonly used to identify
Mesopotamia: despotism.

Postcolonial critiques have pointed to how the
process of imperialism was not limited to the
overt economic and political activities of Western
governments in colonised lands. An entire
system of classification through the arts and
sciences was necessary for the success of the
imperial enterprise in the East and Africa.[1]
Mesopotamian archaeological practices must be
considered within this system, not only because
this field concerns a region that was of

geopolitical interest to the West, but because of its crucial place within the metanarrative of human culture. Archaeology, like other human sciences such as anthropology and history, allowed a European mapping of the subjugated terrain of the Other. While ethnography portrayed the colonised native as a savage requiring Western education and whose culture needed modernisation, archaeology and its practices provided a way of charting the past of colonised lands.

Mesopotamian archaeology is a discipline concerned with defining a particular past, and a particular culture within this past, and like in other archaeological or historical enterprises two of the basic constituents structuring the discursive practices of this discipline are space and time. These ontologically "obvious" measures are not neutral in archaeological practices. In fact, if we apply Heideggerian terms, it is within this structure of space and time that "Mesopotamia" was revealed as a Being-in-the-world. As an ontic phenomenon therefore, Mesopotamia is prefigured by the temporal structure of European metahistorical narrative. In other words, as I aim to show here, "Mesopotamia," as archaeologists generally think of this culture today, is a discursive formation.

The relationship of power to praxis in archaeological research has received some attention in recent years (Hodder *et al.* 1995; Shanks and Tilley 1987). Issues such as the promotion of one historical interpretation over another, or the focus on one sector of society at the expense of all others, have been confronted and discussed at great lengths by a number of scholars. In this chapter, it is not my intention to liberate a "true" Mesopotamian past from the power of Western representation. Rather, by analysing Mesopotamia as a phenomenon within Western archaeological discourse I hope to show how a particular Mesopotamian identity was required for the narrative of the progress of civilisation as an organic universal event. My intention then is to question the ontological or, rather, ontic concept of Mesopotamia as it has been determined by Western archaeological discourse, and to consider the ideological components of this phenomenon. In other words, I would like to open up the field of politicising inquiry in archaeology to consider Mesopotamia not as a factual historical and geographical entity waiting to be studied, excavated and interpreted according to one set

of conventions or another, but as a product of the poetics of a Western historical narrative.

For Mesopotamian archaeology, scholarly considerations of the relationship between politics and archaeology has meant two things only: (a) interpreting the material and textual remains from ancient Iraq primarily as manifestations of political propaganda of Babylonian and Assyrian kings and, more recently, (b) pointing to the Iraqi Baathist regime's use of the pre-Islamic past for propagandist purposes. We, as Mesopotamian archaeologists, do not question the nature of our discipline, its parameters, and its interpretive strategies. I do not use the word "we" because I am a Middle Eastern scholar educated in the West. Eastern archaeologists work within the same parameters and according to the same interpretive models as Western archaeologists, due to the fact that archaeology is a Western discipline that only became instituted in Middle Eastern countries while they were under European rule. As a "high cultural" activity and a humanist discipline we do not question its institutional character or presence. Mesopotamian scholarship assumes that the colonial context of its creation is irrelevant except as a distant, indirectly related, historical event. This attitude is not limited to archaeologists of Western origins. Therefore, Mesopotamian archaeologists, regardless of nationality, have been slow to reflect on the circumstances under which the constitution of the field of Mesopotamian archaeology occurred, and how its textual practices have formed ancient "Mesopotamia" as an area of modern knowledge.

On the level of the overtly political and ideological, ancient history and archaeology have certainly been areas of contestation as in, for example, Palestine/Israel and Cyprus. However, it is not only such geographical areas and histories that can be contested. In this chapter I would like to define and contest another terrain: the conceptual territory which functions in the production of Western culture as narration.

Space and Despotic Time

During the second half of the nineteenth century the myth of Mesopotamia as the origin of Western civilisation became institutionalised into the Western humanist tradition. This modern humanist field of knowledge is a "metatemporal" teleological discourse based upon the concept of culture as an organic natural whole; one that encompassed the entirety of the world. Time, in this cultural narrative, is visualised according to this organic structure and its potential evolution. The past was seen as a necessary part of the present Western identity and, its place in the serial development to the present, of paramount importance.

Michel de Certeau has defined the act of historical writing as a perpetual separation and suturing of the past and present (de Certeau 1975). In the case of Mesopotamia, the cut and suture are not limited to the separation and adhesion of past and present time as abstract phenomenological concepts. This reconstructive historical act has severed "Mesopotamia" from any geographical terrain in order to weave it into the Western historical narrative. In the standardised orthodox text book accounts of Middle Eastern history, Sumerian, Babylonian and Assyrian cultures can have absolutely no connection to the culture of Iraq after the seventh century AD. Instead, this past is grafted onto the tree of the progress of civilisation, a progress that by definition must exclude the East, as its very intelligibility is established by comparison with an Other. The Otherness of the Oriental past, however, plays a double role here. It is at once the earliest phase of a universal history of mankind in which man makes the giant step from savagery to civilisation, and it is an example of the unchanging nature of Oriental cultures.

In historical scripture, then, the Mesopotamian past is the place of world culture's first infantile steps: first writing, laws, architecture and all the other firsts that are quoted in every student handbook and in all the popular accounts of Mesopotamia. These "firsts" of culture are then described as being "passed" as a "torch of civilisation" to the Graeco-Roman world. If Mesopotamia is the cradle of civilisation, and civilisation is to be understood as an organic universal whole, then this Mesopotamia represents human culture's infancy. Already by the 1830s, even before the start of scientific excavations in the Near East, Hegel's lectures on the philosophy of history defined this area as the site of the infancy of human civilisation

(Hegel 1956: 105). European historical writing had provided an interpretive framework in which the development of history was likened to the growth of the human organism, and in which the cradle of that organism was the East. When Mesopotamian material remains actually came to be unearthed in the decades following Hegel's lectures this evolutionary model was firmly in place. Therefore, Mesopotamian archaeological finds were interpreted according to a pre-established model. Conversely, architectural structures, visual and textual representations, as well as every other aspect of culture, were used to confirm a model of progress that had been established before these same cultural remains had been unearthed.

The temporal organisation of this evolution of human civilisation puts Mesopotamia into the distant primeval past of mankind, a time that is both "ours" (i.e. the West's) and that of a barbaric, not yet civilised, civilisation. Thus, the temporal placement of "Mesopotamia" also determines the spatial organisation required for this system to function. In terms of geographical land, Mesopotamia is not to be associated with Iraq as it can only inhabit a temporal, not a terrestrial, space. Thus, in this case, the will to power which is often turned to the production of history, has established as historical fact the development of culture as one Olympic relay with its starting point in a place that needs to remain in the realm of the West, although its savagery can never be totally overcome.

However, the Western historical narrative is not a coherent discourse which merely uses the East as the origins of civilisation for its own political ends, in the sense of appropriation of land, history, or the declaration of cultural and moral superiority; nor does the ancient Orient simply appear within this narrative as a representation of Otherness. The exercise of power may often work on the level of the consciously political. But at the same time, academic discourse as an apparatus of power, with its metaphoricity and rhetoric, is a matrix in which unconscious desire also manifests itself symptomatically. The representation of the ancient Near East within the Western historical narrative then is not limited to overt racial comparison and hierarchisation through linear time; it is also a form of control and fixing of that uncanny, terrifying and unaccountable time: at once "ours" and Other.[2]

In the simplest terms, if the earliest 'signs of civilisation' were unearthed in an Ottoman province inhabited primarily by Arabs and Kurds, how was this to be reconciled with the European notion of the progress of civilisation as one organic whole? Civilisation had to have been passed from ancient Mesopotamia and Egypt to Greece. Therefore, the contemporary inhabitants of this area had to be dissociated from this past, and this unruly ancient time was brought within the linear development of civilisation. However, as a sort of primeval European past it was also construed at the same time as an era of despotism and decadence and, paradoxically, Orientalist notions of nineteenth-century Eastern culture, systems of government and economy were projected backwards in time and applied also to Babylonia and Assyria. From within this matrix of control, the unruly despotic past continues to resurface in descriptive language and interpretive methods.

The structuring of historical time is not only a teleological device. It is my contention here that this temporal framework is necessary for the operations of taxonomy which were so crucial for the colonialist project. It has often been stated that in the evolutionary process of civilisation the telos is equivalent to the West. Countless texts from the Western historical tradition describe how civilisation was passed from the Near East through Greece and Rome to the modern West and this is hardly a point of contention any longer. However, it is my belief that this unilinear time also acts as an organising device for a taxonomy of political systems which are then aligned racially to particular past cultures that are, in turn, seen as the developmental steps of the human cultural organism.

According to Montesquieu, the so-called founder of political science, there are three species of government: the republic, the monarchy and despotism. The republic was the ideal government of Classical antiquity and monarchy that of the West. Despotism, according to Montesquieu, is the government of most Asian countries and, as Louis Althusser has pointed out, the first feature of despotism in Montesquieu's definition is the fact that it is a political regime which has no structure, no laws and lacks any social space. Montesquieu

represents despotism as "the abdication of politics itself" hence its paradoxical character as a political regime which does not exist, as such, but is the constant temptation and peril of other regimes (Althusser 1972: 82). According to Althusser's description of Montesquieu's characterisation, despotism is "space without places, time without duration" (ibid.: 78).

Despotism's timeless quality then explains how latter day Middle Eastern despots can be converged with a primeval past world.[3] Mesopotamia therefore exists within despotic time as the mythical time of despotism or civilisation's unruly malformed past. I have discussed this abstraction in my previous work (Bahrani 1995) and will address it further below. However, first I would like to focus upon how the process of *naming* the historical region in question was so indispensable for its placement within the Western cultural narrative – because, as we have learned from the ancient Mesopotamians, a thing does not exist until it is named.

Name and Being

The earliest European interest in the remains of the ancient cities of Babylon and Assyria stemmed from the desire for the validation of the Bible as an historically accurate document. As early as the twelfth century AD, Western travellers such as Benjamin of Tudela and Petahiah of Ratisbon attempted to identify remains of cities around the area of the city of Mosul in northern Iraq mentioned in the Old Testament. However, it was not until the seventeenth and eighteenth centuries that a number of European travellers began to record their attempts at the identification of ancient sites, sometimes with illustrations of those sites accompanying the written descriptions. The first organised archaeological expeditions or missions in Mesopotamia began in the mid-nineteenth century. This is also the time that a number of terms came to be applied to this geographical locale: Mesopotamia, the Near East, and the Middle East. While the latter two names were interchangeable originally, and encompassed a larger geographical terrain, Mesopotamia became instituted as the name of the pre-Islamic civilisation of the region that under Ottoman rule was known as Iraq.

This name, Iraq, had already-long been in use by the local inhabitants of the region by the time of the writings of the geographer Yakut al Rumi (born 1179 AD/575 AH [Anno Hijra]) and the early tenth century AD (4th century AH) descriptions of the region by Ibn Hawkal.[4]

The terms "Middle East" and "Near East" came into use in Europe and North America in order to identify more clearly the vast geographical terrain that had previously been referred to simply as the Orient, an area that encompassed basically the whole of Asia and northern Africa. In order to distinguish what was nearer to Europe, in a time when European interest in this vast area was intensified, a closer definition of what Europe was dealing with became necessary. The term "Near East," which was first applied at the end of the nineteenth century, soon fell out of general usage. Nevertheless, it has survived until today primarily as a designation for the same geographical locus in the pre-Islamic period, for the place named the Middle East. This is especially true in academic literature produced in the United States. The name "Middle East" was coined in 1902 by the American naval historian, Alfred Thayer Mahan, for whom the center of this region for military strategic purposes was the Persian Gulf (Lewis 1994: 3). In this way a distinction came to be made between the region before and after the advent of Islam that implied the death of one civilisation and its replacement and eradication by another. Within this disciplinary organisation the term that came to be the acceptable name for Iraq in the Pre-Islamic period was "Mesopotamia." This revival of a name applied to the region in the European Classical tradition came to underscore the Babylonian/Assyrian position within the Western historical narrative of civilisation as the remoter, malformed, or partially formed, roots of European culture which has its telos in the flowering of Western culture and, ultimately, the autonomous modern Western man. Thus the term Mesopotamia refers to an atemporal rather than a geographical entity, which is, in the words of the renowned Mesopotamian scholar, A. Leo Oppenheim (1964), a "Dead Civilisation." This civilisation had to be entirely dissociated, by name, from the local inhabitants and contemporary culture

in order to facilitate the portrayal of the history of human civilisation as a single evolutionary process with its natural and ideal outcome in the modern West.

The distinguished American scholar of Middle Eastern history, Bernard Lewis, tells us that only "two of the peoples active in the ancient Middle East had survived with a continuing identity and memory and with a large impact on the world. The Greeks and Jews were still Greeks and Jews and still knew Greek and Hebrew; in these ancient yet living languages, they had preserved the immortal works of religion and literature, which passed into the common inheritance of mankind" (Lewis 1994: 10). Therefore, according to this still commonly held view, the "torch of civilisation" was passed from Mesopotamia to Europe via the two "Eastern ethnicities" that are acceptable to the West: Greeks and Jews. Paradoxically, in the two main sources of the Western cultural narrative, Classical texts and the Bible, the Assyrians and Babylonians and their successors, the Persians, are the hostile Other, presenting a constant threat to the political freedom of democracy and the worship of the true God. The earliest archaeological expeditions to Mesopotamia then were unambiguous in defining the purposes of their mission. Since human civilisation was thought to originate in Mesopotamia, and this civilisation was transferred from the East to the West, the two justifications for the archaeological expeditions were repeatedly stated as being the search for the "roots" of Western culture and to locate the places referred to in the Old Testament.[5]

This obsessive desire to disassociate the past of the region from its present and to present it instead as a primitive stage in the evolution of mankind facilitated the concept of "Mesopotamia" as the rightful domain of the West, both in a historical and a geopolitical sense. A separation and division of (Sumerian, Babylonian, and Assyrian) cultures and an exclusion of the later history of the region was successfully articulated through the act of naming.

The acquisition of monuments and works of art that were shipped to London, Paris and Berlin in the mid-nineteenth century was thus not seen solely, or even primarily, as the appropriation of historical artefacts of Iraq but as the

remains of a mythical pre-European past. Mesopotamian cultural remains unearthed in the first
days of archaeological exploration then served to
illustrate how the modern West had evolved
from this stage of the evolution, and that Biblical
accounts were true, thus that the Judeo-Christian God was the true God. Yet these were certainly not the only needs that dictated the
archaeological endeavour in Mesopotamia.
And, more importantly, the European concepts
that formed "Mesopotamia" are not limited to
the earliest days of archaeological work in the
region. It is even more important to realise that
the construction of a "Mesopotamia" within the
discourse of nineteenth-century colonialism is
not a thing of the past. The structure of this
colonialist discipline continues virtually unchanged today, and remains all but unquestioned.

The most recent and comprehensive engagement of Mesopotamian scholarship with the
issues of imperialism and Orientalism, with the
"construction" of the field of Mesopotamian
archaeology during the height of Western imperialism, was the 1990 conference "The Construction of the Ancient Near East" (Gunter 1992).
The participants, however, confined themselves
to the workings of the field of Ancient Near Eastern studies – whether publications, excavations,
funding – to pre-World War II Europe and North
America, and maintained that the field today is
untainted by any political power interests.
Mathew Stolper seems to be the exception when
he says, "The European literary and intellectual
history that shaped the study of the ancient Near
East is not to be separated from political history"
(Stolper 1992: 20). More significantly, however,
although the contributors refer to the "construction" of the discipline during the period of Western imperialism, the major consensus seems to be
that Near Eastern archaeology is the "stepchild of
imperialism," thus having only an indirect relation to it, and that it was never used as a tool of
imperial power (Cooper 1992: 133). A reading of
the papers presented at this conference indicates
that the silence in Mesopotamian studies regarding the colonial context of the field is not an
oversight. The issue has indeed been brought
up, but only so that it may be dismissed.

While conferences, such as the one organised
at the Smithsonian, and articles written by a
handful of scholars attempt to engage with issues
of Orientalism and colonialism these endeav-
ours, especially in the area of Mesopotamian
archaeology, have been limited to positivist historical documentation of the origins of the discipline in the late nineteenth and early twentieth
centuries. There has been no engagement with
issues such as representation, cultural translation, or prevalent paradigms of discourse,
which have been major areas of focus in related
academic disciplines. Although there has been
some concern with the recording of the events
that occurred in the earliest days of Mesopotamian archaeology, there has been a decided lack
of questioning of the (internalised) structure of
the field and its practices. The rhetoric of objectivity and realism is today still operative in Mesopotamian archaeology. However, what I find
equally disturbing is that now this objectivity is
at times presented in the guise of politically
correct "post-colonial" approaches that are alternatives to the hegemonic mainstream of the
discourse.

The superficial incorporation of the vocabulary of dissent from the margins into the hegemonic discourse of the center without any
reassessment or awareness of the epistemological boundaries of the discipline only serves
to neutralise and deflect, thereby allowing the
central system of practice to remain dominant
and effective. In Gramsci's sense of the word,
hegemony is not ideology and manipulation.
Hegemony constitutes the limits of common
sense for people, and even forms a sense of
reality (Gramsci 1987; Williams 1973). Thus,
the vague references to Orientalism and imperialism in the contemporary discourse of Mesopotamian archaeology have only served to
further validate the status quo and preserve
the conventional epistemological limits of the
field. It seems that a principle of silent exclusion
is in operation, barring any real oppositional
views through the adoption of their vocabulary
into the central dominant discourse.[6] Therefore, this mimicry and subsequent neutralisa-
tion of counter-hegemonic terms within the
parameters of hegemony are decoys of sorts
that lure the possible danger to the integrity of
the discipline by deflecting any oppositional
realities.[7]

Time of the Despots

Once identified and placed within a Western matrix of knowledge, "Mesopotamia" as the cradle of civilisation began to be reduced to characteristics that were identifiable by and recognisable to (scientifically) trained archaeological research. A number of powerful abstractions, not unlike those upon which ethnographers depended in order to get to the "heart" of a culture more rapidly, graphed a diagram for Mesopotamian archaeological practices. Components of this framework were a priori summaries of the East that discerning scholars could access through objective inquiry into every realm of culture. However, if we analyse this "value-neutral" research on the level of the mimetic description of the data we can see that the creative distortion inherent in all mimesis, as Aristotle describes it, forms a dominant mode of discourse. And, furthermore, this discursive mode is heavily dependent upon the prefiguration of the master tropes of metaphor, metonymy and synecdoche for its prosaic mimetic image of antiquity.[8] In metaphor, which is literally "transfer," a figure of speech is used in which a name or descriptive word is transferred to an object or action through analogy or simile. Metonymy, "name change," works through displacement. The part of a thing may be substituted for the whole, cause for effect or agent for act, whereas synecdoche (regarded by some as a form of metonymy) uses a part to symbolise a quality presumed to inhere to the whole (White 1973).

The main recurring tropical or hologramic abstraction in the textual practices of Mesopotamian archaeology is that of despotic rule. Working within the rhetorical boundaries and signifying processes of essentialising metonymy and synecdoche, scholarship has further identified a despotic Mesopotamia as a historical fact, and it is this abstraction of despotism that has allowed Mesopotamia to assume its position as a non-place. The abstract immediacy of Mesopotamia as a despotic entity is found in all manner of archaeological interpretation regarding this culture, from agricultural production to religion, and recurs repeatedly in descriptions of the arts and architecture [...]. Decay, violence, inertia and excess, all characteristics of despotic lands

in Montesquieu's classification, are abstractions through which Mesopotamian culture is represented. Here, I focus on how despotism resurfaces in the form of metaphor, metonymy and synecdoche in the descriptions of aesthetic traditions and artistic genres of Mesopotamian culture. An early example can be seen in the writings of James Fergusson, the architect who worked with Austen Henry Layard in reconstructing the Assyrian palaces:

> Khorsabad formed a period of decay in Assyrian art ... but this is even more striking when we again pass over eight centuries of time and reach Persepolis, which is as much inferior to Khorsabad as that is to Nimrud. In Persepolis, the artists do not seem to have been equal to attempting portrayal of an action, and scarcely even of a group. There are nothing but long processions of formal bass reliefs of kingly state. (Fergusson 1850: 363–4)

In this passage decay and repetitive inertia are characteristics of an architecture that is metaphorically defined for us, in Montesquieu's terms, as despotic. Such a viewpoint published in London in 1850, during the period of British colonial expansion in the East, should come as no surprise. However, abstractions of decay, repetition, inertia and despotism appear more often than not in descriptions of Mesopotamian material culture today. In a whole series of articles and books, Assyrian art – wall reliefs, free standing monuments and entire buildings – has been interpreted as despotic (e.g. Pittman 1996; Winter 1981). For instance, in a recent study of Sennacherib's palace, an entire building is interpreted as an oppressive propagandistic building (Russell 1991: 267). The architectural structure of the palace is described metaphorically as possessing the awesome magnificence of all oriental despots and the power to reduce troublemakers to submission, both in Assyria proper and in distant lands. Synecdochally here, consciously political propaganda is the part of Mesopotamian cultural practices taken to stand for the whole, integrating the entirety. The ideology of despots has clearly become a handy ethnographic abstraction through which archaeologists can get to "the heart" of Mesopotamian culture and describe its aesthetic practices more easily and quickly than if they were to accept the possibility of a certain amount of variation of purpose or means in the cultural production of this despotic non-place.

Political rhetoric and propaganda were certainly important components of Assyrian and Babylonian cultural production. In fact, I argue that no representation, regardless of its country of manufacture, can be entirely separated from politics and ideology. But all manifestations of Mesopotamian culture have been reduced through essentialising metaphors, synecdochally and metonymically, into one identity. While sculpture and architecture created under royal patronage were no doubt infused with some form of propaganda, many other factors went into their creation besides the consciously political. Reading all Mesopotamian cultural remains as nothing more nor less than the propagandist utterances of the king reduces this Mesopotamian identity to the epiphenomenon of articulate ideology and thus serves the rhetorical strategy of "Oriental despotism." In this way, current scholarship repeats and diffuses the prototypes of imperialism. Through the power of writing, abstractions that are colonial in principle are left intact.

This kind of essentialising metonymic and synecdochal representation does not take place solely in text. Since the mid-nineteenth century objects collected from Mesopotamian archaeological sites by Western travellers, adventurers or archaeologists have been displayed in Western museums as a metonymic visual presence of that culture. The categorisation of these objects, and their display in Berlin, Paris and London, in museums that were built or enlarged specifically for that purpose, was unquestionably part and parcel of the Western imperial project in the East in the nineteenth century. At the British Museum, the original installation of the Assyrian finds was advertised to the general public as both an antiquarian object of study and a national prize or trophy (Bohrer 1994; Jenkins 1992). Today, a metonymic method of display continues to be utilised in museums for Mesopotamian (and other Near Eastern) antiquities. A group of Mesopotamian royal monuments, including the famous Stele of Naramsin, formed the main focus of an exhibition entitled "The Royal City of Susa" at the Metropolitan Museum of Art in

New York in 1992. These monuments had been mutilated and carried to Iran by the Elamites in the twelfth century BC. According to the established tradition in scholarship, the didactic material and the catalogue entries expressed horror at this act of theft and destruction. Oriental violence and cruelty was seen as a valid explanation for these actions (Bahrani 1995). "Stolen" works of art from Babylonia were placed directly in the central space of the galleries, as the main focus of the exhibition and as a prime example of, in this case, Elamite cultural practices.

Further, what is interesting for my purposes here is that neither the didactic material in the exhibit, nor the wall maps, made mention of the words Iraq or Iran. The reasoning behind this was, no doubt, that only the ancient names should be represented in a "high cultural" institution. However, I shall venture to say here that this is not common practice with exhibits representing ancient Western cultures within the same institution, nor others like it in this country. The museum and its representation of alien cultures is clearly not a value-neutral domain since this is the arena in which information and representations of other cultures are disseminated to the general public. The deliberate omission of the names Iran and Iraq from these maps and descriptions have only added to the general conception of this area as a non-place, and further strengthened the disassociation of the past and present of a particular geographical region (one which, whether relevantly or irrelevantly happened to be at the moment either at war, or without diplomatic relations to the United States), while paradoxically presenting these cultures as typically "Oriental."

My insistence on the political ramifications of this exhibition through its omission of names from the map may seem unwarranted or at best misguided; however, references to it in the popular press and leading newspapers in the United States indicate that its message was successfully deployed and understood. The following is an excerpt from an article published in the *Houston Chronicle* after a US air attack on Iraq:

Before initiating his pre-inaugural raids on Iraq [Clinton] should have visited the exhibition at New York's Metropolitan Museum of Art called 'The Royal City of Susa.' Had he attended the exhibit, he would have seen that, like Saddam Hussein, the kings and queens of ancient Mesopotamia lived in mortal fear of losing face before their enemies. (Makiya 1993)

The writer clearly associated an oppressive antique despotism with the dictatorship of Saddam Hussein, although confusing Iranian for Mesopotamian artefacts in his comparison. This is hardly surprising considering the exclusion of the names from the exhibition maps and descriptive texts. The omission of the names and the confluence of Iran and Iraq as one despotic entity is traceable to an established Western concept of the East which is still intact from the days of Montesquieu – namely, that everything East of the Mediterranean is one vast oppressive country. Because of the omission of the names and the nature of the display, the writer, Kanan Makiya, came away from this exhibition with a general vague notion of violence and oppression which he was able to apply generically and racially to Middle Eastern dictatorship – the contemporary oriental despotism.

The Extraterrestrial Orient

The creation of a historical narrative in which space and time became transcendental horizons for the Being, Mesopotamia was part of the larger discursive project through which Europe attempted its mastery of the colonised. The narrative of the progress of civilisation was an invention of European imperialism, a way of constructing history in its own image and claiming precedence for Western culture. But this narrative of world civilisation is a representation and one which necessarily requires what is described by Adorno and Horkheimer, as "the organised control of mimesis" (1944: 180). The economy of rhetorical structures in this mimetic

organisation certainly depended upon prefigurative tropological languages. However, it also involved a metaphysical cartography that provided a conceptual terrain necessary for the narration. And the charting of an extraterrestrial Mesopotamia was essential for the success of this representational enterprise. Edward Said points out that "in the history of colonial invasion, maps are always first drawn by the victors, since maps are instruments of conquest. Geography is therefore the art of war" (Said 1996: 28). Historical cartography is also drawn according to the requirements of the victorious, and archaeology is instrumental in the mapping of that terrain.

Likewise, representation in archaeological writing is not a duplication of reality: it is a mimetic activity that cannot be neatly separated from questions of politics and ideology. The ancient Greeks were well aware that mimesis always involves distortion but by some transposition we have come to think of mimesis as an exact realistic copy.[9] In the *Poetics*, Aristotle defines representation as differing in three ways: in object, manner, and means of representation. The first is the thing or action which is represented, the second is the way in which it can be represented, and the last is the medium of representation. While the choices involved in the first and last aspect of representation are addressed in Mesopotamian archaeological theory, the second remains mostly disregarded, any mention of it construed as a radical subversive act. The image of Mesopotamia, upon which we still depend, was necessary for a march of progress from East to West, a concept of world cultural development that is explicitly Eurocentric and imperialist. Perhaps the time has come that we, Middle Eastern scholars and scholars of the ancient Middle East both, dissociate ourselves from this imperial triumphal procession and look toward a redefinition of the land in between.

Notes

1 The bibliography on this subject is vast but see Said (1993).

2 For the application of the Freudian concept of the uncanny to historiographic analysis see

especially M. de Certeau (1975); H. K. Bhabha (1994).

3 As an example of this type of scholarship see Lewis (1996).

4   Encyclopaedia of Islam (1938), vol. 2, part 1 (H–J), Leiden: E. J. Brill, 515–19.

5   In 1898, for example, the Deutsche Orient-Gesellschaft stated that these were the reasons for the newly established journal, *Orientalistische Literaturzeitung*, vol. 1(2), 36, 1898.

6   See Raymond Williams (1973: 3–16) for the concept of the deflection of oppositional "emergent" cultures by the hegemonic center. See also Edward Said, "Opponents, Audiences, Constituencies and Community" in *The Politics of Interpretation*, W. J. T. Mitchell (ed.), pp. 7–32.

7   Similar critiques have been made regarding the assimilation of postcolonial theory into what Stephen Slemon calls "an object of desire for critical practice: as a shimmering talisman that in itself has the power to confer political legitimacy onto specific forms of institutionalized labor" (Slemon 1994).

8   These are three of four master tropes defined and analysed by Hayden White in his *Metahistory* (1973). See also Paul Ricoeur (1984) for the function of mimesis in historical writing.

9   The current usage of the term in the English language according to *The Oxford English Dictionary* refers to very close, accurate, resemblance.

References

Adorno, T. and Horkheimer, M. (1944) *Dialectic of Enlightenment* (trans. J. Cumming 1972), New York: Herder & Herder.

Althusser, L. (1972) *Montesquieu, Rousseau, Marx* (trans. B. Brewster 1982), London: Verso.

Bahrani, Z. (1995) "Assault and Abduction: The Fate of the Royal Image in the Ancient Near East," *Art History* 18, 3: 363–82.

Bhabha, H. K. (1994) *The Location of Culture*, London: Routledge.

Bohrer, F. N. (1994) "The Times and Spaces of History: Representation, Assyria, and the British Museum" in D. J. Sherman and I. Rogoff (eds) *Museum Culture*, Minneapolis: University of Minnesota Press.

Cooper, J. S. (1992) "From Mosul to Manila: Early Approaches to Funding Ancient Near Eastern Studies Research in the United States" in A. C. Gunter (ed.) *The Construction of the Ancient Near East, Special Issue of Culture and History* 11, Copenhagen: Academic Press, pp. 133–59.

de Certeau, M. (1975) *The Writing of History* (trans. T. Conley 1988), New York: Columbia University Press.

Fergusson, J. (1850) *The Palaces of Nineveh and Persepolis Restored: An Essay in Ancient Assyrian and Persian Architecture*, Delhi: Goyal Offset Printers (reprinted 1981).

Gramsci, A. (1987) *The Prison Notebooks* (ed. and trans. Q. Hoare and G. Nowell Smith), New York: International Publishers.

Gunter, A. C. (ed.) (1992) *The Construction of the Ancient Near East, Special Issue of Culture and History* 11, Copenhagen: Academic Press.

Hegel, G. W. F. (1956) *The Philosophy of History* (trans. J. Sibree), New York: Dover Publications.

Heidegger, M. (1962) *Being and Time* (trans. J. Macquarrie and E. Robinson), New York: HarperCollins.

Hodder, I. *et al.* (eds) (1995) *Interpreting Archaeology: Finding Meaning in the Past*, London: Routledge.

Jenkins, I. (1992) *Archaeologists and Aesthetes*, London: British Museum Publications.

Lewis, B. (1994) *The Shaping of the Modern Middle East*, New York: Oxford University Press.

Lewis, B. (1996) *The Middle East: A Brief History of the Last 2000 Years*, New York: Scribner.

Makiya, K. (1993) "Put an End to Saddam, Just Make Him Lose Face," *Houston Chronicle*, January 31.

Mitchell, W. J. T. (1983) *The Politics of Interpretation*, Chicago: University of Chicago Press.

Oppenheim, A. L. (1964) *Mesopotamia, Portrait of a Dead Civilization*, Chicago: The University of Chicago Press.

Pittman, H. (1996) "The White Obelisk and the Problem of Historical Narrative in the Art of Assyria," *The Art Bulletin* LXXVIII, 2: 334–55.

Ricoeur, P. (1984) *Time and Narrative* (trans. K. McLaughlin and D. Pellauer), Chicago: The University of Chicago Press.

Russell, J. M. (1991) *Sennacherib's Palace Without Rival at Nineveh*, Chicago: The University of Chicago Press.

Said, E. W. (1978) *Orientalism*, New York: Vintage Books.

Said, E. W. (1993) *Culture and Imperialism*, New York: Vintage Books.

Said, E. W. (1996) *Peace and its Discontents*, New York: Vintage Books.

Shanks, M. and Tilley, C. (1987) *Re-Constructing Archaeology: Theory and Practice*, London: Routledge.

Slemon, S. (1994) "The Scramble for Post-colonialism" in C. Tiffin and A. Lawson (eds) *De-Scribing*

Empire: Post-Colonialism and Textuality, London: Routledge.

Stolper, M. W. (1992) "On Why and How," in A. C. Gunter (ed.) *The Construction of the Ancient Near East, Special Issue of Culture and History* 11, Copenhagen: Academic Press, pp. 13–22.

White, H. (1973) *Metahistory*, Baltimore, MD: Johns Hopkins University Press.

Williams, R. (1973) "Base and Superstructure in Marxist Cultural Theory," *New Left Review* 82: 3–16.

Winter, I. J. (1981) "Royal Rhetoric and the Development of Historical Narrative in Neo-Assyrian Reliefs," *Visual Communication* 7, 2: 2–38.

Confronting Colonialism
The Mahican and
Schaghticoke Peoples and Us

Russell G. Handsman and
Trudie Lamb Richmond

*The fact nevertheless remains: archaeologists have no informants. We cannot see the past from
the ancients' cultural perspective because they cannot tell us what that might have been.*
(*Lewis Binford*, Data, Relativism and Archaeological Science)

*We have been discouraged from remembering anything but what the missionaries wanted us to
remember. But it's time to read between the lines of the white man's history books. (Dorothy
Davids, Mahican historian)*

More than 40 years ago, in July of 1951, James
Davids, together with his wife and four of their
five children, traveled from Bowler, Wisconsin,
to Stockbridge, Massachusetts, to visit the homeland of his ancestors. During their stay, they
spent several hours in the historical room of
the community library gathering information
about Mahican Indian history. They made visits
to traditional burying grounds and to the graves
of respected clan leaders. The Davids family also
toured the Mission House museum on Main
Street, where they discovered in a back room,
carefully protected under glass, a two-volume
English bible originally given to the Mahican
people of Stockbridge in 1745 by Sir Francis

Russell G. Handsman and Trudie Lamb Richmond,
"Confronting Colonialism: The Mahican and Schaghticoke
Peoples and Us," pp. 87–118 from Peter R. Schmidt and
Thomas C. Patterson (eds) *Making Alternative Histories:
The Practice of Archaeology and History in Non-Western
Settings* (Santa Fe: School of American Research Press,
1995). Reprinted with permission of SAR Press.

Ayscough, chaplain to the Prince of Wales
(*Berkshire Eagle*, 31 July 1951).

When forced in the 1780s to relocate for some
30 years among the Oneida Iroquois in New
Stockbridge, New York, the Mahicans who had
decided to leave their homeland took their bibles
with them. For the next 150 years, as they jour-
neyed westward along what is now remembered as
the Stockbridge Trail of Tears, the books went
along, well cared for and kept in an oak chest. At
each new campsite and settlement, in Ohio,
Indiana, Illinois, and Wisconsin, the bibles were
taken up and read from, a visible reminder of the
Mahicans' constant struggle to survive and of their
continuing cultural identity. Too, the bibles served
to connect the Mahican community in their diaspora to the ancestral homeland in western Massachusetts. The Mahicans' reverence for their bibles
was mentioned by a visitor to their 1830s community on the Fox River in Wisconsin: "I saw yesterday a Bible in their church, which is saved in a kind
of ark of the covenant and is one of the finest Bible
exemplars I ever saw" (*Stockbridge Bible*, p. 13).[1]

The bibles were looked after continuously over the next century, even as Mahican communities fragmented, relocated, and rejoined in response to local racism, acts of violence, and shifting federal and state policies. Sometime after 1911, the bibles were placed for safekeeping in a local Presbyterian church in Wisconsin. In 1930, this church's dwindling and predominantly non-native congregation voted unanimously to sell the bibles and an associated pewter communion set for $1,000. The buyer was Mabel Choate, who was establishing a museum in Stockbridge, Massachusetts, as a memorial to her parents and to John Sergeant, one of the founders of the 1730s mission to the Mahican Indians. Choate had restored and then lived in the house once inhabited by Sergeant's family; in 1948 she deeded the house and all its contents, including the bibles, to the Trustees of Reservations, who own and operate the Mission House museum today.

The Mahican community living in and around Red Springs and Bartelme townships, Wisconsin, in the 1930s knew nothing of the sale of their bibles. During the Great Depression years, which saw the dramatic decline of the state's logging industry, many Mahicans were unemployed and threatened with foreclosure on their houses (Mochon 1968:206). Some elders remembered and spoke of the bibles; others lost track of where they had been placed, assuming they were in a bank vault in nearby Shawano. It was even rumored that the Smithsonian Institution had them. So when James Davids returned from Stockbridge with the news of his discovery, his neighbors responded with excitement and anger as well as many unanswered questions. Decades later, in the 1960s and early 1970s, other Mahican families made the trip east to visit the ancestral homelands. Each group returned talking of its excitement and happiness at seeing "these books that our ancestors used over and over through their tedious and dangerous and bitter years of having to leave home after home" (*Stockbridge Bible*, p. 12).

"And We're Going to Get Our Bibles Back"

The Stockbridge Mahican Tribal Council wrote to the directors of the Trustees of Reservations in 1975, formally requesting the return of the bibles and communion set to "their rightful owners." In reply, the organization stated that custody of the Mahicans' cultural patrimony could not be relinquished without a court decree because the bibles had been given to the trustees by Mabel Choate to be held for "the benefit of the public." Throughout the next 15 years, as Mahican people continued their efforts, the validity of their claims, as well as the moral responsibilities of the trustees, was debated and written about in both communities.

Even as final resolution drew closer, some Mahicans remained understandably cautious, impatient, and skeptical. It was obvious to them that their bibles would be repatriated only because their claim of ownership was supported by clearly incontestable and legally compelling evidence. An inscription inside the first volume reads, in part, that the bibles were given for "the use of the Congregation of Indians, at or near Housatonnoc in a vast wilderness . . . and [are] to remain to the use of the successors, of those Indians, from Generation to Generation" (*Stockbridge Bible*, p. 1). Without this explicit language – suppose the inscription had been lost or destroyed as the Mahicans were continually displaced? – their legitimate ownership could easily have been dismissed as a traditional belief or story and thus made to seem inadmissible in court.

Imagine that such a legal struggle did take place and that historians and anthropologists were called upon to testify about the continuities in Mahican traditions, the contested meanings of the bibles, and the cultural survival of native peoples in New England. What might have been heard? Considering what has happened in similar circumstances (see Clifford 1988) and what has been written to date, some authorities would have talked about acculturation and assimilation instead of resistance, positing the idea that the Stockbridge Mahicans had "abandoned many aboriginal cultural patterns" long before the 1730s (Mochon 1968:213). Or they would have spoken of factionalism instead of persistent efforts to maintain a native identity (Brasser 1978; Mochon 1968). Few would have been willing to admit under oath that colonialist practices, sometimes based upon wrongheaded anthropological and archaeological models, continue to marginalize and misrepresent the lives and experiences of Indian people. There might also have been witnesses who insisted that the traditional histories of native peoples are seldom "factually" supportable or "truthful" (in Washburn's words [1987]). In effect, the long-term existence and cultural integrity of the Mahican people would have been disputed and quite possibly undermined. Thus, their desire to have the bibles returned might have been represented as a spurious and ingenuine act undertaken by people whose claims to an Indian identity were at best, in the words of James Clifton (1990), a "recent cultural invention."

Seen in this way, the Mahicans' persistent effort toward the return of their bibles becomes yet another chapter in an almost 500-year history of prejudice and alienation. This sort of struggle is well known to the Mahican people and their kin, as are the cultural memories through which they preserve and share a knowledge of how their ancestors survived colonialism, maintained and enriched living traditions, and nurtured an enduring identity in place after place, homeland after homeland (Lamb Richmond 1994; Mochon 1968). It is their words and voices that can tell us what might have happened and that will teach us how to see and confront the interpretive silences between the lines of history and a rigorously written scientific archaeology.

What follows is an initial effort to think and write alternative, unofficial "counterhistories" of and against colonialism in New England. Our goal is to illuminate the lives and experiences of native people while challenging how those same lives and experiences are so often still misrepresented. We use, necessarily, a critical, confrontational voice because these misrepresentations are much more than mistakes to be corrected or failures to be forgiven. The writing of history and the doing of archaeology continue to affect (and disrupt) the lives and futures of native people and thus to impact everyone committed to building more open, culturally democratic communities.

"After the Chuh-ko-thuk, or White People, Settled Amongst Them"

Beyond the bibles themselves, the conflict just sketched encompasses history and alternative

histories: New England history (and anthropology), for generations written almost exclusively by non-native people, and traditional histories written and remembered for far longer by Mahican people who, it seems, have always had to contest a dominant history and its misrepresentations – they call it "reading between the lines." For instance, a 1991 article in the popular *Berkshire Magazine* (Ericson 1991), although appropriately titled "The Latest of the Mahicans" (thereby correcting the myth of extinction nurtured by James Fenimore Cooper and later by Hollywood writers), dismissively characterizes eighteenth-century native society as disrupted, disoriented, and politically unstable (see Brasser 1974, 1978 for a scholarly confirmation of this story). Considering this historical background, the article continues, it is not surprising that Mahican Indians so willingly participated in John Sergeant's "novel experiment" to build a "civilized," bicultural Christian community in a six-square-mile village called Stockbridge. There, the writer enthuses, native people were to be "protected from further corruption" while being taught by white families the "skills they would need to prosper in an irrevocably changing world" (Ericson 1991:21).

By ignoring obvious evidence of Mahican resistance to and persistent concerns about their being missionized and resettled (Axtell 1985: 196–204; Mynter 1987), Ericson implies that the Indian people of Stockbridge willingly participated in the colonialist efforts while renouncing their traditions and beliefs. Moreover, because John Sergeant's character and sociopolitical purposes are left unexamined in the article – he did, after all, speak incessantly of the need to "root out their vicious habits" and "promote humanity among them" (Sergeant 1743) – the dark and disturbing forces of colonialism remain hidden from contemporary view.

With these silences, Ericson's article remains faithful to the ways in which histories of Berkshire communities and other Massachusetts towns have been written for more than 150 years. Beginning in 1829 with a county history compiled by an association of Congregational ministers and continuing for the next century (see Jones 1854; MacLean 1928; Smith 1869; Taylor 1882), Stockbridge missionaries are celebrated for their successes in Christianizing and educating the Indians and thus transforming them into "respectable and industrious citizens" (Taylor 1882:67). At the same time, the hard work and self-reliant individualism of the colonial settlers, mostly men, are pointedly praised, often by contrast to the character of the Indians, who are usually stereotyped as "savage, uncivilized, and lazy" (Smith 1869: 43–45) or as speaking only in a "parrot fashion" because of "limited brain power" (Sedgwick and Marquand 1939:1–24).

Baneful representations like these were common in the community histories written throughout western Massachusetts during the later nineteenth and early twentieth centuries. A study of such histories in the Connecticut River valley, east of the Berkshire region (Handsman 1991b), reveals a set of adjectives used redundantly to describe Native Americans: warlike, treacherous, lazy, thieving, quarrelsome, constantly drunk. Consistently Indians were portrayed as people unable to profit from the benefits of civilization brought to them by men like John Sergeant of Stockbridge.

Many of these histories were written after 1850 as the communities of western Massachusetts were urbanized and industrialized (Merchant 1989). Between 1860 and 1900, for example, the population of Great Barrington increased almost 100 percent while that of Pittsfield grew more than 150 percent. By 1895, both towns had become commercial and industrial centers (Wilkie and Tager 1991:35–36). At the same time, the cultural landscapes of western Massachusetts became increasingly diverse as large numbers of immigrants came to work as unskilled laborers and skilled craftsmen in Berkshire manufactories. Foreign-born workers accounted for more than half the labor force in the region's paper mills by 1870; 10 years later, almost one-third of such workers were native-born of foreign parents (McGaw 1987:290–93). Prejudice against these newcomers was common. W. E. B. DuBois wrote of his African-American childhood in Great Barrington as a time when the Irish, their Catholicism, and their "dirty, stinking slums" were the target of everyone else's jokes and ridicule: "The racial angle was more clearly defined against the Irish than against me," he remembered (DuBois 1940:563).

Nevertheless, these newcomers persisted. As their numbers and wealth grew throughout western Massachusetts, they increasingly challenged the political power and social status of the white middle class, affluent gentry farmers, and wealthy factory owners. In response, this elite turned to the past and made obvious the "bravery and contributions" of each town's early colonial settlers, in order to legitimize their class positions and policies. Beginning in 1844 with the Berkshire Jubilee (Birdsall 1959:314–22) and continuing into the 1930s, when many communities celebrated their bicentennials through historic pageants (Glassberg 1990), the elites systematically glorified the colonial past while making explicit their genealogical connections to those who lived then. In a supplement to the history of Great Barrington (MacLean 1928), for example, biographical notes about an early colonial aristocracy were inextricably mixed with those of their descendants – the merchants, manufacturers, and bankers who wanted to control the town's economic destiny. Indeed, the chapters concerning "notable citizens of the past" spoke only of men who were native-born, old-time New Englanders.

As the identity of the elites was now explicitly joined to that of the colonialists, it was necessary for them to do more than simply honor their ancestors. They also felt compelled to defend, or at least explain away, the colonists' more reprehensible actions. The result was that the histories of Mahican peoples in the Berkshires were hidden and denied. Some writers, for example, arrogantly insisted that the Native American presence there was impermanent and sparse, beyond even the "ordinary meagreness of Indian populations" (Smith 1869:43). Saying the same thing differently, a 1926 history of western Massachusetts confidently described pioneer Berkshire County as an unbroken wilderness of dense, undisturbed forests (Lockwood et al. 1926). Some historians, however, told a somewhat different story (Taylor 1882).

Charles Taylor of Great Barrington (1882), himself a dedicated avocational archaeologist, stated that although there were few Indians in the Berkshires at the time of colonial settlement, their numbers "formerly had been quite numerous." Furthermore, he argued, Indian peoples had dwelt here "for a very long term of years," as evidenced "by their many places of interment" and by the "great numbers of their utensils" that are still found by local residents. The pottery fragments, numerous burials, a bedrock corn mortar and stone pestle, and the stone fishing weir preserved near a local factory were all unquestionable evidence for him of the prehistoric existence of a "very considerable Indian population" (Taylor 1882:50–52). According to Taylor, however, none of these archaeological sites could have been occupied and used by Mahican people because their presence did not substantially predate that of the colonists. He insisted, in fact, that there were only eight or ten Mahican families in the entire southern Berkshires when the Stockbridge Mission was founded in 1734.

By thus underrepresenting the number of native people, as well as denying their early and continuing presence, Berkshire County's historians argued that their colonial ancestors settled lands only sparsely occupied and scarcely used. And because there were so few Mahican Indians living there in the early eighteenth century, or so they argued, the effects of colonial settlement on native people were assumed to have been both negligible and short-lived.

This same, seemingly trustworthy argument had been used somewhat earlier by Charles Allen, attorney general of Massachusetts, in his 1870 *Report on the Stockbridge Indians*. Writing in response to a petition from Stockbridge Mahicans living in Wisconsin, Allen (1870:3) dismissed their request for an allowance, declaring that the state had already, and for a long time, aided the Mahicans "by its watchful guardianship." The state must not make itself responsible for land deeds given earlier for which little or no consideration was paid. It did not really matter, Allen argued, that the country was never rightfully obtained. After all, long before the colonial settlement of the Berkshires, the Mahicans "had become reduced in number and scattered" (Allen 1870:23).

Significantly, such nineteenth-century misrepresentations are now being corroborated and thus made to seem more scientifically valid and objective through two archaeological models of late prehistoric and post-contact land use and settlement proposed for the Berkshires. In one study (Shaw et al. 1987), early Mahican peoples are redefined as Connecticut River Algonkians who occupied and used the lands of the

Berkshires only on a seasonal basis for hunting and gathering. The second model tries to interpret the undeniable and highly visible historic Mahican settlement around Stockbridge as a recently arrived community of native people whose purpose was to procure beaver pelts for sale at trading posts along the Connecticut and Hudson rivers (see project summaries in Hasenstab 1989:5–6).

Among Mahican peoples, counterhistories, both oral and written, have existed for a long time. In 1734, as John Sergeant traveled north to begin his work in Stockbridge, his Mahican Indian interpreter-guides stopped along the Housatonic River somewhat north of the Massachusetts border. There they walked into the woods until they reached a "large heap of stones," already, according to Sergeant, more than ten cart-loads in size. As was their custom, the Mahicans placed more stones on this memorial pile every time they passed (Butler 1946). When questioned by Sergeant, they explained that "their fathers used to do so, and they do it because it was the custom of their fathers" (Hopkins 1753:11; Taylor 1882:44–48).

Somewhat later, in the 1790s, another body of Mahican oral tradition was recounted to Hendrick Aupaumut, himself a Stockbridge Mahican, presumably by elders then living among the Oneida Iroquois (Belknap and Morse 1796). These stories told of the ancient origins of the Mahicans and spoke of how their ancestors came to the traditional homelands in eastern New York and western Massachusetts a long time ago. There they found abundant game and fish and rich planting fields: "They seldom felt much want and were very well contented." After "the chuh-ko-thuk, or white people, settled amongst them," the story continues, "they were subject to many disorders and began to decay" (Jones 1854: 15–16). Unlike the town histories written so frequently after 1850, the Mahican traditions make obvious and confront the catastrophic effects of colonialist policies of expansion and occupation. The very fact that such oral histories and cultural memories continued to exist and to be passed on to succeeding generations also means that the Mahicans had not renounced or repudiated their traditions as desired by John Sergeant.

Illuminating the Hidden Histories of Homelands

Although the colonialist image of an occupied and untamed wilderness persists today, in reality there were a series of ancestral Mahican homelands spread along the entire length of the Housatonic River valley in the seventeenth century. The numerous burials and communal cemeteries frequently disturbed by nineteenth-century farmers and house builders in Great Barrington (Nicholas and Mulholland 1987:22–33; Taylor 1882:50–54) indicate that the core of one such homeland was located along the river between that town's center and Stockbridge. Additional homeland cores, including that associated with the Weantinock Indian homeland in New Milford (Figure 24.1), are situated along the river in northwestern Connecticut and were the focus of the Fort Hill project, a long-term archaeological

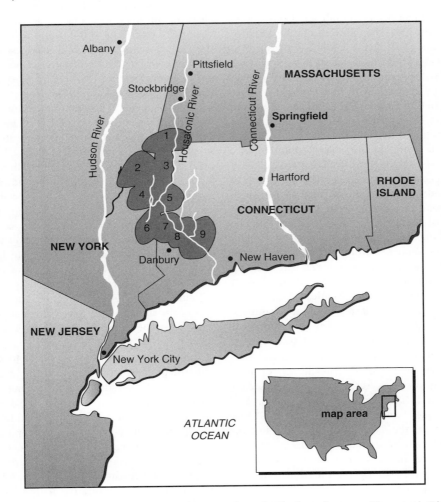

Figure 24.1 Some of the traditional Native American homelands along the upper Housatonic River. Key: 1, the Mahican homeland, where Skatehook was, around Sheffield, Massachusetts; 3, homeland of the Indian people of present-day Sharon and Salisbury, Connecticut; 5, the ancestral Schaghticoke homeland around Kent, Connecticut, where the Schaghticoke reservation is located today; 7, the Weantinock homeland, focus of the Fort Hill project; 8, one of the Pootatuck Indian homelands in present-day Southbury, Connecticut, where the traditional settlement of Pootatuck Wigwams was located. The other homelands were occupied by Mahican and Paugassett peoples, kin of the Schaghticoke and Weantinock.

study undertaken by the American Indian Archaeological Institute between 1987 and 1992 (Handsman 1990, 1991a).

As happened in the Berkshires, the long-term presence of Indians in northwestern Connecticut was denied by nineteenth-century historians, who, using John DeForest's imagery (1851:45–68), characterized the region as a wilderness frontier. The misrepresentation endures today (Handsman and Silberman 1991). Two 1987 maps showing "tribal locations" in 1625 still leave this part of Connecticut empty and uninhabited (Eisenhardt 1987; Lavin 1987). In addition, a recent archaeological study in Canaan, midway between New Milford and Stockbridge, insists that the area was "little used by various groups of Indians" in later prehistory (Connecticut Archaeological Survey 1989). Yet archaeological signs of long and enduring settlement traditions are common throughout the region. The Edward H. Rogers collection from greater New Milford, once housed at the American Indian Archaeological Institute, contains numerous triangular points of chert and quartz, drilled and incised pendants, and clay pipes recovered from plowed fields earlier in the twentieth century. Together with the cultural memories of the valley's First Peoples and clues gathered from archival documents, these archaeological assemblages are helping make more visible the ancestral homelands of the Weantinock and their Mahican kin.

Typically, the core of each homeland was more than ten square miles in extent and contained one or two important settlement places, often located at long-used fishing sites. There, clan ceremonies and elders' councils were held. Extensive cornfields were nearby, as were sacred sites such as cemeteries, memorial piles, and sweat lodges used for curing (Butler 1945). Throughout the core area and surrounding spaces of each homeland stood dozens of wigwams, alone, in pairs, or in small hamlets not very different in size from a traditional meeting place (Handsman 1990).

The people who lived in a homeland were joined to one another and to their kin in other homelands by enduring social and economic relations organized and mediated through a system of matrilineal descent (Brasser 1974:6–9). The principles of matrilineality were still central to Mahican everyday life in the eighteenth

century and were therefore commonly observed, though not well understood, by John Sergeant. For example, after seeing one family quarrel, he reported that "the parting of man and wife is a very common thing." In such cases, "'tis their law [the Mahicans'] that the children and all household stuff belong to the woman.... The man, according to their custom, has no right to the children, any more than any other person whatever" (in Hopkins 1911:45).

Among the Mahicans, and presumably among all their kin along the Housatonic River, there were three matriclans – the Bear, the Wolf, and the Turtle – whose social connectedness was, in the words of Hendrick Aupaumut, "ever united as one family" (Jones 1854:22). In every homeland, each clan was probably represented by localized segments: a dozen or more households, with members from perhaps all three clans, would have inhabited larger settlements while smaller groups of wigwams might be lived in primarily by one clan. Thus clan relations were localized within and around homelands as well as regionalized well beyond each homeland. An extensive network of paths linking people belonging to the same clans was used, for example, by those living in the Weantinock homeland to visit kin and participate in clan ceremonies in Mahican homelands in eastern New York and western Massachusetts.

John Sergeant himself recognized the importance of the enduring relations within and among clans when he reported that "it is a custom among the Indians not to proceed in any affair of importance [such as the decision to permit Sergeant to settle with them] till they have the consent of the several Clans belonging to the Nation" (quoted in Mochon 1968: 192). Through such close and enduring clan relations and the political alliances nurtured by them, it was both symbolically and actually possible for native people to communicate up and down the length of the Housatonic River. There is a long-standing tradition among the native people of the Housatonic Valley that describes this practice: "The Indians of New Milford were on friendly terms with the Schaghticokes of Kent, the Pomeraugs [the Pootatuck] of Woodbury, the Bantams of Litchfield, and the Weantanaugs [a local Mahican group] of Salisbury. It is said that by a system of calls that could be heard from one mountain-top station to another and repeated, an alarm could be conveyed down the [upper Housatonic] river in three hours" (quoted from a traditional story reprinted in the *New Milford Times*, 2 October 1924).

The origins of many traditional homelands and the clan relations that wove them together lie in the distant past. More than 3,000 years ago, native people throughout southern New England began to settle into some areas more permanently than they had previously (a pattern of increased sedentism) while intensifying trade networks and formalizing social relations across the region (Dincauze 1990). Long-used locations on the landscape, such as traditional fishing places, became sites of sacred activity as communal cemeteries were created and then used by successive generations (Handsman 1991b:16–21). Caches of finely chipped bifaces, sometimes made from "exotic" lithic materials, were often placed with the dead or deposited in nearby freshwater springs to mark the symbolic importance of these places. The caches themselves were continually exchanged between clans or clan leaders to cement their social obligations and political alliances (Loring 1985). Somewhat later, these sacred sites and traditional meeting places became the cores of ancestral homelands that are remembered and visited today.

Metichawon, located along the falls at the junction of the Housatonic and Still rivers in the Weantinock homeland, was used as a traditional fishing site and sacred place long before the coming of white people. Archaeological evidence suggests that this locality began to be visited, at first perhaps on a seasonal basis, more than 3,000 years ago. Over successive millennia, settlements became more permanent; by the seventeenth century Metichawon was the residence of one of the Weantinocks' important clan leaders. Today, this long-term pattern of settlement and sacredness is represented by an extensive archaeological record covering more than 50 acres (Handsman 1991a).

The archaeological visibility of places such as Metichawon, like that of the memorial piles built across Indian New England, is evidence of how the cultural meanings of homelands have survived for thousands of years. Yet despite the enduring importance of homelands to Indian people, their cultural meanings and historical presence are often obscured or ignored by regional archaeologists. For example, when New England archaeologists study the late prehistoric period (between 1,000 and 1,500 years ago), they rarely write about ancestral homelands. Instead, one reads stories about decreased mobility, changes in the utilization of habitats, or the intensification of trade networks (Feder 1984; Lavin 1988; McBride and Bellantoni 1982). Indian people themselves are rarely mentioned. Indeed, the language of scientific analysis and interpretation is so dehumanized that it becomes easy to forget that the archaeological record represents the memories and heritages of living people.

I wish I could think of a better term to provide for gathering. Because when people think of gathering, well, we're going to gather berries or we're going to gather nuts. . . . And it's not given the importance that it should be given, because in terms of – I mean, the women were responsible for the gathering of plants; they had to know a great deal. . . . My grandmother had a lot of knowledge, for example, about plant life and how they were used in terms of medicines and foods and things. And I know some of these things. —Trudie Lamb Richmond[2]

That very same archaeological language can also prevent or inhibit the exploration of continuing traditions of settlement and land use in ancestral homelands. Archaeologists normally assume that Mahican peoples and their kin, including the Schaghticoke and Weantinock, lived in centrally located, nucleated villages of between three and sixteen bark-covered long houses and dome-shaped wigwams; population levels varied between 45 and 260 people (Brasser 1978; Snow 1980: 88–90, 319–35). Such settlements are understood to be well above the threshold of archaeological visibility. Yet New England archaeologists have only rarely discovered late prehistoric villages (Thorbahn 1988), and their maps of regional site densities strongly suggest that many interior regions in southern New England were either unoccupied or used solely on a seasonal basis between 1,000 and 300 years ago (see Thomas 1976 for an important exception).

But in the Weantinock homeland there were no large nucleated or stockaded villages. Instead, numerous small hamlets, paired wigwams, and isolated houses were present everywhere. Even the traditional meeting places located in the homeland's core were small, consisting of a few wigwams and one long council house inhabited by a respected clan leader. One of the conceptual and methodological challenges of the Fort Hill project was to develop a systematic approach to the archaeology of these almost invisible settlements. Excavations in 1986 at the late prehistoric Weantinoge site along the Still River in Brookfield clarified the issue of size and spatial organization (Handsman and Maymon 1987). The artifact density there was low, and an initial sampling interval in excess of 10 meters would have missed the site. Features uncovered during block excavations, including pits, ash lenses, and post molds, suggested that between one and three wigwam floors were present in less than 600 square meters. The Weantinock homeland once contained dozens of such settlements.

Fieldwork in 1990 provided an additional opportunity to study the archaeological scale of Weantinock Indian wigwams. By excavating closely spaced lines of test pits across a terrace of the Still River, a previously unknown, late prehistoric settlement (site 96–026) was discovered. This site is represented by thin-walled, well-fired pottery sherds, chert and quartz tools, and features including post molds and charcoal stains. Shovel testing at site 96–026 was conducted in two successive phases, during which the sampling interval between transects was reduced from 10 meters to 5. This resulted in the identification of a second wigwam floor or group of floors, suggesting that even a "tight" testing interval of 7 to 10 meters may not ensure the discovery of such settlements (Handsman 1990). Unless New England archaeologists revise their conceptual models of Native American settlement and the field methodologies reflected by them, our maps will continue to misrepresent traditional homelands as wilderness areas, scarcely occupied and barely used.

By the early eighteenth century, affordable land in many parts of colonial New England was becoming scarce as affluent merchants and farmers continually enlarged the size and value of their private holdings. Wealthy landowners, often acting in concert with speculators as well as with scarcely propertied people, petitioned the General Courts of Massachusetts and Connecticut for permission to explore poorly known "frontier" regions (Akagi 1924). Although the colonists' maps of these areas did not show native settlements, most would-be explorers realized that these lands were already occupied. So long as the petitioners could show evidence that they had incontestable "deeds" from Native Americans, however, colonial courts routinely permitted them to form groups of proprietors who would then decide how the lands of each new town were to be divided and used.

In reality, the documents the colonists (and later historians) referred to as deeds were often carefully worded agreements to share the use of homelands and resources. In them, native people consistently reserved for themselves the rights to collect firewood, hunt and fish, use their planting fields, and even build wigwams on the colonists' common pastures (Handsman 1991b: 19–21; Wright 1905). In a 1724 "deed," Mahican people in the southern Berkshires agreed to allow colonists to use a "certain tract upon the Housatonic River" while reserving some lands for themselves, including the locality they called "Skatehook," a traditional meeting place and sacred site (Taylor 1882:15–16). Almost 40 years later, many of the same Mahicans sent a petition to the Massachusetts legislature protesting a 1762 act that had authorized the formation and public sale of 10 new townships in the Berkshires. "They were the owners of the lands in question," the Mahicans insisted, reminding the colonists that neither "they nor their ancestors had ever been at war with the English or dispossessed of said lands" (Taylor 1882:72; also see Wright 1905:116–19, 184–87). A committee was appointed to "inquire further into the Indians' title"; its report said the Mahican Indians could not offer "sufficient evidence" to support their claims. A recommendation was made and it was so ordered that a sum of 1,000 pounds be made available to keep the Indians "quiet and in good temper" (Taylor 1882:73). In this way the proprietors and settlers of the Berkshires hoped to persuade Mahican peoples to forget and abandon the homelands where the bones of their ancestors were buried.

Similar histories of colonialist appropriation and native resistance were being played out almost simultaneously in the homelands of the Weantinock and their kin along the Housatonic in northwestern Connecticut (Handsman 1990; Wojciechowski 1985). For example, in 1737 the colonial legislature authorized the establishment of six new towns in northwestern Connecticut. Fifty shares of each town were then sold at public auction to speculators as well as to those who planned to resettle (Akagi 1924:197–99; Grant 1972). In less than five years, local Mahicans – long-time, permanent residents of the region – began to complain that they were being defrauded of "their reserved and unsold lands," of which they were the proper owners. After a visit to northwestern Connecticut, a legislative committee reported that there had been no deception involved; the Indians had simply "misunderstood the bargain." Although 50 acres were subsequently reserved for native use, the conflicts continued for almost 10 years. In 1751, colonial settlers in the town of Sharon wrote to the General Assembly expressing their concern over the uneasiness of some Mahicans who were "very angry with those [colonialists] who are the rightful owners of the land" (Sedgwick 1898:36–40).

Earlier, in the beginning of the eighteenth century, the first colonial settlers had arrived in the Weantinock homeland in New Milford. Soon after, in 1702–1703, a deed was signed in which the Weantinock people reserved for themselves "the use of their present planting field and a privilege of fishing at the Falls," the place known traditionally as Metichawon (Wojciechowski 1985:135–36). Even after they were dispossessed of much of their homeland, Weantinock people continued to travel to Metichawon to fish for eels and shad, using the privilege they had reserved for themselves. In the 1770s, local residents formed the Cove Fishing Company. Shareholders were guaranteed a place along the river for spring fishing. Native people were not shareholders; nevertheless, they continued to fish at the falls until 1877, when the building of a dam in the lower Housatonic irreparably injured the shad fishing upstream. The settlement of damages between the Housatonic Water Company and the Cove Fishing Company never mentioned the rights of the Weantinock and their kin (Handsman 1991a:6).

In the early eighteenth century, the Weantinock planting fields covered dozens of acres along the Housatonic; today the fields are a well-preserved archaeological site opposite present-day New Milford village (Carlson and Handsman 1993). Used primarily for corn, these extensive fields probably were worked by both clans and local communities according to traditional calendars based on the lunar cycle. Native people would have set the corn seed in late spring, formed the hills in early summer, celebrated the arrival of the newly ripening green corn in late summer, and harvested the crops in early fall, storing large surpluses for exchange and ceremonial feasts (Butler 1948; Lamb Richmond 1989; Thomas 1976). In the fields, Weantinock elders would have reminded their children of the communal values of working together and sharing, telling them the story of how corn had once grown from the body of a loving woman:

Glooskap and the First Mother

After the first man and woman became husband and wife a long time ago, there came a famine. The woman asked her husband to take her life and draw her body around an open field. He was hesitant, but after talking with Glooskap, the great teacher, did as she said. The man drew her body until the flesh was worn away, and in the middle of the field they buried her bones. When seven moons had gone by and the husband came again to that place, he saw it all filled with beautiful tall plants. The fruits of the plants tasted sweet and he called it *Skarmunal*, corn. (Anastas 1973:12–14)

Soon after the signing of the 1702–1703 deed, the Weantinocks' planting fields began to be taken away. In the first decade of colonial settlement, the proprietors subdivided the better-drained floodplain soils into tiers of four-and-a-half-acre to five-acre lots. Fifteen acres, ironically called "the land improved by the Indians," were reserved for native use. But even this parcel was soon appropriated and divided into 20 individual pieces, each smaller than an acre. Before 1730 – less than three decades after initial colonization – the Weantinock and their kin no longer had access to their ancestral planting fields.

Throughout southwestern Massachusetts and northwestern Connecticut this history of colonialism was repeated over and over as the eighteenth century continued. As they were alienated from their traditional planting fields, as mills and dams were built, disturbing long-used fishing sites, and as pigs and cattle were allowed to graze freely in marshes and groves of nut trees, native peoples were being forced to abandon their homelands.

"According to Our Law and Custom"

That Native Americans sometimes consciously decided to continue living in their ancestral homelands is a fact seldom mentioned in town histories or in the writings of colonial historians today (Merrell 1989). Yet even as parts of Mahican and Weantinock homelands were appropriated, surveyed, divided, and fenced, some native people resisted by making themselves less visible, resettling their families and communities beyond the fringes of colonial settlements (Handsman 1989). Less accessible settings such as the tops of ridge lines and small upland valleys became new home sites. Often such places were in disputed areas along the borders between the colonies of Massachusetts or Connecticut and New York, far removed from administrative centers. Because, at least initially, no one colony had systematic knowledge of or control over these lands, or access to the resources in them, those who lived there – Native Americans, African Americans, and others who were dispossessed – often survived as cohesive multicultural communities into the twentieth century (Feder 1994; Wetherbee and Taylor 1986).

Such localities had long been familiar to Indian people; their paths had traversed them for centuries, linking hamlets in the valleys to locations where raw materials (stone outcrops), food resources (groves of nut trees and sugar maples), or medicinal herbs had been gathered for generations. In these newly occupied places, Native Americans could continue to live within or close to ancestral homelands without making their presence known – unless they so desired.

The existence of such historic communities cannot be documented with any certainty from the records and maps of the colonialists. Similarly, material signs of their presence are either unrecognized or misinterpreted today by those who continue to assume that Native Americans were not an integral part of New England's social landscape after the early 1700s. Yet archaeological sites representing just such enduring traditions of settlement have already been excavated and can be used to aid in the recognition of further evidence. For example, the limited assemblage recovered from the Pootatuck Wigwam site (130–27), located along the Housatonic River in Southbury, Connecticut, includes native-made ceramics, well-worn quartz tools, pieces of cut-up copper or brass kettles reshaped into pendants, gun flints perhaps reused as scrapers, and European ceramics (primarily salt-glazed stonewares and lead-glazed red earthenwares from broken cups and mugs). Normally archaeologists would assume that this assemblage represented a prehistoric lithic scatter overlain by and mixed with historic artifacts redeposited from nearby colonial farmsteads. Oral tradition and a wealth of archival documents, however, make clear that Pootatuck Wigwams was a well-known traditional meeting place and a sacred site (like Metichawon) occupied by clan relations of the Weantinock people in the late seventeenth and eighteenth centuries (McBride 1989). According to Cothren (1854:108–109), "in the 19th century, an elderly native woman, then living among her kin at the Schaghticoke reservation, would travel to Southbury to visit the site of Pootatuck Wigwams and the graves of her ancestors. As she stood along the riverbank with tears on her face, she would say. 'There, there is Pootatuck.'"

At the Wigwams site, Pootatuck people continued to live and work as their ancestors had, at the same time interacting with colonial farmers, traders, and trappers who had been a steadily growing presence in the valley for almost a century (Wojciechowski 1985:46–48, 113–31). When seen in this context, the site's supposedly mixed archaeological assemblage actually represents evidence of periodic contacts with colonists and the selective acceptance and integration of modified colonial artifacts into everyday life (see Rubertone 1989). Examples include the cutting up of trade kettles to provide raw materials for pendants and the reuse of gunflints as woodworking tools. The numerous quartz tools were probably made and used predominantly by Pootatuck women and elders, whose interactions with colonists were much less frequent. Indeed, this tool assemblage could even be seen as representing a strategy of resistant accommodation in which some Pootatucks consciously turned away from the colonists' world – modifying locally available stone cobbles for knives and scrapers instead of acquiring metal tools to use – while others maintained contacts necessary for economic survival. Seen this way, the archaeological record at Pootatuck Wigwams cannot be read as a history of gradual social assimilation and cultural loss. Instead, the site can be interpreted as an important and highly visible center for native resistance and the continuation of living traditions, a place whose significance was well remembered by later generations.

Significantly, very similar assemblages have been recovered from the nearby Weantinock homeland along the route of a recently constructed gas pipeline. At least eight sites located in three adjacent towns produced artifact inventories reminiscent of that from Pootatuck Wigwams, including quartz and chert tools, Native American ceramics, and pieces of lead-glazed stonewares (data abstracted from Cassedy et al. 1991). Without hesitation, the project archaeologists interpreted these assemblages as representing prehistoric campsites or lithic reduction stations mixed with "scatters of historic refuse associated with the agricultural use of the land" (quoted from the summary of site 270A-4-1 in Cassedy et al. 1991). Some of these sites, however, can undoubtedly be interpreted as eighteenth-century homesteads or wigwams occupied by Weantinock people who refused to leave their homeland despite the losses they had suffered.

Other Native Americans did leave, moving to other homelands to live with their kin, often in places of long-standing traditional importance. As native communities in these places slowly increased in size, they became more visible to colonial governments and land companies, who, in turn, wanted to implement policies of assimilation and resettlement. In 1734, John Sergeant began missionizing in one of the Mahican homelands centered along the Housatonic River in southern Berkshire County, Massachusetts. Although later community historians paternalistically celebrated his efforts to bring civilization and Christianity to the Indians, both Sergeant and his financial backers (the New England Company) knew better. Well aware of the interconnectedness of Mahican peoples in the Berkshires and eastern New York, they hoped to extend their influence and that of the Massachusetts colony into disputed territory while establishing economic hegemony over the region's resources and lands (Mandell 1982:5–11). John Sergeant himself argued in 1749 that the educating of this "barbarous, uncultivated people" would prove to be a "means of engaging them more firmly in the British interest" (quoted in Hopkins 1911:148–49).

When John Sergeant first arrived, some of the Mahicans inhabited two small meeting places, each identified with a respected clan leader, and others lived dispersed throughout the homeland in hamlets consisting of three to five wigwams and a small garden. For the next 15 years, until his death, Sergeant continually railed against this tradition of settlement, which did not permit him sufficient control over or daily contact with the Indians. No sooner had he arrived, in fact, than Sergeant (see Hopkins 1753:9–10) insisted that the Mahicans "come together in one place" in order that the Sabbath be better attended and native children "taught on week days." Although a "public house" was built and then encircled by "small huts" (wigwams), Mahican people did not forget their customary obligations or repudiate their traditions. They insisted on "retiring to their own places" in late winter to do maple sugaring and again in late spring to plant and nurture their corn (Axtell 1985:198; Brasser 1978:207; Hopkins 1911:23, 25, 28). Native men were absent more frequently, hunting and trapping in distant parts of the homeland and working on Dutch farmsteads. The food acquired when hunting and the goods men received from their furs or labor, combined with what was grown, caught in the rivers, and gathered by others, provided adequate support for many Mahican families. They in turn could preserve some degree of social separation and cultural autonomy despite the missionary's efforts.

It soon became obvious that Mahican traditions were going to persist, so in 1735 John Sergeant and others developed a plan to establish a mission settlement (the Stockbridge Indian Mission) "in the great meadow above the mountain," where all the Indians could live and work as farmers together (Hopkins 1753:43–51). In order to accomplish this, it was necessary to effect transfers of lands involving Massachusetts colonists, Dutch settlers, and the Mahicans. At a meeting in April 1735, a clan leader expressed some concern: his people could not show clear title for some of the lands being considered for exchange. "If anyone should insist upon anything more than the testimony of living witnesses," Umpachense confessed, "they could prove no title at all." However, he went on, "their [the Mahicans'] titles were good, according to their law and custom in such cases" (Hopkins 1753:49). Despite assurances from Colonel John Stoddard, who, when he died in the 1750s, had become one of the region's wealthiest merchants and gentleman farmers (Sweeney 1984: 233), the Mahican leader was not convinced. What would happen in the future, he wondered, if the children of the colonialists forgot the land "was in great measure given them" and assumed a "superiority over" native people? "What security," he asked, could the Mahicans have "that their children would be free?" (Hopkins 1753:50).

His concerns proved real. Although Mahicans made up a clear majority of Stockbridge's population well past 1760, colonists had gained political control of the town and its elected offices by 1750 (Mandell 1982:20–30). Legislation was passed in the 1760s by the General Court of Massachusetts permitting the English settlers of Stockbridge to tax themselves "exclusive of the Indian inhabitants," thereby sanctioning the division of Sergeant's bicultural community into two unequal parts (Mandell 1982:28). During this same period, as moneys once received from the New England Company and other supporters diminished and as their traditional sources of income and food were denied them, the indebtedness of Mahican peoples rose dramatically (Canning 1894; Mandell 1992:240–44). Increasingly they were forced to sell their lands to discharge debts. Between 1762 and 1772, one-half of all the Mahicans' land in Stockbridge was

acquired by colonists (Mandell 1992:245). By 1783, there was little land left to return to after the American Revolution, in which half of Stockbridge's Mahican men lost their lives fighting for the patriots.

The conflict between the indigenous tradition of living apart in homelands, while being woven together by clans, and the colonial aim of resettling Indian people and thus bringing them under control was central to the cant of conquest and resistance in eighteenth-century New England. Connecticut's colonial government attempted to terminate the enduring tradition through legislation. A 1717 act for the more "effectual well ordering" of Indian peoples declared, "Measures shall be used to form villages of the natives, wherein the several families of them should have suitable portions of the land appropriated to them, so that the said portions shall descend from the father to his children, the more to encourage them to apply themselves to husbandry" (reprinted in Kittrie and Wedlock 1986:28). Their purposes, almost identical to those of John Sergeant and his associates (Axtell 1985:196–204; Jones 1854:62–66; Sergeant 1743), were obvious: to redefine and destroy customary communal matriclan relations and to nurture and intensify dependency relationships by creating settlements that would become instrumental to the establishment and workings of formally recognized reservations (Kawashima 1969). Yet such villages were already being created by Indian people in Connecticut and, ironically, were destined to become centers of resistance and cultural survival.

The place known to the Mahicans as Pishgachtigok or Scaticook, along the Housatonic River just south of present-day Kent, Connecticut, was probably an important meeting and fishing site before the early 1700s. As Weantinock and other native peoples living in the so-called "Western Lands" were alienated from their planting fields by the colonists, some families resettled at Scaticook, joining kin who had lived there for generations. Pishgachtigok was at the center of a traditional homeland which overlapped that of the Weantinock (Figure 24.1). By the early 1740s, the still growing native community there had attracted the attention of Moravian missionaries, who built stone churches at Scaticook and in several nearby Mahican homelands (Beaver 1988:432–33; Brasser 1974:34–35). The Moravians were strangers to New England and thus could rightly claim to be innocent of earlier acts of dispossession and genocide. They were welcomed by traditional leaders, including a man named Gideon Mauwee, especially because they seemed more intent on quietly bringing their beliefs to those who were "disposed to hearken to them" than in converting and "civilizing" entire communities (Axtell 1985:265; Orcutt 1882:132–46).

For almost 20 years, Moravian missionaries preached the gospel at Scaticook, even as the native community continued to maintain and nurture its living traditions (Lamb Richmond 1987, 1994). On numerous occasions, evening services in the church were canceled or poorly attended because traditional ceremonies were being conducted in nearby sweat lodges. As happened at Stockbridge, Schaghticoke people were often absent from the settlement, living beyond the "missionary gaze" in winter hunting camps or visiting kin in nearby Mahican homelands. A series of paths linked the Schaghticoke and Moravian community at Pishgachtigok to other such mission settlements to the west and north, including Shekomeko (near Pine Plains, New York) and Wechquadnack (on Indian Pond near Sharon, Connecticut), where their Mahican kin continued to live. These same paths were used by John Sergeant when he traveled south to preach among the native people in Sharon and Salisbury in northwestern Connecticut, as well as by Schaghticoke people when they went north to attend clan ceremonies and council meetings in Massachusetts. In 1756, after a land sale threatened to cut off one of their traditional paths "into ye Woods" and beyond, the "Chief Sachem and others of the Scaticook Tribe" petitioned the General Assembly to appoint a committee to look into their claims, "that all our grievances may be redressed." They wrote of their patriotism and peacefulness, reminding the government of how they had willingly "encouraged the settlement of English near us by selling our lands for very trifling sums" (quotations from the petition in Wojciechowski 1985:146–47).

Sometimes the Moravians sought to interfere with and disrupt native traditions. The missionaries suggested, for example, that the Schaghticoke organize their labor differently. Instead of entire families moving into the woods to build canoes, perhaps only a few men should go while others gathered raw materials needed for making splint baskets and brooms. For the most part, these ideas were rejected because the Schaghticoke "had always worked together" (Lamb Richmond 1987:135).

In the decades following the establishment of the Moravian mission, the colonial presence in Kent increased substantially; by 1777 there were almost 300 more adult men living in the town than in 1739–40. During this period, many farms began to produce surpluses for resale in local and regional markets (Grant 1972:31–54). Agrarian land uses intensified, as did mining, milling, and lumbering activities. A traveler in 1780 observed, "I have never traveled [in Kent] three miles without meeting a new settlement." Yet "four years ago one might have traveled ten miles in the woods without seeing a single habitation" (quoted in Grant 1972:40). The emergence of agrarian capitalism in Kent and surrounding towns meant that native people now had less access to their traditional fishing sites and planting fields and to the woods where they once hunted and trapped.

These problems were not entirely new. In the early 1750s, the Schaghticoke wrote to the General Assembly complaining that they did not have enough planting ground, their ancestral fields having been appropriated by Kent settlers for use as common pasture: "Your petitioners [the Schaghticoke] have been possessed of a considerable quantity of land of which the white people have got from them and of late the county has surveyed it in Order as [we] apprehend to dispose thereof. [We] have at present for Eighteen Families but a small piece fit for planting which lies between the Haustenick [Housatonic] River and Pachgatgoch Hill which is not sufficient for them to raise corn upon" (1752 petition in Wojciechowski 1985:145, brackets ours).

These changes were also apparent to the Moravians, who encouraged Schaghticoke and Mahican people to manufacture useful household items such as wood-splint baskets, brooms, and wooden bowls (Figure 24.2), arguing that their sale would provide additional income necessary for survival (Brasser 1975).

(a)

(b)

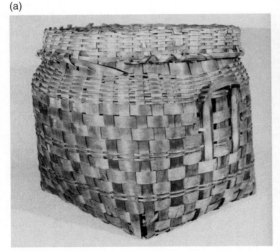 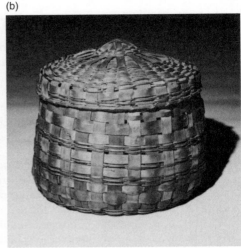

Figure 24.2 Early nineteenth-century wood-splint baskets made by Jacob Mauwee, Schaghticoke (top), and Molly Hatchet, a Paugussett from farther south on the Housatonic River. Native basketmakers used distinctive techniques of weaving and decoration to represent groups and community identitites. (Photos: Collections of the New Milford Historical Society and the American Indian Archaeological Institute.)

In addition, the income would permit native people to become less dependent on their colonial neighbors, whom the Moravians considered intemperate and unscrupulous.

But the production and exchange of wood-splint baskets had another meaning for the Schaghticoke. When given as gifts, in the way caches of finely chipped bifaces were once exchanged, baskets became a way for native people to build and sustain connections with kin who now had to live apart, dispersed throughout the Housatonic Valley (Handsman and McMullen 1987). The mission records from Pishgachtigok (Fliegel 1970) contain numerous references to canoe loads of baskets and brooms being paddled down the river. Along the way, native people would stay over with their clan relations, stop at old meeting places now unused, and visit sacred sites where the bones of their ancestors were buried. Some went as far as Stratford, Connecticut, to the mouth of the Housatonic, where today their splint baskets are preserved in the collections of local historical societies.

The Schaghticoke traditions of making and exchanging splint baskets continued through the nineteenth and into the twentieth centuries (Lamb Richmond 1987). Eunice Mauwee (Figure

24.3), a well-known basketmaker and descendant of the eighteenth-century community leader Gideon Mauwee, lived at Scaticook for most of her life. In 1852, at more than 90 years of age, she spoke of her strong attachment to that place, saying that she did "not wish to leave it for a single day."[3] Her gravestone still stands in the small cemetery along the River Road, part of the Schaghticoke Indian reservation in Kent, Connecticut (Handsman and Williamson 1989:33–34).

"That's why it Means so Much to be a Part of Schaghticoke"

In March 1953, the judiciary committee of the General Assembly of Connecticut held public hearings in Hartford concerning a proposed bill whose stated purposes were "to end the second class citizenship of the state's few remaining Indians" and thus "reduce the administrative burden" of state agencies. In response to questions, Clayton Squires of the state welfare department explained why his agency wanted a mandate to redistribute reservation lands. "We have more and more demands," he said, "from people [of color, whom he refused to

Figure 24.3 Eunice Mauwee, Schaghticoke (1756–1860). Those who live on the present-day reservation remember Eunice Mauwee as "the grandmother of us all," because the main Schaghticoke families today can all trace genealogical connections to her and her descendants.

acknowledge as Indians] to be allowed to build on these reservations and from my investigation they are not the type of citizens we want."[4] If passed and signed into law, the bill would have authorized the dispersal of communally owned lands reserved long ago for native peoples. Some parcels would have been sold at public auction, others incorporated into state forests and parks. The cultural assimilation of the indigenous Indian peoples of Connecticut would thus have been hastened (Bee 1990:194–96). As the hearing ended, the bill's supporters remained seated. The 25 or so non-Indians in opposition stood, joining the Schaghticoke, Golden Hill Paugussett, and Mashantucket Pequot people at the rear of the room. The Indians had listened silently as others dismissed their heritage and traditions, declaring that their presence on ancestral lands was no longer relevant, affordable, or meaningful. The bill died in committee.

Some 37 years later, across the street from the state capitol, the Supreme Court of Connecticut heard arguments in 1990 in a case involving the Schaghticoke people. What began as a local dispute over logging and consensus politics within the reservation community became a highly visible and closely watched legal struggle. Connecticut's then attorney general asked the Supreme Court to overturn an appellate decision and restore the state's authority to regulate what happened on the reservation. Although they did not participate in the proceedings, the Schaghticoke wanted the decision to stand, insisting it supported their struggle to achieve sovereignty. The attorney general stated that "there [were] no facts in the record" to support the contention that "a bona fide Schaghticoke tribe has existed since 1790"; nor was there any evidence of "cohesiveness" or "common interests" within the community. Neither had the Schaghticoke people petitioned the federal government "to acknowledge they exist." In an earlier appearance before the appellate court, the attorney general had argued (wrongly) that the Schaghticoke had no permanent place of settlement until 1752, when the colonial government reserved some land at Scaticook for native use.[5]

After review, the Connecticut Supreme Court, in March 1991, remanded the case to the appellate court and then the original trial court, with clearly stated instructions that the judges involved must determine whether the "Schaghticoke Indians are still a tribe" and whether "they have in the past and presently continue to exercise some form of tribal sovereignty." "The record is devoid of evidence," the justices wrote, "as to whether the tribe is still, or has ever been, a cohesive ethnic unit."[6] Thus in 1991, as in 1953 and the later nineteenth century, the Schaghticoke people were told they could have no identity save that given to or forced upon them. Nor could they have any pasts save the ones written and remembered by others. Their living traditions and their cultural memories and stories about resistance would have no legal standing. Their voices, speaking of the place once called Pishgachtigok, would be denied and marginalized as they continued to make a new place for themselves and for their histories.

Schaghticoke is a harmonious balance of mountainous terrain, thickly forested hills and swamplands; of rocky ledges and streams. And everywhere there are healing plants just waiting for those who know where to look. At one time the air was filled with the sounds of the pounding of ash logs for basket splints. It takes a lifetime to make a basket; a lifetime of growing, of creating and of sharing, to shape what is in your heart; a lifetime filled with customs and traditions. That knowledge is not always visible to the eye. It is so deeply buried in the past. But sometimes only a heartbeat away. There are rare, precious moments when I am privileged to glimpse some of this. That's why it means so much to be a part of Schaghticoke. (Trudie Lamb Richmond, Schaghticoke, quoted in Handsman and Williamson 1989:34)

Conflicts like those between the Schaghticoke Indians and the state of Connecticut or between the Stockbridge-Munsee people and the Trustees of Reservations are often viewed as involving only indigenous people and "the law." But nowadays, struggles for equality and against systematized prejudice increasingly involve the domains of science, cultural politics, knowledge, and writing (Gordimer 1988; Said 1985). In these struggles, which will continue long after 1992 and the supposed "end of history," there is both space and need for scholars to take responsibility for their work and actions and for the consequences of them. Rather than continuing to declare our innocence, we need to see and confront the ways in which our words and actions contribute to the silencing and dispossessing of other people.

Working against colonialism in the future means that we have to interrogate, challenge, and break apart the emerging ideology of cultural difference. This ideology of difference obscures and deflects our critical gaze so that relations between different cultural traditions are not easily seen as matters involving hierarchy, alienation, domination, and control. Instead, the ideology implies that the very real inequalities in power between peoples in the Americas are simply a matter of differing points of view, requiring that we need only learn to be more respectful and tolerant of the "stories" others wish to tell.

As we confront the ideology of cultural difference – the political philosophy of colonialism

today – we who are archaeologists will also be helping to open new understandings of Native American history. Archaeologists can help map and thus make visible the cultural landscapes and social relations of ancestral homelands. We can, for example, help document the persistent presence of Mahican peoples in their homelands, countering the myth of abandonment and cultural extinction by exploring historic wigwam and house sites while searching for all the wood-splint baskets that undoubtedly remain hidden and unrecognized in museum collections throughout the Berkshires (Handsman 1994). By learning to do archaeologies of resistant accommodations and living traditions, we will help create a much-needed long-term perspective for understanding the significance of the Mahicans' struggle to get their bibles back.

Some people in Stockbridge, Massachusetts, today dismiss that struggle and the continuing visits by Mahican people from Wisconsin as the work of activists who only recently decided to remember their Indianness and reclaim their heritage. For a long time, they insist, Mahicans were uninterested in their own pasts and histories. There is little truth in these words. In the early nineteenth century, two Mahican Indians "from the far west" came to Stockbridge to visit "the graves and hunting grounds of their ancestors." While there, they visited the mountain where John Sergeant and the Mahican guides had stopped in 1734. The ancient memorial pile could no longer be seen, having been thrown down and desecrated in the late eighteenth century. Nevertheless, "after standing for some time thoughtfully and in silence," each of the Mahicans "cast a stone upon the spot and turned away" (Taylor 1882:47–48).

Today, when Mahican families travel to Stockbridge, they always visit this place on the mountain. They leave behind piles of stones they have brought from their new homelands in Wisconsin. And they gather stones to take back west, where they are placed on coffee tables and mantles and used as doorstops in their homes. Others of these stones end up in the Arvid E. Miller Memorial Library and Museum, where they can now be seen next to the Stockbridge bibles, which have been returned.

Notes

1 The quotation and related background information concerning the bibles' history and the Mahicans' struggle to have them returned are from *The Stockbridge Bible* (1981), a collection of oral histories, extracts from newspapers and correspondence, and selections from books, compiled and published by the Stockbridge-Munsee Historical Committee, Stoughton, Wisconsin.

2 The testimony by Trudie Lamb Richmond is from an oral history interview, "Native American Gathering," collected and transcribed by Jeremy Brecher for Connecticut Public Radio in January 1989. A copy of the transcription and taped show are on file at Connecticut Public Radio, Hartford.

3 From David T. Lawrence's "Biographical Sketch of Eunice Mauwee" (1852), manuscript collection (81808) of the Connecticut Historical Society, Hartford, Connecticut.

4 The testimony of Clayton Squires and background information on the 1953 bill can be found in Minutes of the Hearings before the Judiciary Committee, 1953, volume II, pp. 423–27, Connecticut State Library, Hartford. Relevant newspaper clippings and correspondence are in records of the State Welfare Department, Record Group 19, Box 4, State Archives, Connecticut State Library.

5 The background and legal arguments related to the Schaghticoke case can be found in the following documents: for the appellate review, see (1) "Schaghticoke Indians of Kent, Connecticut v. Keith Potter et al. (7919)," a 1989 consolidated brief and related appendix filed by the attorney general, state of Connecticut, and Leslie A. Carothers, commissioner of environmental protection, with the Appellate Court of the State of Connecticut, Judicial District of Litchfield; and (2) the majority opinion in the above-named case written by Judge Lavery, released on May 16, 1990. For the State Supreme Court review, see (1) "Schaghticoke Indians of Kent, CT v. Keith Potter et al. (14005)," a 1990 consolidated brief and related appendix filed by the attorney general, state of Connecticut, and Leslie A. Carothers, commissioner of environmental protection, with the Supreme Court of the state of Connecticut; and (2) consolidated brief and related appendix for the above-named case written by William R. Breetz et al. as amicus curiae, Supreme Court of the state of Connecticut. Newspaper accounts include "Connecticut Indian Land in Legal Quandary," *New York Times*, 10 July 1990; "State Power over Indian Tribe in Kent Is Challenged in Ruling," *Litchfield County Times*, 13 July 1990; "Court to tribe: It's all yours," *News Times of Danbury*, 15 July 1990; and "Day in Court Nears for Kent Indians," *Litchfield County Times*, 2 November 1990.

6 The text of the Connecticut Supreme Court decision in "Schaghticoke Indians of Kent, Connecticut, Inc. v. Keith Potter et al." can be found in *Connecticut Reports*, volume 217. See *Connecticut Law Journal*, 5 March 1991.

References

1967 *Regiones de refugio*. Ediciones Especiales, no. 46. Mexico, D.F.: Instituto Indigenista Interamericano.

Akagi, Roy H. 1924 *The town proprietors of the New England colonies: A study of their development, organization, activities and controversies, 1620–1770*. Philadelphia: University of Pennsylvania Press.

Allen, Charles 1870 *Report on the Stockbridge Indians to the Legislature, Massachusetts: House document no. 13*. Boston: Wright and Potter.

Anastas, Peter 1973 *Glooskap's children*. Boston: Beacon Press.

Axtell, James 1985 *The invasion within: The contest of cultures in colonial North America*. New York: Oxford University Press.

Beaver, R. Pierce 1988 "Protestant churches and the Indians." In *Handbook of North American Indians*, vol. 4, ed. W. Washburn, 430–58. Washington, D.C.: Smithsonian Institution Press.

Bee, Robert L. 1990 "Connecticut's Indian policy: From testy arrogance to benign bemusement." In *The Pequots in southern New England: The fall and rise of an American Indian nation*, eds. L. M. Hauptman and J. D. Wherry, 194–214. Norman: University of Oklahoma Press.

Belknap, Jeremy, and Jedidiah Morse 1796 "Report on the Oneida, Stockbridge and Brotherton Indians." Originally published in *Collections of the Massachusetts Historical Society*, first series, 5: 12–32. Reprinted 1955 in *Indian Notes and Monographs*, no. 54. New York: Museum of the American Indian, Heye Foundation.

Birdsall, Richard D. 1959 *Berkshire County: A cultural history*. New Haven: Yale University Press.

Brasser, Ted J. 1974 *Riding on the frontier's crest: Mahican Indian culture and culture change*. Ethnology Division Paper no. 13. Ottawa: National Museum of Man.

Brasser, Ted J. 1975 *A basketful of Indian culture change.* Ethnology Division Paper no. 22. Ottawa: National Museum of Man.

Brasser, Ted J. 1978 "Mahican." In *Handbook of North American Indians, vol. 15: Northeast,* ed. B. Trigger, 198–212. Washington, D.C.: Smithsonian Institution Press.

Butler, Eva L. 1945 "Sweat-houses in the southern New England area." *Bulletin of the Massachusetts Archaeological Society* 6:11–15.

Butler, Eva L. 1946 "The brush or stone memorial heaps of southern New England." *Bulletin of the Archaeological Society of Connecticut* 19:2–11.

Butler, Eva L. 1948 "Algonkian culture and the use of maize in southern New England." *Bulletin of the Archaeological Society of Connecticut* 22:3–39.

Canning, E. W. B. 1894 "Indian land grants in Stockbridge." *Collections of the Berkshire Historical and Scientific Society* 5:45–56.

Carlson, Claire, and Russell G. Handsman 1993 "The Fort Hill project. Recovering buried histories: Archaeology at the Weantinock Indian planting fields." *Newsletter of the Conference on New England Archaeology* 12(1):1–2.

Cassedy, Daniel F., Elise Manning, Bruce Sterling, Christopher Hohman, Tracy Millis, and Mark Rees 1991 *Iroquois gas transmission system: Phase II archaeological evaluations, vol. 4: Connecticut.* Atlanta: Garrow and Associates.

Clifford, James 1988 "Identity in Mashpee." In his *The predicament of culture: Twentieth-century ethnography, literature, and art,* 277–346. Cambridge, Mass.: Harvard University Press.

Clifton, James A. 1990 "The Indian story: A cultural fiction." In *The invented Indian: Cultural fictions and government policies,* ed. J. A. Clifton, 29–47. New Brunswick, NJ: Transaction Publishers.

Connecticut Archaeological Survey 1989 *An archaeological survey of Bridge #2425 over the Hollenbeck River in Canaan, Connecticut.* Project report 511, prepared for the Connecticut Department of Transportation. New Britain: Connecticut Archaeological Survey.

Cothren, William 1854 *History of ancient Woodbury, Connecticut,* vol. 1. Waterbury, Conn.: Bronson Brothers.

DeForest, John W. 1851 *History of the Indians of Connecticut from the earliest known period to 1851.* Hartford, Conn.: William James Hammersley.

Dincauze, Dena F. 1990 "A capsule prehistory of southern New England." In *The Pequots in southern New England: The fall and rise of an American Indian nation,* eds. L. M. Hauptman and J. D. Wherry, 19–32. Norman: University of Oklahoma Press.

DuBois, W. E. B. 1940 "Dusk of dawn: An essay toward an autobiography of a race concept." In his *Writings,* 549–802. Reprinted 1986 with notes by Nathan Huggins. New York: Library of America.

Eisenhardt, Evelyn 1987 *On the trail of Connecticut's woodland Indians.* History on the Go! Workbook Series, no. 5. Hartford: Connecticut Historical Society.

Ericson, Jody 1991 "The latest of the Mahicans." *Berkshire Magazine* 9(6):18–27.

Feder, Kenneth L. 1984 "Pots, plants, and people: The late Woodland period of Connecticut." *Bulletin of the Archaeological Society of Connecticut* 47:99–111.

Feder, Kenneth L. 1994 *A village of outcasts: Historical archaeology and documentary research at the Lighthouse site.* Mountain View, Calif.: Mayfield Publishing Company.

Fliegel, Carl John, compiler 1970 *Index to the records of the Moravian mission among the Indians of North America.* New Haven, Conn.: Research Publications, Inc.

Glassberg, David 1990 *American historical pageantry: The uses of tradition in the early twentieth century.* Chapel Hill: University of North Carolina Press.

Gordimer, Nadine 1988 "The essential gesture." In *The essential gesture: Writing, politics and places,* ed. Stephen Clingman, 285–300. New York: Alfred A. Knopf.

Grant, Charles S. 1972 *Democracy in the Connecticut frontier town of Kent.* New York: W. W. Norton.

Handsman, Russell G. 1989 "Algonkian wigwams: An invisible presence, political spaces." *Artifacts* 17(4):19–21. Washington, Conn.: American Indian Archaeological Institute.

Handsman, Russell G. 1990 "The Weantinock Indian homeland was not a 'desert.'" *Artifacts* 18(2): 3–7.

Handsman, Russell G. 1991a "What happened to the heritage of the Weantinock people." *Artifacts* 19(1):3–9.

Handsman, Russell G. 1991b "Illuminating history's silences in the 'Pioneer Valley.'" *Artifacts* 19(2): 14–25.

Handsman, Russell G. 1994 "Challenging history's myths in the Berkshires: Mahican Indian people and the Bidwell House acreage." Research report prepared for the Bidwell House Museum, Monterey, Massachusetts.

Handsman, Russell G., and Ann McMullen 1987 "An introduction to woodsplint basketry and its interpretation." In *A key into the language of woodsplint baskets,* eds. A. McMullen and R. G. Handsman, 16–35. Washington, Conn.: American Indian Archaeological Institute.

Handsman, Russell G., and Jeffrey H. Maymon 1987 "The Weantinoge site and an archaeology of ten centuries of native history." *Artifacts* 15(4):4–11.

Handsman, Russell G., and Neil Silberman 1991 "John DeForest and US: Critical perspectives on the archaeological alienation of Palestinian and Algonkian Indian histories." Paper presented at the annual meeting of the Society for Historical Archaeology, Richmond, Va.

Handsman, Russell G., and Lynne Williamson 1989 "As we tell our stories: Living traditions and the Algonkian peoples of Indian New England." *Artifacts* 17(4):4–34.

Hanson, Norwood Russell 1958 *Patterns of discovery.* Cambridge: Cambridge University Press.

Hasenstab, Robert 1989 "Workshop on field sampling methods and modeling, held at the CNEA annual meeting, April 9, 1988, Sturbridge, Massachusetts." *Newsletter of the Conference on New England Archaeology* 8(1):3–6.

Heye, George G. 1921 "A Mahican wooden cup." *Indian Notes and Monographs* 5(2):15–18. New York: Museum of the American Indian, Heye Foundation.

Hopkins, Samuel 1753 *Historical memoirs, relating to the Housatunnuck Indians.* Boston: S. Kneeland.

Hopkins, Samuel 1911 "Historical memoirs relating to the Housatonic Indians." *The Magazine of History with Notes and Queries* vol. 5, extra numbers 17–20. Reprinted 1972. New York: Johnson Reprint Corporation.

Jones, Electa F. 1854 *Stockbridge, past and present, or records of an old mission station.* Springfield, Mass.: Samuel Bowles and Company.

Kawashima, Yasu 1969 "Legal origins of the Indian reservation in colonial Massachusetts." *American Journal of Legal History* 13:42–56.

Kittrie, Nicholas N., and Eldon D. Wedlock, eds. 1986 *The tree of liberty: A documentary history of rebellions and political crime in America.* Baltimore, Md: Johns Hopkins University Press.

Lamb Richmond, Trudie 1987 "Spirituality and survival in Schaghticoke basket-making." In *A key into the language of woodsplint baskets*, eds. A. McMullen and R. G. Handsman, 126–43. Washington, Conn.: American Indian Archaeological Institute.

Lamb Richmond, Trudie 1989 "'Put your ear to the ground and listen.' The wigwam festival is the green corn ceremony." *Artifacts* 17(4):24–26. Washington, Conn.: American Indian Archaeological Institute.

Lamb Richmond, Trudie 1994 "A native perspective of history: The Schaghticoke nation, resistance and survival." In *Enduring traditions: The native peoples of New England*, ed. Laurie Weinstein, 103–12. Westport, Conn.: Bergin and Garvey.

Lavin, Lucianne 1987 "Connecticut's native Americans: Weathering the storm of European contact." *Discovery* 20(2):2–9. New Haven, Conn.: Yale Peabody Museum.

Lavin, Lucianne 1988 "Coastal adaptations in southern New England and southern New York." *Archaeology of Eastern North America* 16:101–20.

Lockwood, John H., E. N. Bagg, W. S. Carson, H. E. Riley, E. Boltwood, and W. L. Clark, eds. 1926 *Western Massachusetts: A history, 1636–1925*, vol. 1. New York: Lewis Historical Publishing Company.

Loring, Stephen 1985 "Boundary maintenance, mortuary ceremonialism and resource control in the early Woodland: Three cemetery sites in Vermont." *Archaeology of Eastern North America* 13:93–127.

McBride, Kevin 1989 "Pootatuck Wigwams: Overview of its historic significance and archaeological values." Nomination form for the National Register of Historic Places, prepared for review by the Connecticut Historical Commission, Hartford.

McBride, Kevin, and Nicholas F. Bellantoni 1982 "The utility of ethnohistoric models for understanding late Woodland-contact culture change in southern New England." *Bulletin of the Archaeological Society of Connecticut* 45:51–64.

McGaw, Judith A. 1987 *Most wonderful machine: Mechanization and social change in Berkshire paper making, 1801–1853.* Princeton, NJ: Princeton University Press.

MacLean, George Edwin 1928 *History of Great Barrington, Massachusetts, part II extension: 1882–1922.* Great Barrington: Town of Great Barrington.

Mandell, Daniel R. 1982 "Change and continuity in a Native American community: Eighteenth century Stockbridge." M.A. thesis, Department of History, University of Virginia, Charlottsville.

Mandell, Daniel R. 1992 "Behind the frontier: Indian communities in eighteenth-century Massachusetts." Ph.D. dissertation, Department of History, University of Virginia, Charlottesville.

Merchant, Carolyn 1989 *Ecological revolutions: Nature, gender, and science in New England.* Chapel Hill: University of North Carolina Press.

Merrell, James H. 1989 "Some thoughts on colonial historians and American Indians." *William and Mary Quarterly* 46(1):94–119.

Mochon, Marion Johnson 1968 "Stockbridge – Munsee cultural adaptations: 'Assimilated Indians.'" *Proceedings of the American Philosophical Society* 112(3):182–219.

Mynter, Ken 1987 "Leaving New England: The Stockbridge Indians." In *Rooted like the ash trees: New England Indians and the land*, rev. ed., R. Carlson, 30–32. Naugatuck, Conn.: Eagle Wing Press.

Nicholas, George P., and Mitchell T. Mulholland 1987 *Archaeological locational survey of the Housatunnuk at Skatehook in Sheffield, Massachusetts.* Report from University of Massachusetts Archaeological Services, no. 70. Amherst, Massachusetts.

Orcutt, Samuel 1882 *The Indians of the Housatonic and Naugatuck valleys.* Hartford, Connecticut: Case, Lockwood, and Brainard. Reprinted 1972. Stratford, Connecticut: John E. Edwards.

Rubertone, Patricia E. 1989 "Archaeology, colonialism, and 17th-century native America: Towards an alternative interpretation." In *Conflict in the archae-ology of living traditions,* ed. R. Layton, 32–45. One World Archaeology Series. London: Unwin Hyman.

Said, Edward W. 1985 "Opponents, audiences, con-stituencies, and community." In *Postmodern culture,* ed. H. Foster, 135–59. London: Pluto Press.

Sedgwick, Charles F. 1898 *General history of the town of Sharon, Litchfield County, Connecticut.* Amenia, New York: Charles Walsh.

Sedgwick, Sarah Cabot, and Christina Sedgwick Mar-quand 1939 *Stockbridge, 1739–1939: A chronicle.* Great Barrington, Mass.: Barrington Courier.

Sergeant, John 1743 *Letter to Dr. Colman of Boston (con-taining a proposal for a more effectual method for the education of Indian children).* Boston: Rogers and Fowle.

Shaw, Leslie C., Ellen-Rose Savulis, Mitchell T. Mulhol-land, and George P. Nicholas 1987 *Archaeological locational survey in the central Berkshires, Pittsfield, Massachusetts.* Report no. 18. Amherst, Mass.: Uni-versity of Massachusetts Archaeological Services.

Smith, J. E. A. 1869 *The history of Pittsfield, Massachu-setts, from the year 1734 to the year 1800.* Boston: Lee and Shepard.

Snow, Dean R. 1980 *The archaeology of New England.* New York: Academic Press.

Sweeney, Kevin M. 1984 "Mansion people: Kinship, class, and architecture in western Massachusetts in the mid eighteenth century." *Winterthur Portfolio* 19(4): 231–55.

Taylor, Charles J. 1882 *History of Great Barrington, Massachusetts.* Great Barrington, Mass.: Clark W. Bryan.

Thomas, Peter A. 1976 "Contrasting subsistence strat-egies and land use as factors for understanding Indian–White relations in New England." *Ethnohis-tory* 23(1): 1–18.

Thorbahn, Peter F. 1988 "Where are the late Woodland villages in southern New England?" *Bulletin of the Massachusetts Archaeological Society* 49(2):46–57.

Washburn, Wilcomb E. 1987 "Distinguishing history from moral philosophy and public advocacy." In *The American Indian and the problem of history,* ed. Calvin Martin, 91–97. New York: Oxford University Press.

Wetherbee, Martha, and Nathan Taylor 1986 *Legend of the bushwacker basket.* Sanbornton, NH: Martha Wetherbee Basket Shop.

Wilkie, Richard W., and Jack Tager, eds. 1991 *Historical atlas of Massachusetts.* Amherst: University of Massachusetts Press.

Wojciechowski, Franz L. 1985 *The Paugussett tribes: An ethnohistorical study of the tribal interrelationships of the Indians in the lower Housatonic River area.* Nijmegen, Netherlands: Department of Cultural and Social Anthropology, Catholic University of Nijmegen.

Wright, Harry Andrew, ed. 1905 *Indian deeds of Hamp-den County.* Springfield, Mass.: Privately printed.

Part VIII

Heritage, Patrimony, and Social Justice

WHO OWNS THE PAST? WHO OWNS ANTIQUITY? WHO OWNS NATIVE CULTURE? These are all recent titles of popular books on heritage and cultural patrimony (Brown 2003; Fitz Gibbon 2005; Cuno 2008). They all share in the idea of global or universal heritage. From this perspective, the past is a non-renewable resource that must be protected for the benefit of all people (Atwood 2004). The looting of the past is thus a crime against humanity. Global heritage is also an argument for the role of the universal museum, examples being the Louvre, the British Museum, and the Prado, whose purpose is to serve as cultural repositories for the world. Lying beneath this argument is the neoliberal view that the principles of Western market economics are universal and that they are applicable to the past and to antiquities. However, it is possible to juxtapose against these titles other titles such as *The Ethics of Collecting Cultural Property*, *Grave Injustice*, *Against Cultural Property*, and *Collecting Colonialism* that interrogate the idea of ownership and place the practice of collecting within a historical and cultural context (Messenger 1989; Gosden and Knowles 2001; Fine-Dare 2002; Carman 2005). The social constitution of the past is not monolithic and, indeed, varies considerably across cultures and through time. Not only is the past present as we talk about it and use it for our various contemporary purposes, but, for some cultures, there is no clear dividing line between the two since the past actively intervenes in the present (Layton 1989).

The ideas of cultural heritage and patrimony are intimately bound to the rise of the nation-state. This is because nation-states legitimize themselves by selectively representing the past in ways that emphasize their own continuity, inevitability, and legitimacy. Nation-states historically have wielded heritage as a weapon to delegitimize indigenous populations in areas they wished to colonize. Cultural resource management and heritage management are not neutral practices. While they now serve the interests of multiple publics (McManamon 1991), they do so in ways that almost always yield to the pressures of economic development. In addition, there are issues of the control of knowledge in which the past is translated into a bureaucratic language that requires professional administrators, thereby distancing people from their pasts

(Hollowell 2006). Even today, the legacy of colonialism expressed in the language of heritage continues to frame the political relations between nation-states and indigenous peoples. In North America, for example, the entire Federal recognition process revolves around the ability of tribal nations to document their own political and cultural continuity (Miller 2003; Miller 2004; Raibmon 2005). Nation-states also deploy cultural heritage to distinguish themselves from each other and to assert their sovereignty. This process can be seen in the prominent debates between England and Greece over the Parthenon marbles (Hamilakis 1999) and between Peru and the United States over the Machu Picchu collection at Yale University (Salvatore 2003).

Increasingly, cultural heritage discourse is becoming linked to social justice issues. This was violently brought to the fore by recent global events, particularly the destruction of the Bamiyan Buddhas in Afghanistan in 2001 (Meskell 2002; Colwell-Chanthaphonh 2003) and the looting of the Baghdad Museum in Iraq in 2003 (Pollock 2003). While arguments for the preservation of world heritage were immediately put forth by the museum community, statements of concern for the safety and security of the Afghan and Iraqi people were slower in coming. As Meskell observes, these discourses are of different representational orders and should not, therefore, be confused. These issues have led to the establishment of Archaeologists for Global Justice (AGJ) (www.shef.ac.uk/archaeology/global-justice.html). This organization is led by archaeologists based at the University of Sheffield and was inspired by the actions of Archaeologists Against the War in opposing British involvement in the Iraq conflict. The idea of forming AGJ was publicly proposed during a session entitled "An Eternal Conflict? Archaeology and Social Responsibility in the Post-Iraq World" convened at the Theoretical Archaeological Group (TAG) conference in 2005.

Social justice issues are also implicated in the development of community-based archaeology. There is an emerging international focus on multivocality and an appreciation of the importance of integrating contemporary indigenous views of the past. These insights are part of the commitment to a more equitable or democratic archaeology. At the same time, community advocates and indigenous rights activists have challenged the academy to "give back" to communities with which they have traditionally worked. Their efforts have led to new legal protections, such as the Native American Graves Protection and Repatriation Act (Fine-Dare 2002), as well as new ethical codes (Zimmerman 2002; Meskell and Pels 2005). There are now growing numbers of collaborations between descendant communities and archaeologists on heritage and social issues in North America, Australia, and New Zealand (e.g. Peck et al. 2003; Smith et al. 2003: Smith and Jackson 2006; Colwell-Chanthaphonh and Ferguson 2008; Silliman 2008).

One of the most sophisticated critics of the nation-state is Arjun Appadurai. His chapter is the product of an interview for the *Journal of Social Archaeology* conducted with Ian Hodder, Ashish Chada, Trinity Jackman, and Chris Whitmore. He begins with the proposition that the nation-state today is in crisis and suggests that it is no longer the only player with claims to sovereignty. The nation-state is only one among many entities, including transnational corporations and grass-root interests groups, that are part of our increasingly globalized world. This, as we noted in the introduction to Part VII, is a point also made by Hardt and Negri (2000), who claim that the nation-state is being replaced by Empire, an amorphous global system of transnational corporations and institutions. The conclusion to draw here is that if the nation-state is in crisis, then so too must cultural heritage be in crisis. For Appadurai, the politics of the past is "stretching and deepening in lots of ways as more people become bi-national, multi-national or diasporic." He makes the point that professional archaeology is tied to state institutions, national institutions, and the ruling political party and it plays a critical role in the economy of forgetting and remembering (see also Patterson 1995).

Appadurai regards local knowledge as a contingent process linked to globalization. He notes that there are certain moments in history when the production of the local involves a complex trafficking in knowledge. In some cases, this trafficking can be less hybrid and less negotiated, while in others it is more conscious and deliberate. In this latter case, the goal is often to produce a local that is more lasting and credible. Museums are, of course, the *locus classicus* for the deliberate construction of heritage. There is thus a tension between so-called "universal museums," like the British Museum which contains the Parthenon marbles, and local museums, like the new Parthenon Museum in Athens, which has copies of those same marbles on display. The Greek government is actively seeking the return of the originals (Hamilakis 1999). Appadurai then raises the question of whether museums should be about history or about heritage. He suggests that heritage is more fixed and essentialist, while history is more open and mobile. He wonders, however, how museums might address history when their very materiality and disciplinary basis predispose them to a consideration of heritage. Here Meskell in her chapter provides a partial answer by suggesting that a shift from a focus on sites and buildings to a concern with the multiple manifestations and uses of the past over time might more effectively accommodate living communities.

Appadurai makes an intriguing argument about the agency of heritage and the social construction of the past. He notes that there are some forms of heritage that seemingly do not require the elimination of other heritages. They are tolerant and respectful of cultural diversity. However, there are other forms of heritage that are predatory. They are based upon the idea that one particular heritage is paramount and multiple heritages cannot coexist. Appadurai is particularly interested in investigating the contexts in which some identities and heritages come to be predatory. This observation about predatory and non-predatory heritage is similar in some respects to Habermas's view of the colonization of the lifeworld. According to Habermas (1989), the colonization of the lifeworld refers to the extension of instrumental rationality into more and more spheres of life. It negatively affects those processes that serve to reproduce the lifeworld across generations by disrupting the transmission of cultural knowledge and values, eroding the basis for social norms, solidarity, and sense of community, and interfering with socialization processes related to the formation of personal identity and character.

Lynn Meskell exposes some of the uncomfortable relationships underpinning archaeology, tourism, and politics. Tourism is first and foremost a business. It packages culture and the past in strategic ways to make them desirable to potential consumers. This packaging is accomplished through the use of a variety of tropes, the most common of which is exoticism. Meskell also notes that tourism is commonly regarded as a good thing and as valuable in facilitating economic development. But the reality on the ground is less clear. Tourism has a number of negative consequences for local communities. Meskell notes that the economic revenues are often less than anticipated. In Egypt, for example, only 22 to 25 percent of the international tourist expenditures remain in the country. Meskell also draws attention to how the tourist industry privileges certain parts of Egyptian history: the Pharaonic past is uniformly highlighted over the Islamic present. The post-Pharaonic period is interpreted to signify the "decline of Egypt," and this has negated tourist interest and scholarly attention.

Meskell then discusses the village of Gurna as a compelling case where the dead past is valued over the living present. Gurna is a village of approximately 1,300 families living immediately above the Tombs of the Nobles near the famous Valley of the Kings. Most of the villagers make their living from tourism and farming. In 1948, the Egyptian government sought to relocate the villagers and establish the village of New Gurna along the Nile. This resettlement was unsuccessful and the villagers returned to their original homes. Meskell quotes the head of the Luxor City Council as saying in 1998 that "you can't afford to have this heritage wasted because of informal houses being built in an uncivilized manner." In 2006, the Egyptian government again sought to relocate the villagers. However, this attempt failed as well and only four families moved. Meskell is especially critical of those Egyptologists who have weighed in on the debate and claimed that the presence of the modern village is "disastrous to the survival of the tombs" and leads to "theft, erosion, building and vandalism." She is also critical of the ICOMOS site management plan since while it acknowledges the existence of the villagers, it limits their rights in expanding their homes and managing agricultural water. She concludes that violence, both real and symbolic, has been done to the Gurnawis, and that this is a direct consequence of the privileging of the global over the local.

In 1997, Gurna was again in the news, but this time because a Muslim extremist group killed 58 foreigners and four Egyptians at the Temple of Hatshepsut. This massacre received worldwide coverage and the media emphasized the fact that tourists were explicitly targeted. The media failed to note, however, that this attack was not an isolated case. Earlier in the year, there were separate attacks on tourists outside their hotel near Giza and in a tourist bus in front of the Cairo Museum. Meskell notes that the British newspapers used the Hatshepsut incident to link the Middle East to violence and terrorism, and that some writers took this as an opportunity to demonize Islam. This perspective both stereotyped Islam as extremist and ignored the Gurnawis' public condemnation of the Islamic militants. Although Meskell doesn't explicitly make this point, it is interesting to speculate that the extensive media coverage may also have been a result of the convergence of two factors: wealthy foreign tourists and a world heritage site. Meskell quotes Simon Jenkins, a *Times* reporter, as saying "Monday's massacre on the site of that city [Thebes] saw a new Assyrian terror, from fanatical opponents of Islamic reform. But whereas Ashurbanipal terrorised by laying waste to an entire city, the death squads of al-Gamaa al-Islamiya needed only to machine-gun a busload of Western tourists: A dead Westerner is a media ticket to ride" and "the Temple of Hatshepsut no longer 'belongs' to Egypt, but to the world." Left out of this florid rhetoric is any consideration of the local people.

Michael Blakey explores the practice of an ethnically responsible science in the context of the controversy surrounding the African Burial Ground in New York City. In 1990, the General Services Agency (GSA) hired Historic Conservation and Interpretation (HCI), a contract archaeology firm, to write the archaeological portion of an environmental impact report for a property located at 290 Broadway, where it planned to build a $276 million, 34-story office tower and adjoining four-story pavilion. The HCI report identified the area as part of the "old Negroes Burial Ground." After purchasing the land, the GSA hired HCI to conduct archaeological testing. The archaeologists subsequently discovered the skeletal remains of more than 400 African men, women, and children. This finding immediately challenged the popular view that there was no slavery in colonial New York.

As the excavation proceeded, the GSA inadvertently ignited a controversy that played out on the national stage. The GSA failed to notify the local African American community of its plans and its leaders protested the excavations on the grounds that their concerns were not being addressed. Owing to the accidental destruction of some of the burials during excavation, State Senator David Patterson established an oversight committee to monitor the work. Of particular concern was the lack of an appropriate research design. Additional problems included adequate notification and the proper storage of the human remains. These concerns led Representative Gus Savage, Chair of the House Subcommittee on Public Buildings and Grounds, to shut down the excavations. The GSA then hired Michael Blakey, a professor at Howard University, to create a research design and serving as the director of bioanthropological research program studying the human remains.

Blakey draws his inspiration from critical theory. This is the theoretical approach associated with neo-Marxist philosophers and reinterpreted by numerous black scholars as critical race theory. For Blakey, critical theory has the potential to reveal some of the ways in which sociocultural and ideological factors shape scientific and other scholarly work. He notes that Euro-American history has typically ignored African Americans except in the context of slavery, a category of labor. This has had the effect of dehumanizing African Americans, reducing them to a monolithic category and denying them their diverse lived experiences. Blakey also notes that in his own field of physical anthropology, scholars have participated in the creation of a racist ideology.

One of Blakey's most important contributions is his discussion of how public engagement transformed the project. He acknowledges two clients: the GSA, which funded the research; and the descendant community, which was most affected by the work. He notes that while both have legitimate interests, the descendant community is the ethical client in the sense that its views need to be privileged. This approach is congruent with the ethical policies of the American Anthropological Association and is based upon the power asymmetry between the two clients. Blakey presented a draft research design to the local African American community and others for comment. Among the things he learned in the consultation process was that the African American community preferred that the human remains be referred to as "Africans" or "enslaved Africans," rather than as "slaves." This is an important distinction and acknowledges that Africans were not only slaves, they were complex human beings who had a prior existence in Africa before their enslavement and who resisted slavery psychologically, politically, and militarily. This perspective led to the renaming of the old Negroes Burial Ground as the African American Burial Ground.

Audrey Horning examines heritage as social action in Northern Ireland and the Republic of Ireland. Irish society is divided today into Roman Catholic (nationalist) and Protestant (unionist) traditions and both consider themselves to be a threatened minority. Horning notes that historical memory and representational practices play a key role in the perpetuation of these views. Loyalists murals employ images of events such as the "massacre" of Protestant settlers during the Irish Rebellion of 1641, the Siege of Derry in 1689, and the subsequent victory of King Billy at the Battle of the Boyne in 1690. Nationalist murals, meanwhile, often use the Great Hunger of the 1840s to suggest a British policy of genocide. These images were used to justify violence against the unionists in "The Troubles" that began in 1968.

Horning advocates an ethical and nuanced archaeology committed to fostering positive and informed discourse that questions the assumptions underpinning a deeply divided society. But she notes that archaeologists who seek to question dichotomous histories do so at a real personal risk. The public is hyper-sensitized to even the slightest hint of partisanship. Even the name one chooses to use for one of Northern Ireland's largest settlements, Derry/Londonderry, has political implications. In this context, archaeologists studying post-medieval sites often focus on the archaeological process or local history as a means of encouraging cross-community dialogue and participation. The challenge is to identify the "stakeholders" and relevant communities, and consider the role of the "audience" in determining the archaeological agenda.

References

Atwood, Roger, 2004 Stealing History: Tomb Raiders, Smugglers and the Looting of the Ancient World. New York: St. Martin's Press.

Brown, Michael F., 2003 Who Owns Native Culture? Cambridge, MA: Harvard University Press.

Carman, John, 2005 Against Cultural Property: Archaeology, Heritage and Ownership. London: Duckworth.

Colwell-Chanthaphonh, Chip, 2003 Dismembering/ Disremembering the Buddhas. Journal of Social Archaeology 3(1):75–98.

Colwell-Chanthaphonh, Chip, and T. J. Ferguson, eds., 2008 Collaboration in Archaeological Practice: Engaging Descendant Communities. Lanham, MD: AltaMira.

Cuno, James, 2008 Who Owns Antiquity? Museums and the Battle over Our Ancient Heritage. Princeton: Princeton University Press.

Fine-Dare, Kathleen S., 2002 Grave Injustice: The American Indian Repatriation Movement and NAGPRA. Lincoln: University of Nebraska Press.

Fitz Gibbon, Kate, ed., 2005 Who Owns the Past? Cultural Policy, Cultural Property, and the Law. New Brunswick, NJ: Rutgers University Press.

Gosden, Chris, and Chantal Knowles, 2001 Collecting Colonialism: Material Culture and Colonial Change. Oxford: Berg.

Habermas, Jürgen, 1989 The Theory of Communicative Action, vol. 2. Lifeworld and System: A Critique of Functionalist Reason. Boston: Beacon Press.

Hamilakis, Yannis, 1999 Stories from Exile: Fragments from the Cultural Biography of the Parthenon (or "Elgin") Marbles. World Archaeology 31(2):303–320.

Hardt, Michael, and Antonio Negri, 2000 Empire. Cambridge, MA: Harvard University Press.

Hollowell, Julie, 2006 Moral Arguments on Subsistence Digging. In The Ethics of Archaeology: Philosophical Perpsectives on Archaeological Practice. Chris Scarre and Geoffrey Scarre, eds. Pp. 69–93. Cambridge: Cambridge University Press.

Layton, Robert, 1989 Who Needs the Past?: Indigenous Values and Archaeology. London: Unwin Hyman.

McManamon, Francis P., 1991 The Many Publics for Archaeology. American Antiquity 65(1):121–130.

Meskell, Lynn, 2002 Negative Heritage and Past Mastering. Anthropological Quarterly 75:557–574.

Meskell, Lynn, and Peter Pels, 2005 Embedding Ethics. Oxford: Berg.

Messenger, Phyllis M., 1989 The Ethics of Collecting Cultural Property: Whose Culture? Whose Property? Albuquerque: University of New Mexico Press.

Miller, Bruce G., 2003 Invisible Indigenes: The Politics of Nonrecognition. Lincoln: University of Nebraska Press.

Miller, Mark E., 2004 Forgotten Tribes: Unrecognized Indians and the Federal Acknowledgement Process. Lincoln: University of Nebraska Press.

Patterson, Thomas C., 1995 Towards a Social History of Archaeology in the United States. Fort Worth, TX: Harcourt Brace.

Peck, Trevor, Evelyn Siegfried, and Gerald A. Oetelaar, eds., 2003 Indigenous People and Archaeology. Proceedings of the 32nd Annual Chacmool Conference. Calgary: The Archaeological Association of the University of Calgary.

Pollock, Susan, 2003 The Looting of the Iraq Museum: Thoughts on Archaeology in a Tme of Crisis. Public Archaeology 3:117–124.

Raibmon, Paige, 2005 Authentic Indians: Episodes of Encounter from the Late Nineteenth-Century Northwest Coast. Durham, NC: Duke University Press.

Salvatore, Ricardo D., 2003 Local versus Imperial Knowledge: Reflections on Hiram Bingham and the Yale Peruvian Expedition. Nepantia: View from the South 4(1):67–80.

Silliman, Stephen W., ed., 2008 Collaborative Archaeology at the Trowel's Edge: Learning and Teaching in Indigenous Archaeology. Tucson: University of Arizona Press.

Smith, Claire, and Gary Jackson, 2006 Decolonizing Indigenous Archaeology: Developments from Down Under. American Indian Quarterly 30(3–4): 311–349.

Smith, Laurajane, Anna Morgan, and Anita van der Meer, 2003 Community-Driven Research in Cultural Heritage Management: The Waanyi Women's History Project. International Journal of Heritage Studies 9(1):65–80.

Zimmerman, Larry, 2002 A Decade after the Vermillion Accord: What Has Changed and What Has Not. In The Dead and Their Possessions: Repatriation in Principle, Policy and Practice. Cressida Fforde, Jane Hubert, and Paul Turnbull, eds. Pp. 91–98. London: Routledge.

The Globalization of Archaeology and Heritage

A Discussion with Arjun Appadurai

One aspect of social archaeology is the historical and contemporary use of archaeology within nationalist movements. And yet, many would argue today that there are increasingly global processes that undermine the nation-state and its sovereign ownership of the national past. In his book *Modernity at Large* (1996), Arjun Appadurai dwells on issues of globalization and the relationship between modernity and tradition. For these reasons it was felt that a discussion with him might help to explore the contemporary role of a social archaeology devoted to that topic. Appadurai is also known to archaeologists for his work on material culture in *The Social Life of Things* (1986). So in sitting down to this interview we were interested in examining the broad question of the role of archaeology and material culture studies in a changing world, and in exploring links between social archaeology and wider interdisciplinary debates. The following discussion took place at Stanford University on 14 April 2000 between Arjun Appadurai, Ashish Chadha, Ian Hodder, Trinity Jackman and Chris Witmore.

TJ: It has been argued that the development of the discipline of archaeology was directly

Arjun Appadurai, "The Globalization of Archaeology and Heritage: A Discussion with Arjun Appadurai," pp. 35–49 from *Journal of Social Archaeology* 1 (2002). Reprinted with permission of Sage.

linked to the rise of nationalism and the spread of colonialism. In *Modernity at Large*, you write that the nation-state is entering a period of 'terminal crisis' and that culture is increasingly becoming an arena for conscious choice, justification and representation, the latter often to multiple and spatially dislocated audiences. If this process is coming about, do you see the 'politics of the past' becoming more intense as claims to the past increasingly proliferate? Or, do you think this fluidity and spatial dislocation will neutralize and de-politicize the past? Finally, what role do you imagine archaeology playing in these changes?

AA: My views have not changed but have become slightly more nuanced on the matter of the crisis of the nation-state. I think in *Modernity at Large* I might have overstated the terminality of the nation-state because I wanted to point to certain issues, but clearly the empirical evidence is mixed as to what exactly is going on. I still believe that there is a crisis. The question is what is the nature of that crisis. Now, I would say it's not a matter of a yes/no, terminus/ non-terminus, ending/non-ending, kind of apocalyptic debate, yet I am not convinced by the explanation that the nation-state is simply changing: this explanation is too banal, for it's always changing. I certainly think that there is a widening of the field of sovereignty. I would still argue that as corporations, grass-roots interest groups and the like have become more powerful, the nation-state is no longer the only player with large-scale claims to sovereignty. It must contend with being only one player among many. That seems to me certain. Whether it means the nation-state literally ends is another matter but I'm certainly ready to consider this possibility. I often say to people that the nation-state did not receive an eternal contract but developed historically, as archaeologists know, and can come and go. The question of what would constitute signs of a terminal crisis is an open question, but I would love to ask this question to those individuals who say the nation-state is alive and well.

So I think there is a crisis, and a complication of sovereignty, and that there is a question of multiple sovereignties etc. but I would not simply assert that the end of the nation-state is here, in a way I at least occasionally imply in the book. There is a normative impulse there too, and that impulse remains, as I'm not sure that the nation-state is the most desirable form for the management of large-scale human affairs. Its downside is, on the whole, more striking than its up-side. That is the background to the question of whether the reorganization of the experience and the structures of space and time will have a diffusing effect on the politics of the past or whether will they intensify it. At the moment, in so far as we can read the evidence, we see very little sign that the politics of the past are disappearing. I think they are stretching and deepening in lots of ways as more people become bi-national, multi-national or diasporic. The coherence of location and recollection cannot be taken for granted. A question that particularly interests me now apropos the nation-state is the shifting relationship between the politics of remembering and the politics of forgetting. Some people stress the business of remembering and that's quite justified for a lot of these groups, but not enough attention has been paid to the economy of forgetting and remembering in any given place or situation or in any given national space. In that economy, the nation-state plays a significant role in so far that it significantly controls the apparati through which the economy of remembering and forgetting is configured. The nation-state is in this respect a powerful player; media obviously plays a powerful independent role through documentaries, fiction, history channels, and popular memory and diasporic memory practices all join to complicate this field. Specific mechanisms for remembering and forgetting are still crucial to the national inflection of this economy. Here archaeology plays a vital role as it always has.

Professional archaeology is intimately tied to state institutions, national institutions and the ruling political party; as we saw during the recent World Archaeology Conference in Delhi[1] even the question of how archaeology could enter the space of conversation reminded us that archaeology is a key site through which the apparatus of nations can reflect the politics of remembering. It still remains very salient. In short, in so far as archaeology professionally remains very closely tied in many countries to what Étienne Balibar would call 'producing the people' it remains a critical player in the economy of remembering and forgetting. At some risk of exaggeration we could say that we must invert our weighting of the crude politics of erasure, of forgetting as opposed to that of recovery and remembering. The spatial diffusion of identities surely complicates the field within which the work of archaeology as a national discipline by and large exists.

AC: I ask this question in the context of recent reports about the targeting by right-wing archaeologists, government officials and academicians, of secular sites of Mughal India such as the Fatehpur Sikri which are claimed to be built upon destroyed Hindu temples. You mention in your book *Modernity at Large* that the diasporic community has played an important role along with electronic media in the withering of the nation-state, and has been responsible for the weakening of the hyphen between the nation and the state. How would you then explain the recent increase in NRI (Non-Resident Indian) funding to the Sangh Parivar organizations, whose politics are directly contributing to the strengthening of the nation, and of the state, especially when they are actively reinterpreting the past and denying any multivocality, thus contributing to the opposite of the effect that you talk about?

AA: Again, I would probably reformulate that in a less total form than the metaphor 'withering' would suggest. I do think that it is possible to go too far in one direction with the information on the NRIs. Though the NRI factor is important, no one has shown how important it is, i.e. does the Sangh Parivar fundamentally rely on it? Is it just an add-on? Who needs whom more? Do the NRIs need them more or does the Sangh Parivar need the NRIs more?

Obviously, there are many worrisome developments in the history of India in the 150 years, arguably in the last 400 to 500 years, in the relations between 'Hindus' and 'Muslims'. These developments continued through the colonial period, etc., through the Partition and finally have been woven into the party politics of the present. So there is what in *Modernity at Large* I would have called a history as well as a genealogy to this relationship. The genealogy may look out to the NRI phenomena, but the history does not. My cautionary statement would be to not over-emphasize the salience of what the NRIs are doing or what the BJP (Bharatiya Janata Party) and its allies are doing. These activities may be very important for the NRIs, but I think that it is essential to ask exactly who within this vague category they are important to and in what precise NRI project such interests come to be important.

Once you ask that question, it connects to the earlier part of your query, which concerns the issue of space. Some of these activities are profoundly bifocal and seem clearly to be about what Benedict Anderson calls 'long-distance nationalism'. He has parenthetically suggested that such interventions are somewhat illegitimate and have often got to do with a reproduction of cultural practices driven by anxieties about identity here in the United States, or wherever the non-resident Indian may be, in England, Hong Kong, etc. My conception of a diasporic public sphere does not generate such draconian criticisms of long-distance nationalism.

It is not clear to me how one can read these processes in terms of contemporary Indian politics, in particular the question of the nation and the state in India. How can we be sure what is being fortified? How can we be sure what is being advanced? In fact, is it the project of the Indian nation that is being advanced, or is the effort to delete other histories, other groups (Muslims notably) actually producing new crises of hegemony in India? It is not self-evident that these inputs are simply fortifying, consolidating and drowning everything else. They might, in fact, be complicating the task of producing a hegemonic consensus in India.

As far as the state is concerned, on the other side of the hyphen, so to speak, it is even less clear what NRI support, whether fiscal or otherwise, means to the Sangh Parivar. What is the value of their support to the project of the state, broadly speaking, to development, to the theory of justice, to state economics? I am inclined to think that the issue is less the question of NRIs (though they are surely a part of it), than the contradiction, which is now very widespread but takes a particular form in India and elsewhere, between the opening of the market and the closing of national cultural space. The BJP-led coalition that rules India is certainly involved in this contradiction. Just the other day, we saw that the Indian Minister of Commerce and Industry, Murasoli Maran, has announced that there will be a flood of new opportunities for the middle classes to buy consumer goods, without licenses and restrictions. So, the market is opening wide, while the space for cultural plurality is shrinking. This perspective is related to the kind of argument about globalization that people like Samuel Huntington and Benjamin Barber and others have made. But I think we need a more complex picture of how the opening of markets relates to cultural closure, and here we should focus on the market ideology of the ruling coalition, in which the NRI story is a part, but certainly not the entire story.

Going back to the beginning of your question. I think it is clear that there is a continuing, but not very apparent, pressure on a party like the BJP, as they open the market, to find new ways of establishing their credentials as the trustees of cultural sovereignty, of cultural purity, cultural authenticity. This guardianship acts in their favor because they are caught between the pressure of their commercial supporters to favor liberalization, but also to account to their hardline ideological supporters, notably the RSS (Rashtriya Swayamsevak Sangh) for their pro-Hindu credentials. And one option is certainly to move towards some kind of mono-ethnic nationalism, which can then become xenophobic and even turn genocidal.

I think that there is a story to be told about the actual politics of the monuments and the politics of the 'layering', so to speak, and the narrative of the layer. Underneath the material presence of Islamic ruins is a whole living material world of human monuments, and the earlier narrative of submergence is now being complemented with a narrative of destruction, the narrative of a project of architectural submergence that the Muslims had allegedly undertaken, which has to be unpeeled from the top to reveal a kind of landscape. This politics of layers brings together contemporary spatial politics, such as the demolitions of slums, with the deep politics of monuments and archaeology.

This relationship is part of what I am struggling with now in Bombay. In some sense, urban spaces, increasingly, are being re-inscribed as national spaces or national

soil, and a lot of the practices of ethnic rioting and violence in Bombay can be seen as violent practices of spatial re-inscription, so that, to take one example from the rumors that spread during the ethnic riots of 1992–93, the coastline of Bombay needs protection against the Pakistanis – a kind of implosion of two landscapes. So where does the story of the temples and the mosques, the double layer, with the Hindu layer underneath, fit into this global project, particularly that of reconstructing urban spaces? Which people are ritually and politically mobilized to be associated with the kind of ethnic violence which occurred in Bombay? This kind of re-writing of cities as national spaces, requiring protection, requiring fortification, requiring defense and so on, is constantly occurring. Something is moving between the centers and the borders. From this point of view, you can view the Babri Masjid as the center in the national imagination and military borders, territorial borders and the recent war with Pakistan as borders. And somewhere in between, there are these cities, which are not the centers, but where you can re-play the Babri Masjid story, by attacking a mosque in Bombay. In this, there is not just the simple replication of the events but also a complicated rewriting of these spaces as markedly national, not just as routine components of the national.

So, to return to the question of NRIs. We need to distinguish between the question of the NRIs, which is important in its own right, the question of whether or not the BJP is deepening its own crisis in regard to economic opening and cultural closure, and the question of the politics of trying to find an undisturbed Hindu layer through archaeological practices. I would pull these questions slightly apart and not bring them together very tightly yet.

CW: We recently had a member of a local Native American tribe, Otis Parish (Kashaya Pomo), as a visitor to Stanford who, along with his community, is overseeing a set of unique excavations upon tribal land along a stretch of the Californian coastline just north of San Francisco. This community has taken traditional scientific methods of archaeological excavation, which are seen as universalizing, and made them 'safe' in a hybridized form through the incorporation of ritual. Here we have an example, in the context of archaeology, of a blending of local tradition and science as a facet of modernity. Concomitantly, the story that is being brought to light is one of continuity with the past. Is it possible to address the question of how notions of the theory of rupture, transition and fracture between modernity and tradition, explicit in your work *Modernity at Large*, can be understood and articulated in such a situation where that distinction is purposely blurred? In this particular case the global/local dynamic can also be highlighted since this is a local issue, which is broadcast globally through the Internet.

AA: That is a very interesting and challenging question in two or three different ways. On the one hand, it speaks to a kind of basic dilemma in anthropology and in the humanities and social sciences more generally. We keep deconstructing the idea of the primordial and the primordialist thesis. Yet all sorts of groups act on the assumption that their peoplehood is primordially real. We can say that there is something wrong with the latter view, that it is a form of false consciousness that ethnic or religious groups such as the Serbs or the Hindus may have. People seem to operate without questioning how they transfer 'things' from the historical to the non-historical and thus, somehow, to the physical, hardwired, biological, racial, etc. So people faced with peculiarly modern dilemmas tell a story about who 'we' are which is time-deep, unambiguous and primordial. My response to this point of view is that both the question and the answer are very modern.

There are certain questions that never arise except under these conditions of modernity. A specific example is the question of long-term materially certified authenticity. Some kind of tribal or other identity itself only arises under the conditions of

modern debate about who you are, what your claims are and where you would stake them; and again the nation-state affects the terms of this debate in a specific way. This is due to the fact that it has, in the US for example, put into place the idea that genuine claims to certain forms of community have to be anchored in some kind of spatial sovereignty. Once you have that argument in place then claims to some type of special standing or autonomy, as in the case of most Native American groups, have to be somehow connected up to a story of spaces that are 'ours' over the long run, stories of originality. It is not just that the answer and the ways of answering rely on modernity, but that the question too comes out of debates about who we are and what our claims are, which in turn could not have happened except under the conditions of modernity.

I sense something else in your question of why this orientation to deep-time exists. It is the question of continuity vs. rupture. One could say that certain tropes of continuity and certain ways of materializing continuity, which would bring archaeology into the picture, become particularly salient under conditions of rupture. Here it is only *when* the question of peopleness comes into play, that the national and the archaeological, as mediated by the social sciences more generally, seem to acquire special relations. It is not so much the case that the question is modern and the answer is traditional: I think both are from the same sort of conditions. This is not the kind of debate about deep continuity that you might find, I think, if you had access to inscriptional records from the thirteenth century. You would get other statements about who we are, why we are special and so on, but you would not get this notion of deep-time, unbroken continuity and so on. Such discourses may be themselves historical, and modern.

CW: In the historical situation I was referring to before, approximately 150 years ago a Russian trading post was founded upon this stretch of coast, which opened up these indigenous populations to the outside world through the fur trade. Processes of globalization present at that time had a profound impact upon their conception of identity and understandings of tradition. Believing these contacts to be dangerous, they eventually closed themselves off from the outside world and only in the 1950s did they again make contact. Extreme caution toward the outside world has been a practice for over a century with this tribe. And so when I mentioned how this community dealt with the universalizing process of the scientific method, something that can be associated with modernity and the global, I wished to play upon that dynamic where the global is brought into, utilized and made necessarily safe in a local context through ritual and then is projected back globally through the Internet. This invention of a 'local tradition' is not only heavily influenced by the global but is meant to have influence globally.

AA: The invention of tradition argument does not invite one adequately to ask whether people invent tradition as they please, just like history. And the answer is *no*. They invent it under conditions that are themselves historical. In this case you are pointing to one set of conditions where there is an expanding world and then a shrinking world so that depending on the group in question they are not in a linear progression, but work in ebbs and flows.

Amitav Ghosh, in his book *In an Antique Land* (1992), suggests that we are less cosmopolitan now than we were in the pre-modern epoch in the region of the Indian Ocean. It is an interesting argument and for someone like me it is very challenging. This is not because I have a linear evolutionary view, but I have not known very well how to engage with earlier cosmopolitanisms, earlier global contacts and divisions. I am now trying to reconnect *The Social Life of Things* argument to the *Modernity at Large* essays. I see there is something important to do in reconnecting the idea of commodities and the realities of their movement explicitly to the

arguments found in *Modernity at Large*. For a long time. I had not quite seen that *Modernity at Large* is very much animated by the same sorts of impulses as in *The Social Life of Things*.

IH: One of the themes that was very interesting in the Otis Parrish example was that he was taking the scientific archaeological methods and embedding them in rituals, so that the excavation would take place in the context of, for example, prayer or dance. That raises the wider issue of how we deal with different forms of knowledge, including non-academic forms of knowledge, and how we provide institutional arrangements for better dialogue. The Parrish example is about science and ritual knowledge coming together. I wonder whether you could say something more general about the problems of dealing with different forms of knowledge, perhaps specifically in relation to the past, museums and heritage and how we can provide structures to deal with these sorts of relationships.

AA: I am glad that you highlighted that interesting dimension. I can enter into the debate about multiple knowledges through the idea in the last chapter of *Modernity at Large* about the production of locality. The question is 'what are the kinds of conditions under which locality is produced?' Sometimes it is produced with explicitly hybridizing techniques like the ones that have been mentioned. In such cases the aim is to produce the local, but it is found expedient or compelling to do so by bringing in the discourse of science. Science is introduced into a space which was otherwise separate from it in order to more fully, more plausibly, more attractively and more credibly, perhaps to a wider public sphere, produce the local.

So for me one part of the scaffolding for considering multiple knowledges would be the conditions under which locality is produced. There is a set of historical conditions, at different points in time and space, in which the production of the local involves a quite complicated traffic in knowledges. Sometimes that traffic seems thinner or less stressed, less hybrid, less negotiated. But in the particular case you mention there is a more conscious negotiation in order at the end of the day to somehow both produce a local that is more durable and is also produced in a way that is more credible. The claims are made through a certified apparatus of truth, which is what archaeology in this case is taken to be. It is taken to somehow ratify or sustain the production of a pattern that might otherwise seem more vulnerable.

Important issues surround efforts to conserve, materialize, record and represent heritages for broad publics. One angle on that might be the distinction that my friend and colleague Valentine Daniel (1996) makes in his recent book on Sri Lankan ethnic violence between history and heritage. He tries to speak of these as two modalities associated with Sri Lankans and Tamils as they apprehend the past of that island, and he makes a very sharp normative, or ideal-typic, break between the two, while recognizing that leakages between them do occur. Such distinctions are salient to the question of museum building practices at the end of this century and concern, among other things, whether museums should properly be speaking about history or about heritage? In Val Daniel's terms, heritage becomes a more fixed, a more worrisome and more essentialist notion, and history becomes more open and more mobile. If museums are going to be about history, how can this be achieved when their very materiality as well as the disciplines which produce them conduce to the other type of typological fixity?

There is another angle on these issues that I would like to bring out. I am thinking here of issues such as the contestation of the past, archaeology as a discipline, museums as institutions. I am also thinking of the retrieval of the material, and of the fact that nation-states or, in the broadest sense, national imaginations require (as Fredric Jameson might put it) signatures of the visible, and that museums and archaeology

as a practice are about signatures of the visible. I think we have choices both in what archaeology does in its practices as a discipline and in what museums that are driven by excavation can do.

I want to make just one point about this that I think deserves development. In the general business of retrieving the past, remembering, materializing that memory and further commemorating it, leads directly to the business of the nation, and in does so through certain regimes or techniques of truth provided mainly by archaeology. This process, and I think this is not just true of history but of all social practices of recollection, ties into my interest in ethnic violence and returns to the question of what large-scale violence is about, whether in Eastern Europe or India or Rwanda or anywhere else. In such contexts, there are forms of recollection that do not seem to require the elimination of other memories, and there are other forms of recollection which seem more, to use a term I am trying to develop, predatory. That is, they seem to be premised on that idea that for them to subsist something else must go. So one of my big concerns now is why certain identities, which are parts of pairs or sets which have been in some form of workable juxtaposition at a certain point in time, become predatory. Why does one of them, or sometimes both, become animated by the idea that there is only room for one of them? When and under what circumstances does this happen?

This is a broad and challenging comparative question. But with regard to archaeology and museums, it seems to me one could ask whether a particular exercise in excavation or in documentation or in museumization is going by its form and nature to tend towards predation, which is to say the exclusion of others. How can one organize things so that there is an opening of memory in which there is room for others, for contesting perspectives and so on? I have no clear idea about how one might put items into an exhibit hall in such a way as to discourage predation. That is a complex question for museum curators, but in principle it seems to me to be one consideration to be taken up. One can look at opening exhibits to debate. One can look at using modern information technologies in a non-superficial manner in so-called interactive exhibits. There are many such possibilities, but unless you have good answers to the central question, even excellent answers to exhibit presentation issues will not make museums benign places.

IH: We could go on and talk about 'origins' because very often issues concerning the display of the past get linked to the question of origins. There I think we would have to think through whether it is possible to claim an origin without excluding, and whether the search for origins is not always predatory.

But can I move on to our final topic which is to do with the authentic. I would like to bring up the idea of the commodification of the past and the role that is playing in globalization. You talk in *Modernity at Large* about the past being placed into museums, and the past becoming less a *habitus* and more a choice. One can go from there to wider questions of choice in the marketing of nostalgia, and to ideas of pastiche and depthlessness. But archaeologists often observe that many people today remain absolutely absorbed in the past as real and authentic. The search for the authentic, however much commodification goes on, is very strong. So tourists will ask 'is this produced by indigenous people?', and 'who exactly produced it; how authentic is it?' and so on. There is a fascination with the authentic which is not necessarily reducible to nationalism. The public point of view is not always 'this is my...'. Rather visitors or tourists say 'I want to have the real thing' and they presume that 'real' things have higher market value. I wondered if you could make sense of this fascination for the authentic in a very highly commodified world where the past too has become commodified.

AA: The whole field of the authentic in whatever domain, in tourism or whatever else, is very important to continue to study. I have different kinds of responses. One is that just as particular kinds of authentication through tradition are parts of particularly modern debates about identity that may not have occurred before, likewise the pursuit of the signature – 'who really made this' – arises under the empire of the commodity. The endless effort to singularize, as my colleague Igor Kopytoff would say, occurs because of the constant expansion of the empire of the commodity so that the two (the singular and the commodity) are like scorpions in a bottle constantly feeding off each other. I have begun to write a little essay on the gift in the age of the commodity, playing with the idea of what gifting in this context might mean. In a fully commodified culture, what gift is there that has any singularity to it? Who could possibly make a singular gift other than by cutting off their hands or something like that? Even then it is not clear what you would have to do to be absolutely singular. So the force that you refer to is perfectly understandable in such a context.

I think there are two choices here and I am not sure how one might referee or arbitrate between them. One is to say that the urge you describe is strictly accounted for by the energy of its other, and tourism is the perfect case in that people want precisely to be only there themselves, wanting the unspoilt place. The eternal trope of the travel journals is 'this place is unspoilt, so go find it'. The place then will thus no longer be unspoilt but still you got there first. So the two things are literally two sides of the one coin. But I think there is another way to think about these tensions which is both more benign and more worrisome. This is when one says that there is a metaphysics of presence and recollection and rootedness which is independent of the question of the commodity. That is, people are always seeking to anchor themselves in a relatively unmediated material world that sustains their sense of themselves, their cultural worlds, their modes of signification. It is in that world that the world of the commodity intervenes. So there is an endless search for the margins, for the place where the commodity is not yet king, where one is slightly free of it. In such places one may feel, not entirely without justification, that one has found the signature, found the maker, nailed the case so to speak. Such a space would not be produced by the working of the commodity but would be seen as residual but free of the relentless expansion of commodification.

I don't know how one would arbitrate between these views and I have a feeling one cannot do so deductively. One would have to look at the practice. One would have to look at the actor or the institution and analyze the claims that are being made, the practices, the justifications and the debates and then assign them to one or the other situation. I could accept that some groups, especially some groups that have to struggle for the means of cultural survival, attach themselves to this or that object, space, monument etc. in a manner that is precisely not predatory, which is only about survival and dignity, which does not require someone else to disappear. I am perfectly prepared to see that exercise and that effort as not driven by the dynamics of the commodity. It is driven by something else that may have its own dangers from a Foucauldian perspective – that is it may be humanistic in a limited way. But it would not have the problem of being just the other of the commodity. So, briefly, I am less inclined than I and others would have been five or ten years ago to see authenticity always invariably as the sign of something else negative. Now I am prepared to see that there may be legitimate strivings for connections to the material world and to the past.

In the whole business of identity and ethnicity and so on which preoccupies me now and which is not at all unconnected to the materialities of mosques and destructions of collections, heritage and so on, I have come to see that there are processes and projects of identity building which are fundamentally future-driven. They are 'projects', you might say. And there are the others that are fundamentally driven by the past, at least in their self-understanding. My sense is that

those that are projected usually are likely not to be predatory. But those that are excessively driven by the past tend to crowd others out. Why this should be so is not clear to me.

IH: I am digging in Turkey at the moment. When tourists visit this 9000-year-old site, quite a number of them stay quite a long time. Some have worked hard reading about the site, or it may have a religious value to them. It's a site where the Goddess is supposed to originate. They get a feeling of authentic association with that place even though they have only been there a short period of time. Such diasporic tourists have a sense of locality which is global. They move around as part of their holidays or their searching lives, creating a sense of an authentic relationship with the past in a number of different localities. They put together a story of themselves which is a product of that tour through the past or through time and space. One begins to get this notion of people constructing multiple authentic identities on a global scale. This observation then problematizes the opposition between the global and the local in relation to the past in a very clear way. And then of course there are many imagined communities, like groups in Europe who think they are Native Americans. There are people constructing real authentic relationships with the past that are very separate from them, which are very multiple, and they can move through them. They construct their sense of identity by putting all that together in complex ways.

AA: I have not reflected very much about that kind of experience, that kind of authentication, but the mediating term there would be 'lifestyle'. That is, you acquire a lifestyle, a way of being, assuming the time and money and leisure, in which the delinkage of a single location from a single authentic history is now made possible. But the worry about it is that there is something fundamentally unstable, frivolous or over-privileged about it. That is always the worry about these kinds of complex

Bohemian habits of self-authentication. They are dubious because they are so restricted.

IH: Of course the ability to travel and tourism are restricted, but there are nowadays huge numbers involved in a variety of income groups.

AA: I am very sympathetic to that fact, but I think that the more complex experiential aggregation of memories in relation to places and so on requires more than travel; it requires a whole series of other things. Not that the growing practices of travel are always elitist or exclusive (in the age of mass tourism) but I think they are necessarily partial and occasional experiences. I do not think their specialness disqualifies them in any way. It just opens the question of what kind of requirements are there for having this experience. But you are quite right, in that whatever these experiences are, if one takes them seriously they open other ways to connect space, history, materiality.

IH: It is perhaps important to consider travel as a mechanism and metaphor for relating to the past in order to try and get away from the idea that someone owns the past.

AA: Yes, the property dimension is a little bit connected to something I tried to develop up to a point a long time ago in a completely different context. This is the idea of the past as a scarce resource. In 1981 I published an essay based on my research on a temple and its history, in the British journal *Man*. That debate about the past happens within certain normative parameters. It was a sort of anti-Malinowski argument. One could, of course, think about the past as a boundless resource, endlessly open to variety, elaboration, re-invention and social empowerment. But if indeed the past is a scarce resource, because its construction is subject to cultural as well as material constraints, this means that the economy which governs the production of the past has to be examined even more critically. Specifically, since the most violent social dramas of recent times have involved those contexts in which the material past has been converted into national or ethnic property, it may be helpful to encourage more plural appropriations of the past, such as those encouraged by tourism and travel. So we find ourselves on the horns of our largest contemporary dilemma: whether to be slaves in the empire of the commodity or puppets in the shadow of the state. Recognizing that the past does have an economy, and debating the forms and functions of that economy, may yet point to a way out of this impasse. And archaeology, always and legitimately concerned about the material past, may hold a large part of the answers for an ethics and a politics appropriate to this ambiguous future.

Note

1 The third World Archaeological Conference was hosted in New Delhi by the Archaeological Society of India in December 1994.

References

Appadurai, A. (1981) 'The Past as a Scarce Resource', *Man* (N.S.) 6(2): 201–19.

Appadurai, A., ed. (1986) *The Social Life of Things: Commodities in Cultural Perspective*. Cambridge: Cambridge University Press.

Appadurai, A. (1996) *Modernity at Large: Cultural Dimensions of Globalization*. Minneapolis: University of Minnesota Press.

Daniel, E. V. (1996) *Charred Lullabies: Chapters in an Anthropology of Violence*. Princeton: Princeton University Press.

Ghosh, A. (1992) *In an Antique Land*. London: Granta Publishers.

26

Sites of Violence
Terrorism, Tourism, and Heritage in the Archaeological Present

Lynn Meskell

Locating and materializing ethics in archaeology remains a relatively recent undertaking in part because of the illusion that the subjects of our research are dead and buried and our research goals are paramount. Archaeologists have traditionally operated on the assumption that they are not implicated in the representation and struggles of living peoples and that all such political engagement is negatively charged. Field praxis and the production of heritage sites and their ramifications have only recently come to be considered serious research loci (Fotiadis 1993; Meskell 1998, 2002b; Politis 2001; Scham and Yahya 2003). It has also taken time to persuade archaeologists that ours is a subjective and political enterprise that is far from agenda-free. The primacy of positivist archaeology, particularly in North America, has postponed a sustained disciplinary engagement with ethical discourse (Meskell 2002a). But a new generation of archaeologists is increasingly aware of both the centrality and the embedded nature of ethics (Blundell 1998; Byrne 2003; Colwell-Chanthaphonh 2003a, 2003b; Shepherd 2003; Watkins 2001). We are also witnessing a greater convergence between archaeological and ethnographic practices – field projects in which the two disciplines

Lynn Meskell, "Sites of Violence: Terrorism, Tourism, and Heritage in the Archaeological Present," pp. 123–46 from Lynn Meskell and Peter Pels (eds) *Embedding Ethics* (Oxford: Berg, 2005). Reprinted with permission of Berg Publishers c/o A C Black.

are combined and practitioners with interests in all dimensions of cultural heritage, past and present.

This chapter explores the entwined politics of archaeology in Egypt, specifically around the village of Gurna (West Bank, Luxor), where the preservation of ancient monuments has taken precedence over the needs of the living. It charts political developments over the past decade including government directives for the creation of an open-air archaeological museum and the local community's resistance to its forced relocation. Tensions between the archaeological community, the government, and locals about ethical issues of looting and preservation have been juxtaposed with the use of state-sanctioned violence toward the Gurnawis. As a result, the community has mobilized to create its own museum, which celebrates Gurna's recent past and architectural traditions rather then focusing on its pharaonic heritage. This alternative construction of heritage de-privileges the famous New Kingdom tombs upon which the modern community is situated and expresses concern for the villagers' economic livelihood and traditions. This effectively inverts the prioritizing of past over present that is dominant in the nation-state's vision of heritage and modernity. The chapter also examines a key episode in the ongoing violence surrounding Luxor, the massacre at the Temple of Hatshepsut in 1997. Since tourism and terrorism have come to be inextricably linked in recent years, the discussion fore-grounds the tensions surrounding presentation of the pharaonic past at the expense of later periods in Egyptian history, specifically that of Islamic Egypt. In examining the Egyptian tourist industry and its role in national development, one can see how performing the past has proven a necessary, albeit fraught, endeavor in the context of Islamic nationhood.

More generally, I hope to expose the ramifications of an unthinking attitude toward archaeological heritage, especially for archaeologists working outside their own countries, and its implications for local communities that may fall outside the boundaries of the national imaginary. Archaeologists have been eager to tackle issues of politics and nationalism in the past decade but less inclined to venture onto the slippery terrain of intranational struggles and the connections between diverse groups and constructions of heritage. The latter have local and global impacts upon the practices of tourism, another critical area that has been neglected by archaeologists (see Blundell 1998; Logan and Leone 1997; Meskell 2001; Odermatt 1996), remaining the purview of anthropologists and sociologists (see, for example, Boniface and Fowler 1993; Castañeda 1996; Chambers 1997; Edensor 1998; Franklin and Crang 2001; Herbert 1995; Kirshenblatt-Gimblett 1998; MacCannell 1992, 2000, 2001; Rojek and Urry 1997; Urry 1990). An emergent literature in tourist studies foregrounds the importance of archaeological places as the sites around which narratives of heritage and identity fuse. Drawing on examples from Egypt, specifically the village of Gurna, I attempt to show the interconnectedness between heritage, tourism, and violence at both the real and the symbolic level, suggesting that archaeologists must become more cognizant of their roles in broader political spatialities. An emergent ethics in archaeology must tackle archaeology, heritage, tourism, and national modernity as they coalesce in the countries in which we work and live.

Heritage and Modernity in Ethical Context

A concern with ethics should ideally inflect all modes of archaeological praxis, including fieldwork, publication, education, stewardship, preservation, and, axiomatically, all archaeological engagements with the historical legacies of other communities. One way to ensure responsible archaeology at home and, to some degree, abroad is by crafting codes or guidelines for good practice. Ethical codes and programmatic statements have traditionally been developed under the auspices of national bodies such as the Society for American Archaeology (SAA) in the United States and the Australian Archaeological Association (AAA) in Australia, where local issues of indigeneity are paramount (Lilley 2000; Lynott and Wylie 2000). Yet a genealogy of ethics highlights the dearth of writing on the conduct of archaeology in foreign countries, where practitioners and situational interests take on more complex layerings. How are issues of representation reconciled when archaeologists are separated but not disentangled from the construction and effects of national heritage? I have noted elsewhere that problems inhere in the global legislation and classificatory regulations surrounding the notion of "world heritage" (Meskell 2002b). One consistent theme emerges throughout: all engagements surrounding archaeological heritage must be examined in context.

Archaeologists are gradually starting to interrogate the discipline's public face, specifically our responsibilities to many different constituencies. At issue are the discursive technologies of the self as academician and fieldworker in a variety of contexts – most notably in foreign domains. Archaeologists have rather different concerns from ethnographers, who have long been instrumental in the service of the state, particularly in times of war and counterinsurgency (Pels 1999:110–111). Although the latter have always maintained a higher profile, archaeologists have been similarly involved in politics through negotiations with governments, World Bank consultants, tourist agencies, heritage brokers, local communities, and myriad individuals. It is no longer possible to speak simply of the dual relationship between the researcher and the data – the "dead subjects" of an archaeological past. In an archaeological present we confront influential third parties with authoritative values and protocols. Whether we are involved to the same degree as our anthropological colleagues is difficult to determine, since so little historiographical critique has emerged. Under the influence of postprocessualism the older vision of "pure" academic research has been occluded by political realities including the indigenization of archaeology, the passage of the Native American Graves Protection and Repatriation Act, the Balkan crisis, and the Gulf War (Meskell 2002a). Within the disciplinary context of anthropology, Pels (2000:163) has identified the possibility of an emergent ethics no longer tied to a specific community but entangled in a much larger, more pervasive network. Strathern (2000a:280) takes this farther, arguing that while "anthropological models of society and culture once provided a cue to the conduct of encounters, now such encounters are to be governed by professional protocols which create altogether different kinds of interacting subjects."

Ethics is essentially a theory of social relations rather than a transcendent entity or body of facts. What we see in heritage legislation is a utilitarian ethic that operates as a standard for judging public action, aiming to satisfy the majority's preferences (Goodin 1991:241, 245). Individual utilities are aggregated into an overall measure of social utility that has obvious shortcomings, among them an assumed comparability of individuals. This assumption gives rise to problems when cultural difference is interpolated, as it is in the heritage sphere. This has serious consequences for the production of ethical codes, because such codification can represent inert knowledge rather than knowledge produced in response to the context of application (Pels 1999:113). We must acknowledge the shifting nature of global political contexts, most recently demonstrated in the deployment of archaeological sites and materials for political purposes in Afghanistan and Iraq. Numerous attempts to regulate archaeology and archaeologists have been made by the Society for American Archaeology (SAA), the International Committee on Archaeological Heritage Management (ICAHM), the Society of Professional Archaeologists (SOPA), and others (Scham 1998:304). These codes or guidelines are not redundant; rather, they constitute a locus for further interrogation – texts produced at specific times and places that signify certain practices and mentalities. Ethics and politics are inseparable, and therein lies the danger; they are

peculiarly local. When we consider legislating internationally or creating mandates that would have an impact on living communities in other cultural contexts, dialogue and negotiation are key (for an excellent example, see Colwell-Chanthaphonh and Ferguson 2004). Essentially we need to be vigilant in self-monitoring, self-evaluation, and the sharpening of our moral sense.

In the field of heritage there has been considerable debate over the moral and political implications of the words "property," "patrimony," "heritage," "resources," and "treasures," and while the term "cultural heritage" is objectionable to some because of its implicit moral claims, it may be expedient when discussing the ethics of studying, owning, and preserving the past (Messenger 1999:254). In uncritically subscribing to certain dominant ethical perspectives surrounding the heritage of other cultures we are espousing *ethical absolutism* – imposing a single system on local moral values. An alternative position could be described as *moral relativism,* which acknowledges cultural difference and context and opposes interference with other cultures' moralities: different societies legitimately follow different rules (Buckle 1991:173). Relinquishing our power to intervene in the affairs of others may have uncomfortable repercussions, and some of our aesthetic determinations will inevitably be compromised. The most recent example of this conflict can be seen in the Taliban's destruction of the Bamiyan Buddhas and the resulting outcry from Western commentators (Colwell-Chanthaphonh 2003a; Gamboni 2001; Meskell 2002b).

International charters concerning heritage coalesce around three constructs: rights of ownership, rights of access, and rights of inheritance. The notion of rights was ostensibly propounded by the likes of Grotius and Locke, but whereas the eighteenth-century notion was protective and negative, attempting to limit the power of governments over their subjects, the modern concept includes rights to various forms of welfare. The latter actually justifies the extension of government in the pursuit of social wealth, comfort, or economic advantage (Almond 1991:260). Legal rights and moral rights are not necessarily coterminous, and some purely legal rights can be deleterious to the individual. And what of the rights of others, especially those with whom we disagree? If a right can be linked to prohibiting interference by others, rights can be read as benefits that are open to many, among them diverse communities with variant beliefs and perspectives.

The creation of heritage is a culturally generative act that is intrinsically political. Heritage consultants and archaeologists could be said to invent culture and, in the process, constitute heritage (Hufford 1994:5). Heritage itself has a history and mirrors the divisions of the world formulated by academies and other cultural and scientific institutions. Legislative measures from the 1960s and 1970s designated three arenas: (1) nature (natural species and ecosystems), (2) the built environment (artifacts, buildings, sites, and districts), and (3) folk life/culture (living artistic expressions and traditional communities). Each sphere had its professionals, legislative mandates, public and private supporters, and assorted goals and visions (Hufford 1994:2). However, some forms of heritage take precedence over others, some types of folk life or culture are deemed undesirable, and particular sites are privileged over communities with their own living cultures. Heritage is iterated and enforced by the multinational bodies with which archaeologists frequently interact. The most powerful organizations, such as UNESCO, the International Council on Monuments and Sites (ICOMOS), or the World Bank, are multinational in structure, but Western member states are usually responsible for establishing procedures. Nawal El Saadawi (1997:56) insists that the wave of violence surrounding tourism in Egypt can be linked to the neocolonialist operations of United Nations organizations and development agencies including the General Agreement on Tariffs and Trade, the World Bank, and the International Monetary Fund. Decision making may be orchestrated at the national or the global level, while the serious consequences are most often experienced at the local level.

It could be argued that the construct of "global world heritage" is, in part, a remnant of colonialism. Intimately tied to an Enlightenment project of exploration and knowledge, preserving and showcasing global heritage is always construed as serving a "common good" that purportedly fulfills universal aims. Archaeology is deeply imbued with colonialist residues.

Benedict Anderson demonstrated decades ago that while colonial regimes in South Asia sought to link monumental archaeology and tourism, promoting an image of the state as guardian of local tradition, ultimately archaeological spaces operated as performative regalia for the colonizers (Anderson 1983:181–182). Colonizing the monumentality of the past – a process that has its roots in bygone centuries – has served to separate countries such as India and Egypt from their past glories and future potentials in the service of the ruling empire. Egypt and its riches are still seen as a global resource and hence responsibility, involving heritage managers, conservators, planners, funding bodies, and international organizations. However, archaeologists today occupy the positions of facilitator and manager, this time in the service of Egypt as a modern nation. Some might claim that we also facilitate our academic ventures; none of us should forget that we are making a living from archaeology (Pyburn and Wilk 2000:79).

Foundational to colonial imperatives was the notion that subject cultures required management and regimes for articulating, mapping, and controlling resources such as their monumental past. Following these directives, individuals and organizations still insist that modern Egyptians are incapable of managing these resources, that they must be effectively administered and controlled by the West. Although ultimate decision making resides with the Egyptian antiquities service, it relies heavily on international archaeological investment for both fieldwork and preservation. One example is the effort of UNESCO and German engineers to relocate Abu Simbel after the construction of the Aswan High Dam. UNESCO's funding of the Nubia Museum in Aswan is another high-profile initiative that has become embroiled in controversy over questions of ethnicity, citizenship, and transnational culture (Smith 1999). Organizations such as UNESCO and the World Bank make recommendations and implement schemes that assign patrimony to certain groups and situate the extant traditions of groups, whether Nubians or Gurnawis, in new relationships that produce new notions of humanity's "common cultural foundation." This removes the local and undermines difference in the service of the global. Heritage sites act as markers that signify the identity of the place and its rank within the scheme of world heritage. And the prime mover for these designations is commonly international tourism, which ultimately universalizes culture and society within an implicitly Western framework (Lanfant, Allcock, and Bruner 1995). As archaeologists and heritage practitioners, we are entering a new era of accountability in which we are increasingly answerable to an ever-expanding web of institutions and individuals (Strathern 2000b), not least the foreign communities in which we work.

Touring Places and the Spaces of Resistance

In 1991 Egypt reformed its economic system to embrace liberalization and privatization, including deregulation and financial stimuli to attract private-sector interest. The Egyptian minister for tourism and civil aviation claimed that the government's pricing policy reflected market forces, and, with the floating of the Egyptian pound, the country has been able to keep prices low, making travel to Egypt for foreigners attractive (Jenner and Smith 1993:134). The early 1990s also witnessed major changes in the operations of the Egyptian state tourism organization. A tourism development unit was created with funding from UN agencies, the World Bank, private banks, and the Ministry of Tourism. The World Bank and the Egyptian government undertook a joint project to develop a US$300 million fund to preserve the environment in the face of tourist development (Jenner and Smith 1993:140–141). Despite its accounting for only 1.2 percent of the gross domestic product, tourism remains Egypt's largest single source of foreign exchange earnings (approximately 23 percent), generating around US$3 billion annually in 1998–2000 and employing 145,000 people (Huband 2001:134). Since the political instability and violence of the early 1990s the market has been inclined toward specific sectors: the young budget traveler, the diver, and the domestic traveler.

The tourist industry combines services, culture, and ethnicity and results in a product that unifies and packages society, culture, and identity. It exploits cultural heritage as a resource to be maximized (Lanfant, Allcock, and Bruner

1995:98–99). In numerous tourism publications, economists seek to quantify these elusive sociocultural factors in their cost-benefit analyses, but economic changes are commonly imputed to be positive and sociocultural ones negative, thereby widening the gap between the two (Lanfant, Allcock, and Bruner 1995:109). For the people of Egypt, the economic benefits of tourism are often less than anticipated. North American and Western European companies are responsible for the majority of the tourist investment in the developing world, and this is by no means a charitable venture; the transnationals involved retain the bulk of this tourist expenditure, only 22–25 percent of the retail price remaining in the host country (Urry 1990:64–65). Thus we have to ask whether many developing countries have alternatives to tourism as a development strategy. While there are serious economic as well as social costs, in the absence of alternatives developing countries have little choice but to develop their attractiveness as objects of the gaze of tourists from North America, Western Europe, and Japan. According to Urry (1990:132), the sovereignty of the consumer and trends in popular taste combine to transform the museum's social role. As we will see in the case of the planned open-air museum at Gurna, the overwhelming mass of the population will inevitably be excluded, and this exclusion is linked to a transformation of the nature of citizenship. People who live in a particular place have enjoyed certain rights and duties by virtue of that residence; citizenship has been not just a matter of national rights and duties but also a matter of locality (Urry 1995:220). While heritage politics generally concerns the local, the specificities of place, it is by no means removed from broader spatialities. Sanctioned heritage becomes part of national imaginings (Jacobs 1996:36), and local sites are heavily involved in global processes of commodification. The politics of identity is undeniably also a politics of place and thus an unbounded geography of difference and contest.

There are real tensions in the state's attempts to embrace Western tourism on a grand scale – to reap the rewards of its revenues and provide an experience for foreigners that neither detracts from the glories of the past nor subjects visitors to the harsh realities of Egypt's socioeconomic deprivations and the anti-Western sentiments of a militant minority. Thus, in situating archaeology and its relationship to the modern Egyptian state in global terms, several themes emerge. First, the concept of touring modern Egypt is constructed primarily around a privileging of its Pharaonic and, to a lesser degree, its Classical antecedents. Pharaonic Egypt is reified more than its later hybrid counterparts. The state and many archaeologists who have worked within its boundaries tend to describe Egypt not in terms of a historical continuum but as a series of unrelated parts forming a chain of "decline." Periods later than the Pharaonic are underappreciated and understudied. This reductive strategy affects archaeologists and their research agendas as well as tourists and governmental tourist authorities. As Fahim (2001:10–11) puts it, modern Egypt is still represented as

> two contrasting cultures that co-existed side by side: one was ancient and great while the modern way of life was still medieval and backward. It is ironic to observe that this dual presentation of Egypt's cultural image that dominated the writings of most nineteenth-century European travellers is still used by both European and Egyptian travel agencies to promote tourism and attract individuals and groups to visit Egypt today. I view this practice as alarmingly counter-productive because of the potential conflict of interest between the local and foreign tourist industries and the country's aspirations and efforts to present its image in the eyes and minds of its own people and the outside world as an integrated culture, rather than a polarised one with its potentially serious social and political implications.

As have many developing countries, Egypt has employed cultural tourism as a means to modernization, transforming its heritage into a tourist product and profit-making capital. This entails a cultural involution in which it must construct its future by clinging to its unique past. Thus modern Egypt has to return to its Pharaonic heritage in order to construct a suite of tourist-recognized symbols of identity (Lanfant, Allcock, and Bruner 1995:105). What can archaeologists do in this situation? They can focus their work on the full spectrum of Egyptian history, including all its disparate and divergent groups through time, and they can

work more closely with various communities and become more proactive in the tourist sphere. Caroline Simpson (2000, 2001), for example, a sometime resident of Gurna, has helped to promote a new vision of the Gurnawis' modern history through the establishment of a heritage center called Gurna Discovery. It seems to me an embarrassment to the discipline that it was left to a nonarchaeologist to facilitate the positive presentation of this previously disenfranchised group.

Archaeology can be productively used in the service of indigenous groups by reconstructing heritage that has been lost through conquest and deprivation, and, as Pyburn and Wilk (2000:79) submit, "archaeologists can also offer real support for developing tourism, jobs, crafts industries, self-respect, education, and public awareness.... Educational outreach must go beyond attempts to instill a preservation ethic in school-age children." Here again we see that heritage, tourism, and local politics are inseparable. In Egypt as in many places, tourists' desire for authenticity induces them to compromise the physical stability of heritage sites, eroding their symbolic value in the process. Tourist authorities should be educated to consider travel not simply in commercial terms but as an opportunity to initiate a cultural dialogue between residents and visitors; learning how to be a responsible tourist should be integral to learning how to be a tourist (El-Din 1999:1). Moreover, the tourism industry exploits archaeology for commercial gain and should therefore promote better direct communication with professional archaeologists, and archaeologists must become willing to enter into such dialogue (Herscher and McManamon 2000:50). All stakeholders must communicate more with each other, whether they participate in government, tourist, heritage, or archaeological spheres or happen to dwell among the ancients.

Dead Subjects and Living Communities

Within the archaeological community it has long been said that, because of the impact of Islam, the Egyptian people have no special relationship with antiquity and are largely uninterested in knowing about their past, much less in preserving it. This suggestion assumes a single, normative set of relationships with the past and allows Western scholars to continue their current practices in Egypt in time-honored ways. Gurna is a case in point (Meskell 2001; van der Spek 1998). Timothy Mitchell (2002:chap. 6) has explored the complex machinations between the Egyptian government and one local community involving the forced relocation of the Gurnawis, the tourist trade, and the development of an open-air museum. He focuses upon the desperate attempts of the local people to reclaim their homes and their only source of income. This struggle involves diverse local groups and top-down global pressures stemming from notions of shared world heritage. Having excavated in the Valley of the Nobles for several field seasons, I understand the threat of destruction, the escalating pressures of tourism, and the fractious relationships between archaeologists, tourists, and Gurnawis. As archaeologists we become part of the tourist spectacle. Groups of visitors trekking to the famed tomb of Sennefer would see us working in the courtyard of an adjacent tomb and begin photographing us, asking us questions (typically "Have you found any gold?") or breaching the security cordon to enter the excavation area. We too became part of a tour that they had paid for, and many felt that they had a right to see archaeology performed.

Archaeologists are an important part of the political mix. The professional Egyptologists of Luxor have been instrumental in offering human-impact assessments at Gurna. Not surprisingly, they have opposed the "deleterious impact of the village upon the stability and preservation of the tombs [due to] theft, erosion, building, and vandalism," arguing that the presence of a community here is "disastrous to the survival of the tombs" (van der Spek 1998). Both Egyptologists and tourism officials continue to describe Gurna as an ancient Egyptian landscape, devoid of its living community and its own unique heritage, again reiterating the fantasy that *our subjects are dead*. Privileging the ancients has been further reinforced by several ICOMOS recommendations released in June 2001: that the plan for the site should identify (1) the archaeological areas that must be explored and protected, (2) the houses that should be conserved and the conditions

(building materials, management of water, etc.) required to allow some residents to continue living in the village, (3) visiting trails and the use of those constructions that would be left vacant pending the assessment of the potential for important archaeological strata, and (4) the appropriate location of functions and activities that are not compatible with the safeguarding of the site (commerce, etc.).

The situation at Gurna has not been resolved. We are being asked to prioritize the dead over the living, and this has uncomfortable repercussions. Western intervention has a long, complex and unpleasant history. "Archaeology cleared the way for excavation and tourism by evicting villagers from homes in the temples of Luxor and Edfu. ... The uneven personal and regional benefits and costs of tourism, the tensions between insensitive tourists and conservative villagers, folk-beliefs about the fertility-inducing power of antiquities, and the antipharaonism of Islamist purists are all pieces of an as yet little-known puzzle" (Reid 1985:139–140).

Relocating the people of Gurna has been a governmental imperative for decades. In the past ten years state authorities have deployed bulldozers, armed police officials, tourism investors, and U.S. and World Bank consultants, and the heritage industry has made use of violence in pursuit of its goals. In one attempt at relocation four people were killed and another twenty-five or more were injured. In 1998 the head of the Luxor City Council was quoted in *Al-Ahram* as saying that the shantytown of Old Gurna would have to be depopulated because "you can't afford to have this heritage wasted because of informal houses being built in an uncivilized manner" (see also Mitchell 2002:196). Yet Gurna is not an isolated instance. The Egyptian government has also tried to move families away from the pyramid at Meidum, the temples in Esna and Edfu, and the Great Pyramids in Giza. Some years ago officials succeeded in removing from Gurna some thirteen hundred families who lived in traditional mud-brick houses directly on top of the four hundred Tombs of the Nobles, a major tourist attraction. Many of these Gurnawis are now housed in newly built concrete buildings in a nearby village set up largely by Egypt's armed forces. While some may see this as a step toward modernization, the concrete constructions are less well-suited to the Egyptian climate than traditional ones and could be perceived as alienating in specific context. It is clear that violence, both real and symbolic, has been done to the Gurnawis, ironically in the name of their own national heritage. The global remains privileged territory.

It has long been held that for Luxor to reach its full heritage (read tourist) potential, the village of Gurna would have to be depopulated. In 1982 the World Bank hired U.S. consultants to devise plans for enhancing tourist revenues; the same group had been hired for the same purpose in 1953. This revenue was to be derived from the promotion of high-end tourism: the development of luxury hotels and Nile cruise ships. The government then spent US$60 million, more than half of it borrowed from the World Bank to pay for foreign expertise, on certain improvements (Mitchell 2002:196). The preferred visitor management scheme aimed to promote the physical separation of tourists from the local community by means of separate transportation, restaurants, and shops. For instance, one of the plans included an enclosed visitor center, complete with restaurant and shops, that shielded tourists from any unnecessary engagement with the Gurnawis. Another plan involved an elevated walkway over one village, allowing visitors to move from their luxury coaches to adjacent archaeological sites while avoiding the village. The tourists would literally walk above the villagers, making concrete the perceived hierarchical distinction between foreigners and locals. To date, neither of these plans has come to fruition.

A striking parallel is the forced relocation of the Bidul Bedouin, who once lived in caves at the site of Petra, Jordan. The Jordanian government positioned the Bedouin as remnants of a premodern era whose lifeways were at odds with a new vision of modernity. In Fabian's terms, any discourse that marks the "primitive" is one that already precludes observation or study: it is a temporal concept employed as a distancing device between observer and observed. While the Bidul (similarly to the Gurnawi) could be marketed as a tourist attraction, they embodied troubling temporal notions concerning "progress," "evolution," and "modernity" (Massad 2001:73–79). The image of the nation is often

apprehended through the tourist gaze. Cultural tourism relies on the existence of difference, and while modern nation-states suppress cultural difference within their borders they are eager to market their ethnic minorities for tourism revenue (Crick 1994:6). Ultimately, however, the government's plan had always involved their permanent removal. Strategies for relocating the Bidul since the 1960s have included ideas about returning them to farming (again, similarly to the Gurnawi situation) so that Petra could become an open-air tourist museum free from the incursions of its native inhabitants. In the 1970s there was armed resistance against the government's initiatives, and in the 1980s a permanent settlement was built for the Bidul (Massad 2001:79). Both Luxor and Petra were deemed too central to their nations' identity and heritage to have these indices of modernity undermined by an undesirable group and its particular lifeways.

While problems abound, ethical solutions remain scarce on the ground. One tactical shift that might alleviate tensions between communities would focus on conserving "history" rather than simply historic sites. The tendency of conventional conservation approaches to naturalize historic resources (Hufford 1994:6–7) reflects a purist notion of the past that also serves to dehistoricize them, divorcing them from their other histories and contemporary interpolations. Heritage is not the same as history: "Heritage is history processed through mythology, ideology, nationalism, local pride, romantic ideas, or just plain marketing into commodity" (Schouten 1995:21). By shifting attention from *sites* and *structures* to a more dynamic conception of the past, including its multiple manifestations and uses through time, we might more fully appreciate and accommodate living communities. Since touring historic sites involves a particular experience of the materiality of the past, it might similarly encompass contemporary spheres of interaction that could include local residents, archaeologists, and other interest groups. On the one hand, this is more akin to an "archaeology within anthropology" approach. Such an approach should find special support from North American archaeology, since it is already housed within anthropology departments. On the other hand, this perspective finds resonance in innovative trends in tourism research that demarcate heterogeneous tourist space as a multipurpose space in which boundaries are blurred and a wide range of activities and people may coexist. Such a space provides stages where transitional identities may be performed alongside the everyday actions of residents, passersby, and workers (Edensor 2001:64), what might be deemed a "heterotopia" in Foucauldian terms. In sum, conserving multiple histories rather than simply the site, including many lines of heritage rather than privileging a singular story line, is one way of ameliorating the contention inherent in situations such as those described in Egypt and Jordan (see also Scham and Yahya 2003 on Palestine). Adopting a more inclusive, more anthropological approach to the archaeological past in which past and present act productively for a greater number of stakeholders and audiences will accommodate contemporary concerns and communities within an inclusive framework of cultural and temporal difference.

Tourism and Terrorism on the West Bank

Gurna was a major tourist center until an attack on the Temple of Hatshepsut by Muslim extremists in November 1997 took the lives of fifty-eight foreigners and four Egyptians. Local people are reported to have chased the gunmen armed only with sticks and then spat at their bodies as they were brought down from the surrounding hills. Some are said to have wanted to burn the militants' bodies in their disgust: "They were so ugly. They were not from here. They were not Egyptians. They were mad, evil, not God's people. ... They were others, alien, not like us" (interviews conducted with Caroline Simpson, November 19, 1997). Many Egyptians who were interviewed by the foreign press distanced themselves from the terrorist attack, declaring that it did not represent Muslim sentiments and could never be condoned. The attack severely damaged Egypt's lucrative tourism industry. Figures from Egypt's tourist authority show a drop of 12.8 percent, equating to a decline of 56.8 percent in numbers of tourist nights spent in Egypt. From 1997 to 1998 revenue fell from US$3.7 billion to $2.5 billion (Travel Industry World Yearbook

1998–1999:131). While a few Egyptologists reported the news on various web sites, the topic did not fuel further discussion; it was considered an extreme instance in an escalating series of attacks on tourists over the past few years. This silence is part of a wider malaise in Egyptology as a discipline. Egyptologists have convinced themselves that they have little to do with the lived experience of people like the Gurnawis. They remain outside the processes at work, processes that they are deeply involved in by the nature of their work and the very subject matter of archaeology.

The 1997 massacre is a nodal point in political, religious, economic, social, and spatial terms. This violent assault on one of the most iconic monuments of the pharaonic past was directed primarily against tourists. The visual spectacle of the temple's space has long been recognized and it is similarly celebrated as a performance space: the opera Aïda is often performed there, and in fact President Hosni Mubarak himself had attended a performance there a month before the attack. The temple's history became part of the media coverage, as Swain (1997) reports: "Some of the worst savagery took place at the sanctuary of Anubis, the ancient god of embalming and the dead who is represented by the head of a jackal. Blood and pieces of human flesh stuck to the walls and high ceiling as the terrorists shot and slashed at their victims with knives, making the chamber with its beautiful bas-reliefs look like a primitive slaughterhouse." Ancient grandeur and modern savagery is a common bifurcation in the media's construction of Egypt, with the decline of civilization due to the impact of Islam alluded to throughout.

The Temple of Hatshepsut is a major tourist site and a popular stopping point on the journey to Luxor (Figure 26.1). Reports from the Egyptian authorities suggested that the attack was primarily aimed at the police and security forces, but this was generally assumed to be a government strategy to allay fears and minimize damage to the tourist industry. There had been similar attacks in April 1997, when militants shot nineteen Greek tourists, believing them to be Israelis, outside their hotel near the Giza pyramids. Another terrorist assault occurred in Cairo in September of that year. Gunmen ambushed

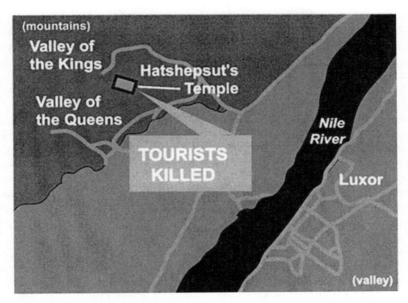

Figure 26.1   The Luxor area, showing the location of the 1997 attack.

another tourist bus in front of the Cairo Museum, killing nine tourists and wounding another nineteen. This famous place, which houses the treasures of Tutankhamun and thousands of other archaeological masterpieces, is a key tourist site for almost every visitor to Egypt. Clearly tourists were the prime targets, ensuring global coverage for the militant cause and maximum damage to the national economy and worldwide profile. A leaflet found in the fatal stomach wound of one Japanese tourist at Hatshepsut's temple read *No Tourists in Egypt – Omar Abdel-Rahman's Squadron of Havoc and Destruction* (Sennott 1997). The Gemaa Islamiya's leader, Talaat Fuad Qasim, interviewed in 1995, called tourism "an abomination, a means by which prostitution and AIDS are spread by Jewish women tourists" (*Economist* 1997). It has been claimed that between 1992 and 1997 some one thousand Egyptians – police, officials, Coptic Christians, and left-wing intellectuals – were also killed.

The press coverage in Britain and the United States in 1997 focused heavily on two themes: tourism and terrorism. The first is couched in terms of Egypt's financial decline as a result of damage to its second-largest source of foreign economic injection. British newspapers used the Luxor incident to brand the Middle East as the locus of political violence and terrorism, and some writers demonized Islam in a manner that could only be described as racist and Orientalist. Walter Ellis (1997) of the *Sunday Times* declared that "right from the beginning Islam was associated with violence." These are sentiments that resurfaced after the events of September 11 in a wave of retaliations against Muslims in the United States and also in Europe and Australia. Islam as a religion has no specific agenda against touring or tourists. On the contrary, there is much in Islam that implicitly and explicitly accepts the notion of travel and encourages it; an obvious example is the pilgrimage to the holy sites of Mecca and Medina. Why, then, have tourists become such a attractive target? Heba Aziz (1995:93) argues that in Upper Egypt there is an enormous gap between tourism development (such as Nile cruises) and the development in the area itself and that the tourist industry actively promotes this phenomenon as an attraction. In many developing countries the socioeconomic inequalities between hosts and guests are extreme, and the atmosphere of relaxation and indulgence is set against poverty and desperation without any obvious benefits in terms of local development or employment opportunities.

In such inflamed contexts tourism introduces the behavior of a wasteful society into the midst of the society of want (Aziz 1995:93). Tourists in their luxury ghettos are the most visible signifiers of Western domination; the wealth and comfort of the "have" societies is juxtaposed with all the moral, religious, and social values of the "want" society. Perhaps unsurprisingly, a large percentage of the Muslim activists are clustered in Upper Egypt, where tourism proliferates; 83.5 percent of the particularly militant activists are younger than twenty-five years old, and the majority belong to a low socioeconomic group (Aziz 1995:94). This disenfranchised group has targeted tourism as a symbol of the new global economy and their exclusion from its benefits while similarly wounding Mubarak's government in terms of its international profile.

Apart from blatant anti-Muslim sentiment, colonial incursions into Egypt were also foregrounded in the subsequent media frenzy. Britain's most conservative newspaper, the Times, reported that "Britain has a special relationship with the Valley of the Kings, where almost exactly 75 years age – on November 30, 1922 – The Times was first to tell the world of the discovery of the tomb of Tutankhamen by Howard Carter and the Earl of Carnarvon" (Murphy 1997:3). In the same issue an article entitled "Blood on the Nile" proclaimed the "shame of ordinary Egyptians that a country that was the cradle of civilisation should now be associated with such barbarity." The invocation of this familiar trope – the cradle of civilization – highlights the paternalistic and colonialist implications of considering the nation's infancy its crowning achievement. In Orientalist fashion, this suggests that these countries of the Middle East have never surpassed their early glories and that the torch of civilization has since passed to Europe. The most offensive coverage of the massacre in the Times, by Simon Jenkins (1997), drew heavily on stereotypes of Oriental despotism and violence:

> When the Assyrian warrior Ashurbanipal descended on Thebes in the 7th century BC, he razed it to the ground. This first great terrorist boasted that he took the entire city. . . . Monday's massacre on the site of that city saw a new

Assyrian terror, from fanatical opponents of Islamic reform. But whereas Ashurbanipal terrorised by laying waste to an entire city, the death squads of al-Gamaa al-Islamiya needed only to machine-gun a busload of Western tourists: A dead Westerner is a media ticket to ride.

He went on to appropriate Egypt as an extension of the known world of England: "We know these places. The path to the Sphinx, the Corniche at Luxor, the drive to the Valley of the Kings are corners of a foreign field that have become forever England. Machine gun us there and you machine gun us in our own backyard, surrounded by cultural family and friends." This sentiment was transferred to Egypt's monuments, too, in the language of global world heritage. Jenkins argues that the Temple of Hatshepsut "no longer 'belongs' to Egypt, but to the world. It is being restored by European archaeologists with UNESCO money. To the fundamentalist, Luxor is a cultural colony, occupied by the armies of world tourism." Foreign intervention in the form of USAID, the World Bank, UNESCO, and so on, is seen as a means of appropriating, controlling, and owning Egypt's cultural resources as part of a shared global property (Meskell 2002b). Inevitably this property is wrested from Egypt and incorporated into Western heritage. Jenkins's article was illustrated by a cartoon depicting two pyramids composed entirely of the bodies of slain tourists that was both insensitive and insightful, combining national heritage, archaeology, tourism, and violence before the colonialist gaze.

Performing Ancient Egypt

Severing ties with antiquity underscores all narratives about a contemporary lack of interest in the past and inflects both tourist and heritage practice in Egypt. It serves as an implicit acknowledgment that modern and ancient Egyptians share no lineage whatsoever and that the former are simply the recalcitrant caretakers of the latter's legacy, "minding the store" in metaphoric and literal terms – explicitly cashing in on a past that has little relevance within a predominantly Muslim Egypt. All of these tensions come to the fore in the shape of one very

Figure 26.2 Ancient agricultural enactment from the Pharaonic Village, Cairo.

famous tourist locale in Egypt, Cairo's premier theme park, the Pharaonic Village (Figure 26.2). Here tensions over religion, nation, authenticity, and performance of the past by both "colonized" and "colonizer" are enunciated. As a heritage locus for the *longue durée* of Egyptian history, the Pharaonic Village evinces the latent problems in attracting tourists to later periods, undoubtedly because they do not traditionally tour Christian and Islamic sites and are therefore lack the knowledge and interest required to make history heritage.

Dr. Hassan Ragab spent ten years and over US$6 million creating the Pharaonic Village, which was opened in 1984. The official web site for the village claims that ancient Egypt is "brought to life by an incredible group of actors and actresses, faithful and exact reproductions of buildings, clothing, and lifestyles ... to create the most precise *living* recreation of the golden days of Pharaonic Egypt" (http://touregypt.net/village). The village covers 150,000 square meters at Ya'aqoob Island, Giza, close to downtown Cairo. It is claimed that some three hundred people supposedly live in an "ancient Egyptian atmosphere and practice various agricultural and industrial activities with the same tools and implements used in antiquity." Claims with regard to authenticity are paramount. Official

web sites declare that while "the city of Cairo surrounds the island, not a trace of it penetrates the thick wall of trees planted around the island," thus screening the vestiges of modern life and making visitors feel as if they had gone back five thousand years in history.

Tourists usually visit the site as part of organized package tours and are transported through the island village on barges moving along canals, accompanied by a fixed soundtrack in a specific language. Since groups are confined to their boats, their movements and sightlines are deliberately restricted. The tourist gaze is directed solely toward the costumed actors as they perform their repetitive roles. Visitors are screened from viewing the mundane objects of modern life in Cairo: brick walls, construction zones, and other scenes of everyday life such as young men fishing on the Nile. Timing is also tightly controlled; the staged vignettes of life, such as the threshing of grain or boat building, are performed in quick succession. Many of the workers look complacent or dejected at the futility of the repetitive simulacra (Slyomovics 1989). Perhaps even more disruptive are the moments when actors, breaking out of their designated roles, wave back at the tourists or ask them if they want additional photos. There is something wonderful about these resistances, which offer

Figure 26.3   Tour guide with tourists and performer at the Pharaonic Village, Cairo.

relief from the monotony of the staged acts. The uncomfortable modalities of power are suddenly thrown into sharp relief or perhaps even inverted as the objects of the gaze disrupt the aura and distance that the tourist desires. As Urry (1990:66–67) argues,

> The tourist gaze is structured by culturally specific notions of what is extraordinary and therefore worth viewing. This means that the services provided, which may of course be incidental to the gaze itself, must take a form which does not contradict or undermine the quality of the gaze, and ideally should enhance it. This in turn poses, as we shall see, immense problems of management of such industries, to ensure that the service provided by the often relatively poor paid service workers is appropriate to the almost sacred quality of the visitors' gaze on some longed-for and remarkable tourist site.

Tourists are also asked to perform at the Pharaonic Village, but they do not assume the roles of "ordinary people" as do their local counterparts. Rather, they are dressed and photographed as ancient pharaohs and queens, fulfilling additional colonial desires about power, beauty, and otherness. The absurdity of middle-aged European and Japanese tourists' living out their

fantasies of being Rameses or Cleopatra needs little explication. Such forms of cultural tourism are strongly influenced by the longing to experience otherness, a desire that developed during the colonial era (Edensor 1998:22). Being photographed in luxurious, quasi-royal settings provides another means of purchasing and consuming visual property and specific cultural histories: no one dresses up as an agricultural laborer or a weaver. And there are additional difficulties over authenticity with regard to the pharaonic clothing worn by the participants, particularly for women. The representation of pharaonic life is restricted by the confines of Islamic protocols, with the result that the actors' garments form a strange hybrid of modern styles and ancient motifs (Figure 26.3). The coherence of most tourist (and host) performances depends on their being performed in such specific "theaters."

Several years ago it was decided to integrate Islamic history into the narrative experience of the Pharaonic Village. After visiting the United States, Abdel-Salam Ragab felt that Westerners did not have a clear picture of Islam. One employee stated that "Islamic culture is part of Egypt's history, and therefore we found it suitable to have it included alongside the pharaonic." Another argued that "the aim of this museum is to educate everybody about this great civilization. The image of Islam abroad is that of fundamentalists and terrorists. People should know that this is not correct, and that Islam has a glorious history and civilization, and that it produced great philosophers and scientists" (http://www.ahram.org.eg/weekly/1998/393/tr1.htm). Here again tourism and terrorism are conjoined in the specter of Islamic fundamentalism, again an inflamed association in the aftermath of September 11. But, sadly, few Western tourists are interested in the Muslim museum or, for that matter, the Coptic museum, and most choose to skip those parts of the tour. Visitors want to see how the pyramids were built or what a nobleman's house was like; they do not care to see how more recent (perhaps, oddly, less familiar) Egyptian histories are articulated and presented. Given that both appear very late on the tour, it is not surprising that many feel exhausted and overwhelmed by another history lesson with which they feel unconnected. While many visitors may have been exposed to pharaonic Egyptian materials in the Metropolitan, the Louvre, and the British Museum, few may have been educated about Late Antique or Muslim culture and history. These periods certainly lack the essential exoticism that marks ancient Egypt as the quintessential *other*.

Conclusions

The terrain covered in this chapter is necessarily messy. Archaeology cannot remain inviolate, since it inhabits a number of domains – landscapes, ethnoscapes, finanscapes, mediascapes, and ideoscapes, to use Appadurai's (1990:296) familiar taxonomy. Archaeological materials and practitioners are instrumental in the production and marketing of heritage sites, working with diverse governments and communities and ultimately providing the raw materials for a burgeoning global tourist economy. The past is also instrumental in political debates, from local-level community tensions as witnessed at Gurna to the more insidious agendas at the global level evidenced by the media coverage of the 1997 attacks. While phrases such as "global village" may seem appropriate, given that expansionary industrial capitalism and modern communications technology have unified the world and set in train various processes of cultural homogenization, they mask the continued inequitable reality of localism – of cultural and ethnic particularism – in the contemporary world (Crick 1994:6). Tourists and archaeologists both participate in colonialist and Orientalist fantasies while touring Egypt. And, while it may appear to be an excessive claim, El Saadawi (1997: 168–169) suggests that "Egyptology is an example of cultural genocide or terrorism, in which a whole nation and its civilization and philosophy are violently reduced to a few stones or ruins ... [to be] looked at by tourists." In developing nations such as Egypt, specialized archaeological and conservation expertise may be wanting, but we must question whether the advantages of Western technology give us *rights* (legal or moral) to the heritage of others. With future funds and training, indigenous Egyptology may attain additional control over its own past and thereby challenge the West's ideological monopoly (Wood 1998: 192). The impossibility is extricating archaeology from the dense web of consequences that it inspires. Archaeologists are both products and producers of the political, and herein lies the primary reason for our engagement with ethics.

Archaeologists are arbiters of the past for myriad stakeholders and communities, and by virtue of the discipline's ventriloquism we occupy the important and responsible role of translator for past cultures and individuals. Yet how that role is defined and performed is negotiable. Traditionally, archaeologists have presented themselves as "trustees" of the past, albeit without explicit acknowledgment, in both legal and practical arenas, but their role is more akin to the contractor's. As Scham (1998:302–303) proposes, there is much to be derived from the notion of the archaeologist as trustee – someone required to defend property from adverse interests. By the nature of our destructive work, we are placed in the unique position of informed interpreters with access to the past in the present. This confers upon us a particular burden different from that of historians, who can repeatedly reconstitute past events. Our position diverges from that of ethnographers, too, since their interpretive constructions are changeable (premised on theoretical positionality) and rarely susceptible to the popular deployment of archaeology's materiality. Beyond heuristics, archaeological remains are more than objects of memory: they are instantiated in the present and in present-day politics.

Politics and ethics are two sides of the same coin: both are constructed and need to be understood contextually. Ethics is neither neutral nor value-free, although it retains a deceptively positive aura. Ethical discourse has only recently reached archaeology, and, while national codes have been a topic of growing interest in the United States, Canada, Australia, England, and elsewhere, they cannot simply be extrapolated to archaeological practice in foreign contexts. Few have even considered this a salient issue, particularly those who work in the shadow of empire, as in Egypt. Archaeologists cannot uncritically impose Western liberal, economic rationalist, or preservationist values upon all other cultural milieus. Moreover, ethics should properly occupy a shifting terrain, one that is

under constant negotiation with divergent interest groups. This promises to make field practice more complex, since archaeologists will need to be more cognizant and considerate of other parties, specifically local governments and communities (Moser et al. 2002). We will have to consult, collaborate, negotiate, incorporate, and be willing to forgo our own research agendas – something archaeologists have been reluctant to do. Undoubtedly, archaeological practice will be fraught – more complex and conflictual – and attuned to a critical, postmodern vision of ethics. Constructions of heritage may then emerge as more networked and developmental. Heritage as a disciplinary locus may then be redefined, giving serious weight to living communities and shared histories rather than merely the physical sites that have traditionally been prioritized. Through this convergence we can address our ethical responsibility in the contemporary world, helping archaeology to move beyond the paradigm of dead subjects toward a new vision of lived histories.

References

Almond, B. 1991. Rights. In *A companion to ethics*, edited by Peter Singer, 259–269. Oxford: Blackwell.

Anderson, Benedict. 1984. *Imagined communities: Reflections on the origins and spread of nationalism.* London: Verso.

Appadurai, Arjun. 1990. Disjuncture and difference in the global cultural economy. In *Global culture: Nationalism, globalization, and modernity*, edited by M. Featherstone, 295–310. London: Sage Publications.

Aziz, Heba. 1995. Understanding attacks on tourists in Egypt. *Tourism Management* 16:91–95.

Blundell, Geoff 1998. Rand, rock art, and resources: Tourism and our indigenous heritage. *Rock Art* 4–6:15–16.

Boniface, P., and P. J. Fowler. 1993. *Heritage and tourism in "the global village."* London: Routledge.

Buckle, S. 1991. Natural law. In *A companion to ethics*, edited by Peter Singer, 161–174. Oxford: Blackwell.

Byrne, Dennis. 2003. Nervous landscapes: Race and space in Australia. *Journal of Social Archaeology* 3:169–193.

Castañeda, Quetzil. 1996. *In the museum of Maya culture: Touring Chichén Itzá.* Minneapolis: University of Minnesota Press.

Colwell-Chanthaphonh, Chip. 2003a. Dismembering/ disremembering the Buddhas: Renderings on the Internet during the Afghan purge of the past. *Journal of Social Archaeology* 3:75–98.

Colwell-Chanthaphonh, Chip. 2003b. Signs in place: Native American perspectives of the past in the San Pedro Valley of southeastern Arizona. *Kiva* 69:5–29.

Colwell-Chanthaphonh, Chip, and T. J. Ferguson. 2004. Virtue ethics and the practice of history: Native Americans and archaeologist along the San Pedro Valley of Arizona. *Journal of Social Archaeology* 4.

Crick, Malcolm. 1994. *Resplendent sites, discordant voices: Sri Lankans and international tourism.* Chur: Harwood Academic Publishers.

Economist. 1997. Bloodbath at Luxor. November 20.

Edensor, Tim. 1998. *Tourists at the Taj: Performance and meaning at a symbolic site.* New York: Routledge.

El-Din, M. S. 1999. Plain talk. *Al-Ahram Weekly Online.* http://www/weekly.ahram.org.

Ellis, Walter. 1997. In the name of Allah. *Sunday Times,* November 23.

El Saadawi, Nawal. 1997. *The Nawal El Saadawi reader.* New York: Zed Books.

Fahim, H. M. 2001. European travelers in Egypt. In *Travellers in Egypt*, edited by Paul Starkey and Janet Starkey, 7–11. London: Tauris Parke.

Fotiadis, Michalis. 1993. Regions of the imagination: Archaeologists, local people, and the archaeological record in fieldwork, Greece. *Journal of European Archaeology* 1:151–170.

Franklin, A., and M. Crang. 2001. The trouble with tourism and travel theory? *Tourist Studies* 1:5–22.

Gamboni, D. 2001. World heritage: Shield or target? *Conservation: The Getty Conservation Institute Newsletter* 16:5–11.

Goodin, R. E. 1991. Utility and the good. In *A companion to ethics*, edited by Peter Singer, 241–248. Oxford: Blackwell.

Herbert, David T., ed. 1995. *Heritage, tourism and society*. London: Mansell.

Herscher, E., and F. P. McManamon. 2000. Public education and outreach: The obligation to educate. In *Ethics in American archaeology*, edited by Mark I. Lynott and Alison Wylie. Washington, D.C.: Society for American Archaeology.

Huband, M. 2001. *Egypt: Regional leader and global player, a market for the 21st century*. London: Euromoney Books.

Hufford, Mary. 1994. Introduction: Rethinking the cultural mission. In *Conserving culture: A new discourse on heritage*, edited by Mary Hufford, 1–11. Urbana: University of Illinois Press.

Jacobs, Jane M. 1996. *Edge of empire: Postcolonialism and the city*. London: Routledge.

Jenkins, Simon. 1997. Hysteria calls the shots. *Times*, November 19.

Jenner, P., and C. Smith. 1993. *Tourism in the Mediterranean*. London: Economist Intelligence Unit.

Kirshenblatt-Gimblett, Barbara. 1998. *Destination culture: Tourism, museums, and heritage*. Berkeley: University of California Press.

Lanfant, Marie-Françoise, John B. Allcock, and Edward M. Bruner, eds. 1995. *International tourism: Identity and change*. London: Sage.

Lilley, Ian, ed. 2000. *Native title and the transformation of archaeology in the postcolonial world*. Oceania Monographs 50. Sydney: University of Sydney.

Logan, G., and M. P. Leone. 1997. Tourism with race in mind: Annapolis, Maryland, examines its African-American past through collaborative research. In *Tourism and culture: An applied perspective*, edited by Erve Chambers, 129–146. Albany: State University of New York Press.

Lynott, Mark J., and Alison Wylie, eds. 2000. *Ethics in American archaeology*. Washington, D.C.: Society for American Archaeology.

MacCannell, Dean. 1992. *Empty meeting grounds: The tourist papers*. London: Routledge.

MacCannell, Dean. 2000. Cultural tourism. *Conservation: The Getty Conservation Institute Newsletter* 15:24–27.

MacCannell, Dean. 2001. Tourist agency. *Tourist Studies* 1:23–37.

Massad, Joseph A. 2001. *Colonial effects*. New York: Columbia University Press.

Meskell, Lynn M., ed. 1998. *Archaeology under fire: Nationalism, politics, and heritage in the Eastern Mediterranean and the Middle East*. London: Routledge.

Meskell, Lynn M., ed. 2001. The practice and politics of archaeology in Egypt. In *Ethics and anthropology: Facing future issues in human biology, globalism, and cultural property*, edited by Anne-Marie Cantwell, Eva Friedlander, and Madeleine Tramm, 146–169. New York: New York Academy of Sciences.

Meskell, Lynn M., ed. 2002a. The intersection of identity and politics in archaeology. *Annual Review of Anthropology* 31:279–301.

Meskell, Lynn M., ed. 2002b. Negative heritage and past mastering in archaeology. *Anthropological Quarterly* 75:557–574.

Messenger, Phyllis Mauch, ed. 1999. *The ethics of collecting cultural property*. Albuquerque: University of New Mexico Press.

Mitchell, Timothy. 2002. *Rule of experts: Egypt, technopolitics, modernity*. Berkeley: University of California Press.

Moser, S., D. Glazier, S. Ballard, J. Phillips, L. N. el Nemer, M. S. Mousa, S. Richardson, A. Conner, and M. Seymour. 2002. Transforming archaeology through practice: Strategies for collaborative archaeology and the Community Archaeology Project at Quseir, Egypt. *World Archaeology* 34:220–248.

Murphy, M. 1997. Lure of ancient capital of the pharaohs. *Times*, October 19.

Odermatt, P. 1996. Built heritage and the politics of representation: Local reactions to the appropriation of the monumental past in Sardinia. *Archaeological Dialogues* 3:95–136.

Odermatt, P. 2001. *IRB guidebook*. Washington, D.C.: U.S. Department of Health and Human Services. http://ohrp.osophs.dhhs.gov/irb_guidebook.html.

OSP (Office of Sponsored Projects), University of California, Santa Cruz. 2000. *Draft guidelines of the Committee for Protection of Human Subjects, UCSC Institutional Review Board*. http://www.ucsc.edu/osp/hsirb.html.

Pagden, Anthony. 1995. *Lords of all the world: Ideologies of empire in Spain, Britain, and France, c. 1500–c. 1800*. New Haven and London: Yale University Press.

Pagden, Anthony. 1998. The genesis of "governance" and Enlightenment conceptions of the cosmopolitan world order. *International Social Science Journal* 50 (155):7–15.

Passmore, John. 1974. *Man's responsibility for nature*. New York: Scribner.

Pastor Fasquelle, Rodolfo. 1989. *Biografía de San Pedro Sula: 1536–1954*. San Pedro Sula: DIMA.

Pels, Peter. 1999. Professions of duplexity: A prehistory of ethical codes in anthropology. *Current Anthropology* 40:101–136.

Pels, Peter. 2000. The trickster's dilemma: Ethics and the technologies of the anthropological self. In *Audit cultures: Anthropological studies in accountability, ethics, and the academy,* edited by Marilyn Strathern, 135–172. London and New York: Routledge.

Politis, Gustavo. 2001. On archaeological praxis, gender bias, and indigenous peoples in South America. *Journal of Social Archaeology* 1:90–107.

Pyburn, K. Anne, and Richard Wilk. 2000. Responsible archaeology is applied anthropology. In *Ethics in American archaeology,* edited by Mark J. Lynott and Alison Wylie. Washington, D.C.: Society for American Archaeology.

Reid, Donald. M. 1985. Indigenous Egyptology: The decolonization of a profession? *Journal of the American Oriental Society* 105:233–246.

Rojek, Chris, and John Urry, eds. 1997. *Touring cultures: Transformations of travel and theory.* London: Routledge.

Scham, Sandra A. 1998. Mediating nationalism and archaeology: A matter of trust? *American Anthropologist* 100:301–308.

Scham, Sandra A., and Adel Yahya. 2003. Heritage and reconciliation. *Journal of Social Archaeology* 3:399–416.

Schouten, F. 1995. Heritage as historical reality. In *Heritage, tourism, and society,* edited by David T. Herbert, 21–31. New York: Mansell.

Sennott, C. M. 1997. Egyptian tourist attack leaves 71 dead: Government puts blame on Islamic militants. *Boston Globe,* November 18.

Shepherd, Nick. 2003. "When the hand that holds the trowel is black ...": Disciplinary practices of self-representation and the issue of "native" labour in archaeology. *Journal of Social Archaeology* 3:334–351.

Simpson, Caroline. 2000. Modern Qurna: Pieces of an historical jigsaw. Paper presented at the Theban Necropolis Colloquium, British Museum, London.

Simpson, Caroline. 2001. Qurna discovery on the move. *Theban Panoramas' News* 4:1–3.

Slyomovics, Susan. 1989. Cross-cultural dress and tourist performance in Egypt. *Performing Arts Journal* 33–34:139–150.

Smith, Elizabeth A. 1999. "Primitive other" or "our distant ancestors"? Nubian identity in tourism in Egypt. MA thesis, New York University.

Stewart, C. Neal, Jr. 2003. Press before paper: When media and science collide. *Nature Biotechnology* 21:353–354.

Stocking, George W., ed. 1983. *Observers observed: Essays on Ethnographic Fieldwork.* Madison: University of Wisconsin Press.

Strathern, Marilyn. 2000a. Accountability and ethnography. In *Audit cultures: Anthropological studies in accountability, ethics, and the academy,* edited by Marilyn Strathern. London and New York: Routledge.

Strathern, Marilyn. 2000b. New accountabilities. In *Audit cultures: Anthropological studies in accountability, ethics, and the academy,* edited by Marilyn Strathern. London and New York: Routledge.

Swain, J. 1997. Terror at the Temple. *Sunday Times,* November 23.

Travel Industry World Yearbook. 1998–1999. *Egypt.* New York: Child and Waters.

Urry, John. 1990. *The tourist gaze.* London: Sage Publications.

Urry, John. 1995. *Consuming places.* London: Sage Publications.

van der Spek, Kees. 1998. Dead mountain versus living community: The Theban Necropolis as cultural landscape. In *Proceedings of the Third International Seminar Forum UNESCO: University and Heritage,* edited by W. S. Logan, C. Long, and J. Martin, 176–182. Melbourne: Deakin University Press.

Watkins, Joe. 2000. *Indigenous archaeology: American Indian values and scientific practice.* Walnut Creek, CA: AltaMira Press.

Wood, M. 1998. The use of the pharaonic past in modern Egyptian nationalism. *Journal of the American Research Center in Egypt* 35:179–196.

An Ethical Epistemology of Publicly Engaged Biocultural Research

Michael L. Blakey

The New York African Burial Ground was redis-covered in 1989 during preparations for the con-struction of a 34 story Federal office building for the United States General Services Administra-tion (GSA)(Ingle et al. 1990). To mitigate the destruction of cultural resources as required by law, a full-scale archaeological excavation con-ducted by HCI (Historic Conservation and Interpretation) and John Milner Associates pre-ceded the building project. The excavation and construction site on the Burial Ground is located at Foley Square, in the city block bounded by Broadway, Duane, Reade, and Elk streets in Lower Manhattan, one block north of City Hall.

Archaeological excavation and building con-struction began during the summer of 1991 and ended in the summer of 1992 when the US Congress called for work on the site to cease in response to the public demand to properly memorialize, and, ultimately, learn about the people buried there. A research team was assem-bled at Howard University beginning in April of 1992. The task of this team was post-excavation analysis, laboratory work, and interdisciplinary studies. This paper examines the interaction of

Michael L. Blakey, "An Ethical Epistemology of Publicly Engaged Biocultural Research," pp. 17–28 from Junko Habu, Clare Fawcett, and John M. Matsunaga (eds) *Evalu-ating Multiple Narratives: Beyond Nationalist, Colonialist, Imperialist Archaeologie*s (New York: Springer, 2008). Reprinted with permission.

ethics and theory during the 12 years in which the project's scientific pursuits interfaced with public interests. The research team of the W. Montague Cobb Biological Anthropology Laboratory at Howard University, and eight other universities affiliated with the project have studied the skeletal remains of 419 indivi-duals representing eighteenth-century African captives and their descendants.

The approach taken to the organization and interpretation of data from the African Burial Ground involves four main elements. How these elements of theory have come to guide our par-ticular research program are discussed in this chapter. These theoretic principles are also gen-eralizable and may be extended to a broader range of research projects than are entailed in our study of the African Burial Ground. The four elements are as follows:

1   Critical theory in the vindicationist vein allows the sociocultural and ideological influences on research interpretations to be scrutinized, while seeking socially empower-ing factual information through scientific and other scholarly research. The fundamental principle rests upon acknowledging that political and ideological implications are intrinsic to science and history, and that choices about these are unavoidable (Blakey 1996, 1998a; Douglass 1999 [1854]). The pervasive incorporation of African

diasporic intellectural traditions of this kind into the dialog around New York's African Burial Ground opened a special opportunity for applying this long-standing critical view of historical knowledge to a bioarchaeological study. Many brands of "critical theory" have emerged in recent decades, including neo-Marxist and postmodernist thought in American and European archaeology. The synthesis of criticism that emerges in this case is, in its mainstream, part of the evolved understandings of the social and political embeddedness of history and anthropology among African diasporans (see Drake 1980; Harrison & Harrison 1999). Yet as participants in the intellectual development of a broader "Western" world, such critical thought connects with other intellectual traditions whose experience has led to compatible insights.

2 Public engagement affords the communities, most affected by a research program, a key role in the design and use of research results. A respect for pluralism and the ethics of working with groups of people who historiography puts at risk of social and psychological harm recommends an acknowledgment of this community's right to participate in research decisions. Scholars balance accountability to such communities with responsibility to standards of evidential proof or plausibility that defines the role of scholars. The goal of this collaboration is not simply ethical. By drawing upon broader societal ideas and interests, public engagement affords opportunities for advancing knowledge and its societal significance. The democratization of knowledge involved here is not predicated on the inclusion of random voices, but on democratic pluralism that allows for a critical mass of ideas and interests to be developed for a bioarchaeological site or other research project, based on the ethical rights of descendant or culturally affiliated communities to determine their own well-being.

3 Multiple data sets (or lines of evidence) provide a crosscheck on the plausibility of results. Results may be rejected, accepted, or recombined into newly plausible "stories" about the past based on how diverse results of different methods compete or reconfigure as a complex whole. The required multidisciplinary experts engage in a "conversation" that produces interdisciplinary interpretations of the archaeological population. Diverse expertise provides for recognition of a subject matter that might otherwise go unnoticed by the individuals and in the communities under study. By revealing multiple dimensions of human subjects, this approach can produce characterizations of even skeletal individuals that more nearly resemble the complexities of human experience than are possible in simple, reductionist descriptions.

4 An African diasporic frame of reference was selected as a context for the New York population. This framework provides a connection both to an Atlantic world political economy and a transatlantic cultural history that is more reflective of the causal conditions existing throughout the life cycle of members of this eighteenth-century community than was the local Manhattan context of enslavement. The broader diasporic context of the New York population's lives also adds to an understanding of the population as more fully human than is afforded by a local context of enslavement. Non-African diasporic research might also circumscribe, differently, the scope of time and space required to examine a sufficiently large political economic system and social history to begin to explain how, what, and why its subject came to be.

Critical Theory

African diasporic intellectuals have, since late slavery, acknowledged the intrinsically political implications of anthropology and history with which they were confronted. Indeed, the historical record of American physical anthropology has continued to demonstrate that the physical anthropologists with the most emphatic interest in "objectivity" have nonetheless participated in the creation of racial and racist ideology (Blakey 1987, 1996; Gould 1981; Rankin-Hill & Blakey 1994). White supremacist notions are supported when representations of blacks are so shallow and biological as to denude them of human characteristics and motivations. As racialized "black slaves," African diasporic populations may be removed from culture and history, an objectification that some view as consistent with the ideals of Western science. Here it is both the biological categorization of identity (race) and the omission of history and culture that deny humanity to these historic populations.

While this process dehumanizes the black past, Euro-American history is also transformed to one in which Africans are not recognizable as people. They become instead a category of labor, the instruments or "portmanteau organisms" of whites (see Crosby 1986) that are therefore not readily identified with as the subjects of human rights abuses. These aspects, even of description, transform American history. Douglass, in 1854, asks scholars to simultaneously take sides and be fair to the evidence. This is different from Enlightenment notions of objectivity, because it is accepted that science and history will always be subjective to current biases and interests. How can one take a position and be fair to the evidence? One conceptualization of the purpose of historical research that may not violate either of these goals is the assumption that research into the diasporic past is not simply the pursuit of new knowledge. Indeed, diasporic traditions of critical scholarship have assumed that the search is for the reevaluation of old, politically distorted, and conveniently neglected knowledge about black history.

The research design of the African Burial Ground project asserts that the motivation to correct these distortions and omissions will drive the research effort in part. This understanding of the ideological nature of the construction of history allows our team to scrutinize data more critically than were we to assume ownership of special tools for neutral knowledge. We need to be more circumspect and aware of how our interpretations may be used and influenced by societal interests beyond the academy walls. Our criticism holds, as an assumed goal, the societally useful rectification of a systematically obscured African-American past. The fact that New York's African Burial Ground should not have existed from the standpoint of the basic education of most Americans supports the need for a critical and corrective approach to archaeology. The history of the northern colonies, of New York, is characterized as free and largely devoid of blacks. That, of course, is untrue. The history that denies the presence of blacks and of slavery in places where these actually did profoundly exist is not accidental. Such a history must be deliberately debated. Yet societal interests also influence our alternative interpretations and they may influence policy and social action. We are screwing around with other people's identities. Who are we as individual scientists to decide how to formulate our research plans relative to such potentially powerful societal effects?

Public Engagement

While we are responsible for our epistemological choices, it is perhaps inappropriate for researchers to make those choices in isolation. The epistemological choices – i.e., the choice of ways of knowing the past by virtue of the selection of research questions, theories and analytical categories – are also the justifiable responsibility of the broader communities whose lives are most affected by the outcome of research. This recognition of the potential for a democratization of knowledge merges epistemological concerns with ethical ones. The communities with which we work – living descendants or culturally affiliated groups – have an ethical right to be protected from harm resulting from the conduct of research. The American Anthropological Association Statement on Professional Responsibility and Ethics, the World Archaeological Congress Ethical Statement, and the new ethical principals of the American Association of Physical Anthropologists, which largely recapitulates the former, are key examples of this ethical standard (see Lynott & Wylie 1995 for an extensive discussion of ethics in American archaeology). Communities have a stake in how research is conducted if it might impact them negatively or positively.

The National Historic Preservation Act of the United States allows the public a say in whether research will be done at all and Native American Graves Protection and Repatriation Act (NAGPRA) legislation gives federally recognized Native Americans and Pacific Islanders rights to determine the disposition of their ancestral remains and sacred objects. Many archaeologists and physical anthropologists have resisted these ethical and legal obligations, arguing that the autonomous authority of researchers needs to be protected for the sake of objectivity and the proper, expert stewardship of knowledge about our past. That position is based on assumptions that are inconsistent with our critical theoretical observations of intrinsic cultural embeddedness of science that have informed the activist scholarship in the diaspora. If science is subjective to social interests, it seems fair, at least in the American cultural ethos, to democratize the choice of those interests that scientists will pursue. Since the people most affected are also to be protected, it is least patronizing for anthropologists to enter into a research relationship with descendant communities by which those communities protect themselves by participating in the decisions regarding research design. Indeed, a "publicly engaged" anthropology of this kind has been proposed by a panel of leading anthropologists who have linked the practice to American values of democratic participation and pluralism (Blakey et al. 1994; Forman 1994). Hodder (1999) has considered "multivocality" as representing the value of a plurality of perspectives for the development of archaeological programs, and distinguishes pluralism from relativism. At the African Burial Ground, we found useful and exciting paths of inquiry as well as elevated scrutiny of evidential proof when naive objectivity was replaced by ethics. It is interesting to consider that the idea of objective methods capable of revealing universal truths may have served to obscure the need for ethics or accountability to nonscientific considerations in the pursuit of knowledge.

Our project has conceived two types of clientage: the descendant community most affected by our research (the ethical client) and the GSA that funds the research (the business client). While both clients have rights that should be protected, the ethical requirements of the field privilege the voices of descendants. Descendants have the right to refuse research entirely and the researcher's obligation is to share what is known about the potential value of bioarchaeological studies. Our project received permission to present a draft research design to African Americans and others interested in the site. Our purpose was to elicit comment, criticism, and new ideas and questions to which the descendant community was most interested in having answers. The result of this public vetting process is, we believe, a stronger research design with more interesting questions

than would have likely come from researchers alone. A sense of community empowerment, in contrast to the preexisting sense of desecration, was fostered by our collaboration. Permission to conduct research according to the resulting design was granted by both clients. Public pressure in support of a more comprehensive research scope than usually afforded such projects resulted from the fact that research questions interested them and that they claimed some ownership of the project. Thus research directions, an epistemological concern, were fostered by public involvement, an ethical concern. The queries produced by the engagement process were condensed to four major research topics:

1 the cultural background and origins of the population;
2 the cultural and biological transformations from African to African-American identities;
3 the quality of life brought about by enslavement in the Americas;
4 the modes of resistance to slavery.

In the application of this approach to an "ethical epistemology" (an ethemology?), experience has shown that conflict, social conflict, can be part and parcel of public engagement. When meeting in a state government auditorium in Harlem while vetting the research design in 1993, the panel of researchers was confronted by some African Americans who objected to our references to slavery in Africa, insisting that slavery had never existed there. We were able to convey familiarity with what we considered to be a reflection of the concern of some African Americans that the Euro-American community's frequent references to African slavery were often meant to suggest that Africans were responsible for the slave trade. That tack gave an apologetic spin that abdicates the responsibility of Europeans and Euro-Americans (the "demand" side of the trade) for American slavery. There was also sensitivity to the all-too-frequent false notion that those brought to the Americas were "slaves" in Africa rather than free people who had been captured and "enslaved." With recognition of this understanding and of differences and similarities between chattel and African household slavery, our requirement as scholars was, nonetheless, to indicate that we would refer to slavery in Africa because of the material evidence for its existence there. It was the community's right to decide whether or not it would encourage scholars to conduct research on the African Burial Ground or to involve only religious practitioners or provide some other treatment. If the project was to be involved, it was to be involved as scholars and that meant standing on evidence. It is significant too that the diasporic scholars on the panel had knowledge of the kinds of critique (not just emotional sensitivity) that had informed the concern over the suggestions of African slavery and could respond that attempts would be made to maintain an awareness, in the course of our work, of previous misuses by other scholars of the fact of slavery in Africa. This we did.

The project leadership was strongly urged to refer to the Africans of colonial New York as "Africans" or "enslaved Africans" rather than slaves. This recommendation upon deliberation and discussion seemed cogent and not inconsistent with material facts. The critical consideration of the community representatives was that "slave" was the objectified role that Europeans and American whites had sought to impose. The Africans themselves, while clearly subject in large part to the conditions of the role of "slave," had often both previous experience and self-concepts that were as complex human beings "who had their own culture before they came here" and who resisted slavery psychologically, politically, and militarily according to material facts. Thus we agreed that we represented the perspectives of slaveholders by using the dehumanizing definition of the people we were to study as slaves, when "enslaved African" reasonably emphasized the deliberate imposition of a condition upon a people with a culture. Similarly we accepted, as did the State and Federal agencies, the renaming of the "Negroes Burying Ground" to the African Burial Ground for reasons similar to the use of "enslaved Africans." And Sherrill Wilson found it in the course of background research for the National Historic Landmarks Designation of the site that Africans named their institutions "African" in New York City as soon as they obtained the freedom to put such nomenclature on record in the early nineteenth century.

This case is exemplary of the value of the process of public engagement and the deliberation,

potential conflict, and reasonable compromise that were often involved. The purpose was to find a synthesis of scholarship and community interests, if a synthesis could be found. These deliberations rest upon trust which is as much established by a demonstration of the integrity of scholarship as it is by the researcher's recognition of the community's ultimate right to determine the disposition of its ancestral remains. Choice of language was one of the most emphatic contributions of the community which did not seem as comfortable with questioning some of the technical aspects of methodology. Invasive methods were discussed and accepted as required to answer the important question of origins that has long been keenly important to African Americans. Family roots and branches were deliberately severed by the economic expediencies and psychological control methods of slavery.

Another community emphasis of importance to the course of the research project was the insistence on including African and Caribbean research in our geographical and cultural scope and on extending the temporal parameters back to the Dutch period when, despite the lack of historical reference, the cemetery might have been used. These ideas helped move the project's research questions and choice of expertise toward the African and diasporic scope that become immensely important for recognizing the specific artifactual, genetic, and epidemiological effects of the cemetery and its population. Furthermore, our team's adherence to the observations of African suppliers of a Euro-American driven transatlantic trade in human captives positioned us properly to receive a senior delegation of the Ghanaian National House of Chiefs who regretfully acknowledged the involvement of some past leaders.

An example of conflict with the project's business client, the GSA, is found in the project's adherence to agreements that the Federal Agency had made on the scope of research, including DNA and chemical studies, that it would begin to reverse 5 years into the study. There seemed to be other attempts to contain or reduce the project by limiting the scope of newsletter mailing or the project and community input into memorialization projects such as the interpretive center. In each case the project leaders returned to the public forum and were brought as com-munity advisors to legislators in New York and on Capitol Hill to make these efforts transparent to the public. Congressmen and community members were able to reiterate their support by letter and verbally to the GSA, which over the course of the project indicated that it was turn-ing the project around and getting it back on track four times, interspersed each time by at least a year of obstruction by a variety of means, usually the elimination of funding. As a partly academically based project, it was possible to continue with alternative funding to meet with the descendant community and govern-ment leaders without fear of loss of the next contract, and the often overwhelming evidence of GSA's inconsistency with its legal require-ments to which it had previously agreed would ultimately bring the agency back to the public to restart the project from the point where it had been when the impediments were put into effect. Although many aspects of the research design (Howard University & John Milner Associates 1993) were ultimately not funded, the integrity of the researchers' relationship to the ethical client was maintained by standing with the com-munity and insisting that the GSA carry through with its commitments. The GSA was not allowed to summarily disregard its legal obligations or promises to the black community once its build-ing had been built, and would have to return to fund aspects of the research and memorialization that it had tabled, sometimes over a period of years. This project's leadership refused to give our business client anything other than our best and honest advice.

Were this project not linked to community interests there might have been fewer conflicts with the federal agency. On the other hand, com-munity engagement (and to some extent the presence of what Congressman Savage called the "obstinacy" of the governmental agency) defined much of the significance of the project that would represent descendant community empo-werment. Part of that empowerment came to be shown by the community's resolve and effective opposition to desecration by a white leadership of a large federal governmental agency of the United States (see Harrington 1993). On the other hand, the project's ability to withstand attempts to arbitrarily end the project is the

result of having a strong base of support in the general public and among legislators represen-ting them. Funding, even under these terms, was adequate for a broad scope of work demon-strated in the current report and two others.

Finally, the project was designed to utilize a biocultural and biohistorical approach and rejected race estimation in favor of culturally salient categories of ethnic origin using DNA, craniometry, archaeological artifacts and features, as well as the available historical record. We had no need of reinforcing the concept of race through our research especially when that con-cept obscures the cultural and historical identity of those who are made subject to its classifica-tion. Moreover, new molecular technologies and specialists in African mortuary data could put us on the trail of ethnic groups with discernable histories. Having acquired the project against the competitive efforts of a forensic team that emphasized its customary use of racing method-ology, an effort in their defense was successfully solicited in which over 50 physical anthropo-logists wrote to the GSA, usually supporting the forensic approach to racing (Cook 1993; Epperson 1997, 1999).

Indeed, a number of these letters and com-ments suggested that the use of DNA, chemistry, and cultural traits such as dental modification could be of no value in determining origins. Without the backing of the descendant commu-nity that was far more interested in social and cultural history than racial classification, the project would not have been able to, as it did, say "no" to the vast majority of physical anthro-pologists who demonstrated a lack of support to the project's business client.

The essential point here is that the questions and approaches that have driven the research of the New York African Burial Ground Project were produced by a public process of empower-ment that involved distinct supporters and detractors. What we have been able to accom-plish for present evaluation and future develop-ment has been the result of protracted struggle with those who customarily expect to control this kind of contracted research to create a research enterprise that is not repugnant to the African-American community. But it is also a project of unusual epistemological complexity. As a result, the project has had an impact upon both the scientific community and public discussions of human rights and reparations for slavery (see Blakey 1998a, 1999b, 2001; La Roche & Blakey 1997). Six documentary films and frequent and lengthy textbook references to the New York African Burial Ground Project (Johnson 1999; Parker Pearson 1999; Thomas 1998 and others) also suggest that the project has raised interesting issues for a broad range of people.

Multiple Data Sets

Multidisciplinary expertise was repeatedly shown to be essential in our attempts to answer the project's major questions regarding the origins, transformations, quality of life, and modes of resistance. Examining a question such as the origin of the population with different sets of data such as genetics, anthropometry, material culture, history, and chemistry was valuable because:

1   Verification of the plausibility of findings on the part of a particular specialized method or set of data is provided in the form of complementary or conflicting results from an alternative data set. Contrasting results were at least as useful as complementary data because these would raise new questions and possibilities about interpretation or the need for methodological development. Biological data (such as molecular genetics) have often been privileged over cultural and historical data. We found genetics data, read in isolation of other information, to lead to erroneous conclusions relative to more verifiably accurate cultural and historical evidence. We do not privilege the biological data, but are benefited from the discussion among the differing results that led us to mutually plausible conclusions. Metaphorically, one voice allowing the floor with impunity can easily make false representations without there being any means of evaluation or accountability. Where there are several voices in a dialogue about facts, the standards of plausibility are elevated by the accountability that the facts generated by each method have to one another. This sort of "discussion" among different data sets become a means, if not of objectivity, of raising standards of plausibility and of fostering a dialectical process by which new research directions would emerge.

2   Multidisciplinary research allows us to recognize more diverse dimensions of the individual biographies and community histories than any one discipline could allow us to "see" in the data. By assessing layers of origins data, for example, we construct the population in terms of its demography, pathology, genetics, cultural influences on burial practices, environmental exposures in teeth, religious history, and art that allow the construction of a more complex human identity at the site. A fraction of these disciplines would have produced a fraction of the richer human qualities we worked to understand because observations are largely limited to the specialized knowledge and research tools required to make them.

3   This disciplinary breadth, inclusive of biology, culture, and history, makes possible the kind of political economic analysis in which we are interested as biocultural anthropologists. The biological data are interpreted in relation to the population's social, political, and economic history. Yet some studies will rely on evolutionary theory while remaining historical in their attempt to discover cultural origins with biological evidence. There needs to be a "tool kit" of theories for purposes of different research questions. The break with tradition here is that such an approach is not in search of a unifying theory that physical anthropology and human evolution are not synonymous.

Diasporic Scope

The descendant community had been forceful in its insistence upon our examination of the African backgrounds for the New York population. Their idea was that these were people with a culture and history that preceded their enslavement and which continued to influence them even in captivity. We found the African and Caribbean connections important for understanding the site in many ways. We would require archaeologists, historians, and biologists with expertise and experience in research in all three areas.

Similar to the value of multidisciplinary resources of the project, the diasporic scope of expertise allowed us to find meaningful evidence where narrower expertise could not have "seen" it. The use of quartz crystals as funerary objects required an African archaeological background whereas Americanist archaeologists might have assigned them no meaning (see Perry 1999); the heart-shaped symbol, believed to be of Akan origin and meaning (see Ansa 1995), was assumed to have a European, Christian meaning in the absence of anyone who could recognize an Akan adinkra symbol. Thus the geographical and cultural connections to the site are enlarged by the diasporic scope of the researchers.

Bioarchaeological projects are often limited to very localized special and temporal contexts of interpretation. Were this project to have limited its scope of interpretation to New York City's history (or to the cemetery itself) the African Burial Ground would have revealed a New York population understood for the immediate conditions of its members' enslavement, or less. A larger international context reveals a cultural background for these captives, an ebb and flow of migration between different environments and social conditions, shifting demographic structures related to a hemispheric economy, and the interactions of people and environments that changed over the course of the life cycle to impact their biology in multiple unhealthy ways. By understanding these African captives as people from societies of their own who were thrust into enslavement in an alien environment, perhaps their human experience can be more readily identified. This at least was the expressed goal in meetings of descendant community members that informed the research design. And of course the desire to reach back and critically examine that experience is motivated by the scope of interests of an African diaspora "concept" that has traditionally included a vindicationist approach to black history that stands against Eurocentric historical apologetics.

A variety of other, specific theories (or explanations relating specific observations to generalizable systems within which they have meaningful implications for us) have been applied to explain particular phenomena observed at the African Burial Ground. The above approaches, however, form the most general framework of our analyses. The meta-theoretical approach described above comprises a process for generating the questions we ask, for assessing the reasons why we are asking those questions, and for making choices about theory with which the information is organized to answer those questions. They are also perhaps the most unique to our situation in which these approaches emerged as special opportunities to resolve problems and contradictions met with at the site. The principles and processes I have described are often likely to be, nonetheless, generalizable and can be usefully extended for bioarchaeological work in many kinds of situations, not to be limited to this site or to African diasporic bioarchaeology.

Final Comment

It has been rewarding to see, now about a quarter century after Joan Gero and I organized the first session on "The Socio-Politics of Archaeology" at the Society for American Archaeology meetings in Minneapolis (see Gero et al. 1983) and with the further inspiration, of the first World Archaeological Congress in Southampton in 1986, the need of practitioners of our field to grapple with the fact of our humanity has begun to be taken seriously enough to produce new ways of knowing the past. One hopes for qualitative change. As for New York's African Burial Ground, our project anthropologists have shared the pleasure of engagement with a community in a battle for the dignity of a desecrated and belittled cemetery, a place that would be established as a new United States National Monument in the summer of 2006.

References

Ansa, K. O. (1995). Identification and validation of the Sankofa symbol. *Update*, 1, 3.

Blakey, M. L. (1987). Skull doctors: Intrinsic social and political bias in the history of American physical anthropology; with special reference to the work of Ales Hrdlicka. *Critique of Anthropology*, 7, 7–35.

Blakey, M. L. (1996). Skull doctors revisited. In L. Reynolds & L. Lieberman (Eds.), *Race and Other*

Misadventures: Essays in Honor of Ashley Montagu in His Ninetieth Year (pp. 64–95). New York: General Hall. Inc.

Blakey, M. L. (1998a). Beyond European enlightenment. In A. H. Goodman & T. L. Leatherman (Eds.), *Building a New Biocultural Synthesis: Political-Economic Perspectives on Human Biology* (pp. 379–405). Ann Arbor: University of Michigan Press.

Blakey, M. L. (1998b). The New York African Burial Ground project: An examination of enslaved lives, a construction of ancestral ties. *Transforming Anthropology*, 7(1), 53–58.

Blakey, M. L. (2001). Bioarchaeology of the African Diaspora in the Americas: Its origins and scope. *Annual Review of Anthropology*, 30, 387–422.

Blakey, M. L., Dubinskas, F., Forman, S., MacLennan, C., Newman, K. S., Peacock, J. L., Rappaport, R. A., Velez-Ibanez, C. G., & Wolfe, A. W. (1994). A statement to the profession: the American Anthropological Association Panel on Disorders of Industrial Societies. In S. Forman (Ed.), *Diagnosing America: Anthropology and Public Engagement* (pp. 295–311). Michigan: University of Michigan Press.

Cook, K. (1993). Black bones, white science: The battle over New York's African Burial Ground. *Village Voice*, 4 May, 23–27.

Crosby, A. (1986). *Ecological Imperialism: the Biological Expansion of Europe 900–1900.* Cambridge: Cambridge University Press.

Douglass, F. (1999) [1854]. Claims of the Negro ethnologically considered, commencement speech at Western Reserve University, Cleveland, OH. In P. S. Foner (Ed.), *Frederick Douglass: Selected Speeches and Writings* (pp. 282–297). Chicago: Lawrence Hill Books.

Drake, St.C. (1980). Anthropology and the Black experience. *The Black Scholar*, 11, 2–31.

Epperson, T. W. (1997). The politics of "race" and cultural identity at the African Burial Ground excavations, New York City. *World Archaeological Bulletin*, 7, 108–117.

Epperson, T. W. (1999). The contested commons: archaeologies of race, repression, and resistance in New York City. In M. P. Leone & P. B. Potter, Jr. (Eds.), *Historical Archaeologies of Capitalism* (pp. 81–110), New York: Plenum.

Forman, S. (Ed.), (1994). *Diagnosing America: Anthropology and Public Engagement.* Ann Arbor: University of Michigan Press.

Gero, J., Lacy, D., & Blakey, M. (Eds.), (1983). *The Socio-Politics of Archaeology.* Research Report No. 23. Amherst: University of Massachusetts, Department of Anthropology.

Gould, S. J. (1981). *The Mismeasure of Man.* New York: Norton & Company.

Harrington, S. P. M. (1993). Bones and bureaucrats. *Archaeology*, 46(2), 28–38.

Harrison, F. V., & Harrison, I. (1999). *African American Pioneers in Anthropology.* Chicago: University of Illinois Press.

Hodder, I. (1999). *The Archaeological Process: An Introduction.* Oxford: Blackwell Publishers.

Howard University & John Milner Associates, (1993). *Research Design for Archeological, Historical, and Bioanthropological Investigations of the African Burial Ground (Broadway Block) New York, New York.*

Ingle, M., Howson, J., & Edward, R. S. (1990). *A Stage 1A Cultural Resource Survey of the Proposed Foley Square Project in the Borough of Manhattan, New York, New York.* Edwards and Kelcey Engineers, Inc., and the General Services Administration. Newton, NJ: Historic Conservation and Interpretation, Inc.

Johnson, M. (1999). *Archaeological Theory: An Introduction.* Oxford: Blackwell Publishers.

La Roche, C. J., & Blakey, M. L. (1997). Seizing intellectual power: The dialogue at the New York African Burial Ground. *Historical Archaeology*, 31, 84–106.

Lynott, M. J., & Wylie, A. (Eds.), (1995). *Ethics in American Archaeology: Challenges for the 1990s.* Washington D.C.: Society for American Archaeology.

Parker Pearson, M. (1999). *The Archaeology of Death and Burial.* College Station: Texas A&M University Press.

Perry, W. (1999). *Landscape Transformations and the Archaeology of Impact: Social Disruption and State Formation in Southern Africa.* Normal, IL: Illinois State University.

Rankin-Hill, L. M., & Blakey, M. L. (1994). W. Montague Cobb: Physical anthropologist, anatomist, and activist. *American Anthropologist*, 96, 74–96.

Thomas, D. H. (1998). *Archaeology* (3rd edition). Fort Worth: Harcourt College Publishers.

Cultures of Contact, Cultures of Conflict?

Identity Construction, Colonialist Discourse, and the Ethics of Archaeological Practice in Northern Island

Audrey Horning

Introduction

Current trends in the archaeology of formerly colonized regions specifically highlight the concerns of indigenous and descendant communities in addressing the ethics of archaeological practice in the modern world. In most formerly colonized regions, there is clearly an imbalance of power yet to be addressed, and in places like Australia and South Africa in particular, archaeologists have immersed themselves in efforts to validate the concerns of historically disenfranchised communities, and in some instances, to promote their agendas (e.g. Harrison 2002; Harrison, Greer, and McIntyre-Tamwoy 2002). The ethics of practice, while hardly straightforward, have a clear focus. Such advances in indigenous rights and involvement in archaeology are critically important and of significant import and impact for 21st-century archaeological practice. But the situation in Northern Ireland is not quite so 'black and white.'

Contemporary identity in Northern Ireland is fragile, complicated, and fragmented. The modern

Audrey Horning, "Cultures of Contact, Cultures of Conflict? Identity Construction, Colonialist Discourse, and the Ethics of Archaeological Practice in Northern Ireland," pp. 107–33 from *Stanford Journal of Archaeology* 5 (2007). Copyright © Audrey Horning 2007. Reprinted with the kind permission of the author.

division of society into two 'traditions', Roman Catholic/nationalist and Protestant/unionist, is rooted in the fraught interactions of native Irish, English, and Scots during the 17th-century Plantation period when British control was made manifest by importation of loyal Protestant settlers. Archaeological evidence from the period readily contradicts essentialist notions of 'the two traditions,' yet in terms of self perception both communities currently view themselves as constituting a distinct and threatened minority. What do we do when faced with a paradoxical situation where all communities self-identify as potentially marginalized and dispossessed? Arguably, by focusing on the ambiguity and complexity inherent in contemporary Irish society as rooted in the relations of the last 500 years, there are lessons for other contested places where contact breeds conflict and creates culture(s).

In looking at the ethics of archaeological practice in Northern Ireland, and also in the Republic of Ireland, I want to reflect not only on the potential of a critical, inclusive archaeology to positively impact upon a divided society, but I also want to analyze more explicitly how we, as professionals, make decisions about inclusivity and exclusivity. Not just how we select 'passive' audiences, but how we aim to identify those active groups generically and awkwardly labeled 'stakeholders.' To what extent do these stake-holders (be they real or constructed) determine, direct, constrain, or broaden our practice? How do we address the validity of competing histor-ical narratives while acknowledging our own biases? Before addressing these issues, however, it is necessary to examine the tangled roots of contemporary conflict in Northern Ireland and to evaluate the advantages and disadvantages of applying postcolonial theory (broadly defined as approaches which seek to redress historic imbalances) to its interpretation.

Background

The roots of contemporary conflict in Northern Ireland lie in the expansion of English, and sub-sequently British, control over Ireland in the 16th and 17th centuries. While England main-tained a degree of political and economic control over Ireland since the Anglo-Norman invasions of the 12th century, the Reformation, fears of Spain, and the increasing commodification of nature inherent in what Immanuel Wallerstein's labeled the capitalist world system (Wallerstein 1974), conspired in the strengthening of England's grip on the island. After a prolonged war in Munster which ended in 1583, Queen Elizabeth instituted a policy of planting English settlers on 400,000 acres of forfeited land, build-ing upon earlier efforts to secure protection for Dublin through the creation of English enclaves in what are today Counties Laois and Offaly. The remainder of Ireland, however, did not submit to English authority until the defeat of Hugh O'Neill in 1603 (Canny 2001).

When James VI of Scotland ascended to the English throne in 1603, England was well posi-tioned to profit from its authority over Ireland. The "flight of the earls" of Tyrone and Tyrcon-nell in 1607 resulted in the forfeiture of the six counties of Armagh, Cavan, Coleraine, Donegal, Fermanagh, and Tyrone to the Crown. James I (VI) began to plant the newly acquired lands, along with nearby Antrim and Down, in an effort to replace the native population with loyal British subjects. Land grants were made to individual 'undertakers,' often loyal soldiers. To help fund this Ulster Plantation initiative, James compelled the Livery Companies of London (the

medieval merchant guilds) to finance part of the effort, repaying the companies with grants of land in the newly created county of London-derry. By 1630, the Companies had collectively contributed between £60,000 and £70,000 to build and protect their settlements, located in what was considered to be the wildest and most vulnerable part of Ulster (Bardon 1992; Canny 2001; Curl 1986; Gillespie 1993; Loeber 1991; Moody 1939; Robinson 1984).

The ambitious aims of the Ulster Plantation, however, were never fully achieved. Native Irish residents were never wholly displaced, and the incoming British settlers never constituted a powerful, unified elite. Political uncertainty and involvement in the War of the Three Kingdoms (better known by the wholly inaccurate label of the English Civil War) in the mid-17th century ensured that the ambitious goals of the planta-tion scheme, in terms of landholding and urban development, were never achieved. Protestant control over the affairs of Ireland was not assured until after the Williamite Wars of 1688–1690, when the Catholic James II was unsuccess-ful in challenging the royal claim of the Protestant William of Orange (Canny 2001; Kennedy 1996; Ohlmeyer 1993).

Yet historical memories of the 17th century are invoked by both traditions to illustrate and underscore ongoing conflict, as reflected in the internationally recognized tradition of mural painting (Jarman 2002). Loyalist murals employ images and memories of symbolic events such as the 'massacre' of Protestant settlers during the Irish Rebellion of 1641, the 1689 Siege of Derry, and the subsequent victory of King Billy at the Battle of the Boyne in July of 1690. Polemical tracts celebrate the achievements of "peace-loving and industrious" Protestants, who intro-duced "habits of order and industry" to Ireland during the Plantation, "where before there had been only robbers' castles, miserable huts, and mud cabins" (Dunleath 1914). By contrast, Republican communities lament the Flight of the Earls (sometimes termed Flight of the Gaelic Nobility to lessen the emphasis upon the English title of Earl), and recall with bitterness the 'massacre' of Catholic Irish in Drogheda and Wexford by Cromwell's soldiers in 1649.

Moving beyond the 17th century, nationalist murals employ imagery from the Great Hunger of the 1840s to suggest a deliberate policy of genocide on the part of the British government (a perception encouraged largely by the persistent Famine memory of the Irish American Diasporic community). Representations of these events serve to justify the violence that characterized the most recent conflict, which began in 1968 and is colloquially termed 'The Troubles.' Over 3,000 deaths have been attributed to the Troubles. In light of the overall population size of Northern Ireland – approximately 1.7 million people – the ratio is roughly equivalent to half a million deaths in the United States (McLernon et al. 2003). Adding a further level of complexity to understandings of contemporary Northern Irish society is the often downplayed reality that a disproportionate amount of Troubles-related violence was suffered by Protestant and Catholic working-class communities. For example, examination of the 2,763 deaths that occurred in the first 20 years of the Troubles reveals that "areas of the Province that are materially disadvantaged have also experienced disproportionately high levels of violence" (Coulter 1999: 72; McKeown 1989: 50). Scholarly as well as political debate over whether or not 'The Troubles' are best understood as the result of economic, social, or religious tensions is heated, ongoing, and unlikely to be resolved. However the contemporary conflict is understood, its legacy has left an indelible mark upon the people of the province and particularly upon how they are perceived externally.

While the distinct nature of the two traditions is open to question, it is clear that in terms of self perception, both communities view themselves as constituting a threatened minority. As the Catholic population continues to rise in the North, unionist fears of the inevitability of a united Catholic Ireland increase, exacerbated by the growing alienation of unionists from the remainder of the United Kingdom. While strong links still exist between Scotland and Northern Ireland, some English people seem to be unaware that Northern Ireland remains part of the United Kingdom (by way of anecdotal evidence, when I moved to England I was repeatedly told when trying to open a bank account that the fact I already had a Northern Ireland bank account was irrelevant to my application as the account

was in a 'foreign' country). Forty-seven percent of Northern Ireland's population self-identify as British (74 percent of Protestants and 12 percent of Catholics self identify as British, 2004 *Northern Ireland Life and Times Survey,* www.ark.ac.uk/nilt/2004/) yet would be labeled as Irish or perhaps Northern Irish outside the boundaries of the province (Nic Craith 2002: 131–132).

By contrast, Catholic Northern Irish may be increasing numerically, but they themselves are often viewed suspiciously by many in the Republic of Ireland (Nic Craith 2002: 145). Despite the ambiguities experienced by both communities, the majority of works purporting to explore the topic of Irish identity – scholarship which draws heavily upon postcolonial theory – is the assumption that the historical and contemporary experiences of the Catholic nationalist community equate to subalternity (eg. Garner 2004; Graham 2001; Graham and Kirkland 1999; Kiberd 1997; cf. Gramsci 1971; Spivak 1988). But to identify any community as somehow more subaltern than another effectively constitutes a political statement. Arguably, if anyone in Northern Ireland could be classified as subaltern it is the working-class communities on both sides of the community divide which truly qualify.

Ireland as Postcolonial?

To analyze the potential contribution of postcolonial approaches to Ireland's historical archaeology necessitates a critical examination of basic concepts, as well as considering who benefits from the imposition of postcoloniality on the Republic of Ireland and Northern Ireland. To be postcolonial presumably requires first being colonial. So, how do we define colonialism, and is it the best framework for understanding the archaeology of early modern and modern Ireland? To answer these questions requires balancing the disparate and often heated arguments of scholars in the fields of Irish history, anthropology, cultural theory, geography, politics, and economics, while also considering the broader Atlantic context – especially in light of the trend towards an ideology of a global historical archaeology (eg. Orser 1996). It has not been difficult for scholars to make the case that the

Republic of Ireland is 'postcolonial' by its own definition following the struggle for independence in the early 20th century. The potential of understanding the archaeology of the 26 counties of the Republic through the lens of colonialism is being tested by Charles Orser's work in Roscommon and Sligo (Orser 1996; 2004), the work of postgraduate students in Dublin, Galway, and Cork, and Jim Delle's attempt to draw parallels with Jamaica (Delle 1999). Elsewhere I have critiqued Delle for drawing stark, simplistic parallels between the experience of enslaved Afro-Jamaicans and Irish Catholics in his effort to "outline a spatial theory which can be used to compare the material culture of colonial episodes in disparate temporal and spatial contexts" (Horning 2006a; cf. Delle 1999: 115).

While comparative colonialism may be a useful framework for examining the archaeology of the Republic of Ireland, in any application of colonialism to Irish history the elephant in the room is inevitably Northern Ireland. Imposing the rhetoric of postcolonialism on the North merely drives the wedge of dichotomization between the 'two traditions' deeper. In the North, unionists and some historians employ the close relationship between medieval England and Ireland in questioning a colonial past. By contrast, 'de-colonization' remains a central platform of Sinn Féin ideology, which therefore places the incendiary label of 'colonizer' or 'settler' onto present-day Ulster Protestants, a problematic label that is often uncritically accepted by social scientists (eg. D. Miller 1998). Not only does the label imply a straightforward colonial history, but it also ignores the perspective of those who point to the strong connections between the western isles of Scotland and the north of Ireland stretching back into the Neolithic period. Some of the more extreme claims promote the idea of the Scots as the original Irish (based upon a loose reading of Iron Age evidence relating to a tribe named the Cruthín) to promote the greater claims of the Ulster Scots protestants to the land of the north of Ireland. According to one such tract, "the ancient people of Ulster – the Cruthín – began a migration to Lowland Scotland after their defeat at the hands of the Gaels at the battle of Moira in 637 AD" (Hume 1986: 12). By this logic, Scots who

participated in the Plantation were reclaiming their ancestral lands. While I am not particularly sympathetic to some of these claims, I very much believe that as practitioners, we have an ethical responsibility to the people we study and the communities in which we work that includes recognizing the power and seriousness of multiple narratives. The interests of local communities may not be well served by an overemphasis upon simplistic models of colonialism and postcolonialism, coupled with the muting effects of a global historical archaeology, which assumes an often adversarial and always uneven relationship between colonized and colonizer. Not only are the interests of contemporary populations not well served by stark models, neither are those of the original participants in what was a murky process riven with uncertainty, insecurity, and incompletion.

While Declan Kiberd (1997: 81) overtly celebrates the Irish as "the first English-speaking people ... to attempt a programme of decolonization," the Republic of Ireland's active participation in the European Union has concomitantly spurred a rejection of the colonial model of Irish history in favor of models of European state development (cf. Ruane 1992). In asking "How does this [Irish] self-image of exceptional suffering and victimhood, which belongs primarily to the nationalist community in Ireland, look when viewed in comparative terms?", historian Liam Kennedy finds little evidence to support the postcolonial formulation. Kennedy clearly enjoys his role as a revisionist, celebrating the fact that "historians have a tendency to spoil a good story" (Kennedy 1996: 187). Yet it is the tenacity of the stories, and the strength of perceptions of colonialism that nevertheless remain paramount in the construction of contemporary identities, and therefore must be recognized and potentially deconstructed in public discourse.

To use colonialism as a lens requires that we recognize the spotty, complicated, non-inevitability of the process, and to view colonialism, in the words of Stephen Howe (2000: 110) as "a patchwork quilt, an enormously varied set of forms of rule and domination, largely the product of improvisation and full of internal contradictions and strains, rather than a deliberately constructed global system." Static treatises on the nature of colonialism presume a binary opposition between colonizer and colonized (not unlike the two traditions model), which offer little to considerations of the complexity of Irish identities. Recognition of the ambiguous structures of early modern colonialism centuries takes us closer to addressing the ambiguities of identity formation. Any examination of colonialism has to acknowledge that social relations are never purely colonial, in the sense of being firmly rooted in exploitation.

Education, Memory, and Multiple Histories

Over the last decade, I have taught the archaeology of British expansion – 'colonialism' – in the United States, Northern Ireland, and, most recently and currently, England. In each land, historical understandings of the colonial process, and, more critically, its legacy, vary wildly. The word 'colonial' in America's Chesapeake region is swaddled in patriotic rhetoric, the violence, uncertainties, and unresolved conflicts deliberately forgotten. In suggesting back in 1993 – on the basis of pretty incontrovertible archaeological evidence – that Virginia's 17th-century capital Jamestown was actually a bit of a non-functioning dump filled with garbage and abandoned buildings, I did not endear myself to tradition-minded Virginia archaeological patrons (Horning [...] 1995; 2000; 2006b; 2006c). Supporting the notion that Jamestown and its scant citizens were actually more English in culture and outlook than proto-American also seems to have fallen on deaf ears, as official rhetoric associated with the 2007 anniversary of Jamestown's founding emphasized the site as the 'birthplace of America' – exactly as celebrated in 1957. Despite calls by native and African American leaders to consider the multiple legacies of the Jamestown settlement, President George Bush overtly employed the word 'celebrate' in his keynote speech at the 13 May, 2007 commemorative assembly at Jamestown Island, stating "... we celebrate the 400th anniversary of Jamestown to honor the beginnings of our democracy" (www.dailypress.com May 13). Given the current political climate in the United States, with its intensification of nationalism and

protectionism, this is hardly surprising – but it does not bode well for the ongoing struggle of some of Virginia's First People to gain Federal recognition and thus a degree of empowerment through the Native American Graves Protection and Repatriation Act (NAGPRA).

Academic discussions of the colonial process in the Chesapeake (outside of Jamestown) have begun to focus on creolization, emphasizing shared elements and creativity within colonial society (eg. Mouer 1993; Mouer et al 1999). Similar emphasis upon cultural creativity can be found in Chris Gosden's general examination of the archaeology of colonialism (Gosden 2004). American students find this relatively 'positive' view of the creativity of the colonial encounter far more palatable than one that emphasizes the violence and discord of colonial entanglements, such as those presented by Carmel Schrire (1996) and Martin Hall (2000) for South Africa. It is not difficult to ascribe these contrasting views of the colonial encounter to contemporary politics and historical memories in both lands.

By contrast, I have found English students to be uncomfortable with discussing any aspect of colonialism, initially unable to disassociate themselves from feeling implicated in the process. Lacking a diachronic conception of the process of European expansion over the last 500 years, owing to the theme-based approach of secondary school history curricula, the students struggle to break away from their episodic knowledge of Victorian imperialism to consider the ambiguities of Elizabethan and Jacobean exploration and colonization. Furthermore, unlike American and Irish students, they are wholly unaccustomed to considering a linkage between early modern British expansion and the unsettled socio-political realities of the 21st century. In discussing history teaching in Northern Ireland, Barton and McCully note that "teaching history in a society that has experienced violent and on-going conflict, at least partially as a consequence of contested views of national identity, presents significant challenges for educators" (Barton and McCully 2003: 107). Oddly, in my experience, teaching history where people have no sense of it at all may be more of a challenge, particularly when introducing concepts such as memory, identity, multiple histories, and the inextricable linkage between past, present, and future.

Northern Irish students from both traditions at the University of Ulster had a far more sophisticated, critical, and, perhaps unfortunately, realistic approach than either the English or American students that I have taught. The Northern Irish students politely listened to my fervent efforts to introduce concepts such as creolization and Gosden's 'creativity,' and they readily accepted the archaeological evidence for the sharing of a material culture by 'natives' and 'newcomers' and the significant daily relations that implies. They saw it all, they recognized it all, they could even intellectually situate themselves as products of this process. Yet they also understood that in contemporary Northern Ireland, the reality of a shared material culture in the 17th century, and by extension the lack of clearly definable cultural differences between the two traditions, seemingly matters very little. In a land where only four percent of schoolchildren are educated in an integrated environment, sectarian narratives of the past remain deeply rooted (Barton and McCully 2003; Nic Craith 2003). Ingrained, externally imposed patterns of belief about social relations concurrently bolster and dismiss a colonial past.

More unfortunate is the fact that the students' understanding of the irrelevancy of the complexity of past experiences in considering modern dichotomous identities is reflected in the astonishing lack of historical knowledge prevalent in a range of sociological writings about the Northern Ireland 'problem.' By focusing solely on the contemporary conflict, the potentially subversive impact of a deeper historical understanding is ignored. For example, in an otherwise sophisticated discussion of memory in Northern Ireland, McLernon et al. completely misconstrue the history that is being remembered. The authors state "... after the emergence of Protestantism in England, the controlling English swamped the Catholic faith in Ireland and the identity of the Irish people. ... by the 18th century the colonists occupied 95 percent of the land which they had confiscated from the natives ..." (McLernon et al. 2003: 126). This statement may resonate with a particularly nationalist view of the past, but it is factually incorrect and in the charged climate of Northern Ireland, is dangerous. English

control over Ireland was never absolute, nor was Catholicism ever obliterated, nor did the complex of multivalent Irish identities ever diminish in the absolute fashion implied.

If we are ever to go beyond merely assessing the importance of historical memory to altering its results, surely we need to re-examine the efficacy or inefficacy of the remembered histories. Here at last is a socially engaged role for archaeology, an opportunity to capitalize upon the often inherent interest of the public in the idea of archaeology, which can lead to a surprising exchange of information and interpretation. Unlike most social scientists immersed in studying contemporary Northern Ireland, our work is physical and publicly visible. In the seeming tangibility of archaeological data, in the incontrovertible physicality of Irish-made pottery found in an 17th-century English village, lies the power to spark a rethinking of narratives. The power is held not by the archaeologists interpreting the significance of the material, but by the non-specialist and how they choose to account for the physical evidence in front of their eyes. It is not for us to control this process, while at the same time judicious, respectful direction may be the course most appropriate for the past and for the present.

Towards Ethical Engagement in Uncomfortable Histories

Negotiating the landscapes of identity and politics in both Northern Ireland and the Republic of Ireland within the framework of comparative colonial archaeology is dependent upon the development and implementation of an ethical and publicly inclusive practice. An ethical and nuanced archaeology of early modern Ireland must not only acknowledge but must prioritize the role of archaeology in fostering positive and informed discourse to challenge the assumptions which reify a deeply divided society. Our challenge as academic archaeologists is to not only be well-versed in our intellectual familiarity with the writings of postcolonial theorists, or our knowledge of primary documentary sources and material culture, or our understanding of stratigraphy and construction sequences, but to possess a willingness and an ability to engage disparate publics in a discourse. Furthermore, as I have argued elsewhere, we must recognize the valid concerns of private sector field archaeologists and accept the responsibilities of our 'privileged' position as researchers (Horning 2006a). We must put our time into developing a nuanced and inclusive practice – an effort that is often denied to even our most concerned and self-aware compatriots in the time-pressured and constrained environment of development-driven rescue archaeology.

Part of the process, as everywhere, is to embark on the difficult process of identifying 'stakeholders' and interested/affected communities, and consider the relevance and role of the 'audience' in determining the archaeological agenda. I have chosen to prioritize the relationship with local communities in my work in the case studies to follow. However, it has to be acknowledged that throughout the Republic of Ireland (in contrast to Northern Ireland), the audience for 'heritage' is not only local communities, but also tourists. Specifically, American tourists. More specifically, the millions of Americans who claim Irish ancestry. As the peace dividend pays out in Northern Ireland, this trend is likely to creep past the border, with a concomitant effect on the character of local history presentations. Already the voyeuristic practice of 'Troubles Tourism' attracts many foreign visitors, who cruise along in black taxis or minibuses through the embattled neighborhoods of working-class Belfast. Armed with their assumptions as well as their cameras, visitors are treated to the spectacle of murals, 'peace' lines, the Holy Cross primary school, and the graves of Hunger Strikers in Milltown cemetery (Jarman 2002). The significance of memory amongst Diasporic groups has long been acknowledged by scholars, some of whom celebrate the connections, and some of whom lament the connections – witness the oft-repeated satirical phrase coined by Kerby Miller regarding "the loud communal whine" of Irish American politics (K. Miller 1985).

In considering the audience for his studies of Famine-era rural life in the west of Ireland, American historical archaeologist Charles Orser acknowledges the influence and role of the Irish Diasporic community: "The descendant community encompasses a global cohort of thousands of people who were forcibly evicted from their homes as a direct result of landlord power. Many of these men and women find themselves living in North America and elsewhere simply because their ancestors were dispossessed in Ireland" (Orser 2004: 174). Yet motives for emigration are always complex. This characterization of the Famine-period emigration to North America (according to one estimate, approximately eight million Irish emigrated between 1801 and 1892 [Fitzpatrick 1984; see also Foster 2002 for a critique of Famine scholarship]) as wholly derived from landlord evictions ignores the movement of urban residents as well as small landholders, overstates the numbers of evictions, and does not take into account the historiography on wider European population movements during the 19th century. As a characterization of the entirety of Irish emigration to North America, it overlooks the movement of substantial numbers of Ulster Protestants during the 18th century. No matter how solid an Irish American's genealogical associations may be, in terms of daily life and identity, the actual connections of fifth- and sixth-generation Irish Americans to the Famine-era Irish sites are at best visceral and at worst imagined. Irish Americans already approach Ireland from a position of privilege. Shouldn't their external, Diasporic concerns be secondary to those of the people currently in the 'homeland'?

Like Delle, Orser (1996; 2005) also endeavors to draw parallels between the Irish experience and that of the African Diaspora in referencing his experience working at Palmares in Brazil, and in considering the racialization of the Irish in the 19th century. However, the experience of enslavement, and the psychological impact of being classed as property, cannot be viewed as equivalent to the experience of a rural peasant, no matter how difficult the life of an Irish tenant farmer may have been, how much economic and political inequity they suffered, and however they may have been described by contemporary chroniclers. Despite the clever arguments of Ignatiev (1996), discussing the experiences of enslaved Africans as articulating with the experiences of the Irish Diaspora runs the risk of being unself-reflexive and potentially deeply offensive. While in no way equating the experiences of the African Diaspora with that of the Irish, I would also argue against prioritizing the concerns of African American visitors to Ghana who are uncomfortable with the preservation of the Elmina slave trading post – while acknowledging the validity of the visitors' complaints (see Kahnpeyeng and DeCorse 2004). In the end, their economic power and hence louder voice should not overturn the local decision to commemorate the complex occurrences at a site which undeniably witnessed much bloodshed, heartache, and unresolved cultural anxieties.

While I can question Orser's choice of stakeholders for his archaeological projects, at least he identifies them. A quick scan of publications produced by the well-funded Discovery Programme for archaeological research in the Republic of Ireland reveals no consideration of the audience for these projects, reliant instead on a presumption of value rather than sailing into the uncharted territory of asking 'why'? Elsewhere, it would appear that heritage professionals intentionally decry the power of a public, any public, as witness the rather astonishing statement in the poorly illustrated, densely-packed 713-page tome *The Heritage of Ireland* which baldly states on the first page that "the interests of Ireland's heritage are perhaps best served … [by entrusting] its advancement to people suitably equipped to discharge this responsibility" (Buttimer, Rynne and Guerin 2004: vii). Bolstered by exceptionally strong legislation protecting historic sites, few seem to outwardly question the public value of heritage, although this debate is beginning to occur in the Republic of Ireland owing to public interest in the impact of a motorway scheme on the archaeological landscape of the Hill of Tara, itself a potent nationalist symbol.

Postcolonialism and the Presentation of Heritage in the Republic of Ireland

Before returning specifically to the ethics of practice in Northern Ireland, I would like to tarry a little longer in the Republic of Ireland to illustrate the power of a nationalist-derived, Irish American voice. The abandoned cottages which dot the landscape of the west of Ireland serve as an ever-present reminder of the impact of emigration and concomitant memories of poverty, discord, and to some, cultural oppression. Emotive survivals such as the Deserted Village of Slievemore (Figure 28.1), on Achill Island, Co. Mayo, appeal to visitors infused with Kennedy's MOPE (Most Oppressed People Ever) syndrome (Kennedy 1996: 121), while more locally the site inspires discomfort and disinterest. Surprisingly little documentation seems to exist about those who dwelt in the village following its 18th-century establishment. The Deserted Village has been archaeologically investigated since 1991 under the aegis of the Achill Archaeological Field School, founded by Achill native Theresa McDonald, who began the project initially more interested in the Neolithic activity underlying the post-medieval village. In 2004 and 2005, I directed fieldwork in the village for two twelve-week training excavations principally attended by paying American students. We took a household archaeology approach, focusing specifically upon the potential of the material culture associated with the 19th-century village to inform our understandings of daily life during a period of undeniable political, economic, and social turmoil, and instituted a series of public open days (McDonald and Horning 2004; Horning and Brannon 2005).

Probably the most intriguing aspect of the village is the disjuncture between presumptive memory and archaeological reality. Visitors to the village encounter the stark and empty husks of long-abandoned houses. No great leap of imagination is required to visualize the depopulation as a direct result of the Great Hunger. Indeed, Famine memory is strong on Achill, particularly in relation to the activities of the Protestant Achill Mission at Dugort, established at the foot of Slievemore Mountain. The Mission and its founder Reverend Edward Nangle are popularly understood as buying converts (derided as 'jumpers' or 'soupers') with food relief (McDonald 1997, 1998; McNally 1973). Whatever the truth of these tales, Achill undoubtedly was hit hard by the Famine. However, archaeological evidence from the Deserted Village makes it clear that occupation continued throughout and following the Famine period. Despite perception and even memory, the Deserted Village was not deserted until the end of the 19th century, with continued use (albeit seasonal) into the 1940s.

Figure 28.1   Deserted Village, Slievemore, Achill Island, Co. Mayo. Although the archaeological record indicates that these dwellings were still in use into the 20th century, the site evokes received memories about the Famine and the trauma of 19th-century emigration amongst visitors. Public open days associated with the Achill Archaeological Field School aimed to challenge these perceptions employing the archaeological evidence. Photograph by the author.

Over the two seasons, we excavated one half of a single unit byre dwelling along with its adjacent garden. Evidence for daily practice is plentiful. Sandy patches in the well-turned soils in the potato rigs suggests the enrichment of the soil through the use of seaweed and provide testament to the routine labor of women. Investigation of the interior of the dwelling revealed how the past occupants altered the original uniform house plan to suit their own purposes (Horning and Brannon 2005). While 18th- and 19th-century descriptions of the west of Ireland expound upon the dearth of material possessions and a lack of interaction with a so-called outside world, the piece-plotted artifact assemblage is replete with decorated tea wares (principally English and Scottish spongewares), manufactured glass, and commercial food jars and cans. Such findings from Slievemore give the lie not only to the 19th-century commentators, but also to mythical notions about the west of Ireland existing in some sort of arrested medieval Gaelic manner until the policies of the British government conspired to eradicate the last vestiges of the true Irish through starvation. I hasten to add that possession of tea wares does not ameliorate

the genuine economic and political inequities at play on Achill, but it should force us to re-evaluate our black-and-white understanding of the rural Irish experience, putting some color and complexity back into the lives of the Slievemore villagers even if it is not what people who come to the site today expect to find.

In his excavations at Ballykilcline, Co. Roscommon, Charles Orser encountered similar ceramic assemblages, noting that "such a large relative percentage of English-made ceramic vessels at the house sites of the Narys was unexpected." Orser suggests that "the purchase of English ceramics may have been conceptualized as an act of covert resistance on the part of the Ballykilcline tenants," to explain why "they willingly bought into the economic system being pressed around the world under the auspices of the same colonial power that sought to dominate them" (Orser 2004; 74–75). Given the documented acts of resistance to rent-paying attempted by these tenant families, perhaps that was indeed their motivation for buying decorated teawares. But is the consumption of tea in the 19th century inherently a colonialist imposition? A century after its introduction to Ireland, it must have become something quite different. Like 'new' habits and material culture anywhere, it is subsumed and subverted into an operational vocabulary. Why couldn't the Slievemore villagers have conceived of teawares – mainly produced in the potteries of Glasgow (and thus arguably Scottish) – not as alien or foreign, or 'English', but as familiar and desirable? Given the outward similarity of their stone cabins, perhaps variety and color on the table served to demarcate individuals and families, and to highlight each family's ability to share hospitality. I have yet to be convinced that the most efficacious means of interpreting the archaeology of 19th-century Ireland is the black-and-white, adversarial rhetoric of resistance predicated upon essentialised notions of cultural identity and traditional folklife, which themselves are based upon dominant nationalist narratives of Irish history.

Such nationalist narratives impact upon the interpretation of material culture beyond the very few excavations which examine the 19th century. Not far from Achill Island, the National Museum of Ireland recently opened up the Museum of Country Life, highlighting its impressive folklife collections, in the market town of Castlebar, Co. Mayo. Located in the former Turlough House Park, once owned by the Fitzgerald family, the Museum of Country Life aims to "portray the lives of ordinary people who lived in rural Ireland in the period 1850–1950. Emphasis is placed on the continuity of lifestyles, which were established for several hundred years and which lasted well into the 20th century." One of the permanent exhibits addresses *Romanticism and Reality* and is described in museum publicity as follows: "Life in rural Ireland is popularly portrayed as simple and romantic. The reality was different. Life was a struggle and survival depended on a detailed knowledge of landscape and environment, on craft, skill and ingenuity. This way of life changed little over many hundreds of years and continuity is evident in the similarities between recently-made objects and their counterparts made long ago" (http://www.museum.ie/ countrylife/overview.asp). The hard if inventive lives of the country folk are presented in clear contrast with those of the Fitzgeralds (descendants of 12th-century Anglo-Norman 'colonizers') in the high Victorian gothic Turlough House.

Displays highlight crafts such as furniture making, thatching, vernacular boat construction, and basketry, with images from windswept Achill Island and other west coast locales providing a backdrop which emphasizes isolation. Hardship is overtly defined in light of the colonial relationship with Britain, with the underlying theme of an essential Irishness that ultimately triumphed through Independence.

While the museum's interpretation is geared, in part, to remind today's materially rich Irish population of the sacrifices of their ancestors, the interpretation is also readily understood by a Diasporic visitor, weaned on stories of oppression tempered by eventual triumph on the golden shores of America. Like a superficial reading of the Deserted Village, the exhibits play into accepted histories and memories. Sadly, the complexities of the lives of now deceased Irish rural families and communities have been intentionally erased in favor of this one-dimensional portrayal, a calculated useable past which dehumanizes and obliterates. Irish country folk, we must believe, never even had the choice to buy English and Scottish teawares, regardless if such an act exemplified a desire to engage in rituals of hospitality, or rituals of resistance. The archaeological records of 19th-century Slievemore and 19th-century Ballykilcline might as well not exist at all.

Heritage as Social Action in Northern Ireland

Archaeologists practicing in Northern Ireland who aim to question similarly stark, dichotomous histories do so while operating in a world marked by political uncertainties with Plantation-era roots, where public discourse over colonialism can entail genuine personal risk. Drawing immediate and overt links between past and present risks losing the attention of a public hyper-sensitized to even the slightest hint of partisanship, in a land where even the name you choose to use for one of Northern Ireland's largest settlements, Derry/Londonderry, is construed as a statement of political allegiance. As noted by one archaeologist in response to a questionnaire I sent out to colleagues in Northern Ireland, some archaeologists try to avoid the period altogether: "many practitioners barely register the post-medieval period as being of archaeological interest, or are nervous of the historical and political baggage that comes with it" (Anon. 2001). In such a climate, those archaeologists who are interested in post-medieval sites often opt to privilege the archaeological process or local history in site interpretation. This approach should be seen as intentional and sensitive; a means of ensuring maximum cross-community engagement in a non-threatening fashion and in a manner where the door is at least opened for further critical discourse (Horning 2006a).

While never overtly political in expression, texts relating to the archaeological heritage of Northern Ireland often evoke an intended audience and a hoped-for outcome. For example, in the Foreword to the monumental study of the maritime archaeology of Strangford Lough, then Minister of the Environment Dermot Nesbitt wrote "our archaeologists have developed the theme of maritime archaeology in a holistic way to examine not just wrecks but all aspects of maritime culture, social, political, economic, and religious" (Nesbitt in McErlean et al 2003: xix). Emphasis on holism and religions is intentional, as Nesbitt continues on to recall how the visit of the tall ships to Belfast in 1991 "gave us a glimpse of normality in those troubled times and what life might be like if we work together as a society" (ibid.). Heritage in this instance is viewed, perhaps naïvely, as a means of encouraging inclusion and cooperation, and the audience is clearly that of Northern Ireland.

Encouraging cross-community interest and participation in archaeology in Northern Ireland is aided by the general public interest in heritage, whatever role that heritage plays in community narratives. In directing the Movanagher Village Project in 1998, an excavation at an abandoned 17th-century Londonderry Plantation village, I was encouraged if initially surprised by the level of public interest as well as the ready cooperation of the media. Having unearthed evidence for significant interaction between native Irish and English and Scots settlers in what was designed to be an exclusive plantation village, we were able to invite local schoolchildren and adults from both communities to consider the evidence for themselves. Radio and television were employed to reach a wider audience. One of the more notable findings was evidence for a partially-earthfast Irish vernacular dwelling exhibiting a subrectangular plan, central open hearth, and swept floor located within the village (Horning 2001). Material culture found in association with this structure included English border ware and North Devon gravel-tempered utilitarian ceramics alongside hand-built Irish everted rim ware, suggestive of daily interaction. That such interactions were complicated and clearly not always benign is evident in the presence of spent lead shot and musket balls.

Whatever the meaning of the Movanagher material culture in the past, it must be remembered that these plantation sites continue to exist in the present, with their meanings and associations renegotiated and reconsidered by each generation. In Co. Tyrone, the stark walls of the ruinous Castle Caulfield tower above the small village bearing the same name. Constructed by an optimistic Sir Toby Caulfield between 1611–1616, Castle Caulfield was an ambitious H-plan Jacobean mansion boasting wide windows (even at ground level) and massive, soaring chimney stacks, defended only by a previously existent late medieval guardhouse (Jope 1958; Brannon 1999). The choice of style over defense was soon regretted, as rebel forces laid waste to the structure in 1641. Today, the site is maintained by the Department of the Environment, who face an uphill battle to combat the spraying of loyalist graffiti in hidden spaces within the ruin (Figure 28.2). Does this graffiti indicate that the site is being reclaimed as a protestant bastion? Or are the taggers unaware of the history of the site, content to spray their slogans on any conveniently concealed location – where its significance lies more in accomplishing a forbidden act than in making a publicly visible statement?

Elsewhere, continuity of association is more overt. Situated just outside of the village of Dungiven, Co. Derry/Londonderry, lie the impressive ruins of a 12th-century Augustinian Priory, itself built upon the site of an early medieval monastery. Adjacent to the site of the priory (Figure 28.3), in state care, is a holy well (the central depression in a bullaun stone, and referred to as the wart well), and rag tree where each fluttering strip of cloth attests to the seeking of a 'cure' for a variety of ills, a living tradition presumed to be of great antiquity. Little seems to and initiatives emphasize only the pre-plantation history of the site, even though government signage at the site clearly addresses its plantation history (see for example http://www.loughfoyleferry.com/dungiven_priory.htm).

A nearby plantation monument that has been recognized and recast by a local community is the Vintner's Company bawn and manor house at Bellaghy (Horning 2006a). Public outreach during the excavation and restoration of the bawn encouraged locals from the predominantly nationalist community to reconsider the role and meaning of the site, long perceived as Protestant territory (Brannon 2002). Through a government and local partnership, the restored Bellaghy Bawn now houses the Seamus Heaney Centre, celebrating the life and poetry of the local hero, while incorporating exhibits acknowledging the Plantation history of the site and the village. This conscious, locally-determined re-imagining of the bawn's appropriate function, coupled with the multiplicity of meanings inherent in the physical and spatial realities of the site, exemplifies the dynamism which characterizes colonial entanglements.

Finally, another archaeological project which is endeavoring to reinstate and investigate the complexity of the process and personal experiences of the Ulster Plantation is an ongoing investigation of an upland landscape in Goodland Townland, Co. Antrim. On this windswept site above the waters of Murlough Bay lie the traces of what may have been a plantation village occupied not by Protestant settlers, but by Roman Catholic Scots from Islay and the Mull of Kintyre in Scotland, part of an effort by the Catholic grant holder Randall McDonnell to maintain his power in north Antrim during the reign of James I (Horning 2004; Horning and Brannon 2004).

Conclusion

Current trends in historical archaeology emphasize the centrality of capitalism and colonial discourse in examining commonalties in the archaeologies of fictive worlds such as the British Atlantic. Yet far from informing archaeological practice, overly simplistic incorporation of postcolonial approaches in comparative archaeologies can impede our ability to disentangle the

Figure 28.2 Loyalist graffiti (Ulster Volunteer Force, a paramilitary organization) on a gatehouse door lintel of the 17th-century Castle Caulfield, Co. Tyrone. Does the graffiti signify ownership and association with the plantation history of the building, or is it merely a convenient locale for sectarian expression? Photograph by the author.

have changed at this site, sacred to the Gaelic population for over one thousand years: continuity of Gaelic life made materially manifest? Looking more closely at the site, however, a series of unusual foundations are appended to the south and east. Unearthed in excavations in the 1980s, these walls are the remains of an O'Cahan tower house and the later bawn and castle of Sir Edward Doddington, designated 'first farmer' of the Skinner's Company Proportion within the Londonderry plantation (Brannon and Blades 1980). While the pre-plantation, pre-Reformation history of the site appears reclaimed, the muted but nonetheless highly visible traces of Doddington's stronghold may provide the first spark for a meaningful discourse about history, identity, and memory. In the meantime, however, local tourism brochures

Figure 28.3 Rag tree and holy well at Dungiven Priory and Bawn, Co. Derry/Londonderry. Although there are substantial traces of the plantation-period occupation of this site, local community understandings of the site emphasize the pre-Reformation history of the priory and the evidence for continuity of Gaelic folk traditions. Photograph by the author.

complexities of the colonial experience. Contemporary implications and memories of 'colonial' entanglements vary wildly and remain contested in historical, political, economic, and popular understandings of the Irish past. With the exception of a brief, and to some degree unsuccessful, period in the early 17th century, the development of Ireland does not truly adhere to a colonial model as it would be understood in North America, Africa, or India. At the same time, ideas of colonialism pervade and structure identity, north and south. In the Republic of Ireland, the pace of development is bringing destruction of the post-medieval heritage in direct contravention to the aims of the National Monument Act and despite the hard work of individual archaeologists and organizations such as the Irish Post-Medieval Archaeology Group (Brannon and Horning 2005; Donnelly and Horning 2002; Horning and ÓBaoill 2000). As clearly illustrated by the nationalist tone of the displays at the National Museum of Country Life, assumptions about a colonial past not only infuse daily life in the Republic, but also reify the beliefs of the Diasporic community. The insights of postcolonial scholarship can aid in our understanding of modern Ireland, but only if we approach such scholarship with a nuanced,

fulsome understanding of Irish historiography and a recognition of the potential of visible, physical archaeological practice to not only deconstruct simplistic models of colonizer versus colonized, but to engage an Irish public who are in danger of sacrificing the experiences of their ancestors to the insecure and myopic machinations of postcolonial political posturing.

By contrast, the unsettled nature of social relations in the north of Ireland is reflected in the ongoing debate over how to treat the built heritage of the Troubles. Should Army bases be destroyed and all traces removed? What ought to be the fate of the Maze prison, scene of the Hunger Strikes and arguably, the centre of the cooperation between Republican and Loyalist prisoners which permitted the Belfast Agreement of 1998 (Brannon 2001; McAtackney 2005). Like the power-sharing executive, decisions will have to strike a balance, with the preservation of a perceived nationalist monument balanced by the preservation of a unionist monument (Brannon 2001; Jarman 2002). However fallacious the divisions may be, the maintenance and continued existence of these discursive sites at least contain the seeds for negotiation, remembrance, and reconciliation.

References

Anon. Respondent to questionnaire. Questionnaire and responses in possession of the author, University of Leicester, 2001.

Bardon, Jonathan. *A History of Ulster*. Belfast: Blackstaff Press, 1992.

Barton, Kevin and Alan McCully. "History Teaching and the Perpetuation of Memories: the Northern Ireland Experience." In *The Role of Memory in Ethnic Conflict* edited by Ed Cairns and Míchaél Roe, 107–124. New York: Palgrave Macmillan, 2003.

Brannon, Nick. "Archives and Archaeology: The Ulster Plantations in the Landscape." In *Old and New Worlds* edited by R. L. Michael and G. Egan, 97–105. Oxford: Oxbow Press, 1999.

Brannon, Nick. "Built Heritage, 'The Troubles', and Military Archaeology in Northern Ireland." Paper read at the 2001 Annual Meeting of the Society for Historical Archaeology, January 10–13, Long Beach, California, 2001.

Brannon, Nick. "The Role of the Environment and Heritage Service in Northern Ireland Archaeology." *Antiquity* 76, no. 292 (2002): 557–561.

Brannon, Nick and Brooke Blades. "Dungiven Bawn Re-Edified." *Ulster Journal of Archaeology* 43 (1980): 91–96.

Brannon, Nick and Audrey Horning. "Post-Medieval Archaeology – It Hasn't Gone Away, You Know." *Archaeology Ireland* 19, no. 2 (2005): 16–17.

Buttimer, Neil, Colin Rynne, and Helen Guerin. *The Heritage of Ireland*. Cork: Collins Press, 2000.

Canny, Nicholas. *Making Ireland British: 1580–1650*. Oxford: Oxford University Press, 2001.

Coulter, Colin. *Contemporary Northern Irish Society*. London: Pluto Press, 1999.

Curl, James Stephens. *The Londonderry Plantation 1609–1914*. London: Phillimore, 1986.

Delle, James "Extending Europe's Grasp: An Archaeological Comparison of Colonial Spatial Process in Ireland and Jamaica." In *Old and New Worlds* edited by R. L. Michael and G. Egan, 106–116. Oxford: Oxbow Press, 1999.

Donnelly, Colm J. and Audrey J. Horning. "Post-Medieval and Industrial Archaeology in Ireland: an Overview." *Antiquity* 76, no. 292 (2002): 557–561.

Dunleath, Rt. Hon. Lord. *Important Bits of Irish History*. Privately printed, 1914.

Fitzpatrick, D. *Irish Emigration, 1801–1921*. Dublin, 1984.

Foster, Roy F. *The Irish Story: Telling Tales and Making it Up in Ireland*. Oxford: Oxford University Press, 2002.

Garner, Steve. *Racism in the Irish Experience*. London: Pluto Press, 2004.

Gillespie, Raymond. "Explorers, Exploiters and Entrepreneurs: Early Modern Ireland and its Context, 1500–1700." In *An Historical Geography of Ireland* edited by Brian J. Graham and Lindsay J. Proudfoot, 123–157. London: Academic Press, 1993.

Gosden, Christopher. *Archaeology and Colonialism: Cultural Contact from 5000 BC to the Present*. Cambridge: Cambridge University Press, 2004.

Graham, Colin. *Deconstructing Ireland*. Edinburgh: Edinburgh University Press, 2001.

Graham, Colin and Richard Kirkland (eds.). *Ireland and Cultural Theory: The Mechanics of Authenticity*. London: Macmillan Press, 1999.

Gramsci, Antonio. *Selections from the Prison Notebooks and the Study of Philosophy* London, 1971.

Hall, Martin. *Archaeology and the Modern World: Colonial Transcripts in South Africa and the Chesapeake*. London: Routledge, 2000.

Harrison, Rodney. "Shared Histories and the Archaeology of the Pastoral Industry in Australia." In *After Captain Cook: The Archaeology of the Recent Indigenous Past in Australia* edited by R. Harrison and C. Williamson, 37–58. Sydney University Archaeological Methods Series 8. Sydney: Archaeological Computing Laboratory, University of Sydney, 2002.

Harrison, Rodney, Shelley Greer and Susan McIntyre-Tamwoy. "Community-based Archaeology in Australia." *World Archaeology* 34, no. 2 (2002): 265–287.

Horning, Audrey J. *A Verie Fit Place to Erect a Great Cittie: Comparative Contextual Analysis of Archaeological Jamestown* PhD dissertation, University of Pennsylvania, Philadelphia. Ann Arbor, Michigan: University Microfilms, 1995.

Horning, Audrey J. "Urbanism in the Colonial South: The Development of Seventeenth-Century Jamestown." In *Urban Archaeology in the South* edited by Amy Young, 52–68. Tuscaloosa: University of Alabama Press, 2000.

Horning, Audrey J. "'Dwelling Houses in the Old Irish Barbarous Manner': Archaeological Evidence for Gaelic Architecture in an Ulster Plantation Village." In *Gaelic Ireland c. 1250–1650: Land, Lordship and Settlement* edited by P. J. Duffy, D. Edwards, and E. FitzPatrick, 375–396. Dublin: Four Courts Press, 2001.

Horning, Audrey J. "Archaeological Explorations of Cultural Identity and Rural Economy in the North of Ireland: Goodland, Co. Antrim." *International Journal of Historical Archaeology* 8, no. 3 (2004): 199–215.

Horning, Audrey J. "Archaeology, Conflict, and Contemporary Identity in the North of Ireland: Implications for Theory and Practice in Comparative Archaeologies of Colonialism." *Archaeological Dialogues* 13, no. 2 (2006a): 183–199.

Horning, Audrey J. "English Towns on the Periphery: Seventeenth-Century Town Development in Ulster and the Chesapeake." In *Cities in the World* edited by Adrian Green and Roger Leech, 61–81. London: Maney, 2006b.

Horning, Audrey J. "Archaeology and the Construction of America's Jamestown." *Post-Medieval Archaeology* 40, no. 1 (2006c): 1–27.

Horning, Audrey J. and Nick Brannon. "Rediscovering Goodland: Neolithic Settlement, Booley Site, or Lost Scottish Village?" *Archaeology Ireland* 18, no. 4 (2004): 28–31.

Horning, Audrey J. and Nick Brannon. *Survey of the Prehistoric and Historic Landscape of Slievemore, Interim Report 2005.* Submitted to the Department of the Environment, Republic of Ireland, 2005.

Horning, Audrey J. and Ruairí ÓBaoill. "Post Medieval Archaeologists Descend on Belfast." *Archaeology Ireland* 14, no. 2 (2000).

Howe, Stephen. *Ireland and Empire: Colonial Legacies in Irish History and Culture.* Oxford: Oxford University Press, 2000.

Hume, David. "Remembering Ferguson and our Culture." *New Ulster* 12 (1986): 11–12.

Ignatiev, Noel. *How the Irish Became White.* London: Routledge Press, 1996.

Jarman, Neil. "Troubling Remnants: Dealing with the Remains of Conflict in Northern Ireland." In *Matériel Culture: The Archaeology of Twentieth-Century Conflict* edited by J. Schofield, W. G. Johnson, and C. M. Beck, 281–295. London: Routledge Press, 2002.

Jope, Edward Martyn. "Castlecaulfield, Co. Tyrone." *Ulster Journal of Archaeology* 21 (1958): 107–108.

Kanhpeyeng, B. W. and Christopher DeCorse 2004. "Ghana's Vanishing Past: Development, Antiquities, and the Destruction of the Archaeological Record." *African Archaeological Review* 21, no. 2 (2004): 89–128.

Kennedy, Liam. *Colonialism, Religion, and Nationalism in Ireland.* Belfast: Institute of Irish Studies, Queen's University Belfast, 1996.

Kiberd, Declan. "Modern Ireland: Postcolonial or European?". In *Not on Any Map: Essays in Postcoloniality and Cultural Nationalism* edited by S. Murray. Exeter: University of Exeter Press, 1997.

Loeber, R. *The Geography and Practice of English Colonisation from 1534 to 1609.* Group for the Study of Irish Historic Settlement. Athlone, 1991.

McAtackney, L. "What can Archaeology Tell Us About the Maze Site?" *Archaeology Ireland* 19, no. 1 (2005): 22–25.

McDonald, Theresa. *Achill Island: Archaeology, History, Folklore.* Tullamore: I.A.S. Publications, 1997.

McDonald, Theresa. "The Deserted Village, Slievemore, Achill Island, Co. Mayo." *International Journal of Historical Archaeology* 2, no. 2 (1998): 73–112.

McDonald, Theresa and Audrey J. Horning, *Survey of the Prehistoric and Historic Landscape of Slievemore, Interim Report 2004.* Submitted to the Department of the Environment, Republic of Ireland, 2004.

McErlean, Thomas, Rosemary McConkey, Wes Forsythe. *Strangford Lough: An Archaeological Survey of the Maritime Cultural Landscape.* Belfast: Blackstaff, 2003.

McLernon, Francis, Ed Cairns, Christopher A. Lewis, and Miles Hewstone. "Memories of Recent Conflict and Forgiveness in Northern Ireland." In *The Role of Memory in Ethnic Conflict* edited by Ed Cairns and Míchaél D. Roe. New York: Palgrave Macmillan, 2003.

McNally, Kenneth. *Achill.* Newton Abbot: David and Charles, 1973.

Miller, David. "Colonialism and Academic Representation of the Troubles." In *Rethinking Northern Ireland* edited by David Miller. New York: Longman, 1998.

Miller, Kerby A. *Emigrants and Exiles: Ireland and the Irish Exodus to North America.* Oxford: Oxford University Press, 1985.

Moody, T. W. *The Londonderry Plantation.* Belfast: William Mullan and Son, 1939.

Mouer, L. Daniel. "Chesapeake Creoles: the Creation of Folk Culture in Colonial Virginia." In *The Archaeology of Seventeenth Century Virginia* edited by T. R. Reinhart and D. J. Pogue, 105–166. Special Publication No. 30 of the Archaeological Society of Virginia. Richmond: Dietz Press, 1993.

Mouer, L. Daniel, Mary Ellen N. Hodges, Stephen. R. Potter, Susan. L. H. Renaud, Ivor Noël Hume, Dennis J. Pogue, Martha W. McCartney, and Thomas E. Davidson. "Colonoware Pottery, Chesapeake Pipes, and 'Uncritical Assumptions.'" In *I, Too, Am America Archaeological Studies of African-American Life* edited by T. Singleton, 75–115. Charlottesville: University Press of Virginia, 1999.

Nic Craith, Mairéad. *Plural Identities Singular Narratives: the Case of Northern Ireland.* New York: Bergahn Books, 2002.

Nic Craith, Mairéad. *Culture and Identity Politics in Northern Ireland.* London: Palgrave, 2003.

Ohlmeyer, Jane. 1993. *Civil War and Restoration in the Three Stuart Kingdoms.* Cambridge: Cambridge University Press, 1993.

Orser, Charles Jr. *A Historical Archaeology of the Modern World.* New York: Plenum Press, 1996.

Orser, Charles, Jr. "Archaeological Interpretation and the Irish Diasporic Community." In *Places in Mind: Public Archaeology as Applied Anthropology* edited by Paul Shackel and Erve Chambers. London: Routledge Press, 2004.

Orser, Charles, Jr. 2005. "The Material Implications of Colonialism in Early Nineteenth-Century Ireland." In *Was Ireland a Colony? Economics, Politics and Culture in Nineteenth-Century Ireland* edited by Terrence McDonough, 66–86. Dublin: Irish Academic Press, 2005.

Robinson, Philip. *The Plantation of Ulster.* Dublin: Gill and Macmillan, 1984.

Ruane, Joseph. "Colonialism and the Interpretation of Irish Historical Development." In *Approaching the Past: Historical Anthropology through Irish Case Studies* edited by M. Silverman and P. H. Gullivan. New York: Columbia University Press, 1992.

Schrire, Carmel. *Digging through Darkness.* Charlottesville: University Press of Virginia, 1996.

Spivak, Gayatri Chakravorty. "Can the Subaltern Speak?" In *Marxism and the Interpretation of Culture* edited by C. Nelson and L. Grossberg, 271–313. London: Macmillan, 1988.

Wallerstein, Immanuel. *The Modern World System: Capitalist Agriculture and the Origins of a European World Economy in the Sixteenth Century.* New York: Academic Press, 1974.

Part IX

Media, Museums, and Publics

ONE OF THE KEY CHARACTERISTICS OF THE POSTMODERN WORLD is the global proliferation of new forms of media and information technologies, including websites, podcasts, blogs, Facebook, MySpace, YouTube, Twitter, Skype, and so on. At one level, this is an exciting new development. Never before have so many people had such easy access to information and such opportunities to share information with others. Google is digitizing the libraries of the University of Michigan, Harvard University, Stanford University, Oxford University, and the New York Public Library to make them available online. Wikipedia has established a new collaborative process for creating a web-based encyclopedia that is continually evolving. Twitter is providing real-time microblogging, which was particularly important during the protests and violence following the 2009 Iranian elections as the only means of on-the-ground communication to the world. It is now possible to Skype with family, friends, and colleagues anywhere in the world in real time. Our sense of time and space is shrinking.

But, at another level, this proliferation of media technologies raises some very serious ethical, moral, and legal concerns yet to be resolved. These concerns include copyright issues, proprietary knowledge, digital piracy, professional expertise, and our very experience of the world (Strangelove 2005; Poster 2006; van Dijck 2007). Should all information be freely available, or is there some knowledge (such as pornography or bomb-making techniques) that should be restricted for the public good? How has the democratization of information affected the status of the professional? How do we evaluate the quality of the information on the Internet? In what ways are these new technologies reconfiguring the ways in which we interact with each other? What are the relationships between virtual reality and lived experience? How are the media impacting archaeology and our sense of the past in the present? These questions seem to validate Jean Baudrillard's (1995) claim that in postmodern society the distinction between reality and representation breaks down and that human experience is largely a simulation of reality, rather than an experience of reality itself.

Historically, archaeology and the popular media have had a long and complex relationship (Clark and Brittain 2007; Kulik 2007). Archaeology, broadly defined, has been and continues to be a popular topic in television, movies, and print (Holtorf 2005, 2007). This is one of the reasons it is so commonly used in advertising campaigns (Holtorf 2005; see Talalay's chapter). This exposure has greatly increased public awareness of and interest in archaeology. However, it has also led to some problematic stereotypes and serious misunderstandings. The popular media tend to exoticize the past, to highlight differences rather than identify similarities. They also tend to foment controversy between archaeologists and between professionals and "alternative" or "fringe" archaeologists for increased ratings. While it is true that the profession has not effectively addressed the social meanings of alternative archaeologies (Harrold and Eve 1987; Williams 1991), the media generally privilege entertainment value over educational content in what has been called "infotainment" (Brittain and Clark 2007:22). Part of the problem, it must be admitted, lies with ourselves as archaeologists. With some notable exceptions (e.g. Brian Fagan), we have not been particularly sophisticated in using the media to convey our results to the public and different interest groups. Rather than using the media for public outreach, we have allowed the popular media to control the popular representation of archaeology. The communication of our results to the public is an integral part of the archaeological process (Sabloff 1998, 2008; Hodder 1999). Fortunately, the profession is addressing this situation and there is today growing professional participation in such venues as the *Time Team* (and *Time Team America*) and *History Detectives* TV series, and the Discovery, Archaeology, National Geographic, and History channels on cable TV.

As the media explosion has increased public awareness of archaeology and history in general, there has been an accompanying rise of groups who identify with religious practices that place them in contentious positions with both indigenous groups and the professional heritage community. The growth of neo-shamanism in the West, for example, has met with condemnation from the Fourth World Association because of what they perceive as attempts to compromise the sovereignty of indigenous nations, their history and imagery (Layton and Wallace 2006:52–53). Developments such as these are the logical outgrowth of the democratization of archaeology and the growth of heritage-based tourism. In some cases, the media have played an active role in highlighting the claims of groups who have argued for access to heritage sites on the grounds of religious practice. The neo-druids of Britain have employed the Internet to argue their case for access to Stonehenge. When Barbara Bender (1998) explored the history and possible interpretations of Stonehenge, she included a dialogue with neo-druids. This approach has been replicated by Ian Hodder (1999) at Çatalhöyük with members of the Goddess movement. These are examples of how digital technology has been employed to accommodate voices beyond those of just the archaeologist. Not surprisingly, this kind of multivocality raises considerable challenges, as both Bender and Hodder note.

New media and information technologies are impacting the global museum community in a variety of profound ways (Pollock and Zemans 2007). The museum community, here defined as art museums, anthropology museums, craft museums, history museums, folk-life museums, and technology museums, are now rethinking their standard exhibition practices to take advantage of these new technologies and promote a more interactive visitor experience. Ironically, this emphasis on new technology is coming precisely at a time when resources are drying up due to the global financial crisis of 2008. Museums are struggling to find new sources of revenue as their visitation decreases and endowments shrink in size. After all, why go to a museum when you can call up its exhibits and collections on a website, unless you can get something more? Many museums are saving money by mounting shows using existing collections that have never before been exhibited. In addition, the very authority of museums as cultural institutions is being challenged (Corsane 2005; Kohlstedt 2005; Leaman 2006; Pollock and Zemans 2007). Museums have been critiqued as bastions of elite culture and as the purveyors of a neoliberal agenda. This has stimulated a pragmatic move toward increased relevance. There is a new museum ethic emerging that sees museums not as passive repositories of things, but as active participants in society, taking on controversial issues in order to highlight injustices and promote cross-cultural understanding.

Sonya Atalay's chapter is a thoughtful critique of the new National Museum of the American Indian (NMAI) on the mall in Washington, DC. The NMAI opened to the public on September 21, 2004 to great fanfare (Lonetree and Cobb 2008). It is the first national museum dedicated to the preservation, study, and exhibition of the Native peoples and cultures from across the Americas. Established by an act of Congress in 1989, the museum collaborates with Native communities to protect and foster their cultures by reaffirming their traditions and beliefs, encouraging contemporary artistic expression, and empowering Native voices. The museum's collections were assembled largely from the holdings of the Museum of the American Indian, Heye Foundation in New York City and include more than 800,000 objects. The collections span all major culture areas of the Americas, representing virtually all tribes of the United States, most of those of Canada, and a significant number of cultures from Central and South America as well as the Caribbean.

The museum also incorporates a Virtual Museum Workshop where Native students learn to use modern technologies to create engaging virtual exhibitions that represent the students' own cultures. Workshop participants digitize objects in the museum's collections, process the photographs on a computer, and create interactive images that may be rotated or magnified on-screen. The students also research the objects using materials from the NMAI and Smithsonian Institution libraries, and write labels for them that can be used to create virtual exhibitions. Demonstrations, performances, and Native language elements are often added using digital audio or video documentation. The students' work is then featured in the NMAI Resource Centers, the students' schools, and/or tribal museums and cultural centers. Past workshops have helped to create a virtual tour of the "Our Universes" gallery.

As an Anishinaabeg woman trained in archaeology, Atalay expresses a series of conflicting reactions to the new museum. On the one hand, she notes that the NMAI represents a dramatic change in museology; it seeks nothing less than to give Native peoples the power to control their own representation and heritage at the national level. In this sense, the NMAI is an example of an ethical and socially just museum practice since it benefits Native communities at the same time as it educates the wider American public and global community about Native peoples. But, on the other hand, Atalay argues that it misses an important opportunity to represent the past and present struggles of Native peoples. It fails to address Western colonization and to depict its devastating and lasting effects on Native communities. Atalay acknowledges that to take this on would be a challenging project and one fraught with dangers. And yet it cannot be avoided. This critique was also made by the American Indian Movement in a flyer circulated at the museum's opening. Floyd Red Crow Westerman, Dennis Banks, Clyde Bellecourt, and Vernon Bellecourt protested the new museum on the grounds that it failed to engage with Native American genocide.

Media are implicated not only in education, but also in the commercialization of the past (Holtorf 2007). Lauren Talalay's chapter is a pioneering study of how the marketing industry has used the past as a commodity in its advertising campaigns to create desire. She notes that there is a long history of using archaeological imagery in Western society to shape consumer behavior, going back as far as the early 19th century. After the discovery of Tutankhamun's tomb in 1922, the Egyptian past was heavily marketed in the selling of luxury goods such as perfume, beer, cigarettes, and cigars. As Talalay notes, advertising works on multiple levels, but precisely how it does so is hotly debated. There is broad agreement that ads typically distill complex issues into simple narratives. They are effective because they play into social and psychological questions of "ambition, snobbery, glamour, luxury, fantasy, fear, health and social acceptance."

Talalay identifies two modes by which "archaeoadverts" address the relationship between the past and present. The first of these is the intentional blurring of the boundary between antiquity and modernity. In this case, images are used to erase time differentials. Talalay cites as an example an Absolut Vodka ad, which transforms the vodka bottle into a Greek column of the Ionic order. Here the vodka brand is lent a sense of cosmopolitanism and sophistication through its association with ancient Greece. The second mode is the opposition of antiquity and modernity. Talalay gives as an example a Famous Amos Chocolate Chip Cookie Company ad which positions the cookie on a Doric column on which the name "Famous Amos" is inscribed in pseudo-Greek letters. This ad works because of the juxtaposition of the past and present to create the notion of fame.

Of special interest is Talaly's discovery that certain ancient cultures tend to be privileged in modern Western advertising. In particular, images of Egypt, Greece, and Rome are more commonly used than either European or New World images. Talalay suggests that representations of the Pyramids, the Parthenon, and the Coliseum are the products of empire and encode subtle and implicit symbols of power. There is important variation within the use of these images and specific stereotypes are at work. Egyptian images are typically associated with death, mystery, eternity, and the exotic. Greek images are linked to artistic achievement and philosophical thought as the roots of Western identities. Finally, Roman images are associated with warfare, games, and architectural feats.

There is a growing appreciation that a democratic archaeology must be accountable to multiple publics. In his chapter, Ian Hodder examines the uses of the past by different interest groups at the famous Neolithic village of Çatalhöyük. He notes that the past matters, but it matters to different people in different ways. He classifies the various interests into two broad categories that are usually considered to be in opposition with one another. The first is the global international economy, which promotes commercialization and homogenization, where cultural differences are regarded as pastiche; he terms this the "past as play." The second are the local economies that favor multiple identities, ethnicities, and nationalities, where cultural differences matter; he labels this the "past as passion." He then critiques this classification, suggesting it should not be seen as one of opposition, since both categories can coexist in various strategies and often interact in complex ways.

As an example of this interaction, Hodder cites the politics surrounding the annual Çumra agricultural festival. In 1996, the local mayor of Çumra petitioned the Ankara officials to establish a Çatalhöyük museum in the town. He also renamed the local festival the Çumra Çatalhöyük festival and incorporated a film and slide show by the Çatalhöyük archaeological team. Hodder was initially surprised by this public endorsement of pre-Islamic archaeology by an Islamic nationalist. However, he recognized that some of this support was certainly due to the fact that the project brought in resources by attracting international tourism and providing employment for local villagers. But it was also the case that the mayor's own political ambitions were served by the museum proposal and festival. He became the center of media attention and the host of various political dignitaries. The coexistence of different strategies is demonstrated by the content of his speeches. He emphasized the national importance of the site to Turkey as the birthplace of Anatolian civilization. At the same time, he stressed its international significance and characterized it as a world heritage site. Hodder sees this as a strategic accommodation of the global and the local.

Hodder and his Çatalhöyük team have made sophisticated use of media to communicate information and promote dialogue with different publics. They have developed a state-of-the art website (Hodder 2009) where raw data are published for all to see, prior to their being synthesized and interpreted. One of the innovative aspects of the website is its Public Forums, which include News and Updates, Public Discussion, and Requests, Complaints, and Suggestions. A particularly interesting exchange took place between Hodder and advocates of the Goddess movement. Many members of the movement expressed a strong desire to learn about women's roles at Çatalhöyük. Hodder acknowledged a shared interest in this question, but demonstrated some of the complexities in archaeological interpretation. He singled out the importance of separating the role of women in mythology and symbolism from the roles of women in daily life, since these can mutually support one another or alternatively contradict one another. These new media thus allow members of the public to interact with the team members about topics of mutual interest.

The democratization of knowledge raises particularly challenging issues with respect to intellectual property (IP). George Nicholas and

Kelly Bannister's chapter is a pathbreaking consideration of IP issues in archaeology. Following Jay Dratler (1994:1–2), they define intellectual property as "intangible personal property in creations of the mind." They note that intellectual property issues are topics of growing interest in academia and other contexts that involve Indigenous communities. This is especially the case for ethnobiology and the commercialization of native medicinal plants (Mgbeoji 2006). There are, however, emerging tensions between national and international laws protecting cultural and intellectual property and notions of Indigenous cultural knowledge and heritage. While ownership is not a Western concept, concepts of Indigenous ownership are not given legal status in most countries. Nicholas and Bannister conclude that archaeology will not move beyond its colonialist practices unless it actively seeks to understand the underlying issues of ownership and control of material and intellectual property as related to Indigenous cultural knowledge and heritage.

Nicholas and Bannister and their colleague Julie Hallowell have recently established the Intellectual Property Issues in Cultural Heritage (IPinCH) project as an international research initiative to promote the fair and equitable exchange of knowledge relating to archaeology (Nichols 2009a, 2009b). This initiative now consists of 50 scholars and 25 partnering organizations and is funded by Social Sciences and Humanities Research Council of Canada. The goals of the project are to document the diversity of principles, interpretations, and actions related to intellectual property issues in cultural heritage worldwide; to analyze the many implications of these situations; to generate more robust theoretical understandings as well as best practices; and to make these findings available to stakeholders. The project seeks to work with Aboriginal communities, professional organizations, and government agencies to help develop and refine appropriate theories, principles, policies, and practices.

References

Baudrillard Jean, 1995 Simulacra and Simulation. Ann Arbor: University of Michigan Press.

Bender, Barbara, 1998 Stonehenge: Making Space. Oxford: Berg.

Brittain, Marcus, and Timothy Clark, 2007 Introduction: Archaeology and the Media. In Archaeology and the Media. Timothy Clark and Marcus Brittain, eds. pp. 11–65. Walnut Creek, CA: Left Coast Press.

Clark, Timothy, and Marcus Brittain, eds., 2007 Archaeology and the Media. Walnut Creek, CA: Left Coast Press.

Corsane, Gerald, ed., 2005 Heritage, Museums, and Galleries: An Introductory Reader. London: Routledge.

Dratler, Jay, 1994 Licensing of Intellectual Property. New York: Law Journal Seminars Press.

Harrold, Francis B., and Raymond A. Eve, eds., 1987 Cult Archaeology and Creationism: Understanding Pseudoscientific Beliefs about the Past. Iowa City: University of Iowa Press.

Hodder, Ian, 1999 The Archaeological Process: An Introduction. Oxford: Blackwell.

Hodder, Ian, 2009 Çatalhöyük website: www.catalhoyuk.com, accessed August 27, 2009.

Holtorf, Cornelius, 2005 From Stonehenge to Las Vegas: Archaeology as Popular Culture. Walnut Creek, CA: AltaMira Press.

Holtorf, Cornelius, 2007 Archaeology is a Brand: The Meaning of Archaeology in Contemporary Popular Culture. Oxford: Archaeopress.

Kohlstedt, Sally Gregory, 2005 Thoughts in Things: Modernity, History and North American Museums. Isis 96(4):586–601.

Kulik, Karol, 2007 A Short History of Archaeological Communication. In Archaeology and the Media. Timothy Clark and Marcus Brittain, eds. pp. 111–124. Walnut Creek, CA: Left Coast Press.

Layton, Robert, and Gillian Wallace, 2006 Is Culture a Commodity? In The Ethics of Archaeology: Philosophical Perspectives on Archaeological Practice. Chris Scarre and Geoffrey Scarre, eds. pp. 46–68. Cambridge: Cambridge University Press.

Leaman, Oliver, 2006 Who Guards and Guardians? In The Ethics of Archaeology: Philosophical Perspectives on Archaeological Practice. Chris Scarre and Geoffrey Scarre, eds. Pp. 32–45. Cambridge: Cambridge University Press.

Lonetree, Amy, and Amanda J. Cobb, eds., 2008 The National Museum of the American Indian: Critical Conversations. Lincoln: University of Nebraska Press.

Mgbeoji, lkechi, 2006 Global Biopiracy: Patents, Plants, and Indigenous Knowledge. Vancouver: UBC Press.

Nicholas, George, ed., 2009a IPinCH Newsletter 1(1).

Nicholas, George, 2009b Intellectual Property Issues in Cultural Heritage (IPinCH) website: http://cgi.sfu.ca/~ipinch/cgi-bin/, accessed August 27, 2009.

Pollock, Griselda, and Joyce Zemans, 2007 Museums after Modernism: Strategies of Engagement. New York: Wiley-Blackwell.

Poster, Mark, 2006 Information Please: Culture and Politics in the Age of Digital Machines. Durham, NC: Duke University Press.

Sabloff, Jeremy A., 1998 Communication and the Future of Archaeology. American Anthropologist 100(4):869–875.

Sabloff, Jeremy A., 2008 Archaeology Matters: Action Archaeology in the Modern World. Walnut Creek, CA: Left Coast Press.

Strangelove, Michael, 2005 The Empire of the Mind: Digital Piracy and the Anti-Capitalist Movement. Toronto: University of Toronto Press.

Van Dijck, José, 2007 Mediated Memories in the Digital Age. Palo Alto, CA: Stanford University Press

Williams, Stephen, 1991 Fantastic Archaeology: The Wild Side of American Prehistory. Philadelphia: University of Pennsylvania Press.

No Sense of the Struggle
Creating a Context for Survivance at the NMAI

Sonya Atalay

Museums, collecting, anthropology, and archaeology were developed within, and are deeply entrenched in, a Western epistemological frame work and have histories that are strongly colonial in nature.[1] As with most contemporary fields of study, these areas of research and practice are fully steeped in Western ways of knowing, naming, ordering, analyzing, and understanding the world. Indigenous people, both outside and within the academy, along with a number of non-Indigenous scholars globally, have struggled long and hard to bring the Western and colonial nature of these fields to the foreground. They have worked to bring us to the place we are today, where such statements are acknowledged (by most scholars) and where those who want to continue working to change these disciplines in positive ways have a space to do so.

The National Museum of the American Indian (NMAI) is one of those spaces. The NMAI attempts to profoundly change the practice of museology and the role of Indigenous people in museums on a grand scale. In some ways it is successful in its mission, yet other areas leave room for improvement. This piece focuses on the latter, and in it I offer critiques of the exhibits on display during the museum's opening on

Sonya Atalay, "No Sense of the Struggle: Creating a Context for Survivance at the NMAI," pp. 597–618 from *The American Indian Quarterly* 30:3–4 (2006). Reprinted with permission of the University of Nebraska Press.

September 21, 2004. Although the substance of this article is primarily critique and suggestions for improvement of the NMAI's exhibits, I want to be clear in stating that, in writing it, my aim is ultimately to support the NMAI because I believe so strongly in its aims, mission, and efforts and in the profound power it has to speak to so many people about us – our lives, our communities, our struggles, and our rights as Native people of sovereign nations. I strongly believe that along with the NMAI's gift of voice, which is the result of financial, political, and community support from Native people, the U.S. government, and both private and corporate donors, the museum also carries a serious responsibility to (re)present our stories to its several million visitors each year, both U.S. citizens and an increasingly large global audience.

My perspective is as a Native person (Ojibwe) who has academic training and research experience in archaeology, heritage studies, and public anthropology. My research focuses on Indigenous archaeology and the ways in which Native people in North America, along with Indigenous and local people globally, have positively influenced and continue to change the discipline of archaeology. I am not a specialist in museums exclusively, but museums are a critical part of heritage studies, and I have thought deeply for many years about issues of Indigenous heritage – about our pasts and the role of the past in the present. I've strived both to critique Western

NO SENSE OF THE STRUGGLE

archaeological and anthropological practices and to develop models in which to do things better, as I feel that for practices to move forward and improve dialogue and critique are crucial first steps that must be followed by practical models and ideas for change.[2]

Critical engagement, critique, and suggestions for improved practice are prominent themes in much of my own research, which attempts to decolonize archaeology and make it a more ethical and socially just practice that benefits the Indigenous and local communities it studies. In its creation and execution, the NMAI shares some of the aims of Indigenous archaeology. The NMAI consulted and worked closely with Native communities from throughout North and South America, moving beyond standard contemporary museum practices on a grand scale to create a museum and a process of operation that listens intently to the voices and concerns of Indigenous people. In these efforts, the NMAI joins a growing number of smaller, tribal museums in allowing Native people the power to control their own representation and heritage. The NMAI attempts to create an ethical and socially just museum practice – one that benefits Native communities while it also educates the wider American and global community about Native peoples.

The aims of the NMAI overlap in many ways with my own research goals; however, while my work will likely reach only a limited group of scholars, students, and non-academic publics, the messages within the walls of the NMAI will reach a far larger audience. Thus the NMAI has the potential to engender substantial transformations in the way diverse publics think and feel about the Native people of this hemisphere. In its role as a public educator, the NMAI literally has the ability to touch and influence the hearts and minds of millions – the voting citizens of our country and others, who are increasingly asked to vote on issues that directly affect the daily lives of Native people such as tribal gaming, land and water issues, and fishing and hunting legislation. Visitors to the NMAI include school board members who approve curricula and textbooks that teach about "Columbus discovering America in 1492," and they are the senators, judges, and government leaders who write and have the power to approve legislation such as the proposed changes to NAGPRA and intellectual

and cultural property rights law.[3] Important audiences for the NMAI also include many of our own Native children and grandchildren, from both reservation communities and urban areas. In my experience as an educator, I've found that Native youth are keenly aware of contemporary Native American life. They know that we're *still here*, but they are often less knowledgeable of the experiences and struggles our ancestors endured to bring us to this point and of the battles and accomplishments of Native leaders of [the twentieth] century. These stories of struggle and adversity provide inspiration and pride by building a context for understanding our ability to not only survive but thrive in the contemporary world.

In this article, I continually emphasize the educational role of the NMAI, the messages it presents to multiple audiences, and the level at which it successfully engages those audiences. This is because, in walking through the exhibits on opening day, I constantly found myself thinking of exactly how much is at stake in the exhibit halls of the NMAI. Museums play a critical role in painting a picture of the people, communities, and cultures they portray; they create a resonant "take-home" message for visitors. In this way museums shape the public mindset and have an effect on policy in this country and internationally. This is a particularly important role for the NMAI, as it attempts (and rightly so) to remove authority from museums that present Native people only through a Western, anthropological gaze.[4] As the NMAI claims to (re)present Native Americans in their own voices and perspectives, many will look to the exhibits of the NMAI as the authority on Native people, replacing traditional anthropological interpretations and representations of Native Americans with those presented in the NMAI.

In many ways, this marks a hard-won victory for the empowerment of Indigenous peoples to control, represent, and maintain sovereignty over their own cultural heritage. For several decades, amid struggles with archaeologists and anthropologists, Native people have reiterated the importance of the past in the present and the connection of contemporary research and representations of our communities and heritage for the future well-being of our people.[5] In regaining control over our own heritage and having both the power and opportunity to represent it on such a truly grand scale as a museum on the National Mall of the U.S. capital, it is critical that we remain cognizant of the effects that representations of our cultures, history, and heritage have on future generations. From this vantage point, the NMAI holds a tremendous responsibility to Native people, not only in the past and present, but also quite literally for future generations as well. It is with a profound respect for our ancestors and a deep concern for those of future generations that I examined carefully and have thought critically about the exhibits in the NMAI and write this article.

The NMAI's Mission

As stated on the NMAI website, the museum's mission is as follows:

> The National Museum of the American Indian shall recognize and affirm to Native communities and the non-Native public the historical and contemporary culture and cultural achievements of the Natives of the Western Hemisphere by advancing – in consultation, collaboration, and cooperation with Natives – knowledge and understanding of Native cultures, including art, history, and language, and by recognizing the museum's special responsibility, through innovative public programming, research and collections, to protect, support, and enhance the development, maintenance, and perpetuation of Native culture and community.[6]

In this mission statement, the NMAI clearly defines its audience as both Native and non-Native publics. Through its exhibitions, the NMAI aims to "recognize and affirm" both historical and contemporary Native cultures, as well as "advancing" knowledge and understanding of those cultures, including the history and cultural achievements of Native peoples. Elsewhere, W. Richard West Jr., the museum's founding director, points out that the NMAI is, "the only national institution in the United States whose exclusive mandate covers the entirety of the native cultures of this hemisphere."[7] This is quite an ambitious mission, and the challenges inherent in attempting to cover the numerous and diverse cultures living in such a large

geographic area, over such a vast period of time, were certainly substantial. There were numerous views to be included and considered and a myriad of thoughts and desires to be accommodated, as both George Horse Capture and Duane Blue Spruce highlight when describing their experiences in the early consultation process with Native communities during the planning stages of the NMAI.[8] Consultation took on many forms, including surveys, interviews, and visits to Native communities throughout the hemisphere. The efforts to incorporate this input productively and to then decide what the organizing principles and themes of the museum would be were certain to have been quite challenging.

While I am aware that much of the organization of the display context in the museum was generated in consultation with Native people and communities, I am unclear on how the *tone* of the exhibits was determined. I use the word "tone" because I've found it difficult to find another word to express what I noticed repeatedly about the NMAI's exhibits. As I explored the galleries on opening day, I was powerfully struck and sadly disappointed by the lack of struggle portrayed in both the text and images present on the exhibition floor. Furthermore, I found that the messages about colonization and its devastating and continual effects on Native communities were benign. In the ways I detail more fully in the following sections, there was a noticeable lack of hard-hitting critique of the process and effects of colonization in Native communities.

Agency and Victimization

Postcolonial theorists have pointed out that colonization is never simply a one-way process in which a victim is acted upon by a colonizing individual or force.[9] Binary and unidimensional representations of colonization are vastly oversimplified and remove the agency of the actors involved, particularly for those portrayed as colonized "victims." Such complexity of interaction was certainly the case in the colonization of North America. Native people were not simply passive receivers of colonial actions; they actively resisted repeated attempts of cultural, spiritual, and physical genocide and simultaneously had profound effects and influence upon colonial settler populations and governments.

Native agency and the ways in which Native people actively worked to create and change their lives and circumstance are presented repeatedly in the NMAI's Our Peoples exhibits. Aesthetically beautiful displays offer celebrations of accomplishments and agency of Native people – a goal that I support fully. However, the presentation of these accomplishments is hollow because the exhibits do not offer visitors the context of struggle necessary to appreciate these victories and the ultimate survival of Indigenous communities of North America as sovereign, self-determining nations. The NMAI's goal in presenting Native American history in such a way may have been to give power and agency to Native people and simultaneously to represent to an international audience Native accomplishments and ability to adapt and change in the contemporary world. However, I argue that the Our People exhibits do not do justice to nor adequately (re)present Native history, because they fail to inform and educate the visitor by not *effectively* presenting information and experiences to appreciate and respect the continued existence of Native cultures. Certainly the agency of Native people, in the past and present, is critical to highlight in any telling of Native history, present, and future. However, we do not honor our ancestors and their struggles and sacrifices if we ignore or fail to tell the stories of extreme brutalization, struggle, and suffering that they endured and overcame. Agency is indisputably vital, and representing Native people as passive victims is not only damaging but inaccurate. However, in teaching and presenting the history of Native America, the choice is not one between binaries of active agent or passive victim. Native history can be skillfully presented in ways that demonstrate the horrors of colonization across this hemisphere yet portray the agency of courageous children, strong women, brave elders, and spirited leaders who struggled to resist the decimation of their worlds. Sadly, the NMAI missed opportunities to provide powerful, nuanced versions of Native American history that would have emotional resonance for the visitor and add appreciably to their knowledge about Native life and experience.

Guns and Bibles

The Our Peoples gallery offers several examples of such missed opportunity. One of the focal points of that gallery is a large display of guns, all pointed in one direction, toward the display of gold in the adjacent panel (Figure 29.1). A portion of the text inside the gun case reads:

> Why Guns? Guns are everywhere in the Native past. Like Christianity and foreign governments, they weave a thread of shared experience that links Native people across the hemisphere. Native desire to adopt new goods drove early encounters between Indians and Europeans. Indigenous people gave up some technologies – pottery, stone, knives, and leather clothing – and adopted brass kettles, metal tools, and eventually, guns. Europeans increased their manufacture capacity to meet the needs of the new American market. Native people made guns their own, using the new technology as they used all new technologies: to shape their lives and future.[10]

Such a reading of these weapons that were used to slaughter, rape, and maim our ancestors is upsetting and outrageous. It literally brought tears to my eyes to read it as I thought about what the countless warriors, women, and children who were slaughtered by those very guns would have said in reading that text panel. Is the agency given to those ancestors by museum curators worth the massive loss in terms of impact and opportunity for knowledge and education? What do visitors gain from viewing that case? What message do they take away with them?

I argue that in order to be effective and to educate audiences, the guns need to be contextualized in a much different way. The curatorial staff must find a way to give the visitor a sense of the extreme terror inflicted by those guns and the creative and courageous efforts of Native people to use these weapons in order to protect their families, land, and communities. In a time when discussions of terrorism are rampant, these guns might have offered an appropriate and effective way to push back the clock of terrorism in the United States – to remind museum visitors that the first major act of terrorism on this land did not occur on September 11, 2001, and that

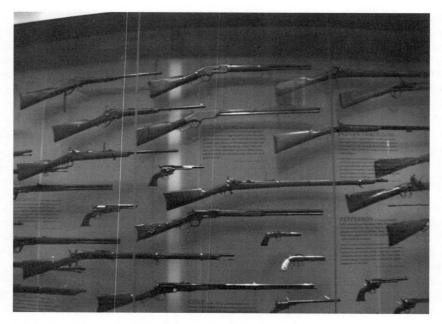

Figure 29.1   Guns display in the Our Peoples gallery. Photo by the author.

acts of aggression and the infliction of mass casualties in this country did not begin at the bombing of Pearl Harbor. This would have been an excellent opportunity to educate several million people a year on the facts surrounding this country's foundation on acts of extreme terror, biological warfare, and genocide against civilian women and children.

Recently a t-shirt has become popular at pow-wows and in Native communities. The t-shirt has a photo of Geronimo and several other Native men holding guns, and the text reads, "Homeland Security: Fighting Terrorism since 1492" (Figure 29.2). Colleen Lloyd (Tsa-la-gi/Tuscarora) created the Homeland Security t-shirt and sells it, along with other products carrying the same image and message, on her website (www.westwindworld.com). This t-shirt effectively and simply communicates volumes about our history as Native people. It gives agency to the men pictured and demonstrates the ways in which they used a foreign object and, to use the words of the NMAI's guns text panel, "made it their own." It brings the past into the present, providing historical context to contemporary events in a way that is humorous yet

hard-hitting, powerful yet non-offensive. The t-shirt carries the tone of decolonization – a message that the NMAI is sorely lacking.

The NMAI's discussion of religion in the Our Peoples gallery is another example of missed opportunity. The religion case, located directly behind the guns case, has a series of Bibles that were translated into different Native languages (Figure 29.3). The text panel for this case reads, in part,

> Why bibles? Christianity weaves a thread of shared experience that links Native People across the hemisphere. Wherever Europeans went, they spread the gospel. This wall features more than 100 bibles, translated into nearly 75 indigenous languages. Such translation is a testament to the tireless efforts Christians have made to convert Indians since 1492. Today the majority of Native peoples call themselves Christian. It is a story not only of choice, but also of adaptation, destruction, resistance and survivance.[11]

As in the guns case discussed earlier, the desire to portray the agency of Native people is obvious, but it is made at the expense of utilizing this

Figure 29.2   Showing t-shirts, "Homeland Security: Fighting Terrorism since 1492." Photo by Colleen Lloyd.

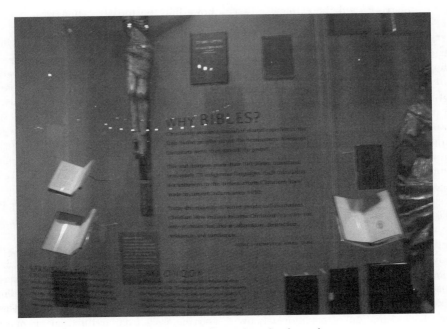

Figure 29.3   Religion case in the Our Peoples gallery. Photo by the author.

space to portray Christianity as a powerful agent of colonization, one that Native people fought harshly against. While this text panel does briefly mention the destruction involved in Christianizing Native people, in viewing this display and reading the accompanying text, one does not get a sense of the range of struggles that Native people endured to keep their own spiritual practices alive. The Ghost Dance, the slaughter at Wounded Knee, the illegality of the Sundance, and the great lengths Native people went to in order to preserve their traditional spiritual practices are not emphasized. Instead, as in the guns case, the curators chose to give a large space in the gallery to a group of objects that were not made by Native people but were used to control them. At the same time, the display minimizes the role (or reading) of the Bibles as artifacts of colonization.

Curatorial staff might have more appropriately chosen to display the translated Bibles in a way that re-contextualized or re-interpreted them, making clear the intimate connections and multiple threads of action involved. Such threads include contemporary celebrations of the survival (indeed resurgence) of traditional Native spiritual knowledge and practices, dramatic efforts of Christians and government to destroy or silence such knowledge, creative and courageous routes of Native and non-Native people to preserve it, and the extreme misbalance of power embedded in all of this. While the text panel (quoted earlier) mentions "adaptation, destruction, and survivance," it does not offer or effectively communicate a view that problematizes Christian leaders' attempts at spiritual genocide and the powerful impact of shame, language destruction, and fear that accompanied it. The irony of the Bibles and their translation into Native languages during the same period in which Native children were punished, even beaten, for speaking their language is another point left unexplored in the galleries of the NMAI.

While there is disappointingly little in this display that problematizes for the visitor the inherent power relations involved in Christianizing Native people and the literal demonizing of traditional practices, the gallery adjacent to this one, titled Our Universes, presents various forms of traditional Native American spiritual practices. However, the celebration of traditional knowledge displayed in the Our Universes gallery also lacks emphasis on the connection of the past struggles our ancestors endured to preserve spiritual practices for present and future generations.

Presenting paradoxes and agency in discussions of Christianity and Indigenous people may be challenging, but there are examples where it has been done in a large, national museum context. One such example is from the Australian Museum, the national museum in Sydney, Australia. In their discussion of the changing practices of the Australian Museum and its representations of Indigenous cultures, Jim Sprecht and Carolyn MacLulich mention the Pieces of Paradise exhibit of 1988, which related to cultures of the Pacific Islands. In there review of the Gogodala section of the exhibit, Sprecht and MacLulich note that the exhibits highlight the presentation of Indigenous resistance and cultural revitalist movements in reaction to the, "oppressive practices of fundamentalist Christian groups."[12] Sadly, in dramatic contrast the NMAI chose not to highlight Native resistance. In presenting Native history in Our Peoples, NMAI curators had ample opportunity to educate visitors about any of the multiple resistance efforts undertaken by Native people against the powerful forces of Christianization. Native agency and survivance could have been powerfully portrayed in that way, but instead curators made the choice to provide visitors with benign representations of guns, churches, and governments.

At the NMAI it is not only historical struggles that are benign, absent, or difficult for viewers to access due to lengthy text panels but also more contemporary issues of confrontation such as present-day battles and victories to repatriate our ancestors and the sacred objects lost during colonization. Highlighting this topic would have brought the struggle for spiritual sovereignty into the twenty-first century through an exhibit focused on the Native American Graves Protection and Repatriation Act (NAGPRA). This is particularly relevant for a national museum that will have a large non-Native audience, as the case of the Ancient One (Kennewick Man) has been widely reported in the mainstream media, making national newspaper headlines, as well as the cover of Time and Newsweek magazines, and has even been featured in an episode of 60 Minutes.[13] Furthermore, efforts in Indian country have been ongoing to amend and improve the NAGPRA legislation to address critical issues such as so-called unaffiliated remains and the very definition of "Native American" under the law.[14] Legislation to amend NAGPRA was recently introduced by former Senator Ben Nighthorse

Campbell (R-Colorado), and such an exhibit at the NMAI could have played a critical role in helping Native communities educate both Native and non-Native publics about the importance of this legislation as a matter of human rights, religious freedom, and cultural property law.

Along the same lines, the museum might have developed a critical view of the process of collecting, display, and representation of Native objects, culture, and heritage. However such critical engagement with and hard-hitting critique of Western intellectual traditions is sorely lacking. Closely related to these topics, and similarly lacking in the NMAI's exhibits, is any mention of cultural and intellectual property rights and a discussion of who has the right to control, utilize, and profit from Indigenous knowledge, symbols, images, and other areas of intangible heritage (i.e., stories, songs, dances). All of these are crucial and relevant issues for Native people today that will continue to play an important role in our communities for generations, and each involves a strong intellectual tradition of Indigenous scholarship and leadership. Yet the visiting public to the NMAI will have no chance to engage with these issues and to take home with them ideas about the various Native perspectives relating to such critical topics.

Context for Survivance

My primary critique with the displays at the NMAI is that they provide the visitor with no sense of the struggle that Native people faced as a result of European colonization. Within the Our Peoples gallery, the NMAI introduces the important concept of "survivance." This is a term developed by Anishinaabe scholar Gerald Vizenor. In defining the concept of survivance, Vizenor states, "survivance ... is more than survival, more than endurance or mere response; the stories of survivance are an active presence.... The native stories of survivance are successive and natural estates; survivance is an active repudiation of dominance, tragedy, and victimry."[15] Vizenor goes on to further discuss this concept, and throughout the book *Fugitive Poses: Native American Indian Scenes of Absence and Presence*, he provides examples of what he refers to as "stories of native survivance."[16] One

of the powerful examples Vizenor provides is that of Dr. Charles Eastman. Eastman was living on Pine Ridge in South Dakota on December 29, 1890, when the Seventh Cavalry massacred ghost dancers and their families at Wounded Knee. In his writings, Eastman describes the massacre and his attempts to find and help any survivors.[17] He writes, "Fully three miles from the scene of the massacre we found the body of a woman completely covered with a blanket of snow, and from this point on we found them scattered along as they had been relentlessly hunted down and slaughtered while fleeing for their lives."[18] Eastman goes on to describe the women, elderly, and children whom the Seventh Cavalry had ruthlessly maimed and slaughtered.

In his discussion of Eastman, Vizenor describes the work that Eastman and his wife, Elaine Goodale, did as they lectured and wrote about "the horror at Wounded Knee." Vizenor goes on to explain the important work that Eastman did as a "name giver" and the central role such work played in helping Native people with land claims and cash settlements. Vizenor describes the writing and work of Eastman saying,

> He encircled the horrors of that massacre in stories of native courage and survivance. That sense of presence, rather than absence or aversion, is natural reason and a source of native identities. The doctor enunciated his visions, memories, and totemic creations as an author. Clearly, his autobiographical stories are native survivance not victimry.[19]

It is my understanding from this and many other notable examples in Vizenor's work that the concept of survivance is not about avoiding or minimizing the horrors and tragedy of colonization. It includes agency and Native presence but does not refuse stories of struggle, particularly those that create a context for understanding and appreciating the creative methods of resistance and survival in the face of such unimaginable turmoil. In my understanding of survivance, Native people are active, present agents whose humanity is emphasized as their responses to struggle are poignantly portrayed. Presenting the horror, injustice, and multi-faceted aspects of Native peoples' struggles while simultaneously highlighting their active engagement and resistance to such onslaughts is not to portray Native people as victims. One cannot appreciate and experience the power of Native survivance if the stories and memories of our histories are not placed within the context of struggle.

The museum specifically mentions and describes the concept of survivance on one of the text panels in the Our Peoples gallery. The panel reads:

> Survivance: Native societies that survived the firestorm of Contact faced unique challenges. No two situations were the same, even for Native groups in the same area at the same time. But in nearly every case, Native people faced a contest for power and possessions that involved three forces – guns, churches, and governments. These forces shaped the lives of Indians who survived the massive rupture of the first century of Contact. By adopting the very tools that were used to change, control, and dispossess them, Native peoples reshaped their cultures and societies to keep them alive. This strategy has been called survivance.[20]

I agree with the words of this text panel and am particularly pleased with the point made about diversity of challenges, even within the same community. The power of the tripartite forces of "guns, churches, and governments" is also critical, and it is central to discussions of power relations between and among Natives and non-Natives. These are important aspects of Native survivance; however, at the NMAI, and in any museum or other telling of Native histories, there can be no stories of survivance without an understanding of extreme struggle and survival in the face of horrific circumstance. Comments by the museum's founding director, W. Richard West Jr., reflect the museum's choice to not focus on the hard-hitting stories of colonization. West told the *Washington Post*:

> Here's what I want everyone to understand. As much and as important as that period of history is, it is at best only about 5 percent of the period we have been in this hemisphere. We do not want to make the National Museum of the American Indian into an Indian Holocaust Museum…. You have to go beyond the story of the tragedy and the travesty of the past 500 years. What we are talking about in the end is cultural survivance. We are still here.[21]

The message that "we are still here" is indeed an important one, and it is one that is effectively and beautifully demonstrated in the NMAI's exhibits. However, as I argued and demonstrated earlier, the exhibits do not offer visitors the context to understand and appreciate Native survivance.

Controversies surrounding the importance of bringing Native people's voice and experience to bear in tellings of Indigenous history occur often in archaeology, my primary field of specialization. Native and non-Native archaeologists, particularly those who are engaged with Indigenous, public, and community archaeology, are exploring more effective methods of involving descendent communities and a range of stakeholders in archaeological research designs and practices and finding ways to make such work relevant and beneficial for Indigenous and local communities. Similarly, both Native and non-Native people involved in the area of Indigenous archaeology are continually facing the challenge of bringing Native voices to bear in the "peopling of the past" and in effective and ethical ways of including Native voices, collaborating with Native people, and making our work relevant in Native communities. Indigenous archaeologists have pointed out that archaeological research should not only focus on precontact periods but that archaeology must also contribute to decolonization by providing physical evidence of the process of colonization, the dramatic effects it had on our communities, and the changes and adaptations Native people made as a result. One of the important goals is to present the public with alternative views to the benign language and interpretations that mainstream archaeologists have put forth for periods of "culture contact." Yet how can we expect this of non-Native archaeologists, when the messages in the exhibits of the NMAI, which presumes to speak for Native people, do not themselves take on this challenge?

Public Audiences

Exhibitions are designed with audiences in mind, and those at the NMAI are no different. As highlighted earlier in this paper, the NMAI has consistently described its audiences as including both Native and non-Native visitors.

The NMAI has also been explicit about the critical role of consultation and the importance of giving up authority and including Native voices on the exhibit floor. However, as Steven D. Lavine points out, "If exhibition makers are simple facilitators, they still have to decide which version of the past to articulate."[22] Making such decisions can be quite difficult, even when only addressing the needs of *one* community.[23] The challenges are compounded when the aim of the museum is to (re)present diverse cultural groups to a range of audiences, as is the ambitious mission of the NMAI.[24]

In his discussion of the growing industry of cultural tourism and the role that museums play in this area, Greg Richards points out the importance of anticipating and meeting the needs of the visitor.[25] He also demonstrates what visitors expect and desire when they visit a museum, stating: "People are increasingly looking for an 'experience' when they visit museums and other attractions," and their basic motivation is often to learn and experience new things.[26] Richards's research from 1999 indicates that 70 percent of museum-going interviewees stated that learning was an "important motivation for their visit."[27] This research indicates not only that people visit museums in search of being educated on some topic but also that they want to experience something and engage in a meaningful way with museum exhibits. Richards demonstrates why it is "increasingly important to provide a total visitor experience that satisfies not just the passive tourist gaze, but that engages the senses."[28] Therefore the *experience* of the museum is critical, and its exhibits must hold resonance for visitors if they are to provide new knowledge that visitors will actively incorporate into their previous understandings. Providing new knowledge to visitors is particularly important at the NMAI precisely because Native Americans have been so vastly stereotyped and essentialized by people around the globe.

As both Constance Perin and Paulette M. McManus point out, museum professionals do not assume they have a unitary public, and they are increasingly attempting to reach visitors who will engage with the museum in very different ways. Some will browse the exhibits visually, others will read all the text carefully, and yet others will engage with the exhibits using a combination of reading and visual skills.[29] McManus points to the limited time that visitors spend engaging with museum exhibits and reading the text carefully. Her research on a large exhibition about cultural relativism indicated that visitors spent six minutes and thirty-five seconds in each gallery, with an average of four minutes and fifty seconds spent in front of exhibits themselves. With this in mind, it is critical that written and visual communication effectively convey the intended messages and main themes of the exhibit.

Aside from the way in which visitors experience the exhibits and the time they spend engaging with the text and displays, visitors to the NMAI are quite diverse culturally. As discussed earlier, audiences to the NMAI are both Native and non-Native, and they will also include a large non-American audience. Richards demonstrates the growing tendency of tourists to visit museums as part of their vacation travel.[30] Washington DC is a major tourist attraction, and the National Mall is one of the city's primary tourist destinations. The NMAI will thus not only see millions of American tourists each year but will also benefit from the overall growth of the cultural tourism industry that will bring increasing numbers of foreign visitors through the doors of the museum. To effectively communicate a message to the "streakers" (those who quickly walk through and predominantly visually browse exhibits), the "strollers" (those who engage with displays for a longer period of time exploring both visual and textual materials), and the "readers" (those who take more time and read all the text presented in an exhibit) requires sophisticated layering in museum displays and demands the attention of experienced curatorial staff with the highest level of expertise in museology practice.[31]

I strongly and emphatically agree that Native people from diverse backgrounds, communities, and experiences – women, elders, men, children, spiritual and political leaders, activists, and intellectuals from locations across the hemisphere – should all be consulted and involved in the creation of the NMAI's (re)presentations of Native cultures. Native stories and experiences must be clearly presented in a way that has impact and resonance with the audience, for there is so much at stake in these exhibits. Future generations will feel the direct effects of the impressions, lessons, and messages that visitors take home with them in their hearts and minds.

There is no doubt that the NMAI curatorial staff faced a great challenge in trying to effectively communicate messages and information to accommodate the varied needs of such a diverse public audience. Sprecht and MacLulich describe one such challenge in their work in developing exhibits for the Indigenous Australians: Australia's First Peoples gallery in the Australian Museum in Sydney.[32] They describe how focus groups and evaluations produced "widely divergent reactions." Sprecht and MacLulich state: "Indigenous respondents felt that the exhibitions would not be sufficiently hard-hitting, whereas non-indigenous people said that it would be too confrontational." This must have been an issue that the NMAI grappled with as well, perhaps even more so since, unlike the Australian Museum, the NMAI has a primary commitment to being a Native place and a mission to collaborate, consult, and cooperate with Native people. Even before accepting the position as director of the NMAI, W. Richard West Jr. had concerns about Native and non-Native audiences. In his essay in *Spirit of a Native Place: Building the National Museum of the American Indian*, West says,

> Before I accepted that honor, and challenge, [as founding director of the museum] I asked myself not only how the museum could become a place where Native peoples could say who we are, but also whether the larger culture would be willing to accept such an institution. Clearly, I decided that it would.[33]

While I appreciate the challenges expressed here, I argue that the primary concern of the NMAI should be with effectively presenting accurate portrayals of Native histories, regardless of whether the larger culture is "willing to accept" it. The NMAI must provide a context for visitors to experience the meaning of our survivance, and all the painful, triumphant, inspiring, resistant, horrific truths encompassed in it – even though such portrayals are confrontational or difficult. In fact, I would argue that such

presentations must be confrontational and challenge the visitor to experience Native histories in a way they unfortunately cannot find in the educational system of this country, in mainstream media portrayals of Native life, and in all the stereotyped messages and lessons of victimry and noble savagery incessantly present in mainstream American life. It is not only celebratory messages of our success and presence in the contemporary world that will touch the visitor's spirit at the deeper, more personal level of their humanity but also the day-to-day experiences of struggle and survivance. This does not mean that visitors must be hit over the head with stories of victimization and oppression. Shallow messages of victimry have been the mainstay of information presented to American and global audiences for centuries.

What is needed at the NMAI is collaborative museum exhibit design that incorporate the voice and views of Native communities to present real, heart-felt, complex histories and experiences that are not relegated to only celebration while glossing over the hard-hitting realities that rob visitors of an entire range of emotions and limits their ability to connect, on a basic human level, to Native people. More than anything else, the NMAI must demonstrate to non-Native and Native audiences that we are not two-dimensional cut-outs of victimry or triumph but that we are human and that, as others do, we have a range of stories to tell. Many of our stories are happy songs of revival and strength; others are sad or difficult and instructive of the shadows of colonization that still loom and continue to challenge our communities.

We, as Native peoples, have many stories to tell. We have a unique way of viewing the world, and it is one that has been severely affected by colonization yet is ever changing and resilient. Bringing Native voices to the foreground to share these experiences and worldviews is a critical part of readjusting the power balance to ensure that Native people control their own heritage, representation, and histories. If we wish to share these experiences and histories with each other and a non-Native audience, hoping to foster and protect them and to raise awareness and respect for them, then we must take seriously the job of educating and the important role of effective communication in the exhibits of the NMAI. We must expect that the galleries will not only celebrate our presence but also value and honor the sense of struggle, as it is such struggle that provides a context for understanding and truly appreciating our survivance.

Notes

1 The terms "Western" and "Indigenous" are used throughout this article to denote very broad, general groups of people and communities, each of which in itself encompasses a great deal of complexity and diversity of views. While I assume that the reader is aware of the categories that I refer to, I want to be clear that by using these broad categorizations in an attempt to present this argument from a general perspective, I do not intend to insinuate that either term refers to a monolithic, homogeneous group with rigid and clearly defined epistemologies and worldviews, but rather each includes a great deal of diversity.

2 For examples of both critiques and models for a changed practice in archaeology see Sonya Atalay, "Domesticating Clay/Engaging with 'They': Anatolian Daily Practice with Clay and Public Archaeology for Indigenous Communities," PhD dissertation, University of California, 2003; Sonya Atalay, "Gikinawaabi: Knowledge Production and Social Science Research from an Indigenous Perspective," Queens University, Belfast, Ireland, 2003; Sonya Atalay, "Multiple Voices for Many Ears in Indigenous Archaeological Practice" (conference paper, Society for American Archaeology, Montreal, 2004).

3 Native American Graves Protection and Repatriation Act of 1991. For more information on proposed changes see http://www.indianz.com/News/2004/004562.asp.

4 George Horse Capture, "The Way of the People," in Spirit of a Native Place: Building the National Museum of the American Indian, ed. Duane Blue Spruce, 42–43 (Washington, DC: National Geographic Society, 2004).

5 The literature on this topic is now quite extensive, but some of the critical texts to consult include Thomas Biolsi and Larry J. Zimmerman, Indians and Anthropologists: Vine Deloria Jr. and the Critique of Anthropology (Tucson: University of Arizona Press, 1997); Vine Deloria Jr., Custer Died for Your Sins: An Indian Manifesto (London: Macmillan, 1969); Devon A. Mihesuah, ed., Repatriation Reader: Who Owns American Indian Remains? (Lincoln: University of Nebraska Press, 2000); George P. Nicholas, "Seeking the End of Indigenous Archaeology," paper presented at the

5th World Archaeological Congress, Washington, DC, 2003; George P. Nicholas and Thomas D. Andrews, eds., At a Crossroads: Archaeology and First Peoples in Canada (Burnaby, BC: Archaeology Press, 1997); James Riding-In, "Our Dead Are Never Forgotten: American Indian Struggles for Burial Rights and Protections," in "They Made Us Many Promises": The American Indian Experience, 1524 to the Present, ed. Philip Weeks, 291–323 (Wheeling, IL: Harlan Davidson, 2002); James Riding-In, "Repatriation: A Pawnee's Perspective," in Mihesuah, Repatriation Reader, 106–120; Linda Tuhiwai Smith, Decolonizing Methodologies: Research and Indigenous Peoples (New York: St. Martin's Press, 1999).

6 The NMAI website lists the museum's mission: http://www.nmai.si.edu/subpage.cfm?subpage=press&second=mission.

7 Quoted in Tom Hill and Richard W. Hill Sr., eds., Creation's Journey: Native American Identity and Belief (Washington, DC: Smithsonian Institution Press, 1994).

8 Duane Blue Spruce, "An Honor and a Privilege," in Blue Spruce, Spirit of a Native Place, 15–29; Horse Capture, "The Way of the People," in Blue Spruce, Spirit of a Native Place, 30–45.

9 Chris Gosden, Archaeology and Colonialism (Cambridge: Cambridge University Press, 2004); Robert J. C. Young, Postcolonialism: An Historical Introduction (Oxford: Blackwell Publishing, 2001); Ania Loomba, Colonialism/Postcolonialism (London: Routledge, 1998).

10 This text is attributed to Paul Chaat Smith and Ann McMullen, 2003.

11 This text is attributed to Gerald McMasters, NMAI, 2003.

12 Jim Sprecht and Carolyn MacLulich, "Changes and Challenges: The Australian Museum and Indigenous Communities," in Archaeological Displays and the Public: Museology and Interpretation, ed. Paulette M. McManus, 39–63 (London: Archetype Publications, 2000).

13 60 Minutes, October 25, 1998; Newsweek, April 26, 1999; Michael D. LeMonick, "Bones of Contention: Scientists and Native Americans Clash over a 9,300-Year-Old Man with Caucasoid Features," Time, October 14, 1996; D. Preston, "The Lost Man," New Yorker, June 19, 1997.

14 For more information on proposed changes, see "Two-Word Change to NAGPRA Pending in Senate," http://www.indianz.com/News/2004/004562.asp.

15 Gerald Vizenor, *Fugitive Poses: Native American Indian Scenes of Absence and Presence* (Lincoln: University of Nebraska Press, 1998), 15.

16 Vizenor, *Fugitive Poses*, 18.

17 Charles Eastman, *From the Deep Woods to Civilization* (Lincoln: University of Nebraska Press, 1977); Charles Eastman, *Indian Boyhood* (New York: Dover, 1971).

18 Eastman, *From the Deep Woods to Civilization*, 111.

19 Vizenor, *Fugitive Poses*, 18.

20 Paul Chaat Smith, NMAI 2003.

21 Joel Achenbach, "Within These Walls, Science Yields to Stories," *Washington Post*, September 19, 2004.

22 Steven D. Lavine, "Audience, Ownership, and Authority: Designing Relations between Museums and Communities," in *Museums and Communities: The Politics of Public Culture*, ed. Ivan Karp, Christine Mullen Kreamer, and Steven D. Lavine, 137–157 (Washington, DC: Smithsonian Institution Press, 1992), 142.

23 For a discussion of this see Lavine, "Audience, Ownership, and Authority." Also see the following for further discussion and examples: Gerald T. Conaty, "Glenbow's Blackfoot Gallery: Working Towards Co-Existence," in *Museums and Source Communities: A Routledge Reader*, ed. Laura L. Peers and Alison K. Brown, 227–241 (New York: Routledge, 2003); Nancy J. Fuller, "The Museum as a Vehicle for Community Empowerment: The Ak-Chin Indian Community Ecomuseum Project," in Karp, Kreamer, and Lavine, *Museums and Communities*, 327–365; Jane Peirson Jones, "The Colonial Legacy and the Community: The Gallery

33 Project," in Karp, Kreamer, and Lavine, *Museums and Communities*, 221–241; Stephanie Moser et al, "Transforming Archaeology through Practice: Strategies for Collaborative Archaeology and the Community Archaeology Project at Queseir, Egypt," in Peers and Brown, *Museums and Source Communities*, 208–226.

24 Lavine, "Audience, Ownership, and Authority," also discusses some of the challenges. Karp, Kreamer, and Lavine, *Museums and Communities*; McManus, *Archaeological Displays*; and Peers and Brown, *Museums and Source Communities*, each provide examples of museums that attempt to represent diverse Indigenous or local communities; each aims to reach Indigenous and non-Indigenous visitors from both national and international audiences.

25 Greg Richards, "Cultural Tourism," in McManus, *Archaeological Displays and the Public*, 1–11.

26 Richards, "Cultural Tourism," 4.

27 Richards, "Cultural Tourism."

28 Richards, "Cultural Tourism," 8.

29 George F. Macdonald, "Change and Challenge: Museums in the Information Society," in Karp, Kreamer, and Lavine, *Museums and Communities*, 158–181; Constance Perin, "The Communicative Circle: Museums as Communities," in Karp, Kreamer, and Lavine, *Museums and Communities*, 182–220.

30 Richards, "Cultural Tourism."

31 For a description of these terms and a discussion of layering museum displays see Perin, "The Communicative Circle."

32 Sprecht and MacLulich, "Changes and Challenges," 58.

33 W. Richard West Jr., "As Long as We Keep Dancing: A Brief Personal History," in Blue Spruce, *Spirit of a Native Place*, 54.

The Past as Commodity
Archaeological Images in Modern Advertising

Lauren E. Talalay

Introduction

The subject of archaeology and popular culture has attracted increasing scholarly attention during the last decade, with themes varying from movies and fiction to political cartoons and stamps (e.g. Day, 1997; Solomon, 1998; Foss, 1999; Hamilakis, 2000; Jensen and Wieczorek, 2003; MacDonald and Rice, 2003; Holtorf, 2005). Rarely discussed, however, is the topic of archaeology and advertising, which may seem to be an obvious target of inquiry. When discussions do appear, they are usually embedded within larger concerns (e.g. Brier, 2004) and are often more descriptive than analytic (e.g. Schnitzler, 2003). Advertisers, however, have long deployed archaeological references in shaping consumer perceptions and behaviours. Images of ancient Egypt, for example, began to emerge in the early 19th century. By the first few decades of the ensuing century, magazines such as *Ladies' Home Journal* and *Companion* were running eye-catching advertisements (ads) that depicted Egyptian princesses enticing women to buy rejuvenating soaps and lotions (Figure 30.1). Following the discovery of King Tutankhamun's tomb in 1922, advertisers took full advantage of the

Lauren Talalay, "The Past as Commodity: Archaeological Images in Modern Advertising," pp. 205–216 from *Public Archaeology* 3 (2004). Reprinted with permission of Maney Publishing.

insatiable appetite for all things Egyptian. Trademark images and ads for perfume, beer, cigarettes and cigars were filled with portrayals of pyramids, obelisks, camels and temples, often represented with a hefty dose of poetic licence (Brier, 2004: 19–21). Today, the pyramids remain a mainstay for promoting Camel cigarettes, and exotic archaeological settings continue to appear in both print media and television advertisements, persuading consumers to purchase everything from cookies to computers.

Given the ubiquity of advertising in Western society, it is instructive to explore the nature and meanings of these 'archaeoadverts', with an eye to how they shape and reflect public consciousness about the past and archaeology. In a first and small step towards deconstructing these ads, I have selected examples from the last two decades taken from popular North American magazines that portray Old World archaeological sites and artefacts. I do not consider 'archaeoadverts' from South American, Asian or European publications – a sub-set that probably would have generated slightly different questions and inferences. The sample is used to address several overarching questions within the context of Western, especially North American, culture: What popular preconceptions about archaeology and the archaeological record do advertisers believe are most effective in their campaigns? What kind of 'authority' do modern consumers grant to antiquity? How permeable are the

Figure 30.1   Palmolive – Colgate Palmolive (1910).

boundaries between past and present? And do archaeologists unwittingly collude in perpetuating some of the detrimental stereotypes projected by these ads? Each of the ads discussed conceals multiple narratives about archaeology and ancient culture, but all are bound by common notions of archaeological identities and the power of the past.

This paper focuses on print advertising of the last 20 years; it does not focus on campaigns in other visual media, such as television, nor does it situate these ads within the larger, and indeed interesting, context of archaeology in fiction and movies. The article begins with a short introduction to the origins and evolution of print advertising, followed by a brief discussion of advertising's role in mediating social identities. The particular advertisements used in this study are presented in section three, while the last two sections consider, respectively, the ways in which the past and the present are manipulated and the implications of these ads for the public discourse on archaeology.

The Origins of Advertising

Advertising, as we recognize it in Western culture, did not begin until the 17th century (Dyer, 1982: 15). Other forms of marketing, proclamation and publicity have no doubt existed for millennia, but the highly visual commercialization of goods and products that we associate with 'modern' ads is a fairly recent occurrence. The roots of that phenomenon, however, stretch back approximately 300 years, to the first appearance of newspapers in England.

Newspapers, or mercuries as they were then called, began regular production in the large towns of Britain during the mid 17th century. Merchants and traders needed reliable details on consumer prices and stocks, and the public found the papers an invaluable resource for notices of fairs and markets. Serving the growing interests and needs of an increasingly literate 'middle class', mercuries also became an important vehicle for advertising, carrying small ads on patent medicines and 'miraculous' cures. Scourges such as the 1665 plague in England considerably boosted the sales (and advertisements) of these medicines, as street posters, handbills and news ads proliferated, promising an array of medical help including 'Anti-pestilential Pills' and 'The Only True Plague-water'. Aimed at wealthy clients who frequented British coffee houses where newspapers were available, these ads were invariably text-based. Over time, the rhetoric evolved from conventional recommendations to more persuasive forms of propaganda (Dyer, 1982: 15–17).

In 18th-century England literacy grew steadily, as did leisure time, amongst the middle class. Newspaper and publishing trades flourished, the volume of ads increased and, for the first time, newspapers targeted a female readership. Unlike modern advertisements, none of these early ads, which typically hawked wigs, tea, coffee, books, wine, purges and cosmetics, was illustrated. Pictorial ads appeared fairly late (in America, for example, a ban on illustrated advertisements was not lifted until 1895). By the turn of the 19th century, however, papers and magazines in both Europe and America were filled with impressive images (some by established painters), slogans and catch phrases. Advertisements seemed to be everywhere: theatre safety curtains displayed ads and an American food company even erected a signboard halfway up the White Cliffs of Dover. But critics eventually began to decry the lack of truth in advertising, as well as the rounds of unpleasant accusations amongst rival merchants. In 1898 the Society for the Checking of Abuses in Public Advertising was founded, and its adherents began what has become an enduring debate over how to judiciously balance 'good taste' against the demands of commerce (Dyer, 1982: 17, 32–37; for an excellent summary of the early history and development of advertising, see Dyer, 1982: 15–69).

As the 20th century progressed, advertising underwent radical transformations, initially driven by the use of the new 'science of psychology' (Dyer, 1982: 43; Scott, 1904; 1916), which was later augmented by market and motivational research as well as applications of various computer techniques. Today, message- and icon-based promotions continually bombard us, emanating from billboards, fliers, posters, magazines, books, radio, television, movies and the Internet – at least one source estimates that in the USA alone the average person is exposed to 500–1,000 commercial messages every day (Arens, 2002: 58). Allegedly, the next wave will include interactive promotions on plasma screens (Perina, 2003) – a far cry from what some believe to be the first simple advertisement printed in English in the *Imperial Intelligencer* of 1648 (Scott, 1904: 29).

Advertising, Social Identity and Visual Communication

The evolution of advertising, perfunctorily outlined above, harbours several themes, not least the communicative and 'performative' aspects of the enterprise (for discussions on advertisements as communication and performance see, e.g. Dyer, 1982; Leiss et al., 1986; Davidson, 1992; Campbell, 1997; Cronin, 2000). Those analysts who view advertising within a communication or semiological model argue that, through the use of rhetoric and symbols, advertisements help mediate and construct social identities. Most people claim, however, that they remain unaffected by advertising and regard ads as

mendacious, trivial and idiotic (Dyer, 1982: 72). Denials notwithstanding, it is hard to escape the conclusion that ads *do* reflect and shape the consumer world of Western cultures, spur the drive to buy not just *things* but *values*, and foster a general sense of social belonging for many people (Davidson, 1992: 123). Although advertising is also about promoting the corporate image of a company and establishing a rhetoric of legitimation for that business and its products (Cronin, 2000: 41), it is intimately linked to cultural identities. As Mary Douglas (1982: 24) argued more than two decades ago, '... mass goods represent culture ... they are an integral part of that process of objectification by which we create ourselves as an industrial society: our identity, our social affiliations, our lived everyday practice'. Advertisements create an environment in which goods are explicitly equated with how we choose to structure our lives, our lifestyles, our consumption and our values.

Precisely how ads help mediate and configure social identities, however, is complex and much contested in the literature. Advertising works on multiple levels and there are several axes along which advertisements can be analysed. Despite disagreements, scholars tend to categorize ads in clusters that are often based on which 'sense of self' an ad appeals to. The most oft-cited categories are social ambition, snobbery, glamour, luxury, fantasy, fear, health and social acceptance (see, e.g. Inglis, 1972: 75–103; Davis, 1991: 142–168). Marketers, not surprisingly, also undertake extensive research on target audiences, often classified by age, class, gender, sex, race, etc. (see, e.g. Davis, 1991: 103–124). In addition, there are various explorations into the use of compelling images, effective language and rhetoric (see, e.g. Gombrich, 1962; Durand, 1970; Barthes, 1977; Dyer, 1982: 158–187) and what are known as central and peripheral routes of persuasion (Arens, 2002: 145–146). Although discussion of these topics is outside the scope of this paper, it is important to note in the context of this article that the visual discourse of advertising employs reductionistic and essentializing vocabularies. Like many cartoons, print ads have only a single frame in which to deliver a message. As Hamilakis (2000: 59) observes in his recent discussion of political cartoons, their power lies 'in summing up in a condensed form a view, idea or preconception' that is materialized by easily recognizable images. Also, like political cartoons, the images in an advertisement must cull from stereotypes and conform to preconceptions in order to be successful. The 'archaeoadverts' analysed below adhere to these formulae – they employ a limited range of stereotypes, play upon simplified preconceptions and use visual vocabularies that are easily accessible to most Western consumers.

Advertising and the Identities of Ancient Culture

If we accept that advertisements have made an art out of appealing to consumers' sense of self, fantasies and social ambitions, several questions follow: Which cultures and what kinds of archaeology have become part of current public discourse? How are archaeology and the past manipulated within the contexts of print advertisements?

Certain ancient cultures appear to be privileged in modern Western advertising: namely, Egypt, Greece and, to some extent, Rome. Visual references to well-known archaeological images or discoveries in Europe such as Stonehenge and Lascaux appear less frequently and New World images from Mayan, Aztec, Pre-Columbian and Palaeo-Indian sites are rare. The archaeologies of the Near and Far East are virtually non-existent, possibly because these civilizations are considered too 'other' to be easily accessible or decoded by modern Western consumers. It is also possible that advertisers are hesitant to 'demean' archaeological monuments that have powerful religious associations for the host countries (a taboo that may be even more potent in our post-11 September 2001 era). The most popular images, such as the Pyramids, the Parthenon or the Coliseum, are immediately recognizable, associated with notions of Empire, and serve as subtle and implicit symbols of power.

The condensed and formulaic language of print advertising demands that Greek, Roman and Egyptian civilizations must be reduced to simplistic categories. Greece tends to be associated with ideas of class, style and the traditions of intellectual thought; Egypt with death, eternity, mystery and the exotic; and Rome with mayhem, warfare, aggression and great

architectural feats. Clearly, these are not necessarily correct, let alone nuanced views of these societies, but the modern consumer does not expect 'truth' in advertising. And advertising is, after all, a rhetoric of persuasion, not a narrative of instruction.

For example, the Estée Lauder Company employed a perfume ad in the mid-1980s showing an elegantly dressed woman perched seductively on a stylish table surrounded by several 'Classical' sculptures, including an Aphrodite type and a nude male. Inset on the lower right side of this full-sized glossy ad is a perfume bottle labelled 'Private Collection'. As consumers, we are, presumably, supposed to think that we are viewing the exclusive office or home of a wealthy private collector. The perfume, the woman and the Classical Greek sculptures create iconographic conventions that signify high art, money, sophistication and power. Greek elements were apparently selected to exude an aura of urbanity and elegance. I suspect that the intended message would probably have failed, or at least been very different, if the advertisers had chosen, for example, artefacts from Egypt, the Near East or Mesoamerica.

Greek stereotypes are not, however, limited to the culture's artistic legacy. Other ads seem to link ancient Greece to the notions of philosophical thought and the roots of Western intellectual identities. The producers of a mid-1980s Benson & Hedges advertisement, for example, chose to place a Socratic-type bust between a young man and a woman. The woman, who balances two books and a pair of eyeglasses, looks adoringly at the man who contemplates, cigarette in hand, the Greek bust. As the ad states: 'She likes the ancient philosophers', while for the hapless man, 'It's all Greek to him'. Clearly, she is meant to be seen as the intelligent member of the pair. Regardless of their respective IQs, however, the advertisers want us to know that '... there's one taste they agree on: Benson & Hedges'. This ad 'speaks', amongst other things, to the consumer's more rational side, and rationality is subtly proposed as a quintessential Greek trait.

A slightly more obscure use of Classical elements comes from the Quintus Corporation, which specializes in computer software. The ad's narrative informs us that the success of any company hinges on a fully integrated customer service system. As the text suggests, 'Only parts that fit together seamlessly elevate customer service to a work of art'. To illustrate the concept, the advertisers show, in an upper register, an array of disembodied arms and hands, allegedly from Classical sculptures. A much smaller image on the middle left side depicts a complete 'integrated' nude male, again recognizable as deriving from the Classical world, broadly defined. While disembodied images from other cultures could no doubt have worked, the purposeful selection of Classical figures underscores not only the accessibility of these works to many Western viewers, but also the notion that the Greeks represent the embodiment of intelligence, high art and rational thought – traits that should be associated with Quintus, as they were in the previous ads for Estée Lauder and Benson & Hedges.[1]

Roman images, on the other hand, tend to be coupled with brawn, not brains, architectural feats rather than intellectual skills, and warfare and games. A recent series of ads from Decon Studrails Company, a North American construction company, suggests that with the proper studrails even you can (as the ads state) 'build Rome in a day'. The well-designed rails will ensure that your job site won't 'look like a battlefield'. These ads tend to be fairly text-heavy, but invariably include archaeological images of columns or fragments of artistic reliefs depicting Romans busily engaged in construction work. A similar concept is suggested by a recent advert announcing the newly expanded Caesar's Palace in Las Vegas. In this ad, a striking blue-coloured rendition of a Roman sculptural relief portraying soldiers building a wall provides the background for the ironic words, 'Oh, by the way, we've finished our little add-on'. Again, the Romans are portrayed as builders par excellence, who command great forces of labour.

Advertisements that call upon Egyptian archaeology for inspiration rely on very different core elements: tombs, hieroglyphs, pyramids and the notion of exotic treasures. An ad from 2000 for the Audi allroad quattro car exploits the public's conception that Egypt is rugged and mysterious, a place where transforming adventure awaits all who visit. The journal-like entry on the top of the promotion, which positions the new car in the midst of the Pyramids, reads, 'The

Figure 30.2 Johnnie Walker and Son (1985).

Eastern desert. June 1. The first time I made my own road, spoke a language I didn't know, got lost on purpose, measured time in cups of mint tea'. At the lower right-hand side, a road sign reads 'Pavement Ends' and, underneath the image, the advertiser's creators have written 'life begins'. The Audi creation is a complex and layered ad, which allows the viewer to glance casually at the image in order to receive the intended message or read through the text and savour, as it were, the more exotic and 'profound' aspects of life's potentials. If, as some scholars argue, visual media have replaced storytelling in our society, then this visually impressive ad provides a good example of how a single-frame image with minimal text can effectively narrate a story, with one eye to the past and one to the future.

In the world of advertising, Egyptian tombs inevitably yield valuable long-lost treasures. The next two ads are carefully structured to suggest that an archaeologist, adventurer or tomb robber, while not visible in the frame, lurks just around the corner. In a 1985 Johnnie Walker ad (Figure 30.2), which depicts an Egyptian tomb painting, several tribute bearers march, single file, toward a seated Pharaoh. Each carries a precious gift for the powerful ruler. One of the gift givers is highlighted by what we are meant to assume is an archaeologist's or perhaps a tomb robber's torch. The illuminated gift bearer proffers not the usual fare but a bottle of Johnnie Walker Red Scotch – an offering truly fit for a king (in this life or the next). In a second ad, a computer, on which is written the word 'Ra!', peeks out from behind an opening that was destructively cut into a painted Egyptian tomb wall. Two kneeling figures, one of Anubis, the other of a royal figure or perhaps a god, bracket the computer. Both figures raise their right arms high. This ad, at least to my mind, is difficult to deconstruct. Although Ra is a well-known Egyptian god, I am not sure why his particular name appears on the computer screen. Nor am I clear about why the designers chose the particular postures of the two painted figures: are they meant to reflect a subtle 'meta-sign' indicating victory at the moment of discovery? Is the word 'Ra' intended as a reference to the interjection 'rah!', a common cry of celebration at sports events? In either case, we are again led to believe that an archaeologist or, in this case, possibly a looter has just exposed this magnificent long-hidden treasure.

It is not surprising that the same cultural simplifications of Rome, Egypt and Greece are reflected in print ads for the highly popular computer games based on these ancient societies. In fact, ads for ancient games form a significant and instructive sub-set within the world of advertising and archaeology. Marketers and designers have already established the nature of the society targeted by the game; the print advertisement merely encapsulates the character of the culture. The following brief comments on magazine adverts for four games serve as typical examples.

An ad for the game 'SPQR' reads: '29 senators murdered. A saboteur loose in the city. Martial law declared. Flood, fire, and riots. Just another day in Rome, AD 205'. The text lies superimposed on a stone relief depicting a body-strewn Roman battlefield. A similar view of the Romans as consummate yet brutal game-players is projected in a two-page magazine advertisement for EA Sports digital games. On one page, a major league American baseball player is shown swinging at a lightning fast pitch to home plate. On the facing page, carved into an ancient stone façade, are the words 'Crushicus Longimus Ballimus'. The text below the fake Latin inscription urges the consumer to purchase the game, but only if he or she is an aggressive competitor, an equal to the ancient Roman sportsmen.

An ad for the Egyptian game 'Pharaoh' is well in line with preconceptions that popular culture seems to associate with life on the ancient Nile. The ad reads: 'Build a kingdom. Rule the Nile. Live Forever'. The requisite images of the Pyramids and the Sphinx dominate the centre of the page, and the text below exhorts the player to '... Immerse yourself in the grandeur of ancient Egypt, the mysterious kingdom beside the river Nile ... Pass along your legacy from generation to generation, creating an empire and a bloodline built only for a Pharoah'. Grandeur, timelessness and immortality are clearly foregrounded in both the images and accompanying text.

More contemplative and allied with popular stereotypes of ancient Greece is an ad for the game 'Zeus'. Spread out over three pages of carefully chosen images, some of which are clearly Greek, others Roman and still others imaginary, the ad asks: 'How will your city turn out – Doric, Ionic, Corinthian or Ruined? How will your citizens turn out – athletic, poetic, artistic or sadistic? And finally, who will your city attract – heroes, fiends, gods, or monsters?'. There are no references here to the promise of immortality, as in the Egyptian game. According to this advert, a typical Greek city, whose fate is controlled by the great Zeus, might entice fiends and monsters (as in ancient Rome), but it will also attract artists, poets, intellects, and heroes – elements of society that don't seem to populate the gaming industry's vision of the Roman and Egyptian worlds.

Each of these three ancient societies has been necessarily reduced to a prescriptive shorthand that belies the complexity of the cultures. The exotic is appropriated from Egypt, the cultured from Greece and the technical ingenuity from Rome. Reducing the cultures to stereotypes helps cast the civilizations as both intriguing but not too alien, and accessible but not too familiar. As some ethnographers (e.g. Sutton, 1998) have observed in other contexts, the past becomes 'domesticated' in order to be consumed, in this case by popular Western culture.

Curiously, ads depicting archaeologists at work are rare, a surprising fact in light of the enormous popularity of Indiana Jones and his more recent female counterpart, Lara Croft. Since the late 1930s, moviegoers have been entertained by cinematic images of archaeologists at work. The image of the archaeologist, however, has not remained static. From the 1930s to the 1980s the silver screen was filled with portrayals of bookish, scholarly archaeologists beset by poison darts and revivified mummies (Solomon, 1998: 93; see also Day, 1997). In contrast, George Lucas' Indiana Jones, who first burst onto the screen in 1981, was an action hero and romantic adventurer. Like his predecessors, he was not without scholarly credentials, but Jones was bent on saving the vanishing past, appearing at times more like a looter than a legitimate archaeologist. My search so far has suggested that the popularity of Indiana Jones did not take hold in printed advertising in the 1980s. Only a few ads depict archaeologists (usually male) at work, often with pith helmets, trowelling off millennia of dirt and dust to reveal, for example, an ancient mosaic of a cigarette pack or an old concrete sewage pipe with a modern logo still intact (Arch-Theory list, 1999). Although I have not seen the following ad from Australian television, one response from an email thread on the Arch-Theory list describes an Indiana-type appearing in an ad for Schweppes. The archaeologist opens the lid of an ancient container, exposes a mummy, races off to inform his colleagues and, in the process, knocks over a bottle of Schweppes. The contents spill over the mummified corpse, which is transformed into a beautiful, exotic woman.

Clearly, the image of archaeologists at work carries overtones of danger, discovery, the search for exotic treasures and travel to distant lands. It is, however, an image that appears less frequently than the actual archaeological monuments or sites.

Past and Present in Archaeoadverts

Although the advertisements discussed above sell an array of products, they share common modes for connecting the past and the present. Specifically, the designers of these 'archaeoadverts' craft at least two different types of relationship between the contemporary and the historical: on the one hand, the boundaries between antiquity and modernity are purposely rendered permeable, and on the other, the two temporal settings are consciously set in opposition. Usually both techniques are used in a single advert, creating an interesting temporal tension.

The melding of the two temporalities – past and present – is accomplished by cleverly contracting or erasing the time differentials. While the archaeological images are recognized as durable relics that have emerged intact from long-term history, their juxtaposition with daily activities shrinks the time depth. The enormous chasms in space and time are eroded by visual or conceptual connections that bond the ancient artefact or monument with the modern product. This technique is especially effective in a 1995 ad for Absolut Vodka, where the modern and readily recognized icon of Absolut Vodka is transmuted into an ancient monument. Many viewers are probably unaware that the Pyramids are several thousand years old or that the Parthenon was built millennia after the great Egyptian structures. Indeed, the precise chronological details are irrelevant. What is important is that the artefacts and monuments are old enough to be somewhat mystifying and unusual, but not so old as to be incomprehensible or irrelevant in the grand scheme of contemporary life. Advertisers are no doubt aware that without skilful visual and textual engineering, which partially erases or at least blurs the time differentials between past and present, these types of ads would be much less effective (Hamilakis, 2000, notes a similar phenomenon amongst recent political cartoons in Greece).

If we probe a little deeper, however, it is arguable that the success of these 'archaeoadverts' derives from an explicit tension between the two different temporalities. While past and present are meant to merge or at least overlap in these narratives, the readers of these 'texts' recognize, on some fundamental level, that the archaeological images are linked to an enduring sense of time while the commodities are tethered to ephemeral contexts. From the consumer's viewpoint, the archaeological depictions reflect larger than life symbols that retain a permanency of meaning. On the other hand, the modern products, whose connection to the past is used to *imply* their timelessness, cannot legitimately claim transcendent meaning. Rather, whatever meanings or values the merchandise may embody, they are contingent on modern consumer whims, desires, values and beliefs. These two different temporalities – the sustained and the impermanent – thread through all 'archaeoadverts' and help explain why these ads can be compelling.

In addition, there are other ways to view the alliances of 'old' and 'new' in these advertisements. While it may seem, on the surface, that the past and the present are 'equal partners', it is the uncontested authority and evocativeness of the past that furnishes these commercials with power. On balance, it is archaeology that captures the public imagination, not the modern commodity. Moreover, it is often the unexpected or humorous matching of the old with the new that renders these adverts effective. Props from the ancient world can provide a setting that is somewhat at odds with the modern world, creating either an arresting or comical appearance. For example, in a humorous ad for Famous Amos cookies the confection is elevated to a work of art by placing the oversized biscuit on a Classical column. And, in another ad from AT&T, the well-known AT&T business logo is transformed into a timeless image by placing it as the centrepiece of an ancient Egyptian stone relief. Held by a striding male, the round, ball-like AT&T logo, which resembles an oversized hieroglyph, is framed by a series of carved hieroglyphs and proffered as an offering by the tribute bearer. A 1985 ad by Timex also effectively juxtaposes the old with the new, but here it is a gold Timex watch (the design of which is inspired by the Step Pyramid of Zoser) resting in the sand amidst other pieces of Egyptian exotica: a piece of ancient papyrus, an (allegedly) old Egyptian clay flask and a simple beaded bracelet. Presumably the viewer will associate the antiquity, durability and storied quality of Zoser and his great structure with the resilience and intriguing design of this Timex watch. As the ad says, this is a watch 'that tells a story, not just the time'.

A visually well-constructed advertisement from Xerox goes one step further – there are no explicit modern images in this depiction. The two-page ad portrays an ancient vase containing a series of papyrus scrolls, reminiscent of the Dead Sea Scrolls. Highlighting these scrolls is an 'off-stage' light illuminating the find. The text reads 'Ancient Dilemma. Sometimes we file knowledge away so well it gets lost forever. Stop putting your knowledge in hard-to-find places. Get a Xerox document centre system and scan it all to your company website. Now everyone can find what they need to know, when they need it. Keep the conversation going. Share the knowledge'. The partnership between past and present is carefully parsed in this ad – the written text alludes to the modern world, the iconography to the archaeological record. The continuity between the two worlds is, however, seamless: people from earlier societies struggled, just like us, with organizational problems. The possible allusion to the Dead Sea Scrolls is significant – it suggests that we (or more precisely, one's company) is acquiring, storing and disseminating knowledge that is potentially as vital.

We can also deconstruct these advertisements on another level that, I suspect, has much more relevance for archaeologists than for the general public. Namely, the ad designers often dismiss archaeological authenticity. Although the pyramids [in the Audi allroad quattro ad] seem to be based on archaeological reality, as are the sculptural fragments in the Quintus ad described above, advertisements more often portray a semblance of the authentic image, be it an ancient wall painting, papyrus, pot or sculpture. The authority of these ads does not depend on what is real or what is fake, what is genuine or what is an approximation of the genuine. Indeed, the ancient image can be a fairly poor imitation of the original or even a cartoon version of a monument and still be persuasive. Unlike political cartoons (Hamilakis, 2000: 60–61) or satirical images, which occasionally delight in ridiculing the masses for their taste in replicas rather than the 'real thing', these ads need only *evoke* a recognizable reference to an ancient monument or artefact in order to be effective.

Some Implications of Modern Advertising for Archaeology

The foregoing analysis of overarching themes and techniques in modern 'archaeoadverts' provides a good vantage point from which to discuss the implications of these ads for our profession. Pertinent ideas outlined by the late Roland Barthes afford useful guidelines. Barthes, who had an enduring interest in the 'rhetoric of the image', was one of the first scholars to accord mass culture the richness and complexity that we often ascribe to high art. Barthes believed that it was possible to read the trivia of daily life in great detail – no object, image or text was purely functional. Rather, it contained an array of supplementary meanings or connotations that often masked the real structures of life, especially the need of those in power to foster conformity and maintain the status quo. Advertisements, which held a particular interest for Barthes, were part of a vast constructed social reality that was passed off as 'natural', when, in fact, it concealed deeper and sometimes disturbing insights into the historical and social origins of our lives. Barthes' observations about the *Blue Guide*, (well known travel guides, published since 1918, that focus on art, architecture and history), which are cited by Davidson in his discussion of advertising in the postmodern age (1992), are particularly apt in the current context:

> For the 'Blue Guide' men exist as 'types'. In Spain, for instance, the Basque is an adventurous sailor, the Levantine a light-hearted gardener, the Catalan a clever tradesman ... The ethnic reality of Spain is thus reduced to a ... nice neat *commedia dell'arte*, whose improbable typology serves to mask the real spectacle of conditions, classes and professions. (Barthes, 1973: 75)

As noted above, ads, out of necessity, fall into this reductionist mode. The abridged definitions are saturated with references to what ad-men and ad-women assume we know about the world (Davidson, 1992: 9). In the case of archaeology, ad designers seem to think that consumers possess limited knowledge about archaeology, archaeologists and specific cultures. Whether these perceptions reflect misleading categories or invented identities (as might be defined by archaeologists or ancient historians) is not the concern of advertisers. Rather, ad designers need 'totemic' images and highly condensed visual vocabularies that maintain the worlds of archaeology and antiquity as static and essentialized entities – archaeologists regularly travel to exotic lands, uncover (or sometimes loot) glorious treasures and study unidimentional societies. Several abstract notions are stabilized by those simplifications: ancient Greece can continue to be cast historically as our intellectual and artistic epicentre, Rome as our decadent and architecturally ingenious ancestral home and Egypt, which lies on the periphery of Western cultural history, as a source of the exotic and mystifying 'other'.

Although advertisements are rarely intended as educational messages, it is still useful to ask whether these stereotypes are harmful to our profession. Should we simply dismiss these ads as light-hearted and often humorous images that enliven our icon-laden and overly commercialized world? If we cannot escape the totalizing narratives of ads, what kinds of universalizing categories might we prefer to see?

Not surprisingly, the answers are complex. On the one hand, these 'archaeoadverts' create a positive force. Consumed by a diverse audience, they help construct and maintain ongoing public interest in antiquity, certainly a benefit for archaeologists. Equally important, they tether the past to the present, casting antiquity in a relevant relationship to the modern world. As the social geographer David Lowenthal notes: 'However depleted by time and use, relics remain essential bridges between then and now. They confirm or deny what we think of [the past], symbolize or memorialize communal links over time, and provide archaeological metaphors that illuminate the process of history and memory' (Lowenthal, 1985: xxiii). In the world of modern advertising, the past, to some extent, can be reclaimed by the present.

On the other hand, many of these ads convey messages that I, as an archaeologist, find disturbing. In the Audi advert [...], for example, the car is situated amidst the most famous sacred landscape of ancient Egypt. An ad for a Mercury Tracer profanes an equally well-known ancient icon, the Athenian Acropolis. Produced as a cartoon strip, the Mercury ad takes us through several frames as the car fluidly careens down the steps of the Parthenon, thereby demonstrating the superior solid body construction and suspension of the Tracer. Admittedly, both scenarios belong more to the realm of fantasy than reality but the seeding of these sub-texts into the public consciousness is troubling. I would argue that these images function as destructive messages within public discourse, subtly condoning the desecration of cultural heritage.

The Ra! computer ad discussed above communicates an equally troublesome concept, although this time the topic seems to be the lure of looting. The intimation of looting may make good advertising copy, but it undermines the careful efforts of archaeologists who strenuously battle to curtail the destructive behaviours of treasure hunters. The disturbing elements of the Estée Lauder advert are more understated. The covert message is that private archaeological collections are a desirable goal in a happy and powerful life. A complicated topic, private collecting has long fuelled the trafficking in illicit antiquities. Ads such as the Estée Lauder example subtly applaud such behaviour. Admittedly, I look at these ads through an archaeological lens, but I am sure that many of the meta-messages broadcast in these examples are not lost on members of the lay public, regardless of their professions, economic status or knowledge of archaeology.

Conclusion

Although new technologies may eventually alter advertising's techniques and promotional strategies, I suspect that the 'hijacking' (Schnitzler, 2003) of images from antiquity will retain its currency in the future. Indeed, the recent rash of films set in the ancient world (or, for example, Pepsi's lavish new television commercial replicating the Roman Coliseum, with Britney Spears and the teeming masses of Rome) suggests that the public is still readily engaged with the past. No doubt, the public's 'consumption' of antiquity will continue to embrace only a limited roster of motifs and monuments (spectacular new archaeological discoveries notwithstanding). As noted above, advertising – once described as the 'louche opiate of our times' (Davidson, 1992:1) – depends on synecdochical rhetoric. Easily recognized images that accord with simplified notions of past cultures or stereotypical ideas about our profession will not be ousted soon from the public market place. On the one hand, I am sympathetic with archaeological purists who would likely condemn the lack of nuanced projections and accuracy in most current adverts or those ads that broadcast detrimental meta-messages. On the other hand, I also support the notion that advertisers, who reach an enormous global audience, should continue to seed antiquity into public discourse, even if those images are not entirely satisfactory and tend to trivialize the past. Certainly, some of the examples cited above could benefit from a heavy dose of 'editing'. But these images do keep the past alive and connected to our present and fractious lives. While more responsible ads would be preferable, I am not hopeful that any advertising firm will soon launch an archaeologically conscious campaign. That aim, however, would provide an interesting 'brand' and challenge for the right company.

Rather than offer an orthodox summary here, I prefer to conclude by engaging the reader in an exercise. Given the above discussion, it is instructive to try our own hand at 'archaeoadvertising': what kind of advertisements would we, as archaeologists, want to create, particularly in light of important global issues such as the illicit traffic in antiquities, looting, repatriation and cultural destruction? Might the Energizer Bunny use his unfailing torch to catch a looter red-handed? Would an ad company take the risk of capitalizing on the troubling image of the exploded Bamiyan Buddhas by summoning the strength of super glue, with a tag line that reads 'For some jobs even super glue can't help; for everything else there is always KRAZY GLUE'. Could cultural preservation be whimsically associated with Zip Lock bags encasing monuments or artefacts? As anyone who attempts this exercise will quickly realize, it is no simple task to create an advertisement that simultaneously satisfies the demands of corporate culture and the discipline of archaeology.

Note

1 One of the reviewers of this paper suggested a valid alternative reading of this particular ad: the use of the name Quintus, together with the style of the logo – a large 'Q' inset within a square – evokes ancient Rome rather than Greece. As the reviewer notes, while the advert plays on the idea of fragmentation, it also aims to convey the need for organization, perhaps hinting at a Roman military sub-text.

References

Arch-Theory List archives.archives-arch-theory@jlscmail.ac.uk (accessed May 1999, entry 11).

Arens, W.F. *Contemporary Advertising.* (8th edn.) McGraw-Hill/Irwin, Boston, MA (2002).

Barthes, R. *Mythologies.* (Trans. Annette Lavers.) Hill & Wang, New York (1973).

Barthes, R. Rhetoric of the image. In *Image, Music, Text.* (Ed. and trans. Stephen Heath.) Fontana, London (1977).

Brier, B. Egyptomania! *Archaeology* 57(1) (2004) 16–22.

Campbell, C. When the meaning is not a message: a critique of the consumption as communication thesis. In Nava, M., Blake, A., MacRury, I. and Richards, B. (eds) *Buy This Book: Studies in advertising and consumption.* Routledge, London (1997) 340–351.

Cronin, A. *Advertising and Consumer Citizenship: Gender, images and rights.* Routledge, London (2000).

Davidson, M.P. *The Consumerist Manifesto: Advertising in postmodern times.* Routledge, London (1992).

Davis, R.D. *False Teeth to a Chicken: Products, advertising & you.* International Publishing Corporation, Chicago IL (1991).

Day, D.H. *A Treasure Hard to Attain: Images of archaeology in popular film with a filmography.* The Scarecrow Press, Inc., London (1997).

Douglas, M. Goods as a system of communication. In Douglas, M. *In the Active Voice.* Routledge & Kegan Paul, Boston, MA (1982) 16–33.

Durand, J. Rhétorique et image publicitare. *Communications* 15 (1970) 70–95.

Dyer, G. *Advertising as Communication.* Methuen, New York (1982).

Foss, C. Postal propaganda. *Archaeology* 52(2) (1999) 70–71.

Gombrich, E.H. *Art and Illusion.* Princeton University Press, Princeton, NJ (1962).

Hamilakis, Y. No laughing matter: antiquity in Greek political cartoons. *Public Archaeology* 1 (2000) 57–72.

Holtorf, C. *From Stonehenge to Las Vegas. Archaeology as popular culture.* Alta Mira Press, [2005], Walnut Creek, CA; see also http://members.chello.se/cornelius/

Humbert, J.-M., Pantazzi, and Zeigler, C.M. (eds) *Egyptomania: Egypt and Western art 1730–1930.* Réunion des Musée Nationaux, Paris; National Gallery of Canada, Ottawa (1994).

Inglis, F. *The Imagery of Power: A critique of advertising.* Heinemann, London (1972).

Jensen, I. and Wiezorek, A. (eds) *Dino, Zeus, und Asterix.* Zeitzeuge Archäologie in Werbung, Kunst, und Alltag heute. Langenweißbach (2003).

Leiss, W., Kline, S. and Jhally, S. *Social Communication in Advertising: Persons, products, and images of well-being.* Methuen, New York (1986).

Lowenthal, D. *The Past is a Foreign Country.* Cambridge University Press, Cambridge (1985).

MacDonald, S. and Rice, M. (eds) *Consuming Ancient Egypt.* UCL, London (2003).

Perina, K. Advertising: virtual mind reading coming soon to a theater near you. *Psychology Today* 36 (March–April, 2003) 78.

Schnitzler, B. Hijacked images: ancient Egypt in French commercial advertising. In MacDonald, S. and Rice, M. (eds) *Consuming Ancient Egypt.* UCL, London (2003) 165–173.

Scott, W.D. The psychology of advertising. *Atlantic Monthly* 93 (1904) 29–36.

Scott, W.D. *The Theory and Practice of Advertising.* Small, Maynard & Co., Boston, MA (1916).

Solomon, J. Decades of make believe. *Archaeology* September/October (1998) 92–95.

Sutton, D. *Memories Cast in Stone: The relevance of the past in everyday life.* Berg, Oxford (1998).

31

The Past as Passion and Play
Çatalhöyük as a Site of Conflict in the Construction of Multiple Pasts

Ian Hodder

Introduction

This article will include 'thick descriptions' of the site at Çatalhöyük as viewed from different perspectives. Recent work at the site has quickly become embroiled in a maelstrom of conflicting interpretations. 'The past matters', but to different people in different ways. The past can be erased or it can be forgotten, later to be picked up and reused with new meanings. The variety of currents in the Near East make this a complex and highly charged process. But it is all too easy to take a distanced stance which is itself part of the appropriation of the past for intellectual gain. Any analysis of the socio-politics of the past in the Eastern Mediterranean is itself a construction, an intellectualisation, an appropriation. This chapter attempts to counter this process by attempting to describe thickly the processes through which a particular site has become engaged in a practical struggle.

An underlying theme is that the kaleidoscope of interests that have converged on Çatalhöyük can be grouped into two broad categories, themselves a product of an underlying tension

Ian Hodder, "The Past as Passion and Play: Çatalhöyük as a Site of Conflict in the Construction of Multiple Pasts," pp. 124–39 from Lynn Meskell (ed.) *Archaeology under Fire: Nationalism, Politics and Heritage in the Eastern Mediterranean and Middle East* (London: Routledge, 1998). Reprinted with permission of Taylor and Francis UK.

between, on the one hand, a global and multinational commercialism and homogenisation which views cultural difference as play and pastiche and, on the other hand, an increasingly fragmented world of competing identities, ethnicities and nationalisms within which the past *matters* very directly. 'Hotel Çatalhöyük' may be a long way from 'Hotel Auschwitz', but it raises some of the same concerns about the clash between, on the one hand, the past as play, postmodern façade, commodity, resource, and, on the other hand, the past as passion, depth, history, ownership. It is argued that these two dimensions of experience of the past in the Near East interact in complex ways and that the past as commodity and as Oriental theme park does not undermine the use of the past in political engagement when local communities, as at Çatalhöyük, become re-engaged in their history.

The Archaeological Discourse

It is too easy, and at least to some extent incorrect, to say that archaeologists have excavated in the Near East in order to elucidate the prehistory and history of that region. Archaeological interpretation of the Near East has also been embedded within a Western construction which opposes the East or Orient as 'other'. The prehistory of the Near East has been constructed in a 'play of difference' within academic discourse.

As Said (1978) has shown more generally, the Orient has been constructed as the Other of Europe. Especially in the nineteenth and twentieth centuries the Orient came to be seen as stagnant and despotic in order to define the democratic dynamism of Europe (see Bahrani, Chapter 23, this volume). In the writing of the prehistory of Europe and the Near East these are not abstract ideas. In a very concrete way they came to define the dominant discourse of European prehistory as exemplified in its most important practitioner, V. G. Childe. In the Preface to the first edition of the *Dawn of European Civilisation* (1925), Childe said that his theme was the 'foundation of European civilisation as a peculiar and individual manifestation of the human spirit.' In Europe 'we can recognise already these very qualities of energy, independence and inventiveness which distinguish the western world from Egypt, India and China.' To Childe, the opposition between Europe and the Orient was especially clear in the Bronze Age because, unlike the Orient, 'European metalworkers were free. They were not tied to any one patron or even to a single tribal society. They were producing for an intertribal if not an international market.'

To exemplify the opposition in the Bronze Age, Childe compared Crete with Egypt and despotic Mesopotamia. He described

the modern naturalism, the truly occidental feeling for life and nature that distinguish Minoan vase paintings and frescoes. Beholding these charming scenes of games and processions, animals and fishes, flowers and trees, we breathe already a European atmosphere. Likewise in industry the absence of the unlimited labourpower at the disposal of a despot necessitated a concentration on the invention and elaboration of tools and weapons that foreshadows the most distinctive feature of European civilisation.

Thus, the Near East was seen as the cradle from which agriculture and civilisation initially spread. But the main developments which laid the foundations for a dynamic, and ultimately capitalist, society took place in Europe during the Bronze Age. The Near East may have been the 'cradle' from which the 'birth' took place, but the Orient never 'grew up' (see Bahrani,

Chapter 23, this volume). In Childe's view it became stagnant and despotic – it became the 'Other' of Europe, its inverse.

Anatolia has been placed in a difficult position in the traditions of research influenced by Childean Orientalism. Anatolia is not within the cradle but neither is it in the European centre of regrowth. As Özdoğan (1995: 27) points out, 'areas to the north of the Taurus range, the high plateau of Anatolia, are regarded as still being outside of the "nuclear zone".' One clear consequence of this has been the lack of theoretical discussion about the development of Neolithic societies in Anatolia. Equally, there has been a lack of serious attempt to look for sites in Anatolia and known site densities remain low for many areas and periods. Further, 'it is of interest to note that even after the recovery of Hacilar, Çatal Höyük and Asikh in central Anatolia, these sites were considered for some time as trading posts for obsidian and salt trade, and not as indicators of a developing Neolithic culture on the Anatolian plateau' (ibid.: 28). There were similar implications of this Anatolian 'blindness' for the chronologies of Anatolia and Southeastern Europe. 3,000 BC had been set as the start of sedentary life in both areas. But with the large-scale application of C14 dates in Europe, the dates of Southeastern early Neolithic sites were pushed back 2–3,000 years. 'However no one considered the impact of the change in datings on the chronology of central Anatolian cultures' (ibid.). Renfrew's (1973) discussion of calibrated C14 dates created a 'fault-line' between Europe and Asia. The effect was to focus attention on developments in Europe at the expense of those in Anatolia. The latter remained caught uncomfortably between the emergent developments in Southeastern Europe and the long sequence of cultural developments in the Near East.

More recently Özdoğan (1995) has argued for a different Neolithic sequence in central Anatolia and for strong links between central Anatolia and Europe in the Chalcolithic. In the work by Turkish archaeologists such as Ufuk Esin (1991) at Asikh Höyük and Refik Duru (1992) in the Burdur areas we begin to obtain a clear picture of a central Anatolian sequence which belies a simple Orient/Occident opposition. 'Central Anatolia should neither be considered as a nuclear nor as a marginal zone to the low lands of the Near East, but as a distinct cultural formation zone, developing on different lines from the Near East' (Özdoğan 1995: 54).

The Global and the Local

Research at Çatalhöyük and other work in central Turkey can help to counteract the Europe/Orient set of differences. But these archaeological examples are part of a wider movement which now challenges that opposition. The new discourse is globalism. 'Globalization has rendered much of the discussion of East and West in orientalism redundant' (Turner 1994: 183). The Orient was constructed as 'other'. With globalisation 'others' have become less strange and have been imported into all societies as a result of human mobility, migration and tourism. 'Otherness has been domesticated' (ibid.). With the collapse of communism and the traditional oppositions of cold-war politics of the post-war era, Islam may function as a substitute for the dangers of communism. But Islam is increasingly part of the 'inside' of the Western world. For example, the Rushdie affair in Britain forced a debate about the recognition that Britain was now a multicultural society. In Germany, Turkish migrants now pose a significant social issue. Globalisation has created a variety of traditions within a given community.

Turner sets up a very clear contrast between Islamic fundamentalism and the commercial processes of late capitalism. He argues that Islamic fundamentalism rejects modernist secularism because of its lack of coherent values and because of its gross inequalities of wealth and power (1994: 88). Fundamentalism has created an anti-consumerist ethic of moral purity based upon classical Islamic doctrine (ibid.: 92). The corruption of pristine faith is going to be brought about by Tina Turner, Coca-Cola and Ford (ibid.: 10). This erosion of faith 'has to be understood in terms of how the diversity of commodities and their global character transform in covert and indirect fashion the everyday beliefs of the mass of the population' (ibid.: 17).

Certainly, to the extent that Çatalhöyük has been threatened by antiquities dealing there are grounds for an opposition between commercialism and fundamentalist and nationalist concerns. The excavations in the early 1960s were closed by the Turkish state for a number of reasons, including problems with the conservation of wall paintings and sculpture. But at least some of the reasons for the closure concerned the purported disappearance of artefacts from the site and the involvement of James Mellaart in the 'Dorak Affair'. The latter involved the disappearance of a claimed 'treasure' of Bronze Age artefacts from northwest Anatolia. Recently the Turkish state has been successful in gaining the return of the Lydian treasure from the Metropolitan Museum in New York. Attempts are being made to return the Schliemann treasure to Troy [...]. All these instances foster a sense of national heritage and an assertion of Turkish identity in the face of the colonial encounter and in reaction against the pillaging of the extraordinarily rich and diverse antiquities of Turkey.

There are other ways in which commercialism might be thought to confront and erode Islamic fundamentalism. The site at Çatalhöyük is located in a traditionally conservative area, largely rural and with minimal technological development. More recently, massive irrigation schemes funded by international agencies have led to the rapid development of large-scale agro-industry. Yet the local population around the site tends to be traditional, conservative and strongly religious. The renewed work at the site and the project's plans for the future might be seen as opening up this local world to new commercial interests. The site guard, Sadettin, has applied for official permission to build a shop at the site to serve the increasing numbers of tourists. There are plans for T-shirts and a range of products. Several artists have asked to be given the right to make 'tasteful' objects derived from, but not replicating, the prehistoric finds for sale at the site, in Turkey, and in the USA. Travel agencies in Istanbul, Britain and USA vie with each other to organise special-interest tours. Plans are being developed for a museum and visitor centre at the site, and for international travelling exhibits of the art. Carpet dealers in Konya use designs from Çatalhöyük, or legitimated by books concerning Çatalhöyük (e.g. Mellaart et al. 1989), in order to enhance their sales. In Istanbul, a Turkish designer,

Rifat Özbek, shows clothes modelled by Linda Evangelista and which incorporate the Çatalhöyük 'Mother Goddess' image. These clothes appear in *Hello* Magazine (January 1991) and demonstrate the ways in which the site can become involved in a global commercial market. These commercial opportunities are certainly taken up locally and nationally in Turkey and they have the potential to transform Islamic fundamentalist belief.

But other experiences suggest that such an opposition between a global commercialism and Islamic fundamentalism are overly simplistic. The relationships between the Çatalhöyük project and the local mayor (Çumra belediye baskani), especially with regard to the 1996 local agricultural festival, illustrate the complexities well.

The mayor in Çumra is at present (since 1995) a member of the MHP party – Islamic but primarily nationalist. The rhetoric of the party is at times anti-Europe, anti-foreign involvement and anti-secular. At times it was difficult working with local officials who might be members of the MHP or the religious Refah party (banned in 1997). Some would very pointedly not shake hands with female members of the team, especially on Fridays, since such contact would mean washing again in preparation for the mosque. Our English-speaking Eurocentric friends in Istanbul were always surprised that we got on so well with the Mayor. In our early years at the site he helped us with accommodation in Çumra, with equipment and materials.

He always embraced me and showed the greatest of respect. In 1995 he asked us for some photographs, especially of the naked 'Mother Goddess' to put in the foyers of all the hotels in Çumra and in neighbouring districts. The belediye had its own hotel in Çumra. Inside it was full of Islamic religious references in its decor. Guests had to remove their shoes at the door. In such a context large images of the 'Mother Goddess' seemed so inappropriate, especially in a town in which all women always remained covered in public. Why did the Mayor want to do this?

The contradictions increased. In 1996 the Mayor made a formal proposal to the authorities in Ankara to set up a Çatalhöyük museum in Çumra itself. In the same year he announced to us that he wanted to call his annual agricultural festival the Çumra Çatalhöyük Festival. We were to provide a film and slide show, which we did, to a large and attentive audience. After the slide show the Mayor started handing out prizes for the best tomatoes and melons. I was embarrassed suddenly to be called on to the stage to be honoured and embraced in my turn, and presented with a plaque.

Why this public endorsement? What was the public advantage? After all, here is a foreign team digging a pre-Islamic site which confronts Islamic teaching both in its use of images and in its specific representations of women. Certainly the naked images are only acceptable because of their non-Islamic context. But the project clearly introduces commercialism and Western attitudes. Why should it be so overtly embraced by an Islamic nationalist from a political party on the far right? Part of the answer is simply that our work brings money into the region, it increases employment, and it encourages tourism. It contributes to economic development and helps to gain a popular vote. It was for these reasons that the Mayor wanted to build a museum in Çumra – so that tourists would come to the town as well as to the site, twelve kilometres away. But also, more personally, the Mayor finds himself, as a result of the project, the centre of media attention and the host to political figures who visit the site from Konya and Ankara. His wider political ambitions are served.

The Mayor's rhetoric at public occasions involving the site deals with the contradictions in subtle ways. Çatalhöyük, he says, is a site of great national significance. It is the source of Anatolian civilisation. And yet it belongs to the world. Its knowledge is for everyone, without boundaries. We wish to give it to the world. The international scientific interest shows the importance of Anatolian civilisation.

The Mayor continues, 'Çatalhöyük is for all humanity'. When I tell my Turkish friends in Istanbul about this they gasp, 'Did he really say that?' And in many ways his strategy is risky. There is all the reason in the world for him to be distrustful of us. There are many local people in the Çumra area who remember what happened in the 1960s, who blame the archaeologists, and who are suspicious of renewed foreign contacts. The site and its imagery might be seen as confronting Islamic traditionalists. And yet, overall, he has decided, at least for the moment, that it is in his interests to support, embrace and even promote the project.

In the above instance, rather than a simple opposition between Islamic groups and religion and the international and commercial components of the project, we see subtle ways in which adjustments are made in order to achieve specific aims, such as increased employment and political status. At least in Turkey some accommodation between the global and the Islamic is clearly possible. The same is true in the following example.

> Women, their heads covered, their shoulders weighed from a long day's labour in the fields, are driven past the site at high speed in the backs of the trucks of their menfolk. Some of their sons and husbands are working as labourers on the new excavations. I asked for some women to work at the site but the menfolk refused to let them go. The younger women have been taught in school that Çatalhöyük is the origin of Anatolian civilisation, the origin of Cybele, the Earth Mother. The posters of the bare-breasted Mother Goddess seem very alien. 'The site is full of images, our menfolk say. It must be pre-Islamic'.
>
> The women from the village confide in some of the women from the foreign team in their midst. In fact there is a remarkable and immediate rapport between the women – an embracing and incorporating of women, just because they are women. They confide that their men are very hard; they give the women little freedom, little money. It is a hard life. But in the end, after two years of negotiating, the men say the wives and daughters can work at the site after all. Perhaps they have grown to trust the foreigners. But, most likely, the men, the families, want the money. When the local people are paid, some of the women find it difficult even to sign their name, and they refuse to take the money – their husbands take it for them.

So, in this local case, men gradually accept the need to allow change in the actions of and attitudes towards the women in the community. Women and men locally turn a blind eye to the naked 'Mother Goddess'. If it brings tourists and jobs so much the better (say some men); if it brings us wages so much the better (say the women). Indeed, local attitudes seem to change in a number of ways.

Local attitudes to the past in the Çatalhöyük area are being studied by David Shankland (1996). Folk knowledge sees the mounds as liminal. They are the landmarks that define the boundaries between communities. They are also the dwelling places of the spirits of the dead. At night the lights of the spirits can sometimes be seen as they travel from one mound to another. There is archaeological evidence that the Çatalhöyük mound was used as a cemetery from the Hellenistic period onwards. We excavated Byzantine graves on the East mound. And yet this tradition associating the mounds with the dead does not prevent the excavation by local communities of soil and clay from the mounds for building materials. Indeed the walls of the buildings in the local villages are full of sherds deriving from the mounds. Perhaps this practical use and the tradition of digging help to explain the acceptance of our own archaeological work at the mounds.

Shankland argues that this local folk knowledge is not matched by an in-depth historical understanding of the site. Although the site is mentioned in primary schools in connection with the origins of Anatolian civilisation, there is little knowledge of historical sequences beyond a simple pre-Islamic–Islamic opposition. He argues that it is for this reason that there has been little response to the Open Days organised for the local communities during our digging seasons.

On the other hand, I have been struck by the degree of fascination and interest when I have organised tours of the site for our workers. Their eyes wide at the images, and bubbling with questions, comments and parallels with their own lives, houses and artefacts, they are excited by ideas about interpretations of the site. Far from being alienated from their past by this engagement within a global system of universal scientific knowledge, their sense of local identity and community seems enlivened and strengthened.

> There are deep cuts across both East and West mounds at Çatalhöyük, paths worn by centuries of feet toiling from village to village in the Konya Plain. And there is a lone Islamic gravestone on the East mound, marking the burial place of a

fallen woman, so the story goes. These mounds had a local meaning, a 'fork' (çatal) in their daily pathways. But now these routes and graves are cut off by a fence, locked gate and guards. The site has been taken over by the state and is being excavated by foreign teams with lasers and computers. Bus-loads of Goddess tourists from California engage in debates with the foreign archaeologists about matriarchies.

But is it quite so confrontational? The notion of a simple opposition between local and global knowledge is undermined by the complexity of social and cultural currents at all levels in Turkish life. One such complexity derives from the division within Turkish politics between those who favour closer links with Europe and who welcome the recent Customs Union, and those who are suspicious of such links. The latter views are associated with fundamentalist and nationalist currents of thought. But the Turkish groups who have become most involved in the Çatalhöyük project tend to be very Eurocentric. The individuals involved tend to live in Istanbul, have often had an élite English-speaking education, and have often spent part of their lives in Europe or the USA. The Istanbul 'Friends of Çatalhöyük' organisation which has been successful in raising funds for the project comes largely from this group. Those people from Istanbul who come to the site include highly articulate, professional and well-to-do Turks, fascinated by our work and by its implications. They like the idea that in prehistory there were many cultural links between Anatolia and Europe. They are enthralled by the project's use of new scientific techniques and of the Web. Some organise and take part in the Goddess Tours. They are part of a global community.

The first time it happened we were all very much taken aback. We did not know what was happening. A message had come to the dig house that the leader of the Istanbul Friends was bringing a group of people to the site, as part of a tour of Turkey. Would we meet them in the local restaurant in Çumra that evening?

Most of the team went – about twenty of us at that time. We were ushered into a room with a long table around which about thirty middle-aged women, and a few men, were sitting. We were arranged amongst them. Alcohol is not allowed in public places in Çumra. But they provided a cocktail of cherry juice hiding vodka. The questions began. Why were we digging the site? Did we believe that men had been allowed into Çatalhöyük? Had we found evidence of the Goddess? Did we not realise that the bull's heads represented Her reproductive organs? What did the female members of the team think about my androcentric interpretations? How were their voices heard?

The following day they came to the site. They were interested in our work, but they also stood in a circle and held hands and prayed. Afterwards they seemed genuinely moved. They said the presence of the Goddess was very strong. You could feel Her coming up through the earth.

The Goddess Tours have become regular since then, although often occurring at times when we are not at the site. The participants are largely professional women from the USA, but they include women from Europe. And it is into this world that some of the Istanbul Friends easily fit. Indeed, some of the Friends from Istanbul were instrumental in tabling a motion at the Beijing UN Conference on Women which named Çatalhöyük as the spiritual centre of the Goddess Movement in Turkey and in the world.

The global character of these New Age Mother Goddess, Ecofeminist and Gaia Movements may confront traditional Islamic attitudes to women, but there are undoubtedly significant sections of élite Istanbul society that welcome such links outside Turkey and use them for their own purposes. Since Atatürk, the commitment to secularism has been a central, if recently diminishing, focus of political life in Turkey. Istanbul in particular is a social and cultural metropolis of enormous size and diversity. There are many shades of accommodation between secularism and fundamentalism. The old intellectual élite is global in perspective and contributes to a political debate which is complex and multi-stranded.

When a group of the Istanbul 'Friends' association came to the site I could see they were angry, despite their politeness and support. They disliked the new dig house. It was unimaginative, dull, functional, not appropriate to such an important site. And worst of all, it was painted bright green! They decided they would not help fund the construction of the dig house. I was disappointed. I needed their help.

The dig house, an ambitious version of an architectural genre found on many sites in the Near East, had been designed by an architect in the local museum service in Konya. Most of his previous work had dealt with the restoration of the wonderful Seljuk architecture in and around that city. The design was approved by the local ancient monuments board. I had contracted a builder from Konya who was strongly recommended by the local museums service. He turned out to be a great pleasure to work with. I respected and liked him enormously and trusted him completely. He chose green because the colour is identified with Islam. He and his family, like many in Konya, were strongly religious.

It was anathema to some of the Istanbul visitors that the dig house should be painted green. It seemed inappropriate. But I decided not to bow to their demands that we repaint the building. It seemed important to respect local Islamic sensitivities in this case.

In other examples, too, it is possible to show local resistance to the global interests of Istanbul Turks or international commercial or New Age movements. For instance, the Istanbul Friends have started a clever and very successful campaign to 'Lend a Hand to Çatalhöyük' which involves giving handprint certificates (based on a Çatalhöyük wall painting) to donors. One proposal is that a long wall be built at the site on which donors can make their handprints. For the moment, this move has been resisted because of local concerns about site preservation. Perhaps the clearest example of the interaction between these different currents of interest in the site is the following:

One of the commercial sponsors of the project is an international credit card company. With its Istanbul-based PR firm, this company is genuinely interested in supporting the project while at the same time making use of its commercial potential. For example, during press visits we all wear hats with the company logo, and a replica of the 'Mother Goddess' with the company name is handed out to clients at receptions in Istanbul. The company sees a particular link to Çatalhöyük

because I argued that obsidian could be seen as the first 'credit card'. Members of the team laughed when I told them and the obsidian specialist was embarrassed. Perhaps I was embarrassed, too, but I justified my compliance by arguing that obsidian was exchanged widely (like credit cards) and that ethnographically artefacts such as obsidian can come to act as media for exchange, and exchange involves setting up debt (and thus credit) between the giver and receiver.

In the end this global commercialising process would have an impact locally. The company wanted to set up an exhibit in the museum which showed the development of 'credit cards' from the first obsidian to the latest credit cards with micro-chips. I could not help but see the, probably unintended, outcome of this. Turkey is seeing a massively expanding market for credit cards, but the main take-up is in the urban centres. In rural areas there has been less impact. The exhibit and the message about prehistoric credit cards might not only legitimate the modern company's claim to be concerned with Turkish culture but also might encourage local interest and take-up.

Nevertheless, the support of the company was genuine and very much needed if the project was going to be able to continue and have any longterm benefit for local identity, tourism, employment and social change.

I wanted to hold a ceremony at the site to open the dig house. I invited the Minister of Culture as well as local and national politicians. The Minister of Culture had recently changed to be a member of Refah, the religious fundamentalist party. I wanted our sponsors to come to thank them. Indeed, the Minister of Culture would unveil a plaque listing their support. This 'photo-opportunity' was rejected by the credit card company which decided it did not want to be associated in this way with the Refah party. Here, commerce and Islam confronted each other and the former stood down.

In the end the Minister did not attend and sent his Director General of Monuments and Museums. The European Ambassador also came. West and East, secular and religious, met and talked at a podium decked out in a Turkish flag by the Mayor. The speeches described the importance of the project and I presented the buildings to the Turkish state. But the currents of differing meanings, strategies and interpretations were rife.

In all the political manoeuvring, the site and the local concerns seemed to play little role. They seemed overrun by global processes and oppositions. But on the other hand, the Mayor and other local officials made their speeches too and there was considerable coverage in the local press. Black Mercedes, flags flapping at high speed, swept in clouds of dust. Armed guards surrounded the mound, and out got the national officials. They came and went, involved in their own strategies. Local people had to be bussed in to create a crowd at the ceremony – a true 'rent-a-crowd'. The local people seemed to understand the motives behind the show for what it was. They tolerated the event as long as it meant they could continue to work, make money, and follow their own strategies. The ceremony, and the national, fundamentalist and global strategies in which it was enmeshed, was necessary if their own lives were to continue to change in ways they, from different points of view, wanted.

Thus, there is no simple opposition between global knowledge and interests and a local and fundamentalist Islam. New Age Women's Movements are received differently in different communities, national and local, in Turkey. In the local villages around Çatalhöyük and in Çumra people participate differentially and purposefully. They are not simply duped into being 'globalised'. People have to be bussed to the opening ceremony. A blind eye is turned to the naked Goddess in the visitor centre at the site. Locally, women may obtain their own wages and the Mayor follows his political ambitions. Locally, men and women use the past in their own ways. They may be drawn into a global process but they use that process locally in complex ways, rejecting some aspects and emphasising others. Change occurs, but in a complex and diverse way. It is no longer an issue of monolithic blocks, as in Europe versus the Orient, secular versus fundamentalist religion. Rather, there is a diversity of global and local experiences and responses within which Çatalhöyük is embroiled.

A Reflexive Moment

So far I have written in terms of an overall argument about the shift from East versus West to global versus local and I have made the point that local interests are not entirely taken over by global processes. All this, even my use of narrative 'thick descriptions', is situated within an academic discourse which might seem to be far removed from the events I am describing. I have constructed the events in a particular way because of my own interests. Indeed any analysis of heritage in the East Mediterranean is 'at a remove'; a past appropriated for intellectual gain. There are two points I wish to make about this process. The first deals with disjunction between the controlled and structured description or text and the contingent process. The second deals with the need to recognise that the archaeologist is not a disinterested observer but part of the process.

Our own emphasis on 'discourse' within the 'discipline' underlies the account I have given. I have written as if the processes I have been describing could be observed, channelled, controlled. Any attempt to write about how the Çatalhöyük past is used, and any attempt to write about how the past matters in the East Mediterranean cannot help but reduce historical processes to an organised scheme or flow. In the following account I want to demonstrate the limitations of this view.

It ranks as one of the worst days in my life. I ended up stunned, bitter, angry and deeply depressed about whether the project would continue.

The day had started so well. The credit card company had arranged an elaborate and expensive press trip to the site. In the morning between fifty and sixty newspaper and TV reporters turned up at the site. During the day the tours all went extremely well. Members of the team were dutifully wearing their promotional hats. The project was coming over as exciting and important. It was getting great coverage. The sponsors and the PR firm were happy. After all, this press day was to be the main return on their investment this year. There had to be a lot of good press coverage and it looked as if there would be.

A few reporters had left and I was relaxing for a moment before the rest departed, when a member of the team came to say that a small bead had disappeared from one of our laboratories. It was one of the objects that had been on display and despite the continual presence of three team members the object had disappeared. The government representatives were told. They called the police. The reporters were searched and held at the site for three hours before being allowed to leave.

Rumours started flying, but so many people could have taken it. There had been so many people there that day. I suddenly saw that in this one event, this one instant, the whole project could flounder. Despite all the planning, all the effort over five years could be undone in one brief act. After all, the site had been closed in the 1960s partly because of incidents in which artefacts disappeared. Would this event play into the hands of local or national groups who objected to the international or foreign character of the project? Even if a permit did continue to be granted, would we be able to gain sponsorship again? Indeed, in the following days the national press printed stories with headlines such as 'Scandal at dig of the century'. How could we ever get sponsorship again? I began to feel that, for one reason or another, the project might have difficulty continuing.

As it turned out, the press coverage during and after the event was very supportive. The papers started carrying positive accounts of the project which did not mention the theft of the bead. The sponsors continued their support and the central government authorities did their best to recover the bead. The damage seems to have been, at the time of writing, marginal. But in that moment and in the days immediately afterwards I feared the worst and I saw how fragile was the negotiated position for all players in the Çatalhöyük project. Everything happened so quickly and in such a variety of directions that the outcome was unpredictable. Structure met conjuncture (Sahlins 1981) and no amount of discursive understanding of East/West, global/local, or even structure/conjuncture could determine or control the way in which things would go.

Such a critique of academic discourse in the context of archaeology and heritage in the East Mediterranean does not imply that the archaeologist should stand at a distance from the processes in which she or he is involved. Indeed this is the second point I wish to make about the need to be reflexive when gazing at, and encapsulating in theoretical discourse, the role of the

past in the East Mediterranean. Since the writing and the discourse have effects, there is a need for positive engagement. In the events just described, I did write letters, get on the phone, make visits, increase security in the stores and laboratories and so on. While such activities could not control the way things went, they perhaps contributed, from a particular standpoint, to what was, is and will be an ongoing negotiation between different and changing interests.

As other examples of the need to move beyond the passive gaze to positive engagement, decisions had to be made, choices had to be taken, about whether to remove the green paint on the dig house. Equally, complex as the issues are, I felt it was important to push for the employment of women at the site. It was necessary, in these examples, to 'take sides'. The same has to be said even in the most 'open' and multivocal discourses. The results of the project are being placed on the Web and resources are being channelled into a variety of interactive and presentation media. These include hypertext (Thomas 1996; Tringham 1996). The aim here is to open the data from the site to multiple audiences, to allow different experiences of the site, to allow discovery in a range of different channels. But it is clear that there is no such thing as open multivocality. A certain level of knowledge is required to participate in hypertext presentations. And certainly the links and nodes are created by the producer of the hypertext. One has to make choices about what audiences are aimed at and what messages are to be given. As much as the Web and hypertext allow a greater diversity and openness of communication, the onus remains on the producer and writer to be reflexive about the impact of 'the text' in the world.

The same point can be extended to the writing of the present article. It could be argued that at least some of what I have written here might offend the groups involved in an ongoing archaeological and heritage project. I have taken the decision to say some things here because I believe that the issues are important and that our experience at Çatalhöyük might help to draw attention to the need for debate about the role of archaeology in a Near East which is involved in processes of globalisation. I have not said other things here because of the need to respect the perspectives of some of the groups and individuals involved. As noted above, I cannot predict the outcome of this intervention in what is a complex process. But I do assert the need to monitor the results of statements and to engage actively from a particular standpoint.

Conclusion

Both in the academic debate about the prehistory of Anatolia and Çatalhöyük and in the practices of public engagement with the site, the old oppositions between Europe and the Orient or between secularism and religious fundamentalism are transcended by the processes of globalism and fragmentation. Çatalhöyük is caught in a maelstrom of perspectives and special interests. These are global in scale. But they are also highly diverse and fragmented, extending from carpet dealers in Konya and New York, to ecofeminists in San Francisco, to women in the local village near Çatalhöyük. Some of these engagements are highly commercial and disinterested – the past as play, the Orient as theme park. Others are motivated by specific highly charged interests. But passion and play are not opposed in some simple opposition. In the global process they interact and feed off each other in myriad ways, equally emboldening and undermining the other.

I have talked in this chapter of the 'team' working at Çatalhöyük. It may not be too much to say that I am no longer sure what the team is. The boundaries of those who do or do not work on the project are difficult to define. Certainly there are the named individuals who have permits to excavate at the site. But some specialists on the project do not visit the site. And many I have asked to contribute from around the world in order to, for example, help interpret the art have no close involvement with the core 'team'. And then what should I make of a psychoanalyst

from California with a particular perspective on the art who publishes an article about the site in the *New Scientist*? Or what should I make of an aboriginal artist from South Africa who wishes to come and work at the site to model her female sculptures? She also wants to contribute to our work. And since the site data are on the Web, what should I make of all those who write in and make their suggestions, or who write their own articles about the site based on our data, and contribute to 'our' understanding of the site? And what should I make of it if people take our data from the Web and change them and create a new alternative database of their own? Such things are at least potentially feasible. Rather than there being a well-bounded 'team' working on the project, Çatalhöyük is involved in a global process of interpretation. The 'team' is global. And I would argue it has to be if the divergent special interests are to be given access to the site. It is not possible to deny that contemporary information technologies allow an enormous dispersal of information so that numerous special interest groups can form and define themselves through an engagement. But so too there are many groups who do not have access to the technologies or to the knowledge necessary to use them. The fragmentation within and across the globalisation processes needs to be reflexively engaged with.

As much as those involved in the project may try to foster plurality and multivocality, the communication does not take place on a level playing-field. The techniques used on the site, from virtual reality to the sieving of micro-residues, promote a particular vision within the kaleidoscope. There is no solution to the paradoxes. Any attempt to 'make sense of it all', including the opposition between 'play' and 'passion', is itself a construct. It is for this reason that I have included so many 'thick descriptive' narratives in this chapter. It is only in the concrete moments of engagement that the socio-politics of Çatalhöyük take their form.

References

Childe, V. G. (1925) *The Dawn of European Civilisation*, London: Kegan Paul.

Duru, R. (1992) 'Höyücek Kazilari 1989', *Belleten* 61: 551–66.

Esin, U. (1991) 'Salvage excavations at the pre-pottery site of Asikh Höyük in Central Anatolia', *Anatolica* 17: 123–74.

Mellaart, J., Hirsch, U. and Balpinar, B. (1989) *The Goddess from Anatolia*, Rome: Eskanazi.

Özdoğan, M. (1995) 'Neolithic in Turkey: the status of research', in *Readings in Prehistory. Studies Presented to Halet Çambel*, Istanbul: University of Istanbul, pp. 41–60.

Renfrew, A. C. (1973) *Before Civilization*, London: Jonathan Cape.

Sahlins, M. (1981) *Historical Metaphor and Mythical Reality*, Ann Arbor: University of Michigan Press.

Said, E. W. (1978) *Orientalism*, London: Routledge and Kegan Paul.

Shankland, D. (1996) 'Çatalhöyük: the anthropology of an archaeological presence', in I. Hodder (ed.) *On the Surface: Çatalhöyük 1993–95*, Cambridge: McDonald Institute for Archaeological Research and British Institute of Archaeology at Ankara, pp. 349–58.

Thomas, S. (1996) 'On-line hypertext in site interpretation', paper presented at TAG conference, Liverpool 1996.

Tringham, S. (1996) 'The use of hypertext in site interpretation', paper presented at TAG conference, Liverpool 1996.

Turner, B. S. (1994) *Orientalism, Postmodernism and Globalism*, London: Routledge.

Copyrighting the Past?
Emerging Intellectual Property Rights Issues in Archaeology

George P. Nicholas and Kelly P. Bannister

"Intellectual property" is defined by Dratler (1994:1–2) as "intangible personal property in creations of the mind." Intellectual property rights are legal rights to precisely defined kinds of knowledge. In general, intellectual property laws "protect a creator's expression in artistic and literary works, the proprietary technology in inventions, the words and symbols used to identify products and services and the aesthetic aspects of product designs" (Cassidy and Langford 1999:1).

Intellectual property rights are a rapidly expanding topic of discussion in academic and other circles and a major issue in ethnobotanical and other research involving Indigenous communities.[1] Interested parties represent a convergence of natural and social scientists from government, academia, and industry, members of Indigenous communities, lawyers, corporate representatives, environmentalists, and others. Key concerns expressed by these diverse parties relate to the sociocultural, ethical, and economic aspects of current intellectual property rights legislation, among them the implications of patenting higher life forms (e.g., CBAC 2001, 2003). For the most part, archaeologists have

George P. Nicholas and Kelly P. Bannister, "Copyrighting the Past? Emerging Intellectual Property Rights Issues in Archaeology," pp. 327–50 from *Current Anthropology* 45:3 (2004). Reprinted with permission of the University of Chicago Press.

yet to find themselves thrust into this complex milieu. We argue that archaeologists should examine whether and in what ways intellectual-property-rights-related issues are relevant to their research, particularly when claims to such rights may be made by Indigenous peoples affected by that research.

The absence of archaeologists from the intellectual property rights debate may be linked to the complexity of the issues and to the challenges of defining "intellectual property" beyond the realm of technological innovation with commercial application. Such is the case with living systems, where what qualifies as intellectual property and is protectable by law is continually being debated and tested, often in the courts.[2] Of particular relevance to archaeology is the application of the idea of intellectual property rights to the protection of the cultural knowledge and property[3] of Indigenous societies. This application is complicated by a lack of consistent terminology across interested or affected parties, Indigenous and non-Indigenous alike. For example, what is it that needs protecting and from whom? As Mann (1997:1) notes, "No one definition [of indigenous knowledge] has been universally endorsed or accepted by either Aboriginal or non-Aboriginal peoples in Canada. What is clear, however, is that indigenous knowledge as a concept concerns information, understanding, and knowledge that reflects symbiotic relationships between individuals, communities, generations, the physical environment and other living creatures, and the spiritual relationships of a people." Likewise, according to the Union of British Columbia Indian Chiefs (Hampton and Henderson 2000:ii), "There is no universally accepted definition for cultural property.... Most academic commentators assert that Indigenous knowledge issues are stretching the existing legal categories so that only a fuzzy line exists between intellectual, spiritual and culture rights." The foregoing largely concerns living people, but what of deceased societies? Archaeological research involving Indigenous societies tends to blur past and present.

National and international laws protecting cultural and intellectual property are often seen as inconsistent with emerging views on what aspects of Indigenous cultural knowledge and heritage require protection. According to Battiste and Henderson (2000:145), the problem involves "negotiating with the modern concept of property" in that Eurocentric legal approaches "treat all thought as a commodity in the artificial market" whereas Indigenous societies tend to see property as "a sacred ecological order" that should not be commodified. They suggest further (p. 250) that intellectual property laws have

> problems dealing with forms of knowledge in the area of high art or high technology (e.g., computer software and biotechnology). The major push for amendment of the law comes from the top, so that areas such as computer technology or biogenetic engineering are receiving a lot of attention, and the law is gradually being altered to accommodate these forms of knowledge. Culture and knowledge on the "bottom" – where Indigenous knowledge is so often situated – tend to be ignored.

The perceived inadequacy of applying existing laws to the protection of Indigenous cultural knowledge and heritage has led to recommendations for the expansion of legal definitions and protection mechanisms and calls for alternative and complementary nonlegal ones. For example, Janke (1998:3) proposes the term "Indigenous cultural and intellectual property rights" to refer to "Indigenous people's rights to their heritage," wherein "heritage comprises all objects, sites and knowledge, the nature or use of which

has been transmitted or continues to be transmitted from generation to generation, and which is regarded as pertaining to a particular Indigenous group or its territory." Artifacts, archaeological sites, and some types of information generated by archaeological research clearly fit this definition. In fact, there is a notable similarity between a statement from Hampton and Henderson's discussion paper that "generally, cultural property is anything exhibiting physical attributes assumed to be the results of human activity" (2000:ii) and definitions of an archaeological site as "any place where objects, features, or ecofacts manufactured or modified by human beings are found" (Fagan 1997:478) and "any place where material evidence exists about the human past" (Thomas 1998:95).

In this paper we explore the concept of Indigenous cultural and intellectual property rights in an archaeological context. The central questions posed are: What relevance do intellectual property rights have to archaeology? What forms do these rights take? How might future claims to intellectual property affect archaeology? We begin by describing the "products" of archaeological research and explaining what they represent in a contemporary sociocultural context. We assess the level of protection of these products provided by existing legislation (specifically, cultural heritage acts) and the potential of current intellectual property protection mechanisms to augment that protection. Our focus is on knowledge and its physical manifestations (such as images and "art") that are derived from or otherwise pertain to the past.

We consider also whether and in what way our understanding of these emerging issues in archaeology can be informed by trends in related disciplines such as anthropology and ethnobotany. One possibility is that Indigenous peoples may seek control of the knowledge and other products of archaeological research conducted in their traditional lands – perhaps much as they have of the results of ethnobotanical research on their traditional knowledge and plant medicines (Bannister 2000, Bannister and Barrett n.d., Brush and Strabinsky 1996, Greaves 1994, Posey and Dutfield 1996). In our final section we turn to this related academic field for insights and comparative examples.

The scope of this paper ranges from local to international. Our examples are drawn from Canada (particularly British Columbia, where intellectual property rights are an important topic in current treaty negotiations), the United States, Australia, and elsewhere. The implications for archaeology are of regional significance and global interest.

Michael Brown's (1998) article "Can Culture Be Copyrighted?" provides an initial point of reference for our discussion.[4] Copyright is one of several legal instruments under statutory and common law that can be used to enforce exclusive rights in the marketplace in creations that meet certain legal criteria (i.e., novelty and material fixedness). In particular, copyright protects the physical expression of ideas but not the ideas themselves or any substantive or factual information. Ownership of copyright is established by the author's fixing the work in a material form and is used to protect rights to novel literary, artistic, dramatic, or musical works (as well as computer software). Protection is for a limited term (e.g., in Canada, the life of the author plus 50 years).[5] Rather than suggesting that copyright is the only – or the most appropriate – tool for protecting rights to intellectual property in archaeology, our title questions the common perception that this is the case. Other forms of intellectual property protection that may be relevant to archaeology include patent, trademark, industrial design, and trade secret.[6] Arguably, some of these mechanisms already have approximations in Indigenous societies – for example, family or clan ownership of songs, stories, or motifs and possession by healers of specialized medicinal knowledge that is not widely shared within the community. While ownership is not a Western[7] concept, these examples of Indigenous ownership are not given legal status in most countries. It is important to distinguish between creations that are legally protectable under current legislation and those that are not. Opportunities or pressure (internal or external) to exploit ownership rights and privileges for commercial purposes present challenges to many Indigenous communities – particularly elders, traditional healers, storytellers, and other knowledge holders, who must often reconcile their reservations about sharing cultural knowledge with the wider society

(thereby contributing to recognition and potential commercial development, as well as misappropriation or misuse) with cultural beliefs and responsibilities that embody sharing. Such challenges are complicated by a widespread lack of understanding of what can and cannot be legally protected. Archaeology will not move beyond being a colonialist enterprise unless it actively seeks to understand the underlying issues of ownership and control of material and intellectual property as related to cultural knowledge and heritage.

Material property issues have certainly arisen in archaeology and will continue to frame key aspects of the discipline. Especially contentious are the repatriation of artifacts and reburial of human remains (e.g., Bray 2001, Ferguson 1996, Mihesuah 2000, Rose, Green, and Green 1996). Issues related to intellectual property have been less prominent,[8] although trends in other fields suggest that this will soon change. This is particularly true in former colonized lands such as the Americas, Africa, and Australia, where the archaeological record is mostly the product of the ancestors of the present Indigenous population(s) and not that of the dominant culture. Archaeological research in the latter context is often seen as appropriating Indigenous knowledge and rights or affecting the sanctity of Indigenous beliefs – even when the archaeologists involved believe that they are working to the benefit of Indigenous communities.

The Products of Archaeological Research and Their Protection

Archaeology is the study of human behavior and history through material culture. It is concerned with what happened in the past, when it happened, and the processes by which things changed and with the application of that knowledge in the modern world. The archaeological record is made up of both the individual and the cumulative responses of humans to a suite of social, demographic, cultural, and environmental opportunities over the course of hours, years, or millennia. Archaeologists seek to discover and explain this record and the cultural diversity it represents. The products of archaeological research thus constitute scientific knowledge in the sense of understanding the (past) world in new ways and at the same time reflect the knowledge of Indigenous cultures. Archaeology is also very much a contemporary socio-cultural phenomenon that seeks to locate, create, classify, objectify, interpret, and present the past in ways that reflect the particular views of its practitioners (see Pinsky and Wylie 1995).[9] A key concern in contemporary archaeology is the degree of participation and control that Indigenous peoples have over the archaeological *process*. In Canada, for example, control issues have centered on the limitation of access to sites in traditional territories by way of a permit system (e.g., Denhez 2000). Little attention has been paid to the *products* of archaeological research.

Aside from unearthed artifacts, what is it that archaeological research produces? In its many forms, archaeology establishes chronology and precontact history (as a supplement or a corollary to oral history) and illuminates the processes by which things have changed. Specific products of archaeological research take the form of site reports, site, artifact, and feature descriptions and classifications, radiocarbon dates, and faunal remains, among other materials. These are analyzed to produce information on past technologies, dietary patterns, land-use patterns, environmental settings, demographic trends, social relationships, and other topics. Such studies may have a very short-term focus (e.g., reconstruction of life at a particular time and place) or a very long-term focus (e.g., shifts in dietary practices over millennia). A central question raised by consideration of intellectual property rights is whose property these products are and how they are protected.

The lack of explicit consideration of these issues in archaeology to date is partly the result of a societal perception that the outcomes of archaeology have limited practical application. While information of substantial public value may be produced, archaeologists often have difficulty communicating the contemporary relevance of their field.[10] Intellectual property rights issues may be especially relevant in cases where the benefits of archaeological research are based directly upon Indigenous cultural knowledge, such as the recognition and restoration of raised-field farming (Erickson 1998) and *chinampas* farming (Coe 1964) in Central and

South America. In such cases, the issues faced by archaeologists may include (1) publication and ownership of copyright in books, reports, and articles, (2) access to, public disclosure of, and ownership of copyright in photographs of artifacts, (3) fiduciary duties related to the secrecy of sacred sites, which could also include copyright in maps, (4) ownership, secrecy, and publication of traditional knowledge that may result from archaeological research, and (5) ownership of, copyright in, or trademarks related to the artifacts, designs, or marks uncovered during archaeological research.

Archaeological sites represent the major physical manifestation of cultural heritage for all human societies. Despite broad concerns with preserving sites, buildings, and objects of historical or cultural value, the degree of preservation and protection varies from country to country and between different states, provinces, and territories. In the United States, for example, there is extensive federal cultural heritage legislation, but archaeological sites on private property are generally not protected (Patterson 1999). The Native American Graves Protection and Repatriation Act (NAGPRA), which protects human remains and "associated funerary objects, unassociated funerary objects, sacred objects, and cultural patrimony," also excludes private property.[11] In Canada, federal legislation is very limited, with most heritage protection being conducted at the provincial level. For example, under the British Columbia Heritage Conservation Act of 1996, all archaeological sites, whether on public or private lands, are protected in principle. There is no provision for site identification surveys for all proposed developments, and therefore many sites are lost. Likewise, artifacts are not covered and are openly bought, sold, or traded at flea markets, auctions, and other venues.[12] Whatever the level of legislated heritage protection, protection of archaeological materials in the United States and Canada is based exclusively on the notion of physical property (e.g., artifacts and sites).

General legislation protecting intellectual property is, however, extensive in both countries. Thus, it is worth exploring intellectual property rights from the perspective of determining whether any aspect of them offers additional protection to archaeological resources and/or provides new avenues that Indigenous peoples can pursue to protect their cultural and intellectual property. Certain products of archaeological fieldwork and research are the result of the creative works of past Indigenous societies. Do they qualify as intellectual property in a legal sense? Should the descendants[13] of those responsible for the archaeological record have rights to that record?

To date, applications of intellectual property rights in fields closely related to archaeology such as anthropology and ethnobotany have largely been concerned with protecting traditional knowledge and the related biological resources (see Bannister 2000, Bannister and Barrett n.d., Brush and Stabinsky 1996, Greaves 1994, Posey and Dutfield 1996). Is access to a site by archaeologists any different from access to traditional knowledge and plant resources by ethnobotanists? From the point of view of archaeology, traditional knowledge can be understood as incorporating historic/modern land-use and health practices, oral and written histories, and expressions of worldview. One reason that little attention has been paid to archaeology may be that only limited material expressions of potential intellectual property are preserved in the archaeological record and even that material tends to be so old as to make issues of ownership moot from a legal perspective. For example, Brown (1998:196) notes,[14]

> The principal goal of intellectual property laws ... is to see that information enters the public domain in a timely fashion while allowing creators, be they individuals or corporate groups, to derive reasonable financial and social benefits from their work. Once a work enters the public domain, it loses most protections. I am free to publish *Uncle Tom's Cabin* or to manufacture steel paper clips without paying royalties to their creators, whose limited monopoly has expired. The same principle applies to prehistoric petroglyphs or to the "Mona Lisa," both of which have become part of our common human heritage, whatever their origins.

Brown's comments raise two important points that require further examination. First, many Indigenous groups simply do not accept that their archaeological past is first and foremost part of a shared human heritage – at least at the expense of their claims to it. Second, intellectual property protection has a limited time span after which the intellectual property becomes part of the public domain. If "time" is considered largely a Western construct (Gould 1987, Zimmerman 1987), the phenomenon it represents may be perceived differently in Indigenous cultures. In Western society time is viewed as linear and worldview is characterized by a series of clear dichotomies: past/present, real/supernatural, male/female, good/evil, and so on. In many Indigenous societies, however, not only is there greater flexibility in classifying the world but the basic conception of time may be significantly different (e.g., Williams and Mununggurr 1989).[15] Where there is no cognitive separation between past and present, ancestral spirits are part of the present. This conceptual difference requires us to avoid an exclusively Western orientation in interpreting prehistoric lifeways (as in evaluating site significance and the implications for cultural resource management practices), and this presents a major challenge to the fundamentals of intellectual property law. In other words, the petroglyphs that Brown refers to may be *timeless*. Thus, intellectual property laws that are constrained by Western conceptions of time may be severely limited in utility and appropriateness to Indigenous cultures.

Given the products of archaeological research, what are potential points of concern with regard to intellectual property rights? If other academic disciplines are any indication, the concerns of the descendants of the people responsible for the archaeological record may include appropriation, misrepresentation, or misuse of knowledge, loss of control of knowledge, and loss of access to the products of research or their benefits. Non-Indigenous researchers,[16] for their part, fear loss of control, censorship, or restrictions on use of knowledge – concerns that relate to suppression of academic freedom and restrictions on publication, which, in turn, may affect academic credentials, promotion, and continued research funding. The issues are not limited to efforts of Indigenous peoples to control their own past but also surface in religious contexts. In Israel, archaeology and related research have been severely limited by objections of ultra-Orthodox Jewish groups over the sanctity of human remains. As a result of a 1994 ruling by the Israeli Attorney General, all human remains must be "immediately handed over to the ministry of religious affairs for reburial" (Balter 2000:35). This has effectively halted most physical anthropology, and it extends to remains not affiliated with the modern Israeli population, including early human remains.

The issue of censorship will likely be raised more frequently as Indigenous peoples in many parts of the world regain greater control over their affairs. Academics are often complacent about their "freedom" until it is threatened. With freedom, however, comes responsibility. Most problems relating to publication of archaeological data can likely be avoided with some conscientious forethought and proactive effort. For example, where the potential for conflict exists, researchers will do well to work closely with community participants from the start and make clear what the project goals and products will be. Researchers should also be clear about how the products of their research may constitute intellectual property and whose property this will be.

Claire Smith (1994:96) offers the following position:

> My view is that Barunga people have the right to censor any aspect of my research that they find distressing or offensive. However, in order to avoid extensive censoring of the research I designed its parameters in consultation with them. Having done this, I do not believe that Barunga people have the right to decide whether the research as a whole should be published, unless we had negotiated this provision prior to the research being undertaken.... Nor do I agree with some Aboriginal people who maintain that results of research should be owned by indigenous people.... In my opinion the intellectual property arising from the research belongs to the researchers involved though they have an overriding responsibility not to offend the people with whom they work.

The question raised is whether the intellectual value or creative contribution of the cultural knowledge being disclosed exceeds that of the research or transcription process. This issue is at the heart of editorial control, restrictions on publication, and claims to intellectual property.

Who owns the intellectual property arising from the research is in some cases institution- or funder-specific. The policies of most academic institutions may be characterized generally as "institution as owner" or "inventor as owner," the former clearly limiting the discretionary power of an individual researcher on the matter (Bannister 2003).

The desire of many Indigenous peoples to control or censor information about their past may have two triggers. One is the largely political motivation to regain control over their own affairs; the other is a response to the unwillingness of some archaeologists to listen to and/or integrate Indigenous perspectives and interpretations into their own. As Whiteley (1997:203) notes, "Archaeologists ... have more often than not systematically excluded the knowledge and interpretations of living Pueblo descendants – as they have with non-Western indigenous peoples worldwide.... The intellectual grounds for exclusion, particularly in the now-old 'new archaeology,' exalt cold 'scientific analysis' of mute material remains over indigenous oral histories: Natives need not apply." Essentially, the validity of the power inequities inherent in the conventional academic research approach (i.e., the archaeologist as expert on Indigenous culture) is in dispute. It is instructive to examine some commonalities between academic and Indigenous communities in the general concerns noted previously. The ultimate risk to both sides is *loss of control* of knowledge. An obvious tension between the different actors exists in terms of the importance, potential utility, and meaning of knowledge. In archaeology at least, this tension is better understood when knowledge is seen as both part of cultural *property* and integral to cultural *identity*. From this perspective, the appropriation and commodification of knowledge acquire added complexity, and control of knowledge becomes vital to cultural integrity.

Archaeological Research Products as Cultural and Intellectual Property

Every human society is the embodiment of a particular system of knowledge. The cultural knowledge possessed by contemporary Indigenous societies is part of a compendium of wisdom that extends back through time, a significant portion of which is represented in archaeological materials and information. This information not only reflects what happened and when it happened in the past but is symbolic of cultural identity and worldview still important to many of the descendants of the sites' creators. Archaeological sites thus constitute not only cultural property but intellectual creations, raising questions of how archaeologically derived knowledge contributes to cultural identity and what aspects of cultural identity qualify as intellectual property. Here we are referring not to archaeological approaches to cultural identity (i.e., using archaeology to define ethnicity [e.g., Shennan 1989]) but rather to the appreciation of archaeological material as a component of cultural identity (Jones 1997) that makes the products of archaeology potential forms of intellectual property. Archaeological sites and materials fit the above-mentioned definitions of Indigenous cultural and intellectual property proposed by Janke (1998) and Hampton and Henderson (2000) in their contributions to cultural identity, worldview, cultural continuity, and traditional ecological knowledge.

Cultural identity

Archaeological artifacts and sites have long served as symbols of national identity worldwide. Stonehenge is not only one of the best-known archaeological sites in the world but also strongly associated with British identity (see Golding 1989). When Rhodesia gained independence in 1980 and became Zimbabwe, it took its new name from an archaeological site and chose as its national symbol a carved soapstone bird from that site. In many parts of the world, Aboriginal communities relocated by government mandate, epidemics, or other factors have retained a strong association with their former homes, whether through occasional visits or through oral histories (e.g., Kritsch and André 1997, Myers 1986). Artifacts and heirlooms also play a vital role in the identity of Indigenous peoples, serving as a link both to past generations and to the systems of knowledge that sustained them. This may help to explain the widespread use of, for example, arrowheads – objects that have likely not been in use for a

century or more – in the contemporary logos of many Aboriginal groups in North America.

Aboriginal peoples may choose to represent themselves or seek confirmation of their cultural identity by continuing to use (or, in some cases, adopting) precontact objects or traditions (e.g., Merrill, Ladd, and Ferguson 1992). These may include architecture, traditional foods and cooking practices, and rock art imagery. In the Interior Plateau of British Columbia, the image of the semisubterranean pit house (Figure 32.1) is widely used by the Secwepemc (or Shuswap) people on letterhead, signage (Figure 32.2), sweatshirts, and promotional items. Full-scale reconstructions of pit houses are found in Aboriginal heritage parks and communities; some individuals have even built and seasonally use their own pit houses. Underground pit-cooking (a practice well-documented in the archaeological record) continues, although only infrequently, and pit-cooked food is prized (Peacock 1998). Pictographs are also widely viewed by Secwepemc and other Plateau peoples as an important part of their heritage (e.g., York, Daly, and Arnett 1993), although no new ones have been painted for many generations. Among other things, pictographs provide an expression of worldview and clear indications of a distinctive Aboriginal presence in the landscape.

Worldview

Certain types of archaeological sites and artifacts, such as pictographs, petroglyphs, medicine wheels, vision quest sites, and burial sites, have long been associated with the worldviews of Indigenous peoples. While few of these are still in use today, those that are reflect continued use since precontact times; offerings are left at sacred places today much as they have been for possibly millennia (e.g., Andrews and Zoe 1997). In Australia, the National Aboriginal Sites Authorities Committee distinguishes two types of Aboriginal sites: (1) archaeological sites, whose significance is defined "on the basis of scientific enquiry and general cultural and historical values," and (2) "sites which are the tangible embodiment of the sacred and secular traditions of the Aboriginal peoples of Australia." It is noted that the latter sites may include the former and that the "relative significance of these sites may only be

Figure 32.1   Reconstructed pit house, Secwepemc Museum and Heritage Park, Kamloops, B.C. (photo G. Nicholas).

Figure 32.2   Example of stylized pit house used as the logo of the Secwepemc Museum, Kamloops, B.C. (photo G. Nicholas).

determined by the Aboriginal custodians" (Ritchie 1993:233).

The role of these types of sites is not necessarily static but reinterpreted or even augmented to meet current needs. Dreamtime sites are places in the landscape where ancestral beings went about creating the land and all it contained, including themselves (see Stanner 1998). To

Aboriginal Australians, the Dreaming is a timeless phenomenon relayed through oral traditions linked to specific places and objects. While most of these tell how things came into being, they also reflect contemporary issues. As noted by Chatwin (1987:12), almost anything "can have a Dreaming. A virus can be a Dreaming. You can have a chickenpox Dreaming, a rain Dreaming, a desert-orange Dreaming, a lice Dreaming. In the Kimberleys they've now got a money Dreaming." Contemporary influences on traditions are also found in North America. Offerings left at sacred places often include tobacco, pebbles, and food, as well as coins and other "modern" items. Such versatility is also seen in rock art, which may include both an objective record of life in the past (e.g., animals seen) and a subjective one (e.g., personal visions, dreams, magic). These images may be interpreted differently today from when they were created.[17] In some places, the tradition continues of repainting or even painting over old images (e.g., Chaloupka 1986).

Mortuary practices and the treatment of human remains are also expressions of worldview, and the reburial issue goes to the core of worldview and cultural identity in indigenous societies everywhere (e.g., Bray 2001, Carmichael et al. 1994, Davidson, Lovell-Jones, and Bancroft 1995, Zimmerman 1997). Cemeteries have long been important places in the cultural landscape and served as territorial markers. Some cemeteries have been in use for thousands of years (O'Neill 1994). Such locations are of importance to the associated contemporary Indigenous communities and may also play a significant role in land claims and political movements.

Cultural continuity

Cultural continuity may be reflected in the occupation of the same lands for millennia, in the retention of the technologies used in the past to produce the same household goods (e.g., ceramics in the American Southwest), and in other ways (e.g., Jones 1997). Archaeological sites serve as important personal and societal touchstones (i.e., as links between past and present) that reaffirm basic values and provide a sense of place. This is indicated by Chase's (1989:17) observations on the significance of precontact archaeological sites for North

Queensland Aboriginal people in Australia. In cases where the colonial experience and a century or more of acculturation have dramatically changed the lives of Aboriginal peoples, there often remain core cultural values that indicate the persistence of traditional beliefs and worldview. These may take the form, for example, of a strong emphasis on family values and respect for community elders.

The strong connection between cultural continuity and Indigenous claims to land and cultural or archaeological materials has significant implications for the recognition of ownership in matters of repatriation and reburial. However, the continuity may sometimes be more apparent than real; as a result of population movements in the distant past or historic federal tribal relocation and the often capricious nature of tribal boundary recognition, one group may occupy a territory that contains the archaeological record of another. Even in central Australia, where until recently the effects of colonialism were limited, the degree of relatedness between the Aboriginal Australian groups mapped by Tindale (1974) and their late Pleistocene predecessors in the area merits examination.

Where cultural discontinuities are recognized in the archaeological record, residents of the area may deal with this information in different ways. For example, the group may lack any concrete knowledge of earlier residents and accept the entirety of the local archaeological record as its own; some Secwepemc people insist that their ancestors *always* lived in pit houses and harvested salmon when the archaeological record suggests that these are later Holocene developments (Nicholas 2003). Alternatively, the newcomers may recognize the legacy of an earlier occupation and integrate knowledge of ancient unrelated beings into their histories and worldviews as Hamann (2002) has documented for Mesoamerica. Finally, the group may consciously co-opt the archaeological record for cultural or political reasons, as is the case with current Navajo claims to Anasazi archaeological sites.

Traditional ecological knowledge

"Traditional ecological knowledge" has been described as an Indigenous system of knowledge that is based on observation, testing, and replicated results and therefore directly comparable with "science." Berkes (1993:3) defines the term as "a cumulative body of knowledge and beliefs, handed down through generations by cultural transmission, about the relationship of living beings (including humans) with one another and with their environment. [It] is an attribute of societies with historical continuity in resource use practices; by and large, these are non-industrial or less technologically advanced societies, many of them Indigenous or tribal." Traditional systems of knowledge have become an important subject of intellectual property rights (e.g., Simpson 1999) and are increasingly recognized by both Indigenous and non-Indigenous people as a manifestation of the acquired knowledge of particular Indigenous societies. This body of knowledge includes not only the intellectual tradition itself (i.e., the information preserved and transmitted) but also the traditional use sites that are the geographic expression of that knowledge.

Archaeological sites by any definition are traditional use sites, and therefore the knowledge represented at these sites is worth considering in the context of cultural and intellectual property. Various types of sites (e.g., fish weirs) represent the operation or practice of past land-use and resource-harvesting practices that, in turn, are the embodiment of traditional ecological knowledge, while those of a particular region collectively reflect compositional and distributional changes that occurred over millennia as past occupants responded to shifts in the natural and social environment. Traditional ecological knowledge is also frequently used by archaeologists to locate archaeological sites (e.g., Greer 1997). Site information is typically obtained through interviews with elders and community members or from published ethnographies.

Should intellectual components of the archaeological record such as these be protected as proprietary? If so, by whom? No explicit protection exists under any provincial or state heritage protection mechanisms in Canada or the United States. Most archaeologists, in fact, may not recognize an intellectual component at all. However, the situation is likely very different for those with a vested interest in their own heritage sites. In Australia, for example, Aboriginal peoples have expressed concern that "the focus

of cultural heritage laws is on tangible cultural heritage, such as specific areas, objects, and sites. The intangible aspects of a significant site, such as its associated stories, songs, and dreaming tracks, are not protected" (Janke 1998:xxiv; also Roberts 2003). Even if an intellectual component is recognized, an argument may be made that the great age of most archaeological sites puts this information in the realm of shared heritage, thus making its exploitation legally acceptable. In the following section we return to the two-sided issue of control of knowledge in archaeology and evaluate threats to Indigenous cultural and intellectual property rights through appropriation and commodification – taking and affixing a price to what many would consider inalienable and priceless.

Appropriation and Commodification of the Past

Appropriation and commodification of cultural knowledge and property affect the cultural identity and integrity of contemporary Indigenous societies. Should cultural knowledge and property be protected from such exploitation? If so, should protection be from outside interests only or from all users, including Indigenous peoples themselves? Mutability (distortions) and transferability (easy dissemination) may be reasons to explore the usefulness of intellectual property mechanisms for protecting some aspects of cultural knowledge and property from exploitation. But what if Indigenous groups want to exploit their own past for commercial gain?[18] Should intellectual property laws be used discriminately to protect the past – to support Indigenous rights? We do not address these important and complicated questions here. Rather, our aim is to raise issues and outline potential consequences of appropriation and commodification of artifacts and information with the intention of informing and stimulating discussion in this growing area of concern.

Artifacts

The collection of antiquities extends back in time for thousands of years (Trigger 1989:27–72). Today, however, the acquisition of antiquities, often by illegal or unethical means, is occurring at unprecedented rates to satisfy the growing interest of collectors and museums in historic or prehistoric items that are prized for their age, rarity, exoticness, or "Aboriginalness." Sometimes Indigenous peoples themselves contribute to the appropriation and commodification of artifacts; the often impoverished Indigenous Central and South Americans known as *huaqueros* loot tombs and sell the artifacts to support their families: "Many of Latin America's indigenous peoples see themselves as the legitimate heirs to both seeds and artifacts, which are conceived of as ancestor's gifts, given to humanity by real or mythological patrons to be harvested, or excavated, as it were, by later generations" (Matsuda 1998:88). "Subsistence digging" also occurs in North America (Hollowell 2003, Staley 1993), and its profits may provide the means of acquiring the knowledge or skills that allow Aboriginal people to improve their circumstances. Zimmer (2003:306–7), for example, reports: "Once a young [Native] woman brought a newly-found artifact to show me, an ivory animal worth many thousands of dollars on the market. 'I know I shouldn't sell this, Julie,' she said, 'but it will help pay for my college education.'" Subsistence digging is not limited to Aboriginal peoples, as is evidenced by the *tombaroli* of Italy and pothunters in the United States, and in some cases Indigenous subsistence diggers do not consider the archaeological remains part of their culture.

The appropriation and commodification of artifacts may also take less obvious forms. For example, reproductions of artifacts in various media and the public dissemination of information, objects, and images derived from the archaeological record are often found among the technologically assisted and mass-produced products introduced into modern society. These include images of artifacts and sites, sometimes including those cherished by or sacred to past or present Indigenous peoples, that appear on postcards, T-shirts, and billboards and in magazine advertisements, books, and films. For example, Sherwin-Williams uses images of the Upper Paleolithic Lascaux Cave paintings to sell house paint, and AT&T digitally inserts its logo into Egyptian tomb carvings. Through these advertisements, the past is appropriated and commodified in the sense that it is marketed in ways parallel to other, original or more contemporary ideas and resources.

Appropriation and commodification are accompanied by the objectification of the past – a focus on artifacts rather than on the people behind them. In a book on the pictographs of British Columbia, Corner (1968:1) states that "the freedom to wander unrestricted through the rugged and beautiful Kootenay country made me appreciate the feelings of the Indians, and created an intense interest in their life and culture." He goes on to report that "a diligent search of the recorded data on pictographs in North America failed to reveal a simple key that would unlock the mystery of what these fascinating paintings really mean,"[19] overlooking the possibility that contemporary Aboriginal peoples could have assisted him in this effort.

Although anthropologists and archaeologists ought to be more sensitive than others to issues of cultural appropriation and commodification, they, too, sometimes assume that ancient objects become divorced from contemporary cultural impacts when they enter the public domain. When a seated-figurine bowl was illustrated on the program cover of the 1992 Northwest Anthropology Conference, several First Nations individuals in attendance considered this use inappropriate because such bowls still have spiritual value. A similar bowl was illustrated by Winter and Henry (1997) but only with the permission of the Saanich Native Heritage Society. Perhaps the most common example of such appropriation is the use of artifacts and rock art imagery as part of the cover designs of books and journals.[20] If permission to reproduce such artifacts is sought, it is generally from the museum that today curates or owns them.

In marketing the past, the accomplishments of earlier societies are not only removed from their original physical and cultural context but sometimes otherwise altered. The transformation of the unique into the commonplace radically changes the value of things. For centuries, the great Renaissance frescoes of Europe could be viewed only from inside the buildings in which they were painted. Addressing this point, John Berger (1977:19) writes: "Originally paintings were an integral part of the building for which they were designed.... The uniqueness of every painting was once part of the uniqueness of the place where it resided.... When the camera reproduces a painting, it destroys the uniqueness of its image. Or, more exactly, its meaning multiplies and fragments into many meanings." Berger is writing here of Western art, but his comments pertain also to Indigenous representations, both historic and prehistoric. The same is true of the Upper Paleolithic cave paintings of Lascaux and of Native American rock art, all of which were previously part of fixed landscapes.

Regardless of the original intention of their creators, the appreciation of these representations is very different when they are widely disseminated – and perhaps even altered – through a variety of media. The following anecdote (from Nicholas) illustrates how easy it is to alter an idea expressed in tangible form, how little control we have over dissemination of the original idea, and how difficult it is to make proprietorial claims of an intellectual nature in various high-tech media:

> About ten years ago I was preparing a lecture on hunter-gatherer economy. I was thinking about "access to the means of production" and other ideas influenced by the work of Karl Marx while making overhead transparencies of !Kung hunters. The next thing I knew, the old boy's head had been pasted onto a hunter's body and then onto an Upper Paleolithic "Venus" figurine. Soon after, I sent copies of this inspired artwork to several colleagues, including Martin Wobst of the University of Massachusetts–Amherst, where I had completed my Ph.D. Last year I learned from Wobst that my Venus/Marx figure had appeared on a T-shirt prepared for the 25th anniversary of the department. I was amused and honored that this late-night whimsy had its 15 minutes of fame. However, in thinking about IPR issues, I began to wonder where the design on this shirt might ultimately end up. Perhaps an enterprising entrepreneur, seeing someone wearing it, will decide to create a series of T-shirts featuring famous people on Venus-figurine bodies.

The unauthorized appropriation of Aboriginally produced images, whether ancient or modern, has been a topic of discussion in Australia for some time (see Johnson 1996). Much attention has been given to the theft of Aboriginal design, particularly those created by contemporary Aboriginal artists. Still another dimension of this relates to the theft of intellectual property through the appropriation of Aboriginal art. Brown (1998:219) notes that in a recent legal case in Darwin the plaintiffs were "asking the federal court to recognize the clan's economic and moral rights in the artist's graphic designs, rights tied to the clan's territory and ritual knowledge." At least some pictographs and petroglyphs in North America represent graphic designs tied to traditional territories and the ritual knowledge of past people whose descendants may still occupy that territory. These designs may subsequently appear in books and other media,[21] seldom with attribution to the traditional peoples concerned.

Even when there is approval by Aboriginal persons for the publication of such images or interpretations thereof, is the approval at the level of family, community, tribe, or nation? In some cases it may be Aboriginal peoples themselves that commodify the past. For example, the native people of St. Lawrence Island, Alaska, have been digging and selling artifacts from their ancestral sites for many years (see Hollowell 2003, Hollowell-Zimmer 2001, Staley 1993, Zimmer 2003). However, as Zimmer (2003:307) notes, "Perhaps a Euro-American notion in which objects of material culture are venerated as 'heritage' is somewhat foreign to a people whose heritage is performed and experienced in daily practices like speaking their own language, whaling, eating Native foods, and drum-dancing *sans* tourists."

Appropriation of the North American archaeological record has been facilitated by Indigenous and non-Indigenous parties alike. One example involves the Zia Pueblo sun symbol. Zia Pueblo has demanded $73 million from the state of New Mexico for the use of its *Zia* sun symbol on the state flag. The symbol, adopted by the state in 1925, had been developed by Harry Mera, a physician and anthropologist at the Santa Fe Laboratory of Anthropology, on the basis of a pot on display in the museum that had been made by an anonymous Zia potter in the late 1800s (Healy 2003). (The symbol had likely appeared much earlier.) Another example concerns the cancellation of a mural of images from Pottery Mound ruin commissioned for the new archaeology building at the University of

New Mexico in deference to objections raised by
Acoma Pueblo. Pottery Mound is an 800-year-
old site near Albuquerque that was excavated in
the 1950s and 1960s. The Acoma admit that their
ancestors had nothing to do with the artwork at
the site. A statement by the muralist, Tom Baker,
raises an important point beyond the issue of
political correctness: "Public Mound images
were excavated by a taxpayer-supported institution on public land, and thus are public property" (Duin 2003).

Information

What has occurred with material property is also
occurring with the know-how of Indigenous
peoples. Knowledge that was once restricted to
specific cultural systems has now been made
widely available, seldom because of decisions of
the communities themselves. Immense public
interest in things Aboriginal has for centuries
prompted collection, study, and even imitation
of Native curios and lifeways. This interest is
increasingly specialized through fields like
anthropology, which aims to understand the
totality of humankind through detailed studies
of selected societies, often in collaboration with
representatives of those societies. In some cases
information recorded by anthropologists has
been of immense value to community members
decades later; that collected and published by
Franz Boas (1897, 1969 [1930]) has aided the
Kwakiutl of British Columbia in restoring
aspects of their ceremonies that had been out-
lawed in 1885 (Holm 1990). Until the Indian Act
was revised in 1951, it was illegal to hold certain
ceremonies; individuals or communities who
persisted were often jailed and their masks,
regalia, and other items confiscated.[22] For the
almost 70 years in which they were banned,
potlatches and Winter Dances continued
secretly, but many of their components were
changed or lost in the process. The detailed
information collected by Boas and his assistant
George Hunt has thus become a vital source for
those interested in restoring the ceremonies to
their original form. Intellectual aspects of cultural property and cultural identity have been
appropriated and sometimes commodified in
various ways, including traditional use studies,
use of human remains, cultural reconstructions

of life (i.e., cultural tourism/living museums),
and applications of archaeological research
results to modern problems.

TRADITIONAL USE STUDIES

In British Columbia between 1995 and 2000,
provincially funded "traditional use studies"
provided Aboriginal communities with the
"opportunity" to identify and map the cultural
resources in their territories systematically.[23]
Through these studies, site-specific biological
and cultural information on traditional activities
was compiled by the participating community
and/or hired consultants. As part of the associated "sharing agreement," the resulting data were
submitted to the Provincial Heritage Registered
Database for use in the government's natural-
resource management decisions. Information-
sharing agreements were established through a
memorandum of understanding between the
province and the Aboriginal community as part
of the final phase of the study (i.e., *after* the data
had been compiled), but an interim sharing
agreement (signed by all parties *prior* to the
initial phase of the project) was required for
final project funding. Sharing agreements
addressed the storage and distribution of inventory data, confidentiality and security, and continued reporting and management of
information (Markey 2001:71). Issues of data
ownership and intellectual property rights were
not specifically addressed – a serious omission
that was recognized by many First Nations and
made them unwilling to participate because of
uncertainty about the future use of the data. In
her critical analysis of the traditional use study
as a model for data gathering and interpretation
of traditional ecological knowledge in British
Columbia, Markey (2001:14) concludes that
such studies "continue to produce inventory-
based data, reflecting minimal concern for
Aboriginal perspectives and knowledge by taking
cultural information out of context."

APPROPRIATION OF HUMAN REMAINS

The Kennewick Man controversy (Chatters
2000, Preston 1997) has become a landmark
case on the disposition of prehistoric human
remains. Aboriginal groups in the Northwest
have argued in the courts since 1996 that the
remains of this 9,000-year-old individual should

be repatriated and reburied under the provisions of the NAGPRA, which states that Aboriginal human remains must be turned over to the representative Aboriginal group where affinity can be determined. A group of archaeologists has countered that because of their great age these remains cannot be related to the Aboriginal groups laying claim to them and has sued the U.S. government for the right to study them (*Bonnichsen v United States*, 969 F Supp 628 [1997])[24] – essentially asserting themselves as the rightful owners or stewards of the information contained in the skeletal remains. In September 2000 a federal judge ruled that the remains were to be turned over to the tribal claimants. The case was subsequently appealed. In August 2002 U.S. Magistrate John Jelderks ruled that the skeletal remains could be studied by the archaeologists. The ultimate fate of the remains and the information they embody is uncertain; an appeal of the decision is planned by the tribal claimants.[25] This case has obvious implications for the appropriation of material property and, pending the results of legal decisions on ancestry and custodianship, may raise issues of intellectual property in relation to the appropriation of Indigenous worldview.

RECONSTRUCTION OF INDIGENOUS LIFEWAYS
Cultural tourism has become a significant industry worldwide, and living museums and theme parks are widespread. Many of these include reenactments of life in the past utilizing speech and people in period clothing to represent both the colonizers and the colonized. The "best" of these include or are led by bearers of the culture involved,[26] but some of them blatantly exploit and stereotype Indigenous peoples. Living museums allow visitors to take home the experience of an "authentic" (and safe) encounter with the Other. There is also today a proliferation of Aboriginal heritage parks, tours, workshops, and "experiences" that are Aboriginally conceived, developed, and run.[27] The way in which Aboriginal communities choose to present themselves is critical to whether the experience is appreciated by visitors as one of cultural education and sharing or criticized as cultural "prostitution."

Other examples are worth noting. The German Indian clubs (Calloway, Gmunden, and Zantop

2002, Robbins and Becher 1997–98) consist of individuals who "play Indian" at several removes from the Native Americans they emulate [...]. Going a step farther, the Smokis of the American Southwest have actually appropriated and violated Hopi ceremonies. Founded in 1921 by white businessmen, the Smokis put on public performances that are essentially parodies of the Hopi Snake Dance (Whitely 1997:178). Added to threats to the sanctity of, loss of access to, or destruction of sacred places (e.g., Mt. Graham, Arizona) and the commodification of religious objects, symbolism, and artifacts (Pearlstone 2000, 2001, Whiteley 1997), these activities leave little of the cultural knowledge and property of Southwestern Indigenous peoples unscathed.

APPLICATIONS OF ARCHAEOLOGICAL RESEARCH
Two types of archaeologically derived information have particular relevance in the modern world.[28] The first is information derived from studies of long-term shifts in subsistence practices or settlement patterns, which can be used to evaluate the potential impact of climate change on modern populations. The second is information on prehistoric technology. Both types may be appropriated and commodified.

One example of the development of new ideas through archaeologically obtained knowledge of prehistoric technology is the use of obsidian blades as surgical scalpels. Obsidian was widely utilized for stone blade production in many parts of the world. Aware that such blades had an edge up to 1,000 times sharper than surgical steel, Payson Sheets (1989) developed obsidian scalpels for use in eye surgery, where the sharper edge promotes faster healing and reduces scarring. Even though stone blade production was practiced by virtually all past human societies, this technology was potentially patentable because it represented a new use.[29] Other modern flint-knappers had observed how quickly obsidian cuts healed, but Sheets was the first to capitalize on it. Another example is the reintroduction of raised-field farming techniques by Clark Erickson and his colleagues as a means of assisting native communities to improve their agricultural yields. There is extensive archaeological evidence of raised fields throughout Central and South America (Parsons and Denevan

1967), but this technology appears to have fallen out of use until it was promoted by Erickson and his colleagues (Erickson 1998). This is not the case with the *chinampas*, a type of raised-field farming constructed in swamps (Coe 1964), that were the economic basis of the Aztec economy in Mexico and of other societies in Central and South America and have continued to be used to the present and introduced into new areas. Does the reintroduction of forgotten raised-field farming represent intellectual property? If so, for whom – the archaeologists or the descendants of the people who developed the technology in the first place? Erickson's (2000) more recent work on precontact artificial fisheries in the Bolivian Amazon suggests yet another area of potentially commercially valuable Indigenous knowledge.

So far we have explored the notion that some products of archaeological research represent cultural and intellectual property according to Janke's (1998) definition and outlined some of the ways in which archaeologically derived knowledge has been appropriated or commodified. We next focus on the means by which Indigenous peoples are seeking (or may seek in future) to regain control over this knowledge through existing legal rights, including intellectual property ownership mechanisms.

Who Owns the Future?

"Everyone now speaks of their culture," says Sahlins (1999:x), "precisely in the context of national or international threats to its existence. This does not mean a simple and nostalgic desire for teepees and tomahawks or some such fetishized repositories of a pristine identity. A 'naïve attempt to hold peoples hostage to their own histories,' such a supposition, Terence Turner remarks, would thereby deprive them of history. What the self-consciousness of 'culture' does signify is the demand of the peoples for their own space within the world cultural order." A strong association between cultural knowledge and cultural identity is reflected not only in a society's material culture (e.g., the pit house in Interior British Columbia) but in the intellectual aspects of cultural traditions. Language, for example, is a very important contributor to Indigenous cultural identity (see Maffi 2000). Given the

strength of this association, it is clear why control of knowledge is at the heart of the issue – not simply for economic reasons but because control is integral to the definition or restoration of cultural identity for present and future Indigenous societies.

It can be argued that whoever owns (or controls records of) the past also owns or otherwise shapes the future of that past. Archaeologists have, to date, controlled the dissemination of information derived from the archaeological record through publication practices, restriction of access to site locations, and other means. While this management of knowledge has done much to help preserve archaeological resources, it has had several drawbacks. For one, much information has been kept from Indigenous communities, often inadvertently. Since archaeologists are in the position to choose what they will or will not publish, information potentially useful to Indigenous peoples may simply not be available because it fell outside of the interests of the investigator and was not pursued. Access to knowledge is obviously the first of several key steps in establishing control of it. Yet publication itself is a double-edged sword in terms of sharing research findings versus protecting knowledge from third-party exploitation (see Bannister 2000, Bannister and Barrett 2001, n.d., Laird et al. 2002). Beyond simply relying on heritage protection legislation, is it possible to increase Indigenous control of cultural knowledge and property through existing intellectual property laws and complementary nonlegal tools? If so, what are the implications for future archaeological research? In this final section, we explore several current examples that may begin to elucidate answers to these complex questions.

Control through contracts and local protocols for research

Examples of Indigenous groups' seeking to control access to and/or use of their past are definitely on the rise. Brown (1998:194) cites a 1994 letter to several museums from the chair of the Hopi Tribe that "states the tribe's interest in all published or unpublished field data relating to the Hopi, including notes, drawings, and photographs, particularly those dealing with religious matters." He notes also that

the Hopi initiative was soon followed by a declaration issued by a consortium of Apache tribes
demanding exclusive decision-making power
and control over Apache "cultural property,"
here defined as "all images, text, ceremonies,
music, songs, stories, symbols, beliefs, customs,
ideas and other physical and spiritual objects
and concepts" relating to the Apache, including
any representations of Apache culture offered by
Apache or non-Apache people (Inter-Apache
Summit on Repatriation 1995:3).

An important question to consider is to what
degree archaeological research products might
be included here.

Local Indigenous protocols are increasingly
being used as the basis for research contracts or
agreements between the communities and outside
researchers. Protocols have been developed by
many Aboriginal groups in British Columbia,
and some require a permit in lieu of one issued
by the B.C. Heritage Branch under the Heritage
Conservation Act. The Sto:lo Nation, for example,
states: "We hereby declare that all artifacts recovered from our traditional campsites, ceremonial
sites, villages, burial grounds and archaeological
sites are the rightful property of the Sto:lo people"
(quoted in Mohs 1987:169). The protocol of the
Cultural Resources Management Department
(CRMD) of the Kamloops Band, Secwepemc
Nation, contains even more inclusive terms and
provisions for an archaeological permitting system, stating that "all data, maps, journals, and
photographs, and other material generated
through or as a result of the study are the exclusive
property of the Band," that "there shall be joint
copyright between the Permittee and the Band over
any such publications, unless otherwise agreed
between the parties," and that "all material found
or generated by the proponent as a result of heritage investigations shall be deemed the property of
the Kamloops Indian Band." How effective is this
agreement, and what rights are ceded upon signing? The provisions of the archaeological permit
refer to physical property/results but do not specifically mention intellectual property ownership
aside from "joint copyright." The provisions do,
however, specifically include "data," and the fact
that the term is not defined enables the Kamloops
Band to interpret it broadly, perhaps allowing some
forms of intellectual property to be included.

Should such permits explicitly include reference to intellectual property rights? If so, is it
possible or likely that at some point a contemporary Aboriginal group will lay claim to a major
archaeological site and exercise exclusive control
over the site name, images of the artifacts, or
related items? What if there are competing interests due to overlapping land claims (e.g., Franklin and Bunte 1994)? These are complex control
issues that have yet to arise. It is important to
note, however, that regaining control, such as
repatriation of human remains, is often just the
beginning of a series of related challenges; control
of knowledge or resources without the capacity to
manage them can have significant consequences.
As Winter and Henry (1997:222) note,

> An associated issue is the intrinsic power of
> excavated materials. While the [Saanich] Society
> has a responsibility for the preservation of arti-
> facts of cultural, artistic, and historical value to
> the Saanich people, in some cases it is difficult to
> accept such objects. Some artifacts carry with
> them a constellation of responsibilities. To ac-
> cept care of certain artifacts brings onerous cul-
> tural and spiritual obligations. Some need
> extensive ritual care. Some artifacts may only
> be returned to individuals who are culturally
> appropriate by reason of family, lineage, gender,
> or initiation. Such people may not be available,
> or may not be willing to personally undertake
> the effort and personal expense.

Control through intellectual property ownership mechanisms

Beyond contractual approaches to controlling
Indigenous cultural and intellectual property,
existing intellectual property ownership tools
are beginning to be employed. Academic
researchers are increasingly required to negotiate
issues related to publication, including standard
copyright issues (authorship and moral rights),
editorial control (restrictions on publication),
and benefit sharing. For example, "joint copyright between the Permittee and the Band" for all
resulting publications is required by the heritage
investigation permit of the Kamloops Indian
Band referred to above. With most archaeological publications, copyright is held by the
publishers. With greater collaboration between
archaeologists and Aboriginal communities,

publishers will need to accommodate the need for more flexible copyright arrangements. This is already under way with some ethnobotany publications (e.g., Turner 1997, 1998). Furthermore, some archaeologists have turned over copyright to the Indigenous peoples with whom they work (e.g., Roberts 2002). Sharing or transferring copyright may require (and benefit from) review by the community collaborator(s) prior to publication – an extension of existing concepts of peer review to include community experts. Such collaborative approaches to publication, however, often require additional time. Another issue is copyright ownership and access to photographs of Aboriginal designs, which raises the question which of these is the true creation or artistic work, the design or the photograph. Here one could suggest a parallel with the patenting of isolated and purified plant chemicals by drug companies that use cultural knowledge as a guide; which creativity is most deserving of protection, the laboratory manipulation or the original knowledge?

Trademark is also gaining recognition as a potentially useful legal tool for protecting Indigenous images and designs. For example, several members of Pauktuutit, a Canadian Inuit women's organization, are currently examining how a variation on trademark that they term a "cultural property mark" might be employed to protect the *amauti*, an innovative traditional form of clothing with both practical and holistic attributes. The concept of a cultural property mark is similar to a trademark but would apply to the collective knowledge of Indigenous peoples rather than the knowledge of individuals or corporations (Blackduck 2001*a,b*). Aboriginal groups in British Columbia such as the Cowichan Band Council have registered certain words as "certification marks" (another form of trademark) for commercial use. For example, "Cowichan," "Genuine Cowichan," and "Genuine Cowichan Approved" are registered for use in the marketing of handmade clothing created by Coast Salish knitters using traditional materials, methods, and patterns.[30] These marks have potential application in the protection or promotion of other aspects of cultural heritage. While trademark use typically involves protection of exclusive rights to an image intended for commercial purposes, defensive uses of

trademark law have been documented. In February 2000 the Snuneymuxw Nation successfully registered some ancient petroglyphs in their traditional territory as "official marks" to prevent their being copied and reproduced by anyone for any purpose, arguing that they are sacred and copying them for any reason would be sacrilegious (Associated Press 2000, Tanner 2000). The Comox Indian Band has protected the place-name of a sacred site, Queneesh,[31] as an official mark.

Patents may seem unrelated to archaeological research. At the molecular level, however, archaeological research may involve the recovery of ancient DNA, a potentially patentable material.[32] DNA has, for example, been extracted from 8,000-year-old brain tissue (Doran et al. 1986). Access to and study of DNA from contemporary populations is a very contentious issue, in part because it brings up serious issues of privacy and prior informed consent but also because the genetic information derived through analysis may be seen as a valuable commodity. Given that human genetic material is patentable in Canada, the United States, and many European countries, one can speculate that if, for example, ancient DNA from prehistoric human remains were to play a critical role in informing future medical treatments for contemporary diseases there might be important issues to be resolved regarding both cultural heritage and intellectual property rights. At best, intellectual property and other laws offer a piecemeal approach to protecting certain aspects of cultural heritage. This contrasts with the blanket approach that Brown (2003:209) calls "total heritage protection" and describes as "a benign form of quarantine that safeguards all elements of cultural life. Entire cultures would thus be defined as off-limits to scrutiny and exploitation. Within this sheltering umbrella, communities would remain free to devise appropriate ways to defend their philosophical or scientific or artistic achievements." He points out the contradictions inherent in this approach (pp. 217–18):

> To defend indigenous peoples, it promotes official boundaries that separate one kind of native person from another, and native persons from non-native ones, thereby threatening the fluidity of ethnic and family identities typically found in

aboriginal communities. In the name of defending indigenous traditions, it forces the elusive qualities of entire civilizations – everything from attitudes and bodily postures to agricultural techniques – into ready-made legal categories, among which "heritage" and "culture" are only the most far-reaching. In the interest promoting diversity, Total Heritage Protection imposes procedural norms that have the paradoxical effect of flattening cultural difference.

While much of the recent intellectual property rights discussion has centered on the use or expansion of existing legal mechanisms, Brown (1998:199) contends that this strategy serves primarily to "convert information into property" but that "property discourse *replaces* [emphasis ours] what should be extensive discussion on the moral implications of exposing Native people to unwanted scrutiny, on the one hand, and sequestering public-domain information, on the other." We strongly support Brown's call (p. 202) for "public discussion about mutual respect and the fragility of native cultures in mass societies." Given that the establishment of an adequate process for such a dialogue has been slow, however, we suggest that the existing legal and nonlegal protection mechanisms discussed herein merit consideration.

Cultural prospecting? Lessons from other disciplines

Non-Indigenous archaeologists have long held a monopoly on the recovery of prehistoric materials and scientific knowledge of past peoples. In general, they have also profited the most from archaeological research in the sense of creating personal careers and building their professional field. Indeed, archaeological exploration of the past could be viewed as cultural prospecting, parallel to biodiversity prospecting. This being the case, are there lessons to be gleaned from the current intellectual property rights debate in ethnobotany? Archaeology is based on physical evidence that is often seen as lacking in contemporary value. In contrast, the intellectual contributions (e.g., language, traditional plant knowledge) of living Indigenous societies are integral to ethonobotany and are in many cases highly regarded in contemporary human and

environmental health applications. Some archaeological research products are protected by federal, state, or provincial laws. While such legislation appears to be inadequate to protect cultural and intellectual property, it is often supplemented by well-developed local protocols, contracts, and/or permit systems. By comparison, no provincial or federal policy in Canada specifically limits access to or use of ethnobotanical knowledge or plant biodiversity on public lands. The ethnobotanical research policies and guidelines that have been developed are mainly institutionally derived (i.e., university, industry, professional society). Relevant international statements and declarations are emerging (e.g., *Kari-Oca Declaration* 1992, *Mataatua Declaration* 1993), but protocols developed by Indigenous groups themselves are largely recent developments.[33]

Through publication of their data, archaeologists increase access to the historical record, as archaeological information is often not readily available to communities. Not surprisingly, copyright relating to the publication of results has been largely perceived as the main intellectual property issue, although there is the potential for patent issues and trademark applications are emerging. Indeed, if marketers can seek and often gain legal protection of "proprietary" phrases, symbols, names, and even odors (see Brown 2003:76), then the notion of Indigenous peoples' seeking protection for medicine wheels, rock art, or other aspects of their cultural heritage cannot be viewed as outlandish or unprecedented. In ethnobotany, by comparison, publication raises important issues (see Bannister and Barrett n.d., 2001, Laird et al. 2002), but copyright is viewed as inadequate protection in that it serves only to limit the *physical reproduction* of published works rather than protecting their intellectual components. Copyright is also very difficult to monitor or enforce. Patents are the mechanisms of choice for researchers interested in protecting intellectual property rights to "inventions" with commercial potential based on traditional plant knowledge. Ethnobotanists are increasingly having to consider patent issues and trade secrecy (fiduciary duty) in connection with traditional medicines or foods.

Significant differences between archaeology and ethnobotany are obvious in the types of information sought and the ways in which that information is utilized. Archaeology and ethnobotany approach intellectual property issues from opposite ends of the spectrum – archaeology from the *material* record of *past* culture with supposed *limited* present use and ethnobotany from the *intellectual* aspects (and related biological resources) of *living* (or recently living) peoples with perceived *high* contemporary value. Perhaps the two disciplines can inform one another. Archaeologists have the potential to become leaders in dealing with issues of intellectual property rights in their own field by becoming aware of debates in related disciplines and considering their implications.

Costewardship of the future

Unless archaeologists consider the implications of existing intellectual property laws and the subject matter that might lead to intellectual property disputes (e.g., publication of academic research, fiduciary duties with regard to secret knowledge, reproduction of images of cultural artifacts or symbols, use of traditional knowledge derived from archaeological digs) they may be caught unawares by restrictions on data access or use imposed on them by tribes that have gained legal rights or developed the capacity to conduct research on their own. The situation is analogous in some respects to the events leading up to drafting of the NAGPRA.

For decades professional archaeologists and their antiquarian predecessors were complacent about the recovery and treatment of human skeletal remains, assuming that they had the unlimited right to claim these precontact materials for their own use and that Native Americans had little or no interest in those materials (see Thomas 2000 for overview). Those who held this view were "shocked and outraged" by the ease of passage of this powerful piece of legislation (e.g., Meighan 1992).

We advocate a more active role for archaeologists working with Indigenous peoples (or on Indigenous territories) in considering the implications of their research. We believe that solutions to disputes between archaeologists (or archaeology) and tribes will be found in the recognition of what archaeological knowledge means and what *control* of that knowledge means beyond simply economics or professional rewards and advancement. There must be recognition of ethical obligations at both the individual and the collective level. Adopting participatory research approaches, supporting meaningful collaboration with Indigenous colleagues, sharing decisionmaking responsibilities and benefits in research processes and outcomes, and working cooperatively with all those who have an interest in Indigenous cultural heritage will be key to identifying, understanding, and addressing the conflicts that may arise in claiming ownership of the past.

Notes

1 We use "Aboriginal," "Indigenous," and "Native" interchangeably. "Aboriginal" tends to be used more commonly in Canada and Australia. In Canada it includes First Nations, Métis, and Inuit.

2 See, for example, *Harvard College v Canada* (Commissioner of Patents) 2002 SCC 76. File No. 28155 December 5 (http://www.texum.umontreal.ca/csc-scc/en/pub/2002/vol4/html/2002scr4_0046.html) and the reexamination of U.S. Plant Patent No. 5,751, the "Da Vine Patent" on the Amazonian rain-forest plant *Banisteriopsis caapi*, issued June 17, 1986, to Loren S. Miller and rejected by the U.S. Patent and Trademark Office on November 3, 1999 (CIEL 1999).

3 Bell and Patterson (1999:206) define "Aboriginal cultural property" as "movable objects that have sacred, ceremonial, historical, traditional, or other

purposes integral to the culture of a First Nations community and may be viewed as collective property of an Aboriginal people" and continue: "Aboriginal perspectives on identification of cultural property and persons with authority to alienate or convey such property may vary in accordance with the laws, traditions and property systems of the claimant group."

4 This theme is expanded upon in Brown's book *Who Owns Native Culture?* (2003), which is highly recommended as a comprehensive review and discussion of many key issues.

5 Copyright Act. R.S., c. C-30, s. i, Canada (http://laws.justice.gc.ca/en/C-42/37844.html).

6 A patent is the right to exclude others for a defined period of time (e.g., 20 years in Canada) from making, using, or selling an invention that involves

a new process, structure, or function. A trademark is a word, symbol, picture, or group of these used to distinguish the products or services of one individual, organization, or company from those of another. An industrial design protects the shape, pattern, or ornamentation of an industrially produced object. A trade secret is practical knowledge that has commercial value, provides a competitive advantage, and is not widely known (Industry Canada 1995, Posey and Dutfield 1996, Stephenson 1999).

7   However limited the term is, we use "Western" here in its usual colonial/post-colonial sense, as in the distinction between "the West and the Rest" (Sahlins 1976).

8   Asch (1997) has examined the issue of ownership of cultural property in an archaeological context but not that of intellectual property rights per se.

9   We are very much aware that archaeology has frequently been conducted in the context of an unequal power relationship in which descendant communities have had little participation or say. This has been true for Native Americans (e.g., Jemison 1997, Watkins 2000) and African-Americans (e.g., McDavid 2002, Singleton 1995). The situation has changed notably in recent years (see e.g., the Code of Ethics of the World Archaeological Congress).

10 For example, the long-term study and excavation of landfills in the United States by William Rathje has demonstrated their ineffectiveness and contributed to their redesign (Rathje 1991, Rathje and Murphy 1992). Carlson's (1995) study of fish remains from archaeological sites in northeastern North America correlates the substantial – and anomalous – historic salmon population with the Little Ice Age cooling, thereby explaining why many expensive salmon restoration projects may be unlikely to reach projected goals.

11 "Cultural patrimony" is "an object having ongoing historical, traditional, or cultural importance central to the Native American group or culture" (NAGPRA 1990:sec. 2).

12 Export of artifacts out of the province is prohibited by the British Columbia Heritage Conservation Act, while the export of many materials out of Canada is regulated or prohibited by the Cultural Property Export and Import Act.

13 We must be careful about making assumptions as to who the descendants of a particular population are. In the Kennewick Man case, there is little scientific evidence that the 9,000-year-old skeletal remains can be directly related to modern Umatilla and other claimants. In the case of the Navajo claim to association with Anasazi sites,

archaeological data indicate that it is the Pueblo tribes that are strongly linked to those sites, the Navajo having moved into the Southwest only relatively recently.

14 The "Mona Lisa," however, is owned by the Louvre and may not be entirely in the public domain in a copyright sense. The museum controls access to it and access to quality reproductions. Petroglyphs have been trademarked (as official marks) in British Columbia and therefore are not necessarily part of our common human heritage.

15 Morris (1984:11), for example, notes that "ancient peoples believed that time was cyclic in character," ignoring the fact that many contemporary Aboriginal peoples also believe this.

16 Concerns faced by Indigenous researchers would presumably include some elements from both of these points of view and be further influenced by whether they were members of the communities in which they were working. Such individuals may also expose themselves to criticism for having "sold out."

17 This is likely the case with the Nlaka'pamux elder Annie York's interpretation of pictographs in her band territory in the Interior Plateau of British Columbia (York, Daly, and Arnett 1993). The degree to which her interpretations of imagery match those of its creators hundreds or thousands of years ago is debatable (Nicholas 2001).

18 This is but one facet of a larger and more difficult question: If a group "owns" or controls its cultural heritage, should it not have the freedom to do what it wishes with it? Many who agree in principle with this reasoning are dismayed when it is put into practice (for example, when repatriated human remains are reburied).

19 While many Aboriginal people had commented on the appropriateness of Corner's book, the recent publication of another book on British Columbia rock art (Nankivell and Wyse 2003), this one including GPS locations, has raised the ire of some First Nations.

20 Including *American Antiquity, Australian Archaeology,* the *Canadian Journal of Archaeology, Latin American Antiquity,* the *Mid-Continental Journal of Archaeology,* and *Northeast Anthropology.*

21 The cover of *Australian Archaeology* shows two stylized human figures that are based on but not direct copies of rock art images. Amy Roberts (personal communication, 2001) notes that Aboriginal people have complained but thinks that this "has to do with the figures' being naked." In 2000, the Australian Archaeological Association membership voted to keep the design.

22 Many of these materials became part of the collections of the National Museum of Man and the Royal Ontario Museum, among others (Lohnse and Sundt 1990:92).

23 These land-use and occupancy studies (cancelled in 2002) were a product of British Columbia government policy responses to legal obligations in land-use management as defined by the Court of Appeal in *Delgamuukw v The Queen (1993)* (Culhane 1998). The goal of the program was "to inventory TUS data to provide the province and industry with the tools to facilitate meaningful consultation with participating First Nations in land use planning" as well as to "[assist] First Nations participating in the treaty process, [and develop] cultural education and capacity" (http://www.for.gov.bc.ca/aab/int_msrs/pim_tus.htm).

24 D. Ore, cited in the final court brief (http://www.kennewick-man.com/documents/doi.html).

25 Non-Aboriginal organizations have also made claims, including the Asatru Folk Assembly, which insists that the remains are those of an ancient European: "the Asatru Folk Assembly ... practices an ancient religion known as Asatru, with roots in northern Europe.... Asatru emphasizes the spiritual importance of ancestral bonds. Since Kennewick Man may well be related to modern-day people of European descent, the AFA filed suit in 1996 in federal court to prevent the U.S. government from giving the skeleton to local Indian tribes, and to ensure the remains were studied and results released to the public" (http://www.runestone.org/kmfact.html).

26 For example, those of African-American slaves at Colonial Williamsburg (Virginia) offered through an interpretive program called "The Other Half Tour."

27 For example, Xà:ytem (Hatzic Rock) and Tla-o-qui-aht cultural tours by Tla-ook Adventures in British Columbia and the co-managed Kakadu National Park in Australia.

28 Archaeological information is also relevant to other realms, such as education.

29 On the basis of a search of the U.S. Patent Office database (http://www.uspto.gov/patft/) and personal communication with a representative of Fine Science Tools Inc., a Vancouver-based company that currently sells "Stone Age scalpels" made from obsidian (http://finescience.com/fst/ScalpelsKnives/10110-01.html), we conclude that obsidian scalpels were not patented.

30 Canadian Intellectual Property Office web site (http://strategis.ic.gc.ca/SSG/0792/trdp079217400e.html).

31 Canadian Intellectual Property Office web site (http://strategis.ic.gc.ca/SSG/0908/trdp090857300e.html).

32 For example, deCODE Genetics of Delaware has been creating databases of Icelanders' genes and their medical and genealogical records. The company cross-references these data and markets them and other bioinformatics software products to drug developers (Industry Standard web site [http://www.thestandard.com/companies/dossier/0,1922,276205,00.html]). DeCODE "will license the genes that it discovers (all of which it intends to patent) to drugmakers only if they agree to provide medicines developed as a result to all Icelanders without charge" (Gibbs 1998). The Mannvernd Association for Ethics in Science and Medicine in Iceland is opposing the databases through a lawsuit on the grounds that they violate human rights (http://mannvernd.is).

33 Examples of protocols or guidelines developed by indigenous groups include *Guidelines for Respecting Cultural Knowledge (Alaska Native Knowledge Network)* (http://www.ankn.uaf.edu/standards/knowledge.html), *Mi'kmaq Research Principles and Protocols* (http://mrc.uccb.ns.ca/mci/default.htm), *Code of Ethics for Researchers Conducting Research Concerning the Ktunaxa Nation* (http://www.law.ualberta.ca/research/aboriginalculturalheritage/casestudies.htm), and '*Namgis First Nation Guidelines for Visiting Researchers/Access to Information* (http://www.law.ualberta.ca/research/aboriginalculturalheritage/casestudies.htm).

References

Andrews, T. D., and J. B. Zoe. 1997. "The *Idaà* trail: Archaeology and the Dogrib cultural landscape, Northwest Territories, Canada," in *At a crossroads: Archaeologists and First Peoples in Canada*. Edited by G. P. Nicholas and T. D. Andrews, pp. 160–77. Burnaby, B.C.: Archaeology Press.

Asch, M. 1997. "Cultural property and the question of underlying title," in *At a crossroads: Archaeologists and first peoples in Canada*. Edited by G. P. Nicholas and T. D. Andrews, pp. 266–71. Burnaby, B.C.: Archaeology Press.

Associated Press. 2000. Indian band applies for trademark on ancient petroglyphs. February 16.

Balter, M. 2000. Archaeologists and rabbis clash over human remains. *Science* 287:34–35.

Bannister, K. 2000. Chemistry rooted in cultural knowledge: Unearthing the links between antimicrobial properties and traditional knowledge in food and medicinal plant resources of the Secwepemc (Shuswap) Aboriginal Nation. Ph.D. diss., University of British Columbia, Vancouver, B.C., Canada.

Bannister, K. 2003. Use of traditional knowledge of Aboriginal peoples for university research: An analysis of academic ethics and research policies in British Columbia, Canada. Commissioned report prepared for the Biodiversity Convention Office for submission to the Convention on Biological Diversity Article 8j. Hull. Quebec.

Bannister, K., and K. Barrett. 2001. Challenging the status quo in ethnobotany: A new paradigm for publication may protect cultural knowledge and traditional resources. *Cultural Survival Quarterly* 24(4):10–13.

Bannister, K., and K. Barrett. n.d. "Weighing the proverbial 'ounce of prevention' versus the 'pound of cure' in a biocultural context: A role for the precautionary principle in ethnobiological research," in *Ethnobotany and conservation of biocultural diversity*. Edited by T. J. Carlson and L. Maffi. Advances in Economic Botany 15.

Battiste, M., and J. (S.) Y. Henderson. 2000. *Protecting indigenous knowledge and heritage: A global challenge*. Saskatoon: Purich Publishing.

Bell, C. E., and R. K. Patterson. 1999. Aboriginal rights to cultural property. *International Journal of Cultural Property* 8:167–211.

Berger, J. 1977. *Ways of seeing*. New York: Viking Penguin.

Berkes, F. 1993. "Traditional ecological knowledge in perspective," in *Traditional ecological knowledge: Concepts and cases*. Edited by J. T. Inglis, pp. 1–10. Ottawa: Canadian Museum of Nature.

Blackduck, A. 2001*a*. Protecting Inuit clothing designs: Pauktuutit looks to Panama for legal model. *Nunatsiaq News* [Iqaluit], May 25, Iqaluit. http://www.nunatsiaq.com/nunavut/nvt10525_091.

Blackduck, A. 2001*b*. Pauktuutit to continue work on Amauti protection: Rankin workshop impresses federal officials. *Nunatsiaq News* [Iqaluit], June 1.

Boas, F. 1897. The social organization and the secret societies of the Kwakiutl Indians. *Report of the U.S. National Museum for 1895*, pp. 311–738. Washington, D.C.

Boas, F. 1969 (1930). *The religion of the Kwakiutl Indians*. New York: AMS Press.

Bray, T. L. Editor. 2001. *The future of the past: Archaeologists, Native Americans, and repatriation*. New York: Garland.

Brown, M. F. 1998. Can culture be copyrighted? *Current Anthropology* 39:193–222.

Brown, M. F. 2003. *Who owns native culture?* Cambridge: Harvard University Press.

Brush, S., and D. Stabinsky. 1996. *Valuing local knowledge: Indigenous people and intellectual property rights*. Washington, D.C.: Island Press.

Calloway, C. G., G. Gmunden, and S. Zantop. 2002. *Germans and Indians: Fantasies, encounters, projections*. Lincoln: University of Nebraska Press.

Carlson, C. C. 1995. "The (in)significance of Atlantic salmon in New England," in *New England's creatures: 1400–1900*. Edited by P. Benes, pp. 1–10. Cambridge: Boston University Press.

Carmichael, D. L., J. Hubert, B. Reeves, and A. Schanche. Editors. 1994. *Sacred sites, sacred places*. New York: Routledge.

Cassidy, M., and J. Langford. 1999. *Intellectual property and Aboriginal people: A working paper*. Ottawa: Indian and Northern Affairs Canada.

CBAC (Canadian Biotechnology Advisory Committee). 2001. Biotechnological intellectual property and the patenting of higher life forms. Consultation Document, Ottawa. http://www.cbac-cccb.ca/IPConsult_eng.htm.

CBAC (Canadian Biotechnology Advisory Committee). 2003. Higher life forms and the Patent Act. Advisory Memorandum, February 24. http://cbac-cccb.ca/epic/internet/incbac-cccb.nsf/vwGeneratedInterE/ahoo217e.html.

Chaloupka, G. 1986. *Burrunguy, Nourlangie Rock*. Darwin: Northart.

Chase, A. K. 1989. "Perceptions of the past among North Queensland Aboriginal people: The intrusion of Europeans and consequent social change," in *Who needs the past? Indigenous values and archaeology*. Edited by R. Layton, pp. 169–79. London: Unwin Hyman.

Chatters, J. C. 2000. The recovery and first analysis of an Early Holocene human skeleton from Kennewick, Washington. *American Antiquity* 65:291–316.

Chatwin, B. 1987. *The songlines*. New York: Penguin Books.

CIEL (Centre for International Environmental Law). 1999. US Patent Office admits error, rejects patent claim on sacred "ayahuasca" plant. Centre for International Environmental Law press release, November 4. http://www.ciel.org/Biodiversity/AyahuascaRejectionPR.html.

Coe, M. 1964. The chinampas of Mexico. *Scientific American* 211(1):90–98.

Corner, J. 1968. *Pictographs (Indian rock paintings) in the interior of British Columbia*. Vernon, B.C.: Wayside Press.

Davidson, I., C. Lovell-Jones, and R. Bancroft. Editors. 1995. *Archaeologists and aborigines working together*. Armidale: University of New England Press.

Denhez, M. 2000. *Unearthing the law: Archaeological legislation on lands in Canada*. Ottawa: Archaeological Services Branch, Parks Canada.

Doran, G. H., D. N. Dickel, W. E. Ballinger Jr., O. F. Agee, P. J. Laipis, and W. W. Hauswirth. 1986.

Anatomical, cellular, and molecular analysis of 8,000-yr-old human brain tissue from the Windover archaeological site. *Nature* 323:803–6.

Dratler, J. 1994. *Licensing of intellectual property.* New York: Law Journal Seminars-Press.

Duin, J. 2003. Tribes veto Southwest mural. *Washington Times,* February 18. http://www.thomasbakerpaintings.com/Washington%20Times%20article.

Erickson, C. L. 1998. "Applied archaeology and rural development: Archaeology's potential contribution to the future," in *Crossing currents: Continuity and change in Latin America.* Edited by M. Whiteford and S. Whiteford, pp. 34–45. Upper Saddle River, N.J.: Prentice-Hall.

Erickson, C. L. 2000. An artificial landscape-scale fishery in the Bolivian Amazon. *Nature* 408:190–93.

Fagan, B. M. 1997. 9th edition. *In the beginning: An introduction to archaeology.* New York: Longman.

Ferguson, T. J. 1996. Native Americans and the practice of Archaeology. *Annual Reviews in Anthropology* 25:63–79.

Franklin, R., and P. Bunte. 1994. "When sacred land is sacred to three Tribes: San Juan Paiute sacred sites and the Hopi-Navajo-Paiute suit to partition the Arizona Navajo reservation," in *Sacred sites, sacred places.* Edited by D. L. Carmichael, J. Hubert, B. Reeves, and F. Schanche, pp. 245–58. London: Routledge.

Gibbs, W. W. 1998. Natural born guinea pigs: A start-up discovers genes for tremor and psoriasis in the DNA of inbred Icelanders. *Scientific American* (online). http://www.sciam.com/1998/0298issue/0298techbus3.html.

Golding, F. N. 1989. "Stonehenge – past and future," in *Archaeological heritage management in the modern world.* Edited by H. F. Cleere, pp. 256–64. London: Unwin Hyman.

Gould, S. J. 1987. *Time's arrow, time's cycle: Myth and metaphor in the discovery of geological time.* Cambridge: Harvard University Press.

Greaves, T. 1994. *Intellectual property rights for indigenous peoples: A sourcebook.* Oklahoma City: Society for Applied Anthropology.

Greer, S. 1997. "Traditional knowledge in site recognition," in *At a crossroads: Archaeologists and First Peoples in Canada.* Edited by G. P. Nicholas and T. D. Andrews, pp. 145–59. Burnaby, B.C.: Archaeology Press/Simon Fraser University Press.

Hamann, B. 2002. The social life of pre-sunrise things: Indigenous Mesoamerican archaeology. *Current Anthropology* 43: 351–82.

Hampton, E., and S. Henderson. 2000. "Discussion paper on indigenous knowledge and intellectual property: Scoping the definitions and issues (executive summary)," in *Protecting knowledge: Traditional resource rights in the new millennium,* pp. i–vi. Vancouver, B.C., Canada.

Healy, D. 2003. The flag of Zia Pueblo. http://users.aol.com/Donh523/navapage/zia.htm.

Hollowell, J. J. 2003. Digging for "old things": Perspectives on a legal market for archaeological materials from Alaska's Bering Strait. Ph.D. diss., Indiana University, Bloomington, Ind.

Hollowell-Zimmer, J. J. 2001. Intellectual property protection for Alaska native arts. *Cultural Survival Quarterly* 24(4).

Holm, B. 1990. "Kwakiutl: Winter ceremonies," in *Handbook of North American Indians,* vol. 7, *Northwest Coast.* Edited by W. Suttles, pp. 378–86. Washington, D.C.: Smithsonian Institution Press.

Industry Canada. 1995. *Canadian patent law.* Canadian Intellectual Property Office, Hull, Que., Canada.

Inter-Apache Summit on Repatriation. 1995. Inter-Apache policy on repatriation and the protection of Apache culture. MS.

Janke, T. 1998. *Our culture. Our future. Report on Australian indigenous cultural and intellectual property rights.* Surrey Hills, N.S.W.: Australian Institute of Aboriginal and Torres Strait Islander Commission/Michael Frankel.

Jemison, G. P. 1997. "Who owns the past?" in *Native Americans and archaeologists: Stepping stones to common ground.* Edited by N. Swidler, K. E. Dongoske, R. Anyon, and A. S. Downer, pp. 57–63. Walnut Creek: AltaMira Press.

Johnson, V. 1996. *Copyrites: Aboriginal art in the age of reproductive technologies (Touring exhibition 1996 catalogue).* Sydney: National Indigenous Arts Advocacy Association and Macquarie University Press.

Jones, S. 1997. *The archaeology of ethnicity: Constructing identities in the past and present.* New York: Routledge.

Kritsch, I. D., and A. M. André. 1997. "Gwich'in traditional knowledge and heritage studies in the Gwich'in settlement area," in *At a crossroads: Archaeologists and first peoples in Canada.* Edited by G. P. Nicholas and T. D. Andrews, pp. 125–44. Burnaby, B.C.: Archaeology Press/Simon Fraser University Press.

Laird, S. A., M. N. Alexiades, K. P. Bannister, and D. A. Posey. 2002. "Publication of biodiversity research results and the flow of knowledge," in *Biodiversity and traditional knowledge: Equitable partnerships in practice.* Edited by S. A. Laird, pp. 77–101. London: Earthscan.

Lohnse, E. S., and F. Sundt. 1990. "History of research: Museum collection," in *Handbook of North American Indians,* vol. 7, *Northwest Coast.* Edited by W. Suttles, pp. 88–97. Washington, D.C.: Smithsonian Institution Press.

McDavid, C. 2002. Archaeologies that hurt, descendants that matter: A pragmatic approach to collaboration in the public interpretation of African-American archaeology. *World Archaeology* 34:303–13.

Maffi, L. 2000. Language preservation vs. language maintenance and revitalization: Assessing concepts, approaches, and implications for the language sciences. *International Journal of the Sociology of Language* 142:175–90.

Mann, H. 1997. Intellectual property rights, biodiversity, and indigenous knowledge: A critical analysis in the Canadian context. Report submitted to the Canadian Working Group on Article 8(j) of the Convention on Biological Diversity.

Markey, N. 2001. Data "gathering dust": An analysis of traditional use studies conducted within Aboriginal communities in British Columbia. MA. thesis, Department of Sociology and Anthropology, Simon Praser University, Burnaby, B.C., Canada.

Matsuda, D. 1998. The ethics of archaeology, subsistence digging, and artifact looting in Latin America: Point, muted counterpoint. *International Journal of Cultural Property* 7:89–97.

Meighan, C. W. 1992. Some scholar's views on reburial. *American Antiquity* 57:704–10.

Merrill, W. L., E. J. Ladd, and T. J. Ferguson. 1992. The return of the *ahayu:da*: Lessons for repatriation from Zuni Pueblo and the Smithsonian Institution. Current Anthropology 34:523–67.

Mihesuah, D. A. 2000. *Repatriation reader: Who owns American Indian remains?* Lincoln: University of Nebraska Press.

Mohs, G. 1987. Spiritual sites, ethnic significance, and native spirituality: The heritage and heritage sites of the Sto:lo Indians of British Columbia. M.A. thesis, Department of Archaeology, Simon Fraser University, Burnaby, B.C., Canada.

Morris, R. 1984. *Time's arrows*. New York: Simon and Schuster.

Myers, F. R. 1986. *Pintupi country, Pintupi self: Sentiment, place, and politics among Western Desert Aborigines*. Washington, D.C.: Smithsonian Institution Press.

Nagpra (*Native American Graves Protection and Repatriation Act*). 1990. http://www.usbr.gov/nagpra/naglaw.htm.

Nankivell, S., and D. Wyfe. 2003. *Exploring B.C.'s pictographs: A guide to native rock art in the British Columbia interior*. Burnaby, B.C.: Mussio Ventures.

Nicholas, G. P. 2001. The past and future of Indigenous archaeology: Global challenges, North American perspectives, Australian prospects. *Australian Archaeology* 52:29–40.

Nicholas, G. P. 2003. "Understanding the present, honoring the past," in *Indigenous peoples and archaeology*. Edited by T. Peck, E. Siegfried, and G. Oetelaar. Calgary: University of Calgary Archaeological Association.

O'Neill, G. 1994. Cemetery reveals complex aboriginal society. *Science* 264:1403.

Parsons, J., and W. Denevan. 1967. Pre-Columbian ridged fields. *Scientific American* 217(1):92–101.

Patterson, T. C. 1999. *A social history of anthropology in the United States*. New York: Berg.

Peacock, S. 1998. Putting down roots: The emergence of wild food production on the Canadian Plateau. Ph.D. diss., University of Victoria, Victoria, B.C., Canada.

Pearlstone, Z. 2000. Mail-order "katsinam" and the issue of authenticity. *Journal of the Southwest* 42:801–32.

Pearlstone, Z. 2001. *Katsina: Commodified and appropriated images of Hopi supernaturals*. Los Angeles: UCLA Fowler Museum of Cultural History.

Pinsky, V., and A. Wylie. 1995. *Critical traditions in contemporary archaeology: Essays in the philosophy, history, and socio-politics of archaeology*. Albuquerque: University of New Mexico Press.

Posey, D. A., and G. Dutfield. 1996. *Beyond intellectual property rights: Toward traditional resource rights*. Ottawa: IDRC.

Preston, D. 1997. The lost man. *New Yorker*, June 16, pp. 70–81.

Rathje, W. L. 1991. Once and future landfills. *National Geographic*, May, pp. 116–34.

Rathje, W. L., and C. Murphy. 1992. *Rubbish! The archaeology of garbage*. New York: HarperCollins.

Ritchie, D. 1993. "Principles and practice of site protection laws in Australia," in *Sacred sites, sacred places*. Edited by D. L. Carmichael, J. Hubert, B. Reeves, and A. Schanche, pp. 227–44. London: Routledge.

Robbins, A., and M. Becher. 1997–98. "Karl May Festival," in *German Indians*. Photographic display at Leslie Tonkanow Artworks and Projects, New York. http://robbecher.www4.5omegs.com/TonkanowGlimagesframe.html.

Roberts, A. 2002. *Indigenous South Australian perspectives of archaeology project report*. Adelaide: Department of Archaeology, Flinders University.

Roberts, A. 2003. Knowledge, power, and voice: An investigation of indigenous South Australian perspectives of archaeology. Ph.D. diss., Flinders University, Adelaide, Australia.

Rose, J. C., T. J. Green, and V. D. Green. 1996. NAGPRA is forever: Osteology and the repatriation of skeletons. *Annual Review of Anthropology* 25:81–103.

Sahlins, M. 1976. *Culture and practical reason*. Chicago: University of Chicago Press.

Sahlins, M. 1999. What is anthropological enlightenment? Some lessons of the twentieth century. *Annual Reviews in Anthropology* 29:i–xxiii.

Sheets, P. D. 1989. "Dawn of a new Stone Age in eye surgery," in *Applying anthropology: An introductory reader*. Edited by A. Poloefsky and P. J. Brown, pp. 113–15. Mountain View, Calif.: Mayfield.

Shennan, S. Editor. 1989. *Archaeological approaches to cultural identity*. London: Unwin Hyman.

Simpson, L. R. 1999. The construction of traditional ecological knowledge: Issues, implications, and insights. Ph.D. diss., University of Manitoba, Winnipeg, Manitoba, Canada.

Singleton, T. A. 1995. The archaeology of slavery in North America. *Annual Review of Anthropology* 24:119–40.

Smith, C. E. 1994. Situating style: An ethnoarchaeological study of social and material context in an Australian Aboriginal artistic system. Ph.D. diss., University of New England, Armidale, Australia.

Staley, D. P. 1993. St. Lawrence Island's subsistence diggers: A new perspective on human effects on archaeological sites. *Journal of Field Archaeology* 20:347–55.

Stanner, W. H. H. 1998. "The dreaming," in *Traditional Aboriginal society*, 2d edition. Edited by W. H. Edwards, pp. 227–38. South Yarra: Macmillan Australia.

Stephenson, D. J., Jr. 1999. "A practical primer on intellectual property rights in a contemporary ethnoecological context," in *Ethnoecology: Situated knowledge/located lives*. Edited by V. Nazarea, pp. 230–48. Tucson: University of Arizona Press.

Tanner, A. 2000. Image problem. *The Province* [Gabriola Island, B.C.], February 13.

Thomas, D. H. 1998. 3d edition. *Archaeology*. Fort Worth: Harcourt Brace.

Thomas, D. H. 2000. *Skull wars: Kennewick man, archaeology, and the battle for Native American identity*. New York: Basic Books.

Tindale, N. B. 1974. *Aboriginal tribes of Australia: Their terrain, environmental controls, distribution, limits, and proper names*. Canberra: Australian National University Press.

Trigger, B. G. 1989. *A history of archaeological thought*. New York: Cambridge University Press.

Turner, N. J. 1997 (1978). Revised edition. *Food plants of interior First Peoples*. Vancouver: University of British Columbia Press/Victoria: Royal British Columbia Museum.

Turner, N. J. 1998 (1979). Revised edition. *Plant technology of British Columbia first peoples*. Vancouver: University of British Columbia Press/Victoria: Royal British Columbia Museum.

Watkins, J. 2000. *Indigenous archaeology: American Indian values and scientific practice*. Walnut Creek: AltaMira Press.

Whiteley, P. 1997. "The end of anthropology (at Hopi)?" in *Indians and anthropologists: Vine Deloria Jr. and the critique of anthropology*. Edited by T. Biolsi and L. J. Zimmerman, pp. 177–208. Tucson: University of Arizona Press.

Williams, N. M., and D. Mununggurr. 1989. "Understanding Yolngu signs of the past," in *Who needs the past? Indigenous values and archaeology*. Edited by R. Layton, pp. 70–83. London: Unwin Hyman.

Winter, B., and D. Henry. 1997. "The *Sddlnewhala* bowl: Cooperation or compromise?" in *At a crossroads: Archaeology and First Peoples in Canada*. Edited by G. P. Nicholas and T. D. Andrews, pp. 214–23. Burnaby, B.C.: Archaeology Press/Simon Fraser University Press.

York, A., R. Daly, and C. Arnett. 1993. *They write their dreams on the rock forever: Rock writings in the Stein River valley of British Columbia*. Vancouver: Talonbooks.

Zimmer, J. J. 2003. "When archaeological artifacts are commodities: Dilemmas faced by native villages of Alaska's Bering Strait," in *Indigenous peoples and archaeology: Proceedings of the 32nd Chacmool conference*. Edited by T. Peck, E. Siegfried, and G. Oetelaar, pp. 298–312. Calgary: Archaeological Association of the University of Calgary.

Zimmerman, L. 1987. The impact of concepts of time and past on the concept of archaeology: Some lessons from the reburial issue. *Archaeological Review of Cambridge* 6(1):42–50.

Zimmerman, L. 1997. "Remythologizing the relationship between Indians and archaeologists," in *Native Americans and archaeologists: Stepping stones to common ground*. Edited by N. Swidler, K. Dongoske, R. Anyon, and A. Dower, pp. 44–56. Walnut Creek: AltaMira Press.

Index